T0142042

Lecture Notes in Computer Science   13091

Founding Editors

Gerhard Goos
Karlsruhe Institute of Technology, Karlsruhe, Germany
Juris Hartmanis
Cornell University, Ithaca, NY, USA

Editorial Board Members

Elisa Bertino
Purdue University, West Lafayette, IN, USA
Wen Gao
Peking University, Beijing, China
Bernhard Steffen ⓘ
TU Dortmund University, Dortmund, Germany
Gerhard Woeginger ⓘ
RWTH Aachen, Aachen, Germany
Moti Yung ⓘ
Columbia University, New York, NY, USA

More information about this subseries at https://link.springer.com/bookseries/7410

Mehdi Tibouchi · Huaxiong Wang (Eds.)

Advances in Cryptology – ASIACRYPT 2021

27th International Conference on the Theory
and Application of Cryptology and Information Security
Singapore, December 6–10, 2021
Proceedings, Part II

 Springer

Editors
Mehdi Tibouchi 🆔
NTT Corporation
Tokyo, Japan

Huaxiong Wang 🆔
Nanyang Technological University
Singapore, Singapore

ISSN 0302-9743   ISSN 1611-3349   (electronic)
Lecture Notes in Computer Science
ISBN 978-3-030-92074-6   ISBN 978-3-030-92075-3   (eBook)
https://doi.org/10.1007/978-3-030-92075-3

LNCS Sublibrary: SL4 – Security and Cryptology

© International Association for Cryptologic Research 2021
This work is subject to copyright. All rights are reserved by the Publisher, whether the whole or part of the material is concerned, specifically the rights of translation, reprinting, reuse of illustrations, recitation, broadcasting, reproduction on microfilms or in any other physical way, and transmission or information storage and retrieval, electronic adaptation, computer software, or by similar or dissimilar methodology now known or hereafter developed.
The use of general descriptive names, registered names, trademarks, service marks, etc. in this publication does not imply, even in the absence of a specific statement, that such names are exempt from the relevant protective laws and regulations and therefore free for general use.
The publisher, the authors and the editors are safe to assume that the advice and information in this book are believed to be true and accurate at the date of publication. Neither the publisher nor the authors or the editors give a warranty, expressed or implied, with respect to the material contained herein or for any errors or omissions that may have been made. The publisher remains neutral with regard to jurisdictional claims in published maps and institutional affiliations.

This Springer imprint is published by the registered company Springer Nature Switzerland AG
The registered company address is: Gewerbestrasse 11, 6330 Cham, Switzerland

Preface

Asiacrypt 2021, the 27th Annual International Conference on Theory and Application of Cryptology and Information Security, was originally planned to be held in Singapore during December 6–10, 2021. Due to the COVID-19 pandemic, it was shifted to an online-only virtual conference.

The conference covered all technical aspects of cryptology, and was sponsored by the International Association for Cryptologic Research (IACR).

We received a total of 341 submissions from all over the world, and the Program Committee (PC) selected 95 papers for publication in the proceedings of the conference. The two program chairs were supported by a PC consisting of 74 leading experts in aspects of cryptology. Each submission was reviewed by at least three PC members (or their sub-reviewers) and five PC members were assigned to submissions co-authored by PC members. The strong conflict of interest rules imposed by IACR ensure that papers are not handled by PC members with a close working relationship with the authors. The two program chairs were not allowed to submit a paper, and PC members were limited to two submissions each. There were approximately 363 external reviewers, whose input was critical to the selection of papers.

The review process was conducted using double-blind peer review. The conference operated a two-round review system with a rebuttal phase. After the reviews and first-round discussions the PC selected 233 submissions to proceed to the second round and the authors were then invited to provide a short rebuttal in response to the referee reports. The second round involved extensive discussions by the PC members.

Alongside the presentations of the accepted papers, the program of Asiacrypt 2021 featured an IACR distinguished lecture by Andrew Chi-Chih Yao and two invited talks by Kazue Sako and Yu Yu. The conference also featured a rump session which contained short presentations on the latest research results of the field.

The four volumes of the conference proceedings contain the revised versions of the 95 papers that were selected, together with the abstracts of the IACR distinguished lecture and the two invited talks. The final revised versions of papers were not reviewed again and the authors are responsible for their contents.

Via a voting-based process that took into account conflicts of interest, the PC selected the three top papers of the conference: "On the Hardness of the NTRU problem" by Alice Pellet-Mary and Damien Stehlé (which received the best paper award); "A Geometric Approach to Linear Cryptanalysis" by Tim Beyne (which received the best student paper award); and "Lattice Enumeration for Tower NFS: a 521-bit Discrete Logarithm Computation" by Gabrielle De Micheli, Pierrick Gaudry, and Cécile Pierrot. The authors of all three papers were invited to submit extended versions of their manuscripts to the Journal of Cryptology.

Many people have contributed to the success of Asiacrypt 2021. We would like to thank the authors for submitting their research results to the conference. We are very grateful to the PC members and external reviewers for contributing their knowledge and expertise, and for the tremendous amount of work that was done with reading papers and contributing to the discussions. We are greatly indebted to Jian Guo, the General Chair, for his efforts and overall organization. We thank San Ling and Josef Pieprzyk, the advisors of Asiacrypt 2021, for their valuable suggestions. We thank Michel Abdalla, Kevin McCurley, Kay McKelly, and members of IACR's emergency pandemic team for their work in designing and running the virtual format. We thank Chitchanok Chuengsatiansup and Khoa Nguyen for expertly organizing and chairing the rump session. We are extremely grateful to Zhenzhen Bao for checking all the LATEX files and for assembling the files for submission to Springer. We also thank Alfred Hofmann, Anna Kramer, and their colleagues at Springer for handling the publication of these conference proceedings.

December 2021   Mehdi Tibouchi
                                                                Huaxiong Wang

Organization

General Chair

Jian Guo   Nanyang Technological University, Singapore

Program Committee Co-chairs

Mehdi Tibouchi   NTT Corporation, Japan
Huaxiong Wang   Nanyang Technological University, Singapore

Steering Committee

Masayuki Abe
Lynn Batten
Jung Hee Cheon
Steven Galbraith
D. J. Guan
Jian Guo
Khalid Habib
Lucas Hui
Nassar Ikram
Kwangjo Kim
Xuejia Lai
Dong Hoon Lee
Satya Lokam
Mitsuru Matsui (Chair)
Tsutomu Matsumoto
Phong Nguyen

Dingyi Pei
Duong Hieu Phan
Raphael Phan
Josef Pieprzyk (Vice Chair)
C. Pandu Rangan
Bimal Roy
Leonie Simpson
Huaxiong Wang
Henry B. Wolfe
Duncan Wong
Tzong-Chen Wu
Bo-Yin Yang
Siu-Ming Yiu
Yu Yu
Jianying Zhou

Program Committee

Shweta Agrawal	IIT Madras, India
Martin R. Albrecht	Royal Holloway, University of London, UK
Zhenzhen Bao	Nanyang Technological University, Singapore
Manuel Barbosa	University of Porto (FCUP) and INESC TEC, Portugal
Lejla Batina	Radboud University, The Netherlands
Sonia Belaïd	CryptoExperts, France
Fabrice Benhamouda	Algorand Foundation, USA
Begül Bilgin	Rambus - Cryptography Research, The Netherlands
Xavier Bonnetain	University of Waterloo, Canada
Joppe W. Bos	NXP Semiconductors, Belgium

Wouter Castryck	KU Leuven, Belgium
Rongmao Chen	National University of Defense Technology, China
Jung Hee Cheon	Seoul National University, South Korea
Chitchanok Chuengsatiansup	The University of Adelaide, Australia
Kai-Min Chung	Academia Sinica, Taiwan
Dana Dachman-Soled	University of Maryland, USA
Bernardo David	IT University of Copenhagen, Denmark
Benjamin Fuller	University of Connecticut, USA
Steven Galbraith	The University of Auckland, New Zealand
María Isabel González Vasco	Universidad Rey Juan Carlos, Spain
Robert Granger	University of Surrey, UK
Alex B. Grilo	CNRS, LIP6, Sorbonne Université, France
Aurore Guillevic	Inria, France
Swee-Huay Heng	Multimedia University, Malaysia
Akinori Hosoyamada	NTT Corporation and Nagoya University, Japan
Xinyi Huang	Fujian Normal University, China
Andreas Hülsing	Eindhoven University of Technology, The Netherlands
Tetsu Iwata	Nagoya University, Japan
David Jao	University of Waterloo and evolutionQ, Inc., Canada
Jérémy Jean	ANSSI, France
Shuichi Katsumata	AIST, Japan
Elena Kirshanova	I. Kant Baltic Federal University, Russia
Hyung Tae Lee	Chung-Ang University, South Korea
Dongdai Lin	Institute of Information Engineering, Chinese Academy of Sciences, China
Rongxing Lu	University of New Brunswick, Canada
Xianhui Lu	Institute of Information Engineering, Chinese Academy of Sciences, China
Mary Maller	Ethereum Foundation, UK
Giorgia Azzurra Marson	NEC Labs Europe, Germany
Keith M. Martin	Royal Holloway, University of London, UK
Daniel Masny	Visa Research, USA
Takahiro Matsuda	AIST, Japan
Krystian Matusiewicz	Intel Corporation, Poland
Florian Mendel	Infineon Technologies, Germany
Nele Mentens	Leiden University, The Netherlands, and KU Leuven, Belgium
Atsuko Miyaji	Osaka University, Japan
Michael Naehrig	Microsoft Research, USA
Khoa Nguyen	Nanyang Technological University, Singapore
Miyako Ohkubo	NICT, Japan
Emmanuela Orsini	KU Leuven, Belgium
Jiaxin Pan	NTNU, Norway
Panos Papadimitratos	KTH Royal Institute of Technology, Sweden

Alice Pellet–Mary	CNRS and University of Bordeaux, France
Duong Hieu Phan	Télécom Paris, Institut Polytechnique de Paris, France
Francisco Rodríguez-Henríquez	CINVESTAV, Mexico
Olivier Sanders	Orange Labs, France
Jae Hong Seo	Hanyang University, South Korea
Haya Shulman	Fraunhofer SIT, Germany
Daniel Slamanig	AIT Austrian Institute of Technology, Austria
Ron Steinfeld	Monash University, Australia
Willy Susilo	University of Wollongong, Australia
Katsuyuki Takashima	Waseda University, Japan
Qiang Tang	The University of Sydney, Australia
Serge Vaudenay	EPFL, Switzerland
Damien Vergnaud	Sorbonne Université and Institut Universitaire de France, France
Meiqin Wang	Shandong University, China
Xiaoyun Wang	Tsinghua University, China
Yongge Wang	UNC Charlotte, USA
Wenling Wu	Institute of Software, Chinese Academy of Sciences, China
Chaoping Xing	Shanghai Jiao Tong University, China
Sophia Yakoubov	Aarhus University, Denmark
Takashi Yamakawa	NTT Corporation, Japan
Bo-Yin Yang	Academia Sinica, Taiwan
Yu Yu	Shanghai Jiao Tong University, China
Hong-Sheng Zhou	Virginia Commonwealth University, USA

Additional Reviewers

Behzad Abdolmaleki
Gorjan Alagic
Orestis Alpos
Miguel Ambrona
Diego Aranha
Victor Arribas
Nuttapong Attrapadung
Benedikt Auerbach
Zeta Avarikioti
Melissa Azouaoui
Saikrishna Badrinarayanan
Joonsang Baek
Karim Baghery
Shi Bai
Gustavo Banegas
Subhadeep Banik

James Bartusek
Balthazar Bauer
Rouzbeh Behnia
Yanis Belkheyar
Josh Benaloh
Ward Beullens
Tim Beyne
Sarani Bhattacharya
Rishiraj Bhattacharyya
Nina Bindel
Adam Blatchley Hansen
Olivier Blazy
Charlotte Bonte
Katharina Boudgoust
Ioana Boureanu
Markus Brandt

Anne Broadbent
Ileana Buhan
Andrea Caforio
Eleonora Cagli
Sébastien Canard
Ignacio Cascudo
Gaëtan Cassiers
André Chailloux
Tzu-Hsien Chang
Yilei Chen
Jie Chen
Yanlin Chen
Albert Cheu
Jesús-Javier Chi-Domíguez
Nai-Hui Chia
Ilaria Chillotti
Ji-Jian Chin
Jérémy Chotard
Sherman S. M. Chow
Heewon Chung
Jorge Chávez-Saab
Michele Ciampi
Carlos Cid
Valerio Cini
Tristan Claverie
Benoît Cogliati
Alexandru Cojocaru
Daniel Collins
Kelong Cong
Craig Costello
Geoffroy Couteau
Daniele Cozzo
Jan Czajkowski
Tianxiang Dai
Wei Dai
Sourav Das
Pratish Datta
Alex Davidson
Lauren De Meyer
Elke De Mulder
Claire Delaplace
Cyprien Delpech de Saint Guilhem
Patrick Derbez
Siemen Dhooghe
Daniel Dinu
Christoph Dobraunig

Samuel Dobson
Luis J. Dominguez Perez
Jelle Don
Benjamin Dowling
Maria Eichlseder
Jesse Elliott
Keita Emura
Muhammed F. Esgin
Hulya Evkan
Lei Fan
Antonio Faonio
Hanwen Feng
Dario Fiore
Antonio Florez-Gutierrez
Georg Fuchsbauer
Chaya Ganesh
Daniel Gardham
Rachit Garg
Pierrick Gaudry
Romain Gay
Nicholas Genise
Adela Georgescu
David Gerault
Satrajit Ghosh
Valerie Gilchrist
Aron Gohr
Junqing Gong
Marc Gourjon
Lorenzo Grassi
Milos Grujic
Aldo Gunsing
Kaiwen Guo
Chun Guo
Qian Guo
Mike Hamburg
Ben Hamlin
Shuai Han
Yonglin Hao
Keisuke Hara
Patrick Harasser
Jingnan He
David Heath
Chloé Hébant
Julia Hesse
Ryo Hiromasa
Shiqi Hou

Lin Hou
Yao-Ching Hsieh
Kexin Hu
Jingwei Hu
Zhenyu Huang
Loïs Huguenin-Dumittan
Arnie Hung
Shih-Han Hung
Kathrin Hövelmanns
Ilia Iliashenko
Aayush Jain
Yanxue Jia
Dingding Jia
Yao Jiang
Floyd Johnson
Luke Johnson
Chanyang Ju
Charanjit S. Jutla
John Kelsey
Taechan Kim
Myungsun Kim
Jinsu Kim
Minkyu Kim
Young-Sik Kim
Sungwook Kim
Jiseung Kim
Kwangjo Kim
Seungki Kim
Sunpill Kim
Fuyuki Kitagawa
Susumu Kiyoshima
Michael Klooß
Dimitris Kolonelos
Venkata Koppula
Liliya Kraleva
Mukul Kulkarni
Po-Chun Kuo
Hilder Vitor Lima Pereira
Russell W. F. Lai
Jianchang Lai
Yi-Fu Lai
Virginie Lallemand
Jason LeGrow
Joohee Lee
Jooyoung Lee
Changmin Lee

Hyeonbum Lee
Moon Sung Lee
Keewoo Lee
Dominik Leichtle
Alexander Lemmens
Gaëtan Leurent
Yannan Li
Shuaishuai Li
Baiyu Li
Zhe Li
Shun Li
Liang Li
Jianwei Li
Trey Li
Xiao Liang
Chi-Chang Lin
Chengjun Lin
Chao Lin
Yao-Ting Lin
Eik List
Feng-Hao Liu
Qipeng Liu
Guozhen Liu
Yunwen Liu
Patrick Longa
Sebastien Lord
George Lu
Yuan Lu
Yibiao Lu
Xiaojuan Lu
Ji Luo
Yiyuan Luo
Mohammad Mahzoun
Monosij Maitra
Christian Majenz
Ekaterina Malygina
Mark Manulis
Varun Maram
Luca Mariot
Loïc Masure
Bart Mennink
Simon-Philipp Merz
Peihan Miao
Kazuhiko Minematsu
Donika Mirdita
Pratyush Mishra

Tomoyuki Morimae
Pratyay Mukherjee
Alex Munch-Hansen
Yusuke Naito
Ngoc Khanh Nguyen
Jianting Ning
Ryo Nishimaki
Anca Nitulescu
Kazuma Ohara
Cristina Onete
Jean-Baptiste Orfila
Michele Orrù
Jong Hwan Park
Jeongeun Park
Robi Pedersen
Angel L. Perez del Pozo
Léo Perrin
Thomas Peters
Albrecht Petzoldt
Stjepan Picek
Rafael del Pino
Geong Sen Poh
David Pointcheval
Bernardo Portela
Raluca Posteuca
Thomas Prest
Robert Primas
Chen Qian
Willy Quach
Md Masoom Rabbani
Rahul Rachuri
Srinivasan Raghuraman
Sebastian Ramacher
Matthieu Rambaud
Shahram Rasoolzadeh
Krijn Reijnders
Joost Renes
Elena Reshetova
Mélissa Rossi
Mike Rosulek
Yann Rotella
Joe Rowell
Arnab Roy
Partha Sarathi Roy
Alexander Russell
Carla Ráfols

Paul Rösler
Yusuke Sakai
Amin Sakzad
Yu Sasaki
Or Sattath
John M. Schanck
Lars Schlieper
Martin Schläfer
Carsten Schmidt
André Schrottenloher
Jacob Schuldt
Jean-Pierre Seifert
Yannick Seurin
Yaobin Shen
Yixin Shen
Yu-Ching Shen
Danping Shi
Omri Shmueli
Kris Shrishak
Hervais Simo Fhom
Luisa Siniscalchi
Daniel Smith-Tone
Fang Song
Pratik Soni
Claudio Soriente
Akshayaram Srinivasan
Douglas Stebila
Damien Stehlé
Bruno Sterner
Christoph Striecks
Patrick Struck
Adriana Suarez Corona
Ling Sun
Shi-Feng Sun
Koutarou Suzuki
Aishwarya T.
Erkan Tairi
Akira Takahashi
Atsushi Takayasu
Abdul Rahman Taleb
Younes Talibi Alaoui
Benjamin Hong Meng Tan
Syh-Yuan Tan
Titouan Tanguy
Alexander Tereshchenko
Adrian Thillard

Emmanuel Thomé
Tyge Tiessen
Radu Titiu
Ivan Tjuawinata
Yosuke Todo
Junichi Tomida
Bénédikt Tran
Jacques Traoré
Ni Trieu
Ida Tucker
Michael Tunstall
Dominique Unruh
Thomas Unterluggauer
Thomas van Himbeeck
Daniele Venturi
Jorge Villar
Mikhail Volkhov
Christine van Vredendaal
Benedikt Wagner
Riad Wahby
Hendrik Waldner
Alexandre Wallet
Junwei Wang
Qingju Wang
Yuyu Wang
Lei Wang
Senpeng Wang
Peng Wang
Weijia Wang
Yi Wang

Han Wang
Xuzi Wang
Yohei Watanabe
Florian Weber
Weiqiang Wen
Nils Wisiol
Mathias Wolf
Harry H. W. Wong
Keita Xagawa
Zejun Xiang
Jiayu Xu
Luyao Xu
Yaqi Xu
Shota Yamada
Hailun Yan
Wenjie Yang
Shaojun Yang
Masaya Yasuda
Wei-Chuen Yau
Kazuki Yoneyama
Weijing You
Chen Yuan
Tsz Hon Yuen
Runzhi Zeng
Cong Zhang
Zhifang Zhang
Bingsheng Zhang
Zhelei Zhou
Paul Zimmermann
Lukas Zobernig

Contents – Part II

Enhanced Public-Key Encryption and Time-Lock Puzzles

Real-World Protocols

Physical Attacks, Leakage and Countermeasures

Secure and Efficient Software Masking on Superscalar Pipelined Processors

Barbara Gigerl[1(✉)], Robert Primas[1(✉)], and Stefan Mangard[1,2(✉)]

[1] Graz University of Technology, Graz, Austria
{barbara.gigerl,robert.primas,stefan.mangard}@iaik.tugraz.at
[2] Lamarr Security Research, Graz, Austria

Abstract. Physical side-channel attacks like power analysis pose a serious threat to cryptographic devices in real-world applications. Consequently, devices implement algorithmic countermeasures like masking. In the past, works on the design and verification of masked software implementations have mostly focused on simple microprocessors that find usage on smart cards. However, many other applications such as in the automotive industry require side-channel protected cryptographic computations on much more powerful CPUs. In such situations, the security loss due to complex architectural side-effects, the corresponding performance degradation, as well as discussions of suitable probing models and verification techniques are still vastly unexplored research questions.

We answer these questions and perform a comprehensive analysis of more complex processor architectures in the context of masking-related side effects. First, we analyze the RISC-V SweRV core—featuring a 9-stage pipeline, two execution units, and load/store buffers—and point out a significant gap between security in a simple software probing model and practical security on such CPUs. More concretely, we show that architectural side effects of complex CPU architectures can significantly reduce the protection order of masked software, both via formal analysis in the hardware probing model, as well as empirically via gate-level timing simulations. We then discuss the options of fixing these problems in hardware or leaving them as constraints to software. Based on these software constraints, we formulate general rules for the design of masked software on more complex CPUs. Finally, we compare several implementation strategies for masking schemes and present in a case study that designing secure masked software for complex CPUs is still possible with overhead as low as 13%.

Keywords: Masking · Verification · Side-channel analysis · SweRV · Glitches · Application-level processors · Coco · Probing model

1 Introduction

Cryptographic primitives are primarily designed to withstand mathematical attacks in a black-box setting. However, as soon as these primitives are deployed in the real world, they find themselves in a grey-box setting in which an attacker

© International Association for Cryptologic Research 2021
M. Tibouchi and H. Wang (Eds.): ASIACRYPT 2021, LNCS 13091, pp. 3–32, 2021.
https://doi.org/10.1007/978-3-030-92075-3_1

may observe additional physical side-channel information, such as instantaneous power consumption that can be used to extract secrets like cryptographic keys. One particularly powerful example of such a side-channel attack, differential power analysis (DPA), was introduced in 1999 by Kocher et al. [27]. In this type of attack, the adversary observes a device's power consumption while encrypting several known plaintexts, and can then extract sensitive information using statistical analysis.

The typical approach of protecting against these attacks is to implement algorithmic countermeasures, like masking [6,9,14,22,25,34]. The main idea of masking is to make computations independent from the actually processed data. For this purpose, masking schemes split input and intermediate variables of cryptographic computations into $d + 1$ random shares such that observations of up to d shares do not reveal any information about the native (unmasked) value. The security of such dth-order protected computations relies, amongst others, on the assumption of independent leakage, i.e., independent computations result in independent leakage [33]. However, many academic works in the past have shown that such assumptions are typically not satisfied on ordinary CPUs, for example, memory transitions in the register file or RAM can leak the Hamming distance between two shares [2,15,21,28,32]. In general, one can work around these problems using two different strategies. Works like [7,20,21,32] show that one can design dedicated masked software implementations that take specific characteristics of the microprocessor into account, e.g., by never processing shares of the same variable in immediate succession. Alternatively, one can follow the *lazy engineering* approach, accept a certain loss of masking protection order due to architecture side-effects and compensate for that by using a protection order that is higher than theoretically required. This strategy was more formally analyzed by Balasch et al. [2] who also formulated the so-called order reduction theorem. This theorem states that, when considering simple register-based CPU architectures, the security of a dth-order masked software implementation reduces to $\lfloor \frac{d}{2} \rfloor$-th order if transition-based leakage is taken into account.

Building efficient and correct masked software implementations is generally difficult since one either needs to (1) carefully patch implementations for specific microprocessors [7,21,32], or (2) invest in masking orders that are a lot higher than required [2]. In both cases, the runtime of the resulting masked software implementations is significantly increased and subsequent manual leakage assessments are needed to confirm that the performed modifications have the desired effect, which is a quite labor-intensive and error-prone task. This situation becomes only ever more difficult with increasing processor complexity. For example, the effects of multiple ALU pipeline stages, forwarding logic, superscalar building blocks, caches, and complex logic for handling loads/stores on masked software implementations have not been analyzed in this detail before. One reason for that might be the sheer complexity of application-level processors that usually consist of superscalar building blocks and multi-stage pipelines. On such processors, identifying and understanding masking related side-effects can barely be done manually anymore. Here, automated analysis methods that can give concrete conditions under which masked software implementations can guarantee a certain protection order on such CPUs are more relevant then ever.

In this context, a recent work by Gigerl et al. [20] studies the simple IBEX core with COCO, a tool that can verify the correct execution of masked software implementations on given CPU netlists, while considering all possible architectural side effects. Simply speaking, COCO treats an entire CPU design as a hardware circuit and then tracks all the shares of executed masked software implementations over several cycles using methods that are inspired by REBECCA [13]. One result of their analysis is a slightly modified *secured* IBEX core on which masked software implementations can preserve their theoretic protection order in practice if a few simple software constraints are followed. While this result is certainly interesting for applications like smart cards where low computing power is sufficient, many other IoT or automotive use cases require the usage of significantly more powerful processors. This raises a number of questions about the performance, as well as the theoretic and practical security of masked software on more complex CPUs.

Our Contribution. We answer these questions by providing the following contributions:

- We generate several generic higher-order masked cryptographic software implementations using Tornado and show with COCO that there is little hope that such implementations can even provide 1st-order protection on more complex CPU cores. We demonstrate this based on the dual-issue 9-stage RISC-V SweRV core.
- In addition to the formal analysis of COCO, we perform gate-level simulations to demonstrate that architecture-based glitch effects are visible in practice and reduce the security of masked software by multiple orders. This points out a significant gap between security in the simple software probing model and practical security, and further motivates the verification of masked software on concrete CPU netlists in a more hardware focused probing model.
- We then further analyze the components of SweRV that do not exist in simpler cores, identify new problems, and discussed possible solutions in software or hardware.
- Based on this analysis, we formulate more general rules for designing masked software that takes into consideration properties such as the pipeline length, the amount of execution units, or architectural buffers. We also present arguments why relying on the *lazy engineering* approach alone, as proposed by [2], does not seem viable anymore in case of more complex CPUs.
- Finally, we present a case study that compares how efficiently our derived software constraints can be met with different implementation strategies. Maybe somewhat surprisingly we show that, with knowledge about a processors netlist, one can build secure and efficient masked software for SweRV-like cores with overhead as low as 13%.

Outline. In Sect. 2 we cover relevant background on masking and the verification of masking, including the basic working principles of COCO and Tornado. In

Sect. 3, we describe the evaluation setup for the analysis of more complex CPUs with COCO, present some initial verification results and describe the significance of these in a practical evaluation. In Sect. 4, we present a detailed analysis of SweRV architecture, describe all hardware components that can pose problems to masked software implementations and propose viable solutions. In Sect. 5, we list the generic software constraints and evaluate their overhead in Sect. 6. We conclude our work in Sect. 7.

Open Source. We plan to publish both, our modified SweRV core, as well as the corresponding software implementations that are used in this paper on github[1].

2   Background

2.1   Masking

Masking has become one of the first-choice measures to defeat power-analysis attacks on algorithmic level. In general, masking is a secret-sharing technique which splits intermediate values of a computation into $d + 1$ shares. The shares are uniformly random, such that an attacker who observes up to d shares cannot infer any information about the underlying native value. A dth-order Boolean masking scheme splits a native variable s into $d + 1$ random shares $s_0 \ldots s_d$, such that $s = s_0 \oplus \ldots \oplus s_d$. The values $s_0 \ldots s_{d-1}$ are chosen uniformly at random while $s_d = s_0 \oplus \ldots \oplus s_{d-1} \oplus s$. Consequently, each share s_i is uniformly distributed and statistically independent of the native value s.

Implementing linear functions when designing masked cryptographic implementations is trivial, as they can simply be computed on each share individually. However, non-linear functions (S-boxes) are not as simple, since computations involve multiple shares of a native value at the same time, which is more difficult to implement in a secure and correct manner. Therefore, the main interest in literature lays on masked implementations of non-linear functions [6,9,14,22,23,25,34]

2.2   Formal Verification of Masking

In general, masked implementations must ensure that each intermediate value of a computation is statistically independent of any native values. The verification of this property is usually done with the help of a security model that specifies the abilities of an attacker. Typically, it is assumed that the ability of the attacker is to place a certain amount of probes in a computation, that allow monitoring concrete values at those locations.

Formal Verification of Hardware Implementations. The *classical probing model* by Ishai et al. [25] is the most commonly used security model for masked hardware circuits and it's accuracy in modeling real world attacks has been confirmed by many works [18,35]. Here, an attacker is allowed to place up to d probes at any

---

[1] https://github.com/barbara-gigerl/sw-masking-swerv.

location in a circuit, which can be used to observe the corresponding gates/wires permanently. A masked hardware implementation is considered dth-order secure if an attacker cannot learn any information about the native values by combining all d observations. Examples of tools that can verify classical probing security for cryptographic hardware implementations are REBECCA [13], `Silver` [26], and `maskVerif` [3]. These tools are mainly tailored to the verification of masked hardware (ASIC/FPGA) implementations. `maskVerif` does offer some support for software implementations but (1) can only deal with code that is written in a special intermediate language, and (2) only considers simple CPU side-effects such as register overwrites.

Formal Verification of Software Implementations. On software side, the research community has also published many methods and tools to automatically generate or verify masked software implementations [4,5,8,17,29,45]. More recently, Belaïd et al. proposed Tornado [10], a tool that takes a high-level description of an unmasked cryptographic function, generates a corresponding (any-order) masked C implementation, and verifies its probing security. Tornado's verification itself is based on tightPROVE+, an extension of tightPROVE [9]. tightPROVE+ performs the verification of masked software in the *register probing model*. This model allows an attacker to place probes on individual words of a processor's register file, and to use them for one cycle each during the execution of a masked software implementation. Hereby, it is assumed that the probed registers cause independent leakage, in other words, no additional potential side effects of a processors architecture, such as glitches or register overwrites, are considered [33].

More precise verification tools, that e.g. also cover transition leakage have been presented in [1,7,40], while with COCO, Gigerl et al. have recently presented a tool that can verify the correctness of masked software implementations while considering possible architectural side effects of a given CPU netlist [20].

2.3   Coco

COCO is a tool for the co-design and co-verification of masked software implementations on CPU netlists [20]. It formally verifies the security of (any-order) masked assembly implementations that are executed on concrete CPUs, defined by gate-level netlists. COCO's verification strategy is inspired by REBECCA but extended in a way such that the verification of masked software, when running on hardware, is converted into a pure hardware verification problem. This involves not only the addition of control-flow awareness but also several performance improvements since entire CPUs are usually significantly larger designs, when compared to pure hardware implementations of cryptographic functions. COCO does not only capture transition-based effects, but in principle any glitch-related hardware side-effects that can be derived from a CPU netlist. This is also formalized in the so-called *time-constrained probing model*, in which an attacker can use each probe to measure any specific gate/wire for the duration of one clock cycle that can be chosen independently for each probe.

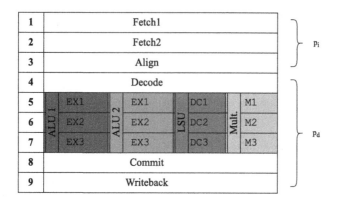

Fig. 1. Pipeline stages of SweRV [42]

Verification Flow. In the following, we briefly outline the workflow of Coco, broken into multiple steps. Steps **A** and **B** explain how the execution of software can be combined with an otherwise purely hardware-focused verification method. Step **C** then describes the application of Coco in a bit more detail.

A. Yosys [44] is used to parse the given CPU design into a gate-level netlist. The masked assembly implementation together with the netlist is then given to Verilator [36], which produces a cycle-accurate simulation of the execution in form of an *execution trace*. The execution trace contains concrete values of all CPU control signals during the software execution.

B. Registers or memory locations in the CPU netlist receive annotations (labels) that indicate the location of shares and randomness at the start of the software execution.

C. The CPU netlist, execution trace, initial labeling and desired verification order is given to the verifier, which propagates the labels through the CPU netlist, for as many cycles as the software execution takes. In case Coco detects that a specific gate in the netlist leaks information about a native value (by observing a combination of shares of the same native value), e.g. due to implementation mistakes or architectural side-effects, the exact gate in the netlist and the execution cycle is reported as a leak. For a more detailed description of this verification method we refer to the original publication [20].

2.4   RISC-V SweRV Core

The SweRV processor family [37] was first introduced by Western Digital in 2019 and designed for data-intensive applications like storage controllers and industrial IoT. As of today, there are three different variants of the processor: the EH1, the EH2 and the EL2 [43]. The EH1 features a 32-bit superscalar 9-stage pipeline, while the EH2 basically adds a second thread with a dedicated register file and instruction fetch buffer. The EL2 is a smaller version of the EH1 with only 4 pipeline stages and one execution unit.

In our experiments, we use the SweRV EH1 core[2], which implements the RISC-V RV32IMC instruction set and has nine pipeline stages [42], as sketched in Fig. 1. The first three pipeline stages (Fetch1, Fetch2, Align) are responsible for loading instructions from the instruction memory and storing them into the fetch buffer. In the Decode stage, the instructions are decoded and prepared for execution. The execution happens in pipeline stages 5–7, either in the Load-Store unit (DC1,DC2,DC3), the multiplication unit (M1, M2, M3) or the ALUs (EX1, EX2, EX3). The EH1 core has a dual-issue pipeline, which means that in each clock cycle, the processor can decode two instructions and send them to two different ALUs. In the last two pipeline stages, Commit (EX4) and Writeback (EX5), the final result is stored in the register file. There are several peripherals attached to the core via an AXI4 bus, including the SRAM and instruction and data closely-coupled memories. The core operates in-order, except for loads which might get executed earlier when the value is needed in the pipeline.

According to Western Digital, the SweRV EH1 core can be operated at frequencies of up to 1 GHz [41] and its performance can be compared to an ARM Cortex A15, making it outperform other RISC-V processors like the Berkely BOOM core [38]. This makes EH1 an interesting target to analyze the effects of more complex CPU architectures on masked software implementations. Another reason why we chose SweRV EH1 is Coco's current requirement of CPU designs to be written in Verilog or SystemVerilog.

3   Generic Masked Software on SweRV

In this section we perform an initial analysis of generic (higher-order) masked software implementations on the SweRV EH1 core and show that, even after applying the same hardware modifications as proposed for IBEX in [20], a more complex CPU architecture introduces additional problems that can reduce the protection of masked software by several orders. In Sect. 3.1, we describe a few small hardware modifications that we carry over from Gigerl et al.'s *secured* IBEX to SweRV, that would otherwise lead to identical problems on SweRV. In Sect. 3.2 we describe modifications we made to Coco's verification flow itself so that it can better handle CPU designs that are significantly larger than IBEX. In Sect. 3.3, we generate generic, up to 4th-order masked software implementations of the Keccak S-box using Tornado, verify their execution on the *secured* SweRV using Coco, and conclude that there is little hope that such implementations can achieve even just 1st-order protection. Finally, we present additional empirical evidence of the impact of architectural glitches on masked software via several gate-level timing simulations in Sect. 3.4.

3.1   Modifications of SweRV

Gigerl et al. have analyzed the simple 32-bit RISC-V IBEX core in terms of software masking-related side effects. As a result of their analysis, they pointed out

---

[2] https://github.com/chipsalliance/Cores-SweRV.

three hardware components that can cause unintended combinations of shares during the execution of masked software implementations that are completely invisible from software perspective: the register file, the Arithmetic Logic Unit (ALU), and the Load-Store unit (LSU). Not surprisingly, the SweRV core has similar problems, which is why we briefly discuss how we map these proposed hardware fixes from IBEX to the SweRV core in the following. The resulting *secured* SweRV core will then serve as the base of our further analysis. We expect that the total area overhead of the hardware modifications for the SweRV core is very similar to the IBEX core as analyzed in [20], which was about 2kGe. Since the SweRV core is much larger, this overhead is insignificant.

We use SweRV core commit `499378d0c67ab11965` as the baseline for our modifications. For our analysis, we disable closely-coupled memories for instructions and data, but enable the instruction cache. We do this since (1) the instruction cache is large enough to hold all implementations that we intend to test, (2) we want to analyze the "worst-case" in which the CPU can fetch instructions without delay, thereby achieving the maximal possible amount of instructions (and side-effects) in the pipeline stages. Hence, when running a verification with COCO, we execute each software implementation twice, once to load it into the instruction cache from instruction memory, and once to perform the actual verification.

Register File. Ordinary register file implementations consist of a group of register words (32 × 32bit for RV32IMC) plus addressing logic for reading two words and writing one word within one clock cycle. This addressing logic is usually implemented via multiplexer trees that select source and destination registers depending on the currently decoded instruction. As previously shown for IBEX, these selector signals are usually calculated by combinatorial logic within the same cycle as the actual read/write event. Consequently, within a single clock cycle, differences in signal propagation delays can cause glitches on these selector signals, which in return can cause a read/write port to unreliably switch between multiple register words until the selector signals at all multiplexers are stable[3]. This is problematic for masked software implementations as they hold many shares in the register file that must be kept strictly separated from each other.

The proposed solution for this problem is to replace multiplexer trees with OR trees while introducing a one-hot encoded gating mechanism for each value that is calculated in the previous clock cycle and buffered in a additional register [20]. This mechanism ensures that glitches on a read/write port can only ever happen between the operand of two consecutive instructions. In the SweRV core, we face the same problems and fix these by applying the same register gating concept. The main difference here is the fact that SweRV features four read and three write ports, compared to IBEX's two read and one write port. Gating the read and write ports for SweRV works almost straightforward, except

---

[3] Even if the selector signals were stable, e.g. by calculating and buffering them in the previous clock cycle, there is still no guarantee that this signal arrives at all multiplexers in stable condition in the next clock cycle due to different wire lengths.

for the third write port, which is used for data from the memory, and requires a dedicated solution (cf. Sect. 4.2).

Concurrent ALU Computations. Cores like IBEX and SweRV always concurrently calculate simple operations like AND, XOR, ADD, SHIFT in the execution stage and later only forward the result that is actually needed by the currently executed instruction. This is not a problem for most masking techniques, however there do exist some masking techniques that store individual shares of the a native value in the same register word [6]. This is okay as long as all computations keep the individual bits of a register word separate from another, e.g., by performing only bit-wise operations such as AND and XOR. Operations such as ADD or SHIFT on the other side do combine bits of individual operands and can thus create side-channel leakage, even if the results of these computations are ultimately discarded.

The suggested solution for the IBEX core is to implement a gating mechanism that ensures that only the intended computation is performed. This mechanism can also be easily carried over from IBEX to SweRV.

Data Memory. Storing shares in the data memory leads to similar problems with glitches in the addressing logic as for the register file. In theory, one could again use the same one-hot encoded gating mechanism as discussed before, however, this approach does not scale well for the large address ranges that are required for data memory. Consequently, Gigerl et al. propose a trade-off that consists of using only partially one-hot encoded addresses for data memory which can be implemented with an area overhead that is indeed negligible when compared to the area of SRAM blocks themselves. The downside of this trade-off is that only memory words within certain address ranges (blocks) are properly separated from each other. This is sufficient as long as a block is large enough to hold all the shares that need to be kept isolated from each other during the execution of masked software implementations.

We apply the same LSB one-hot address encoding to SweRV's data memory. Since the SweRV core reads 64 bit from the memory in one cycle instead of 32-bit, we gate memory words on 64-bit granularity.

3.2 Modifications of Coco

In this section we briefly outline modifications that we have made to Coco's verification workflow so that it can better handle large CPU designs. These modifications first and foremost reduce SweRV's circuit size which in return also significantly reduces Coco's verification runtime.

Removal of Unused Logic. As mentioned before, we ensure that instructions can be directly loaded from the instruction cache during Coco's verification. We only ever use the slower instruction memory in a read-only fashion to fill the instruction cache and can, for the pure purpose of Coco's verification, remove any unused logic that would allow writes to data memory, which reduces the circuit size by about 29%.

Control Wire Tagging. The initial version of COCO effectively treats each wire of a CPU netlist equally and does not distinguish control from data wires. In reality, only a small fraction of wires can actually affect the data that is processed by a masked software implementation in such a way that side-channel related problems could occur. Therefore, we adapted COCO such that it is possible to tag wires as explicit *control* signals. During the verification, COCO will then simply ignore these wires instead of applying the laborious process of constructing empty SAT equations for them. Clearly, this tagging needs to be done carefully such that we do not later overlook any architecture side-effects during COCO's verification. Since manual tagging of individual wires is infeasible for entire CPU designs, we instead only do this in a course-grained manner and only in cases where we can easily deduce that there will be no consequences for the processed data of software with constant (data-independent) control flow. More precisely, we tag the instruction memory, instruction cache and signals depending solely on those as control signals automatically.

3.3   Initial Analysis of the SweRV Core

In this section we present our initial analysis of several higher-order masked software implementations on the *secured* SweRV core that already includes all hardware modifications that were proposed in the previous analysis of IBEX [20]. First, we use Tornado to generate generic, up to 4th-order masked C implementations of the Keccak S-box that are formally verified in Tornado's register probing model, meaning that an attacker observing up to d intermediate values (of the algorithm) is not allowed to learn information about native values. We then analyze the execution of these implementations on SweRV using COCO to get an impression of how many more issues can be detected in COCO's time-constrained probing model, in which an attacker, able to observe up to d wires/gates in the CPU netlist throughout one clock cycle each, is not allowed to learn information about native values.

Since COCO can only deal with assembly implementations by default, we create an assembly wrapper around the Tornado-generated C functions and adapt the work flow accordingly. We then analyze these implementations using COCO, while targeting the verification of 1st-order protection. Unfortunately, the verification results show that none of the tested implementations can even reach just 1st-order protection. Upon first inspection of the reported problems, we can see that multiple additional issues still exist within SweRV that can significantly reduce the protection order of our tested software implementations. For example, the forwarding logic in SweRV's 9-stage pipeline is reported by COCO as one of the main culprits for the loss of multiple protection orders in the time-constrained probing model.

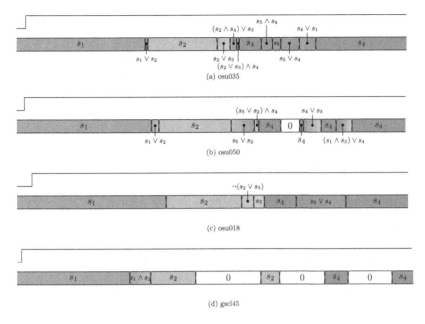

Fig. 2. Value of wire fwd_data at the beginning of a clock cycle for four different standard cell libraries. $s_1 \dots s_5$ denote up to five of the shares that are visible in this experiment due to architectural glitch effects. Since the analyzed time window in each plot is different (due to different propagation delays) we have applied suitable horizontal scalings to improve readability. The time before the rising clock edge is always 10ps.

3.4   Empirical Evaluation

In order to empirically confirm the problems identified by Coco in the SweRV core, we perform and analyze gate-level simulations in this section. More concretely, we perform gate-level timing simulations of the forwarding logic within SweRV's pipeline (see Fig. 3) using multiple cell libraries to better illustrate how problems in the time-constrained probing model can relate to practical problems. Our evaluation reveals that glitches in the forwarding logic can lead to independent occurrences of up to five shares on one wire within one clock cycle, and combined occurrences of up to three shares at the same time. We note that while the exact behaviour of glitches strongly depends on the used standard cell library, all of our tested standard cell libraries report leaks leading to a reduction in the masking order between three and five.

Setup. We use signal traces from the post-synthesis simulations of the SweRV core netlist. The synthesis process maps logic gates in the netlist to suitable cells in the standard cell library, which defines the exact behavior and delay of each cell. We investigate and compare four different open-source cell libraries[4], osu035, osu018, osu050, and gscl45nm. The mapping process is performed by Yosys [44], before running the simulation with Modelsim to obtain an execution trace of our test program.

The same test program is used in all four evaluation scenarios. The test program works with a native value split into 10 shares, which corresponds to a 9th-order masked implementation. First, the test program executes 10 instructions, each operating on exactly one share. This effectively stores each share to its own register in a specific pipeline stage. Second, the test program executes an instruction referring to a previously computed result, which sends the shares in the pipeline registers to the bypass logic, which finally forwards the correct share to the ALU. It should be noted that the program is correctly masked on algorithmic level because exactly one share is processed per instruction.

Results. Figure 2 shows what information an attacker can observe by probing the wire `fwd_data` in SweRV's forwarding logic for the duration of one clock cycle using different cell libraries. Each plot additionally shows the corresponding clock signal and contains marks that indicate at which point in time a specific share (or combination of shares) is visible until the value of the wire has stabilized. Since the analyzed time window in each plot is different (due to different propagation delays) we have applied suitable horizontal scalings to improve readability.

From these plots we can see that an attacker can always observe at least three shares (Fig. 2d), and at most five shares (Fig. 2-c) within one clock cycle when probing the `fwd_data` wire. Sometimes, shares do not appear independently, but also in combination with other shares. For example, in Fig. 2a, the attacker first observes s_1, and then s_1 in combination with s_2. Note that both, the occurrence of multiple shares independently within one cycle, or the occurrence of combinations of shares at any point in time breaks the assumption of independent leakage.

Clearly, this evaluation is not exhaustive. Every technology, every cell library, and every different placement of a design, leads to different timing properties and differences in the exact leakage. Also concrete ASIC or FGPA prototypes are just instances of particular configurations. The exact quantification of the leakage, i.e. determining the number of traces that are needed for exploitation in a particular configuration, is not in the scope of this paper. In fact, it is also

---

[4] https://github.com/RTimothyEdwards/qflow/tree/master/tech.

not clear if it would be possible to find a representative configuration and setup that would allow more than making a statement on leakage for one particular realization in one particular setup. A worst case setup would be a library with delay settings that lead to the observation even all 10 shares in a single clock cycle.

Instead of focusing on more specific instances, the focus of our analysis in this section was on showing that problems identified using COCO actually lead to critical signal transitions in the design. Given the empirical confirmation of critical signal transitions, we therefore use COCO as a reference for the identification of critical design elements in the design of SweRV. With COCO we are able to formulate a generalized statement about the security of a masked software implementation in the time-constrained probing model, which is independent of a specific technology or platform.

4 Analysis of Problems on SweRV

As shown in our previous analysis of generic (higher-order) masked software implementations, the hardware components of more complex CPUs can cause a significant reduction in the protection order. In this section, we discuss these problematic components in the *secured* SweRV core that already has the IBEX-patches applied (cf. Sect. 3.1). We divide these problems into *big* and *small* problems, based on how many shares may be combined, since, as we show later in Sect. 5, one can follow different strategies to deal with them. A component causes a *big* problem when more than two shares can be potentially combined. A *small* problem indicates that a component can combine at most two shares. For each potential leakage source, we discuss the options of making further modifications in hardware or shifting this problem as a constraint to masked software implementations.

4.1 Pipelines and Execution Units

The dual-issue SweRV EH1 core features nine pipeline stages and can process two instructions per clock cycle. Accordingly, the fetch/decode stages (1–4) can handle multiple instructions at the same time, the execution/writeback stages (5–9) exist twice, while the lesser used multiply (5–7) and load/store stages (5–7) exist only once (c.f. Fig. 1). The dual issue design also requires a register file with four read ports and three write ports. Since symmetric cryptographic software implementations are usually implemented with constant (data independent) control flow, which is also the case for all our tested software implementations, only the later execution/writeback stages (5–9) get in touch with actual data and can thus cause potential side-channel related problems.

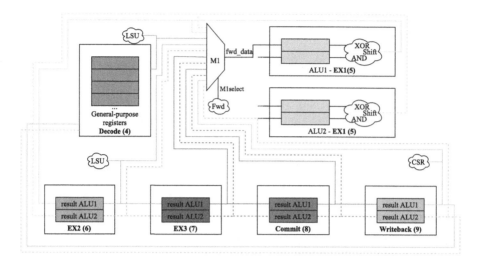

Fig. 3. Pipeline stages 4–9 in SweRV. Shares reside in the register file (■), are then sent to the ALU (■) before being buffered in pipeline registers (■, ■, ■, ■). Forwarding values from the pipeline registers to the ALU is possible in each stage and handled by the multiplexer M1, and the respective select signal M1select.

A typical optimization in pipelined CPU designs is the usage of forwarding logic, also known as bypass-logic, that can redirect the result of an instruction from a later pipeline stage to a previous stage without needing to wait for the result to be written into the register file. Forwarding significantly reduces the occurrence of pipeline stalls in cases where one instruction uses an operand that was only just calculated by the previous instruction. In the context of masking, this architectural design causes problems in two different points.

Figure 3 shows a simplified depiction of SweRV's pipeline stages 4–9. The multiplexer M1 is responsible for selecting which data is used as input for EX1, the first of the execution stages. This data either comes from the register file (GPR), the (LSU), or from any of the later execution stages due to forwarding logic. The select signal of this multiplexer, M1select, is computed in the respective pipeline stage from combinatorial logic and is therefore susceptible for glitches. Consequently, an attacker probing the output of M1, fwd_data, could, in the worst case, observe all of M1's possible inputs within one clock cycle until the select signal stabilizes. This means that if multiple shares of the same native value are in different pipeline registers, a combination of those can be observed at fwd_data in the same clock cycle. On top of that, since two different instructions are executed by SweRV at the same time, fwd_data can also combine data from the other execution unit. Exactly this problem was also seen in our empirical evaluation in Sect. 3.4.

In software, special care is also needed for control transfer instructions like conditional jumps. The instructions beq, bne, blt and bge perform conditional branches on data but are typically not used in (symmetric) cryptographic implementations to avoid potential timing side channels. Still, they can be used together with the unconditional jump instructions jal and jalr to implement loops or function calls. In the context of masking, these instructions can cause problems which are invisible via e.g. the control flow graph of the software. Since the SweRV core decodes two instructions per cycle, the jump is potentially decoded with the instruction which comes code-wise after it. If this instruction operates on shares, and there are still shares of the same native value in the pipeline, a leak occurs, before the CPU realizes a change in the instruction pointer caused by the branch two cycles later. The instructions in these two cycles must be unrelated instructions, which requires in total four unrelated instructions.

Possible Hardware Solutions. One could first consider to solve this problem in hardware by using a trick similar to the one used to prevent unintended glitches in the multiplexer tree of the register file. For example, one could gate the output of each pipeline register with a bit indicating whether the respective value should be forwarded back to the first execution stage (5) or not. This would further require individual gate-bits to be glitch-free, i.e., to be computed in the previous clock cycle and buffered in a register. The problem with pre-computing gate-bits is that those values are typically only available in the same cycle like the forwarding signal. One can overcome this problem by introducing additional pipeline stages in between the execution stage, however, this would significantly impact the overall performance of the core, also in cases where ordinary non-masked software is executed. Since we do not consider such a performance degradation to be a viable option, we next explore if those problems can better be dealt with on software-level.

Possible Software Solutions. For a masked software implementation to not be affected by the side-effects of SweRV's forwarding logic, it must ensure that at no time there are two or more shares corresponding to the same native value in any execution stage of either execution unit. For example, if we consider the execution of two instructions, each of which uses a different share of the same native value, then one would need to ensure that there are $2 \times 6 + 1$ unrelated instructions between them. Hereby, an amount of 6 instructions is needed to clear all execution stages (5–9) of one execution unit, that then has to be doubled since SweRV has two execution units in total. Unrelated instructions are instructions processing data unrelated to any share (for example a nop), or shares from another native value.

While such a software constraint can significantly decrease the performance of masked software implementations, it is a solution that does not impact the performance of ordinary non-masked software. Nevertheless, as we will show later in Sect. 6, it is still possible to implement efficient masked software implementations fulfilling this constraint if the right masking/implementation techniques are used.

Software Constraints for ALU Operations

- *(Pipeline Stages and Execution Units)*. Two instructions using different shares of the same native value must be separated by $6 \times 2 + 1$ unrelated instructions. *Combination of up to 13 shares possible (big problem)*.
- *(Control transfer instructions)*. Control transfer instructions, which are preceded by instructions processing shares, must be followed by 4 unrelated instructions. *Combination of up to 4 shares possible (big problem)*.

4.2   Management Components of Data Memory

The SweRV core manages communication to the data memory via the Load-Store unit (LSU). The LSU is a component between the CPU and the memory to ensure low memory latency by providing buffers and a dedicated pipeline for store operations. Our analysis shows, that the LSU Bus Buffer, responsible for saving values of recent loads or stores, similar to a data cache, turns out to be a major source of leakage which potentially combines multiple shares (*big* problem). Furthermore, the dedicated store pipeline, components in the data memory interface, back-to-back memory accesses and the dedicated register file write port for memory accesses potentially combine two shares (*small* problems). For each of these problems, we discuss possible solutions in hardware and software.

LSU Bus Buffer. Since data memory is connected to the SweRV core over an AXI4 bus, which can potentially introduce a considerable amount of latency, the LSU implements the so-called the LSU Bus Buffer, which works in principle like a small data cache. The LSU Bus Buffer consists of eight elements that are used to temporarily store the values of recent load or store events. Each element additionally stores the target address, an age, and a state, since the LSU uses a state machine to manage the buffer entries. Initially, all element states are set to *Idle*, meaning that they are ready to receive data, and their age is set to 0. While executing the memory access, the state and age are updated accordingly, until the memory access is finished and the element enters the *Idle* state again. However, the element is not removed from the buffer until the buffer is full and the oldest element is overwritten.

In the context of masked software implementations two problems arise in the LSU Bus Buffer. First, it is problematic if one share of a native value in the buffer and is overwritten with its counterpart, which might happen, e.g., when loading two shares from the data memory. This is not only a problem for load operations within short succession but can also occur if these operations are far apart since buffer elements are not cleared once their state goes back to *Idle*. Second, if multiple shares of the same native value are stored in the buffer at the same time but at different locations, one can observe similar side-effects as originally described for ordinary register files (c.f. Sect. 3.1). The second problem could in principle be solved in hardware by applying a similar gating mechanism as for

```
1   # Reset state/age of buffer elements
2   fence
3   # Load share 1 from address 0x20
4   lw x1, 0x20
5   # Reset state/age of buffer elements
6   fence
7   # Dummy overwrite of buffer element 1
8   lw x0, (x0)
9   # Reset state/age of buffer elements
10  fence
11  # Load share 2 from address 0x40
12  lw x2, 0x40
```

Fig. 4. Example of flushing the LSU buffer to clear it from shares

the register file. However, in case of the LSU buffer, such a solution requires an additional register layer for pre-computing stable one-hot encoded signals, which decreases the performance of all software.

Instead, we can solve this problem on software-level by ensuring that the buffer holds at most one share per native value, which additionally prevents the problem of overwriting shares. When doing so, we could ideally target individual elements of the buffer such that a share can easily be overwritten with dummy data whenever needed. However, the LSU buffer is completely invisible from a programmer's perspective, which is also why there is no easy way to manipulate specific elements from software side. The choice of which buffer element is overwritten is determined by the element age, which depends not only on time, but also instruction dependencies, data addresses and the element state. While one could formulate a software constraint that takes all of these factors into consideration, we do not consider this a worthwhile solution due to complexity. Instead, we propose a software solution utilizing RISC-V's fence, that while introducing a 2–5 cycle overhead for each usage, is significantly easier to use in a correct way. In general, a fence can be used to ensure a certain order of memory operations by stalling the CPU pipeline unless previous load/store operations are finished. For the LSU Bus Buffer this means that all buffer elements are set to *Idle* with age 0. However, the stored values are not cleared, which must be done manually by executing load/store instructions dealing with unrelated data. The fence ensures that these loads and stores are inserted consecutively into the buffer, i.e., starting at the first slot and ending at the last slot, finally overwriting all buffer elements. It is recommended to place a second fence after this load/store sequence, before loading or storing further shares. Figure 4 shows a short exemplary code snipped, in which a share is stored in the buffer and later cleared.

Store Pipeline Stages. Before being stored to memory, data values pass through three dedicated pipeline stages in the LSU (c.f. Fig. 1), which are exclusively updated when a store happens. A share used as an operand in a store instruction will therefore hang in the pipeline until it is overwritten by the data of the next store. This is problematic if the data of the next store is a share from the same native value. In order to avoid this problem, it is sufficient to ensure that at least one unrelated store operation is performed between two stores that transfer two shares of the same native value.

Data Memory Interface. SweRV reads 8 bytes from the external data memory module in one cycle, and then selects the parts which are effectively needed according to the load address and load instruction (`lw`, `lh` or `lb`). Glitches in the selection signal can lead to problems if two shares of a native value are stored in the same 8-byte data memory word. A hardware gating mechanism is again not viable since it would increase latency, which is why we suggest to store shares of the same native value not within the same 8-byte word.

Back-to-Back Memory Accesses. SweRV is able to execute memory accesses in a back-to-back fashion, i.e., in two consecutive cycles. Given a data memory layout that utilizes partially one-hot encoded addresses (c.f. Sect. 3.1), an additional problem can occur if shares s_i, s_j are stored in block $b1$ at indices i, j respectively, and one accesses unrelated data at indices i, j in another block $b2$ in two consecutive cycles. The output of $b1$, even though ignored, will switch from s_i to s_j in two consecutive cycles. Preventing this kind of leakage can be done by paying special attention to the block indices during each memory access, or reserving one "neutral" index within blocks that never holds any shares and thus can be used for inserting a dummy load.

Register File Gating for Data from Memory. Register file write ports of the SweRV core need to be gated by a stable gate bit (c.f Sect. 3.1). Computing the gate bit is straightforward for all write ports except for the one dedicated to data loaded from memory, since it depends on a potentially glitching write enable signal derived from the LSU bus buffer entries. First, we gate the write data with the stable register write address only, which means the preliminary gate bit is set for all registers which have loads pending in the LSU bus buffer. In the next cycle, the write enable value is then used to select the final, correct write register. This solution requires the software to ensure that no other pending load in the LSU bus buffer writes to a register, which contains another share from the same native value.

Software Constraints for Memory Operations

- *(LSU Bus Buffer).* Two memory accesses processing two shares must be separated by a `fence`, followed by a load of unrelated data, followed by a `fence`. *Combination of up to* **8** *shares possible (* **big** *problem).*
- *(Store Pipeline Stages).* Two stores storing two shares must be separated by a `fence`, followed by a store of unrelated data, followed by a `fence`. *Combination of up to* **2** *shares possible (* **small** *problem).*

- *(Data Memory Interface)*. Shares must be stored in the same memory block, but not within an 8-byte word.
  Combination of up to 2 shares possible (small problem).
- *(Back-to-back memory accesses)*. Either one 8-byte region per block at index i is not used to store shares and between any two loads, a load to this region is performed, or if a share s_i is stored at index i and s_j is stored at index j in a block, no back-to-back accesses to any addresses mapping to index i and j are performed.
  Combination of up to 2 shares possible (small problem).
- *(Write port 2 of the register file)*. If a share s_i is stored in register x_i and s_j is stored in memory, then there must not exist another load at the same time which writes to register x_i.
  Combination of up to 2 shares possible (small problem).

5 Deriving Generic Software Rules

In this section, we propose generic rules for the design of masked software implementations that are intended to run on more complex CPUs like SweRV. These rules take into account features like pipeline length, the number of execution units, and the size of load/store buffers, and are based on the software constraints defined in Sect. 4. We also discuss the *lazy engineering* approach by Balasch et al. [2] and demonstrate that, while entirely relying on this approach in our setting is not recommended, it can still be a worthwhile trade-off that can eliminate many smaller problems, that would otherwise all need be dealt with in software.

5.1 Generic Rules for Masked Software

A CPU can be described by numerous characteristics, ranging from the architecture width to register file size to cache sizes. Our analysis in Sect. 4 shows that, when considering the implementation of masked software implementations, the following characteristics are especially important:

- The amount of pipeline stages p
- The amount of execution units e
- The size of data buffers.

Pipelines and Execution Units. Forwarding logic, also known as bypass-logic, is a common optimization in pipelined CPUs which we identify to be a big problem for masked software implementations. In the worst case, each pipeline stage forwards its current content to the first stage, where it can be effectively combined with data from all stages due to glitches. Assuming a pipeline length $p = p_i + p_d$, where p_i is the number instruction fetch stages and p_d is the number of decode/execute stages (processing actual data), this problem can be avoided by ensuring that at least $p_d + 1$ unrelated instructions are executed between any two instructions processing the shares of the same native value. We have observed this problem on the SweRV core ($p_i = 3$, $p_d = 6$) but it also affects simpler cores such as the CV32E40P (formerly known as RI5CY) that is roughly comparable to an ARM Cortex M4 [31]. This core features a 4-stage pipeline ($p_i = 1$, $p_d = 3$), and would therefore still require a "padding" with four unrelated instructions.

On top of that, more powerful CPUs like SweRV often feature a super-scalar architecture, including e.g. a dual-issue pipeline, that allows executing two instructions per clock cycle. This is achieved by having e execution units in parallel, all of which have their own fetch/decode/execute stages. In those cases, forwarding is not only possible between stages of the same execution unit but also across them. This additionally increases the required amount of padding to $e \times p_d + 1$.

Data Buffers and Caches. Besides pipeline stages, another big problem for masked software implementations is the existence of data buffers that are invisible from a programmers perspective. Defining generic rules for these components is somewhat harder as their exact behavior can differ quite a lot depending on their concrete implementation. However, typically when considering SweRV's LSU buffer or many other cache designs, these components can cause shares to essentially get stuck at certain locations within the CPU where they then represent an additional source of leakage from this time onward. While such problems can be resolved in hardware, e.g. as shown for the register file (c.f. Sect. 3.1), this is only really a viable option in cases where these hardware modifications do not increase latency, which is also why we need to deal with SweRV's LSU buffer side effects in software. In general one needs to ensure that, whenever a share is transferred over an unmodified buffer, none of the other buffer entries contain shares that correspond to the same native value. How this can be achieved is implementation dependent. In the easier case, a mechanism to clear the buffer contents could be implemented in hardware, which is however not always efficient since it would also affect unmasked data. In the harder case, one has to make use of dummy loads/stores to clear all unwanted values.

Rules. Here we summarize the most important rules for masked software on application-level processors. As we explain in Sect. 5.2, many of the other smaller problems are probably better dealt with using the "lazy engineering" approach.

R1 Two instructions processing shares from the same native value must be separated by $e \times p_d + 1$ unrelated instructions.
R2 Whenever a share is transferring through a buffer, none of the other buffer entries must contain shares that correspond to the same native value.

Naturally, at this point one could also ask how these rules would look like on even more complex CPUs with multi-level caches, out-of-order execution, or speculative memory accesses. For example, the 64-bit out-of-order RISC-V BOOM core would be a potential target for further analysis. However, when considering the analysis of such CPUs we currently see quite a few problems that are not necessarily easy to overcome. First, out-of-order execution will violate our assumption of having software with constant control flow, meaning that verifying a program's execution once might not be indicative of future runs. Second, the effects of, e.g., large cache hierarchies will likely cause problems where corresponding software constraints would become too complex to implement with reasonable effort and overhead. Nevertheless, we argue that physical attacks like power analysis are most relevant only for devices in the range from microprocessors to application processors. An attacker having physical access to a desktop/server could anyway use other methods, like cold boot attacks, to compromise a system more efficiently.

5.2   The Cost of Lazily Engineering

Until now, the verification of masked software implementations is mostly done using rather simple security models like the value-based or register-based leakage model. While such models are certainly useful to detect some problems, many other works also show that processors do emit leakage that is not captured by these models [2,19,21,28,32]. Balasch et al. [2] formalize this behaviour in their order-reduction theorem, which states that on simple CPUs, the security of dth-order masked software in the value-based leakage model reduces to $\lfloor \frac{d}{2} \rfloor$-th order in the transition-based leakage model. In other words, as a rule-of-thumb for a "lazy" software engineer, they suggest to double the security-order of a masked implementation to achieve the desired security-order in a model that more accurately reflects reality.

   While these works focus on rather simple microprocessors, our analysis has shown that on more complex application-level processors, the reduction of security order can be significantly higher. When deriving the expected security reduction of *lazy engineering* on application-level processors, the main point to consider is the component that can potentially combine the most shares. In the case of our modified SweRV this component would be the forwarding logic of the CPU pipeline. According to our generic rules, a processor executing algorithmically correct masked software, might combine up to $e \times p_d + 1$ shares in its pipeline. Consequently, without any further assumptions, the CPU could create all combinations of any choice of $e \times p_d + 1$ shares, which corresponds to an order reduction of $\lfloor \frac{d}{e \times p_d + 1} \rfloor$.

   To give a concrete example, when relying entirely on lazy engineering, one would in theory require at least a 13th-order masked implementation for actual 1st-order security on SweRV in the time-constrained probing model. While we do not expect an easily exploitable order reduction this large when performing physical power measurements of SweRV (c.f. Sect. 3.4), we also want to stress that these architectural side effects should not be underestimated. For example, works like [28] show that, already on simple microprocessors, a generic 2nd-order masked software implementations can very well loose both of its protection orders in practice. If we add to that the fact that SweRV's architecture has the potential to unintentionally combine many more shares at many more locations, one can expect that quite a few masking orders will also be required in case

Table 1. Runtime comparison of masked software implementations on the SweRV core. Plain implementations do not consider software constraints, and thus lose all protection orders. Secure implementations are handcrafted for SweRV, consider all required constraints, and can thus preserve their claimed protection order. NOPs indicate the required amount of nop's or dummy loads/stores. Testcases marked with *reg.* do not perform any memory accesses, i.e., all data is in the register file at the beginning/end of the computation.

Name	Input shares	Fresh randomness	Plain implementations		Secure implementations			
			Cycles	Instructions	Cycles	Instructions	NOPs	Verification runtime
Tornado-generated implementations								
ISW Keccak S-box	10 × 32 bit	5 × 32 bit	163	330	–			
ISW Keccak S-box, 2nd order	15 × 32 bit	15 × 32 bit	1272	810	–			
ISW Keccak S-box, 3rd order	20 × 32 bit	30 × 32 bit	2124	1121	–			
ISW Keccak S-box, 4th order	25 × 32 bit	50 × 32 bit	4406	3309	–			
AND Gate Implementations								
DOM AND *reg.* [23]	4 × 32 bit	32 bit	10	8	33	48	40	1.4 m
ISW AND *reg.* [25]	4 × 32 bit	32 bit	10	8	32	48	40	57 s
TI AND *reg.* [30]	4 × 32 bit	-	14	15	37	54	39	1.1 m
Trichina AND *reg.* [39]	4 × 32 bit	32 bit	9	8	34	46	38	1.28 m
DOM AND *reg.*, 2nd order [23]	6 × 32 bit	3 × 32 bit	20	21	86	148	127	3.2 m
DOM AND *reg.*, 3rd order [23]	8 × 32 bit	6 × 32 bit	33	42	250	295	235	9.6 m
Serial/Parallel implementations								
DOM Keccak S-box *reg.*, serial [24]	10 × 32 bit	5 × 32 bit	83	95	240	418	333	8.4 m
DOM Keccak S-box *reg.*, parallel	10 × 32 bit	5 × 32 bit	36	60	81	144	79	3.7 m
DOM Keccak S-box, serial [24]	10 × 32 bit	5 × 32 bit	174	140	550	624	464	22.38 m
DOM Keccak S-box, 2nd order, serial	15 × 32 bit	15 × 32 bit	283	250	2050	1465	283	1.5 h
Threshold implementations								
TI Keccak S-box, *reg.*	15 × 32 bit	–	66	105	72	126	15	3.5 m
TI Ascon (1 round)	15 × 64 bit	–	721	863	1621	1153	290	1.18 h

of SweRV. Given that masking imposes a runtime overhead that is quadratic in the masking order, such very high-order implementations might however still not be a desirable solution, especially in automotive applications with real-time requirements. As we show later, in such cases, we recommend utilizing lazy engineering only for eliminating small problems while tackling big problems using more effective implementation/masking strategies that we describe in Sect. 6.

6 Evaluation

In this section we demonstrate that, despite the fact that cores like SweRV can cause significant problems for masked software implementations in general, one can still design fine-tuned, secure versions with very small overhead. First, we explain how one can use a *parallel* instead of the usual *serial* coding strategy to significantly reduce the performance impact of software constraints that require a separation between processing shares of the same native value. We then explain how one can utilize Threshold masking schemes, and by extension also the core idea of lazy engineering, to design masked software for SweRV that is secure, efficient, and easy to implement. More concretely, we show that the runtime overhead of e.g. a masked Keccak S-box implementation providing 1st-order security on SweRV, when compared to a corresponding implementation ignoring all software constraints, can be as little as 13%.

Evaluation Setup. All of our tested implementations are hand-written assembly code, except for the Tornado-generated C implementations that are compiled with the compiler flag -O1. For the verification and performance benchmarks we used the cycle accurate simulation of SweRV's netlist within Coco. Coco itself was executed on a 64-bit Linux operating system on an Intel Core i7-7600U CPU with a clock frequency of 2.70 GHz and 16 GB of RAM. We configure SweRV with data memory ranging from 256 byte to 2 KB, adapted as required by the respective testcase. The instruction memory and instruction cache is configured to be 2KB for each test case.

The SweRV configuration using 256 byte of data memory, after applying the optimizations described in Sect. 3.2, results in a circuit with 420 000 gates, of which 108 000 are registers and 97 000 are non-linear gates. A detailed breakdown of these numbers can be found in Appendix A. This makes the hardware design of SweRV orders of magnitudes larger than the IBEX design which was studied in [20], and consisted of only 27 000 gates.

Software Implementation Package. To measure the overhead imposed by different software constraints, we construct a comprehensive set of masked software implementations. First, we take a look at several examples of masked AND gates, which represent the simplest non-linear function (degree 2). More concretely, we analyze 1st-order implementations of the Ishai-Sahai-Wagner (ISW) AND [25], the Trichina AND [39], the Threshold Implementation (TI) AND [30], and up to 3rd-order masked variants of the Domain Oriented Masking (DOM) AND [23].

We then investigate masked S-box implementations which represent the non-linear layer within symmetric cryptographic computations, and use masked AND-gates as basic building blocks. Here, we focus on 1st- and 2nd-order masked implementations of the Keccak S-box, which has a prominent use in the SHA-3 hash function. Furthermore, we provide TI variants of the Keccak S-box [11], as well as one complete round (linear + non-linear layer) of the Ascon cipher [16].

In Table 1 we list *plain* implementations, which are correct in the value-based leakage model, but do not consider any of SweRV's software constraints, and are thus also not secure on this core when verified by Coco in the time-constrained probing model. In contrast, *secure* implementations fulfill all required constraints can thus be verified successfully for their claimed protection order on SweRV. For each implementation, we report SweRV's execution runtime in cycles, as well as the number of executed instructions. Additionally, for secure implementations, we report the number of unrelated instructions (NOPs), that are needed to achieve the required amount of time separation between the processing of shares of the same native value, as stated by the individual software constraints.

6.1   Serial Vs. Parallel Implementations

Many modern symmetric cryptographic primitives have a mathematical description based on simple Boolean functions that can be easily mapped into a corresponding software/hardware implementation. For example, the Keccak S-box (as used in SHA-3) operates on a state consisting of five *lanes*, each of which is combined with two other lanes using a sequence of simple AND, XOR, and NOT operations to compute the corresponding output lane. The most straightforward way of implementing this S-box in software is to take a set of three lanes, processing them, storing the resulting output lane, and repeating these steps until the computation of all five output lanes is finished.

If we now consider a masked implementation, where each input/output lane is represented by two (or more) shares, the same implementation strategy can be used, except for the fact that the sequence of Boolean operations needs to be adapted such that (1) shares of the same native value (lane) are never directly combined, (2) the (native) output is still the same. If we further consider a software constraint that requires a certain amount of unrelated instructions between processing shares of the same native value, one can imagine that additional nop instructions will need to be introduced for this purpose. Alternatively, one could consider a *parallel* implementation, where one interleaves the computation of the five output lanes such that nop's can be replaced with computations on shares of other lanes. We give an example that illustrates the runtime difference between serial and parallel implementations in Appendix B. This runtime difference is also quite visible in Table 1. For example, the parallel DOM Keccak S-box implementation (81 cycles) is three times faster than its serial counterpart (240 cycles).

One potential downside of parallel implementations is the fact that they increase the maximum amount of intermediate values that need to be kept track of. Especially in case of higher-order masked implementations, a processor's register file might not be large enough to hold this increased amount of intermediate values. The resulting register spilling then requires additional load/store operations that also need to comply with software constraints and can thus eliminate any potential gain of this approach. To illustrate the overhead of memory operations, we have included a serial implementation of the Keccak S-box that initially loads all shares from memory and computes the S-box. If we compare the runtime of this implementation (550 cycles) to the serial implementation that performs computations without intial memory operations (240 cycles), we can observe a runtime overhead of about factor two.

6.2   Threshold Implementations

Threshold implementations (TI) [30], is a provable secure masking scheme that splits non-linear functions into multiple incomplete *component functions*. More concretely, in TI, each component function fulfills the non-completeness property, meaning that its computation is independent of at least one of its input shares. One consequence of incompleteness is that TI schemes require computations with at least three shares in order to provide 1st-order security. At the same time, this incompleteness guarantees that any combination of intermediate values during the computation of one component function can combine at most two out of three shares of any native value, therefore leaving 1st-order security intact.

In the context of implementing secure and efficient masked software implementations for SweRV, TI turns out to be beneficial in two ways. First, the "lazy" characteristic of TI allows us to ignore all *small* problems that can combine at most two shares. Second, a TI description of Keccak, for example as shown in [12], also gives a description of three S-box component functions, each of which only contain instructions that operate on an incomplete set of shares. Hence, when implementing TI Keccak in software, one can calculate the linear layer in sequence for each share, and the non-linear layer in sequence for each component function. Then, one only really needs to pay attention to *big* problems when switching the calculation from one component functions to another. This significantly simplifies the software development process as *big* problems can only really occur twice per Sbox computation.

In Table 1, we show a TI implementation of the Keccak S-box (72 cycles) which has almost no overhead compared to the corresponding plain implementation (66 cycles). Compared to a plain parallel DOM implementation, the overhead of a secure TI implementation is still only a about a factor of two, while being at lot easier to implement. With TI Ascon, we also present runtimes of implementations that compute an entire cipher round (linear + non-linear layer). The choice of using Ascon for this comparison is motivated by the fact that Ascon uses a S-box very similar to Keccak, and a linear layer that is significantly easier to implement in assembly than in case of Keccak. From the reported numbers we can see that only 290 additional nops are needed to make this implementation conform to the required software constraints. While the cycle count of the secure implementation is still about twice as large as in the plain case, we want to stress that most of this overhead ($\approx$900 cycles) is due to software constraints for data memory since three shares of Ascon's state do not quite fit into the register file anymore.

7   Conclusion

In this work, we have performed a comprehensive analysis of more complex CPU architectures in the context of masking-related side effects. First, we showed that on cores like SweRV, there exists a significant gap between security in a simple software probing model and practical security for masked software. We underlined this point both via a formal analysis in the hardware probing model and via empirical analysis based on gate-level timing simulations. We then further analyzed the components of SweRV in the hardware probing model, identified new problems, and discuss possible solutions in terms of software constraints. Ultimately, while there exist many hardware components that can reduce the security of masked software due to architectural side-effects, we show that there only exist a few components that could reduce the security of masking schemes by multiple orders. Hence, when considering the implementation of efficient masked software for such CPUs, we recommend to use a combination of TI/lazy engineering to deal with small problems while only addressing the few large problems directly in the software implementation. In that case, the performance overhead of software constraints can be as low as 13% while the resulting implementation can be fully formally verified on our *secured* SweRV in the hardware probing model. If 2nd-order protection is desired, one could again rely on TI/lazy engineering for small problems, here however the additional cost of this approach might not justify this convenience anymore. When aiming for even higher protection orders, one likely needs to consider all software constraints directly in the implementation to keep the runtime overhead manageable.

Acknowledgements. This work was supported by the TU Graz LEAD project "Dependable Internet of Things in Adverse Environments", and the Austrian Research Promotion Agency (FFG) via the K-project DeSSnet, which is funded in the context of COMET – Competence Centers for Excellent Technologies by BMVIT, BMWFW, Styria and Carinthia, and via the FERMION project (grant nr 867542).

Appendix A

See Fig. 5.

```
1   # Shares lane 0: x2, x3              1   # Shares lane 0: x2, x3
2   # Shares lane 1: x4, x5              2   # Shares lane 1: x4, x5
3   # ...                                3   # ...
4   # Randomness: x12, x13, x14, x15, x1 4   # Randomness: x12, x13, x14, x15, x16
5   # Lane 0                             5   # NOT
6   not x17, x2                          6   not x17, x2
7   and x24, x17, x5                     7   not x18, x4
8   xor x24, x24, x12                    8   not x19, x6
9   and x25, x3, x4                      9   not x20, x8
10  xor x25, x25, x12                    10  not x21, x10
11  and x27, x17, x4                     11  #DOM-AND - Instr 1
12  xor x27, x27, x24                    12  and x22, x17, x5
13  and x28, x3, x5                      13  and x23, x18, x7
14  xor x28, x28, x25                    14  and x24, x19, x9
15  xor x27, x27, x10                    15  and x25, x20, x11
16  xor x28, x28, x11                    16  and x26, x21, x3
17  # Lane 1                             17  #DOM-AND - Instr 2
18  not x17, x4                          18  xor x22, x22, x12
19  and x24, x17, x7                     19  xor x23, x23, x13
20  xor x24, x24, x13                    20  xor x24, x24, x14
21  and x25, x5, x6                      21  xor x25, x25, x15
22  ...                                  22  xor x26, x26, x16
23  #Lane 2                              23  #DOM-AND - Instr 3
24  ...                                  24  ...
```

Fig. 5. Comparison between serial and parallel DOM Keccak S-box

Appendix B

See Table 2.

Table 2. Circuit size of the SweRV core (256 byte of data memory, 2 KB of instruction memory/cache) before and after optimization (Removal of unused instruction memory logic)

	Raw circuit	Optimized circuit
Registers	108 129	108 043
Linear Gates	8 828	8 708
Non-linear Gates	133 415	97 222
Not-Gates	3 518	3 248
Multiplexers	335 294	203 107
Total	**589 188**	**420 332**

References

1. Athanasiou, K., Wahl, T., Ding, A.A., Fei, Y.: Automatic detection and repair of transition- based leakage in software binaries. In: Christakis, M., Polikarpova, N., Duggirala, P.S., Schrammel, P. (eds.) NSV/VSTTE -2020. LNCS, vol. 12549, pp. 50–67. Springer, Cham (2020). https://doi.org/10.1007/978-3-030-63618-0_4
2. Balasch, J., Gierlichs, B., Grosso, V., Reparaz, O., Standaert, F.-X.: On the cost of lazy engineering for masked software implementations. In: Joye, M., Moradi, A. (eds.) CARDIS 2014. LNCS, vol. 8968, pp. 64–81. Springer, Cham (2015). https://doi.org/10.1007/978-3-319-16763-3_5
3. Barthe, G., Belaïd, S., Cassiers, G., Fouque, P.-A., Grégoire, B., Standaert, F.-X.: maskVerif: automated verification of higher-order masking in presence of physical defaults. In: Sako, K., Schneider, S., Ryan, P.Y.A. (eds.) ESORICS 2019. LNCS, vol. 11735, pp. 300–318. Springer, Cham (2019). https://doi.org/10.1007/978-3-030-29959-0_15
4. Barthe, G., Belaïd, S., Dupressoir, F., Fouque, P.-A., Grégoire, B., Strub, P.-Y.: Verified proofs of higher-order masking. In: Oswald, E., Fischlin, M. (eds.) EUROCRYPT 2015. LNCS, vol. 9056, pp. 457–485. Springer, Heidelberg (2015). https://doi.org/10.1007/978-3-662-46800-5_18
5. Barthe, G., et al.: Strong non-interference and type-directed higher-order masking. In: Weippl, E.R., Katzenbeisser, S., Kruegel, C., Myers, A.C., Halevi, S. (eds.) Proceedings of the 2016 ACM SIGSAC Conference on Computer and Communications Security, Vienna, Austria, 24–28 October 2016, pp. 116–129. ACM (2016)
6. Barthe, G., Dupressoir, F., Faust, S., Grégoire, B., Standaert, F.-X., Strub, P.-Y.: Parallel implementations of masking schemes and the bounded moment leakage model. In: Coron, J.-S., Nielsen, J.B. (eds.) EUROCRYPT 2017. LNCS, vol. 10210, pp. 535–566. Springer, Cham (2017). https://doi.org/10.1007/978-3-319-56620-7_19
7. Barthe, G., Gourjon, M., Grégoire, B., Orlt, M., Paglialonga, C., Porth, L.: Masking in fine-grained leakage models: construction, implementation and verification. IACR Cryptology ePrint Archive **2020**, 603 (2020)

8. Bayrak, A.G., Regazzoni, F., Novo, D., Ienne, P.: Sleuth: automated verification of software power analysis countermeasures. In: Bertoni, G., Coron, J.-S. (eds.) CHES 2013. LNCS, vol. 8086, pp. 293–310. Springer, Heidelberg (2013). https://doi.org/10.1007/978-3-642-40349-1_17

9. Belaïd, S., Benhamouda, F., Passelègue, A., Prouff, E., Thillard, A., Vergnaud, D.: Private multiplication over finite fields. In: Katz, J., Shacham, H. (eds.) CRYPTO 2017. LNCS, vol. 10403, pp. 397–426. Springer, Cham (2017). https://doi.org/10.1007/978-3-319-63697-9_14

10. Belaïd, S., Dagand, P.É., Mercadier, D., Rivain, M., Wintersdorff, R.: Tornado: automatic generation of probing-secure masked bitsliced implementations. In: Canteaut, A., Ishai, Y. (eds.) EUROCRYPT 2020. LNCS, vol. 12107, pp. 311–341. Springer, Cham (2020). https://doi.org/10.1007/978-3-030-45727-3_11

11. Bertoni, G., Daemen, J., Peeters, M., Assche, G.V.: The keccak reference (2011)

12. Bilgin, B., Daemen, J., Nikov, V., Nikova, S., Rijmen, V., Van Assche, G.: Efficient and First-Order DPA resistant implementations of KECCAK. In: Francillon, A., Rohatgi, P. (eds.) CARDIS 2013. LNCS, vol. 8419, pp. 187–199. Springer, Cham (2014). https://doi.org/10.1007/978-3-319-08302-5_13

13. Bloem, R., Gross, H., Iusupov, R., Könighofer, B., Mangard, S., Winter, J.: Formal verification of masked hardware implementations in the presence of glitches. In: Nielsen, J.B., Rijmen, V. (eds.) EUROCRYPT 2018. LNCS, vol. 10821, pp. 321–353. Springer, Cham (2018). https://doi.org/10.1007/978-3-319-78375-8_11

14. De Cnudde, T., Reparaz, O., Bilgin, B., Nikova, S., Nikov, V., Rijmen, V.: Masking AES with $d+1$ shares in hardware. In: Gierlichs, B., Poschmann, A.Y. (eds.) CHES 2016. LNCS, vol. 9813, pp. 194–212. Springer, Heidelberg (2016). https://doi.org/10.1007/978-3-662-53140-2_10

15. Coron, J.-S., Giraud, C., Prouff, E., Renner, S., Rivain, M., Vadnala, P.K.: Conversion of security proofs from one leakage model to another: a new issue. In: Schindler, W., Huss, S.A. (eds.) COSADE 2012. LNCS, vol. 7275, pp. 69–81. Springer, Heidelberg (2012). https://doi.org/10.1007/978-3-642-29912-4_6

16. Dobraunig, C., Eichlseder, M., Mendel, F., Schläffer, M.: Ascon v1.2. submission to the ceasar competition (2016). https://ascon.iaik.tugraz.at/files/asconv12.pd. Accessed 4 Feb 2021

17. Eldib, H., Wang, C., Schaumont, P.: Formal verification of software countermeasures against side-channel attacks. ACM Trans. Softw. Eng. Methodol. **24**(2), 11:1–11:24 (2014)

18. Faust, S., Rabin, T., Reyzin, L., Tromer, E., Vaikuntanathan, V.: Protecting circuits from leakage: the computationally-bounded and noisy cases. In: Gilbert, H. (ed.) EUROCRYPT 2010. LNCS, vol. 6110, pp. 135–156. Springer, Heidelberg (2010). https://doi.org/10.1007/978-3-642-13190-5_7

19. Gao, S., Marshall, B., Page, D., Oswald, E.: Share-slicing: friend or foe? IACR Trans. Cryptogr. Hardw. Embed. Syst. **2020**(1), 152–174 (2020)

20. Gigerl, B., Hadzic, V., Primas, R., Mangard, S., Bloem, R.: Coco: co-design and co-verification of masked software implementations on CPUs. In: 30th USENIX Security Symposium, USENIX Security 2021 (2021)

21. de Groot, W., Papagiannopoulos, K., de La Piedra, A., Schneider, E., Batina, L.: Bitsliced Masking and ARM: friends or foes? In: Bogdanov, A. (ed.) LightSec 2016. LNCS, vol. 10098, pp. 91–109. Springer, Cham (2017). https://doi.org/10.1007/978-3-319-55714-4_7

22. Gross, H., Mangard, S.: Reconciling $d + 1$ masking in hardware and software. In: Fischer, W., Homma, N. (eds.) CHES 2017. LNCS, vol. 10529, pp. 115–136. Springer, Cham (2017). https://doi.org/10.1007/978-3-319-66787-4_6

23. Groß, H., Mangard, S., Korak, T.: Domain-oriented masking: compact masked hardware implementations with arbitrary protection order. In: Proceedings of the ACM Workshop on Theory of Implementation Security, TIS@CCS 2016 Vienna, Austria, October 2016, p. 3. ACM (2016)
24. Groß, H., Schaffenrath, D., Mangard, S.: Higher-order side-channel protected implementations of KECCAK. In: Euromicro Conference on Digital System Design, DSD 2017, Vienna, Austria, 30 August–1 September 2017, pp. 205–212. IEEE Computer Society (2017)
25. Ishai, Y., Sahai, A., Wagner, D.: Private circuits: securing hardware against probing attacks. In: Boneh, D. (ed.) CRYPTO 2003. LNCS, vol. 2729, pp. 463–481. Springer, Heidelberg (2003). https://doi.org/10.1007/978-3-540-45146-4_27
26. Knichel, D., Sasdrich, P., Moradi, A.: SILVER – statistical independence and leakage verification. In: Moriai, S., Wang, H. (eds.) ASIACRYPT 2020. LNCS, vol. 12491, pp. 787–816. Springer, Cham (2020). https://doi.org/10.1007/978-3-030-64837-4_26
27. Kocher, P., Jaffe, J., Jun, B.: Differential power analysis. In: Wiener, M. (ed.) CRYPTO 1999. LNCS, vol. 1666, pp. 388 397. Springer, Heidelberg (1999). https://doi.org/10.1007/3-540-48405-1_25
28. Meyer, L.D., Mulder, E.D., Tunstall, M.: On the effect of the (micro)architecture on the development of side-channel resistant software. IACR Cryptol. ePrint Arch. **2020**, 1297 (2020)
29. Moss, A., Oswald, E., Page, D., Tunstall, M.: Compiler assisted masking. In: Prouff, E., Schaumont, P. (eds.) CHES 2012. LNCS, vol. 7428, pp. 58–75. Springer, Heidelberg (2012). https://doi.org/10.1007/978-3-642-33027-8_4
30. Nikova, S., Rechberger, C., Rijmen, V.: Threshold implementations against side-channel attacks and glitches. In: Ning, P., Qing, S., Li, N. (eds.) ICICS 2006. LNCS, vol. 4307, pp. 529–545. Springer, Heidelberg (2006). https://doi.org/10.1007/11935308_38
31. OpenHW Group: Openhw group cv32e40p user manual: pipeline details. https://cv32e40p.readthedocs.io/en/latest/pipeline/. Accessed 26 Jan 2021
32. Papagiannopoulos, K., Veshchikov, N.: Mind the gap: towards secure 1st-order masking in software. In: Guilley, S. (ed.) COSADE 2017. LNCS, vol. 10348, pp. 282–297. Springer, Cham (2017). https://doi.org/10.1007/978-3-319-64647-3_17
33. Renauld, M., Standaert, F.-X., Veyrat-Charvillon, N., Kamel, D., Flandre, D.: A formal study of power variability issues and side-channel attacks for nanoscale devices. In: Paterson, K.G. (ed.) EUROCRYPT 2011. LNCS, vol. 6632, pp. 109–128. Springer, Heidelberg (2011). https://doi.org/10.1007/978-3-642-20465-4_8
34. Reparaz, O., Bilgin, B., Nikova, S., Gierlichs, B., Verbauwhede, I.: Consolidating masking schemes. In: Gennaro, R., Robshaw, M. (eds.) CRYPTO 2015. LNCS, vol. 9215, pp. 764–783. Springer, Heidelberg (2015). https://doi.org/10.1007/978-3-662-47989-6_37
35. Rivain, M., Prouff, E.: Provably secure higher-order masking of AES. In: Mangard, S., Standaert, F.-X. (eds.) CHES 2010. LNCS, vol. 6225, pp. 413–427. Springer, Heidelberg (2010). https://doi.org/10.1007/978-3-642-15031-9_28
36. Snyder, W.: Verilator. https://www.veripool.org/wiki/verilator. Accessed 2 Feb 2021
37. Marena, T.: Western digital: the journey of risc-v implementation (2019). https://documents.westerndigital.com/content/dam/doc-library/en_us/assets/public/western-digital/collateral/white-paper/article-journey-of-RISC-V-implementation.pdf. Accessed 16 Jan 2021

38. The Regents of the University of California: Riscv-boom: the load/store unit (LSU). https://docs.boom-core.org/en/latest/sections/load-store-unit.html. Accessed 27 Jan 2021

39. Trichina, E.: Combinational logic design for AES subbyte transformation on masked data. IACR Cryptol. ePrint Arch. **2003**, 236 (2003)

40. Wang, J., Sung, C., Wang, C.: Mitigating power side channels during compilation. In: Dumas, M., Pfahl, D., Apel, S., Russo, A. (eds.) Proceedings of the ACM Joint Meeting on European Software Engineering Conference and Symposium on the Foundations of Software Engineering, ESEC/SIGSOFT FSE 2019, Tallinn, Estonia, 26–30 August 2019, pp. 590–601. ACM (2019)

41. Western Digital: Risc-v: high performance embedded swerv core microarchitecture, performance and chips alliance. https://riscv.org/wp-content/uploads/2019/04/RISC-V_SweRV_Roadshow-.pdf. Accessed 16 Jan 2021

42. Western Digital: Risc-v swerv eh1 programer's reference manual. https://github.com/chipsalliance/Cores-SweRV/blob/master/docs/RISC-V_SweRV_EH1_PRM.pdf. Accessed 16 Jan 2021

43. Western Digital: Risc-v and open source hardware address new compute requirements (2019). https://documents.westerndigital.com/content/dam/doc-library/en_us/assets/public/western-digital/collateral/tech-brief/tech-brief-western-digital-risc-v.pdf. Accessed 16 Jan 2021

44. Wolf, C.: Yosys open synthesis suite. http://www.clifford.at/yosys/. Accessed 2 Feb 2021

45. Zhang, J., Gao, P., Song, F., Wang, C.: SCInfer: refinement-based verification of software countermeasures against side-channel attacks. In: Chockler, H., Weissenbacher, G. (eds.) CAV 2018. LNCS, vol. 10982, pp. 157–177. Springer, Cham (2018). https://doi.org/10.1007/978-3-319-96142-2_12

Fault-Injection Attacks Against NIST's Post-Quantum Cryptography Round 3 KEM Candidates

Keita Xagawa[3]($\boxtimes$), Akira Ito[1]($\boxtimes$), Rei Ueno[1,2]($\boxtimes$), Junko Takahashi[3]($\boxtimes$), and Naofumi Homma[1,4]($\boxtimes$)

[1] Tohoku University, 2-1-1 Katahira, Aoba-ku, Sendai-shi 980-8577, Japan
{ito,homma}@riec.tohoku.ac.jp, rei.ueno.a8@tohoku.ac.jp
[2] PRESTO, Japan Science and Technology Agency, 4-1-8 Honcho, Kawaguchi, Saitama 332-0012, Japan
[3] NTT Social Informatics Laboratories, 3-9-11 Midori-cho, Musashino-shi, Tokyo 180-8585, Japan
{keita.xagawa.zv,junko.takahashi.fc}@hco.ntt.co.jp
[4] CREST, Japan Science and Technology Agency, 4-1-8 Honcho, Kawaguchi, Saitama 332-0012, Japan

Abstract. We investigate *all* NIST PQC Round 3 KEM candidates from the viewpoint of fault-injection attacks: Classic McEliece, Kyber, NTRU, Saber, BIKE, FrodoKEM, HQC, NTRU Prime, and SIKE. All KEM schemes use variants of the Fujisaki-Okamoto transformation, so the equality test with re-encryption in decapsulation is critical.

We survey effective key-recovery attacks when we can skip the equality test. We found the existing key-recovery attacks against Kyber, NTRU, Saber, FrodoKEM, HQC, one of two KEM schemes in NTRU Prime, and SIKE. We propose a new key-recovery attack against the other KEM scheme in NTRU Prime. We also report an attack against BIKE that leads to leakage of information of secret keys.

The open-source pqm4 library contains all KEM schemes except Classic McEliece and HQC. We show that giving a single instruction-skipping fault in the decapsulation processes leads to skipping the equality test *virtually* for Kyber, NTRU, Saber, BIKE, and SIKE. We also report the experimental attacks against them. We also report the implementation of NTRU Prime allows chosen-ciphertext attacks freely and the timing side-channel of FrodoKEM reported in Guo, Johansson, and Nilsson (CRYPTO 2020) remains, while there are no such bugs in their NIST PQC Round 3 submissions.

Keywords: Post-quantum cryptography · NIST PQC standardization · KEM · The Fujisaki-Okamoto transformation · Fault-injection attacks

© International Association for Cryptologic Research 2021
M. Tibouchi and H. Wang (Eds.): ASIACRYPT 2021, LNCS 13091, pp. 33–61, 2021.
https://doi.org/10.1007/978-3-030-92075-3_2

1   Introduction

1.1   Background

Key encapsulation mechanism: Public-key encryption (PKE in short) allows us to send a message secretly without a pre-shared secret key [30,67,73], which is a fundamental task of cryptography. PKE consists of three algorithms; a key-generation algorithm that generates a public key and a secret key, an encryption algorithm that takes a message and a public key as input and outputs a cipher-text, and a decryption algorithm that takes a secret key and a ciphertext as input and outputs a message.

Key encapsulation mechanism (KEM in short) is also fundamental crypto-graphic primitive [1,26,72], which can be considered as a variant of public-key encryption (PKE). KEM's encryption algorithm, which we call the encapsulation algorithm, takes a public key as input and outputs a ciphertext and *a key* (or an ephemeral key). KEM's decryption algorithm, which we call the decapsulation algorithm, takes a secret key and a ciphertext as input and outputs a key instead of a message. KEM's sender and receiver share a key instead of a message in the case of PKE. KEM is a versatile primitive and has a lot of applications, e.g., key exchange, hybrid encryption, secure authentication, and authenticated key exchange.

The most standard security notion of KEM is indistinguishability against chosen-ciphertext attacks (IND-CCA security) [26,63]. Since it is hard to con-struct efficient IND-CCA-secure KEMs directly, cryptographers often use the transformations from weakly-secure PKE/KEM into IND-CCA-secure KEM. The Fujisaki-Okamoto (FO) transformation [29,35,36] is one of the transfor-mations often used in the design of IND-CCA-secure PKE/KEM in the random oracle model (ROM). Roughly speaking, the FO transformation transforms an underlying PKE scheme into KEM as follows: Let G and H be two random oracles. A key-generation algorithm of KEM is that of PKE. An encapsulation algorithm on input a public key pk chooses a message m randomly, encrypts it into $ct = \mathsf{Enc}(pk, m; \mathsf{G}(m))$, where Enc is an encryption algorithm of PKE and the randomness of encryption is computed as $\mathsf{G}(m)$, and outputs a ciphertext ct and a key $K = \mathsf{H}(m)$. A decapsulation algorithm on input sk and ct decrypts ct into $m' = \mathsf{Dec}(sk, ct)$, where Dec is a decryption algorithm of PKE, re-encrypts m' into $ct' = \mathsf{Enc}(pk, m'; \mathsf{G}(m'))$, and outputs a key $K = \mathsf{H}(m')$ if $ct = ct'$ and a rejection symbol otherwise.

Post-quantum cryptography: Scalable quantum computers will threaten classi-cal public-key cryptography since Shor's algorithm on a quantum machine solves factorization and discrete logarithms efficiently [71]. The recent progress in devel-oping quantum machines motivates us to replace classical public-key cryptog-raphy with post-quantum cryptography (PQC). Hence, in the past decade, the security proofs of the FO transformation and its variants have been extended to those in the quantum random oracle model (QROM) [19] to show the security against *quantum* polynomial-time adversary. See e.g., [17,42,47,48,52,69,76].

Moreover, in 2016, NIST PQC standardization called for proposals on PKE/KEM and signatures as the basic primitives[1]. In 2020, NIST selected four finalists and five alternate candidates for KEM in Round 3 [6]. All use the FO-like transformations to construct IND-CCA-secure KEMs in the (Q)ROM.

Fault-injection attacks: In the real world, the decapsulation algorithm is implemented physically. Hence, investigations into side-channel attacks (SCA) [50,51] and fault-injection attacks (FIA) [16,20] against proposed KEMs are strongly promoted by NIST. The attacks' targets are recovery of an ephemeral key of a given ciphertext or a secret key of a given public key. We call the former and the latter ephemeral-key-recovery attack and key-recovery attack, respectively.

We focus on FIA against KEM and review the scenario of it. Suppose that an adversary can inject faults into a decapsulation machine that contains a secret key. In this situation, it is natural to think the adversary has the machine itself (e.g., decapsulation machines in card, sensor, robot, and TV box) and uses it freely because the adversary can physically access the machine. Hence, the adversary can decrypt any ciphertexts and recover the corresponding ephemeral key of the target ciphertext. Thus, if we consider FIA, ephemeral-key-recovery attacks are not so important.

On the other hand, recovery of secret key via FIA is non-trivial and interesting, because the key-recovery attack logically breaks a tamper-resilient memory by extracting the secret from it. In addition, once one obtains a secret key from a decapsulation machine, one can copy the machine. Thus, we examine how FIA leads to a key-recovery attack.

There are a lot of techniques to make decapsulation faulty; shooting a LASER to set/reset a bit of SRAM [74], injecting a clock or power glitch [11,33,68], using electromagnetic (EM) pulses [41]. (Un)fortunately, an injection of fault often fails to obtain an expected result, say, a skip of an instruction of the assembly code. Thus, the less number of faults in a single run of decapsulation an attack requires, the better. Especially, we are interested in *single-fault* key-recovery attacks.

Skipping-the-equality-test attack: In the FO-like transformations, the decapsulation algorithm given a ciphertext ct first decrypts the ciphertext into m', re-encrypts it into ct', and returns $K = H(m', \mathsf{aux})$ if $ct = ct'$ and pseudorandom value $K = H(s, \mathsf{aux})$ or the rejection symbol $\perp$ otherwise, where H is a hash function modeled by a random oracle, aux depends on pk and ct, and s is a secret value.

By injecting a fault carefully, we could force the decapsulation machine to *skip* the equality test $ct = ct'$ and return $K = H(m', \mathsf{aux})$ always, where $m' = \mathsf{Dec}(sk, ct)$. This enables us to implement a plaintext-checking oracle on input guess m_{guess} and ciphertext ct by checking if $K = H(m_{\mathsf{guess}}, \mathsf{aux})$ or not and a key-mismatch oracle on input guess K_{guess} and ciphertext ct by checking if

---

[1] https://csrc.nist.gov/Projects/post-quantum-cryptography/post-quantum-cryptography-standardization/Call-for-Proposals.

$K = K_{\text{guess}}$ or not. Such oracles would enable an adversary to mount a key-recovery attack against KEM.

Fault-injection attack against pre-quantum KEMs: Factoring/RSA-based PKE/KEM is vulnerable against FIA. For example, safe-error attacks [79,80] are effective to guess a bit of secret key. They are also applicable to Discrete-logarithm (DL)-based PKE/KEM. DL-based PKE/KEM has several attack surfaces vulnerable to FIA. See, for example, invalid point/curve attacks [8,15,18, 75].

We note that the existing key-recovery FIAs do not target the equality test of the FO transformation. It is not known whether this plaintext-checking/key-mismatch oracle (or even decryption oracle) enables us to recover the secret key of the underlying PKE, say, the textbook RSA. (See e.g., [21] and [3].) Thus, the key-recovery FIA against pre-quantum KEMs that skips the equality test are not so explored.

Fault-injection attack against post-quantum KEMs: This situation is changed in post-quantum KEMs. Unfortunately, underlying PKEs in the post-quantum PKE/KEMs are often vulnerable to key-recovery chosen-ciphertext attacks. For example, Hall, Goldberg, and Schneier [40] pointed out message-recovery and key-recovery chosen-ciphertext attacks against the McEliece PKE [55,58] and the Ajtai-Dwork PKE [5], respectively. Fluhrer pointed out that a simple key-exchange scheme based on ring learning with errors (RLWE) is vulnerable to the key-mismatch attack if a user fixes its secret [34]. Galbraith, Petit, Shani, and Ti [37] gave a key-recovery key-mismatch attack against SIDH [28,46] with fixed secret. Therefore, the equality test is an important target of FIA.

Although Pessl and Prokop [60] pointed out that the equality test is 'an obvious faulting target,' we do not know how easily we can mount a skipping-the-equality-test attack by injecting a *single fault* against the implementations in the wild and how effective the skipping-the-equality-test attack is against the NIST PQC Round 3 KEM candidates.

1.2 Our Contribution

We systematically study how effective fault-injection attacks that lead to the skip of the equality test of FO-like transformations are against *all* KEMs in the NIST PQC Round 3 finalists and the alternates: Classic McEliece [7], Kyber [70], NTRU (ntruhps and ntruhrss) [22], Saber [27], BIKE [9], FrodoKEM [57], HQC [4], NTRU Prime (sntrupr and ntrulpr) [14], and SIKE [45]. We summarize our findings in Table 1.

Theoretical analysis: We study whether the underlying PKEs of KEMs are resilient to key-recovery plaintext-checking attacks (KR-PCA) or not, since skipping the equality test enables an adversary to obtain $K = \mathsf{H}(\mathsf{Dec}(sk, ct), \mathsf{aux})$ instead of pseudorandom string or $\perp$ and to implement a plaintext-checking oracle easily.

Table 1. Summary of our findings on NIST PQC Round 3 KEM Candidates (finalists and alternates) and their implementations in pqm4: PCA implies plaintext-checking attack.

Name	Effect of PCA	Attack Surface in pqm4	Effect of FIA in pqm4
Classic McEliece [7]	Unknown	N/A	N/A
Kyber [70]	Key recovery	Skip	Key recovery
NTRU – ntruhps [22]	Key recovery	Skip	Key recovery
NTRU – ntruhrss [22]	Key recovery	Skip	Key recovery
Saber [27]	Key recovery	Skip	Key recovery
BIKE [9]	Key leakage (New)	Skip	Key leakage
FrodoKEM [57]	Key recovery	Timing bug	Key recovery
HQC [4]	Key recovery	N/A	N/A
NTRU Prime – sntrupr [14]	Key recovery	CCA bug	Key recovery
NTRU Prime – ntrulpr [14]	Key recovery (New)	CCA bug	Key recovery
SIKE [45]	Key recovery	Skip	Key recovery

We found that almost all PKEs except the underlying PKE of Classic McEliece leaks information of the decryption key in the presence of plaintext-checking oracle *in vitro*. Our findings are summarized as follows (see also Table 2):

Kyber, NTRU, Saber, FrodoKEM, HQC, sntrupr of NTRU Prime, and SIKE: We survey the literature and found that there are KR-PCAs against the underlying PKEs of Kyber, ntruhps and ntruhrss of NTRU, Saber, FrodoKEM, HQC, sntrupr of NTRU Prime, and SIKE.

ntrulpr of NTRU Prime: We propose a KR-PCA against the underlying PKE of NTRU LPRime (ntrulpr of NTRU Prime) by mimicking the KR-PCAs against the underlying PKEs of Saber and Kyber [44]. See Sect. 4.

BIKE: The underlying PKE of BIKE in round 3 also leaks the secret key's information from the plaintext-checking oracle as QC-MDPC [56] is vulnerable to the KR-PCA proposed by Guo, Johansson, and Stankvoski [39]. However, the change of a decoder algorithm in round 3 makes key-recovery attacks difficult. See the full version.

Classic McEliece: There are no known KR-PCAs against the underlying PKE of Classic McEliece if the decoder in a decryption algorithm rejects invalid plaintexts[2] (We note that the specifications seem to allow the use of any decoder that decodes binary Goppa codes.)

Trade-off: Skipping the equality test enables the adversary to obtain $K = \mathsf{KDF}(m, \mathsf{aux})$ with $m = \mathsf{Dec}(sk, ct)$ rather than the plaintext-checking oracle. Thus, the adversary can check if $m = m_{\mathsf{guess}}$ by checking $K = \mathsf{KDF}(m_{\mathsf{guess}}, \mathsf{aux})$ from *a single faulty experiment*. If the number of candidates of m is small, then

---

[2] The plaintext space is a set of n-dimensional vectors whose Hamming weight is t.

Table 2. Theoretical plaintext-checking attacks and key-mismatch attacks against the underlying PKEs of NIST PQC Round 3 KEM Candidates.

Name	Results
Classic McEliece [7]	Unknown
Kyber [70]	Key recovery [44,61,62,66]
NTRU – ntruhps [22]	Key recovery [31]
NTRU – ntruhrss [22]	Key recovery [81]
Saber [27]	Key recovery [44,62]
BIKE [9]	Key leakage (New, adapted from [39])
FrodoKEM [57]	Key recovery [10,62,66,77]
HQC [4]	Key recovery [44]
NTRU Prime – sntrupr [14]	Key recovery [64]
NTRU Prime – ntrulpr [14]	Key recovery (New, adapted from [10,44,61,62,66,77])
SIKE [45]	Key recovery [37]

we can determine the value of m by an exhaustive search. By using this property, there are trade-offs between the computational cost and the number of faulty experiments in the cases of Kyber, Saber, FrodoKEM, and ntrulpr of NTRU Prime. See the details in Sect. 4 for the case of ntrulpr of NTRU Prime.

Investigation of KEMs in pqm4: We investigate implementation of KEMs in pqm4 [49], which include Kyber, NTRU (ntruhps and ntruhrss), Saber, BIKE, FrodoKEM, NTRUPrime (sntrupr and ntrulpr), and SIKE[3]

NTRU Prime: In the pqm4 implementation of NTRU Prime (sntrupr and ntrulpr), a decapsulation program contains a fatal bug that forces the result of the equality test to be true.[4] Thus, we can mount a chosen-ciphertext attack against them freely. See Subsect. 5.1.

FrodoKEM: In 2020, Guo et al. [38] pointed out that the implementation of FrodoKEM (and HQC) contains a leaky equality test that leaks information of the secret key from the timing side channel and succeeded in mounting a key-recovery attack using the timing information. Although FrodoKEM in Round 3 repaired this leaky equality test, the bug still remains in the pqm4 implementation.[5] See Subsect. 5.2.

Kyber, NTRU, and Saber: They shared a same structure to compute a key. Roughly speaking, decapsulation programs use a flag for the equality test and overwrite the decrypted result m' by a secret seed s if the flag is set. This overwriting is done by a single function call of 'cmov' (conditional-move). (Un)fortunately, we can skip this function call by a single fault and mount FIA. See Subsect. 5.3

---

[3] We use 2021 Jun. 5 version. https://github.com/mupq/pqm4/commit/8d3384d879 b10619c8c36947e4be6ab13ec6d268.

[4] We report it in https://github.com/mupq/pqm4/issues/195.

[5] pqm4 noticed this issue. See https://github.com/mupq/pqm4/issues/161.

BIKE: The decapsulation program of BIKE in pqm4 computes mask, which is -1 or 0 depending on the re-encryption check, and overwrites the decryption result m' by a secret seed s or keep it as "$m' \leftarrow (m' \wedge \neg\mathsf{mask}) \vee (s \wedge \mathsf{mask})$".[6] (Un)fortunately, we identify a single operation such that if we skip the operation, then mask is set to 0 always. Thus, we can skip the overwrite procedure virtually by a single fault. See Subsect. 5.4.

SIKE: The implementation of SIKE in pqm4 simply uses an 'if' statement to overwrite the decrypted result m' by a secret seed s. In the assembly code, this if-then-overwrite is implemented as 'compare' and 'conditional jump'. (Un)fortunately, we can skip this 'conditional jump' by a single fault. See Subsect. 5.5.

Experimental results: On the basis of our findings, we conduct the experimental skip attacks on Kyber, NTRU, Saber, BIKE, and SIKE. The target is STM32F415 whose core is ARM Cortex-M4, which is a de-facto standard platform as NIST suggested. We run 100 fault injections to each scheme and succeeded in injecting faults correctly with 15–50%. See Sect. 6.

1.3 Related Works

For PQC candidates and their implementation, we recommend the reader to read an exhaustive survey written by Howe, Prest, and Apon [43]. Ravi and Roy gave a lecture on SCAs and FIAs against lattice-based PQC candidates [65]. Costello wrote a survey of isogeny-based cryptography [25]. For SCA, FIA, and key-recovery plaintext-checking/key-mismatch attacks against NIST PQC KEM Candidates, see our survey in the full version.

1.4 Organization

Section 2 reviews basic notions and notations. Section 3 reviews the variants of the FO transformation. Section 4 gives a key-recovery attack against ntrulpr of NTRU Prime using plaintext-checking oracle and discusses a trade off between efficiency and the number of queries if we consider the fault-injection attack. Section 5 describes the equality test of KEMs and how we can mount skipping attack. Section 6 reports our experimental results. In the full version, we will review the variants of the FO transformation, the KEM schemes, and KR-PCAs against them. In addition, we will report our key-leakage PCAs against BIKE.

2 Preliminaries

2.1 Notation

A security parameter is denoted by λ. We use the standard O-notations. DPT, PPT, and QPT stand for deterministic polynomial-time, probabilistic polynomial-time, and quantum polynomial-time, respectively. A function $f(\lambda)$ is said to be *negligible* if $f(\lambda) = \lambda^{-\omega(1)}$. We denote a set of negligible functions

---

[6] If mask $= 0$, then we have $m' \leftarrow m'$. Otherwise, we have $m' \leftarrow s$.

by $\mathsf{negl}(\lambda)$. For a statement P (e.g., $r \in [0,1]$), we define $\mathsf{boole}(P) = 1$ if P is satisfied and 0 otherwise.

For a distribution χ, we often write "$x \leftarrow \chi$," which indicates that we take a sample x in accordance with χ. For a finite set S, $U(S)$ denotes the uniform distribution over S. We often write "$x \leftarrow S$" instead of "$x \leftarrow U(S)$." If inp is a string, then "out $\leftarrow$ A(inp)" denotes the output of algorithm A when run on input inp. If A is deterministic, then out is a fixed value and we write "out := A(inp)." We use the notation "out := A(inp; r)" to make the randomness r explicit.

For an odd positive integer q, we define $r' := r \bmod^{\pm} q$ to be the unique element $r' \in [-(q-1)/2, (q-1)/2]$ with $r' \equiv r \pmod{q}$.

2.2   Public-Key Encryption (PKE)

The model for PKE schemes is summarized as follows:

Definition 2.1. *A PKE scheme* PKE *consists of the following triple of polynomial-time algorithms* (Gen, Enc, Dec):

- Gen($1^{\lambda}; r_g$) $\to$ (pk, sk): *a key-generation algorithm that takes as input 1^{λ}, where λ is the security parameter, and randomness $r_g \in \mathcal{R}_{\mathsf{Gen}}$ and outputs a pair of keys (pk, sk). pk and sk are called the encryption key and decryption key, respectively.*
- Enc($pk, m; r_e$) $\to$ ct: *an encryption algorithm that takes as input encryption key pk, message $m \in \mathcal{M}$, and randomness $r_e \in \mathcal{R}_{\mathsf{Enc}}$ and outputs ciphertext $ct \in \mathcal{C}$.*
- Dec(sk, ct) $\to$ $m/\bot$: *a decryption algorithm that takes as input decryption key sk and ciphertext ct and outputs message $m \in \mathcal{M}$ or a rejection symbol $\bot \notin \mathcal{M}$.*

Definition 2.2. *We say a PKE scheme* PKE *is deterministic if* Enc *is deterministic, that is, it takes pk and m and does not take a randomness r_e. DPKE stands for deterministic public-key encryption.*

Plaintext-checking oracle: Since we review and propose key-recovery attacks using plaintext-checking oracle (PCO), we formally review the definition of the plaintext-checking oracle [2,59].

Definition 2.3 (Plaintext-Checking Oracle). *A plaintext-checking oracle* PCO *takes as input a plaintext m and a ciphertext ct and outputs 1 if and only if m is equal to the decrypted result* Dec(sk, ct). *That is,* PCO(m, ct) := $\mathsf{boole}(m = \mathsf{Dec}(sk, ct))$.

2.3   Key Encapsulation Mechanism (KEM)

The model for KEM schemes is summarized as follows:

Definition 2.4. *A KEM scheme* KEM *consists of the following triple of polynomial-time algorithms* (Gen, Encaps, Decaps):

- $\mathsf{Gen}(1^\lambda; r_g) \to (pk, sk)$: *a key-generation algorithm that takes as input* 1^λ, *where* λ *is the security parameter, and randomness* $r_g \in \mathcal{R}_{\mathsf{Gen}}$ *and outputs a pair of keys* (pk, sk). pk *and* sk *are called the encapsulation key and decapsulation key, respectively.*
- $\mathsf{Encaps}(pk; r_e) \to (ct, K)$: *an encapsulation algorithm that takes as input encapsulation key* pk *and randomness* $r_e \in \mathcal{R}_{\mathsf{Encaps}}$ *and outputs ciphertext* $ct \in \mathcal{C}$ *and key* $K \in \mathcal{K}$.
- $\mathsf{Decaps}(sk, ct) \to K/\bot$: *a decapsulation algorithm that takes as input decapsulation key* sk *and ciphertext* ct *and outputs key* K *or a rejection symbol* $\bot \notin \mathcal{K}$.

Key-mismatch oracle: We review the key-mismatch oracle, which is an analogue of the plaintext-checking oracle for PKE.

Definition 2.5. [Key-Mismatch Oracle]. *A key-mismatch oracle* KMO *takes as input a key* K *and a ciphertext* ct *and outputs* 1 *if and only if* K *is equal to the decapsulated result* $\mathsf{Decaps}(sk, ct)$. *That is,* $\mathrm{KMO}(K, ct) := \mathsf{boole}(K = \mathsf{Decaps}(sk, ct))$.

3   Variants of the Fujisaki-Okamoto Transformation

We review the variants of the FO transformation that are used by NIST PQC Round 3 candidate KEMs: $\mathsf{FO}^{\cancel{\bot}}$ in this section and $\mathsf{FO}^{\cancel{\bot}\prime}$, $\mathsf{FO}^{\cancel{\bot}\prime\prime}$, $\mathsf{HFO}^\bot$, $\mathsf{HFO}^{\cancel{\bot}}$, SXY, and $\mathsf{HU}^{\cancel{\bot}}$ in the full version. Let $\mathsf{PKE} = (\mathsf{Gen}, \mathsf{Enc}, \mathsf{Dec})$ be a PKE, whose ciphertext space is $\mathcal{C}_{\mathsf{PKE}}$. If PKE is probabilistic, then $\mathcal{R}_{\mathsf{Enc}}$ denotes the randomness space of Enc. Let $\{0, 1\}^{k(\lambda)}$ be the key space of KEM.

3.1   FO with Implicit Rejection

$\mathsf{FO}^{\cancel{\bot}}$ transforms a weakly-secure probabilistic PKE into IND-CCA-secure KEM, where the identifier "$\cancel{\bot}$" implies *implicit rejection* [42]. This variant is used by BIKE and SIKE.

Let $\{0, 1\}^{\ell(\lambda)}$ be the plaintext space of PKE. Let $\mathsf{G} \colon \{0, 1\}^* \to \mathcal{R}_{\mathsf{Enc}}$ and $\mathsf{H} \colon \{0, 1\}^{\ell(\lambda)} \times \mathcal{C}_{\mathsf{PKE}} \to \{0, 1\}^{k(\lambda)}$ be hash functions modeled by the random oracles. The $\mathsf{FO}^{\cancel{\bot}}$ is summarized as Fig. 1. Assuming the IND-CPA security of PKE, the obtained KEM scheme is IND-CCA-secure in the QROM (see e.g., [52]).

Remark 3.1. BIKE and SIKE do *not* test whole re-encryption check. Roughly speaking, their encryption algorithm Enc is separable into two algorithms Enc_1 and Enc_2. Enc_1 takes pk and randomness r and outputs c_1 and $k \in \{0, 1\}^{\ell(\lambda)}$. Enc_2 takes m and k and outputs $c_2 := k \oplus m$.

Using this property, BIKE omits the re-encryption check. Concretely speaking, k in BIKE's Enc_1 is computed as $k := \mathsf{H}(r)$, where H is a hash function modeled by the random oracle. BIKE's Dec internally obtains r' and checks the

Gen(1^λ)	Encaps(pk)	Decaps($\overline{sk}, ct$), where $\overline{sk} = (sk, pk, s)$
$(pk, sk) \leftarrow$ Gen(1^λ)	$m \leftarrow \{0,1\}^{\ell(\lambda)}$	$m' := $ Dec(sk, ct)
$s \leftarrow \{0,1\}^{\ell(\lambda)}$	$r := $ G(m) // for BIKE	$r' := $ G(m') // for BIKE
$\overline{sk} := (sk, pk, s)$	$r := $ G(m, pk) // for SIKE	$r' := $ G(m', pk) // for SIKE
return ($pk, \overline{sk}$)	$ct := $ Enc($pk, m; r$)	$ct' := $ Enc($pk, m'; r'$)
	$K := $ H(m, ct)	if $ct = ct'$, then return $K := $ H(m', ct)
	return (K, ct)	else return $K := $ H(s, ct)

Fig. 1. KEM := FO$^{\not\perp}$[PKE, G, H] for BIKE and SIKE.

validity of c_1. It then retrieves $m' := c_2 \oplus $ H(r') and checks the validity of the ciphertext by checking $r' = $ G(m') or not.

SIKE's Decaps performs the test $c_1' = c_1$ but omits the test $c_2' = c_2$. Since Dec retrieves $m' := c_2 \oplus k$ *deterministically*, we do not need to check the equality of c_2 and c_2'.

4   Key-Recovery Plaintext-Checking Attack Against ntrulpr of NTRU Prime

We propose a new key-recovery attack using plaintext-checking oracle against ntrulpr of NTRU Prime [14]. NTRU LPRime (ntrulpr) is a variant of the LPR PKE [54] and has a similar structure to Kyber and Saber. We mimic the KR-PCA against Kyber and Saber proposed by Băetu et al. [10] and Huguenin-Dumittan and Vaudenay [44].

ntrulpr of NTRU Prime: NTRU LPRime has parameter sets $p, q, w, \delta, \tau_0, \tau_1, \tau_2$, and τ_3. We note that $q = 6q' + 1$ for some q' and $q \geq 16w + 2\delta + 3$. For concrete values, see Table 3.

Table 3. Parameter sets of ntrulpr of NTRU Prime

parameter sets	p	q	w	δ	τ_0	τ_1	τ_2	τ_3
ntrulpr653	653	4621	252	289	2175	113	2031	290
ntrulpr761	761	4591	250	292	2156	114	2007	287
ntrulpr857	857	5167	281	329	2433	101	2265	324
ntrulpr953	953	6343	345	404	2997	82	2798	400
ntrulpr1013	1013	7177	392	450	3367	73	3143	449
ntrulpr1277	1277	7879	429	502	3724	66	3469	496

Let $\mathcal{R} := \mathbb{Z}[x]/(x^p - x - 1)$ and $\mathcal{R}_q := \mathbb{Z}_q[x]/(x^p - x - 1)$. Let $\mathcal{S} := \{a = \sum_{i=0}^{p-1} a_i x^i \in \mathcal{R} \mid a_i \in \{-1, 0, +1\}, $ HW(a) $= w\}$, a set of "short" polynomials.

Table 4. The PCO's behaviors

sk_i	$\mathsf{PCO}(\vec{1}_{256}, ct_0)$	$\mathsf{PCO}(\vec{1}_{256}, ct_1)$
1	1	1
0	1	0
−1	0	0

For $a \in [-(q-1)/2, (q-1)/2]$, define $\mathsf{Round}(a) = 3 \cdot \lceil a/3 \rceil$.[7] For a polynomial $A = \sum_i a_i x^i \in \mathcal{R}_q$, we define $\mathsf{trunc}(A, l) = (a_0, \ldots, a_{l-1}) \in \mathbb{Z}_q^l$. For $C \in [0, q)$, define $\mathsf{Top}(C) = \lfloor (\tau_1(C + \tau_0) + 2^{14})/2^{15} \rfloor$. For $T \in [0, 16)$, define $\mathsf{Right}(T) = \tau_3 T - \tau_2 \in \mathbb{Z}_q$. For $a \in \mathbb{Z}$, define $\mathsf{Sign}(a) = 1$ if $a < 0$, 0 otherwise.

The underlying CPA-secure PKE scheme[8] works as follows:

- $\mathsf{Gen}(pp)$: Generate $A \leftarrow \mathcal{R}_q$ and $sk \leftarrow \mathcal{S}$. Compute $B := \mathsf{Round}(A \cdot sk)$. Output $pk := (A, B)$ and sk.
- $\mathsf{Enc}(pk, \mu \in \{0,1\}^{256})$: Choose $t \leftarrow \mathcal{S}$ and output

$$(U, V) := \left(\mathsf{Round}(t \cdot A), \mathsf{Top}(\mathsf{trunc}(t \cdot B, 256) + \mu(q-1)/2)\right).$$

- $\mathsf{Dec}(sk, (U, V))$: Compute $r := \mathsf{Right}(V) - \mathsf{trunc}(sk \cdot U, 256) + (4w+1) \cdot \vec{1}_{256} \in \mathbb{Z}^{256}$ and outputs $m := \mathsf{Sign}(r \bmod^{\pm} q)$.

4.1 Key-Recovery Attack

We mainly follow the KR-PCAs against Kyber and Saber in Baetu et al. [10] and Huguenin-Dumittan and Vaudenay [44], but we need some tweaks. Roughly speaking, to determine the i-th coefficient of sk, their attack queries $(a, b \cdot x^i)$ with constant a and b and a candidate plaintext, because in the case of Kyber and Saber, the dimension of V is the same as that of the base ring. However, ntrulpr truncates tB to reduce redundancy, so we need to modify the query ciphertext. Note that we can *shift* the effect of sk_i into *constant coefficient* by multiplying x^{p-i}. That is, for $i - 1, \ldots, p - 1$ and $sk - sk_0 + sk_1 x + \ldots sk_{p-1} x^{p-1} \in \mathcal{R}$, we have

$$x^{p-i} \cdot sk = sk_i + (sk_i + sk_{i+1})x + (sk_{i+1} + sk_{i+2})x^2 + \cdots + (sk_{p-1} + sk_0)x^{p-i}$$
$$+ sk_1 x^{p-i+1} + sk_2 x^{p-i+2} + \cdots + sk_{i-1} x^{p-1}.$$

Using this relation, we show the following two lemmas:

Lemma 4.1 (For general $i \in [1, p)$). *Let $c = \tau_2 - (4w+1)$, $b = \lfloor (c-1)/6 \rfloor \cdot 3$ and $t_\beta = \lfloor (\beta b + c - 1)/\tau_3 \rfloor$ for $\beta \in \{0, 1\}$. Let us consider our test ciphertext $ct_\beta = (b \cdot x^{p-i}, (t_\beta, 0, \ldots, 0))$ for $\beta \in \{0, 1\}$ and candidate plaintext $\vec{1}_{256}$. Then, we have the relations between the i-th coordinate of decryption key and the behavior of PCO as in Table 4.*

---

[7] When $q = 6q' + 1$, $\mathsf{Round}([-(q-1)/2, (q-1)/2]) \in [-(q-1)/2, (q-1)/2]$.
[8] 'NTRU LPRime Core' in the specification.

Proof. The decryption algorithm computes $r = \mathsf{Right}\big((t_\beta, 0, \ldots, 0)\big) - \mathsf{trunc}\big(sk \cdot b \cdot x^{p-i}, 256\big) + (4w+1) \cdot \vec{1}_{256}$. Expanding this, we have

$$
\begin{cases}
r_0 = \tau_3 t_\beta - b \cdot sk_i - c, \\
r_j = -b \cdot (sk_{i+j-1 \bmod p} + sk_{i+j \bmod p}) - c & (j = 1, 2, \ldots, \min\{256, p-i\}) \\
r_j = -b \cdot sk_{j-(p-i) \bmod p} - c & (j = p-i+1, \ldots, \min\{256, p-1\}).
\end{cases}
$$

Recall that $sk_i \in \{-1, 0, +1\}$ for all i since sk is in $\mathcal{S}$. Thus, we have $r_j \in \{-2b-c, -b-c, -c, b-c, 2b-c\}$ for $j = 1, \ldots, 256$. Since we set $b = \lfloor (c-1)/6 \rfloor \cdot 3 \leq (c-1)/2$, we have $-2b - c > -2c$ and $2b - c < 0$. Fortunately, we have $-2c = -2\tau_2 - 8w - 2 \geq -(q-1)/2$ for all parameter sets. Thus, r_j's are decoded into 1 for $j = 1, \ldots, 256$.

Let us consider r_0. We have

$$
r_0 = \tau_3 t_\beta - b \cdot sk_i - c > 0 \iff (\tau_3 t_\beta - c)/b > sk_i
$$

By our setting, if $t_\beta = t_0$ (and t_1), then $(\tau_3 t_\beta - c)/b$ is slightly smaller than 0 (and 1) for all parameter sets, respectively. In addition, we have $\tau_3 t_1 + b - c \leq (q-1)/2$ for all parameter sets. Therefore, r_0 for t_0 is decoded into 0 if and only if $sk_i < 0$ and r_0 for t_1 is decoded into 0 if and only if $sk_i < 1$. This completes the proof. $\qquad\square$

By a similar argument, we have the following lemma on sk_0.

Lemma 4.2 ($i = 0$). *Let* $c = \tau_2 - (4w+1)$, $b = \lceil (c-1)/6 \rceil \cdot 3$ *and* $t_\beta = \lfloor (\beta b + c - 1)/\tau_3 \rfloor$ *for* $\beta \in \{0, 1\}$. *Let us consider our test ciphertext* $ct_\beta = (b, (t_\beta, 0, \ldots, 0))$ *and candidate plaintext* $\vec{1}_{256}$. *Then, we have the relations between the constant term of decryption key and the behavior of PCO as in Table 4.*

Using the above lemmas, we can determine sk_i for $i = 0, \ldots, p-1$ by testing $2p$ queries with the PCO.

4.2   Trade-Off

We observe that an adversary can obtain $K' = \mathsf{H}(m', ct)$ by skipping the equality test instead of the equality of K' and K_{guess} or the equality of m' and m_{guess}. Therefore, the adversary can check if $m' = m_{\mathsf{guess}}$ or not by computing $K_{\mathsf{guess}} = \mathsf{H}(m_{\mathsf{guess}}, ct)$ by itself. This enables the adversary to determine ℓ coefficients of the secret key at once by sacrificing the computational efficiency.

For simplicity, we let $\ell = 2^k < 256$.

Determine $sk_{y\ell}, \ldots, sk_{y\ell+\ell-1}$ *for* $y = 0, \ldots, 256/\ell - 1$: Let us determine ℓ coefficients $sk_{y\ell}, \ldots, sk_{y\ell+\ell-1}$ of sk at once, where $y = 0, \ldots, 256/\ell - 1$. Suppose that we query two ciphertexts

$$
ct_\beta = (U, V_\beta) = (b, (\overbrace{0, \ldots, 0}^{y\ell}, \overbrace{t_\beta, \ldots, t_\beta}^{\ell}, \overbrace{0, \ldots, 0}^{256-(y+1)\ell}))
$$

for $\beta \in \{0,1\}$. The decryption algorithm computes $r = \mathsf{Right}(V_\beta) - \mathrm{trunc}(sk \cdot b, 256) + (4w+1) \cdot \vec{1}_{256}$. Expanding this, we have

$$
r_j = \begin{cases} \tau_3 t_\beta - b \cdot sk_j - c & (j = y\ell, \ldots, y\ell + \ell - 1) \\ -b \cdot sk_j - c & (j = 0, \ldots, y\ell - 1, (y+1)\ell, \ldots, 256). \end{cases}
$$

By using the argument in the proof of Lemma 4.1, r_j's are decoded into 1 for $j = 0, \ldots, y\ell - 1, (y+1)\ell, \ldots, 256$. We also have, for $j = y\ell, \ldots, y\ell + \ell - 1$, r_j for t_1 is decoded into 0 if and only if $sk_i < 0$ and r_j for t_2 is decoded into 0 if and only if $sk_i < 1$.

Seeing $K = \mathsf{H}(m', ct_\beta)$ where $m' = \mathsf{Dec}(sk, ct_\beta)$, we compute $K_{\mathsf{guess}} = \mathsf{H}(m_{\mathsf{guess}}, ct_\beta)$ for $m_{\mathsf{guess}} = \vec{1}_{y\ell} \| m'' \| \vec{1}_{256-(y+1)\ell}$ for all $m'' \in \{0,1\}^\ell$ and determine sk_j for $j = y\ell, \ldots, y\ell + \ell - 1$.

Determine $sk_{y\ell}, \ldots, sk_{y\ell + \ell - 1}$ for $y = 256/\ell, \ldots, \lfloor p/\ell \rfloor$: Suppose that we have determined $y\ell$ coefficients $sk_0, \ldots, sk_{y\ell - 1}$ for some $y \in \{256/\ell, \ldots, \lfloor p/\ell \rfloor\}$. Let us determine ℓ coefficients $sk_{y\ell}, \ldots, sk_{y\ell + \ell - 1}$ at once: Let $t_\beta = \lfloor (\beta b + c - 1)/\tau_3 \rfloor$ for $\beta \in \{-1, 0, 1, 2\}$. Suppose that we query four ciphertexts

$$
ct_\beta = (U, V_\beta) = \big(b \cdot x^{p-y\ell-1}, (0, \overbrace{t_\beta, \ldots, t_\beta}^{\ell}, \overbrace{0, \ldots, 0}^{256-\ell-1}) \big)
$$

for $\beta \in \{-1, 0, 1, 2\}$. The decryption algorithm computes $r = \mathsf{Right}(V_\beta) - \mathrm{trunc}(sk \cdot bx^{p-y\ell-1}, 256) + (4w+1) \cdot \vec{1}_{256}$. Expanding this, we have

$$
r_j = \begin{cases} -b \cdot sk_{y\ell-1} - c & (j = 0) \\ \tau_3 t_\beta - b \cdot (sk_{y\ell+j-2 \bmod p} + sk_{y\ell+j-1 \bmod p}) - c & (j = 1, 2, \ldots, \ell) \\ -b \cdot (sk_{y\ell+j-2 \bmod p} + sk_{y\ell+j-1 \bmod p}) - c & (j = \ell+1, \ldots, \min\{256, p - y\ell\}) \\ -b \cdot sk_{j-(p-i) \bmod p} - c & (j = \min\{256, p - y\ell + 1\}, \ldots, 256). \end{cases}
$$

By using the argument in the proof of Lemma 4.1, r_j's are decoded into 1 for $j = 0$ and $j = \ell+1, \ldots, 256$.

Let us consider r_j for $j = 1, \ldots, \ell$. We have

$$
r_j = \tau_3 t_\beta - b \cdot (sk_j + sk_{j+1}) - c > 0 \iff (\tau_3 t_\beta - c)/b > sk_j + sk_{j+1}.
$$

By our setting, $(\tau_3 t_\beta - c)/b$ is slightly smaller than β for all parameter sets, respectively. In addition, we have $-(q-1)/2 \leq \tau_3 t_\beta - 2b - c$ and $\tau_3 t_\beta + 2b - c \leq (q-1)/2$ for all parameter sets. Therefore, r_j for t_β is decoded into 0 if and only if $sk_i < \beta$.

Seeing $K' = \mathsf{H}(m', ct_\beta)$ where $m' = \mathsf{Dec}(sk, ct_\beta)$, we compute $K_{\mathsf{guess}} = \mathsf{H}(m_{\mathsf{guess}}, ct_\beta)$ for $m_{\mathsf{guess}} = 1 \| m'' \| \vec{1}_{256-\ell-1}$ for all $m'' \in \{0,1\}^\ell$ and determine $sk_{y\ell+j-2} + sk_{y\ell+j-1} \in \{-2, -1, 0, 1, 2\}$ for $j = 1, \ldots, \ell$. Since we know $sk_{y\ell-1}$, we can determine $sk_{y\ell}, \ldots, sk_{y\ell+\ell-1}$ sequentially.

5 Skipping the Equality Test by Skipping a Single Instruction

In this section, we describe the fault-injection attack on the equality checking of each KEM implementation. First, we examine the implementation of pqm4 [49] for each scheme and discuss the possibility of skipping the equivalence test. To identify the instructions to be skipped, we cross-compiled the C code in pqm4 with GCC 8.3.1 running on Debian bullseye. The compilation options were basically according to pqm4, with "-O3" as an optimization option.

We do not mention the attacks on Classic McEliece and HQC in this section because pqm4 does not include their ARM Cortex M4-optimized code. Hereafter, we describe the possibility of skip attacks on NTRU Prime, FrodoKEM, Kyber, Saber, NTRU, BIKE, and SIKE.

If the reader is unfamiliar to Arm Cortex M4, please see the manual[9].

5.1 NTRU Prime – CCA Bug

The functions in the C code related to the FO-like transformation are `crypto_kem_dec`, `Decap`, and `Ciphertexts_diff_mask`.[10] Figure 2 shows the source code of NTRU Prime's comparison in pqm4. Note that we omit the `crypto_kem_dec` function as it just calls `Decap`.

Let us consider how `Ciphertexts_diff_mask` computes the return value. It initializes the `uint16` variable `differentbits` as 0. After some computations, it outputs `((-1)-((differentbits-1)>>31))` in line 17. The value is initialized as 0 and *unchanged* before the return value is computed; these computations only involve `differentbits2`. Thus, we eventually obtain 0 as the result of `(-1)-((0-1)>>31)` and `ciphertexts_diff_mask` always outputs 0.

`Decap` first decrypts $r := \mathsf{Dec}(sk, c)$ in line 13 and encodes it into `r_enc` and re-encrypts it into `cnew` in line 14. In line 15, `mask` is always 0, since `Ciphertexts_diff_mask` always returns 0 as we explained. Thus, `r_enc`, which is the result of faulty decryption, is unchanged, and `Decap` always sets `k` as the result of `H(1,r_enc,c)`. This means that there is no re-encryption check and the implementation opens the attack surface of chosen-ciphertext attacks.

5.2 FrodoKEM – Timing Attack

The decapsulation of FrodoKEM is performed in the `crypto_kem_dec` function.[11] Figure 3 shows the source code of the equality test in the function. From the

---

[9] https://developer.arm.com/documentation/100166/0001. See https://developer.arm.com/documentation/100166/0001/Programmers-Model/Instruction-set-summary/Table-of-processor-instructions?lang=en for instruction set.

[10] The source code of these functions is https://github.com/mupq/pqm4/blob/master/crypto_kem/sntrup761/m4f/kem.c.

[11] https://github.com/mupq/pqm4/blob/master/crypto_kem/frodokem640shake/m4/kem.c.

```
1  static int Ciphertexts_diff_mask(const unsigned char *c,
2                                    const unsigned char *c2)
3  {
4    uint16 differentbits = 0;
5    int len = Ciphertexts_bytes+Confirm_bytes;
6
7    int *cc = (int *)(void *)c;
8    int *cc2 = (int *)(void *)c2;
9    int differentbits2 = 0;
10   for (len-=4 ;len>=0; len-=4) {
11     differentbits2 = __USADA8((*cc++),(*cc2++),differentbits2);
12   }
13   c = (unsigned char *)(void *) cc;
14   c2 = (unsigned char *)(void *) cc2;
15   for (len &= 3; len > 0; len--)
16     differentbits2 =__USADA8((*c++),(*c2++),differentbits2);
17   return ((-1)-((differentbits-1)>>31));
18 }
```

```
1  static void Decap(unsigned char *k,const unsigned char *c,
2                                     const unsigned char *sk)
3  {
4    const unsigned char *pk = sk + SecretKeys_bytes;
5    const unsigned char *rho = pk + PublicKeys_bytes;
6    const unsigned char *cache = rho + Inputs_bytes;
7    Inputs r;
8    unsigned char r_enc[Inputs_bytes];
9    unsigned char cnew[Ciphertexts_bytes+Confirm_bytes];
10   int mask;
11   int i;
12
13   ZDecrypt(r,c,sk);
14   Hide(cnew,r_enc,r,pk,cache);
15   mask = Ciphertexts_diff_mask(c,cnew);
16   for (i = 0;i < Inputs_bytes;++i)
17     r_enc[i] ^= mask&(r_enc[i]^rho[i]);
18   HashSession(k,1+mask,r_enc,c);
19 }
```

Fig. 2. NTRU Prime's comparison in pqm4.

source code, this function uses the memcmp function with && to compare the ciphertext and the re-encryption result. This indicates that the current implementation is still vulnerable to the timing attack by Guo et al. [38].

```
// Is (Bp == BBp & C == CC) = true
if (memcmp(Bp, BBp, 2 * PARAMS_N * PARAMS_NBAR) == 0 &&
      memcmp(C, CC, 2 * PARAMS_NBAR * PARAMS_NBAR) == 0) {
    // Load k' to do ss = F(ct || k')
    memcpy(Fin_k, kprime, CRYPTO_BYTES);
} else {
    // Load s to do ss = F(ct || s)
    memcpy(Fin_k, sk_s, CRYPTO_BYTES);
}
shake(ss, CRYPTO_BYTES, Fin, CRYPTO_CIPHERTEXTBYTES
                                + CRYPTO_BYTES);
```

Fig. 3. FrodoKEM's comparison in pqm4

5.3 Kyber, Saber, and NTRU – cmov

In this subsection, we describe the skip attacks on Kyber, Saber, and NTRU among the finalists. The basic idea of the skip attacks on these implementations is identical, and thus we describe the case of Saber as an example to explain the skip attack procedure. Figure 4 shows the `crypto_kem_dec` function that performs the decapsulation of FO transformation[12].

The `crypto_kem_dec` function performs re-encryption using the `indcpa_kem_enc_cmp` function at line 14 and stores the comparison results of the ciphertext and the re-encryption result into a variable `fail`. If these ciphertexts are not the same, `fail` becomes 1 and, if they are the same, `fail` becomes 0. At line 16, the `cmov` substitutes a random value for `kr` when `fail` is 1. Note here that the hash value calculated from the decrypted result is stored in the variable `kr` before `cmov` is called, and this means that we can perform a key-recovery attack by skipping the call of `cmov` even when `fail` is 1.

Figure 5 shows the assembly code corresponding to the call of `cmov`. This program first calls the `sha3_256` function at line 1, prepares the arguments of `cmov` at line 4–7, calls `cmov` at line 8, and finally prepares the arguments and call the `sha3_256` function at line 10–14. From this code, we notice that Saber can be attacked by skipping `bl cmov` at line 8 using fault injection. In addition to Saber, NTRU and Kyber also use `cmov` in the same manner, and therefore, this attack can be applied to all of them.

---

[12] https://github.com/mupq/pqm4/blob/master/crypto_kem/saber/m4f/kem.c.

```
1        int crypto_kem_dec(uint8_t *k, const uint8_t *c,
2                                         const uint8_t *sk)
3   {
4       uint8_t fail;
5       uint8_t buf[64];
6       uint8_t kr[64]; // Will contain key, coins
7       const uint8_t *pk = sk + SABER_INDCPA_SECRETKEYBYTES;
8       const uint8_t *hpk = sk + SABER_SECRETKEYBYTES - 64;
9                           // Save hash by storing h(pk) in sk
10
11      indcpa_kem_dec(sk, c, buf);
12      memcpy(buf + 32, hpk, 32);
13      sha3_512(kr, buf, 64);
14      fail = indcpa_kem_enc_cmp(buf, kr + 32, pk, c);
15      sha3_256(kr + 32, c, SABER_BYTES_CCA_DEC);
16      cmov(kr, sk + SABER_SECRETKEYBYTES - SABER_KEYBYTES,
17                              SABER_KEYBYTES, fail);
18      sha3_256(k, kr, 64);
19      return (0);
20  }
21
```

Fig. 4. Saber's comparison in pqm4

```
1        bl   sha3_256
2   .LVL26:
3   .loc 1 79 3 is_stmt 1 view .LVU62
4       uxtb   r3, r7
5       add r1, r4, #1536
6       add r0, sp, #64
7       movs   r2, #32
8       bl   cmov
9   .LVL27:
10      .loc 1 82 3 view .LVU63
11      movs   r2, #64
12      mov r0, r6
13      add r1, sp, r2
14      bl   sha3_256
```

Fig. 5. Assembly code of Saber's comparison in pqm4

5.4   BIKE – for Loop

We describe the skip attack on BIKE in this subsection. Figure 6 shows the C code of BIKE's comparison in the decapsulation[13]. We also show secure_cmp function and secure_l32_mask function in Fig. 7. Line 4–7 in Fig. 6 compares

---

[13] https://github.com/mupq/pqm4/blob/master/crypto_kem/bikel1/m4f/kem.c.

the hash value of the original message and that of the decrypted message from the ciphertext. Then, if they are equal, the `for` block at line 12–15 stores the decrypted message into `m_prime.raw[i]`. Therefore, the goal of the fault-injection attack is to store the decrypted message even when these hash values differ. For this purpose, we need to force the variable `mask` to be 0.

Figure 8 shows the assembly code corresponding to the line 6–11 in the C code to explain the position of a fault injection. Line 1–30 and line 31–44 in the assembly code correspond to line 6 and line 11 in the C code, respectively. The operation we need to skip for a key-recovery attack is "`ldr r2, [sp, #20]`" at line 33 in this assembly code for the following reason.

Before line 33 in the assembly code, the `r2` register is used in "`cmp r2, #0`" at line 26. This corresponds to "`return (0 == res);`" at line 11 in `secure_cmp` function (Fig. 7). Therefore, at this time, the `r2` register contains the value of the `res` variable. The value of the `r2` register does not become 0 from the attack assumption because the value of the `res` variable is not 0 when the two arguments of `secure_cmp` are not equal. Thus, the `r2` register must be a non-zero value if line 33 in the assembly code is skipped. After line 33, the value of the `r2` register is used at line 41. This line corresponds to line 9 in the `secure_132_mask` function (Fig. 7). The `secure_132_mask` function compares the two arguments `v1` and `v2` and returns 0 when `v1 < v2` holds. `mask` becomes 0 when `v2` is not 0 because `v1` is 0 as shown in Fig. 6. Meanwhile, we note that the variable `v2` does not become 0 when we skip line 33 in the assembly code because the `r2` register corresponds to the `v2` variable. From the above, we can fix `mask` to 0 by the fault injection, and thus the key-recovery attack is possible.

5.5   SIKE – Simple if

This subsection describe the skip attack on SIKE. Figure 9 and Fig. 10 shows the C code and its assembly of the comparison process in the FO transformation[14].

The target of fault injection in C code is the `if` statement at line 4–6. The assembly code in Fig. 10 corresponds to the `if` statement. The process of condition in the `if` statement at line 4 in the C code corresponds to line 1–3 in the assembly code. In the assembly code, "`bl memcmp`" compares the variables `c0_` and `ct`. If they differ, "`cbnz r0, .L500`" performs a jump to line 23. Note that, even if we jump to line 23, the procedure comes back to line 4 because of "`b .L495`" at line 33. In other words, line 23–33 in the assembly code correspond to the process in the `if` block at line 5 in the C code. Thus, we can perform the skip attack on SIKE by injecting a fault into "`cbnz r0, .L500`" at line 3.

---

[14] https://github.com/mupq/pqm4/blob/master/crypto_kem/sikep434/m4/sike.inc.

```
1   // Check if H(m') is equal to (e0', e1')
2   // (in constant-time)
3   GUARD(function_h(&e_tmp, &m_prime));
4   success_cond = secure_cmp(PE0_RAW(&e_prime),
5                             PE0_RAW(&e_tmp), R_BYTES);
6   success_cond &= secure_cmp(PE1_RAW(&e_prime),
7                             PE1_RAW(&e_tmp), R_BYTES);
8
9   // Compute either K(m', C) or K(sigma, C) based on the
10  //                                success condition
11  mask = secure_l32_mask(0, success_cond);
12  for(size_t i = 0; i < M_BYTES; i++) {
13    m_prime.raw[i] &= u8_barrier(~mask);
14    m_prime.raw[i] |= (u8_barrier(mask) & l_sk.sigma.raw[i]);
15  }
```

Fig. 6. BIKE's comparison in pqm4.

```
1   _INLINE_ uint32_t secure_cmp(IN const uint8_t *a,
2                                IN const uint8_t *b,
3                                IN const uint32_t size)
4   {
5     volatile uint8_t res = 0;
6
7     for(uint32_t i = 0; i < size; ++i) {
8       res |= (a[i] ^ b[i]);
9     }
10
11    return (0 == res);
12  }
```

```
1   // Return 0 if v1 < v2, (-1) otherwise
2   _INLINE_ uint32_t secure_l32_mask(IN const uint32_t v1,
3                                     IN const uint32_t v2)
4   {
5     // If v1 >= v2 then the subtraction result is 0^32||(v1-v2).
6     // else it is 1^32||(v2-v1+1).
7     // Subsequently, negating the upper
8     // 32 bits gives 0 if v1 < v2 and otherwise (-1).
9     return ~((uint32_t)(((uint64_t)v1 - (uint64_t)v2) >> 32));
10  }
```

Fig. 7. secure_cmp and secure_l32_mask function of BIKE in pqm4.

```
 1  .L26:
 2      .loc 1 69 5 is_stmt 1 view .LVU627
 3      ldrb    r2, [r5, #1]!
 4  .LVL169:
 5      .loc 1 69 9 view .LVU629
 6      ldrb    r4, [r1, #1]!
 7      ldrb    r3, [sp, #18]
 8      eors    r2, r2, r4
 9      orrs    r3, r3, r2
10      .loc 1 68 3 view .LVU630
11      cmp     r0, r5
12      .loc 1 69 9 view .LVU631
13      strb    r3, [sp, #18]
14  .LVL170:
15      .loc 1 68 3 view .LVU632
16      bne     .L26
17  .LBE629:
18      .loc 1 72 3 is_stmt 1 view .LVU633
19  .LVL171:
20      .loc 1 72 13 is_stmt 0 view .LVU634
21      ldrb    r2, [sp, #18]
22  .LBE628:
23  .LBE627:
24      .loc 2 278 16 view .LVU635
25      ldr     r3, [sp, #20]
26      cmp     r2, #0
27      ite     ne
28      movne   r3, #0
29      andeq   r3, r3, #1
30      str     r3, [sp, #20]
31      .loc 2 282 3 is_stmt 1 view .LVU636
32      .loc 2 282 10 is_stmt 0 view .LVU637
33      ldr     r2, [sp, #20]
34  .LVL172:
35  .LBB630:
36  .LBI630:
37      .loc 1 113 19 is_stmt 1 view .LVU638
38  .LBB631:
39      .loc 1 140 3 view .LVU639
40      .loc 1 140 37 is_stmt 0 view .LVU640
41      rsbs    r2, r2, #0
42      sbc     r3, r3, r3
43      .loc 1 140 10 view .LVU641
44      mvns    r5, r3
```

Fig. 8. Assembly code of BIKE's comparison in pqm4

```
1  // Generate shared secret ss <- H(m||ct)
2  //                      or output ss <- H(s||ct)
3  EphemeralKeyGeneration_A(ephemeralsk_, c0_);
4  if (memcmp(c0_, ct, CRYPTO_PUBLICKEYBYTES) != 0) {
5      memcpy(temp, sk, MSG_BYTES);
6  }
7  memcpy(&temp[MSG_BYTES], ct, CRYPTO_CIPHERTEXTBYTES);
8  shake256(ss, CRYPTO_BYTES, temp,
9                  CRYPTO_CIPHERTEXTBYTES+MSG_BYTES);
```

Fig. 9. SIKE's comparison in pqm4

```
1      bl   memcmp
2      .loc 5 88 8 view .LVU4945
3      cbnz    r0, .L500
4  .L495:
5      .loc 5 91 5 is_stmt 1 view .LVU4946
6      mov r1, r4
7      add r0, sp, #508
8      mov r2, #346
9      bl   memcpy
10     .loc 5 92 5 view .LVU4947
11     mov r0, r8
12     add r2, sp, #492
13     mov r3, #362
14     movs    r1, #16
15     bl   shake256
16     .loc 5 94 5 view .LVU4948
17     .loc 5 95 1 is_stmt 0 view .LVU4949
18     movs    r0, #0
19     add sp, sp, #856
20     .cfi_remember_state
21     .cfi_def_cfa_offset 24
22     pop {r4, r5, r6, r7, r8, pc}
23  .L500:
24     .cfi_restore_state
25     .loc 5 89 9 is_stmt 1 view .LVU4950
26     ldr r0, [r5]
27     ldr r1, [r5, #4]
28     ldr r2, [r5, #8]
29     ldr r3, [r5, #12]
30     add r5, sp, #492
31     .loc 5 89 9 is_stmt 0 view .LVU4951
32     stmia    r5!, {r0, r1, r2, r3}
33     b    .L495
```

Fig. 10. Assembly code of SIKE's comparison in pqm4

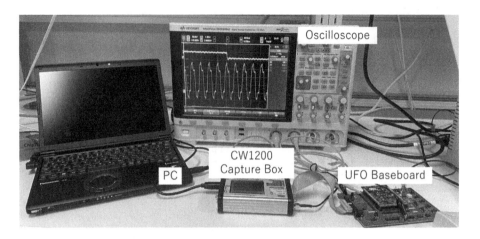

Fig. 11. Experimental setup overview.

Table 5. Numbers of failures and successes when we conducted 100 skip attacks on each scheme

Name	# failures	# Successes	# required queries	Expected time [s]
Kyber – Kyber512	60	52	5908	626
NTRU – ntruhps2048509	74	46	2235	384
Saber – LightSaber	33	33	15515	1,567
BIKE – Bike1	49	34	-	-
SIKE – sikep434	30	15	1787	19,478

6   Experimental Attacks

In this section, we conduct the experimental skip attacks on the pqm4 implementation of the above mentioned KEM schemes. The target schemes in this section are Kyber, NTRU, Saber, BIKE, and SIKE, which were shown to be attackable by a single fault injection in the previous section. In this experiment, we used the parameters of the security level 1 for all schemes.

6.1   Setup

Figure 11 shows the experimental environment. The target chip under attack is an STM32F415 microcontroller with an ARM Cortex M4 core, which is a de-facto standard platform to evaluate software implementation of schemes running in NIST's PQC process. The target device is mounted on a ChipWhisperer cw308 UFO baseboard, which enables us to perform fault-injection attacks using a glitchy clock. The ChipWhisperer cw1200 capture box is used to generate the base clock, and the clock frequency was set to 24 MHz. The glitch parameters for instruction skipping were searched by sweeping the parameters to find the one that successfully skips the instruction. We use the implementation in pqm4 for each KEM scheme, and "O3" was specified as an optimization option during compilation.

6.2 Results

Table 5 reports the experimental results of the proposed skip attacks. In Table 5, we show the number of times when a fault occurred on the device and the number of successful instruction skips when we performed 100 fault injections for each scheme. Also, the table shows the number of required queries to recover the secret key from each scheme using fault injection.[15,16] These required query numbers are calculated by multiplying the minimum required number of queries for a key-recovery attack and the inverse of the success rate of a skip attack. We only omitted the number of required queries for the case of BIKE in this table because it is difficult to fully recover the secret key. We also show the expected time to recover the secret key for each scheme. From the table, we confirm that the probability of a successful attack was about 15–50%, and there is a difference in the probability of successful attacks among Saber, Kyber, and NTRU, although the fault-injection capability is almost the same. This would be because of the difference in instructions before and after the call of the cmov function that affects the state of pipeline registers in the microcontroller.

In addition, in this experiment, the injected faults did not always cause a single instruction skip as expected and sometimes crashed the device, which led to a non-negligible cost for an oracle access. A similar phenomenon was also observed in [60] in fault-injection attacks on lattice KEMs using ChipWhisperer, and more sophisticated equipment for fault injection should achieve higher attack stability.

7   Countermeasure

Default fail: The one of major countermeasures is the 'default fail' technique, which initiates a variable with the fail result and if a condition is satisfied then the variable is overwritten by the sensitive data [32].

Recall Saber's decapsulation in Fig. 4: We want to compute $K = \mathsf{H}(\bar{K}', \mathsf{H}(ct))$ or $\mathsf{H}(s, \mathsf{H}(ct))$ depending on the re-encryption test result, where $\bar{K}'$ is computed from the decrypted result m' and pk and s is a secret seed. If we skip the function call of cmov, then $\bar{K}'$ in kr is unchanged and we obtain $K = \mathsf{H}(\bar{K}', \mathsf{H}(ct))$ as the faulty decapsulation result. According to the 'default fail' technique, we put a secret seed s as the *default* value of kr and apply cmov to overwrite s by $\bar{K}'$

---

[15] In practice, we may need more queries than the values shown in the table, because the value of the secret key may occasionally carry an error due to an inserted fault. For simplicity, we ignore such situations here.

[16] On Saber and Kyber, we have trade-offs between the number of expected queries and efficiency. In this table, we use $\ell = 1$.

depending on the value `flag`. (In addition, we will need to clear the original $\bar{K}'$.) If it was, then skipping `cmov` results in $K = \mathsf{H}(s, \mathsf{H}(ct))$ irrelevant to the decrypted result m'.

Moreover, a concrete assembly-level implementation of conditional branch resistant to single instruction skipping by default fail was presented in [32]. Their countermeasure enables that sensitive instruction(s) should be performed only if a condition is surely tested and satisfied. In other words, if the condition test is skipped by a single-fault attack, the implementation with their countermeasure always outputs the rejection.

Instruction duplication: The other major countermeasures is the 'assembly-level instruction duplication' technique: If every instructions are duplicated carefully, then a single-fault instruction skipping attack is ineffective. See, e.g., [12] for the effectiveness and cost.

Random delay: Random delays are yet another major countermeasure of fault-injection analysis. If a random delay is inserted, then it is hard to determine the timing for injecting a fault. See, e.g., [24] for such technique.

8   Conclusion

From the viewpoint of fault-injection attacks, we have investigate *all* NIST PQC Round 3 KEM candidates, which use variants of the FO transformation. We survey effective key-recovery attacks if we can skip the equality test.

We found the existing key-recovery attacks against Kyber, NTRU, Saber, FrodoKEM, HQC, and SIKE (Table 2). We have proposed a new key-recovery attack against ntrulpr of NTRU Prime. We also pointed out trade-offs between the number of queries and computational costs when the target is Kyber, Saber, or ntrulpr. We also reported attacks against sntrupr of NTRU Prime and BIKE that lead to leakage of information of secret keys.

The open-source pqm4 library contains Kyber, NTRU, Saber, BIKE, FrodoKEM, NTRU Prime, and SIKE. We show that giving a single instruction-skipping fault in the decapsulation processes leads to skipping the equality test *virtually* for Kyber, NTRU, Saber, BIKE, and SIKE. We also report the implementation of NTRU Prime allows chosen-ciphertext attacks freely and the timing side-channel of FrodoKEM reported in Guo et al. [38] remains.

Finally, we have reported the experimental attacks against Kyber, NTRU, Saber, BIKE, and SIKE on pqm4. We also discuss possible countermeasures.

Acknowledgment. The authors would like to thank to anonymous reviewers of Asiacrypt 2021 for their helpful and insightful comments.

References

1. ISO/IEC 18033-2:2006 information technology – security techniques – encryption algorithms – part 2: asymmetric ciphers (2006). https://www.iso.org/standard/37971.html

2. Abdalla, M., Benhamouda, F., Pointcheval, D.: Public-key encryption indistinguishable under plaintext-checkable attacks. In: Katz, J. (ed.) PKC 2015. LNCS, vol. 9020, pp. 332–352. Springer, Heidelberg (2015). https://doi.org/10.1007/978-3-662-46447-2_15
3. Aggarwal, D., Maurer, U.: Breaking RSA generically is equivalent to factoring. In: Joux, A. (ed.) EUROCRYPT 2009. LNCS, vol. 5479, pp. 36–53. Springer, Heidelberg (2009). https://doi.org/10.1007/978-3-642-01001-9_2
4. Aguilar Melchor, C., et al.: HQC. Technical report, National Institute of Standards and Technology (2020)
5. Ajtai, M., Dwork, C.: A public-key cryptosystem with worst-case/average-case equivalence. In: STOC 1997, pp. 284–293. ACM Press, May 1997
6. Alagic, G., et al.: NISTIR 8309: status report on the second round of the NIST post-quantum cryptography standardization process, July 2020
7. Albrecht, M.R., et al.: Classic McEliece. Technical report, National Institute of Standards and Technology (2020)
8. Antipa, A., Brown, D., Menezes, A., Struik, R., Vanstone, S.: Validation of elliptic curve public keys. In: Desmedt, Y.G. (ed.) PKC 2003. LNCS, vol. 2567, pp. 211–223. Springer, Heidelberg (2003). https://doi.org/10.1007/3-540-36288-6_16
9. Aragon, N., et al.: BIKE. Technical report, National Institute of Standards and Technology (2020)
10. Băetu, C., Durak, F.B., Huguenin-Dumittan, L., Talayhan, A., Vaudenay, S.: Misuse attacks on post-quantum cryptosystems. In: Ishai, Y., Rijmen, V. (eds.) EUROCRYPT 2019, Part II. LNCS, vol. 11477, pp. 747–776. Springer, Cham (2019). https://doi.org/10.1007/978-3-030-17656-3_26
11. Barenghi, A., Bertoni, G., Perrinello, E., Pelosi, G.: Low voltage fault attacks on the RSA cryptosystem. In: FDTC 2009. IEEE Computer Society (2009)
12. Barenghi, A., Breveglieri, L., Koren, I., Pelosi, G., Regazzoni, F.: Countermeasures against fault attacks on software implemented AES: effectiveness and cost. In: WESS 2010 (2010)
13. Bellare, M. (ed.): CRYPTO 2000, LNCS, vol. 1880. Springer, Heidelberg, August 2000. https://doi.org/10.1007/3-540-44598-6
14. Bernstein, D.J., et al.: NTRU Prime. Technical report, National Institute of Standards and Technology (2020)
15. Biehl, I., Meyer, B., Müller, V.: Differential fault attacks on elliptic curve cryptosystems. In: Bellare [13], pp. 131–146 (2000)
16. Biham, E., Shamir, A.: Differential fault analysis of secret key cryptosystems. In: Kaliski, B.S. (ed.) CRYPTO 1997. LNCS, vol. 1294, pp. 513–525. Springer, Heidelberg (1997). https://doi.org/10.1007/BFb0052259
17. Bindel, N., Hamburg, M., Hövelmanns, K., Hülsing, A., Persichetti, E.: Tighter proofs of CCA security in the quantum random oracle model. In: Hofheinz, D., Rosen, A. (eds.) TCC 2019, Part II. LNCS, vol. 11892, pp. 61–90. Springer, Cham (2019). https://doi.org/10.1007/978-3-030-36033-7_3
18. Blömer, J., Günther, P.: Singular curve point decompression attack. In: FDTC 2015, pp. 71–84. IEEE Computer Society (2015)
19. Boneh, D., Dagdelen, Ö., Fischlin, M., Lehmann, A., Schaffner, C., Zhandry, M.: Random oracles in a quantum world. In: Lee, D.H., Wang, X. (eds.) ASIACRYPT 2011. LNCS, vol. 7073, pp. 41–69. Springer, Heidelberg (2011). https://doi.org/10.1007/978-3-642-25385-0_3
20. Boneh, D., DeMillo, R.A., Lipton, R.J.: On the importance of eliminating errors in cryptographic computations. J. Cryptol. 14(2), 101–119 (2001)

21. Boneh, D., Venkatesan, R.: Breaking RSA may not be equivalent to factoring. In: Nyberg, K. (ed.) EUROCRYPT 1998. LNCS, vol. 1403, pp. 59–71. Springer, Heidelberg (1998). https://doi.org/10.1007/BFb0054117
22. Chen, C., et al.: NTRU. Technical report, National Institute of Standards and Technology (2020)
23. Cheon, J.H., Takagi, T. (eds.): ASIACRYPT 2016, Part I. LNCS, vol. 10031. Springer, Heidelberg (2016). https://doi.org/10.1007/978-3-662-53887-6
24. Coron, J.-S., Kizhvatov, I.: An efficient method for random delay generation in embedded software. In: Clavier, C., Gaj, K. (eds.) CHES 2009. LNCS, vol. 5747, pp. 156–170. Springer, Heidelberg (2009). https://doi.org/10.1007/978-3-642-04138-9_12
25. Costello, C.: The case for SIKE: a decade of the supersingular isogeny problem. Cryptology ePrint Archive, Report 2021/543 (2021). https://eprint.iacr.org/2021/543
26. Cramer, R., Shoup, V.: Design and analysis of practical public-key encryption schemes secure against adaptive chosen ciphertext attack. SIAM J. Comput. $33(1)$, 167–226 (2003)
27. D'Anvers, J.P., et al.: SABER. Technical report, National Institute of Standards and Technology (2020)
28. De Feo, L., Jao, D., Plût, J.: Towards quantum-resistant cryptosystems from supersingular elliptic curve isogenies. J. Math. Cryptol. $8(3)$, 209–247 (2014)
29. Dent, A.W.: A designer's guide to KEMs. In: Paterson, K.G. (ed.) Cryptography and Coding 2003. LNCS, vol. 2898, pp. 133–151. Springer, Heidelberg (2003). https://doi.org/10.1007/978-3-540-40974-8_12
30. Diffie, W., Hellman, M.E.: New directions in cryptography. IEEE Trans. Inf. Theory $22(6)$, 644–654 (1976)
31. Ding, J., Deaton, J., Schmidt, K., Vishakha, Zhang, Z.: A simple and practical key reuse attack on NTRU cryptosystem. Cryptology ePrint Archive, Report 2019/1022 (2019). https://eprint.iacr.org/2019/1022
32. Endo, S., Homma, N., Hayashi, Y., Takahashi, J., Fuji, H., Aoki, T.: A multiple-fault injection attack by adaptive timing control under black-box conditions and a countermeasure. In: Prouff, E. (ed.) COSADE 2014. LNCS, vol. 8622, pp. 214–228. Springer, Cham (2014). https://doi.org/10.1007/978-3-319-10175-0_15
33. Endo, S., Sugawara, T., Homma, N., Aoki, T., Satoh, A.: An on-chip glitchy-clock generator for testing fault injection attacks. J. Crypt. Eng. $1(4)$, 265–270 (2011)
34. Fluhrer, S.: Cryptanalysis of ring-LWE based key exchange with key share reuse. Cryptology ePrint Archive, Report 2016/085 (2016). https://eprint.iacr.org/2016/085
35. Fujisaki, E., Okamoto, T.: Secure integration of asymmetric and symmetric encryption schemes. In: Wiener [78], pp. 537–554 (1999)
36. Fujisaki, E., Okamoto, T.: Secure integration of asymmetric and symmetric encryption schemes. J. Cryptol. $26(1)$, 80–101 (2013)
37. Galbraith, S.D., Petit, C., Shani, B., Ti, Y.B.: On the security of supersingular isogeny cryptosystems. In: Cheon and Takagi [23], pp. 63–91 (2016)
38. Guo, Q., Johansson, T., Nilsson, A.: A key-recovery timing attack on post-quantum primitives using the Fujisaki-Okamoto transformation and its application on FrodoKEM. In: Micciancio, D., Ristenpart, T. (eds.) CRYPTO 2020, Part II. LNCS, vol. 12171, pp. 359–386. Springer, Cham (2020). https://doi.org/10.1007/978-3-030-56880-1_13
39. Guo, Q., Johansson, T., Stankovski, P.: A key recovery attack on MDPC with CCA security using decoding errors. In: Cheon and Takagi [23], pp. 789–815 (2016)

40. Hall, C., Goldberg, I., Schneier, B.: Reaction attacks against several public-key cryptosystem. In: Varadharajan, V., Mu, Y. (eds.) ICICS 1999. LNCS, vol. 1726, pp. 2–12. Springer, Heidelberg (1999). https://doi.org/10.1007/978-3-540-47942-0_2

41. Hayashi, Y., Homma, N., Sugawara, T., Mizuki, T., Aoki, T., Sone, H.: Non-invasive trigger-free fault injection method based on intentional electromagnetic interference. In: Proceedings of The Non-Invasive Attack Testing Workshop - NIAT 2011, September 2011

42. Hofheinz, D., Hövelmanns, K., Kiltz, E.: A modular analysis of the Fujisaki-Okamoto transformation. In: Kalai, Y., Reyzin, L. (eds.) TCC 2017, Part I. LNCS, vol. 10677, pp. 341–371. Springer, Cham (2017). https://doi.org/10.1007/978-3-319-70500-2_12

43. Howe, J., Prest, T., Apon, D.: SoK: how (not) to design and implement post-quantum cryptography. In: Paterson, K.G. (ed.) CT-RSA 2021. LNCS, vol. 12704, pp. 444–477. Springer, Cham (2021). https://doi.org/10.1007/978-3-030-75539-3_19

44. Huguenin-Dumittan, L., Vaudenay, S.: Classical misuse attacks on NIST round 2 PQC. In: Conti, M., Zhou, J., Casalicchio, E., Spognardi, A. (eds.) ACNS 2020, Part I. LNCS, vol. 12146, pp. 208–227. Springer, Cham (2020). https://doi.org/10.1007/978-3-030-57808-4_11

45. Jao, D., et al.: SIKE. Technical report, National Institute of Standards and Technology (2020)

46. Jao, D., De Feo, L.: Towards quantum-resistant cryptosystems from supersingular elliptic curve isogenies. In: Yang, B.-Y. (ed.) PQCrypto 2011. LNCS, vol. 7071, pp. 19–34. Springer, Heidelberg (2011). https://doi.org/10.1007/978-3-642-25405-5_2

47. Jiang, H., Zhang, Z., Chen, L., Wang, H., Ma, Z.: IND-CCA-Secure key encapsulation mechanism in the quantum random oracle model, revisited. In: Shacham, H., Boldyreva, A. (eds.) CRYPTO 2018, Part III. LNCS, vol. 10993, pp. 96–125. Springer, Cham (2018). https://doi.org/10.1007/978-3-319-96878-0_4

48. Jiang, H., Zhang, Z., Ma, Z.: Key encapsulation mechanism with explicit rejection in the quantum random oracle model. In: Lin, D., Sako, K. (eds.) PKC 2019, Part II. LNCS, vol. 11443, pp. 618–645. Springer, Cham (2019). https://doi.org/10.1007/978-3-030-17259-6_21

49. Kannwischer, M.J., Rijneveld, J., Schwabe, P., Stoffelen, K.: pqm4: post-quantum crypto library for the ARM Cortex-M4 (2021). https://github.com/mupq/pqm4

50. Kocher, P.C.: Timing attacks on implementations of Diffie-Hellman, RSA, DSS, and other systems. In: Koblitz, N. (ed.) CRYPTO 1996. LNCS, vol. 1109, pp. 104–113. Springer, Heidelberg (1996). https://doi.org/10.1007/3-540-68697-5_9

51. Kocher, P.C., Jaffe, J., Jun, B.: Differential power analysis. In: Wiener [78], pp. 388–397 (1999)

52. Kuchta, V., Sakzad, A., Stehlé, D., Steinfeld, R., Sun, S.-F.: Measure-rewind-measure: tighter quantum random oracle model proofs for one-way to hiding and CCA security. In: Canteaut, A., Ishai, Y. (eds.) EUROCRYPT 2020, Part III. LNCS, vol. 12107, pp. 703–728. Springer, Cham (2020). https://doi.org/10.1007/978-3-030-45727-3_24

53. Lindner, R., Peikert, C.: Better key sizes (and attacks) for LWE-based encryption. In: Kiayias, A. (ed.) CT-RSA 2011. LNCS, vol. 6558, pp. 319–339. Springer, Heidelberg (2011). https://doi.org/10.1007/978-3-642-19074-2_21

54. Lyubashevsky, V., Peikert, C., Regev, O.: On ideal lattices and learning with errors over rings. In: Gilbert, H. (ed.) EUROCRYPT 2010. LNCS, vol. 6110, pp. 1–23. Springer, Heidelberg (2010). https://doi.org/10.1007/978-3-642-13190-5_1

55. McEliece, R.J.: A public-key cryptosystem based on algebraic coding theory. The deep space network progress report 42–44, Jet Propulsion Laboratory, California Institute of Technology, January/February 1978. https://ipnpr.jpl.nasa.gov/progress_report2/42-44/44N.PDF

56. Misoczki, R., Tillich, J., Sendrier, N., Barreto, P.S.L.M.: MDPC-McEliece: new McEliece variants from moderate density parity-check codes. In: ISIT 2013, pp. 2069–2073. IEEE (2013)

57. Naehrig, M., et al.: FrodoKEM. Technical report, National Institute of Standards and Technology (2020)

58. Niederreiter, H.: Knapsack-type cryptosystems and algebraic coding theory. Prob. Control Inf. Theory **15**(2), 159–166 (1986)

59. Okamoto, T., Pointcheval, D.: REACT: rapid enhanced-security asymmetric cryptosystem transform. In: Naccache, D. (ed.) CT-RSA 2001. LNCS, vol. 2020, pp. 159–174. Springer, Heidelberg (2000). https://doi.org/10.1007/3-540-45353-9_13

60. Pessl, P., Prokop, L.: Fault attacks on CCA-secure lattice KEMs. IACR TCHES **2021**(2), 37–60 (2021). https://tches.iacr.org/index.php/TCHES/article/view/8787

61. Qin, Y., Cheng, C., Ding, J.: An efficient key mismatch attack on the NIST second round candidate Kyber. Cryptology ePrint Archive, Report 2019/1343 (2019). https://eprint.iacr.org/2019/1343

62. Qin, Y., Cheng, C., Zhang, X., Pan, Y., Hu, L., Ding, J.: A systematic approach and analysis of key mismatch attacks on CPA-secure lattice-based NIST candidate KEMs. Cryptology ePrint Archive, Report 2021/123 (2021). https://eprint.iacr.org/2021/123

63. Rackoff, C., Simon, D.R.: Non-interactive zero-knowledge proof of knowledge and chosen ciphertext attack. In: Feigenbaum, J. (ed.) CRYPTO 1991. LNCS, vol. 576, pp. 433–444. Springer, Heidelberg (1992). https://doi.org/10.1007/3-540-46766-1_35

64. Ravi, P., Ezerman, M.F., Bhasin, S., Chattopadhyay, A., Roy, S.S.: Will you cross the threshold for me? - Generic side-channel assisted chosen-ciphertext attacks on NTRU-based KEMs. Cryptology ePrint Archive, Report 2021/718 (2021). https://eprint.iacr.org/2021/718

65. Ravi, P., Roy, S.S.: Side-channel analysis of lattice-based PQC candidates. NIST PQC Round 3 Seminars (2021). https://csrc.nist.gov/projects/post-quantum-cryptography/workshops-and-timeline/round-3-seminars

66. Ravi, P., Roy, S.S., Chattopadhyay, A., Bhasin, S.: Generic side-channel attacks on CCA-secure lattice-based PKE and KEMs. IACR TCHES **2020**(3), 307–335 (2020). https://tches.iacr.org/index.php/TCHES/article/view/8592

67. Rivest, R.L., Shamir, A., Adleman, L.M.: A method for obtaining digital signatures and public-key cryptosystems. Commun. Assoc. Comput. Mach. **21**(2), 120–126 (1978)

68. Saha, D., Mukhopadhyay, D., RoyChowdhury, D.: A diagonal fault attack on the advanced encryption standard. Cryptology ePrint Archive, Report 2009/581 (2009). https://eprint.iacr.org/2009/581

69. Saito, T., Xagawa, K., Yamakawa, T.: Tightly-secure key-encapsulation mechanism in the quantum random oracle model. In: Nielsen, J.B., Rijmen, V. (eds.) EUROCRYPT 2018, Part III. LNCS, vol. 10822, pp. 520–551. Springer, Cham (2018). https://doi.org/10.1007/978-3-319-78372-7_17

70. Schwabe, P., et al.: CRYSTALS-KYBER. Technical report, National Institute of Standards and Technology (2020)

71. Shor, P.W.: Algorithms for quantum computation: discrete logarithms and factoring. In: 35th FOCS, pp. 124–134. IEEE Computer Society Press, November 1994
72. Shoup, V.: Using hash functions as a hedge against chosen ciphertext attack. In: Preneel, B. (ed.) EUROCRYPT 2000. LNCS, vol. 1807, pp. 275–288. Springer, Heidelberg (2000). https://doi.org/10.1007/3-540-45539-6_19
73. Singh, S.: The Code Book. Fourth Estate (1999)
74. Skorobogatov, S.P., Anderson, R.J.: Optical fault induction attacks. In: Kaliski, B.S., Koç, K., Paar, C. (eds.) CHES 2002. LNCS, vol. 2523, pp. 2–12. Springer, Heidelberg (2003). https://doi.org/10.1007/3-540-36400-5_2
75. Takahashi, A., Tibouchi, M.: Degenerate fault attacks on elliptic curve parameters in openssl. In: Euro S&P 2019, pp. 371–386. IEEE (2019)
76. Targhi, E.E., Unruh, D.: Post-quantum security of the Fujisaki-Okamoto and OAEP transforms. In: Hirt, M., Smith, A. (eds.) TCC 2016-B, Part II. LNCS, vol. 9986, pp. 192–216. Springer, Heidelberg (2016). https://doi.org/10.1007/978-3-662-53644-5_8
77. Vacek, J., Václavek, J.: Key mismatch attack on ThreeBears, Frodo and Round5. In: Hong, D. (ed.) ICISC 2020. LNCS, vol. 12593, pp. 182–198. Springer, Cham (2021). https://doi.org/10.1007/978-3-030-68890-5_10
78. Wiener, M. (ed.): CRYPTO 1999. LNCS, vol. 1666. Springer, Heidelberg (1999). https://doi.org/10.1007/3-540-48405-1
79. Yen, S.M., Joye, M.: Checking before output may not be enough against fault-based cryptanalysis. IEEE Trans. Comput. 49(9), 967–970 (2000)
80. Sung-Ming, Y., Kim, S., Lim, S., Moon, S.: A countermeasure against one physical cryptanalysis may benefit another attack. In: Kim, K. (ed.) ICISC 2001. LNCS, vol. 2288, pp. 414–427. Springer, Heidelberg (2002). https://doi.org/10.1007/3-540-45861-1_31
81. Zhang, X., Cheng, C., Qin, Y., Ding, R.: Small leaks sink a great ship: an evaluation of key reuse resilience of PQC third round finalist NTRU-HRSS. Cryptology ePrint Archive, Report 2021/168 (2021). https://eprint.iacr.org/2021/168. To appear in ICICS 2021

Divided We Stand, United We Fall: Security Analysis of Some SCA+SIFA Countermeasures Against SCA-Enhanced Fault Template Attacks

Sayandeep Saha[1(✉)], Arnab Bag[1(✉)], Dirmanto Jap[2(✉)],
Debdeep Mukhopadhyay[1(✉)], and Shivam Bhasin[2(✉)]

[1] Department of Computer Science and Engineering, IIT Kharagpur,
Kharagpur, India
{sahasayandeep,abag,debdeep}@iitkgp.ac.in
[2] Temasek Labs, Nanyang Technological University, Singapore, Singapore
{djap,sbhasin}@ntu.edu.sg

Abstract. Protection against Side-Channel (SCA) and Fault Attacks (FA) requires two classes of countermeasures to be simultaneously embedded in a cryptographic implementation. It has already been shown that a straightforward combination of SCA and FA countermeasures are vulnerable against FAs, such as Statistical Ineffective Fault Analysis (SIFA) and Fault Template Attacks (FTA). Consequently, new classes of countermeasures have been proposed which prevent against SIFA, and also includes masking for SCA protection. While they are secure against SIFA and SCA individually, one important question is whether the security claim still holds at the presence of a combined SCA and FA adversary. Security against combined attacks is, however, desired, as countermeasures for both threats are included in such implementations.

In this paper, we show that some of the recently proposed combined SIFA and SCA countermeasures fall prey against combined attacks. To this end, we enhance the FTA attacks by considering side-channel information during fault injection. The success of the proposed attacks stems from some non-trivial fault propagation properties of S-Boxes, which remains unexplored in the original FTA proposal. The proposed attacks are validated on an open-source software implementation of Keccak with SIFA-protected χ_5 S-Box with laser fault injection and power measurement, and a hardware implementation of a SIFA-protected χ_3 S-Box through gate-level power trace simulation. Finally, we discuss some mitigation strategies to strengthen existing countermeasures.

Keywords: Fault Attack · Side-channel · Masking

An extended version with supplementary material is available at https://eprint.iacr.org/2020/892.

© International Association for Cryptologic Research 2021
M. Tibouchi and H. Wang (Eds.): ASIACRYPT 2021, LNCS 13091, pp. 62–94, 2021.
https://doi.org/10.1007/978-3-030-92075-3_3

1   Introduction

Implementation-centric attacks on cryptographic primitives are one of the greatest practical threats to secure communication. The core idea behind such attacks is to exploit the physical properties of implementations, which often correlate with the secret. Especially for embedded and IoT devices, such physical properties are easily accessible to an adversary. Most of the implementation attacks are quite challenging to prevent, and there is a continuous effort for building suitable countermeasures against such exploits.

Side-Channel Attacks (SCA) [1–3] and Fault Attacks (FA) [4,5] are the two most established classes of implementation attacks. An SCA adversary exploits the fact that the power consumption or electromagnetic (EM) radiation from a cryptographic implementation is correlated with the computation. Passive eavesdropping on these signals may lead to the recovery of the secret. An FA adversary, on the other hand, actively perturbs the computation and exploit the faulty responses to derive the secret. Controlled transient perturbation of the computation, as required for FA, is feasible for both hardware and software implementations. Some popular means of injecting such controlled faults include clock/voltage glitching [6], EM radiation [7], and laser injection [8]. Over the years, the injection mechanisms have improved significantly, which allows an adversary to inject even at a bit-level precision with very high repeatability [7,8].

Several countermeasures have been proposed for both SCA and FA prevention. In the context of SCA, the most prominent class of countermeasures is the masking [9–12]. Loosely speaking, masking aims to remove the dependency between the power/EM signals and the cryptographic computation by randomizing each execution. This randomization is achieved by realizing secret sharing at the circuit-level. More precisely, masking schemes randomly split each variable x into multiple variables $x^1, x^2, \cdots, x^{d+1}$ called *shares* of x, which satisfies the invariant $x^1 \star x^2 \star \cdots \star x^{d+1} = x$. Here $\star$ denotes some operations. A function $f()$ operating on x (and maybe some other variables y, z, $\cdots$) is also split into multiple component functions $f_1, f_2, \cdots f_m$ such that $\star$ combination of the outcomes from these functions matches with the actual outcome of f. In order to perform the SCA on such an implementation, the adversary must combine the information from all $d + 1$ shares of a variable. No proper subset of the shares of a target variable leak information about the variable. Breaking such schemes thus requires a statistical analysis with d-th order moment and the data complexity (i.e. the number of encryptions required) of the attacks increases almost exponentially with the statistical order d.

FA countermeasures use some form of redundancy in computation to detect the presence of a fault. Upon detection of a fault, the cipher output is either muted or randomized. The redundancy is realized either in time/space or as information redundancy in the form of Error-Correcting Codes (ECC) [6]. Furthermore, the fault detection operation is either applied at the end of each round, or the end of the complete encryption operation. Such countermeasures are found to be effective for many of the fault models with an exception for so-called *ineffective faults*. Ineffective faults are those faults which may or may not corrupt

Attack	Breaks Simple SCA-FA Countermeasure	Breaks SCA-SIFA Countermeasure	Remarks
SIFA	✓	✗	No middle round attack
FTA	✓	✗	Middle round attack possible
SCA-FTA	✓	✓	**Middle round attack possible**

the output depending upon the value(s) of some intermediate variable(s). The Statistical Ineffective Fault Attacks (SIFA) [13,14] and Fault Template Attacks (FTA) [7], which exploit the data-dependency of ineffective faults, can successfully bypass most of the detection-based countermeasures. To prevent SIFA, finegrained error correction on shares is suggested [15], so that the data-dependency of fault ineffectivity is mitigated. Another alternative is to modify the S-Box implementations so that every fault becomes effective [16]. In such cases, error detection at the end of computation becomes sufficient for SIFA prevention.

Most of the (if not all) unprotected cryptographic primitives (without loss of generality, in this work we consider symmetric key primitives only) are vulnerable against SCA and FA. It is thus desirable that such primitives include countermeasures for both the attack classes. Recently, there have been multiple proposals which combine masking with some FA countermeasure to prevent both SCA and FA [15–17]. However, an interesting question still remains – do these schemes provide protection while both SCA and FA are applied simultaneously? This question is important as both SCA and FA countermeasures incur significant cost in terms of area and timing, and a user would expect protection from both threats (even simultaneously) if countermeasures for both are present. While many of the existing countermeasure proposals already show vulnerability to SIFA, there exist some recent proposals [15,16,18,19] preventing SIFA.

1.1 Our Contributions

The aim of this work is to show that certain implementations (more precisely, those described in [16] and [15]) containing both SCA and FA countermeasures are still insecure against combined SCA-FA attacks, even if they explicitly include SIFA protection. In order to show this, we enhance the recently proposed FTA attacks by considering side-channel leakage in the presence of faults, and constructing fault templates based on that leakage. More precisely, we exploit side-channel leakage from the detection and correction operations in the presence of faults. The main cause behind the success of SCA enhanced FTA (referred as SCA-FTA in this work) is that *output differentials of an S-Box leak information about the input of the S-Box, if the fault location is fixed (that means the input differential is fixed.)*. Using this fact, we can expose intermediate states of a symmetric key primitive, even if it includes FA, SCA and certain SIFA countermeasures[1]. Such exploitation of detection and correction operations raises an important question – how to perform error detection/correction without causing new vulnerabilities? We discuss a potential way to address this issue at the end.

While performing attacks on masked implementations, one has to be careful about the statistical order of the leakage. Any attack involving SCA leakage, having a statistical order beyond the claimed SCA security order, is considered as trivial. We carefully take this issue into consideration and show that the proposed attacks do not violate the SCA security margins of the targets. For example, we designate an attack on a first-order secure implementation as *efficient*, only if the attack is also first order in terms of SCA analysis. SCA-FTA can efficiently attack the target implementations even if they have higher-order masking, with single-bit fault along with SCA leakage of an order lower than the masking.

As an interesting outcome of this work, we found that the *non-completeness* property present in certain masking schemes plays an important role behind the success and failure of the attacks. This observation is crucial as it may help in constructing countermeasures. However, in this paper, we do not explore the countermeasures in detail and only present a short guideline in this context.

In order to validate our ideas, we utilize different masked S-Boxes. To theoretically validate the attacks against SIFA-secure implementations we choose one example presented in [16] on χ_3 S-Box [20]. To practically validate our idea, we choose the open-source SIFA-protected Keccak implementation with χ_5 S-Box (an extension of the χ_3 S-Box) due to [16], and target this using laser fault injection and power measurements. Furthermore, to understand the impact of the attack on a hardware-level SCA-leakage scenario, we validate one of our attack over a hardware implementation of the SIFA secure χ_3 S-Box [16] through fault simulation and power-trace simulation. Our trace simulation flow uses commercial tools such as VCS, Design Compiler, and PrimeTime-PX from Synopsys[2].

It is worth mentioning that previous works have also proposed combined SCA and FA attacks on protected implementations. Notable among them are [21–23], where the error detection operation at the last round was targeted for extracting the fault differential through SCA. However, none of these attacks works for the cases where error detection is performed on masked data[3]. SCA-FTA works in such a context. Moreover, SIFA countermeasures combined with masking were

---

[1] It is worth noting that SIFA and FTA break certain countermeasures which directly combine masking and detection/infection. SCA-FTA can also break them by measuring the SCA leakage while computing the correctness of the ciphertext. However, in this paper, we only discuss some SIFA countermeasures, which are secure against SIFA and classical FTA.

[2] These tools are under registered trademarks of Synopsys Inc.

[3] We note that the combined attack in [21] exploits the fact that error detection is often performed on unmasked data even if the rest of the computation is masked. They extracted the Hamming weight (HW) of unmasked ciphertext differentials through side-channel and exploited it. It was pointed out in [21] that this attack can be mitigated if the detection is performed on masked data. In this paper, we show that SCA-FTA works even while the detection/correction is performed on masked data.

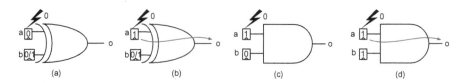

Fig. 1. Fault activation and propagation with stuck-at-0 fault: (a) No fault activation; (b) Fault activation and propagation for XOR; (c) Fault activation but no propagation for AND; (d) Fault activation and propagation for AND.

never been analyzed in such combined attack contexts. No fault templates were constructed to exploit information leakage from different fault locations in these attacks, which is also new in SCA-FTA. Finally, unlike previous attacks, our attacks are applicable to the middle rounds not requiring any ciphertext access (if there are error detection/correction at the middle rounds such as in [15]). Appendix E (ref. supplementary material) presents a comparative discussion on SCA-FTA and the related attacks.

The rest of the paper is organized as follows. We begin with presenting the preliminary ideas of fault-induced SCA leakage in Sect. 2. The SCA-FTA attack is proposed next with application to unmasked implementations in Sect. 3. Section 4 presents attacks on masked implementations and two recently proposed SIFA countermeasures. We summarize the practical evaluations in Sect. 5, with details given in the supplementary material (Appendix F). A brief discussion on a candidate countermeasure strategy is presented in Sect. 6. Finally, we conclude in Sect. 7. A discussion on the impact of SCA-FTA on some other countermeasures is presented in Appendix G in the supplementary material[4].

2   Fault-Induced SCA Leakage

2.1   Faults and Combinational Circuits

A faulty outcome in a combinational circuit is a result of two consecutive events, namely, *Fault Activation* and *Fault Propagation*. Given an internal net[5] i in a combinational circuit $\mathcal{C}$, fault activation event assigns i with a value x such that i carries complement of x (i.e. $\bar{x}$) in the presence of a fault in i, and x, otherwise. On the other hand, fault propagation is an event which takes place when the impact of an activated fault is observed at some output net of the circuit $\mathcal{C}$. The goal of an Automatic Test Pattern Generation (ATPG) algorithm is to figure out test vectors which can activate and propagate a fault happening at some internal net i to the output, leading to the detection of that fault. Detection of a fault depends on the test vector and the location of the faulty net in $\mathcal{C}$.

---

[4] Code for validating the attacks has been published at https://github.com/sayandeep-iitkgp/SCA-FTA.

[5] In this paper, we use the terms wire and net interchangeably.

The most important observation in this context is the location and input-dependency of fault detection for a given combinational circuit. This data-dependency has also been utilized in the original FTA and SIFA. The data dependency stems from the fact that fault propagation through basic gates is data-dependent. To further explain this, we consider the XOR and the AND gates shown in Fig. 1. The activation of the fault in any of the inputs of these gates depends upon the current value assigned to the input. For example, if we consider a stuck-at-0 fault, the target input net must be assigned to a value 1 in order to activate the fault (ref. Fig. 1(b), (c), (d)). However, in the case of bit-flip faults, the fault activation happens with certainty and does not depend on the value in the net. The fault propagation depends on the type of the gate. In the case of an XOR gate, the fault propagation happens whenever there is a fault activation in one of the input nets[6] (Fig. 1(b)). In contrast, fault propagation in an AND gate is dependent on the fault activation, and the values assigned to the other non-faulty input nets of the gate. More precisely, fault propagation requires all the other input nets to have a value 1 (also called the *non-controlling* value for an AND gate; Fig. 1(d)). Similar impacts can be observed for OR gates where the non-controlling value is 0. To summarize, our observations are as follows:

1. Stuck-at faults at an input net of an XOR gate only leak the value at the faulty net by means of fault activation. Fault propagation in XOR gate happens with certainty whenever there is a fault at an input.
2. Bit-flip faults at an XOR gate input does not leak the input value as the activation is not data-dependent.
3. Both stuck-at and bit-flip faults leak input values of an AND gate through fault propagation, except the value of the faulty net in case of bit-flip faults.

Most of the fault-induced leakages in combinational circuits are caused by the three abovementioned conditions. In the original FTA proposal, a gate input (during some intermediate computation of a cipher) is exposed to the adversary based on whether the ciphertext is correct or faulty. Knowledge of correctness does not require the adversary to have the ciphertexts explicitly. Moreover, depending on the underlying fault propagation patterns in the target implementation, the FTA adversary forms *fault templates* over a device under her control. Later it can use these templates to target a similar device with an unknown key. In contrast, SIFA attacks require access to the correct ciphertexts. The SIFA countermeasures we are going to analyze, however, prevents such data-dependent fault propagations to the ciphertexts. Attacking them thus requires some more properties of fault propagations to be taken into consideration. In the next subsection, we analyse the impact of fault propagation for multi-output combinational circuits, which is important for developing the SCA-enhanced FTA. Without loss of generality, we shall mostly use bit-flip faults.

---

[6] Note that here we restrict ourselves to the cases where only one input net is faulty.

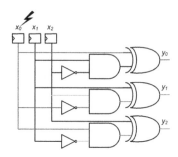

Fig. 2. Fault propagation through χ_3 S-Box for a bit-flip fault at x_0. The wires through which the fault propagates without data dependency are shown in red. The data-dependent propagation is shown in blue. For each AND gate, the input controlling the propagation is shown in green. (Color figure online)

2.2 Fault Propagation in Multi-output Combinational Circuits

Combinational circuits, in general, contain *fan-outs*[7] as well as multiple outputs. Depending on the structure of the circuit, the fault location, and the input value an injected fault may corrupt one or multiple of these outputs. Interestingly, there exists a data and fault location-dependent pattern of output corruption for a given multi-output circuit. To explain this we consider the circuit shown in Fig. 2 which is the χ_3 S-Box from [20]. Note that we specifically consider an S-Box here as they are going to be the primary attack targets in the rest of the paper. The logic expressions corresponding to each output of χ_3 are given as:

$$y_0 = x_0 + x_1\overline{x_2} , \qquad y_1 = x_1 + x_2\overline{x_0} , \qquad y_2 = x_2 + x_0\overline{x_1} \qquad (1)$$

Here x_0, x_1, x_2 denote the input bits of the S-Box and y_0, y_1, y_2 represent the output bits. x_0 and y_0 denote the Most Significant Bits (MSB) of the input and output, respectively. Without loss of generality, we consider a bit-flip fault at the input x_0. The fan-outs allow the fault to propagate to all three output logic expressions. However, the propagation patterns depend on the inputs. One may observe that the fault always propagates to the output y_0 irrespective of the inputs. This is because the fault model is bit-flip and x_0 exists linearly in the expression of y_0 (i.e. x_0 is the input of an XOR gate). However, y_1 gets corrupted only if $x_2 = 1$. Similarly, y_2 is faulty only if $x_1 = 0$.

The fault patterns corresponding to each input pattern of the S-Box is shown in Table 1 for the above-mentioned fault location. The patterns leak the values of x_1 and x_2, hence resulting in an entropy reduction of 2 bits for the S-Box input. No information is leaked for x_0. As a result of 2-bit entropy loss, there are only two inputs corresponding to each fault pattern (ref. Table 2). Choosing any other fault injection point, (say x_1) would leak the value of x_0. Data-dependent

---

[7] A fan-out is a structure where one net drives the input of multiple gates. The driver net is called the *fan-out stem* and the inputs driven by the *fan-out stem* are called *fan-out branches*.

Table 1. Inputs and Corresponding Fault Patterns for χ_3 S-Box for a bit-flip fault at x_0. 'F' denotes faulty and 'C' denotes correct output bit.

x_0	x_1	x_2	y_0	y_1	y_2
0	0	0	F	C	F
0	0	1	F	F	F
0	1	0	F	C	C
0	1	1	F	F	C
1	0	0	F	C	F
1	0	1	F	F	F
1	1	0	F	C	C
1	1	1	F	F	C

Table 2. Distinct fault patterns and the inputs causing them for bit-flip fault at x_0 of χ_3

y_0	y_1	y_2	Input
F	C	F	(0, 4)
F	F	F	(1, 5)
F	C	C	(2, 6)
F	F	C	(3, 7)

output fault patterns exist for most of the existing S-Box constructions. The key reason behind this data-dependency is the non-linearity which is essential for any S-Box. However, the amount of entropy loss may vary depending on the S-Box structure. To illustrate this, we consider the 4-bit S-Box from the block cipher PRESENT [24] given as follows:

$$
\begin{aligned}
y_0 &= x_0x_1x_3 + x_0x_2x_3 + x_0 + x_1x_2x_3 + x_1x_2 + x_2 + x_3 + 1 \\
y_1 &= x_0x_1x_3 + x_0x_2x_3 + x_0x_2 + x_0x_3 + x_0 + x_1 + x_2x_3 + 1 \\
y_2 &= x_0x_1x_3 + x_0x_1 + x_0x_2x_3 + x_0x_2 + x_0 + x_1x_2x_3 + x_2 \\
y_3 &= x_0 + x_1x_2 + x_1 + x_3
\end{aligned}
\tag{2}
$$

Here x_0, x_1, x_2, x_3 are the inputs and y_0, y_1, y_2, y_3 are outputs. x_0 and y_0 are the Most Significant Bits (MSB) of the input and output, respectively. A fault in x_0 in this case propagates to y_0 only if $x_1x_3 + x_2x_3 + 1 = 1$ ($x_1x_3 + x_2x_3 + 1 = 0$, otherwise). Similarly, y_1 gets corrupted if $x_1x_3 + x_2x_3 + x_2 + x_3 + 1 = 1$, and y_2 gets corrupted if $x_1x_3 + x_1 + x_2x_3 + x_2 + 1 = 1$. Simplification of such equations results in the exposure of x_1, x_2 and x_3 if $(x_1 + x_2) = 1$ (that is an entropy reduction of 3 bits). If $(x_1 + x_2) = 0$, an entropy reduction of 2 bits happen for x_1, x_2, x_3 with constraints $(x_1 + x_2) = 0$ and $(x_2 + x_3) = 0$ (or $(x_2 + x_3) = 1$). Table 3 shows the distinct fault patterns at the output and inputs causing them.

Table 3. Distinct fault patterns and the inputs causing them for bit-fault at x_0 in PRESENT S-Box

y_0	y_1	y_2	y_3	Input
F	C	F	F	(1, 6, 9, 14)
F	F	C	F	(4, 12)
C	F	F	F	(5, 13)
F	F	F	F	(0, 7, 8, 15)
F	C	C	F	(2, 10)
C	C	F	F	(3, 11)

Table 4. DDT for PRESENT

$\delta_i \backslash \delta_o$	0	1	2	3	4	5	6	7	8	9	10	11	12	13	14	15
0	16	0	0	0	0	0	0	0	0	0	0	0	0	0	0	0
1	0	0	0	4	0	0	0	4	0	4	0	0	0	4	0	0
2	0	0	0	2	0	4	2	0	0	0	2	0	2	2	2	0
3	0	2	0	2	2	0	4	2	0	0	2	2	0	0	0	0
4	0	0	0	0	0	4	2	2	0	2	2	0	2	0	2	0
5	0	2	0	0	2	0	0	0	0	2	2	2	4	2	0	0
6	0	0	2	0	0	0	2	0	2	0	0	4	2	0	0	4
7	0	4	2	0	0	0	2	0	2	0	0	0	2	0	0	4
8	0	0	0	2	0	0	0	2	0	2	0	4	0	2	0	4
9	0	0	2	0	4	0	2	0	2	0	0	0	2	0	4	0
10	0	0	2	2	0	4	0	0	2	0	2	0	0	2	2	0
11	0	2	0	0	2	0	0	0	4	2	2	2	0	2	0	0
12	0	0	2	0	0	4	0	2	2	2	2	0	0	0	2	0
13	0	2	4	2	2	0	0	2	0	0	2	2	0	0	0	0
14	0	0	2	2	0	0	2	2	2	2	0	0	2	2	0	0
15	0	4	0	0	4	0	0	0	0	0	0	0	0	0	4	4

The entropy losses due to data-dependency of output differentials can also be explained by means of the Differential Distribution Table (DDT) of an S-Box. Let us consider the DDT of PRESENT S-Box depicted in Table 4. Referring to the fault location x_0 from the previous paragraph (which is the MSB), the input differential between the correct input nibble X and faulty input nibble X_f becomes $\delta_i = X + X_f = 8$. The output differentials (δ_o) corresponds to the fault patterns at the output ("F" denotes 1 and "C" denotes 0). In the δ_i-th (shaded) row of the DDT, there are only 6 non-zero cells indicating *only 6 distinct output differentials are possible if a fault is injected at x_0*. Furthermore, there are 4 cells with value 2 indicating that *for 4 of the possible output differentials there are only 2 possible input values (that is an entropy loss of 3 bits for a 4-bit S-Box input)*. Finally, there are 2 cells with 4 input values indicating an entropy loss of 2 bits corresponding to those output differentials. The output differentials are directly linked with the constraints we derived in the last paragraph using the concept of fault propagation (i.e. output differentials decide the right-hand side of each constraint equation). Even though we link the data-dependency of output differentials with DDT, in the rest of the paper, we shall continue giving explanations in terms of fault propagation only as it seems more intuitive. However, it is worth mentioning that similar (albeit complex) explanations can be given in terms of DDT as well.

Table 5. HW of fault patterns and inputs causing them (for bit-flip fault at x_0 in χ_3)

HW	State
1	(2, 6)
2	(0, 4, 3, 7)
3	(1, 5)

Table 6. HW of fault patterns and inputs causing them (for bit-flip fault at x_0 in PRESENT S-Box)

HW	State
2	(2, 10, 3, 11)
3	(1, 6, 9, 14, 4, 12, 5, 13)
4	(0, 7, 8, 15)

2.3 The Role of SCA Leakage

It is clear from the last subsection that the knowledge of the output fault patterns of an S-Box leads to the leakage of its inputs. However, an important question still remains – how to track down the output fault patterns in a cipher implementation. In case of an unprotected implementation, it is straightforward for several Substitution-Permutation Network (SPN) constructions (such as AES or PRESENT) if the faults are injected at the inputs of the last round S-Boxes. This is because the attacker can obtain both correct and the faulty ciphertexts in this case. However, in this paper, we are mainly interested in protected implementations. For simplicity, let us first consider only FA protected implementations. Almost every FA-protected implementation incorporates time/space/information redundancy to detect the injected faults. Without loss of generality, we consider simple time/space redundancy where the cryptographic computation is performed at least two times and the end results are checked for mismatch. In the case of mismatch, no ciphertext (or maybe a randomized ciphertext) is returned. The check can also be incorporated in a per-round manner [25]. Such checks are usually performed by computing bitwise XOR between the actual and the redundant states followed by a bitwise OR to detect a nonzero XOR computation in case of a fault.

2.3.1 SCA Leakage from Detection

The bitwise XOR operation performed in several detection-based countermeasures leak information about the fault differential at the S-Box output. Referring to Table 2 and Table 3, a faulty ("F") output bit implies that the XOR outcome is 1, and a correct bit implies the XOR outcome is 0. An adversary capable of observing SCA leakage during fault injection can obtain some function of this output differential through the traces. More precisely, the adversary can obtain a $\mathcal{L} = HW(\delta_o) + \mathcal{N}$ where $\mathcal{L}$ is the observed SCA leakage, HW is the Hamming weight, and $\mathcal{N}$ denotes a Gaussian noise. Although the leakage of HW results in some information loss from δ_o, some entropy reduction for the S-Box input still takes place. To understand this, once again we refer to the fault patterns and the corresponding S-Box inputs from Table 2 and Table 3. In case of Table 2, a HW value 1 indicates that the input is in the set $(2, 6)$, HW value 2 indicates that the input belongs to the set $(0, 4, 3, 7)$, and HW value 3 indicates the input is in $(1, 5)$. This is consolidated in Table 5. Similar mappings can be constructed for Table 3 (ref. Table 6). *Clearly, even in the absence of faulty ciphertexts, the S-Box inputs can be exposed, which may lead to key or state recovery attacks.*

3 SCA-FTA: The SCA-Enhanced FTA

The last section motivates the importance of output differentials of S-Boxes and how they can be observed through SCA leakage. In this section, we exploit this observation for constructing practical attacks on block ciphers or other symmetric key primitives like hash functions. The proposed SCA-FTA attack is more powerful than original FTA in the sense that it can work even if information leakage due to fault ineffectivity does not reach the ciphertexts. **We assume an adversary who can inject a fault and measure the power traces at the same time, but not necessarily in the same clock cycles. Moreover, the adversary has full control over a test device for profiling which he can study extensively, and decide his fault-positions, injection-parameters, and build templates. Finally, the number of injections and the count of wires probed (through SCA leakage) in a specific clock cycle must be less than the defined security orders of the target with respect to faults and SCA**[8]. For the sake of explanation, we first describe the attack on an unmasked implementation with FA countermeasure. In Sect. 4, we apply SCA-FTA on SCA-SIFA countermeasures.

3.1 The Template Attack

The main assumption behind template attacks (whether side-channel template or fault template) is that an attacker can extensively profile a device similar to the target device. Such attacks consist of two phases:

3.1.1 Offline Phase (Template Building)
In the offline phase the adversary gathers information from a device (similar to the target), for which it has the complete knowledge and control of the secrets. The main idea is to construct an informed model, which can be utilized to derive the secret from a target device during the actual attack. Formally, a template in SCA-FTA can be described as a mapping $T : S_{\mathcal{F}} \to \mathcal{X}$, where an $s \in S_{\mathcal{F}}$ is a tuple described as $s = \langle \mathcal{G}_1(\mathcal{O}_{fl_1}), \mathcal{G}_2(\mathcal{O}_{fl_2}), \cdots, \mathcal{G}_M(\mathcal{O}_{fl_M}) \rangle$. Each $\mathcal{O}_{fl_i}$ denotes a set of SCA traces (power or EM) under the influence of fault injections at location fl_i and each $\mathcal{G}_i$ is a function extracting some statistic values according to some leakage model from these traces. The range set $\mathcal{X}$ represents a part of the secret intermediate state (for example, value of a byte/nibble).

At this point, it is important to compare the templates of SCA-FTA to the templates of original FTA. In original FTA proposal, the observables were the

---

[8] That is, for an implementation claiming protection against single-fault, not more than one fault is injected in each encryption. Similarly, for a first-order SCA secure implementation, only first-order attacks are performed.

Table 7. Template (noise-free) for unmasked FA-protected PRESENT considering average HW values as leakages.

fl_1	fl_2	fl_2	fl_3	State
2.0	3.0	2.0	3.0	(10)
4.0	2.0	2.0	2.0	(0, 15)
3.0	3.0	2.0	2.0	(12, 14)
4.0	2.0	3.0	3.0	(7)
2.0	2.0	3.0	3.0	(3)
3.0	2.0	2.0	2.0	(4, 13)
4.0	3.0	2.0	3.0	(8)
3.0	2.0	3.0	2.0	(1, 5)
3.0	2.0	2.0	3.0	(6, 9)
2.0	2.0	2.0	3.0	(2, 11)

correctness of the computation at the end. In contrast, we use the side-channel leakage from the computation under the influence of faults. Similar to the FTA, SCA-FTA also compiles information from multiple fault locations. For both the attacks, only one fault location is excited per encryption. However, a key difference between the two attacks is that while original FTA can only exploit the information whether an encryption is faulty or not at the end of computation, SCA-FTA can utilize fault information even from internal computation through SCA leakage. The difference with SCA template attacks is that while SCA templates are usually formed on the intermediate state values, templates in SCA-FTA are formed on the leakage from error-handling logic. Further, as we show for the masked implementations, SCA-FTA does not construct any template on the masks. In contrast, SCA template attacks result in higher-order attacks that leak information through templates built on higher-order-moments (hardware) or thought templates on both the mask and the state values (software).

3.1.2 Attack Phase (Template Matching)

In the online phase, the adversary injects faults at the predefined locations (from the template building phase) $\langle fl_1, fl_2, \cdots, fl_M \rangle$ on a target device with an unknown secret. The secret is recovered by first constructing an $s \in S_{\mathcal{F}}$ from the observables, and then using the mapping defined in $\mathcal{T}$.

In the next few subsections, we continue describing the SCA-FTA attacks on unmasked implementations.

3.2 Attacking Unmasked FA-Secure Implementations

Exploiting the ideas developed in the previous sections, here we present the first concrete realization of SCA-FTA. We consider an unmasked implementation of

Algorithm 1. *BUILD_TEMPLATE*

Input: Target implementation C, Faults $fl_1, fl_2, ..., fl_M, num_{ob}$
Output: Template $\mathcal{T}$
   $\mathcal{T} := \emptyset$
   $w :=$ GET_SBOX_SIZE()   ▷ Get the width of the S-Box
   for $(0 \leq x \leq 2^w)$ **do**   ▷ The key is known and fixed here and $x = p + k$
      $s := \emptyset$
      for each $fl \in \{fl_1, fl_1, ..., fl_M\}$ **do**
         $\mathcal{O}_{fl} := \emptyset$
         for num_{ob} observations **do**
            $y_f := C(x)^{fl}$ ▷ Inject fault in one copy of the S-Box for each execution
            $y_c := C(x)$
            $\mathcal{O}_{fl} := \mathcal{O}_{fl} \cup$ SCA_LEAKAGE(y_f, y_c) ▷ Leakage from the fault detection operation
         end for
         $s := s \cup \mathcal{G}(\mathcal{O}_{fl})$ ▷ We consider the same function $\mathcal{G}$ for all trace sets.
      end for
      $\mathcal{T} := \mathcal{T} \cup \{(s, x)\}$
   end for
   Return $\mathcal{T}$

PRESENT with fault detection at the end of encryption. Since the detection step is present at the end of the computation, we target the last round S-Box computation with faults. **The plaintext is kept fixed in this attack.** The aim of the attacker here is to extract the inputs to the last round S-Box layer of PRESENT. We also assume that the correct ciphertext corresponding to the plaintext is available to the attacker.

3.2.1 Template Building

It has already been shown in Sect. 2.3.1 that HW of the output differential leaks information for a given fault location. However, the entropy loss may not be sufficient with a single fault location for efficiently recovering the S-Box inputs via template matching. **The trick for further entropy reduction is to combine information from multiple fault locations, with only one location faulted per encryption.** The fault locations chosen in this specific experiment on PRESENT are $fl_1 = x_0$, $fl_2 = x_1$, $fl_3 = x_2$ and $fl_4 = x_3$, where x_is are inputs to the PRESENT S-Box (Eq. (2)). In all the cases, we inject bit-flip faults.

For the sake of explanation, we illustrate the attack here for a noise-free case, where the HW of the detection operation is considered as the SCA leakage. However, the algorithms will be described considering the actual noisy scenario (and they do not vary significantly from the noise-free cases). The template building algorithm is described in Algorithm 1 for a single S-Box. For each input value and fault location, the output differential is observed through SCA leakage. For the noise-free case, we represent this information as HW of the output differentials, which is obtained from the XOR operations of the detection step. Hence, each $s \in \mathcal{S}_\mathcal{F}$ is a tuple $s = \langle \mathcal{G}_1(\mathcal{O}_{fl_1}), \mathcal{G}_2(\mathcal{O}_{fl_2}), \mathcal{G}_3(\mathcal{O}_{fl_3}), \mathcal{G}_4(\mathcal{O}_{fl_4}) \rangle$, with $\mathcal{O}_{fl_i}$ containing traces corresponding to the fault location fl_i. Each $\mathcal{G}_i$ here corresponds to the mean and standard deviation (or mean vector and covariance matrix if multiple-points are considered for template building) over some leaky points at the traces from a $\mathcal{O}_{fl_i}$ set (that is all $\mathcal{G}_i$s are the same and denoted as

---

Algorithm 2. *MATCH_TEMPLATE*

Input: Protected cipher with unknown key C_k, Faults $fl_1, fl_2, ..., fl_M$, Template $\mathcal{T}$, num_{ob}

Output: Set of candidate correct states x_{cand}

$\quad x_{cand} := \emptyset$ ▷ Set of candidate states

$\quad w := \text{GET\_SBOX\_SIZE}()$

$\quad s' := \emptyset$

$\quad \textbf{for each } fl \in \{fl_1, fl_2, \cdots fl_M\} \textbf{ do}$

$\quad\quad \mathcal{O}_{fl} := \emptyset$

$\quad\quad \textbf{for } num_{ob} \textbf{ observations do}$

$\quad\quad\quad y_f := C(x)^{fl}$ ▷ Inject fault in one copy of the S-Box for each execution

$\quad\quad\quad y_c := C(x)$

$\quad\quad\quad \mathcal{O}_{fl} := \mathcal{O}_{fl} \cup \text{SCA\_LEAKAGE}(y_f, y_c)$ ▷ Leakage from the fault detection operation

$\quad\quad \textbf{end for}$

$\quad\quad s' := s' \cup \underset{s[fl]; s \in \mathcal{S}_{\mathcal{F}}}{\arg\max}\ L(s[fl], \mathcal{O}_{fl})$

$\quad \textbf{end for}$

$\quad x_{cand} := x_{cand} \cup \{\mathcal{T}(\underset{s \in \mathcal{S}_{\mathcal{F}}}{\arg\min}\ Dist(s, s'))\}$ ▷ $Dist$ implies Euclidean distance

$\quad \textbf{Return } x_{cand}$

$\mathcal{G}$). For the noise-free cases, we store the average HW values only.[9] The range set $\mathcal{X}$ in the templates consists of suggestions for a nibble value. The template corresponding to the noise-free case is shown in Table 7. However, such noise-free templates are just for illustration purposes and actual templates consider both fault injection and SCA noise (Algorithm 1, 2, 4 and 5).

3.2.2   Template Matching

In the online phase of the attack, the fault injections are performed at fl_1, fl_2, fl_3 and fl_4. The attacker acquires traces $\mathcal{O}_{fl_i}$ corresponding to each fault location. However, the template matching here is not a simple table lookup (except for the noise-free case). Here we consider each $s \in \mathcal{S}_{\mathcal{F}}$ and check which one of them is statistically closest to the traces obtained in the online phase. For the traces corresponding fault location fl_i ($1 \leq i \leq M$), we perform a *log-likelihood-estimation* (LLE) considering each s_i ($s = \langle s_i \rangle_{i=1}^{i=M}$) as follows:

$$L(s_i, \mathcal{O}_{fl_i}) = \sum_{j=0}^{j=|\mathcal{O}_{fl_i}|} \log(\mathbb{P}[\mathcal{O}_{fl_i}[j]; \mathbf{m_{s_i}}, \sigma_{\mathbf{s_i}}]) \tag{3}$$

Here L denotes the log-likelihood function, $\mathcal{O}_{fl_i}[j]$ denote traces from the set $\mathcal{O}_{fl_i}$. $\mathbb{P}$ is the Gaussian probability density function. $\mathbf{m_{s_i}}$ and $\sigma_{\mathbf{s_i}}$ denote the mean (resp. mean vector) and standard deviation (resp. covariance matrix) stored in s_i. They are the outcomes of $\mathcal{G}_i$ during template building. The s_i having the highest log-likelihood value is considered to be the correct one for the obtained traces. After finding out the highest s_i for every fault location fl_i, we construct an s' combining all s_i suggestions, which should match with exactly one $s \in \mathcal{S}_{\mathcal{F}}$.

---

[9] Note that, in order to perform template construction in a noisy environment, we might need to store the covariance matrix of the traces as well. However, using the covariance matrix for template building and matching does not mean that the attack is second-order. Clear evidence of this fact is that in a noise-free case here, we can construct the template on mean values of leakage.

Note that, in some cases, an exact match for s' may not be obtained due to noise. In those cases, we select an s from the template for which the maximum number of s_i have matched. One way of doing this matching is to compute Euclidean distance between s' and each $s \in \mathcal{S}_\mathcal{F}$. The s with minimum distance gives the correct answer. Algorithm 2 presents the template matching. An alternative template matching algorithm is given in Appendix A (supplementary material).

Key Recovery: The template building and matching steps described above, target one S-Box at a time. In order to extract a complete round key, one needs to extract the complete intermediate state of the cipher under consideration. In the present context, the attack requires 4 distinct fault locations per S-Box and hence $16 \times 4 = 64$ distinct fault locations. For serialized hardware implementations and software implementations, where one S-Box is called multiple times, finding out injection locations for a single S-Box is sufficient. To cover all S-Boxes, it is sufficient to change the timing (i.e. clock cycles) of injections. Furthermore, considering the ciphertext as known, recovering the S-Box inputs of the penultimate round may result in complete key recovery. However, referring to the templates shown in Table 7, the recovered keys are not unique as for half of the patterns we get multiple suggestions. Even considering this we found that the round key complexity after attacks vary roughly from 2^8 to 2^9 for an entire round of PRESENT, which is fairly reasonable. The required number of injections (and thus the number of traces per location) also depends upon the noise incurred during experiments. One may note that noise can come from two distinct sources here – the fault injection and the SCA measurements. Noise in fault injections may occur due to injections at undesired locations and missed injections. **We used a fault noise probability of around 0.38–0.40 for simulation. For SCA noise, we found that the standard deviation values (covariance, while multiple points are considered together) of measurements may vary up to 3.061 in practical setups with hardware targets.** We deliberately add noise with the HW values according to these noise parameters. The attack roughly requires 105–180 traces per fault location. Roughly 11,000 traces were sufficient for recovering the last round state of PRESENT.

Middle Round Attacks: The proposed SCA-FTA attack works equally well for middle-round attacks like the original FTA. However, in this case, the cipher must perform redundancy checks in a per-round manner, which is true for several countermeasure implementations such as [25]. Moreover, some of the recently proposed countermeasures against SIFA performs error correction in a per-round manner [15]. However, for all these cases, the attacker must recover two consecutive states in order to extract the key. The number of fault locations gets doubled in this case.

From the next section onward, we shall focus on attacks on masked implementations with FA countermeasures. In SCA-FTA, where there is an SCA component in the attack, evaluation against masking becomes crucial. Moreover, any SCA and FA secure implementation is supposed to be protected against a combined adversary as well, which increases the relevance of the study we are going to make in the following sections.

4   Analyzing Combined SCA and SIFA Countermeasures

We begin this section with a brief (informal) overview of masking schemes and their security. Subsequently, we present the SCA-FTA attacks on implementations having both SCA and SIFA countermeasures. We note that the original FTA proposal already covers implementations having masking and FA countermeasures without SIFA protection only with faults. It is worth mentioning that SCA-FTA would also work for those SIFA and FTA vulnerable cases, as they have no protection against data-dependent fault propagation to the output. **However, SIFA countermeasures try to prevent data-dependency of fault propagation to the ciphertexts. We, thus, specifically focus on two recently proposed SIFA countermeasures [16] and [15], which also include masking. The goal is to verify whether the mechanisms implemented in these countermeasures for preventing SIFA are also sufficient in terms of SCA-FTA, or not.**

4.1   A Brief Overview of Masking

Masking is the most popular and well-studied countermeasure against SCA attacks. The main idea behind Boolean masking is to split the data into multiple random shares such that their addition over $GF(2^n)$ returns the actual value. Every function which processes over the data is also split into multiple component functions. The basic requirement of masking is the statistical independence of each intermediate signal from the unshared inputs and outputs.

Security of a masking scheme is often formalized in terms of the *probing model* introduced in [26]. The main idea behind probing model is that an adversary is allowed to probe only a fixed number of wires (denoted as protection order d) at a time within the circuit. *A circuit is called d-th order probing secure if the adversary gains no information about an unshared value even while it probes up to d wires, simultaneously. In masking schemes d-th order security is ensured if the adversary cannot gain any information even by probing d shares corresponding to a single (unshared) bit.* It was demonstrated in [27] that there indeed exists a relationship between the probing model and the statistical order of Differential Power Analysis (DPA). In fact, it was shown in [28], that there exists an exponential relationship between the protection order and the number of leakage traces required for revealing the secret.

Splitting (we also denote it as *sharing*) a function into multiple components for operating over input shares is the most critical part of masking. While sharing linear functions over $GF(2^n)$ is trivial, sharing nonlinear functions require special care. This is because implementations of shared nonlinear functions may result in (unwanted) combining of input shares causing leakage. As a simple example of how nonlinear functions are shared, we consider a 2-share AND gate as follows:

$$q^0 = x^0 y^0 + (x^0 y^1 + (x^1 y^0 + (x^1 y^1 + z))), \qquad q^1 = z \qquad (4)$$

Here $q = q^0 + q^1 = xy$, $x = x^0 + x^1$ and $y = y^0 + y^1$. x^0, x^1, y^0, y^0 denote the input shares, z denotes a random bit, and q^0 and q^1 denote the output shares. This basic gate should be secure against first-order attacks under the d-probing model (in order to know x^0, x^1, y^0, y^0 or q^0, q^1 the adversary must simultaneously probe two shares of any of the unshared bit). However, in the presence of physical defaults such as glitches, this shared AND gate shows first-order leakage [29]. This is due to the fact that the extra power consumption of XOR gates due to glitches indirectly combines the input shares.

Over the years, several masking schemes have been proposed to alleviate the problems with glitches. The most prominent among them are the Threshold Implementations (TI) [9], which introduces four fundamental properties for ensuring security, namely *correctness*, *uniformity* (or *input uniformity*), *non-completeness*, and *output uniformity*. In particular, the non-completeness property ensures security against glitches. The main idea of non-completeness is that *none of the output share expressions (i.e. component functions) contains all the input shares of a bit*. While this provides protection against glitches, it also causes a rapid increase in the number of shares. The output uniformity property ensures that while cascading multiple TI sub-blocks, each sub-block can have a uniformly random sharing it its input. The uniformity of input is essential for security. Maintaining output uniformity is, however, not straightforward (especially for higher-order TI) as it depends on the function to be shared as well as the sharing that has been adopted. In the Consolidated Masking Schemes (CMS) [10], the issue with output uniformity was alleviated by introducing *refreshing gadgets* at the output of each S-Box which requires extra fresh randomness. XORing some of the output shares also work in some cases for maintaining uniformity. The requirement of extra randomness, however, increases the randomness complexity. Since the last couple of years, there has been a constant effort for reducing the randomness complexity of masking. Some notable mentions are the Domain-Oriented Masking (DOM) [11] and Unified-Masking Scheme (UMA) [12]. In the rest of the paper, we shall mainly give examples based on TI and DOM implementations. However, our observations would also extend to other derivatives of these schemes such as UMA and PINI [30]. **All of our attacks consider the masks to be unknown and varying randomly, while the plaintext is held fixed.** Moreover, *we consider an attack to be efficient only if it can be performed by respecting the probing security bounds of the target implementation while exploiting the SCA traces. For example, for a first-order secure implementation, we only consider a first-order SCA-FTA attack as efficient (first-order SCA-FTA means that the statistical analysis on the SCA traces is first-order).*

4.2   Leakage from Masking and Error Detection

We begin our discussion with DOM AND gates. There exists two variants of DOM AND gates, namely DOM-*independent* (abbreviated DOM-*indep*) and DOM-*dependent* (abbreviated DOM-*dep*). We analyze both of these variants. We also consider that each DOM AND is instantiated two times. The end results of them are unmasked and XOR-ed together for correctness check. If the XOR returns 1, it indicates an incorrect computation[10].

Without loss of generality, we first consider the DOM-*indep* gate with first-order protection. The construction is depicted in Fig. 3(a) with the fault location. We also present the test construction used for error detection in Fig. 3(b). The faults considered here are bit-flip faults in the input registers of the DOM gate. Let us consider the Boolean expression for the DOM-*indep* as follows:

$$q^0 = a^0b^0 + (a^0b^1 + z), \quad q^1 = a^1b^1 + (a^1b^0 + z) \tag{5}$$

Here each input bit a and b is shared as $a = a^0 + a^1$ and $b = b^0 + b^1$. z denotes a random bit. The output shares are denoted as q^0 and q^1 (actual output $q = q^0 + q^1$). Given a fault is injected at a^0, it can be observed that the fault affects the computation of two AND gates. For a^0b^0, the fault only propagates to the AND gate output only if $b^0 = 1$ (else there is no fault propagation). Similarly, the fault in a^0b^1 propagates only if $b^1 = 1$. The XORing of z does not have any impact on fault propagation. On the other hand, the last XOR operation before the output of q^0 propagates the fault to q^0 if only one of a^0b^0 or a^0b^1 has a faulty outcome. Otherwise, if both a^0b^0 and a^0b^1 are faulty, the fault gets cancelled at this XOR gate. Overall, *the output bit q^0 becomes faulty, only if $(b^0+b^1) = b = 1$. Otherwise, there is no fault at q^0*. One should also note that no fault propagation happens at q^1. Therefore, during error check, the detection circuit results in an outcome 1 only if the input $b = 1$. Hence, the value of b gets exposed even while the adversary is allowed to inject a single bit-flip at a shared value. A similar situation occurs when we inject the fault at b^0 (or at any other input share except z). However, in this case, the value of bit a is exposed. Another important observation for fault injection at b^0 is that the fault, in this case, propagates to both q^0 and q^1. However, the combined outcome (i.e. $q = q^0 + q^1$) only becomes faulted if $a = 1$. In this case, either q^0 or q^1 is faulted depending on the mask.

The observation regarding the DOM-*indep* AND is valid for higher-order cases as well. To illustrate this, we consider the expression for higher-order DOM-*indep* gates as follows:

$$q^0 = a^0b^0 + (a^0b^1 + z_0) + (a^0b^2 + z_1) + (a^0b^3 + z_3) + \cdots$$
$$q^1 = (a^1b^0 + z_0) + a^1b^1 + (a^1b^2 + z_2) + (a^1b^3 + z_4) + \cdots$$
$$q^3 = (a^2b^0 + z_1) + (a^2b^1 + z_2) + a^2b^2 + (a^2b^3 + z_5) + \cdots \tag{6}$$
$$\vdots \qquad\qquad \vdots \qquad\qquad \vdots$$

Here each input bit a and b is shared as $a = a^0 + a^1 + a^2 + \cdots$ and $b = b^0 + b^1 + b^2 + \cdots$. Each z_i, on the other hand, denotes a random bit. It can be observed that for a fault injection at a^0, the fault propagates to q^0 only if $(b^0 + b^1 + b^2 + \cdots) = 1$. No fault propagation happens at other output bits.

---

[10] Note that, unmasking can be dangerous if error-checking is performed in the middle rounds. It is often adopted while error checking is performed at ciphertext-level to reduce the number of check operations [16].

Hence, our attacks remain valid even for higher-order DOM-*indep* AND gates, as the resulting leakage in this case is first-order. **More precisely, we need to probe only one output wire q^0 (even though the DOM gate can be of any arbitrary masking order).** The observations can also be extended for DOM-*dep* constructions (see Appendix B in the supplementary material).

One interesting observation in this context is the difference between the fault propagation patterns for the inputs a and b. As described in the previous examples, an injection at a^0 reveals b only through the output q^0. No other output bit gets corrupted in this case. This is true if the fault is injected at any share of a. However, if a share of b is corrupted, the fault propagation happens to all the outputs q^i. In other words, to gain information regarding a, all the output shares q^i must be combined. Although for the error checking construction we are considering here (the outputs are unmasked before check) fault propagation to all output shares is not an issue for SCA-FTA, it will become critical for attack efficiency in certain other cases as we show in the next section.

4.3   Leakage from Detection on Shared Values

It is an interesting question whether the attacks proposed in the previous subsection also work if the detection operation is performed before unmasking. The construction under consideration is shown in Fig. 3(c). One consideration, in this case, is that the sharing in both the main and redundant copies should be equal (that is the masks are equal in the main and the redundant copies). Such redundancy in masking has been considered in many recent works such as [15,19].

Loosely speaking, the main idea behind the proposed attacks is to monitor wires in the error detection (or correction as we show later) unit for information leakage. If the detection operation is performed on masked values, the error may potentially propagate to multiple shares of the same output bit. For example,

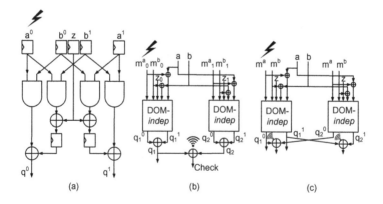

(a)   (b)   (c)

Fig. 3. (a) DOM-*indep*; (b) DOM-*indep* with error detection after unmasking. Two copies of the DOM gate use different randomness.; (c) DOM-*indep* with error detection on shares. Two copies of the DOM gate use same randomness.

considering the first-order DOM-*indep* AND gate form the previous subsection, if the fault is injected in b^0, it propagates through both the output shares q^0 and q^1 leaking a. a can only be recovered while fault information from both q^0 and q^1 are combined. Note that shares are never combined internally by construction until the ciphertext. In the present case, while the check operation is performed per share, *combining the information of both q^0 and q^1 by the attacker essentially indicates probing two wires corresponding to different shares of a single bit in a first-order implementation.* This is undesired as it violates the SCA security assumptions of first-order secure implementations. The attack is not *efficient.*

However, a different situation occurs for the other case, while a fault is injected in any share of a (say a^0) of the DOM-*indep* AND gate. As already pointed out in the previous subsection, the fault here only propagates through one of the q^is leaking b. *Probing only a single share (i.e. the detection corresponding to a share) of the actual output q here leaks the information about the unshared bit b.* This is clearly an efficient attack as we can still extract information while being restricted within the security bound of the masking scheme. *Moreover, we corrupt only a single redundant branch of computation in this case. Hence, the attack works as it is, even while the degree of redundancy is increased.*

One observation here is that while b can be retrieved with a single fault and single wire probe, a cannot be retrieved in this way. However, it is not of serious concern in SCA-FTA attacks which can combine information from different fault locations (injected at different executions). For practical applications such as S-Boxes, a single bit may have fan-out to multiple gate inputs. Hence, if it is not possible to recover a bit from a specific gate due to the aforementioned restrictions, it might become possible with high probability from another gate. Indeed it depends on the structure of the circuit under consideration. However, as we shall show later in Sect. 4.5, it is practically feasible to recover every input bit of an S-Box even with all the restrictions. In the next subsection, we discuss the consequence of using bit-level error correction on the leakage.

4.4 Leakage from Correction on Shares

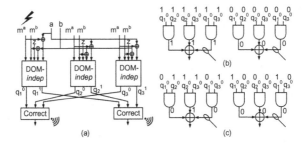

Fig. 4. (a) Construction for error correction on share values (i.e. before unmasking); Leakage from majority voting based error correction: (b) Wire values for correct inputs; (c) Wire values for faulty inputs. Faulty input bits are shown in red. Correct inputs are in blue. Intermediate bits are shown in green. (Color figure online)

Recently, error correction has been considered in multiple proposals as a potential countermeasure against SIFA [15, 18, 19]. The main intuition behind using error correction is that correcting every error (possibly with some bound in the number of corrected bits) removes the dependency between intermediate data and the correct ciphertexts, hence preventing SIFA. Here we show that in the presence of SCA and faults, some correction circuits may leak information.

Figure 4(a) depicts the configuration we consider in this case. The error correction here is considered on each share of a bit [15]. For single-bit correction, we thus need to maintain 3 copies of the same bit. The logic diagram of the correction circuit is shown in Fig. 4(b), (c). The attack described in the last subsection (detection on shared values) applies here directly if this error correction circuit leaks. In order to show the leakage from error correction circuit we consider the situations depicted in Fig. 4(b), (c), where the first copy of a bit is carrying the fault. There can be two correct input configurations for this circuit – $(0, 0, 0)$ or $(1, 1, 1)$ (ref. Fig. 4(b)). Similarly, in the presence of a fault in the first copy, there are two faulty input configurations – $(1, 0, 0)$ or $(0, 1, 1)$ (ref. Fig. 4(c)). *Now consider probing the output of the AND gate computing $q_1^0 q_3^0$ (shown with a probe in the figures). In the presence of a fault, this output never toggles and remains stuck at a value 0 (ref. Fig. 4(c)). In contrast during correct computation, this wire toggles randomly Fig. 4(b). This creates an exploitable first-order SCA leakage for a first-order implementation by distinguishing when error correction happens from when it does not happen.*

It is worth mentioning that the attack described here on DOM-*indep* AND also applies to its higher-order variants and all variants of DOM-*dep* AND gates. While this is tempting, it is still important to see whether these attacks also apply to more complex constructions like S-Boxes. In the next subsection, we show that the attacks apply equally well for S-Boxes, and it has a strong consequence on some recently proposed SIFA countermeasures.

4.5 Leakage from SIFA Countermeasures

Several countermeasures have been proposed in recent past to protect against SIFA attacks. SIFA attacks also exploit the fact that activation and propagation of faults through digital circuits are data-dependent. As a result, a fault may remain ineffective (i.e. does not corrupt output) for certain data values and may become effective (i.e. corrupts output) for some other values. The ineffectivity of faults result in correct ciphertexts, which are used by SIFA for key extraction. The aim of SIFA countermeasures is to break this dependency between ineffective faults and ciphertexts. This can be achieved in two different ways – 1) either by ensuring that every fault propagates to the output; or 2) by letting no fault propagation to the output at all. The first approach has been adopted in [16] using error detection, and the second approach has been utilized in [15] by means of error correction in each share. Below we briefly describe both of these approaches. Note that both of these schemes also include masking and hence, are supposed to provide combined security. Masking also helps in preventing SIFA while the faults do not corrupt the intermediate computation of the S-Boxes [15].

4.5.1   Analysis of the Countermeasure in [16]

SIFA Protection with Error Detection [16]*:* The idea of this protection mechanism is to ensure that a fault at any of the shares at any point (i.e. even at intermediate locations) of computation surely propagates to at least one of the S-Box outputs. There are two different ways proposed in [16] for implementing this philosophy. The first one uses Toffoli gates for implementing the entire S-box, while the second one modifies the S-Box construction itself. Both constructions ensure that *whenever there is a fault in any of the intermediate net (wire) of the S-box, it propagates to at least one of the outputs with probability 1.* This *mandatory fault propagation* indeed prevents SIFA attacks as every fault (more precisely, single-bit faults as considered in [16]) injected to the S-Box results in a faulty outcome, which gets muted at the final detection phase. Moreover, the final fault detection operation is performed by unmasking the ciphertexts (to save the number of checks).

Leakage Due to Faults: Without loss of generality, we begin our discussion with a DOM-based construction proposed in [16] (ref. Algorithm 3). The main fact we utilize is that *even though the construction ensures the corruption of at least one S-Box output bit for any single-bit fault, there are other outputs for which the fault still shows data-dependent ineffectivity.* We show this referring to the construction in Algorithm 3. This is a 2-shared version χ_3 S-Box. The actual input bits (a, b and c) are shared into (a^0, a^1), (b^0, b^1), and (c^0, c^1), respectively. The output shares are given as (r^0, r^1), (s^0, s^1), and (t^0, t^1). Following the notations from [16], each variable with a "prime" (i.e. "$'$") in its superscript denotes the *clone* of the actual variable. For example, $b^{0'}$ denotes a clone of b^0. Each clone denotes a *fan-out* branch. Furthermore, the variables R_r and R_t denote random bits, and T_0, T_1, T_2 and T_3 denote temporary variables. Finally, each variable $\bar{v}$ denotes the complement of variable v.

Algorithm 3. *SIFA-PROTECTED* χ_3 [16]

Input: $(a^0, a^1, b^0, b^1, \mathbf{c}^0, c^1)$

Output: $(r^0, r^1, s^0, s^1, t^0, t^1)$

1: $R_s \leftarrow R'_r + R'_t$

2: $T_0 \leftarrow \overline{b^{0'}c^{1'}}$; $T_2 \leftarrow a^{1'}b^{1'}$

3: $\mathbf{T_1} \leftarrow \overline{\mathbf{b^{0'}c^{0'}}}$; $T_3 \leftarrow a^{1'}b^{0'}$

4: $r^0 \leftarrow T_0 + R'_r$; $t^1 \leftarrow T_2 + R'_t$

5: $r^0 \leftarrow r^0 + T_1$; $t^1 \leftarrow t^1 + T_3$

6: $\mathbf{T_0} \leftarrow \overline{\mathbf{c^{0'}a^{1'}}}$; $T_2 \leftarrow b^{1'}c^{1'}$

7: $\mathbf{T_1} \leftarrow \overline{\mathbf{c^{0'}a^{0'}}}$; $\mathbf{T_3} \leftarrow \mathbf{b^{1'}c^{0'}}$

8: $s^0 \leftarrow T_0 + R'_s$; $r^1 \leftarrow T_2 + R_r$

9: $s^0 \leftarrow s^0 + T_1$; $r^1 \leftarrow r^1 + T_3$

10: $T_0 \leftarrow \overline{a^{0'}b^{1'}}$; $T_2 \leftarrow c^{1'}a^{1'}$

11: $T_1 \leftarrow \overline{a^{0'}b^{0'}}$; $T_3 \leftarrow c^{1'}a^{0'}$

12: $t^0 \leftarrow T_0 + R_t$; $s^1 \leftarrow T_2 + R_s$

13: $t^0 \leftarrow t^0 + T_1$; $s^1 \leftarrow s^1 + T_3$

14: $r^0 \leftarrow r^0 + a^0$; $t^1 \leftarrow t^1 + c^1$

15: $s^0 \leftarrow s^0 + b^0$; $r^1 \leftarrow r^1 + a^1$

16: $\mathbf{t^0} \leftarrow \mathbf{t^0} + \mathbf{c^0}$; $s^1 \leftarrow s^1 + b^1$

17: **Return**$(r^0, r^1, s^0, s^1, t^0, t^1)$

Table 8. Template (noise-free) for masked χ_3 S-Box (error detection on unmasked value)

$fl_1 = c^0$	$fl_2 = b^0$	$fl_3 = a^1$	State
2.0	2.0	2.0	(0, 7)
2.0	3.0	1.0	(1)
3.0	2.0	1.0	(5)
1.0	3.0	2.0	(3)
3.0	1.0	2.0	(4)
2.0	1.0	3.0	(6)
1.0	2.0	3.0	(2)

Let us assume that the input c^0 has been chosen as a fault location and we consider bit-flip fault model. It can be observed that this fault corrupts 4 expressions of Algorithm 3 involving AND gates – the first expression in line 3, the first expression in line 6, and the first and the second expression in line 7. c^0 is also directly XOR-ed with t^0 in the first expression of line 16. Furthermore, the AND operations $\overline{c^{0'}a^{1'}}$ (line 6) and $\overline{c^{0'}a^{0'}}$ (line 7) are combined in s^0 as $s^0 = (\overline{c^{0'}a^{1'}} + R'_s) + \overline{c^{0'}a^{0'}}$ (line 8, 9). Since s^0 is an output bit and s^0 does not combine with any other faulty bit in the rest of the S-Box computation, *the output bit s^0 becomes faulty only if $a^{1'} + a^{0'} = a^1 + a^0 = a = 1$. One should also note that the same fault also propagates to the outputs r^0 and r^1 leaking b. However, in this case the value of b can be recovered only when error information of r^0 and r^1 are combined. To summarize, leakage of a does not require combination of error information because the fault only affects s^0, while leakage of b requires combination of error information for both r^0 and r^1 because fault propagates to both shares.* Finally, there is a mandatory fault propagation to t^0 as c^0 is XOR-ed with this bit at the end of computation. In a similar fashion, fault injections at input b^0 reveals the value of c through the output bit r^0, and the value of a through the bits t^0 and t^1. Finally, a last injection location at a^1 reveals b through t^1 and c through s^0 and s^1. One should note that for each fault location there is an output bit for which the fault propagation is mandatory. However, the location of this bit changes with the fault location. For example, location c^0 induces mandatory propagation at t^0, and location b^0 results in mandatory propagation at s^0. Each of the output bits can have mandatory fault propagation depending on the fault location for this implementation.

As described in [16], we first consider that the ciphertext outputs are unmasked before the error checking operation. Constructing a template based on the above-mentioned fault locations results in the leakage of the input. **In the actual attack (and in all subsequent attacks described in this paper), we keep the plaintext fixed during the template matching phase. However, the masks vary randomly. One should note that we corrupt only a single location per execution of the cipher and combine the outcomes from multiple executions together to build and match the templates.** The template building and matching algorithms, in this case, are very similar to that of Algorithm 1 and Algorithm 2 and we do not repeat it here. The noise-free template based on HW values from the detection operation is shown in Table 8. In the presence of both SCA and fault injection-related noise, the attack requires roughly 170–235 injections per fault location (hence those many traces) during template matching, and roughly 400–510 injections for an entire S-Box.

One interesting observation, in this case, is that for single fault injection, an adversary can gain information regarding both of the (unmasked) input bits it leaks. For example, if fault is injected at c^0, adversary can extract a through s and b through r. This is because the output bits are unmasked before check, so the information in r^0 and r^1 are combined by construction. From the probing model perspective, another injection at b^0 (which leaks c and a) thus should be sufficient for revealing the entire unmasked input of the S-Box. However, in our attack, we consider a situation where the HW of all the XOR computations in the detection circuit is leaked simultaneously. This seems more practical in hardware implementations due to the parallelization present there. So far the probing security is concerned, only two fault locations seem sufficient for this case. However, due to the information loss caused by the HW computation, the first template in Table 8 returns two value suggestions.

Attack on Error Detection on Shares: A tempting question in the present context is whether or not error detection on masked data would prevent the proposed attack, or make it *inefficient* in terms of probing security. As we see, the answer is negative. To elaborate, we consider the masked χ_3 S-Box once again, now with error detection at each share. One important consequence of such error checking is that the masks in the original and redundant computation have to be the same. *Respecting the probing security, we consider that only a single wire can be probed. More precisely, we allow the attacker to only probe a single specific wire from the XOR gate outputs in the error detection circuit.*

Let us, for illustration, consider the case when the fault location is at c^0. It can be observed that the adversary can only extract the value of a by probing the error detection logic corresponding to the bit s^0. Notably, it cannot extract b as it requires probing of both the shares r^0 and r^1 (i.e. their error detection logic). Probing two shares of a wire in a first-order implementation violates probing security. Nevertheless, considering the two other fault locations (b^0 and a^1), the adversary can extract all the (unmasked) S-Box input bits without violating

Algorithm 4. *BUILD_TEMPLATE*

Input: Target implementation C, Faults $fl_1, fl_2, ..., fl_M, num_{ob}$
Output: Template $\mathcal{T}$
$\quad \mathcal{T} := \emptyset$
$\quad w := \text{GET\_SBOX\_SIZE}()$ $\qquad\qquad\qquad\qquad\qquad$ ▷ Get the width of the S-Box
$\quad \textbf{for } (0 \leq x \leq 2^w) \textbf{ do}$ $\qquad\qquad$ ▷ The key is known and fixed here and $x = p + k$
$\quad\quad s := \emptyset$
$\quad\quad \textbf{for each } fl \in \{fl_1, fl_1, ..., fl_M\} \textbf{ do}$
$\quad\quad\quad \mathcal{O}_{fl} := \emptyset$
$\quad\quad\quad \textbf{for } num_{ob} \textbf{ observations do}$ $\qquad\qquad\qquad\qquad$ ▷ Masks vary randomly
$\quad\quad\quad\quad y_f := C(x)^{fl}$ $\qquad\quad$ ▷ Inject fault in one copy of the S-Box for each execution
$\quad\quad\quad\quad y_c := C(x)$
$\quad\quad\quad\quad \mathcal{O}_{fl} := \mathcal{O}_{fl} \cup \text{SCA\_LEAKAGE}(y_f, y_c)$ $\qquad$ ▷ Leakage from the fault detection operation
$\quad\quad\quad \textbf{end for}$
$\quad\quad\quad \mathcal{O}_{fl} := \text{CAL\_Group\_AVG}(\mathcal{O}_{fl})$ ▷ Divide the trace set into groups and calculate average trace
per group.

$\qquad\qquad s := s \cup \mathcal{G}(\mathcal{O}_{fl})$ $\qquad\qquad\qquad$ ▷ We consider the same function $\mathcal{G}$ for all trace sets.
$\quad\quad \textbf{end for}$
$\quad\quad \mathcal{T} := \mathcal{T} \cup \{(s, x)\}$
$\quad \textbf{end for}$
$\quad \textbf{Return } \mathcal{T}$

Algorithm 5. *MATCH_TEMPLATE*

Input: Protected cipher with unknown key C_k, Faults $fl_1, fl_2, ..., fl_M$, Template $\mathcal{T}, num_{ob}$
Output: Set of candidate correct states x_{cand}
$\quad x_{cand} := \emptyset$ $\qquad\qquad\qquad\qquad\qquad\qquad\qquad\qquad$ ▷ Set of candidate states
$\quad w := \text{GET\_SBOX\_SIZE}()$
$\quad s' := \emptyset$
$\quad \textbf{for each } fl \in \{fl_1, fl_2, \cdots fl_M\} \textbf{ do}$
$\quad\quad \mathcal{O}_{fl} := \emptyset$
$\quad\quad \textbf{for } num_{ob} \textbf{ observations do}$ $\qquad\qquad\qquad\qquad\qquad$ ▷ Masks vary randomly
$\quad\quad\quad y_f := C(x)^{fl}$ $\qquad\qquad$ ▷ Inject fault in one copy of the S-Box for each execution
$\quad\quad\quad y_c := C(x)$
$\quad\quad\quad \mathcal{O}_{fl} := \mathcal{O}_{fl} \cup \text{SCA\_LEAKAGE}(y_f, y_c)$ $\qquad$ ▷ Leakage from the fault detection operation
$\quad\quad \textbf{end for}$
$\quad\quad \mathcal{O}_{fl} := \text{CAL\_Group\_AVG}(\mathcal{O}_{fl})$ $\qquad$ ▷ Divide the trace set into groups and calculate average trace
per group

$\qquad s' := s' \cup \underset{s[fl]; s \in S_{\mathcal{F}}}{\arg \max} \ L(s[fl], \mathcal{O}_{fl})$
$\quad \textbf{end for}$
$\quad x_{cand} := x_{cand} \cup \{\mathcal{T}(\underset{s \in S_{\mathcal{F}}}{\arg \min} \ Dist(s, s'))\}$ $\qquad$ ▷ *Dist* implies Euclidean distance

$\quad \textbf{Return } x_{cand}$

---

the probing security restrictions. Hence, the proposed construction is not secured
even while error detection on masked data is considered. The noise-free template
corresponding to this attack is described in Table 9. One interesting observation
here is that the template in Table 9 is better than the template in Table 8 in the
sense that it can uniquely determine each input value. This, however, does not
contradict the probing security and the attack described is still first-order. An
explanation for this is given in the supplementary material (Appendix D).

The template building and template matching algorithms for detection on
masked values are similar to Algorithm 1 and 2 with some subtle changes. The
changes are driven by the fact that corresponding to a fault injection, the output
fault patterns may partially vary (ref. Appendix D). *In other words, we may have
multiple HW values corresponding to a single fault location and input value.*
This is not problematic in a noise-free situation as we consider the average HW
values in templates. However, for noisy situations with real traces, in many

Table 9. Template (noise-free) for masked χ_3 S-Box (error detection on shares)

$fl_1 = c^0$	$fl_2 = b^0$	$fl_3 = a^1$	State
3.0	3.0	3.0	(7)
2.0	2.0	2.0	(0)
2.0	3.0	2.0	(1)
3.0	3.0	2.0	(5)
2.0	3.0	3.0	(3)
3.0	2.0	2.0	(4)
3.0	2.0	3.0	(6)
2.0	2.0	3.0	(2)

Table 10. Template (noise-free) for masked χ_3 S-Box (error correction on shares)

$fl_1 = c^0$	$fl_2 = b^0$	$fl_3 = a^1$	State
7.0	6.0	6.0	(3)
6.0	6.0	7.0	(5)
7.0	6.0	7.0	(1)
6.0	6.0	6.0	(7)
7.0	7.0	7.0	(0)
6.0	7.0	6.0	(6)
7.0	7.0	6.0	(2)
6.0	7.0	7.0	(4)

cases, the template matching requires multiple SCA traces corresponding to the same intermediate value for a high-confidence decision. In case there are multiple fault patterns (occurring randomly with the variation of masks), such matching becomes challenging. Fortunately, the variation in fault patterns for a given input value is not very high (corresponding to a given fault location). As a result, *the mean value of the traces (over different fault patterns) for different input values remain fairly distinguishable.* Accordingly, we modify the template building and matching algorithms. During template matching, we gather several traces corresponding to a fault location and divide them into multiple small groups (subsets). Next, the averaged traces are computed for each group. During the log-likelihood estimation step in template matching, these averaged traces are utilized (as the group averages should be almost identical for each input value and fault location). The modified template building and matching algorithms are shown in Algorithm 4 and Algorithm 5, respectively.

The number of encryptions required for the proposed attack varies with the amount of noise present in the experiment. Similar to the other cases described previously, here we consider a FA noise with noise probability 0.38–0.40. The SCA noise is considered up to covariance value of 3.061. In the presence of such noise, the attack requires roughly 360–520 traces per fault location (that is those many fault injections per location) during template matching. Some other variants of SIFA protections were also proposed in [16]. For the sake of completeness, we discuss them in the supplementary material (Appendix G). The next subsection describes attacks on another SIFA countermeasure proposed recently using error correction.

4.5.2 Analysis of the SIFA Countermeasure in [15]

SIFA Protection with Error Correction: The proposal in [15] describes two different models for SIFA faults. In the first model (SIFA-1), a biased bit-flip fault is assumed to be injected in the state. As it was shown, masking is a potential countermeasure for SIFA in this case. However, masking cannot provide any protection against SIFA if the faults corrupt the intermediate computations of S-Boxes. Bit-flip faults (not necessarily biased) inside the masked S-Boxes are termed as SIFA-2 faults. As a protection against such faults, the work in [15] proposed bit-level error correction at the end of each S-Box. The overall scheme, which is called *Transform-and-Encode* maintains 3 copies of each share and performs a majority-voting based error correction for achieving single-bit SIFA security. It was also claimed that *the combination of any masking scheme and error correction mechanism would work for preventing SIFA.*

Leakage Due to Faults: Without loss of generality, we construct an instance of *Transform-and-Encode* with the same masked χ_3 S-Box we have considered so far. Instead of error detection, we now use error correction for each share. It has already been shown in Sect. 4.4, that majority-vote based error correction circuits leaks information on whether any correction has happened or not. With this property of error correction logic, the attack becomes a straightforward extension of the attack described in the previous section for error detection on shared values. The attack algorithms remain similar to Algorithm 4 and Algorithm 5. *Instead of HW of all the XOR outputs in detection step, in this case we consider the HW of all the output wires of the AND gates in the error correction stage to abstract the leakage (ref. Fig. 4(b)(c) & Table 10).* In the presence of noise the attack requires roughly 880–1085 encryptions per fault location. *Another important observation for this countermeasure construction is that it also enables middle round attacks given the correction operations are present at each round.*

So far, in this paper, we have only considered masked S-Boxes based on DOM principle. A natural question is whether the attacks still apply on other masking paradigms such as TI [9]. In the next subsection, we present examples on TI implementations which are found vulnerable against the SCA-FTA strategy.

4.6 Leakage from TI S-Boxes

The TI constructions require that each component function (i.e. output share) of any given nonlinear function should be *non-complete*. In order to achieve non-completeness, it ensures that no component function contains all the shares of a single variable. The cost of strictly imposing non-completeness is a rapid increase in the share count for increasing degree of nonlinearity and security order. More precisely, the number of input shares for higher-order security is given as $s_{in} \geq t \times d+1$, where t is the degree of the function under consideration, d is the security order, and s_{in} is the count of input shares. The number of output shares (that is the count of component functions) $s_{out} \geq \binom{s_{in}}{t}$. However, later work on TI, such as Consolidated Masking Scheme (CMS) [10] has shown that these share requirements can be reduced to $d + 1$ shares for d-th order security. They proposed careful selection of component functions with more computation steps, and, most importantly, the introduction of registers between different computation steps to avoid the accidental combination of shares.

One important step in TI implementations is *compression* of shares [10]. In many cases, the number of output shares become larger than the number of input shares, and in order to maintain composability some of the output shares are XOR-ed together to reduce the number of shares (keeping the number of input and output shares equal). This is also useful in maintaining *output uniformity*, which is also an essential property of TI. Before combining the shares, it is important to add a register layer to prevent the propagation of glitches. Further, as proposed in CMS [10], a *refreshing layer* is also required before share compression in many cases in order to maintain the output uniformity.

The issue that arises with TI is due to this share compression. *In many cases, the share compression does not explicitly maintain the non-completeness any more. Rather the glitch resistance is achieved by introducing registers before share compression* [31]. While this does not create any problem for SCA security as the register layer is suggested before share compression, it can be exploited by SCA-FTA in certain cases. In order to elaborate this, we consider the function $d = ab + c$.[11] A valid non-complete sharing for this function is given as follows:

$$d^0 = a^0 b^0 + c^0, \qquad d^1 = a^0 b^1, \qquad d^2 = a^1 b^0 + c^1, \qquad d^3 = a^1 b^1 \quad (7)$$

The number of input shares in this case is 2 ((a^0, a^1) and (b^0, b^1)) and number of output shares is 4 (d^0, d^1, d^2, d^3). In order to reduce the number of shares, a valid compression option in this case is $e^0 = d^0 + d^1$ and $e^1 = d^2 + d^3$. This compression also maintains the output uniformity. Further, this compensates the violation of non-completeness by introducing a register layer before the compression. However, *if a fault is induced in a^0, it propagates to e^0 only if $b^0 + b^1 = b = 1$*. This enables SCA-FTA attack if the error detection/correction is performed at the output shares e^0 and e^1. A single probe to the detection/correction circuit at e^0 would be sufficient for revealing b in this case.

Leakage in Higher-Order TI: One should note that the abovementioned issue with share compression also persists for higher-order TI implementations. In order to show this concretely, we consider the second-order secure SIMON implementation from [31]. Once again, the function under consideration is $d = ab + c$. The TI equations in this case are:

$$
\begin{aligned}
d^0 &= c^1 + a^1 b^1 + a^0 b^1 + a^1 b^0, & d^1 &= c^2 + a^2 b^2 + a^0 b^2 + a^2 b^0, \\
d^2 &= c^3 + a^3 b^3 + a^0 b^3 + a^3 b^0, & d^3 &= c^0 + a^0 b^0 + a^0 b^4 + a^4 b^0, \\
d^4 &= c^4 + a^4 b^4 + a^1 b^4 + a^4 b^1, & d^5 &= a^1 b^3 + a^3 b^1, \\
d^6 &= a^1 b^2 + a^2 b^1, & d^7 &= a^2 b^3 + a^2 b^4 + a^3 b^4, \\
d^8 &= a^3 b^2 + a^4 b^2 + a^4 b^3
\end{aligned}
\quad (8)
$$

Here the inputs have 5 shares and output have 9 shares. The equations for share compression are given as:

$$e^0 = d^0 + d^5, \qquad e^1 = d^1 + d^6, \qquad e^2 = d^2 + d^7, \qquad e^3 = d^3 + d^8, \qquad e^4 = d^4 \quad (9)$$

---

[11] This example is due to [10].

In case of a fault injection at a^4, if the attacker probes the error detection/correction modules corresponding to e^3 and e^4 the outputs become faulted only if $b^0 + b^1 + b^2 + b^3 + b^4 = b = 1$. An adversary can easily combine the leakage of these two wires (e^3 and e^4) and extract the information. In this case, *the security of a second-order secure implementation is violated only with two probes which indicates an efficient attack according to our terminology.* In a nutshell, SCA-FTA can violate many existing combined SCA and FA protection schemes, which are based on detection/correction, and involves masking. Also, SCA-secure composable gadgets, such as probe-isolating-non-interference (PINI) [30], falls prey to SCA-FTA (ref. Appendix C in the supplementary materiel).

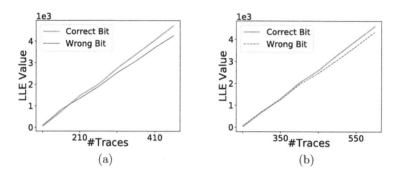

Fig. 5. LLE variation for recovering one bit from the SIFA-protected χ_5 S-Box. Fault is injected at one of the shares (share e^0) of the LSB of the S-Box input; (a) detection on unshared values; (b)detection on shared values.

5 Practical Validation

So far, in this paper, we have abstracted the SCA leakage as HW of multiple wires in the error detection/correction circuits. However, practical validation is also necessary in this regard. We practically validated the proposed attacks on an open-source software implementation of SIFA-protected Keccak implementation provided with [16]. To validate our claims we only add the error-detection circuits at the end, and no other customization has been made. Two types of detection operation were evaluated – detection on unshared (actual) values as suggested in [16], and detection over shared values. The faults were injected using laser-pulses, while the SCA leakages were measured through power consumption. It was found that recovering each bit requires roughly 210–220 traces for detection over unmasked values (shown through variation in LLE values in Fig. 5(a)), and 320 to 350 traces for detection over masked values (ref. Fig. 5(b)). Total 5 distinct injection locations in the code were utilized while the clock cycle of injection was varied for choosing different S-Boxes. Further, in order to understand the feasibility of the attacks on hardware implementations, we performed a gate-level power-trace simulation approach. The simulated faults were bit-flip. Experiments were performed on a shared χ_3 S-Box hardware with error correction.[12] Detailed experiments are presented in the supplementary material (Appendix F).

6   Discussion on Probable Fixes

In Sect. 4.6, we pointed out that the compression layer of TI is responsible for the attack. *In the context of faults, the compression of shares violates the non-completeness property of TI. Compensating non-completeness violation with registers does not work for faults*[13]. *Unlike glitches, a faulty value can propagate through registers causing share combination which enables SCA-FTA.* A natural question, that arises in this context is – can we maintain security if there is no compression layer? At least for some cases, we found that the answer is positive. *More precisely we found that if the error detection/correction is performed before the compression operation, the security can still be maintained.*

A Secure Instantiation of the Countermeasure in [15]*:* As an example of the aforementioned claim, we refer to a concrete instantiation of the *Transform-and-Encode* framework called AntiSIFA [15]. AntiSIFA proposes a single-bit SIFA protected scheme along with first-order masking for PRESENT. The masking was realized with the first-order TI for PRESENT in [33]. Although the generic framework *Transform-and-Encode* is found to be insecure against SCA-FTA, this specific construction is found to be secure. To understand why this is secure, we need to consider the first-order TI implementation of PRESENT S-Box [33]. The implementation first decomposes the S-Box S into two quadratic sub-functions F and G such that $S(x) = F(G(x))$. Next, both F and G are shared with 3 input and 3 shares each (no compression).

Let us consider a part of the shared F function which corresponds to a single (unmasked) output bit if the S-Box. The corresponding equations are given as:

$$\begin{aligned}
f_{10} &= x_1^2 + x_2^2 x_0^2 + x_2^2 x_0^3 + x_2^3 x_0^2 \\
f_{20} &= x_1^3 + x_2^3 x_0^3 + x_2^1 x_0^3 + x_2^3 x_0^1 \\
f_{30} &= x_1^1 + x_2^1 x_0^1 + x_2^1 x_0^2 + x_2^2 x_0^1
\end{aligned} \tag{10}$$

Here f_{10}, f_{20} and f_{30} denote the output shares of S-Box output f_0. Each x_j^i denote the i-th share of the jth input bit. *Now let consider a fault at the bit x_0^2. While this indeed leaks information about $x_2 = x_2^1 + x_2^2 + x_2^3$ the leakage happens through outputs f_{10} and f_{30} and error-correction is performed at the end of both wires. Even for any other input bit, the leakage would always happen through two wires and the correction operation is performed for both the wires. Such fault propagation takes place as each of the output shares are non-complete.*

---

[12] While attacks on hardware implementations are feasible and have been validated in practice [32], the effort to attack will be much higher than microcontrollers due to noise, required fault injection capability, and any present parallelism.

[13] It works for preventing glitch leakages, as glitch cannot propagate through registers.

As a result, one cannot attack this implementation without violating the first-order probing security claims. A similar situation takes place for the combined security schemes introduced in [19] (called NINA), where the error correction is performed at the output of each product term of a masked AND gate (each product term on shares is non-complete). **These observations indicate that even for TI implementations where share compression is essential, performing error detection or correction on non-complete combinational paths before share compression may provide security against SCA-FTA.** Further investigation and development of a generic and provable countermeasure based on this observation is left as a future work. It is worth mentioning that certain other countermeasures such as CAPA [34] and Friet [35] also prevent SCA-FTA attacks for slightly different reasons. They have been discussed in Appendix G in the supplementary material. Re-keying [36] schemes can also be useful if the key generation can be made attack resilient.

7   Conclusion

Modern cryptographic implementations utilize special algorithmic measures to protect against SCA and FA attacks. A reasonable expectation is that implementations containing both countermeasures would also prevent against combined attacks. In this paper, we show and practically validate that this is not the case, even for some implementations which include both masking and SIFA countermeasures. A novel combined attack strategy called SCA-FTA has been proposed for exploiting these vulnerabilities. The proposed attacks can exploit information leakage form the error detection/correction logic (though side-channel) even if the detection/correction is performed over masked data. Finally, we note that the non-completeness property of certain masking implementations can play a crucial role in preventing the proposed attacks. A potential future work in this regard can be further analysis of both the attack and the prevention approach.

Acknowledgements. Debdeep Mukhopadhyay acknowledges the support from Department of Science and Technology, Government of India through the Swarna-jayanti Fellowship. Dirmanto Jap and Shivam Bhasin acknowledge the support from the Singapore National Research Foundation ("SOCure" grant NRF2018NCR-NCR002-0001).

References

1. Kocher, P., Jaffe, J., Jun, B.: Differential power analysis. In: Wiener, M. (ed.) CRYPTO 1999. LNCS, vol. 1666, pp. 388–397. Springer, Heidelberg (1999). https://doi.org/10.1007/3-540-48405-1_25
2. Chari, S., Rao, J.R., Rohatgi, P.: Template attacks. In: Kaliski, B.S., Koç, K., Paar, C. (eds.) CHES 2002. LNCS, vol. 2523, pp. 13–28. Springer, Heidelberg (2003). https://doi.org/10.1007/3-540-36400-5_3
3. Oswald, E., Mangard, S.: Template attacks on masking—resistance is futile. In: Abe, M. (ed.) CT-RSA 2007. LNCS, vol. 4377, pp. 243–256. Springer, Heidelberg (2006). https://doi.org/10.1007/11967668_16

4. Boneh, D., DeMillo, R.A., Lipton, R.J.: On the importance of checking cryptographic protocols for faults. In: Fumy, W. (ed.) EUROCRYPT 1997. LNCS, vol. 1233, pp. 37–51. Springer, Heidelberg (1997). https://doi.org/10.1007/3-540-69053-0_4

5. Biham, E., Shamir, A.: Differential fault analysis of secret key cryptosystems. In: Kaliski, B.S. (ed.) CRYPTO 1997. LNCS, vol. 1294, pp. 513–525. Springer, Heidelberg (1997). https://doi.org/10.1007/BFb0052259

6. Patranabis, S., Chakraborty, A., Mukhopadhyay, D., Chakrabarti, P.P.: Fault space transformation: countering biased fault attacks. In: Patranabis, S., Mukhopadhyay, D. (eds.) Fault Tolerant Architectures for Cryptography and Hardware Security. CADM, pp. 183–195. Springer, Singapore (2018). https://doi.org/10.1007/978-981-10-1387-4_9

7. Saha, S., Bag, A., Basu Roy, D., Patranabis, S., Mukhopadhyay, D.: Fault template attacks on block ciphers exploiting fault propagation. In: Canteaut, A., Ishai, Y. (eds.) EUROCRYPT 2020. LNCS, vol. 12105, pp. 612–643. Springer, Cham (2020). https://doi.org/10.1007/978-3-030-45721-1_22

8. Agoyan, M., et. al.: How to flip a bit? In: IEEE IOLTS, pp. 235–239. IEEE (2010)

9. Nikova, S., Rechberger, C., Rijmen, V.: Threshold implementations against side-channel attacks and glitches. In: Ning, P., Qing, S., Li, N. (eds.) ICICS 2006. LNCS, vol. 4307, pp. 529–545. Springer, Heidelberg (2006). https://doi.org/10.1007/11935308_38

10. Reparaz, O., Bilgin, B., Nikova, S., Gierlichs, B., Verbauwhede, I.: Consolidating masking schemes. In: Gennaro, R., Robshaw, M. (eds.) CRYPTO 2015. LNCS, vol. 9215, pp. 764–783. Springer, Heidelberg (2015). https://doi.org/10.1007/978-3-662-47989-6_37

11. Groß, H., Mangard, S., Korak, T.: Domain-oriented masking: compact masked hardware implementations with arbitrary protection order. IACR Cryptol. ePrint Arch. **2016**, 486 (2016)

12. Gross, H., Mangard, S.: Reconciling d + 1 masking in hardware and software. In: Fischer, W., Homma, N. (eds.) CHES 2017. LNCS, vol. 10529, pp. 115–136. Springer, Cham (2017). https://doi.org/10.1007/978-3-319-66787-4_6

13. Dobraunig, C., et. al.: SIFA: exploiting ineffective fault inductions on symmetric cryptography. TCHES **2018**, 547–572 (2018)

14. Dobraunig, C., Eichlseder, M., Gross, H., Mangard, S., Mendel, F., Primas, R.: Statistical ineffective fault attacks on masked AES with fault countermeasures. In: Peyrin, T., Galbraith, S. (eds.) ASIACRYPT 2018. LNCS, vol. 11273, pp. 315–342. Springer, Cham (2018). https://doi.org/10.1007/978-3-030-03329-3_11

15. Saha, S., et. al.: A framework to counter statistical ineffective fault analysis of block ciphers using domain transformation and error correction. IEEE Trans. Inf. Forensics Secur. **15**, 1905–1919 (2019)

16. Daemen, J., et al.: Protecting against statistical ineffective fault attacks. TCHES **2020**, 508–543 (2020)

17. Schneider, T., Moradi, A., Güneysu, T.: ParTI – towards combined hardware countermeasures against side-channel and fault-injection attacks. In: Robshaw, M., Katz, J. (eds.) CRYPTO 2016. LNCS, vol. 9815, pp. 302–332. Springer, Heidelberg (2016). https://doi.org/10.1007/978-3-662-53008-5_11

18. Shahmirzadi, A.R., Rasoolzadeh, S., Moradi, A.: Impeccable circuits II. IACR Cryptology ePrint Archive **2019** (2019)

19. Dhooghe, S., Nikova, S.: My gadget just cares for me - how NINA can prove security against combined attacks. In: Jarecki, S. (ed.) CT-RSA 2020. LNCS, vol. 12006, pp. 35–55. Springer, Cham (2020). https://doi.org/10.1007/978-3-030-40186-3_3

20. Daemen, J., Hoffert, S., Assche, G.V., Keer, R.V.: The design of Xoodoo and Xoofff. IACR Trans. Symmetric Cryptol. **2018**(4), 1–38 (2018)
21. Roche, T., Lomné, V., Khalfallah, K.: Combined fault and side-channel attack on protected implementations of AES. In: Prouff, E. (ed.) CARDIS 2011. LNCS, vol. 7079, pp. 65–83. Springer, Heidelberg (2011). https://doi.org/10.1007/978-3-642-27257-8_5
22. Lomné, V., Roche, T., Thillard, A.: On the need of randomness in fault attack countermeasures-application to AES. In: FDTC, pp. 85–94. IEEE (2012)
23. Saha, S., et. al.: Breaking redundancy-based countermeasures with random faults and power side channel. In: FDTC, pp. 15–22 (2018)
24. Bogdanov, A., et al.: PRESENT: an ultra-lightweight block cipher. In: Paillier, P., Verbauwhede, I. (eds.) CHES 2007. LNCS, vol. 4727, pp. 450–466. Springer, Heidelberg (2007). https://doi.org/10.1007/978-3-540-74735-2_31
25. Guo, X., Mukhopadhyay, D., Jin, C., Karri, R.: Security analysis of concurrent error detection against differential fault analysis. J. Crypt. Eng. **5**(3), 153–169 (2014). https://doi.org/10.1007/s13389-014-0092-8
26. Ishai, Y., Sahai, A., Wagner, D.: Private circuits: securing hardware against probing attacks. In: Boneh, D. (ed.) CRYPTO 2003. LNCS, vol. 2729, pp. 463–481. Springer, Heidelberg (2003). https://doi.org/10.1007/978-3-540-45146-4_27
27. Faust, S., Rabin, T., Reyzin, L., Tromer, E., Vaikuntanathan, V.: Protecting circuits from leakage: the computationally-bounded and noisy cases. In: Gilbert, H. (ed.) EUROCRYPT 2010. LNCS, vol. 6110, pp. 135–156. Springer, Heidelberg (2010). https://doi.org/10.1007/978-3-642-13190-5_7
28. Chari, S., Jutla, C.S., Rao, J.R., Rohatgi, P.: Towards sound approaches to counteract power-analysis attacks. In: Wiener, M. (ed.) CRYPTO 1999. LNCS, vol. 1666, pp. 398–412. Springer, Heidelberg (1999). https://doi.org/10.1007/3-540-48405-1_26
29. Mangard, S., Schramm, K.: Pinpointing the side-channel leakage of masked AES hardware implementations. In: Goubin, L., Matsui, M. (eds.) CHES 2006. LNCS, vol. 4249, pp. 76–90. Springer, Heidelberg (2006). https://doi.org/10.1007/11894063_7
30. Cassiers, G., Standaert, F.X.: Trivially and efficiently composing masked gadgets with probe isolating non-interference. IEEE Trans. Inf. Forensics Secur. **15**, 2542–2555 (2020)
31. Shahverdi, A., Taha, M., Eisenbarth, T.: Lightweight side channel resistance: threshold implementations of Simon. IEEE Trans. Comput. **66**(4), 661–671 (2016)
32. Dutertre, J.M., et. al.: Laser fault injection at the CMOS 28 nm technology node: an analysis of the fault model. In: FDTC, pp. 1–6 (2018)
33. Poschmann, A., et al.: Side-channel resistant crypto for less than 2,300 GE. JoC **24**(2), 322–345 (2011)
34. Reparaz, O., et al.: CAPA: the spirit of beaver against physical attacks. In: Shacham, H., Boldyreva, A. (eds.) CRYPTO 2018. LNCS, vol. 10991, pp. 121–151. Springer, Cham (2018). https://doi.org/10.1007/978-3-319-96884-1_5
35. Simon, T., et al.: FRIET: an authenticated encryption scheme with built-in fault detection. In: Canteaut, A., Ishai, Y. (eds.) EUROCRYPT 2020. LNCS, vol. 12105, pp. 581–611. Springer, Cham (2020). https://doi.org/10.1007/978-3-030-45721-1_21
36. Dobraunig, C., Koeune, F., Mangard, S., Mendel, F., Standaert, F.-X.: Towards fresh and hybrid re-keying schemes with beyond birthday security. In: Homma, N., Medwed, M. (eds.) CARDIS 2015. LNCS, vol. 9514, pp. 225–241. Springer, Cham (2016). https://doi.org/10.1007/978-3-319-31271-2_14

Efficient Leakage-Resilient MACs Without Idealized Assumptions

Francesco Berti[1,2](✉), Chun Guo[3,4,5](✉), Thomas Peters[1](✉), and François-Xavier Standaert[1](✉)

[1] UCLouvain, ICTEAM/ELEN/Crypto Group, Louvain-la-Neuve, Belgium
{thomas.peters,fstandae}@uclouvain.be
[2] TU Darmstadt, Germany, CAC - Applied Cryptography, Darmstadt, Germany
francesco.berti@tu-darmstadt.de
[3] School of Cyber Science and Technology, Shandong University,
Qingdao 266237, Shandong, China
chun.guo@sdu.edu.cn
[4] Key Laboratory of Cryptologic Technology and Information Security
of Ministry of Education, Shandong University, Qingdao 266237,
Shandong, China
[5] State Key Laboratory of Information Security, Institute of Information
Engineering, Chinese Academy of Sciences, Beijing 100093, China

Abstract. The security proofs of leakage-resilient MACs based on symmetric building blocks currently rely on idealized assumptions that hardly translate into interpretable guidelines for the cryptographic engineers implementing these schemes. In this paper, we first present a leakage-resilient MAC that is both efficient and secure under standard and easily interpretable black box and physical assumptions. It only requires a collision resistant hash function and a single call per message authentication to a Tweakable Block Cipher (TBC) that is unpredictable with leakage. This construction leverages two design twists: large tweaks for the TBC and a verification process that checks the inverse TBC against a constant. It enjoys beyond birthday security bounds. We then discuss the cost of getting rid of these design twists. We show that security can be proven without them as well. Yet, a construction without large tweaks requires stronger (non idealized) assumptions and may incur performance overheads if specialized TBCs with large tweaks can be exploited, and a construction without twisted verification requires even stronger assumptions (still non idealized) and leads to more involved bounds. The combination of these results makes a case for our first pragmatic construction and suggests the design of TBCs with large tweaks and good properties for side-channel countermeasures as an interesting challenge.

1 Introduction

Ever since its introduction by Dziembowski and Pietrzak [20], leakage-resilient cryptography has been characterized by a quest towards the best tradeoff between weak physical assumptions and efficient cryptographic constructions.

© International Association for Cryptologic Research 2021
M. Tibouchi and H. Wang (Eds.): ASIACRYPT 2021, LNCS 13091, pp. 95–123, 2021.
https://doi.org/10.1007/978-3-030-92075-3_4

Finding good abstractions to limit the informativeness of the leakage function, that can be fulfilled by hardware engineers while also enabling sound security proofs, is a typical example of this challenge. Current assumptions range from various types of "bounded leakage", as comprehensively discussed in [21], to simpler solutions leveraging the scarce use of "strongly protected components", modeled as leak-free in [33]. Unsurprisingly, the most efficient (symmetric) constructions in the literature leverage such strong (idealized) assumptions [6].

While avoiding idealized assumptions is of general interest in cryptography, it is even more desirable in leakage-resilient cryptography, since perfectly ensuring a physical assumption may not be possible, or only at prohibitive cost. For example, instantiating a (128-bit) leak-free component would require masking it at very high security orders, leading to significant performance overheads [22], while security against $< 2^{80}$ measurements may be sufficient for a majority of applications. So despite proofs relying on a leak-free component are a useful guide towards efficient constructions with good leakage properties, interpreting their security bounds in terms of concrete requirements for cryptographic engineers (e.g., in terms of a level of protection to reach in practice) remains difficult.

Given this state-of-the-art, the design of leakage-resilient MACs appears as a first natural target. As put forward by Micali and Reyzin, ensuring unpredictability in the presence of leakage is significantly easier than ensuring indistinguishability in the presence of leakage [32]. This observation led the authors of [10] to propose authenticated encryption schemes for which the integrity holds even if the vast majority of its (ephemeral) secrets are leaked in full to the adversary: a model that we next denote as the "unbounded leakage model". Yet, these authenticated encryption schemes (and follow ups next listed as related works) still rely on the scarce utilization of a leak-free component.

An intermediate step towards getting rid of the leak-free component has been made by Berti et al. [8]: it shows that it is possible to replace this leak-free component by a (tweakable) block cipher ensuring "strong unpredictability with leakage". The idea of basing MAC security on unpredictable ciphers is not new. To the best of our knowledge, it dates back to [1] and has been revisited in [18,19,36]. Its leakage generalization is specially appealing since such a game-based definition can then be verified/falsified by evaluation laboratories. Yet, the results in [8] still rely on a random oracle assumption, which seems mostly due to the difficult interaction between an unpredictable (tweakable) block cipher and the hash part of their constructions. As for the leak-free component, such an idealized assumption is in general undesirable, and possibly even more when leakage comes into play. So the main question we tackle in this work is: *can we design leakage-resilient MACs without idealized assumptions (i.e., no leak-free component nor random oracles)?* We answer it positively by exhibiting efficient constructions for which the leakage security holds in the unbounded leakage model, only requiring strong unpredictability with leakage for their tweakable block cipher and (more or less) standard properties for their hash function.

More precisely, our contributions are threefold:

We first propose a pragmatic construction (next denoted as LR-MAC1) that takes advantage of simple design twists. The starting observation for this purpose is that the HTBC construction in [8] performs the verification by checking whether an inverted Tweakable Block Cipher (TBC) matches the output of a hash function. By changing this verification and checking whether the inverted TBC equals a constant (e.g., zero) value, we avoid the difficult interaction between the hash function and the TBC that has led this previous work to rely on a random oracle assumption. We then show that if the construction is instantiated with a TBC having $2n$-bit tweaks, it provides tight and beyond-birthday security bounds, under standard assumptions (namely, strong unpredictability with leakage for the TBC and collision-resistance for the hash function). While this construction positively answers our question, it still relies on two design twists, namely a TBC with $2n$-bit tweaks and the introduction of a constant value in the verification process. So we complement our first pragmatic constructions by two other designs aiming to clarify whether these twists are necessary.

Our second design (next denoted as LR-MAC2) is a variant of LR-MAC1 that only relies on TBCs having n-bit tweaks. We show that it is possible to maintain leakage security without idealized assumptions with this simpler building block. However, designs reaching this goal currently need to rely on two calls to the TBC, which is in general more expensive than a single call to a TBC with $2n$-bit tweaks if a specialized TBC can be used [27]. Besides, the best construction we reach also requires a less standard (yet non idealized) assumption on its hash function (namely, collision-resistance for one half of its output). The latter may therefore require more rounds in the instances of hash functions it uses.

Eventually, we revisit the leakage security of the HTBC design (which does not use a constant value in its verification), analyzed in [8] under a random oracle assumption. We show that such a construction can be proven secure without this idealized assumption, but at the cost of more involved bounds and stronger (still non idealized) assumptions for the hash function than LR-MAC2.

Overall, the combination of our observations regarding LR-MAC2 and HTBC strengthen the interest of the pragmatic LR-MAC1 solution, and suggest the design of TBCs with $2n$-bit tweaks and good properties to be protected via masking as natural design targets for leakage-resilient modes of operation.

Related Works. Leakage-resilient MACs have first been proposed by Hazay et al. [25] and Martin et al. [31], but imply higher performance overheads than the symmetric constructions we consider in this work. The first leakage-resilient MACs based on symmetric building blocks were proposed in [33,34]. Several (TBC-based or permutation-based) leakage-resilient authenticated encryption schemes have been proposed and embed a leakage-resilient MAC for their integrity guarantees, e.g., [9,14–16,23,24,30]: they all rely on idealized assumptions to some extent (see [6] for an overview). The specific issue of comparing values (e.g., tags) in a leakage-resilient manner is discussed in [11,17].

2   Background

Notations. With $\{0,1\}^n$ (resp., $\{0,1\}^*$), we denote the set of all strings of length n (resp., all finite-length strings). With $|\mathcal{X}|$, we denote the size of the set $\mathcal{X}$.

In some arguments, we denote by n the security parameter, $\mathsf{negl}(n)$ negligible functions and $\mathsf{poly}(n)/\mathsf{superpoly}(n)$ polynomial/super-polynomial functions.

2.1   Primitives: Hash Functions and TBC

Our schemes use hash functions and TBCs. For hash functions, the minimum property we require is collision-resistance, which we recall next:

Definition 1. *Let* $\mathsf{H} : \mathcal{HK} \times \{0,1\}^* \to \mathcal{X}$ *be a hash function.* H *is* (t, ϵ)-collision resistant (CR) *if for every t-bounded adversary* A*, the probability that* $\mathsf{A}(s)$ *outputs a pair of distinct inputs* $(m^0, m^1) \in (\{0,1\}^*)^2$*, such that* $\mathsf{H}_s(m^0) = \mathsf{H}_s(m^1)$ *and* $m^0 \neq m^1$*, is bounded by* ϵ*, with* $s \xleftarrow{\$} \mathcal{HK}$ *picked uniformly at random with:*

$$\Pr[s \xleftarrow{\$} \mathcal{HK}, \mathsf{A}(s) \Rightarrow (m^0, m^1) \in (\{0,1\}^*)^2 \text{ s.t. } m^0 \neq m^1, \mathsf{H}_s(m^0) = \mathsf{H}_s(m^1)] \leq \epsilon.$$

We will sometimes require range-oriented preimage resistant hash functions:

Definition 2. *Let* $\mathsf{H} : \mathcal{HK} \times \{0,1\}^* \to \mathcal{X}$ *be a hash function.* H *is* (t, ϵ)-range-oriented preimage resistant (rpre) *if, for every t-bounded adversary* A*:*

$$\Pr[s \xleftarrow{\$} \mathcal{HK}, y \xleftarrow{\$} \mathcal{X}, \mathsf{A}(s,y) \Rightarrow m \in \{0,1\}^* \text{ s.t. } \mathsf{H}_s(m) = y] \leq \epsilon.$$

Properties of rpre Hashing. Following [2], a hash function can be characterized by a table of preimage computing probabilities.

Definition 3. *Let* A *be an adversary against the preimage resistance of a hash function, then the associated success probability matrix* $M \in [0,1]^{|\mathcal{HK}| \times |\mathcal{X}|}$ *is:*

$$M_{s,y} = \Pr_{\mathsf{A}(s,y) \Rightarrow m}\big[\mathsf{H}_s(m) = y\big],$$

defined entry-wise where $s \in \mathcal{HK}$ *and* $y \in \mathcal{X}$*, and where the probability is taken over the random coins of* A*.*

Consider a hash function $\mathsf{H} : \mathcal{HK} \times \{0,1\}^* \to \mathcal{X}$ and an arbitrary adversary A. The intuition is that the preimage for some "weak" points in $\mathcal{X}$ may be easily computable. But if H is range-oriented preimage resistant, then the total number of such "weak" points should be limited. To formalize this idea, for any $s \in \mathcal{HK}$, we define a set for such "weak" points as:

$$\mathcal{WP}(s, \mathsf{A}) = \Big\{ y \in \mathcal{X} : \Pr_{\mathsf{A}(s,y) \Rightarrow m}\big[\mathsf{H}_s(m) = y\big] = \mathsf{poly}(n)^{-1} \Big\}. \qquad (1)$$

With the above definition, we are able to establish the following claim.

Lemma 1. *If* H *is range-oriented preimage resistant, then with high probability, the size of the set* $\mathcal{WP}(s, \mathsf{A})$ *of "weak" images is polynomial with:*

$$\Pr\big[s \xleftarrow{\$} \mathcal{HK} : |\mathcal{WP}(s, \mathsf{A})| = \mathsf{superpoly}(n)\big] = \mathsf{negl}(n).$$

Proof. To see this, we expand the expression as follows:

$$\Pr[s \xleftarrow{\$} \mathcal{HK}, y \xleftarrow{\$} \mathcal{X}, \mathsf{A}(s,y) \Rightarrow m \in \{0,1\}^* \text{ s.t. } \mathsf{H}_s(m) = y],$$

$$= \sum_{s \in \mathcal{HK}} \frac{1}{|\mathcal{HK}|} \sum_{y \in \mathcal{X}} \frac{1}{|\mathcal{X}|} \Pr[\mathsf{A}(s,y) \Rightarrow m \in \{0,1\}^* \text{ s.t. } \mathsf{H}_s(m) = y],$$

$$\geq \sum_{s \in \mathcal{HK}} \frac{1}{|\mathcal{HK}|} \sum_{y \in \mathcal{WP}(s,\mathsf{A})} \frac{1}{|\mathcal{X}|} \cdot \mathsf{superpoly}(n),$$

$$\geq \sum_{s \in \mathcal{HK}, |\mathcal{WP}(s,\mathsf{A})| = \mathsf{superpoly}(n)} \frac{1}{|\mathcal{HK}|} \frac{|\mathcal{WP}(s,\mathsf{A})|}{|\mathcal{X}|} \cdot \mathsf{superpoly}(n),$$

$$\geq \Pr\left[s \xleftarrow{\$} \mathcal{HK} : |\mathcal{WP}(s,\mathsf{A})| = \mathsf{superpoly}(n)\right] \cdot \frac{\mathsf{superpoly}(n)}{|\mathcal{X}|}. \tag{2}$$

By this, if $\Pr\left[s \xleftarrow{\$} \mathcal{HK} : |\mathcal{WP}(s,\mathsf{A})| = \mathsf{superpoly}(n)\right]$ is not $\mathsf{negl}(n)$, then Eq. (2) cannot be negligible, contradicting the range-oriented preimage resistance assumption. The claim thus follows. $\square$

Thanks to Lemma 1, it *may* be feasible to decide the set $\mathcal{WP}(s,\mathsf{A})$ for any adversary A and any seed s. In Sect. 5, Theorem 3, this result will allow us to assume that the set $\mathcal{WP}(s,\mathsf{A})$ for the hash function used in our design is computable in Probabilistic Polynomial-Time (PPT).

For TBC, the minimum property we require is strong pseudorandomness:

Definition 4 (stPRP). *A tweakable block cipher* $\mathsf{F} : \mathcal{K} \times \mathcal{TW} \times \{0,1\}^n \to \{0,1\}^n$ *is a* (q,t,ϵ)-*strong tweakable pseudorandom permutation (stPRP) if* $\forall (k,tw) \in \mathcal{K} \times \mathcal{TW}, \mathsf{F}_k^{tw} : \{0,1\}^n \to \{0,1\}^n$ *is a permutation and if for every* (q,t)-*adversary* A, *the advantage :*

$$\mathsf{Adv}_\mathsf{F}^{\mathsf{stPRP}}(\mathsf{A}) := \left| \Pr\left[\mathsf{A}^{\mathsf{F}_k(\cdot,\cdot),\mathsf{F}_k^{-1}(\cdot,\cdot)} \Rightarrow 1\right] - \Pr\left[\mathsf{A}^{\mathsf{f}(\cdot,\cdot),\mathsf{f}^{-1}(\cdot,\cdot)} \Rightarrow 1\right] \right|,$$

is upper bounded by ϵ, *where* k *and* f *are chosen uniformly at random from their domains, namely* $\mathcal{K}$ *and the space* $\mathcal{TPERM}(\mathcal{TW}, \{0,1\}^n)$ *of tweakable permutations (i.e., the space of functions* $\mathsf{f} : \mathcal{TW} \times \{0,1\}^n \to \{0,1\}^n$ *s.t.* $\forall tw \in \mathcal{TW}, \mathsf{f}(tw,\cdot) : \{0,1\}^n \to \{0,1\}^n$ *is a permutation). The adversary can do at most* q' *queries to the first oracle and* $q - q'$ *queries to the second one for any* $q' \leq q$.

For simplicity, an (n,n,n)-TBC is a TBC with $\mathcal{K} = \mathcal{TW} = \{0,1\}^n$.

2.2 MAC (Message Authentication Code)

We recall the definition of Message Authentication Code (MAC) as follows:

Definition 5. *A MAC is a triple* $\Pi = (\mathsf{Gen}, \mathsf{Mac}, \mathsf{Vrfy})$ *where:*

Gen. *The key-generation algorithm* Gen *picks a key in the keyspace* $\mathcal{K}$.

Mac. *The tag-generation algorithm* Mac *takes as input a couple* $(k, m) \in \mathcal{K} \times \{0, 1\}^*$ *and outputs a tag* $\tau \leftarrow \mathsf{Mac}_k(m)$ *from the tag space* $\mathcal{TAG}$.

Vrfy. *The verification algorithm* Vrfy *takes as input a triple* (k, m, τ) *in* $\mathcal{K} \times \{0, 1\}^* \times \mathcal{TAG}$ *and outputs either* "$\top$" *("accept") or* "$\bot$" *("reject").*

We require correctness: $\forall (k, m) \in \mathcal{K} \times \{0, 1\}^*$, $\mathsf{Vrfy}(k, m, \mathsf{Mac}(k, m)) = \top$.

Since we will only consider the security for MACs in the presence of leakage, we omit the security definition in the black-box model (that is, when there is no leakage). This definition can be found in many works, for example [29].

2.3   Leakage Models and Security Definitions with Leakage

Notations. When an adversary has access not only to the outputs of an oracle but also to its leakage, we denote it with A^{OL}. In this case, queries to the oracle OL on input x are answered with $y = \mathsf{O}(x)$ and the leakage $\mathsf{l}_\mathsf{O} := \mathsf{L}_\mathsf{O}(x)$. If the oracle is keyed with the key k, we write the leakage function as $\mathsf{L}_\mathsf{O}(x; k)$. Finding good abstractions to restrict L_O is in general a hard problem [21].[1]

Strong Unforgeability with Leakage (sUF-L2). We start by introducing the security for MACs in the presence of leakage. We want that it is hard to forge valid tags even having access to the leakage of the tag-generation and the verification algorithms (that is, finding a fresh and valid couple message tag (m, τ) such that $\mathsf{Vrfy}_k(m, \tau) = \top$ should be hard). We use the sUF-L2 definition of Berti et al. [8] for this purpose, which we recall next:

Definition 6 (sUF-L2). *A* MAC $=$ (Gen, Mac, Vrfy) *with tag-generation leakage function* L_M *and verification leakage function* L_V *is* $(q_L, q_M, q_V, t, \epsilon)$-*strongly existentially unforgeable against chosen message and verification attacks with leakage in the tag-generation and the verification (sUF-L2) if for all* (q_L, q_M, q_V, t)-*adversaries* A^L, *we have:*

$$\Pr\left[\mathsf{FORGEL2}^{\mathsf{suf\text{-}vcma\text{-}L2}}_{\mathsf{MAC}, \mathsf{L}_M, \mathsf{L}_V, \mathsf{A}} \Rightarrow 1\right] \leq \epsilon,$$

where the $\mathsf{FORGEL2}^{\mathsf{suf\text{-}vcma\text{-}L2}}$ *experiment is defined in Table 1.*

For simplicity, we consider the verification query induced by the final output of the adversary as the $(q_v + 1)th$ verification query.

---

[1] Adversaries are sometimes allowed to "model" the leakage. For this purpose, we grant them access to the oracle L. This oracle is peculiar since it allows the adversary to make queries not only on inputs x but also of keys k' of its choice.

Table 1. The FORGEL2$^{\text{suf-vcma-L2}}$ experiment.

The FORGEL2$^{\text{suf-vcma-L2}}_{\text{MAC},L_M,L_V,A^L}$ experiment	
Initialization:	Oracle MacL$_k(m)$:
$\quad k \leftarrow$ Gen	$\quad \tau = \text{Mac}_k(m)$
$\quad \mathcal{S} \leftarrow \emptyset$	$\quad \mathcal{S} \leftarrow \mathcal{S} \cup \{(m,\tau)\}$
	$\quad$ Return $(\tau, L_M(m;k))$
Finalization:	
$\quad (m,\tau) \leftarrow A^{L,\text{MacL}_k(\cdot),\text{VrfyL}_k(\cdot,\cdot)}$	Oracle VrfyL$_k(m,\tau)$:
$\quad$ If $(m,\tau) \in \mathcal{S}$ or $\perp = \text{Vrfy}_k(m,\tau)$	$\quad$ Return
$\quad\quad$ Return 0	$\quad\quad (\text{Vrfy}_k(m,\tau), L_V(m,\tau;k))$
$\quad$ Return 1	

The Unbounded Leakage Model. We next need to specify the functions we will use for L_M and L_V. Based on the aforementioned difficulty to restrict the leakage in a meaningful manner, we first follow the observation made in [33] that it is possible to implement leakage-resilient cryptographic functionalities so that the execution of most underlying building blocks can leak in an unrestricted manner. The resulting "leveled implementations" only require a few calls to a strongly protected component (frequently modeled as leak-free) to ensure the desired security property (here, sUF-L2). So we will next consider the unbounded leakage model, where the leakage function yields all the internal states produced during each execution of the scheme under investigation, at the exclusion of the strongly protected components that are used to manipulate long-term secrets. More precisely, in the unbounded leakage model:

- Unprotected building blocks leak their inputs, outputs and keys in full;
- Building blocks with strongly protected implementation leak their inputs and outputs in full and their key only leaks in a restricted manner.

In practice, the only strongly protected component we will use in our construction is a TBC, and we next specify how its leakage will be restricted by asking implementers to ensure its strong unpredictability with leakage.

Strong Unpredictability with Leakage (sUP-L2). Unpredictability is among the simplest requirements for (tweakable) block ciphers. As mentioned in introduction, its application in leakage-resilient cryptography is appealing since it corresponds to a game-based definition that can directly be tested by an evaluation laboratory. We next give its definition which formalizes that it should be hard for an adversary to find a triple (tw, x, y) which is fresh and valid (i.e., $y = F_k^{tw}(x)$) even if the leakage function $L = (L_{\text{Eval}}, L_{\text{Inv}})$ associated to an implementation of the TBC can be queried, with $L_{\text{Eval}}(tw, x; k)$ (resp. $L_{\text{Inv}}(tw, z; k)$) the leakage resulting from the computation of $F_k(tw, x)$ (resp., $F_k^{-1}(tw, z)$).

Definition 7 (sUP-L2). *A tweakable block cipher* $\mathsf{F} : \mathcal{K} \times \mathcal{TW} \times \{0,1\}^n \to \{0,1\}^n$ *with leakage function pair* $\mathsf{L} = (\mathsf{L_{Eval}}, \mathsf{L_{Inv}})$ *is* $(q_L, q_E, q_I, t, \epsilon)$-*strongly unpredictable with leakage in evaluation and inversion (sUP-L2), or* $(q_L, q_E, q_I, t, \epsilon)$-*sUP-L2, if for any* (q_L, q_E, q_I, t)-*adversary* A, *we have:*

$$\Pr[\mathsf{sUP\text{-}L2_{A,F,L}} \Rightarrow 1] \leq \epsilon,$$

where the sUP-L2 *experiment is defined in Table 2, and* A^L *makes at most* q_L *(offline) queries to* L *(used to model the leakage, cf. Footnote 6).*

When the adversary has access only to the $\mathsf{l_e}$ oracle, the TBC is *unpredictable with leakage* (as previously defined by Dodis and Steinberger [18]).[2]

Table 2. Strong unpredictability with leakage in evaluation and inversion.

The sUP-L2$_{A,F,L}$ experiment.	
Initialization:	Oracle LEval(tw, x):
$k \xleftarrow{\$} \mathcal{K}$	$z = \mathsf{F}_k(tw, x)$
$\mathcal{L} \leftarrow \emptyset$	$\mathsf{l_e} = \mathsf{L_{Eval}}(tw, x; k)$
	$\mathcal{L} \leftarrow \mathcal{L} \cup \{(x, tw, z)\}$
Finalization:	Return $(z, \mathsf{l_e})$
$(x, tw, z) \leftarrow \mathsf{A}^{\mathsf{L}, \mathsf{LEval}(\cdot,\cdot), \mathsf{LInv}(\cdot,\cdot)}$	
If $(x, tw, z) \in \mathcal{L}$	Oracle LInv(tw, z):
Return 0	$x = \mathsf{F}_k^{-1}(tw, z)$
If $z = \mathsf{F}_k(tw, x)$	$\mathsf{l_i} = \mathsf{L_{Inv}}(tw, z; k)$
Return 1	$\mathcal{L} \leftarrow \mathcal{L} \cup \{(x, tw, z)\}$
Return 0	Return $(x, \mathsf{l_i})$

Concretely, this assumption is significantly closer to practice than idealized ones. In particular, breaking it requires one to fully compute the value of the block cipher on a new point with non-trivial probability [18]. Therefore, we expect that satisfying unpredictability with leakage mainly requires protecting the long-term key, and that testing block cipher implementations against side-channel key recovery attacks, which is the current focus of evaluation laboratories [4], should give a good indication of their unpredictability with leakage.

---

[2] Degabriele et al. give an alternative definition in [14]. The main difference is that the set of inputs ($\mathcal{S}$ in their definition, $\mathcal{L}$ in ours) is not increased for inputs X for which only the leakage is observed, while we always give access to both the primitive's output and their leakage. Hence, this definition cannot be satisfied in the unbounded leakage model as we aim, since the adversary can then get a valid tag in full. (Their motivation was also different from ours and specially tailored for analyzing constructions leveraging leakage-resilient PRFs).

3   Design and Analysis of **LR-MAC1**

In this section, we present LR-MAC1, which is sUF-L2 in the unbounded leakage model, assuming a collision-resistant hash function and a sUP-L2 TBC.

The main design idea used by LR-MAC1 is to avoid that a value obtained by leakage in verification may be used for a future forgery. This happened in the HTBC leakage-resilient MAC of [8] because the output of an (inverse) TBC is compared with a hash value $h = H(m)$. As illustrated in Fig. 1, LR-MAC1 prevents this by doing the verification check with a fixed value that does not depend on the message m. In this figure, strongly protected components are in gray, unprotected components are in white, inputs and outputs of the scheme (together with values that can be computed publicly from them) are in green, intermediate values that leak (in an unbounded manner in our case) are in orange and long-term secrets manipulated by strongly protected components are in red.

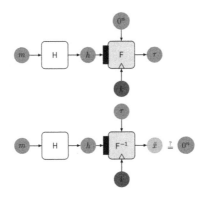

Fig. 1. LR-MAC1. (Color figure online)

Concretely, the hash of the message is used only as a tweak of the TBC, while the input of the TBC is always a fixed value (i.e., 0^n). In decryption, we check if the inverse of the tag $\tilde{x} := F_k^{-1}(\tau)$ is 0^n. This way, even an unbounded leakage during an invalid verification cannot lead to efficient forgeries since $\tilde{x}$ cannot be reused (contrary to what happens for HTBC). Moreover, since the hash of the message h is used only as a tweak, there is no target to find a preimage (without producing a collision). As a result, a verification query $\mathsf{Vrfy}_k(m, \tau) \to \top$ immediately results in a forgery $\big(H_s(m), 0^n, \tau\big)$, which does not rely on the distribution of $H_s(m)$. This eliminates the necessity of the random oracle in our proofs. The detailed specifications of LR-MAC1 can be found in Algorithm 1.

3.1   **sUF-L2-Security of LR-MAC1**

We now prove that LR-MAC1 is sUF-L2 in the unbounded leakage model.

Algorithm 1. The LR-MAC1 algorithm.

It uses a strongly protected TBC $F : \mathcal{K} \times \mathcal{TW} \times \{0,1\}^n \to \{0,1\}^n$ and a hash function
$H : \mathcal{HK} \times \{0,1\}^n \to \mathcal{TW}$.

- Gen
  - $k \xleftarrow{\$} \mathcal{K}$
  - $s \xleftarrow{\$} \mathcal{HK}$
- $\mathsf{Mac}_k(m)$:
  - $h = H_s(m)$
  - $\tau = F_k^h(0^n)$
  - Return τ
- $\mathsf{Vrfy}_k(m, \tau)$:
  - $h = H_s(m)$
  - $\tilde{x} = F_k^{h,-1}(\tau)$
  - If $\tilde{x} == 0^n$ Return $\top$
  - Else Return $\bot$

Unbounded leakage specification. Before assessing the sUF-L2 of LR-MAC1, we
have to define the leakage that an adversary can collect:

- $L_M(m; k)$ returns $\mathsf{LEval}(0^n, h; k)$ with $h = H_s(m)$.[3]
- $L_V(m, \tau; k)$ returns $\tilde{x}$ and $\mathsf{LInv}(\tau, h; k)$ with $h = H_s(m)$.

Our main result for LR-MAC1 is then formalized by the following theorem:

Theorem 1. *Let* H *be a* $(t_1, \epsilon_{\mathsf{CR}})$-*collision resistant hash function. Let* F *be a*
$(q_L, q_M, q_V, t_2, \epsilon_{\mathsf{sUP\text{-}L2}})$-sUP-L2 *TBC. Then,* LR-MAC1 *is* (q_M, q_V, t, ϵ)-sUF-L2-
secure in the unbounded leakage model with:

$$\epsilon \leq \epsilon_{\mathsf{CR}} + (q_V + 1)\, \epsilon_{\mathsf{sUP\text{-}L2}},$$

with $t_1 = t + (q_M + q_V + 1)t_H + (q_M + q_V)(t_F + t_{L(F)})$ *and* $t_2 = t + (q_M + q_V + 1)t_H$,
where t_H *is the time needed to execute once the hash function* H, t_F *is the time
needed to execute once the TBC* F *and* $t_{L(F)}$ *is the time needed to collect the
leakage of one execution of the TBC* F.

Proof. We use a sequence of games. To make the proof simpler, we give only a
sketch of the adversaries used. Details are in the ePrint version of the paper.

Game 0. Let Game 0 be the sUF-L2 game where the (q_M, q_V, t)-adversary A^L
tries to produce a forgery when she plays against LR-MAC1. Let E_0 be the event
that the adversary wins the game (i.e., the output of the game is 1).

Game 1. Game 1 is Game 0 except that we abort if there is a collision in the
hash function. Let E_1 be the event that the adversary wins the game.

---

[3] h can be computed by the adversary since the key s of the hash function is public.

Transition between Game 1 and Game 2. Clearly, Game 0 and Game 1 are identical if the following event HC (*Hash Collision*) does not happen:[4]

$$HC := \{\exists i,j \in \{1,...,q_M\}\cup\{1,...,q_V+1\} \text{ with } i \stackrel{\%}{=} j \text{ s.t. } h^i = h^j \text{ and } m^i \neq m^j\}.$$

To compute this event, we build a t_1-CR-adversary B.

The t_1-CR-adversary B is an adversary playing against the hash function, based on A, which does the hash queries induced by the queries of A and then correctly computes the answer for A. At the end of the game, B sees if her hash queries have produced a collision. If it is the case, she outputs it. This adversary needs time $t + (q_M + q_V + 1)t_H + (q_M + q_V)(t_F + t_{L(F)})$.

Bounding $|\Pr[E_0] - \Pr[E_1]|$. Observe that if event HC happens, B wins. Note that B simulates correctly Game 0 for A^L. Since B is a t_1-adversary and H is a (t_1, ϵ_{CR})-collision resistant hash function, we can bound:

$$|\Pr[E_0] - \Pr[E_1]| \leq \epsilon_{CR}.$$

Game 2. Game 2 is Game 1 except that we abort if one verification query (or the final one) made by A is fresh and valid. Let E_2 be the event that the adversary wins the game (i.e., the output of the game is 1).

Transition between Game 1 ad Game 2. We build a sequence of $q_V + 2$ games: Game 1^0,...,Game 1^{q_V+1} as follows.

Game 1^j. Game 1^j is Game 1 where we abort if one of the first j verification queries is fresh and valid. Thus, Game 1^0 is Game 1 while Game 1^{q_V+1} is Game 2. Let E_1^j be the event that the adversary wins the game.

Transition between Game 1^j and Game 1^{j+1}. Clearly, Game 1^j and Game 1^{j+1} are identical if the $j+1$-th verification query is either invalid or not fresh. If this query is fresh and valid, we say that event GT^j (Good Tag) happens. In order to bound the probability that event GT^j happens we build a $(q_L, q_{Eval}, q_{Inv}, t_2)$-sUP-L2-adversary C^j against F as follows.

The $(q_L, q_{Eval}, q_{Inv}, t_2)$-sUP-L2-adversary C^j has to find a valid triple (x, tw, y) for F_k which is fresh and valid. She simulates Game 1^j for A until the $j + 1$th verification query. Then, when A asks his $j + 1$-th verification query on input $(m^{q_V+1}, \tau^{q_V+1})$, C^j computes (1) $h^{j+1} = H_s(m^{j+1})$, and (2) she outputs $(0^n, h^{j+1}, \tau^{j+1})$. This takes time t_H. In total, C^i does at most q_L query to L, q_M to LEval and $j \leq q_v$ to LInv. She needs time at most $t + (q_M + j + 1)t_H \leq t_2$.

Bounding $|\Pr[E_1^j] - \Pr[E_1^{j+1}]|$. Note that C^i simulates correctly Game 1^j for A^L. Since C^j is a (q_L, q_M, q_V, t_2)-adversary and F is $(q_L, q_M, q_V, t_2, \epsilon_{sUP-L2})$-sUP-L2, we can bound:

---

[4] $i \stackrel{\%}{=} j$ means that if i comes from a tag-generation query and j from a verification query, or vice-versa, then they are considered differently.

$$|\Pr[E_1^j] - \Pr[E_1^{j+1}]| \leq \Pr[GT^{j+1}] \leq \epsilon_{\mathsf{sUP\text{-}L2}}.$$

Bounding $\big|\Pr[E_1] - \Pr[E_2]\big|$. Iterating we can bound:

$$\big|\Pr[E_1] - \Pr[E_2]\big| \leq \sum_{j=0}^{q_V} \big|\Pr[E_1^j] - \Pr[E_1^{j+1}]\big| \leq (q_V + 1)\epsilon_{\mathsf{sUP\text{-}L2}}.$$

Concluding the Proof. Since the probability of E_2 is 0, we can conclude the proof putting everything together:

$$\Pr[E_0] = \sum_{i=0}^{1} \big|\Pr[E_i] - \Pr[E_{i+1}]\big| + \Pr[E_2] = \epsilon_{\mathsf{CR}} + (q_V + 1)\epsilon_{\mathsf{sUP\text{-}L2}} + 0.$$

3.2   Instantiation and Concrete Security

Built upon a "good enough" hash function, the term ϵ_{CR} is expected to be in $O(t_1^2/2^{|\mathcal{TW}|})$. On the other hand, the term $\epsilon_{\mathsf{sUP\text{-}L2}}$ depends on the concrete side-channel strength of the TBC implementation. Since we have a birthday bound only on the size of the tweak space $\mathcal{TW}$ and not on the block space $\mathcal{B} = \{0,1\}^n$, a natural idea is to use a TBC with the tweak space bigger than the block space. For example, a good instantiation would be to use SHA256 as hash function and Deoxys-384 (which has a 128-bit block and 256-bit tweak [28]) as TBC. In this case, finding a collision requires the computation of around 2^{128} hash functions, and therefore, the $(q_V + 1)\epsilon_{\mathsf{sUP\text{-}L2}}$ term dominates the bound.[5]

4   Design and Analysis of LR-MAC2

In this section, we question the possibility to design a leakage-resilient MAC with a (more standard) TBC design having only n-bit tweaks rather than $2n$ for LR-MAC1. We show that this is achievable at the cost of a second call per message authentication to the TBC and by requiring an additional property of the hash function that we develop after the description of the scheme. Our security analysis also holds without idealized assumption.

4.1   Description of LR-MAC2

To get high security we start again from $\mathsf{H}_s(m) = u\|v$, where $u, v \in \{0,1\}^n$, as illustrated in Fig. 2. As in HTBC, we first compute $\mathsf{F}_k^v(u)$ with $k = k_1$ to get a value dependent on both n-bit strings u and v. To verify the validity of a tag τ for message m, we know that we should rely on a TBC inversion call to avoid leaking useful information about the good tag if (m, τ) is actually an invalid message-tag pair. However, we also have to circumvent the difficulty encountered when dealing with the verification of HTBC tags, as discussed in the introduction.

---

[5] In the black box setting (i.e., without leakage), the security of this construction is beyond birthday since $(q_V + 1)\,\epsilon_{\mathsf{sUP\text{-}L2}} \leq \epsilon_{\mathsf{sPRP}} + \frac{q_V + 1}{2^{128} - q_M - q_V}$, which is optimal.

That means that we should use our second TBC call in such a way that the equality check must not directly involve either u or v (so, a half hash value) and an output of the TBC (thus requiring to rely on a backwards computation). As a result, we need a serial evaluation of the TBC calls to compute a tag, e.g., as $\tau = \left(\mathsf{F}^v_{k_2} \circ \mathsf{F}^v_{k_1}\right)(u)$, with an equality check performed in the middle to compare $\mathsf{F}^v_{k_1}(u)$ and $\mathsf{F}^{v,-1}_{k_2}(\tau')$ in the verification for a candidate tag τ'.

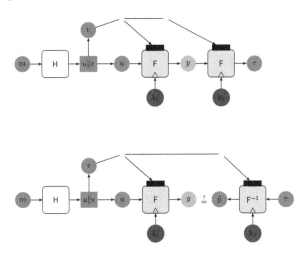

Fig. 2. LR-MAC2.

Up to switching the role between u and v, we now explain why $\mathsf{F}^v_{k_2} \circ \mathsf{F}^v_{k_1}$ is the good choice beyond the fact that using only a secret key primitive for the equality check allows us to learn what is computed and when, contrarily to the hash function. Since F_{k_2} and F_{k_1} are independent instances of the TBC, using the same tweak still enable us to use the output of one call against each other. The advantage of re-using the same tweak is twofold. First, we can easily partition all the queries with respect to v, the "lower half" of $\mathsf{H}_s(m) = u\|v$. This avoids considering many intermediate cases in the proof since with another computation of the form $\mathsf{F}^u_{k_2}$, with tweak u, we would have to deal with many "crossed" half hashes like $u_1\|v_1$, $u_1\|v_2$, $u_2\|v_1\ldots$ Second, given v, $\mathsf{F}^v_{k_2} \circ \mathsf{F}^v_{k_1}$ is a permutation between u and τ. We will see that this also simplifies the distribution of the potential forgeries, which in turn improves the security bound.

The complete specification of LR-MAC2 is given in Algorithm 2.

Single key version. For the sake of simplicity, we described LR-MAC2 with two uniform and independent keys. However, with some extra work we can rely on a single secret key k. The careful reader will have noted that we cannot derive k_1 and k_2 from F_k as the TBC is only unpredictable with leakage, and not pseudorandom with leakage which is a controversy assumption in the standard model. So the keys k_1 and k_2 will not have the right distribution to assume that F_{k_1} and F_{k_2} are themselves unpredictable with leakage. Nevertheless, the

---

Algorithm 2. The LR-MAC2 algorithm.

It uses a strongly protected TBC $F : \mathcal{K} \times \mathcal{TW} \times \{0,1\}^n \to \{0,1\}^n$ and a hash function $H : \mathcal{HK} \times \{0,1\}^* \to \{0,1\}^{2n}$.

- Gen
  - $k = (k_1, k_2) \xleftarrow{\$} \mathcal{K}^2$
  - $s \xleftarrow{\$} \mathcal{HK}$
- $\mathsf{Mac}_k(m)$:
  - $u \| v \xleftarrow{n} \mathsf{H}_s(m)$
  - $y = \mathsf{F}_{k_1}^v(u)$
  - $\tau = \mathsf{F}_{k_2}^v(y)$
  - Return τ
- $\mathsf{Vrfy}_k(m, \tau)$:
  - $u \| v \xleftarrow{n} \mathsf{H}_s(m)$
  - $y = \mathsf{F}_{k_1}^v(u)$
  - $\tilde{y} = \mathsf{F}_{k_2}^{v,-1}(\tau)$
  - If $y == \tilde{y}$ Return $\top$
  - Else Return $\bot$

---

other known alternatives work. We can either assume that the TBC supports one more bit-tweak, i.e., tweaks of size $n+1$, or we can drop one bit of v in order to force in both cases the use of a domain separation bit in the tweaks between the two calls of the TBC. For completeness, we depict the construction where we compute $\tau = \mathsf{F}_k^{v\|1} \circ \mathsf{F}_k^{v\|0}(u)$ in the ePrint version of this work.

4.2 Half Multi-collision Resistance

It is natural to combine a double output length hash function $\mathsf{H}_s(m) = h = u\|v \in \{0,1\}^{2n}$ with an (n, n, n)-TBC F to target high MAC unforgeability. But since the hash value h is too long it cannot be used directly, and we split it into two n-bit pieces u and v to input $\mathsf{F}_k^v(u)$, for instance, where k is the n-bit key. The values u and v thus have distinct purposes in the design and it is equally natural to investigate the properties of both halves separately. At high level, this therefore requires that $\mathsf{H}_s = \mathsf{H}_s^1 \| \mathsf{H}_s^2$ comes with additional guarantees for H_s^1 and H_s^2, which can be seen as a strengthened security requirement for H_s.

General purpose standard hash functions should be as close as possible to public random functions. Since our goal is to avoid relying on idealized assumption, we will use the intuition that H_s^1 and H_s^2 should be asymptotically as good as H_s. That is, even if in practice hash functions are built for a precise output-length (e.g., 256 bits), it just corresponds to asking that H_s^1 and H_s^2 are 128-bit output-length secure (enough) hash functions.

Obviously, we cannot simply concatenate any two 128-bit output collision resistant hash functions to build H_s and hope boosting the collision resistance of the resulting construction, say, up to 2^{96} queries or more. Still, $\mathsf{H}_s^1(m) = u$ and $\mathsf{H}_s^2(m) = v$ have to behave as securely as possible and we can expect them to be range-oriented/second/... preimage resistant and/or collision resistant up to $2^{64\theta}$ queries, for some $\theta \in (0,1)$ as close as possible to 1.

Building some good hash $H_s = H_s^1 \| H_s^2$ enjoying additional "half-security" is out of the scope of this paper, and this additional requirement will be part of the discussion confirming the interest of the pragmatic LR-MAC1 construction at the end of the section. Yet, we see the independent security of H_s^1 and H_s^2 as a valuable asset and a natural target as many constructions might benefit from using the two halves u and v of h at different places in a cryptographic scheme, leading to a better overall security. We assume that it could be ensured by standard constructions, at the cost of slightly increased parameters.

Among the usual security guarantees of hash functions we can ask for the halves H_s^i, for $i = 1, 2$, we require the hardness of computing many collisions on H_s^2. Bounding the probability of multi-collisions is reminiscent of deriving beyond-birthday security from symmetric (T)BC-based constructions of MAC or AEAD in the ideal-cipher model. In our construction, $H_s^2(m) = v$ is used as a tweak and we want to have a probability that decreases fast in the number of additional colliding v-values. By controlling the probability of multi-collisions on H_s^2, we will have only few messages m_i in the adversarial view such that $H_s(m_i) = u_i \| v$ for distinct u_i (otherwise we have a collision on the full H_s). That is, few possible preimages of F_k^v for any chosen v to compute a forgery.

We follow [7] to define a natural notion of multi-collision resistance before adapting it to the "half output" case as we require for our proofs.

Definition 8. *Let* $H : \mathcal{HK} \times \{0,1\}^* \rightarrow \{0,1\}^n$ *be a hash function, and* $\mu \geq 2$ *be an integer. We say that* H *is* μ-*multi collision resistant if, for any efficient adversary* A*, there is a negligible function* negl *such that:*

$$\Pr_{\substack{s \leftarrow \mathcal{HK} \\ m_1,\ldots,m_\mu \leftarrow A(s)}} \left[\forall i,j \in [\mu] : i \neq j \rightarrow m_i \neq m_j \wedge H_s(m_i) = H_s(m_j) \right] \leq \mathsf{negl}(n).$$

We further say that H *is multi collision resistant if there is a value* $\mu \geq 2$ *such that* H *is* μ-*multi collision resistant.*

If H is modeled as a random oracle, H is clearly μ-multi collision resistant for any $\mu \geq 2$. In the standard model, H might only be multi collision resistant from some lower bound, say $\mu \geq 10$ or $\mu \geq n/4$. Still, if H is μ-multi collision resistant it is also μ'-multi collision resistant, for any $\mu' \geq \mu$. We elaborate more on the possible behavior of μ in relation with a decreasing family of negligible functions to derive more concrete bounds in Sect. 4.4, after the security analysis.

We now simply define the *half multi-collision resistance* of $H_s : \{0,1\}^* \mapsto \{0,1\}^{2n}$ as the multi-collision resistance of H_s^1 or H_s^2, where $H_s = H_s^1 \| H_s^2$.

Definition 9. *Let* $H : \mathcal{HK} \times \{0,1\}^* \rightarrow \{0,1\}^{2n}$ *be a hash function, and define* $H^i : \mathcal{HK} \times \{0,1\}^* \rightarrow \{0,1\}^n$*, for* $i = 1, 2$*, such that for any* $s \leftarrow \mathcal{HK}$ *and any message* $m \in \{0,1\}^*$*, we have* $H_s(m) = H_s^1(m) \| H_s^2(m)$*. We say that* H *is* half multi-collision resistant *for* $i = 1, 2$ *if* H^i *is multi-collision resistant. To avoid indexes, if* $i = 1$*, we also say that* H *is* upper-*half multi-collision resistant, and, if* $i = 2$*, that* H *is* lower-*half multi-collision resistant.*

Assuming that H satisfies this notion is a falsifiable assumption.

4.3 Security Analysis of LR-MAC2

Unbounded leakage specification. Before assessing the sUF-L2 security of LR-MAC2, we have to define the leakage that an adversary can collect:

- $L_M(m; k)$ returns $(y, \mathsf{LEval}(v, u; k_1), \mathsf{LEval}(v, y; k_2))$, where $u\|v \xleftarrow{n} H_s(m)$ and the intermediate value $y = F^v_{k_1}(u)$ is given.
- $L_V(m, \tau; k)$ returns $(y, \tilde{y}, \mathsf{LEval}(v, u; k_1), \mathsf{LInv}(v, \tau; k_2))$, where $u\|v \xleftarrow{n} H_s(m)$, and the intermediate values $y = F^v_{k_1}(u)$ and $\tilde{y} = F^{-1,v}_{k_2}(\tau)$ are given.

Our main result for LR-MAC2 is then formalized by the following theorem:

Theorem 2. *Let* $H : \mathcal{HK} \times \{0,1\}^* \to \{0,1\}^{2n}$ *be a* $(t_1, \epsilon_{\mathsf{CR}(2n)})$*-collision resistant hash function and* $(t_1, \epsilon_{\mu\text{-}\mathsf{CR}(n)})$*-$\mu$-lower-half multi-collision resistant, for some* $\mu \geq 2$. *Let* F *be a* $(q_L, q_{\mathsf{Eval}}, q_{\mathsf{Inv}}, t_2, \epsilon_{\mathsf{sUP-L2}})$*-strongly unpredictable with leakage* TBC*, then, LR-MAC2 is* $(q_L, q_M, q_V, t, \epsilon)$*-sUF-L2 with:*

$$\epsilon \leq \epsilon_{\mathsf{CR}(2n)} + \epsilon_{\mu\text{-}\mathsf{CR}(n)} + 2\mu q_V \epsilon_{\mathsf{sUP-L2}},$$

where $q_{\mathsf{LF}} \leq q_{\mathsf{LF}}$, $q_{\mathsf{Eval}} \leq q_M + q_V + 1$, $q_{\mathsf{Inv}} \leq q_V$, $t_1 \leq t + (q_M + q_V + 1)t_\mathsf{H} + 2(q_M + q_V)(t_\mathsf{F} + t_{\mathsf{L(F)}})$, *and* $t_2 \leq t + (q_M + j + 1)t_\mathsf{H} + (q_M + q_V + 1)(t_\mathsf{F} + t_{\mathsf{L(F)}})$.

Below, we give a detailed sketch of the proof. We defer the full proof to the ePrint version of the paper and discuss the security bound in Sect. 4.4.

Proof (Sketch). To simplify our exposition, we assume the adversary gets the unbounded leakage without being explicit. Let (m, τ) be the first valid message-tag pair involved in a verification query which can be used by the adversary as a forgery. That is, the pair (m, τ) is *fresh* at the time of that verification query in the sense that it was never involved in an earlier verification query and (m, τ) is not the result of any previous tag-generation query for m. Given such a fresh and valid pair, let $u\|v \xleftarrow{n} H_s(m)$, $y = F^v_{k_1}(u)$ and $\tilde{y} = F^{-1,v}_{k_2}(\tau)$. Below, we consider different cases depending on whether the TBC triples (v, u, y) for k_1 and $(v, \tilde{y}, \tau)$ for k_2 have already been defined before the verification query of (m, τ) or not. We note that if the computation of $\tau = F^v_{k_2}(\tilde{y})$ occured before (necessarily in a tag-generation query) our second triple is already defined.

F_1 The triples (v, u, y) for k_1 and $(v, \tilde{y}, \tau)$ for k_2 have not been defined yet.
F_2 The triple (v, u, y) for k_1 has already been defined, while $(v, \tilde{y}, \tau)$ for k_2 has not been defined yet.
F_3 Conversely, the triple (v, u, y) for k_1 has not been defined yet, while $(v, \tilde{y}, \tau)$ for k_2 has already been defined.
F_4 Both triples (v, u, y) for k_1 and $(v, \tilde{y}, \tau)$ for k_2 have already been defined. We split that case into three sub-cases:
  F_{41} Both triples (v, u, y) for k_1 and $(v, \tilde{y}, \tau)$ for k_2 have been defined in the same tag-generation or verification query.

F_{42} The triple (v, u, y) for k_1 was defined in some query (of any type) precedent to the one in which $(v, \tilde{y}, \tau)$ was defined for k_2.

F_{43} The triple $(v, \tilde{y}, \tau)$ for k_2 was defined in some query (of any type) precedent to the one in which (v, u, y) was defined for k_1.

We now give intuition about how we bound the probability of these events. The main difficulty arises in F_4, where would like to rely on the sUP-L2 security of the TBC. In F_{42} (resp., F_{43}), we would like to use the second-call triple $(v, \tilde{y}, \tau)$ (resp., the first-call triple (v, u, y)) as our winning prediction against the TBC. The trouble comes while we should avoid querying an evaluation/inversion that settles all the triples associated to (m, τ) as defined, in which case the attack will not be successful (to win the triple must not be defined). Fortunately, half-multi-collisions on v allow detecting the potential triples for which we have to be careful. Since their amounts are bounded by μ, unless H is not lower-half multi-collision resistant, we only get an additional factor μ in $\epsilon_{\text{sUP-L2}}$ for each case.

F_1 We build a sUP-L2 adversary against the TBC, conceptually against the "second call" F_{k_2}. It picks $k_1 \xleftarrow{\$} \mathcal{K}$ for itself and simulates the computation of F_{k_2} by querying its own TBC oracle. In the verification query (m, τ), it computes y itself and outputs (v, y, τ) as its prediction. Given that (m, τ), the probability that this event occurs is bounded by $\epsilon_{\text{sUP-L2}}$.

F_2 We build a sUP-L2 adversary against the TBC as in the case of F_1.

F_3 We build a sUP-L2 adversary against the TBC, conceptually against the "first call" F_{k_1}. It picks $k_2 \xleftarrow{\$} \mathcal{K}$ for itself and simulates the computation of F_{k_1} by querying its own TBC oracle. In the verification query (m, τ), it computes $\tilde{y}$ itself and outputs $(v, u, \tilde{y})$ as its prediction. Given that (m, τ), the probability that this event occurs is bounded by $\epsilon_{\text{sUP-L2}}$.

F_4 This case is less straightforward. We deal with its sub-cases independently.

   F_{41} Let (m', τ') be the message-tag pair involved in the earlier query that defines (v, u, y) and $(v, \tilde{y}, \tau)$. Then, $\tau' = \tau$ (regardless of the query type).

   F_{411} If $m^i = m$, it contradicts the freshness of (m, τ). This case is void.

   F_{412} If $m^i \neq m$, since the defined triples implies $u \| v \xleftarrow{n} \mathsf{H}(m')$, we found a collision. The probability that this event occurs is bounded by ϵ_{CR}.

   F_{42} Let (m^i, τ^i) be the message-tag pair involved in the earlier query that defines (v, u, y) for k_1 and (m^j, τ^j) be the message-tag pair involved in a subsequent query that defines $(v, \tilde{y}, \tau)$ for k_2, and both (regardless of their respective type of query) occurring before our (m, τ). By the meaning of the triples, we have $u \| v \xleftarrow{n} \mathsf{H}(m^i)$ and $\tau^j = \tau$, and we can assume that $m^i = m$ as we already dealt with collisions. However, we note that $\tau^i \neq \tau$ and $m^j \neq m$ as otherwise it would contradict the freshness of (m, τ). So (m^i, τ^i) must be an invalid pair in a verification query as well as (m^j, τ^j) (if it is valid it can only be a tag-generation query by definition of (m, τ), but then $u^j = \mathsf{F}_{k_1}^{v, -1} \circ \mathsf{F}_{k_2}^{v, -1}(\tau^j) = \mathsf{F}_{k_1}^{v, -1} \circ \mathsf{F}_{k_2}^{v, -1}(\tau) = u$).[6] This implies

---

[6] The choice to reuse v as the only tweak of the TBC in our design is crucial. With distinct tweaks the security bound will be much more loose. Among other advantages, here, we only have to deal with the verification queries.

that we already have a lower-half 2-multi-collision on v. Indeed, we see that $\mathsf{H}_s^2(m^i) = \mathsf{H}_s^2(m^j)$ with $m^i \neq m^j$.

Then, to avoid defining the second-triple $(v, \tilde{y}, \tau)$ we must use it as a winning prediction against the TBC at the time the query (m^j, τ^j) is made. Moreover, the situation will be the same with any subsequent query (m^j, τ^j) before (m, τ) where the second-triple is given by $(v, \tilde{y}, \tau)$, i.e., $v^l = v$, $\tau^l = \tau$ and distinct m^l (otherwise it is a repeating query).

We can bound the probability of all these events given (m^i, τ^i). Each time a new verification query is made for some (m^l, τ^l) such that $m^i \neq m^l$ and $v^i = v^l$ (we include $l = j$ here), for the at most $\mu - 1$ possible cases, we make an hybrid on the ordered such l, and a reduction to the sUP-L2 experiment against the TBC in the "second call" by picking k_1 and outputting the prediction (v^i, y^i, τ^l) (while the TBC oracle is called for all the previous verification queries to emulate the second MAC call).

F_{43} We are in the same case as case F_{42} with the difference that the query (m^j, τ^j) defining $(v, \tilde{y}, \tau)$ for k_2 is made before the query (m^i, τ^i) defining (v, u, y) for k_1. Since our argument showing that these queries in F_{42} are of verification type and the input pairs are invalid does not depend on which query happens before, we are exactly in the dual situation where we somehow switched the first-call and the second-call.

We can bound the probability of all these events given (m^j, τ^j). Each time a new verification query is made for some (m^l, τ^l) such that $m^l \neq m^j$ and $v^l = v^j$ (we include $l = i$ here), for the at most $\mu - 1$ possible cases, we make an hybrid on the ordered such l, and a reduction to the sUP-L2 experiment against the TBC in the "first call" by picking k_2 and outputting the prediction $(v^j, u^l, \tilde{y}^j)$ (while the TBC oracle is called for all the previous verification queries to emulate the second MAC call).

In the full proof, we first deal with the collision resistance of H_s and the μ-multi-collision resistance of H_s^2. For the events F_{42} and F_{43} we of course do not know when we will be in face of the queries (m^i, τ^i) and (m^j, τ^j) which could define the triples of the first potential forgery (m, τ). However, by considering all the verification queries as potentially being (m^i, τ^i) or (m^j, τ^j) that defines the first triple of (m, τ), we cover all the cases with a term like $2\mu q_V \epsilon_{\mathsf{sUP-L2}}$. That way, we also cover the case that (m, τ) might be any of the verification queries. Indeed, once we analyze a potential (m^i, τ^i) or (m^j, τ^j), we will consider all the next verification queries sharing v^i or v^j among which all the possible (m, τ) lie when F_{42} or F_{43} occur. In the remaining case, it is straightforward to deal with F_1, F_2 and F_3. Overall, we find $[2(\mu - 1)q_V + q_V + 1]\epsilon_{\mathsf{sUP-L2}}$ for the TBC term.

4.4 Deriving Concrete Bounds

Deriving concrete bounds from asymptotic security is not an easy task in the standard model. However, we can argue why it is realistic to assume the existence of building blocks which will confer high security to LR-MAC2. Since the sUP-L2 of the TBC can be argued in the same lines as in the rest of the paper, we next focus on the stronger properties that we require for the hash function.

Multi-collision Resistant Hashing. The security bound shows that it is reasonable to take $\mu \in O(n)$ without blowing up the term related to the unpredictability of the TBC. Moreover, increasing μ can only decrease the probability of finding more and more multi-collisions. Indeed, μ-multi collision resistance implies $(\mu + 1)$-multi collision resistance. And, even it the definition does not imply that the negligible probability decreases when μ increases, it is reasonable to assume so for "good" hash functions, as for SHA2 or SHA3.

In the ROM, it is a well-known fact that n-multi collision resistance allows up to $q \approx 2^n/n$ hash queries. Of course, we will not assume in the standard model that H remains secure up to that number of evaluations. However, it might be the case that H is $3n$-multi collision resistant up to $q \approx 2^{96}$, which is much less demanding and fully compatible with our other terms in our security bound.

As another justification, Berti et al. [9, Lemma 5] proved that the Merkle-Damgård iteration of the Hirose's DBL compression function [26] gives rise to a half-multi-collision resistant hash function in the ideal cipher model.

Multi-collision Independence. By more closely mimicking the behavior of random functions, we derive another relaxed notion that could be realized without idealized assumption on half outputs of H. This is a stronger definition than the (half-) multi-collision resistance notion, but it offers a way to more accurately model a decreasing negligible functions' family depending on the multi-collision parameter μ. This allows us to soundly analyze how the negligible functions related to a (half-) μ-multi-collision resistant hash function H might become better and better as μ grows, as expected from any "good" hash function, and without relying on any ideal argument. Of course, the decreasing rate in μ can be much slower than a truly random function but our security bounds of LR-MAC2 shows how comfortable we are to increase μ even in a leakage setting.

First, we recall a result of [35] showing that for a random function with 2^n possible outputs, the multi-collision event $\mathsf{MultiColl}(2^n, q) \geq \mu$ that at least $\mu \geq 2$ inputs give a same output among a total of q function evaluations satisfies:

$$\Pr[\mathsf{MultiColl}(2^n, q) \geq \mu] \leq \frac{1}{2^{n(\mu-1)}} \binom{q}{\mu}.$$

Since the right-hand side is also bounded by $q^\mu/2^{n(\mu-1)}$, we can simplify this result by saying that any additional collision comes at a marginal probability of $\approx q/2^n$ starting from the standard collision bound $q^2/2^n$, where $\mu = 2$.

Definition 10. *Let* $\mathsf{H} : \mathcal{HK} \times \{0,1\}^* \to \{0,1\}^n$ *be a hash function. We say that* H *is* θ-*powerwise collision independent if, for* $s \leftarrow \mathcal{HK}$, *the probability that an efficient adversary* $\mathsf{A}(s)$ *making at most* q *hash evaluations computes at least* μ *distinct* $m_1, \ldots, m_\mu \in \{0,1\}^*$ *such that* $\mathsf{H}_s(m_1) = \ldots = \mathsf{H}_s(m_\mu)$ *is bounded by:*

$$2^n \left(\frac{q^{1+\theta}}{2^n} \right)^\mu,$$

with $\mu \geq 2$, $0 \leq \theta \leq 1$. The factor $q^{1+\theta}/2^n$ is the marginal collision probability and θ is called the non-idealization power. We say that H is multi-collision independent if it is θ-powerwise collision independent for some $\theta \in (0,1)$.

If the non-idealization power is null, the hash function is a random function and the marginal collision probability matches the one discussed above.

We stress that finding a μ-multi-collision for any $\mu \geq 2$ gives the same chance of finding "one more" collision in the sense of a $(\mu + 1)$-multi-collision. Said otherwise, the marginal collision probability is independent of the number of multi-collisions already found, hence the name. For instance, finding more multi-collisions does not help in finding even more multi-collisions. This might be seen as a strong collision resistant flavor as the hash function should resist further collision attacks even if some previous attacks already succeeded. However, standard hash functions should fulfill such a collision resilient condition. At least, they have to offer a graceful degradation and, in particular, given a collision it should not become easy to find some others. Still, we require here that the degradation factor be constant, given the security parameter n and the non-idealization power θ. But we might only have a middle non-idealization power $\theta = 1/2$. In that case, the collision probability (i.e., the 2-multi-collision) is only upper-bounded by $q^3/2^n$ ensuring collision security up to $q \approx 2^{42}$, for $n = 128$. Nevertheless, we can reach the 20-multi-collision security up to $q \approx 2^{81}$. By letting $\theta = 1/\rho$, we can reach the n-multi-collision security up to $q \approx 2^{n\rho/(1+\rho)}$.

We now simply define half-multi-collision independence of $H_s : \{0,1\}^* \mapsto \{0,1\}^{2n}$ as the multi-collision independence of H_s^1 or H_s^2, where $H_s = H_s^1 \| H_s^2$.

Definition 11. Let $H : \mathcal{HK} \times \{0,1\}^* \to \{0,1\}^{2n}$ be a hash function, and define $H^i : \mathcal{HK} \times \{0,1\}^* \to \{0,1\}^n$, for $i = 1, 2$, such that for any $s \leftarrow \mathcal{HK}$ and any message $m \in \{0,1\}^*$, we have $H_s(m) = H_s^1(m) \| H_s^2(m)$. We say that H is half-multi-collision independent for $i = 1, 2$ if H^i is multi-collision independent. To avoid indexes, if $i = 1$, we also say that H is upper-half-multi-collision independent, and, if $i = 2$, that H is lower-half-multi-collision independent.

Armed with this stronger theoretical background, we can re-evaluate the security of LR-MAC2 in the light of the non-idealization power θ, assuming that H is lower-half-multi-collision independent (where H_s^2 outputs tweaks). Let us first recall the security bound $\epsilon_{\text{CR}(2n)} + \epsilon_{\mu\text{-CR}(n)} + 2\mu q_V \epsilon_{\text{sUP-L2}}$ of Theorem 2, and assume that $\epsilon_{\text{sUP-L2}}$ supports 2^{85} (online) queries, for $n = 128 = 2^7$. Setting $q_V = 2^{75}$ then allows us to take $\mu = 2^8$. That means that if the number of evaluation of H remains below 2^{90}, the non-idealization power could be $\theta = 2/5$ for H_s^2 since $\epsilon_\mu \leq 2^{128}(2^{90\cdot7/5}/2^{128})^{256} < 2^{-128}$, even if H_s^2 would only be (2-multi-) collision resistant up to $2^{63/(1+\theta)} = 2^{45}$ hash evaluations.

So overall, we conclude this section by observing that LR-MAC2 could provide strong leakage resilience guarantees. Yet, on the one hand, it requires stronger assumptions which, despite not idealized, are less standard than the collision resistance that LR-MAC1 requires. On the other hand, it also requires two calls to a TBC with n-bit tweaks which, as mentioned in introduction, should in general be more expensive than one call to a TBC with $2n$-bit tweaks if specialized constructions can be used. We note there are constructions that achieve the same leakage-resilience guarantees without half collision resistance, but the best solution we are aware of (given in the ePrint version of the paper) requires three TBC calls for this purpose. So despite theoretically interesting, we believe these results also amplify the pragmatic interest of using large tweaks.

5   Analysis of **HTBC**

In this section, we finally show that the popular Hash-then-PRF MAC construction is provable without idealized assumptions in a leakage setting. For consistency with the LR-MAC1 and LR-MAC2 constructions, we focus on the Hash-then-TBC scheme described in Fig. 3 and specified in Algorithm 3.

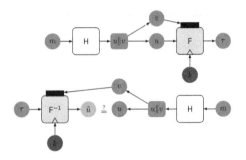

Fig. 3. Hash-then-TBC.

Algorithm 3. The HTBC algorithm.

It uses a strongly protected TBC $\mathsf{F} : \mathcal{K} \times \{0,1\}^n \times \{0,1\}^n \to \{0,1\}^n$ and a hash function $\mathsf{H} : \mathcal{HK} \times \{0,1\}^n \to \{0,1\}^{2n}$.

- Gen
    - $k \xleftarrow{\$} \mathcal{K}$
    - $s \xleftarrow{\$} \mathcal{HK}$
- $\mathsf{Mac}_k(m)$:
    - $u\|v = \mathsf{H}_s(m)$
    - $\tau = \mathsf{F}_k^v(u)$
    - Return τ
- $\mathsf{Vrfy}_k(m, \tau)$:
    - $u\|v = \mathsf{H}_s(m)$
    - $\tilde{u} = \mathsf{F}_k^{v,-1}(\tau)$
    - If $\tilde{u} == u$ Return $\top$
    - Else Return $\bot$

5.1   A First Analysis in the Standard Model

The security proof requires the hash H to be collision resistant and range-oriented preimage resistant. A stronger (and less standard) assumption is *weak image set computable*, that is, there exists a PPT algorithm M that outputs the set $\mathcal{WP}(s, A)$ defined in Eq. (1) for any s and A. By Lemma 1, for range-oriented preimage resistant hash functions it is feasible to output the set $\mathcal{WP}(s, A)$ in PPT. We will serve more intuitions on this assumption at the end of this section.

The assumption of *weak image set computability* admittedly renders the concrete security analysis hard to interpret. As a result, below we eschew the concrete security approach (which is followed by Theorems 1 and 2) in favor of the *asymptotic approach*. We justify this choice by the fact that the goal of this section is to show a theoretical possibility, potentially opening a path towards more advanced and concrete analyzes in the future.

Theorem 3. *Let the hash function H be collision resistant, range-oriented preimage resistant, and weak image set computable. Let F be a TBC that is sUP-L2. Then, HTBC is sUF-L2-secure in the unbounded leakage model.*

Proof. In the unbounded leakage model, all the intermediate computations leak (except the long-term key). Wlog, we assume that the forgery adversary A has been "normalized". That is, before making every oracle query, A outputs the list of all images $\mathcal{S}(s) \subseteq \{0,1\}^n$ for which she knows the preimage. Clearly, this cannot decreases the success probability of A. Moreover, this only induces a polynomial blow-up in A's running time: $\mathcal{S}(s)$ must be polynomial, as otherwise A gets a superpolynomial number of input/output relations $H_s(m) = y$ and would be able to break the collision resistance of H.

To prove the theorem, we follow a sequence of games.

Game 0. Let Game 0 be the sUF-L2 game where the adversary A^L tries to produce a forgery when she plays against HTBC. Let E_0 be the event that the adversary wins the game; that is, the output of the game is 1.

Game 1. Game 1 is Game 0, except that we abort if there is a full collision in the hash function. Clearly, Game 0 and Game 1 are identical if the following event *HC* (*Hash collision*) does not happen: $HC := \{\exists i, j \in \{1, ..., q_M\} \cup \{1, ..., q_V + 1\}$ with $i \overset{\%}{\neq} j$ s.t. $h^i = h^j$ and $m^i \neq m^j\}$ (see Footnote 4). Since H is collision resistant, we have $\Pr[\text{Game } 0 \Rightarrow 1] \approx \Pr[\text{Game } 1 \Rightarrow 1]$.

Linking to Unpredictability. To complete the argument, we exhibit a predictor B against F_k using an adversary A that forges in Game 1. In detail, B picks a hash seed s uniformly at random, passes s to A and simulates Game 1 against A. B also picks an index $\ell \overset{\$}{\leftarrow} \{1, ..., q_v + 1\}$ at random. Assume that A outputs the forgery (m^*, τ^*) at the end of the game, where $H_s(m^*) = u^* \| v^*$.

Now, if Game 1 outputs 1, i.e., $\mathsf{VrfyL}_k(m^*, \tau^*)$ returns $\top$ at the end, then the probability that the ℓ-th verification query $\mathsf{VrfyL}_k(m^{(\ell)}, \tau^{(\ell)})$ constitutes the first time $(\mathsf{F}_k^{v^*})^{-1}(\tau^*)$ is queried is at least $1/q_v$. It can be seen that either of the following bad events necessarily occurred during the game:

- Case 1: intuitively, at some time, the oracle $(\mathsf{F}_k^{v^*})^{-1}(\tau^*)$ returns a target u^* and A later solves its preimage $\mathsf{H}_s(m^*) = u^* \| v^*$; or,
- Case 2: intuitively, at some time, A has been aware of the relation $\mathsf{H}_s(m^*) = u^* \| v^*$, and the oracle $(\mathsf{F}_k^{v^*})^{-1}(\tau^*)$ later returns a target $u' = u^*$.

But B cannot predict which case will be encountered. Fortunately, in either case the number of candidates for $(\mathsf{F}_k^{v^*})^{-1}(\tau^*)$ is polynomial, and thus B can simply take a union. In more detail:

If the first case is encountered, then the concatenation $u^* \| v^*$ of the returned target $u^* = (\mathsf{F}_k^{v^*})^{-1}(\tau^*)$ and the tweak v^* necessarily falls in the set $\mathcal{WP}(s, \mathsf{A})$ (otherwise A won't be able to solve the preimage). Then, since we assumed that the set $\mathcal{WP}(s, \mathsf{A})$ is computable given s and A, the predictor B could make a guess u' among $\mathcal{WP}(s, \mathsf{A})$ and take (v^*, u', τ^*) as a forgery for F_k.

If the second case is encountered, then as we assumed that A always outputs the list $\mathcal{S}(s)$ of all images that she knows the preimage, the predictor B could make a guess u' among $\mathcal{S}(s)$ and takes (v^*, u', τ^*) as a forgery for F_k.

By the above, the predictor B first runs the algorithm M to obtain $\mathcal{WP}(s, \mathsf{A})$, and then reads the set $\mathcal{S}(s)$ from A's outputs. B then picks $u' \xleftarrow{\$} \mathcal{WP}(s, \mathsf{A}) \cup \mathcal{S}(s)$ uniformly and outputs (v^*, y', τ^*) as a forgery for F_k.

Summing over the two cases, the success probability of B is at least:

$$
\begin{aligned}
&\left(\frac{\Pr[\text{Game } 1 \Rightarrow 1]}{q_v + 1} \right) \cdot \left(\frac{\Pr[\text{Case } 1]}{|\mathcal{WP}(s, \mathsf{A})| + |\mathcal{S}(s)|} + \frac{\Pr[\text{Case } 2]}{|\mathcal{WP}(s, \mathsf{A})| + |\mathcal{S}(s)|} \right), \\
\geq\ &\left(\frac{\Pr[\text{Game } 1 \Rightarrow 1]}{q_v + 1} \right) \cdot \left(\Pr[\text{Case } 1] + \Pr[\text{Case } 2] \right) \cdot \frac{1}{|\mathcal{WP}(s, \mathsf{A})| + |\mathcal{S}(s)|}, \\
=\ &\frac{\Pr[\text{Game } 1 \Rightarrow 1]}{(q_v + 1)(|\mathcal{WP}(s, \mathsf{A})| + |\mathcal{S}(s)|)}.
\end{aligned}
\tag{3}
$$

By the unpredictability assumption on F, the final term $\Pr[\text{Game } 1 \Rightarrow 1]/(q_v + 1)(|\mathcal{WP}(s, \mathsf{A})| + |\mathcal{S}(s)|)$ should be negligible, which means $\Pr[\text{Game } 1 \Rightarrow 1] = \mathsf{negl}(n)$. This complete the proof. $\qquad\square$

Discussion. To facilitate understanding, we provide further intuition on the proof of Theorem 3. A first impression may suggest the infeasibility to decide and output the weak set $\mathcal{WP}(s, \mathsf{A})$ since the seed space is exponential, which (seems) to gain support from the formalism of collision resistant hashing. However, this intuition is incorrect: the seed space being exponential does not *necessarily* mean the computation is infeasible. In particular, it may be easy to derive $\mathcal{WP}(s, \mathsf{A})$ from the seed, or even seed-independent (i.e., the algorithm does not necessarily need to keep a table for all the seeds) as we now detail.

First, assume using a keyed random oracle $\mathsf{RO} : \mathcal{HK} \times \{0,1\}^* \rightarrow \{0,1\}^{2n}$ as the hash function. In this case, $\Pr_{\mathsf{A}(s,y)\Rightarrow m}\left[\mathsf{RO}_s(m) = y\right]$ is negligible for all $y \in \{0,1\}^{2n}$, meaning that $\mathcal{WP}(s,\mathsf{A}) = \emptyset$. By this, the probability that Case 1 in the proof occurs is negligible (which is indeed the case, as the probability is in $O(q/2^n)$, with q the number of adversarial RO queries). On the other hand, the "normalized" adversary A simply outputs its RO query/response list before the ℓ-th verification query, and this could be used to predict $(\mathsf{F}_k^v)^{-1}(\tau)$.[7].

Let us now assume using a keyed SHA3 variant (denoted sha) producing 256-bit hash digests. According to known cryptanalytic results, for any A with running time t, $\Pr_{\mathsf{A}(s,y)\Rightarrow m}\left[\mathsf{sha}_s(m) = y\right] = O(t/2^{256})$ for all $y \in \{0,1\}^{256}$, meaning that $\mathcal{WP}(s,\mathsf{A})$ remains $\emptyset$ in some sense.

On the one hand, it seems that the number of SHA3 input/output pairs that could be derived in time t is only $O(t)$, and the "normalized" adversary A simply outputs a list of $O(t)$ input/output pairs. On the other hand, the double-block-length hash function Tandem-DM has a "weak" image 0 that is easily invertible [3]. If Tandem-DM is used, then $\mathcal{WP}(s,\mathsf{A}) = \{0\}$, the size of which is just 1. Further consider the keyed hash $\mathsf{KeyedTDM}_s(M) = \mathsf{Tandem\text{-}DM}(M) \oplus s$. Despite being contrived, for this instructive example the weak set $\mathcal{WP}(s,\mathsf{A}) = \{s\}$ which is seed-dependent but very easy to derive.

Note that we do not need the hash function to be non-malleable. The proof follows even if the hash admits the weakness that $\mathsf{H}_s(m \oplus \delta_1) = \mathsf{H}_s(m \oplus \delta_1) \oplus \delta_2$ for *a specific pair* of differences (δ_1, δ_2) and *any* m: in this case, the number of "known" input/output pairs remains in $O(t)$. We additionally remark that:

- the weak image set computability assumption doesn't contradict the range-oriented preimage resistant assumption, because the latter concerns with random images that are unlikely to fall in $\mathcal{WP}(s,\mathsf{A})$;
- this assumption doesn't contradict the collision resistant assumption either, because weak images don't necessarily have multiple preimages.

Finally, we note that our proof approach easily extends to the constructions of Hash-then-block cipher of [11] and Hash-then-PRF (enhanced with the leakage-resilient value comparison tricks [17]). It is also intriguing to ask whether more "common" assumptions on hashing could suffice, e.g., even the UCE hashing [5] or some weak form of correlation intractable hashing [12,13]. We leave the investigation of these alternative approaches for future investigations.

5.2   Towards Another Analysis

As an opening, we eventually discuss whether adapting the security proofs of [8] could lead to another analysis. The simplest solution for this purpose is to find the appropriate assumption on H that could hold in the standard model to replace the random oracle. This is also what is done in the previous analysis but we next suggest another (stronger) possibility that is simple to express.

---

[7] The latter trick was also used in [8].

Essentially, what we need from the hash function H is that any *targeted* image y that has never been defined yet by computing $H(x)$ for some x is still unattainable. Of course, by computing $H(x)$ for a fresh input x we always attain a new image with overwhelming probability, unless we find a collision. Obviously, all the undefined images cannot be our targets. So, the main difficulty is to define a natural meaning of *targets* that can be chosen *adaptively* by the adversary. This is where the new definition will anyway be less standard than usual pre-image resistance. But this is precisely what we need in the security proof of HTBC to adapt [8]. Indeed, let $\tilde{u} = \mathsf{F}_k^{v,-1}(\tau)$, and let us consider again the cases where either $\tilde{u}\|v$ was already computed from $H(m)$ for some m or it was not. In the first case, if we know that $H(m) = \tilde{u}\|v$ has already been computed in the unforgeability game, we can easily build an adversary against TBC and compute a prediction. In the second case, if we know that $\tilde{u}\|v$ was never defined as an output of H, then we want to define $\tilde{u}\|v$ as a target. That means that if we know which hashing has already been computed, we can adaptively define a set of targets of polynomial size. Since the number of TBC calls is bounded by the number of queries against the unforgeability of HTBC, knowing which value is already a defined image of H is precisely what we need, and what is done in the random oracle model. Still, we do not need to have uniformly random output.

As a consequence, as long as H is half-multi-collision independent or even half-multi-collision resistant as defined in Sect. 4, since the proof in [8] already needs such kind of assumption even if it comes for free from the random oracle, the proof can go through if we require H to satisfy the notion of *essentially preimage resistance* which precisely models the hardness of computing a pre-image of a single target among any polynomial set of targets that can be adaptively updated by the adversary before trying to find it.

Essentially-pre-image resistance would simply model which hashing is already defined or not and maintain the list of targets that the adversary announced she will try to attack. To do so, even if the hash function is a public-key primitive, we should demand that computing hash values requires "querying" H even if the hash values are computed *faithfully* (without any other restriction about the distribution of the outputs). Hashing becomes interactive in that model but *only* for the sake of defining fresh targets and nothing else. The interaction does not occur in practice: it is just a way to soundly define what are the fresh targets and to avoid trivial attacks in the standard model.

It is easy to see that for any Turing Machine A without interaction with H, we can build a Turing Machine A' that explicitly returns all the inputs it uses for H, and directly after the output of that computation. Based on this discussion, we can see that the security of HTBC can be essentially good.

6 Conclusions

This paper describes and analyzes three leakage-resilient MACs that can be proven based on minimum physical assumptions (namely the unpredictability of a TBC with leakage) and more or less standard (anyway non idealized) black box assumptions for their hash part. We believe these results make an important step in building cryptographic primitives enabling strong security against side-channel attacks at limited cost, by leveraging the leveled implementation concept. The constructions we analyze range from pragmatic to theoretically more involved. The difficulty to maintain tight bounds with minimum assumptions when getting rid of the design twists used in our pragmatic solution (i.e., large tweaks for the TBC and a verification process that checks the inverse TBC against a constant) confirms that selecting good assumptions is critical for such constructions, as generally observed in cryptography but possibly even more with leakage. Avoiding idealized assumptions is important in this respect, since they make it impossible to translate security proofs and bounds into concrete requirements for the engineers implementing the corresponding schemes.

These results suggest different tracks for further investigations. In view of the limited overheads that its design twists imply, further instantiating the LR-MAC1 construction and designing a TBC with large tweaks that is suited to side-channel countermeasures appears as a practically relevant goal. In parallel, investigating whether the performances' and assumptions' gaps between LR-MAC1 and the LR-MAC2 or HTBC constructions can be tightened is an interesting question as well (for example using some of the directions outlined at the end of Sect. 5). Eventually, extending our results to sponge-based constructions (e.g., ISAP-MAC [15]) is another challenge that would deserve attention: we expect that such an analysis will require some adaptation and different assumptions. For example, secure authentication in this case cannot directly work in the unbounded leakage model, as per the recent work of Dobraunig and Menning [17]. The same holds for extending the quest for leakage-resilient constructions without idealized assumptions from MACs to (authenticated) encryption schemes.

Acknowledgments. We thank the ASIACRYPT 2021 reviewers for their insightful feedback. Francesco Berti was founded by the Emmy Noether Program FA 1320/1-1 of the German Research Foundation (DFG). Chun Guo was supported in parts by the Program of Taishan Young Scholars of the Shandong Province, the Program of Qilu Young Scholars (Grant No. 6158008996 3177) of Shandong University, the National Natural Science Foundation of China (Grant No. 62002202), and the Shandong Nature Science Foundation of China (Grant No. ZR2020MF053). Thomas Peters and François-Xavier Standaert are research associate and senior research associate of the Belgian Fund for Scientific Research (F.R.S.-FNRS). This work has been funded in parts by the EU through the ERC project SWORD (724725).

References

1. An, J.H., Bellare, M.: Constructing VIL-MACs from FIL-MACs: message authentication under weakened assumptions. In: Wiener, M. (ed.) CRYPTO 1999. LNCS, vol. 1666, pp. 252–269. Springer, Heidelberg (1999). https://doi.org/10.1007/3-540-48405-1_16

2. Andreeva, E., Stam, M.: The symbiosis between collision and preimage resistance. In: Chen, L. (ed.) IMACC 2011. LNCS, vol. 7089, pp. 152–171. Springer, Heidelberg (2011). https://doi.org/10.1007/978-3-642-25516-8_10
3. Armknecht, F., Fleischmann, E., Krause, M., Lee, J., Stam, M., Steinberger, J.: The preimage security of double-block-length compression functions. In: Lee, D.H., Wang, X. (eds.) ASIACRYPT 2011. LNCS, vol. 7073, pp. 233–251. Springer, Heidelberg (2011). https://doi.org/10.1007/978-3-642-25385-0_13
4. Azouaoui, M., et al.: A systematic appraisal of side channel evaluation strategies. In: van der Merwe, T., Mitchell, C., Mehrnezhad, M. (eds.) SSR 2020. LNCS, vol. 12529, pp. 46–66. Springer, Cham (2020). https://doi.org/10.1007/978-3-030-64357-7_3
5. Bellare, M., Hoang, V.T., Keelveedhi, S.: Instantiating random oracles via UCEs. In: Canetti, R., Garay, J.A. (eds.) CRYPTO 2013. LNCS, vol. 8043, pp. 398–415. Springer, Heidelberg (2013). https://doi.org/10.1007/978-3-642-40084-1_23
6. Bellizia, D., et al.: Mode-level vs. implementation-level physical security in symmetric cryptography. In: Micciancio, D., Ristenpart, T. (eds.) CRYPTO 2020. LNCS, vol. 12170, pp. 369–400. Springer, Cham (2020). https://doi.org/10.1007/978-3-030-56784-2_13
7. Berman, I., Degwekar, A., Rothblum, R.D., Vasudevan, P.N.: Multi-collision resistant hash functions and their applications. In: Nielsen, J.B., Rijmen, V. (eds.) EUROCRYPT 2018. LNCS, vol. 10821, pp. 133–161. Springer, Cham (2018). https://doi.org/10.1007/978-3-319-78375-8_5
8. Berti, F., Guo, C., Pereira, O., Peters, T., Standaert, F.-X.: Strong authenticity with leakage under weak and falsifiable physical assumptions. In: Liu, Z., Yung, M. (eds.) Inscrypt 2019. LNCS, vol. 12020, pp. 517–532. Springer, Cham (2020). https://doi.org/10.1007/978-3-030-42921-8_31
9. Berti, F., Guo, C., Pereira, O., Peters, T., Standaert, F.: Tedt, a leakage-resist AEAD mode for high physical security applications. IACR Trans. Cryptogr. Hardw. Embed. Syst. **2020**(1), 256–320 (2020)
10. Berti, F., Koeune, F., Pereira, O., Peters, T., Standaert, F.: Ciphertext integrity with misuse and leakage: definition and efficient constructions with symmetric primitives. In: AsiaCCS, pp. 37–50. ACM (2018)
11. Berti, F., Pereira, O., Peters, T., Standaert, F.: On leakage-resilient authenticated encryption with decryption leakages. IACR Trans. Symmetric Cryptol. **2017**(3), 271–293 (2017)
12. Canetti, R., Chen, Y., Reyzin, L., Rothblum, R.D.: Fiat-Shamir and correlation intractability from strong KDM-secure encryption. In: Nielsen, J.B., Rijmen, V. (eds.) EUROCRYPT 2018. LNCS, vol. 10820, pp. 91–122. Springer, Cham (2018). https://doi.org/10.1007/978-3-319-78381-9_4
13. Canetti, R., Goldreich, O., Halevi, S.: The random oracle methodology, revisited. J. ACM **51**(4), 557–594 (2004)
14. Degabriele, J.P., Janson, C., Struck, P.: Sponges resist leakage: the case of authenticated encryption. In: Galbraith, S.D., Moriai, S. (eds.) ASIACRYPT 2019. LNCS, vol. 11922, pp. 209–240. Springer, Cham (2019). https://doi.org/10.1007/978-3-030-34621-8_8
15. Dobraunig, C., et al.: Isap v2.0. IACR Transactions of Symmetric Cryptology **2020**(S1), 390–416 (2020)
16. Dobraunig, C., Mennink, B.: Leakage resilience of the duplex construction. In: Galbraith, S.D., Moriai, S. (eds.) ASIACRYPT 2019. LNCS, vol. 11923, pp. 225–255. Springer, Cham (2019). https://doi.org/10.1007/978-3-030-34618-8_8

17. Dobraunig, C., Mennink, B.: Leakage resilient value comparison with application to message authentication. In: Canteaut, A., Standaert, F.-X. (eds.) EUROCRYPT 2021. LNCS, vol. 12697, pp. 377–407. Springer, Cham (2021). https://doi.org/10.1007/978-3-030-77886-6_13

18. Dodis, Y., Steinberger, J.: Message authentication codes from unpredictable block ciphers. In: Halevi, S. (ed.) CRYPTO 2009. LNCS, vol. 5677, pp. 267–285. Springer, Heidelberg (2009). https://doi.org/10.1007/978-3-642-03356-8_16

19. Dodis, Y., Steinberger, J.: Domain extension for MACs beyond the birthday barrier. In: Paterson, K.G. (ed.) EUROCRYPT 2011. LNCS, vol. 6632, pp. 323–342. Springer, Heidelberg (2011). https://doi.org/10.1007/978-3-642-20465-4_19

20. Dziembowski, S., Pietrzak, K.: Leakage-resilient cryptography. In: FOCS, pp. 293–302. IEEE Computer Society (2008)

21. Fuller, B., Hamlin, A.: Unifying leakage classes: simulatable leakage and pseudoentropy. In: Lehmann, A., Wolf, S. (eds.) ICITS 2015. LNCS, vol. 9063, pp. 69–86. Springer, Cham (2015). https://doi.org/10.1007/978-3-319-17470-9_5

22. Goudarzi, D., Rivain, M.: How fast can higher-order masking be in software? In: Coron, J.-S., Nielsen, J.B. (eds.) EUROCRYPT 2017. LNCS, vol. 10210, pp. 567–597. Springer, Cham (2017). https://doi.org/10.1007/978-3-319-56620-7_20

23. Guo, C., Pereira, O., Peters, T., Standaert, F.: Towards low-energy leakage-resistant authenticated encryption from the duplex sponge construction. IACR Trans. Symmetric Cryptol. **2020**(1), 6–42 (2020)

24. Guo, C., Standaert, F., Wang, W., Yu, Y.: Efficient side-channel secure message authentication with better bounds. IACR Trans. Symmetric Cryptol. **2019**(4), 23–53 (2019)

25. Hazay, C., López-Alt, A., Wee, H., Wichs, D.: Leakage-resilient cryptography from minimal assumptions. In: Johansson, T., Nguyen, P.Q. (eds.) EUROCRYPT 2013. LNCS, vol. 7881, pp. 160–176. Springer, Heidelberg (2013). https://doi.org/10.1007/978-3-642-38348-9_10

26. Hirose, S.: Some plausible constructions of double-block-length hash functions. In: Robshaw, M. (ed.) FSE 2006. LNCS, vol. 4047, pp. 210–225. Springer, Heidelberg (2006). https://doi.org/10.1007/11799313_14

27. Jean, J., Nikolić, I., Peyrin, T.: Tweaks and keys for block ciphers: the TWEAKEY framework. In: Sarkar, P., Iwata, T. (eds.) ASIACRYPT 2014. LNCS, vol. 8874, pp. 274–288. Springer, Heidelberg (2014). https://doi.org/10.1007/978-3-662-45608-8_15

28. Jean, J., Nikolic, I., Peyrin, T., Seurin, Y.: Deoxys v1. 41. CAESAR Competition, Final Portfolio (2016)

29. Katz, J., Lindell, Y.: Introduction to Modern Cryptography, Second Edition. CRC Press (2014)

30. Krämer, J., Struck, P.: Leakage-resilient authenticated encryption from leakage-resilient pseudorandom functions. In: Bertoni, G.M., Regazzoni, F. (eds.) COSADE 2020. LNCS, vol. 12244, pp. 315–337. Springer, Cham (2021). https://doi.org/10.1007/978-3-030-68773-1_15

31. Martin, D.P., Oswald, E., Stam, M., Wójcik, M.: A leakage resilient MAC. In: Groth, J. (ed.) IMACC 2015. LNCS, vol. 9496, pp. 295–310. Springer, Cham (2015). https://doi.org/10.1007/978-3-319-27239-9_18

32. Micali, S., Reyzin, L.: Physically observable cryptography. In: Naor, M. (ed.) TCC 2004. LNCS, vol. 2951, pp. 278–296. Springer, Heidelberg (2004). https://doi.org/10.1007/978-3-540-24638-1_16

33. Pereira, O., Standaert, F., Vivek, S.: Leakage-resilient authentication and encryption from symmetric cryptographic primitives. In: CCS, pp. 96–108. ACM (2015)

34. Schipper, J.: Leakage-resilient authentication. Master's thesis (2011)
35. Suzuki, K., Tonien, D., Kurosawa, K., Toyota, K.: Birthday paradox for multi-collisions. In: Rhee, M.S., Lee, B. (eds.) ICISC 2006. LNCS, vol. 4296, pp. 29–40. Springer, Heidelberg (2006). https://doi.org/10.1007/11927587_5
36. Zhang, L., Wu, W., Wang, P., Zhang, L., Wu, S., Liang, B.: Constructing rate-1 MACs from related-key unpredictable block ciphers: PGV model revisited. In: Hong, S., Iwata, T. (eds.) FSE 2010. LNCS, vol. 6147, pp. 250–269. Springer, Heidelberg (2010). https://doi.org/10.1007/978-3-642-13858-4_14

DEFAULT: Cipher Level Resistance Against Differential Fault Attack

Anubhab Baksi[1]([✉]), Shivam Bhasin[2]([✉]), Jakub Breier[3]([✉]),
Mustafa Khairallah[1]([✉]), Thomas Peyrin[1]([✉]), Sumanta Sarkar[4]([✉]),
and Siang Meng Sim[5]([✉])

[1] Nanyang Technological University, Singapore, Singapore
ANUBHAB001@e.ntu.edu.sg, {mustafa.khairallah,thomas.peyrin}@ntu.edu.sg
[2] Temasek Labs NTU, Singapore, Singapore
sbhasin@ntu.edu.sg
[3] Silicon Austria Labs, Graz, Austria
jbreier@jbreier.com
[4] University of Warwick, Coventry, UK
sumanta.sarkar@warwick.ac.uk
[5] DSO National Laboratories, Singapore, Singapore
crypto.s.m.sim@gmail.com

Abstract. Differential Fault Analysis (DFA) is a well known cryptanalytic technique that exploits faulty outputs of an encryption device. Despite its popularity and similarity with the classical Differential Analysis (DA), a thorough analysis explaining DFA from a designer's point-of-view is missing in the literature. To the best of our knowledge, no DFA immune block cipher at an algorithmic level has been proposed so far. Furthermore, all known DFA countermeasures somehow depend on the device/protocol or on the implementation such as duplication/comparison. As all of these are outside the scope of the cipher designer, we focus on designing a primitive which can protect from DFA on its own. We present the first concept of cipher level DFA resistance which does not rely on any device/protocol related assumption, nor does it depend on any form of duplication. Our construction is simple, software/hardware friendly and DFA security scales up with the state size. It can be plugged before and/or after (almost) any symmetric key cipher and will ensure a non-trivial search complexity against DFA. One key component in our DFA protection layer is an SBox with linear structures. Such SBoxes have never been used in cipher design as they generally perform poorly against differential attacks. We argue that they in fact represent an interesting trade-off between good cryptographic properties and DFA resistance. As a proof of concept, we construct a DFA protecting layer, named DEFAULT-LAYER, as well as a full-fledged block cipher DEFAULT. Our solutions compare favorably to the state-of-the-art, offering advantages over the sophisticated duplication based solutions like impeccable circuits/CRAFT or infective countermeasures.

Keywords: Differential fault attack · Protection · SBox · Differential attack · DEFAULT

© International Association for Cryptologic Research 2021
M. Tibouchi and H. Wang (Eds.): ASIACRYPT 2021, LNCS 13091, pp. 124–156, 2021.
https://doi.org/10.1007/978-3-030-92075-3_5

1   Introduction

Fault Attacks (FA) are considered strong implementation threats rendering many ciphers vulnerable. Unlike classical cryptanalysis, which assumes no interference with the internal operations of a cipher, in the case of FA the attacker has more control over the device where the cipher is currently being executed. As a result, among other options, he is able to suddenly alter an external input to the device (such as voltage level, EM radiation, heat, etc.), forcing it to run under sub-optimal condition. This type of condition can result in incorrect (*faulty*) output from the device. This faulty output may then help the attacker to gain information about the secret key. FA gained much popularity among the security/cryptography researchers and has been deployed to analyze a variety of ciphers.

When it comes to analyzing symmetric key cryptographic primitives, the most popular choice for FA is generally the *Differential Fault Analysis* or *Differential Fault Attack* (DFA) [15]. DFA is very powerful: almost all (if not all) block ciphers which are considered secure with respect to classical attacks have been shown to be vulnerable to DFA. Note that, to the best of our knowledge, no cipher has yet been designed to have a natural DFA immunity, although there were no shortage of new cipher proposals or new DFA countermeasures in recent years.

The crux of this situation is, as we observe, a lack of theoretical results towards designing DFA-resistant primitives, akin to its classical counterpart, the *Differential Analysis* (DA). Cipher designers have been very careful to design DA resistant ciphers, but not much attention has been given to design a DFA-resistant cipher. Indeed, designing a DFA-resistant cipher looks like a very difficult task as the attacker has enormous power in this setting.

The usual DFA protections lie outside the domain of cipher design. At one end, some device/protocol level technique is used, while at the other end, duplication based protection is used (see Sect. 2.2 for more details). Duplication based countermeasures assume that the fault can alter the execution within a predesignated boundary. Thereafter, a comparison (which can be direct or with an error-detection code) between the two executions is used to detect a fault. Since device/protocol level solutions are beyond the control of the cipher designer, the best option to ensure DFA protection is duplication[1]. Given this scenario, our work analyzes this problem and proposes a new type of solution, which is able to ensure a non-trivial search complexity for the attack when using DFA, solely based on the cipher construction itself. We use the basic design strategy and components of the lightweight block cipher GIFT-128 [11] and thus manage to keep our design within low-cost performance figures. Note that the DFA protection mechanism could be costly and that our design does not need duplication or any protocol level countermeasure, we believe our work opens up a new genre of low-cost DFA countermeasure.

Our Contributions. In this work, in order to offer natural DFA protection, we explore the potential offered by the SBox, one of the basic building blocks of

---

[1] It may still be argued that duplication based protections cannot be guaranteed at the cipher design level, and hence off-limit to a cipher designer.

symmetric-key cryptography algorithms. As the SBox is generally the only non-linear component in a cipher, it is naturally vulnerable to DFA (as DFA does not work on a linear component, whereas it works very well on a non-linear one). In a nutshell, strong linearity makes it hard to attack a cipher with DFA, but too much linearity will of course render a cipher either insecure or not efficient. The designer's goal is therefore to try to find a good trade-off.

Since a secure cipher cannot be constructed by using only linear components, we naturally focus on finding a building block that is somewhat in the middle ground between an SBox and a linear function. Unsurprisingly, the middle ground lies in a weak class of SBoxes, whose members behave like a linear function in some aspects, more precisely by allowing the presence of so-called *Linear Structures* (LS). Such SBoxes have properties which are generally considered undesirable for a cipher construction, which leads to a paradoxical situation: an SBox which is more resistant against differential attacks is weaker against DFA, while those which are more resistant against DFA are considered weaker against differential attacks.

To circumvent this situation, we propose to maintain the main cipher to be protected (which is presumably secure against classical attacks) untouched, but to add two keyed permutations as additional layers before and after it, respectively. These keyed permutations present a special structure that renders DFA non-trivial on them, naturally allowing the entire construction to be DFA resistant. Indeed, assuming a certain fault model for DFA, the attacker has to attack the first or last rounds of the overall cipher to make the attack work. At the same time, the classical security of the construction, which is guaranteed by the main cipher, will not be hampered.

To validate our claims, we propose an SPN-based construction of a 128-bit keyed permutation L, DEFAULT-LAYER, using a 4×4 SBox that contains 3 LS. We show that this keyed permutation can provide safeguard against DFA up to a non-trivial search complexity ($2^{n/2}$ for an n-bit block cipher). DEFAULT-LAYER is hardware/software friendly and any variant of L with a multiple of 16-bit can be constructed (we recommend it to be at least 128-bit). As the DFA security scales up with the size of L (which does not happen for classical ciphers), if a 256-bit variant of L is used it will effectively provide a DFA security of (at least) 2^{128} computations. In fact, by playing with the number of LS in the SBox chosen, it is even possible to find trade-offs that go beyond $2^{n/2}$ security.

The idea of our keyed permutation is then extended to a complete SPN-based cipher DEFAULT. It uses a specially crafted component DEFAULT-CORE (which does not have security against DFA) between two DEFAULT-LAYER instances (to provide DFA security), in a hope of overall improved performances compared to a full-fledged cipher sandwiched between two DEFAULT-LAYER blocks. Indeed, DEFAULT-CORE will provide the extra classical security that is lacking with only two DEFAULT-LAYER instances.

Using duplication on GIFT-128 cipher, either in the spatial or the temporal domain, as a reference countermeasure for benchmarking (as duplication is a widely adopted fault protection method in commercial products), we note that DEFAULT incurs similar overheads, both in hardware and software. Yet, DEFAULT has the advantage of resisting a higher number of faults when compared to duplication. In retrospect, our solution can be considered lightweight compared to more sophisticated duplication countermeasures (such as infection or error-detecting codes). Infective countermeasures can have $\approx 3\times$ cost increase when compared to the basic implementation [10]. Moreover, we note that the recent block cipher CRAFT [14] and FRIET [39] based on error detection codes, leads to a $2.45\times$ overhead when protecting against single bit faults at the output and scales even higher for protecting against more faults. CRAFT is proposed as a block cipher with fault protection as a prime target, designed with carefully chosen components that incur lower overhead when protected with error detection codes. FRIET is proposed as a permutation with built-in fault detection based on error-detection code (like parity-check). DEFAULT, on the other hand, explores an alternative methodology to design a cipher with natural DFA resistance and is not limited to a specific number of faults.

As an independent contribution, we also study how to model a cipher which has an SBox with linear structures when searching for differential and linear bounds using automated tools.

Outline. We give some background on DFA, explain our fault model and provide preliminaries on SBoxes properties and notations in Sect. 2. Then, we explain how SBoxes with linear structures can provide some DFA resistance in Sect. 3. We describe our DFA protection component DEFAULT-LAYER and our entire cipher proposal DEFAULT (based on DEFAULT-CORE) in Sect. 4. The rationale behind the cipher structure and components is provided in Sect. 5, while detailed DFA and classical cryptanalysis is performed in Sect. 6, MILP modeling in Sect. 7. Finally, implementations and benchmarks of our designs are given in Sect. 8 and we conclude in Sect. 9.

2 Background and Preliminaries

2.1 Differential Fault Attacks in a Nutshell

As already mentioned, DFA is closely related to DA. In a classical DA, a difference is introduced in plaintexts (resp., ciphertexts) at the beginning of the cipher encryption (resp. decryption). Detecting the expected output difference requires large amount of data, where the data complexity is inversely proportional to the differential probability. Cipher designers often prove security against DA by showing that the probability of any differential trail is too low for launching a DA.

In comparison, in DFA the input difference is inserted in the form of a transient fault and can be applied anytime during the course of the encryption/decryption. In practice, faults are injected near the end of the cipher execution, effectively bypassing most of the rounds designed to resist DA when compounded. This difference propagates through only a handful of non-linear components, and based on the output differential value, the adversary is able to reduce the key search space significantly.

The cryptanalysis procedure in DFA consists of two orthogonal terms, namely, fault complexity (the number of faulty encryptions) and search complexity (computational/memory complexity required). The general trend is to reduce the fault complexity while keeping the search complexity within an acceptable limit.

2.2   Differential Fault Attack Protections

The state-of-the-art DFA countermeasures can be broadly classified into the following categories [6]:

1. A separate, dedicated device that detects (and takes precaution) [25] or a shield that blocks any potential source of a fault.
2. The underlying communication protocol between Alice and Bob ensures that a fault does not occur with a significant probability. This can be ensured, e.g., by assuming a small portion of the circuit is protected by other means [7].
3. Duplicate the cipher execution followed by implicit/explicit check for the equality of the executions, so-called *duplicated computations*. One may refer to [10] for a study of such countermeasures. Redundancy at the component level may also be introduced, possibly with error detection/correction codes [2].
4. Use mathematical solutions to render DFA ineffective/inefficient.

One may notice that the countermeasures in above-mentioned categories 1 and 2 are basically engineering solutions and generally outside the scope of cryptography design. In a slight contrast, category 3 is somewhat close to what a cipher designer can specify. Yet, identical faults in the duplicated computations will result in no differences between the outputs and treated as if no fault is injected. This tricks the countermeasure to release the faulty output, and works against state-of-the-art countermeasures like infection [10]. Although relatively hard to achieve in practice, this type of attack was shown to be feasible in [38] and we refer to it as *duplicate fault*. While the device could be protected by using different encodings for the two executions of the cipher, such methods usually add additional performance cost. We also mention that sophisticated duplication countermeasures may require additional components as well as an external source of randomness [10].

Our work falls under category 4, together with countermeasures like impeccable circuits [2]/CRAFT [14] and FRIET [39]. The authors of [2] proposed an efficient DFA protection mechanism based on error detection codes and this idea was later extended to a block cipher, named CRAFT. CRAFT employs error detection codes, which have different performance figures and fault coverage depending on the underlying code. Any fault injection that successfully alters the output beyond the detectable bound will make the DFA protection of CRAFT ineffective. In comparison, our construction is free from such limitation (more details in Sect. 6.4).

2.3   Our Claim

Novel Idea Against DFA. At a higher level, most of the countermeasures, including CRAFT, FRIET and duplicated computation, aim at *fault detection* which could be fooled by stronger equipment that makes the faults go undetected. In comparison, we aim at *fault resilience*[2], meaning we allow the faults to propagate and even output faulty ciphertexts, but the amount of information that an adversary can learn from them is limited: *we impose a lower bound on the search complexity of DFA*. Even with stronger equipment access, an adversary cannot overcome the lower bound of the search complexity. In addition, our design is completely at the algorithmic level, scalable, can be applied to existing ciphers and does not require an additional source of randomness. These features make our proposal different from infection-like countermeasures [10] which further corrupt the injected faults and need a source of randomness for a provable security [12].

Analysis Methods. Instead of enumerating the various fault models and fault attacks, we consider how an attack gains sensitive information, i.e., the analysis method. We can broadly categorise the analysis methods into two types:

1. Deduce information from the differential values of the executions.
2. Deduce information from the statistical bias of the executions.

The fundamental reason why our design increases the search complexity of DFA is due to the larger number of solutions for any given differential (details in Sect. 3). Hence, for attacks that gain information from the differential values (analysis method 1), it is not going to be as effective. We believe that our design could actually provide protection beyond DFA. In a broader sense:

Our design can protect against DFA and any form of FA that deduces information from the differential values of the executions.

Other attacks that exploit information leakages from statistical biases under analysis method 2 are beyond our focus. We provide more discussions in Sect. 6.5.

2.4 Difference Distribution Table and Related Properties

A *Difference Distribution Table* (DDT) is an analysis table used in DA. For an $n \times n$ SBox S, it is basically the $2^n \times 2^n$ matrix, where the row δ $(= 0, 1, \ldots, 2^n - 1)$ and column Δ $(= 0, 1, \ldots, 2^n - 1)$, denoted as $\mathrm{DDT}_S[\delta, \Delta]$, stores the number of solution(s) x for $S(x) \oplus S(x \oplus \delta) = \Delta$. Notice that $\mathrm{DDT}_S[0, 0] = 2^n$ as $S(x) \oplus S(x \oplus 0) = 0$ holds for all x. The maximum entry at the DDT of S, except the case $\delta = \Delta = 0$, is called the *Differential Uniformity* (DU).

In order for an SBox to be better resistant against DA, the (non-zero) maximal values in the DDT have to be small, otherwise DA will be more effective. Thus, symmetric-key cryptography designers almost exclusively look for SBoxes which have smaller values in the DDT. However, the situation for DFA is completely opposite. Here, if the (non-zero) DDT values are small, then the attacker has fewer solutions for the unknown input when collecting faulty outputs. Thus, she is able to narrow down the search space more efficiently: a DDT with smaller

---

[2] The term "fault injection resilience" was first introduced in [24].

(non-zero) values will make the DFA easier. Hence, we see that the strategy to thwart DA is exactly opposite to that of DFA. This paradoxical situation is among the challenges to build a cipher level DFA protection.

We call SBoxes S_1 and S_2 *Affine Equivalent* (AE) if there exist two affine permutations A_1 and A_2 such that $S_2 = A_1 \circ S_1 \circ A_2$. AE SBoxes have the same DDT up to a permutation. Therefore, differential uniformity is invariant under affine equivalence, so are the other cryptographic properties like non-linearity, algebraic degree, etc. It is to be noted that the affine equivalence classification of all 4×4 SBoxes has been completed already—there are 302 such classes. We follow the class representative SBoxes given in [19, Chapter 5.4.2]. For a more compact representation, an element $\alpha \in \mathbb{F}_2^n$ will be denoted by its corresponding integer value from $[0, 2^n - 1]$.

Definition 1 ($S_\alpha\langle\delta\rangle$). *For the SBox S, the fault δ and the value α, the set of solutions of the equation $S(x) \oplus S(x \oplus \delta) = S(\alpha) \oplus S(\alpha \oplus \delta)$ is the set $S_\alpha\langle\delta\rangle$.*

Notice that, both α and $\alpha \oplus \delta \in S_\alpha\langle\delta\rangle$. Basically, the cardinality of $S_\alpha\langle\delta\rangle$ gives the entry of the DDT at the δth row which contains α, which is at the column $\Delta = S(\alpha) \oplus S(\alpha \oplus \delta)$. By applying fault δ, the attacker cannot identify α from other elements which belong to $S_\alpha\langle\delta\rangle$.

Definition 2 ($\text{MinF}_S(\alpha)$). *For an $n \times n$ SBox S with input α,*

$$MinF_S(\alpha) = \begin{cases} -1 & \text{if } \bigcap_{\delta=1}^{2^n-1} S_\alpha\langle\delta\rangle \neq \{\alpha\}; \\ t & \text{where } t = \min k \text{ such that } \bigcap_{i=1}^{k} S_\alpha\langle\delta_i\rangle = \{\alpha\}. \end{cases}$$

Hence $\text{MinF}_S(\alpha) = -1$ means, no matter what fault values that an attacker chooses, she will be left with more than one choice for α. Also notice that, if $\text{MinF}_S(\alpha) \neq -1$, then it must be ≥ 2.

Definition 3 (MinF_S). *Given an $n \times n$ SBox S, MinF_S is defined as:*

$$MinF_S = \begin{cases} \max_{0 \leq \alpha \leq 2^n - 1} MinF_S(\alpha) & \text{if } MinF_S(\alpha) \neq -1, \forall \alpha \in \{0, 1 \dots, 2^n - 1\}; \\ -1 & \text{otherwise.} \end{cases}$$

The subscript S is dropped if understood from context.

The interpretation of MinF_S can be stated as: given an SBox S, it is the lower bound on the number of faults required to uniquely solve any input.

Definition 4 (Linear Structure). *For $F : \mathbb{F}_2^n \to \mathbb{F}_2^n$, an element $a \in \mathbb{F}_2^n$ is called a linear structure of F if for some constant $c \in \mathbb{F}_2^n$, $F(x) \oplus F(x \oplus a) = c$ holds $\forall x \in \mathbb{F}_2^n$.*

Note that the set of all linear structures of F denoted as $\mathcal{L}(F)$ forms a subspace of $\mathbb{F}_2^n$ and is termed as the *linear space* of F. If $F : \mathbb{F}_2^n \to \mathbb{F}_2^n$ has a (non-zero) linear structure then 2^n becomes an entry in the corresponding DDT. In that case $\text{DU} = 2^n$, thus F performs worst against differential attacks compared to all F's that do not have a (non-zero) linear structure.

Definition 5 (Coordinate Function and Component Function). *Suppose* $F : \mathbb{F}_2^n \to \mathbb{F}_2^n$ *is defined as* $F(x) = (f_0(x), \ldots, f_{n-1}(x))$ *for all* $x \in \mathbb{F}_2^n$, *where* $f_i : \mathbb{F}_2^n \to \mathbb{F}_2$ *for* $i = 0, \ldots, n-1$. *Then each* f_i *is called a coordinate function of* F. *Furthermore, the linear combinations of* f_i's *are called the component functions of* F.

Definition 6 (Non-linearity). *The non-linearity of the Boolean function* $f : \mathbb{F}_2^n \to \mathbb{F}_2$ *is the minimum distance of* f *to the set of all affine functions. Furthermore, the non-linearity of* $F : \mathbb{F}_2^n \to \mathbb{F}_2^n$ *is the minimum of the non-linearities of all the component functions of* F.

3   Characterizing SBoxes in View of DFA

From now on, we implicitly assume that neither δ or Δ is 0 and that an SBox S is a permutation. We denote $\Delta(\alpha, \delta)$ the output difference for input value α and input difference δ.

Theorem 1. *Let* $S(x) \oplus S(x \oplus \delta) = \Delta(\alpha, \delta)$ *have a solution* $x = \alpha$. *Further, let* a *be a (non-zero) linear structure of* S. *Then,* $(\alpha \oplus a)$ *is also a solution of* $S(x) \oplus S(x \oplus \delta) = \Delta(\alpha, \delta)$, *i.e., the coset* $\alpha \oplus \mathcal{L}(S)$ *is a subset of solutions of* $S(x) \oplus S(x \oplus \delta) = \Delta(\alpha, \delta)$. *So,* $MinF_S = -1$.

Proof. As a is a linear structure of S, we have that $S(x) \oplus S(x \oplus a)$ is constant. Taking derivative with respect to δ, $\forall x$ we get $S(x) \oplus S(x \oplus a) \oplus S(x \oplus \delta) \oplus S(x \oplus a \oplus \delta) = 0$. Using $x = \alpha$, $S(\alpha) \oplus S(\alpha \oplus \delta) \oplus S(\alpha \oplus a) \oplus S(\alpha \oplus a \oplus \delta) = 0$ $\implies$ $S(\alpha \oplus a) \oplus S(\alpha \oplus a \oplus \delta) = S(\alpha) \oplus S(\alpha \oplus \delta) = \Delta(\alpha, \delta)$. Hence, $(\alpha \oplus a)$ is also a solution of $S(x) \oplus S(x \oplus \delta) = \Delta(\alpha, \delta)$. $\square$

Theorem 1 gives an interesting insight regarding DFA resistance in SBoxes. If an SBox has a (non-trivial) linear structure, then it is not possible to find the input to the SBox just by analyzing the effect of faults, no matter how many faults are injected. In such cases, the attacker has to search exhaustively among the set of solutions to find the proper input. This increases the search complexity associated with DFA.

Lemma 1 (Converse of Theorem 1). *For the input* α *to* S, *if* $\alpha \oplus a$ *is a solution of* $S(x) \oplus S(x \oplus \delta) = \Delta(\alpha, \delta)$ *for all input differences* δ, *then* a ($\neq 0$) *is a linear structure of* S.

Remark 1. Theorem 1 and Lemma 1 are valid for all (non-trivial) linear structure(s) of S. In other words, the larger the number of (non-trivial) linear structures, the larger the number of candidates that will be in the intersection of solution sets of all faults.

Lemma 2. *Suppose* S_1 *and* S_2 *are two* $n \times n$ *SBoxes having* ℓ_1 *and* ℓ_2 *linear structures (including the trivial linear structure 0) respectively, then the* $2n \times 2n$ *SBox* (S_1, S_2) *will have* $\ell_1 \ell_2$ *linear structures (including the trivial linear structure* $(0, 0)$*).*

Lemma 3. *Suppose* $F : \mathbb{F}_2^n \rightarrow \mathbb{F}_2^n$ *to be any function and* $L : \mathbb{F}_2^n \rightarrow \mathbb{F}_2^n$ *to be linear. Then* $L \circ F$ *and* F *have the same number of linear structures.*

Theorem 2. *Assume that the SBox* S *does not have any (non-zero) linear structure and that* $S(x) \oplus S(x \oplus \delta) = \Delta(\alpha, \delta)$ *has exactly* $2m + 2$ *solutions. Then there exist* $m + 2$ *faults* $\{\delta, \delta', \delta_1, \ldots, \delta_m\}$ *such that the system of equations*

$$S(x) \oplus S(x \oplus \delta) = \Delta(\alpha, \delta), \qquad S(x) \oplus S(x \oplus \delta') = \Delta(\alpha, \delta'),$$
$$S(x) \oplus S(x \oplus \delta_1) = \Delta(\alpha, \delta_1), \quad \ldots, \quad S(x) \oplus S(x \oplus \delta_m) = \Delta(\alpha, \delta_m)$$

has a unique solution. Hence, $MinF_S(\alpha) \leq m + 2$.

From Theorem 2, we see that it is possible to uniquely recover the input/output value of each SBox with no more than $DU_S/2 + 1$ faults (unless there is a linear structure) when attacking the last round. This gives a provable upper bound on the number of faults the attacker needs per SBox (if faults values are judiciously chosen) in order the find out its input uniquely, given that the SBox does not have a linear structure.

Corollary 1. (From Theorem 2). $MinF_S \leq \dfrac{DU_S}{2} + 1.$

Remark 2. Although it is theoretically possible, we could not find any 4-bit SBox with $MinF_S = 3$ (refer to Corollary 1). Whether or not this is a tight bound is left open for future research.

The proof for the Lemmas and Theorems can be found in the long version of this article [8], together with other relevant results and examples.

Remark 3. Lemma 2 and Lemma 3 give another interesting view-point: if an unkeyed SPN permutation is constructed by repeating an SBox with l LS m times (in each round), then the total number of linear structures for the super SBox (which is the round function) is l^m.

In order to better visualize the effect of DFA security with respect to the number of linear structures for SPN ciphers (for a given SBox size), we present detailed information in Table 1 for varying state sizes[3]. Note that the last cases (i.e., a 4×4 SBox with 4 and an 8×8 SBox with 128 linear structures) is the theoretical limit for DFA protection (as any more LS would imply that the SBox is linear). Hence, in theory we can achieve DFA security up to 2^{64} (for a 128-bit state) or 2^{128} (for a 256-bit state) using 4-bit SBoxes; and 2^{112} (for a 128-bit state) or 2^{224} (for a 256-bit state) using 8-bit SBoxes. As a proof of concept, our instantiation of this DFA protection layer will use a 4-bit SBox with 4 LS (which can provide DFA security of 2^{64} computations) and it is described in Sect. 4.

---

[3] DFA security refers to the remaining key search complexity after the fault(s) have been injected.

4   Construction of DFA Resistant Layer and Cipher

With the background given in Sect. 2, we first look at the problem of maximizing the fault complexity. Note that fault complexity is the highest when the fault is injected at the last round. Usually, for an SPN block cipher, three faults per SBox are sufficient as most block ciphers use an SBox with DU = 4 (except for GIFT SBox [11], where DU is 6). In fact, in many cases, only two faults are needed to solve for any input. For example, for the SBoxes chosen in AES [33], PRESENT [16], SKINNY-64 [13] and GIFT [11], the fault values $\{1, 6\}$ are sufficient to retrieve all inputs uniquely. Thus, it seems hard to force the fault complexity to increase significantly.

Table 1. DFA security for SPN ciphers depending on the number of linear structures in the SBox. Our design DEFAULT-LAYER will use a 4×4 SBox with 4 linear structures for a state size of 128 bits, hence ensuring a 2^{64} DFA security.

<table>
<tr><td colspan="3">(a) 4×4 SBox</td><td colspan="3">(b) 8×8 SBox</td></tr>
<tr><td rowspan="2">♯ LS</td><td>State</td><td>DFA</td><td rowspan="2">♯ LS</td><td>State</td><td>DFA</td></tr>
<tr><td>Size</td><td>Security</td><td>Size</td><td>Security</td></tr>
<tr><td rowspan="2">2</td><td>128</td><td>2^{32}</td><td rowspan="2">8</td><td>128</td><td>2^{48}</td></tr>
<tr><td>256</td><td>2^{64}</td><td>256</td><td>2^{96}</td></tr>
<tr><td rowspan="2">4</td><td>128</td><td>2^{64}</td><td rowspan="2">64</td><td>128</td><td>2^{96}</td></tr>
<tr><td>256</td><td>2^{128}</td><td>256</td><td>2^{192}</td></tr>
<tr><td></td><td></td><td></td><td rowspan="2">128</td><td>128</td><td>2^{112}</td></tr>
<tr><td></td><td></td><td></td><td>256</td><td>2^{224}</td></tr>
</table>

4.1   Ad-hoc DFA Protection Layer (DEFAULT-LAYER)

Our approach is to tackle the problem of increasing the search complexity instead. This means that we give the attacker the power to apply as many faults as she wants in total, but the search space for the analysis should remain very large. As we already pointed out (Theorem 1), if an SBox S has non-zero linear structure(s), then the attacker will not be able to uniquely identify the input. Thus, she has to enumerate the remaining key candidates from the input difference – output difference relation.

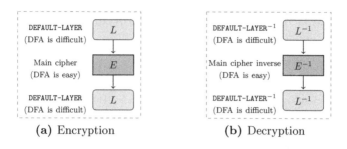

Fig. 1. Main cipher augmented by DEFAULT-LAYER to resist DFA

Now, using an SBox with a linear structure is generally considered undesirable for a block cipher design, as it makes the classical differential attacks easier (as explained in Sect. 2.4). Hence, we arrive at a paradoxical situation: if we want to design a cipher with better resistance against DFA, it becomes weak against classical attacks; and vice-versa. In order to find a middle ground, where the cipher is strong against both DFA and classical attacks, we propose the concept of prepending/appending an extra layer (that uses SBoxes with linear structures) to the underlying cipher (henceforth referred to as *"main cipher"*). Figure 1 visually represents the idea. The layer L, which we name as DEFAULT-LAYER and describe in Sect. 4.3, is prepended and appended to the main cipher E, as in Fig. 1(a). For decryption, L^{-1} is both prepended and appended to the main cipher inverse (shown in Fig. 1(b)), since the ciphertext $C = L \circ E \circ L(P)$, and the decryption $L^{-1} \circ E^{-1} \circ L^{-1}(C) = (L^{-1} \circ E^{-1} \circ L^{-1}) \circ (L \circ E \circ L)(P) = P$. The idea is that the underlying cipher E will have desirable protection against classical attacks, while the additional layer L will be used to thwart DFA. Since for DFA the attacker has to slowly peel off the outer rounds of the cipher, we only have to protect these rounds against DFA, while the inner cipher will provide all the security we expect from a block cipher in the black-box model (adding a layer L will not weaken its security).

As we assume the attacker can target both the encryption and decryption processes, the model described here can thwart DFA on both. If we assume a constrained model for the attacker, for example where the decryption is done at a server which is physically protected such that it cannot be accessed (as in [7, Section III]), then the prepended layer L in Fig. 1(a) and the appended layer L^{-1} in Fig. 1(b) can be removed, which will result in better performance.

4.2   Extension to a Full-Fledged Cipher (DEFAULT)

Aside from an ad-hoc layer which is able to protect any cipher from DFA, it is also possible to construct a full-fledged block cipher. This is done by sandwiching the so-called DEFAULT-CORE (this is another keyed permutation described in Sect. 4.4) with DEFAULT-LAYER. The DEFAULT-CORE contains an SBox that is especially resistant to classical linear attacks, and DEFAULT-LAYER uses an SBox that contains linear structures to resist DFA and its variants. Hence DEFAULT consists of 2 components (for both the encryption and decryption), as can be seen in Fig. 1(a), replacing E with DEFAULT-CORE.

DEFAULT-CORE also follows a construction similar to GIFT-128, but we do not reuse GIFT-128 permutation exactly as core permutation because we want to maximize the security against linear attacks, even if that results in relatively low security against differential attacks (which will be partially provided by the DEFAULT-LAYER layers anyway). Thus, we do not use LS SBox, but in contrary we will use an SBox with excellent linear approximation table (LAT) properties.

Therefore, the advantage of using DEFAULT instead of simply a classical cipher protected with DEFAULT-LAYER layers, is that since DEFAULT-CORE has been designed to be especially strong against linear attacks, we can reduce the number of cryptographic operations globally. In other words, we believe DEFAULT strikes a better balance in terms of security/efficiency, while using a classical cipher with DEFAULT-LAYER probably comes with some performance overkill (DEFAULT-LAYER will provide extra differential attack resistance on top of the main cipher, which was not needed since the cipher is assumed to be secure already).

4.3 Construction of DEFAULT-LAYER

We detail the 128-bit version of our proposed DFA protecting layer (DEFAULT-LAYER). It can be used to protect 128-bit block ciphers, but we emphasize that it can be adapted to any block size that is a multiple of 16.

DEFAULT-LAYER is a 28-round keyed permutation[4] that receives a 128-bit message as the state $X = b_{127}b_{126}\ldots b_0$, where b_0 is the least significant bit, and a 128-bit key. The state can also be expressed as $X = w_{31}\|w_{30}\|\ldots\|w_0$, where w_i is a 4-bit nibble word. We do not describe the inverse layer here for the sake of brevity, but it can be trivially derived. The round function (denoted by $\mathcal{R}$ henceforth) of DEFAULT-LAYER consists of 4 steps (in order): SubCells—applying a 4-bit SBox to the state, PermBits—permute the bits of the state (same as in GIFT-128 [11]), AddRoundConstants—XORing a 6-bit constant as well as another bit to the state (same as in GIFT-128), and AddRoundKey—XORing the round key to the state.

SubCells. It uses the 4-bit LS SBox $S = 037ED4A9CF18B265$. This SBox is applied to every nibble of the state: $w_i \leftarrow S(w_i), \forall i \in \{0, \ldots, 31\}$.

PermBits. The bit-permutation is the same as the permutation P_{128} in GIFT-128, which maps bits from bit position i of the internal state to bit position $P_{128}(i)$: $b_{P_{128}(i)} \leftarrow b_i, \forall i \in \{0, ..., 127\}$.

AddRoundConstants. A single bit "1" and a 6-bit round constant C = $c_5c_4c_3c_2c_1c_0$ are XORed into the cipher state at bit position 127, 23, 19, 15, 11, 7 and 3 respectively: $w_{127} = w_{127} \oplus 1$, $w_{23} = w_{23} \oplus c_5$, $w_{19} = w_{19} \oplus c_4$, $w_{15} = w_{15} \oplus c_3$. Table 2 shows the round constants (6-bit) for DEFAULT-CORE and DEFAULT-LAYER. At each round the value is encoded into a 6-bit word and XORed to the cipher state, with c_0 being the least significant bit.

---

[4] We avoid calling it a "cipher" as it is a DFA protecting layer used on top of an actual cipher.

Table 2. Round constants for DEFAULT

	Round Constants	♯
DEFAULT-CORE	1, 3, 7, 15, 31, 62, 61, 59, 55, 47, 30, 60, 57, 51, 39, 14, 29, 58, 53, 43, 22, 44, 24, 48, 33, 2, 5, 11	28
DEFAULT-LAYER	1, 3, 7, 15, 31, 62, 61, 59, 55, 47, 30, 60, 57, 51, 39, 14, 29, 58, 53, 43, 22, 44, 24, 48	24

AddRoundKey. A round key k is bitwise XORed to the state: $b_i \leftarrow b_i \oplus k_i^j, \forall i \in \{0, ..., 127\}$.

Key Schedule. The 128-bit master key K is used to generate four 128-bit subkeys K_0, K_1, K_2 and K_3 as follows: $K_0 = K$ and $K_{i+1} = \mathcal{R}'(\mathcal{R}'(\mathcal{R}'(\mathcal{R}'(K_i))))$ for $i \in [0, 1, 2]$, where $\mathcal{R}'$ denotes the $\mathcal{R}$ round function with no AddRoundKey layer and with the AddRoundConstants layer changed to only XORing a single bit "1" at bit position 127. Alternatively, $\mathcal{R}'$ can be seen as the $\mathcal{R}$ function with an all-zero round key and an all-zero round constant. Then, these four subkeys are used to generate the round keys as follows: for round i with $i \geq 0$, the subkey $K_{i \bmod 4}$ is used as round key input for AddRoundKey.

4.4 Construction of DEFAULT-CORE (and DEFAULT)

In order to design the full-fledged cipher, we need to describe the middle part of the cipher (DEFAULT-CORE), for which the SBox does not have any (non-zero) linear structure. The design of the core is much alike to the DEFAULT-LAYER (hence omitted here for the sake of brevity), except for the SBox, and it has 24 rounds. The SBox of choice here is 196F7C82AED043B5, based on its very desirable cryptographic properties against linear attacks (see Sect. 7.2 for details). In a nutshell, the overall design of DEFAULT consists of: DEFAULT-LAYER (28 rounds), followed by DEFAULT-CORE (24 rounds), followed by another DEFAULT-LAYER (28 rounds). Hence DEFAULT is an SPN block cipher with heterogeneous round structure, consisting of 80 rounds. Therefore, in comparison with time-duplicated GIFT-128 (which contains 80 rounds in total), DEFAULT has the same number of rounds. As for the round counter, we use the same from GIFT-128, which is refreshed at the beginning of DEFAULT-LAYER/DEFAULT-CORE.

5 Design Rationale

The goals of our DEFAULT-CORE/DEFAULT-LAYER designs are clear: (1) to protect against DFA, (2) applicable to different state sizes as well as to wide variety of symmetric key ciphers, and (3) simple and lightweight. During its design, various choices have been made and we discuss those here.

5.1   Design Philosophy

SPN vs Feistel Network. Our first decision was to choose between SPN and Feistel network. Although implementing the inverse of Feistel construction is simple and does not require the inverse of its f-function, the non-linearity is introduced to only half of its state in each round and hence usually requires more rounds (though lighter rounds) to achieve the desired security margin. On the other hand, SPN introduces non-linearity to the entire state and thus requires lesser rounds in general. Study is also simpler, so we chose to start with SPN.

Bit Permutation vs Rotational-XOR Diffusion vs Word-Mixing Diffusion. For SPN constructions, the diffusion layer is usually either a bit permutation (like in PRESENT and GIFT), a rotational-XOR layer (like in SMS4 [20], ASCON [22]), or a word-mixing diffusion (like in AES and SKINNY). Although the latter two provide a stronger diffusion, they can be costly in hardware and non-trivial to adopt to different block sizes as it might lead to quite different descriptions. In hardware, the bit permutation is basically free to implement as it consists simply of circuit wiring. Moreover, from the design strategy of GIFT, we see that a bit permutation can be adjusted to various state sizes. Therefore, we choose bit permutation over other choices of diffusion layer.

5.2   Structure of the DEFAULT PermBits

We recall here the structure of the PRESENT and GIFT bit permutations as this will be useful later to understand our security guarantees. There are essentially two levels of permutation within the PRESENT or GIFT bit permutation: the group mapping and the SBox grouping.

Group Mapping. The mapping of the output bits from a group of 4 SBoxes to another group of 4 SBoxes in the next round. This is the main difference between the PRESENT and GIFT permutation. For 4-bit SBoxes, we denote the 4 bits as bit 0, 1, 2 and 3, where bit 0 is the least significant bit. Within a group, the PRESENT permutation sends the 4 output bits from the ith SBox (index from 0) to bit i of the 4 SBoxes in the next round, forming a symmetrical structure. Due to this symmetrical structure, PRESENT has many symmetrical differential characteristics for a given fixed input and output differences, which results in a higher differential probability (similar situation for the linear cryptanalysis case). On the other hand, the GIFT permutation sends bit i from the output of the jth SBox (index from 0) to the bit i of the lth SBox in the next round, where $l = i - j \mod 4$. Since bit i of an SBox output is always mapped to bit i of another SBox, it makes the analysis on the propagation of the differences easier and breaks the symmetry. Therefore, we choose GIFT group mapping.

SBox Grouping. The partitioning of the SBoxes into the groups of 4 SBoxes. The SBox grouping for the 64-bit block ciphers PRESENT and GIFT-64 are the same, and the designers of GIFT extended the idea to construct SBox grouping for 128-bit block size. Similar to [11], we denote the SBoxes in round i as $S_0^i, S_1^i, \ldots, S_{g-1}^i$, where $g = n/4$ for block size n. These SBoxes can be grouped in 2 different ways - the Quotient Q and Remainder R groups, defined as $Qx = \{S_{4x}, S_{4x+1}, S_{4x+2}, S_{4x+3}\}$ and $Rx = \{S_x, S_{q+x}, S_{2q+x}, S_{3q+x}\}$, where $q = g/4$, $0 \leq x \leq q - 1$. The SBox grouping simply maps SBoxes from Qx^i to Rx^{i+1}, where within this group the 16-bit mapping is defined as the group mapping described above. This is the adaptable component of the bit permutation, as one can see that the SBox grouping is well-defined as long as n is a multiple of 16.

5.3   Selection of the DEFAULT SBoxes

Here we describe the selection process of the LS SBox (used in DEFAULT-LAYER) and the non-LS SBox (used in DEFAULT-CORE) providing high resistance against linear attacks. A summary of various properties of our chosen SBoxes together with SBoxes from other lightweight ciphers (PRESENT, SKINNY-64 and GIFT) are shown in Table 3.

As for the size of the SBox, we decided to choose 4-bit. Although there are better (in terms of DFA security) 8-bit SBoxes (see Table 1), we chose the 4-bit SBoxes for the following main reasons: (1) to lower the cost (similar to GIFT [11]), (2) making the MILP modelling (described in Sect. 7) more efficient as generating the same for 8-bit SBoxes could be costly [41].

Table 3. Properties of the DEFAULT (LS, Non-LS), PRESENT, SKINNY-64 and GIFT 4-bit SBoxes. DBN is differential branch number, LBN is linear branch number, LS are the linear structures, DU is the differential uniformity, AD is the algebraic degree of the coordinate functions and NL is the non-linearity.

		DBN	LBN	LS	DU	AD		NL
						max	min	
DEFAULT LS	037ED4A9CF18B265	3	3	0, 6, 9, f	16	2	1	0
DEFAULT Non-LS	196F7C82AED043B5	2	2	0	8	3	2	4
PRESENT [16]	C56B90AD3EF84712	3	2	0	4	3	2	4
SKINNY-64 [13]	C6901A2B385D4E7F	2	2	0	4	3	2	4
GIFT [11]	1A4C6F392DB7508E	2	2	0	6	3	2	4

LS SBox. From the list of 302 affine equivalence (AE) classes of SBoxes by De Cannière [19], there are 10 AE classes with non-zero linear structures. Among these 10 AE classes, 8 of them (#293—#300) have only one non-zero linear structure, AE class #301 has three non-zero linear structures and the last AE class #302 is fully linear (contains the identity permutation). To maximize the number of linear structures and yet to use a non-linear permutation, we chose the AE class #301 (the representative for this AE class in [19] is 1032456789ABCDEF).

Within this class, we chose an SBox with the following criteria (HW denoting Hamming weight):

1. Both differential and linear branch number 3.
2. Zero diagonal in the DDT and LAT (except $(0,0)$).
3. In the DDT, $\forall \delta_i \in \mathbb{F}_2^4 \setminus \{0\}$, if $(\delta_i, \delta_o) = 16$, then $HW(\delta_i) \geq 2$, $HW(\delta_o) \geq 2$.
4. In the LAT, $\forall \alpha_i \in \mathbb{F}_2^4 \setminus \{0\}$, if $(\alpha_i, \alpha_o) = 8$, then $HW(\alpha_i) + HW(\alpha_o) \geq 4$.

In other words, first we try to optimize the differential and linear diffusion with branch number 3. Next, we avoid enabling 1-round iterative differential or linear patterns (hence we look for empty diagonals). Then, for any probability 1 differential transition, we make sure that the input and output difference Hamming weight is at least 2 (we could not find an SBox for which such transitions necessarily happen with $HW(\delta_i) \geq 3$, or $HW(\delta_o) \geq 3$, or $HW(\delta_i) + HW(\delta_o) \geq 5$). Lastly, for any full linear transition, we select an SBox that will maximize the Hamming weight of the input and output values. The two last criteria are basically trying to maximize the number of active SBoxes before and after a probability 1 differential or a full linear transition. In total, we found 240 SBoxes candidates that satisfy our selection criteria and we ended up choosing SBox 037ED4A9CF18B265.

Any of these 240 SBoxes, combined with our DEFAULT-LAYER bit permutation, ensures the following properties: for any 5-round differential characteristic,

(P1) there are at least 10 active SBoxes,
(P2) if there are exactly 10 active SBoxes, then each of these active SBoxes has differential probability 2^{-1} (which totals to 2^{-10}),
(P3) if there exists one active SBox with differential probability 1, then there are at least 12 other active SBoxes with differential probability 2^{-1} each (which totals to 2^{-12}).

We give a general intuition on how the selection criteria facilitates these properties (we actually do not really need to prove these properties, since we will later be using automated tools to guarantee bounds on the differential characteristics probability in Sect. 7). First, observe that all the 240 SBoxes will ensure that $\forall \delta, \Delta \in \mathbb{F}_2^4 \setminus \{0\}$,

(C1) if $\text{DDT}_S[\delta, \Delta] > 0$, then $HW(\delta) + HW(\Delta) \geq 3$,
(C2) if $\text{DDT}_S[\delta, \Delta] = 16$, then $HW(\delta) + HW(\Delta) \geq 4$,
(C3) if $\text{DDT}_S[\delta, \Delta] = 16$, then $HW(\delta) \geq 2$ and $HW(\Delta) \geq 2$.

Then, from (C1) one can prove that there will be at least 10 active SBoxes over 5 rounds (P1) (in Fig. 2(a)), which is basically Theorem 1 in [16]. By (C2) and the first case in the proof of Theorem 1 in [16], one can show that for such a 10-active SBoxes differential characteristic, none of these SBoxes (in Fig. 2(a)) can have a differential probability 1 (P2). If there exists an SBox with differential probability 1, again by (C1) and (C2), there are at least 13 active SBoxes (see Fig. 2(b)). Criterion (C3) enforces that only 1 of these 13 active SBoxes can potentially have differential probability 1 (P3).

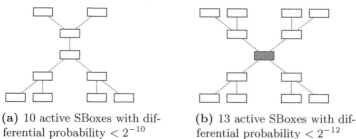

(a) 10 active SBoxes with differential probability $< 2^{-10}$

(b) 13 active SBoxes with differential probability $< 2^{-12}$

Fig. 2. 5-round differential characteristics (solid lines are active bits, white boxes are active SBoxes and red box is SBox with differential probability 1) (Color figure online)

From these properties, we can (conservatively) estimate that the probability of any differential characteristic drops by at least a factor of 2^2 for every additional round.

Non-LS SBox. For this SBox candidate, we focused on the linearity of the SBox as linear attacks will be the most difficult part to protect. Among the 33 AE classes with the lowest maximum linear bias 2^{-2}, the AE classes #32 (represented by C0A23547691B8DEF) and #33 (represented by D0A23547691BC8EF) have the least number of non-zero entries in the LAT. Statistically speaking, this gives us a higher chance of finding linear branch number 3 SBoxes. However, every 4×4 SBox with linear branch number 3 has at least one non-trivial linear structure (belonging to the AE classes #294, #297, #298, #300, #301, #302 of [19]). Hence, we tried several of those SBoxes and obtained the corresponding linear bias bounds using the automated technique described in Sect. 7. However, the bounds we obtained were not good enough. Thus, our next strategy was to select an SBox with the following linear properties:

1. $\sharp\{((\alpha_i, \alpha_o)) \mid HW(\alpha_i) = HW(\alpha_o) = 1, (\alpha_i, \alpha_o) \neq 0\} = 1$.
2. Zero diagonal in the LAT (except $(0,0)$).
3. $\sharp\{((\alpha_i, \alpha_o)) \mid HW(\alpha_i) + HW(\alpha_o) = 3, (\alpha_i, \alpha_o) = \pm 4\} = 13$.
4. $\sharp\{((\alpha_i, \alpha_o)) \mid HW(\alpha_i) + HW(\alpha_o) = 3, (\alpha_i, \alpha_o) = \pm 2\} = 6$.

In other words, first we limit the number of Hamming weight $1 \to 1$ transitions to 1^5. Next, we avoid having a 1-round iterative linear pattern. Lastly, we minimize the number of possible Hamming weight $1 \to 2$ and $2 \to 1$ transitions. This is to encourage faster and wider propagation of the linear trail. We finally choose the SBox 196F7C82AED043B5 from the AE class #32.

We note that other considerations could be incorporated in addition to the ones mentioned in this section, such as side-channel attacks resilient criteria [27], but we believe this falls out of the scope of our research that tries to focus on natural immunity to DFA.

---

[5] In [36], the authors show that, under their BOGI+ paradigm, when there are at least 9 consecutive rounds, having only 1 Hamming weight $1 \to 1$ transition is a sufficient condition to achieve a theoretic bound of at least 2 active SBoxes per round.

5.4 Unbiased Linear Structures

We need an extra security criterion: each bit of the linear structures of S as well as S^{-1} must be unbiased. This is to avoid certain undesirable property of the linear layer. If we assume that the linear structures for S are $\{0, 1, 2, 3\}$, the two MSBs are always 0. One such SBox is 1032456789ABCDEF (the representative for class #301 in [19]). It has the property that if the first two bits of its input are known uniquely, then the first two bits of its output are also known uniquely. The attacker may be able to leverage this property by attacking the penultimate round of the cipher/protection layer, with attacking the last round. This issue does not arise when each bit of the linear structures is unbiased (in which case the attacker is not able to find any bit uniquely). In our chosen LS SBox, the linear structures being $\{0, 6, 9, f\}$, and that of the inverse SBox being $\{0, 5, a, f\}$, this criterion is indeed satisfied.

6 Security Analysis

Conducting security analysis on DEFAULT is quite different from conducting security analysis on block ciphers, despite having similar structure. This is because DEFAULT-LAYER is built on top of an existing (and presumably secure against classical attacks) cipher and only assists in providing the desired security against DFA, while DEFAULT-CORE is used in conjunction with two instances of DEFAULT-LAYER. Although classical attacks do not pose any threat against DEFAULT-LAYER, some cryptanalytic techniques could still be applied to DEFAULT through DFA. For instance, suppose an attacker injects faults to the output of the main cipher, this difference will only propagate through the DEFAULT-LAYER and not the entire cipher, creating some form of differential attack on the DEFAULT-LAYER itself. Thus, we need to ensure that DEFAULT-LAYER is not vulnerable to classical attacks that could bypass the main cipher using DFA and target DEFAULT-LAYER directly. The desired security for the classical attacks are summarized in Table 4 and security evaluation against such attacks are done subsequently in Sect. 6.2. Detailed discussion on the classical attacks are omitted here for brevity, but interested readers may find it for example in [11, Section 4]. It may be noted that more precise differential and linear bounds are presented in Sect. 7. The security against DFA and side-channel attacks are evaluated subsequently (Sect. 6.1 and Sect. 6.3, respectively).

Table 4. Security requirement of DEFAULT against classical attacks

	DEFAULT-LAYER	DEFAULT-CORE
Differential, Algebraic	2^{64} Search Complexity	–
Integral, Impossible Diff.	–	No Distinguisher
Linear	2^{32} Search Complexity	2^{64} Search Complexity
Invariant Subspace	–	2^{128} Search Complexity

As DEFAULT comprises of DEFAULT-CORE and (two layers of) DEFAULT-LAYER, we specify which component we are analyzing and for which cryptanalysis technique. The analysis is summarized in Table 5.

Table 5. Security analysis of DEFAULT

	DEFAULT-LAYER (28-rounds)	DEFAULT-CORE (24-rounds)	DEFAULT (80-rounds)	Ref.
Differential Fault Attacks (64-bit Security)				
On DEFAULT-LAYER	2^{64}	Bypassed	2^{64}	Section 6.1
On DEFAULT-CORE	$\geq 2^{64}$	Negligible	$> 2^{64}$	
Double Fault		Not applicable		
Classical Cryptanalysis (128-bit Security)				
Differential	$\geq 2^{64}$	$> 2^{24}$ (Trivial)	$> 2^{128}$	Section 6.2
Linear	$> 2^{40}$	$> 2^{128}$	$> 2^{128}$	
Impossible Diff.	Main cipher	Not vulnerable	Not vulnerable	
Invariant Subspace	Main cipher	Not vulnerable	Not vulnerable	
Algebraic	Main cipher	Not vulnerable	Not vulnerable	

6.1 Differential Fault Attacks

First, we look at DFA on DEFAULT-LAYER, when it is used as a protection layer for other block ciphers. Next, we look at DFA on DEFAULT-CORE or other block ciphers with DEFAULT-LAYER as protection layer.

DFA on DEFAULT-LAYER. Our chosen SBox has 3 non-trivial linear structures: $6, 9, f$. Hence, for any input $\alpha \in \{0, \ldots, f\}$, the attacker cannot uniquely identify which among $\{\alpha, \alpha \oplus 6, \alpha \oplus 9, \alpha \oplus f\}$ is the actual input to the SBox. In other words, the attacker will be able to identify one partition of the input: $\{\{0, 6, 9, f\}, \{1, 7, 8, e\}, \{2, 4, b, d\}, \{3, 5, a, c\}\}$, but will not be able to identify which particular input is correct. Similarly for the output of the SBox, due to the linear structures, the attacker will only able to identify the partition to be one of these $\{\{0, 5, a, f\}, \{1, 4, b, e\}, \{2, 7, 8, d\}, \{3, 6, 9, c\}\}$ and not a particular output.

In the last round attack of DEFAULT-LAYER, the attacker has to inject faults and analyze each of the 32 SBoxes independently. That means, for each SBox she has to do a brute-force search of 4, leading to a total search complexity of $4^{32} = 2^{64}$.

DFA on DEFAULT-CORE or other block ciphers with DEFAULT-LAYER. Alternatively, the adversary could still try to launch DFA on the main cipher by injecting fault(s) to the last round of it and hope that it will propagate nicely through DEFAULT-LAYER. If so, it boils down to whether the adversary can distinguish the output difference from the main cipher with less than 2^{64} effort, otherwise it is better off attacking DEFAULT-LAYER directly (2^{64}). Using MILP, we found that the maximum differential probability of DEFAULT-LAYER is upper bounded by 2^{-64} (details in Sect. 7.2). Thus, the attack complexity is too high and this alternative strategy is not worthwhile.

Information-Combining DFA on DEFAULT-LAYER. An attacker could apply DFA on multiple rounds and hope to combine these learnt information to further reduce the number of key candidates. For instance, targeting the last two rounds of DEFAULT, or the first and last round of DEFAULT through DFA on both the encryption and decryption processes. Such a possibility was first identified for a previous version of DEFAULT by a reviewer from CRYPTO 2021 and ASIACRYPT 2021 and later confirmed independently by a team of researchers [31]. In order to avoid this attack vector, we have designed a special key schedule for DEFAULT.

First, assume an idealized DEFAULT-LAYER variant where all round keys are independent, which can basically be seen as defining a new component DEFAULT-LAYER with a much larger key input size (128-bit of key material per round). In this variant, since a fresh new round key is added at every round, the information-combining attack becomes useless for the attacker.

The goal of the key schedule in DEFAULT is therefore to mimic the behaviour of this idealized variant for a reasonable performance cost. Namely, we use 4 entire DEFAULT rounds to generate the next round key, which is chosen to ensure full diffusion. Then, we limit the number of distinct round keys to 4 (for performance), since our analysis shows that combining information throughout 4 rounds is very difficult.

We note that more conservative options could be selected for the key schedule, with an obvious performance cost during the round key precomputation: for example one could have 8 distinct rounds keys (instead of 4) and/or use more entire DEFAULT rounds to generate the next round key.

6.2 Classical Cryptanalysis

In the following, we apply classical cryptanalysis techniques on DEFAULT. Recall that DEFAULT has a sandwich structure with two DEFAULT-LAYER layers and a DEFAULT-CORE layer in the middle. For most of the cryptanalysis considered, it will be sufficient to show that DEFAULT-CORE is resistant against the attack.

Differential Cryptanalysis. Using MILP, we found that the maximum differential probability of DEFAULT-LAYER is upper bounded by 2^{-64} (details in Sect. 7.2). Since there are two layers of DEFAULT-LAYER, we already show that there is no meaningful differential characteristic tracing across two layers of DEFAULT with differential probability more than 2^{-128}. In addition, DEFAULT-CORE has 24 rounds and any differential characteristic will involve at least 1 active SBox per round. Thus, this trivially adds an additional factor of 2^{-24} to any differential characteristic. In summary, DEFAULT is not susceptible to differential cryptanalysis.

Linear Cryptanalysis. Using MILP, we found that the absolute linear bias of 11-round DEFAULT-CORE is upper bounded by 2^{-33} (details in Sect. 7.2). Thus, with a simple concatenation of two 11-round linear characteristics, we can show that there is no meaningful 22-round linear characteristic in DEFAULT-CORE. In addition, there are two layers of DEFAULT-LAYER, which will only make the linear cryptanalysis even harder to realise (even though linear structures are present in the SBox). In summary, DEFAULT is not susceptible to linear cryptanalysis.

Impossible Differential Attacks. We considered the possible effect of impossible differential attacks against DEFAULT-CORE. As proposed in [37], we generated MILP instances (Sect. 7) for all $\binom{128}{1} \times \binom{128}{1} = 16384$ differentials with both the input and output differences of Hamming weight 1 on DEFAULT-CORE and check if any of these instances were infeasible, which implies impossible differential. For the 7th round, we observe all instances are feasible (i.e., no impossible differential exists). Therefore, following the philosophy of [37], we believe the full-round DEFAULT-CORE is secure against impossible differential attacks.

Invariant Subspace Attacks. In order to simplify the analysis of invariant subspace attacks, we assume that any (affine) subspaces are preserved over the entire DEFAULT-LAYER, the PermBits and AddRoundConstants step. Thus, we focus on subspace transition over the SubCells step in DEFAULT-CORE, namely the non-LS SBoxes layer.

There is no dimension 3 (affine) subspace transition, and among the dimension 2 transitions most of them can only propagate up to 3 rounds, except one: $5 \oplus \{0, 2, \mathsf{c}, \mathsf{e}\} \rightarrow 0 \oplus \{0, 2, \mathsf{c}, \mathsf{e}\}$. Notice that this affine subspace will be preserved over the AddRoundKey step if each nibble of the round key belongs to $\{5, 7, 9, \mathsf{b}\}$.

Suppose each nibble of K_i belongs to $\{5, 7, 9, \mathsf{b}\}$. During the key schedule update (again we assume that the subspace is preserved over PermBits and AddRoundConstants), we have $(\mathcal{R}')^4(\{5, 7, 9, \mathsf{b}\}) \rightarrow \{7, 4, \mathsf{d}, 8\}$. K_{i+1} will break the subspace structure unless all nibbles of K_i are 5, resulting in all nibbles of K_{i+1} to be 7. However in the next update, all nibbles of K_{i+2} will be 4 $\notin$ $\{5, 7, 9, \mathsf{b}\}$. Thus, we believe that no (affine) subspace can be preserved for more than 3 rounds and DEFAULT is not vulnerable to invariant subspace attacks.

Algebraic Attacks. In order to evaluate the security of DEFAULT-CORE against algebraic attacks, we checked its algebraic properties using Sage[6]. We are able to represent DEFAULT-CORE as Boolean expressions up to 4-rounds. We have observed that the minimum number of monomials is 11101, at least 97 variables (out of 128) are involved and the minimum algebraic degree is 8. Furthermore, computing bounds on the maximum algebraic degree for different number of rounds according to the degree estimate given in [17], we can hope to reach maximum degree 127 after 8 rounds.

---

[6] http://www.sagemath.org/.

Integral Attacks. Suppose an attacker repeats the encryption multiple times and injects all possible differential fault values to a specific word in the output of the main cipher. This is similar to collecting a set of inputs (more precisely the output from the main cipher) with specific structure to launch an integral attack. Such model is reported in [34] and [35, Chapter 6.3].

This model is a special case of DFA where all possible faults are considered. Since the attacker does not get any extra information by using all possible faults, DEFAULT-LAYER (and hence DEFAULT) is resistant against it.

As for DEFAULT-CORE, we could reuse some of the security analysis of GIFT-128 for our design. In particular, the designers of GIFT evaluated the longest integral distinguisher for GIFT-128 using the (bit-based) division property [42] to be 11 rounds, and concluded that GIFT-128 is secure against integral attacks. Since DEFAULT-CORE has 28 rounds, we believe that DEFAULT-CORE is secure against integral attacks.

Using the SOLVATORE tool [23], we could find a distinguisher for DEFAULT-LAYER till 12 rounds. Beyond this, no solution is returned in a reasonable time.

6.3   Protection Against Side-Channel Attacks

In essence, DEFAULT-LAYER/DEFAULT is simply a bit permutation based SPN block cipher and, as such, usual side-channels attacks might apply on it. Usual countermeasures such as masking can of course be applied on DEFAULT.

We point out that protecting DEFAULT against side-channels attacks should not make DFA easier. An additional feature of the DEFAULT-LAYER SBox is that it has lower number of AND operations compared to the usual SBoxes used in other cipher designs, hence making it easier to mask [29]. One might argue that the large number of rounds of DEFAULT or DEFAULT-LAYER would be problematic, but implementation trade-offs would partially avoid this issue (implementing 2 or 4 rounds per clock cycle would greatly improve the throughput while moderately increase the area).

6.4   Comparison with CRAFT, FRIET and Duplicated Computation

As stated earlier, CRAFT, FRIET and duplication are the most relevant countermeasures when comparing with DEFAULT. Under a single fault adversary, duplication and DEFAULT are all secure against DFA. CRAFT in itself does not protect against DFA but is designed with a consideration to make it cost effective when integrating error detection codes. CRAFT only protects against faults that are detectable by the deployed error detection code and remains vulnerable to faults outside the detection capability. For an error detection codes with minimum distance d (*i.e.* minimum distance between distinct codewords), CRAFT can detect faults altering up to $t(= d - 1)$ cells[7] at once (within one cycle). Note that for low cost equipment where injected faults are often random, the probability of

---

[7] The "cell" is adopted from the CRAFT paper [14] referring to the word size.

getting a fault which is beyond the detection limit of error detection code is non-negligible. With precise fault injection equipment, an adversary could inject specific difference large enough ($\geq t$ cells) to change the code to another valid code and fool the error detection mechanism trivially. On the contrary, DEFAULT is not bounded by any such t.

FRIET adopts a parity check code to detect a *single-limb*[8] fault in the computation. Similar to CRAFT, for faults that alter more than one limb are beyond the detection limit. Again, DEFAULT is not bounded by any such limb.

Regarding duplicate faults, CRAFT claims no security. Duplicated computation was demonstrated to be broken by injecting two identical faults in the redundant execution using state of the art fault injection equipment [38]. DEFAULT is not vulnerable to DFA under duplicate faults as it does not rely on redundancy.

6.5 Other Fault Attacks

Although we do not claim security against attacks that uses analysis method 2, for completeness we discuss the security of our design against some of such attacks.

Fault Altering Control/Algorithm Flow. Since our solution is at algorithm level and does not rely on any engineering solutions, it is natural that our security claim holds under the assumption of the correctness of our algorithm. Therefore, we do not claim security against faults that alter the execution sequence of the algorithm. An accomplished attacker could hypothetically skip the execution of DEFAULT-LAYER completely with a control flow fault and can target the main cipher with standard DFA.

Hypothetical Multiple Precision Fault Attacks. Consider a *multiple precision fault attack* where the adversary injects a fault to introduce a specific difference just before an SBox and another difference right after the same SBox in an attempt to precisely cancel the difference. When the cancellation is successful, it will result in the same output as a fault-free execution, and the adversary can obtain the possible solutions for that SBox. While this is not effective against our LS SBoxes, it could still target the main cipher which typically does not have any LS. Feasibility of such precise multiple faults have never been demonstrated. In addition, this attack falls under analysis method 2 which is outside of our fault model.

Precise Bit Flipping Attacks. A single bit flip on a specific bit, though much harder to achieve, has been reported in practice by lasers [3]. Despite its precision, bit precision DFA (equivalent to injecting a Hamming weight 1 difference) will still be ineffective against our design. As described in Sect. 6.1, any input α will still lead to multiple solutions thanks to our LS SBox.

---

[8] The "limb" refers to an array of bits within the internal state of FRIET.

Assume that the adversary can target the logic gate component of the SBox, there could be a statistical attack, but again, we do not make claims against attacks that fall under analysis method 2.

Other Non-DFA Models. The *Safe Error Attack* (SEA) [26,43,44] model has been proposed which utilizes the cases where the faulty and non-faulty outputs are the same. Among the SEA models, one particular model is known as *Ineffective Fault Attack* (IFA) [18]. Another type of fault attack uses statistical information on the output distribution as it has become biased because of fault injection [32,45]. Such analysis often are based upon hostile fault models like stuck-at, permanent or persistent faults which assume a stronger attacker, specially stuck-at faults which are widely used in the fault analysis literature [21,32]. Stuck-at faults in electronic devices are generally related to defects in devices either at manufacturing or due to high-energy radiation in space electronics. Injecting stuck-at fault intentionally for malicious purpose requires expensive equipment like precise lasers, ion beams, etc. and thus considered under strong adversary capability . In comparison, bit flips or random faults are relatively easier to realise with simple fault injection equipment. A hybrid model – *Statistical Ineffective Fault Attack* (SIFA) [21] is proposed. It relies on both ineffective fault and statistical information of the computation. All these attacks exploit information leakages from statistical biases under analysis method 2, which is beyond our focus. If needed, specialized countermeasures can be used [5,9].

7   Automated Bounds for Differential and Linear Attacks

In [30], the authors present a method to find optimal differential and linear characteristics based on *Mixed Integer Linear Programming* (MILP), which is then tuned to work with bit permutation based block ciphers in [41].

Indeed, our special SBox with linear structures has probability 1 differential transitions (resp., $\pm 1/2$ linear bias). For the differential case, the above mentioned approach will always yield an MEDP bound of $\epsilon_d = 1$ (1 is raised to the power of an integer), which naturally signifies the smallest possible protection against differential attacks (the attack succeeds with only one chosen input difference or two chosen inputs). In case of linear cryptanalysis, it can be shown that the overall bias ϵ_l, considering only $\pm 1/2$ biases (and assuming mutual independence of the biases), is $1/2$. This is obtained by substituting $\epsilon_i = 1/2 \ \forall i$ in [40, Lemma 3.1]. Similar to the differential case, this also leads to the smallest protection against linear attack (the attack succeeds with roughly $1/\epsilon_l^2 = 4$ known inputs). Naturally, we need to devise a way to count precisely the number of probability $1/2$ differential transitions and $\pm 1/4$ linear biases.

To overcome this problem, we devise a new strategy which is inspired from the concept of *indicator constraint* used in linear programming (also known as the *big M* method), where a large constant M is chosen.

The details of our strategy and description of the MILP modeling can be found in the long version of this article [8].

7.1   Optimizations

Using the idea described in previous section, we construct the MILP problems and attempt to solve them using the Gurobi[9] solver. Being inspired from [28], we use redundancy in the MILP constraints. Using redundant constraints together with the usual constraints does not change the problem description, but could make the execution faster. As for the choice of the heuristics, we use the idea of *Convex Hull* (CH) [41].

For the differential case, we use the complete set of the CH inequalities, while for the linear case we use the greedy algorithm to select a subset of the complete set of the CH inequalities. The details on generation of the CH inequalities and the greedy algorithm can be found in [41]. We observe that using the heuristics the solution time can be improved by almost a factor of 10 compared to the respective cases where no heuristic was used. For more details on the heuristics, refer to [4].

7.2   Results

For the LS SBox (used in `DEFAULT-LAYER`), the bounds obtained from the corresponding MILP programs are: 2^{-4} at the 5th round for linear, and 2^{-20} at the 7th round for differential. This translates to around 2^8 computations for 5 rounds against classical linear attacks and around 2^{20} computations against differential attacks. Hence, we believe 28 rounds of `DEFAULT-LAYER` is enough to provide a security level of 2^{64} computations against classical differential attacks and of 2^{32} computations against classical linear attacks.

As explained in Sect. 6.2, we only consider the security against the classical linear attack against `DEFAULT-CORE`. For the non-LS SBox (used in `DEFAULT-CORE`) 196F7C82AED043B5, the bound obtained from the MILP program for the linear case is 33.00 at the 11th round. Hence, the linear cryptanalysis security at 11 rounds of `DEFAULT-CORE` is around 2^{66} computations. Hence, we conclude `DEFAULT` ensures the required DFA security (of 2^{64} computations) and also the required classical security (of 2^{128} computations).

Table 6. Differential and linear bounds (in $-\log_2$ notation) for LS and non-LS SBoxes

(a) LS SBox: 037ED4A9CF18B265

Rounds	1	2	3	4	5	6	7
Diff.	0	0	2	6	10	15	20
Linear	0	0	0	1	4	-	-

(b) Non-LS SBox: 196F7C82AED043B5

Rounds	1	2	3	4	5	6	7	8	9	10	11
Linear	1	2	4	6	8	12	16	20	25	30	33

More results regarding this can be found in Table 6 (Table 6(a) for differential and linear bounds for the LS SBox037ED4A9CF18B265 and Table 6(b) for linear

---

[9] https://www.gurobi.com/.

bounds for the non-LS SBox196F7C82AED043B5), as obtained from the MILP instances. Those results are obtained from a workstation with 16× Intel Xeon E7-8880 physical cores (shared among multiple users), running Gurobi 8.1 on 64-bit Ubuntu 18.04. Due to the time taken by the solver, it would be difficult to compute the bounds beyond the ones given in Table 6, at least with the current modelling (and with our computing resource).

8   Performance

In this part we state benchmarks for hardware and software implementations of DEFAULT. Comparison is done with GIFT-128 and a duplication-protected GIFT-128 which runs the same computation twice (in space or time) and compares the output. The output is released only if both computations produce same ciphertext, otherwise it is suppressed. This is the so-called *detective countermeasure* [10]. As a side note, it can be mentioned that the current academic researches have drifted away from the simple detective countermeasure towards more sophisticated error detection code-based or infection-based countermeasures, which would incur higher overheads. If such a sophisticated countermeasure is taken into account, DEFAULT provides much better performance.

8.1   Hardware Benchmark

The area and throughput for DEFAULT, GIFT-128 and AES are given in Table 7. We also provide the same for GIFT-128 and AES when protected with spatial or temporal duplication, or with DEFAULT-LAYER. The code is written in Verilog, and synthesized on Synopsys Design Compiler J-2019 on the TSMC 65nm standard cell library using compile_ultra. The area is given in gate equivalents. The throughput is computed for 2 GHz clock frequency. We assume the round keys are precomputed for all implementations. The implementations of DEFAULT and the protected ciphers are available online[10]. For GIFT-128 with DEFAULT-LAYER, we implemented two versions. The first (v1) is a simple combination of DEFAULT-LAYER with main cipher, while the second one (v2) takes advantage of the structural similarities between GIFT-128 and DEFAULT-LAYER. For AES, we noticed that the area required to implement DEFAULT-LAYER is small compared to the size of the AES circuit. Besides, the AES circuit is the bottleneck for clock frequency. Hence, we experimented with 3 different architectures for DEFAULT-LAYER i.e. one round (×1), two round (×2) and four rounds (×4) unrolled per clock cycle. In order to put our results into perspective, we implemented two versions of the simple duplication countermeasure for AES and GIFT-128. The first version is temporal duplication, where the cipher is implemented once and called twice, then the outputs are compared. The second version is spatial duplication, where two instances of cipher are computed in parallel followed by final comparison.

---

[10] https://github.com/mustafa-khairallah/default.

Table 7. ASIC Synthesis Results on the TSMC 65 nm library.

Design	Area (GE)	Cycles	Throughput (Mbps)
DEFAULT-LAYER	1786	28	9143
DEFAULT	2377	80	3200
GIFT-128 + DEFAULT-LAYER (v1/v2)	2410	96	2667
GIFT-128	1584	40	6400
GIFT-128 temporal duplication	2608	81	3160
GIFT-128 spatial duplication	3680	41	6244
AES + DEFAULT-LAYER (×1)	15692	67	3821
AES + DEFAULT-LAYER (×2)	16861	39	6564
AES + DEFAULT-LAYER (×4)	18889	25	10240
AES	14451	11	23273
AES temporal duplication	15475	23	11130
AES spatial duplication	29414	12	21333

Our results show that for GIFT-128, the area needed to add the DEFAULT-LAYER is small, where the area needed for the full design is similar to that of DEFAULT, while the throughput drops by a factor of 2.4×. The area of our design is significantly smaller than both types of duplication. This takes advantage of the similarities between GIFT-128 and DEFAULT, where they share the linear layer and storage, while differing in only the sbox.

For AES, the cost for adding DEFAULT-LAYER (×1) to AES is also small, while the DEFAULT-LAYER (×4) architecture leads to the highest throughput. Unlike GIFT-128, the differences between AES and DEFAULT-LAYER lead to a smaller advantage over duplication. Temporal duplication behaves better than AES +DEFAULT-LAYER, while spatial duplication have much higher throughput but at the cost 55% larger area. While the AES duplication countermeasure is competitive in terms of performance, the drawbacks of simple duplications were discussed in details in Sect. 6.4, which we believe justifies the cost of our countermeasure.

We have also synthesized our implementations for the Xilinx Kintex 7 FPGA. We fixed the clock frequency to 200 MHz. Due to the nature of FPGA look-up tables (LUTs), they are sometimes under-utilized. This makes it possible to add extra functionality or extra flip-flops to the design for almost no cost. The results are given in Table 8. Our results show that the DEFAULT-LAYER can be added to GIFT-128 for no extra LUTs or flip-flops. The throughput drops by a factor of 2.4×. Both types of duplication lead to drop in throughput and increase in both LUTs and flip-flops.

Table 8. FPGA Synthesis Results on Kintex 7.

Design	Cycles	LUT	FF	Throughput (Mbps)
DEFAULT-LAYER	28	256	128	914.3
DEFAULT	80	256	128	320.0
GIFT-128 + DEFAULT-LAYER v1	96	358	128	266.7
GIFT-128 + DEFAULT-LAYER v2	96	256	128	266.7
GIFT-128	40	256	128	640.0
GIFT-128 temporal duplication	81	384	256	316.0
GIFT-128 spatial duplication	41	640	256	624.4
AES + DEFAULT-LAYER (×1)	67	918	128	382.1
AES + DEFAULT-LAYER (×2)	39	964	128	656.4
AES + DEFAULT-LAYER (×4)	25	1204	128	1024.0
AES	11	528	128	2327.3
AES temporal duplication	23	656	256	1113.0
AES spatial duplication	12	1184	256	2133.3

In the case of duplication for AES, the ×1, ×2 and ×4 unrolled architectures of DEFAULT-LAYER have larger overhead compared to duplication. While duplication is about twice as efficient as our solution when it comes to AES, this is only specific to AES as its base line cost is relatively reduced on FPGAs, taking advantage of the large LUTs available. Moreover, the security features of DEFAULT compared to duplication still makes it interesting for AES on FPGAs.

8.2 Software Benchmark

The software benchmarks for GIFT-128, duplicated GIFT-128 (in time) and DEFAULT are given in Table 9. The relative overheads compared to GIFT-128 are shown within parenthesis. The clock cycles were measured by utilizing time() function from time.h library in C, by averaging over multiple executions. Program was running on a single core. Compiler optimizations were disabled to produce a consistent result. Note that the main purpose of this benchmark is to show the relative performance compared to GIFT in the same setting. It can be seen that the code size for DEFAULT is slightly more compared to duplicated GIFT-128, but at the same time DEFAULT is faster. We would also like to note that a new efficient software representation of GIFT was published recently [1], called the fixslicing technique, drastically reducing the cycles needed for encryption on ARM Cortex-M family of microcontrollers. The fixsliced implementation of DEFAULT would have very similar per-round performances as GIFT-128, as the permutation is the same (which is what the fixslicing technique is trying to optimize), while the Sboxes have similar cost. Overall, we expect the overheads to be similar as it scales accordingly to the number of rounds. Generally, this scaling would apply to other optimizations as well.

Table 9. Software benchmarking for `DEFAULT` and `GIFT-128` with/without duplication

		Intel Xeon Silver 4215	Arm Cortex A-53
Speed (Cycles/Bytes)	`GIFT-128`	9.7 (1.000×)	61.3 (1.000×)
	`GIFT-128` Duplicated	21.9 (2.258×)	124.4 (2.029×)
	`DEFAULT`	19.2 (1.979×)	121.9 (1.989×)
Code Size (Bytes)	`GIFT-128`	6624 (1.000×)	5593 (1.000×)
	`GIFT-128` Duplicated	6859 (1.035×)	5818 (1.040×)
	`DEFAULT`	8024 (1.211×)	7085 (1.267×)

9   Conclusion and Future Works

In this paper, we presented the first theoretical study on SBoxes with respect to their properties against differential fault attacks. We observe that DFA works as a simplified model of differential attacks, yet the properties of an SBox which makes DFA harder, will make DA easier, and vice-versa. Our findings enabled us to propose the first cipher-level countermeasure against DFA. Our construction does not incur too much overhead and is competitive with state-of-the-art in terms of performances, while protecting against a larger spectrum of faults. The core idea is to use a special SBox with linear structures, so that when trying all possible fault values, the attacker is not able to narrow down the search space below square root bound. This work opens up a new paradigm of symmetric-key cipher design, by studying SBoxes with LS, which has not been explored much yet.

Below we summarize the advantages and limitations of our proposal.

+ **First cipher-level protection.** This solves the concern raised against existing DFA countermeasures (Sect. 2.2). In particular, we remove the DFA protection from the hand of the cipher implementer to the cipher designer.
+ **Scalable to (almost) all symmetric-key primitives as an ad-hoc layer.** Using `DEFAULT-LAYER`, the basic concept we propose can be scaled to ensure a non-trivial DFA security on any symmetric-key primitive. We give a proof of concept for 128-bit state size, but it can be easily adapted to handle any state size that is multiple of 16 bits (by adjusting the number of rounds).
+ **Possibility to get a non-trivial DFA security.** The particular instantiation we propose offers up to $2^{n/2}$ DFA security where $n \geq 128$ is the state size of a block cipher (without jeopardizing its classical security). However, this is not a maximum limit as can be seen from Table 1. Note that, attack complexity of $2^{n/2}$ can be considered impractical for fault attacks.
+ **Protected against duplicate faults .** `DEFAULT` is not vulnerable to duplicate faults, unlike duplication based countermeasure. This remains true regardless of the number of faults, unlike some error detection based protection where faults are not detected beyond a certain coverage.

+ **Extension to any FA that uses differential analysis method.** The use of LS Sboxes increases the number of solutions for any given differential, which makes any attack under analysis method 1 harder.

+ **No need for external randomness/protected device.** The commonly referred infective countermeasure [10] uses an external source of randomness. For the protocol level countermeasures, such as [7], a part of the device is assumed to be off limit to the attacker due some device level protection. In our case, there is neither a need for an external source of entropy nor a specially protected device.

− **Not full DFA security.** It is technically possible to achieve almost full DFA security (such as 2^{112} for a 128-bit state, see Table 1). However, it does not seem possible to achieve a full state-size DFA security by this methodology.

We believe our work opens up a new research direction for ciphers that are resilient against fault attacks, here are a few potential open problems that would be interesting to explore in the future. One can look for a self-inverse SBox that fits our criteria to reduce the hardware cost when both the layer and its inverse are implemented in the same circuit. As the LS SBox has fewer AND operations, future ciphers could be designed while leveraging this. Finally, a solution that would combine fault protection with side-channel resistance would be extremely valuable. On the attack side, it would be interesting to study how far one could go with a combined side-channel analysis/DFA against DEFAULT.

Acknowledgments. We would like to thank the anonymous referees for their helpful comments, especially with regards to information combining attacks.

References

1. Adomnicai, A., Najm, Z., Peyrin, T.: Fixslicing: A New GIFT Representation. IACR Cryptology ePrint Archive **2020**, 412 (2020)
2. Aghaie, A., Moradi, A., Rasoolzadeh, S., Shahmirzadi, A.R., Schellenberg, F., Schneider, T.: Impeccable circuits. Cryptology ePrint Archive, Report 2018/203 (2018)
3. Agoyan, M., Dutertre, J.M., Mirbaha, A.P., Naccache, D., Ribotta, A.L., Tria, A.: How to flip a bit? In,: IEEE 16th International On-Line Testing Symposium. IEEE **2010**, pp. 235–239 (2010)
4. Baksi, A.: New insights on differential and linear bounds using mixed integer linear programming (full version). Cryptology ePrint Archive, Report 2020/1414 (2020)
5. Baksi, A., Bhasin, S., Breier, J., Chattopadhyay, A., Kumar, V.B.Y.: Feeding Three Birds With One Scone: A Generic Duplication Based Countermeasure To Fault Attacks (Extended Version). Cryptology ePrint Archive, Report 2020/1542 (2020)
6. Baksi, A., Bhasin, S., Breier, J., Jap, D., Saha, D.: Fault attacks in symmetric key cryptosystems. Cryptology ePrint Archive, Report 2020/1267 (2020)
7. Baksi, A., Bhasin, S., Breier, J., Khairallah, M., Peyrin, T.: Protecting block ciphers against differential fault attacks without re-keying (extended version). Cryptology ePrint Archive, Report 2018/085 (2018)

8. Baksi, A., Bhasin, S., Breier, J., Peyrin, T., Sarkar, S., Sim, S.M.: DEFAULT: Cipher Level Resistance Against Differential Fault Attack. Cryptology ePrint Archive, Report 2021/712 (2021)
9. Baksi, A., Kumar, V.B.Y., Karmakar, B., Bhasin, S., Saha, D., Chattopadhyay, A.: A novel duplication based countermeasure to statistical ineffective fault analysis. In: Information Security and Privacy - 25th Australasian Conference, ACISP (2020)
10. Baksi, A., Saha, D., Sarkar, S.: To infect or not to infect: a critical analysis of infective countermeasures in fault attacks. J. Cryptogr. Eng. **10**(4), 355–374 (2020)
11. Banik, S., Pandey, S.K., Peyrin, T., Sasaki, Y., Sim, S.M., Todo, Y.: GIFT: a small present - towards reaching the limit of lightweight encryption. CHES **2017**, 321–345 (2017)
12. Barbu, G., et al.: A high-order infective countermeasure framework. In: FDTC 2021 (2021)
13. Beierle, C., et al.: The SKINNY Family of Block Ciphers and Its Low-Latency Variant MANTIS. In: Robshaw, M., Katz, J. (eds.) CRYPTO 2016. LNCS, vol. 9815, pp. 123–153. Springer, Heidelberg (2016). https://doi.org/10.1007/978-3-662-53008-5_5
14. Beierle, C., Leander, G., Moradi, A., Rasoolzadeh, S.: CRAFT: lightweight tweakable block cipher with efficient protection against DFA attacks. IACR Trans. Symmetric Cryptol. **2019**(1), 5–45 (2019)
15. Biham, E., Shamir, A.: Differential fault analysis of secret key cryptosystems. In: Kaliski, B.S. (ed.) CRYPTO 1997. LNCS, vol. 1294, pp. 513–525. Springer, Heidelberg (1997). https://doi.org/10.1007/BFb0052259
16. Bogdanov, A., et al.: PRESENT: An Ultra-Lightweight Block Cipher. In: Paillier, P., Verbauwhede, I. (eds.) CHES 2007. LNCS, vol. 4727, pp. 450–466. Springer, Heidelberg (2007). https://doi.org/10.1007/978-3-540-74735-2_31
17. Boura, C., Canteaut, A., De Cannière, C.: Higher-order differential properties of KECCAK and *Luffa*. In: Joux, A. (ed.) FSE 2011. LNCS, vol. 6733, pp. 252–269. Springer, Heidelberg (2011). https://doi.org/10.1007/978-3-642-21702-9_15
18. Clavier, C.: Secret external encodings do not prevent transient fault analysis. CHES **2007**, 181–194 (2007)
19. De Cannière, C.: Analysis and Design of Symmetric Encryption Algorithms. Katholieke Universiteit Leuven, Belgium, PhD thesis (2007)
20. Diffie, W., (translators), G.L.: SMS4 Encryption Algorithm for Wireless Networks. Cryptology ePrint Archive, Report 2008/329 (2008)
21. Dobraunig, C., Eichlseder, M., Korak, T., Mangard, S., Mendel, F., Primas, R.: SIFA: exploiting ineffective fault inductions on symmetric cryptography. IACR Trans. Cryptogr. Hardw. Embed. Syst. **2018**(3), 547–572 (2018)
22. Dobraunig, C., Eichlseder, M., Mendel, F., Schläffer, M.: Ascon. CAESAR Final Portfolio (2014). https://ascon.iaik.tugraz.at/
23. Eskandari, Z., Kidmose, A.B., Kölbl, S., Tiessen, T.: Finding integral distinguishers with ease. Cryptology ePrint Archive, Report 2018/688 (2018)
24. Guilley, S., Sauvage, L., Danger, J., Selmane, N.: Fault injection resilience. In: FDTC 2010, pp. 51–65 (2010)
25. He, W., Breier, J., Bhasin, S., Miura, N., Nagata, M.: Ring oscillator under laser: potential of PLL-based countermeasure against laser fault injection. In: FDTC 2016, pp. 102–113. IEEE (2016)
26. Joye, M., Quisquater, J., Yen, S., Yung, M.: Observability analysis - detecting when improved cryptosystems fail. CT-RSA **2002**, 17–29 (2002)

27. Lerman, L., Veshchikov, N., Picek, S., Markowitch, O.: On the construction of side-channel attack resilient S-boxes. In: Guilley, S. (ed.) COSADE 2017. LNCS, vol. 10348, pp. 102–119. Springer, Cham (2017). https://doi.org/10.1007/978-3-319-64647-3_7

28. Li, L., Wu, W., Zheng, Y., Zhang, L.: The Relationship between the Construction and Solution of the MILP Models and Applications. Cryptology ePrint Archive, Report 2019/049 (2019)

29. Mangard, S., Oswald, E., Popp, T.: Power Analysis Attacks. Springer, Boston (2007). https://doi.org/10.1007/978-0-387-38162-6

30. Mouha, N., Wang, Q., Gu, D., Preneel, B.: Differential and linear cryptanalysis using mixed-integer linear programming. In: Wu, C.-K., Yung, M., Lin, D. (eds.) Inscrypt 2011. LNCS, vol. 7537, pp. 57–76. Springer, Heidelberg (2012). https://doi.org/10.1007/978-3-642-34704-7_5

31. Nageler, M., Dobraunig, C., Eichlseder, M.: Information-combining differential fault attacks on DEFAULT (Draft). Personal Communication, September 2021

32. Ghalaty, N.F., Bilgiday Yuce, P.S.: Analyzing the efficiency of biased-fault based attacks. Cryptology ePrint Archive, Report 2015/663 (2015)

33. National Institute of Standards and Technology (NIST): ADVANCED ENCRYPTION STANDARD (AES) (2001)

34. Phan, R.C.-W., Yen, S.-M.: Amplifying side-channel attacks with techniques from block cipher cryptanalysis. In: Domingo-Ferrer, J., Posegga, J., Schreckling, D. (eds.) CARDIS 2006. LNCS, vol. 3928, pp. 135–150. Springer, Heidelberg (2006). https://doi.org/10.1007/11733447_10

35. Sakiyama, K., Sasaki, Y., Li, Y.: Security of Block Ciphers - From Algorithm Design to Hardware Implementation. Wiley (2015)

36. Sarkar, S., Sasaki, Yu., Sim, S.M.: On the design of bit permutation based ciphers. In: Aoki, K., Kanaoka, A. (eds.) IWSEC 2020. LNCS, vol. 12231, pp. 3–22. Springer, Cham (2020). https://doi.org/10.1007/978-3-030-58208-1_1

37. Sasaki, Y., Todo, Y.: New impossible differential search tool from design and cryptanalysis aspects - revealing structural properties of several ciphers. EUROCRYPT **2017**, 185–215 (2017)

38. Selmke, B., Heyszl, J., Sigl, G.: Attack on a DFA protected AES by simultaneous laser fault injections. FDTC **2016**, 36–46 (2016)

39. Simon, T., et al.: FRIET: an authenticated encryption scheme with built-in fault detection. In: Canteaut, A., Ishai, Y. (eds.) EUROCRYPT 2020. LNCS, vol. 12105, pp. 581–611. Springer, Cham (2020). https://doi.org/10.1007/978-3-030-45721-1_21

40. Stinson, D.R.: Cryptography - Theory and Practice. Discrete Mathematics and its Applications Series, CRC Press, Boca Raton (2006)

41. Sun, S., Hu, L., Wang, P., Qiao, K., Ma, X., Song, L.: Automatic security evaluation and (related-key) differential characteristic search: Application to Simon, present, Lblock, DES(L) and other bit-oriented block ciphers. ASIACRYPT **2014**, 158–178 (2014)

42. Todo, Y.: Structural evaluation by generalized integral property. EUROCRYPT **2015**, 287–314 (2015)

43. Yen, S., Joye, M.: Checking before output may not be enough against fault-based cryptanalysis. IEEE Trans. Comput. **49**(9), 967–970 (2000)

44. Sung-Ming, Y., Kim, S., Lim, S., Moon, S.: A countermeasure against one physical cryptanalysis may benefit another attack. In: Kim, K. (ed.) ICISC 2001. LNCS, vol. 2288, pp. 414–427. Springer, Heidelberg (2002). https://doi.org/10.1007/3-540-45861-1_31

45. Zhang, F., et al.: Persistent fault analysis on block ciphers. IACR Trans. Cryptogr. Hardw. Embed. Syst., 150–172 (2018)

Dynamic Random Probing Expansion with Quasi Linear Asymptotic Complexity

Sonia Belaïd[1]($\boxtimes$), Matthieu Rivain[1]($\boxtimes$), Abdul Rahman Taleb[1,2]($\boxtimes$), and Damien Vergnaud[2,3]($\boxtimes$)

[1] CryptoExperts, Paris, France
{sonia.belaid,matthieu.rivain,abdul.taleb}@cryptoexperts.com
[2] Sorbonne Université, CNRS, LIP6, 75005 Paris, France
damien.vergnaud@lip6.fr
[3] Institut Universitaire de France, Paris, France

Abstract. The masking countermeasure is widely used to protect cryptographic implementations against side-channel attacks. While many masking schemes are shown to be secure in the widely deployed probing model, the latter raised a number of concerns regarding its relevance in practice. Offering the adversary the knowledge of a fixed number of intermediate variables, it does not capture the so-called horizontal attacks which exploit the repeated manipulation of sensitive variables. Therefore, recent works have focused on the *random probing model* in which each computed variable leaks with some given probability p. This model benefits from fitting better the reality of the embedded devices. In particular, Belaïd, Coron, Prouff, Rivain, and Taleb (CRYPTO 2020) introduced a framework to generate random probing circuits. Their compiler somehow extends base gadgets as soon as they satisfy a notion called *random probing expandability* (RPE). A subsequent work from Belaïd, Rivain, and Taleb (EUROCRYPT 2021) went a step forward with tighter properties and improved complexities. In particular, their construction reaches a complexity of $\mathcal{O}(\kappa^{3.9})$, for a κ-bit security, while tolerating a leakage probability of $p = 2^{-7.5}$.

In this paper, we generalize the random probing expansion approach by considering a dynamic choice of the base gadgets at each step in the expansion. This approach makes it possible to use gadgets with high number of shares –which enjoy better asymptotic complexity in the expansion framework– while still tolerating the best leakage rate usually obtained for small gadgets. We investigate strategies for the choice of the sequence of compilers and show that it can reduce the complexity of an AES implementation by a factor 10. We also significantly improve the asymptotic complexity of the expanding compiler by exhibiting new asymptotic gadget constructions. Specifically, we introduce RPE gadgets for linear operations featuring a quasi-linear complexity as well as an RPE multiplication gadget with linear number of multiplications. These new gadgets drop the complexity of the expanding compiler from quadratic to quasi-linear.

Keywords: Random probing model · Masking · Side-channel security · RPE

© International Association for Cryptologic Research 2021
M. Tibouchi and H. Wang (Eds.): ASIACRYPT 2021, LNCS 13091, pp. 157–188, 2021.
https://doi.org/10.1007/978-3-030-92075-3_6

1 Introduction

Implementations of cryptographic algorithms may be vulnerable to the powerful *side-channel attacks*. The latter exploit the power consumption, the electromagnetic radiations or the temperature variations of the underlying device which may carry information on the manipulated data. Entire secrets can be recovered within a short time interval using cheap equipment.

Among the several approaches investigated by the community to counteract side-channel attacks, *masking* is one of the most deployed in practice. Simultaneously introduced by Chari, Jutla, Rao, and Rohatgi [12] and by Goubin and Patarin [16] in 1999, it consists in splitting the sensitive variables into n random shares, among which any combination of $n - 1$ shares does not reveal any secret information. When the shares are combined by bitwise addition, the masking is said to be *Boolean*. In this setting, the linear operations can be very easily implemented by applying on each share individually. Nevertheless, non-linear operations require additional randomness to ensure that any set of less than n intermediate variables is still independent from the original secret.

To reason on the security of masked implementations, the community has introduced so-called *leakage models*. They aim to define the capabilities of the attacker to formally counteract the subsequent side-channel attacks. Among them, the *probing model* introduced in 2003 by Ishai, Sahai, and Wagner [18] is probably the most widely used. In a nutshell, it assumes that an adversary is able to get the exact values of up to a certain number of intermediate variables. The idea is to capture the difficulty of learning information from the combination of noisy variables. Despite its wide use by the community [7,13,14,20,21], the probing model raised a number of concerns regarding its relevance in practice [5,17]. It actually fails to capture the huge amount of information resulting from the leakage of all manipulated data. As an example, it typically ignores the repeated manipulation of identical values which would average the noise and remove uncertainty on secret variables (see horizontal attacks [5]). Another model, the *noisy leakage model* introduced by Prouff and Rivain and inspired from [12], offers an opposite trade-off. Although it captures well the reality of embedded devices by assuming that all the data leaks with some noise, it is not convenient to build security proofs. To get the best from both worlds, Duc, Dziembowski, and Faust proved in 2014 that a scheme secure in the probing model is also secure in the noisy leakage model [15]. Nevertheless, the reduction is not very tight in the standard probing model (considering a constant number of probes) since the security level decreases as the size of the circuit increases (*i.e.* a secure circuit C in the probing model is also secure in the noisy model but loses at least a factor $|C|$, where $|C|$ is the number of operations in the circuit).

The reduction from [15] relies on an intermediate leakage model, referred to as *random probing model*. The latter benefits from a tight reduction with the noisy leakage model which becomes independent of the size of the circuit. In a nutshell, it assumes that every wire in the circuit leaks with some constant leakage probability. This leakage probability is somehow related to the amount of side-channel noise in practice. A masked circuit is secure in the random probing model whenever its random probing leakage can be simulated without knowledge of the underlying secret data with a negligible simulation failure. In addition to the attacks already captured by the probing model, the random probing model further encompasses the powerful *horizontal attacks* which exploit the repeated manipulations of variables in an implementation.

To the best of our knowledge, five constructions tolerate a constant leakage probability so far [1,3,4,9,10]. The two former ones [1,4] use expander graphs and do not make their tolerated probability explicit. In the third construction [3], Ananth, Ishai, and Sahai develop an expansion strategy on top of multi-party computation protocols. According to the authors of [9], their construction tolerates a leakage probability of around 2^{-26} for a complexity of $\mathcal{O}(\kappa^{8.2})$ with respect to the security parameter κ. Finally, the two more recent constructions [9,10] follow an expansion strategy on top of masking gadgets achieving the so-called *random probing expandability* (RPE) notion. In a nutshell, every gate in the original circuit is replaced by a corresponding gadget for some chosen number of shares. The operation is repeated until the desired security level is achieved. The improved gadgets of [10] make it possible to tolerate of leakage probability of $2^{-7.5}$ for a complexity of $\mathcal{O}(\kappa^{3.9})$.

Our contributions. In this paper, we push the random probing expansion strategy one step further by analyzing a dynamic choice of the base gadgets. While the expanding compiler considered in [9,10] consists in applying a compiler CC composed of base RPE gadgets a given number of times, say k, to the input circuit: $\widehat{C} = \mathrm{CC}^{(k)}(C)$, we consider a dynamic approach in which a new compiler is selected at each step of the expansion from a family of base compilers $\{\mathrm{CC}_i\}_i$. This approach is motivated by the generic gadget constructions introduced in [10] which achieve the RPE property for any number of shares n. While the asymptotic complexity of the expanding compiler decreases with n, the tolerated leakage probability p also gets smaller with n, which makes those constructions only practical for small values of n. We show that using our dynamic approach we can get the best of both worlds: our dynamic expanding compiler enjoys the best tolerated probability as well as the best asymptotic complexity from the underlying family of RPE compilers $\{\mathrm{CC}_i\}_i$. We further illustrate how this approach can reduce the complexity of a random probing secure AES implementation by a factor 10 using a dynamic choice of the gadgets from [10].

This first contribution further motivates the design of asymptotic RPE gadgets achieving better complexity. While the asymptotic constructions introduced in [10] achieve a quadratic complexity, we introduce new constructions achieving quasi-linear complexity. We obtain this result by showing that the quasi-linear refresh gadget from Battistello, Coron, Prouff, and Zeitoun [6] achieves a *strong random probing expandability* (SRPE) which makes it a good building block for linear RPE gadgets (addition, copy, multiplication by constant). We thus solve a first issue left open in [10]. With such linear gadgets, the complexity bottleneck of the expanding compiler becomes the number of multiplications in the multiplication gadget, which is quadratic in known RPE constructions. We then provide a new generic construction of RPE multiplication gadget featuring a linear number of multiplications. We obtain this construction by tweaking the probing-secure multiplication gadget from Belaïd, Benhamouda, Passelègue, Prouff, Thillard, and Vergnaud [8]. As in the original construction, our RPE gadget imposes some constraint on the underlying finite field. We demonstrate that for any number of shares there exist a (possibly large) finite field on which our construction can be instantiated and we provide some concrete instantiations for some (small) number of shares.

Using our new asymptotic gadget constructions with the dynamic expansion approach we obtain random probing security for a leakage probability of $2^{-7.5}$ with asymptotic complexity of $\mathcal{O}(\kappa^2)$. Moreover, assuming that the constraint on the finite field from our multiplication gadget is satisfied, we can make this asymptotic complexity arbitrary close to $\mathcal{O}(\kappa)$ which is optimal. In practice, this means that securing circuits defined on large field against random probing leakage can be achieved at a sub-quadratic nearly-linear complexity.

2   Preliminaries

Along the paper, we shall use similar notations and formalism as [9]. In particular, $\mathbb{K}$ shall denote a finite field. For any $n \in \mathbb{N}$, we shall denote $[n]$ the integer set $[n] = [1, n] \cap \mathbb{Z}$. For any tuple $x = (x_1, \ldots, x_n) \in \mathbb{K}^n$ and any set $I \subseteq [n]$, we shall denote $x|_I = (x_i)_{i \in I}$. Any two probability distributions D_1 and D_2 are said ε-close, denoted $D_1 \approx_\varepsilon D_2$, if their statistical distance is upper bounded by ε, that is

$$\mathsf{SD}(D_1; D_2) := \frac{1}{2} \sum_x |p_{D_1}(x) - p_{D_2}(x)| \leq \varepsilon ,$$

where $p_{D_1}(\cdot)$ and $p_{D_1}(\cdot)$ denote the probability mass functions of D_1 and D_2.

2.1   Linear Sharing, Circuits, and Gadgets

In the following, the n-*linear decoding* mapping, denoted LinDec, refers to the function $\mathbb{K}^n \to \mathbb{K}$ defined as

$$\mathsf{LinDec} : (x_1, \ldots, x_n) \mapsto x_1 + \cdots + x_n ,$$

for every $n \in \mathbb{N}$ and $(x_1, \ldots, x_n) \in \mathbb{K}^n$. We shall further consider that, for every $n, \ell \in \mathbb{N}$, on input $(\widehat{x}_1, \ldots, \widehat{x}_\ell) \in (\mathbb{K}^n)^\ell$ the n-linear decoding mapping acts as

$$\mathsf{LinDec} : (\widehat{x}_1, \ldots, \widehat{x}_\ell) \mapsto (\mathsf{LinDec}(\widehat{x}_1), \ldots, \mathsf{LinDec}(\widehat{x}_\ell)) .$$

Definition 1 (Linear Sharing). *Let* $n, \ell \in \mathbb{N}$. *For any* $x \in \mathbb{K}$, *an* n-*linear sharing of* x *is a random vector* $\widehat{x} \in \mathbb{K}^n$ *such that* $\mathsf{LinDec}(\widehat{x}) = x$. *It is said to be uniform if for any set* $I \subseteq [n]$ *with* $|I| < n$ *the tuple* $\widehat{x}|_I$ *is uniformly distributed over* $\mathbb{K}^{|I|}$. *A* n-*linear encoding is a probabilistic algorithm* LinEnc *which on input a tuple* $x = (x_1, \ldots, x_\ell) \in \mathbb{K}^\ell$ *outputs a tuple* $\widehat{x} = (\widehat{x}_1, \ldots, \widehat{x}_\ell) \in (\mathbb{K}^n)^\ell$ *such that* $\widehat{x}_i$ *is a uniform* n-*sharing of* x_i *for every* $i \in [\ell]$.

An *arithmetic circuit* on a field $\mathbb{K}$ is a labeled directed acyclic graph whose edges are *wires* and vertices are *arithmetic gates* processing operations on $\mathbb{K}$. We consider circuits composed of gates from some base $\mathbb{B} = \{g : \mathbb{K}^\ell \to \mathbb{K}^m\}$, *e.g.*, addition gates, $(x_1, x_2) \mapsto x_1 + x_2$, multiplication gates, $(x_1, x_2) \mapsto x_1 \cdot x_2$, and copy gates, $x \mapsto (x, x)$. A *randomized arithmetic circuit* is equipped with an additional random gate which outputs a fresh uniform random value of $\mathbb{K}$.

In the following, we shall call an *(n-share, ℓ-to-m) gadget*, a randomized arithmetic circuit that maps an input $\widehat{x} \in (\mathbb{K}^n)^\ell$ to an output $\widehat{y} \in (\mathbb{K}^n)^m$ such that $x = \mathsf{LinDec}(\widehat{x}) \in \mathbb{K}^\ell$ and $y = \mathsf{LinDec}(\widehat{y}) \in \mathbb{K}^m$ satisfy $y = g(x)$ for some function g.

Definition 2 (Circuit Compiler). *A circuit compiler is a triplet of algorithms* $(\mathsf{CC}, \mathsf{Enc}, \mathsf{Dec})$ *defined as follows:*

- CC *(circuit compilation) is a deterministic algorithm that takes as input an arithmetic circuit C and outputs a randomized arithmetic circuit $\widehat{C}$,*
- Enc *(input encoding) is a probabilistic algorithm that maps an input $x \in \mathbb{K}^\ell$ to an encoded input $\widehat{x} \in \mathbb{K}^{\ell'}$,*
- Dec *(output decoding) is a deterministic algorithm that maps an encoded output $\widehat{y} \in \mathbb{K}^{m'}$ to a plain output $y \in \mathbb{K}^m$,*

which satisfy the following properties:

- **Correctness:** *For every arithmetic circuit C of input length ℓ, and for every $x \in \mathbb{K}^\ell$, we have*

$$\Pr\left(\mathsf{Dec}(\widehat{C}(\widehat{x})) = C(x) \mid \widehat{x} \leftarrow \mathsf{Enc}(x)\right) = 1 \;, \; \text{where } \widehat{C} = \mathsf{CC}(C).$$

- **Efficiency:** *For some security parameter $\kappa \in \mathbb{N}$, the running time of $\mathsf{CC}(C)$ is* $\mathrm{poly}(\kappa, |C|)$, *the running time of $\mathsf{Enc}(x)$ is* $\mathrm{poly}(\kappa, |x|)$ *and the running time of $\mathsf{Dec}(\widehat{y})$ is* $\mathrm{poly}(\kappa, |\widehat{y}|)$, *where* $\mathrm{poly}(\kappa, \ell) = \mathcal{O}(\kappa^{e_1} \ell^{e_2})$ *for some constants e_1, e_2.*

2.2 Random Probing Security

Let $p \in [0, 1]$ be some constant leakage probability parameter, a.k.a. the *leakage rate*. In the *p-random probing model*, an evaluation of a circuit C leaks the value carried by each wire with a probability p, all the wire leakage events being mutually independent.

As in [9], we formally define the random-probing leakage of a circuit from the two following probabilistic algorithms:

- The *leaking-wires sampler* takes as input a randomized arithmetic circuit C and a probability $p \in [0, 1]$, and outputs a set W, denoted as

$$W \leftarrow \mathsf{LeakingWires}(C, p) \;,$$

where W is constructed by including each wire label from the circuit C with probability p to W (where all the probabilities are mutually independent).

– The *assign-wires sampler* takes as input a randomized arithmetic circuit C, a set of wire labels W (subset of the wire labels of C), and an input $\boldsymbol{x}$, and it outputs a $|W|$-tuple $\boldsymbol{w} \in \mathbb{K}^{|W|}$, denoted as

$$\boldsymbol{w} \leftarrow \mathsf{AssignWires}(C, W, \boldsymbol{x}) \ ,$$

where $\boldsymbol{w}$ corresponds to the assignments of the wires of C with label in W for an evaluation on input $\boldsymbol{x}$.

Definition 3 (Random Probing Leakage). *The p-random probing leakage of a randomized arithmetic circuit C on input $\boldsymbol{x}$ is the distribution $\mathcal{L}_p(C, \boldsymbol{x})$ obtained by composing the leaking-wires and assign-wires samplers as*

$$\mathcal{L}_p(C, \boldsymbol{x}) \overset{id}{=} \mathsf{AssignWires}(C, \mathsf{LeakingWires}(C, p), \boldsymbol{x}) \ .$$

Definition 4 (Random Probing Security). *A randomized arithmetic circuit C with $\ell \cdot n \in \mathbb{N}$ input gates is (p, ε)-random probing secure with respect to encoding Enc if there exists a simulator Sim such that for every $\boldsymbol{x} \in \mathbb{K}^\ell$:*

$$\mathsf{Sim}(C) \approx_\varepsilon \mathcal{L}_p(C, \mathsf{Enc}(\boldsymbol{x})) \ . \tag{1}$$

2.3 Random Probing Expansion

In [3], Ananth, Ishai and Sahai proposed an *expansion* approach to build a random-probing-secure circuit compiler from a secure multi-party protocol. This approach was later revisited by Belaïd, Coron, Prouff, Rivain, and Taleb who formalize the notion of *expanding compiler* [9].

The principle of the expanding compiler is to recursively apply a base compiler, denoted CC and which simply consists in replacing each gate of $\mathbb{B}$ in the input circuit by the corresponding gadget. Assume we have n-share gadgets G_g for each gate g in $\mathbb{B}$. The base compiler CC simply consists in replacing each gate g in these gadgets by G_g and by replacing each wire by n wires carrying a sharing of the value. We thus obtain n^2-share gadgets by simply applying CC to each gadget: $G_g^{(2)} = \mathsf{CC}(G_g)$. This process can be iterated an arbitrary number of times, say k, to an input circuit C:

$$C \xrightarrow{\ \mathsf{CC}\ } \widehat{C}_1 \xrightarrow{\ \mathsf{CC}\ } \cdots \xrightarrow{\ \mathsf{CC}\ } \widehat{C}_k \ .$$

The first output circuit $\widehat{C}_1$ is the original circuit in which each gate g is replaced by a base gadget G_g. The second output circuit $\widehat{C}_2$ is the original circuit C in which each gate is replaced by an n^2-share gadget $G_g^{(2)}$. Equivalently, $\widehat{C}_2$ is the circuit $\widehat{C}_1$ in which each gate is replaced by a base gadget. In the end, the output circuit $\widehat{C}_k$ is hence the original circuit C in which each gate has been replaced by a k-expanded gadget and each wire has been replaced by n^k wires carrying an (n^k)-linear sharing of the original wire.

The expanding compiler achieves random probing security if the base gadgets verify a property called *random probing expandability* [9]. We recall hereafter the original definition of the random probing expandability (RPE) property for 2-to-1 gadgets.

Definition 5 (Random Probing Expandability [9]**).** *Let* $f : \mathbb{R} \to \mathbb{R}$. *An n-share 2-to-1 gadget* $G : \mathbb{K}^n \times \mathbb{K}^n \to \mathbb{K}^n$ *is* (t, f)-*random probing expandable (RPE) if there exists a deterministic algorithm* Sim_1^G *and a probabilistic algorithm* Sim_2^G *such that for every input* $(\widehat{x}, \widehat{y}) \in \mathbb{K}^n \times \mathbb{K}^n$, *for every set* $J \subseteq [n]$ *and for every* $p \in [0, 1]$, *the random experiment*

$$W \leftarrow \mathsf{LeakingWires}(G, p)$$

$$(I_1, I_2, J') \leftarrow \mathsf{Sim}_1^G(W, J)$$

$$out \leftarrow \mathsf{Sim}_2^G(W, J', \widehat{x}|_{I_1}, \widehat{y}|_{I_2})$$

ensures that

1. *the failure events* $\mathcal{F}_1 \equiv (|I_1| > t)$ *and* $\mathcal{F}_2 \equiv (|I_2| > t)$ *verify*

$$\Pr(\mathcal{F}_1) = \Pr(\mathcal{F}_2) = \varepsilon \quad and \quad \Pr(\mathcal{F}_1 \wedge \mathcal{F}_2) = \varepsilon^2 \tag{2}$$

   with $\varepsilon = f(p)$ *(in particular* $\mathcal{F}_1$ *and* $\mathcal{F}_2$ *are mutually independent)*,
2. J' *is such that* $J' = J$ *if* $|J| \leq t$ *and* $J' \subseteq [n]$ *with* $|J'| = n - 1$ *otherwise*,
3. *the output distribution satisfies*

$$out \stackrel{id}{=} \left(\mathsf{AssignWires}(G, W, (\widehat{x}, \widehat{y})), \widehat{z}|_{J'}\right) \tag{3}$$

where $\widehat{z} = G(\widehat{x}, \widehat{y})$.

The RPE notion can be simply extended to gadgets with 2 outputs: the Sim_1^G simulator takes two sets $J_1 \subseteq [n]$ and $J_2 \subseteq [n]$ as input and produces two sets J_1' and J_2' satisfying the same property as J' in the above definition (w.r.t. J_1 and J_2). The Sim_2^G simulator must then produce an output including $\widehat{z}_1|_{J_1'}$ and $\widehat{z}_2|_{J_1'}$ where $\widehat{z}_1$ and $\widehat{z}_2$ are the output sharings. The RPE notion can also be simply extended to gadgets with a single input: the Sim_1^G simulator produces a single set I so that the failure event $(|I| > t)$ occurs with probability ε (and the Sim_2^G simulator is then simply given $\widehat{x}|_I$ where $\widehat{x}$ is the single input sharing). We refer the reader to [9] for the formal definitions of these variants.

Although the requirement of mutual independence for the failure events might seem strong, it can be relaxed which leads to the notion of *weak random probing expandability*. It is shown in [9] that this weaker notion actually implies the RPE notion for some ε which is derivable from the (joint) probability of the failure events.

The authors of [10] eventually introduced a tighter version the RPE security property, namely the tight random probing expandability (TRPE). In this setting, the failure events are re-define as $\mathcal{F}_j \equiv (|I_j| > \min(t, W))$. Both RPE and TRPE notions can be split into two sub-notions (that are jointly equivalent to the original one) corresponding to the two possible properties of J' in Definition 5. Specifically, in (T)RPE1, the set J is constrained to satisfy $|J| \leq t$ and $J' = J$, while in (T)RPE2, J' is chosen by the simulator such that $J' \subseteq [n]$ and $|J'| = n - 1$.

2.4 Complexity of the Expanding Compiler

Consider circuits with base of gates $\mathbb{B} = \{g_1, \ldots, g_\beta\}$ for which we have n-share RPE gadgets $\{G_g\}_{g \in \mathbb{B}}$. Further denote G_{random} the n-share random gadget which generates n independent random values as a random n-sharing as well as CC the circuit compiler based from those gadgets. To each gadget a complexity vector is associated $N_G = (N_{g_1}, \ldots, N_{g_\beta}, N_r)^{\mathsf{T}}$ where N_{g_i} stands for the number of gates g_i and N_r for the number of random gates in the gadget G. Then the *compiler complexity matrix* M_{CC} is the $(\beta + 1) \times (\beta + 1)$ matrix defined as

$$M_{\mathsf{CC}} = \left(N_{g_1} \mid \cdots \mid N_{g_\beta} \mid N_{G_{\text{random}}} \right) \quad \text{with} \quad N_{G_{\text{random}}} = (0, \ldots, 0, n)^{\mathsf{T}} \ .$$

Given a circuit C with complexity vector N_C (which is defined as the gate-count vector as for gadgets), compiling it with the base gadgets gives a circuit $\widehat{C}$ of complexity vector $N_{\widehat{C}} = M_{\mathsf{CC}} \cdot N_C$. It follows that the kth power of the matrix M gives the gate counts for the level-k gadgets as:

$$M_{\mathsf{CC}}^k = \underbrace{M_{\mathsf{CC}} \cdots M_{\mathsf{CC}}}_{k \text{ times}} = \left(N_{g_1}^{(k)} \mid \cdots \mid N_{g_\beta}^{(k)} \mid N_{G_{\text{random}}}^{(k)} \right) \quad \text{with} \quad N_{G_{\text{random}}}^{(k)} = \begin{pmatrix} 0 \\ \vdots \\ 0 \\ n^k \end{pmatrix}$$

where $N_{g_i}^{(k)}$ are the gate-count vectors for the level-k gadgets $G_{g_i}^{(k)}$. Let us denote the eigen decomposition of M_{CC} as $M_{\mathsf{CC}} = Q \cdot \Lambda \cdot Q^{-1}$, we get

$$M_{\mathsf{CC}}^k = Q \cdot \Lambda^k \cdot Q^{-1} \quad \text{with} \quad \Lambda^k = \begin{pmatrix} \lambda_1^k & & \\ & \ddots & \\ & & \lambda_{\beta+1}^k \end{pmatrix}$$

where λ_i are the eigenvalues of M_{CC}. We then obtain an asymptotic complexity of

$$|\widehat{C}| = \mathcal{O}\left(|C| \cdot \sum_{i=1}^{\beta+1} |\lambda_i|^k \right) = \mathcal{O}\left(|C| \cdot \max(|\lambda_1|, \ldots, |\lambda_{\beta+1}|)^k \right)$$

for a compiled circuit $\widehat{C} = CC^{(k)}(C)$.

The complexity of the expanding compiler can be further expressed in terms of the target random probing security level κ. This complexity is related to the notion of *amplification order* that we recall hereafter.

Definition 6 (Amplification Order)

– Let $f : \mathbb{R} \to \mathbb{R}$ which satisfies

$$f(p) = c_d \, p^d + \mathcal{O}(p^{d+\varepsilon})$$

as p tends to 0, for some $c_d > 0$ and $\varepsilon > 0$. Then d is called the amplification order of f.

– Let $t > 0$ and G a gadget. Let d be the maximal integer such that G achieves (t, f)-RPE for $f : \mathbb{R} \to \mathbb{R}$ of amplification order d. Then d is called the amplification order of G (with respect to t).

We stress that the amplification order of a gadget G is defined with respect to the RPE threshold t. Namely, different RPE thresholds t are likely to yield different amplification orders d for G (or equivalently d can be thought of as a function of t).

As shown in [9], the complexity of the expanding compiler relates to the (minimum) amplification order of the gadgets composing the base compiler CC. If the latter achieve (t, f)-RPE with an amplification order d, the expanding compiler achieves $(p, 2^{-\kappa})$-random probing security with an expansion level k such that $f^{(k)}(p) \leq 2^{-\kappa}$, which yields a complexity blowup of

$$|\widehat{C}| = \mathcal{O}(|C| \cdot \kappa^e) \quad \text{with} \quad e = \frac{\log N_{\max}}{\log d} \tag{4}$$

where

$$N_{\max} = \max \; \mathsf{eigenvalues}(M_{\mathsf{CC}}) , \tag{5}$$

where $\mathsf{eigenvalues}(\cdot)$ returns the tuple of eigenvalues (or modules of eigenvalues in case of complex numbers) of the input matrix.

Let us slightly explicit the complexity with the 3-gate base $\mathbb{B} = \{\text{add, mult, copy}\}$ as used in [9,10]. Considering that multiplication gates are solely used in the multiplication gadget $(N_{G_{\text{add}},m} = N_{G_{\text{copy}},m} = 0)$ which is the case in the constructions of [9,10], it can be checked that (up to some permutation) the eigenvalues satisfy

$$(\lambda_1, \lambda_2) = \mathsf{eigenvalues}(M_{ac}) , \quad \lambda_3 = N_{G_{\text{mult}},m} \quad \text{and} \quad \lambda_4 = n$$

where M_{ac} is the top left 2×2 block matrix of M_{CC}

$$M_{ac} = \begin{pmatrix} N_{G_{\text{add}},a} & N_{G_{\text{copy}},a} \\ N_{G_{\text{add}},c} & N_{G_{\text{copy}},c} \end{pmatrix}$$

where $N_{x,y}$ denotes the number of gates x in a gadget y, with m for the multiplication, a for the addition, and c for the copy. We finally get

$$|\widehat{C}| = \mathcal{O}(|C| \cdot N_{\max}^k) \quad \text{with} \quad N_{\max} = \max(\mathsf{eigenvalues}(M_{ac}), N_{G_{\text{mult}},m}, n) . \tag{6}$$

As an illustration, the expanding compiler from [10] satisfies $N_{\max} = 3n^2 - 2n$ and $d = \frac{\min(t+1, n-t)}{2}$ which yields an asymptotic complexity of $\mathcal{O}(\kappa^e)$ with

$$e = \frac{\log(3n^2 - 2n)}{\log(\lfloor (n+1)/4 \rfloor)}$$

which tends to 2 as n grows. In comparison, in this work, we shall achieve a quasi-linear complexity, i.e., $N_{\max} = \mathcal{O}(n \log n)$.

2.5   Tolerated Leakage Rate

Finally, we recall the notion of *tolerated leakage rate* which corresponds to the maximum value p for which we have $f(p) < p$. This happens to be a necessary and sufficient condition for the expansion strategy to apply with (t, f)-RPE gadgets.

In practice, the tolerated leakage rate should be measured on concrete devices and fixed accordingly. Hence the motivation to exhibit gadgets which tolerate a high probability to cover any setting. So far, the asymptotic constructions provide a trade-off between tolerated leakage rate and complexity. However, we only know how to compute the former for small numbers of shares and the bounds for larger values are not tight.

As an illustration, the instantiation proposed in [9] tolerates a leakage probability up to $2^{-7.80}$, while the instantiation of [10] tolerates $2^{-7.50}$, both for 3-share base gadgets.

3   Dynamic Random Probing Expansion

As recalled in Sect. 2, the principle of the expanding compiler is to apply a base circuit compiler CC which is composed of base gadgets –one per gate type in the circuit– several times, say k, to the input circuit: $\widehat{C} = \mathsf{CC}^{(k)}(C)$. The level of expansion k is chosen in order to achieve a certain desired security level κ such that $f^{(k)}(p) \leq 2^{-\kappa}$.

In this section, we generalize this approach to choose the circuit compiler dynamically at the different steps of the expansion. Let $\{\mathsf{CC}_i\}_i$ be a family of circuit compilers, the *dynamic expanding compiler* for this family with respect to the expansion sequence $k_1, \dots k_\mu$, is defined as

$$\widehat{C} = \mathsf{CC}_\mu^{k_\mu} \circ \mathsf{CC}_{\mu-1}^{k_{\mu-1}} \circ \dots \cdots \circ \mathsf{CC}_1^{k_1}(C) . \tag{7}$$

The idea behind this generalization is to make the most from a family of RPE compilers $\{\mathsf{CC}_i\}_i$ which is defined with respect to the number of shares n_i in the base gadgets. If we assume that each compiler CC_i with n_i shares achieves the maximum amplification order $d_i = \frac{n_i+1}{2}$, then the benefit of using a compiler with higher number of shares is to increase the amplification order and thus reduce the number of steps necessary to achieve the desired security level κ. On the other hand, the tolerated leakage rate of existing constructions decreases with n_i. As we show hereafter, a dynamic increase of n_i can ensure both, the tolerated leakage rate of a small n_i and the better complexity of a high n_i.

3.1   Dynamic Expanding Compiler

We formally introduce the dynamic expanding compiler hereafter.

Definition 7 (RPE Compiler). *Let* $\mathbb{B} = \{g : \mathbb{K}^\ell \to \mathbb{K}^m\}$ *be an arithmetic circuit basis. Let* $n_i, t \in \mathbb{N}$, *and let* $\{G_g\}_{g \in \mathbb{B}}$ *be a family of* (t, f_g)-*RPE* n_i-*share gadgets for the gate functionalities in* $\mathbb{B}$. *The RPE compiler* CC_i *associated to* $\{G_g\}_{g \in \mathbb{B}}$ *is the circuit compiler which consists in replacing each gate from a circuit over* $\mathbb{B}$ *by the corresponding gadget* G_g. *Moreover,*

- *the* expanding function *of* CC_i *is the function* f_i *defined as*

$$f_i : p \mapsto \max_g f_g(p)$$

- *the* amplification order *of* CC_i *is the integer* d_i *defined as*

$$d_i = \min_g d_g$$

where d_g *is the amplification order of* f_g,

- *the* gadget complexity *of* CC_i *is the integer* s_i *defined as*

$$s_i = \max_g |G_g|$$

where $|G_g|$ *denotes the number of wires in the gadget* G_g,

- *the* tolerated leakage rate *of* CC_i *is the real number* $q_i \in [0, 1)$ *such that* $f_i(p) < p$ *for every* $p < q_i$.

In the following, we state the security and asymptotic complexity of the dynamic expanding compiler. We start with a formal definition of this compiler:

Definition 8 (Dynamic Expanding Compiler). *Let* $\{\mathsf{CC}_i\}_i$ *be a family of RPE compilers with numbers of shares* $\{n_i\}_i$. *The dynamic expanding compiler for* $\{\mathsf{CC}_i\}_i$ *with expansion levels* $k_1, \ldots, k_\mu$, *is the circuit compiler* $(\mathsf{CC}, \mathsf{Enc}, \mathsf{Dec})$ *where*

1. *The input encoding* Enc *is a* $\left(\prod_{i=1}^\mu n_i^{k_i} \right)$-*linear encoding.*
2. *The output decoding* Dec *is the* $\left(\prod_{i=1}^\mu n_i^{k_i} \right)$-*linear decoding mapping.*
3. *The circuit compilation is defined as*

$$\mathsf{CC}(\cdot) = \mathsf{CC}_\mu^{k_\mu} \circ \mathsf{CC}_{\mu-1}^{k_{\mu-1}} \circ \ldots \cdots \circ \mathsf{CC}_1^{k_1}(\cdot) .$$

The following theorem states the random probing security of the dynamic expanding compiler. The proof of the theorem is very similar to the proof of RPE security (Theorem 2) from [9]. The main difference is that at each level of the expansion, we can use a different expanding compiler with different sharing orders. Besides that, the proof follows the same baselines as in [9]. The proof is provided in the full version of this paper.

Theorem 1 (Security). *Let* $\{\mathsf{CC}_i\}_i$ *be a family of RPE compilers with expanding functions* $\{f_i\}_i$. *The dynamic expanding compiler for* $\{\mathsf{CC}_i\}_i$ *with expansion levels* $k_1, \ldots, k_\mu$ *is* (p, ε)-*random probing secure with*

$$\varepsilon = f_\mu^{k_\mu} \circ \cdots \circ f_1^{k_1}(p) .$$

We now state the asymptotic complexity of the dynamic expanding compiler in the next theorem. The proof is given in the full version of this paper.

Theorem 2 (Asymptotic Complexity). *Let* $\{CC_i\}_i$ *be a family of circuit compilers with complexity matrices* $\{M_{CC_i}\}_i$. *For any input circuit* C, *the output circuit* $\widehat{C} = CC_\mu^{k_\mu} \circ \cdots \cdots \circ CC_1^{k_1}(C)$ *is of size*

$$|\widehat{C}| = |C| \cdot \mathcal{O}\left(\prod_{i=1}^{\mu} \lambda_i^{k_i}\right) \quad \text{with} \quad \lambda_i := \max \text{ eigenvalues}(M_{CC_i}) . \tag{8}$$

In the following, we shall call λ_i as defined above, the *eigen-complexity* of the compiler CC_i. We shall further call the product $\prod_{i=1}^{\mu} \lambda_i^{k_i}$ the *complexity blowup* of the dynamic expanding compiler. We note that minimizing the complexity blowup is equivalent to minimizing the log complexity blowup, which is

$$\sum_{i=1}^{\mu} k_i \cdot \log_2(\lambda_i) . \tag{9}$$

3.2   General Bounds for Asymptotic Constructions

The following theorem introduces general bounds on the tolerated leakage rate and the expanding function of an RPE compiler with respect to its amplification order and gadget complexity. The proof of the theorem is given in the full version of this paper.

Theorem 3. *Let* CC_i *be an RPE circuit compiler of amplification order* d_i *and gadget complexity* s_i. *The tolerated leakage rate* q_i *of* CC_i *is lower bounded by*

$$q_i \geq \bar{q}_i := \frac{1}{e}\left(\frac{1}{2e}\right)^{\frac{1}{d_i-1}}\left(\frac{d_i}{s_i}\right)^{1+\frac{1}{d_i-1}} \tag{10}$$

For any $p < \bar{q}_i$, *the expanding function* f_i *of* CC_i *is upper bounded by*

$$f_i(p) \leq 2\binom{s_i}{d_i}p^{d_i} \leq 2\left(\frac{e \cdot s_i}{d_i}\right)^{d_i} p^{d_i} . \tag{11}$$

The lower bound $\bar{q}_i$ on the tolerated leakage rate quickly converges to the ratio $e^{-1} \cdot d_i/s_i$ as d_i grows. In other words, an RPE compiler family $\{CC_i\}_i$ indexed by the number of shares n_i of its base gadgets tolerates a leakage probability which is linear in the ratio between its amplification order d_i and its complexity s_i. For known families of RPE compilers from [10] this ratio is in $\mathcal{O}(1/n_i)$.

From Theorem 3, we obtain the following bound for the composition $f_i^{(k)}$. The proof of the corollary is given in the full version of this paper.

Corollary 1. *Let* CC_i *be an RPE compiler of expanding function* f_i, *amplification order* d_i *and gadget complexity* s_i. *For any* $p < \bar{q}_i$ *as defined in* (10), *we have*

$$f_i^{(k)}(p) \leq \left[2 \binom{s_i}{d_i} \right]^{\left(1 + \frac{1}{d_i - 1}\right) d_i^{k-1}} p^{d_i^k} \leq \left[\left(\frac{2^{\frac{1}{d_i}} e s_i}{d_i} \right)^{\left(1 + \frac{1}{d_i - 1}\right)} p \right]^{d_i^k} .$$

The following lemma gives an explicit lower bound on the expansion level $\{k_i\}_i$ to reach some arbitrary target probability $p_{out} = 2^{-\kappa_{out}}$ from a given input probability $p_{in} = 2^{-\kappa_{in}}$ by applying $\mathsf{CC}_i^{(k_i)}$.

Lemma 1. *Let* $p_{in} = 2^{-\kappa_{in}} < q_i$ *and* $p_{out} = 2^{-\kappa_{out}} \in (0, 1]$. *For any integer* k_i *satisfying*

$$k_i \geq \log_{d_i}(\kappa_{out}) - \log_{d_i}(\kappa_{in} - \Delta_i)$$

with

$$\Delta_i := \left(1 + \frac{1}{d_i - 1}\right) \left(\frac{1}{d_i} + \log_2 \left(\frac{e s_i}{d_i}\right)\right)$$

we have

$$f_i^{(k_i)}(p_{in}) \leq p_{out} = 2^{-\kappa_{out}} .$$

In the above lemma, Δ_i represents a lower bound for κ_{in} which matches the upper bound $\bar{q}_i$ of $p_{in} = 2^{-\kappa_{in}}$. Assuming that s_i and d_i are both monotonically increasing with i, we get that the threshold Δ_i tends towards $\log_2 \left(\frac{e s_i}{d_i}\right)$.

From Lemma 1, we further get that the cost induced by the choice of the compiler CC_i to go from an input probability p_{in} to a target output probability p_{out} is

$$k_i \cdot \log_2(\lambda_i) \geq \frac{\log_2(\lambda_i)}{\log_2(d_i)} \left(\log_2(\kappa_{out}) - \log_2(\kappa_{in} - \Delta_i) \right) \tag{12}$$

(in terms of the log complexity blowup (9)). Note that this upper bound is tight: it could be replaced by an equality at the cost of ceiling the term between parentheses (*i.e.* the term corresponding to k_i). We further note that the above equation is consistent with the complexity analysis of the expanding compiler provided in [9]. Indeed going from a constant leakage probability $p_{in} = p$ to a target security level $p_{out} = 2^{-\kappa}$ by applying k_i times a single RPE compiler CC_i, we retrieve a complexity of $\mathcal{O}(\kappa^e)$ with $e = \frac{\log_2(\lambda_i)}{\log_2(d_i)}$.

Equation (12) shows that using CC_i to go from input probability p_{in} to output probability p_{out} induces a log complexity cost close to

$$\frac{\log_2(\lambda_i)}{\log_2(d_i)} \left(\log_2(\kappa_{out}) - \log_2(\kappa_{in}) \right)$$

provided that κ_{in} is sufficiently greater than Δ_i. So given the latter informal condition, it appears that the parameter i minimizing the ratio $\frac{\log_2(\lambda_i)}{\log_2(d_i)}$ gives the best complexity.

Application. For the asymptotic construction introduced in [10], the RPE compiler CC_i features

- an amplification order $d_i = \mathcal{O}(n_i)$,
- a gadget complexity $s_i = \mathcal{O}(n_i^2)$,
- an eigen-complexity $\lambda_i = \mathcal{O}(n_i^2)$.

For such a construction, the ratio $\frac{\log_2(\lambda_i)}{\log_2(d_i)}$ is decreasing and converging towards 2 as n_i grows. On the other hand, Δ_i tends to $\log_2(n_i)$ which implies that CC_i should only be applied to an input probability lower than $\frac{1}{n_i}$.

3.3   Selection of the Expansion Levels

In this section, we investigate the impact of the choice of the expansion levels k_i on the complexity of the dynamic expanding compiler. We first assess the asymptotic complexity obtained from a simple approach and then provide some application results for some given gadgets.

   In the following CC_0 shall denote an RPE compiler with constant parameters while $\{CC_i\}_{i \geq 1}$ shall denote a family of RPE compilers indexed by a parameter i. We do this distinction since the goal of the CC_0 compiler shall be to tolerate the highest leakage rate and to transit from a (possibly high) leakage probability p to some lower failure probability p_i which is in turn tolerated by at least one compiler from $\{CC_i\}_i$.

A Simple Approach. We consider a simple approach in which the compiler CC_0 is iterated k_0 times and then a single compiler CC_i is iterated k_i times. The complexity blowup of this compiler is $\lambda_0^{k_0} \lambda_i^{k_i}$. The first expansion level k_0 is chosen to ensure that the intermediate probability $p_i := f_0^{(k_0)}(p)$ is lower than $\bar{q}_i$ (the lower bound on the tolerated leakage rate of CC_i from Theorem 3). Then k_i is chosen so that $f_i^{(k_i)} \leq 2^{-\kappa}$.

   Concretely, we set $\kappa_i := \Delta_i + 1$ which, by Lemma 1, gives

$$k_0 = \left\lceil \log_{d_0}(\Delta_i + 1) - \log_{d_0}(\log_2(p) - \Delta_0) \right\rceil , \tag{13}$$

and

$$k_i = \left\lceil \log_{d_i}(\kappa) \right\rceil = \mathcal{O}\left(\log_{d_i}(\kappa) \right) . \tag{14}$$

   For some constant leakage probability p and some start compiler CC_0 with constant parameters, we get $k_0 = \mathcal{O}\left(\log_{d_0}(\Delta_i) \right)$ giving an asymptotic complexity blowup of

$$\mathcal{O}\left(\lambda_0^{k_0} \lambda_i^{k_i} \right) = \mathcal{O}\left(\Delta_i^{e_0} \kappa^{e_i} \right) \quad \text{with} \quad e_0 = \frac{\log_2(\lambda_0)}{\log_2(d_0)} \quad \text{and} \quad e_i = \frac{\log_2(\lambda_i)}{\log_2(d_i)} . \tag{15}$$

Then for any choice of i we get an asymptotic complexity blowup of $\mathcal{O}\left(\kappa^{e_i} \right)$ which is the same asymptotic complexity as the standard expanding compiler with base compiler CC_i. On the other hand, our simple dynamic compiler $CC_i^{(k_i)} \circ CC_0^{(k_0)}$ tolerates the same leakage rate as CC_0.

Using this simple approach we hence get the best of both worlds:

- a possibly inefficient RPE compiler CC_0 tolerating a high leakage rate q_0,
- a family of RPE compilers $\{CC_i\}_i$ with complexity exponent $e_i = \frac{\log_2(\lambda_i)}{\log_2(d_i)}$ decreasing with i.

We stress that for monotonously increasing λ_i and d_i, the asymptotic complexity of our simple approach is $\mathcal{O}(\kappa^e)$ where e can be made arbitrary close to $\lim_{i\to\infty} \frac{\log_2(\lambda_i)}{\log_2(d_i)}$.

Application. To illustrate the benefits of our dynamic approach, we simply get back to the experimentations on the AES implementation from [9]. The authors apply either a 3-share or 5-share compiler repeatedly until they reach their targeted security level. While using the 5-share compiler reduces the tolerated probability, we demonstrate that we can use both compilers to get the best tolerated probability as well as a better complexity.

Figure 1 illustrates the trade-offs in terms of achieved security level and complexity of the expansion strategy when using different compilers at each iteration of the expansion. Starting from a tolerated leakage probability p ($2^{-7.6}$ on the left and $2^{-9.5}$ on the right), the empty bullets (○) give this trade-off when only the 3-share compiler is iterated. In this case, the final security function ε from Theorem 1 is equal to $f_3^{(k_3)}(p)$ if we consider f_3 to be the failure function of the 3-share compiler, for a certain number of iterations k_3 which is written next to each empty bullet on the figure. On the other hand, the black bullets (●) represent the trade-offs achieved in terms of complexity and security levels while combining both compilers with different numbers of iterations. In this case, we start the expansion with a certain number of iterations k_3 of the 3-share compiler, and then we continue with k_5 iterations of the 5-share compiler of failure function f_5, the final compiled circuit is then random probing secure with $\varepsilon = f_5^{(k_5)}(f_3^{(k_3)}(p))$ for $p \in \{2^{-7.6}, 2^{-9.5}\}$. The number of iterations of the compilers is written next to each black bullet in the format k_3-k_5.

For instance, starting from the best tolerated probability $2^{-7.6}$, the static compiler from [9,10] requires 11 applications of the 3-share compiler to achieve a security level of at least 80 bits. This effort comes with an overall complexity of $10^{17.52}$. Using our dynamic approach, we can combine the 3-share and the 5-share to achieve this 80 bits security level for the same tolerated probability but with a complexity of $10^{16.04}$. That would require 7 iterations of the 3-share compiler and 2 iterations of the 5-share compiler. Starting from the same leakage probability, a security level of at least 128 bits is achieved also with 11 applications of the 3-share compiler with a complexity of $10^{17.52}$. In order to achieve at least the same security, we would need more iterations of both compilers in the dynamic approach. With 7 iterations of the 3-share compiler and 3 iterations of the 5-share compiler, we get a complexity of $10^{17.62}$ which is very close to the complexity of

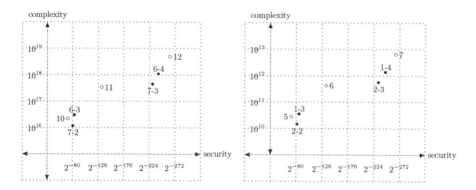

Fig. 1. Complexity of random probing AES for different security levels for a tolerated probability of $2^{-7.6}$ (left) or $2^{-9.5}$ (right).

the 3-share application alone, while achieving a security level of 231 bits. That is, we almost double the security level achieved using 11 iterations of the 3-share compiler with an almost equal complexity. For a tolerated probability of $2^{-7.6}$ and at least 128 bits of security, note that 11 applications of the 3-share compiler yield a security order of 2^{-135} while both other trade-offs directly yield security orders of 2^{-242} (6 iterations of 3-share and 4 iterations of 5-share) and 2^{-231} (7 iterations of 3-share and 3 iterations of 5-share), with one less iteration they would be below 128 bits, which explains their more important complexity. The same behavior can be observed with a starting tolerated leakage probability of $2^{-9.5}$ on the right.

The above results motivate the next contributions of this paper, namely finding RPE compilers which achieve the maximal amplification orders and which benefit from good asymptotic complexity (*i.e.* gadgets defined for any number of shares n with amplification order increasing with n) in order to optimize the security-efficiency trade-off and to tolerate the best possible leakage probability. We showed this far that the tolerated leakage probability decreases with an increasing number of shares n. So if we want to tolerate the best leakage probability, we would start with a few iterations of a compiler with a small number of shares and which tolerates a good leakage probability (which can be computed for instance with the verification tool VRAPS [9]), typically a 3-share construction. Meanwhile, after a few constant number of iterations, we can change to a different compiler which benefits from a better asymptotic complexity (as explained above with our simple approach). In the constructions from [10], the bottleneck in terms of asymptotic complexity was from the linear gadgets (addition and copy). Thanks to the quasilinear refresh gadget we introduce later in this paper, the bottleneck becomes the multiplication gadget (with n^2 multiplications), which we also improve in the following sections under some conditions on the base field.

4   Linear Gadgets with Quasi-Linear Complexity

In a first attempt, we aim to reduce the complexity of the linear gadgets that are to be used in our dynamic compiler.

In [10], the authors provide new constructions of generic addition and copy gadgets, using a refresh gadget G_{refresh} as a building block. The construction works for any number of shares and the authors prove the RPE security of the gadgets based on the security of G_{refresh}. In a nutshell, given a n-share refresh gadget G_{refresh}, the authors construct a copy gadget G_{copy} which on input sharing $(a_1, \ldots, a_n)$, outputs the sharings

$$\Big(G_{\text{refresh}}(a_1, \ldots, a_n), G_{\text{refresh}}(a_1, \ldots, a_n) \Big) \tag{16}$$

with two independent executions of G_{refresh}. The authors also construct an addition gadget G_{add} which, on input sharings $(a_1, \ldots, a_n)$ and $(b_1, \ldots, b_n)$, first refreshes the inputs separately, then outputs the sharewise sum of the results

$$\Big(G_{\text{refresh}}(a_1, \ldots, a_n) + G_{\text{refresh}}(b_1, \ldots, b_n) \Big). \tag{17}$$

If the refresh gadget G_{refresh} is TRPE of amplification order d, the authors show that G_{copy} is also TRPE of amplification order d, and G_{add} is TRPE of amplification order at least $\lfloor d/2 \rfloor$.

While the copy gadgets from [10] achieve an optimal amplification order, this is not the case yet for addition gadgets and we first aim to fill this gap. Precisely, we introduce a new property which, when satisfied by its inherent refresh gadget G_{refresh}, makes the addition gadget TRPE with the same amplification order as G_{refresh}. We then prove that this new property is actually satisfied by the refresh gadget from [6] which has quasi-linear complexity $\mathcal{O}(n \log n)$ in the sharing order n. Using this refresh gadget as a building block, we obtain linear gadgets G_{add} and G_{copy} with quasi-linear complexities.

Constructions of Linear Gadgets from a Stronger Building Block. We first define our new property (as a variant of properties defined in [9,10]) which proves to be a useful requirement for refresh gadgets when used as a building block of linear gadgets.

Definition 9 (*t*-Strong TRPE2). *Let G be an n-share 1-input gadget. Then G is t-Strong TRPE2 (abbreviated t-STRPE2) if and only if for any set J' of output shares indices and any set W of internal wires of G such that $|W| + |J'| \leq t$, there exists a set J of output share indices such that $J' \subseteq J$ and $|J| = n - 1$ and such that the assignment of the wires indexed by W together with the output shares indexed by J can be perfectly simulated from the input shares indexed by a set I of cardinality satisfying $|I| \leq |W| + |J'|$.*

Remark 1. This new property directly implies the TRPE2 property with maximal amplification order introduced in [10]. Recall that G is t-TRPE2 with maximal amplification order if and only if for any set W of probed wires such that

$|W| < \min(t+1, n-t)$, there exists a set J of output shares indices such that $|J| = n - 1$ and such that an assignment of the wires indexed by W and the output shares indexed by J can be jointly perfectly simulated from input shares indexed in a set I such that $|I| \leq |W|$.

Having a refresh gadget which satisfies the property from Definition 9 results in tighter constructions for generic addition gadgets as stated in Lemma 2. Its proof is given in the full version of this paper.

Lemma 2. *Let $G_{refresh}$ be an n-share refresh gadget and let G_{add} be the addition gadget described in Eq. (17). Then if $G_{refresh}$ is (t, f)-TRPE for any $t \leq n - 1$ of amplification order $d \geq \min(t+1, n-t)$ and $G_{refresh}$ is $(n-1)$-STRPE2, then G_{add} is (t, f')-RPE (resp. (t, f')-TRPE) for any $t \leq n-1$ for some f' of amplification order $\min(t+1, n-t)$.*

Instantiation of Linear Gadgets with Quasi-Linear Refresh Gadget. A refresh gadget with $\mathcal{O}(n \log n)$ complexity was introduced in [6]. In a nutshell, the idea is to add a linear number of random values on the shares at each step, to split the shares in two sets to apply the recursion, and then to add a linear number of random values again. The algorithmic description of this refresh gadget can be found in [6] or in the full version of the present paper. It was proven to be $(n-1)$-SNI in [6]. In Lemma 3, we show that this gadget is also (t, f)-TRPE of amplification order $\min(t+1, n-t)$ and that it satisfies $(n-1)$-STRPE2. The proof is given in the full version of this paper.

Lemma 3. *Let $G_{refresh}$ be the n-share refresh gadget described above from [6]. Then $G_{refresh}$ is (t, f)-TRPE for some function $f : \mathbb{R} \to \mathbb{R}$ of amplification order $d \geq \min(t+1, n-t)$. $G_{refresh}$ is additionally $(n-1)$-STRPE2.*

Hence, we can instantiate the generic copy and addition gadgets described in (16) and (17) using the above refresh gadget as $G_{refresh}$. We thus obtain RPE gadgets G_{add} and G_{copy} enjoying optimal amplification order in quasi-linear complexity $\mathcal{O}(n \log n)$.

Regarding the asymptotic complexity of the expanding compiler, the eigenvalues λ_1, λ_2 from Sect. 2 are hence now both in $\mathcal{O}(n \log n)$. At this point, only the quadratic number of multiplications in the multiplication gadget still separates us from a compiler of quasi-linear complexity. We tackle this issue in the next section by constructing a generic multiplication gadget. We finally end up with a full expanding compiler with quasi-linear asymptotic complexity.

5 Towards Optimal Multiplication Gadgets

In what follows we should distinguish two types of multiplication gates: regular two-operand multiplications on $\mathbb{K}$, that we shall call bilinear multiplications, and multiplications by constant (or scalar multiplications) which have a single input operand and the constant scalar is considered as part of the gate description.

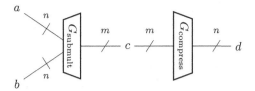

Fig. 2. n-share multiplication gadget G_{mult} from two subgadgets G_{submult} and G_{compress}

In previous works [9,10], the number of bilinear multiplications is the prominent term of the expanding compiler's complexity. While the most deployed multiplication gadgets (*e.g.*, [18]) require a quadratic number of bilinear multiplications in the masking order, the authors of [8] exhibited a probing secure higher-order masking multiplication with only a linear number of bilinear multiplications. Their construction, which applies on larger fields, is built from the composition of two subgadgets G_{submult} and G_{compress}, as described in Fig. 2. In a nutshell, on input sharings $\widehat{a}$ and $\widehat{b}$, the subgadget G_{submult} performs multiplications between the input shares of $\widehat{a}$ and $\widehat{b}$ as well as linear combinations of these products and it outputs a m-sharing $\widehat{c}$ of the product $a \cdot b$ where $m \geq n^1$. Next, the compression gadget G_{compress} compresses the m-sharing $\widehat{c}$ back into an n-sharing $\widehat{d}$ of the product $a \cdot b$.

The authors of [8] instantiate this construction with a sub-multiplication gadget which performs only $\mathcal{O}(n)$ bilinear multiplications and with the compression gadget from [11]. In addition to bilinear multiplications their sub-multiplication gadget additionally requires a quadratic number of linear operations (*i.e.*, addition, copy, multiplications by a constant) and random generation gates.

In the following, we rely on the construction [8] with its gadget G_{submult} which offers a linear number of bilinear multiplications to build a more efficient RPE multiplication gadget. In order to use it in our expanding compiler, we integrate an additional gate for the multiplication by a constant and discuss the resulting asymptotic complexity. We additionally demonstrate that the compression gadget of [8] is not $(n-1)$-SNI as claimed in the paper, and show that we can rely on other simple and more efficient compression gadgets which satisfy the expected properties.

5.1   Global Multiplication Gadget

We first define two new properties that G_{submult} and G_{compress} will be expected to satisfy to form a (t, f)-RPE multiplication gadget with the maximum amplification order from the construction [8].

Contrary to the usual simulation notions, the first *partial*-NI property distinguishes the number of probes on the gadget, and the number of input shares

---

[1] In case of a sharewise multiplication for instance, we would have $m = n^2$.

that must be used to simulate them. It additionally tolerates a *simulation failure* on at most one of the inputs (*i.e.*, no limitation on the number of shares for the simulation).

Definition 10 ((s, t)-partial NI). *Let G be a gadget with two input sharings $\widehat{a}$ and $\widehat{b}$. Then G is (s,t)-partial NI if and only any the assignment of any t wires of G can be perfectly simulated from shares $(a_i)_{i \in I_1}$ of $\widehat{a}$ and $(b_i)_{i \in I_2}$ of $\widehat{b}$ such that $|I_1| \leq s$ or $|I_2| \leq s$.*

The second property is a variant of the classical TRPE property that we refer to as *comp-TRPE*.

Definition 11 ((t, f)-comp-TRPE). *Let G be a 1-to-1 gadget with m input shares and n output shares such that $m > n$. Let $t \leq n - 1$ and $d = \min(t + 1, n - t)$. Then G is (t, f)-comp-TRPE if and only if for all set of internal wires W of G with $|W| \leq 2d - 1$, we have:*

1. *$\forall J, |J| \leq t$ a set of output share indices of G, the assignment of the wires indexed by W and the output shares indexed by J can be jointly perfectly simulated from the input shares of G indexed by a set I, such that $|I| \leq |W|$.*

2. *$\exists J', |J'| = n - 1$ a set of output share indices of G, such that the assignment of the wires indexed by W and the output shares indexed by J' can be jointly perfectly simulated from the input shares of G indexed by a set I, such that $|I| \leq |W|$.*

Similarly to what was done in [8] for the SNI property, we can prove that the composition of a gadget G_{submult} and G_{compress} which satisfy well chosen properties results in an overall multiplication gadget which is (t, f)-RPE specifically for any $t \leq n - 1$ achieving the maximum amplification order $d = \min(t + 1, n - t)$. This is formally stated in Lemma 4 which proof is given in the full version of this paper.

Lemma 4. *Consider the n-share multiplication gadget of Fig. 2 formed by a 2-to-1 multiplication subgadget G_{submult} of m output shares and a 1-to-1 compression gadget G_{compress} of m input shares such that $m > n$. Let $t \leq n - 1$ and $d = \min(t + 1, n - t)$. If*

- *G_{submult} is $(d - 1)$-NI and $(d - 1, 2d - 1)$-partial NI,*
- *G_{compress} is (t, f)-comp-TRPE,*

then the multiplication gadget G_{mult} is (t, f)-RPE of amplification order d.

5.2   Construction of G_{compress}

In a first attempt, we analyze the compression function that was introduced in [11] and used to build a multiplication gadget in [8]. As it turns out not to be SNI or meet our requirements for the expanding compiler, we exhibit a new and also more efficient construction in a second attempt.

G_{compress} from [8,11]. The authors of [8] use the $[m : n]$-compression gadget introduced in [11] for any input sharing m, using a $[2n : n]$-compression sub-gadget as a building block. In a nutshell, it first generates an *ISW*-refresh of the zero n-sharing $(w_1, \ldots, w_n)$. Then, these shares are added to the input ones $(c_1, \ldots, c_n)$ to produce the sequence of output shares $(c_1 + w_1, \ldots, c_n + w_n)$.

The compression gadget is claimed to be $(n-1)$-SNI in [8]. However, we demonstrate that it is not with the following counterexample. Let $n > 2$ and $i \in [n]$. We consider the set composed of a single output share of the compression procedure $J = \{(c_i + w_i) + c_{n+i}\}$ and the set of probes on the internal wires $W = \{w_i\}$. For the compression to be 2-SNI, we must be able to perfectly simulate both the wires in W and J with at most $|W| = 1$ share of the input $\hat{c}$. However, we can easily observe that $(c_i + w_i) + c_{n+i} - w_i = c_i + c_{i+n}$ requires the two input shares c_i and c_{i+n} to be simulated, which does not satisfy the 2-SNI property. In conclusion, the above gadget is actually not SNI, and interestingly it is not sufficient either for our construction, *i.e.* it does not satisfy Definition 11. This observation motivates our need for a new compression gadget which satisfies the necessary property for our construction.

New Construction for G_{compress}. In Algorithm 1, we exhibit a new $[m : n]$-compression technique using an m-share refresh gadget G_{refresh} as a building block. We demonstrate in Lemma 5 that this new compression gadget satisfies the necessary properties for our construction as long as $m \geq 2n$. The proof is given in the full version of this paper.

Algorithm 1: $[m : n]$-compression gadget

Input : $(c_1, \ldots, c_m)$ such that $m \geq 2n$, m-share refresh gadget G_{refresh}
Output: $(d_1, \ldots, d_n)$ such that $\sum_{i=1}^{n} d_i = \sum_{i=1}^{m} c_i$
$K \leftarrow \lfloor m/n \rfloor$;
$(c'_1, \ldots, c'_m) \leftarrow G_{\text{refresh}}(c_1, \ldots, c_m)$;
$(d_1, \ldots, d_n) \leftarrow (c'_1, \ldots, c'_n)$;
for $i = 1$ to $K - 1$ **do**
    $(d_1, \ldots, d_n) \leftarrow (d_1 + c'_{1+i \cdot n}, \ldots, d_n + c'_{n+i \cdot n})$;
end
for $i = 1$ to $m - K \cdot n$ **do**
    $d_i \leftarrow d_i + c'_{i+K \cdot n}$;
end
return $(d_1, \ldots, d_n)$;

Lemma 5. *Let $G_{compress}$ be the $[m : n]$-compression gadget from Algorithm 1 such that $m \geq 2n$. If $G_{refresh}$ is $(m-1)$-SNI and $(m-1)$-STRPE2, then $G_{compress}$ is (t, f)-comp-TRPE (Definition 11).*

As shown in Sect. 4, the refresh gadget from [5] is actually $(m-1)$-SNI and $(m-1)$-STRPE2 for any sharing order m. This gadget can then be used as a building block for the $[m:n]$-compression gadget, giving it a complexity of $\mathcal{O}(m \log m)$ and satisfying the necessary properties. In addition, this further provides an improvement over the complexity of the proposed gadget in [8] which has a complexity of $\mathcal{O}(\lfloor \frac{m}{n} \rfloor n^2)$ (because it performs a n-share ISW-refreshing $\lfloor \frac{m}{n} \rfloor$ times, see [8] for more details on the algorithm).

5.3   Construction of G_{submult}

To complete the construction of the overall multiplication gadget, we now exhibit relevant constructions for G_{submult}. We first rely on the construction from [8] which happens to achieve the desired goal in some settings. While all the cases are not covered by the state-of-the-art proposal, we then slightly modify the construction to meet all our requirements. Both constructions rely on linear multiplications that are not included yet on the expanding compiler. We thus start with a construction for this additional linear gadget that we further denote G_{cmult}.

Construction for G_{cmult}. We give a natural construction for G_{cmult} in Algorithm 2 which simply multiplies each input share by the underlying constant value and then applies a (t, f)-RPE refresh gadget G_{refresh}. Basically, with a (T)RPE refresh gadget G_{refresh}, we obtain a (T)RPE linear multiplication gadget G_{cmult} as stated in Lemma 6. The proof is given in the full version of the paper.

Algorithm 2: n-share multiplication by a constant

Input : sharing $(a_1, \ldots, a_n)$, constant value $\hat{c}$, n-share refresh gadget G_{refresh}
Output: sharing $(d_1, \ldots, d_n)$ such that $d_1 + \cdots + d_n = c.(a_1 + \ldots + a_n)$
$(b_1, \ldots, b_n) \leftarrow (c.a_1, \ldots, c.a_n)$;
$(d_1, \ldots, d_n) \leftarrow G_{\text{refresh}}((b_1, \ldots, b_n))$;
return $(d_1, \ldots, d_n)$;

Lemma 6. *Let $G_{refresh}$ be a (t, f)-(T)RPE n-share refresh gadget of amplification order d. Then G_{cmult} instantiated with $G_{refresh}$ is (t, f')-(T)RPE of amplification order d.*

Relying on an additional gate for the linear multiplication does not impact the security analysis and the application of the compilation, but it modifies the complexity analysis of the expanding compiler. From the analysis given in Sect. 2.4, a complexity vector is associated to each base gadget $N_G = (N_a, N_c, N_{cm}, N_m, N_r)^{\mathsf{T}}$ where N_a, N_c, N_{cm}, N_m, N_r stand for the number of addition gates, copy gates, constant multiplication gates, (bilinear) multiplication gates and random gates respectively in the corresponding gadget. The matrix M_{CC} is now a 5×5 square matrix defined as

$$M = \left(N_{G_{\mathrm{add}}} \mid N_{G_{\mathrm{copy}}} \mid N_{G_{\mathrm{cmult}}} \mid N_{G_{\mathrm{mult}}} \mid N_{G_{\mathrm{random}}} \right)$$

including, for each vector, the number of linear multiplications. Five eigenvalues $\lambda_1, \lambda_2, \lambda_3, \lambda_4, \lambda_5$ are to be computed, $i.e.$, one more compared to the expanding compiler in the original setting.

We can consider as before that multiplication gates are solely used in G_{mult} ($N_{G_{\mathrm{add}},m} = N_{G_{\mathrm{copy}},m} = N_{G_{\mathrm{cmult}},m} = 0$) and that constant multiplication gates are eventually solely used in G_{cmult} and G_{mult} ($N_{G_{\mathrm{add}},cm} = N_{G_{\mathrm{copy}},cm} = 0$) which is the case in the constructions we consider in this paper. It can be checked that (up to some permutation) the eigenvalues satisfy

$$(\lambda_1, \lambda_2) = \mathsf{eigenvalues}(M_{ac}) \ , \quad \lambda_3 = N_{G_{\mathrm{cmult}},cm} \ , \quad \lambda_4 = N_{G_{\mathrm{mult}},m} \quad \text{and} \quad \lambda_5 = n$$

where M_{ac} is the top left 2×2 block matrix of M_{CC}

$$M_{ac} = \begin{pmatrix} N_{G_{\mathrm{add}},a} & N_{G_{\mathrm{copy}},a} \\ N_{G_{\mathrm{add}},c} & N_{G_{\mathrm{copy}},c} \end{pmatrix} \ .$$

We get two complexity expressions for the expansion strategy

$$|\widehat{C}| = \mathcal{O}\left(|C| \cdot N_{\max}^{k}\right) \tag{18}$$

with $N_{\max} = \max(\mathsf{eigenvalues}(M_{ac}), N_{G_{\mathrm{cmult}},cm}, N_{G_{\mathrm{mult}},m}, n)$ and with the security parameter κ

$$|\widehat{C}| = \mathcal{O}\left(|C| \cdot \kappa^{e}\right) \quad \text{with} \quad e = \frac{\log N_{\max}}{\log d} \ .$$

Note that exhibited construction for the linear multiplication gadget requires $N_{G_{\mathrm{cmult}},cm} = n$ linear multiplications. Hence $\lambda_3 = N_{G_{\mathrm{cmult}},cm} = \lambda_5 = N_{G_{\mathrm{random}},r} = n$ and the global complexity (18) can be rewritten as

$$|\widehat{C}| = \mathcal{O}\left(|C| \cdot N_{\max}^{k}\right) \quad \text{with} \quad N_{\max} = \max(\mathsf{eigenvalues}(M_{ac}), N_{G_{\mathrm{mult}},m})$$

if the number of multiplications is greater than n. The asymptotic complexity of the RPE compiler is thus not affected by our new base gadget G_{cmult}. We now describe our constructions of G_{submult}.

G_{submult} from [8]. The authors of [8] provide a $(n-1)$-NI construction for G_{submult} which outputs $2n-1$ shares while consuming only a linear number of bilinear multiplications in the masking order. We first recall their construction which relies on two square matrices of $(n-1)^2$ coefficients in the working field. As shown in [8], these matrices are expected to satisfy some condition for the compression gadget to be $(n-1)$-NI. Since we additionally want the compression gadget to be $(d-1, 2d-1)$-partial NI, we introduce a stronger condition and demonstrate the security of the gadget in our setting.

Let $\mathbb{F}_q$ be the finite field with q elements. Let $\gamma = (\gamma_{i,j})_{1 \le i,j < n} \in \mathbb{F}_q^{(n-1) \times (n-1)}$ be a constant matrix, and let $\delta = (\delta_{i,j})_{1 \le i,j < n} \in \mathbb{F}_q^{(n-1) \times (n-1)}$ be the matrix defined by $\delta_{i,j} = 1 - \gamma_{j,i}$ for all $1 \le i, j < n - 1$. G_{submult} takes as input two n-sharings a and b and outputs the following a $(2n - 1)$-sharing c such that:

- $c_1 = \left(a_1 + \sum_{i=2}^{n}(r_i + a_i)\right) \cdot \left(b_1 + \sum_{i=2}^{n}(s_i + b_i)\right)$
- $c_i = -r_i \cdot \left(b_1 + \sum_{j=2}^{n}(\delta_{i-1,j-1}s_j + b_j)\right)$ for $i = 2, \ldots, n$
- $c_{i+n-1} = -s_i \cdot \left(a_1 + \sum_{j=2}^{n}(\gamma_{i-1,j-1}r_j + a_j)\right)$ for $i = 2, \ldots, n$

where r_i and s_i are randomly generated values for all $2 \le i \le n$. It can be easily checked that G_{submult} performs $2n - 1$ bilinear multiplications, and that it is correct, i.e. $\sum_{i=1}^{2n-1} c_i = \sum_{i=1}^{n} a_i \cdot \sum_{i=1}^{n} b_i$.

In [8], the authors prove that a gadget is $(n - 1)$-NI if one cannot compute a linear combination of any set of $n - 1$ probes which can reveal all of the n secret shares of the inputs and which does not include any random value in its algebraic expression. We refer to [8] for more details on this result.

Based on this result, the authors demonstrate in [8], that G_{submult} is $(n-1)$-NI if the matrices γ and δ satisfy Condition 1 that we recall below.

Condition 1 (from [8]). *Let $\ell = (2(n - 1) + 4) \cdot (n - 1) + 1$. Let $I_{n-1} \in \mathbb{F}_q^{(n-1) \times (n-1)}$ be the identity matrix, $0_{x \times y} \in \mathbb{F}_q^{x \times y}$ be a matrix of zeros (when $y = 1$, $0_{x \times y}$ is also written 0_x), $1_{x \times y} \in \mathbb{F}_q^{x \times y}$ be a matrix of ones, $D_{\gamma,j} \in \mathbb{F}_q^{(n-1) \times (n-1)}$ be the diagonal matrix such that $D_{\gamma,j,i,i} = \gamma_{j,i}$, $T_{n-1} \in \mathbb{F}_q^{(n-1) \times (n-1)}$ be the upper-triangular matrix with just ones, and $T_{\gamma,j} \in \mathbb{F}_q^{(n-1) \times (n-1)}$ be the upper-triangular matrix for which $T_{\gamma,j,i,k} = \gamma_{j,i}$ for $i \le k$:*

$$I_{n-1} = \begin{pmatrix} 1 & 0 & \ldots & 0 \\ 0 & 1 & & 0 \\ \vdots & & \ddots & \vdots \\ 0 & \ldots & 0 & 1 \end{pmatrix} \qquad D_{\gamma,j} = \begin{pmatrix} \gamma_{j,1} & 0 & \ldots & 0 \\ 0 & \gamma_{j,2} & & 0 \\ \vdots & & \ddots & \vdots \\ 0 & \ldots & 0 & \gamma_{j,n-1} \end{pmatrix}$$

$$T_{n-1} = \begin{pmatrix} 1 & 1 & \ldots & 1 \\ 0 & 1 & & 1 \\ \vdots & & \ddots & \vdots \\ 0 & \ldots & 0 & 1 \end{pmatrix} \qquad T_{\gamma,j} = \begin{pmatrix} \gamma_{j,1} & \gamma_{j,1} & \ldots & \gamma_{j,1} \\ 0 & \gamma_{j,2} & & \gamma_{j,2} \\ \vdots & & \ddots & \vdots \\ 0 & \ldots & 0 & \gamma_{j,n-1} \end{pmatrix}$$

We define the following matrices (with $n' = n - 1$):

$$L = \begin{pmatrix} 1 & \mathbf{0}_{1\times n'} & \mathbf{0}_{1\times n'} & \mathbf{0}_{1\times n'} & \mathbf{0}_{1\times n'} & \cdots & \mathbf{0}_{1\times n'} & \mathbf{1}_{1\times n'} & \mathbf{1}_{1\times n'} & \cdots & \mathbf{1}_{1\times n'} \\ \mathbf{0}_{n'} & \mathbf{I}_{n'} & \mathbf{0}_{n'\times n} & \mathbf{I}_{n'} & \mathbf{I}_{n'} & \cdots & \mathbf{I}_{n'} & \mathbf{T}_{n'} & \mathbf{T}_{n'} & \cdots & \mathbf{T}_{n'} \end{pmatrix}$$

$$M = \begin{pmatrix} \mathbf{0}_{n'} & \mathbf{0}_{n'\times n} & \mathbf{I}_{n'} & \mathbf{I}_{n'} & \mathbf{D}_{\gamma,1} & \cdots & \mathbf{D}_{\gamma,n'} & \mathbf{T}_{n'} & \mathbf{T}_{\gamma,1} & \cdots & \mathbf{T}_{\gamma,n'} \end{pmatrix}$$

Condition *1* is satisfied for a matrix γ *if for any vector $v \in \mathbb{F}_q^{\ell}$ of Hamming weight* $\mathsf{hw}(v) \leq n - 1$ *such that $L \cdot v$ contains no coefficient equal to 0 then* $M \cdot v \neq \mathbf{0}_{n-1}$.

In the above condition, the matrices $\mathbf{L}$ and $\mathbf{M}$ represent the vectors of dependencies for each possible probe. All the probes involving shares of $\hat{a}$ for matrix γ (and symmetrically shares of $\hat{b}$ for matrix δ) are covered in the columns of $\mathbf{L}$ and $\mathbf{M}$. Namely, the first column represents the probe a_0. As it does not involve any random, it results in a zero column in $\mathbf{M}$. The next columns represents the probes a_i, then the probes r_i. They are followed by columns for the probes $(a_i + r_i)$, then $(a_i + \gamma_{j-1,i-1}r_i)$ (for $2 \leq j \leq n$), then $a_1 + \sum_{i=2}^{k}(r_i + a_i)$ (for $2 \leq k \leq n$), and finally then $a_1 + \sum_{j=2}^{n}(\gamma_{i-1,j-1}r_j + a_j)$ (for $2 \leq i \leq n$ and $2 \leq k \leq n$). The above condition means that there is no linear combination of $(n-1)$ probes which can include the expression of all of the input shares, and no random variable.

From this result and by the equivalence between non-interference and tight non-interference developed in [8], we conclude that G_{submult} is $(d-1)$-NI for $d = \min(t+1, n-t)$ for any $t \leq n-1$. Lemma 4 also requires G_{submult} to be $(d-1, 2d-1)$-partial NI to get an overall RPE multiplication gadget. For G_{submult} to satisfy this second property, we need to rely on a stronger condition for matrices γ and δ that we present in Condition 2.

Condition 2. *Let $z = (2(n-1) + 4).(n-1) + 1$. Let $I_{n-1} \in \mathbb{F}_q^{(n-1)\times(n-1)}$, $\mathbf{0}_{\ell\times n} \in \mathbb{F}_q^{\ell\times n}$, $\mathbf{1}_{\ell\times n} \in \mathbb{F}_q^{\ell\times n}$, $\mathbf{D}_{\gamma,j} \in \mathbb{F}_q^{(n-1)\times(n-1)}$, $\mathbf{T}_{n-1} \in \mathbb{F}_q^{(n-1)\times(n-1)}$, $\mathbf{T}_{\gamma,j} \in \mathbb{F}_q^{(n-1)\times(n-1)}$ and L and M the same matrices as defined in Condition 1*

Condition 2 is satisfied for a matrix γ if and only if for any vector $v \in \mathbb{F}_q^z$ of Hamming weight $\mathsf{hw}(v) \leq n - 1$, *and for any $i_1, \ldots, i_K \in [z]$ such that $v_{i_1} \neq 0, \ldots, v_{i_K} \neq 0$ and the corresponding columns $i_1, \ldots, i_K$ in L and in M have no zero coefficient (i.e. there are K probes of the form $a_1 + \sum_{i=2}^{n}(r_i + a_i)$ or $a_1 + \sum_{j=2}^{n}(\gamma_{i-1,j-1}r_j + a_j)$ for any $i \in \{2, \ldots, n\}$), if $M.v = 0$, then we have* $\mathsf{hw}(L \cdot v) \leq \mathsf{hw}(v) - K$.

Based on this new condition, we can prove our second property G_{submult}, as stated in Lemma 7. The proof is given in the full version of this paper.

Lemma 7. *Let $t \leq n - 1$ such that either n is even or $t \neq \lfloor \frac{n-1}{2} \rfloor$ and let $d = \min(t+1, n-t)$. Let G_{submult} the multiplication subgadget introduced in [8]. If both matrices γ and δ satisfy Condition 2, then G_{submult} is $(d-1)$-NI and $(d-1, 2d-1)$-partial NI.*

The condition on t and n on Lemma 7 implies that the maximum amplification order for the multiplication gadget cannot be achieved for an odd number of shares (since the maximum order is reached when $t = \lfloor \frac{n-1}{2} \rfloor$). This is not a proof artifact but a limitation of the gadget G_{submult} with respect to the new $(d-1, 2d-1)$-partial NI property. We can easily show that under this extreme conditions on t and n, we have $2d - 1 = n$. If we consider the instantiation of G_{submult} for $n = 3$ input shares, we obtain the following $2n - 1 = 5$ output shares:

$$c_1 = (a_1 + (r_2 + a_2) + (r_3 + a_3)) \cdot (b_1 + (s_2 + b_2) + (s_3 + b_3))$$
$$c_2 = -r_2 \cdot (b_1 + (\delta_{1,1} \cdot s_2 + b_2) + (\delta_{1,2} \cdot s_3 + b_3))$$
$$c_3 = -r_3 \cdot (b_1 + (\delta_{2,1} \cdot s_2 + b_2) + (\delta_{2,2} \cdot s_3 + b_3))$$
$$c_4 = -s_2 \cdot (a_1 + (\gamma_{1,1} \cdot r_2 + a_2) + (\gamma_{1,2} \cdot r_3 + a_3))$$
$$c_5 = -s_3 \cdot (a_1 + (\gamma_{2,1} \cdot r_2 + a_2) + (\gamma_{2,2} \cdot r_3 + a_3))$$

To prove the $(d-1, 2d-1)$-partial NI property, we need to ensure that any set of at most $2d - 1 = 3$ probes can be perfectly simulated from at most $d - 1 = 1$ shares of one of the input and any number of shares from the other one. However, the three probes on c_1, c_3, c_4 reveal information on each of their sub-product. In particular, $(a_1 + (r_2 + a_1) + (r_3 + a_3))$ (from c_1), r_3 (from c_3) and $(a_1 + (\gamma_{1,1} \cdot r_2 + a_2) + (\gamma_{1,2} \cdot r_3 + a_3))$ (from c_4) would reveal $\hat{a}$. Similarly, $(b_1 + (s_2 + b_2) + (s_3 + b_3))$ (from c_1), $(b_1 + (\delta_{2,1} \cdot s_2 + b_2) + (\delta_{2,2} \cdot s_3 + b_3))$ (from c_3) and s_2 (from c_4) would reveal $\hat{b}$. Hence, the gadget is not $(d-1, 2d-1)$-partial NI. This counterexample with 3 shares can be directly extended to any odd number of shares.

This counterexample motivates a new construction for G_{submult} which would cover all values for n and t. In the following, we slightly modify the construction from [8] to achieve the maximum amplification order in any setting.

Remark 2. The current construction of G_{submult} outputs $m = 2n - 1$ shares, which does not satisfy the requirement $m \geq 2n$ shares for the compression gadget. Nevertheless, it is enough to add an artificial extra share c_{2n-1} equal to zero between both building blocks. In particular, the compression gadget (and subsequently and the refresh gadget) does not expect the input sharing to be uniform to achieve the stated security properties.

New Construction for G_{submult}. As stated earlier, Lemma 7 does not hold for G_{submult} in the case where n is odd and $t = (n-1)/2$. In order to cover this case, we propose a slightly modified version of G_{submult} with two extra random values r_0 and s_0. In this version, we let $\gamma = (\gamma_{i,j})_{1 \leq i,j \leq n} \in \mathbb{F}_q^{n \times n}$ be a constant matrix, and let $\delta \in \mathbb{F}_q^{n \times n}$ be the matrix defined by $\delta_{i,j} = 1 - \gamma_{i,j}$. The sub-gadget G_{submult} outputs $2n + 1$ shares:

- $c_1 = \left(\sum_{i=1}^{n} (r_i + a_i) \right) \cdot \left(\sum_{i=1}^{n} (s_i + b_i) \right)$

- $c_{i+1} = -r_i \cdot \left(\sum_{j=1}^{n} (\delta_{i,j} s_j + b_j) \right)$ for $i = 1, \ldots, n$
- $c_{i+n+1} = -s_i \cdot \left(\sum_{j=1}^{n} (\gamma_{i,j} r_j + a_j) \right)$ for $i = 1, \ldots, n$

where r_i and s_i are randomly generated values. It can be easily checked that G_{submult} now performs $2n + 1$ bilinear multiplications, and that it is correct, i.e. $\sum_{i=1}^{2n+1} c_i = \sum_{i=1}^{n} a_i \cdot \sum_{i=1}^{n} b_i$.

We now need the following slightly modified version of Condition 2 on γ and on δ, which instead of considering a linear combination of at most $n-1$ probes as in Condition 2, considers up to n probes:

Condition 3. *Let $z = (2n+4) \cdot n$. Let $I_n \in \mathbb{F}_q^{n \times n}$ be the identity matrix, $0_{\ell \times n} \in \mathbb{F}_q^{\ell \times n}$ be the matrix of zeros, $1_{\ell \times n} \in \mathbb{F}_q^{\ell \times n}$ be the matrix of ones, $D_{\gamma,j} \in \mathbb{F}_q^{n \times n}$ be the diagonal matrix such that $D_{\gamma,j,i,i} = \gamma_{j,i}$, $T_n \in \mathbb{F}_q^{n \times n}$ be the upper triangular matrix with just ones, $T_{\gamma,j} \in \mathbb{F}_q^{n \times n}$ be the upper triangular matrix such that $T_{\gamma,j,i,k} = \gamma_{j,i}$ for $i \leq k$. We define the following matrices:*

$$L = \begin{bmatrix} I_n & | 0_{n \times n} | & I_n & | & I_n & | & \cdots & | & I_n & | & T_n & | & T_n & | & \cdots & | & T_n \end{bmatrix}$$
$$M = \begin{bmatrix} 0_{n \times n} & | & I_n & | & I_n & | D_{\gamma,1} | & \cdots & | D_{\gamma,n} | & T_n & | T_{\gamma,1} | & \cdots & | T_{\gamma,n} \end{bmatrix}$$

Then we say that γ satisfies Condition 3 if and only if

- *for any vector $v \in \mathbb{F}_q^z$ of Hamming weight $\text{hw}(v) \leq n$,*
- *for any $i_1, \ldots, i_K \in [z]$ such that $v_{i_1} \neq 0, \ldots, v_{i_K} \neq 0$ and the corresponding columns $i_1, \ldots, i_K$ in L and in M have no zero coefficient (i.e. there are K probes of the form $a_0 + \sum_{i=1}^{n-1} (r_i + a_i)$ or $a_0 + \sum_{j=1}^{n-1} (\gamma_{i,j} r_j + a_j)$ for any $i = 0, \ldots, n-1$),*

if $M \cdot v = 0$, then we have $\text{hw}(L \cdot v) \leq \text{hw}(v) - K$.

Under this new condition, we obtain the following result, whose proof is available in the full version.

Lemma 8. *Let $t \leq n - 1$ and $d = \min(t + 1, n - t)$. Let G_{submult} as defined above with n-share inputs. If both matrices γ and δ satisfy Condition 3, then G_{submult} is $(d-1)$-NI and $(d-1, 2d-1)$-partial NI.*

Remark 3. The number of output shares $m = 2n + 1$ of G_{submult} satisfies the constraint required by G_{compress} in Algorithm 1 ($m \geq 2n$). We can thus use the compression gadget G_{compress} exactly as described in the algorithm on the input sharing $(c_0, \ldots, c_{2n})$, instantiated with the $\mathcal{O}(n \log n)$ refresh gadget from Sect. 4. Since the multiplication sub-gadget G_{submult} requires $\mathcal{O}(n)$ random values and G_{compress} requires $\mathcal{O}(n \log n)$ random values from the refresh gadget, the overall multiplication gadget G_{mult} also requires a quasi-linear number of random values $\mathcal{O}(n \log n)$.

5.4   Instantiations

We first state the existence of a matrix γ which satisfies Condition 3 over any finite field $\mathbb{F}_q$ for q large enough (with $\log(q) = \Omega(n \log n))^2$. The proof technique follows closely the proof of [8, Theorem 4.5] and makes use of the non-constructive "probabilistic method". Specifically, it states that if one chooses γ uniformly at random in $\mathbb{F}_q^{n \log n}$, the probability that the matrix γ satisfies Condition 3 is strictly positive, when q is large enough. It is important to note that the proof relies on probability but the existence of a matrix γ which satisfies Condition 3 (for q large enough) is guaranteed without any possible error.

Theorem 4. *For any $n \geq 1$, for any prime power q, if γ is chosen uniformly in $\mathbb{F}_q^{n \times n}$, then*

$$\Pr[\gamma \text{ satisfies Condition 3}] \geq 1 - 2 \cdot (12n)^n \cdot n \cdot q^{-1} .$$

In particular, for any $n \geq 1$, there exists an integer $Q = \mathcal{O}(n)^{n+1}$, such that for any prime power $q \geq Q$, there exists a matrix $\gamma \in \mathbb{F}_q^{n \times n}$ satisfying Condition 3.

As when γ is uniformly random, so is δ, Theorem 4 immediately follows from the following proposition and the union bound.

Proposition 1. *For any $n \geq 1$, for any prime power q, if γ is chosen uniformly in $\mathbb{F}_q^{n \times n}$, then*

$$\Pr[\gamma \text{ satisfies Condition 3}] \geq 1 - (12n)^n \cdot n \cdot q^{-1} .$$

In particular, for any $n \geq 1$, there exists an integer $Q = \mathcal{O}(n)^{n+1}$, such that for any prime power $q \geq Q$, there exists a matrix $\gamma \in \mathbb{F}_q^{n \times n}$ satisfying Condition 3.

The proof of this proposition is very technical but follows essentially the proof of the analogous [8, Proposition 4.6]. It is provided in the full version of this paper.

In [8], Belaïd et al.. presented examples of matrices which satisfy their condition for 2 shares and 3 shares. Karpman and Roche [19] proposed afterwards new explicit instantiations up to order $n = 6$ over large finite fields and up to $n = 4$ over practically relevant fields such as $\mathbb{F}_{256}$. It is worth mentioning that the matrices proposed in [19] are actually incorrect (due to a sign error) but this can be easily fixed and we check that matrices obtained following [19] also achieves our Condition 3. These matrices for 3, 4 and 5 shares are provided in the full version of this paper.

---

[2] Such large finite fields may actually be useful to build efficient symmetric primitives (see for instance MiMC [2]).

6   Improved Asymptotic Complexity

In the previous sections, we exhibit the construction of a multiplication gadget G_{mult} which performs a linear number of multiplications between variables, and a quadratic number of multiplications by a constant operations. Using the results of Lemmas 5, 8 and 4, the constructed multiplication gadget is RPE and achieves the maximum amplification order $\lfloor \frac{n+1}{2} \rfloor$ for any number of shares n.

Using the three linear gadgets proposed in Sect. 4 (G_{add}, G_{copy}, G_{cmult}) with the $\mathcal{O}(n \log n)$ refresh gadgets, and the proposed construction of the multiplication gadget G_{mult}, we get an expanding compiler with a complexity matrix M_{CC} of eigenvalues:

$$(\lambda_1, \lambda_2) = (n, 6n \log(n) - 2n) \,, \quad \lambda_3 = n \,, \quad \lambda_4 = 2n + 1 \quad \text{and} \quad \lambda_5 = n.$$

Hence we have $N_{\max} = 6n \log(n) - 2n = \mathcal{O}(n \log n)$.

Figure 3 illustrates the evolution of the complexity exponent with respect to the number of shares n, for the best construction provided in [10] with quadratic complexity for an expanding compiler (orange curve), and our new construction with quasi-linear complexity (pink curve). While the best construction from [10] yields a complexity in $\mathcal{O}(|C| \cdot \kappa^e)$ for e close to 3 for reasonable numbers of shares, the new expanding compiler quickly achieves a sub-quadratic complexity in the same settings.

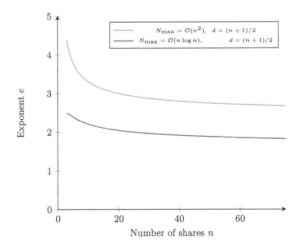

Fig. 3. Evolution of the complexity exponent $e = \log(N_{\max})/\log(d)$ with respect to the number of shares n. The orange curve matches the instantiation from [10] with quadratic asymptotic complexity ($N_{\max} = \mathcal{O}(n^2)$); the pink curve matches the new construction with quasi-linear asymptotic complexity ($N_{\max} = \mathcal{O}(n \log n)$). (Color figure online)

7 Conclusion

In this paper we have put forward a dynamic expansion strategy for random probing security which can make the most of different RPE gadgets in terms of tolerated leakage probability and asymptotic complexity. We further introduce new generic constructions of gadgets achieving RPE for any number of shares n. When the base finite field of the circuit meets the requirement of our multiplication gadget, the asymptotic complexity of the obtained expanding compiler becomes arbitrary close to linear, which is optimal.

As for concrete instantiations, our small example on the AES demonstrates the benefits of our dynamic approach. Namely, it provides the best tolerated probability (from the best suited compiler) while optimizing the complexity using higher numbers of shares. Using two compilers with 3 and 5 shares instead of a single one already reduces the complexity by a factor 10.

To go further in the concrete use of our expanding compiler, future works could exhibit explicit constructions of matrices with (quasi)constant field size for our multiplication gadget. One could also investigate further designs of RPE multiplication gadgets with linear number of multiplications for arbitrary fields. Another interesting direction is to optimize the tolerated leakage probability for a set of (possibly inefficient) small gadgets to be used as starting point of the expansion in our dynamic approach before switching to more (asymptotically) efficient RPE gadgets.

References

1. Ajtai, M.: Secure computation with information leaking to an adversary. In: Fortnow, L., Vadhan, S.P. (eds.) 43rd ACM STOC, pp. 715–724. ACM Press (June 2011)
2. Albrecht, M., Grassi, L., Rechberger, C., Roy, A., Tiessen, T.: MiMC: efficient encryption and cryptographic hashing with minimal multiplicative complexity. In: Cheon, J.H., Takagi, T. (eds.) ASIACRYPT 2016, Part I. LNCS, vol. 10031, pp. 191–219. Springer, Heidelberg (2016). https://doi.org/10.1007/978-3-662-53887-6_7
3. Ananth, P., Ishai, Y., Sahai, A.: Private circuits: a modular approach. In: Shacham, H., Boldyreva, A. (eds.) CRYPTO 2018, Part III. LNCS, vol. 10993, pp. 427–455. Springer, Cham (2018). https://doi.org/10.1007/978-3-319-96878-0_15
4. Andrychowicz, M., Dziembowski, S., Faust, S.: Circuit compilers with $O(1/\log(n))$ leakage rate. In: Fischlin, M., Coron, J.-S. (eds.) EUROCRYPT 2016, Part II. LNCS, vol. 9666, pp. 586–615. Springer, Heidelberg (2016). https://doi.org/10.1007/978-3-662-49896-5_21
5. Battistello, A., Coron, J.-S., Prouff, E., Zeitoun, R.: Horizontal side-channel attacks and countermeasures on the ISW masking scheme. In: Gierlichs, B., Poschmann, A.Y. (eds.) CHES 2016. LNCS, vol. 9813, pp. 23–39. Springer, Heidelberg (2016). https://doi.org/10.1007/978-3-662-53140-2_2

6. Battistello, A., Coron, J.-S., Prouff, E., Zeitoun, R.: Horizontal side-channel attacks and countermeasures on the ISW masking scheme. Cryptology ePrint Archive, Report 2016/540 (2016). https://eprint.iacr.org/2016/540
7. Belaïd, S., Benhamouda, F., Passelègue, A., Prouff, E., Thillard, A., Vergnaud, D.: Randomness complexity of private circuits for multiplication. In: Fischlin, M., Coron, J.-S. (eds.) EUROCRYPT 2016, Part II. LNCS, vol. 9666, pp. 616–648. Springer, Heidelberg (2016). https://doi.org/10.1007/978-3-662-49896-5_22
8. Belaïd, S., Benhamouda, F., Passelègue, A., Prouff, E., Thillard, A., Vergnaud, D.: Private multiplication over finite fields. In: Katz, J., Shacham, H. (eds.) CRYPTO 2017, Part III. LNCS, vol. 10403, pp. 397–426. Springer, Cham (2017). https://doi.org/10.1007/978-3-319-63697-9_14
9. Belaïd, S., Coron, J.-S., Prouff, E., Rivain, M., Taleb, A.R.: Random probing security: verification, composition, expansion and new constructions. In: Micciancio, D., Ristenpart, T. (eds.) CRYPTO 2020, Part I. LNCS, vol. 12170, pp. 339–368. Springer, Cham (2020). https://doi.org/10.1007/978-3-030-56784-2_12
10. Belaïd, S., Rivain, M., Taleb, A.R.: On the power of expansion: more efficient constructions in the random probing model. In: Canteaut, A., Standaert, F.-X. (eds.) EUROCRYPT 2021, Part II. LNCS, vol. 12697, pp. 313–343. Springer, Cham (2021). https://doi.org/10.1007/978-3-030-77886-6_11
11. Carlet, C., Prouff, E., Rivain, M., Roche, T.: Algebraic decomposition for probing security. Cryptology ePrint Archive, Report 2016/321 (2016). https://eprint.iacr.org/2016/321
12. Chari, S., Jutla, C.S., Rao, J.R., Rohatgi, P.: Towards sound approaches to counteract power-analysis attacks. In: Wiener, M. (ed.) CRYPTO 1999. LNCS, vol. 1666, pp. 398–412. Springer, Heidelberg (1999). https://doi.org/10.1007/3-540-48405-1_26
13. Coron, J.-S., Prouff, E., Rivain, M., Roche, T.: Higher-order side channel security and mask refreshing. In: Moriai, S. (ed.) FSE 2013. LNCS, vol. 8424, pp. 410–424. Springer, Heidelberg (2014). https://doi.org/10.1007/978-3-662-43933-3_21
14. Coron, J.-S., Rondepierre, F., Zeitoun, R.: High order masking of look-up tables with common shares. Cryptology ePrint Archive, Report 2017/271 (2017). https://eprint.iacr.org/2017/271
15. Duc, A., Dziembowski, S., Faust, S.: Unifying leakage models: from probing attacks to noisy leakage. In: Nguyen, P.Q., Oswald, E. (eds.) EUROCRYPT 2014. LNCS, vol. 8441, pp. 423–440. Springer, Heidelberg (2014) https://doi.org/10.1007/978-3-642-55220-5_24
16. Goubin, L., Patarin, J.: DES and differential power analysis the "Duplication" method. In: Koç, Ç.K., Paar, C. (eds.) CHES 1999. LNCS, vol. 1717, pp. 158–172. Springer, Heidelberg (1999). https://doi.org/10.1007/3-540-48059-5_15
17. Groß, H., Stoffelen, K., De Meyer, L., Krenn, M., Mangard, S.: First-order masking with only two random bits. In: Bilgin, B., Petkova-Nikova, S., Rijmen, V. (eds.) Proceedings of ACM Workshop on Theory of Implementation Security Workshop, TIS@CCS 2019, London, UK, November 11, 2019, pp. 10–23. ACM (2019)
18. Ishai, Y., Sahai, A., Wagner, D.: Private circuits: securing hardware against probing attacks. In: Boneh, D. (ed.) CRYPTO 2003. LNCS, vol. 2729, pp. 463–481. Springer, Heidelberg (2003). https://doi.org/10.1007/978-3-540-45146-4_27
19. Karpman, P., Roche, D.S.: New instantiations of the CRYPTO 2017 masking schemes. In: Peyrin, T., Galbraith, S. (eds.) ASIACRYPT 2018, Part II. LNCS, vol. 11273, pp. 285–314. Springer, Cham (2018). https://doi.org/10.1007/978-3-030-03329-3_10

20. Rivain, M., Prouff, E.: Provably secure higher-order masking of AES. In: Mangard, S., Standaert, F.-X. (eds.) CHES 2010. LNCS, vol. 6225, pp. 413–427. Springer, Heidelberg (2010). https://doi.org/10.1007/978-3-642-15031-9_28
21. Schramm, K., Paar, C.: Higher order masking of the AES. In: Pointcheval, D. (ed.) CT-RSA 2006. LNCS, vol. 3860, pp. 208–225. Springer, Heidelberg (2006). https://doi.org/10.1007/11605805_14

Multiparty Computation

Homomorphic Secret Sharing for Multipartite and General Adversary Structures Supporting Parallel Evaluation of Low-Degree Polynomials

Reo Eriguchi[1,3]([☒]) and Koji Nuida[2,3]([☒])

[1] The University of Tokyo, Tokyo, Japan
reo-eriguchi@g.ecc.u-tokyo.ac.jp
[2] Kyushu University, Fukuoka, Japan
nuida@imi.kyushu-u.ac.jp
[3] National Institute of Advanced Industrial Science and Technology, Tokyo, Japan

Abstract. Homomorphic secret sharing (HSS) for a function f allows input parties to distribute shares for their private inputs and then locally compute output shares from which the value of f is recovered. HSS can be directly used to obtain a two-round multiparty computation (MPC) protocol for possibly non-threshold adversary structures whose communication complexity is independent of the size of f. In this paper, we propose two constructions of HSS schemes supporting parallel evaluation of a single low-degree polynomial and tolerating multipartite and general adversary structures. Our multipartite scheme tolerates a wider class of adversary structures than the previous multipartite one in the particular case of a single evaluation and has exponentially smaller share size than the general construction. While restricting the range of tolerable adversary structures (but still applicable to non-threshold ones), our schemes perform ℓ parallel evaluations with communication complexity approximately $\ell/\log \ell$ times smaller than simply using ℓ independent instances. We also formalize two classes of adversary structures taking into account real-world situations to which the previous threshold schemes are inapplicable. Our schemes then perform $\Omega(m)$ parallel evaluations with almost the same communication cost as a single evaluation, where m is the number of parties.

Keywords: Homomorphic secret sharing · General adversary structure · Parallel evaluation

1 Introduction

This paper concerns a large-scale multiparty computation (MPC), in which the number m of parties are considerably large, e.g., $m = 1000$ [25]. We also aim at realizing parallel evaluation of a single low-degree polynomial (or SIMD operations) [9,19]. That setting practically appears in privacy-preserving statistics and machine learning. A fundamental analysis such as linear regression can be

© International Association for Cryptologic Research 2021
M. Tibouchi and H. Wang (Eds.): ASIACRYPT 2021, LNCS 13091, pp. 191–221, 2021.
https://doi.org/10.1007/978-3-030-92075-3_7

expressed as an m-variate polynomial of constant degree [11,24]. We should involve a large number of inputs to make analysis results useful. Furthermore, amortized communication cost is important if the same analysis is performed on different data sets.

The privacy requirement is specified by an adversary structure Δ, a family of all possible corrupted subsets of the whole set P. Although Δ may contain all strict subsets, the all-but-one corruption is an unrealistically strong setting. Moreover, the only possible solution in that setting would be using fully homomorphic encryption (FHE) [21,32] or general-purpose MPC (e.g., [3,13,23]). The existing FHE schemes are based on a narrow class of assumptions and their concrete efficiency leaves much to be desired. General-purpose MPC results in considerably large communication complexity proportional to the function description size, which is $O(m^d)$ for a degree-d polynomial. It is then important to improve performance by focusing on practical adversary structures. For example, many real-world situations are expressed by multipartite adversary structures [18], in which P is divided into L parts P_j and whether each subset X is in Δ is determined by $(|X \cap P_1|, \ldots, |X \cap P_L|)$.

Homomorphic secret sharing (HSS) [6] allows m parties to distribute shares for their inputs and then locally compute output shares from which the output of a function is recovered. HSS offers protection against bounded collusion and can be constructed from weak assumptions, such as the intractability of the Diffie-Hellman problem [14], or even information-theoretically. It is directly used to obtain a two-round MPC protocol whose point-to-point communication cost is linear in its share size, which is independent of the function description size.

There are several constructions of HSS schemes. The packed secret sharing scheme [19] is an information-theoretic scheme that generalizes Shamir's scheme [31] to support parallel evaluation, the scheme of [17] is an information-theoretic one for multipartite adversary structures, and the schemes of [26,30] are computational variants of Woodruff and Yekhanin's scheme [34] and the CNF scheme [2], respectively, which tolerate wider classes of adversary structures.

However, they do not give a satisfactory solution to practical non-threshold adversary structures Δ. The schemes [19,26] need to set a corruption threshold to the *maximum* size of $X \in \Delta$ and then are inapplicable if Δ contains *at least one* set of size exceeding their tolerable thresholds. The construction [30] is applicable to any adversary structure but results in exponentially large share size for multipartite ones. In addition, Δ is practically much smaller than maximally tolerable adversary structures of [17,26,30][1]. Then, the previous schemes satisfy unnecessarily strong privacy requirements and would limit the possibility of parallel evaluation. In summary, we need to construct HSS schemes tailored to given non-threshold adversary structures to tolerate corruptions in real-world situations and also to improve the amortized communication cost.

---

[1] Here, a maximally tolerable adversary structure of an HSS scheme means Δ such that the scheme cannot tolerate $\Delta \cup \{X\}$ for any $X \notin \Delta$.

1.1   Our Results

We propose HSS schemes for multipartite and general adversary structures assuming k-HE, homomorphic encryption for polynomials of degree $k = O(1)$. Our technical novelty is applying the packing technique of [19] to the non-threshold schemes [17,30]. It is especially not straightforward to apply it to [30], which does not involve polynomial interpolation.

HSS for Multipartite Adversary Structures. Let Δ be an L-partite adversary structure and N be the number of all vectors associated with maximal sets of Δ (Table 1). When performing ℓ parallel evaluations of a degree-d polynomial, the input and output share sizes of our scheme are $O(N \log(m + \ell))$ and $O(\log(m + \ell))$, respectively, omitting polynomial factors of the security parameter λ. Note that $N = O(m^L)$ and L is practically small, e.g., $L = 2$ [18]. As a result, we obtain an MPC protocol for Δ whose communication complexity is logarithmic in ℓ and is approximately $\ell/\log \ell$ times smaller than [17] while the range of tolerable Δ degrades as ℓ increases (Fig. 1 (left)). Our scheme for $\ell = 1$ tolerates a wider class of adversary structures than [17]. By setting $L = 1$, we obtain a threshold HSS scheme (Table 2). Given k, d, and m, its tolerable threshold is strictly larger than [19]. Compared to [26], there is a trade-off between thresholds and share sizes. If a threshold t is smaller than $t^* = \lceil (k+1)m/d-1 \rceil$, our scheme can perform $\ell \leq t^* - t$ parallel evaluations with communication cost $\ell/\log \ell$ times smaller than [26].

Table 1. Comparison of HSS schemes for an L-partite adversary structure Δ supporting ℓ parallel evaluations of a degree-d polynomial. Let $\Pi = (P_j)_{j \in [L]}$ be an L-partition of P, $\{a_1, \ldots, a_N\}$ be the collection of $(|X \cap P_j|)_{j \in [L]}$ for all maximal sets X, and $\Phi^{\Pi}(P) = (|P_j|)_{j \in [L]}$ (see Sect. 3.3). Define $\epsilon_{k,d}(\Delta) = \min\{|(k+1)\Phi^{\Pi}(P) - (a_{i_1} + \cdots + a_{i_d})|_{\infty} : 1 \leq i_1 \leq \ldots \leq i_d \leq N\}$, where $|v|_{\infty} = \max_{j \in [L]}\{\max\{v_j, 0\}\}$ for $v = (v_j)_{j \in [L]} \in \mathbb{Z}^L$.

Reference	[17]	Ours (Corollary 2)
Condition on Δ	$\epsilon_{0,d}(\Delta) > 0$	$\epsilon_{k,d}(\Delta) > d(\ell - 1)$
Input share size	$O(\ell N \log m)$	$O(N \log(m + \ell))$
Output share size	$O(\ell \log m)$	$O(\log(m + \ell))$
Assumption	–	k-HE

Table 2. Comparison of HSS schemes for a threshold adversary structure supporting ℓ parallel evaluations of a degree-d polynomial.

Reference	[19]	[26]	Ours (Corollary 1)
Threshold	$m/d - \ell$	$(k+1)m/d - 1$	$(k+1)m/d - \ell$
Input share size	$O(\log(m + \ell))$	$O(\ell \log m)$	$O(\log(m + \ell))$
Output share size	$O(\log(m + \ell))$	$O(\ell \log m)$	$O(\log(m + \ell))$
Assumption	–	k-HE	k-HE

HSS for General Adversary Structures. Let Δ be an adversary structure and N be the number of all maximal sets of Δ (Table 3). For ℓ parallel evaluations, the input and output share sizes of our scheme are $O(N\log(m+\ell))$ and $O(\log(m+\ell))$, respectively, omitting poly[λ] factors. Note that our scheme is applicable only to Δ such that $N = \text{poly}[m]$ to guarantee polynomial computational complexity while $N = O(2^m)$ in the worst case. Nevertheless, as shown below, there is an interesting class of adversary structures even if $N = O(m)$. We obtain an MPC protocol for Δ whose communication complexity is logarithmic in ℓ and is $\ell/\log\ell$ times smaller than [30] while the range of tolerable Δ degrades as ℓ increases (Fig. 1 (right)).

Table 3. Comparison of HSS schemes for a general adversary structure Δ supporting ℓ parallel evaluations of a degree-d polynomial. Let N be the number of all the maximal sets $\{B_1, \ldots, B_N\}$ and $\mathbf{1}_m$ is the all-ones vector. Let $\mathbf{a}_i \in \mathbb{Z}^m$ be such that the j-th entry is 1 if $j \in B_i$ and otherwise 0. Define $\delta_{k,d}(\Delta) = \min\{|(k+1)\mathbf{1}_m - (\mathbf{a}_{i_1} + \cdots + \mathbf{a}_{i_d})|_+ : 1 \le i_1 \le \ldots \le i_d \le N\}$, where $|\mathbf{v}|_+ = \sum_{j \in [m]} \max\{v_j, 0\}$ for $\mathbf{v} = (v_j)_{j \in [m]} \in \mathbb{Z}^m$.

Reference	[30]	Ours (Corollary 3)
Condition on Δ	$\delta_{k,d}(\Delta) > 0$	$\delta_{k,d}(\Delta) > (d+1)(\ell-1)$
Input share size	$O(\ell N)$	$O(N\log(m+\ell))$
Output share size	$O(\ell)$	$O(\log(m+\ell))$
Assumption	k-HE	k-HE

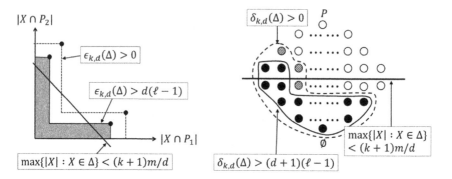

Fig. 1. Conceptual comparison between the threshold constraint, $\epsilon_{k,d}(\Delta) > 0$, and $\epsilon_{k,d}(\Delta) > d(\ell-1)$ for a 2-partite adversary structure (left) and between the threshold constraint, $\delta_{k,d}(\Delta) > 0$, and $\delta_{k,d}(\Delta) > (d+1)(\ell-1)$ for a general adversary structure (right). The circles to the right show the subsets of P ordered with respect to inclusion.

Formalization of Practical Adversary Structures. We formalize two classes of adversary structures and show advantages of our schemes over [17,19,26,30].

- Unbalanced 2-partite adversary structure: For parameters τ, σ and a 2-partition $\Pi = (P_1, P_2)$, we define a Π-partite adversary structure which contains all subsets X of size at most τm satisfying either $|X \cap P_1| \leq \sigma m$ or $|X \cap P_2| \leq \sigma m$. We suppose a situation in which an adversary belongs to either of the two parts and corrupts at most τm parties as in the threshold adversary structure but he is only able to corrupt σm parties from the other part. Our multipartite scheme can be applied to parameters τ, σ to which the threshold schemes [19, 26] cannot. It supports $\ell = O(m)$ parallel evaluations and decreases communication cost by $O(m)$ times compared to [17].
- Adversary structure induced by a random graph: For a graph on m parties (vertices), we define an adversary structure which contains the neighborhood of j for all vertices j, i.e., a subset of all vertices adjacent to j including j itself. That captures a situation in which an adversary is one of parties and corrupts all adjacent parties in the graph. We show that for a random graph whose edges occur independently with probability p, our HSS scheme for general adversary structures can be applied with high probability. Under certain parameter settings, our scheme supports $\ell = O(m)$ parallel evaluations and decreases communication cost by $O(m/\log m)$ times compared to [30]. The threshold schemes [19, 26] cannot be applied with high probability.

1.2   Related Work

There are packing methods of homomorphic encryption which packs many elements into a single ciphertext [12, 32] and it may be used to reduce the share size of [26, 30]. However, packing methods asymptotically reducing ciphertext size are based on the LWE assumption or the one that implies FHE.

Under the LWE assumption, spooky encryption [15] provides an HSS scheme for the adversary structure containing all strict subsets. The schemes [5–7] assume the client-server model, in which input parties have to trust and give sensitive information related to their inputs to a small number of external servers. They are only applied to $m = O(1)$ and not suited to our setting.

The authors of [26] show an MPC protocol with preprocessing whose online communication complexity is independent of the function description size. In the plain model, however, it ends up communication complexity linear in the description size since the preprocessing phase is jointly executed by input parties.

2   Technical Overview

In this section, we provide an overview of our constructions of HSS schemes. We give more detailed descriptions and security proofs in the following sections.

2.1   Adjusting the ILM Compiler [26] to Parallel Evaluation

The authors of [26] propose a compiler, which we call the ILM compiler, that converts an information-theoretic HSS (IT-HSS) scheme with *recovery information* to an HSS scheme using k-HE. In an IT-HSS scheme with recovery information, the decoding algorithm Dec needs to use auxiliary information to compute an output of a function. Our technical contributions are constructions of IT-HSS schemes supporting parallel evaluation, from which our HSS schemes are obtained by the ILM compiler. However, the original compiler assumes a single evaluation and a naive generalization ends up in output shares whose size is proportional to the number of evaluations. We need to consider in more detail an algebraic property of the IT-HSS scheme that the compiler assumes.

Specifically, to apply the ILM compiler, the output of Dec has to be expressed as $\boldsymbol{a}^\top \boldsymbol{y}$, where $\boldsymbol{y}$ is a vector representing an output share of the IT-HSS scheme and $\boldsymbol{a}$ is a vector whose entries are degree-k polynomials of recovery information. This is why the ILM compiler successfully works by letting a new sharing algorithm output ciphertexts $\widetilde{\boldsymbol{a}}$ for $\boldsymbol{a}$ and letting a new evaluation algorithm compute a ciphertext for $\boldsymbol{a}^\top \boldsymbol{y}$ from $\boldsymbol{y}$ and $\widetilde{\boldsymbol{a}}$. For ℓ parallel evaluations, the output of Dec is expressed as $\boldsymbol{A}\boldsymbol{y}$ using a matrix $\boldsymbol{A} = (\boldsymbol{a}_1, \ldots, \boldsymbol{a}_\ell)^\top$ whose entries are degree-k polynomials of recovery information. However, if the IT-HSS scheme only satisfies this algebraic property, an output share consists of ℓ ciphertexts for $\boldsymbol{a}_i^\top \boldsymbol{y}$, whose size is proportional to ℓ. We require a more involved property that the output of Dec is expressed as $\boldsymbol{C}\boldsymbol{A}\boldsymbol{y}$ using $\boldsymbol{A} = (\boldsymbol{a}_1, \ldots, \boldsymbol{a}_h)^\top$ whose entries are degree-k polynomials of recovery information and an ℓ-by-h constant matrix $\boldsymbol{C}$. Then, an output share consists of h ciphertexts for $\boldsymbol{a}_i^\top \boldsymbol{y}$ and the decoding procedures can be done by only using public information $\boldsymbol{C}$. An important feature is that the output share size is constant (ignoring poly$[\lambda]$ factors) if we can choose h independent of ℓ.

2.2   HSS for Multipartite Adversary Structures

As a warm-up, we construct an HSS scheme for threshold adversary structures by applying the ILM compiler to a variant of the packed secret sharing scheme [19] whose recovery information is derivatives of an interpolating polynomial. That construction is a natural generalization of the IT-HSS scheme [26,34], which is a variant of Shamir's scheme using derivatives as recovery information. Specifically, we fix $m+\ell$ points $\zeta_1, \ldots, \zeta_m, \eta_1, \ldots, \eta_\ell$. For a threshold t and a vector of ℓ inputs $\boldsymbol{x}$, the sharing algorithm chooses a random polynomial φ of degree $t + \ell - 1$ such that $(\varphi(\eta_i))_{i\in[\ell]} = \boldsymbol{x}$, and set input shares as $(\varphi(\zeta_j))_{j\in[m]}$ and recovery information as the derivatives of φ of the up to k-th order on the ζ_j's. Since the degree of the interpolating polynomial is at most $d(t + \ell - 1)$ after evaluating a degree-d polynomial, the decoding succeeds if $d(t + \ell - 1) < (k + 1)m$ due to Hermite interpolation [33].

To deal with an L-partite adversary structure, we recall the HSS scheme [17], which decompose it to many threshold sub-structures and combines Shamir's schemes realizing them. We replace Shamir's schemes used there with the above variant of the packed scheme. In our resulting scheme, an input vector $\boldsymbol{x}$ can be additively split into $\boldsymbol{x}_1, \ldots, \boldsymbol{x}_N$, where N is the number of the sub-structures, and each $\boldsymbol{x}_u$ is shared by using the above threshold scheme. We can evaluate a degree-d polynomial if each monomial $\boldsymbol{x}_{u_1} * \cdots * \boldsymbol{x}_{u_d}$ is recovered by parties in some part of the L parts, where $*$ denotes the element-wise product. This is actually the case if the number of parties in some part exceeds a certain threshold relating to the degree of the interpolating polynomial for $\boldsymbol{x}_{u_1} * \cdots * \boldsymbol{x}_{u_d}$, which is formalized as the condition in Table 1.

Then, we can apply the ILM compiler to that IT-HSS scheme with recovery information. However, there still remains a problem of *context hiding*, which guarantees that output shares reveal nothing beyond the output value and is necessary for an application to MPC. Using a technique similar to [27], an HSS scheme for a single evaluation can be made context-hiding by modifying output shares so that they add up to the single output value and re-randomizing them by an additive sharing of zero. To output ℓ values, however, that solution results in communicating ℓ output shares each of which is an additive share of each output value. We observe that the set of all possible consistent output shares is a translation of a subspace W in a linear space V by an element $v \in V$ relating to the output values. Thus, we can re-randomize output shares by adding a random element from W, which can be predistributed in the sharing phase without increasing the share size asymptotically.

2.3   HSS for General Adversary Structures

Our starting point is the HSS scheme [30], which is the result of applying the ILM compiler to the CNF scheme [2]. In their scheme for Δ, a scalar input x is additively split into N elements x_u, where N is the number of all maximal sets of Δ and an index u corresponds to the u-th maximal set B_u. Then, an input share for the j-th party consists of x_u for all u with $j \notin B_u$ and his recovery information consists of x_u for all u with $j \in B_u$. To deal with a vector $\boldsymbol{x}$, we use the packing technique of [19], which is not straightforward since the above procedures do not involve polynomial interpolation. Specifically, we additively split $\boldsymbol{x}$ into N vectors $\boldsymbol{x}_u$ and distribute shares for $\boldsymbol{x}_u$ using the packed secret sharing among parties not in B_u instead of simply sending a copy of $\boldsymbol{x}_u$. That is, for each $u \in [N]$, the sharing algorithm chooses a random polynomial φ_u of degree $\ell - 1$ such that $(\varphi_u(\eta_i))_{i \in [\ell]} = \boldsymbol{x}_u$. It sets an input share for the j-th party as $\varphi_u(\zeta_j)$ for all u with $j \notin B_u$ and his recovery information as $\varphi_u(\zeta_j)$ for all u with $j \in B_u$ and some derivatives of φ_u on ζ_j for all $u \in [N]$. The input share size increases logarithmically in ℓ since each party receives elements from a field of size at least $m + \ell$.

The above scheme can evaluate a degree-d polynomial if for $\boldsymbol{u} = (u_1, \ldots, u_d) \in [N]^d$, sufficiently many values and derivatives of $\varphi_{u_1} \cdots \varphi_{u_d}$ is computed from input shares and degree-k polynomials of recovery information due to Hermite interpolation. However, this solution falls short of preventing the output share size from increasing linearly in ℓ since the coefficients in Hermite interpolation formula to compute $(\varphi_{u_1} \cdots \varphi_{u_d})(\eta_i)$ depend on $i \in [\ell]$ and hence parties need to send output shares separately for each $i \in [\ell]$. Instead, we introduce public polynomials $p_{\boldsymbol{u}}$ for all $\boldsymbol{u} \in [N]^d$ such that $p_{\boldsymbol{u}}(\eta_i) = 1$ for all $i \in [\ell]$ and that the values and derivatives of $g = \sum_{\boldsymbol{u} \in [N]^d} p_{\boldsymbol{u}} \varphi_{u_1} \cdots \varphi_{u_d}$ is computed from input shares and degree-k polynomials of recovery information. The condition in Table 3 comes from a sufficient condition for such polynomials to exist. An important feature is that the number of the values and derivatives of g to be communicated is independent of ℓ and that the decoding algorithm locally recovers g (and hence $g(\eta_i)$ for all $i \in [\ell]$) from them. Now, that scheme can perform ℓ parallel evaluations while the share size is logarithmic in ℓ. On the other hand, it has to pay the cost of degrading the range of tolerable adversary structures as ℓ increases since the degree of the interpolating polynomial g becomes higher.

3 Preliminaries

Notations. Let $\mathbb{Z}_+$ and $\mathbb{R}_+$ denote the sets of all non-negative integers and all non-negative real numbers, respectively. For $\ell \in \mathbb{N}$, define $[\ell] = \{1, \ldots, \ell\}$ and $[0..\ell] = \{0\} \cup [\ell]$. The power set of a set X is denoted by 2^X and X^m is the Cartesian product of m copies of X. Let $\mathbb{F}$ be a finite field or the ring of integers $\mathbb{Z}$. The vector $\mathbf{1}_m \in \mathbb{F}^m$ is the one whose entries are all one. The i-th component of $\boldsymbol{v} \in \mathbb{F}^m$ is denoted by $\boldsymbol{v}(i)$. If $\mathbb{F} = \mathbb{Z}$, define $|\boldsymbol{v}|_+ = \sum_{i \in [m]} \max\{\boldsymbol{v}(i), 0\}$ and $|\boldsymbol{v}|_\infty = \max_{i \in [m]}\{\max\{\boldsymbol{v}(i), 0\}\}$. For $\boldsymbol{v}, \boldsymbol{w} \in \mathbb{Z}^m$, we write $\boldsymbol{v} \preceq \boldsymbol{w}$ if $\boldsymbol{v}(i) \leq \boldsymbol{w}(i)$ for any $i \in [m]$ and $\boldsymbol{v} \prec \boldsymbol{w}$ if $\boldsymbol{v} \preceq \boldsymbol{w}$ and $\boldsymbol{v} \neq \boldsymbol{w}$. Let $f \in \mathbb{F}[X_1, \ldots, X_n]$ be an n-variate polynomial over $\mathbb{F}$. We say that f is a degree-k polynomial if its total degree is at most k. For $\ell \in \mathbb{N}$ and $(\boldsymbol{x}_1, \ldots, \boldsymbol{x}_n) \in (\mathbb{F}^\ell)^n$, we define $\mathcal{P}_\ell(f, (\boldsymbol{x}_1, \ldots, \boldsymbol{x}_n)) = (f(\boldsymbol{x}_1(j), \ldots, \boldsymbol{x}_n(j)))_{j \in [\ell]}$. Define the differential operator $\mathcal{D}$ as $(\mathcal{D}\varphi)(X) = \sum_i i c_i X^{i-1}$ for $\varphi = \sum_i c_i X^i \in \mathbb{F}[X]$. We assume $\mathcal{D}^0 \varphi = \varphi$. For two random variables R_1 and R_2 over a set $\mathcal{U}$, we write $R_1 \approx R_2$ if the statistical distance $\mathbb{SD}(R_1, R_2) = (1/2) \sum_{u \in \mathcal{U}} |\Pr[R_1 = u] - \Pr[R_2 = u]|$ is negligible in a security parameter. We write $u \leftarrow_{\$} \mathcal{U}$ if u is randomly chosen from $\mathcal{U}$.

3.1 Hermite Interpolation

We recall Hermite interpolation [33], which generalizes Lagrange interpolation in that it recovers a polynomial using its derivatives and values on given points.

Proposition 1 ([33]). *Let $m, k \in \mathbb{N}$ and $r_j \in [0..k]$ for $j \in [m]$. Let $\mathbb{F}$ be a prime field such that $|\mathbb{F}| \geq \max\{m, k+1\}$. Let $\zeta_1, \ldots, \zeta_m$ be m distinct elements of $\mathbb{F}$. Let $y_{j,w} \in \mathbb{F}$ for each $j \in [m]$ and $w \in [0..r_j]$. Then, there exists a unique polynomial $g \in \mathbb{F}[X]$ such that $\deg g < \sum_{j \in [m]}(r_j + 1)$ and $\mathcal{D}^w g(\zeta_j) = y_{j,w}$ for all $j \in [m]$ and $w \in [0..r_j]$. Furthermore, g can be written as $g(X) = \sum_{j=1}^m \sum_{w=0}^{r_j} A_{j,w}(X) y_{j,w}$ using some polynomials $A_{j,w}$ of degree less than $\sum_{j=1}^m (r_j + 1)$ whose coefficients are independent of the $y_{j,w}$'s.*

We require that $\mathbb{F}$ is a prime field such that $|\mathbb{F}| \geq k + 1$ to guarantee that $w!$ for all $w \in [k]$, which appear as denominators in Hermite interpolation formula, have inverses in $\mathbb{F}$. Let $\ell \in \mathbb{N}$ and assume that $|\mathbb{F}| \geq \max\{m + \ell, k + 1\}$. Let $\zeta_1, \ldots, \zeta_m, \eta_1, \ldots, \eta_\ell$ be $m + \ell$ distinct elements of $\mathbb{F}$, $\boldsymbol{\zeta} = (\zeta_1, \ldots, \zeta_m) \in \mathbb{F}^m$, and $\boldsymbol{\eta} = (\eta_1, \ldots, \eta_\ell) \in \mathbb{F}^\ell$. Applying Proposition 1 to the case of $r_1 = \cdots = r_m = k$ implies an $\mathbb{F}$-linear map $\mathsf{Hermite}_{\boldsymbol{\zeta}, \boldsymbol{\eta}} : \mathbb{F}^{(k+1)m} \to \mathbb{F}^\ell$ such that for any polynomial $g \in \mathbb{F}[X]$ of degree less than $(k+1)m$, it holds that $\mathsf{Hermite}_{\boldsymbol{\zeta}, \boldsymbol{\eta}}((\boldsymbol{z}_j)_{j \in [m]}) = (g(\eta_i))_{i \in [\ell]}$, where $\boldsymbol{z}_j = (\mathcal{D}^w g(\zeta_j))_{w \in [0..k]}$ for $j \in [m]$.

3.2   Homomorphic Encryption

We recall the notion of homomorphic encryption for degree-k polynomials.

Definition 1 (Homomorphic Encryption (HE)). *A homomorphic encryption scheme* $\mathsf{HE} = (\mathsf{KGen}, \mathsf{Enc}, \mathsf{Eval}, \mathsf{Dec})$ *for degree-k polynomials over* $\mathbb{F}$, *k-HE for short, consists of the following PPT algorithms:*

- $\mathsf{KGen}(1^\lambda)$: *Given the security parameter* 1^λ, *the key generation algorithm outputs a public key* pk *and a secret key* sk.
- $\mathsf{Enc}(\mathsf{pk}, \boldsymbol{x})$: *Given the public key* pk *and a message* $\boldsymbol{x} \in \mathbb{F}^n$ *for some* $n = \mathsf{poly}[\lambda]$, *the encryption algorithm outputs a ciphertext* $\boldsymbol{c} \in \mathcal{C}^n$ *in some ciphertext space* $\mathcal{C}$.
- $\mathsf{Eval}(\mathsf{pk}, f, \boldsymbol{c})$: *Given the public key* pk, *(a description of) a degree-k polynomial* $f \in \mathbb{F}[X_1, \ldots, X_n]$, *and a ciphertext* $\boldsymbol{c} \in \mathcal{C}^n$ *for some* $n = \mathsf{poly}[\lambda]$, *the evaluation algorithm outputs a ciphertext* $c' \in \mathcal{C}$.
- $\mathsf{Dec}(\mathsf{sk}, \boldsymbol{c})$: *Given the secret key* sk *and a ciphertext* $\boldsymbol{c} \in \mathcal{C}^n$ *for some* $n = \mathsf{poly}[\lambda]$, *the decryption algorithm outputs a plaintext* $\boldsymbol{x} \in \mathbb{F}^n$.

As in [27,30], we consider the standard notions of compactness, correctness, IND-CPA security, circuit privacy [8], and their multi-key variants. We provide the formal definitions in the full version. We focus on small $k = O(1)$, for which it is not known how k-HE can be bootstrapped [21] into FHE. For $k \in \{1, 2\}$, there exist efficient k-HE schemes [1,4,11,16,20,29]. For general $k = O(1)$, k-HE schemes can be constructed from the LWE assumption with smaller parameters than those which imply FHE, and therefore concretely efficient. There exist several multi-key HE schemes in the literature [10,28].

3.3   Adversary Structures

Let $P = [m]$ for $m \in \mathbb{N}$. A family Δ of subsets of P is monotonically decreasing if $A \in \Delta$ and $A \supseteq B$ imply $B \in \Delta$ for any $A, B \subseteq P$. We call a monotonically decreasing family of subsets of P an adversary structure on P. A set $A \in \Delta$ is called maximal if $A \subsetneq B$ implies $B \notin \Delta$ for any $B \subseteq P$. Let $\Pi = (P_1, \ldots, P_L)$ be an L-partition of P, i.e., $P_i \cap P_j = \emptyset$ for $i \neq j$ and $P = \bigcup_{j \in [L]} P_j$. A permutation τ on P is called a Π-permutation if $\tau(P_j) = P_j$ for any $j \in [L]$. An adversary structure Δ is called Π-partite [18] if $\tau(B) \in \Delta$ for any $B \in \Delta$ and any Π-permutation τ. There is a geometric representation of Π-partite adversary structures. Let $\Phi^\Pi : 2^P \to \mathbb{R}^L$ be a map defined by $\Phi^\Pi(X) = (|X \cap P_j|)_{j \in [L]}$. A Π-partite adversary structure Δ is uniquely determined by $\Phi^\Pi(\Delta)$. Note that, if $\boldsymbol{a} \in \Phi^\Pi(\Delta)$ and $\boldsymbol{a} \succeq \boldsymbol{b}$, then $\boldsymbol{b} \in \Phi^\Pi(\Delta)$ for any $\boldsymbol{a}, \boldsymbol{b} \in \Phi^\Pi(2^P)$. Thus, any Π-partite adversary structure Δ is uniquely determined only by specifying $\max \Phi^\Pi(\Delta) := \{\boldsymbol{a} \in \Phi^\Pi(\Delta) : \boldsymbol{a} \prec \boldsymbol{b} \preceq \Phi^\Pi(P) \Rightarrow \boldsymbol{b} \notin \Phi^\Pi(\Delta)\}$. For a real number τ with $0 \leq \tau \leq 1$, the threshold adversary structure $\mathcal{T}_\tau^m$ is defined by $\mathcal{T}_\tau^m = \{A \subseteq P : |A| \leq \tau m\}$. Note that $\mathcal{T}_\tau^m$ is Π-partite for any partition Π.

3.4 Homomorphic Secret Sharing

We provide the definition of homomorphic secret sharing in the public-key setup model [27]. Homomorphic secret sharing can be defined in the multi-key setting and then lifted to the plain model [6] as described below. In addition, we here distinguish between clients holding inputs and servers performing evaluation. However, this is only for simplicity of the syntax and descriptions of schemes. In its application to MPC, we suppose that clients themselves do evaluation of a function as well as sharing of their inputs.

Definition 2 (Homomorphic Secret Sharing (HSS)). *Suppose that there are n inputs and m servers. A homomorphic secret sharing scheme consists of four PPT algorithms* HSS = (KGen, Share, Eval, Dec):

- $(\mathsf{pk}, \mathsf{sk}) \leftarrow \mathsf{KGen}(1^\lambda)$: *Given the security parameter 1^λ, the key generation algorithm outputs a public key* pk *and a secret key* sk.
- $(\mathsf{in}_j^{\langle i \rangle})_{j \in [m]} \leftarrow \mathsf{Share}(\mathsf{pk}, i, \boldsymbol{x}^{\langle i \rangle})$: *Given the public key* pk, *an index $i \in [n]$, and an input $\boldsymbol{x}^{\langle i \rangle} \in \mathcal{X}$, the sharing algorithm outputs input shares $(\mathsf{in}_j^{\langle i \rangle})_{j \in [m]}$.*
- $\mathsf{out}_j \leftarrow \mathsf{Eval}(\mathsf{pk}, j, f, (\mathsf{in}_j^{\langle i \rangle})_{i \in [n]})$: *Given the public key* pk, *an index $j \in [m]$, (a description of) a function $f : \mathcal{X}^n \to \mathcal{Y}$, and the shares of the j-th server $(\mathsf{in}_j^{\langle i \rangle})_{i \in [n]}$, the evaluation algorithm outputs an output share out_j.*
- $y \leftarrow \mathsf{Dec}(\mathsf{sk}, (\mathsf{out}_j)_{j \in [m]})$: *Given the secret key* sk *and output shares $(\mathsf{out}_j)_{j \in [m]}$ from all servers, the decoding algorithm outputs y.*

The efficiency measures $\alpha = \alpha(n, m, \log |\mathcal{X}|)$ and $\beta = \beta(n, m, \log |\mathcal{Y}|)$ are the lengths of input and output shares, respectively (omitting poly$[\lambda]$ *factors). That is,* $\mathsf{in}_j^{\langle i \rangle} \in \{0, 1\}^{\alpha \cdot \mathsf{poly}[\lambda]}$ *and* $\mathsf{out}_j \in \{0, 1\}^{\beta \cdot \mathsf{poly}[\lambda]}$ *for any $i \in [n]$ and $j \in [m]$.*

Definition 3 (Correctness). *Let $\mathbb{F}$ be a finite field. An n-input m-server HSS scheme* HSS *is said to support ℓ parallel evaluations of degree-d polynomials over $\mathbb{F}$ if each input is a vector $\boldsymbol{x}^{\langle i \rangle} \in \mathbb{F}^\ell$ and the following holds: for any $\lambda \in \mathbb{N}$, any $n, m \in$* poly$[\lambda]$, *any $(\mathsf{pk}, \mathsf{sk}) \leftarrow \mathsf{KGen}(1^\lambda)$, any degree-$d$ polynomial $f \in \mathbb{F}[X_1, \ldots, X_n]$, any n-tuple of inputs $(\boldsymbol{x}^{\langle i \rangle})_{i \in [n]} \in (\mathbb{F}^\ell)^n$, any shares $(\mathsf{in}_j^{\langle i \rangle})_{j \in [m]} \leftarrow$* Share$(\mathsf{pk}, i, \boldsymbol{x}^{\langle i \rangle})$ *for $i \in [n]$, and any $\mathsf{out}_j \leftarrow \mathsf{Eval}(\mathsf{pk}, j, f, (\mathsf{in}_j^{\langle i \rangle})_{i \in [n]})$ for $j \in [m]$, it holds that* $\Pr\left[\mathsf{Dec}(\mathsf{sk}, (\mathsf{out}_j)_{j \in [m]}) = \mathcal{P}_\ell(f, (\boldsymbol{x}^{\langle 1 \rangle}, \ldots, \boldsymbol{x}^{\langle n \rangle}))\right] \geq 1 - \mathsf{negl}(\lambda)$.

It is sufficient for the HSS scheme to evaluate degree-d polynomials that is *homogeneous*, i.e., polynomials written as the sum of degree-d monomials. This is because we can pad any monomial of degree $d' < d$ with $d - d'$ copies of a dummy variable X_0. We set the corresponding input to $\boldsymbol{x}^{\langle 0 \rangle} = (1, \ldots, 1) \in \mathbb{F}^\ell$ and the shares of $\boldsymbol{x}^{\langle 0 \rangle}$ to some predetermined ones. For that reason, we assume in the following that a polynomial to be evaluated is homogeneous.

The security of an HSS scheme guarantees that collusion of servers in $B \in \Delta$ cannot guess inputs of clients from their input shares.

Definition 4 (Security). *Let Δ be an adversary structure on the set of servers. An n-input m-server HSS scheme* HSS *is said to satisfy Δ-privacy if for* *any PPT algorithm* $\mathcal{A} = (\mathcal{A}_0, \mathcal{A}_1)$, *there exists a negligible function* $\mathsf{negl}(\lambda)$ *such that for any* $\lambda \in \mathbb{N}$, $|\Pr[\mathsf{Security}^0_{\mathcal{A},\mathsf{HSS}} = 1] - \Pr[\mathsf{Security}^1_{\mathcal{A},\mathsf{HSS}} = 1]| < \mathsf{negl}(\lambda)$, *where* $\mathsf{Security}^b_{\mathcal{A},\mathsf{HSS}}$ *is defined in Fig. 2 (left) for* $b \in \{0,1\}$.

We use the shorthand (n, m, ℓ, d, Δ)-HSS to refer to n-input m-server homomorphic secret sharing that supports ℓ parallel evaluations of degree-d polynomials and satisfies Δ-privacy. Note that an $(n, m, 1, d, \Delta)$-HSS scheme HSS_1 with efficiency measures α_1 and β_1 can be trivially extended to an (n, m, ℓ, d, Δ)-HSS scheme HSS_ℓ with efficiency measures $\alpha = \ell\alpha_1$ and $\beta = \ell\beta_1$ by simply running ℓ independent instances of HSS_1.

The notion of context hiding [1] assures that the output client learns nothing beyond the output of the computation.

Definition 5 (Context Hiding). *An* (n, m, ℓ, d, Δ)-*HSS scheme* HSS *is said to be context-hiding if for any PPT algorithm* $\mathcal{A} = (\mathcal{A}_0, \mathcal{A}_1)$, *there exists a PPT algorithm* S_{HSS} *and a negligible function* $\mathsf{negl}(\lambda)$ *such that for any* $\lambda \in \mathbb{N}$, $|\Pr[\mathsf{ContextHiding}^0_{\mathcal{A},S_{\mathsf{HSS}},\mathsf{HSS}} = 1] - \Pr[\mathsf{ContextHiding}^1_{\mathcal{A},S_{\mathsf{HSS}},\mathsf{HSS}} = 1]| < \mathsf{negl}(\lambda)$, *where* $\mathsf{ContextHiding}^b_{\mathcal{A},S_{\mathsf{HSS}},\mathsf{HSS}}$ *is defined in Fig. 2 (right) for* $b \in \{0,1\}$.

$\underline{\mathsf{Security}^b_{\mathcal{A},\mathsf{HSS}}(1^\lambda):}$

$(\mathsf{pk}, \mathsf{sk}) \leftarrow \mathsf{KGen}(1^\lambda)$

$(\boldsymbol{x}_0, \boldsymbol{x}_1, B \in \Delta, \mathsf{state}) \leftarrow \mathcal{A}_0(\mathsf{pk})$

$(\mathsf{in}_1, \ldots, \mathsf{in}_m) \leftarrow \mathsf{Share}(\mathsf{pk}, \boldsymbol{x}_b)$

$b' \leftarrow \mathcal{A}_1(\mathsf{state}, (\mathsf{in}_j)_{j \in B})$

return b'

$\underline{\mathsf{ContextHiding}^b_{\mathcal{A},S_{\mathsf{HSS}},\mathsf{HSS}}(1^\lambda):}$

$(\mathsf{pk}, \mathsf{sk}) \leftarrow \mathsf{KGen}(1^\lambda)$

$(f, \boldsymbol{x}^{\langle 1 \rangle}, \ldots, \boldsymbol{x}^{\langle n \rangle}, \mathsf{state}) \leftarrow \mathcal{A}_0(\mathsf{pk})$

if $b = 0$ **then**

  $(\mathsf{in}_1^{\langle i \rangle}, \ldots, \mathsf{in}_m^{\langle i \rangle}) \leftarrow \mathsf{Share}(\mathsf{pk}, i, \boldsymbol{x}^{\langle i \rangle}), \ \forall i \in [n]$

  $y_j \leftarrow \mathsf{Eval}(\mathsf{pk}, j, f, (\mathsf{in}_j^{\langle i \rangle})_{i \in [n]}), \ \forall j \in [m]$

else

  $(y_1, \ldots, y_m) \leftarrow S_{\mathsf{HSS}}(1^\lambda, \mathsf{pk}, f(\boldsymbol{x}^{\langle 1 \rangle}, \ldots, \boldsymbol{x}^{\langle n \rangle}))$

endif

$b' \leftarrow \mathcal{A}_1(\mathsf{state}, (y_1, \ldots, y_m))$

return b'

Fig. 2. Security and context hiding experiments for HSS

The authors of [26] introduce the notion of information-theoretic HSS with recovery information, which is an intermediate primitive for constructing HSS in the sense of Definition 2. That variant guarantees that a secret is protected against unbounded adversaries but the decoding algorithm requires auxiliary information to compute the output of a function.

Definition 6 (Information-Theoretic HSS with Recovery Information). *An* (n, m, ℓ, d, Δ)-*IT-HSS scheme with recovery information consists of three algorithms* $\mathsf{HSS} = (\mathsf{Share}, \mathsf{Eval}, \mathsf{Dec})$:

- $(\text{in}_j^{\langle i \rangle}, \text{rec}_j^{\langle i \rangle})_{j \in [m]} \leftarrow \text{Share}(i, \boldsymbol{x}^{\langle i \rangle})$: *Given an input index $i \in [n]$ and an input $\boldsymbol{x}^{\langle i \rangle}$, the sharing algorithm outputs a set of input shares $(\text{in}_j^{\langle i \rangle})_{j \in [m]}$ and recovery information $(\text{rec}_j^{\langle i \rangle})_{j \in [m]}$.*

- $\text{out}_j \leftarrow \text{Eval}(j, f, (\text{in}_j^{\langle i \rangle})_{i \in [n]})$: *Given an index $j \in [m]$, (a description of) a degree-d polynomial f, and the shares of the j-th server $(\text{in}_j^{\langle i \rangle})_{i \in [n]}$, the evaluation algorithm outputs an output share out_j.*

- $y \leftarrow \text{Dec}((\text{out}_j)_{j \in [m]}, (\text{rec}_j^{\langle i \rangle})_{i \in [n], j \in [m]})$: *Given output shares $(\text{out}_j)_{j \in [m]}$ and recovery information $(\text{rec}_j^{\langle i \rangle})_{i \in [n], j \in [m]}$, the decoding algorithm outputs y.*

The definition of correctness is the same as Definition 3 except that Dec is allowed to take the recovery information as input. The definition of security is the same as Definition 4 except that the adversary $\mathcal{A}$ is unbounded.

Application to MPC. Any (m, m, ℓ, d, Δ)-HSS scheme has a direct application to m-input MPC for an adversary structure Δ. Assume that there are m input parties each holding their private inputs $\boldsymbol{x}^{\langle i \rangle}$ and a distinguished output party. For an m-variate degree-d polynomial f, consider the following protocol:

1. The output party generates $(\text{pk}, \text{sk}) \leftarrow \text{KGen}(1^\lambda)$ and publishes pk.
2. For $i \in [m]$, the i-th input party computes $(\text{in}_j^{\langle i \rangle})_{j \in [m]} \leftarrow \text{Share}(\text{pk}, i, \boldsymbol{x}^{\langle i \rangle})$ and sends $\text{in}_j^{\langle i \rangle}$ to the j-th input party for all $j \in [m]$.
3. For $j \in [m]$, the j-th input party computes $\text{out}_j \leftarrow \text{Eval}(\text{pk}, j, f, (\text{in}_j^{\langle i \rangle})_{i \in [n]})$ and sends it to the output party.
4. The output party outputs $y \leftarrow \text{Dec}(\text{sk}, (\text{out}_j)_{j \in [m]})$.

The Δ-privacy of the HSS scheme guarantees that an adversary corrupting a subset X of input parties such that $X \in \Delta$ cannot guess the inputs of parties not in X. In addition, if the scheme is context-hiding, the output party obtains nothing beyond $\mathcal{P}_\ell(f, (\boldsymbol{x}^{\langle 1 \rangle}, \dots, \boldsymbol{x}^{\langle n \rangle}))$. The individual communication complexity between input parties themselves is $\alpha \cdot \text{poly}[\lambda]$ and each input party sends an output share of length $\beta \cdot \text{poly}[\lambda]$ to the output party. Hence, the total communication complexity is at most $(\alpha m^2 + \beta m) \cdot \text{poly}[\lambda]$.

Multi-key HSS. As shown in [27], the syntax of HSS can be easily generalized to the multi-key settings by extending the evaluation algorithm so that all servers take as input all public keys of the participating input clients, the decoding algorithm takes as input all the corresponding secret keys. While the definition of security is unchanged and is required to hold for each secret key, the definitions of correctness and context hiding are extended accordingly. According to [27], multi-key HSS can be generically lifted to the plain model [6] requiring no public-key setup by simply letting input clients locally generate key pairs, adding their public keys and m-out-of-m additive shares of their secret keys to input shares, and letting servers relay the additive shares to an output client. Therefore, by instantiating it with a multi-key HSS scheme, we can lift the above MPC protocol to the plain model without increasing the order of communication complexity.

4 Adjusting the ILM Compiler to Parallel Evaluation

The ILM compiler [26] converts an IT-HSS scheme with recovery information to an HSS scheme based on HE. Although it originally assumes a single evaluation of polynomials, we can generalize the ILM compiler so that it is applicable to IT-HSS schemes supporting ℓ parallel evaluations. As shown in Sect. 2.1, that generalization is not trivial in that we need to consider in more detail an algebraic expression of the decoding algorithm to obtain an HSS scheme whose output share size is not proportional to ℓ.

Proposition 2. *Let* HSS_0 *be an* (n, m, ℓ, d, Δ)-*IT-HSS scheme and* HE *be an IND-CPA secure k-HE scheme. Assume that* HSS_0 *satisfies the following:*

- *An input share* $\mathsf{in}_j^{\langle i \rangle}$ *is a vector* $\boldsymbol{s}_j^{\langle i \rangle} \in \mathbb{F}^\alpha$.
- *Each piece of recovery information* $\mathsf{rec}_j^{\langle i \rangle}$ *is a vector* $\boldsymbol{r}_j^{\langle i \rangle} \in \mathbb{F}^\rho$.
- *An output share* out_j *is a vector* $\boldsymbol{y}_j \in \mathbb{F}^\beta$.
- $\mathsf{HSS}_0.\mathsf{Dec}((\mathsf{out}_j)_{j \in [m]}, (\mathsf{rec}_j^{\langle i \rangle})_{i \in [n], j \in [m]})$ *outputs* $\sum_{j \in [m]} \boldsymbol{C}_j(\boldsymbol{A}_j \boldsymbol{y}_j + \boldsymbol{b}_j)$, *where* $\boldsymbol{C}_j$ *is a constant ℓ-by-h matrix over $\mathbb{F}$ for some h, $\boldsymbol{A}_j$ is an h-by-β matrix whose entries are degree-k polynomials of $(\boldsymbol{r}_j^{\langle i \rangle})_{i \in [n]}$ over $\mathbb{F}$, and $\boldsymbol{b}_j$ is an h-dimensional vector whose entries are degree-k polynomials of $(\boldsymbol{r}_j^{\langle i \rangle})_{i \in [n]}$.*

Then, there exists an (n, m, ℓ, d, Δ)-*HSS scheme* HSS *with efficiency measures* $\alpha' = \alpha \log |\mathbb{F}| + \rho$ *and* $\beta' = h$.

Proof. For $j \in [m]$, write $\boldsymbol{A}_j = (\boldsymbol{p}_{j,1}, \ldots, \boldsymbol{p}_{j,h})^\top$, $\boldsymbol{b}_j = (q_{j,1}, \ldots, q_{j,h})^\top$, where $\boldsymbol{p}_{j,w}$ is a β-dimensional vectors of polynomials of $(\boldsymbol{r}_j^{\langle i \rangle})_{i \in [n]}$ and $q_{j,w}$ is a polynomial of $(\boldsymbol{r}_j^{\langle i \rangle})_{i \in [n]}$. In Fig. 3, we define HSS following the framework in [26].

$\mathsf{HSS.KGen}(1^\lambda)$:

$(\mathsf{pk}, \mathsf{sk}) \leftarrow \mathsf{KGen}(1^\lambda)$

return $(\mathsf{pk}, \mathsf{sk})$

$\mathsf{HSS.Share}(\mathsf{pk}, i, \boldsymbol{x}^{\langle i \rangle})$:

$(\boldsymbol{s}_j^{\langle i \rangle}, \boldsymbol{r}_j^{\langle i \rangle})_{j \in [m]} \leftarrow \mathsf{HSS}_0.\mathsf{Share}(i, \boldsymbol{x}^{\langle i \rangle})$

$\boldsymbol{u}_j^{\langle i \rangle} \leftarrow \mathsf{HE.Enc}(\mathsf{pk}, \boldsymbol{r}_j^{\langle i \rangle}), \forall j \in [m]$

$\mathsf{in}_j^{\langle i \rangle} = (\boldsymbol{s}_j^{\langle i \rangle}, \boldsymbol{u}_j^{\langle i \rangle}), \forall j \in [m]$

return $(\mathsf{in}_j^{\langle i \rangle})_{j \in [m]}$

$\mathsf{HSS.Eval}(\mathsf{pk}, j, f, (\mathsf{in}_j^{\langle i \rangle})_{i \in [n]})$:

$\boldsymbol{y}_j \leftarrow \mathsf{HSS}_0.\mathsf{Eval}(j, f, (\boldsymbol{s}_j^{\langle i \rangle})_{i \in [n]})$

$\nu_{j,w} = \boldsymbol{p}_{j,w}^\top \boldsymbol{y}_j + q_{j,w}, \forall w \in [h]$

$d_{j,w} \leftarrow \mathsf{HE.Eval}(\mathsf{pk}, \nu_{j,w}, (\boldsymbol{u}_j^{\langle i \rangle})_{i \in [n]}), \forall w \in [h]$

return $\mathsf{out}_j = (d_{j,w})_{w \in [h]}$

$\mathsf{HSS.Dec}(\mathsf{sk}, (\mathsf{out}_j)_{j \in [m]})$:

$\boldsymbol{d}_j = \mathsf{HE.Dec}(\mathsf{sk}, \mathsf{out}_j), \forall j \in [m]$

return $\displaystyle\sum_{j \in [m]} \boldsymbol{C}_j \boldsymbol{d}_j$

Fig. 3. Compiler from HSS_0 to HSS based on HE

To see correctness, observe that $d_{j,w}$ in the evaluation algorithm of HSS is a ciphertext that decrypts to $\boldsymbol{p}_{j,w}(\boldsymbol{r}_j^{\langle 1 \rangle}, \ldots, \boldsymbol{r}_j^{\langle n \rangle})^\top \boldsymbol{y}_j + q_{j,w}(\boldsymbol{r}_j^{\langle 1 \rangle}, \ldots, \boldsymbol{r}_j^{\langle n \rangle})$ since each entry of $\boldsymbol{p}_{j,w}$ and $q_{j,w}$ are degree-k polynomials. Hence, it holds that $\boldsymbol{d}_j = A_j\boldsymbol{y}_j + \boldsymbol{b}_j$ and the correctness of HSS_0 implies that $\sum_{j\in[m]} C_j\boldsymbol{d}_j = \mathcal{P}_\ell(f, (\boldsymbol{x}^{\langle 1\rangle},\dots,\boldsymbol{x}^{\langle n\rangle}))$. As in [26], the security of HSS follows from the information-theoretic security of HSS_0 and the IND-CPA security of HE. An input share $\mathsf{in}_j^{\langle i\rangle}$ consists of $\boldsymbol{s}_j^{\langle i\rangle} \in \mathbb{F}^\alpha$ and a ciphertext for $\boldsymbol{r}_j^{\langle i\rangle} \in \mathbb{F}^\rho$. An output share out_j consists of h ciphertexts. Therefore, the correctness of α' and β' follows. $\qquad\square$

The computational complexity of HSS.Share is that of HSS_0.Share plus $m\rho\cdot$ poly$[\lambda]$. The computational complexity of HSS.Eval is that of HSS_0.Eval plus $\beta(n\rho)^k h\cdot$ poly$[\lambda]$. Here, we assume that $\mathsf{HE.Eval}(f,\cdot)$ can be computed in time $|f|\cdot$ poly$[\lambda]$ for a function f whose description size is $|f|$. The computational complexity of HSS.Dec is $m\ell h\cdot$ poly$[\lambda]$.

Note that we can obtain a multi-key HSS scheme by replacing the HE scheme with the corresponding multi-key variant.

5   Warm-Up: HSS for Threshold Adversary Structures

As a warm-up, we construct an IT-HSS scheme with recovery information for a threshold adversary structure $\mathcal{T}_\tau^m$. Let $n, m, \ell, d, k \in \mathbb{N}, \tau \in \mathbb{R}_+$, and set $t = \lfloor \tau m\rfloor \in \mathbb{Z}_+$. We fix $m + \ell$ distinct elements $\zeta_1,\dots,\zeta_m, \eta_1,\dots,\eta_\ell$ of $\mathbb{F}$ and set $\boldsymbol{\zeta} = (\zeta_j)_{j\in[m]}$ and $\boldsymbol{\eta} = (\eta_j)_{j\in[\ell]}$. The sharing algorithm on input $\boldsymbol{x}^{\langle i\rangle} \in \mathbb{F}^\ell$ chooses a random polynomial $\varphi^{\langle i\rangle}$ such that $\boldsymbol{x}^{\langle i\rangle} = (\varphi^{\langle i\rangle}(\eta_j))_{j\in[\ell]}$ and $\deg\varphi^{\langle i\rangle} \le t + \ell - 1$. It sets input shares as $\mathsf{in}_j^{\langle i\rangle} = \varphi^{\langle i\rangle}(\zeta_j)$ and recovery information as $\mathsf{rec}_j^{\langle i\rangle} = ((\mathcal{D}^w\varphi^{\langle i\rangle})(\zeta_j))_{w\in[k]}$. The $\mathcal{T}_\tau^m$-privacy is straightforward since input shares are equivalent to shares of the packed secret sharing scheme [19], which reveal nothing about $\boldsymbol{x} \in \mathbb{F}^\ell$ as long as the number of shares is at most t.

Consider the simplest case of $f = X_1\cdots X_d$. Then, $\mathcal{P}_\ell(f, (\boldsymbol{x}^{\langle 1\rangle},\dots,\boldsymbol{x}^{\langle n\rangle})) = \boldsymbol{x}^{\langle 1\rangle} * \cdots * \boldsymbol{x}^{\langle d\rangle} = (g(\eta_j))_{j\in[\ell]}$, where $*$ denotes the element-wise product and $g = \varphi^{\langle 1\rangle}\cdots\varphi^{\langle d\rangle}$. For $j \in [m]$ and $w \in [0..k]$, the chain rule implies

$$\mathcal{D}^w g(\zeta_j) = \sum_{\substack{e\in\mathbb{Z}_+^d:\\ e_1+\cdots+e_d=w}} \frac{w!}{e_1!\cdots e_d!} \prod_{\substack{\kappa\in[d]:\\ e_\kappa=0}} \varphi^{\langle\kappa\rangle}(\zeta_j) \prod_{\substack{\kappa\in[d]:\\ e_\kappa>0}} (\mathcal{D}^{e_\kappa}\varphi^{\langle\kappa\rangle})(\zeta_j). \qquad (1)$$

The j-th server computes and outputs $\prod_{\kappa:e_\kappa=0} \varphi^{\langle\kappa\rangle}(\zeta_j)$ for all w, e with $\sum e_\kappa = w$ from its input shares. Then, the output client computes $\prod_{\kappa:e_\kappa>0}(\mathcal{D}^{e_\kappa}\varphi^{\langle\kappa\rangle})(\zeta_j)$ for all j, w, e from recovery information. Combining them with output shares, he obtains $\boldsymbol{z}_j = (\mathcal{D}^w g(\zeta_j))_{w\in[0..k]}$ and computes $\mathsf{Hermite}_{\zeta,\eta}((\boldsymbol{z}_j)_{j\in[m]}) = (g(\eta_j))_{j\in[\ell]}$ if $d(t + \ell - 1) < (k+1)m$.

To apply the ILM compiler, we have to check whether an output of the decoding algorithm has the form specified in Proposition 2. Indeed, each piece of recovery information is a vector $\boldsymbol{r}_j^{\langle i\rangle} \in \mathbb{F}^\rho$ for $\rho = k$ and an output share is a vector $\boldsymbol{y}_j$ whose dimension β is the number of all the pairs (w, e) such that $w \in [0..k]$ and $\sum_\kappa e_\kappa = w$, i.e., $\beta \le k2^{k+d}$. In view of Eq. (1), $\mathcal{D}^w g(\zeta_j)$ is a degree-1 polynomial of $\prod_{\kappa:e_\kappa=0}\varphi^{\langle\kappa\rangle}(\zeta_j)$ for all e such that $\sum_\kappa e_\kappa = w$. Furthermore, the coefficient of each $\prod_{\kappa:e_\kappa=0} \varphi^{\langle\kappa\rangle}(\zeta_j)$ is a degree-k polynomial of $(r_j^{\langle i\rangle})_{i\in[n]}$ since $|\{\kappa \in [d] : e_\kappa > 0\}| \leq w \leq k$. Therefore, z_j can be expressed as $A_j y_j + b_j$ using a $(k+1)$-by-β matrix A_j and $(k+1)$-dimensional vector b_j whose entries are degree-k polynomials of $(r_j^{\langle i\rangle})_{i\in[n]}$. Since $\mathsf{Hermite}_{\zeta,\eta}((z_j)_{j\in[m]})$ is linear in $(z_j)_{j\in[m]}$, the output of Dec can be expressed as $\sum_{j\in[m]} C_j(A_j y_j + b_j)$ using some constant ℓ-by-$(k+1)$ matrices C_j. In summary, we have the following theorem. Since it is a special case of Theorem 2, we omit the formal proof here.

Theorem 1. *Let $n,m,\ell,d,k \in \mathbb{N}$. Let $\tau \in \mathbb{R}_+$ and $t = \lfloor \tau m \rfloor \in \mathbb{Z}_+$. Let $\mathbb{F}$ be a prime field such that $|\mathbb{F}| \geq \max\{m+\ell, k+1\}$. Assume that $(k+1)m - dt > d(\ell-1)$. Then, there exists an $(n,m,\ell,d,\mathcal{T}_\tau^m)$-IT-HSS scheme HSS_0 with recovery information that satisfies the properties in Proposition 2 for $\alpha = 1$, $\rho = k$, $\beta = n^d k 2^{k+d}$, and $h = k+1$.*

By applying the ILM compiler in Proposition 2, assuming a k-HE scheme HE, we obtain an $(n,m,\ell,d,\mathcal{T}_\tau^m)$-HSS scheme HSS with efficiency measures $\alpha = \log |\mathbb{F}| + k$ and $\beta = k + 1$. To make computational complexity polynomial in λ, we assume that $n,m \in \mathsf{poly}[\lambda]$ and $k,d \in O(1)$ since the most costly part is the evaluation algorithm, whose time complexity is $n^{d+k} k^{k+1} 2^{k+d} \cdot \mathsf{poly}[\lambda]$.

Since the ILM compiler does not provide context hiding in general, we add re-randomizing procedures to the sharing and evaluation algorithms of the compiled scheme HSS. Specifically, an output share of HSS computed by the j-th server consists of $k+1$ ciphertexts $(d_{j,w})_{w\in[0..k]}$ of HE each of which decrypts to $\mathcal{D}^w g(\zeta_j)$ for a polynomial g of degree less than $(k+1)m$ such that $(g(\eta_j))_{j\in[\ell]} = \mathcal{P}_\ell(f, (x^{\langle 1\rangle}, \ldots, x^{\langle n\rangle}))$. We modify the sharing algorithm so that the first client (on behalf of all clients) additionally generates a polynomial θ such that $\deg(\theta) < (k+1)m$ and $(\theta(\eta_j))_{j\in[\ell]} = \mathbf{0}$, and sends $(\mathcal{D}^w \theta(\zeta_j))_{w\in[0..k]}$ to the j-th server for each $j \in [m]$. Accordingly, the j-th server executes the evaluation algorithm of HSS to obtain $(d_{j,w})_{w\in[0..k]}$ and then using $(\mathcal{D}^w \theta(\zeta_j))_{w\in[0..k]}$, outputs $k+1$ ciphertexts $(d'_{j,w})_{w\in[0..k]}$ each of which decrypts to $(\mathcal{D}^w g'(\zeta_j))_{w\in[0..k]}$, where $g' = g + \theta$. In this modified scheme HSS', the output shares are ciphertexts of values and derivatives of g', which is uniformly distributed over the set $\{\widetilde{g} \in \mathbb{F}[X] : \deg(\widetilde{g}) < (k+1)m \wedge (\widetilde{g}(\eta_j))_{j\in[\ell]} = \mathcal{P}_\ell(f, (x^{\langle 1\rangle}, \ldots, x^{\langle n\rangle}))\}$. Combined with the circuit-privacy of HE, the output shares can be simulated only from $\mathcal{P}_\ell(f, (x^{\langle 1\rangle}, \ldots, x^{\langle n\rangle}))$. In summary, we have the following result. Again, we omit the formal proof here since Corollary 1 is a special case of Corollary 2.

Corollary 1. *Using the notations in Theorem 1, assume that $n, m \in \mathsf{poly}[\lambda]$ and $k, d \in O(1)$. Assuming a k-HE scheme HE, there exists an $(n,m,\ell,d,\mathcal{T}_\tau^m)$-HSS scheme HSS with efficiency measures $\alpha = \log |\mathbb{F}| + k$ and $\beta = k+1$. Furthermore, if HE is circuit-private, there exists a context-hiding $(n,m,\ell,d,\mathcal{T}_\tau^m)$-HSS scheme HSS' with efficiency measures $\alpha = (k+2)\log |\mathbb{F}| + k = O(\log(m+\ell))$ and $\beta = k+1 = O(1)$.*

To lift the above result to the plain model, it is sufficient to replace the HE scheme with the corresponding multi-key variant. We can instantiate the m-input

MPC protocol in Sect. 3.4 with the threshold HSS scheme in Corollary 1 and then the communication complexity is $O(m^2 \log(m + \ell))$.

6   HSS for Multipartite Adversary Structures

We show a construction of IT-HSS schemes with recovery information for multipartite adversary structures.

Theorem 2. *Let* $n, m, \ell, d, k, L \in \mathbb{N}$. *Let* Π *be an* L-*partition of the set* P *of* m *servers. Let* Δ *be a* Π-*partite adversary structure on* P *and* $\max \Phi^\Pi(\Delta) = \{a_1, \ldots, a_N\}$. *Let* $\mathbb{F}$ *be a prime field such that* $|\mathbb{F}| \geq \max\{m + \ell, k+1\}$. *Assume that* Δ *satisfies the condition*

$$\forall (u_1, \ldots, u_d) \in [N]^d : |(k + 1)\Phi^\Pi(P) - (a_{u_1} + \cdots + a_{u_d})|_\infty > d(\ell - 1). \quad (2)$$

Then, the scheme HSS_0 *described in Fig. 4 is an* (n, m, ℓ, d, Δ)-*IT-HSS scheme with recovery information that satisfies the properties in Proposition 2 for* $\alpha = N$, $\rho = Nk$, $\beta = n^d N^d k 2^{k+d}$, *and* $h = k + 1$.

Proof. Since $|(k + 1)\Phi^\Pi(P) - (a_{u_1} + \cdots + a_{u_d})|_\infty > d(\ell - 1)$ for any $(u_1, \ldots, u_d) \in [N]^d$, there is a map $\psi : [N]^d \to [L]$ such that $(k + 1)|P_v| > a_{u_1}(v) + \cdots + a_{u_d}(v) + d(\ell-1)$ for any $(u_1, \ldots, u_d) \in [N]^d$ and $v = \psi(u_1, \ldots, u_d)$.

To see correctness, let $f(X_1, \ldots, X_n) = \sum_{i \in [n]^d} c_i X_{i_1} \cdots X_{i_d}$. Using the notations in Fig. 4, for any input $\boldsymbol{x}^{\langle 1 \rangle}, \ldots, \boldsymbol{x}^{\langle n \rangle} \in \mathbb{F}^\ell$, it holds that

$$\begin{aligned}
\mathcal{P}_\ell(f, (\boldsymbol{x}^{\langle 1 \rangle}, \ldots, \boldsymbol{x}^{\langle n \rangle})) &= \sum_{\boldsymbol{u} \in [N]^d} \sum_{i \in [n]^d} c_i \boldsymbol{x}_{u_1}^{\langle i_1 \rangle} * \cdots * \boldsymbol{x}_{u_d}^{\langle i_d \rangle} \\
&= \sum_{v=1}^L \sum_{\boldsymbol{u} \in \psi^{-1}(v)} \sum_{i \in [n]^d} c_i \boldsymbol{x}_{u_1}^{\langle i_1 \rangle} * \cdots * \boldsymbol{x}_{u_d}^{\langle i_d \rangle} \\
&= \sum_{v=1}^L (g_v(\eta_j))_{j \in [\ell]},
\end{aligned}$$

where $*$ denotes the element-wise product and $g_v = \sum_{\boldsymbol{u} \in \psi^{-1}(v)} \sum_{i \in [n]^d} c_i \varphi_{u_1, v}^{\langle i_1 \rangle} \cdots \varphi_{u_d, v}^{\langle i_d \rangle}$. It holds that

$$\mathcal{D}^w g_v = \sum_{\boldsymbol{u} \in \psi^{-1}(v)} \sum_{i \in [n]^d} \sum_{\substack{e \in \mathbb{Z}_+^d : \\ e_1 + \cdots + e_d = w}} \frac{w!}{e_1! \cdots e_d!} c_i (\mathcal{D}^{e_1} \varphi_{u_1, v}^{\langle i_1 \rangle}) \cdots (\mathcal{D}^{e_d} \varphi_{u_d, v}^{\langle i_d \rangle})$$

and hence $y_{j,w} = (\mathcal{D}^w g_{v_j})(\zeta_j)$ for any $j \in [m]$ and $w \in [0..k]$. Since the degree of g_v is at most $\max_{\boldsymbol{u} \in \psi^{-1}(v)} \{a_{u_1}(v) + \cdots + a_{u_d}(v) + d(\ell - 1)\} < (k + 1)|P_v|$, we have $\mathsf{Hermite}_{\zeta_v, \eta}((z_j)_{j \in P_v}) = (g_v(\eta_j))_{j \in [\ell]}$. Therefore, $\sum_{v \in [L]} \mathsf{Hermite}_{\zeta_v, \eta}((z_j)_{j \in P_v}) = \mathcal{P}_\ell(f, (\boldsymbol{x}^{\langle 1 \rangle}, \ldots, \boldsymbol{x}^{\langle n \rangle}))$.

Notations.
- Parameters $n, m, \ell, d, k, L \in \mathbb{N}$.
- An L-partition $\Pi = (P_1, \ldots, P_L)$ of the set of m servers.
- A Π-partite adversary structure Δ and $\max \Phi^\Pi(\Delta) = \{a_1, \ldots, a_N\}$.
- A prime field $\mathbb{F}$ such that $|\mathbb{F}| \geq \max\{m + \ell, k + 1\}$.
- $m + \ell$ distinct elements $\zeta_1, \ldots, \zeta_m, \eta_1, \ldots, \eta_\ell \in \mathbb{F}$, $\boldsymbol{\zeta}_v = (\zeta_j)_{j \in P_v}$ for $v \in [L]$, and $\boldsymbol{\eta} = (\eta_1, \ldots, \eta_\ell)$.
- A map $\psi : [N]^d \to [L]$ such that $(k+1)|P_v| > a_{u_1}(v) + \cdots + a_{u_d}(v) + d(\ell - 1)$ for any $(u_1, \ldots, u_d) \in [N]^d$ and $v = \psi(u_1, \ldots, u_d)$.
- For $j \in [m]$, a set

$$
S_j = \left\{ (\boldsymbol{i}, \boldsymbol{u}, w, \boldsymbol{e}) : \begin{array}{l} \boldsymbol{i} = (i_1, \ldots, i_d) \in [n]^d, \ \boldsymbol{u} = (u_1, \ldots, u_d) \in \psi^{-1}(v_j), \\ w \in [0..k], \ \boldsymbol{e} = (e_1, \ldots, e_d) \in \mathbb{Z}_+^d \text{ s.t. } e_1 + \cdots + e_d = w \end{array} \right\}.
$$

$\mathsf{Share}(i, \boldsymbol{x}^{\langle i \rangle})$. Given an index $i \in [n]$ and an input $\boldsymbol{x}^{\langle i \rangle} \in \mathbb{F}^\ell$:

1. Choose $\boldsymbol{x}_u^{\langle i \rangle} \in \mathbb{F}^\ell$, $u \in [N]$ at random such that $\boldsymbol{x}^{\langle i \rangle} = \sum_{u \in [N]} \boldsymbol{x}_u^{\langle i \rangle}$.
2. For each $u \in [N]$ and $v \in [L]$, choose $\varphi_{u,v}^{\langle i \rangle} \in \mathbb{F}[X]$ at random such that $\boldsymbol{x}_u^{\langle i \rangle} = (\varphi_{u,v}^{\langle i \rangle}(\eta_j))_{j \in [\ell]}$ and $\deg(\varphi_{u,v}^{\langle i \rangle}) \leq a_u(v) + \ell - 1$.
3. For each $j \in [m]$, set

$$
\mathsf{in}_j^{\langle i \rangle} = (\varphi_{u,v_j}^{\langle i \rangle}(\zeta_j))_{u \in [N]} \text{ and } \mathsf{rec}_j^{\langle i \rangle} = ((\mathcal{D}\varphi_{u,v_j}^{\langle i \rangle})(\zeta_j), \ldots, (\mathcal{D}^k \varphi_{u,v_j}^{\langle i \rangle})(\zeta_j))_{u \in [N]},
$$

where $v_j \in [L]$ is the unique index such that $j \in P_{v_j}$.
4. Output $(\mathsf{in}_j^{\langle i \rangle}, \mathsf{rec}_j^{\langle i \rangle})_{j \in [m]}$.

$\mathsf{Eval}(j, f, (\mathsf{in}_j^{\langle i \rangle})_{i \in [n]})$. Given an index $j \in [m]$, a polynomial $f = \sum_{\boldsymbol{i} \in [n]^d} c_{\boldsymbol{i}} X_{i_1} \cdots X_{i_d}$ where $c_{\boldsymbol{i}} \in \mathbb{F}$, and input shares $(\mathsf{in}_j^{\langle i \rangle})_{i \in [n]}$, output

$$
\mathsf{out}_j = \left(c_{\boldsymbol{i}} \prod_{\kappa : e_\kappa = 0} \varphi_{u_\kappa, v_j}^{\langle i_\kappa \rangle}(\zeta_j) : (\boldsymbol{i}, \boldsymbol{u}, w, \boldsymbol{e}) \in S_j \right).
$$

$\mathsf{Dec}((\mathsf{out}_j)_{j \in [m]}, (\mathsf{rec}_j^{\langle i \rangle})_{i \in [n], j \in [m]})$. Given output shares $(\mathsf{out}_j)_{j \in [m]}$ and recovery information $(\mathsf{rec}_j^{\langle i \rangle})_{i \in [n], j \in [m]}$:

1. For each $j \in [m]$ and $w \in [0..k]$, compute

$$
y_{j,w} := \sum_{\substack{\boldsymbol{i}, \boldsymbol{u}, \boldsymbol{e}: \\ (\boldsymbol{i}, \boldsymbol{u}, w, \boldsymbol{e}) \in S_j}} \frac{w!}{e_1! \cdots e_d!} \left(c_{\boldsymbol{i}} \prod_{\kappa : e_\kappa = 0} \varphi_{u_\kappa, v_j}^{\langle i_\kappa \rangle}(\zeta_j) \right) \left(\prod_{\kappa : e_\kappa > 0} (\mathcal{D}^{e_\kappa} \varphi_{u_\kappa, v_j}^{\langle i_\kappa \rangle})(\zeta_j) \right).
$$

2. Letting $\boldsymbol{z}_j = (y_{j,w})_{w \in [0..k]}$, output $\sum_{v \in [L]} \mathsf{Hermite}_{\boldsymbol{\zeta}_v, \boldsymbol{\eta}}((\boldsymbol{z}_j)_{j \in P_v})$.

Fig. 4. An (n, m, ℓ, d, Δ)-IT-HSS scheme with recovery information for an L-partite adversary structure Δ

An input share is an N-dimensional vector, each piece of recovery information is an Nk-dimensional vector $r_j^{\langle i \rangle}$, and an output share out_j is an $|S_j|$-dimensional vector y_j. It follows from the definition of S_j that $|S_j| \leq n^d \cdot N^d \cdot k \cdot 2^{k+d} =: \beta$. Each $y_{j,w}$ computed by Dec is a degree-1 polynomial with respect to out_j. The degree of $y_{j,w}$ with respect to $(\mathsf{rec}_j^{\langle i \rangle})_{i \in [n]}$ is at most the maximum of $|\{\kappa \in [d] : e_\kappa > 0\}|$ over all $e = (e_1, \ldots, e_d) \in \mathbb{Z}_+^d$ such that $e_1 + \cdots + e_d = w$ and hence is at most $w \leq k$. Therefore, $z_j = (y_{j,w})_{w \in [0..k]}$ can be expressed as $A_j y_j + b_j$ using a $(k+1)$-by-β matrix A_j and $(k+1)$-dimensional vector b_j whose entries are degree-k polynomials of $(r_j^{\langle i \rangle})_{i \in [n]}$. Since $\sum_{v \in [L]} \mathsf{Hermite}_{\zeta_v, \eta}((z_j)_{j \in P_v})$ is linear with respect to $(z_j)_{j \in [m]}$, the output of Dec can be expressed as $\sum_{j \in [m]} C_j(A_j y_j + b_j)$ using some constant ℓ-by-$(k+1)$ matrices C_j.

To see Δ-privacy, we show that for any $x, x' \in \mathbb{F}^\ell$ and $B \in \Delta$, the distributions of input shares $(\mathsf{in}_j)_{j \in B}$ for x and $(\mathsf{in}'_j)_{j \in B}$ for x' are identical. Since $\Phi^\Pi(B) \preceq a_i$ for some $i \in [N]$, there exist L polynomials $\theta_1, \ldots, \theta_L \in \mathbb{F}[X]$ such that for all $v \in [L]$, $\deg(\theta_v) \leq a_i(v) + \ell - 1$, $(\theta_v(\eta_j))_{j \in [\ell]} = x' - x$, and $\theta_v(\zeta_j) = 0$ for any $j \in P_v \cap B$. We have a bijection between randomness used by Share on input x and randomness used by Share on input x' such that the shares of B are the same under this bijection. Indeed, we map any random polynomials $(\varphi_{u,v})_{u \in [N], v \in [L]}$ generated by Share on input x to $(\varphi'_{u,v})_{u \in [N], v \in [L]}$ where $\varphi'_{u,v} = \varphi_{u,v} + \theta_v$ if $u = i$ and $v \in [L]$, and otherwise $\varphi'_{u,v} = \varphi_{u,v}$. Then, $(\varphi'_{u,v})_{u \in [N], v \in [L]}$ provide consistent shares for x' and the shares of B resulting from $(\varphi'_{u,v})_{u \in [N], v \in [L]}$ are the same as the ones resulting from $(\varphi_{u,v})_{u \in [N], v \in [L]}$. $\square$

By applying the ILM compiler in Proposition 2, we obtain an HSS scheme for multipartite adversary structures. To guarantee context hiding, we have to add certain re-randomizing procedures.

Corollary 2. *Using the notations in Theorem 2, assume that $n, m \in \mathsf{poly}[\lambda]$, $k, d \in O(1)$, and $N \in \mathsf{poly}[\lambda]$. Assuming a (resp. multi-key) k-HE scheme HE, there exists an (n, m, ℓ, d, Δ)-HSS scheme HSS (resp. in the plain model) with efficiency measures $\alpha = N \log |\mathbb{F}| + Nk$ and $\beta = k + 1$. Furthermore, if HE satisfies circuit privacy, there exists a context-hiding (n, m, ℓ, d, Δ)-HSS scheme HSS' (resp. in the plain model) with efficiency measures $\alpha = (N + k + 1) \log |\mathbb{F}| + Nk = O(N \log(m + \ell))$ and $\beta = k + 1 = O(1)$.*

Proof. In view of Proposition 2 and Theorem 2, we obtain an (n, m, ℓ, d, Δ)-HSS scheme HSS with efficiency measures $\alpha = N \log |\mathbb{F}| + Nk$ and $\beta = k + 1$.

We make HSS context-hiding by adding re-randomizing procedures to the sharing and evaluation algorithms. Using the notations in the proof of Theorem 2, we can see that in HSS, the sharing algorithm executed by the i-th client outputs ciphertexts $c_j^{\langle i \rangle} = (\mathsf{HE.Enc}(\mathsf{pk}, \mathcal{D}^w \varphi_{u,v_j}^{\langle i \rangle}(\zeta_j)))_{u \in [N], w \in [0..k]}$ for $j \in [m]$. The evaluation algorithm executed by the j-th server outputs $k + 1$ ciphertexts $(d_{j,w})_{w \in [0..k]}$ each of which decrypts to $y_{j,w} = (\mathcal{D}^w g_{v_j})(\zeta_j)$ for $w \in [0..k]$, where g_v is a polynomial of degree less than $(k+1)|P_v|$. Note that there are degree-k polynomials $\nu_{j,w}$ (whose coefficients depend on $(\varphi_{u,v_j}^{(i)}(\zeta_j))_{u\in[N]}$) such that $d_{j,w} = \mathsf{HE.Eval}(\mathsf{pk}, \nu_{j,w}, (\boldsymbol{c}_j^{\langle 1\rangle}, \ldots, \boldsymbol{c}_j^{\langle n\rangle}))$ (see Fig. 3).

We fix any client, say, $i = 1$. If the input index is $i = 1$, we let the sharing algorithm additionally generate random polynomials $(\theta_v)_{v\in[L]}$ such that $\deg(\theta_v) < (k+1)|P_v|$ for all $v \in [L]$ and $\sum_{v\in[L]}(\theta_v(\eta_j))_{j\in[\ell]} = \mathbf{0}$. Then, it sends $k+1$ field elements $y'_{j,w} = (\mathcal{D}^w\theta_{v_j})(\zeta_j)$ for $w \in [0..k]$ to the j-th server in addition to an input share $\mathsf{in}_j^{\langle 1\rangle}$ of HSS. We do not modify the procedures for the other clients. Accordingly, the size of input shares are now $\alpha = (N+k+1)\log|\mathbb{F}| + Nk$. When executing the evaluation algorithm of HSS, the j-th server outputs $k+1$ ciphertexts $(d'_{j,w})_{w\in[0..k]}$ each of which decrypts to $y_{j,w} + y'_{j,w} = (\mathcal{D}^w g'_{v_j})(\zeta_j)$ where $g'_v = g_v + \theta_v$. More precisely, the j-th server computes $d'_{j,w} \leftarrow \mathsf{HE.Eval}(\mathsf{pk}, \nu_{j,w}(\cdot) + y'_{j,w}, (\boldsymbol{c}_j^{\langle 1\rangle}, \ldots, \boldsymbol{c}_j^{\langle n\rangle}))$ for all $w \in [0..k]$.

In this modified HSS scheme HSS', the output client receives $k+1$ ciphertexts $(d'_{j,w})_{w\in[0..k]}$ from the j-th server. Now, $d'_{j,w}$ decrypts to $(\mathcal{D}^w g'_{v_j})(\zeta_j)$ and the polynomials g'_v are uniformly random under the constraints $\sum_{v\in[L]}(g'_v(\eta_j))_{j\in[\ell]} = \mathcal{P}_\ell(f, (\boldsymbol{x}^{\langle 1\rangle}, \ldots, \boldsymbol{x}^{\langle n\rangle}))$ and $\deg g'_v < (k+1)|P_v|$. Due to the circuit privacy of HE, the output shares can be simulated from $\mathcal{P}_\ell(f, (\boldsymbol{x}^{\langle 1\rangle}, \ldots, \boldsymbol{x}^{\langle n\rangle}))$. Precisely, let S_{HE} be the simulator for the circuit privacy of HE. Given $\mathcal{P}_\ell(f, (\boldsymbol{x}^{\langle 1\rangle}, \ldots, \boldsymbol{x}^{\langle n\rangle}))$, the simulator $S_{\mathsf{HSS}'}$ randomly chooses polynomials $\widetilde{g}_v$ for $v \in [L]$ such that $\sum_{v\in[L]}(\widetilde{g}_v(\eta_j))_{j\in[\ell]} = \mathcal{P}_\ell(f, (\boldsymbol{x}^{\langle 1\rangle}, \ldots, \boldsymbol{x}^{\langle n\rangle}))$ and $\deg\widetilde{g}_v < (k+1)|P_v|$ for all $v \in [L]$, and then computes $\widetilde{d}_{j,w} \leftarrow S_{\mathsf{HE}}(1^\lambda, \mathsf{pk}, (\mathcal{D}^w\widetilde{g}_{v_j})(\zeta_j))$ for all $j \in [L]$ and $w \in [0..k]$. It finally outputs $((\widetilde{d}_{1,w})_{w\in[0..k]}, \ldots, (\widetilde{d}_{m,w})_{w\in[0..k]})$.

We analyze the distribution of the output of $S_{\mathsf{HSS}'}$. Let $j \in [m]$, $w \in [0..k]$, and $r_{j,w}$ be any fixed field element. The circuit privacy of HE implies that

$$\mathsf{HE.Eval}(\mathsf{pk}, \nu_{j,w}(\cdot) + r_{j,w}, (\boldsymbol{c}_j^{\langle 1\rangle}, \ldots, \boldsymbol{c}_j^{\langle n\rangle})) \approx S_{\mathsf{HE}}(1^\lambda, \mathsf{pk}, y_{j,w} + r_{j,w}),$$

where $\approx$ denotes statistical indistinguishability. Then, we have that

$$(\mathsf{HE.Eval}(\mathsf{pk}, \nu_{j,w}(\cdot) + r_{j,w}, (\boldsymbol{c}_j^{\langle 1\rangle}, \ldots, \boldsymbol{c}_j^{\langle n\rangle})))_{w\in[0..k], j\in[m]}$$
$$\approx (S_{\mathsf{HE}}(1^\lambda, \mathsf{pk}, y_{j,w} + r_{j,w}))_{w\in[0..k], j\in[m]}. \tag{3}$$

Let V be the set from which $(\theta_v)_{v\in[L]}$ is sampled. Note that V is a linear space over $\mathbb{F}$. Since Eq. (3) holds for any fixed elements $r_{j,w}$, we can apply it to $r_{j,w} = y'_{j,w} = \mathcal{D}^w\theta_{v_j}(\zeta_j)$ where $(\theta_v)_{v\in[L]} \leftarrow_\$ V$, and obtain that

$$(d'_{j,w})_{w\in[0..k], j\in[m]} = (\mathsf{HE.Eval}(\mathsf{pk}, \nu_{j,w}(\cdot) + y'_{j,w}, (\boldsymbol{c}_j^{\langle 1\rangle}, \ldots, \boldsymbol{c}_j^{\langle n\rangle})))_{w\in[0..k], j\in[m]}$$
$$\approx (S_{\mathsf{HE}}(1^\lambda, \mathsf{pk}, y_{j,w} + y'_{j,w}))_{w\in[0..k], j\in[m]}. \tag{4}$$

The distribution of $(g'_v)_{v\in[L]}$ is the uniform distribution over an affine space $(g_v)_{v\in[L]} + V := \{(g_v + \theta_v)_{v\in[L]} : (\theta_v)_{v\in[L]} \in V\}$, which is the same as the distribution of $(\widetilde{g}_v)_{v\in[L]}$. Furthermore, the differential operator and the evaluation map are both linear maps over $\mathbb{F}$. Therefore, the distribution of $(\mathcal{D}^w g'_{v_j}(\zeta_j))_{w\in[0..k],j\in[m]}$ induced by $(\theta_v)_{v\in[L]} \leftarrow_\$ V$ is identical to that of $(\mathcal{D}^w \tilde{g}_{v_j}(\zeta_j))_{w\in[0..k],j\in[m]}$ induced by $(\tilde{g}_v)_{v\in[L]} \leftarrow_\$ (g_1,\dots,g_L) + V$. Combined with Eq. (4), we obtain that

$$(d'_{j,w})_{w\in[0..k],j\in[m]} \approx (S_{\mathsf{HE}}(1^\lambda, \mathsf{pk}, \mathcal{D}^w g'_{v_j}(\zeta_j)))_{w\in[0..k],j\in[m]}$$
$$= (S_{\mathsf{HE}}(1^\lambda, \mathsf{pk}, \mathcal{D}^w \tilde{g}_{v_j}(\zeta_j)))_{w\in[0..k],j\in[m]}$$
$$= S_{\mathsf{HSS}'}(1^\lambda, \mathsf{pk}, \mathcal{P}_\ell(f, (\boldsymbol{x}^{\langle 1\rangle},\dots,\boldsymbol{x}^{\langle n\rangle}))).$$

We show that the computational complexity of HSS' is polynomial in the security parameter λ. The most costly step in the sharing algorithm of HSS_0 is sampling random polynomials $\varphi_{u,v}^{\langle i\rangle}$, which can be done in polynomial time in m, N, ℓ by pre-computing and publishing a basis for the linear space

$$\mathcal{L}_{u,v} := \{\varphi_{u,v} \in \mathbb{F}[X] : \deg(\varphi_{u,v}) \le \boldsymbol{a}_u(v) + \ell - 1, \ (\varphi_{u,v}(\eta_j))_{j\in[\ell]} = \boldsymbol{0}\}$$

for each $u \in [N]$ and $v \in [L]$. We have that $\ell = O(m)$ due to the condition (2) and hence the time complexity of that step is polynomial in λ. Since the additional re-randomizing steps of HSS' can also be done in time $\mathsf{poly}[m, N, \ell, \lambda]$, the time complexity of $\mathsf{HSS}'.\mathsf{Share}$ is still polynomial in λ. Next, $\mathsf{HSS}_0.\mathsf{Eval}$ computes $\beta = O(n^d N^d)$ products and $\mathsf{HE}.\mathsf{Eval}$ can be executed by $\mathsf{HSS}'.\mathsf{Eval}$ in time $\beta(n\rho)^k \cdot \mathsf{poly}[\lambda] = O(n^{d+k} N^{d+k}) \cdot \mathsf{poly}[\lambda]$. The time complexity of $\mathsf{HSS}'.\mathsf{Eval}$ is therefore also polynomial in λ. Finally, in view of Proposition 2, $\mathsf{HSS}'.\mathsf{Dec}$ can be done in time $m\ell(k+1) \cdot \mathsf{poly}[\lambda] = \mathsf{poly}[\lambda]$.

We can lift the above scheme to the plain model by replacing the HE scheme with the corresponding multi-key variant.   □

Theorem 1 and Corollary 1 can be recovered by setting $L = 1$ and $\Delta = \mathcal{T}_\tau^m$, in which $\max \Phi^\Pi(\Delta) = \{\lfloor \tau m \rfloor\} \subseteq \mathbb{Z}_+$.

In Table 1 in Sect. 1.1, we have defined $\epsilon_{k,d}(\Delta) := \min\{|(k+1)\Phi^\Pi(P) - (\boldsymbol{a}_{u_1} + \dots + \boldsymbol{a}_{u_d})|_\infty : \forall(u_1,\dots,u_d) \in [N]^d\}$. It can be seen that the condition $\epsilon_{0,d}(\Delta) > 0$ is equivalent to the Q_d property [2], namely there are no d sets in Δ whose union covers the entire set P. The authors of [17] construct an information-theoretic HSS scheme (without recovery information) tolerating a multipartite Q_d-adversary structure. Since $\epsilon_{k,d}(\Delta) > \epsilon_{0,d}(\Delta)$ if $k \ge 1$, our scheme in the particular case of $\ell = 1$ can be viewed as a computational variant of the scheme [17] that tolerates a wider class of Q_d-adversary structures.

We can instantiate the m-input MPC protocol in Sect. 3.4 with the HSS scheme in Corollary 2 and then the communication complexity is $O(Nm^2 \log(m + \ell))$, where ℓ is the number of parallel evaluations. Since $N = O(m^L)$ and L is practically chosen as $L \in \{2,3\}$ [18], it is much smaller than the description size $O(m^d)$ of a polynomial to compute. Furthermore, as shown in Sect. 8, there is still an interesting class of adversary structures even in the case of $N = O(1)$.

7   HSS for General Adversary Structures

We show a construction of IT-HSS schemes with recovery information for general adversary structures.

Theorem 3. *Let $n, m, \ell, d, k \in \mathbb{N}$. Let Δ be an adversary structure on the set P of m servers and $\{B_1, \ldots, B_N\}$ be all maximal sets of Δ. Let $\mathbb{F}$ be a prime field such that $|\mathbb{F}| \geq \max\{m + \ell, k + 1\}$. Assume that Δ satisfies the condition*

$$\forall (u_1, \ldots, u_d) \in [N]^d : |(k+1)\mathbf{1}_m - (\boldsymbol{a}_{u_1} + \cdots + \boldsymbol{a}_{u_d})|_+ > (d+1)(\ell - 1), \quad (5)$$

where $\boldsymbol{a}_u \in \mathbb{Z}^m$ is a vector in which $\boldsymbol{a}_u(j) = 1$ if $j \in B_u$ and $\boldsymbol{a}_u(j) = 0$ otherwise. Then, the scheme HSS_0 described in Fig. 5 and 6 is an (n, m, ℓ, d, Δ)-IT-HSS scheme with recovery information that satisfies the properties in Proposition 2 for $\alpha = O(N)$, $\rho = O(Nk)$, $\beta = n^d N^d k 2^{k+d}$, and $h = k + 1$.

Proof. To see correctness, let $f(X_1, \ldots, X_n) = \sum_{\boldsymbol{i} \in [n]^d} c_{\boldsymbol{i}} X_{i_1} \cdots X_{i_d}$. Using the notations in Fig. 5 and 6, it holds that $\mathcal{P}_\ell(f, (\boldsymbol{x}^{\langle 1 \rangle}, \ldots, \boldsymbol{x}^{\langle n \rangle})) = (g(\eta_j))_{j \in [\ell]}$ for $h_{\boldsymbol{u}} = \sum_{\boldsymbol{i} \in [n]^d} c_{\boldsymbol{i}} \varphi_{u_1}^{\langle i_1 \rangle} \cdots \varphi_{u_d}^{\langle i_d \rangle}$ and $g = \sum_{\boldsymbol{u} \in [N]^d} p_{\boldsymbol{u}} h_{\boldsymbol{u}}$. For $j \in [m]$, $w \in [0..k]$, and $\boldsymbol{u} \in [N]^d$, the chain rule implies $\gamma_{j,\boldsymbol{u},w} = (\mathcal{D}^w h_{\boldsymbol{u}})(\zeta_j)$ if $\mu_{j,\boldsymbol{u}} \leq k - w$, and

$$(\mathcal{D}^w g)(\zeta_j) = \sum_{\boldsymbol{u} \in [N]^d} \sum_{v=0}^{w} \frac{w!}{v!(w-v)!}(\mathcal{D}^{w-v} p_{\boldsymbol{u}})(\zeta_j) \cdot (\mathcal{D}^v h_{\boldsymbol{u}})(\zeta_j)$$

$$= \sum_{\substack{\boldsymbol{u} \in [N]^d: \\ \mu_{j,\boldsymbol{u}} \leq k-w}} \sum_{v=0}^{w} \frac{w!}{v!(w-v)!}(\mathcal{D}^{w-v} p_{\boldsymbol{u}})(\zeta_j) \cdot (\mathcal{D}^v h_{\boldsymbol{u}})(\zeta_j)$$

$$+ \sum_{v'=1}^{w} \sum_{\substack{\boldsymbol{u} \in [N]^d: \\ \mu_{j,\boldsymbol{u}} = k-w+v'}} \sum_{v=0}^{w-v'} \frac{w!}{v!(w-v)!}(\mathcal{D}^{w-v} p_{\boldsymbol{u}})(\zeta_j) \cdot (\mathcal{D}^v h_{\boldsymbol{u}})(\zeta_j)$$

$$+ \sum_{v'=1}^{w} \sum_{\substack{\boldsymbol{u} \in [N]^d: \\ \mu_{j,\boldsymbol{u}} = k-w+v'}} \sum_{v=0}^{v'-1} \frac{w!}{(w-v)!v!}(\mathcal{D}^v p_{\boldsymbol{u}})(\zeta_j) \cdot (\mathcal{D}^{w-v} h_{\boldsymbol{u}})(\zeta_j)$$

$$+ \sum_{\substack{\boldsymbol{u} \subset [N]^d: \\ \mu_{j,\boldsymbol{u}} > k}} \sum_{v=0}^{w} \frac{w!}{(w-v)!v!}(\mathcal{D}^v p_{\boldsymbol{u}})(\zeta_j) \cdot (\mathcal{D}^{w-v} h_{\boldsymbol{u}})(\zeta_j).$$

In the first and second terms of the last equation, $\gamma_{j,\boldsymbol{u},v} = \mathcal{D}^v h_{\boldsymbol{u}}(\zeta_j)$ since $\mu_{j,\boldsymbol{u}} \leq k - w \leq k - v$ and $\mu_{j,\boldsymbol{u}} \leq k - (w - v') \leq k - v$, respectively. Furthermore, in the third and fourth terms, we have $\mathcal{D}^v p_{\boldsymbol{u}}(\zeta_j) = 0$ since $\mu_{j,\boldsymbol{u}} = k - w + v' \geq v' > v$ and $\mu_{j,\boldsymbol{u}} > k \geq w \geq v$, respectively. It then holds that

$$(\mathcal{D}^w g)(\zeta_j) = \sum_{\substack{\boldsymbol{u} \in [N]^d: \\ \mu_{j,\boldsymbol{u}} \leq k-w}} \sum_{v=0}^{w} \frac{w!}{v!(w-v)!}(\mathcal{D}^{w-v} p_{\boldsymbol{u}})(\zeta_j) \cdot \gamma_{j,\boldsymbol{u},v}$$

$$+ \sum_{v'=1}^{w} \sum_{\substack{\boldsymbol{u} \in [N]^d: \\ \mu_{j,\boldsymbol{u}} = k-w+v'}} \sum_{v=0}^{w-v'} \frac{w!}{v!(w-v)!}(\mathcal{D}^{w-v} p_{\boldsymbol{u}})(\zeta_j) \cdot \gamma_{j,\boldsymbol{u},v},$$

Notations.
- Parameters $n, m, \ell, d, k \in \mathbb{N}$.
- The family $\{B_1, \ldots, B_N\}$ of all maximal sets of Δ.
- A prime field $\mathbb{F}$ such that $|\mathbb{F}| \geq \max\{m + \ell, k + 1\}$.
- $m + \ell$ distinct elements $\zeta_1, \ldots, \zeta_m, \eta_1, \ldots, \eta_\ell \in \mathbb{F}$, $\boldsymbol{\zeta} = (\zeta_j)_{j \in [m]}$, and $\boldsymbol{\eta} = (\eta_1, \ldots, \eta_\ell)$.
- For $j \in [m]$ and $\boldsymbol{u} = (u_1, \ldots, u_d) \in [N]^d$, a set $M_{j,\boldsymbol{u}} = \{\kappa \in [d] : j \in B_\kappa\}$ and $\mu_{j,\boldsymbol{u}} = |M_{j,\boldsymbol{u}}|$.
- For $j \in [m]$, a set

$$S_j = \left\{ (\boldsymbol{i}, \boldsymbol{u}, w, \boldsymbol{e}) : \begin{array}{c} \boldsymbol{i} = (i_1, \ldots, i_d) \in [n]^d, \boldsymbol{u} = (u_1, \ldots, u_d) \in [N]^d, \\ w \in [0..k] \text{ s.t. } w \leq k - \mu_{j,\boldsymbol{u}}, \\ \boldsymbol{e} = (e_1, \ldots, e_d) \in \mathbb{Z}_+^d \text{ s.t. } e_1 + \cdots + e_d = w \end{array} \right\}.$$

$\mathsf{Share}(i, \boldsymbol{x}^{\langle i \rangle})$. Given an index $i \in [n]$ and an input $\boldsymbol{x}^{\langle i \rangle} \in \mathbb{F}^\ell$:
1. Choose $\boldsymbol{x}_u^{\langle i \rangle} \in \mathbb{F}^\ell$, $u \in [N]$ at random such that $\boldsymbol{x}^{\langle i \rangle} = \sum_{u \in [N]} \boldsymbol{x}_u^{\langle i \rangle}$.
2. For each $u \in [N]$, choose $\varphi_u^{\langle i \rangle} \in \mathbb{F}[X]$ at random such that $\boldsymbol{x}_u^{\langle i \rangle} = (\varphi_u^{\langle i \rangle}(\eta_j))_{j \in [\ell]}$ and $\deg(\varphi_u^{\langle i \rangle}) \leq \ell - 1$.
3. For each $j \in [m]$, set

$$\mathsf{in}_j^{\langle i \rangle} = (\varphi_u^{\langle i \rangle}(\zeta_j))_{u \in [N]: j \notin B_u} \text{ and}$$
$$\mathsf{rec}_j^{\langle i \rangle} = ((\varphi_u^{\langle i \rangle}(\zeta_j))_{u \in [N]: j \in B_u}, ((\mathcal{D}\varphi_u^{\langle i \rangle})(\zeta_j), \ldots, (\mathcal{D}^k \varphi_u^{\langle i \rangle})(\zeta_j))_{u \in [N]}).$$

4. Output $(\mathsf{in}_j^{\langle i \rangle}, \mathsf{rec}_j^{\langle i \rangle})_{j \in [m]}$.

$\mathsf{Eval}(j, f, (\mathsf{in}_j^{\langle i \rangle})_{i \in [n]})$. Given an index $j \in [m]$ and a polynomial $f = \sum_{\boldsymbol{i} \in [n]^d} c_{\boldsymbol{i}} X_{i_1} \cdots X_{i_d}$ where $c_{\boldsymbol{i}} \in \mathbb{F}$, and input shares $(\mathsf{in}_j^{\langle i \rangle})_{i \in [n]}$, output

$$\mathsf{out}_j = \left(c_{\boldsymbol{i}} \prod_{\substack{\kappa: \\ \kappa \notin M_{j,\boldsymbol{u}}, e_\kappa = 0}} \varphi_{u_\kappa}^{\langle i_\kappa \rangle}(\zeta_j) : (\boldsymbol{i}, \boldsymbol{u}, w, \boldsymbol{e}) \in S_j \right).$$

Fig. 5. The sharing and evaluation algorithms of an (n, m, ℓ, d, Δ)-IT-HSS scheme with recovery information for an adversary structure Δ

Notations. Using the notations in Fig. 5,

  - For $\boldsymbol{u} \in [N]^d$, $p_{\boldsymbol{u}} \in \mathbb{F}[X]$ is the polynomial of minimum degree such that $p_{\boldsymbol{u}}(\eta_i) = 1$ for any $i \in [\ell]$ and $(\mathcal{D}^w p_{\boldsymbol{u}})(\zeta_j) = 0$ for any $w \in [0..k]$ and any $j \in [m]$ with $\mu_{j,\boldsymbol{u}} > w$.

$\mathsf{Dec}((\mathsf{out}_j)_{j\in[m]}, (\mathsf{rec}_j^{\langle i \rangle})_{i\in[n],j\in[m]})$. Given output shares $(\mathsf{out}_j)_{j\in[m]}$ and recovery information $(\mathsf{rec}_j^{\langle i \rangle})_{i\in[n],j\in[m]}$:

1. For each $j \in [m]$ and $w \in [0..k]$, compute

$$
\gamma_{j,\boldsymbol{u},w} := \sum_{\substack{i,e: \\ (i,\boldsymbol{u},w,e)\in S_j}} \frac{w!}{e_1!\cdots e_d!} \left(c_i \prod_{\substack{\kappa: \\ \kappa\notin M_{j,\boldsymbol{u}}, e_\kappa=0}} \varphi_{u_\kappa}^{\langle i_\kappa \rangle}(\zeta_j) \right)
$$

$$
\times \left(\prod_{\substack{\kappa: \\ \kappa\in M_{j,\boldsymbol{u}}, e_\kappa=0}} \varphi_{u_\kappa}^{\langle i_\kappa \rangle}(\zeta_j) \right) \left(\prod_{\kappa:e_\kappa>0} (\mathcal{D}^{e_\kappa} \varphi_{u_\kappa,v_j}^{\langle i_\kappa \rangle})(\zeta_j) \right).
$$

   for all $\boldsymbol{u} \in [N]^d$ such that $\mu_{j,\boldsymbol{u}} \leq k - w$ and compute

$$
y_{j,w} := \sum_{\substack{\boldsymbol{u}\in[N]^d: \\ \mu_{j,\boldsymbol{u}}\leq k-w}} \sum_{v=0}^{w} \frac{w!}{v!(w-v)!} (\mathcal{D}^{w-v} p_{\boldsymbol{u}})(\zeta_j)\gamma_{j,\boldsymbol{u},v}
$$

$$
+ \sum_{v'=1}^{w} \sum_{\substack{\boldsymbol{u}\in[N]^d: \\ \mu_{j,\boldsymbol{u}}=k-w+v'}} \sum_{v=0}^{w-v'} \frac{w!}{v!(w-v)!} (\mathcal{D}^{w-v} p_{\boldsymbol{u}})(\zeta_j)\gamma_{j,\boldsymbol{u},v}.
$$

2. Letting $\boldsymbol{z}_j = (y_{j,w})_{w\in[0..k]}$, output $\mathsf{Hermite}_{\boldsymbol{\zeta},\boldsymbol{\eta}}((\boldsymbol{z}_j)_{j\in[m]})$.

Fig. 6. The decoding algorithm of an (n, m, ℓ, d, Δ)-IT-HSS scheme with recovery information for an adversary structure Δ

which is equal to $y_{j,w}$. For each $j \in [m]$, $w \in [0..k]$, and $\boldsymbol{u} \in [N]^d$, define $c_{w,\boldsymbol{u}} = |\{j \in [m] : \mu_{j,\boldsymbol{u}} > w\}|$, and $\delta_{j,w,\boldsymbol{u}} = 1$ if $\mu_{j,\boldsymbol{u}} \leq w$ and otherwise 0. Proposition 1 implies that $\deg p_{\boldsymbol{u}} \leq \ell - 1 + \sum_{j\in[m]} \mu_{j,\boldsymbol{u}}$. We also have that

$$
\sum_{j\in[m]} \mu_{j,\boldsymbol{u}} = \sum_{w\in[0..k]} c_{w,\boldsymbol{u}}
$$

$$
= (k+1)m - \sum_{j=1}^{m}\sum_{w=0}^{k} \delta_{j,w,\boldsymbol{u}}
$$

$$
= (k+1)m - \sum_{j=1}^{m} \max\{k+1-\mu_{j,\boldsymbol{u}}, 0\}
$$

$$
= (k+1)m - |(k+1)\mathbf{1}_m - (\boldsymbol{a}_{u_1}(j) + \cdots + \boldsymbol{a}_{u_d}(j))|_+.
$$

Hence, the condition (5) implies that $\deg p_u < (k+1)m - d(\ell-1)$. Then, we have $\deg g \le \max_{u \in [N]^d}\{p_u h_u\} < (k+1)m$ and $\mathsf{Hermite}_{\zeta,\eta}((z_j)_{j\in[m]}) = (g(\eta_j))_{j\in[\ell]}$.

An input share $\mathsf{in}_j^{\langle i \rangle}$ is a vector of dimension $N_j := |\{u \in [N] : j \notin B_u\}|$ and each piece of recovery information $\mathsf{rec}_j^{\langle i \rangle}$ is a vector of dimension $N - N_j + Nk$. Since $|S_j| \le n^d \cdot N^d \cdot k \cdot 2^{k+d} =: \beta$, an output share out_j is a vector $\boldsymbol{y}_j \in \mathbb{F}^\beta$. Each $y_{j,w}$ computed by Dec is linear in the $\gamma_{j,u,v}$'s, each of which is in turn a degree-1 polynomial of out_j. The degree of $y_{j,w}$ with respect to $(\mathsf{rec}_j^{\langle i \rangle})_{i\in[n]}$ is at most the maximum of $\mu_{j,u} + |\{\kappa \in [d] : e_\kappa > 0\}|$ over all $\boldsymbol{u} \in [N]^d$ and all $\boldsymbol{e} \in \mathbb{Z}_+^d$ such that $\mu_{j,u} \le k - w$ and $\sum_\kappa e_\kappa = w$, which is at most $(k-w)+w \le k$. Therefore, $\boldsymbol{z}_j = (y_{j,w})_{w\in[0..k]}$ can be expressed as $\boldsymbol{A}_j \boldsymbol{y}_j + \boldsymbol{b}_j$ using a $(k+1)$-by-β matrix $\boldsymbol{A}_j$ and $(k+1)$-dimensional vector $\boldsymbol{b}_j$ whose entries are degree-k polynomials of $(\boldsymbol{r}_j^{\langle i \rangle})_{i\in[n]}$. Since $\mathsf{Hermite}_{\zeta,\eta}((z_j)_{j\in[m]})$ is linear in $(z_j)_{j\in[m]}$, the output of Dec can be expressed as $\sum_{j\in[m]} \boldsymbol{C}_j(\boldsymbol{A}_j \boldsymbol{y}_j + \boldsymbol{b}_j)$ using $\boldsymbol{C}_j \in \mathbb{F}^{\ell\times(k+1)}$.

To see Δ-privacy, we show that for any $\boldsymbol{x}, \boldsymbol{x}' \in \mathbb{F}^\ell$ and $B \in \Delta$, the distributions of $(\mathsf{in}_j)_{j\in B}$ for $\boldsymbol{x}$ and $(\mathsf{in}_j')_{j\in B}$ for $\boldsymbol{x}'$ are identical. We may assume that $B = B_i$ for some $i \in [N]$. There exists a polynomial θ such that $\deg(\theta) \le \ell - 1$ and $(\theta(\eta_j))_{j\in[\ell]} = \boldsymbol{x}' - \boldsymbol{x}$. We then have a bijection between the random strings used by Share on input $\boldsymbol{x}$ and those used by Share on input $\boldsymbol{x}'$ such that the shares of B are the same under this bijection. Indeed, we map any polynomials $(\varphi_u)_{u\in[N]}$ generated by Share on input $\boldsymbol{x}$ to $(\varphi_u')_{u\in[N]}$ where $\varphi_u' = \varphi_u + \theta$ if $u = i$ and otherwise $\varphi_u' = \varphi_u$. Then, $(\varphi_u')_{u\in[N]}$ provide consistent shares for $\boldsymbol{x}'$ and the shares of B resulting from $(\varphi_u')_{u\in[N]}$ are the same as the ones for $(\varphi_u)_{u\in[N]}$ since the j-th share does not contain $\varphi_i'(\zeta_j)$ or $\varphi_i(\zeta_j)$ if $j \in B_i$.   □

By applying the ILM compiler in Proposition 2, we obtain an HSS scheme for a general adversary structure. Again, as in Corollary 2, we have to add similar re-randomizing procedures to guarantee context hiding.

Corollary 3. *Using the notations in Theorem 3, assume that $n, m \in \mathsf{poly}[\lambda]$, $k, d \in O(1)$, and $N \in \mathsf{poly}[\lambda]$. Assuming a (resp. multi-key) k-HE scheme HE, there exists an (n, m, ℓ, d, Δ)-HSS scheme HSS (resp. in the plain model) with efficiency measures $\alpha = N\log|\mathbb{F}| + Nk$ and $\beta = k + 1$. Furthermore, if HE satisfies circuit privacy, there exists a context-hiding (n, m, ℓ, d, Δ)-HSS scheme HSS' (resp. in the plain model) with efficiency measures $\alpha = (N + k + 1)\log|\mathbb{F}| + Nk = O(N\log(m+\ell))$ and $\beta = k + 1 = O(1)$.*

Proof. In view of Proposition 2 and Theorem 3, we obtain an (n, m, ℓ, d, Δ)-HSS scheme HSS with efficiency measures $\alpha = N\log|\mathbb{F}| + Nk$ and $\beta = k + 1$.

We make HSS context-hiding by adding re-randomizing procedures to the sharing and evaluation algorithms. Using the notations in the proof of Theorem 3, the output of the sharing algorithm of HSS on input $\boldsymbol{x}^{\langle i \rangle}$ includes

$$c_j^{\langle i \rangle} = ((\mathsf{HE.Enc}(\mathsf{pk}, \varphi_u^{\langle i \rangle}(\zeta_j)))_{u\in[N]:j\in B_u}, (\mathsf{HE.Enc}(\mathsf{pk}, \mathcal{D}^w\varphi_u^{\langle i \rangle}(\zeta_j)))_{u\in[N],w\in[0..k]})$$

for $j \in [m]$. The evaluation algorithm executed by the j-th server outputs $k+1$ ciphertexts $(d_{j,w})_{w \in [0..k]}$ each of which decrypts to $y_{j,w} = \mathcal{D}^w g(\zeta_j)$ for $w \in [0..k]$. Note that there are degree-k polynomials $\nu_{j,w}$ (whose coefficients depend on $(\varphi_u^{\langle i \rangle}(\zeta_j))_{u \in [N]: j \notin B_u}$) such that $d_{j,w} = \mathsf{HE.Eval}(\mathsf{pk}, \nu_{j,w}, (c_j^{\langle 1 \rangle}, \ldots, c_j^{\langle n \rangle}))$. We fix any client, say, $i = 1$. If the input index is $i = 1$, we let the sharing algorithm generate a random polynomial θ such that $\deg(\theta) < (k+1)m$ and $(\theta(\eta_j))_{j \in [\ell]} = 0$. Then, it sends $k + 1$ field elements $y'_{j,w} = \mathcal{D}^w \theta(\zeta_j)$ for $w \in [0..k]$ to the j-th server in addition to an input share $\mathsf{in}_j^{\langle 1 \rangle}$ of HSS. We do not modify the procedures for the other clients. The size of input shares are now $\alpha = (N + k + 1) \log |\mathbb{F}| + Nk$. When executing the evaluation algorithm of HSS, the j-th server outputs $k+1$ ciphertexts $(d'_{j,w})_{w \in [0..k]}$ each of which decrypts to $y_{j,w} + y'_{j,w} = (\mathcal{D}^w g')(\zeta_j)$ where $g' = g + \theta$. More precisely, the j-th server computes $d'_{j,w} \leftarrow \mathsf{HE.Eval}(\mathsf{pk}, \nu_{j,w}(\cdot) + y'_{j,w}, (c_j^{\langle 1 \rangle}, \ldots, c_j^{\langle n \rangle}))$ for all $w \in [0..k]$.

Given $\mathcal{P}_\ell(f, (x^{\langle 1 \rangle}, \ldots, x^{\langle n \rangle}))$, the simulator $S_{\mathsf{HSS}'}$ randomly chooses a polynomial $\widetilde{g}$ such that $(\widetilde{g}(\eta_j))_{j \in [\ell]} = \mathcal{P}_\ell(f, (x^{\langle 1 \rangle}, \ldots, x^{\langle n \rangle}))$ and $\deg \widetilde{g} < (k+1)m$, and then computes $\widetilde{d}_{j,w} \leftarrow S_{\mathsf{HE}}(1^\lambda, \mathsf{pk}, (\mathcal{D}^w \widetilde{g})(\zeta_j))$ for all $j \in [m]$ and $w \in [0..k]$, where S_{HE} is the simulator for the circuit privacy of HE. It finally outputs $((\widetilde{d}_{1,w})_{w \in [0..k]}, \ldots, (\widetilde{d}_{m,w})_{w \in [0..k]})$. We analyze the distribution of the output of $S_{\mathsf{HSS}'}$. Let $j \in [m]$, $w \in [0..k]$, and $r_{j,w}$ be any fixed field element. The circuit privacy of HE implies that $\mathsf{HE.Eval}(\mathsf{pk}, \nu_{j,w}(\cdot) + r_{j,w}, (c_j^{\langle 1 \rangle}, \ldots, c_j^{\langle n \rangle})) \approx S_{\mathsf{HE}}(1^\lambda, \mathsf{pk}, y_{j,w} + r_{j,w})$, where $\approx$ denotes statistical indistinguishability. Then, we have that

$$(\mathsf{HE.Eval}(\mathsf{pk}, \nu_{j,w}(\cdot) + r_{j,w}, (c_j^{\langle 1 \rangle}, \ldots, c_j^{\langle n \rangle})))_{w \in [0..k], j \in [m]}$$
$$\approx (S_{\mathsf{HE}}(1^\lambda, \mathsf{pk}, y_{j,w} + r_{j,w}))_{w \in [0..k], j \in [m]}. \tag{6}$$

Let V be the set from which θ is sampled. Note that V is a linear space over $\mathbb{F}$. Since Eq. (6) holds for any fixed elements $r_{j,w}$, we can apply it to $r_{j,w} = y'_{j,w} = \mathcal{D}^w \theta(\zeta_j)$ where $\theta \leftarrow_\$ V$, and obtain that

$$(d'_{j,w})_{w \in [0..k], j \in [m]} = (\mathsf{HE.Eval}(\mathsf{pk}, \nu_{j,w}(\cdot) + y'_{j,w}, (c_j^{\langle 1 \rangle}, \ldots, c_j^{\langle n \rangle})))_{w \in [0..k], j \in [m]}$$
$$\approx (S_{\mathsf{HE}}(1^\lambda, \mathsf{pk}, y_{j,w} + y'_{j,w}))_{w \in [0..k], j \in [m]}. \tag{7}$$

The distribution of g' is the uniform distribution over an affine space $g + V := \{g + \theta : \theta \in V\}$, which is the same as that of $\widetilde{g}$. Taking derivatives and substitution are both linear maps over $\mathbb{F}$. Hence, the distribution of $(\mathcal{D}^w g'(\zeta_j))_{w \in [0..k], j \in [m]}$ induced by $\theta \leftarrow_\$ V$ is identical to that of $(\mathcal{D}^w \widetilde{g}(\zeta_j))_{w \in [0..k], j \in [m]}$ induced by $\widetilde{g} \leftarrow_\$ g + V$. Combined with Eq. (7), we obtain that

$$(d'_{j,w})_{w \in [0..k], j \in [m]} \approx (S_{\mathsf{HE}}(1^\lambda, \mathsf{pk}, \mathcal{D}^w g'(\zeta_j)))_{w \in [0..k], j \in [m]}$$
$$= S_{\mathsf{HSS}'}(1^\lambda, \mathsf{pk}, \mathcal{P}_\ell(f, (x^{\langle 1 \rangle}, \ldots, x^{\langle n \rangle}))).$$

We show that the computational complexity of HSS$'$ is polynomial in the security parameter λ. The most costly step in the sharing algorithm of HSS$_0$

is sampling random polynomials $\varphi_u^{\langle i \rangle}$, which can be done in polynomial time in N, ℓ by pre-computing and publishing a basis for the linear space $\mathcal{L}_u := \{\varphi_u \in \mathbb{F}[X] : \deg(\varphi_u) \leq \ell - 1, (\varphi_u(\eta_j))_{j \in [\ell]} = \mathbf{0}\}$ for each $u \in [N]$. We have that $\ell = O(m)$ due to the condition (5) and hence the time complexity of that step is polynomial in λ. Since the additional steps of HSS$'$.Share can also be done in time $\mathsf{poly}[m, N, \ell, \lambda]$, the time complexity of HSS$'$.Share is polynomial in λ. Next, HSS$_0$.Eval computes $\beta = O(n^d N^d)$ products and HE.Eval can be executed by HSS$'$.Eval in time $\beta(n\rho)^k \cdot \mathsf{poly}[\lambda] = O(n^{d+k} N^{d+k}) \cdot \mathsf{poly}[\lambda]$. The time complexity of HSS$'$.Eval is therefore also polynomial in λ. Finally, in view of Proposition 2, HSS$'$.Dec can be done in time $m\ell(k+1) \cdot \mathsf{poly}[\lambda] = \mathsf{poly}[\lambda]$.

We can lift the above scheme to the plain model by replacing the HE scheme with the corresponding multi-key variant. □

Since $N = \mathsf{poly}[\lambda]$ is required, Corollary 3 cannot be applied to adversary structures whose number of all maximal sets is exponential in $m = \mathsf{poly}[\lambda]$, which actually occurs in the worst case. Therefore, Corollary 3 is especially important for the case of $N = \mathsf{poly}[m]$. As shown in Sect. 8, there is still an interesting class of adversary structures even if $N = O(m)$.

We can instantiate the m-input MPC protocol in Sect. 3.4 with the HSS scheme in Corollary 3 and then the communication complexity is $O(Nm^2 \log(m + \ell))$, where ℓ is the number of parallel evaluations. The scheme [30] can be recovered by setting $\ell = 1$. Indeed, at Step 2 of the sharing algorithm in Fig. 5, a possible polynomial $\varphi_u^{\langle i \rangle}$ is only the constant polynomial $\boldsymbol{x}_u^{\langle i \rangle}$ of degree 0. Therefore, $\mathsf{in}_j^{\langle i \rangle}$ at Step 3 consists of $(\boldsymbol{x}_u^{\langle i \rangle})_{u \in [N]: j \notin B_u}$. We can set $\mathsf{rec}_j^{\langle i \rangle}$ as $(\boldsymbol{x}_u^{\langle i \rangle})_{u \in [N]: j \in B_u}$ by removing the other entries since $\mathcal{D}^w \varphi_u^{\langle i \rangle}$ is the zero polynomial for $w \geq 1$. This is exactly the same as the one in [30].

8   Formalization of Practical Adversary Structures

We formalize two classes of non-threshold adversary structures and show advantages of our schemes over the previous schemes [17,19,26,30] in the application to m-input MPC shown in Sect. 3.4. That is, the i-th input party has ℓ kinds of data $\boldsymbol{x}^{\langle i \rangle} = (\boldsymbol{x}^{\langle i \rangle}(1), \ldots, \boldsymbol{x}^{\langle i \rangle}(\ell)) \in \mathbb{F}^\ell$ and an output party wants $\mathcal{P}_\ell(f, (\boldsymbol{x}^{\langle 1 \rangle}, \ldots, \boldsymbol{x}^m))$. We suppose that the degree d is independent of the number of data m. For example, d depends only on the order of approximation for Fisher's linear discriminant analysis [24].

8.1   Unbalanced 2-Partite Adversary Structure

Let $\Pi = (P_1, P_2)$ be a 2-partition and $\tau, \sigma \in \mathbb{R}_+$. Define a Π-partite adversary structure $\mathcal{B}_{\tau,\sigma}^\Pi = \{X \subseteq [m] : |X| \leq \tau m \wedge (|X \cap P_1| \leq \sigma m \vee |X \cap P_2| \leq \sigma m)\}$. The motivation behind $\mathcal{B}_{\tau,\sigma}^\Pi$ is modification of $\mathcal{T}_\tau^m$ so that it takes into account a real-world situation. Suppose that input parties are classified to two organizations P_1, P_2 and an adversary $\mathcal{A}$ is one of the parties. If $\mathcal{A}$ belongs to P_1, then it would be more difficult for $\mathcal{A}$ to corrupt parties in the other organization

P_2 than parties in P_1. We therefore add the constraint $|X \cap P_2| \leq \sigma m$ to the threshold constraint $|X| \leq \tau m$. Similarly, we require $|X \cap P_1| \leq \sigma m$. We show that an HSS scheme for $\mathcal{B}^{\Pi}_{\tau,\sigma}$ is obtained from Corollary 2 under a certain parameter setting. The proof is given in the full version.

Proposition 3. *Let $m \in \mathbb{N}$ be an even number and $\Pi = (P_1, P_2)$ be a 2-partition such that $|P_1| = |P_2| = m/2$. Let $k, d \in \mathbb{N}$ be constants and assume that d is an odd number. Let $\epsilon, \tau, \sigma \in \mathbb{R}_+$ be such that*

$$\frac{d-1}{2d}\tau + \frac{d+1}{2d}\sigma + \epsilon \leq \frac{k+1}{2d} \text{ and } \sigma \leq \tau. \tag{8}$$

and set $\ell = \epsilon m$. Assuming a circuit-private k-HE scheme and a prime field $\mathbb{F}$ with $|\mathbb{F}| \geq \max\{m + \ell, k + 1\}$, there exists a context-hiding $(m, m, \ell, d, \mathcal{B}^{\Pi}_{\tau,\sigma})$-HSS scheme with efficiency measures $\alpha = (k+3)\log|\mathbb{F}| + 2k$ and $\beta = k + 1$.

The threshold schemes [19,26] only tolerate $\mathcal{T}^m_\tau$ and hence inapplicable to $\mathcal{B}^{\Pi}_{\tau,\sigma}$ for $\tau \geq (k+1)/d$. In the scheme [30], the input share size α is exponential in m since the number of all maximal sets of $\mathcal{B}^{\Pi}_{\tau,\sigma}$ is larger than $\binom{m/2}{\sigma m}\binom{m/2}{(\tau-\sigma)m}$. Our scheme can be applied to $\mathcal{B}^{\Pi}_{\tau,\sigma}$ even for τ such that $(k+1)/d \leq \tau < (k+1)/(d-1)$ and the input and output share sizes are only constant numbers of field elements and ciphertexts. Furthermore, if there are sufficiently many input parties, it can support parallel evaluations without increasing communication complexity.

To be more concrete, suppose that there are $m = 1000$ input parties and that a polynomial of degree $d = 5$ is computed on $\ell = 10$ data sets. Assuming a 1-HE scheme (i.e., $k = 1$), we can choose $\epsilon = 0.01$, $\tau = 0.45$, and $\sigma = 0.01$, which means that our scheme can tolerate a collusion X of at most 450 input parties such that $|X \cap P_1| \leq 10$ or $|X \cap P_2| \leq 10$. The point-to-point communication complexity between input parties is 4 field elements plus 2 ciphertexts and each input party sends 2 ciphertexts to an output party. Hence, the total communication complexity is $4m^2$ field elements plus $2m^2 + 2m$ ciphertexts. The schemes [19,26] cannot be applied to this setting since $\tau > 0.4 = (k+1)/d$. Since the scheme of [17] does not support parallel evaluation, the communication complexity increases $\ell = \epsilon m$ times, that is, $4\epsilon m^3$ field elements plus $2\epsilon m^3 + 2\epsilon m^2$ ciphertexts.

8.2   Adversary Structure Induced by a Random Graph

Let $G = ([m], E)$ be a graph on the set of input parties (vertices) and let A_j be the set of all adjacent vertices of $j \in [m]$. We define an adversary structure $\Delta_G = \{X \subseteq [m] : X \subseteq A_j \cup \{j\} \text{ for some } j \in [m]\}$. Note that the number N of all the maximal sets of Δ_G is at most m. The motivation behind Δ_G is a real-world scenario in which an adversary is one of input parties and colludes with all adjacent parties in G. For p with $0 < p < 1$, we consider the probability distribution $\mathcal{G}(m, p)$ [22] over the set of all the graphs on m vertices, in which a random graph is obtained by starting with a set of m isolated vertices and adding every possible edge independently with probability p. We show that for sufficiently large m and G sampled from $\mathcal{G}(m, p)$, an HSS scheme for Δ_G can be obtained from Corollary 3 with high probability. The proof is given in the full version.

Proposition 4. *Let $m, d, k \in \mathbb{N}$ and p be a real number with $0 < p < 1$. Let $\ell \in \mathbb{N}$ be such that $\ell \leq (d+1)^{-1} k (1-p)^d (m-d)$ and $q \in \mathbb{R}_+$ be such that*

$$q \geq 1 - m^d \exp \left(-\frac{2(1-p)^{2d}(m-d)}{(k+1)^2} \right).$$

Assume a circuit-private k-HE scheme and a prime field $\mathbb{F}$ with $|\mathbb{F}| \geq \max\{m + \ell, k+1\}$. If G is sampled from $\mathcal{G}(m, p)$, then with probability at least q, there exists a context-hiding $(m, m, \ell, d, \Delta_G)$-HSS scheme with efficiency measures $\alpha = (m + k + 1) \log |\mathbb{F}| + 2k$ and $\beta = k + 1$.

We demonstrate concrete parameters. Assume a 1-HE scheme, i.e., $k = 1$. Suppose that we want to compute a single polynomial of degree $d = 5$ and that every possible edge occurs with probability $p = 0.45$. Then, if there are $m \geq 50000$ input parties, we can obtain, with probability at least 0.99, an HSS scheme for Δ_G computing the polynomial on $\ell \gtrsim m/200 \geq 250$ different data sets. The threshold schemes [19,26] cannot be applied to this setting since $\Delta_G \not\subseteq \mathcal{T}_\tau^m$ with high probability if $p > \tau$. Precisely, we also show in the full version that if $p = \tau + \epsilon$, the probability that $\Delta_G \subseteq \mathcal{T}_\tau^m$ occurs is at most $\exp(-2(m\epsilon - p + 1)^2/(m-1))$, which converges exponentially to 0 for $m \to \infty$. For the above parameters, if $m \geq 1000$, $\Delta_G \not\subseteq \mathcal{T}_{0.4}^m$ occurs with probability at least 0.99. The scheme [30] can tolerate Δ_G and does not require $|\mathbb{F}| \geq m + \ell$. However, their scheme cannot support parallel evaluation and hence the efficiency measures $\alpha = O(\ell m \log |\mathbb{F}|)$ and $\beta = O(\ell)$ are ℓ times larger than our scheme. As for the assumption on the field size, since statistical analysis and machine learning typically deal with numerical data, we end up to choose a field of size much larger than $m + \ell$ due to another requirement of sufficiently approximating the data.

Acknowledgements. This research was partially supported by JSPS KAKENHI Grant Numbers JP20J20797 and 19H01109, JST CREST JPMJCR19F6 and JPMJCR14D6, and Ministry of Internal Affairs and Communications SCOPE Grant Number 182103105.

References

1. Attrapadung, N., Hanaoka, G., Mitsunari, S., Sakai, Y., Shimizu, K., Teruya, T.: Efficient two-level homomorphic encryption in prime-order bilinear groups and a fast implementation in webassembly. In: Proceedings of the 2018 on Asia Conference on Computer and Communications Security, ASIACCS 2018, pp. 685–697 (2018)

2. Barkol, O., Ishai, Y., Weinreb, E.: On d-multiplicative secret sharing. J. Cryptol. **23**(4), 580–593 (2010)
3. Beaver, D., Micali, S., Rogaway, P.: The round complexity of secure protocols. In: Proceedings of the Twenty-Second Annual ACM Symposium on Theory of Computing, STOC 1990, pp. 503–513 (1990)
4. Boneh, D., Goh, E.-J., Nissim, K.: Evaluating 2-DNF formulas on ciphertexts. In: Kilian, J. (ed.) TCC 2005. LNCS, vol. 3378, pp. 325–341. Springer, Heidelberg (2005). https://doi.org/10.1007/978-3-540-30576-7_18
5. Boyle, E., Couteau, G., Gilboa, N., Ishai, Y., Kohl, L., Scholl, P.: efficient pseudorandom correlation generators: silent OT extension and more. In: Boldyreva, A., Micciancio, D. (eds.) CRYPTO 2019, Part III. LNCS, vol. 11694, pp. 489–518. Springer, Cham (2019). https://doi.org/10.1007/978-3-030-26954-8_16
6. Boyle, E., Gilboa, N., Ishai, Y.: Breaking the circuit size barrier for secure computation under DDH. In: Robshaw, M., Katz, J. (eds.) CRYPTO 2016, Part I. LNCS, vol. 9814, pp. 509–539. Springer, Heidelberg (2016). https://doi.org/10.1007/978-3-662-53018-4_19
7. Boyle, E., Kohl, L., Scholl, P.: Homomorphic secret sharing from lattices without FHE. In: Ishai, Y., Rijmen, V. (eds.) EUROCRYPT 2019, Part II. LNCS, vol. 11477, pp. 3–33. Springer, Cham (2019). https://doi.org/10.1007/978-3-030-17656-3_1
8. Cachin, C., Camenisch, J., Kilian, J., Müller, J.: One-round secure computation and secure autonomous mobile agents. In: Montanari, U., Rolim, J.D.P., Welzl, E. (eds.) ICALP 2000. LNCS, vol. 1853, pp. 512–523. Springer, Heidelberg (2000). https://doi.org/10.1007/3-540-45022-X_43
9. Cascudo, I., Cramer, R., Xing, C., Yuan, C.: Amortized complexity of information-theoretically secure MPC revisited. In: Shacham, H., Boldyreva, A. (eds.) CRYPTO 2018, Part III. LNCS, vol. 10993, pp. 395–426. Springer, Cham (2018). https://doi.org/10.1007/978-3-319-96878-0_14
10. Castagnos, G., Laguillaumie, F.: Linearly homomorphic encryption from DDH. In: Nyberg, K. (ed.) CT-RSA 2015. LNCS, vol. 9048, pp. 487–505. Springer, Cham (2015). https://doi.org/10.1007/978-3-319-16715-2_26
11. Catalano, D., Fiore, D.: Using linearly-homomorphic encryption to evaluate degree-2 functions on encrypted data. In: Proceedings of the 22nd ACM SIGSAC Conference on Computer and Communications Security, CCS 2015, pp. 1518–1529 (2015)
12. Cheon, J.H., et al.: Batch fully homomorphic encryption over the integers. In: Johansson, T., Nguyen, P.Q. (eds.) EUROCRYPT 2013. LNCS, vol. 7881, pp. 315–335. Springer, Heidelberg (2013). https://doi.org/10.1007/978-3-642-38348-9_20
13. Damgård, I., Pastro, V., Smart, N., Zakarias, S.: Multiparty computation from somewhat homomorphic encryption. In: Safavi-Naini, R., Canetti, R. (eds.) CRYPTO 2012. LNCS, vol. 7417, pp. 643–662. Springer, Heidelberg (2012). https://doi.org/10.1007/978-3-642-32009-5_38
14. Diffie, W., Hellman, M.: New directions in cryptography. IEEE Trans. Inf. Theory **22**(6), 644–654 (1976)
15. Dodis, Y., Halevi, S., Rothblum, R.D., Wichs, D.: Spooky encryption and its applications. In: Robshaw, M., Katz, J. (eds.) CRYPTO 2016, Part III. LNCS, vol. 9816, pp. 93–122. Springer, Heidelberg (2016). https://doi.org/10.1007/978-3-662-53015-3_4
16. Elgamal, T.: A public key cryptosystem and a signature scheme based on discrete logarithms. IEEE Trans. Inf. Theory **31**(4), 469–472 (1985)

17. Eriguchi, R., Kunihiro, N.: d-Multiplicative secret sharing for multipartite adversary structures. In: 1st Conference on Information-Theoretic Cryptography (ITC 2020). Leibniz International Proceedings in Informatics (LIPIcs), vol. 163, pp. 2:1–2:16 (2020)
18. Farràs, O., Padró, C., et al.: Ideal secret sharing schemes for useful multipartite access structures. In: Chee, Y.M. (ed.) IWCC 2011. LNCS, vol. 6639, pp. 99–108. Springer, Heidelberg (2011). https://doi.org/10.1007/978-3-642-20901-7_6
19. Franklin, M., Yung, M.: Communication complexity of secure computation (extended abstract). In: Proceedings of the Twenty-Fourth Annual ACM Symposium on Theory of Computing, STOC 1992, pp. 699–710 (1992)
20. Freeman, D.M.: Converting pairing-based cryptosystems from composite-order groups to prime-order groups. In: Gilbert, H. (ed.) EUROCRYPT 2010. LNCS, vol. 6110, pp. 44–61. Springer, Heidelberg (2010). https://doi.org/10.1007/978-3-642-13190-5_3
21. Gentry, C.: Fully homomorphic encryption using ideal lattices. In: Proceedings of the Forty-First Annual ACM Symposium on Theory of Computing, STOC 2009, pp. 169–178 (2009)
22. Gilbert, E.N.: Random graphs. Ann. Math. Stat. **30**(4), 1141–1144 (1959)
23. Goldreich, O., Micali, S., Wigderson, A.: How to play any mental game. In: Proceedings of the Nineteenth Annual ACM Symposium on Theory of Computing, STOC 1987, pp. 218–229 (1987)
24. Graepel, T., Lauter, K., Naehrig, M.: ML confidential: machine learning on encrypted data. In: Kwon, T., Lee, M.-K., Kwon, D. (eds.) ICISC 2012. LNCS, vol. 7839, pp. 1–21. Springer, Heidelberg (2013). https://doi.org/10.1007/978-3-642-37682-5_1
25. Hazay, C., Orsini, E., Scholl, P., Soria-Vazquez, E.: TinyKeys: a new approach to efficient multi-party computation. In: Shacham, H., Boldyreva, A. (eds.) CRYPTO 2018, Part III. LNCS, vol. 10993, pp. 3–33. Springer, Cham (2018). https://doi.org/10.1007/978-3-319-96878-0_1
26. Ishai, Y., Lai, R.W.F., Malavolta, G.: A geometric approach to homomorphic secret sharing. In: Garay, J.A. (ed.) PKC 2021, Part II. LNCS, vol. 12711, pp. 92–119. Springer, Cham (2021). https://doi.org/10.1007/978-3-030-75248-4_4
27. Lai, R.W.F., Malavolta, G., Schröder, D.: Homomorphic secret sharing for low degree polynomials. In: Peyrin, T., Galbraith, S. (eds.) ASIACRYPT 2018, Part III. LNCS, vol. 11274, pp. 279–309. Springer, Cham (2018). https://doi.org/10.1007/978-3-030-03332-3_11
28. López-Alt, A., Tromer, E., Vaikuntanathan, V.: On-the-fly multiparty computation on the cloud via multikey fully homomorphic encryption. In: Proceedings of the Forty-Fourth Annual ACM Symposium on Theory of Computing, STOC 2012, pp. 1219–1234 (2012)
29. Paillier, P.: Public-key cryptosystems based on composite degree residuosity classes. In: Stern, J. (ed.) EUROCRYPT 1999. LNCS, vol. 1592, pp. 223–238. Springer, Heidelberg (1999). https://doi.org/10.1007/3-540-48910-X_16
30. Phalakarn, K., Suppakitpaisarn, V., Attrapadung, N., Matsuura, K.: Constructive t-secure homomorphic secret sharing for low degree polynomials. In: Bhargavan, K., Oswald, E., Prabhakaran, M. (eds.) INDOCRYPT 2020. LNCS, vol. 12578, pp. 763–785. Springer, Cham (2020). https://doi.org/10.1007/978-3-030-65277-7_34
31. Shamir, A.: How to share a secret. Commun. ACM **22**(11), 612–613 (1979)
32. Smart, N.P., Vercauteren, F.: Fully homomorphic SIMD operations. Des. Codes Cryptogr. **71**(1), 57–81 (2012). https://doi.org/10.1007/s10623-012-9720-4

33. Spitzbart, A.: A generalization of Hermite's interpolation formula. Am. Math. Mon. **67**(1), 42–46 (1960)
34. Woodruff, D., Yekhanin, S.: A geometric approach to information-theoretic private information retrieval. In: 20th Annual IEEE Conference on Computational Complexity (CCC 2005), pp. 275–284 (2005)

Improved Single-Round Secure Multiplication Using Regenerating Codes

Mark Abspoel[1]([⊠]), Ronald Cramer[1,2]([⊠]), Daniel Escudero[3]([⊠]),
Ivan Damgård[4]([⊠]), and Chaoping Xing[5]([⊠])

[1] CWI, Amsterdam, Netherlands
{M.A.Abspoel,Ronald.Cramer}@cwi.nl
[2] Leiden University, Leiden, Netherlands
[3] J.P. Morgan AI Research, New York, USA
daniel.escudero@protonmail.com
[4] Aarhus University, Aarhus, Denmark
ivan@cs.au.dk
[5] School of Electronic Information and Electric Engineering,
Shanghai Jiao Tong University, Shanghai, China
xingcp@sjtu.edu.cn

Abstract. In 2016, Guruswami and Wootters showed Shamir's secret-sharing scheme defined over an extension field has a regenerating property. Namely, we can compress each share to an element of the base field by applying a linear form, such that the secret is determined by a linear combination of the compressed shares. Immediately it seemed like an application to improve the complexity of unconditionally secure multiparty computation must be imminent; however, thus far, no result has been published.

We present the first application of regenerating codes to MPC, and show that its utility lies in reducing the number of rounds. Concretely, we present a protocol that obliviously evaluates a depth-d arithmetic circuit in $d + O(1)$ rounds, in the amortized setting of parallel evaluations, with $o(n^2)$ ring elements communicated per multiplication. Our protocol makes use of function-dependent preprocessing, and is secure against the maximal adversary corrupting $t < n/2$ parties. All existing approaches in this setting have complexity $\Omega(n^2)$.

Moreover, we extend some of the theory on regenerating codes to Galois rings. It was already known that the repair property of MDS codes over fields can be fully characterized in terms of its dual code. We show this characterization extends to linear codes over Galois rings, and use it to show the result of Guruswami and Wootters also holds true for Shamir's scheme over Galois rings.

1 Introduction

Secret-sharing is a technique that enables a given secret to be distributed into multiple values, called *shares*, in such a way that certain subsets of these do

---

Work done while Daniel Escudero was at Aarhus University.

© International Association for Cryptologic Research 2021
M. Tibouchi and H. Wang (Eds.): ASIACRYPT 2021, LNCS 13091, pp. 222–244, 2021.
https://doi.org/10.1007/978-3-030-92075-3_8

not leak anything about the secret, whereas certain other subsets completely determine the secret. These techniques are used in a wide range of areas such as distributed storage, cloud computing and multiparty computation, and improving/expanding them in different directions has huge impact in a lot of different domains.

The theory of secret-sharing schemes shares a deep connection with the theory of error-correcting codes, with many results in one domain translating naturally to results in the other. In 2016, Guruswami and Wootters showed that in a certain parameter regime, Reed-Solomon codes have a regenerating property [13], which in terms of secret-sharing can be translated into reconstructing a secret using "incomplete" shares. In this context, we can illustrate this property with the following example.

Consider Shamir's secret-sharing scheme with n shares and t-privacy defined over the binary extension field $\mathbb{F}_{2^m}$, subject to the regime $t < n - 2^{m-1}$. Suppose we are in an interactive scenario, where n parties $P_1, \ldots, P_n$ are connected by pairwise communication channels, with each party having a distinct share. We know Shamir's scheme has $(t + 1)$-reconstruction: the secret can be computed from any subset of $t + 1$ shares. Therefore, if the parties wish to reconstruct the secret value towards one of the parties, say P_1, they can do so by having t other parties send their share, an element in $\mathbb{F}_{2^m}$, to P_1, resulting in $m \cdot t$ bits of communication.

However, it turns out that it suffices for *all* parties to send a *single bit* to P_1, reducing communication by a factor $mt/(n-1)$. To accomplish this, each party P_i applies an $\mathbb{F}_2$-linear *compression function* $\phi_i : \mathbb{F}_{2^m} \to \mathbb{F}_2$ to their share, each of which is chosen such that the n compressed shares jointly determine the secret.

As mentioned before, secret-sharing techniques play a key role in information-theoretic multiparty computation (MPC). In this context, there is a set of participants $P_1, \ldots, P_n$ who want to jointly compute a given function on private data without leaking anything but the output. At a high level, the standard approach consists of letting the parties hold the inputs in secret-shared form, and designing methods to obtain shares of every intermediate step of the computation, until shares of the desired output are reached. At this point, this secret-shared value is reconstructed towards the party who is intended to learn the given output.

Reconstructing secret-shared values is a crucial step in MPC protocols, as this does not only happen in the output phase when the result of the computation must be reconstructed: most MPC protocols require reconstruction of secret-shared values for every non-trivial operation like a multiplication. Given this, it might seem at first sight that the techniques developed by Guruswami and Wootters would immediately improve communication complexity for information-theoretic multiparty computation (MPC). However, so far, a concrete application has remained elusive.[1] There are a number of factors that play into this.

---

[1] When Mary Wootters presented this result to the community in an invited talk of the Beyond TCS workshop affiliated to CRYPTO 2018, she posed the question to the community of what its implications to MPC are. It generated a bit of a buzz,

First, one general observation is that since the reduction in communication is proportional to m, the largest improvement is obtained when m is large. An implication is that since $0 < t < n - 2^{m-1}$, this also means the number of players must be large. Therefore, we restrict ourselves to asymptotic improvements only. In the following, we assume the adversary threshold t is at least linear in n.

Second, even though regenerating codes apply to large fields, the function that we wish to compute via MPC is typically expressed as a circuit over a finite field of small fixed size, such as $\mathbb{F}_2$. Efficient computation over $\mathbb{F}_{2^m}$ to evaluate circuits over $\mathbb{F}_2$ gives us an advantage in the amortized model, where we execute the same circuit many times in parallel with different inputs. In this model, we can obtain a lower amortized communication complexity (per circuit evaluation) by using reverse multiplication-friendly embeddings (RMFEs) [4].

Third, using compressed shares only improves communication for the reconstruction of a secret, and not for secret-sharing a value. This means that we cannot hope to easily improve the standard 2-round protocol for secure multiplication. In more detail, one way to securely multiply secret-shared values x and y is for the parties to consume an additional random secret-shared element r, and reconstruct their share of $\delta := xy - r$ towards one party, who subsequently broadcasts δ. If we assume this broadcast is cheap, the online cost of this secure multiplication is essentially the same as the reconstruction of one secret-sharing. However, as mentioned, regenerating codes will not help us optimize the generation of the random secret-shared r, so the overall protocol still requires $\Omega(n)$ bits of communication[2].

All this leaves only one setting in which we can meaningfully ask if regenerating codes can help: we can consider the tradeoff between the communication complexity and the number of rounds. The multiplication protocol we just considered has complexity $O(n)$ bits, which is asymptotically optimal [10], however, it uses two rounds.[3] It can be modified to use only *a single round*, where each player simply sends his share of δ to all players. But then the complexity increases to $\Theta(n^2)$. In fact, no currently known single-round protocol beats this bound, and we conjecture that it is optimal for the non-amortized setting. Note that in the amortized setting we can use packed secret sharing to get an improved single-round multiplication. However, this only works for a submaximal adversary $t < (1/2 - \varepsilon)n$.

Decreasing the round complexity of secure multiparty computation protocols is a well-motivated goal. Since information-theoretic MPC protocols typically

---

with several members of the community working on it even during the conference, however no result has been published thus far. We remark that other applications to regenerating codes to, for example, leakage-resilience of secret-sharing schemes [3] or side-channel countermeasures have been proposed, but none of these study positive effects in MPC constructions [5].

[2] We could try to get around this using computationally secure pseudorandom secret sharing, but this requires an exponential number of keys in n.

[3] The communication of the king-based protocol is $O(n)$ *field elements* for the maximal adversary $n = 2t + 1$. By incorporating a constant-rate RMFE we can achieve a communication of $O(n)$ *bits*, which is asymptotically optimal [10].

evaluate a circuit gate by gate, they require a number of sequential interactions of at least the round complexity per multiplication times the circuit depth. When the network latency is high, such as in wide area networks, the number of rounds can become the dominant factor in the running time of the protocol. Furthermore, there are even scenarios where *single-round* multiplication is essential.[4] For example, the work of [6] introduces the concept of "fluid MPC protocols", where the set of compute parties changes from one round to the next, enabling secure computation in a dynamic setting such as blockchains. In that work, the authors present a protocol that heavily relies on secure multiplication in a single round, and they leave it as an open problem to obtain a fluid MPC protocol that requires less than $\Theta(n^2)$ bits of communication per multiplication.

Motivated by the above, the question we ask is: can regenerating codes help us to build a one-round secure multiplication protocol in the amortized setting (and for a maximal adversary) where the complexity is $o(n^2)$?

1.1 This Work

In a nutshell, we give an answer in the affirmative to the question above by presenting an MPC protocol that, by making use of regenerating codes, achieves a round complexity that is not only proportional to the multiplicative depth of the circuit, but is essentially equal to it, while keeping sub-quadratic communication complexity in the number of parties. Our protocol achieves statistical security against an active adversary corrupting a minority of the parties. Furthermore, our protocol and techniques are not restricted to finite fields only: they are set in the context of *Galois rings*, which are a natural generalization involving power-of-primes characteristics. All finite fields are Galois rings, but Galois rings also include non-field rings such as $\mathbb{Z}/p^k\mathbb{Z}$, that have gained popularity for MPC recently.

In order to obtain our results, we first show in Sect. 4, as a contribution on its own, that the repair property is equivalent to a condition on the dual code containing a particular subcode. This was already noted in [12] for MDS codes over fields, but we give an alternative proof that extends to arbitrary linear codes over Galois rings. From this characterization, we obtain a generalization of the result of [13], as we show that Shamir's scheme over Galois rings [1] also has the repair property.

As mentioned before, we show that the utility of regenerating codes in information-theoretic MPC lies in reducing the number of rounds, and we obtain the first application of regenerating codes in this domain. Answering the above question, we reduce the communication complexity of single-round secure multiplication from $O(n^2)$ to $O(n^2/\log(n))$ ring elements, while requiring only $d+O(1)$ rounds for a depth-d circuit.

Our results are obtained by using our extended characterization of regenerating codes over Galois rings in order to reconstruct secret-shared values efficiently, together with the standard approach for MPC based on preprocessed

---

[4] We call a single-round protocol one that only requires one round per multiplication layer in the circuit.

multiplication triples. Furthermore, in order to effectively make use of the large-degree Galois ring extension required for regenerating codes to exist, we employ RMFEs [4,8] to compute several copies of the same circuit in parallel, achieving the desired communication complexity for each individual execution (i.e. after dividing by the total number of copies). Whether our results can also be achieved in the non-amortized setting, i.e. when only one execution is required, is left as an open problem. We conjecture, however, that this is not possible, and provide arguments for this in Sect. 5.

In a bit more detail, we first show in Sect. 4.1 that a direct application of our regenerating code characterization, together with standard multiplication protocols based on multiplication triples, yield a single-round multiplication protocol with non-trivial communication complexity, assuming that the degree of the Galois ring extension is large enough. Then, in Sects. 4.2 and 4.3 we show how to leverage the simple protocol described in Sect. 4.1 in order to compute several copies of the same circuit in parallel, which yields our final result. This is achieved, as mentioned before, by making use of RMFEs to pack multiple elements of the base ring into a Galois ring extension element.

Unfortunately, this amortization step is far from trivial. Although, in [4], the authors present a compiler that takes any multiplication protocol over a field extension, and turns it into a multiplication protocol for several parallel multiplication over the corresponding base field, we cannot make use of these techniques directly to obtain our results. This is not only because these techniques are set over fields rather than Galois rings, which is possible to fix [8]. Instead, the main complication comes from the fact our protocol is highly constrained in that it must achieve secure multiplication in *one round*, and the RMFE-based protocol from [4] adds an extra round for each multiplication. This is due to the fact that the actual multiplication protocol needs to do more than just a multiplication in the large field; rather, the real goal of the protocol is to coordinate-wise multiply vectors of values in the small field, and this requires encoding them as elements in the large field, with a re-encoding step after every large field multiplication.

In order to overcome this issue, we show that we can use the same RMFE but encode values in a different manner, which allows us to fit the entire multiplication into a single round. This contribution can be of independent interest, given that it also removes the necessity of re-encoding the output of each multiplication in the original compiler of [4] (plus removing a necessary subdomain check in the input phase to ensure security against active adversaries). Works that make use of these techniques will also benefit from our encoding improvement.

Finally, since our protocol operates by opening secret-shared values using compressed shares, which do not offer any redundancy for detecting errors, consistency in the event of an active adversary may not be guaranteed during the execution of the protocol. In order to ensure that no cheating took place, a single check that aggregates all the multiplications performed during the protocol execution is run at the end, which results in unconditional security with abort. A subtle issue with this approach is that, allowing the parties to inadvertently continue with the execution of the protocol in spite of the adversary injecting errors in some of the multiplications, may harm privacy. To overcome this problem, we make use of multiplication triples in a different way than how it is done traditionally. This is achieved by employing a novel use of *function-dependent preprocessing*, which was already used in [2,11] to improve the communication complexity of MPC protocols. To the best of our knowledge, ours constitutes the first work that identifies this technique to be beneficial for security purposes as well.

Our protocol assumes an honest majority $t < n/2$, and works for the maximal adversary $n = 2t + 1$. Our main result in terms of MPC is described in the theorem below.

Theorem 1. *There exists a family of protocols, indexed by the number of parties $n \to \infty$, that privately computes a depth-d arithmetic circuit over $\mathbb{Z}/p^k\mathbb{Z}$ with abort many times in parallel on different vectors of inputs in $d+O(1)$ rounds, and communicates $o(n^2 \log_2(p))$ bits per multiplication gate. The protocols make use of function-dependent preprocessing and are secure against an active adversary that can corrupt $t < n/2$ parties and can also abort the computation.*

We remark that the communication costs discussed above are asymptotic in terms of the number of multiplication gates of the underlying circuit. If there are M multiplication gates, the cost of evaluating these securely turns out to be $o(n^2 M)$, plus a term $\approx n^2$, which vanishes as $M \to \infty$.

1.2 Related Work

The task of minimizing the number of rounds in unconditionally-secure MPC has not received much attention, at least when compared to the task of minimizing communication. It is a long-standing open problem whether constant-round protocols that are efficient (i.e. have polynomial communication complexity in n for functionalities beyond NC^1) and enjoy information-theoretic security exist. In fact, in [14] a tight relation between this problem and a problem on private information retrieval, considered to be among the most intriguing open problems in complexity theory, was established. Given this, existing unconditionally secure MPC protocols have a number of rounds that grows proportionally to the multiplicative depth of the circuit. One of the first protocols in this direction is the BGW protocol [20], which presents an information-theoretically secure protocol that requires $d+O(1)$ rounds to securely compute a function with multiplicative depth d, but requires $\Omega(n^2)$ communication for each multiplication. More modern protocols with linear communication in the number of parties, such as the popular DN07 protocol [9], but at the expense of requiring $c \cdot d + O(1)$ rounds for some $c > 1$.

To the best of our knowledge, Galois rings have not been considered within the literature of regenerating codes, so there are no related works in this direction. Furthermore, as we stressed in previous paragraphs, applications of regenerating codes to MPC have been elusive until this point. However, even though regenerating codes have not been used for secret-sharing in MPC, there has been a big body of research that makes use of these techniques for secret-sharing in the context of distributed storage. For instance, [17] studies the problem of handling errors and erasures during the data-reconstruction and node-repair operations, and proposes explicit regenerating codes that resist errors and erasures, and show their optimality. Also, in [16] constructions of the so-called Minimum Bandwidth Regenerating (MBR) and Minimum Storage Regenerating (MSR) codes are presented, which are useful for distributed storage. We stress that in works along these lines, secret-sharing is used as a mean to store information, rather than as a method for secure computation, which is the setting we consider in our work.

Finally, we note that there are other constructions of regenerating codes on top of Reed-Solomon codes, which are follow-ups to the original work of Guruswami and Wootters, which is the one we use as a starting point in our work. For instance, in [18], Reed-Solomon codes achieving the so-called cut-set bound are introduced, which represent an improvement over the original construction in terms of savings when performing regeneration. We believe such works would be beneficial for MPC too by following a similar approach as the one we present in our work, and we leave it as future work to explore these potentially fruitful directions.

2   Preliminaries

Galois Rings. All rings that we refer to are commutative and have a multiplicative identity 1. For a ring R and R-modules A, B, we denote by $\mathrm{Hom}_R(A, B)$ the R-module of R-linear maps from A to B.

A Galois ring R is a finite ring such that the set of zero divisors, with 0 added, forms a principal ideal generated by $p \cdot 1$ where $p \in \mathbb{Z}$ is prime. It is a local ring, whose maximal ideal is precisely the ideal (p) of zero divisors. R is isomorphic to the ring $(\mathbb{Z}/p^k\mathbb{Z})[X]/(h(X))$, where k is a positive integer and p is prime, and $h(X) \in (\mathbb{Z}/p^k\mathbb{Z})[X]$ is a monic polynomial such that its reduction modulo p is irreducible in $\mathbb{F}_p[X]$. Conversely, all rings of this form are Galois rings, and a choice of p, k and $m = \deg h(X)$ uniquely defines the Galois ring up to isomorphism, so that we may write $R = \mathrm{GR}(p^k, m)$. The kernel of the unique ring homomorphism $\mathbb{Z} \to R$ is the ideal $(p^k) \subset \mathbb{Z}$, hence the characteristic of R is $\mathrm{char}(R) = p^k$. All finite fields, as well as the rings $\mathbb{Z}/p^k\mathbb{Z}$, are Galois rings.

From the definition it is easy to see that every element of a Galois ring $R = (\mathbb{Z}/p^k\mathbb{Z})[X]/(h(X))$ can be written uniquely as a polynomial of degree at most $m - 1$ and coefficients in $\mathbb{Z}/p^k\mathbb{Z}$. However, another representation that we will find useful in this work is the following.

Theorem 2 (Theorem 14.8 in [19]). *Let $R = \mathrm{GR}(p^k, m)$. There exists $\xi \in R$ of order $p^m - 1$ such that every $c \in R$ can be written uniquely as $c = a_0 + a_1 p + \cdots + a_{k-1}p^{k-1}$, where $a_i \in \{0, 1, \xi, \xi^2, \ldots, \xi^{p^m-2}\}$ for $i = 0, \ldots, k-1$. Moreover, c is a unit if and only if $a_0 \neq 0$, and c is a zero divisor, or zero, if and only if $a_0 = 0$.*

Suppose we have a subring $S \subseteq R$. Then S is a Galois ring with char$(R) =$ char(S), and we call R/S an extension of Galois rings. If $R = \mathrm{GR}(p^k, m)$ and $S = \mathrm{GR}(p^k, n)$, then $n \mid m$. We call m/n the *degree* of the extension, and denote it $[R : S]$. Proofs of the above assertions and more details on Galois rings can be found in [19]. More details on Galois rings in the context of secret sharing and MPC can be found in [1].

Generalized Reed-Solomon Codes. Let t, n be non-negative integers with $t < n$. We denote by $R[X]_{\leq t}$ ($R[X]_{<t}$) the free R-module of polynomials over R of degree at most (strictly less than) t. A sequence of elements $\alpha_1, \ldots, \alpha_n \in R$ is called exceptional if $\alpha_i - \alpha_j$ is a unit for each pair of distinct indices $i \neq j$. There exists an exceptional sequence in R of length p^m (e.g., lift each element of the residue field to R), and this is the maximum length. Given such an exceptional sequence, and a vector of units $(y_1, \ldots, y_n) \in (R^*)^n$, a generalized Reed-Solomon code over R of length n and rank $t + 1$ is an R-submodule $C \subseteq R^n$ given by

$$C = \left\{ (y_1 f(\alpha_1), \ldots, y_n f(\alpha_n)) \mid f \in R[X]_{\leq t} \right\}.$$

Reverse Multiplication-Friendly Embeddings. Let ℓ be a positive integer and write $m := [R : S]$. We denote by S^ℓ the S-module of ℓ copies of S. It is also an S-algebra with respect to the coordinatewise product $*$. An (ℓ, m)-*reverse multiplication-friendly embedding (RMFE) for R/S* is a pair of S-linear maps $\phi : S^\ell \to R$, $\psi : R \to S^\ell$, such that

$$\mathbf{x} * \mathbf{y} = \psi(\phi(\mathbf{x}) \cdot \phi(\mathbf{y}))$$

for all $\mathbf{x}, \mathbf{y} \in S^\ell$.

We are particularly interested in RMFEs for $R/(\mathbb{Z}/p^k\mathbb{Z})$, since they allow us to evaluate parallel circuits over $\mathbb{Z}/p^k\mathbb{Z}$ using MPC over R [4]. Such RMFEs exist, even with the property of being asymptotically good (i.e., with the rate ℓ/m tending to a positive constant). This was shown in the following theorem from [8, Theorem 22].

Theorem 3. *There exists a family of (ℓ, m)-RMFEs, indexed by $m \to \infty$, for the Galois ring extensions $\mathrm{GR}(p^k, m)/(\mathbb{Z}/p^k\mathbb{Z})$ with $\ell = \Omega(m)$.*

Security Model. For the security proofs of our protocol we make use of the UC model for multiparty computation. Details can be found in [7]. Also, we assume that whenever an honest party aborts, all the honest parties abort. This can be assumed without loss of generality given that we assume a broadcast channel, so the abort signals can be transmitted through this medium.

3 Regenerating Codes over Galois Rings

Let R/S be an extension of Galois rings of characteristic p^k, with $S = \mathrm{GR}(p^k, \ell)$ and $R = \mathrm{GR}(p^k, m \cdot \ell)$. Let n be a positive integer, and let $C \subseteq R^{n+1}$ be an R-submodule with coordinates indexed by $0, 1, \ldots, n$. For each index i we denote the projection map onto the i-th coordinate by $\pi_i : C \to R$. We say C is a *regenerating code* if it has the following *repair property*.[5]

Definition 1. *An R-submodule $C \subseteq R^{n+1}$ has* linear repair over S of the 0-coordinate *if for each index $i > 0$ there exists an S-linear map $\phi_i : R \to S$ and a scalar $z_i \in R$, such that for each element $(x_0, x_1, \ldots, x_n) \in C$ it holds that $x_0 = \sum_{i=1}^{n} \phi_i(x_i) \cdot z_i$.*

We now show that the repair property can be fully characterized in terms of the dual code $C^{\perp}$. This was already shown in [12] for MDS codes over fields, but we show it in our setting of 1-dimensional repair of the 0-coordinate, and demonstrate it extends to arbitrary linear codes over Galois rings.

Theorem 4. *Let $C \subseteq R^{n+1}$ be an R-submodule. Then C has linear repair over S of the 0-coordinate if and only if there exists an S-submodule $D_0 \subseteq C^{\perp}$ of the dual code, with the following properties.*

1. $\pi_0(D_0) = R$
2. *For each index $i > 0$ there is some integer j with $0 \le j \le k$, such that $\pi_i(D_0) \cong p^j S$ as S-modules.*

From this characterization, we will below easily derive a generalization of a result of [13], namely that Reed-Solomon codes over *Galois rings* have linear repair. To prove the theorem we use two general lemmas.

Lemma 1. *Let $f : R \to S$ be a surjective S-linear map. For each $\alpha \in R$, let $f_\alpha : R \to S$ denote the S-linear map given by $x \mapsto f(\alpha x)$. Then, the map*

$$R \longrightarrow \mathrm{Hom}_S(R, S)$$
$$\alpha \longmapsto f_\alpha$$

is an S-module isomorphism.

Proof. We observe the map is S-linear. Since $R \cong S^{[R:S]}$ as S-modules, we have that R and $\mathrm{Hom}_S(R, S)$ are two finite sets of the same cardinality. Therefore, it suffices to show injectivity.

Let $\alpha \in R$ be nonzero. By surjectivity of f, there exists $w \in R$ such that $f(w) = 1$. It must hold that w is a unit, otherwise $p^{k-1} = p^{k-1}f(w) = f(p^{k-1}w) = f(0) = 0$. Write $\alpha = p^t u$, where t is an integer with $0 \le t < k$ and $u \in R^*$ is a unit. For $x := u^{-1}w$ we have that $f_\alpha(x) = f(\alpha x) = f(p^t w) = p^t \neq 0$, which shows that f_α is not the zero map. □

Lemma 2. *Let $f : R \to S$ be a surjective S-linear map. Let $x, y \in R$. Then $x = y$ if and only if, for all $\gamma \in R$, we have $f(\gamma x) = f(\gamma y)$.*

---

[5] We only regard 1-dimensional repair of the 0-th coordinate, since we specifically target applications to MPC. In the literature on regenerating codes, the definition typically includes all coordinates and allows for larger messages to be sent.

Proof. For an arbitrary $\gamma \in R$, we have $f(\gamma x) = f(\gamma y)$ if and only if $f((x-y)\gamma) = 0$. The latter holds for all $\gamma \in R$ if and only if f_{x-y} is the zero map, which by Lemma 1 holds if and only if $x - y = 0$. $\qquad\square$

With these two lemmas at hand, we are now ready to give a proof of Theorem 4.

Proof (of Theorem 4). Let $f : R \to S$ be any surjective S-linear map (for example, choose an S-basis of R and project onto the first coordinate). Assume C has linear repair, i.e. there exist maps $\phi_1, \ldots, \phi_n : R \to S$ and elements $z_1, \ldots, z_n \in R$ such that for all $\mathbf{x} = (x_0, x_1, \ldots, x_n) \in C$ we have $x_0 = \sum_{i=1}^{n} \phi_i(x_i)z_i$. By Lemma 2 this equality holds if and only if for all $g \in R$ we have

$$f(gx_0) = f\left(g\sum_{i=1}^{n} \phi_i(x_i)z_i \right) = \sum_{i=1}^{n} f(g\phi_i(x_i)z_i) = \sum_{i=1}^{n} f(gz_i)\phi_i(x_i).$$

Using Lemma 1, we write each $\phi_i(x_i)$ as $f(\beta_i x_i)$, for some $\beta_1, \ldots, \beta_n \in R$, and obtain

$$f(gx_0) = \sum_{i=1}^{n} f(gz_i)f(\beta_i x_i) = \sum_{i=1}^{n} f(f(gz_i)\beta_i x_i) = f\left(\sum_{i=1}^{n} f(gz_i)\beta_i x_i \right).$$

By R-linearity of C we may replace $\mathbf{x}$ by $\gamma\mathbf{x}$ for arbitrary $\gamma \in R$, therefore we may apply Lemma 2 and see equality holds without application of f. Equivalently, the vector $(-g, f(gz_1)\beta_1, \ldots, f(gz_n)\beta_n)$ is in the dual $C^\perp$.

Let D_0 denote the collection of these vectors where g varies over R, and note that $\pi_0(D_0) = -R = R$. Now let $i > 0$ be any index, and consider the projection

$$\pi_i(D_0) = \{f(gz_i)\beta_i \mid g \in R\} = \{f(gz_i) \mid g \in R\}\beta_i.$$

We have that $\{f(gz_i) \mid g \in R\}$ is an S-submodule of S, hence it is an ideal of S, and therefore equal to $p^j S$ for some nonnegative integer j. We can write $\beta_i = p^{j'} u$, where $u \in R^*$ is a unit and j' is some nonnegative integer. Multiplication by u gives an S-module isomorphism $p^{j'} S \cong p^{j'} Su = S\beta_i$. We conclude $\pi_i(D_0) \cong p^{j+j'} S$, and remark that if $j + j' \geq k$ this is equal to $p^k S = 0$, thus proving the forward direction of the theorem.

For the converse, assume we have $D_0 \subseteq C^\perp$ as in the theorem. From the second condition of D_0, we know there exist $\beta_1, \ldots, \beta_n \in R$ such that $\pi_i(D_0) = S\beta_i$ for each index $i > 0$. Now, we choose an S-basis of R, say $b_1, \ldots, b_m \in R$. By the first condition on D_0, we have that for each b_j there exist $\lambda_1^{(b_j)}, \ldots, \lambda_n^{(b_j)} \in S$ such that $\left(-b_j, \lambda_1^{(b_j)}\beta_1, \ldots, \lambda_n^{(b_j)}\beta_n\right) \in D_0$. For each $g \in R$ we may write $g = \sum_{j=1}^{m} g_j b_j$, hence by S-linearity of D_0 there exists a vector in D_0 whose zeroth component is $-g$ and for each index $i > 0$ its i-th component is $\left(\sum_{j=1}^{m} g_j \lambda_i^{(b_j)}\right)\beta_i$. Applying Lemma 1 there exist fixed z_i for each index $i > 0$ such that for all $g \in R$ we have $f(gz_i) = \sum_{j=1}^{m} g_j \lambda_i^{(b_j)}$. We now have that for each $g \in R$, there exists a vector

$$(-g, f(gz_1)\beta_1, \ldots, f(gz_n)\beta_n) \in C^\perp.$$

We can follow the steps of the proof above in reverse direction, and writing $\phi_i(x_i) := f(\beta_i x_i)$ for each index $i > 0$, we conclude for each $(x_0, \ldots, x_n) \in C$ we have that $x_0 = \sum_{i=1}^n \phi_i(x_i) z_i$. $\qquad\qquad\qquad\qquad\qquad\qquad\qquad\qquad\qquad\qquad\square$

We now use our characterization of the repair property to show the result of [13] generalized to Galois rings. Namely, a generalized Reed-Solomon code defined over R has linear repair over S of the coordinate corresponding to the evaluation point 0. To show this we make use of the generalized trace function corresponding to the extension of Galois rings R/S.

An important lemma we will make use of is the following, which is a natural generalization of the equivalent result over fields. A proof of this result can be found, for example, in [15].

Lemma 3. *Let* $\alpha_0, \alpha_1, \ldots, \alpha_n \in R$ *be an exceptional sequence. Let* $\mathbf{y} = (y_0, \ldots, y_n) \in (R^*)^{n+1}$ *be a vector of units, and let* C *be the generalized Reed-Solomon code of rank* $t+1$ *and length* $n+1$ *given by*

$$C = \left\{ (y_0 f(\alpha_0), y_1 f(\alpha_1), \ldots, y_n f(\alpha_n)) \mid f \in R[X]_{\leq t} \right\}.$$

Then the dual of C *is given by the code of length* $n+1$ *and rank* $n-t$ *given by*

$$C^\perp = \left\{ (w_0 f(\alpha_0), w_1 f(\alpha_1), \ldots, w_n f(\alpha_n)) \mid f \in R[X]_{<n-t} \right\},$$

where $w_i = \left(y_i \cdot \prod_{j \neq i} (\alpha_i - \alpha_j) \right)^{-1}$.

Before stating the main theorem of this section, we require a definition. Let $\phi : R \to S$ be the generalized Frobenius automorphism, which is given by

$$a_0 + a_1 p + \cdots + a_{k-1} p^{k-1} \overset{\phi}{\longmapsto} a_0^q + a_1^q p + \cdots + a_{k-1}^q p^{k-1},$$

where $q = p^\ell$ is the cardinality of the residue field of S, and each a_i belongs to $\{0, 1, \xi, \ldots, \xi^{p^{m \cdot \ell} - 2}\}$, with $\xi \in R^*$ a non-zero element of order $p^{m \cdot \ell} - 1$, as guaranteed by Theorem 2. This allows us to define the generalized trace function $\mathrm{Tr} : R \to S$ of the Galois ring extension R/S, which is given by $\mathrm{Tr}(x) = x + \phi(x) + \cdots + \phi^{m-1}(x)$, where ϕ^i stands for ϕ applied i times. It is easy to see that the generalized trace is a S-linear surjective map [19].

With these definitions and the lemma above at hand, we are ready to prove that generalized Reed-Solomon codes over *Galois Rings* have linear repair, as stated in the theorem below.

Theorem 5. *Let* $\alpha_0, \alpha_1, \ldots, \alpha_n \in R$ *be defined as* $\alpha_0 = 0$ *and* $\alpha_i = \xi^{i-1}$ *for* $i = 1, \ldots, n$. *This constitutes an exceptional sequence. Let* $\mathbf{y} = (y_0, \ldots, y_n) \in (R^*)^{n+1}$ *be a vector of units, and let* $t \geq 0$ *be an integer with* $q^{m-1} \leq n - t$. *Then the generalized Reed-Solomon code*

$$C = \left\{ (y_0 f(0), y_1 f(\alpha_1), \ldots, y_n f(\alpha_n)) \mid f \in R[X]_{\leq t} \right\}$$

over R *of length* $n+1$ *and rank* $t+1$, *has linear repair over* S *of the 0-th coordinate.*

Proof. For $g \in R$ define

$$h_g(X) = g + \phi(g)X^{q-1} + \cdots + \phi^{m-1}(g)X^{q^{m-1}-1}.$$

Observe that $h_g(0) = g$ and $\deg h_g(X) < q^{m-1}$. Now, let D_0 be the S-linear code defined as

$$D_0 = \{(w_0 h_g(\alpha_0), \ldots, w_n h_g(\alpha_n)) : g \in R\},$$

where $w_i = \left(y_i \cdot \prod_{j \neq i}(\alpha_i - \alpha_j)\right)^{-1}$. We claim that D_0 satisfies the conditions of Theorem 4. This, from the same theorem, would prove that C has linear repair over S of the 0-th coordinate.

For the first property we need to show that $\pi_0(D_0) = R$, which follows from the fact that $\pi_0(D_0) = w_0 \cdot R \cong R$, since w_0 is a unit. It only remains to show that, for $i = 1, \ldots, n$, $\pi_i(D_0) \cong p^j S$ for some $0 \leq j \leq k$. To see this, first observe that, for every $g \in R$, it holds that $\operatorname{Tr}(g \cdot \xi^j) = \xi^j \cdot h_g(\xi^j)$, which follows from the fact that $\phi^u(g \cdot \xi^j) = \phi^u(g) \cdot (\xi^j)^{q^u}$. From this it follows that $\alpha_i \cdot h_g(\alpha_i) = \operatorname{Tr}(g \cdot \alpha_i)$, or $h_g(\alpha_i) = \operatorname{Tr}(g \cdot \alpha_i)/\alpha_i$, since $\alpha_i \in R^*$. From this, and from the fact that the generalized trace function is surjective, we see that $\pi_i(D_0) = \{w_i h_g(\alpha_i) : g \in R\} = \frac{w_i}{\alpha_i} S \cong S$, since w_i and α_i are both units.

Finally, from Lemma 3, and given that $q^{m-1} \leq n - t$, we see that D_0 is an S-submodule of $C^\perp$. This concludes the proof.   □

Remark 1. If $k = 1$, that is, if R is a field, then the Theorem above would hold even if $\alpha_0, \ldots, \alpha_n \in R$ is *any* exceptional sequence with $\alpha_0 = 0$. For general Galois rings, the requirement that $\alpha_i \in \{1, \xi, \ldots, \xi^{p^d-2}\}$ is crucial for the result to hold. This is because, in general, the relation $\alpha_i \cdot h_g(\alpha_i) = \operatorname{Tr}(g \cdot \alpha_i)$ is not true.

4   Protocols

Let $P_1, \ldots, P_n$ be parties connected by secure pairwise communication channels, as well as a broadcast channel. We develop a protocol that allows the parties to obliviously evaluate an arbitrary arithmetic circuit over $\mathbb{Z}/p^k\mathbb{Z}$ on many vectors of inputs in parallel in $d + O(1)$ rounds, where d is the depth of the circuit. Security is defined against a computationally unbounded adversary that can statically corrupt a minority $t < n/2$ of parties and obtain full control, as well as force the computation to abort.

Let m be a positive integer such that $p^{m-1} \leq n - t$; asymptotically we can find $m = \Omega(\log(n))$. In this section we write $S := \mathbb{Z}/p^k\mathbb{Z}$ and let $R = \operatorname{GR}(p^k, m)$ be the degree-m extension ring of S. Let $[\cdot]$ denote the secret-sharing scheme associated to the rank-$(t + 1)$ length-$(n + 1)$ Reed-Solomon code over R from Theorem 5 with $y_1 = \cdots = y_n = 1$ and some coordinates $\alpha_1, \ldots, \alpha_n \in R$ as in Theorem 5. More precisely, for a secret $x \in R$ we denote by $[x]$ a vector of shares $(x_1, \ldots, x_n) \in R^n$ such that there is a polynomial $f(X) \in R[X]_{\leq t}$ with

$x_i = f(\alpha_i)$ for all i and $f(0) = x$. Whenever we discuss secret-sharings $[x]$, we implicitly mean that each party P_i has the share x_i.

Let $w_0, w_1, \ldots, w_n \in R^*$ be the weights associated to the dual of the Reed-Solomon code above. We can glean explicit compression functions from the proofs of Theorems 4 and 5. Concretely, we set $\phi_i(x_i) = \mathrm{Tr}\left(\frac{w_i x_i}{\alpha_i}\right)$ and $z_i = -\frac{\alpha_i}{w_0}$ for each i. Then, for all share vectors $[x] = (x_1, \ldots, x_n) \in C$, we can reconstruct the secret from the compressed shares as

$$x = \sum_{i=1}^{n} \phi_i(x_i) z_i = -\sum_{i=1}^{n} \mathrm{Tr}\left(\frac{w_i x_i}{\alpha_i}\right) \frac{\alpha_i}{w_0}.$$

4.1 Single-Round Opening and R-Multiplication

The repair property of C allows us to efficiently open secret-shared values.

Protocol 1. Open $[x]$ using compressed shares.
Input: $[x] = (x_1, \ldots, x_n)$.

- -

1. Each party P_j sends its compressed share $\phi_j(x_j)$ to all other parties.
2. Each party calculates $x = \sum_{j=1}^{n} \phi_j(x_j) z_j$, or aborts if any of the shares are missing or malformed.

Protocol 1 communicates $O(n^2 \log |S|)$ bits in one round, which represents an improvement over the current best known (naive) $O(n^2 \log |R|)$ bits.

Note that the compressed shares do not offer error detection. As such, any maliciously corrupted party P_j may send a value different from $\phi_j(x_j)$, which causes a different value $x' \neq x$ to be opened. Moreover, P_j may send a different value to each party and cause different honest parties to compute different values for x'.

To check whether parties have behaved correctly in Protocol 1, we present Protocol 2. In this separate protocol, we are able to batch check many openings at once at constant cost, so this does not affect our per-gate communication.

For the protocol, we assume access to a functionality $\mathcal{F}_{\mathsf{coin}}$ that samples a uniformly random value in R and sends this value to all parties.

Protocol 2. Check whether sharings $\{[x_\ell]\}_{\ell=1}^N$ where opened correctly. Input: sharings $\{[x_\ell]\}_{\ell=1}^N$ and the values $\{x'_\ell\}_{\ell=1}^N$ they were opened to. Note each party may input a different value x'_ℓ.

Broadcast check

Let $m_\ell^{(i)} \in S$ denote the correct compressed share that P_i was supposed to send during the opening of x_ℓ, and let $\hat{m}_\ell^{i \to j} \in S$ denote the value that was actually sent to P_j.

1. The parties perform N calls to $\mathcal{F}_{\text{coin}}$ to get $s_1, \ldots, s_N \in R$.
2. Each party P_i broadcasts $\gamma_i = \sum_{\ell=1}^N s_\ell \cdot m_\ell^{(i)}$.
3. If some P_j detects that $\gamma_i \neq \sum_{\ell=1}^N s_\ell \cdot \hat{m}_\ell^{i \to j}$, then it aborts.

Consistency check

1. The parties perform N calls to $\mathcal{F}_{\text{coin}}$ to get $r_1, \ldots, r_N$.
2. The parties compute $[v] := \sum_{\ell=1}^N r_\ell([x_\ell] - x'_\ell)$. After the broadcast check has passed, the values x'_ℓ are the same for each party.
3. Each party broadcasts their (uncompressed) share of $[v]$.
4. Each party checks whether the received shares of $[v]$ form a correct sharing of 0. If it does not, they abort.

Remark 2. The number of calls to $\mathcal{F}_{\text{coin}}$ in Protocol 2 can be reduced by the following techniques:

- One can re-use the $s_1, \ldots, s_N$ from the broadcast check in the consistency check, that is, the parties can set $r_\ell = s_\ell$ for $\ell = 1, \ldots, N$.
- Instead of using $s_1, \ldots, s_\ell$ as independent random values, the parties can set $s_\ell := s^{\ell-1}$ for one single random value s. This is at the expense of increasing the cheating probability of the adversary by a polynomial factor of N.

We now show that Protocol 2 is statistically secure, and the probability that an adversary successfully cheats is at most $1/p^m$. To get negligible error probability, in practice we can interpret our secret-sharings over, and move $\mathcal{F}_{\text{coin}}$ to, a Galois ring extension K/R of degree d such that dm is larger than the security parameter κ. If N is large, we can even pack d elements of R into K so this can be done at no extra cost [1].

Proposition 1. *After an execution Protocol 2 where no party aborts, we have $x'_\ell = x_\ell$ for all $\ell = 1, \ldots, N$, except with probability at most $1/p^m$.*

Proof. We first show that if no party aborts the broadcast check, then for each corrupt party P_i and each pair of honest parties $P_j, P_{j'}$, we have that $\hat{m}_\ell^{i \to j} = \hat{m}_\ell^{i \to j'}$ for all $\ell = 1, \ldots, N$. We argue by contradiction: assume we have i, j, j', ℓ^* such that $\hat{m}_{\ell^*}^{i \to j} \neq \hat{m}_{\ell^*}^{i \to j'}$. Since P_i is corrupt, it may have introduced a non-zero error ε_i and broadcast $\gamma_i + \varepsilon_i$ instead of γ_i. Since neither P_j nor $P_{j'}$ aborted, we have that

$$\sum_{\ell=1}^{N} s_\ell \cdot \hat{m}_\ell^{i\to j} = \gamma_i + \varepsilon_i = \sum_{\ell=1}^{N} s_\ell \cdot \hat{m}_\ell^{i\to j'}.$$

This implies that $\sum_{\ell=1}^{N} s_\ell \cdot (\hat{m}_\ell^{i\to j'} - \hat{m}_\ell^{i\to j}) = 0$, and since $s_{\ell*} \in R$ is uniformly random and independent of the values sent during the opening, this is satisfied with probability at most p^{-m} [1].

Assume the broadcast check passed, and so each honest party P_j received the same value x'_ℓ for each ℓ. If the consistency check also passed without an abort, we know that in the reconstruction of $[v] := \sum_{\ell=1}^{N} r_\ell([x_\ell] - x'_\ell)$, the opened value is exactly equal to v due to the error-correction properties of Shamir secret-sharing. This implies that $\sum_{\ell=1}^{N} r_\ell(x_\ell - x'_\ell) = 0$, which by similar reasoning to the above implies $x_\ell = x'_\ell$ for all $\ell = 1, \ldots, N$ except with probability at most p^{-m}.   □

With Protocol 1 we can instantiate the secure multiplication of elements in R in one single round. For example, we can use Beaver multiplication triples, which are sharings $([a], [b], [c])$, with a, b independent and uniformly random and $c = ab$. To securely multiply two sharings $[x], [y]$ using a multiplication triple, the parties open (in one round) $u = [x] - [a]$ and $v = [y] - [b]$ and calculate $[xy] = uv + v[a] + u[b] + [c]$. The protocol we will describe below in Sect. 4.2 is a bit more involved than what we sketched above, given that it is our goal to postpone the use of the broadcast channel until all multiplications have been performed, and this turns out to lead to selective failure attacks in which an adversary can learn sensitive information if one uses Beaver triples directly.

Finally, since we insist on a maximal adversary, we cannot use random double sharings instead of multiplication triples. Random double sharings are uniformly random sharings $[r]$, together with a "product sharing" of r, i.e. a share vector in the square code C^2. They have the advantage of allowing for a simpler multiplication protocol, that also extends to the inner product of two secret-shared vectors at no extra cost. The square code C^2 is also Reed-Solomon and therefore could have linear repair. However, the rank of the square code is $2t + 1$, and for the maximal adversary $n = 2t + 1$ we cannot have $p^{m-1} \leq n - 2t = 1.$[6]

4.2 Parallel Multiplications

Let $\phi : S^\ell \to R, \psi : R \to S^\ell$ be an (ℓ, m)-RMFE for the Galois ring extension R/S, with $\ell = O(m)$. We can embed two ℓ-length vectors $\mathbf{x}, \mathbf{y} \in S^\ell$ using ϕ and use multiplication of elements in R to obtain the coordinatewise product $\mathbf{x} * \mathbf{y} = \psi(\phi(\mathbf{x})\phi(\mathbf{y}))$. By secret-sharing $[\phi(\mathbf{x})], [\phi(\mathbf{y})]$ we can therefore use secure multiplication in R as explained above, and then open the result and apply ψ to securely evaluate $\mathbf{x} * \mathbf{y}$.

---

[6] Also note that product sharings do not give error detection, so if we did not insist on a maximal adversary and wanted to use random double sharings, we would have to employ different techniques to get active security.

Unfortunately, this only works for a single multiplication, since in general $\mathbf{x} * \mathbf{y} * \mathbf{z} \neq \psi(\phi(\mathbf{x})\phi(\mathbf{y})\phi(\mathbf{z}))$. The problem is that $\phi(\mathbf{x}) \cdot \phi(\mathbf{y}) \in R$ is not generally contained in the image of ϕ. We get around this problem by "re-encoding" values, as follows.[7]

We encode each input $\mathbf{x} \in S^\ell$ of the circuit by an element in $\psi^{-1}(\mathbf{x}) \in R$. Surjectivity of ψ follows from the definitions of an RMFE hence such an element always exists, though it need not be unique. We proceed to apply the S-linear map $\tau := \phi \circ \psi$, and then multiply the resulting values in R. This allows us to maintain the following invariant: the value on each wire is a vector $\mathbf{x} \in S^\ell$, encoded as $x \in R$ such that $\psi(x) = \mathbf{x}$. This is because if $\mathbf{x}, \mathbf{y} \in S^\ell$ with $\psi(\mathbf{x}) = x$ and $\psi(\mathbf{y}) = y$, then

$$\psi\left(\tau(x)\tau(y)\right) = \psi\left(\phi(\mathbf{x})\phi(\mathbf{y})\right) = \mathbf{x} * \mathbf{y}.$$

Following this invariant, we can define an S-linear secret-sharing scheme of vectors $\mathbf{x} \in S^\ell$, with the share vector given by $[x] \in C$ such that $\psi(x) = \mathbf{x}$. Note that since ϕ, ψ are not in general R-linear (but instead S-linear), parties cannot apply τ to secret-shared values without any interaction.

Our multiplication protocol uses an input-independent offline phase, where secret-shared random elements are generated that are used in the online phase once the inputs are known. The offline phase generates quintuples

$$([a], [b], [\tau(a)], [\tau(b)], [\tau(a)\tau(b)]),$$

where $a, b \in R$ are independent and uniformly random. Because all quintuples can be generated in parallel, the round complexity is not important, and so we can use known techniques. The only requirement is that the generated quintuples are correct; for example, we can use from [1] the protocol `RandElStat` to get pairs $([a], [\tau(a)])$, and combine it with their multiplication protocol to generate the quintuples.

Given a quintuple, the online single-round protocol to compute $[\tau(x)\tau(y)]$ is very similar to using a regular multiplication triple. The parties open $u = [x] - [a]$ and $v = [y] - [b]$ using Protocol 1 and then compute

$$[\tau(x)\tau(y)] = \tau(v)[\tau(a)] + \tau(u)[\tau(b)] + [\tau(a)\tau(b)] + \tau(u)\tau(v).$$

This operation is definitely secure against a passive adversary, however against an active adversary the security is not so clear. Since we postpone the broadcast and consistency checks until the end, an active adversary can introduce additive errors when opening $[u], [v]$, and it can do so at every multiplication throughout the circuit. The question whether this compromises the privacy or not is closely related to the amount of redundancy the compressed shares contain. We leave this question for now, and return to it in Sect. 5.

---

[7] The idea of re-encoding is based on [4], but we have developed an improved encoding that allows us to decrease the number of rounds for a multiplication, and that also allows for a simpler input phase. We explain the differences between the two approaches in Sect. 5.

Our protocol circumvents this issue entirely, by observing that the issue does not arise when using *function-dependent preprocessing* [2]. Whereas Beaver multiplication triples are generic in the sense that the triples are not specific to any particular multiplication gate, with function-dependent preprocessing we generate random sharings tailored to each multiplication gate. Besides sidestepping the issue of security, this also has the advantage that it reduces communication by half, and it allows computing the inner product of two secret-shared vectors at the same communication cost as one secure multiplication.

Recall each wire in our circuit has an associated secret vector $\mathbf{x} \in S^\ell$. We will maintain the invariant that each such vector $\mathbf{x}$ is secret-shared as the tuple $[\![\mathbf{x}]\!] := ([\lambda_x], \mu_x)$, where $\lambda_x \in R$ is a uniformly random element that is secret-shared using the scheme $[\cdot]$, and $\mu_x = x - \lambda_x$ is a publicly known element such that $\psi(x) = \mathbf{x}$. Given λ_x and μ_x, a party can compute $\mathbf{x} = \psi(\mu_x + \lambda_x)$ and recover the secret value. This construction defines an S-linear secret-sharing scheme.

To securely compute $[\![\mathbf{x} * \mathbf{y}]\!]$ from $[\![\mathbf{x}]\!]$ and $[\![\mathbf{y}]\!]$, the parties can proceed as in Protocol 3. We assume a functionality $\mathcal{F}_{\mathsf{prep}}$ that generates the necessary preprocessing material, consisting of the following:

- A shared random value $[\lambda_x]$ for every wire.
- For every multiplication gate with inputs x and y, a quintuple

$$([\lambda_x], [\lambda_y], [\tau(\lambda_x)], [\tau(\lambda_y)], [\tau(\lambda_x)\tau(\lambda_y)]).$$

Generating these sharings can be done in a similar way as the quintuples mentioned above. Note that this data is specific to the topology of the circuit.

Protocol 3. Multiply $[\![\mathbf{x}]\!] = ([\lambda_x], \mu_x)$ and $[\![\mathbf{y}]\!] = ([\lambda_y], \mu_y)$.
Preprocessed: $[\lambda_z]$ and $([\lambda_x], [\lambda_y], [\tau(\lambda_x)], [\tau(\lambda_y)], [\tau(\lambda_x)\tau(\lambda_y)])$ produced by $\mathcal{F}_{\mathsf{prep}}$.

- -

1. Use Protocol 1 to open μ_w towards all parties, where
$\mu_w = \tau(\mu_x)\tau(\mu_y) + \tau(\mu_x)[\tau(\lambda_y)] + \tau(\mu_y)[\tau(\lambda_x)] + [\tau(\lambda_x)\tau(\lambda_y)] - [\lambda_w]$.
2. The parties return the shares $[\![\mathbf{w}]\!] := ([\lambda_w], \mu_w)$.

The reason why this multiplication protocol is private against an active adversary, is the following. The adversary can still tamper with the reconstruction of μ_w by adding some error (perhaps different to every party). However, here this error is independent of any sensitive input and is in fact completely known by the adversary, so intuitively speaking, it does not allow the adversary to learn anything new. Formally speaking, the simulator will be able to extract these errors and emulate the honest parties correctly in the ideal world.

4.3 Secure Parallel Computation

Let f be a function represented by an arithmetic circuit over S. For simplicity and without loss of generality, we assume f is of the form $S^n \to S$, where each input in S is held by one party. We show how to securely evaluate f in parallel ℓ times in Protocol 4 below. Here, let $\mathbf{x}_i \in S^\ell$ be the vector of inputs of party P_i for the ℓ executions of f. Also, let $\mathbf{w}_j \in S^n$ denote the input vector to the j-th execution of f (that is, the i-th entry of $\mathbf{w}_j$ is the j-th entry of $\mathbf{x}_i$).

Our protocol, described below, requires as preprocessing material a random sharing $[r]$ where $r \in \ker(\psi)$, which is used to mask the output before opening. This is required since, due to the invariant, the value that is produced as output is a preimage under ψ of the output vector, but this preimage itself may depend on intermediate values. By masking before opening with an element of the kernel of ψ, we ensure that this preimage is uniform among all possible preimages, which enables the simulator in the proof to emulate this step towards the adversary.

Protocol 4. Obliviously evaluate f on ℓ vectors of inputs $\mathbf{w}_1, \ldots, \mathbf{w}_\ell \in S^n$.
Preprocessing: Random sharing $[r]$, where $r \in \ker(\psi)$.
Output: $f(\mathbf{w}_1), \ldots, f(\mathbf{w}_\ell)$.

- -

Input phase. Let $\mathbf{x}_i \in S^\ell$ be the input from P_i. For each $i = 1, \ldots, n$, the parties do the following.
1. The parties send their shares of $[\lambda_{x_i}]$ to P_i.
2. P_i broadcasts $\mu_{x_i} := x_i - \lambda_{x_i}$, where $\psi(x_i) = \mathbf{x}_i$.
3. Parties set $[\![\mathbf{x_i}]\!] = ([\lambda_{x_i}], \mu_{x_i})$.
Computation phase. The parties process the circuit gate-by-gate, using Protocol 3 and maintaining the invariant of $[\![\cdot]\!]$.
Output phase.
1. The parties run Protocol 2 to verify correctness of all opened values.
2. Let $[\![\mathbf{z}]\!] = ([\lambda_z], \mu_z)$ be the shared output. Each party broadcasts their shares of $[\lambda_z] + [r]$, and the output is defined as $\mathbf{z} = \psi((\lambda_z + r) + \mu_z)$.

The security of our protocol is proved in the following theorem, which in turn proves Theorem 1.

Theorem 6. *Protocol 4 securely computes ℓ copies of the function f in the $(\mathcal{F}_{\mathsf{coin}}, \mathcal{F}_{\mathsf{prep}})$-hybrid model with statistical security with abort against an active adversary.*

Proof. We construct a simulator $\mathcal{S}$ that interacts with an environment $\mathcal{Z}$ and with an MPC functionality in such a way that the environment cannot distinguish between the simulated execution and the real protocol.

The simulator emulates the behavior of the honest parties towards the adversary, as well as emulating the functionalities $\mathcal{F}_{\mathsf{coin}}$ and $\mathcal{F}_{\mathsf{prep}}$. $\mathcal{S}$ begins by generating all the necessary preprocessing material. For the input phase, the simulator receives $\mu_{x_i} := x_i - \lambda_{x_i}$ for each corrupt party P_i, and since $\mathcal{S}$ knows λ_{x_i}, it can recover the inputs $\mathbf{x}_i$, which are then sent to the MPC functionality. For the inputs from the honest parties $\mathcal{S}$ simply uses dummy values.

For the addition gates the simulator simply emulates the local operations on the honest parties. On the other hand, for multiplication gates, $\mathcal{S}$ receives the reduced shares $\phi_i(\mu_{w,i})$ from each corrupt party P_i, corresponding to the secrets $\mu_w = x - \lambda_x$ from the protocol. Here the simulator samples uniformly at random some value $\mu_w \in R$, and sets the honest parties' shares so that they are consistent with this value and with the shares held by the corrupt parties. Then $\mathcal{S}$ opens these (compressed) shares towards the adversary.

Observe that the adversary may cause each corrupt party P_i to send $\phi_i(\mu_{w,i}) + \epsilon_{ij}$ to each honest party P_j, instead of the correct reduced share. As a result, P_j will think that μ_w is actually equal to $\sum_{\ell=1}^{n}(\phi_\ell(\mu_{w,\ell}) + \epsilon_{\ell j}) \cdot z_\ell$. Since the simulator knows the actual shares that the corrupt parties must have sent, it knows the value described above and it can continue emulating the honest parties.[8]

For the output phase the simulator begins by sending an abort signal if there exists a corrupt party P_i and a pair of different honest parties P_j and $P_{j'}$ such that $\epsilon_{ij} \neq \epsilon_{ij'}$, for some multiplication gate. If this is not the case let us denote $\epsilon_i := \epsilon_{ij}$. If $e := \sum_{\ell=1}^{n} \epsilon_\ell \cdot z_\ell \neq 0$, then $\mathcal{S}$ sends an abort signal. Else, $\mathcal{S}$ receives the output from the MPC functionality, samples a random preimage under ψ of this output, sets the shares of the honest parties so that they are consistent with this output and with the corrupt parties' shares, and then emulates the reconstruction protocol by broadcasting the shares corresponding to the honest parties.

Now we argue that the simulation is statistically indistinguishable to the environment from the real execution. The input phase is clearly indistinguishable, as well as the additions as they follow the exact same distribution in both executions. For multiplications, observe that in the real world the adversary only sees $\mu_w = w - \lambda_w$, but since λ_w is uniformly random and unknown to the adversary, then μ_w follows the uniform distribution, which coincides with what the adversary sees in the ideal execution.

The only potential difference lies in the check performed by the parties at the end. In the ideal execution the parties abort if any of the broadcasted values does not match, which is also the case in the real execution except with negligible probability thanks to Proposition 1 combined with the remark about moving to a large Galois ring. □

5   Discussion

Our results demonstrate that regenerating codes can improve the round complexity of MPC protocols, or alternatively, when insisting on a minimum number of rounds they can improve the communication complexity.

Differences with [4]. Our protocol uses techniques from [4] and the generalizations to Galois rings [1,8], but there are a few key differences. Evidently, we have plugged in Protocol 1 to get an efficient single-round opening. But the essential

---

[8] This is precisely what goes wrong if one uses traditional multiplication triples: The error on each honest party's share will depend on the honest parties' inputs, which the adversary cannot simulate.

modification is that we encode vectors in S^ℓ not using ϕ, but using ψ^{-1}. The difference is subtle, but it allows us to combine a multiplication together with ReEncode procedure from [4], that applies the map $\tau = \phi \circ \psi$ to the output of a multiplication, into a single round. The original work also benefits from this approach since it improves the number of rounds, even without using regenerating codes. Additionally, this encoding simplifies correctness of the input phase, since the security of the protocol does not require each wire value to be contained in the image of ϕ.

Active Security of the Quintuple-Based Protocol. The quintuple-based protocol sketched in Sect. 4.2 is passively secure, but it is not clear whether it is private against a malicious adversary that introduces errors. Recall that to multiply $[x]$ and $[y]$, the parties open $u = [x] - [a]$ and $v = [y] - [b]$ using Protocol 1 and then compute $[\tau(x)\tau(y)] = \tau(v)[\tau(a)] + \tau(u)[\tau(b)] + [\tau(a)\tau(b)] + \tau(u)\tau(v)$. Assume without loss of generality that P_1 is honest. Since the adversary may send different compressed shares to different parties, it may cause P_1 to think that u and v are actually equal to $u + \varepsilon$ and $v + \delta$, which causes P_1's share to be equal to the correct share plus

$$e_1 = \tau(\varepsilon)\tau(b)_1 + \tau(\delta)\tau(a)_1 + \tau(u)\tau(\delta) + \tau(v)\tau(\varepsilon) + \tau(\varepsilon)\tau(\delta).$$

Assume the other honest parties learn u and v correctly. Notice that the adversary does not know the value of e_1 as it depends on the unknown values a and b.

Now imagine that as part of the function being computed, $w = \tau(x)\tau(y)$ is fed into another multiplication gate. As part of the protocol, the parties open $u' = [w] - [a']$. Assume for a moment that instead of sending compressed shares, the parties send their full shares. Hence, the adversary receives the share of $w - a'$ from P_1, which is altered by an amount of e_1. However, note that the adversary knows the corrupt parties' shares of $w - a'$, so if all the shares sent by the honest parties happen to be consistent with these shares, then the adversary can conclude that $e_1 = 0$, else, $e_1 \neq 0$ (and in this case the parties abort).

Notice that the adversary knows all values in the expression defining e_1 except for $\tau(a)_1$ and $\tau(b)_1$. Consider for simplicity that $\delta = 0$, so $e_1 = \tau(\varepsilon)\tau(b)_1 + \tau(v)\tau(\varepsilon)$. If ε is such that $\tau(\varepsilon) \in R^*$, knowing whether e_1 is non-zero or not leaks one bit of information about $\tau(b)_1$, namely whether it equals $-\tau(v)$ or not. However, to the adversary, $\tau(a)$ is a function of $\tau(a)_1$, so this leaks information about $\tau(a)$, which in turn leaks information about $\tau(y)$ given that the adversary knows $\tau(v)$ and $v = y - b$.

The attack above assumes that the parties send their full shares, but in the protocol description they send their *reduced* shares. One may think that these reduced shares, since they carry less redundancy than the original shares, may hinder the attack. However, it seems hard to quantify this, since for example a repair scheme with no compression (so ϕ_i is the identity for all i) would be susceptible to the attack above, and it is not clear at what point the compression level is "enough" so that the adversary cannot learn any sensitive information. We leave this for future work.

Lower Bound. We have shown that when amortizing over many parallel multiplications, we can multiply two elements of $\mathbb{Z}/p^k\mathbb{Z}$ in a single round with $o(n^2)$ elements of $\mathbb{Z}/p^k\mathbb{Z}$ communication, in our model of honest majority and unconditional security. To the best of our knowledge, there is no currently known way to achieve $o(n^2)$ complexity without amortization, and we conjecture that this is in fact impossible.

To support this conjecture, we note that a single-round opening of a sharing over any *fixed* Galois ring requires $\Omega(n^2)$ bits of communication. This is because each party must hear from at least t other parties; if not, an adversary could corrupt t parties and learn the secret without opening the value. All multiplication protocols in the preprocessing model rely on opening a value, and the alternative of re-sharing also requires each party to send $\Omega(n)$ shares to the other parties.

Limitation on the Possible Values of n and t. Notice that, once the values for p and k have been set, Theorem 5 implicitly contains certain restrictions on the possible values of t and n. First, we have the bound $p^{\ell \cdot (m-1)} \leq n - t$, but in addition, since we assume that $\alpha_0, \ldots, \alpha_n$ constitutes an exceptional sequence, it must be the case that $n + 1 \leq p^{m \cdot \ell}$. By considering a maximal adversary $n = 2t + 1$, we get that $p^{\ell \cdot (m-1)} - 1 \leq t \leq \frac{p^{\ell \cdot m} - 2}{2}$.

It holds that $\ell = 1$ if $S = \mathbb{Z}/p^k\mathbb{Z}$, but if a larger value of n (or equivalently, t) must be accommodated, ℓ can be chosen to be large enough so that the bounds above are satisfied. This would lead to an equivalent asymptotic result as the one obtained here for secure computation over $\mathrm{GR}(p^k, \ell)$, which can be translated without asymptotic loss into a result for (parallel) computation over $\mathbb{Z}/p^k\mathbb{Z} = \mathrm{GR}(p^k, 1)$ by using, once again, RMFEs, exactly as done in [8].

Acknowledgments. We thank the anonymous Asiacrypt 2021 reviewers for their valuable feedback. Chaoping Xing's research work is partially supported by the NSFC under grant 12031011, Huawei-SJTU joint projects and the National Key Research and Development Project 2020YFA0712300. During his time in Aarhus University, Daniel Escudero was supported by the European Research Council (ERC) under the European Union's Horizon 2020 research and innovation programme under grant agreement No 669255 (MPCPRO).

This paper was prepared for information purposes by the Artificial Intelligence Research group of JPMorgan Chase & Co and its affiliates ("JP Morgan"), and is not a product of the Research Department of JP Morgan. JP Morgan makes no representation and warranty whatsoever and disclaims all liability, for the completeness, accuracy or reliability of the information contained herein. This document is not intended as investment research or investment advice, or a recommendation, offer or solicitation for the purchase or sale of any security, financial instrument, financial product or service, or to be used in any way for evaluating the merits of participating in any transaction, and shall not constitute a solicitation under any jurisdiction or to any person, if such solicitation under such jurisdiction or to such person would be unlawful. 2021 JPMorgan Chase & Co. All rights reserved.

References

1. Abspoel, M., Cramer, R., Damgård, I., Escudero, D., Yuan, C.: Efficient information-theoretic secure multiparty computation over $\mathbb{Z}/p^k\mathbb{Z}$ via Galois rings. In: Hofheinz, D., Rosen, A. (eds.) TCC 2019. LNCS, vol. 11891, pp. 471–501. Springer, Cham (2019). https://doi.org/10.1007/978-3-030-36030-6_19
2. Ben-Efraim, A., Nielsen, M., Omri, E.: Turbospeedz: double your online SPDZ! improving SPDZ using function dependent preprocessing. In: Deng, R.H., Gauthier-Umaña, V., Ochoa, M., Yung, M. (eds.) ACNS 2019. LNCS, vol. 11464, pp. 530–549. Springer, Cham (2019). https://doi.org/10.1007/978-3-030-21568-2_26
3. Benhamouda, F., Degwekar, A., Ishai, Y., Rabin, T.: On the local leakage resilience of linear secret sharing schemes. J. Cryptol. **34**(2), 1–65 (2021)
4. Cascudo, I., Cramer, R., Xing, C., Yuan, C.: Amortized complexity of information-theoretically secure MPC revisited. In: Shacham, H., Boldyreva, A. (eds.) CRYPTO 2018. LNCS, vol. 10993, pp. 395–426. Springer, Cham (2018). https://doi.org/10.1007/978-3-319-96878-0_14
5. Chabanne, H., Maghrebi, H., Prouff, E.: Linear repairing codes and side-channel attacks. IACR Trans. Cryptographic Hardware Embedded Syst. **2018**(1), 118–141 (2018)
6. Choudhuri, A.R., Goel, A., Green, M., Jain, A., Kaptchuk, G.: Fluid MPC: secure multiparty computation with dynamic participants. Cryptology ePrint Archive, Report 2020/754 (2020). https://eprint.iacr.org/2020/754
7. Cramer, R., Damgård, I., Nielsen, J.B.: Secure Multiparty Computation and Secret Sharing. Cambridge University Press, Cambridge (2015). ISBN 9781107043053. www.cambridge.org/de/academic/subjects/computer-science/cryptography-cryptology-and-coding/secure-multiparty-computation-and-secret-sharing?format=HB&isbn=9781107043053
8. Cramer, R., Rambaud, M., Xing, C.: Asymptotically-good arithmetic secret sharing over $Z/(p^\ell Z)$ with strong multiplication and its applications to efficient MPC. Cryptology ePrint Archive, Report 2019/832 (2019). https://eprint.iacr.org/2019/832
9. Damgård, I., Nielsen, J.B.: Scalable and unconditionally secure multiparty computation. In: Menezes, A. (ed.) CRYPTO 2007. LNCS, vol. 4622, pp. 572–590. Springer, Heidelberg (2007). https://doi.org/10.1007/978-3-540-74143-5_32
10. Damgård, I., Larsen, K.G., Nielsen, J.B.: Communication lower bounds for statistically secure MPC, with or without preprocessing. In: Boldyreva, A., Micciancio, D. (eds.) CRYPTO 2019. LNCS, vol. 11693, pp. 61–84. Springer, Cham (2019). https://doi.org/10.1007/978-3-030-26951-7_3
11. Escudero, D., Dalskov, A.: Honest majority MPC with abort with minimal online communication. Cryptology ePrint Archive, Report 2020/1556 (2020). https://eprint.iacr.org/2020/1556
12. Guruswami, V., Wootters, M.: Repairing Reed-Solomon codes. CoRR, abs/1509.04764 (2015). Note, we specifically refer to the version published on arXiv
13. Guruswami, V., Wootters, M.: Repairing Reed-Solomon codes. In: Wichs, D., Mansour, Y. (eds.) Proceedings of the 48th Annual ACM SIGACT Symposium on Theory of Computing, STOC 2016, Cambridge, MA, USA, 18–21 June 2016, pp. 216–226. ACM (2016). https://doi.org/10.1145/2897518.2897525

14. Ishai, Y., Kushilevitz, E.: On the hardness of information-theoretic multiparty computation. In: Cachin, C., Camenisch, J.L. (eds.) EUROCRYPT 2004. LNCS, vol. 3027, pp. 439–455. Springer, Heidelberg (2004). https://doi.org/10.1007/978-3-540-24676-3_26

15. Quintin, G., Barbier, M., Chabot, C.: On generalized Reed-Solomon codes over commutative and noncommutative rings. IEEE Trans. Inf. Theory **59**(9), 5882–5897 (2013)

16. Rashmi, K.V., Shah, N.B., Kumar, P.V.: Optimal exact-regenerating codes for distributed storage at the MSR and MBR points via a product-matrix construction. IEEE Trans. Inf. Theory **57**(8), 5227–5239 (2011)

17. Rashmi, K.V., Shah, N.B., Ramchandran, K., Kumar, P.V.: Regenerating codes for errors and erasures in distributed storage. In: 2012 IEEE International Symposium on Information Theory Proceedings, pp. 1202–1206. IEEE (2012)

18. Tamo, I., Ye, M., Barg, A.: Optimal repair of Reed-Solomon codes: achieving the cut-set bound. In: 2017 IEEE 58th Annual Symposium on Foundations of Computer Science (FOCS), pp. 216–227. IEEE (2017)

19. Wan, Z.-X.: Lectures on Finite Fields and Galois Rings. World Scientific Publishing Company (2003). ISBN 978-9812385048. https://doi.org/10.1142/5350

20. Wigderson, A., Or, M.B., Goldwasser, S.: Completeness theorems for noncryptographic fault-tolerant distributed computations. In: Proceedings of the 20th Annual Symposium on the Theory of Computing (STOC 1988), pp. 1–10 (1988)

Garbling, Stacked and Staggered
Faster k-out-of-n Garbled Function Evaluation

David Heath[✉], Vladimir Kolesnikov[✉], and Stanislav Peceny[✉]

Georgia Institute of Technology, Atlanta, GA, USA
{heath.davidanthony,kolesnikov,stan.peceny}@gatech.edu

Abstract. Stacked Garbling (SGC) is a Garbled Circuit (GC) improvement that efficiently and securely evaluates programs with conditional branching. SGC reduces bandwidth consumption such that communication is proportional to the size of the single longest program execution path, rather than to the size of the entire program. Crucially, the parties expend *increased computational* effort compared to classic GC.

Motivated by procuring a subset in a menu of computational services or tasks, we consider GC evaluation of k-out-of-n branches, whose indices are known (or eventually revealed) to the GC evaluator E. Our stack-and-stagger technique amortizes GC computation in this setting. We retain the communication advantage of SGC, while *significantly* improving computation *and wall-clock time*. Namely, each GC party garbles (or evaluates) the total of n branches, a significant improvement over the $O(n \cdot k)$ garblings/evaluations needed by standard SGC. We present our construction as a garbling scheme.

Our technique brings significant overall performance improvement in various settings, including those typically considered in the literature: e.g. on a 1Gbps LAN we evaluate 16-out-of-128 functions $\approx 7.68\times$ faster than standard stacked garbling.

Keywords: Garbled circuit · Conditional branching · Stacked garbling

1 Introduction

Garbled circuits (GCs) allow two mutually untrusting parties to securely compute arbitrary functions of their private inputs while revealing only the functions' outputs. GC was formalized by [BHR12] as a primitive. It is foundational in secure multiparty computation (MPC).

Research that improves the practical cost of GC, e.g. [NPS99, KS08, BHKR13, KMR14, ZRE15, BMR16], focuses on two metrics:

- *Communication.* GC constructions require that the GC generator G send to the GC evaluator E a large collection of ciphertexts that encode the truth tables for each gate. Reducing the number of required ciphertexts improves network utilization.

© International Association for Cryptologic Research 2021
M. Tibouchi and H. Wang (Eds.): ASIACRYPT 2021, LNCS 13091, pp. 245–274, 2021.
https://doi.org/10.1007/978-3-030-92075-3_9

- *Computation.* Typical GC constructions encode each gate's truth table using a hash function or key derivation function H. Reducing the number of calls to H improves each party's CPU utilization.

Stacked Garbling (or SGC) [HK20c, HK20b] is a recent GC improvement that reduces GC communication consumption for functions that contain *conditional branching*, e.g. as the result of a program if or switch statement. SGC shows that G need not send material proportional to the entire circuit; sending material proportional only to the longest program execution path is sufficient.

While traditionally communication is considered the bottleneck in the GC performance, SGC's communication improvement changed that *status quo*, as it *did not* bring a corresponding computation improvement. In many settings, computation now limits GC performance, sometimes severely (see examples and use cases discussed in our work).

SGC improves evaluation of 1-out-of-n circuits. In this work, we consider a generalization to secure evaluation of k-out-of-n circuits, but with the constraint that the GC evaluator E knows (or learns) the identities of the active branches. Such evaluation is well motivated, see Sect. 1.1. While SGC can be directly employed to solve this problem, the resulting solution is computationally inefficient: we could use the 1-out-of-n SGC solution k times, but this leads to each party (i.e. G and E) garbling each of n branches $O(k)$ times[1]. Already for $k > 3$ computation may overtake communication as the limiting resource (see, e.g., Fig. 6).

This overhead is unfortunate, particularly because standard garbling without stacking does not require this computation overhead. In standard garbling, the generator G simply generates each of the n circuits once and includes a special multiplexer circuit that propagates the output of the k active branches only. Thus each party processes a circuit only $O(n)$ times. However, adopting this approach sacrifices the communication benefit of SGC.

Thus, if we wish to securely evaluate k-out-of-n branches, we must either compromise computation or communication. Fortunately, this dilemma can be resolved, and we can get the best of both above techniques.

In this work, we show that we can retain the communication advantage of SGC, while only garbling an (almost) optimal number of branches. Specifically, like the standard SGC-based approach, we consume communication proportional to only k circuits, while reducing the computation to n garblings by G and $n - k$ garblings by E (compare to the total of SGC's $O(n \cdot k)$ garblings). The resulting wall-clock time improvement is surprisingly significant, with the total runtime almost $k\times$ smaller than SGC for a wide range of parameters (see Sect. 10).

In sum, we note that network bandwidth is a limited resource, and should be consumed with care. At the same time, it is not pragmatic to reduce communication by indiscriminately sacrificing computation: even mainstream CPUs

---

[1] Because of our setting, we consider a corresponding special case of SGC where E knows the active branch; hence to evaluate 1-out-of-n functions, the parties consume only linear work in n. General SGC, where neither party knows the active branch, requires $O(n \log n)$ computation [HK21].

generate GC at the rate only 3× the speed of 1Gbps LAN, and are expensive both in dollar cost and power consumption. Our approach strikes a balance between network utilization and hardware utilization and potentially allows use with cheap, computationally weak devices whose use, e.g. in IoT, is exploding.

Our Setting. We summarize our considered setting.

GC generator G and evaluator E agree on a set of n functions of which k will be evaluated. Both G and E provide input into the functions (common input can be reused across functions).

E knows *a priori* or receives as output from the GC the identity of the k branches. If the active branches are revealed by the GC, then the revelation must be completed before the k-out-of-n conditional can run.

We formalize our approach as a *garbling scheme* [BHR12], not a protocol. Garbling schemes are flexible primitives that can be plugged into a number of cryptographic protocols. For example, our implementation (Sect. 10) uses our scheme to implement a typical constant-round 2PC protocol secure against semi-honest adversaries.

The k-out-of-n branching can be sequentially composed and nested (see discussion in Sects. 7.3 and 7.4).

1.1 Motivation

Consider a server that offers a suite of various services to clients, and suppose that these services have privacy concerns for both the server and client. The client may *a priori* know which services it wishes to request, but may wish that even the choice of services are kept secret. Alternatively, the identity of the provided services might be computed securely, but might be implied by the client's output. In such cases, an efficient k-out-of-n secure computation can allow the server to securely provide k out of its offered n services while learning only the number of requested services k.

As an example, suppose a telehealth company offers services that screen concerned patients for a variety of medical conditions. In this example, both parties may have privacy concerns: the patient may not wish to disclose her health data and the server may use sensitive health data of other individuals to aid in the screening or use proprietary data. The patient may *a priori* know that a number of medical conditions are unlikely to be the source of her symptoms (e.g. it is unlikely that the patient's headaches are caused by athlete's foot). Hence, the client may only wish to be screened for k health conditions out of the possible n. By employing our k-out-of-n construction, the telehealth company can potentially offer its services to the client at a cheaper rate.

We note that high speed networking (e.g., LAN or WiFi modules) are cheap (a few U.S. dollars) and low-power, while even mainstream CPUs are expensive both in cost and power. Thus, our approach is particularly suited for use with cheaper computationally weaker and/or battery-powered devices, whose use, e.g., in IoT, is exploding.

1.2 Contribution

We improve GC evaluation of k-out-of-n functions where the k choices are known (either *a priori* or revealed by the computation) to the GC evaluator E. In particular we:

- Present a modification to Stacked Garbling [HK20b] that retains $O(k)$ communication consumption, but that improves the total number of branch garblings performed by G and E from $O(n \cdot k)$ to only $2n - k$.
- Prove our construction secure as a *garbling scheme* [BHR12]. Garbling schemes can be used as a primitive to instantiate secure protocols, e.g. semi-honest 2PC protocols.
- Implement and experimentally evaluate our approach. The implementation instantiates a semi-honest 2PC protocol. Our experimental results indicate that our computation improvement (and wall clock time!) over standard Stacked Garbling indeed scales with k. For example, for $n = 128$ and $k = 16$ we improve over Stacked Garbling by $\approx 7.68\times$.

1.3 High Level Intuition

Stacked Garbling improves communication needed to evaluate 1-out-of-n circuits by bitwise XORing, or *stacking*, the n GC *materials* needed to evaluate each of the branches. For each inactive branch, E receives a compact seed used to derive all of G's randomness when garbling it. This allows E to securely reconstruct and unstack material for the $n - 1$ inactive branches, so that she can recover the material for the active branch and evaluate normally. Unfortunately, naively extending this technique to k-out-of-n branches incurs factor k increase in the cost to garble and unstack material.

At the highest level, our technique shows that G can send to E k stacks of *linearly independent* combinations of exactly n materials. Crucially, each stack will now contain garblings of both inactive and active branches. The inactive garblings can be easily removed from these k stacks via seeds. The remnants are a collection of k stacks that each contain k active materials. To transform these k stacks into the k materials, we use the linear independence: E uses an optimized form of Gaussian elimination to quickly transform the k stacks into k materials and then uses the results to evaluate the k active circuits.

Because we reuse the same n materials across all k branch evaluations, we reduce garbling computation by factor k. We choose our linear combinations carefully such that this stacking and unstacking can be achieved using only simple XOR operations. Our technique must consume $O(n \cdot k)$ calls to XOR to stack/unstack the linear combinations, but these XOR calls are significantly cheaper than the gate-by-gate construction of circuit garblings. Hence our technique significantly improves performance.

2 Related Work

Stacked Garbling. Ours is in a line of works that improve GC evaluation of conditional branches [KKW17, Kol18, HK20c, HK20b, HK21]. The more recent of these works introduce Stacked Garbling, improving GC communication by up to the program branching factor.

While [HK20b] and [HK21] consider the general case of branching where neither party knows the active branch, [Kol18] and [HK20c] consider special cases where one party knows the branch. Our work builds on [HK20c] which considers the case where E knows the active branch, and we review its technique in Sect. 4.

[Kol18] considers the dual case where G knows the active branch. We briefly explain why we do not instead build on this work.

Firstly, the setting is less flexible, since G, unlike E, cannot non-interactively receive messages from the GC. Hence G must *choose* the active branches. In contrast, our approach allows E to choose the active branches *or alternatively* allows the branches to be chosen by the GC and revealed to E as part of her output.

Secondly, GC players G and E enjoy asymmetric levels of trust: security against malicious E is often trivially attained simply from the authenticity property of GC. Therefore, changing the roles of the MPC participants (e.g. switching Alice from being G to E) results in a corresponding trust model change, which may not be desired. In the context of the motivation discussed in Sect. 1.1, G is more naturally played by the (more trusted) service provider.

Finally, and most importantly, the [Kol18] technique also incurs $O(n \cdot k)$ computation, though for different reasons than [HK20c]. In particular, the technique requires G to simply send to E k GC materials corresponding to the active branches. Upon receiving these, E who does not know the branches, tries to evaluate each branch with each material; hence she evaluates $O(n \cdot k)$ times. When E makes a bad guess, her evaluation results in so-called garbage output labels, which must be discarded in favor of valid output labels. [HK20b] showed that garbage can be collected without additional interaction via a special multiplexer, but constructing the multiplexer requires G to emulate E's bad evaluation. Thus, in this construction, both G and E perform $O(n \cdot k)$ times, and it is not clear how this can be improved. In contrast, the [HK20c] technique allows for an efficient Gaussian elimination technique that we present in this work.

Other Improved Secure Conditional Branching. Outside GC, improved conditional branching has begun to emerge. Although our emphasis is constant round 2PC, we mention these works for completeness.

In the Zero Knowledge setting, some branching improvements have been made. [GGHAK21] developed a compiler for sigma protocols that takes advantage of disjunctive proofs. [BMRS20] developed an efficient interactive ZK proof system that incorporates a stacking optimization. Like our work, [BMRS20] also considers k-out-of-n branching, though their protocol and setting are entirely different.

In the MPC setting, conditional improvements to the classic GMW protocol and to Beaver Triples have been shown [HKP20, HKP21].

Prior Work Motivated by Similar Scenarios. We discuss several prior works, whose setting and motivation is related to ours. These works address different MPC aspects, and we don't compare our work to them, e.g., w.r.t. performance.

Multiple executions of (identical) functions was considered by [HKK+14, LR14]. Both works designed improved cut-and-choose algorithms for batched execution. We can view our work as improving a batched execution of *a subset of different* functions. We note that improvements of bare garbling schemes are more rare than improvements in the richer world of constructions built on garbling schemes.

[KNT06] considered private policy negotiation. Here the negotiation process itself, i.e. determining what data will be revealed under what conditions, is considered privacy-sensitive. One method of policy selection considered in this work involves one player privately evaluating k-out-of-n matching functions. A related question is of multi-factor authentication or policy match check, where authentication (policy check) succeeds if k out of n private conditions hold.

3   Notation and Assumptions

Notation

- G is the GC generator. We refer to G as he/him.
- E is the GC evaluator. We refer to E as she/her.
- κ denotes the computational security parameter (e.g. 128).
- $[n]$ denotes the sequence of natural numbers $0, ..., n-1$.
- We work with vectors/matrices and bitstrings (i.e., vectors of bits). We index vectors and matrices with subscripts and use 0-based indexing, e.g. x_0 or $A_{i,j}$.
- We consider GC evaluation of k-out-of-n circuits:
  - n is the number of branches.
  - k is the number of *target* branches.
  - $\mathcal{C}_i$ is the Boolean circuit that implements branch i.
  - M denotes the vector of n *materials* corresponding to the garbling of each branch. Informally, the material M_i is the collection of encrypted truth tables needed for E to evaluate branch $\mathcal{C}_i$.
  - t denotes the *target set*, which is the set of active branches. Since t always has size k, we treat it interchangeably as a vector of k elements.

Cryptographic Assumptions. Our garbling scheme (Sect. 7) requires only standard assumptions.

Our *implementation* builds on top of the state-of-the-art Boolean circuit half-gates technique [ZRE15] which uses the Free XOR technique [KS08]. Thus our implementation assumes a circular correlation robust hash function H [CKKZ12].

4 Preliminaries – Stacked Garbling [HK20c]

Our work can be viewed as an extension to the Stacked Garbling (SGC) technique [HK20b, HK20c] which improves the communication consumption of GC in the context of conditional branching.

Even though our focus is secure 2PC, not ZK, the most relevant to our work is the technique of [HK20c], which improves GC-based ZK (GCZK). Indeed, their core technique does not actually *require* the simpler ZK setting. Instead, it simply requires that the GC evaluator E knows the identity of each active branch. In such cases, [HK20c] shows that it suffices to send garbled material proportional to the longest conditional branch rather than to the entire circuit.

[HK20c] is built on two ideas:

1. The material produced by garbling each conditional can be handled as a bitstring. This means that materials can be XORed, or *stacked*, with one another to reduce communication.
2. Material can be expanded from a pseudorandom seed. If all random choices used to generate a circuit garbling are derived from a seed, then material is a deterministic expansion of that seed. Thus, a seed is a compact representation of a circuit material.

   As a seed uniquely determines all wire labels in the GC, it is insecure to send material via a seed to the circuit evaluator. However, [HK20c] shows that it is secure to reveal a seed for an *inactive* branch.

Let $\{\mathcal{C}_1, \ldots, \mathcal{C}_n\}$ be a set of conditionally composed circuits. Let $\mathcal{C}_t$ be the active (target) branch and let E know t. G knows each $\mathcal{C}_i$, but does not know and must not learn t.

G chooses n seeds s_i and uses each s_i to garble circuit $\mathcal{C}_i$. The result is a vector of n 'materials' M, which are the collections of encrypted truth tables needed to evaluate the GC. Rather than sending the concatenation of these materials, G instead *stacks* the materials by sending to E the following XOR sum:

$$\bigoplus_i M_i$$

(Shorter materials are padded with trailing zeros such that each material has the same length.) Of course, the XOR sum of the n materials is shorter than the concatenation, and hence SGC greatly reduces communication consumption.

The parties then ensure that E receives the $n-1$ seeds $s_{i \neq t}$ corresponding to each inactive branch. These seeds can be conveyed from G to E via oblivious transfer (OT) or can be conveyed by the GC itself [HK20b][2]. Because E holds these seeds, she can reconstruct each material $M_{i \neq t}$ by simply replaying the actions of G. E now computes:

$$\left(\bigoplus_i M_i \right) \oplus \left(\bigoplus_{i \neq t} M_i \right) = M_t$$

---

[2] Namely, at runtime E will hold garbled labels corresponding to the branch condition t; G can include an encrypted table that allows E to decrypt different seeds depending on the semantic value of t. Thus, E can receive the seeds without additional interaction. This is useful when t is implied by E's output rather than by her input.

Therefore E can recover the material M_t corresponding to the active branch. Crucially, although E successfully recovers the branch material, she never receives the sensitive seed s_t[3]. From here, E can evaluate the active branch normally. We can exit the conditional and continue GC evaluation by including a multiplexer component[4]. Thus, [HK20c] evaluates 1-out-of-n circuits while requiring only enough communication for the single longest circuit.

5   Technical Overview

Let $\mathcal{C}_0, \ldots, \mathcal{C}_{n-1}$ denote n circuits of which k should be evaluated. For sake of example, suppose that $k = 2$; our approach generalizes to arbitrary k. Let α, β denote the indices of the two circuits to be evaluated.

Let us first consider evaluation of circuit $\mathcal{C}_\alpha$. As reviewed in Sect. 4, standard Stacked Garbling [HK20c] allows the GC generator G to first generate each circuit $\mathcal{C}_i$ from a seed s_i. Let M denote the vector of n resulting GC materials (i.e., the collections of encoded gate truth tables). Rather than sending the concatenation of these materials, G instead sends to E the following XOR sum:

$$\bigoplus_i M_i$$

E then receives each seed $s_{i \neq \alpha}$, uses these seeds to regenerate each material $M_{i \neq \alpha}$, and then computes:

$$\left(\bigoplus_i M_i \right) \oplus \left(\bigoplus_{i \neq \alpha} M_i \right) = M_\alpha$$

Thus, E can recover the material for the target branch using communication proportional to only the single longest material. From here, E can use GC input labels to correctly evaluate circuit $\mathcal{C}_\alpha$.

Now, consider evaluation of $\mathcal{C}_\beta$. Unfortunately, the above work cannot be re-used when evaluating $\mathcal{C}_\beta$. Namely, it is *not secure* for G to re-use any above materials M_i: E has already received s_β, and it is not secure for E to hold a seed used to generate evaluated material. Instead, G must start from fresh seeds s_i' and generate fresh materials M'. Similarly, E must receive all seeds $s_{i \neq \beta}'$ and regenerate each material $M_{i \neq \beta}'$. In general, E and G each generate each of n circuits k times.

---

[3] The seed s_t conceptually contains both the material M_t *and* all 'wire labels', and so it is not secure for E to view this seed. If she did, she could decrypt the wires on the active branch. It *is* secure for her to receive seeds on inactive branches because we can ensure that inactive branches hold no semantic values via a *demultiplexer* component [HK20b].

[4] [HK20b] and [HK21], which consider the more general case where neither party knows the active branch, require significant extra computation to generate the multiplexer. This extra computation is needed because E does not know the active branch t, and hence makes "mistakes" during evaluation that need to be cleaned up. [HK20c] and we assume that E does know t, and hence the multiplexer is extremely efficient to generate by simply enumerating a garbled table based on t.

Our Approach. Let us return to the point where G had computed each material M_i, but before any stacking and sending had taken place. We allow the parties to re-use the same n materials M_i to evaluate *all* k target circuits. Thus, we reduce the number of needed materials from $n \cdot k$ to only n.

Our key idea is to view each material M_i as an element in a (very large) finite field $\mathrm{GF}(2^\ell)$. From here, G computes and sends to E k linearly independent combinations of the n materials. For example, when $k = 2$, G sends the following two stacks:

$$M_0 \oplus M_1 \oplus M_2 \oplus \cdots \oplus M_{n-1}$$
$$M_0 \oplus 2 \cdot M_1 \oplus 4 \cdot M_2 \cdots \oplus 2^{n-1} \cdot M_{n-1}$$

The GC then conveys to E (via a garbled gadget) all seeds $s_{i \neq \alpha, \beta}$; hence E can reconstruct all materials $M_{i \neq \alpha, \beta}$. This information suffices for E to perform Gaussian elimination. In particular, E XORs both stacks with (multiples of) her reconstructed materials and hence recovers:

$$M_\alpha \oplus M_\beta$$
$$2^\alpha \cdot M_\alpha \oplus 2^\beta \cdot M_\beta$$

E can now solve for M_α and M_β and then use these materials to securely evaluate $\mathcal{C}_\alpha$ and $\mathcal{C}_\beta$. Crucially, (1) we re-use the same n materials to evaluate all k circuits, (2) we retain SGCs $O(k)$ communication complexity, and (3) we ensure that E does not obtain the seed for any active branch. Hence, we can securely and efficiently evaluate k-out-of-n functions inside the GC.

5.1 Gaussian Elimination via 'Staggering'

In practice, we choose our field $\mathrm{GF}(2^\ell)$ and our linear combinations such that all operations can be implemented by simple XORs. This ensures that we can both stack and unstack material using efficient hardware instructions. Hence, the approach is efficient in practice.

Specifically, the materials in each stack are 'staggered' (see Fig. 1) by multiplying them by some power of two in the field. The powers of two for each stack are chosen such that all stacks are linearly independent combinations of the materials and hence contain sufficient information to unstack. We choose the field $\mathrm{GF}(2^\ell)$ such that even multiplying a material by the largest such power of two will not cause "wrap-around" in the field, and hence no modular reduction is needed to implement multiplication. Formally, if m is the size of the largest material, $\ell \geq m + n \cdot k$ is (more than) sufficient to ensure no modular reduction is needed. From here on, we largely ignore the size of the field and simply assume it is large enough to avoid need for modular reduction.

6 Garbling, Stacked and Staggered

We now formalize the key algorithms for our staggered stacking technique discussed above. Section 7 later hosts these algorithms in a *garbling scheme* [BHR12] such that our technique can be used in GC protocols.

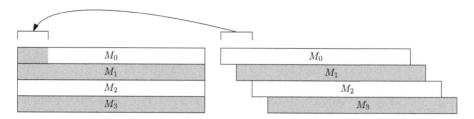

Fig. 1. An example of our staggered stacking for $n = 4$ and $k = 2$. Suppose $\mathcal{C}_0$ and $\mathcal{C}_2$ are the active branches. Hence E reconstructs from seeds inactive branch materials M_1 and M_3. G sends to E two stacks of all material, but the materials in the second stack are "staggered" by prepending materials with varying numbers of zeros. E unstacks (indicated in grey) M_1 and M_3. Notice that E can directly extract the first bits of M_0 from the second stack. She then unstacks these bits from the first stack, allowing her to view the first bits of M_2. By repeatedly unstacking portions of materials from the stacks, E eventually unstacks all k target materials.

PARAMETERS:

- A finite field $\mathbb{F} \triangleq GF(2^\ell)$.
- Number of branches n.
- Number of targets k.
- The stacking matrix $\mathbb{A}$ for n and k (see Definition 1).

INPUT: A vector of materials $M \in \mathbb{F}^n$.
OUTPUT: A vector of stacks of material $S \in \mathbb{F}^k$ where $S \triangleq \mathbb{A} \cdot M$.
PROCEDURE:

$$S \leftarrow 0^k$$
$$\text{for } i \in [k]:$$
$$\quad \text{for } j \in [n]:$$
$$\quad\quad \text{if } \mathbb{A}_{i,j} \neq 0:$$
$$\quad\quad\quad \triangleright \ll \text{denotes bitwise left shift.}$$
$$\quad\quad\quad S_i \leftarrow S_i \oplus (M_j \ll \log \mathbb{A}_{i,j})$$
$$\quad \text{return } S$$

Fig. 2. G's procedure for stacking n materials into k stacks. The procedure implements simple matrix multiplication by the stacking matrix $\mathbb{A}$ (see Definition 1). We take advantage of zeros in $\mathbb{A}$ to reduce the number of needed XOR operations.

Figure 1 depicts the bit-shift interpretation of our staggering technique for $n = 4$ and $k = 2$. We expound on this intuition, formalizing the technique for arbitrary n and k by using our field multiplication interpretation.

PARAMETERS:

- A finite field $\mathbb{F} \triangleq GF(2^\ell)$.
- Number of branches n.
- Number of targets k.
- Maximum material length len $< \ell$.
- The stacking matrix $\mathbb{A}$ for n and k (see Definition 1).

INPUT:

- A set of targets t.
- A vector of stacks $S' \in \mathbb{F}^n$ where materials for inactive branches $C_{i \notin t}$ have been XORed out.

OUTPUT: A vector of materials for the active branches $C_{i \in t}$. I.e., the vector of materials $M_{i \in t} = \text{Strike}(t, \mathbb{A})^{-1} \cdot S'$.

PROCEDURE:

$$\text{delay}_i \triangleq \begin{cases} t_0 \cdot (k-1) & \text{if } i = k-1 \\ \text{delay}_{i+1} + i \cdot (t_{k-j-1} - t_{k-j-2}) & \text{otherwise} \end{cases}$$

out $\leftarrow 0^k$

▷ Iterate through the stacks bit by bit.

for $b \in [\text{len} + \text{delay}_0]$:

    ▷ Iterate through each stack, recovering and unstacking one bit per stack.

    for $i \in k-1, ..., 0$:

        if $\text{delay}_i \leq b < \text{delay}_i + \text{len}$:

            ▷ α denotes the branch index *associated* with stack S_i.

            $\alpha \leftarrow t_{k-i-1}$

            $p \leftarrow b - \text{delay}_i$

            ▷ shift denotes the bit index of the bth bit of M_α.

            shift $\leftarrow \log(A_{i,\alpha}) + p$

            $\text{out}_{i,p} \leftarrow S'_{i,\text{shift}}$

            ▷ Unstack the bit $\text{out}_{i,p}$ from each stack.

            for $i' \in [k]$:

                if $\mathbb{A}_{i',\alpha} > 0$:

                    $\text{shift}' \leftarrow \log(\mathbb{A}_{i',\alpha}) + p$

                    $S'_{i',\text{shift}'} \leftarrow S'_{i',\text{shift}'} \oplus \text{out}_{i,p}$

return out

Fig. 3. Our unstacking algorithm allows E to perform efficient Gaussian elimination and to unstack k materials from k stacks. Strike is defined in Definition 2.

The key object in our formalization is a $k \times n$ matrix which we refer to as the *stacking matrix*. The stacking matrix formalizes the bit shift distance for each material in each stack.

Definition 1 (Stacking Matrix). *Let n be a number of branches and k be a number of targets. The* stacking matrix *for n and k is a $k \times n$ matrix $\mathbb{A}$ whose entries are defined as follows:*

$$\mathbb{A}_{i,j} \triangleq \begin{cases} 0 & \text{if } ((i+j) \bmod n) < k - 1 \\ 2^{i \cdot (i+j+k-1)} & \text{otherwise} \end{cases}$$

The stacking matrix is notationally complex, but its structure can be understood through example:

Example 1 (4×6 stacking matrix). The 4×6 stacking matrix is defined as follows:

$$\mathbb{A} \triangleq \begin{bmatrix} 0 & 0 & 0 & 1 & 1 & 1 \\ 0 & 0 & 1 & 2 & 4 & 0 \\ 0 & 1 & 4 & 16 & 0 & 0 \\ 1 & 8 & 64 & 0 & 0 & 0 \end{bmatrix}$$

Notice that each matrix row has $k - 1$ zeros; other entries are powers of two, and the powers of two increase with the rows. We choose varying rows to ensure linear independence which will be important when allowing E to unstack material.

To stack n materials in M into k stacks S, G simply computes $S \triangleq \mathbb{A} \cdot M$. We choose $\mathbb{A}$ with this matrix-vector multiplication in mind. In particular, (1) we maximize the number of zero entries in the matrix and (2) non-zero entries are powers of two. These properties allow for an efficient algorithm that stacks material using only simple XORs (see Fig. 2).

G then sends the k stacks S to E and E obliviously receives $n - k$ seeds corresponding to the inactive branches. Let t denote the set of active branch identifiers. From here, E reconstructs the $n - k$ inactive materials: she reconstructs each $M_{i \notin t}$. E then constructs the following n element vector M':

$$M' \triangleq \begin{cases} M_i & \text{if } i \notin t \\ 0 & \text{otherwise} \end{cases}$$

Now, E can remove the $n - k$ reconstructed materials from her stacks by computing the following:

$$S' \triangleq S \oplus \mathbb{A} \cdot M'$$

In other words, E shifts each material by the appropriate amount (according to $\mathbb{A}$) before XORing it with each stack. The resulting vector S' contains linear combinations of the k materials $M_{i \in t}$ only.

To define how E transforms these k stacks into the k active branch materials, we first give a helper definition that allows E to remove columns from the stacking matrix $\mathbb{A}$:

Definition 2 (Strike). *Let A be a $k \times n$ matrix and let s be a set of indices such that $|s| < n$. Then $\mathrm{Strike}(s, A)$ is the $k \times (n - |s|)$ matrix that contains all columns in A except those whose index appears in s.*

Example 2 (Strike two columns from 4×6 stacking matrix). Let $\mathbb{A}$ denote the 4×6 stacking matrix and let $s = \{1, 4\}$:

$$\mathrm{Strike}(s, \mathbb{A}) = \begin{bmatrix} 0 & 0 & 1 & 1 \\ 0 & 1 & 2 & 0 \\ 0 & 4 & 16 & 0 \\ 1 & 64 & 0 & 0 \end{bmatrix}$$

Note that the following equality holds:

$$S' = \mathrm{Strike}(\bar{t}, \mathbb{A}) \cdot M_{i \in t}$$

This equality holds simply from the fact that E already removed each inactive branch material from S'.

Thus, to transform the k stacks into the k target materials, E needs to invert $\mathrm{Strike}(\bar{t}, \mathbb{A})$. The stacking matrix $\mathbb{A}$ is designed with this inversion in mind: by construction, any choice of k columns are linearly independent. Thus, our approach allows E to perform Gaussian elimination to unstack any choice of k-out-of-n branches. To complete the unstacking, E computes the following:

$$M_{i \in t} = \mathrm{Strike}(\bar{t}, \mathbb{A})^{-1} \cdot S'$$

Like our stacking procedure (Fig. 2), this unstacking can also be achieved using simple XORs only; see Fig. 3. Unlike our stacking procedure, this unstacking procedure is nontrivial. This may be surprising, since the case for $k = 2$ (e.g. Fig. 1) is quite simple. However, with $k > 2$ the algorithm must carefully coordinate the order in which bits are unstacked. Nevertheless, due to the special case of the matrix $\mathbb{A}$, we can unstack materials using only $O(k^2 \cdot \ell)$ bit XORs, where ℓ is the length of the longest stack.

We explain in greater detail our unstacking algorithm in the following correctness lemma:

Lemma 1 (Unstack Correct). *Upon inputs t and S', the procedure in Fig. 3 indeed computes:*
$$\mathrm{Strike}(\bar{t}, \mathbb{A})^{-1} \cdot S'$$

Proof. By inspection of Fig. 3.

Recall, e.g., from Example 1 that each material is shifted by some amount, according to the stacking matrix $\mathbb{A}$. Our algorithm extracts bits one by one from the stacks. Each stack will be used to recover a single material. In particular, stack i will be used to recover material $M_{t_{k-i-1}}$ We say that stack i is *associated* with material $M_{t_{k-i-1}}$ and with branch $C_{t_{k-i-1}}$.

In the general case, we extract one bit per stack per iteration. However, note that on the first iteration (i.e. before anything has been unstacked), some stacks may have more than one material stacked into the first bit (for reference, see Fig. 1). Therefore, we add a per-stack *delay* which ensures that we do not attempt to recover bits prematurely. For example, in Fig. 1, we must first unstack a bit of material from the second stack before we can recover a bit of material from the first.

We formalize the delay for stack i with the following expression:

$$\text{delay}_i \triangleq \begin{cases} t_0 \cdot (k-1) & \text{if } i = k-1 \\ \text{delay}_{i+1} + i \cdot (t_{k-j-1} - t_{k-j-2}) & \text{otherwise} \end{cases}$$

This delay formalizes the distance between (1) the bit location in the ith stack where its associated material begins and (2) the bit location in the $(i+1)$th stack where its associated material begins. Note that the delay is quite complex because we must account for the fact that some materials (i.e. those for inactive branches) have been *a priori* removed from each stack. The delay for stack i depends on (1) the delay of its neighboring stack $i+1$, (2) the shift distance for stack i which is itself i, and (3) the difference between the indexes of the two target branches associated with stack i and stack $i+1$. Note that the smallest delay occurs for stack $k-1$, which corresponds to the fact that we can start extracting material from this stack first.

Now, view the collection of stacks as a matrix S where $S_{i,j}$ denotes the jth bit of stack i. Consider an arbitrary bit $S_{i,j}$. Before we begin to unstack, this bit is a stacking of (in the general case) k bits from each of the k materials. Therefore, we must ensure that $k-1$ bits from the non-associated materials are each removed before we attempt to extract the bit. This is exactly the purpose of the above delay.

We show that our algorithm ensures bit $S_{i,j}$ is correctly unstacked by considering two cases of the other bits originally in $S_{i,j}$: those associated with stack $r > i$ and those associated with stack $r < i$:

1. Consider a bit b associated with stack $r > i$ originally XORed into $S_{i,j}$. By the time our algorithm attempts to extract $S_{i,j}$, b will have already been unstacked. This is ensured because $\text{delay}_r < \text{delay}_i$ by definition.
2. Consider a bit b associated with stack $r < i$ originally XORed into $S_{i,j}$. By the time our algorithm attempts to extract $S_{i,j}$, b will have already been unstacked. This is ensured because we choose delay according to the shift distance of each stack. Thus, although stack r has longer delay than stack i, its associated material is not shifted as much, and hence it will have already been unstacked.

Thus, we correctly recover each bit $S_{i,j}$, and so Fig. 3 is correct.   □

Thus G conveys k circuit materials at the cost of only $O(n)$ circuit garblings.

7   Stacked and Staggered Garbling Scheme

We formalize our technique as a *garbling scheme* [BHR12] which we call S&S. S&S allows G and E to securely evaluate k-out-of-n functions where E outputs the identity of the evaluated functions.

A garbling scheme is a five-tuple of algorithms:

$$(\mathsf{ev}, \mathsf{Gb}, \mathsf{En}, \mathsf{Ev}, \mathsf{De})$$

These five algorithms specify how G and E handle the GC. Namely, (1) En specifies how G encodes cleartext inputs as input labels, (2) Gb specifies how G constructs the garbled circuit, (3) Ev specifies how E evaluates the garbled circuit and obtains output labels, (4) De specifies how output labels are decoded to cleartext outputs, and (5) ev specifies circuit semantics. En, Gb, Ev, and De should together securely implement ev.

Additionally, [BHR12] formalizes the garbling scheme properties *correctness*, *obliviousness*, *privacy*, and *authenticity* (we provide definitions of these properties as we prove them). By proving our garbling scheme satisfies these properties, we ensure that the scheme may be plugged into GC protocols as a black box.

Underlying Garbling Scheme. Because our focus is conditional evaluation only, we adopt a formalization technique of [HK20c] whereby our scheme focuses *exclusively* on the handling of k-out-of-n branching; we leave the handling of the functions in each branch to another *underlying* garbling scheme which we refer to as Base. S&S may be instantiated with different schemes for Base. Our implementation instantiates Base with the state-of-the-art Boolean-circuit-based half-gates technique [ZRE15].

We require that Base satisfies the [BHR12] properties of *correctness*, *obliviousness*, *privacy*, and *authenticity*. Additionally, [HK21] introduced a property called *strong stackability* which ensures that the garbling scheme produces garbled material that may be safely stacked. We provide their definition of strong stackability; a candidate garbling scheme must satisfy the property to instantiate Base.

Definition 3 (Strong Stackability). *A garbling scheme is* strongly stackable *if:*

1. *For all circuits $\mathcal{C}$ and all inputs x,*

$$(\mathcal{C}, M, \mathsf{En}(e, x)) \overset{c}{=} (\mathcal{C}, M', X')$$

   where $(M, e, \cdot) = \mathsf{Gb}(1^\kappa, \mathcal{C})$, $X' \leftarrow \{0,1\}^{|X|}$, and $M' \leftarrow \{0,1\}^{|M|}$.
2. *The scheme is* projective *[BHR12]. I.e., the input encoding string e and output decoding string d are vectors of pairs of labels.*
3. *There exists an efficient deterministic procedure Color that maps strings to $\{0,1\}$ such that for all $\mathcal{C}$ and all projective label pairs $A^0, A^1 \in d$:*

$$\mathsf{Color}(A^0) \neq \mathsf{Color}(A^1)$$

   where $(\cdot, \cdot, d) = \mathsf{Gb}(1^\kappa, \mathcal{C})$.

4. There exists an efficient deterministic procedure Key *that maps strings to* $\{0,1\}^\kappa$ *such that for all* C *and all projective label pairs* $A^0, A^1 \in d$:

$$\mathrm{Key}(A^0) \parallel \mathrm{Key}(A^1) \overset{c}{=} \{0,1\}^{2\kappa}$$

where $(\cdot, \cdot, d) = \mathsf{Gb}(1^\kappa, C)$.

The first sub-property ensures that GC material looks random, which ensures that E cannot determine the active branch by simply looking at the garbling[5]. Second, properties (2–4) allow our scheme to work with the output labels that emerge when evaluating Base. More precisely, (3) corresponds to the classic point-and-permute technique to reduce the number of PRF calls in evaluating the GC gates. The Color procedure produces a bit that instructs which garbled row to decrypt. (4) allows us to extract a suitable PRF key from each label.

7.1   Garbling Scheme Algorithms

Construction 1 (S&S Garbling Scheme). *Let* Base *denote an underlying garbling scheme that is* correct, oblivious, private, authentic, *and* strongly stackable. S&S *is the tuple of algorithms specified in Fig. 4.*

In Sect. 7.5, we prove Construction 1 *correct, oblivious, private,* and *authentic,* as defined by [BHR12]. Note that Construction 1 is not strongly stackable; see Sect. 7.4 for discussion.

The algorithms in Fig. 4 host our staggering technique (Sect. 6) into a garbling scheme. This hosting is relatively straightforward; we note the more interesting details:

- S&S is a *projective* garbling scheme [BHR12]: i.e., each circuit wire has exactly two possible GC labels. Formally, the input encoding string e and output decoding string d are simple vectors of pairs of GC labels. This means that our procedures En and De are standard, and are implemented as straightforward mappings between cleartext values and garbled labels (i.e., they index e and d).
- S&S handles k-out-of-n branching *only.* We leave the handling of low level details of branch internals to Base. Additionally, our scheme can be hosted inside another garbling scheme in order to sequentially compose multiple k-out-of-n computations (see Sect. 7.3). This way, our formalization can cleanly focus on our contribution without sacrificing expressivity.

---

[5] It may seem strange that we require GC material look random, given that we reveal the active branch to E. However, we need this strong property to meet the [BHR12] definition of obliviousness. Informally, our scheme ensures that the garbling of a circuit provides no information to E. Only once output decoding tables d are revealed to E does E learn the branch conditions, which allow her to evaluate.

$\mathsf{S\&S.Gb}(1^\kappa, \mathcal{C})$:
  $k, \mathcal{C}_0, .., \mathcal{C}_{n-1} \leftarrow \mathcal{C}$
  $T \leftarrow (\{0,1\}^\kappa)^n$
  for $i \in [n]$:
    $M_i, e_i, d_i \leftarrow \mathsf{Base.Gb}[T_i](1^\kappa, \mathcal{C}_i)$
  $e', M_{\mathrm{dem}} \leftarrow \mathrm{GbDem}(T, e_0..e_{n-1})$
  $e \leftarrow T \parallel e'$
  $d', M_{\mathrm{mux}} \leftarrow \mathrm{GbMux}(T, d_0..d_{n-1})$
  $d \leftarrow T, d'$
  $M_{\mathrm{stack}} \leftarrow \mathrm{Stack}(k, M_0, .., M_{n-1})$
  $M \leftarrow M_{\mathrm{dem}} \parallel M_{\mathrm{stack}} \parallel M_{\mathrm{mux}}$
  return M, e, d

$\mathsf{S\&S.Ev}(\mathcal{C}, M, X, t)$:
  $k, \mathcal{C}_0, .., \mathcal{C}_{n-1} \leftarrow \mathcal{C}$
  $M_{\mathrm{dem}}, M_{\mathrm{stack}}, M_{\mathrm{mux}} \leftarrow M$
  $T, X' \leftarrow X$
  $j \leftarrow 0$
  for $i \notin t$:
    $M_i, e_i, d_i \leftarrow \mathsf{Base.Gb}[T_j](1^\kappa, \mathcal{C}_i)$
    $j \leftarrow j + 1$
  $M_{i \in t} \leftarrow \mathrm{Unstack}(t, M_{\mathrm{stack}}, M_{i \notin t})$
  $X_0, .., X_{k-1} \leftarrow \mathrm{EvDem}(t, T, M_{\mathrm{dem}}, X')$
  for $i \in [k]$:
    $Y_i \leftarrow \mathsf{Base.Ev}(\mathcal{C}_{t_i}, M_{t_i}, X_i)$
  $Y \leftarrow \mathrm{EvMux}(t, T, M_{\mathrm{mux}}, Y_0, .., Y_{k-1})$
  return T, Y

$\mathsf{S\&S.ev}(\mathcal{C}, x)$:
  $k, \mathcal{C}_0, .., \mathcal{C}_{n-1} \leftarrow \mathcal{C}$
  $t, x' \leftarrow x$
  $y \leftarrow$ empty-string
  for $i \in [k]$:
    $y \leftarrow y \parallel \mathsf{Base.ev}(\mathcal{C}_{t_i}, x')$
  return t, y

$\mathsf{S\&S.En}(e, x)$:
  $X \leftarrow$ empty-string
  for $i \in [\|x\|]$:
    $X^0, X^1 \leftarrow e_i$
    if $x_i = 0$ then $X_i \leftarrow X^0$;
    else $X_i \leftarrow X^1$;
  return X

$\mathsf{S\&S.De}(d, Y)$:
  $y \leftarrow$ empty-string
  for $i \in [\|Y\|]$:
    $Y^0, Y^1 \leftarrow d_i$
    if $Y_i = Y^0$ then $y_i \leftarrow 0$;
    else if $Y_i = Y^1$ then
      $y_i \leftarrow 1$
    else return $\bot$;
  return y

Fig. 4. Our garbling scheme S&S. The procedure Stack refers to the procedure specified in Fig. 2. The procedure Unstack refers to the procedure described in Sect. 6 whereby E first computes $S' \triangleq S \oplus \mathbb{A} \cdot M'$ and then performs Gaussian elimination via Fig. 3. Our Ev procedure is nonstandard because we pass the set of target branches t as an extra cleartext argument. This models the fact that E knows the targets. T denotes a bitwise encoding of the set t. If T_i encodes zero, then branch $\mathcal{C}_i$ is not active; otherwise $\mathcal{C}_i$ is active. We use the zero encoding for T_i as a seed to garble branch $\mathcal{C}_i$; $\mathsf{Gb}[T_i]$ denotes configuring the randomness in the procedure Gb according to the seed T_i. GbMux and EvMux respectively garble and evaluate the multiplexer component. GbDem and EvDem respectively garble and evaluate the demultiplexer component.

- As written, S&S does not directly support *nested* k-out-of-n computations. We discuss nesting, including explaining how it can be added to our scheme, in greater length in Sect. 7.4. Note that we *can* nest 1-out-of-n oblivious branching inside our scheme by instantiating Base with an existing stacked garbling scheme [HK21].
- Our scheme invokes procedures Stack and Unstack. These procedures use the algorithms in Figs. 2 and 3 to stack and unstack material.

- By convention, the first n bits of input to our circuits encode the target set t. The ith target bit indicates if branch C_i is a target. If branch C_i is a target, then E will obtain an encoding of one for the ith target bit. Each target bit's zero encoding is used as the seed to garble branch C_i. Hence, E can garble inactive branches.
- We add an additional input t to S&S.Ev to model the fact that E knows the target set t. The set t is also formalized as a circuit output. This, again, models the fact that E knows the target set. In particular, this output allows us to prove privacy (see Theorem 3).
- Our top level circuit feeds input to (resp. collects output from) the active branches via a demultiplexer (resp. multiplexer). See below for extended discussion of these gadgets.

7.2   Multiplexer and Demultiplexer

Our construction routes inputs to and collects outputs from the k active branches via a *demultiplexer* and a *multiplexer*. These garbled gadgets are simple, and can be built using standard GC techniques: namely, according to the inputs we build an encrypted function table such that E can decrypt only the appropriate outputs. Both gadgets are similar to the gadgets used in [HK20b, HK21].

For simplicity and because they are constructed in a standard way, we do not fully specify garbled algorithms for these components. However, we do specify the cleartext functions that they compute.

The *demultiplexer* takes as input a target set t and an input string x. For each of the n branches C_i, the demultiplexer computes the following simple function:

$$\mathrm{demux}(t, x) \triangleq \begin{cases} x & \text{if } i \in t \\ \bot & \text{otherwise} \end{cases}$$

Namely, the demultiplexer forwards the input x to each active branch and propagates a garbage value to each inactive branch. In the GC, our demultiplexer encodes $\bot$ values by producing a uniform GC label that is distinct yet indistinguishable from the label's in the encoding string e. This ensures that E does not learn the active branch set t until she sees the output decoding string d, which is needed to show that our scheme is oblivious.

The *multiplexer* takes as input a target set t and n output strings y_i. It concatenates and propagates the output from the k active branches in t:

$$\mathrm{mux}(t, y_0, ..., y_{n-1}) \triangleq y_{t_0} \; || \; ... \; || \; y_{t_{k-1}}$$

7.3   Sequential Composition

As mentioned above, our scheme explicitly handles k-out-of-n branching *only*. Nevertheless, our scheme can be used to achieve more general circuits, where a k-out-of-n conditional may occur multiple times within another circuit (here we cover sequential composition; nested composition is discussed in Sect. 7.4).

To achieve this kind of sequential composition of circuits, i.e. where another circuit appears before and/or after a k-out-of-n conditional, we can host our scheme inside another garbling scheme. This outer scheme can handle the details of threading the outputs from one circuit to inputs of another. Such sequential composition is not hard, and e.g., the formalization of [HK21] can be used with our scheme to achieve sequential composition.

We emphasize that our scheme requires the outer scheme to pass the target set t as a cleartext argument to S&S.Ev. This can be easily achieved in both the case where t is part of E's input or if t is computed by a prior circuit component and released as output to E. Technically, the latter release to E is achieved by including t as formal output, and into the corresponding decoding table d. Because t must be available to E prior to the evaluation of the conditional, (at least) the corresponding portion of d must be available to E during GC evaluation.

7.4 Nested Branching

We do not prove our garbling scheme strongly stackable [HK21]. Indeed, our garbling scheme will not in general work for embedding inside a stacked conditional where neither party knows the target branch. Indeed, to use our construction, E must know in cleartext the target set t. Therefore, if S&S is in an inactive branch, E will obtain a uniformly sampled set t, which may be distinguishable from a real-execution t, which will break SGC properties.

However, it is easy to see that it is secure to nest *our* scheme inside itself, e.g. to allow a tree of k-out-of-n branching: in this case, the above distinguisher does not apply, since E already knows the targets of all outer conditionals.

Unfortunately, the [BHR12] framework is not suitable for proving that nesting our scheme is secure. The problem is that [BHR12] provides no mechanism for revealing *intermediate* circuit values to E. Rather than either losing the modularity of our scheme or performing a complete overhaul to the [BHR12] framework, we instead provide a modular and informal discussion of the changes that would be needed to prove that nesting our scheme is secure.

Our approach to resolving this is the introduction of the notion of *mandatory outputs*, which will play a special role in composition. Namely, each circuit, in addition to having a collection of *regular* outputs, has a second formal collection of *mandatory* outputs. When composing more than one garbling scheme to build up complexity, the outer scheme is required to verbatim forward all mandatory outputs of its inner schemes as its own mandatory outputs. With this change added, we could set each target set t as a mandatory output. This would in particular ensure that E learns the control flow path through k-out-of-n conditionals as required. Since E learns the full path through the conditionals, she can correctly evaluate. Moreover, E's view is simulatable since the control flow path is implied by the mandatory outputs.

As discussed above (Sect. 7.3), these mandatory outputs need to be released over time to E. I.e., to begin evaluating a k-out-of-n conditional, E must know the target set t.

As a final detail, to achieve *obliviousness* (see Definition 5) when nesting branches, our multiplexer and demultiplexer must produce material indistinguishable from uniform strings. This ensures that E cannot learn the active set t before learning the GC decoding string d.

7.5   Proofs

S&S satisfies the [BHR12] definitions of *correctness, obliviousness, privacy,* and *authenticity.* We include definitions and proofs of each of these properties.

Definition 4 (Correctness). *A garbling scheme is* correct *if for all circuits C and all inputs x:*

$$\mathsf{De}(d, \mathsf{Ev}(\mathcal{C}, M, \mathsf{En}(e, x))) = \mathsf{ev}(\mathcal{C}, x)$$

where $(M, e, d) = \mathsf{Gb}(1^\kappa, \mathcal{C})$.

Correctness requires that the garbling scheme algorithms implement the semantics specified by ev.

Theorem 1. *If* Base *is correct and strongly stackable,* S&S *is correct.*

Proof. By the correctness and strong stackability of Base.

S&S.En and S&S.De are straightforward mappings between cleartext values and GC labels and so are trivially correct. Thus the core task is to show that given valid input encodings X corresponding to input x, Gb and Ev jointly ensure an output encoding Y corresponding to $\mathsf{ev}(\mathcal{C}, x)$.

Recall that our scheme handles k-out-of-n conditionals only. The conditional is preceded by a demultiplexer, which routes inputs to active branches, and followed by a multiplexer, which collects outputs from the active branches (see Sect. 7.2).

Recall that for active branch set t, the demultiplexer computes for each branch $\mathcal{C}_i$ the following simple function:

$$\mathrm{demux}(t, x) \triangleq \begin{cases} x & \text{if } i \in t \\ \bot & \text{otherwise} \end{cases}$$

I.e., the input x is routed to each active branch. The demultiplexer (formally GbDem and EvDem) is implemented as a standard garbled gadget built from an encrypted function table and is correct.

The core of our approach is the stacking and unstacking of material. Correctness of this step can be inferred from discussion in Sects. 5 and 6. In short, Gb stacks the n circuit materials by left multiplying the stacking matrix $\mathbb{A}$ (see Definition 1 and Fig. 2). Recall from Fig. 4 that each branch material is constructed using a zero label in the encoding T. Ev computes the inactive branch zero labels and hence can reconstruct and unstack all inactive branch materials. From here, Ev performs Gaussian elimination (via Fig. 3, see Lemma 1) to extract the active branch materials. Thus, Ev correctly unstacks materials. Base is assumed correct, so invoking Base.Ev on correct material yields correct output labels for each active branch.

Finally, Ev routes the outputs of each active branch to the multiplexer (formally GbMux and EvMux). Importantly, Base is assumed strongly stackable, so the Color procedure is available. This allows us to construct the multiplexer as a standard garbled gadget based on point and permute [BMR90]. This gadget implements the following simple function:

$$\text{mux}(t, y_0, ..., y_{n-1}) \triangleq y_{t_0} \parallel ... \parallel y_{t_{k-1}}$$

Hence output labels are properly propagated from the active branches.

S&S is correct.   □

Definition 5 (Obliviousness). *A garbling scheme is oblivious if there exists a simulator $\mathcal{S}_{\text{obv}}$ such that for any circuit $\mathcal{C}$ and all inputs x, the following are indistinguishable:*

$$(\mathcal{C}, M, X) \overset{c}{=} \mathcal{S}_{\text{obv}}(1^\kappa, \mathcal{C})$$

where $(M, e, \cdot) = \text{Gb}(1^\kappa, \mathcal{C})$ and $X = \text{En}(e, x)$.

Obliviousness ensures that the material M and encoded input labels X reveal no information about the input x or about the output $\text{ev}(\mathcal{C}, x)$.

Theorem 2. *If Base is oblivious and strongly stackable, then S&S is oblivious.*

Proof. By constructing an obliviousness simulator $\mathcal{S}_{\text{obv}}$.

$\mathcal{S}_{\text{obv}}$ simply does the following: (1) run $\text{S\&S.Gb}(1^\kappa, \mathcal{C})$ to generate a fresh garbling (M', e', d'), (2) run $\text{S\&S.En}(e', 0)$ to generate X', and (3) output $(\mathcal{C}, M', X')$. In other words, the simulator simply constructs a fresh garbling and encodes the all zeros string. We claim that this simulation is indistinguishable from real.

For our k-out-of-n setting, the most notable point is that the garbling does not leak the target set t. The target set t is disclosed to E by the decoding string d which is not available to the obliviousness distinguisher, so t must be hidden. As an informal aside, obliviousness can be useful when E may never eventually evaluate a particular GC, e.g. in cut-and-choose. Hiding the target set t from E until it is explicitly revealed by d allows our scheme to satisfy obliviousness.

Our scheme composes three subcomponents: the n branches themselves, the multiplexer, and the demultiplexer. We consider each.

Recall (from Sect. 7.2) that the demultiplexer forwards valid input labels to the active branches only; inactive branches are instead given labels that encode $\perp$. The demultiplexer is built as a standard GC gadget, and so it hides the semantic values of its inputs. If branch $\mathcal{C}_i$ is active, then the demultiplexer outputs labels in the encoding string e_i. Each of these encoding strings hold uniform values due to strong stackability (Definition 3). If branch $\mathcal{C}_i$ is inactive, then the demultiplexer instead outputs a uniform string that encodes $\perp$.

Hence, the demultiplexer supports indistinguishability. Both in the real world and the simulation, the demultiplexer maps input labels to uniform labels for every branch.

The branches themselves support obliviousness because their garbling is uniform due to strong stackability. This is crucial, since it means that a distinguisher cannot attempt to unstack material to determine which of the t branches are active.

Finally, the multiplexer trivially supports obliviousness since it is built as a standard GC gadget, and maps uniform input labels (due to strong stackability) to output labels.

Hence the simulation is indistinguishable and S&S is oblivious.   □

Definition 6 (Privacy). *A garbling scheme is* private *if there exists a simulator* $\mathcal{S}_{\mathrm{prv}}$ *such that for any circuit* $\mathcal{C}$ *and all inputs* x, *the following are computationally indistinguishable:*

$$(M, X, d) \stackrel{c}{=} \mathcal{S}_{\mathrm{prv}}(1^\kappa, \mathcal{C}, y),$$

where $(M, e, d) = \mathsf{Gb}(1^\kappa, \mathcal{C})$, $X = \mathsf{En}(e, x)$, *and* $y = \mathsf{ev}(\mathcal{C}, x)$.

Privacy ensures that E, who is given (M, X, d), learns nothing about the input x except what can be learned from the output y.

Theorem 3. *If* Base *is oblivious and strongly stackable,* S&S *is private.*

Proof. We prove privacy by constructing a simulator $\mathcal{S}_{\mathrm{prv}}$.

By Theorem 2, S&S is oblivious, and hence there exists an obliviousness simulator $\mathcal{S}_{\mathrm{obv}}$. $\mathcal{S}_{\mathrm{prv}}$ first runs $\mathcal{S}_{\mathrm{obv}}(1^\kappa, \mathcal{C})$, resulting in a simulated garbling $(\mathcal{C}, M', X')$. From here, $\mathcal{S}_{\mathrm{prv}}$ must construct a decoding string d' that together with M' and X', is indistinguishable from (M, X, d) even given the output y.

We now show how $\mathcal{S}_{\mathrm{prv}}$ simulates d.

$\mathcal{S}_{\mathrm{prv}}$ holds M' and X'; it also knows the set t of the target branches. (Recall by our syntactic convention, t is always included in the output of S&S.) $\mathcal{S}_{\mathrm{prv}}$ uses these strings to invoke $Y' = \mathsf{Ev}(\mathcal{C}, M', X', t)$ and obtains Y', which holds the output labels for all target branches. The key issue is to now simulate d' such that $\mathsf{S\&S.De}(d', Y') = y$. Indeed, if this decoding does *not* hold, then there is clearly a distinguisher. Constructing such d', given Y' and y is easy: $\mathcal{S}_{\mathrm{prv}}$ simply populates the 2-dimensional table of d' with the corresponding to y labels of Y'. It then fills in the remaining slots of d' with simulated labels. Note, here we rely on the property that unseen labels of the GC can be simulated. This holds for standard GC schemes, e.g. half-gates, standard Yao, etc. Hence the multiplexer, which ultimately produces our output labels and is built using such standard techniques, produces simulatable labels.

It is easy to see that this simulation is indistinguishable from the real execution. Indeed, the simulated d' successfully decodes the true output y, and its entries are indistinguishable from the entries of the real d.   □

Definition 7 (Authenticity). *A garbling scheme is* authentic *if for all circuits $\mathcal{C}$, all inputs x, all target sets t, and all poly-time adversaries $\mathcal{A}$ the following probability is negligible in κ:*

$$\Pr\left(Y' \neq \mathsf{Ev}(\mathcal{C}, M, X, t) \wedge \mathsf{De}(d, Y') \neq \bot\right)$$

where $(M, e, d) = \mathsf{Gb}(1^\kappa, \mathcal{C})$, $X = \mathsf{En}(e, x)$, and $Y' = \mathcal{A}(\mathcal{C}, M, X, t)$.

Authenticity ensures that even an adversarial E cannot construct labels that successfully decode except by running Ev as intended.

Theorem 4. *If* Base *is authentic and strongly stackable,* S&S *is authentic.*

Proof. Authenticity follows from the fact that (1) the multiplexer and the demultiplexer are implemented as garbled gadgets using standard GC that is authentic and (2) Base is assumed authentic.

Our proof starts at the end of a circuit and proceeds backwards, at each step showing that $\mathcal{A}$ cannot forge outputs of a circuit component without forging inputs to that component. Thus, $\mathcal{A}$ cannot forge overall circuit outputs without forging overall circuit inputs, and so the circuit is authentic.

Recall that our scheme handles k-out-of-n circuits only, so we need only prove the related subcomponents authentic.

- As stated above, the multiplexer is built as a standard authentic GC gadget. It is authentic.
- The n branches are authentic by assumption on Base. Note that $n - k$ of these branches are *inactive* and $\mathcal{A}$ holds the seeds for each of these branches. Hence, she may forge arbitrary outputs from each inactive branch. However, the logic of the multiplexer component discards inactive branch outputs, so forging values inside inactive branches does not help $\mathcal{A}$ forge outputs of the overall conditional.
- The demultiplexer, like the multiplexer, is a standard authentic GC gadget.

Note that our scheme can compose the three above components because of the strong stackability of Base: namely, our multiplexer and demultiplexer can directly manipulate the wire labels of the base scheme. Strong stackability ensures this manipulation is authentic (resp. correct) by including Key (resp. Color) procedures.

S&S is authentic.   □

8   Application to Zero Knowledge Proofs (ZKP)

We point out an immediate application of our garbling scheme to Zero Knowledge. ZK is a natural application for the setting where the k choices are known to the GC evaluator E (prover in GC-ZK). Our garbling scheme can be directly used in GC-ZK, resulting in a corresponding computation improvement from $O(n \cdot k)$ to only $2n - k$ of symmetric key operations. Unlike the MPC setting, our k-out-of-n branching does not place additional assumptions on the prover; in particular, branching can be placed anywhere in the proof statement. We don't view this as our core contribution, since IT-MAC-based ZK [HK20a, WYKW21, YSWW20, BMRS21, DIO20] overtook GC-ZK in performance in the area of interactive ZK.

9   Implementation and Experimental Setup

We implemented S&S in C++ and used it to instantiate a semi-honest 2PC protocol such that we can evaluate our approach (see Sect. 10).

Implementation Details. We instantiated the underlying garbling scheme Base with [ZRE15]'s state-of-the-art half-gates technique. Our computational security parameter κ is 127: we reserve the 128th bit for the classic permute-and-point technique [BMR90]. We instantiated oblivious transfer, needed to convey input labels from G to E, via the OT extension of [IKNP03] as implemented by EMP [WMK16].

Our formal constructions present our staggering technique at the bit-level. I.e., the stacking matrix $\mathbb{A}$ (Definition 1) staggers stacks by low powers of two. To achieve higher concrete efficiency, our implementation shifts at the word level of our machine. Specifically, we shift materials by multiples of 128 bits. This coarse granularity ensures that the implementation need not even perform bit shifts; we instead simply load from/store to the correct location in memory to implement staggering.

Further low level improvements to our implementation are possible. For example, our current implementation does not *stream* the GC stacks from G to E as they are produced. Instead, we send all stacks in a batch across the network.

Compared Garbling Schemes. To compare the performance of our technique, we implemented two other GC-based techniques for handling k-out-of-n circuits:

1. *Standard Stacked Garbling.* Our primary point of comparison is stacked garbling *without* our staggering optimization. Namely, rather than using Gaussian elimination to extract k materials from k stacks, G separately garbles each of the n circuits k times.

2. *Standard GC.* For further reference, we also instantiate k-out-of-n branching using a basic Boolean circuit with no stacking optimization. This technique consumes communication/computation independent of k[6].

Evaluation Machine. We run both G and E on a single commodity laptop. The laptop runs Ubuntu 20.04 and features an Intel(R) Core(TM) i5-8350U CPU @ 1.70GHz and 16GB RAM. Each party runs on a single thread of execution.

Network Settings. We consider two simulated network settings:

1. *LAN:* A simulated ethernet connection with 1Gbps bandwidth and 2ms round-trip latency.
2. *WAN:* A simulated wide area network connection with 100Mbps bandwidth and 20ms round-trip latency.

Networks are simulated by the `tc` program.

Benchmark. To provide a clean point of comparison, we evaluate the three GC techniques on a program that conditionally evaluates k-out-of-n different instances of SHA-256. It is, of course, unrealistic that each branch would hold the same circuit, but our goal is to capture performance characteristics only. Despite using the same circuit for each branch, we take no shortcuts. For example, we generate the cleartext circuit once for each branch and keep each separately in memory. Similarly, we garble the circuits separately for each branch.

Note that we do not expect our performance to diminish when faced with smaller circuits: our technique is lean as Gaussian elimination is implemented only with XORs. However, traditional stacked garbling must pay cost linear in the number of the conditional's inputs and outputs, and we inherit this cost. Thus, our approach is best applied when the circuits are large in comparison to the total number of inputs/outputs of the conditional.

The SHA-256 circuit has $\approx 9 \times 10^4$ AND gates.

10   Evaluation

We report experimental results obtained when running our system against both standard Stacked Garbling and standard garbled circuits without stacking.

We used all three implementations to handle k-out-of-n circuits where each circuit is SHA-256. We set n to 16 and to 128 and then varied k from 2 to $n-1$. See Sect. 9 for further details on the experimental setup. Figures 5 and 6 plot the results.

---

[6] Technically, a full standard GC implementation would have variable performance in k due to the need to multiplex the branch outputs. For simplicity, our standard GC implementation does not multiplex outputs. This omission yields a small difference in performance that is strictly in favor of the standard technique: the circuit is smaller.

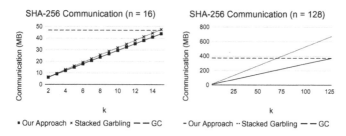

Fig. 5. S&S's and compared schemes' communication consumption as a function of k. The experiments confirm that our technique maintains the communication advantage of stacked garbling [HK20c].

Communication. Recall that our technique improves computation when evaluating k-out-of-n circuits. Figure 5 demonstrates that our method achieves this computation improvement *without* sacrificing communication.

Specifically, our technique has similar communication to the [HK20c]-based method. From the $n = 128$ chart, it is clear that our implementation of standard SGC has higher communication; we discuss why shortly. Technically, our approach's *branch* GC materials are slightly longer than those for the [HK20c]-based method because of our staggering (see e.g. Fig. 1). In the last stack, each material is shifted by $k - 1$ blocks (in practice we shift each material in 128-bit blocks). Assuming all n materials are XORed into each stack, the last material is shifted by $(k-1)(n-1)$ blocks. This is our increase in stack length over [HK20c]. For $k = 15$, this increase is only ≈ 7 KB and is small compared to the size of GC material even for small circuits.

We note and briefly explain the poor communication performance of the SGC protocol, which is particularly evident in the $n = 128$ case of Fig. 5. This is due to the need to manage $k \cdot n$ sets of inputs and outputs, since the k SGC stacks are processed independently. I.e. our standard SGC implementation pays factor k overhead for multiplexers/demultiplexers. We note that it should be possible to reduce the SGC costs to be in line with ours; we did not implement this engineering optimization.

Wall-Clock Time. Figure 6 plots the wall-clock run-time for all three approaches and on both a LAN and a WAN. For $n = 16$, we averaged each data point over 100 runs. For $n = 128$, we averaged each data point over 10 runs.

Our experiments show that we indeed concretely improve computation in both network settings. We greatly reduce computation as compared to the standard Stacked Garbling technique, which must pay significant overhead to regarble each circuit k times. Our run-time improvement over standard garbling without stacking is less pronounced, but recall that our *communication* is significantly improved. Thus, in a sense we achieve the best of both worlds: we capture the low communication utilization of standard Stacked Garbling, but without high computation.

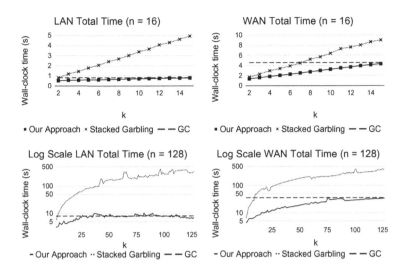

Fig. 6. S&S's and compared schemes' wall-clock runtime on both a WAN and a LAN as a function of k. As k increases, our staggering technique offers much lower computation overhead than standard Stacked Garbling. Hence, we greatly improve in terms of wall clock time. Standard GC without stacking has essentially constant performance because the parties must execute all n branches, regardless of parameter k.

Notice that in both settings, our performance is roughly upper bounded by the performance of standard GC without stacking. Specifically, our wall clock time approaches that of standard garbling as k approaches n. This can be explained by our choice of stacking matrix $\mathbb{A}$: as k approaches n, $\mathbb{A}$ features increasing numbers of zeros, which reduces the cost to both stack and unstack material. In the special case $n = k$, $\mathbb{A}$ features zeros everywhere except on one diagonal, where it is ones (it is a mirror of the identity matrix). Hence in this special case, our scheme and standard GC perform essentially identical actions.

We highlight specific features of the plots in Fig. 6:

- **LAN wall-clock time.** On our moderately fast LAN, we improve over standard Stacked Garbling by $\approx 6.4\times$ for 15-out-of-16 circuits, and by $\approx 46.6\times$ for 127-out-of-128 circuits. We do not achieve $k\times$ improvement for two reasons. First, while we reduce the number of AES invocations from $O(n \cdot k)$ to $O(n)$, to stack and unstack materials both techniques use the same number of XOR operations. Second, both approaches consume the same amount of bandwidth, which cuts into our advantage. When we instead run the 15-out-of-16 experiment on localhost (i.e., without simulating a bandwidth limit) we achieve $\approx 10.8\times$ improvement, much closer to the $15\times$ limit. For 16-out-of-128 circuits and on LAN, we improve over standard Stacked Garbling by $\approx 7.68\times$ and over standard GC by $\approx 4.82\times$.

- **WAN wall-clock time.** On this weaker network, bandwidth consumption becomes a greater concern. Our advantage over standard Stacked Garbling thus decreases, but our advantage over garbling without stacking increases. For 15-out-of-16 branches, we achieve $\approx 2.1\times$ speedup over standard stacked garbling; for 127-out-of-128 branches, we achieve $\approx 10.8\times$ speedup. In a 16-out-of-128 setting, we improve over standard Stacked Garbling by $\approx 7.22\times$ and over standard GC by $\approx 3.44\times$.

Acknowledgments. This work was supported in part by NSF award #1909769, by a Facebook research award, a Cisco research award, by Georgia Tech's IISP cybersecurity seed funding (CSF) award. This material is also based upon work supported in part by DARPA under Contract No. HR001120C0087. Any opinions, findings and conclusions or recommendations expressed in this material are those of the authors and do not necessarily reflect the views of DARPA.

References

[BHKR13] Bellare, M., Hoang, V.T., Keelveedhi, S., Rogaway, P.: Efficient garbling from a fixed-key blockcipher. In: 2013 IEEE Symposium on Security and Privacy, pp. 478–492. IEEE Computer Society Press, May 2013

[BHR12]   Bellare, M., Hoang, V.T., Rogaway, P.: Foundations of garbled circuits. In: Yu, T., Danezis, G., Gligor, V.D. (eds.) ACM CCS 2012, pp. 784–796. ACM Press, October 2012

[BMR90]   Beaver, D., Micali, S., Rogaway, P.: The round complexity of secure protocols (extended abstract). In: 22nd ACM STOC, pp. 503–513. ACM Press, May 1990

[BMR16]   Ball, M., Malkin, T., Rosulek, M.: Garbling gadgets for Boolean and arithmetic circuits. In: Weippl, E.R., Katzenbeisser, S., Kruegel, C., Myers, A.C., Halevi, S. (eds.) ACM CCS 2016, pp. 565–577. ACM Press, October 2016

[BMRS20] Baum, C., Malozemoff, A.J., Rosen, M., Scholl, P.: Mac'n'cheese: Zero-knowledge proofs for arithmetic circuits with nested disjunctions. Cryptology ePrint Archive, Report 2020/1410 (2020). https://eprint.iacr.org/2020/1410.pdf

[BMRS21] Baum, C., Malozemoff, A.J., Rosen, M.B., Scholl, P.: Mac'n'Cheese: zero-knowledge proofs for Boolean and arithmetic circuits with nested disjunctions. In: Malkin, T., Peikert, C. (eds.) CRYPTO 2021. LNCS, vol. 12828, pp. 92–122. Springer, Cham (2021). https://doi.org/10.1007/978-3-030-84259-8_4

[CKKZ12] Choi, S.G., Katz, J., Kumaresan, R., Zhou, H.-S.: On the security of the "Free-XOR" technique. In: Cramer, R. (ed.) TCC 2012. LNCS, vol. 7194, pp. 39–53. Springer, Heidelberg (2012). https://doi.org/10.1007/978-3-642-28914-9_3

[DIO20]   Dittmer, S., Ishai, Y., Ostrovsky, R.: Line-point zero knowledge and its applications. Cryptology ePrint Archive, Report 2020/1446 (2020). https://eprint.iacr.org/2020/1446

[GGHAK21] Goel, A., Green, M., Hall-Andersen, M., Kaptchuk, G.: Stacking sigmas: a framework to compose Σ-protocols for disjunctions. Cryptology ePrint Archive, Report 2021/422 (2021). https://eprint.iacr.org/2021/422.pdf

[HK20a] Heath, D., Kolesnikov, V.: A 2.1 KHz zero-knowledge processor with BubbleRAM. In: Ligatti, J., Ou, X., Katz, J., Vigna, G. (eds.) ACM CCS 2020, pp. 2055–2074. ACM Press, November 2020

[HK20b] Heath, D., Kolesnikov, V.: Stacked garbling. In: Micciancio, D., Ristenpart, T. (eds.) CRYPTO 2020. LNCS, vol. 12171, pp. 763–792. Springer, Cham (2020). https://doi.org/10.1007/978-3-030-56880-1_27

[HK20c] Heath, D., Kolesnikov, V.: Stacked garbling for disjunctive zero-knowledge proofs. In: Canteaut, A., Ishai, Y. (eds.) EUROCRYPT 2020. LNCS, vol. 12107, pp. 569–598. Springer, Cham (2020). https://doi.org/10.1007/978-3-030-45727-3_19

[HK21] Heath, D., Kolesnikov, V.: Logstack: stacked garbling with o(b log b) computation. Cryptology ePrint Archive, Report 2021/531 (2021). https://eprint.iacr.org/2021/531.pdf

[HKK+14] Huang, Y., Katz, J., Kolesnikov, V., Kumaresan, R., Malozemoff, A.J.: Amortizing garbled circuits. In: Garay, J.A., Gennaro, R. (eds.) CRYPTO 2014. LNCS, vol. 8617, pp. 458–475. Springer, Heidelberg (2014). https://doi.org/10.1007/978-3-662-44381-1_26

[HKP20] Heath, D., Kolesnikov, V., Peceny, S.: MOTIF: (almost) free branching in GMW - via vector-scalar multiplication. In: Moriai, S., Wang, H. (eds.) ASIACRYPT 2020. Part III, volume 12493 of LNCS, pp. 3–30. Springer, Heidelberg (2020)

[HKP21] Heath, D., Kolesnikov, V., Peceny, S.: Masked triples. In: Garay, J.A. (ed.) PKC 2021. LNCS, vol. 12711, pp. 319–348. Springer, Cham (2021). https://doi.org/10.1007/978-3-030-75248-4_12

[IKNP03] Ishai, Y., Kilian, J., Nissim, K., Petrank, E.: Extending oblivious transfers efficiently. In: Boneh, D. (ed.) CRYPTO 2003. LNCS, vol. 2729, pp. 145–161. Springer, Heidelberg (2003). https://doi.org/10.1007/978-3-540-45146-4_9

[KKW17] Kennedy, W.S., Kolesnikov, V., Wilfong, G.: Overlaying conditional circuit clauses for secure computation. In: Takagi, T., Peyrin, T. (eds.) ASIACRYPT 2017. LNCS, vol. 10625, pp. 499–528. Springer, Cham (2017). https://doi.org/10.1007/978-3-319-70697-9_18

[KMR14] Kolesnikov, V., Mohassel, P., Rosulek, M.: FleXOR: flexible garbling for XOR gates that beats Free-XOR. In: Garay, J.A., Gennaro, R. (eds.) CRYPTO 2014. LNCS, vol. 8617, pp. 440–457. Springer, Heidelberg (2014). https://doi.org/10.1007/978-3-662-44381-1_25

[KNT06] Kursawe, K., Neven, G., Tuyls, P.: Private policy negotiation. In: Di Crescenzo, G., Rubin, A. (eds.) FC 2006. LNCS, vol. 4107, pp. 81–95. Springer, Heidelberg (2006). https://doi.org/10.1007/11889663_6

[Kol18] Kolesnikov, V.: FreeIF: how to omit inactive branches and implement S-universal garbled circuit (almost) for free. In: Peyrin, T., Galbraith, S. (eds.) ASIACRYPT 2018, Part III. LNCS, vol. 11274, pp. 34–58. Springer, Heidelberg (2018). https://doi.org/10.1007/978-3-030-03332-3_2

[KS08] Kolesnikov, V., Schneider, T.: Improved garbled circuit: free XOR gates and applications. In: Aceto, L., Damgård, I., Goldberg, L.A., Halldórsson, M.M., Ingólfsdóttir, A., Walukiewicz, I. (eds.) ICALP 2008. LNCS, vol. 5126, pp. 486–498. Springer, Heidelberg (2008). https://doi.org/10.1007/978-3-540-70583-3_40

[LR14] Lindell, Y., Riva, B.: Cut-and-choose YAO-based secure computation in the online/offline and batch settings. In: Garay, J.A., Gennaro, R. (eds.) CRYPTO 2014. LNCS, vol. 8617, pp. 476–494. Springer, Heidelberg (2014). https://doi.org/10.1007/978-3-662-44381-1_27

[NPS99] Naor, M., Pinkas, B., Sumner, R.: Privacy preserving auctions and mechanism design. In: Proceedings of the 1st ACM Conference on Electronic Commerce, pp. 129–139. ACM (1999)

[WMK16] Wang, X., Malozemoff, A.J., Katz, J.: EMP-toolkit: efficient multiParty computation toolkit (2016). https://github.com/emp-toolkit

[WYKW21] Weng, C., Yang, K., Katz, J., Wang, X.: Wolverine: fast, scalable, and communication-efficient zero-knowledge proofs for boolean and arithmetic circuits. In: 42nd IEEE Symposium on Security and Privacy (2021)

[YSWW20] Yang, K., Sarkar, P., Weng, C., Wang, X.: Quicksilver: efficient and affordable zero-knowledge proofs for circuits and polynomials over any field. Cryptology ePrint Archive, Report 2021/076 (2020)

[ZRE15] Zahur, S., Rosulek, M., Evans, D.: Two halves make a whole. In: Oswald, E., Fischlin, M. (eds.) EUROCRYPT 2015. LNCS, vol. 9057, pp. 220–250. Springer, Heidelberg (2015). https://doi.org/10.1007/978-3-662-46803-6_8

Better Security-Efficiency Trade-Offs in Permutation-Based Two-Party Computation

Yu Long Chen[1(✉)] and Stefano Tessaro[2(✉)]

[1] imec-COSIC, KU Leuven, Leuven, Belgium
yulong.chen@kuleuven.be
[2] Paul G. Allen School of Computer Science and Engineering,
University of Washington, Seattle, USA
tessaro@cs.washington.edu

Abstract. We improve upon the security of (tweakable) correlation-robust hash functions, which are essential components of garbling schemes and oblivious-transfer extension schemes. We in particular focus on constructions from *permutations*, and improve upon the work by Guo *et al.* (IEEE S&P '20) in terms of security and efficiency.

We present a tweakable one-call construction which matches the security of the most secure two-call construction – the resulting security bound takes form $O((p + q)q/2^n)$, where q is the number of construction evaluations and p is the number of direct adversarial queries to the underlying n-bit permutation, which is modeled as random.

Moreover, we present a new two-call construction with much better security degradation – in particular, for applications of interest, where only a constant number of evaluations per tweak are made, the security degrades as $O((\sqrt{q}p + q^2)/2^n)$. Our security proof relies on the sum-capture theorems (Babai '02; Steinberger '12, Cogliati and Seurin '18), as well as on new balls-into-bins combinatorial lemmas for limited independence ball-throws.

Of independent interest, we also provide a self-contained concrete security treatment of oblivious transfer extension.

Keywords: Correlation-robust hashing · Two-party computation · Provable security

1 Introduction

Secure two-party computation makes intensive use of *symmetric-key* primitives, both in *garbling* [5,26] and *oblivious-transfer (OT) extension* [18] schemes. A common denominator of many such schemes is a special form of hash functions, known as *correlation-robust* (crHF) [18], which is pseudorandom when its input is whitened with a secret key, as well as the stronger notion of a *circular* crHF [8] (ccrHF). Recent works by Guo *et al.* [15,16] initiated the study of the concrete security of crHFs and ccrHFs in the ideal-permutation and cipher models. They

© International Association for Cryptologic Research 2021
M. Tibouchi and H. Wang (Eds.): ASIACRYPT 2021, LNCS 13091, pp. 275–304, 2021.
https://doi.org/10.1007/978-3-030-92075-3_10

also point out that naïve constructions lead to substantial security degradation with the number of *gates* (in the case of garbling) and of *OT instances* (in the case of OT extension). In fact, the authors of [15] leverage this to attack particular instantiations of half-gate garbling [27] with 80-bit security parameters.

MAIN GOALS OF THIS PAPER. This paper presents new (tweakable) crHFs and ccrHFs from *permutations* with substantially improved security-efficiency trade-offs. We give a one-call construction matching the security of the two-call construction from [16], and give a two-call construction with much better security degradation against a limited class of distinguishers sufficient for applications. We also revisit OT extension in concrete-security terms, weakening in particular the security requirements for the underlying crHF.

There are two ways in which our results can be interpreted – one is in terms of constructions from *fixed-key* block ciphers, in the spirit of [4,16]. The other, and perhaps better, interpretation is in terms of constructions from simpler objects, like block-cipher rounds, which we abstract as random permutations to model generic attacks – this is in line with the extensive research program on analyzing symmetric constructions. (We discuss this further below.)

Next, we briefly review the definiton of crHFs, as well as the achievable levels of security, before giving an overview of our results in greater detail.

CORRELATION-ROBUST HASHING. A *tweakable correlation-robust hash function* [16,18] is an efficiently computable two-argument function $H : \{0,1\}^n \times \{0,1\}^t \to \{0,1\}^n$ with the property that the oracle

$$\mathcal{O}_R^{\mathrm{tcr}}(w,t) = H(w \oplus R, t)$$

for a random $R \xleftarrow{\$} \{0,1\}^n$ is indistinguishable from a random function $f : \{0,1\}^n \times \{0,1\}^t \to \{0,1\}^n$. The second argument is the *tweak* – it enables domain separation (i.e., querying the same w on different tweaks should result in independent outputs), but also controls security degradation. To see what this means, note first that if H is a random oracle, then the distinguishing advantage of a q-query distinguisher making p direct queries to H is $\frac{pq}{2^n}$. (The proof is folklore and follows that of the Even-Mansour construction [11].) However, a crucial point is that for many applications we can restrict the distinguisher to make *at most B queries per tweak*, where B can be *very* small (even just $B = 1$) - in this case the advantage is[1]

$$\delta(q,p,B) \leq \frac{Bp}{2^n} . \tag{1}$$

As we show in Sect. 3, for OT extension, it is enough to use $B = 1$. Similarly, $B = 1$ is enough for garbling schemes [15,16]. Moreover, [15] gives a tweakable crHF construction making one call to an ideal cipher with concrete security

$$\delta(q,p,B) \leq \frac{Bp}{2^n} + \frac{(B-1)q}{2^n} .$$

---

[1] The basic idea of the simple proof is that a direct query $H(m,t)$ only helps if $m = w \oplus R$ for one of the B oracle queries (w,t).

In fact, both constructions can be adapted to satisfy *circular* crHF security, which is amenable to half-gate garbling [27] and free-XOR [8].

The above constructions make however fairly strong assumptions – either a monolithic random oracle or a monolithic ideal cipher. In the following, we want to study constructions from simpler primitives.

WHY IS THE PROBLEM HARD? Before moving on, it is worth pointing out that the main technical challenge in the design of secure crHFs is that we are aiming for a secret-key object with no designated secret key input – the secret key is XORed to the actual input, and we cannot change this. This makes crHFs very challenging to build. In particular, one cannot obtain crHFs from tweakable block ciphers directly, since the latter require a designated secret-key input.

Instead, the problem is related to designing related-key secure block ciphers – indeed, if a cipher E is pseudorandom against related-key attacks [6], it is not hard to see that $H(x,t) = E(x,t)$ is a good crHF – our warm-up construction below can indeed be thought as the case where E is the (one-key) Even-Mansour construction with non-linear key schedule from [9]. However, we prove the stronger notion of circular crHF, here, which does not follow generically. Also, our main two-call construction below however does not match any construction from prior works [9,12]. Tessaro [25] introduces related-key key-derivation functions which achieve similar security as (non-tweakable) crHFs, but with the goal of achieving near-optimal security (from random *functions*), and the resulting constructions are quite inefficient. Further, we actually do not know any standard-model construction for such additive (in $\mathbb{F}_{2^n}$) attacks, except under very strong multilinear-map assumptions [1].

THE ONE-CALL CONSTRUCTION. Our first warm-up result is concerned with one-call constructions from a permutation $\pi : \{0,1\}^n \to \{0,1\}^n$. Here, Guo *et al.* (GKWY) [16], proposed a construction – called MMO – which simply outputs $\pi(m) \oplus m$. MMO is not tweakable, and they prove a bound of $\frac{q(q+p)}{N}$. To additionally support a tweak, GKWY propose a two-call construction, called TMMO, while also achieving a similar security bound of $O\left(\frac{q(q+p)}{N}\right)$.

Here, we show that a very simple variant of MMO already achieves the same quantitative security with one single permutation call. Namely,

$$H(m,t) = \pi(m \otimes t) \oplus (m \otimes t),$$

where $\otimes$ stands for multiplication of bit-strings interpreted as elements of $\mathbb{F}_{2^n}$. Clearly, the tweak $t = 0^n$ needs to be excluded, but this is usually not a limitation, and all other tweaks are usable. To achieve tweakable ccrHF security, it is enough to also exclude the tweak $t = 0^{n-1}1$ (i.e., the neutral element of multiplication).

The analysis inherits ideas from tweakable block ciphers [21], however we need to take into account that no secret key can be used other than the one injected implicitly via whitening the input – the core of the security proof (which we carry out using the H-coefficient method [7,23]) relies on the fact that for given input-tweak pairs $\{(w_i, t_i)\}_{i=1,\ldots,q}$, the probability that for some $i \neq j$ we have

$$t_i \otimes (w_i \oplus R) = t_j \otimes (w_j \oplus R)$$

is at most 2^{-n}, over the random choice of R.

THE TWO-CALL CONSTRUCTION. Our more interesting result looks at two-call constructions. Ideally, we would like to obtain a construction improving upon the bound $qp/2^n$, but this is impossible *in general* [16]. However, we show that a positive result is possible if we limit the distinguisher's queries so that (1) the number of queries per tweak is bounded by B, and (2) the tweaks are chosen from a *nice* combinatorial subset $T \subseteq \{0,1\}^t$. We already discussed (1) as being sufficient for applications, but (2) is also not a major restriction – for our instantiation, we need to pick T as a *random* subset, but we can actually *fix* this set once and for all, and re-use it across instances.[2]

Our construction is called FPTP (this stands for Feed-forward Permutation-Tweak-Permutation), and on input $m \in \{0,1\}^n$ and tweak $t \in \{0,1\}^n$, it outputs

$$\text{FPTP}(m,t) = \pi(t \oplus \pi(\sigma(m))) \oplus \sigma(m) .$$

Here, σ is linear, and an *orthomorphism*, i.e., $\sigma(x) \oplus x$ is *also* a permutation. Removing σ, this construction resembles TMMO from [16], but the main (and crucial) difference is that we feed the *input* forward, as opposed to $\pi(m)$.

Assuming T is a good set for which all non-principal Fourier coefficients[3] are sufficiently small (and this is true for a randomly chosen T, as proved e.g. in [3,24]), then any distinguisher as above achieves advantage at most of order

$$\delta(q,p,B) \leq \frac{B\sqrt{qp}}{2^n} + \frac{q^2}{2^n} .$$

against *circular* crHF security. The first term here is significantly better than $qp/2^n$ for small $B < \sqrt{q}$, and in particular we usually want $B = 1$.

One restriction for this result is that it only holds for distinguishers for which inputs to the construction are distinct, even across tweaks. This restriction is strictly speaking not-necessary (we could input $m \otimes t$ instead of m), but in most applications, it is not necessary, and thus decide to opt for presenting this more efficient construction which is only secure under this input restriction. Indeed, in Sect. 3 we give a modified version of OT-extension that only requires security for *distinct* inputs. Moreover, for garbling applications, it is already known that it is sufficient to achieve security for *random* inputs, which are distinct with high probability (up to the birthday bound).

We also note that if we are only concerned with (non-circular) crHF security, then we can drop the map σ. We also give an analysis of our construction in the multi-user setting. We focus on the case of random inputs, which are sufficient for multi-user garbling, as studied in [15].

OT EXTENSION AND CONCRETE SECURITY. We also revisit the concrete security of oblivious-transfer extension [18]. In particular, we follow the angle of [16],

---

[2] Heuristically, one could evaluate a hash function on a fixed subset of inputs to obtain the corresponding tweaks.

[3] I.e., of the characteristic function of the set.

and look specifically at the concrete security of transforming the Δ-random-OT functionality into an OT functionality using tweakable crHFs. We focus specifically on malicious security.

In addition to making the treatment concrete, we show that it is enough to consider a crHF construction which is secure for *distinct* inputs only by slightly modifying the classical transformation. Moreover, we also discuss instantiations from random tweaks (and see that the cost can be kept fairly low if these need to be generated on the fly, for example by recycling them across instances). Indeed, interestingly, we see that despite the common belief, tweaks for active security serve more as a mean of controlling concrete security than to mitigate active attackers that force inputs to be equal across OT instances.

As a result of this, we obtain OT extension making two permutation calls per OT instance, and whose security degrades as $\frac{\sqrt{mp}}{2^n}$, where m is the number of OT instances (assuming $m < 2^{n/2}$). If we have $n = 102$, then we can for example have $m = 2^{32}$, and obtain 80-bit security.

INTERPRETING THE RESULTS. We see this work as part of the general program on understanding the security of cryptographic primitives. One way to think of a random permutation is not as a heuristic property of a complex object, but instead as a black-box abstraction for a component of the scheme that can be leveraged by an attack. In that sense, the simpler the component, the better. So, for example, the permutation could abstract a few rounds of AES (instead of the full AES) – of course proofs in this model should be backed by additional cryptanalysis (as it is always the case with any ideal-model proof).

An alternative interpretation (as in [16]) is that our constructions are instantiated from a fixed-key block cipher (like AES). However, it is not clear this interpretation is the most suitable one – the number of calls need to necessarily increase to obtain better security, and it is hard to beat the one-call construction from [15] – while the latter *does* use re-keying, it has already been shown that with appropriate implementation care, the costs of re-keying can be mitigated (as e.g. in [14]).

1.1 Technical Overview

We give an overview of the main ingredients behind the proof of security for the FPTP construction, which is our main result. To this end, we look at the two-permutation version (i.e., π_1, π_2 are independent permutations), namely the crHF candidate

$$H(m, t) = \pi_2(t \oplus \pi_1(m)) \oplus m .$$

This variant is analyzed in the full version of the paper. Its analysis is somewhat cleaner and pedagogical than the (more relevant) one-permutation version, which however follows similar ideas. Here, we focus also on discussing the proof that the construction is correlation-robust, i.e., we do not consider the circular version.

The full analysis adopts the H-coefficient method [7, 23] – we give some intuition about possible bad interaction transcripts which lead to distinguishing and why they can only occur with probability consistent with the claimed bound in the ideal world. (This is only part of the analysis – we also need to show that the probabilities of a good transcript occurring are similar in the real and ideal worlds.) Note that the discussion here does not exhaust all the bad events, we only discuss the most important ones. Every transcript contains q tweak-input-output triples $(t_1, w_1, z_1), \ldots, (t_q, w_q, z_q)$, where (1) $w_1, \ldots, w_q$ are disjoint and (2) every tweak t_i appears at most B times. Further, we have two sub-transcripts τ_1 and τ_2 of queries to π_1 and π_2, respectively – each containing (at most) p entries of the form (u, v) resulting from either a forward and backward queries to π_1 and π_2, respectively. Then, the key R is also included in the transcript – in the ideal world, in particular, the key $R \xleftarrow{\$} \{0,1\}^n$ is chosen *last* and independently from the interaction so far (as opposed to the real world, where it is chosen first).

CHAINS. One natural way of breaking the construction is to produce a so-called *chain*. One type of such a chain occurs if for a query (t_i, w_i, z_i), there exists one query $(u, v) \in \tau_1$ to π_1 and one query $(u', v') \in \tau_2$ to π_2 such that

$$w_i = u \oplus R , v \oplus t_i = u' .$$

Then, in the real world, we necessarily have $v' \oplus w_i \oplus R = z_i$, whereas in the ideal world this is unlikely to be the case, as the values $z_1, \ldots, z_q$ have been generated randomly and independently.

Now imagine we can bound the number of query pairs $(u, v) \in \tau_1$ and $(u', v') \in \tau_2$ for which $v \oplus u' \in T$ by some number $\phi \leq p^2$. Then, for every such pair, we have a well-defined tweak $t \in T$ such that $v \oplus u' = t$, and the probability that at least one of the queries for tweak t satisfies $w \oplus R = u$ is therefore (by union bound) 2^{-n}, assuming R is chosen last. It turns out that if T is well chosen, then ϕ can be smaller than p^2 – for example, for a randomly sampled set, we can show that roughly $\phi \leq \sqrt{q}p + qp^2/2^n$, using a sum-capture theorem [3,24]. This gives us the desired bound.

OTHER TYPES OF DOUBLE-CHAINS. There are other types of chains that can occur. One accounts to the symmetric case to the above – namely $v' = w_i \oplus R \oplus z_i , v \oplus t_i = v'$. This is handled in a similar manner.

However, we also need to handle a third case, namely one where

$$u = w_i \oplus R , \quad v' = z_i \oplus w_i \oplus R . \tag{2}$$

In particular, the above means that $u \oplus v' = z_i$, where z_i is the output of a random function. Because the values $z_1, \ldots, z_q$ are random, we can use a slightly different sum-capture theorem [10], and by a similar discussion to the above, the number of relevant pairs is also (with high probability) at most $\sqrt{q}p + qp^2/2^n$, and this thus the probability of each pair satisfying additional (2) is at most $\sqrt{q}p/2^n + qp^2/2^{2n}$.

MERGING CHAINS. A final issue that can happen is that, even though no chains are completed, we learn that two chains are bound to *merge*. For example, this means that for two queries (t_i, w_i, z_i) and (t_j, w_j, z_j), for which $w_i \neq w_j$, we can find $(u_1, v_1) \in \tau_1, (u_2, v_2) \in \tau_1$, such that

$$u_1 = w_i \oplus R , \quad u_2 = w_j \oplus R , \quad v_1 \oplus t_i = v_2 \oplus t_j . \tag{3}$$

Then we know we ought to have $z_i \oplus z_j = w_i \oplus w_j$, which is unlikely to be true in the ideal world. It turns out that upper bounding the probability of chains merging is the most involved part of our proof.

To see how this is resolved, fix now a pair of queries (t_i, w_i, z_i) and (t_j, w_j, z_j), and assume that we have a bound L on the number of pairs of permutation queries $(u_1, v_1), (u_2, v_2)$ such that $u_1 \oplus u_2 = w_i \oplus w_j$ and $v_1 \oplus v_2 = t_i \oplus t_j$, then the random choice R will satisfy (3) additionally with probability at most $L/2^n$. In fact, if we can show that for any Δ, Δ' the number of pairs $(u_1, v_1), (u_2, v_2) \in \tau_1$ such that $u_1 \oplus u_2 = \Delta$ and $v_1 \oplus v_2 = \Delta'$ is at most L, then we would get an upper bound of $q^2 L/2^n$ that any such merge occurs.

It turns out that proving such bound L accounts to a balls-into-bins problem, where an adaptive adversary interacts with a random permutation by means of p queries, and then *every pair* of queries $(u_1, v_1), (u_2, v_2)$ results into one of $\binom{p}{2}$ balls being thrown into bin $(u_1 \oplus u_2, v_1 \oplus v_2)$. We will prove that the load of the heaviest bin is, with high probability, small enough (roughly linear in n). This is actually surprising and non-trivial – the main reason is that the $\binom{p}{2}$ balls are not-independent, and the result of an adaptive process, yet their behavior is very similar to the assignment of p^2 random balls into 2^{2n} bins. We give an analysis (of a more general setting) in Sect. 5.2.

2 Preliminaries

For $n \in \mathbb{N}$, we denote by $\{0,1\}^n$ the set of bit strings of length n. For two bit strings $X, Y \in \{0,1\}^n$, we denote by $X \oplus Y$ their bitwise addition and by $X \otimes Y$ the multiplication of the bit strings interpreted as elements of $\mathbb{F}_{2^n}$. For any value Z, we denote by $A \leftarrow Z$ the assignment of Z to the variable A. For any finite set $\mathcal{S}$, we define by $S \xleftarrow{\$} \mathcal{S}$ the uniformly random selection of S from $\mathcal{S}$. For any integers a, b such that $1 \leq b \leq a$, we denote $(a)_b = a \cdot (a-1) \ldots (a-b+1)$ and $(a)_0 = 1$. We denote by $\mathrm{Perm}(n)$ the set of all permutations on $\{0,1\}^n$, and by $\mathrm{Func}(m, n)$ the set of all functions that maps $\{0,1\}^m$ to $\{0,1\}^n$. For $\pi \xleftarrow{\$} \mathrm{Perm}(n)$ and a list $\mathcal{Q}_\pi = \{(x_1, y_1), \ldots\}$, we denote by $\pi \vdash \mathcal{Q}_\pi$ the event that permutation π is consistent with the queries-response tuples in $\mathcal{Q}_\pi$, i.e. that $\pi(x) = y$ for all $(x, y) \in \mathcal{Q}_\pi$.

For any subset $A \subseteq \{0,1\}^n$ such that $|A| = q$, we denote $1_A : \{0,1\}^n \to \{0,1\}$ the characteristic functions of A, namely $1_A(x) = 1$ if $x \in A$ and $1_A(x) = 0$ if $x \notin A$. Given any function $f : \{0,1\}^n \to \mathbb{R}$ and $\alpha \in \{0,1\}^n$, the Fourier coefficient of f corresponding to α is

$$\widehat{f}(\alpha) = \frac{1}{2^n} \sum_{x \in \{0,1\}^n} f(x)(-1)^{\alpha \cdot x},$$

where $\alpha \cdot x$ denotes inner product. The coefficient corresponding to $\alpha = 0^n$ is called the principal Fourier coefficient, all the other ones are called non-principal Fourier coefficients. We define $\Phi(A) = \max \left\{ 2^n \left| \widehat{1}_A(\alpha) \right| : \alpha \in \{0,1\}^n, \alpha \neq 0^n \right\}$.

2.1   Tweakable (Circular) Correlation Robustness Hash Functions

We rely on the multi-instance tweakable correlation robustness (miTCR) and the multi-instance tweakable circular correlation robustness (miTCCR) notion introduced by Guo et al. [15,16].

For $n, t \in \mathbb{N}$, we consider a hash function that takes as input a n-bit message, a t-bit tweak, and returns a n-bit ciphertext. More formally, let $H \colon \{0,1\}^n \times \{0,1\}^t \to \{0,1\}^n$ be a hash function that is based on r n-bit permutations $\pi_1, \ldots, \pi_r$, let $\mathcal{R}$ be a distribution on the message space $\{0,1\}^n$ of H, and define

$$\mathcal{O}_R^{\mathrm{tcr}}(w,t) = H(w \oplus R, t),$$
$$\mathcal{O}_R^{\mathrm{tccr}}(w,t,b) = H(w \oplus R, t) \oplus b \cdot R,$$

for $R \xleftarrow{\$} \mathcal{R}$ and $b \in \{0,1\}$. We will consider both the miTCR and the miTCCR security of H, where we assume that $\pi_1, \ldots, \pi_r \xleftarrow{\$} \mathrm{Perm}(n)$. For the case of the miTCR security, the distinguisher $\mathcal{D}$ is given access to either $(\mathcal{O}_{R_1}^{\mathrm{tcr}}, \ldots, \mathcal{O}_{R_u}^{\mathrm{tcr}}, \pi_1^{\pm}, \ldots, \pi_r^{\pm})$ for $R_1, \ldots, R_u \xleftarrow{\$} \mathcal{R}$, or $(f_1, \ldots, f_u, \pi_1^{\pm}, \ldots, \pi_r^{\pm})$ for $f_1, \ldots, f_u \xleftarrow{\$} \mathrm{Func}(n + t, n)$. Its goal is to determine which oracle it is given access to:

$$\mathbf{Adv}_{H,\mathcal{R}}^{\mathrm{miTCR}}(\mathcal{D}) = \left| \Pr\left[\mathcal{D}^{\mathcal{O}_{R_1}^{\mathrm{tcr}}, \ldots, \mathcal{O}_{R_u}^{\mathrm{tcr}}, \pi_1^{\pm}, \ldots, \pi_r^{\pm}} = 1 \right] - \Pr\left[\mathcal{D}^{f_1, \ldots, f_u, \pi_1^{\pm}, \ldots, \pi_r^{\pm}} = 1 \right] \right|.$$

For the case of the miTCCR security, the distinguisher $\mathcal{D}$ is given access to either $(\mathcal{O}_{R_1}^{\mathrm{tccr}}, \ldots, \mathcal{O}_{R_u}^{\mathrm{tccr}}, \pi_1^{\pm}, \ldots, \pi_r^{\pm})$ for $R_1, \ldots, R_u \xleftarrow{\$} \mathcal{R}$, or $(f_1, \ldots, f_u, \pi_1^{\pm}, \ldots, \pi_r^{\pm})$ for $f_1, \ldots, f_u \xleftarrow{\$} \mathrm{Func}(n + t + 1, n)$. Its goal is to determine which oracle it is given access to:

$$\mathbf{Adv}_{H,\mathcal{R}}^{\mathrm{miTCCR}}(\mathcal{D}) = \left| \Pr\left[\mathcal{D}^{\mathcal{O}_{R_1}^{\mathrm{tccr}}, \ldots, \mathcal{O}_{R_u}^{\mathrm{tccr}}, \pi_1^{\pm}, \ldots, \pi_r^{\pm}} = 1 \right] - \Pr\left[\mathcal{D}^{f_1, \ldots, f_u, \pi_1^{\pm}, \ldots, \pi_r^{\pm}} = 1 \right] \right|.$$

In the both cases the superscript $\pm$ for the π_i's indicates that the distinguisher has bi-directional access. For the miTCCR security, we require that $\mathcal{D}$ never queries both $(w,t,0)$ and $(w,t,1)$ to the same oracle (for any (w,t) couple).

When $u = 1$, we consider the single instance security of H with the distribution $\mathcal{R}$, and we simply denote $\mathcal{D}$'s advantage in distinguishing the real world from random by $\mathbf{Adv}_{H,\mathcal{R}}^{\mathrm{TCR}}(\mathcal{D})$ for the case of tweakable correlation robustness, and by $\mathbf{Adv}_{H,\mathcal{R}}^{\mathrm{TCCR}}(\mathcal{D})$ for the case of tweakable circular correlation robustness.

It is easy to see that the miTCCR (TCCR) notion implies the miTCR (TCR) notion (when b is always zero). In the remainder of this work, we mainly focus on the miTCCR (TCCR) notion, and on hash functions with tweak space $\{0,1\}^n$.

2.2   Universal Hash Functions

For $n \in \mathbb{N}$, let $H \colon \mathcal{K}_h \times \{0,1\}^* \to \{0,1\}^n$ such that for $K_h \in \mathcal{K}_h$, $H_{K_h}(\cdot) = H(K_h, \cdot)$ is called an ϵ-almost XOR universal (ϵ-AXU) hash function [20] if for all distinct $M, M' \in \{0,1\}^*$ and all $C \in \{0,1\}^n$, we have

$$\Pr\left[K_h \xleftarrow{\$} \mathcal{K}_h \colon H_{K_h}(M) \oplus H_{K_h}(M') = C \right] \leq \epsilon.$$

2.3 Linear Orthomorphism

A function $\sigma\colon \{0,1\}^n \to \{0,1\}^n$ is a *linear orthomorphism* if σ (1) linear: $\sigma(x \oplus y) = \sigma(x)\oplus\sigma(y)$; and (2) an orthomorphism: σ is a permutation, and the function $\sigma'(x) = \sigma(x) \oplus x$ is also a permutation. In this work, we will need the following result of [16].

Lemma 1. *Let $\sigma\colon \{0,1\}^n \to \{0,1\}^n$ be a linear orthomorphism and for a distribution $\mathcal{R}$, set $\mathbf{H}_\infty(\sigma(\mathcal{R}) \oplus \mathcal{R}) = -\log\left(\max_{R^*} \Pr_{R \leftarrow \mathcal{R}}[\sigma(R) \oplus R = R^*]\right)$. Then, we have $\mathbf{H}_\infty(\sigma(\mathcal{R}) \oplus \mathcal{R}) = \mathbf{H}_\infty(\mathcal{R})$.*

2.4 Patarin's H-Coefficient Technique

In this work, we use H-coefficient technique by Patarin [23], but we will follow the modernization of Chen and Steinberger [7].

We consider a deterministic distinguisher $\mathcal{D}$ that is given access to either the real world oracle $\mathcal{O}$ or the ideal world oracle $\mathcal{P}$. The distinguisher's goal is to determine which oracle it is given access to and we denote by

$$\mathbf{Adv}(\mathcal{D}) = \left|\Pr\left[\mathcal{D}^{\mathcal{O}} = 1\right] - \Pr\left[\mathcal{D}^{\mathcal{P}} = 1\right]\right|$$

its advantage. We define a transcript τ that summarizes all query-response tuples learned by $\mathcal{D}$ during its interaction with its oracle $\mathcal{O}$ or $\mathcal{P}$. We denote by $X_{\mathcal{O}}$ (resp. $X_{\mathcal{P}}$) the probability distribution of transcripts when interacting with $\mathcal{O}$ (resp. $\mathcal{P}$). We call a transcript $\tau \in \mathcal{T}$ attainable if $\Pr[X_{\mathcal{P}} = \tau] > 0$.

Lemma 2 (H-coefficient Technique). *Consider a deterministic distinguisher $\mathcal{D}$. Define a partition $\mathcal{T} = \mathcal{T}_{\text{good}} \cup \mathcal{T}_{\text{bad}}$, where $\mathcal{T}_{\text{good}}$ is the subset of $\mathcal{T}$ which contains all the "good" transcripts and $\mathcal{T}_{\text{bad}}$ is the subset with all the "bad" transcripts. Let $0 \le \epsilon \le 1$ be such that for all $\tau \in \mathcal{T}_{\text{good}}$:*

$$\frac{\Pr[X_{\mathcal{O}} = \tau]}{\Pr[X_{\mathcal{P}} = \tau]} \ge 1 - \epsilon. \tag{4}$$

Then, we have $\mathbf{Adv}(\mathcal{D}) \le \epsilon + \Pr[X_{\mathcal{P}} \in \mathcal{T}_{\text{bad}}]$.

2.5 Babai's Lemma

Define the following quantity

$$\mu(A, U, V) = |\{(a, u, v) \in A \times U \times V\colon a = u \oplus v\}| .$$

We consider the following lemma of Babai [3].

Lemma 3 (Babai [3] Theorem 4.1). *Let $A, U, V \subseteq \{0,1\}^n$. We have*

$$\mu(A, U, V) \le \frac{|A|\,|U|\,|V|}{2^n} + \Phi(A)\sqrt{|U|\,|V|},$$

As shown in [3,24], when the set A is a randomly chosen subset of $\{0,1\}^n$ of size q, we have $\Phi(A) \le 4\sqrt{2\ln(2^n)q}$, except for probability $4/2^n$. Cogliati and Seurin [10] also showed that when A is a multiset where the elements of A are chosen uniformly at random with replacement, then we have $\Phi(A) \le \sqrt{3nq}$, except for probability $2/2^n$.

Functionality $\mathcal{F}_{\Delta\text{-ROT}}(m,k)$:

Initialization: Inputs:

- Player P_A: $\Delta \in \{0,1\}^k$
- Player P_B: $\perp$.
- Adversary $\mathcal{A}$: If $P_B \in \mathsf{Corr}$, $P : \{0,1\}^k \to \{0,1\}$. Else set P to be the constant 1 predicate.

Return $P(\Delta)$ to $\mathcal{A}$. If $P(\Delta) = 0$, then return abort to P_A, and stop.

Correlation phase. Inputs:

- Player P_A: $\perp$.
- Player P_B: $(x_1, \ldots, x_m) \in \{0,1\}^m$
- Adversary $\mathcal{A}$: $\mathbf{z}_1, \ldots, \mathbf{z}_m \in \{0,1\}^k$.

If $P_A \in \mathsf{Corr}$, then $\mathbf{a}_i \leftarrow \mathbf{z}_i$, $\mathbf{b}_i \leftarrow \mathbf{a}_i \oplus x_i \cdot \Delta$ for all $i \in [m]$.
If $P_B \in \mathsf{Corr}$, then $\mathbf{b}_i \leftarrow \mathbf{z}_i$, $\mathbf{a}_i \leftarrow \mathbf{b}_i \oplus x_i \cdot \Delta$ for all $i \in [m]$.
If $\mathsf{Corr} = \emptyset$ then $\mathbf{b}_i \xleftarrow{\$} \{0,1\}^m$, $\mathbf{a}_i \leftarrow \mathbf{b}_i \oplus x_i \cdot \Delta$ for all $i \in [m]$.
Return $(\mathbf{a}_1, \ldots, \mathbf{a}_m)$ to P_A and $(\mathbf{b}_1, \ldots, \mathbf{b}_m)$ to P_B.

Fig. 1. The Δ-Random-OT functionality $\mathcal{F}_{\Delta\text{-ROT}}(m,k)$. The set Corr takes one of the three values $\emptyset$, $\{P_A\}$, or $\{P_B\}$.

Functionality $\mathcal{F}_{\text{S-OT}}(m,\ell)$:

Inputs:

- Player P_A: $(\mathbf{m}_1^0, \mathbf{m}_1^1), \ldots, (\mathbf{m}_m^0, \mathbf{m}_m^1)$, where $\mathbf{m}_i^b \in \{0,1\}^\ell$ for all $i \in [m]$ and $b \in \{0,1\}$.
- Player P_B: $(x_1, \ldots, x_m) \in \{0,1\}^m$.
- Adversary $\mathcal{A}$: $\perp$

Return $\perp$ to P_A and $(\mathbf{m}_1^{x_1}, \ldots, \mathbf{m}_m^{x_m})$ to P_B.

Fig. 2. The Standard OT functionality $\mathcal{F}_{\Delta\text{-ROT}}(m,\ell)$.

3   A Concrete Security Treatment of OT Extension

Prior work [15] already gives a concrete treatment of garbling from tweakable circular crHFs. As further motivation, we revisit the concrete security of OT extension via correlation-robust hashing, and present a slightly more general protocol that only assumes the underlying function to be secure against distinct inputs. We follow the angle of Guo et al. [16], who gave an asymptotic treatment, and focus on protocols implementing the standard-OT functionality $\mathcal{F}_{\text{S-OT}}$

(cf. Figure 2) from the random-OT functionality $\mathcal{F}_{\Delta\text{-ROT}}$ (cf. Fig. 1), and discuss instantiations from the constructions presented below. Protocols to implement the latter functionality are known, both in the semi-honest and malicious settings [2,18,19].

MODELING 2PC. We give a concrete security definition of (stand-alone) 2PC malicious security. This is a fairly straightforward adaptation of the asymptotic treatment [13], with some notational simplifications that narrow the scope.

Ideal functionalities proceed in rounds of simultaneous inputs, for which they produce (simultaneously) outputs. A functionality $\mathcal{F}$ offers three interfaces – two are to the players P_A and P_B, and the third to the adversary $\mathcal{A}$. Here, we are specifically interested in running a (synchronous) two-party hybrid-model protocol $\Pi = (\Pi_A, \Pi_B)$ accessing a functionality $\mathcal{F}$ and implementing a target functionality $\mathcal{G}$. In each round, either (1) one party sends a message to the other party, or (2) they simultaneously interact with the functionality $\mathcal{G}$. We will distinguish now the *real-world* from the *ideal-world* execution. Both of them are parameterized by a set $\mathsf{Corr} \subsetneq \{\mathsf{P}_A, \mathsf{P}_B\}$ of corrupted parties controlled by the adversary $\mathcal{A}$. (The case $\mathsf{Corr} = \{\mathsf{P}_A, \mathsf{P}_B\}$ is uninteresting, but the case $\mathsf{Corr} = \emptyset$ is needed to define correctness.)

- **Real-world execution.** Initially, we fix the input(s) $x_{\overline{\mathsf{Corr}}}$ of the uncorrupted parties (remember both parties could be uncorrupted). Then, we run the protocol, and the adversary (1) can choose the messages meant to be sent by the corrupted player (if any) in the protocol Π, (2) has access to the player's interface in $\mathcal{F}$, and (3) it has access to $\mathcal{A}$'s dedicated interface in $\mathcal{F}$, as well as to all messages sent in the protocol. Finally, the adversary outputs some value z. We let $\mathsf{REAL}^{\Pi, \mathcal{F}}_{\mathsf{Corr}, \mathcal{A}}(x_{\overline{\mathsf{Corr}}}) = (x_{\overline{\mathsf{Corr}}}, z)$.
- **Ideal-world execution.** Here, we instead supply the input(s) $x_{\overline{\mathsf{Corr}}}$ to the corresponding interfaces of $\mathcal{G}$, and the adversary $\mathcal{A}$ interacts with a simulator $\mathcal{S}$. The latter can use $\mathcal{G}$'s interface for corrupted parties (if any), as well as the adversarial interface. Again $\mathcal{A}$ will produce an output z, and define $\mathsf{IDEAL}^{\mathcal{G}}_{\mathsf{Corr}, \mathcal{A}, \mathcal{S}}(x_{\overline{\mathsf{Corr}}}) = (x_{\overline{\mathsf{Corr}}}, z)$.

We then define

$$\mathbf{Adv}^{(\mathcal{F} \to \mathcal{G})\text{-mpc}}_{\Pi, \mathsf{Corr}}(\mathcal{A}, \mathcal{D}, \mathcal{S}, x_{\overline{\mathsf{Corr}}}) = \Pr\left[\mathcal{D}(\mathsf{REAL}^{\Pi, \mathcal{F}}_{\mathsf{Corr}, \mathcal{A}}(x_{\overline{\mathsf{Corr}}})) = 1\right]$$
$$- \Pr\left[\mathcal{D}(\mathsf{IDEAL}^{\mathcal{G}}_{\mathsf{Corr}, \mathcal{A}, \mathcal{S}}(x_{\overline{\mathsf{Corr}}})) = 1\right].$$

Intuitively, we want to show that for any $\mathcal{A}$, there exists some $\mathcal{S}$, such that $\mathbf{Adv}^{\text{mpc}}_{\mathcal{F}, \mathcal{G}, \Pi, \mathsf{Corr}}(\mathcal{A}, \mathcal{D}, \mathcal{S}, x_{\overline{\mathsf{Corr}}})$ is "negligible." (Of course, we aim for a concrete bound, which we aim to optimize.)

A PROTOCOL. We present and analyze a protocol implementing $\mathcal{F}_{\mathsf{S}\text{-OT}}(m, \ell)$ from $\mathcal{F}_{\Delta\text{-ROT}}(m, k)$ using a (tweakable) correlation-robust hash function $H : \{0,1\}^k \times \{0,1\}^n \to \{0,1\}^\ell$. The protocol differs from the "standard approach" in that H is only required to be secure for *distinct* inputs – this will be instrumental for our instantiation below, as we give high-security constructions which are only secure if the inputs are distinct. The modification is in fact very simple, and relies on using a ϵ-almost XOR universal hash function $\mathsf{AXU} : \mathcal{K} \times [m] \rightarrow \{0,1\}^k$, for a small ϵ. Then, in the i-th OT instance, we invoke H as $H(x \oplus \mathsf{AXU}(K, i), t_i)$ on any input x, where t_i is a tweak associated with the i-th instance. The key K is actually publicly generated by the sender, and revealed to the receiver – the only requirement is that it is chosen after the inputs x to H are determined.

The resulting protocol $\Pi_{OT}^{m,k,\ell}$ is described in Fig. 3. The description assumes that there exists a set of usable tweaks $T = \{t_1, \ldots, t_m\} \subseteq \{0,1\}^n$ for the construction – depending on the instantiation, this set T may need to be chosen carefully.

SECURITY OF THE PROTOCOL. Security against a corrupt sender is trivial and holds perfectly. The next theorem characterizes the *sender security* of Protocol $\Pi_{OT}^{m,k,\ell}$, i.e., the case $\mathsf{Corr} = \{\mathsf{P}_B\}$ where the receiver is corrupted. We target ideal-model security here – i.e., the function H makes calls to an ideal primitive (e.g., a random permutation), and so do $\mathcal{A}$, $\mathcal{D}$ and $\mathcal{S}$. We however assume that P input to $\mathcal{A}$'s interface in $\mathcal{F}_{\Delta\text{-ROT}}(m, k)$ does not make queries to this primitive, though the *choice* of P itself *may* depend adaptively on earlier queries. (This is sufficient to handle existing $\mathcal{F}_{\Delta\text{-ROT}}(m, k)$ protocols.)

To properly handle ideal-model security, the following theorem (proved in the full version of the paper) differs from the work of Guo et al. [16], which as far as we can tell, cannot be used for ideal-model constructions.[4] Here, we instead assume indistinguishability *even if* at the end of the ideal-model interaction, the distinguisher learns the secret shift R (but is otherwise prevented from making any queries, including those to the ideal primitive) – in the ideal model, this shift is simply generated independently of the interaction. We refer to this notion as TCR* security, and we note that our proofs (as most H-coefficient proofs) do give bounds also for TCR* security *for free*, as we include R in the transcripts.

Theorem 1 (Sender-security). *Let* $\mathsf{AXU} : \mathcal{K} \times [m] \rightarrow \{0,1\}^k$ *be ϵ-almost XOR universal. For every adversary $\mathcal{A}$, every distinguisher $\mathcal{D}$, there exists a simulator $\mathcal{S}$ and an adversary $\mathcal{B}$ such that for every $x = ((\mathbf{m}_1^0, \mathbf{m}_1^1), \ldots, (\mathbf{m}_m^0, \mathbf{m}_m^1))$,*

$$\mathbf{Adv}_{\Pi_{OT}^{m,k,\ell}, \{\mathsf{P}_B\}}^{(\mathcal{F}\rightarrow\mathcal{G})-\mathsf{mpc}}(\mathcal{A}, \mathcal{D}, \mathcal{S}, x) \leq \mathbf{Adv}_{H, \{0,1\}^k}^{\mathsf{TCR}^*}(\mathcal{B}) + q^2\epsilon, \qquad (5)$$

where $\mathcal{F} = \mathcal{F}_{\Delta\text{-ROT}}(m, k)$ *and* $\mathcal{G} = \mathcal{F}_{\mathsf{S-OT}}(m, \ell)$. *Here, $\mathcal{B}$ makes m distinct queries, for distinct tweaks. Further, in an ideal model, the number of ideal-primitive queries $p_\mathcal{B}$ of $\mathcal{B}$ satisfies $p_\mathcal{B} = 2(p_\mathcal{A} + p_\mathcal{D}) + p_H$, where $p_\mathcal{A}$ and $p_\mathcal{D}$ are the number of ideal-primitive queries of $\mathcal{A}$ and $\mathcal{D}$'s, respectively, and p_H is the number of ideal-primitive queries in one evaluation of H.*

---

[4] Their proof, for a slightly simpler protocol, is in the standard model and tacitly assumes *non-uniform* tweakable crHF security. Roughly, their proof needs to build an adversary $\mathcal{B}$ for keys chosen from a set $\mathcal{R}$, but this set needs to be fixed non-uniformly – this is problematic in ideal models, because the choice of $\mathcal{R}$ itself depends on the ideal primitive.

Protocol $\Pi_{\mathsf{OT}}^{m,k,\ell}$:

Inputs:

- Player P_A: $(\mathbf{m}_1^0, \mathbf{m}_1^1), \ldots, (\mathbf{m}_m^0, \mathbf{m}_m^1)$, where $\mathbf{m}_i^b \in \{0,1\}^\ell$ for all $i \in [m]$ and $b \in \{0,1\}$.
- Player P_B: $(x_1, \ldots, x_m) \in \{0,1\}^m$.

Protocol:

(1) Player P_A chooses $\Delta \xleftarrow{\$} \{0,1\}^k$, and inputs Δ to $\mathcal{F}_{\Delta\text{-ROT}}(m,k)$. Player P_B inputs $\perp$ to $\mathcal{F}_{\Delta\text{-ROT}}(m,k)$.

(2) Player P_A inputs $\perp$ to $\mathcal{F}_{\Delta\text{-ROT}}(m,k)$ if abort was not output in (1). Player P_B inputs $(x_1, \ldots, x_m)$ to $\mathcal{F}_{\Delta\text{-ROT}}(m,k)$. The players receive respectively $\{\mathbf{a}_i\}_{i \in [m]}$ and $\{\mathbf{b}_i\}_{i \in [m]}$ such that $\mathbf{a}_i \oplus \mathbf{b}_i = \Delta \cdot x_i$ for all $i \in [m]$.

(3) Player P_A chooses $K \xleftarrow{\$} \mathcal{K}$, and computes, for all $i \in [m]$,

$$\mathbf{c}_i^0 \leftarrow H(\mathbf{a}_i \oplus \mathsf{AXU}(K,i), t_i) \oplus \mathbf{m}_i^0;$$
$$\mathbf{c}_i^1 \leftarrow H(\mathbf{a}_i \oplus \Delta \oplus \mathsf{AXU}(K,i), t_i) \oplus \mathbf{m}_i^1 .$$

It then sends $K, \mathbf{c}_1^0, \mathbf{c}_1^1, \ldots, \mathbf{c}_m^0, \mathbf{c}_m^1$ to P_B

(4) Player P_B then computes

$$\mathbf{m}_i^{x_i} \leftarrow H(\mathbf{b}_i \oplus \mathsf{AXU}(K,i), t_i) \oplus \mathbf{c}_i^{x_i}$$

for all $i \in [m]$, and outputs $(\mathbf{m}_1^{x_1}, \ldots, \mathbf{m}_m^{x_m})$. Player P_A outputs $\perp$.

Fig. 3. The OT Protocol.

INSTANTIATION. We give an instantiation of $\Pi_{\mathcal{OT}}^{n,m,n}$ making two permutation calls per instance, using the FPTP1 construction below and Theorem 3. To this end, we also choose a random set of tweaks T of size m, for which $\Phi(T) = O(\sqrt{nm})$, except with probability $O(1/2^n)$ (cf. Sect. 2.5) – this could be fixed a-priori, generated heuristically, and/or chosen randomly in the protocol (in which case the tweaks t_i would be sent along). Moreover, we have efficient constructions of AXU with $\epsilon = 1/2^n$, and the bound thus takes the form $O((\sqrt{mp} + m^2)n/2^n)$, where p is the sum of the numbers of queries to π by $\mathcal{A}$ and $\mathcal{D}$. The construction makes two calls to the permutation per OT instance.

This should be compared with an instantiation using directly a monolithic random oracle (as we claimed in the introduction), or the ideal-cipher construction from [15] – this would achieve security of $O(p/2^n)$, however under a stronger assumption. The term $m^2n/2^n$ in our bounds is not very relevant – we would never be able to scale to m's large enough to be a concern. However, it is a great question to see whether one can improve upon the $\sqrt{m}$ degradation without increasing (or at least, without increasing by much) the number of permutation calls per OT instance.

RANDOM TWEAKS EXTENSION. The usage of random tweaks can increase bandwidth (if the sender chooses them, then they need to be sent over to the receiver). But note that for our context, tweaks are used only for concrete security, and since inputs are already guaranteed to be distinct, we can actually re-use tweaks through a small number r of instances (say $r = 64$), and this would lead to a factor r in the bound, but only a $1/r$ increase in communication complexity.

4   Hash Function Using One Permutation Call

We consider the following hash function, based on one permutation call and one non-linear operation $\otimes$. Let $n \in \mathbb{N}$, and let $\pi \in \mathrm{Perm}(n)$. One can consider a generic hash function construction $H \colon \{0,1\}^n \times \{0,1\}^n \to \{0,1\}^n$ as

$$H[\pi](m, t) = \pi(m \otimes t) \oplus m \otimes t, \tag{6}$$

The security is considered against distinguishers making arbitrary input messages to the construction oracle. For simplicity, we consider the single user security $(u = 1)$.

Theorem 2. *Let $n \in \mathbb{N}$, and consider $H \colon \{0,1\}^n \times \{0,1\}^n \to \{0,1\}^n$ based on permutation $\pi \xleftarrow{\$} \mathrm{Perm}(n)$. For any distinguisher $\mathcal{D}$ making at most q construction queries, and at most p primitive queries to $\pi^\pm$. When the input tweaks are chosen from $\{0,1\}^n \setminus \{0^n\}$ for TCR security, and chosen from $\{0,1\}^n \setminus \{0^n, 0^{n-1}1\}$ for TCCR security, then we have*

$$\mathbf{Adv}_{H,\mathcal{R}}^{\mathrm{TCR}}(\mathcal{D}), \mathbf{Adv}_{H,\mathcal{R}}^{\mathrm{TCCR}}(\mathcal{D}) \le \frac{2qp}{|\mathcal{R}|} + \frac{q^2}{2\,|\mathcal{R}|} + \frac{q^2}{2^{n+1}}. \tag{7}$$

Proof. We only look at the TCCR security in the proof. Let $R \xleftarrow{\$} \mathcal{R}$, $\pi \xleftarrow{\$} \mathrm{Perm}(n)$, and $f \xleftarrow{\$} \mathrm{Func}(2n+1, n)$. Consider any distinguisher $\mathcal{D}$ that has access to two oracles: $(\mathcal{O}_R, \pi^\pm)$ in the real world with

$$\mathcal{O}_R(w, t, b) = H[\pi](w \oplus R, t) \oplus bR = \pi((w \oplus R) \otimes t) \oplus (w \oplus R) \otimes t \oplus bR,$$

or $(f, \pi^\pm)$ in the ideal world. We require that $\mathcal{D}$ is computational unbounded and deterministic. The distinguisher makes q construction queries to $\mathcal{O}_R$ or f such that $t \neq 0^n$ and $t \oplus 0^{n-1}1 \neq 0^n$, and these are summarized in a transcript of the form $\tau_0 = \{(w^{(1)}, t^{(1)}, b^{(1)}, z^{(1)}), \ldots, (w^{(q)}, t^{(q)}, b^{(q)}, z^{(q)})\}$. It also makes p primitive queries to $\pi^\pm$, and these are summarized in transcripts τ_1. We assume that τ_0 and τ_1 do not contain duplicate elements. After $\mathcal{D}$'s interaction with the oracles, but before it outputs its decision, we disclose the random value R to the distinguisher. In the real world, this is the randomness for the message input of construction. In the ideal world, R is a dummy value that is drawn uniformly at random. The complete view is denoted by $\tau = (\tau_0, \tau_1, R)$.

Bad Events. We say that $\tau \in \mathcal{T}_{\mathrm{bad}}$ if and only if there exist construction queries $(w^{(j)}, t^{(j)}, b^{(j)}, z^{(j)})$, $(w^{(j')}, t^{(j')}, b^{(j')}, z^{(j')}) \in \tau_0$ such that $j \neq j'$, and primitive queries $(u, v), (u', v') \in \tau_1$ such that one of the following conditions holds:

$\text{bad}_1: (w^{(j)} \oplus R) \otimes t^{(j)} = u$,

$\text{bad}_2: (w^{(j)} \oplus R) \otimes t^{(j)} \oplus z^{(j)} \oplus b^{(j)} R = v$,

$\text{bad}_3: (w^{(j)} \oplus R) \otimes t^{(j)} = (w^{(j')} \oplus R) \otimes t^{(j')}$,

$\text{bad}_4: (w^{(j)} \oplus R) \otimes t^{(j)} \oplus z^{(j)} \oplus b^{(j)} R = (w^{(j')} \oplus R) \otimes t^{(j')} \oplus z^{(j')} \oplus b^{(j')} R$.

Note that for any attainable transcript τ, $\tau \notin T_{bad}$ implies that τ is a good transcript.

$\mathbf{Pr[X_P \in T_{bad}]}$. We want to bound the probability that an ideal world transcript τ satisfies either of bad_1-bad_4. Therefore, the probability that $\tau \in T_{bad}$ is given by

$$\Pr[\tau \in T_{bad}] \le \sum_{i=1}^{4} \Pr[\text{bad}_i].$$

We first consider the bad event bad_1, which we rewrite as

$$w^{(j)} \otimes t^{(j)} \oplus u = R \otimes t^{(j)}.$$

Since we have $t \ne 0^n$, and $R \leftarrow \mathcal{R}$ is a dummy value generated independently of τ_0 and τ_1, the probability that the above equation holds for fixed j and (u, v) is $1/|\mathcal{R}|$. Summed over all q possible j's and all p possible (u, v)'s, we have

$$\Pr[\text{bad}_1] \le \frac{qp}{|\mathcal{R}|}.$$

The same reasoning applies for bad_2, which we rewrite as

$$w^{(j)} \otimes t^{(j)} \oplus z^{(j)} \oplus v = (t^{(j)} \oplus 0^{n-1} b^{(j)}) \otimes R.$$

Since we have $t \ne 0^n$ and $t \oplus 0^{n-1} 1 \ne 0^n$, the probability that the above equation holds for fixed j and (u, v) is $1/|\mathcal{R}|$ as before. Summed over all q possible j's and all p possible (u, v)'s, we have

$$\Pr[\text{bad}_2] \le \frac{qp}{|\mathcal{R}|}.$$

Now, we consider the bad event bad_3, which we rewrite as

$$w^{(j)} \otimes t^{(j)} \oplus w^{(j')} \otimes t^{(j')} = (t^{(j)} \oplus t^{(j')}) R.$$

Since we have $t \ne 0^n$, if $t^{(j)} = t^{(j')}$, then we must have $w^{(j)} \ne w^{(j')}$, in that case the above equation never holds. If $t^{(j)} \ne t^{(j')}$, then since $R \leftarrow \mathcal{R}$ is a dummy value generated independently of τ_0 and τ_1, the probability that the above equation holds for fixed $j \ne j'$ is $1/|\mathcal{R}|$. Summing over all possible choices of $j \ne j'$, we have

$$\Pr[\text{bad}_3] \le \binom{q}{2} \frac{1}{|\mathcal{R}|}.$$

The same reasoning applies for bad_4, which we rewrite as

$$w^{(j)} \otimes t^{(j)} \oplus w^{(j')} \otimes t^{(j')} \oplus (t^{(j)} \oplus t^{(j')} \oplus 0^{n-1}b^{(j')} \oplus 0^{n-1}b^{(j)})R = z^{(j)} \oplus z^{(j')}.$$

Since the values $z^{(j)}$ and $z^{(j')}$ are generated uniform and independent in the ideal world, the probability that the above equation holds for fixed $j \neq j'$ is $1/2^n$. Summing over all possible choices of $j \neq j'$, we have

$$\Pr[bad_4] \leq \binom{q}{2} \frac{1}{2^n}.$$

Summing the these probabilities, we get

$$\Pr[\tau \in \mathcal{T}_{bad}] \leq \frac{2qp}{|\mathcal{R}|} + \frac{q^2}{2|\mathcal{R}|} + \frac{q^2}{2^{n+1}}. \tag{8}$$

$\Pr[X_{\mathcal{O}} = \tau]/\Pr[X_{\mathcal{P}} = \tau]$. Consider an attainable transcript $\tau \in \mathcal{T}_{good}$. To compute $\Pr[X_{\mathcal{O}} = \tau]$ and $\Pr[X_{\mathcal{P}} = \tau]$, it suffices to compute the probability of oracles that could result in view τ. We first consider the ideal world $\mathcal{P}$, and obtain

$$\Pr[X_{\mathcal{P}} = \tau] = \frac{1}{|\mathcal{R}|} \cdot \frac{(2^n - p)!}{2^n!} \cdot \frac{2^{n(2^{2n+1}-q)}}{2^{n 2^{2n+1}}} = \frac{1}{|\mathcal{R}|} \cdot \frac{1}{(2^n)_p} \cdot \frac{1}{2^{nq}}.$$

The first term corresponds to the number of randomly drawn R values; the second term is the ratio of public random permutations π compliant with τ_1; and the last term is the ratio of random functions $f \in \text{Func}(2n+1, n)$ compliant with τ_0.

Similarly we say that a real world oracle $\mathcal{O}$ is compatible with τ if it is compatible with τ_0 and τ_1. We have

$$\Pr[X_{\mathcal{O}} = \tau] = \frac{1}{|\mathcal{R}|} \cdot \frac{1}{(2^n)_p} \cdot \Pr[\pi \xleftarrow{\$} \text{Perm}(n) \colon \mathcal{O}_R[\pi] \vdash \tau_0 \mid \pi \vdash \tau_1].$$

As before, the first term corresponds to the number of randomly drawn R values; the second term is the ratio of public random permutations π compliant with τ_1; and the last term is the ratio of $\mathcal{O}_R[\pi]$ compliant with τ_0, given that π compliant with τ_1.

Define $\rho(\tau) = \Pr[\pi \xleftarrow{\$} \text{Perm}(n) \colon \mathcal{O}_R[\pi] \vdash \tau_0 \mid \pi \vdash \tau_1]$, we obtain

$$\frac{\Pr[X_{\mathcal{O}} = \tau]}{\Pr[X_{\mathcal{P}} = \tau]} = 2^{nq} \rho(\tau). \tag{9}$$

Since τ is good, all values $\sigma(w^{(j)} \oplus R) \otimes t^{(j)}$ for $(w^{(j)}, t^{(j)}, b^{(j)}, z^{(j)}) \in \tau_0$ are distinct by $\neg bad_3$, and are also distinct from all values u for $(u, v) \in \tau_1$ by $\neg bad_1$. Similarly, all values $\sigma(w^{(j)} \oplus R) \otimes t^{(j)} \oplus z^{(j)} \oplus b^{(j)}R$ for $(w^{(j)}, t^{(j)}, b^{(j)}, z^{(j)}) \in \tau_0$

are distinct by $\neg\mathsf{bad}_4$, and are also distinct from all values v for $(u, v) \in \tau_1$ by $\neg\mathsf{bad}_2$. This clearly implies that

$$\rho(\tau) = \frac{1}{(2^n - p)_q},$$

Processing further from (9), we have

$$\frac{\Pr[X_\mathcal{O} = \tau]}{\Pr[X_\mathcal{P} = \tau]} = \frac{2^{nq}}{(2^n - p)_q} \geq \frac{2^{nq}}{2^{nq}} = 1.$$

$\square$

5   Hash Function Using Two Permutation Calls

We consider the FPTP construction (Feed-forward Permutation- Tweak-Permutation), based on two permutations. Let $n \in \mathbb{N}$, let $\pi_1, \pi_2 \in \mathrm{Perm}(n)$, and let $\sigma \colon \{0, 1\}^n \to \{0, 1\}^n$ be a linear orthomorphism. One can consider a generic hash function construction FPTP $\colon \{0, 1\}^n \times \{0, 1\}^n \to \{0, 1\}^n$ as

$$\mathrm{FPTP}[\pi_1, \pi_2](m, t) = \pi_2(\pi_1(\sigma(m)) \oplus t) \oplus \sigma(m). \tag{10}$$

We will consider the construction for two variants: FPTP2 for the case where π_1, π_2 are independent in the full version of the paper, and FPTP1 for the case where π_1, π_2 are identical in Sect. 5.1. For the both cases, security is considered against distinguishers making distinct or uniform independent input messages to the construction oracle for the case of single user, and against distinguishers making uniform independent input messages to the construction oracles for the case of multi-user. The single user security proof of FPTP1 is given in Sect. 5.3.

5.1   FPTP Based on Two Same Permutations

We prove the security of FPTP1 where $\pi_1 = \pi_2$. Let $n \in \mathbb{N}$, and consider the given set T of the tweaks such that the size of T is ℓ and $\ell \leq q$ (since there are q different tweaks when $B = 1$). We present the following result against distinguishers making distinct input messages to the construction oracle for $u = 1$ (single user security). Recall that $\Phi(A) = \max \left\{ 2^n \left| \widehat{1}_A(\alpha) \right| : \alpha \in \{0, 1\}^n, \alpha \neq 0^n \right\}$ (see Section 2.0).

Theorem 3. *Let $n \in \mathbb{N}$, and consider* FPTP1 $\colon \{0, 1\}^n \times \{0, 1\}^n \to \{0, 1\}^n$ *based on permutation $\pi \xleftarrow{\$} \mathrm{Perm}(n)$, where the input tweaks are chosen from the set T. For any distinguisher $\mathcal{D}$ making at most q construction queries, at most B construction queries per tweak, and at most p primitive queries to $\pi^{\pm}$.*

(a) When $\mathcal{D}$ makes q construction queries with distinct input messages, we have

$$\mathbf{Adv}_{\mathrm{FPTP1}, \mathcal{R}}^{\mathrm{TCCR}}(\mathcal{D}) \leq \frac{7}{2^n} + \frac{(2B + 1)qp^2}{2^n |\mathcal{R}|} + \frac{p\sqrt{3nq}}{|\mathcal{R}|} + \frac{2B\Phi(T)p}{|\mathcal{R}|}$$
$$+ \frac{6nq^2}{|\mathcal{R}|} + \frac{9q^2}{2^{n+1}} + \frac{4q(p + q)(p + 2q)}{2^{2n}}. \tag{11}$$

(b) When $\mathcal{D}$ makes q construction queries with uniform independent input messages, $\mathbf{Adv}^{\mathrm{TCCR}}_{\mathrm{FPTP1},\mathcal{R}}(\mathcal{D})$ is the same as the case of distinct input messages, except that there is an additional $q^2/2^{n+1}$ term.

Note that (11) is dominated by the terms $2B\Phi(T)p/|\mathcal{R}|+9q^2/2^{n+1}$. For $|\mathcal{R}| = 2^n$, and a carefully chosen set T such that $\Phi(T) \leq \sqrt{q}$ (like the one mentioned in the introduction), the security bound in (11) matches with the asymptotic bound given in the abstract and introduction.

Proof. The proof of (a) is given in Sect. 5.3. The proof of (b) follows straightforwardly from Theorem 3 (a), and the fact that two uniform independent values collide with probability at most $q^2/2^{n+1}$ by the birthday bound. $\square$

Let $n \in \mathbb{N}$, and consider the given set $T = T_1 \cup \cdots \cup T_u \subseteq \{0,1\}^n$ of the tweaks such that the size of $T = \ell$ and $\ell \leq q$. We present the following result against distinguishers making uniform independent input messages to the construction oracles for $u > 1$ (multi-user security).

Theorem 4. *Let $n \in \mathbb{N}$, and consider FPTP1: $\{0,1\}^n \times \{0,1\}^n \to \{0,1\}^n$ based on permutation $\pi \xleftarrow{\$} \mathrm{Perm}(n)$, where the input tweaks of i-th oracle are chosen from the set T_i. For any distinguisher $\mathcal{D}$ making at most q/u construction queries with uniform independent input messages to each of its u construction oracles, at most B construction queries per tweak across all oracles, and at most p primitive queries to $\pi^\pm$, we have*

$$\mathbf{Adv}^{\mathrm{miTCCR}}_{\mathrm{FPTP1},\mathcal{R}}(\mathcal{D}) \leq \frac{7}{2^n} + \frac{(2B+1)qp^2}{2^n|\mathcal{R}|} + \frac{p\sqrt{3nq}}{|\mathcal{R}|} + \frac{2B\Phi(T_1 \cup \cdots \cup T_u)p}{|\mathcal{R}|}$$
$$+ \frac{6nq^2}{|\mathcal{R}|} + \frac{10q^2}{2^{n+1}} + \frac{q^2p}{|\mathcal{R}|^2} + \frac{4q(p+q)(p+2q)}{2^{2n}}. \quad (12)$$

The proof is given in the full version of the paper.

We can extend the FPTP construction to process the input $w \otimes t$ instead of w. For plain (non-circular) TCR security, this would give us security under arbitrary inputs. Let call FPTP1* the FPTP1 construction using the input $w \otimes t$, then the TCR security of FPTP1* is given in Theorem 5.

Theorem 5. *Let $n \in \mathbb{N}$, and consider FPTP1*: $\{0,1\}^n \times \{0,1\}^n \to \{0,1\}^n$ based on permutation $\pi \xleftarrow{\$} \mathrm{Perm}(n)$, where the input tweaks are chosen from the set T. For any distinguisher $\mathcal{D}$ making at most q construction queries, at most B construction queries per tweak, and at most p primitive queries to $\pi^\pm$. We have*

$$\mathbf{Adv}^{\mathrm{TCR}}_{\mathrm{FPTP1}^*,\mathcal{R}}(\mathcal{D}) \leq \frac{7}{2^n} + \frac{(2B+1)qp^2}{2^n|\mathcal{R}|} + \frac{p\sqrt{3nq}}{|\mathcal{R}|} + \frac{2B\Phi(T)p}{|\mathcal{R}|}$$
$$+ \frac{q^2(12n+1)}{2|\mathcal{R}|} + \frac{9q^2}{2^{n+1}} + \frac{4q(p+q)(p+2q)}{2^{2n}}. \quad (13)$$

Proof (Sketch). The proof of Theorem 5 is very similar to the proof of Theorem 3, but with a few minor differences. First of all, the bad transcripts analysis remains basically the same, except that $w \otimes t$ needs to be considered instead of w, and this can be modified in a straightforward way. However, there is an additional bad event, namely

$$\exists (w^{(j)}, t^{(j)}, b^{(j)}, z^{(j)}) \neq (w^{(j')}, t^{(j')}, b^{(j')}, z^{(j')}) \in \tau_0 : (w^{(j)} \oplus R) \otimes t^{(j)} = (w^{(j')} \oplus R) \otimes t^{(j')} .$$

This is the same event as bad_3 of the one permutation call construction in (6), hence this event will lead to an extra term $\binom{q}{2}/\mathcal{R}$ in the final bound. Finally, the ratio analysis remains roughly the same. $\square$

5.2   Balls-into-Bins Lemmas

Before we turn to our proofs, we state and prove some generic balls-into-bins lemmas for the setting where an adversary queries a random permutation. These may be of independent interest. We rely below on the following generalized version of the Chernoff bound [17,22], which does not need to assume independence, and instead only requires a weaker direct-product condition.

Theorem 6 (Generalized Chernoff Bound). *Let $X_1, \ldots, X_n \in \{0,1\}$ be random variables such that, for some $\delta \in [0,1]$, $\Pr\left[\bigwedge_{i \in S} X_i = 1\right] \leq \delta^{|S|}$ for every $S \subseteq [n]$. Then, for any $\gamma \in [\delta, 1]$, $\Pr\left[\sum_{i=1}^n X_i \geq \gamma n\right] \leq e^{-nD(\gamma \,\|\, \delta)}$, where $D(\gamma \,\|\, \delta) = \gamma \ln\left(\frac{\gamma}{\delta}\right) + (1 - \gamma) \ln\left(\frac{1-\gamma}{1-\delta}\right)$ is the relative binary entropy function.*

THE INPUT-OUTPUT BALLS-INTO-BINS LEMMA. We assume that an adversary $\mathcal{A}$ makes p adaptive queries to a random permutation $\pi \overset{\$}{\leftarrow} \mathrm{Perm}(n)$, which then defines a transcript $\tau = ((u_1, v_1), \ldots, (u_p, v_p))$ of input-output pairs, i.e., a pair (u_i, v_i) indicates that either $\pi(u_i)$ was queried, returning v_i or $\pi^{-1}(v_i)$ was queried, returning u_i. (Without loss of generality, we assume that these queries are non-redundant, i.e., $u_1, \ldots, u_p$ are distinct.) Further, let $\sigma, \rho \in \mathrm{Perm}(n)$ be *fixed* permutations. We then assign each query (u_i, v_i) to a bin labeled by $\sigma(u_i) \oplus \rho(v_i)$. (I.e., there are 2^n possible bins.) We also define L^{io} as the max load of the bins, and show it is small with high probability. The proof is similar to that of classical balls-into-bins lemmas, but we use Theorem 6 to deal with the adversary's adaptivity and the permutation structure of outputs.

Lemma 4 (Input-Output Balls-into-Bins). *For every $p \leq 2^{n-1}$, let $\mathcal{A}$ be any p-query adversary $\mathcal{A}$ querying an n-bit random permutation, and let L^{io} be as above. Then, for any $\epsilon > 0$, we have $\Pr\left[L^{\mathrm{io}} \geq n \ln(2) + \ln(1/\epsilon) + 2\right] \leq \epsilon$.*

The proof is given in the full version of the paper.

THE XOR BALLS-INTO-BINS LEMMA. We also consider a more complex setting where each (ordered) query *pair* i, j is assigned to one of $(2^n - 1)^2$ bins, each denoted as $B_{\Delta_{\mathrm{in}}, \Delta_{\mathrm{out}}}$, where $\Delta_{\mathrm{in}}, \Delta_{\mathrm{out}} \in \{0,1\}^n \setminus \{0^n\}$. In particular, we fix *four* permutations $\sigma, \sigma', \rho, \rho' \in \mathrm{Perm}(n)$, and the query pair (i, j) is added to the bin with $\Delta_{\text{in}} = \sigma(u_i) \oplus \sigma'(u_i')$ and $\Delta_{\text{out}} = \rho(v_i) \oplus \rho'(v_i')$. We define now L^{xor} as the max load of one of the bins.

We want to show a bound on the load, similar to Lemma 4. The challenge here is that the $p(p-1)$ ball assignments are (1) highly dependent, and (2) defined by an adaptive process, where $\mathcal{A}$ chooses some of the u_i's and of the v_i's. The following lemma shows that, however, their behavior is similar to $p(p-1)$ independent balls thrown into $(2^n-1)^2$ bins.

Lemma 5 (XOR Balls-into-Bins). *For every $p \leq 2^{n-1}$, let $\mathcal{A}$ be any p-query adversary $\mathcal{A}$ querying an n-bit random permutation, and let L^{xor} be defined as above. Then, for any $\epsilon > 0$, we have $\Pr\left[L^{\text{xor}} \geq 4n\ln(2) + 2\ln(1/\epsilon) + 4\right] \leq 2\epsilon$.*

Before we turn to the proof, we note that in the symmetric case where $\sigma = \sigma'$ and $\rho = \rho'$, it is often enough to count unordered pairs $\{i, j\}$ as ball throws, and one can then replace 2ϵ by ϵ, and $4n\ln(2)$ by $2n\ln(2)$.

Proof. Let us fix any $\Delta_{\text{in}}, \Delta_{\text{out}} \in \{0,1\}^n \setminus \{0^n\}$, and one assume $\mathcal{A}$ generates the transcript $\tau = ((u_1, v_1), \ldots, (u_p, v_p))$ of non-redundant queries to the random permutation π. We are interested in the random variable

$$Z^{\Delta_{\text{in}}, \Delta_{\text{out}}} = |\{(i, j) \mid j < i, \ \sigma(u_i) \oplus \sigma'(u_j) = \Delta_{\text{in}}, \ \rho(v_i) \oplus \rho'(v_j) = \Delta_{\text{out}}\}| \ .$$

Also, define $Z_i^{\Delta_{\text{in}}, \Delta_{\text{out}}}$ as the indicator random variable, which is 1 if there exists $j < i$ such that $\sigma(u_i) \oplus \sigma'(u_j) = \Delta_{\text{in}}$ and $\rho(v_i) \oplus \rho'(v_j) = \Delta_{\text{out}}$. (It is 0 otherwise.) Then, note that $Z^{\Delta_{\text{in}}, \Delta_{\text{out}}} = \sum_{i=1}^p Z_i^{\Delta_{\text{in}}, \Delta_{\text{out}}}$, because for each query (u_i, v_i), there is at most one earlier query (u_j, v_j) such that $\sigma(u_i) \oplus \sigma'(u_j) = \Delta_{\text{in}}$ and $\rho(v_i) \oplus \rho'(v_j) = \Delta_{\text{out}}$. Because $p < 2^{n-1}$, and the queries are guaranteed not to be redundant, we have

$$\Pr\left[Z_i^{\Delta_{\text{in}}, \Delta_{\text{out}}} = 1 \mid Z_1^{\Delta_{\text{in}}, \Delta_{\text{out}}} = b_1, \ldots, Z_{i-1}^{\Delta_{\text{in}}, \Delta_{\text{out}}} = b_{i-1}\right] \leq \frac{2}{2^n}, \quad (14)$$

for any $b_1, \ldots, b_{i-1} \in \{0, 1\}$. To see this, assume the i-th query is in the forward direction, for some u_i. Then $Z_i^{\Delta_{\text{in}}, \Delta_{\text{out}}} = 1$ if and only if there exists $j < i$ with $\sigma'(u_j) \oplus \sigma(u_i) = \Delta_{\text{in}}$, and (assuming this is the case) we also have $\rho'(v_j) \oplus \rho(v_i) = \Delta_{\text{out}}$. The latter happens with probability at most $1/(2^n - (i-1)) \leq 2/2^n$. For a query in the backward direction, the argument is entirely symmetric. Then, in turn, (14) implies that for any set $S \subseteq [p]$, we have

$$\Pr\left[\bigwedge_{i \in S} Z_i^{\Delta_{\text{in}}, \Delta_{\text{out}}} = 1\right] \leq \left(\frac{2}{2^n}\right)^{|S|} \ .$$

Theorem 6 yields, for any $k \geq 1$, $\Pr\left[Z^{\Delta_{\text{in}}, \Delta_{\text{out}}} \geq k\right] \leq e^{-p \cdot D(k/p \,\|\, 2/2^n)}$. One can actually show that $D(\gamma \,\|\, \delta) \geq (\gamma - \delta)^2/(2\gamma)$,[5] and this yields

$$p \cdot D(k/p \,\|\, 2/2^n) \geq \frac{p^2(k/p - 2/2^n)^2}{k} \geq \frac{(k-1)^2}{k} > k - 2 \ ,$$

---

[5] For $\gamma \geq \delta$, by looking at the Taylor series, one can show that $f_\delta(\epsilon) = D((1+\epsilon)\delta \| \delta) \geq \epsilon^2 \delta / 2(1+\epsilon)$. This yields the inequality with $\epsilon\delta = (\gamma - \delta)$ and $1 + \epsilon = \gamma/\delta$.

because $2/2^n \leq 1/p$. Thus, with $k = 2n\ln(2) + \ln(1/\epsilon) + 2$, we get

$$\Pr\left[\exists \Delta_{\mathsf{in}}, \Delta_{\mathsf{out}} : Z^{\Delta_{\mathsf{in}}, \Delta_{\mathsf{out}}} \geq k\right] \leq 2^{2n} \cdot 2^{-2n} \cdot \epsilon = \epsilon \ .$$

Similarly, we can define a random variable $W^{\Delta_{\mathsf{in}}, \Delta_{\mathsf{out}}}$ which counts pairs $i < j$ such that $\sigma(u_i) \oplus \sigma'(u_j) = \Delta_{\mathsf{in}}$ and $\rho(v_i) \oplus \rho'(v_j) = \Delta_{\mathsf{out}}$, and conclude that $\Pr\left[W^{\Delta_{\mathsf{in}}, \Delta_{\mathsf{out}}} \geq k\right] \leq 2^{-2n} \cdot \epsilon$. By the union bound,

$$\Pr\left[L^{\mathsf{xor}} \geq 2k\right] \leq \Pr\left[\exists \Delta_{\mathsf{in}}, \Delta_{\mathsf{out}} : Z^{\Delta_{\mathsf{in}}, \Delta_{\mathsf{out}}} \geq k \ \vee \ W^{\Delta_{\mathsf{in}}, \Delta_{\mathsf{out}}} \geq k\right]$$
$$\leq \Pr\left[\exists \Delta_{\mathsf{in}}, \Delta_{\mathsf{out}} : Z^{\Delta_{\mathsf{in}}, \Delta_{\mathsf{out}}} \geq k\right] + \Pr\left[\exists \Delta_{\mathsf{in}}, \Delta_{\mathsf{out}} : W^{\Delta_{\mathsf{in}}, \Delta_{\mathsf{out}}} \geq k\right]$$
$$\leq 2 \cdot 2^{2n} \cdot 2^{-2n} \epsilon = 2\epsilon \ . \qquad \square$$

5.3   Proof of Theorem 3 on FPTP1

Let $R \xleftarrow{\$} \mathcal{R}$, $\pi \xleftarrow{\$} \mathrm{Perm}(n)$, and $f \xleftarrow{\$} \mathrm{Func}(2n+1, n)$. Consider any distinguisher $\mathcal{D}$ that has access to two oracles: $(\mathcal{O}1_R, \pi^{\pm})$ in the real world with

$$\mathcal{O}1_R(w, t, b) = \mathrm{FPTP1}[\pi](w \oplus R, t) \oplus bR = \pi(\pi(\sigma(w \oplus R)) \oplus t) \oplus \sigma(w \oplus R) \oplus bR,$$

or $(f, \pi^{\pm})$ in the ideal world. We require that $\mathcal{D}$ is computational unbounded and deterministic. The distinguisher makes q construction queries to $\mathcal{O}1_R$ or f, and B construction queries per tweak. These are summarized in a transcript of the form $\tau_0 = \{(w^{(1)}, t^{(1)}, b^{(1)}, z^{(1)}), \ldots, (w^{(q)}, t^{(q)}, b^{(q)}, z^{(q)})\}$. It also makes p primitive queries to $\pi^{\pm}$, and these are summarized in transcripts τ_1. We assume that τ_0, and τ_1 do not contain duplicate elements. After $\mathcal{D}$'s interaction with the oracles, but before it outputs its decision, we disclose the random value R to the distinguisher. In the real world, this is the randomness for the message input of the construction. In the ideal world, R is a dummy value that is drawn uniformly at random. The complete view is denoted $\tau = (\tau_0, \tau_1, R)$.

Bad Events. We say that $\tau \in \mathcal{T}_{\mathrm{bad}}$ if there exist construction queries $(w^{(j)}, t^{(j)}, b^{(j)}, z^{(j)}), (w^{(j')}, t^{(j')}, b^{(j')}, z^{(j')}) \in \tau_0$ such that $j \neq j'$, and primitive queries $(u, v), (u', v') \subset \tau_1$ such that one of the following conditions holds:

$\mathrm{bad}_1: \sigma(w^{(j)} \oplus R) = u \ \wedge \ \sigma(w^{(j)} \oplus R) \oplus z^{(j)} \oplus b^{(j)} R = v'$,

$\mathrm{bad}_2: \sigma(w^{(j)} \oplus R) = u \ \wedge \ t^{(j)} \oplus v \oplus u' = 0$,

$\mathrm{bad}_3: t^{(j)} \oplus v \oplus u' = 0 \ \wedge \ \sigma(w^{(j)} \oplus R) \oplus z^{(j)} \oplus b^{(j)} R = v'$,

$\mathrm{bad}_4: \sigma(w^{(j)} \oplus R) \oplus z^{(j)} \oplus b^{(i)} R = \sigma(w^{(j')} \oplus R) \oplus z^{(j')} \oplus b^{(i')} R$,

$\mathrm{bad}_5: \sigma(w^{(j)} \oplus R) = u \ \wedge \ \sigma(w^{(j')} \oplus R) = u' \ \wedge \ v \oplus t^{(j)} = v' \oplus t^{(j')}$,

$\mathrm{bad}_6: \sigma(w^{(j)} \oplus R) \oplus z^{(j)} \oplus b^{(j)} R = v \ \wedge \ \sigma(w^{(j')} \oplus R) \oplus z^{(j')} \oplus b^{(j')} R = v'$
$\qquad \wedge \ u \oplus t^{(j)} = u' \oplus t^{(j')}$,

$\mathrm{bad}_7: \sigma(w^{(j)} \oplus R) = u \ \wedge \ v \oplus t^{(j)} = \sigma(w^{(j')} \oplus R)$,

$\mathrm{bad}_8: \sigma(w^{(j)} \oplus R) \oplus z^{(j)} \oplus b^{(j)} R = v \ \wedge \ u \oplus t^{(j)} = \sigma(w^{(j')} \oplus R) \oplus z^{(j')} \oplus b^{(j')} R.$

Note that for any attainable transcript τ, $\tau \notin \mathcal{T}_{bad}$ implies that τ is a good transcript.

$\Pr[X_{\mathcal{P}} \in \mathcal{T}_{\mathbf{bad}}]$. We want to bound the probability that an ideal world transcript τ satisfies either of bad_1-bad_8. Therefore, the probability that $\tau \in \mathcal{T}_{bad}$ is given by

$$\Pr[\tau \in \mathcal{T}_{bad}] \leq \sum_{i=1}^{8} \Pr[bad_i].$$

We denote

$$U = \{u \in \{0,1\}^n : (u,v) \in \tau_1\}, \quad V = \{v \in \{0,1\}^n : (u,v) \in \tau_1\}.$$

We first consider the bad event bad_1. Using the fact that σ is a linear orthomorphism, we can rewrite bad_1 as

$$\sigma(w^{(j)}) \oplus u = \sigma \circ \sigma'^{-1}\left(\sigma(w^{(j)}) \oplus z^{(j)} \oplus v'\right) = \sigma(R).$$

Here we have $\sigma'(x) = \sigma(x)$ when $b^{(j)} = 0$, and $\sigma'(x) = \sigma(x) \oplus x$ when $b^{(j)} = 1$. We define the sets

$$A^* = \{(\sigma(w^{(1)}) \oplus \sigma \circ \sigma'^{-1}(\sigma(w^{(1)}) \oplus z^{(1)}), \ldots, \sigma(w^{(q)}) \oplus \sigma \circ \sigma'^{-1}(\sigma(w^{(q)}) \oplus z^{(q)})\},$$
$$V' = \{\sigma \circ \sigma'^{-1}(v') : v' \in V\},$$

Then, combining Lemma 3 and the result of Cogliati and Seurin [10], there are $\mu(A^*, U, V')$ possible combinations of $\sigma(w^{(j)}) \oplus \sigma \circ \sigma'^{-1}(\sigma(w^{(j)}) \oplus z^{(j)})$, u and $\sigma \circ \sigma'^{-1}(v')$ that satisfy bad_1. We denote

$$\Omega_1 = \left|\left\{(j, (u,v), (u',v')) \,\Big|\, \sigma(w^{(j)}) \oplus u = \sigma \circ \sigma'^{-1}\left(\sigma(w^{(j)}) \oplus z^{(j)} \oplus v'\right)\right\}\right|.$$

It is easy to see that $\Omega_1 = \mu(A^*, U, V')$. Note that in the ideal world, Ω_1 only depends on f and π. Ω_1 does not depend on the randomness R, which is drawn uniformly at random at the end of the interaction. Hence, for any $C_1 > 0$, we have

$$\Pr[bad_1] \leq \Pr[\mu(A^*, U, V') \geq C_1] + \frac{C_1}{|\mathcal{R}|}.$$

We thus set $C_1 = \frac{qp^2}{2^n} + p\sqrt{3nq}$ and obtain

$$\Pr[bad_1] \leq \frac{2}{2^n} + \frac{qp^2}{2^n |\mathcal{R}|} + \frac{p\sqrt{3nq}}{|\mathcal{R}|}.$$

For the second bad event bad_2, we first consider the right hand side of the bad event. Consider the given set $T \subseteq \{0,1\}^n$ of the tweaks. Then, combining

Lemma 3, there are $\mu(T, U, V)$ possible combinations of $t^{(j)}$, (u, v) and (u', v') that satisfy the second equation of bad$_2$, with

$$\mu(T, U, V) \leq \frac{qp^2}{2^n} + \Phi(T)p.$$

We denote

$$\Omega_2 = \left| \left\{ (j, (u, v), (u', v')) \mid t^{(j)} \oplus u' \oplus v = 0 \right\} \right|.$$

Since there are B construction queries per tweak, we have that $\Omega_2 = B\mu(T, U, V)$. We rewrite the first equation of bad$_2$ as

$$\sigma(w^{(j)}) \oplus u = \sigma(R).$$

By the fact that $R \leftarrow \mathcal{R}$ is a dummy value generated independently of τ_0 and τ_1, the probability that the first equation of bad$_2$ holds for fixed j and (u, v) is $1/|\mathcal{R}|$. We have

$$\Pr[\text{bad}_2] \leq \frac{Bqp^2}{2^n |\mathcal{R}|} + \frac{B\Phi(T)p}{|\mathcal{R}|}.$$

The same reasoning applies for the left hand side of bad$_3$, and we rewrite the second equation of bad$_3$ as

$$\sigma(w^{(j)}) \oplus z^{(j)} \oplus v' = \sigma(R) \oplus b^{(j)}R.$$

If $b^{(j)} = 0$, the probability that the second equation of bad$_3$ holds for fixed j and (u', v') is $1/|\mathcal{R}|$ as before. If $b^{(j)} = 1$, this probability is at most $1/|\mathcal{R}|$ (see Lemma 1). Together, we have

$$\Pr[\text{bad}_3] \leq \frac{Bqp^2}{2^n |\mathcal{R}|} + \frac{B\Phi(T)p}{|\mathcal{R}|}.$$

Now, we consider the bad event bad$_4$, which we rewrite as

$$\sigma(w^{(j)} \oplus w^{(j')}) \oplus (b^{(j')} \oplus b^{(j)})R = z^{(j)} \oplus z^{(j')}.$$

Since the values $z^{(j)}$ and $z^{(j')}$ are generated uniformly and independent in the ideal world, the probability that the above equation holds for fixed $j \neq j'$ is $1/2^n$. Summing over all possible choices of $j \neq j'$, we have

$$\Pr[\text{bad}_4] \leq \binom{q}{2} \frac{1}{2^n}.$$

Next, we consider the bad events bad$_5$ and bad$_6$. The bad event bad$_5$ implies

$$u \oplus u' = \sigma(w^{(j)}) \oplus \sigma(w^{(j')}) \land v \oplus v' = t^{(j)} \oplus t^{(j')}.$$

Now we take $\Delta_{\text{in}} = \sigma(w^{(j)}) \oplus \sigma(w^{(j')})$ and $\Delta_{\text{out}} = t^{(j)} \oplus t^{(j')}$, and by applying Lemma 5, we define L^{xor} as the max load of the bin $B_{\Delta_{\text{in}}, \Delta_{\text{out}}}$. Hence, for any $C_5 > 0$, and by the fact that $R \leftarrow \mathcal{R}$ is a dummy value generated independently of τ_0 and τ_1, the probability that the first two equations of bad_5 hold for a fixed (j, j') couple is $1/|\mathcal{R}|$. By a union bound over all possible choices of $j \neq j'$, we have

$$\Pr[\text{bad}_5] \leq \Pr\left[L^{\text{xor}} \geq C_5\right] + \binom{q}{2} \frac{C_5}{|\mathcal{R}|},$$

Thus, with $C_5 = 2n \ln(2) + \ln(1/\epsilon) \leq 3n$ and with $\epsilon = 1/2^n$, we have

$$\Pr[\text{bad}_5] \leq \frac{1}{2^n} + \binom{q}{2} \frac{3n}{|\mathcal{R}|}.$$

For bad_6, when $b^{(j)} \oplus b^{(j')} = 0$, the analysis is identical as the one of bad_5. We now consider the case when $b^{(j)} = 0 \wedge b^{(j')} = 1$ (the case $b^{(j)} = 1 \wedge b^{(j')} = 0$ is entirely symmetric). We first rewrite the first two equations of bad_6 as

$$\sigma(w^{(j)}) \oplus z^{(j)} \oplus v = \sigma \circ \sigma'^{-1}\left(\sigma(w^{(j')}) \oplus z^{(j')} \oplus v'\right) = \sigma(R),$$

with $\sigma'(x) = \sigma(x) \oplus x$. Then bad_6 implies

$$v \oplus \sigma \circ \sigma'^{-1}(v') = \sigma(w^{(j)}) \oplus z^{(j)} \oplus \sigma \circ \sigma'^{-1}\left(\sigma(w^{(j')}) \oplus z^{(j')}\right) \wedge$$
$$u \oplus u' = t^{(j)} \oplus t^{(j')}.$$

Now we take $\Delta_{\text{in}} = t^{(j)} \oplus t^{(j')}$ and $\Delta_{\text{out}} = \sigma(w^{(j)}) \oplus z^{(j)} \oplus \sigma \circ \sigma'^{-1}\left(\sigma(w^{(j')}) \oplus z^{(j')}\right)$, and by applying Lemma 5 (here we should use the case of $4n \ln(2)$), we get

$$\Pr[\text{bad}_6] \leq \frac{2}{2^n} + \binom{q}{2} \frac{5n}{|\mathcal{R}|}.$$

Finally, we consider the bad events bad_7 and bad_8. The bad event bad_7 implies

$$u \oplus v = \sigma(w^{(j)}) \oplus \sigma(w^{(j')}) \oplus t^{(j)}.$$

Now we take $\Delta = \sigma(w^{(j)}) \oplus \sigma(w^{(j')}) \oplus t^{(j)}$, and by applying Lemma 4, we define L^{io} as the max load of the bin B_Δ. Hence, for any $C_7 > 0$, and by the fact that $R \leftarrow \mathcal{R}$ is a dummy value generated independently of τ_0 and τ_1, the probability that bad_7 holds for a fixed (j, j') couple is $1/|\mathcal{R}|$. By a union bound over all possible choices of $j \neq j'$, we have

$$\Pr[\text{bad}_7] \leq \Pr\left[L^{\text{io}} \geq C_7\right] + \binom{q}{2} \frac{C_7}{|\mathcal{R}|},$$

Thus, with $C_7 = n\ln(2) + \ln(1/\epsilon) \leq 2n$ and with $\epsilon = 1/2^n$, we have

$$\Pr[\mathrm{bad}_7] \leq \frac{1}{2^n} + \binom{q}{2}\frac{2n}{|\mathcal{R}|}.$$

For bad_8, when $b^{(j)} \oplus b^{(j')} = 0$, the analysis is identical as the one of bad_7. We now consider the case when $b^{(j)} = 0 \wedge b^{(j')} = 1$ (the case $b^{(j)} = 1 \wedge b^{(j')} = 0$ is entirely symmetric). We first rewrite bad_8 as

$$\sigma(w^{(j)}) \oplus z^{(j)} \oplus v = \sigma \circ \sigma'^{-1}\left(\sigma(w^{(j')}) \oplus z^{(j')} \oplus u \oplus t^{(j')}\right) = \sigma(R),$$

with $\sigma'(x) = \sigma(x) \oplus x$. Then bad_8 implies

$$\sigma \circ \sigma'^{-1}(u) \oplus v = \sigma(w^{(j)}) \oplus z^{(j)} \oplus \sigma \circ \sigma'^{-1}\left(\sigma(w^{(j')}) \oplus z^{(j')} \oplus t^{(j')}\right).$$

Now we take $\Delta = \sigma(w^{(j)}) \oplus z^{(j)} \oplus \sigma \circ \sigma'^{-1}\left(\sigma(w^{(j')}) \oplus z^{(j')} \oplus t^{(j')}\right)$, and by applying Lemma 4, we get

$$\Pr[\mathrm{bad}_8] \leq \frac{1}{2^n} + \binom{q}{2}\frac{2n}{|\mathcal{R}|}.$$

Summing the these probabilities, we get

$$\Pr[\tau \in \mathcal{T}_{\mathrm{bad}}] \leq \frac{7}{2^n} + \frac{(2B+1)qp^2}{2^n\,|\mathcal{R}|} + \frac{p\sqrt{3nq}}{|\mathcal{R}|} + \frac{2B\Phi(T)p}{|\mathcal{R}|} + \frac{6nq^2}{|\mathcal{R}|} + \frac{q^2}{2^{n+1}}.$$

$\mathbf{Pr}[X_{\mathcal{O}} = \tau]/\mathbf{Pr}[X_{\mathcal{P}} = \tau]$. Consider an attainable transcript $\tau \in \mathcal{T}_{\mathrm{good}}$. To compute $\Pr[X_{\mathcal{O}} = \tau]$ and $\Pr[X_{\mathcal{P}} = \tau]$, it suffices to compute the probability of oracles that could result in view τ. As explained in the proof of Theorem 2, we have

$$\frac{\Pr[X_{\mathcal{O}} = \tau]}{\Pr[X_{\mathcal{P}} = \tau]} = 2^{nq}\rho(\tau). \tag{15}$$

with $\rho(\tau) = \Pr[\pi \xleftarrow{\$} \mathrm{Perm}(n) \colon \mathcal{O}1_R[\pi] \vdash \tau_0 \mid \pi \vdash \tau_1]$.

In order to bound $\rho(\tau)$, we re-group the construction queries in τ_0 according to their collisions with the primitive queries.

$$Q_U = \{(w^{(j)}, t^{(j)}, b^{(j)}, z^{(j)}) \in \tau_0 \colon \sigma(w^{(j)} \oplus R) \in U\},$$
$$Q_V = \{(w^{(j)}, t^{(j)}, b^{(j)}, z^{(j)}) \in \tau_0 \colon \sigma(w^{(j)} \oplus R) \oplus z^{(j)} \oplus b^{(j)}R \in V\},$$
$$Q_0 = \{(w^{(j)}, t^{(j)}, b^{(j)}, z^{(j)}) \in \tau_0 \colon \sigma(w^{(j)} \oplus R) \notin U \wedge \sigma(w^{(j)} \oplus R) \oplus z^{(j)} \oplus b^{(j)}R \notin V\}.$$

We define $|Q_U| = \alpha_1$ and $|Q_V| = \alpha_2$. Note that we have $Q_U \cap Q_V = \emptyset$ by $\neg\mathrm{bad}_1$, $Q_U \cap Q_0 = \emptyset$ and $Q_V \cap Q_0 = \emptyset$ by the definition of Q_U, Q_V, and Q_0.

We denote respectively E_1, E_2, and E_0 the event that $\mathcal{O}1_R[\pi] \vdash Q_U$, Q_V, and Q_0 such that $\rho(\tau) = \rho'(\tau)\rho''(\tau)$, with $\rho'(\tau) = \Pr[E_1 \wedge E_2 \mid \pi \vdash \tau_1]$ and $\rho''(\tau) = \Pr[E_0 \mid E_1 \wedge E_2 \wedge \pi \vdash \tau_1]$.

Lower Bounding $\rho'(\tau)$. At this moment, $\pi \vdash \tau_1$ defines *exactly* p distinct input-output tuples for π. We know that for each $(w^{(j)}, t^{(j)}, b^{(j)}, z^{(j)}) \in Q_U$, there is a unique $(u, v) \in \tau_1$ such that $\sigma(w^{(j)} \oplus R) = u$, and $\pi(\sigma(w^{(j)} \oplus R)) = v$. We define

$$\tilde{U}_2 = \{\pi(\sigma(w^{(j)} \oplus R)) \oplus t^{(j)} : (w^{(j)}, t^{(j)}, b^{(j)}, z^{(j)}) \in Q_U\},$$
$$\tilde{V}_2 = \{\sigma(w^{(j)} \oplus R) \oplus z^{(j)} \oplus b^{(j)} R : (w^{(j)}, t^{(j)}, b^{(j)}, z^{(j)}) \in Q_U\}.$$

Similarly, for each $(w^{(j)}, t^{(j)}, b^{(j)}, z^{(j)}) \in Q_V$, there is a unique $(u, v) \in \tau_1$ such that $\sigma(w^{(j)} \oplus R) \oplus z^{(j)} \oplus b^{(j)} R = v$, and $\pi^{-1}(\sigma(w^{(j)} \oplus R) \oplus z^{(j)} \oplus b^{(j)} R) = u$. Again, define

$$\tilde{V}_1 = \{\pi^{-1}(\sigma(w^{(j)} \oplus R) \oplus z^{(j)} \oplus b^{(j)} R) \oplus t^{(j)} : (w^{(j)}, t^{(j)}, b^{(j)}, z^{(j)}) \in Q_V\},$$
$$\tilde{U}_1 = \{\sigma(w^{(j)} \oplus R) : (w^{(j)}, t^{(j)}, b^{(j)}, z^{(j)}) \in Q_V\}.$$

Note that all values in $\tilde{U}_1$ are distinct since $w^{(j)}$'s are distinct, all values in $\tilde{U}_2$ are distinct by $\neg\text{bad}_5$, $U \cap \tilde{U}_1 = \emptyset$ by $\neg\text{bad}_1$, $U \cap \tilde{U}_2 = \emptyset$ by $\neg\text{bad}_2$, and $\tilde{U}_1 \cap \tilde{U}_2 = \emptyset$ by $\neg\text{bad}_7$; and that all values in $\tilde{V}_1$ are distinct by $\neg\text{bad}_6$, all values in $\tilde{V}_2$ are distinct by $\neg\text{bad}_4$, $V \cap \tilde{V}_1 = \emptyset$ by $\neg\text{bad}_3$, $V \cap \tilde{V}_2 = \emptyset$ by $\neg\text{bad}_1$, and $\tilde{V}_1 \cap \tilde{V}_2 = \emptyset$ by $\neg\text{bad}_8$.

Hence, the event E_1 and E_2 define *exactly* $\alpha_1 + \alpha_2$ new and distinct input-output tuples for π, we have

$$\rho'(\tau) = \frac{1}{(2^n - p)_{\alpha_1 + \alpha_2}}. \tag{16}$$

Lower Bounding $\rho''(\tau)$. At this moment, $\pi \vdash \tau_1$, E_1 and E_2 define *exactly* $p + \alpha_1 + \alpha_2$ distinct input-output tuples for π. Our goal now is to count the number of new and distinct evaluations on π, introduced by the event E_0. Let

$$q' = |Q_0| = q - \alpha_1 - \alpha_2,$$
$$p' = \left|U \cup \tilde{U}_1 \cup \tilde{U}_2\right| = \left|V \cup \tilde{V}_1 \cup \tilde{V}_2\right| = p + \alpha_2 + \alpha_1.$$

To ease the subsequent counting, we rewrite the queries in Q_0 as

$$Q_0 = \{(w_1, t_1, b_1, z_1), \ldots, (w_{q'}, t_{q'}, b_{q'}, z_{q'})\}.$$

For $i = 1, \ldots, q'$, let

$$\bar{U}_1 = \{\bar{u}_{1,1}, \ldots, \bar{u}_{1,q'}\} \quad \text{with} \quad \bar{u}_{1,i} = \sigma(w_i \oplus R),$$
$$\bar{V}_2 = \{\bar{v}_{2,1}, \ldots, \bar{v}_{2,q'}\} \quad \text{with} \quad \bar{v}_{2,i} = \sigma(w_i \oplus R) \oplus z_i \oplus b_i R,$$

Note that by definition of Q_0, the $\bar{u}_{1,i}$'s are distinct and outside $U \cup \tilde{U}_1$, and the $\bar{v}_{2,i}$'s are distinct and outside $V \cup \tilde{V}_2$. Besides that, we also know that $\bar{u}_{1,i}$'s are outside $\tilde{U}_2$ by $\neg\text{bad}_7$, and that $\bar{v}_{2,i}$'s are outside $\tilde{V}_1$ by $\neg\text{bad}_8$.

We define by FRESH the event that the underlying permutation calls to π introduced by the construction queries in Q_0 evaluate on distinct inputs, and we also define $\rho''^*(\tau) = \Pr[E_0 \wedge \text{FRESH} \mid E_1 \wedge E_2 \wedge \pi \vdash \tau_1]$. Note that we have $\rho''(\tau) \geq \rho''^*(\tau)$. Hence it is sufficient to focus on $\rho''^*(\tau)$ instead of $\rho''(\tau)$. Let N_0 be the number of solutions

$$\{\bar{v}_{1,1}, \ldots, \bar{v}_{1,q'}, \bar{u}_{2,1}, \ldots, \bar{u}_{2,q'}\}$$

where $\bar{u}_{2,1}, \ldots, \bar{u}_{2,q'} \notin \bar{U}_1$ and $\bar{v}_{1,1}, \ldots, \bar{v}_{1,q'} \notin \bar{V}_2$ because of the event FRESH. N_0 satisfies the following conditions.

1. $\forall i\colon \bar{v}_{1,i} \oplus t_i = \bar{u}_{2,i}$. There are in total 2^n different choices for each $(\bar{v}_{1,i}, \bar{u}_{2,i})$ couple.
2. Conditions for $\bar{v}_{1,i}$:
   (a) $\forall i\colon \bar{v}_{1,i} \notin (V \cup \tilde{V}_1 \cup \tilde{V}_2 \cup \bar{V}_2)$. This excludes at most $p' + q'$ choices for each $(\bar{v}_{1,i}, \bar{u}_{2,i})$ couple,
   (b) $\forall(i, i')$ and $i' < i\colon \bar{v}_{1,i} \neq \bar{v}_{1,i'}$. This excludes at most $i - 1$ choices for each $(\bar{v}_{1,i}, \bar{u}_{2,i})$ couple.
3. Conditions for $\bar{u}_{2,i}$:
   (a) $\forall i\colon \bar{u}_{2,i} \notin (U \cup \tilde{U}_1 \cup \tilde{U}_2 \cup \bar{U}_1)$. This excludes at most $p' + q'$ choices for each $(\bar{v}_{1,i}, \bar{u}_{2,i})$ couple,
   (b) $\forall(i, i')$ and $i' < i\colon \bar{u}_{2,i} \neq \bar{u}_{2,i'}$. This excludes at most $i - 1$ choices for each $(\bar{v}_{1,i}, \bar{u}_{2,i})$ couple.

Taking into account the conditions (1)–(3), we can bound the number N_0 as

$$N_0 \geq \prod_{i=1}^{q'} \left(2^n - 2p' - 2q' - 2(i-1)\right).$$

All in all, we have that for any of the N_0 possible choices for the solutions $\{\bar{v}_{1,1}, \ldots, \bar{v}_{1,q'}, \bar{u}_{2,1}, \ldots, \bar{u}_{2,q'}\}$ satisfying all conditions, the event E_0 is equivalent to exactly $2q'$ new equations on π. Hence, it follows that

$$\rho''^*(\tau) \geq \frac{N_0}{(2^n - p - \alpha_1 - \alpha_2)_{2q'}}. \tag{17}$$

Combining (15), (16) and (17) and using that $q - q' = \alpha_1 + \alpha_2$., we obtain

$$\frac{\Pr[X_{\mathcal{O}} = \tau]}{\Pr[X_{\mathcal{P}} = \tau]} \geq \frac{N_0 \cdot 2^{nq}}{(2^n - p)_{\alpha_1 + \alpha_2 + 2q'}}$$

$$= \frac{N_0 2^{nq'}}{(2^n - p')_{2q'}} \cdot \frac{2^{nq}}{2^{nq'}(2^n - p)_{\alpha_1 + \alpha_2}}$$

$$\geq \frac{N_0 2^{nq'}}{(2^n - p')_{2q'}} \cdot \frac{2^{n(q-q')}}{2^{n(\alpha_1 + \alpha_2)}} = \frac{N_0 2^{nq'}}{(2^n - p')_{2q'}}. \tag{18}$$

Processing further from (18), we have

$$(18) \geq \frac{\prod_{i=1}^{q'} 2^n \left(2^n - 2p' - 2q' - 2(i-1)\right)}{(2^n - p')_{2q'}}$$

$$= \prod_{i=1}^{q'} \frac{2^n \left(2^n - 2p' - 2q' - 2(i-1)\right)}{(2^n - p' - (i-1))(2^n - p' - q' - (i-1))} \tag{19}$$

We denote $B = p' + (i-1)$ and $C = p' + q' + (i-1)$. The Eq. (19) can be written as

$$(19) = \prod_{i=1}^{q'} \frac{2^{2n} - 2 \cdot 2^n C}{(2^n - B)(2^n - C)}$$

$$= \prod_{i=1}^{q'} \frac{2^{2n} - 2 \cdot 2^n C}{2^{2n} - 2^n B - 2^n C + BC}$$

$$= \prod_{i=1}^{q'} \left(1 - \frac{2^n (C - B) + BC}{2^{2n} - 2^n B - 2^n C + BC}\right) \geq \prod_{i=1}^{q'} \left(1 - \frac{4(C-B)}{2^n} - \frac{4BC}{2^{2n}}\right) \tag{20}$$

where for the last inequality we used $B \leq C = p' + q' + (i-1) \leq 2^n/2$.

Fill in the values of B, C, and $C - B = q'$, and using union bound, we obtain

$$(20) = \prod_{i=1}^{q'} \left(1 - \frac{4q'}{2^n} - \frac{4(p' + (i-1))(p' + q' + (i-1))}{2^{2n}}\right)$$

$$\geq 1 - \frac{4q'^2}{2^n} - \frac{4q'(p' + (i-1))(p' + q' + (i-1))}{2^{2n}}. \tag{21}$$

By definition of p', and q', we have

$$q' \leq q,$$
$$p' + (i-1) \leq p' + q' = p + q,$$
$$p' + q' + (i-1) \leq p' + 2q' \leq p + 2q.$$

Then, we conclude from (21) that

$$\frac{\Pr[X_\mathcal{O} = \tau]}{\Pr[X_\mathcal{P} = \tau]} \geq 1 - \left(\frac{8q^2}{2^{n+1}} + \frac{4q(p+q)(p+2q)}{2^{2n}}\right) =: 1 - \epsilon.$$

Acknowledgments. This work was done at the University of Washington, Seattle, USA, when the first author was visiting there. Yu Long Chen is supported by a Ph.D. Fellowship and a long term travel grant from the Research Foundation - Flanders (FWO). Stefano Tessaro was supported in part by NSF grants CNS-1930117 (CAREER), CNS-1926324, CNS-2026774, a Sloan Research Fellowship, and a JP Morgan Faculty Award. The authors would like to thank the anonymous reviewers for their comments and suggestions.

References

1. Abdalla, M., Benhamouda, F., Passelègue, A.: Algebraic XOR-RKA-secure pseudorandom functions from post-zeroizing multilinear maps. In: Galbraith, S.D., Moriai, S. (eds.) ASIACRYPT 2019. LNCS, vol. 11922, pp. 386–412. Springer, Cham (2019). https://doi.org/10.1007/978-3-030-34621-8_14

2. Gilad, A., Yehuda, L., Thomas, S., Michael, Z.: More efficient oblivious transfer and extensions for faster secure computation. In: Sadeghi, A.Z., Gligor, V.D., Yung, M., (Eds.) ACM CCS 2013, pp. 535–548. ACM Press, November 2013

3. Babai, L.: The fourier transform and equations over finite abelian groups: An introduction to the method of trigonometric sums (lecture notes)

4. Bellare, M., Hoang, V.T., Keelveedhi, S., Rogaway, P.: Efficient garbling from a fixed-key blockcipher. In: 2013 IEEE Symposium on Security and Privacy, pp. 478–492. IEEE Computer Society Press, May 2013

5. Bellare, M., Hoang, V.T., Rogaway, P.: Foundations of garbled circuits. In: Yu, T., Danezis, G., Gligor, V.D. (Eds.) ACM CCS 2012, pp. 784–796. ACM Press, October 2012

6. Bellare, M., Kohno, T.: Hash function balance and its impact on birthday attacks. In: Cachin, C., Camenisch, J.L. (eds.) EUROCRYPT 2004. LNCS, vol. 3027, pp. 401–418. Springer, Heidelberg (2004). https://doi.org/10.1007/978-3-540-24676-3_24

7. Chen, S., Steinberger, J.: Tight security bounds for key-alternating ciphers. In: Nguyen, P.Q., Oswald, E. (eds.) EUROCRYPT 2014. LNCS, vol. 8441, pp. 327–350. Springer, Heidelberg (2014). https://doi.org/10.1007/978-3-642-55220-5_19

8. Choi, S.G., Katz, J., Kumaresan, R., Zhou, H.S.: On the security of the "free-XOR" technique. In: Cramer, R. (ed.) TCC 2012. LNCS, vol. 7194, pp. 39–53. Springer, Heidelberg, March 2012

9. Cogliati, B., Seurin, Y.: On the provable security of the iterated even-mansour cipher against related-key and chosen-key attacks. In: Oswald, E., Fischlin, M. (eds.) EUROCRYPT 2015. LNCS, vol. 9056, pp. 584–613. Springer, Heidelberg (2015). https://doi.org/10.1007/978-3-662-46800-5_23

10. Cogliati, B., Seurin, Y.: Analysis of the single-permutation encrypted davies-meyer construction. Des. Codes Cryptogr. 86(12), 2703–2723 (2018)

11. Even, S., Mansour, Y.: A construction of a cipher from a single pseudorandom permutation. J. Cryptol. 10(3), 151–161 (1997) https://doi.org/10.1007/s001459900025

12. Farshim, P., Procter, G.: The related-key security of iterated even–mansour ciphers. In: Leander, G. (ed.) FSE 2015. LNCS, vol. 9054, pp. 342–363. Springer, Heidelberg (2015). https://doi.org/10.1007/978-3-662-48116-5_17

13. Goldreich, O.: Foundations of Cryptography: Basic Applications, vol. 2. Cambridge University Press, Cambridge (2004)

14. Gueron, S., Lindell, Y., Nof, A., Pinkas, B.: Fast garbling of circuits under standard assumptions. J. Cryptol. 31(3), 798–844 (2018)

15. Guo, C., Katz, J., Wang, X., Weng, C., Yu, Y.: Better concrete security for half-gates garbling (in the multi-instance setting). In: Micciancio, D., Ristenpart, T. (eds.) CRYPTO 2020. LNCS, vol. 12171, pp. 793–822. Springer, Cham (2020). https://doi.org/10.1007/978-3-030-56880-1_28

16. Guo, C., Katz, J., Wang, X., Yu, Y.: Efficient and secure multiparty computation from fixed-key block ciphers. In: 2020 IEEE Symposium on Security and Privacy, pp. 825–841. IEEE Computer Society Press, May 2020

17. Impagliazzo, R., Kabanets, V.: Constructive proofs of concentration bounds. In: Serna, M., Shaltiel, R., Jansen, K., Rolim, J. (eds.) APPROX/RANDOM -2010. LNCS, vol. 6302, pp. 617–631. Springer, Heidelberg (2010). https://doi.org/10.1007/978-3-642-15369-3_46

18. Ishai, Y., Kilian, J., Nissim, K., Petrank, E.: Extending oblivious transfers efficiently. In: Boneh, D. (ed.) CRYPTO 2003. LNCS, vol. 2729, pp. 145–161. Springer, Heidelberg (2003). https://doi.org/10.1007/978-3-540-45146-4_9

19. Keller, M., Orsini, E., Scholl, P.: Actively secure ot extension with optimal overhead. In: Gennaro, R., Robshaw, M. (eds.) CRYPTO 2015. LNCS, vol. 9215, pp. 724–741. Springer, Heidelberg (2015). https://doi.org/10.1007/978-3-662-47989-6_35

20. Krawczyk, H.: LFSR-based hashing and authentication. In: Desmedt, Y.G. (ed.) CRYPTO 1994. LNCS, vol. 839, pp. 129–139. Springer, Heidelberg (1994). https://doi.org/10.1007/3-540-48658-5_15

21. Liskov, M., Rivest, R.L., Wagner, D.: Tweakable block ciphers. J. Cryptol. 24(3), 588–613 (2011)

22. Panconesi, A., Srinivasan, A.: Randomized distributed edge coloring via an extension of the chernoff-hoeffding bounds. SIAM J. Comput. 26(2), 350–368 (1997)

23. Patarin, J.: The "coefficients H" technique (invited talk). In: Avanzi, R.M., Keliher, L., Sica, F. (eds.) SAC 2008, volume 5381 of LNCS, pp. 328–345. Springer, Heidelberg, August 2009. https://doi.org/10.1007/978-0-387-30440-3

24. Steinberger, J.P.: The sum-capture problem for abelian groups. arXiv preprint arXiv:1309.5582 (2013)

25. Tessaro, S.: Optimally secure block ciphers from ideal primitives. In: Iwata, T., Cheon, J.H. (eds.) ASIACRYPT 2015, Part II, volume 9453 of LNCS, pp. 437–462. Springer, Heidelberg, November/December 2015

26. Yao, A.C.C.: How to generate and exchange secrets (extended abstract). In: 27th FOCS, pp. 162–167. IEEE Computer Society Press, October 1986

27. Zahur, S., Rosulek, M., Evans, D.: Two halves make a whole. In: Oswald, E., Fischlin, M. (eds.) EUROCRYPT 2015. LNCS, vol. 9057, pp. 220–250. Springer, Heidelberg (2015). https://doi.org/10.1007/978-3-662-46803-6_8

Two-Round Adaptively Secure MPC from Isogenies, LPN, or CDH

Navid Alamati[1](✉), Hart Montgomery[2](✉), Sikhar Patranabis[3](✉),
and Pratik Sarkar[4](✉)

[1] UC Berkeley and Visa Research, Berkeley, USA
nalamati@visa.com
[2] Fujitsu Research of America, Sunnyvale, USA
hmontgomery@fujitsu.com
[3] ETH Zürich and Visa Research, Zürich, Switzerland
sipatran@visa.com
[4] Boston University, Boston, USA
pratik93@bu.edu

Abstract. We present a new framework for building round-optimal (two-round) *adaptively* secure MPC. We show that a relatively weak notion of OT that we call *indistinguishability OT with receiver oblivious sampleability* (r-iOT) is enough to build two-round, adaptively secure MPC against *malicious* adversaries in the CRS model. We then show how to construct r-iOT from CDH, LPN, or isogeny-based assumptions that can be viewed as group actions (such as CSIDH and CSI-FiSh). This yields the first constructions of two-round adaptively secure MPC against malicious adversaries from CDH, LPN, or isogeny-based assumptions. We further extend our non-isogeny results to the plain model, achieving (to our knowledge) the first construction of two-round adaptively secure MPC against semi-honest adversaries in the plain model from LPN.

Our results allow us to build two-round adaptively secure MPC against malicious adversaries from essentially all of the well-studied assumptions in cryptography. In addition, our constructions from isogenies or LPN provide the first post-quantum alternatives to LWE-based constructions for round-optimal adaptively secure MPC. Along the way, we show that r-iOT also implies non-committing encryption (NCE), thereby yielding the first constructions of NCE from isogenies or LPN.

1 Introduction

Secure multiparty computation (MPC) allows mutually distrusting parties to jointly evaluate functions of their secret inputs in a manner that doesn't reveal any information outside of the final output. More precisely, an MPC protocol involves n parties $P_1, \ldots, P_n$ with private inputs $x_1, \ldots, x_n$ such that, at the end

---

N. Alamati—Most of the work was done while the author was affiliated with UC Berkeley.

S. Patranabis—Most of the work was done while the author was affiliated with ETH Zürich.

© International Association for Cryptologic Research 2021
M. Tibouchi and H. Wang (Eds.): ASIACRYPT 2021, LNCS 13091, pp. 305–334, 2021.
https://doi.org/10.1007/978-3-030-92075-3_11

of the protocol, each party P_i learns an output of the form $f_i(x_1, \ldots, x_n)$ but nothing else about the private inputs of any other party.

MPC has been extensively studied since the 1980s [Yao86, GMW87] and is currently used in practice for a wide variety of applications, such as privacy-preserving studies for social good [LJA+18], privacy-preserving online advertising [IKN+17], distributed key management [unb], and securely instantiating blockchain protocols [CCD+20].

MPC constructions are closely related to (and often based upon) another widely studied primitive called *oblivious transfer* (OT) [Rab05, EGL82]. Informally speaking, an OT protocol involves a *sender* holding two messages m_0 and m_1, and a receiver holding a bit b. At the end of the protocol, the receiver should only learn the message m_b and nothing about m_{1-b}, while the sender should learn nothing about the bit b. Due to its wide range of applications, OT has been studied extensively in a long line of works [NP01, PVW08, BD18, FMV19, DGH+20, LGdSG21, CSW20, ADMP20].

Models and Round Complexity. Given the ubiquity of MPC in cryptography, it is no surprise that MPC protocols have been studied in many different security models. Examples of such models include *semi-honest/malicious* as well as *static/adaptive* adversarial corruptions. MPC has also been studied in a variety of computational models such as the plain model and the common reference string (CRS) model. An important feature of any MPC protocol is its *round complexity* (i.e., the number of rounds of communication between the parties during protocol execution). Minimal round complexity is desirable when communication time dominates computational cost, which is the case in many practical protocols. So, designing *round-optimal* MPC protocols is widely regarded to be an important topic in MPC research.

The Static Corruption Model. In the *static* corruption model for MPC, the adversary is allowed to corrupt a pre-determined set of parties. A long line of works have shown how to design round-optimal MPC protocols in this model from a variety of assumptions in the CRS model [GGHR14, MW16, CPV17a]. Notably, [BL18, GS18] showed how to construct two-round MPC protocols from two-round OT protocols in different security models and computational settings.

In terms of concrete computational assumptions, two-round maliciously secure OT protocols in the static corruption model have been constructed from DDH, QR/DCR, and LWE [NP01, PVW08, HK12, BD18]. More recently, such OT protocols have been designed from the CDH and LPN assumptions [DGH+20], as well as from isogenies of elliptic curves [ADMP20]. To summarize, we can currently build round-optimal maliciously secure MPC in the static corruption model from essentially all of the commonly used computational assumptions.

Limitations of the Static Corruption Model. Unfortunately, the static corruption model for MPC is not strong enough for certain real-world applications. In particular, the static corruption model does not provide security against "hacking attacks" where an adversary might adaptively corrupt parties at different stages of the protocol. For instance, what happens if the adversary seizes control of the parties' machines through backdoor access? Secure erasures of the party's state upon corruption is one possible solution to tackle such an attack. However, it is an impractical solution as argued by [CFGN96] since it requires the party to detect an attack and honestly execute its erasure of internal state. This motivates designing MPC protocols that are secure in the *adaptive* corruption model without relying on secure erasures. In this work we refer to adaptive security in the non-erasure model as adaptive security.

The Adaptive Corruption Model. In the *adaptive* corruption model for MPC, the adversary is allowed to dynamically corrupt any set of parties at any time during the protocol execution. Canetti *et al.* [CDD+04] presented the first formal investigation of the adaptive corruption model for MPC, and the relationships between adaptive security and static security in several models of computation. Garay *et al.* [GWZ09] showed how to construct adaptively secure two-party computation protocols in a generic manner from OT protocols satisfying a weaker notion of *semi-adaptive security*; they also showed how to obtain semi-adaptively secure OT protocols from somewhat non-committing encryption (NCE), which is a weaker variant of standard NCE [CLOS02]. Subsequently, Hazay *et al.* [HV15] showed that adaptively secure MPC protocols can be obtained from minimal assumptions like trapdoor simulatable public key encryption (PKE).

However, the scenario is different once round optimality is taken into consideration. It is currently open to design round-optimal maliciously secure MPC protocols even from certain commonly used computational assumptions such as CDH, LPN and isogeny-based assumptions.[1] Initial works on two round, adaptively secure MPC relied on indistinguishability obfuscation (and other standard assumptions) [CGP15, GP15, CPV17a, CsW19] or assuming secure erasures[2] [CsW19] of the party's internal states.

The work of Benhamouda *et al.* [BLPV18] was the first to show how to construct round-optimal adaptively universal composability (UC) [Can01] secure MPC protocols from certain standard computational assumptions without obfuscation and erasures. More concretely, they established the following:

- Against *semi-honest* adversaries, adaptively UC-secure two-round MPC in the plain model is implied by non-committing encryption (NCE) [CLOS02], which in turn can be built from CDH/DDH, LWE, and RSA [CDMW09].
- Against *malicious* adversaries, adaptively UC-secure two-round MPC in the CRS model can be built from a certain kind of two-round statically secure OT protocol with additional "oblivious sampleability" properties, which in turn can be based on DDH, QR, and LWE.

---

[1] Note that constant round maliciously secure MPC against adaptive corruptions can only be achieved in the CRS model; see [GS12] for results establishing the impossibility of maliciously secure adaptive MPC in the plain model from black-box simulation.

[2] The secure erasures model allows erasing the internal state of an honest party when its gets adaptively corrupted by the adversary. It is a strictly weaker model than the one we consider, where erasing the party's state is not allowed.

The recent work of [CSW20] constructs a two round adaptively secure MPC protocol based on the DDH assumption. It is currently open to construct round-optimal (i.e., two-round) maliciously secure MPC protocols in the adaptive corruption model from commonly studied assumptions such as CDH, LPN and isogeny-based assumptions. In particular, the constructions of Benhamouda *et al.* [BLPV18] crucially rely on certain primitives such as "obliviously sampleable" smooth projective hash functions (SPHFs) and "augmented" non-committing encryption (NCE) that are not known from some or all of these assumptions. More generally, it is not known how to construct such MPC protocols from a *single* generic primitive that can be built from commonly used computational assumptions.

Moreover, there are motivating concerns about efficient quantum computing and adaptive MPC. Currently, the only plausibly post-quantum secure constructions [BLPV18, CsW19] of two-round maliciously secure MPC protocols in the adaptive corruption model are based on LWE. This lack of diversity in post-quantum constructions is potentially concerning since a major advance in lattice cryptanalysis could substantially degrade (or in the worst case, invalidate) the security of LWE-based constructions for all practical parameter sets. Notably, the recent NIST competition to standardize post-quantum cryptosystems [CJL+16, AAAS+19, AASA+20] considers a wider class of post-quantum assumptions, including isogeny-based assumptions. In this paper, we ask the following question:

Can we construct two round adaptively UC-secure MPC protocols from a wider class of assumptions, such as CDH, LPN, and isogeny-based assumptions?

1.1 Our Contributions

We answer this above question in the affirmative. We establish a new route to achieving two round maliciously UC-secure MPC protocols in the adaptive corruption setting that relies on potentially weaker (or "less structured") cryptographic primitives as compared to those used by Benhamouda *et al.* [BLPV18]. We also show how to instantiate these primitives from CDH, LPN, and certain families of isogeny-based assumptions (such as CSIDH [CLM+18] and CSI-FiSh [BKV19]). Our results thus establish the feasibility of realizing adaptively secure MPC from essentially *all* commonly used cryptographic assumptions.

We present our results in the "local" CRS model where every session of protocol execution has a local independently sampled CRS string. This is the same model in which Benhamouda *et al.* [BLPV18] described their constructions and proofs. The only other work [CSW20] in this setting is in the single common random string model, but it is solely based on DDH. We note here that Choi *et al.* [CKWZ13] achieved efficient, adaptively secure, composable OT protocols with a single, global CRS, albeit from a different set of concrete assumptions as compared to what we consider in this paper.

Our Ingredients. Our constructions of two-round, adaptively UC-secure MPC essentially rely on a *single* building block, which we refer to as *indistinguishability OT with receiver oblivious sampleability* (r-iOT). Informally, r-iOT is a

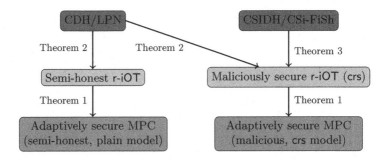

Fig. 1. A simplified overview of our results

two-message OT protocol that satisfies indistinguishability security [DGH+20] against the sender and the receiver in the *static* corruption model, while also satisfying an additional property called "receiver oblivious sampleability". At a high level, this property requires that it is possible to obliviously sample the OT receiver's message (without knowledge of any secret randomness and receiver's choice bit). This property also requires an algorithm for claiming that an honestly generated receiver's message was, in fact, obliviously sampled.

We note that the concept of receiver oblivious sampleable OT was introduced and used in their constructions by Benhamouda *et al.* [BLPV18]. However, our constructions rely on a *strictly weaker* set of properties for our starting r-iOT protocol. First of all, the constructions in [BLPV18] assume that the starting OT protocol satisfies (simulation-based) UC-security against a semi-honest sender and a malicious receiver in the static corruption model. On the other hand, our starting r-iOT protocol is only required to achieve a strictly weaker notion of indistinguishability security, which we subsequently bootstrap all the way to full-fledged UC security via a sequence of transformations. Additionally, the constructions in [BLPV18] assume that the starting OT protocol satisfies *both* receiver and sender oblivious sampleability, while our starting r-iOT protocol is *not* required to satisfy sender oblivious sampleability.

Main Results. Figure 1 summarizes the main results of this paper. Our first main result is a generic construction of UC-secure two-round adaptive MPC from any r-iOT protocol. In somewhat more detail, our first result can be summarized as follows:

Theorem 1 (Informal). *Assuming r-iOT, i.e., a two-message OT protocol that satisfies indistinguishability security and receiver oblivious sampleability against static corruption of the sender/receiver by malicious adversaries in the CRS model (resp. semi-honest adversaries in the plain model), there exists a two-round MPC protocol for any functionality f that satisfies UC security against adaptive corruption of any subset of the parties by malicious adversaries in the CRS model (resp. semi-honest adversaries in the plain model).*

We achieve this result via a sequence of transformations that build progressively stronger OT protocols from weaker ones. These transformations use a number of additional cryptographic primitives, all of which we show can be built in a generic way from any r-iOT protocol in the appropriate model.

Next, we show how to instantiate an r-iOT protocol in various models from a variety of concrete assumptions, including CDH, LPN, and isogeny-based assumptions. In somewhat more details, our second main result can be summarized as follows:

Theorem 2 (Informal). *Assuming CDH or LPN, there exists a construction of* r-iOT *that is secure against malicious adversaries in the CRS model (resp. semi-honest adversaries in the plain model).*

Theorem 3 (Informal). *Under certain isogeny-based assumptions (notably, CSIDH [CLM+18] or CSI-FiSh [BKV19]), there exists a construction of* r-iOT *that is secure against malicious adversaries in the CRS model.*

Our constructions of r-iOT from CDH and LPN build upon previous work due to Döttling *et al.* [DGH+20] that realized UC-secure OT/MPC against static corruptions from the same set of assumptions. Our construction of r-iOT from isogeny-based assumptions is based on a novel usage of the *(restricted) effective group action* framework due to Alamati *et al.* [ADMP20]. In particular, we show how to use a trusted setup to bypass issues around sampling obliviously from the "set" of an effective group action, which is a well-known open problem in the isogeny literature [Pet17, DMPS19, CPV20].[3]

Combined with the previous theorem, we obtain as a corollary the *first* constructions of two-round adaptively UC-secure MPC against malicious adversaries from the same concrete assumptions:

Corollary 1 (Informal). *Assuming CDH, LPN, or certain isogeny-based assumptions (notably, CSIDH [CLM+18] or CSI-FiSh [BKV19]), there exists a two-round MPC protocol for any functionality f that satisfies UC security against adaptive corruption of any subset of the parties by malicious adversaries in the CRS model.*

In summary, we show that it is feasible to construct round-optimal maliciously secure MPC in the adaptive corruption model from essentially all of the commonly used cryptographic assumptions. This essentially closes the gap between the static corruption model and the adaptive corruption model in terms of constructing round-optimal maliciously secure MPC from concrete assumptions. Figure 2 presents a high-level summary of our roadmap from r-iOT to adaptively UC-secure MPC.

---

[3] Unlike CDH or LPN, we do not achieve a construction of r-iOT from isogeny-based assumptions in the plain model. Achieving this seemingly requires new techniques for sampling obliviously from the "set" of an effective group action beyond those used in state-of-the-art isogeny-based cryptography.

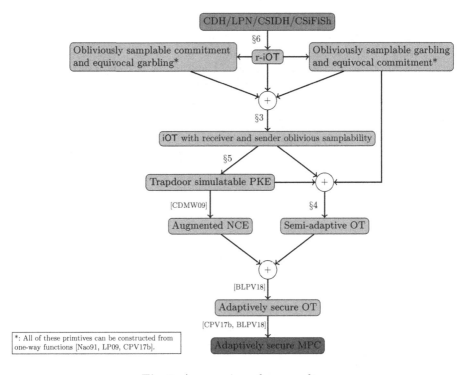

Fig. 2. An overview of our results

Additional Results. Besides our main contributions, we show some additional results that could be of independent interest. In particular, we show that any r-iOT protocol that is secure against semi-honest adversaries implies the existence of a *trapdoor-simulatable* PKE, which in turn is known to imply *non-committing encryption* (NCE) in a generic manner (in fact, it was shown in [CDMW09] that trapdoor-simulatable PKE implies an "augmented" variant of NCE). Due to its wide range of applications, NCE (and its augmented variants) have been studied by a long line of works [CFGN96, CDMW09, CPR17, YKT19, BBD+20].

Theorem 4 (Informal). *Any* r-iOT *that is secure against semi-honest adversaries implies a construction of trapdoor-simulatable PKE.*

Combined with the previous theorem on instantiations of r-iOT from concrete assumptions, and the known implication due to [CDMW09], we obtain as a corollary the *first* constructions (to our knowledge) of (augmented) NCE from LPN or certain isogeny-based assumptions:

Corollary 2 (Informal). *Assuming LPN, there exists a construction of a two round (augmented) non-committing encryption (NCE) scheme.*

Corollary 3 (Informal). *Assuming isogeny-based assumptions such as CSIDH [CLM+18] or CSI-FiSh [BKV19], there exists a construction of a two round (augmented) non-committing encryption (NCE) scheme in the CRS model.*

Complexity Analysis of Our Constructions. Our constructions may be viewed primarily as feasibility results for adaptive OT/MPC, and hence they are not tuned for practical efficiency. For the sake of completeness, we present here an asymptotic complexity analysis of the number of public-key operations used in our constructions. We assume that all messages are κ-bit, where κ is the security parameter. We also assume that the commitment schemes underlying our constructions require $O(\kappa)$ bits of randomness to commit to a bit.

1. Our construction of bit iOT in Sect. 3 requires $O(\kappa)$ executions of the underlying r-iOT protocol.
2. Our construction of trapdoor-simulatable PKE in Sect. 5 requires $O(1)$ executions of the underlying r-iOT protocol.
3. Our construction of semi-adaptive OT in Sect. 4 requires $O(\kappa)$ executions of both the underlying (string) iOT protocol as well as the underlying trapdoor-simulatable PKE scheme.
4. The construction of augmented NCE in [CDMW09] requires $O(\kappa)$ executions of a trapdoor-simulatable PKE scheme.
5. The construction of adaptive OT in [BLPV18] requires $O(1)$ executions of both the underlying semi-adaptive OT protocol and the underlying augmented NCE scheme.

Thus, asymptotically, the construction of adaptive OT based on our proposed framework requires $\mathcal{O}(\kappa^2)$ executions of the bit iOT protocol. This translates to $\mathcal{O}(\kappa^3)$ executions of the underlying r-iOT protocol for a $\mathcal{O}(\kappa)$-bit message. Finally, we analyze the number of public-key operations required in the various instantiations of r-iOT (for $O(\kappa)$-bit messages) from concrete assumptions:

– The construction of r-iOT from CDH (resp., LPN) assumption in [DGH+20] requires $O(\kappa)$ exponentiation operations (resp., LPN-sample generations).
– Our construction of r-iOT from isogeny-based assumptions (more concretely, from restricted effective group actions) in Sect. 6.1 requires $O(\kappa\ell)$ group action computations for any $\ell = \omega(\log \kappa)$.

Outline. The rest of the paper is organized as follows. Section 2 presents notations and definitions for two-round OT protocols in the CRS model. Section 3 describes our construction of two-round iOT with both receiver and sender oblivious sampleability from any two-round r-iOT protocol. Section 4 describes our construction (and proof) of semi-adaptively secure two-round OT from any two-round iOT with both receiver and sender oblivious sampleability. Section 5 presents our construction of trapdoor simulatable PKE (and augmented NCE) from any two-round r-iOT protocol. Section 6 describes our concrete constructions of two-round r-iOT from isogeny-based assumptions, CDH or LPN. Due to lack of space, we defer some additional background material and detailed proofs to the full version of our paper.

2   Preliminaries

In this section, we present some core preliminaries that are integral to our constructions. We defer many definitions and other background with which we expect most readers to be familiar to the full version of our paper.

2.1   Notations

We denote by $a \leftarrow D$ a uniform sampling of an element a from a distribution D. The set of elements $\{1, \ldots, n\}$ is represented by $[n]$. We denote polylog(a) and poly(b) as polynomials in $\log a$ and b respectively. We denote a probabilistic polynomial time algorithm as PPT. We denote the computational security parameter by κ. We denote a negligible function in κ as $\mathsf{neg}(\kappa)$. When a party S gets corrupted we denote it by S^*. Our security proofs are in the Universal Composability (UC) framework of [Can01]. We refer to the original paper for details. We denote computational and statistical indistinguishability by $\overset{c}{\approx}$ and $\overset{s}{\approx}$ respectively. We abbreviate "common reference string" as CRS. Unless otherwise specified, our constructions and proofs are in "local" CRS model. This happens to be the same CRS model in which the prior work due to Benhamouda *et al.* [BLPV18] showed constructions of adaptive MPC protocols with security against malicious adversaries.

2.2   Two-Message Oblivious Transfer in the CRS Model

In this section, we formally define a two-message oblivious transfer (OT) protocol in the common reference string (CRS) model. We then define two security notions for such an OT protocol, namely universal composability (UC) security and a weaker notion of indistinguishability-based security. We first focus on security against static corruptions by a malicious adversary. Subsequently, we discuss different levels of adaptive security.

A two-message OT protocol in the CRS model is a tuple of four algorithms of the form $\mathsf{OT} = (\mathsf{Setup}, \mathsf{OTR}_1, \mathsf{OTS}, \mathsf{OTR}_2)$ described below:

- $\mathsf{Setup}(1^\kappa)$: Takes as input the security parameter κ and outputs a CRS string crs and a trapdoor td.[4]
- $\mathsf{OTR}_1(\mathsf{crs}, b \in \{0,1\})$: Takes as input the crs and a bit $b \in \{0,1\}$, and outputs the receiver's message $\mathsf{M_R}$ and the receiver's internal state st.
- $\mathsf{OTS}(\mathsf{crs}, \mathsf{M_R}, m_0, m_1)$: Takes as input the crs, the receiver's message $\mathsf{M_R}$, a pair of input strings (m_0, m_1), and outputs the sender's message $\mathsf{M_S}$.
- $\mathsf{OTR}_2(\mathsf{crs}, \mathsf{M_S}, b, \mathsf{st})$: Takes as input the crs, the sender's message $\mathsf{M_S}$, a bit b, and receiver's internal state st, and outputs a message string m'.

---

[4] For standard two-message OT protocols, the setup algorithm need not output a trapdoor td, but we include it for certain security properties described subsequently.

Correctness. A two-message OT protocol in the CRS model is said to be correct if for any $b \in \{0,1\}$ and any (m_0, m_1), letting $(\mathsf{crs}, \mathsf{td}) \leftarrow \mathsf{Setup}(1^\kappa)$ and $(\mathsf{M_R}, \mathsf{st}) \leftarrow \mathsf{OTR}_1(\mathsf{crs}, b)$, the following holds with overwhelming probability:

$$\mathsf{OTR}_2(\mathsf{crs}, \mathsf{OTS}(\mathsf{crs}, \mathsf{M_R}, m_0, m_1), b, \mathsf{st}) = m_b.$$

Corruption Models. We consider the following (progressively non-decreasing in strength) adversarial models against any two-message OT protocol:

- *Static Corruption:* The adversary corrupts the parties at the onset of the protocol.
- *Semi-Adaptive Corruption:* The adversary corrupts one party (either the receiver or the sender) adaptively (at any point before/during/after the protocol) and the other party statically at the beginning of the protocol.
- *Adaptive Corruption:* The adversary corrupts both parties adaptively (at any point before/during/after the protocol). This scenario covers the previous corruption cases.

Indistinguishability-Based Security. We also consider a weaker notion of indistinguishability-based security against malicious adversaries in the static corruption setting. This notion is adopted directly from [DGH+20]. A two-message OT protocol $\mathsf{iOT} = (\mathsf{Setup}, \mathsf{iOTR}_1, \mathsf{iOTS}, \mathsf{iOTR}_2)$ satisfies indistinguishability-based security if the following properties hold:

Receiver's Indistinguishability Security. Formally, receiver's indistinguishability security requires that the following holds for any $(\mathsf{crs}, \mathsf{td}) \leftarrow \mathsf{Setup}(1^\kappa)$:

$$(\mathsf{crs}, \mathsf{iOTR}_1(\mathsf{crs}, 0)) \stackrel{c}{\approx} (\mathsf{crs}, \mathsf{iOTR}_1(\mathsf{crs}, 1)).$$

Sender's Indistinguishability Security. Sender's indistinguishability security is defined in [DGH+20] via an experiment $\mathsf{Exp}_{\mathsf{iOT}}^{\mathsf{crs}, r, w, b}(\mathcal{A})$ between a non-uniform PPT adversary $\mathcal{A} = (\mathcal{A}_1, \mathcal{A}_2)$ and a challenger, where the experiment is parameterized by some honestly generated crs, random coins $r \in \{0,1\}^\kappa$, an integer n representing the bitwise length of messages, a bit $w \in \{0,1\}$, and a bit $b \in \{0,1\}$:

$\underline{\mathsf{Exp}_{\mathsf{iOT}}^{\mathsf{crs}, r, w, b}(\mathcal{A})}$:

1. Run $(m_0, m_1, \mathsf{M_R}, \mathsf{st}) \leftarrow \mathcal{A}_1(1^\kappa, \mathsf{crs})$.
2. If $b = 0$, compute $\mathsf{M_S} \leftarrow \mathsf{iOTS}(\mathsf{crs}, \mathsf{M_R}, (m_0, m_1))$.
3. If $b = 1$, compute $\mathsf{M_S} \leftarrow \mathsf{iOTS}(\mathsf{crs}, \mathsf{M_R}, (m'_0, m'_1))$ where $m'_w \leftarrow \{0,1\}^n$ and $m'_{1-w} := m_{1-w}$.
4. Output $s \leftarrow \mathcal{A}_2(\mathsf{st}, \mathsf{M_S})$.

For a given $(\mathsf{crs}, r, w \in \{0,1\})$, we define the advantage $\mathcal{A}_{\mathsf{iOT}}^{\mathsf{crs}, r, w}(\mathcal{A})$ as:

$$\mathsf{Adv}_{\mathsf{iOT}}^{\mathsf{crs}, r, w}(\mathcal{A}) = |\Pr[\mathsf{Exp}_{\mathsf{iOT}}^{\mathsf{crs}, r, w, 0}(\mathcal{A}) = 1] - \Pr[\mathsf{Exp}_{\mathsf{iOT}}^{\mathsf{crs}, r, w, 1}(\mathcal{A}) = 1]|.$$

We say that iOT satisfies sender's indistinguishability security if for any PPT adversary $\mathcal{A}$, $\mathsf{Adv}_{\mathsf{iOT}}^{\mathsf{crs},r,w}(\mathcal{A})$ is negligible in κ for at least one $w \in \{0,1\}$, where the probability is taken over $\mathsf{crs} = \mathsf{Setup}(1^\kappa)$ and $r \leftarrow \{0,1\}^\kappa$.[5]

2.3   iOT with Oblivious Sampleability

We also consider notions of *oblivious sampleability* for indistinguishability-secure two-message OT protocols in the CRS model. An iOT protocol of the form $\mathsf{iOT} = (\mathsf{Setup}, \mathsf{iOTR}_1, \mathsf{iOTS}, \mathsf{iOTR}_2)$ is said to satisfy oblivious sampleability if it supports additional "oblivious sampling" algorithms - $(\widetilde{\mathsf{iOTR}}, \widetilde{\mathsf{iOTS}})$ and the corresponding "randomness inversion" algorithms - $(\widetilde{\mathsf{iOTR}_{\mathsf{Inv}}}, \widetilde{\mathsf{iOTS}_{\mathsf{Inv}}})$ defined as:

- $\widetilde{\mathsf{iOTR}}(\mathsf{crs}; r)$: Outputs an obliviously sampled receiver's message $\mathsf{M_R}$.
- $\widetilde{\mathsf{iOTS}}(\mathsf{crs}, w, m_{1-w}; r)$ Outputs an obliviously sampled sender's message $\mathsf{M_S}$.
- $\widetilde{\mathsf{iOTR}_{\mathsf{Inv}}}(\mathsf{crs}, \mathsf{M_R}, \mathsf{td}, r)$: Outputs randomness $\tilde{r}$ corresponding to an honestly generated receiver message $\mathsf{M_R}$.
- $\widetilde{\mathsf{iOTS}_{\mathsf{Inv}}}(\mathsf{crs}, w, \mathsf{M_S}, \mathsf{td}, r)$: Outputs randomness $\tilde{r}$ corresponding to an honestly generated sender message $\mathsf{M_S}$.

We say that the iOT is obliviously sampleable if it satisfies *both* receiver and sender oblivious sampleability, as defined below.

Receiver Oblivious Sampleability: For any bit $b \in \{0,1\}$, an obliviously sampled receiver's message should be indistinguishable from an honestly generated one, even given the sampling randomness. More formally, we require that for any $(\mathsf{crs}, \mathsf{td}) = \mathsf{Setup}(1^\kappa)$ and any bit $b \in \{0,1\}$, we have $(\mathsf{crs}, \mathsf{M_R}, \hat{r}) \stackrel{c}{\approx} (\mathsf{crs}, \widetilde{\mathsf{M_R}}, \tilde{r})$, where for uniformly random coins $r, \tilde{r} \leftarrow \{0,1\}^\kappa$, we have

$$\mathsf{M_R} = \mathsf{iOTR}(\mathsf{crs}, b; r), \quad \hat{r} = \widetilde{\mathsf{iOTR}_{\mathsf{Inv}}}(\mathsf{crs}, \mathsf{M_R}, \mathsf{td}, r), \quad \widetilde{\mathsf{M_R}} = \widetilde{\mathsf{iOTR}}(\mathsf{crs}, b; \tilde{r}).$$

Sender Oblivious Sampleability: We also require that a corrupt receiver cannot infer whether the sender's message (corresponding to the bit w which is not chosen by the receiver) was obliviously sampled or generated honestly. We consider an adversary $\mathcal{A} = (\mathcal{A}_1, \mathcal{A}_2)$ participating in an experiment $\mathsf{Exp}_{\widetilde{\mathsf{iOT}}}^{\mathsf{crs},r,w,b}(\mathcal{A})$, indexed by a crs, random coins $r \in \{0,1\}^\kappa$, a bit $w \in \{0,1\}$ and a bit $b \in \{0,1\}$:

$\underline{\mathsf{Exp}_{\widetilde{\mathsf{iOT}}}^{\mathsf{crs},r,w,b}(\mathcal{A}):}$

- Run $(m_0, m_1, \mathsf{M_R}, \mathsf{st}) \leftarrow \mathcal{A}_1(1^\kappa, \mathsf{crs}; r)$.
- If $b = 0$, sample randomness $\tilde{r}$ and compute $\mathsf{M_S} \leftarrow \widetilde{\mathsf{iOTS}}(\mathsf{crs}, w, m_{1-w}; \tilde{r})$.

---

[5] This is slightly different from the traditional notion of sender's indistinguishability security for two-message OT; we refer to [DGH+20] for more details.

- If $b = 1$, sample randomness $\hat{r}$, compute $\mathsf{M_S} \leftarrow \mathsf{iOTS}(\mathsf{crs}, \mathsf{M_R}, (m_0, m_1); \hat{r})$ and $\tilde{r} = \widetilde{\mathsf{iOTS}}_{\mathsf{Inv}}(\mathsf{crs}, w, \mathsf{M_S}, \mathsf{td}, \hat{r})$.
- Compute and output $s \leftarrow \mathcal{A}_2(\mathsf{st}, \tilde{r}, \mathsf{M_S})$.

Define the advantage of $\mathcal{A}$ as

$$\mathsf{Adv}_{\widetilde{\mathsf{iOT}}}^{\mathsf{crs},r,w}(\mathcal{A}) = |\Pr[\mathsf{Exp}_{\widetilde{\mathsf{iOT}}}^{\mathsf{crs},r,w,0}(\mathcal{A}) = 1] - \Pr[\mathsf{Exp}_{\widetilde{\mathsf{iOT}}}^{\mathsf{crs},r,w,1}(\mathcal{A}) = 1]|.$$

We say that iOT satisfies sender oblivious sampleability if for any PPT adversary $\mathcal{A}$ and any $w \in \{0, 1\}$, $\mathsf{Adv}_{\widetilde{\mathsf{iOT}}}^{\mathsf{crs},r,w}(\mathcal{A})$ is negligible in κ, where $(\mathsf{crs}, \mathsf{td}) \leftarrow \mathsf{Setup}(1^\kappa)$ and $r \leftarrow \{0, 1\}^\kappa$.

r-iOT. We denote by $\mathsf{r\text{-}iOT} = (\mathsf{Setup}, \mathsf{r\text{-}iOTR}_1, \mathsf{r\text{-}iOTS}, \mathsf{r\text{-}iOTR}_2, \widetilde{\mathsf{r\text{-}iOTR}}, \widetilde{\mathsf{r\text{-}iOTR}}_{\mathsf{Inv}})$, an indistinguishability-secure two-message OT in the CRS model that satisfies receiver oblivious sampleability but *not necessarily* sender oblivious sampleability. Such an OT protocol only needs to support an "oblivious sampling" algorithm $\widetilde{\mathsf{r\text{-}iOTR}}$ (where $\widetilde{\mathsf{r\text{-}iOTR}}$ is defined similar to $\widetilde{\mathsf{iOTR}}$) and the corresponding "randomness inversion" algorithm $\widetilde{\mathsf{r\text{-}iOTR}}_{\mathsf{Inv}}$ (where $\widetilde{\mathsf{r\text{-}iOTR}}_{\mathsf{Inv}}$ is defined similar to $\widetilde{\mathsf{iOTR}}_{\mathsf{Inv}}$) for the receiver.

2.4   Garbling Schemes

A garbling scheme [Yao86, CPV17b] is a tuple $\mathsf{Garble} = (\mathsf{Gb}, \mathsf{En}, \mathsf{Ev})$, described as follows:

- $\mathsf{Gb}(1^\kappa, \mathcal{C}) \rightarrow (\mathsf{GC}, \mathsf{Keys})$: A randomized algorithm which takes as input the security parameter and a circuit $\mathcal{C} : \{0, 1\}^n \rightarrow \{0, 1\}^m$ and outputs a tuple of strings $(\mathsf{GC}, \mathsf{Keys})$, where GC is the garbled circuit and Keys denotes the input-wire labels.
- $\mathsf{En}(x, \mathsf{Keys}) = \mathsf{X}$: a deterministic algorithm that outputs the garbled input X corresponding to input x.
- $\mathsf{Ev}(\mathsf{GC}, \mathsf{X}) = y$: A deterministic algorithm which evaluates garbled circuit GC on garbled input X and outputs y.

We borrow this definition and the associated notations from the work of [CPV17b]. The garbling scheme used in our protocols needs to satisfy standard properties such as correctness and privacy (we refer to [Yao86, CPV17b] for the definitions). We additionally borrow two extra properties from [CPV17b] for our garbling schemes: namely, oblivious sampleability and equivocability, which we define here.

Oblivious Sampleability. Oblivious sampleability allows the garbler to obliviously sample a garbled circuit without the knowledge of the input keys Keys. It also enables an honestly computed garbled circuit to be claimed as obliviously sampled. A garbling scheme $\mathsf{Garble} = (\mathsf{Gb}, \mathsf{En}, \mathsf{Ev})$ is said to satisfy oblivious sampleability if there exist PPT algorithms $\widetilde{\mathsf{Gb}}$ and $\mathsf{Gb}_{\mathsf{Inv}}$ defined as:

- $\widetilde{\mathsf{Gb}}(1^\kappa, \mathcal{C}, y) \to (\widetilde{\mathrm{GC}}, \widetilde{\mathsf{X}})$: A randomized algorithm that outputs an obliviously sampled garbled circuit $\widetilde{\mathrm{GC}}$ and obliviously sampled wire labels $\widetilde{\mathsf{X}}$ such that evaluating $\widetilde{\mathrm{GC}}$ on $\widetilde{\mathsf{X}}$ would yield y as output,
- $\mathsf{Gb}_{\mathsf{Inv}}(r, \mathsf{Keys}, x) \to \widehat{r}$: A randomness inversion algorithm that given some randomness of garbling r, input-wire labels Keys, and an input x, outputs some random coins $\widehat{r}$,

such that for any polynomial-time circuit $\mathcal{C}$ and for all input output pairs (x, y) such that $\mathcal{C}(x) = y$ it holds that

$$(\mathsf{Gb}_{\mathsf{Inv}}(r, \mathsf{Keys}, x), \mathrm{GC}, \mathsf{X}) \overset{c}{\approx} (\widehat{r}, \widetilde{\mathrm{GC}}, \widetilde{\mathsf{X}}),$$

where for random coins $r, \widetilde{r} \leftarrow \{0, 1\}^\kappa$, we have

$$(\mathrm{GC}, \mathsf{Keys}) = \mathsf{Gb}(1^\kappa, \mathcal{C}; r), \quad \mathsf{X} = \mathsf{En}(x, \mathsf{Keys}), \quad (\widetilde{\mathrm{GC}}, \widetilde{\mathsf{X}}) = \widetilde{\mathsf{Gb}}(1^\kappa, \mathcal{C}, y; \widetilde{r}).$$

Equivocal Garbling. Finally, we require the garbled circuit to be equivocal [CPV17b]. It allows a privacy simulator $\mathcal{S}_{\mathrm{GC}}$ to generate a fake garbled circuit $\widetilde{\mathrm{GC}}$ and fake input wire labels $\widetilde{\mathsf{X}}$ that always evaluate to a fixed output. Later, the simulator can open $(\widetilde{\mathrm{GC}}, \widetilde{\mathsf{X}})$ to a particular input x by providing consistent randomness used in the garbling process. We define this as follows: a garbling scheme $\mathsf{Garble} = (\mathsf{Gb}, \mathsf{En}, \mathsf{Ev}, \widetilde{\mathsf{Gb}})$ is said to be equivocal if there exists a pair of PPT algorithms $(\mathcal{S}^1_{\mathrm{GC}}, \mathcal{S}^2_{\mathrm{GC}})$, such that any PPT adversary $\mathcal{A}$ wins the following game with at most negligible advantage:

1. $\mathcal{A}$ gives a circuit $\mathcal{C}$ and an input x to the challenger.
2. The challenger flips a bit b.
   - If $b = 0$: It computes $(\mathrm{GC}, \mathsf{Keys}) \leftarrow \mathsf{Gb}(\mathcal{C}; r)$ and $\mathsf{X} \leftarrow \mathsf{En}(x, \mathsf{Keys})$. It sends $\mathrm{GC}, \mathsf{X}, \mathsf{Keys}, r$ to the adversary $\mathcal{A}$.
   - If $b = 1$: It sets $y = C(x)$. It runs the simulator $(\mathrm{GC}, \mathsf{X}, \mathsf{st}) \leftarrow \mathcal{S}^1_{\mathrm{GC}}(\mathcal{C}, y)$. It runs the simulator $(\mathsf{Keys}, r) \leftarrow \mathcal{S}^2_{\mathrm{GC}}(\mathsf{st}, x)$. It sends $\mathrm{GC}, \mathsf{X}, \mathsf{Keys}, r$ to the adversary $\mathcal{A}$.
3. The adversary outputs a bit b'.

The adversary wins if $b = b'$.

2.5 Additional Cryptographic Primitives

In this section, we define certain additional cryptographic primitives that we require for our constructions: namely, equivocal commitments with oblivious sampleability, and trapdoor simulatable PKE.

Equivocal Commitment. Let $\mathsf{Com} = (\mathsf{Setup}, \mathsf{Com}, \mathsf{Ver}, \mathsf{Equiv})$ be an equivocal commitment scheme in the CRS model as defined in [BLPV18]. We say that Com is *obliviously sampleable* if there exist additional algorithms $(\widetilde{\mathsf{Com}}, \widetilde{\mathsf{Com}}_{\mathsf{Inv}})$ for oblivious commitment generation and randomness inversion, respectively, such that for any $(\mathsf{crs}, \mathsf{td}) = \mathsf{Setup}(1^\kappa)$ and any message m, we have $(c, \widehat{r}) \overset{c}{\approx} (\widetilde{c}, \widetilde{r})$, where

$$c = \mathsf{Com}(\mathsf{crs}, m; r), \quad \widehat{r} = \widetilde{\mathsf{Com}}_{\mathsf{Inv}}(\mathsf{crs}, m, r, \mathsf{td}), \quad \widetilde{c} = \widetilde{\mathsf{Com}}(\mathsf{crs}; \widetilde{r}),$$

for random coins $r, \widetilde{r} \leftarrow \{0,1\}^\kappa$. Such an equivocal commitment scheme with oblivious sampleability can be obtained from one-way-functions [Nao91].

Trapdoor Simulatable PKE. We recall the definition of trapdoor simulatable PKE from [CDMW09]. A trapdoor simulatable PKE scheme in the CRS model is a tuple of the form $(\mathsf{Setup}, \mathsf{Gen}, \mathsf{Enc}, \mathsf{Dec}, \mathsf{oGen}, \mathsf{oEnc})$, where the tuple $(\mathsf{Setup}, \mathsf{Gen}, \mathsf{Enc}, \mathsf{Dec})$ is a standard PKE scheme that is augmented with oblivious sampling algorithms $(\mathsf{oGen}, \mathsf{oEnc})$ and randomness inverting algorithms $(\mathsf{rGen}, \mathsf{rEnc})$. The trapdoor of the setup string allows generating a public key (resp. a ciphertext) honestly and then claiming that the public key (resp. a ciphertext) was obliviously sampled using the rGen (resp. the rEnc) algorithm. Formally, we require that for any message $m \in \{0,1\}^\ell$, letting $(\mathsf{crs}, \mathsf{td}) = \mathsf{Setup}(1^\kappa)$,

$$(\mathsf{pk}, c, \widehat{r}_G, \widehat{r}_E) \overset{c}{\approx} (\widetilde{\mathsf{pk}}, \widetilde{c}, \widetilde{r}_G, \widetilde{r}_E),$$

where for random coins $r_G, r_E, \widetilde{r}_G, \widetilde{r}_E \leftarrow \{0,1\}^\kappa$, we have $(\mathsf{pk}, \mathsf{sk}) = \mathsf{Gen}(\mathsf{crs}; r_G)$, $c = \mathsf{Enc}(\mathsf{crs}, \mathsf{pk}, m; r_E)$, $\widetilde{\mathsf{pk}} = \mathsf{oGen}(\mathsf{crs}; \widetilde{r}_G)$, $\widetilde{c} = \mathsf{oEnc}(\mathsf{crs}; \widetilde{r}_E)$, and

$$\widehat{r}_G = \mathsf{rGen}(\mathsf{crs}, r_G, \mathsf{td}), \quad \widehat{r}_E = \mathsf{rEnc}(\mathsf{crs}, r_G, r_E, m, \mathsf{td}).$$

3   iOT with Oblivious Sampleability from r-iOT

In this section, we present the first generic construction in our overall framework: we show how to build a two-message iOT protocol in the CRS model with *both* oblivious sender and receiver sampleability given a two-message r-iOT protocol (iOT with receiver oblivious sampleability but *not necessarily* sender oblivious sampleability). For simplicity of exposition, we describe the construction in the CRS model against malicious corruptions; the corresponding construction in the plain model against semi-honest corruptions follows analogously.

3.1   Construction Overview and Intuition

We construct a two-message iOT protocol with oblivious sender and receiver sampleability in the CRS model given the following ingredients: (1) a two-message r-iOT protocol in the CRS model, (2) an equivocal garbling scheme, (3) an obliviously sampleable garbling scheme, and (4) an obliviously sampleable commitment scheme (in the CRS model). The latter three schemes are implied by one-way functions (and hence by r-iOT).

A First Attempt. We describe below an initial attempt to build iOT with receiver and sender oblivious sampleability from r-iOT. This simple construction additionally uses a standard garbling scheme and a standard (non-interactive) commitment scheme. Additionally, let $\mathcal{C}[\beta, c](\cdot, \cdot)$ denote a circuit that is hardwired with a bit $\beta \in \{0,1\}$ and a commitment c. It takes as input some randomness r and a message m, and outputs m if c is valid commitment to β using randomness r. Otherwise, it outputs $\perp$ (the circuit $\mathcal{C}$ is also hardwired with the CRS string for the commitment scheme, but we avoid mentioning this explicitly for simplicity of presentation.).

- iOTR$_1$: The receiver uses the commitment scheme to create a commitment c to its input choice bit b under randomness r. The receiver transmits this commitment c to the sender. The receiver also uses the underlying r-iOT protocol to send one r-iOT-receiver message corresponding to each bit of the randomness r (in parallel).
- iOTS: The sender uses the commitment c from the receiver to create two circuits $\mathcal{C}_{0,c}(\cdot, m_0)$ and $\mathcal{C}_{1,c}(\cdot, m_1)$ as described earlier. It then garbles these circuits using the garbling scheme to create a pair of garbled circuits GC_0 and GC_1, along with the corresponding wire labels for their input bits.
  The sender sends across GC_0 and GC_1 to the receiver. In parallel, the sender uses the underlying r-iOT scheme and the r-iOT messages from the receiver to generate one r-iOT-sender message for each pair of wire labels, and also sends all of these across to the receiver.
- iOTR$_2$: The receiver uses the r-iOT-sender messages to recover the wire labels corresponding to its randomness string r for both garbled circuits GC_0 and GC_1. It then evaluates GC_b on r by using the corresponding wire labels to recover the message m_b.

The above approach fails to give us sender's oblivious sampleability. Note that the sender's message has two parts - the garbled circuits (GC_0, GC_1), and the r-iOT-sender messages. Using an *obliviously sampleable garbling scheme* naturally allows oblivious sampleability for the first part of the sender's message. However, it is not clear if the second part of the sender's message can be obliviously sampled since the underlying r-iOT protocol does not necessarily support sender oblivious sampleability.

Our Solution. We address this issue by using *two separate sets* of garbled circuits. The first set of garbled circuits are created using a garbling scheme Garble' that is *obliviously sampleable* [LP09], while the second set of garbled circuits are created using a garbling scheme Garble that is *equivocal* [CPV17b]. The complete solution is described formally in Fig. 3. The oblivious sampling and randomness inversion algorithms are described in Fig. 4.

Theorem 5. *Assuming that: (1) $\pi_{r\text{-}iOT}$ is a two-message r-iOT protocol in the crs_{iOT} model, (2) Com is an obliviously sampleable commitment scheme, (3) Garble is an equivocal garbling scheme, and (4) Garble' is an obliviously sampleable garbling scheme, π_{iOT} is a two-message iOT protocol with sender and receiver oblivious sampleability in the CRS model.*

The formal security proof is deferred to the full version of the paper. We present here a high-level overview of the arguments for indistinguishability security and oblivious sampleability (for both sender and receiver) of our protocol.

Indistinguishability Security (Informal). Arguing receiver's indistinguishability security is again straightforward. Informally, the commitment c computationally hides the receiver's choice bit b because the r-iOT messages sent by the receiver computationally hide the receiver's randomness string r.

π_{iOT}

- **Public Inputs:** $\mathsf{crs}_{\mathsf{iOT}} = (\mathsf{crs}_{\mathsf{r\text{-}iOT}}, \mathsf{crs}_{\mathsf{com}})$ where $\mathsf{crs}_{\mathsf{r\text{-}iOT}}$ and $\mathsf{crs}_{\mathsf{com}}$ are the setup strings of r-iOT and Com respectively.
- **Circuits:** Circuit $\mathcal{C}[c, \mathsf{crs}_{\mathsf{com}}, \beta](r, p) = p$ if $c = \mathsf{Com}(\mathsf{crs}_{\mathsf{com}}, \beta; r)$, else $\mathcal{C}$ outputs $\bot$. Circuit $\mathcal{C}'[\mathsf{crs}_{\mathsf{com}}](c', s, m) = m$ if $c' = \mathsf{Com}(\mathsf{crs}_{\mathsf{com}}, 0; s)$, else it outputs $\bot$.
- **Private Inputs:** S has input bits (m_0, m_1) where $m_0, m_1 \in \{0, 1\}$; R has input choice bit b.
- **Primitives:** Let $\pi_{\mathsf{r\text{-}iOT}} = (\mathsf{r\text{-}iOTR}_1, \mathsf{r\text{-}iOTS}, \mathsf{r\text{-}iOTR}_2, \widetilde{\mathsf{r\text{-}iOTR}})$ denote a receiver obliviously sampleable indistinguishable OT. $(\mathsf{Com}, \widetilde{\mathsf{Com}})$ is an obliviously sampleable commitment scheme. $\mathsf{Garble} = (\mathsf{Gb}, \mathsf{En}, \mathsf{Ev}, \mathcal{S}_{\mathsf{GC}})$ is an equivocal garbling scheme. $\mathsf{Garble}' = (\mathsf{Gb}', \mathsf{En}', \mathsf{Ev}', \widetilde{\mathsf{Gb}}')$ is an obliviously sampleable garbling scheme.

$\mathsf{iOTR}_1(\mathsf{crs}_{\mathsf{iOT}}, b)$:

- R commits to b using randomness r as $c = \mathsf{Com}(b; r)$. Let $|r| = \ell$.
- R computes $\pi_{\mathsf{r\text{-}iOT}}$ receiver messages as $\{\gamma_{0,i}, \gamma_{1,i}\}$ where $\gamma_{b,i} = \mathsf{r\text{-}iOTR}_1(\mathsf{crs}_{\mathsf{r\text{-}iOT}}, r_i)$ and $\gamma_{1-b,i} \leftarrow \widetilde{\mathsf{r\text{-}iOTR}}(\mathsf{crs}_{\mathsf{r\text{-}iOT}})$ for $i \in [\ell]$.
- R sends $\mathsf{M}_{\mathsf{R}} = \left(c, \{\gamma_{0,i}, \gamma_{1,i}\}_{i \in [\ell]}\right)$ as the receiver's message.

$\mathsf{iOTS}(\mathsf{crs}_{\mathsf{iOT}}, \mathsf{M}_{\mathsf{R}}, (m_0, m_1))$:
S runs the following algorithm for $\beta \in \{0, 1\}$:

- S computes $c'_\beta = \mathsf{Com}(0; s_\beta)$. S garbles $(\mathsf{GC}'_\beta, \mathsf{Keys}'_\beta) = \mathsf{Gb}'(1^\kappa, \mathcal{C}'[\mathsf{crs}_{\mathsf{com}}])$. S computes $\{\mathsf{Y}_{\beta,i}\}_{i \in [t+\ell+1]} = \mathsf{En}'(c'_\beta || s_\beta || m_\beta, \mathsf{Keys}'_\beta)$.
- S sets $p_\beta = \{\mathsf{Y}_{\beta,i}\}_{i \in [t]}$ as the garbled input for c'_β corresponding to GC'_β. Let $|p_\beta| = t\kappa$. S garbles another garbled circuit for circuit $\mathcal{C}$ as $(\mathsf{GC}_\beta, \mathsf{Keys}_\beta) = (\mathsf{GC}_\beta, \{\mathsf{X}^0_{\beta,i}, \mathsf{X}^1_{\beta,i}\}_{i \in [\ell+t\kappa]}) = \mathsf{Gb}(1^\kappa, \mathcal{C}[c, \mathsf{crs}_{\mathsf{com}}, \beta])$. Sender sets $\mathsf{X}^p_\beta = \mathsf{En}(p_\beta, \{\mathsf{X}^0_{\beta,i}, \mathsf{X}^1_{\beta,i}\}_{i \in [\ell, \ell+t\kappa]}, \mathsf{Keys}_\beta)$ as the garbled input for p_β corresponding to GC_β.
- S computes $\pi_{\mathsf{r\text{-}iOT}}$ sender messages for receiver's input r in GC_β as $\tau_{\beta,i} = \mathsf{r\text{-}iOTS}(\mathsf{crs}_{\mathsf{r\text{-}iOT}}, \gamma_{\beta,i}, (\mathsf{X}^0_{\beta,i}, \mathsf{X}^1_{\beta,1}))$ for $i \in [\ell]$.

S sends $\mathsf{M}_s = \{\mathsf{M}_{\mathsf{S},\beta}\}_{\beta \in \{0,1\}} = \{\mathsf{GC}_\beta, \mathsf{GC}'_\beta, \{\tau_{\beta,i}\}_{i \in [\ell]}, \mathsf{X}^p_\beta, \{\mathsf{Y}_{\beta,i}\}_{i \in [t,t+\ell]}\}_{\beta \in \{0,1\}}$.

$\mathsf{iOTR}_2(\mathsf{crs}_{\mathsf{iOT}}, \mathsf{M}_{\mathsf{S}}, b)$:

- R computes the wire labels corresponding to commitment randomness r in GC_b as $\mathsf{X}_i = \mathsf{r\text{-}iOTR}_2(\mathsf{crs}_{\mathsf{r\text{-}iOT}}, \tau_{b,i})$ for $i \in [\ell]$. R evaluates GC to receive garbled input U for c'_b corresponding to GC' - $\mathsf{U} = \mathsf{Ev}(\mathsf{GC}, \{\mathsf{X}_i\}_{i \in [\ell+t\kappa]}) = \mathsf{U}$ where $|\mathsf{U}| = t\kappa$.
- R sets $\{\mathsf{Y}_i\}_{i \in [t]} = \{\mathsf{U}_i\}_{i \in t}$ where U_i is the ith chunk of κ bits of U. R outputs $m_b = \mathsf{Ev}'(\mathsf{GC}', \{\mathsf{Y}_i\}_{i \in [t+\ell]})$.

Fig. 3. Constructing iOT with Oblivious Sampleability from r-iOT

To argue sender's indistinguishability security, we point out that the only information about m_{1-b} that the receiver could learn is from the garbled circuit GC'_{1-b}. However, the receiver cannot evaluate GC'_{1-b} to m_{1-b} unless it learns p_{1-b}. As long as the receiver does not learn p_{1-b}, m_{1-b} is computationally hidden by the privacy of the garbling scheme itself. To see why the receiver cannot learn anything about p_{1-b}, observe that the only information about p_{1-b} that

---

$\widetilde{\text{iOTR}}(\text{crs}_{\text{iOT}})$:

R computes $c \leftarrow \widetilde{\text{Com}}(\text{crs}_{\text{com}}; r_{\text{Com}})$ and $\gamma_{\beta,i} \leftarrow \widetilde{\text{r-iOTR}}(\text{crs}_{\text{r-iOT}}; r_{\text{r-iOT},\beta,i})$ for $\beta \in \{0,1\}, i \in [\ell]$. Set $r_{\text{r-iOT}} = \{r_{\text{r-iOT},\beta,i}\}_{\beta \in \{0,1\}, i \in [\ell]}$. R returns $r_{\text{R}} = (r_{\text{Com}}||r_{\text{r-iOT}})$ as the sampling randomness.

$\widetilde{\text{iOTR}}_{\text{Inv}}(\text{crs}, M_{\text{R}}, \text{td} = (\text{td}_{\text{Com}}, \text{td}_{\text{r-iOT}}), r_{\text{R}})$

Denote $r_{\text{R}} = (r_{\text{Com}}||r_{\text{r-iOT}}||b||r)$. Obtain $\widetilde{r_{\text{Com}}} = \widetilde{\text{Com}}_{\text{Inv}}(\text{crs}_{\text{com}}, b, r_{\text{Com}}, \text{td}_{\text{Com}})$ and $\widetilde{r_{\text{r-iOT}}} = \{\text{r-iOTR}_{\text{Inv}}(\text{crs}_{\text{r-iOT}}, \gamma_{\beta,i}, \text{td}_{\text{r-iOT}}, r_{\text{r-iOT},\beta,i})\}_{\beta \in \{0,1\}, i \in [\ell]}$. Return $\tilde{r}_{\text{R}} = (\widetilde{r_{\text{Com}}}||\widetilde{r_{\text{r-iOT}}})$ as the randomness.

$\widetilde{\text{iOTS}}(\text{crs}_{\text{iOT}}, w, m_{1-w}; r_{\text{S}})$:

- S computes $M_{\text{S},1-w}$ correctly corresponding to message m_{1-w} using randomness r_{1-w}.
- For obliviously sampling $M_{\text{S},w}$, S performs the following using randomness r_w: S samples $m_w \leftarrow \{0,1\}$ and obliviously samples garbled circuit as $GC'_w = \widetilde{\text{Gb}}(1^\kappa, \mathcal{C}'[\text{crs}_{\text{com}}], m_w; r_{w,GC'})$. S but correctly garbles $(GC_w, \text{Keys}_w) = \text{Gb}(1^\kappa, \mathcal{C}[c, \text{crs}_{\text{com}}, b]; r_{w,GC})$. Sender samples $\{(X^0_{w,i}, X^1_{w,i})\}_{i \in [\ell]} \leftarrow \{0,1\}^*$ randomly and samples X^p_w and $\{Y_{w,i}\}_{i \in [t,t+\ell]}$ randomly. S computes $\tau_{w,i}$ messages correctly. S sets $M_{s,w} = (GC_w, GC'_w, \{\tau_{w,i}\}_{i \in [\ell]}, X^p_w, \{Y_{w,i}\}_{i \in [t,t+\ell]})$.
- Return $M_{\text{S}} = (M_{\text{S},0}, M_{\text{S},1})$ and randomness $r_{\text{S}} = (r_0||r_1)$.

$\widetilde{\text{iOTS}}_{\text{Inv}}(\text{crs}, w, M_{\text{S}}, \text{td} = \perp, r_{\text{S}})$

- Denote $r_{\text{S}} = (r_0||r_1)$ and set $\widetilde{r_{1-w}} = r_{1-w}$.
- r_w contains the garbling randomness for GC_w, GC'_w and $\{\tau_{w,i}\}_{i \in [\ell]}$ as $r_w = (r_{w,GC}||r_{w,GC'}||r_{w,\text{r-iOT}})$. Set $\widetilde{r_{w,GC}} = r_{w,GC}$, $\widetilde{r_{w,GC'}} = \text{Gb}_{\text{Inv}}(r_{w,GC'}, \text{Keys}'_w, 0^{t+\ell+1})$, where Keys' is the encoding information of GC'. Compute $\widetilde{r_w} = (\widetilde{r_{w,GC}}||\widetilde{r_{w,GC'}}||r_{w,\text{r-iOT}})$.
- Output $\tilde{r}_{\text{S}} = (\tilde{r}_0||\tilde{r}_1)$ and claim that $X^p_w, \{Y_{w,i}\}_{i \in [t,t+\ell]}$ were randomly sampled.

Fig. 4. Oblivious Sampling and Randomness Inversion Algorithms for iOT

the receiver could learn is from the garbled circuit GC_{1-b}. However, the receiver cannot evaluate GC_{1-b} to anything other than $\perp$ since: (1) it cannot prove that c is a commitment to $(1-b)$ under randomness r (this follows from the binding property of the commitment scheme), and (2) it cannot recover any input labels to GC_{1-b} other than those corresponding to r (due to the sender privacy of the underlying r-iOT protocol).

Oblivious Sampleability (Informal). Finally, we argue informally that our new construction satisfies *both* receiver *and* sender oblivious sampleability.

Receiver Oblivious Sampleability. Given that we are starting with an r-iOT protocol that already satisfies receiver oblivious sampleability, arguing receiver oblivious sampleability for our overall construction is straightforward as long as we use a commitment scheme that is obliviously sampleable (this motivates us to use an obliviously sampleable commitment scheme).

Sender Oblivious Sampleability. We now argue that the modified construction also achieves sender oblivious sampleability. To obliviously sample a sender message for the branch $w = (1-b)$, we garble GC_w as per the "real" garbling scheme, but obliviously sample GC'_w (recall that GC'_w is generated using an obliviously sampleable garbling scheme Garble'). The r-iOT messages are computed using the wire labels of GC_w. To demonstrate sampleability, the simulator in the security experiment simply discloses the randomness used in the entire process as the sampling randomness.

The corresponding inversion algorithm takes as input the randomness used for correctly constructing GC_w, GC'_w and r-iOT messages. The simulator can now rely on the oblivious sampleability of the garbling scheme Garble' to claim that GC'_w was, in fact, obliviously sampled. The randomness for the honestly generated r-iOT messages and GC_w is provided as the sampling randomness. This is indistinguishable from an obliviously sampled sender message since in both cases GC_w evaluates to $\perp$.

At this point, we rely on the equivocal property of the garbling scheme Garble to argue that these two cases are indistinguishable since the inputs of GC_w are predetermined from receiver's OT message. This holds true even when the sampling adversary gets all the input wire labels for GC_w from the r-iOT randomness. This is the fundamental reason why we added the extra "layer" of garbling to our protocol. In the formal proof, this argument is a bit more technically involved: we need to also rely on distinguisher dependent simulation techniques [JKKR17,DGH+20]. We refer to the full version of our paper for details.

4   Semi-Adaptive OT from iOT with Oblivious Sampleability

In this section, we show how to build a semi-adaptively simulation-secure two-message OT protocol starting from a two-message iOT protocol with both receiver and sender oblivious sampleability in the static corruption setting. Coupled with our first generic construction from Sect. 3, this completes our roadmap to semi-adaptively simulation-secure two-message OT protocol starting from a two-message r-iOT protocol.

Construction Overview. To generate the receiver OT message, the receiver uses the equivocal commitment scheme to create a commitment c to its choice bit b under some appropriately sampled randomness r. Next, the receiver creates a set of encryptions (e_0, e_1). We need two encryptions instead of one to enable semi-adaptive security (which is discussed later on). The encryption e_b encrypts the commitment randomness r under the trapdoor simulatable PKE scheme using some appropriately sampled randomness s (we explain the intuition for this step subsequently). Meanwhile, $e_{\bar{b}}$ is obliviously sampled. The receiver also creates a set of (parallel) iOT-receiver messages with the bits of r and s as input. The receiver sends across to the sender the commitment c, the encryptions (e_0, e_1) and the iOT-receiver messages.

Upon receiving the receiver's first message, the sender in the semi-adaptive OT protocol uses its input strings m_0 and m_1 to create two circuits (this step is similar to the construction of iOT in Sect. 3). Based on the value of m_β, the garbled circuit GC_β is created.

- If $m_\beta = 1$ then GC_β is obliviously sampled such that it outputs $\bot$.
- Else, for $m_\beta = 0$ the garbled circuit GC_β is of the form (for $\beta \in \{0,1\}$): $C[\beta, c, e_\beta](\cdot, \cdot)$, in the sense that each circuit is hardwired with a bit β, the receiver's commitment c and the receiver's commitment-encryption e_β; each circuit takes as input some randomness r and some randomness s and outputs 0 if all of the following conditions are satisfied: (a) c is a valid commitment to β under randomness r, (b) e_β is a valid encryption of r under randomness s. Otherwise it outputs $\bot$. The sender then garbles these circuits using the garbling algorithm (for $m_\beta = 0$) and oblivious garbling algorithm ($m_\beta = 1$) to create a pair of garbled circuits GC_0 and GC_1, along with the corresponding wire labels for their input bits.

The sender finally sends across GC_0 and GC_1 to the receiver. In parallel, the sender uses the iOT messages from the receiver to generate one iOT-sender message for each pair of wire labels, and also sends all of these to the receiver. The receiver uses the iOT-sender messages to recover the wire labels corresponding to its randomness strings (r, s) for both garbled circuits GC_0 and GC_1. It then evaluates GC_b on r and s by using the corresponding wire labels to recover the correct message m_b (it sets m_b to 0 if the GC_b evaluates to 0; otherwise, it sets m_b to 1).

Detailed Construction. Figure 5 presents a detailed description of our semi-adaptively simulation-secure two-message OT protocol π_{OT} in the CRS model from the following ingredients: (1) a two-message iOT protocol π_{iOT} with both receiver and sender oblivious sampleability in the CRS model and in the static corruption setting, (2) a trapdoor simulatable PKE, (3) an obliviously sampleable garbling scheme Garble, and (4) an equivocal commitment scheme Com (in the CRS model). We state the following theorem.

Theorem 6. *Assuming that: (1) π_{iOT} is a two-message iOT protocol with sender and receiver oblivious sampleability in the CRS model, (2) Com is an equivocal commitment scheme, (3) Garble is a private and an obliviously sampleable garbling scheme, and (4) the PKE scheme is trapdoor simulatable, π_{OT} is simulation-secure in the CRS-model against semi-adaptive malicious corruption of parties.*

The formal security proof is deferred to the full version of the paper. We present below an informal overview of the arguments for static and semi-adaptive security for our constructions.

Security against statically corrupt sender. The commitment c computationally hides the receiver's choice bit b because the encryption (e_0, e_1) computationally hides the receiver's randomness string r used for the commitment, and the iOT

π_{OT}

- **Public Inputs:** $\mathsf{crs}_{OT} = (\mathsf{crs}_{iOT}, \mathsf{crs}_{com})$ where crs_{iOT} and crs_{com} are the setup strings of iOT and Com, respectively. Circuit $C[c, \mathsf{crs}_{com}, \mathsf{crs}_{pk}, \beta, e, \mathsf{pk}](r, s) = 0$ if $c = \mathsf{Com}(\mathsf{crs}_{com}, b; r) \wedge e = \mathsf{Enc}(\mathsf{crs}_{pk}, \mathsf{pk}, r; s)$; otherwise C outputs $\perp$.
- **Private Inputs:** S has input bits (m_0, m_1) where $m_0, m_1 \in \{0,1\}$; R has input choice bit b.
- **Primitives:** Let $\pi_{iOT} = (\mathsf{iOTR}_1, \mathsf{iOTS}, \mathsf{iOTR}_2, \widetilde{\mathsf{iOTR}}, \widetilde{\mathsf{iOTS}})$ denote an iOT with (R, S)-oblivious sampling. Com is an equivocal commitment scheme. pk is the public key of a trapdoor simulatable PKE. Garble $= (\mathsf{Gb}, \mathsf{En}, \mathsf{Ev}, \widetilde{\mathsf{Gb}})$ is an obliviously sampleable garbling scheme.

$\mathsf{OTR}_1(\mathsf{crs}_{OT}, b)$:

- R commits to b using randomness r as $c = \mathsf{Com}(b; r)$.
- R encrypts r using randomness s as $e_b = \mathsf{Enc}(\mathsf{crs}_{pk}, \mathsf{pk}, r; s)$. R samples $e_{\bar{b}} \leftarrow \mathsf{oEnc}(\mathsf{crs}_{pk}, \mathsf{pk})$ obliviously. Let $t = (r\|s)$ denote the commitment and encryption randomness, where $|t| = \ell$.
- R computes $\{\gamma_{0,i}, \gamma_{1,i}\}$ where $\gamma_{b,i} = \mathsf{iOTR}_1(\mathsf{crs}_{iOT}, t_i)$ and $\gamma_{\bar{b},i} \leftarrow \widetilde{\mathsf{iOTR}}(\mathsf{crs}_{iOT})$ for $i \in [\ell]$.
- R sends $M_R = (c, e_0, e_1, \{\gamma_{0,i}, \gamma_{1,i}\}_{i \in [\ell]})$ as the receiver's OT message.

$\mathsf{OTS}(\mathsf{crs}_{OT}, M_R, (m_0, m_1))$:
S runs the following algorithm for $\beta \in \{0,1\}$:

- If $m_\beta = 0$ then S computes the garbled circuit and input encoding as $(\mathsf{GC}_\beta, \{\mathsf{X}^0_{\beta,i}, \mathsf{X}^1_{\beta,i}\}_{i \in [\ell]}) = \mathsf{Gb}(1^\kappa, C[c, \mathsf{crs}_{com}, \mathsf{crs}_{pk}, \beta, e_\beta, \mathsf{pk}])$. S computes the iOT sender messages as $\tau_{\beta,i} = \mathsf{iOTS}(\mathsf{crs}_{iOT}, \gamma_{\beta,i}, (\mathsf{X}^0_{\beta,i}, \mathsf{X}^1_{\beta,i}))$ for $i \in [\ell]$.
- If $m_\beta = 1$ then S obliviously samples garbled circuit as $\mathsf{GC}_\beta = \widetilde{\mathsf{Gb}}(1^\kappa, C[c, \mathsf{crs}_{com}, \mathsf{crs}_{pk}, \beta, e_\beta, \mathsf{pk}], \perp)$. S obliviously samples the iOT sender messages as $\tau_{\beta,i} \leftarrow \widetilde{\mathsf{iOTS}}(\mathsf{crs}_{iOT}, \beta)$ for $i \in [\ell]$.

S sends $M_S = \{\mathsf{GC}_0, \{\tau_{0,i}\}_{i \in [\ell]}, \mathsf{GC}_1, \{\tau_{1,i}\}_{i \in [\ell]}\}$ as the sender's OT message

$\mathsf{OTR}_2(\mathsf{crs}_{OT}, M_S, b)$:

- R computes the wire labels corresponding to commitment and encryption randomness t in GC_b as $\mathsf{Y}_i = \mathsf{iOTR}_2(\mathsf{crs}_{iOT}, \tau_{b,i}, b)$ for $i \in [\ell]$.
- R outputs $m_b = 0$ if $\mathsf{Ev}(\mathsf{GC}, \{\mathsf{Y}_i\}_{i \in [\ell]}) = 0$ else R outputs $m_b = 1$.

Fig. 5. Semi-adaptively Simulation-Secure Oblivious Transfer

messages sent by the receiver computationally hide the receiver's randomness string s for encryption.

A corrupt sender's messages can be extracted by a simulator $\mathcal{S}$. The simulator $\mathcal{S}$ constructs the commitment c in equivocal mode, i.e. $c = \mathsf{Com}(0; r_0) = \mathsf{Com}(1; r_1)$. The encryptions are set as follows - e_0 is an encryption of r_0 under randomness s_0 and e_1 is an encryption of r_1 under randomness s_1. $\mathcal{S}$ runs the two set of iOT messages correctly with input choice bits $t_0 = (r_0\|s_0)$ and $t_1 = (r_1\|s_1)$. Upon obtaining sender's OT message, the simulator decrypts input wire labels for both GC_0 and GC_1. $\mathcal{S}$ evaluates GC_0 and GC_1 to extract m_0 and m_1 respectively.

Security against statically corrupt receiver. A corrupt receiver learns no information about $m_{\bar{b}}$. To see why this is the case, observe that the only information about $m_{\bar{b}}$ that the receiver could learn is from the garbled circuit $GC_{\bar{b}}$. However, the receiver cannot evaluate $GC_{\bar{b}}$ to anything other than $\bot$ since: (1) it cannot prove that c is a commitment to $\bar{b}$ under randomness r (this follows from the binding property of the commitment scheme), (2) it cannot prove that $e_{\bar{b}}$ decrypts to anything other than the commitment randomness r (this follows from the correctness of decryption for the PKE scheme), and (3) it cannot recover any input labels to $GC_{\bar{b}}$ other than those corresponding to r (due to the sender privacy of the underlying iOT protocol). At this point, we invoke the privacy (when $m_{\bar{b}} = 0$) or oblivious sampleability (when $m_{\bar{b}} = 1$) of the garbling scheme to argue that the receiver learns no information about the message $m_{\bar{b}}$. Sender privacy follows from the privacy (when $m_{\bar{b}} = 0$) and oblivious sampleability (when $m_{\bar{b}} = 1$) of the garbling scheme, binding of the commitment scheme and the sender privacy of iOT. A corrupt receiver cannot obtain both wire labels for any input wire of a garbled circuit due to sender privacy of iOT. Given this argument holds, an honestly generated garbled circuit $GC_{\bar{b}}$ is indistinguishable from an obliviously sampled one since in both cases the receiver evaluates $GC_{\bar{b}}$ to $\bot$.

Next, we show a simulator that extracts a corrupt receiver's input. The receiver's input can be extracted using the secret key associated with the public key in the crs. The simulator decrypts e_0 and e_1 to obtain candidate randomness r_0 and r_1. It then checks whether $c = \mathsf{Com}(0; r_0)$ or $c = \mathsf{Com}(1; r_1)$. If both conditions are satisfied then the corrupt receiver has broken the binding property of the commitment scheme. Otherwise, the receiver's choice bit can be uniquely extracted. This completes our overview for static security.

Overview of Semi-adaptive Simulation-Security. Let us denote the set of OT messages for the bth branch (resp. $\bar{b}$th branch) as the bth set(resp. $\bar{b}$th set). Semi-adaptive simulation security considers two corruption scenarios: 1) the receiver gets corrupted post execution and the sender is statically corrupt, or 2) the receiver is statically corrupt and the sender gets corrupted post execution. In either of the cases, the simulator plays the role of the honest party which gets corrupted post-execution. The simulator needs to extract the input of the statically corrupt party. Also, when the honest party gets corrupted post execution, the simulator obtains the input of the honest party. The simulator needs to show randomness for the party such that the randomness is consistent with the party's input. We consider two corruption cases:

1. We first consider the case where the receiver gets corrupted post execution and the sender is statically corrupt. The simulator constructs the receiver OT message as described above. When the receiver gets corrupted post-execution the simulator shows randomness for the construction of e_b and claims that $c = \mathsf{Com}(b; r_b)$. It also claims that $e_{\bar{b}}$ and the iOT sender messages for the $\bar{b}$th set were obliviously sampled. Indistinguishability follows due to the equivocal property of the commitment scheme, the oblivious ciphertext sampleability of the encryption scheme, and the receiver sampleability of iOT.

2. Next we consider the case where the sender gets corrupted post-execution and the receiver is statically corrupted. In this setting the simulator $\mathcal{S}$ extracts the choice bit b from the receiver's OT message. The simulator invokes the OT functionality $\mathcal{F}_{\mathsf{OT}}$ with b to obtain m_b. $\mathcal{S}$ constructs GC_b and the iOT sender messages for the bth set correctly. $\mathcal{S}$ also constructs $\mathsf{GC}_{\bar{b}}$ and iOT sender messages for the $\bar{b}$th set correctly as if $m_{\bar{b}} = 0$. This helps to equivocate the sender's view if $m_{\bar{b}}$ turns out to be 1 when the sender gets corrupted post-execution. We know that the evaluation of $\mathsf{GC}_{\bar{b}}$ always yields $\perp$ since c is not a valid commitment to $\bar{b}$. If the simulator is required to show randomness for $m_{\bar{b}} = 1$ then the simulator claims that $\mathsf{GC}_{\bar{b}}$ and the iOT sender messages for $\bar{b}$th set were obliviously sampled. This is indistinguishable from the real world execution where they were actually obliviously sampled. Thus, we rely on the sender oblivious sampling property of iOT and the oblivious sampling property of the garbling scheme to argue security.

5   Trapdoor Simulatable PKE from r-iOT

In this section, we show that any (two-message) r-iOT protocol implies a trapdoor simulatable PKE. The work of [CDMW09] constructed a two-round augmented NCE protocol from any trapdoor simulatable PKE scheme. This implies that any (two-message) r-iOT protocol implies a two-round augmented NCE protocol.

We actually show that any (two-message) iOT protocol satisfying *both* receiver *and* sender oblivious sampleability implies a trapdoor simulatable PKE. Since we already showed in Sect. 3 that any (two-message) r-iOT protocol implies that a (two-message) iOT protocol satisfying both receiver and sender oblivious sampleability, this yields our desired result.

Our Construction. Let $\mathsf{iOT} = (\mathsf{Setup}_{\mathsf{iOT}}, \mathsf{iOTR}_1, \mathsf{iOTS}, \mathsf{iOTR}_2)$ be an indistinguishability based OT. We construct a trapdoor simulatable PKE as follows:

- $\mathsf{Setup}(1^\kappa)$: Sample and output $(\mathsf{crs}, \mathsf{td}) \leftarrow \mathsf{Setup}_{\mathsf{iOT}}(1^\kappa)$.
- $\mathsf{Gen}(\mathsf{crs})$: Sample $\mathsf{M_R} = \mathsf{iOTR}_1(\mathsf{crs}, 0; \mathsf{rr_R})$ for uniformly sampled receiver randomness $\mathsf{rr_R}$. Output $(\mathsf{pk}, \mathsf{sk}) = (\mathsf{M_R}, \mathsf{rr_R})$.
- $\mathsf{Enc}(\mathsf{crs}, \mathsf{pk} = \mathsf{M_R}, m)$: Sample $m' \leftarrow \{0, 1\}$ and generate the OT sender message $\mathsf{M_S} \leftarrow \mathsf{iOTS}(\mathsf{crs}, \mathsf{M_R}, (m, m'))$. Output the ciphertext $\mathsf{ct} = \mathsf{M_S}$.
- $\mathsf{Dec}(\mathsf{crs}, \mathsf{sk}, \mathsf{ct} = \mathsf{M_S})$: Output $m' = \mathsf{iOTR}_2(\mathsf{crs}, \mathsf{sk}, \mathsf{M_S})$.

Additionally, suppose that iOT is equipped with the oblivious sampling algorithms - $(\widetilde{\mathsf{iOTR}}, \widetilde{\mathsf{iOTS}})$ for the receiver and sender, and the corresponding inverting algorithms - $(\widetilde{\mathsf{iOTR}}_{\mathsf{Inv}}, \widetilde{\mathsf{iOTS}}_{\mathsf{Inv}})$. We design the trapdoor simulatable PKE to have oblivious sampling algorithms (oGen, oEnc) and randomness inverting algorithms (rGen, rEnc) defined as follows:

- oGen(crs; $\widetilde{rr}_G$): Sample $\widetilde{M}_R = \widetilde{iOTR}(crs; \widetilde{rr}_G)$ and output $\widetilde{pk} = \widetilde{M}_R$.
- oEnc(crs; $\widetilde{rr}_E$): Sample $m' \leftarrow \{0,1\}$ and $\widetilde{M}_S = \widetilde{iOTS}(crs, 0, m'; \widetilde{rr}_E)$. Output $\widetilde{ct} = \widetilde{M}_S$.
- rGen(crs, rr_G, td): Generate $M_R = iOTR_1(crs, 0; rr_G)$ and output

$$\widehat{rr}_G = \widetilde{iOTR_{Inv}}(crs, M_R, td, rr_G).$$

- rEnc(crs, m, rr_G, rr_E, td): Generate the following:

$$M_R = iOTR_1(crs, 0; rr_G), \quad M_S = iOTS(crs, M_R, (m, m); rr_E),$$

and output

$$\widehat{rr}_E = \widetilde{iOTR_{Inv}}(crs, M_R, M_S, td, rr_G, rr_E).$$

Correctness of decryption follows immediately from the correctness of the underlying iOT scheme.

Theorem 7. *Our construction of trapdoor simulatable PKE is IND-CPA secure assuming that iOT satisfies indistinguishability security against a semi-honest sender and a semi-honest receiver.*

Theorem 8. *Our construction of trapdoor simulatable PKE satisfies trapdoor oblivious sampleability and randomness inversion assuming that iOT satisfies oblivious receiver and sender sampleability.*

The formal proofs are deferred to the full version of our paper. At a high level, ensuring oblivious sampleability (correspondingly randomness inversion) of the public key and ciphertexts in the resulting trapdoor simulatable PKE are relatively straightforward; one can simply reuse the receiver and sender oblivious sampling (correspondingly randomness inversion) algorithms provided by the iOT for obliviously sampling (correspondingly, inverting the randomness of) the public key and the ciphertext, respectively.

6   Instantiations of R-iOT from Concrete Assumptions

In this section we briefly discuss our instantiations of r-iOT from isogeny-based assumptions, CDH and LPN.

6.1   Instantiation from Isogeny-Based Assumptions

In this section, we show how to construct a two-message r-iOT protocol secure against malicious adversaries in the CRS model from certain isogeny-based assumptions (notably, CSIDH [CLM+18] or CSI-FiSh [BKV19]). We base our construction on the existence of a secure *(restricted) effective group action* (EGA) equipped with appropriate computational hardness assumptions as described in [ADMP20]. We then rely on known instantiations of such a group action from the aforementioned isogeny-based assumptions.

In the rest of the section, we rely on the notations and formal definitions of EGA introduced in [ADMP20]. We refer the reader to [ADMP20] and to the full version of our paper for background material on group actions and EGA. We simply state here that our construction of r-iOT from group actions relies on the existence of a weak pseudorandom EGA, which is essentially the analogue of the DDH assumption in the context of group actions. As pointed out in [ADMP20], a weak pseudorandom EGA can be instantiated from isogeny-based assumptions, such as the decisional CSIDH assumption [CLM+18] and counterpart assumption in the setting of CSI-FiSh [BKV19].

The starting point of our construction of r-iOT is the construction of iOT from any (restricted) EGA proposed originally in [ADMP20]. This construction already satisfies indistinguishability-based security against maliciously corrupted sender and the receiver in the static corruption model. The key feature that this construction does not provide is receiver oblivious sampleability.

It turns out that we could argue that this construction satisfies receiver oblivious sampleability in a straightforward manner if we had the ability to sample obliviously from the "set" of a (restricted) EGA by "hashing into" the set. However, this is a well-known open problem in the isogeny literature and is likely to require fundamentally new ideas beyond state-of-the-art techniques for isogeny-based cryptography (see [Pet17, DMPS19, CPV20] for more details).

Our Construction. Our core technical centerpiece is a workaround for this wherein we settle for a weaker notion of *trapdoor oblivious sampleability* for the "set" of a (restricted) EGA. In other words, while it is hard to obliviously sample a "set" element in the plain model, one can obliviously sample a "set" element given a specially designed trapdoor (corresponding to some public CRS). This is the core idea behind our construction of r-iOT from (restricted) EGA. In view of the inherent restrictions outlined earlier, our workaround only allows us to achieve an r-iOT construction in the CRS model (and not in the plain model). Our construction of r-iOT from any weak pseudorandom (restricted) EGA is summarized in Fig. 6. Note that the sender and receiver algorithms remain unchanged from the original iOT construction due to [ADMP20].

Theorem 9. *Let $(G, X, \star)$ be a weak pseudorandom EGA (as introduced in [ADMP20]). The protocol in Fig. 6 is an r-iOT protocol in the CRS model.*

The formal proof is deferred to the full version of our paper. We provide a proof overview here.

Private Inputs: S has input bits (m_0, m_1); R has input choice bit b.

Primitives: $(G, X, \star)$ is a weak pseudorandom EGA with initial set element x_0 and $H : X^\ell \to \{0, 1\}$ is a pairwise independent hash function.

Setup(1^κ):

- Sample and $g, h \leftarrow G$, and set $x_1 = g \star x_0$ and $x_2 = h \star x_0$.
- Sample $t \leftarrow G$ and compute $y_0 = t \star x_0, y_1 = t \star x_1$ and $y_2 = t \star x_2$.
- Set $\mathsf{crs}_{\text{r-iOT}} = (x_0, x_1, x_2, y_0, y_1, y_2)$ and $\mathsf{td}_{\text{r-iOT}} = (g, h, t)$.

r-iOTR$_1$($\mathsf{crs}_{\text{r-iOT}}, b$): Sample $s \leftarrow G$ and output $\mathsf{M_R}$ computed as follows:

$$\mathsf{M_R} = (u, v) = (s \star x_b, s \star y_b), \quad \mathsf{st} = s.$$

r-iOTS($\mathsf{crs}_{\text{r-iOT}}, \mathsf{M_R}, (m_0, m_1)$): For each $\beta \in \{0, 1\}$, uniformly sample

$$\mathbf{r}_\beta = (r_{\beta,1}, \ldots, r_{\beta,\ell}) \leftarrow G^\ell, \quad \mathbf{b}_\beta = (b_{\beta,1}, \ldots, b_{\beta,\ell}) \leftarrow \{0, 1\}^\ell.$$

For each $i \in [\ell]$ and for each $\beta \in \{0, 1\}$, compute

$$c_{\beta,i} = \begin{cases} r_{\beta,i} \star x_\beta & \text{if } b_{\beta,i} = 0 \\ r_{\beta,i} \star y_\beta & \text{if } b_{\beta,i} = 1 \end{cases}, \quad c'_{\beta,i} = \begin{cases} r_{\beta,i} \star u & \text{if } b_{\beta,i} = 0 \\ r_{\beta,i} \star v & \text{if } b_{\beta,i} = 1. \end{cases}$$

For $\beta \in \{0, 1\}$, define the vectors $\mathbf{c}_\beta, \mathbf{c}'_\beta \in X^\ell$ as:

$$\mathbf{c}_\beta := (c_{\beta,1}, \ldots, c_{\beta,\ell}), \quad \mathbf{c}'_\beta := (c'_{\beta,1}, \ldots, c'_{\beta,\ell}).$$

For $\beta \in \{0, 1\}$, compute $z_\beta = H(\mathbf{c}'_\beta) \oplus m_\beta$, and output the sender message

$$\mathsf{M_S} = ((\mathbf{c}_0, z_0), (\mathbf{c}_1, z_1)).$$

r-iOTR$_2$($\mathsf{crs}_{\text{r-iOT}}, \mathsf{M_S}; \mathsf{st} = s$): Output m_b computed as follows:

$$m_b = H(s \star c_1, \ldots, s \star c_\ell) \oplus z_b.$$

---

r-iOTR̃($\mathsf{crs}_{\text{r-iOT}}$): Sample $s \leftarrow G$ and output $\widetilde{\mathsf{M_R}} = (s \star x_2, s \star y_2)$.

r-iOTR̃$_{\mathsf{Inv}}$ ($\mathsf{crs}_{\text{r-iOT}}, \mathsf{M_R}, \mathsf{td}_{\text{r-iOT}}, \mathsf{rr}$): Represent $\mathsf{rr} = (b||s)$ and $\mathsf{td}_{\text{r-iOT}} = (g, h, t)$. If $b = 0$ then output $\hat{s} = sh^{-1}$, else output $\hat{s} = sgh^{-1}$.

Fig. 6. Construction of r-iOT from weak pseudorandom EGA

Perfect Receiver Privacy. The receiver's choice bit b is perfectly hidden from the point of view of a (computationally unbounded) malicious receiver, even given $\mathsf{crs}_{\text{r-iOT}}$ and $\mathsf{M_R} = (u, v)$. We show this by assuming $b = 1$ (the same argument holds when $b = 0$). If receiver computes (u, v) using randomness s when $b = 1$, then the same (u, v) can be shown as a valid receiver message for $b = 0$ using randomness $s' = sg$. In particular, we have $(u, v) = (sg \star x_0, sg \star y_0)$, since $x_1 = g \star x_0$ and $y_1 = t \star x_1 = tg \star x_0 = g \star (t \star x_0) = g \star y_0$.

Computational Sender Privacy. We show the following that there must be some bit $w \in \{0,1\}$ such that

$$\text{r-iOTS}(\text{crs}_{\text{iOT}}, M_R, (m_0, m_1)) \overset{c}{\approx} \text{r-iOTS}(\text{crs}_{\text{iOT}}, M_R, (m'_0, m'_1)),$$

where $m_{1-w} = m'_{1-w}$ and $m_w \neq m'_w$. We first modify the setup string to $\text{crs}'_{\text{r-iOT}}$ such that $y_0 = t_0 \star x_0$ and $y_1 = t_1 \star x_1$ where $t_0 \neq t_1$. We argue that $\text{crs}_{\text{r-iOT}}$ and $\text{crs}'_{\text{r-iOT}}$ are computationally indistinguishable based on the weak pseudorandomness of EGA.

Next, we argue that under the modified CRS $\text{crs}'_{\text{r-iOT}}$, there must be some bit $w \in \{0,1\}$ such that M_S statistically hides m_w irrespective of the manner in which a malicious receiver generates the message M_R. It allows us to move to a hybrid where the sender's message is modified to m'_w. The proof is very similar to the proof of Lemma 4.10 of [ADMP20].

Finally, we change the setup string back to $\text{crs}_{\text{r-iOT}}$ as in the real protocol. This switch is again computationally indistinguishable based on the weak pseudorandomness of EGA. At this point, the sender's message is distributed as $\text{r-iOTS}(\text{crs}_{\text{iOT}}, M_R, (m'_0, m'_1))$, as desired. We refer to the full version of our paper for the formal proof.

Receiver Oblivious Sampleability. Finally, we claim that an obliviously sampleable receiver's message is distributed identically to an honestly generated message, even given the sampling randomness. In particular:

- If the receiver's choice bit $b = 0$, then $(u, v) = (s \star x_0, s \star y_0)$ generated using randomness s can be claimed as obliviously sampled using randomness $\hat{s} = sh^{-1}$, since $(u, v) = ((sh^{-1}) \star x_2, (sh^{-1}) \star y_2)$.
- If the receiver's choice bit $b = 1$, then $(u, v) = (s \star x_1, s \star y_1)$ generated using randomness s can be claimed as obliviously sampled using randomness $\hat{s} = sgh^{-1}$, since $(u, v) = ((sgh^{-1}) \star x_2, (sgh^{-1}) \star y_2)$.

6.2 Instantiation from CDH or LPN

To instantiate r-iOT from CDH or LPN, we rely on the iOT constructions of [DGH+20]. Specifically, Döttling *et al.* showed that iOT can be constructed from a weaker notion of OT called elementary OT, and they demonstrated instantiations of elementary OT from CDH or LPN assumption. The generic transformation of [DGH+20] is done in two steps: (1) they first show how to build iOT from an intermediate primitive called search OT via parallel repetition (which preserves receiver oblivious sampleability), (2) they show how to construct search OT from elementary OT where the receiver's message in search OT is identical to that of elementary OT.

Since the generic transformation of [DGH+20] does not affect *receiver* oblivious sampleability, it suffices to show that their elementary OT constructions from CDH or LPN *inherently* satisfy the receiver oblivious sampleability property. The corresponding proofs are immediate from the constructions in [DGH+20]. We refer the reader to the full version of our paper for more details.

Acknowledgements. The work of Pratik Sarkar is supported by the DARPA SIEVE project and NSF awards 1931714, 1414119.

References

[AAAS+19] Alagic, G., et al.: Status report on the first round of the NIST post-quantum cryptography standardization process. US Department of Commerce, National Institute of Standards and Technology (2019)

[AASA+20] Alagic, G., et al.: Status report on the second round of the NIST post-quantum cryptography standardization process. US Department of Commerce, NIST (2020)

[ADMP20] Alamati, N., De Feo, L., Montgomery, H., Patranabis, S.: Cryptographic group actions and applications. In: Moriai, S., Wang, H. (eds.) ASIACRYPT 2020, Part II. LNCS, vol. 12492, pp. 411–439. Springer, Cham (2020). https://doi.org/10.1007/978-3-030-64834-3_14

[BBD+20] Brakerski, Z., Branco, P., Döttling, N., Garg, S., Malavolta, G.: Constant ciphertext-rate non-committing encryption from standard assumptions. In: Pass, R., Pietrzak, K. (eds.) TCC 2020, Part I. LNCS, vol. 12550, pp. 58–87. Springer, Cham (2020). https://doi.org/10.1007/978-3-030-64375-1_3

[BD18] Brakerski, Z., Döttling, N.: Two-message statistically sender-private OT from LWE. In: Beimel, A., Dziembowski, S. (eds.) TCC 2018, Part II. LNCS, vol. 11240, pp. 370–390. Springer, Cham (2018). https://doi.org/10.1007/978-3-030-03810-6_14

[BKV19] Beullens, W., Kleinjung, T., Vercauteren, F.: CSI-FiSh: efficient isogeny based signatures through class group computations. In: Galbraith, S.D., Moriai, S. (eds.) ASIACRYPT 2019, Part I. LNCS, vol. 11921, pp. 227–247. Springer, Cham (2019). https://doi.org/10.1007/978-3-030-34578-5_9

[BL18] Benhamouda, F., Lin, H.: k-round multiparty computation from k-round oblivious transfer via garbled interactive circuits. In: Nielsen, J.B., Rijmen, V. (eds.) EUROCRYPT 2018, Part II. LNCS, vol. 10821, pp. 500–532. Springer, Cham (2018). https://doi.org/10.1007/978-3-319-78375-8_17

[BLPV18] Benhamouda, F., Lin, H., Polychroniadou, A., Venkitasubramaniam, M.: Two-round adaptively secure multiparty computation from standard assumptions. In: Beimel, A., Dziembowski, S. (eds.) TCC 2018, Part I. LNCS, vol. 11239, pp. 175–205. Springer, Cham (2018). https://doi.org/10.1007/978-3-030-03807-6_7

[Can01] Canetti, R.: Universally composable security: a new paradigm for cryptographic protocols. In: 42nd FOCS, pp. 136–145. IEEE Computer Society Press, October 2001

[CCD+20] Chen, M., et al.: Multiparty generation of an RSA modulus. In: Micciancio, D., Ristenpart, T. (eds.) CRYPTO 2020. LNCS, vol. 12172, pp. 64–93. Springer, Cham (2020). https://doi.org/10.1007/978-3-030-56877-1_3

[CDD+04] Canetti, R., Damgard, I., Dziembowski, S., Ishai, Y., Malkin, T.: Adaptive versus non-adaptive security of multi-party protocols. J. Cryptol. **17**(3), 153–207 (2004). https://doi.org/10.1007/s00145-004-0135-x

[CDMW09] Choi, S.G., Dachman-Soled, D., Malkin, T., Wee, H.: Improved non-committing encryption with applications to adaptively secure protocols. In: Matsui, M. (ed.) ASIACRYPT 2009. LNCS, vol. 5912, pp. 287–302. Springer, Heidelberg (2009). https://doi.org/10.1007/978-3-642-10366-7_17

[CFGN96] Canetti, R., Feige, U., Goldreich, O., Naor, M.: Adaptively secure multi-party computation. In: 28th ACM STOC, pp. 639–648. ACM Press, May 1996

[CGP15] Canetti, R., Goldwasser, S., Poburinnaya, O.: Adaptively secure two-party computation from indistinguishability obfuscation. In: Dodis, Y., Nielsen, J.B. (eds.) TCC 2015, Part II. LNCS, vol. 9015, pp. 557–585. Springer, Heidelberg (2015). https://doi.org/10.1007/978-3-662-46497-7_22

[CJL+16] Chen, L., et al.: Report on post-quantum cryptography, vol. 12. US Department of Commerce, National Institute of Standards and Technology (2016)

[CKWZ13] Choi, S.G., Katz, J., Wee, H., Zhou, H.-S.: Efficient, adaptively secure, and composable oblivious transfer with a single, global CRS. In: Kurosawa, K., Hanaoka, G. (eds.) PKC 2013. LNCS, vol. 7778, pp. 73–88. Springer, Heidelberg (2013). https://doi.org/10.1007/978-3-642-36362-7_6

[CLM+18] Castryck, W., Lange, T., Martindale, C., Panny, L., Renes, J.: CSIDH: an efficient post-quantum commutative group action. In: Peyrin, T., Galbraith, S. (eds.) ASIACRYPT 2018, Part III. LNCS, vol. 11274, pp. 395–427. Springer, Cham (2018). https://doi.org/10.1007/978-3-030-03332-3_15

[CLOS02] Canetti, R., Lindell, Y., Ostrovsky, R., Sahai, A.: Universally composable two-party and multi-party secure computation. In: 34th ACM STOC, pp. 494–503. ACM Press, May 2002

[CPR17] Canetti, R., Poburinnaya, O., Raykova, M.: Optimal-rate non-committing encryption. In: Takagi, T., Peyrin, T. (eds.) ASIACRYPT 2017, Part III. LNCS, vol. 10626, pp. 212–241. Springer, Cham (2017). https://doi.org/10.1007/978-3-319-70700-6_8

[CPV17a] Canetti, R., Poburinnaya, O., Venkitasubramaniam, M.: Better two-round adaptive multi-party computation. In: Fehr, S. (ed.) PKC 2017, Part II. LNCS, vol. 10175, pp. 396–427. Springer, Heidelberg (2017). https://doi.org/10.1007/978-3-662-54388-7_14

[CPV17b] Canetti, R., Poburinnaya, O., Venkitasubramaniam, M.: Equivocating Yao: constant-round adaptively secure multiparty computation in the plain model. In: Hatami, H., McKenzie, P., King, V. (eds.) 49th ACM STOC, pp. 497–509. ACM Press, June 2017

[CPV20] Castryck, W., Panny, L., Vercauteren, F.: Rational isogenies from irrational endomorphisms. In: Canteaut, A., Ishai, Y. (eds.) EUROCRYPT 2020, Part II. LNCS, vol. 12106, pp. 523–548. Springer, Cham (2020). https://doi.org/10.1007/978-3-030-45724-2_18

[CsW19] Cohen, R., Shelat, A., Wichs, D.: Adaptively secure MPC with sublinear communication complexity. In: Boldyreva, A., Micciancio, D. (eds.) CRYPTO 2019, Part II. LNCS, vol. 11693, pp. 30–60. Springer, Cham (2019). https://doi.org/10.1007/978-3-030-26951-7_2

[CSW20] Canetti, R., Sarkar, P., Wang, X.: Efficient and round-optimal oblivious transfer and commitment with adaptive security. In: Moriai, S., Wang, H. (eds.) ASIACRYPT 2020. LNCS, vol. 12493, pp. 277–308. Springer, Cham (2020). https://doi.org/10.1007/978-3-030-64840-4_10

[DGH+20] Döttling, N., Garg, S., Hajiabadi, M., Masny, D., Wichs, D.: Two-round oblivious transfer from CDH or LPN. In: Canteaut, A., Ishai, Y. (eds.) EUROCRYPT 2020, Part II. LNCS, vol. 12106, pp. 768–797. Springer, Cham (2020). https://doi.org/10.1007/978-3-030-45724-2_26

[DMPS19] De Feo, L., Masson, S., Petit, C., Sanso, A.: Verifiable delay functions from supersingular isogenies and pairings. In: Galbraith, S.D., Moriai, S. (eds.) ASIACRYPT 2019, Part I. LNCS, vol. 11921, pp. 248–277. Springer, Cham (2019). https://doi.org/10.1007/978-3-030-34578-5_10

[EGL82] Even, S., Goldreich, O., Lempel, A.: A randomized protocol for signing contracts. In: Chaum, D., Rivest, R.L., Sherman, A.T. (eds.) CRYPTO'82, pp. 205–210. Plenum Press, New York (1982)

[FMV19] Friolo, D., Masny, D., Venturi, D.: A black-box construction of fully-simulatable, round-optimal oblivious transfer from strongly uniform key agreement. In: Hofheinz, D., Rosen, A. (eds.) TCC 2019, Part I. LNCS, vol. 11891, pp. 111–130. Springer, Cham (2019). https://doi.org/10.1007/978-3-030-36030-6_5

[GGHR14] Garg, S., Gentry, C., Halevi, S., Raykova, M.: Two-round secure MPC from indistinguishability obfuscation. In: Lindell, Y. (ed.) TCC 2014. LNCS, vol. 8349, pp. 74–94. Springer, Heidelberg (2014). https://doi.org/10.1007/978-3-642-54242-8_4

[GMW87] Goldreich, O., Micali, S., Wigderson, A.: How to play any mental game or a completeness theorem for protocols with honest majority. In: Aho, A., (ed.) 19th ACM STOC, pp. 218–229. ACM Press, May 1987

[GP15] Garg, S., Polychroniadou, A.: Two-round adaptively secure MPC from indistinguishability obfuscation. In: Dodis, Y., Nielsen, J.B. (eds.) TCC 2015, Part II. LNCS, vol. 9015, pp. 614–637. Springer, Heidelberg (2015). https://doi.org/10.1007/978-3-662-46497-7_24

[GS12] Garg, S., Sahai, A.: Adaptively secure multi-party computation with dishonest majority. In: Safavi-Naini, R., Canetti, R. (eds.) CRYPTO 2012. LNCS, vol. 7417, pp. 105–123. Springer, Heidelberg (2012). https://doi.org/10.1007/978-3-642-32009-5_8

[GS18] Garg, S., Srinivasan, A.: Two-round multiparty secure computation from minimal assumptions. In: Nielsen, J.B., Rijmen, V. (eds.) EUROCRYPT 2018, Part II. LNCS, vol. 10821, pp. 468–499. Springer, Cham (2018). https://doi.org/10.1007/978-3-319-78375-8_16

[GWZ09] Garay, J.A., Wichs, D., Zhou, H.-S.: Somewhat non-committing encryption and efficient adaptively secure oblivious transfer. In: Halevi, S. (ed.) CRYPTO 2009. LNCS, vol. 5677, pp. 505–523. Springer, Heidelberg (2009). https://doi.org/10.1007/978-3-642-03356-8_30

[HK12] Shai Halevi and Yael Tauman Kalai: Smooth projective hashing and two-message oblivious transfer. J. Cryptol. 25(1), 158–193 (2012). https://doi.org/10.1007/s00145-010-9092-8

[HV15] Hazay, C., Venkitasubramaniam, M.: On black-box complexity of universally composable security in the CRS model. In: Iwata, T., Cheon, J.H. (eds.) ASIACRYPT 2015, Part II. LNCS, vol. 9453, pp. 183–209. Springer, Heidelberg (2015). https://doi.org/10.1007/978-3-662-48800-3_8

[IKN+17] Ion, M., et al.: Private intersection-sum protocol with applications to attributing aggregate ad conversions. Cryptology ePrint Archive, Report 2017/738 (2017). https://eprint.iacr.org/2017/738

[JKKR17] Jain, A., Kalai, Y.T., Khurana, D., Rothblum, R.: Distinguisher-dependent simulation in two rounds and its applications. In: Katz, J., Shacham, H. (eds.) CRYPTO 2017, Part II. LNCS, vol. 10402, pp. 158–189. Springer, Cham (2017). https://doi.org/10.1007/978-3-319-63715-0_6

[LGdSG21] Lai, Y.-F., Galbraith, S.D., Delpech de Saint Guilhem, C.: Compact, efficient and UC-secure isogeny-based oblivious transfer. In: Canteaut, A., Standaert, F.-X. (eds.) EUROCRYPT 2021. LNCS, vol. 12696, pp. 213–241. Springer, Cham (2021). https://doi.org/10.1007/978-3-030-77870-5_8

[LJA+18] Lapets, A., et al.. Accessible privacy-preserving web-based data analysis for assessing and addressing economic inequalities. In: Proceedings of the 1st ACM SIGCAS Conference on Computing and Sustainable Societies, pp. 1–5 (2018)

[LP09] Lindell, Y., Pinkas, B.: A proof of security of Yao's protocol for two-party computation. J. Cryptol. **22**(2), 161–188 (2008). https://doi.org/10.1007/s00145-008-9036-8

[MW16] Mukherjee, P., Wichs, D.: Two round multiparty computation via multi-key FHE. In: Fischlin, M., Coron, J.-S. (eds.) EUROCRYPT 2016, Part II. LNCS, vol. 9666, pp. 735–763. Springer, Heidelberg (2016). https://doi.org/10.1007/978-3-662-49896-5_26

[Nao91] Naor, M.: Bit commitment using pseudorandomness. J. Cryptol. **4**(2), 151–158 (1991). https://doi.org/10.1007/BF00196774

[NP01] Naor, M., Pinkas, B.: Efficient oblivious transfer protocols. In: Rao Kosaraju, S. (ed.) 12th SODA, pp. 448–457. ACM-SIAM, January 2001

[Pet17] Petit, C.: Faster algorithms for isogeny problems using torsion point images. In: Takagi, T., Peyrin, T. (eds.) ASIACRYPT 2017, Part II. LNCS, vol. 10625, pp. 330–353. Springer, Cham (2017). https://doi.org/10.1007/978-3-319-70697-9_12

[PVW08] Peikert, C., Vaikuntanathan, V., Waters, B.: A framework for efficient and composable oblivious transfer. In: Wagner, D. (ed.) CRYPTO 2008. LNCS, vol. 5157, pp. 554–571. Springer, Heidelberg (2008). https://doi.org/10.1007/978-3-540-85174-5_31

[Rab05] Rabin, M.O.: How to exchange secrets with oblivious transfer. Cryptology ePrint Archive, Report 2005/187 (2005). https://eprint.iacr.org/2005/187

[unb] Unbound security. https://www.unboundtech.com

[Yao86] Yao, A.C.C.: How to generate and exchange secrets (extended abstract). In: 27th FOCS, pp. 162–167. IEEE Computer Society Press, October 1986

[YKT19] Yoshida, Y., Kitagawa, F., Tanaka, K.: Non-committing encryption with quasi-optimal ciphertext-rate based on the DDH problem. In: Galbraith, S.D., Moriai, S. (eds.) ASIACRYPT 2019. LNCS, vol. 11923, pp. 128–158. Springer, Cham (2019). https://doi.org/10.1007/978-3-030-34618-8_5

Reverse Firewalls for Adaptively Secure MPC Without Setup

Suvradip Chakraborty[1]($\boxtimes$), Chaya Ganesh[2]($\boxtimes$), Mahak Pancholi[3]($\boxtimes$),
and Pratik Sarkar[4]($\boxtimes$)

[1] IST Austria, Klosterneuburg, Austria
[2] IISc Bangalore, Bengaluru, India
[3] Aarhus University, Aarhus, Denmark
[4] Boston University, Boston, USA

Abstract. We study Multi-party computation (MPC) in the setting of subversion, where the adversary tampers with the machines of honest parties. Our goal is to construct actively secure MPC protocols where parties are corrupted adaptively by an adversary (as in the standard adaptive security setting), and in addition, honest parties' machines are compromised.

The idea of reverse firewalls (RF) was introduced at EUROCRYPT'15 by Mironov and Stephens-Davidowitz as an approach to protecting protocols against corruption of honest parties' devices. Intuitively, an RF for a party $\mathcal{P}$ is an external entity that sits between $\mathcal{P}$ and the outside world and whose scope is to sanitize $\mathcal{P}$'s incoming and outgoing messages in the face of subversion of their computer. Mironov and Stephens-Davidowitz constructed a protocol for passively-secure two-party computation. At CRYPTO'20, Chakraborty, Dziembowski and Nielsen constructed a protocol for secure computation with firewalls that improved on this result, both by extending it to *multi*-party computation protocol, and considering *active* security in the presence of *static* corruptions.

In this paper, we initiate the study of RF for MPC in the *adaptive* setting. We put forward a definition for adaptively secure MPC in the reverse firewall setting, explore relationships among the security notions, and then construct reverse firewalls for MPC in this stronger setting of adaptive security. We also resolve the open question of Chakraborty, Dziembowski and Nielsen by removing the need for a trusted setup in constructing RF for MPC.

Towards this end, we construct reverse firewalls for adaptively secure augmented coin tossing and adaptively secure zero-knowledge protocols and obtain a constant round adaptively secure MPC protocol in the reverse firewall setting without setup. Along the way, we propose a new multi-party adaptively secure coin tossing protocol in the plain model, that is of independent interest.

S. Chakraborty—Received funding from the European Research Council (ERC) under the European Union's Horizon 2020 research and innovation programme (682815 - TOCNeT).

P. Sarkar—Received funding from NSF grants 1931714, 1414119.

© International Association for Cryptologic Research 2021
M. Tibouchi and H. Wang (Eds.): ASIACRYPT 2021, LNCS 13091, pp. 335–364, 2021.
https://doi.org/10.1007/978-3-030-92075-3_12

1 Introduction

The standard definitions of security in cryptographic protocols are under the assumption that honest parties can completely trust the machines that implement their algorithms. However, such an assumption may be unwarranted in the real world. The security guarantees of cryptosystems depend on the adversarial model which, however, often makes idealized assumptions that are not always realized in actual implementations. Several practical attacks in the real-world exploit *implementation* details of an algorithm rather then treating it as a "black-box". In addition, users may be forced to use hardware built by companies with expertise, and software that are mandated by standardization agencies. The capability of the adversary to "tamper" with the implementation is not captured by security models in classical cryptography. This model is not overkill, as we now know by Snowden [4] revelations that one of potential mechanisms for large scale mass surveillance is compromise of security by subversion of cryptographic standards, and tampering of hardware. The threat of an adversary modifying the implementation so that the subverted algorithm remains indistinguishable from the specification in black-box behavior, while leaking secrets was originally studied by Young and Yung as kleptography [33], and in the setting of subliminal channels by Simmons [32]. Since Snowden revelations brought to light actual deployment of such attacks, there is renewed attention, and has led cryptographers to model such tampering in the security definition in order to closely capture real-world concerns.

Reverse Firewalls. The *cryptographic reverse firewall* (RF) framework was introduced by Mironov and Stephens-Davidowitz [28] in the context of designing protocols secure against adversaries that can corrupt users' machines in order to compromise their security. A reverse firewall for a party $\mathcal{P}$ is an external intermediate machine that modifies the incoming and outgoing messages sent by $\mathcal{P}$'s machine. In essence, a reverse firewall sits between a party $\mathcal{P}$ and the external world, and "sanitizes" the messages that are sent and received by $\mathcal{P}$. Note that the party does not put any trust in the RF, meaning that it does not share any secrets with the firewall. This rules out trivial solutions like a trusted RF that simply keeps $\mathcal{P}$'s secrets and runs on $\mathcal{P}$'s behalf. Instead, the goal is for an uncorrupted[1] RF to provide meaningful security guarantees even in the case that an honest party's machine has been tampered with. Consider an arbitrary protocol that satisfies some notions of functionality and security. A reverse firewall for a protocol is said to be *functionality-maintaining* if the resulting protocol (protocol with a firewall for party $\mathcal{P}$) achieves the same functionality as the original protocol. Roughly, the RF should not ruin the functionality of the underlying protocol, in the sense that the protocol with an RF for a party should still work as expected in case no subversion takes place. At the same time, the RF is expected to preserve security. An RF is said to preserve security if the

---

[1] The RF being corrupt is not interesting in the active setting, since the corrupt RF and the other party together can be thought of as the adversary.

protocol *with* the firewall is secure even when an honest party's implementation is tampered with to behave in an arbitrarily corrupt way. Finally, an RF should provide *exfiltration-resistance*, i.e., regardless of how the user's machine behaves, the presence of the RF will prevent the machine from leaking any information to the outside world.

The work of [28] provides a construction of a two-party passively secure computation protocol with a reverse firewall. The recent work of [12] generalizes reverse firewalls for secure computation by showing feasibility of reverse firewalls for Multi Party Computation (MPC). They give a construction of reverse firewalls for secure computation in a stronger and general setting that handles multiple parties, and consider protocols in the malicious security model.

RFs in other settings have been constructed including key exchange and secure message transmission [14,20], oblivious transfer [14,20], digital signatures [2], and zero-knowledge proofs (ZK) [23]. Reverse firewalls has also been used in a practical context in the design of *True2F* [16], a system that is based on a firewalled key generation and ECDSA signature generation with potential applications in cryptocurrency wallets.

1.1   Our Results

In this work, we take forward the study of reverse firewalls in the setting of MPC. We begin by proposing definitions that capture the requirements of an RF for MPC in the presence of *adaptive* corruptions. We then explore relationships among them the notions. Next, we turn our attention to constructing RFs for maliciously secure protocols in the presence of adaptive corruptions. Towards this end, we construct protocols with reverse firewalls for multi-party augmented coin tossing, zero-knowledge, and coin tossing, all in the presence of adaptive corruptions. We then use the above building blocks to construct a maliciously secure MPC in the presence of adaptive corruptions together with a reverse firewall. We further elaborate on the contributions in this work.

On the relationship between definitions. As our first contribution, we revisit the different notions of subversion security for MPC protocols in the presence of RF. The work of [28] defined the notions of *security preservation* (SP) and *exfiltration resistance* (ER) as the properties required from an RF. SP asks that an RF preserve the security properties of the underlying protocol for an honest party even when the honest party's implementation is tampered with. ER is concerned with a type of attack called exfiltration, where an honest party's tampered implementation attempts to leak secrets. A reverse firewall that is exfiltration resistant prevents an adversary from learning secrets even when the honest party's machine is tampered with. Roughly, exfiltration resistance for a party P_i asks that the transcripts produced in the following two ways are *indistinguishable*: (i) by running the protocol with the RF for P_i whose implementation has been arbitrarily subverted and in the presence of other malicious parties, (ii) by running the protocol with the RF for honest implementation of P_i in the presence of other malicious parties. In [28], it was shown that for certain indistinguishability-based security notions like semantic security of an encryption scheme, an exfiltration resistant RF is also security preserving. It was postulated in [28] that, in general, when security requirements are simulation-based, ER *does not* imply SP. Surprisingly, we establish that exfiltration resistance *implies* security preservation for a reverse firewall when the security of the underlying protocol is simulation-based (computational) MPC security. For simulation-based security, this implication was only known for special functionalities like zero-knowledge. Our definitional implication shows that ER is the "right" notion for RF in the MPC setting; for new constructions, we need only construct RFs that are exfiltration resistant for each of the parties, and when all honest parties have an RF, security preservation for the protocol follows in the presence of malicious parties and arbitrary tampering of honest parties' implementations. In the other direction, [28] showed that a security preserving RF is not necessarily ER when the underlying security does not promise privacy.

Reverse firewalls for adaptively secure MPC. The adaptive security notion for an MPC protocol models the realistic threat that an adversary can corrupt a party during the execution of a protocol. Adaptive security is much harder to achieve than static security for MPC. In the reverse firewall setting, capturing a technical formulation of the adaptive security notion requires some care. When a party gets adaptively corrupted, the adversary can learn all of that party's inputs and internal random coins. Consider an MPC protocol where an honest party deploys a firewall; now adaptively corrupting this party amounts to the adversary learning the composed state of the party with its reverse firewall. Typically, for reverse firewalls, security preservation means that the underlying security properties hold even under subversion. In the adaptive security case, we ask that adaptive security holds under subversion, where the adaptive adversary can learn the *composed state* of an adaptively corrupt party. Defining exfiltration resistance in the adaptive case needs some care. Here, we ask that the adversary not be able to distinguish between a tampered implementation of party P and an honest implementation, where the adversary can specify tampered implementations for initially honest parties and corrupt parties adaptively in the execution. While exfiltration resistance is not meaningful anymore once P gets corrupt in the middle of the protocol, our definition asks that up *until the point* that P gets corrupted, exfiltration resistance hold. Intuitively, the definition says that if P gets corrupted in the middle of execution, the adversary can see the composed state of P (the state of P composed with the state of the RF). Even given this state, the adversary should not be able to say if until corruption it was interacting with P composed with RF or $\tilde{P}$ composed with RF, where $\tilde{P}$ is a tampered implementation for P.

We construct reverse firewalls for *maliciously* secure MPC protocols in the presence of *adaptive* corruptions in the plain model. Similar to [12], we consider RFs for functionality-maintaining tampering (see Sect. 3).

Theorem 1. *(Informal) Assuming DDH and LWE assumptions, there exists an $\mathcal{O}(1)$ round actively secure MPC protocol with reverse firewalls that is secure against adaptive corruptions in the* urs *model.*

Later, we generate (Theorem 3) the urs using an adaptively secure coin tossing protocol in the *plain* model based on the Discrete Logarithm (DLOG) and the Knowledge of Exponent (KEA) assumption in a different group. We consider this to be a result of independent interest, and further elaborate on the coin tossing protocol in the technical overview section.

Our approach is to construct an MPC protocol along the lines of GMW [26], and add reverse firewall to this protocol. That is, our construction is essentially an *adaptive compiler*: it takes a semi-honest adaptively secure MPC protocol and runs [26]-like steps in the reverse firewall setting to yield an adaptively secure MPC protocol with reverse firewalls. Towards this, we design adaptively secure protocols for augmented coin tossing and zero-knowledge, and construct reverse firewalls for each of the sub-protocols used in the compiler. Finally, we show that the compiled MPC protocol is adaptively secure in the presence of tampering of honest parties. We state each of the results below.

- *Reverse firewall for ZK:* Zero-knowledge in the presence of subversion have been studied in the form of parameter subversion for NIZK [5], and in the RF setting for a class of interactive protocols called malleable sigma protocols [23]. In this work, we consider interactive ZK since we aim for protocols without setup. Our protocol is a variant of the adaptively secure ZK protocol of [11] which is in the Uniform Random String (urs) model. Finally, we show how to design an RF for this protocol.

Theorem 2. *(Informal) Assuming LWE, there exists a three round actively secure ZK protocol with reverse firewalls that is secure against adaptive corruption of parties in the* urs *model.*

- *Reverse firewall for augmented coin-tossing:* We provide a construction of an adaptively-secure multi-party augmented coin-tossing protocol. Similar to our ZK protocol, our augmented coin-tossing protocol is also in the urs model. The main building block of our augmented coin tossing protocol is an adaptively-secure commitment scheme (in the urs model) which is additively homomorphic over the message and randomness spaces. We then show how to construct an RF for this protocol.

Since our adaptively-secure augmented coin-tossing and ZK protocols are in the urs model, the compiled MPC protocol is also in the urs model. However, in the subversion setting we consider, a trusted setup is not available since a setup is susceptible to subversion too. For instance, the security guarantees of NIZKs completely break down in the face of subversion of the CRS [5]. To circumvent the need for a trusted setup, we show how to generate the urs needed by our adaptively secure MPC protocol securely in the presence of subversion by presenting a multi-party coin tossing protocol with a reverse firewall in the plain model.

Adaptively secure coin tossing in plain model. As a contribution of independent interest, we construct an adaptively secure multi-party coin tossing protocol in the *plain model* under the knowledge of exponent (KEA) assumption. Our use of non-black-box assumptions seems justified, in light of the result of [24] that shows that it is not possible to construct an adaptively secure multi-party protocol with respect to black-box simulators without giving up on round efficiency in the plain model[2]. We use our coin-tossing protocol to generate the urs of our MPC protocol.

Theorem 3. *(Informal) Assuming DLOG, KEA and LWE assumptions, there exists a $\mathcal{O}(1)$ actively secure multi-party coin-tossing protocol that is secure against adaptive corruptions in the plain model.*

We then show how to add reverse firewalls to our adaptively secure coin tossing protocol. Finally, putting everything together, we obtain an *adaptively* secure MPC protocol with reverse firewall in the *plain* model. This resolves the open question posed in [12] of removing the trusted setup assumption in constructing MPC protocols with reverse firewalls.

1.2   Technical Overview

We provide a high-level overview of our construction, which can be viewed as an adaptive compiler for MPC protocols in the RF setting following the blueprint of [26]. The main idea of the [26] compiler is as follows: Each party (i) runs an instance of an augmented multi-party coin-tossing protocol to obtain a uniformly random string that it is committed to, (ii) commits to its input and broadcasts the input commitment to every other party, (iii) runs the underlying semi-honest adaptively secure MPC protocol, while proving in zero-knowledge that the computations have been done correctly. Since our goal is adaptive security, we start with an adaptively secure semi-honest protocol. Our compiler will use adaptively secure augmented coin-tossing and adaptively-secure ZK protocols in the plain model.

Adding reverse firewalls. The protocol outlined above requires randomness in the augmented coin-tossing protocol and the ZK protocol. The rest of the MPC protocol is deterministic given the coins and the randomness of the ZK protocol. We propose an adaptively secure multi-party augmented coin-tossing protocol Π_{coin} and an adaptively secure (input-delayed) ZK protocol Π_{zk}. We then design reverse firewalls for these protocols and show that they provide exfiltration resistance for tampered parties. Then, by invoking our theorem that an exfiltration resistant RF is security preserving, we get that the RFs preserve security of the above protocols. We now explain them in more detail below.

- $\Pi_{\mathsf{a\text{-}coin}}$ *using reverse firewalls*: Our augmented coin-tossing uses the "commit-then-open" paradigm. At the end of this protocol, the initiating party (say, P_i) obtains a random string r_i along with the appropriate decommitment information, whereas all other parties $\{P_j\}_{j \in [n] \setminus i}$ obtain the (same) commitment to r_i. We assume that the message and randomness spaces of the commitment scheme

---

[2] If we had a coin tossing protocol with black-box simulation, we could use it to transform a two round adaptively secure MPC protocol in the URS model [10] to a protocol in the plain model by generating the URS via the coin toss protocol.

form an additive group and the commitment scheme is *additively homomorphic* over these spaces. In the first round, each party $\{P_j\}_{j \in [n] \setminus i}$ sample their own randomness r_j and s_j, commits to the random coin r_j using s_j and broadcasts the commitment $c_j = \mathsf{Com}(r_j; s_j)$. In the second round, party P_i samples its own randomness (r_i, s_i), and broadcasts the commitment $c_i = \mathsf{Com}(r_i; s_i)$ to all other parties. Finally, in the third round all parties $\{P_j\}_{j \in [n] \setminus i}$ broadcast their respective openings (r_j, s_j). Party P_i then obtains the final string as $R = \sum_{k \in [n]} r_k$, and locally computes the commitment c_i as $c = \mathsf{Com}(R; S)$, where $S = \sum_{k \in [n]} s_k$. All other parties can compute the same commitment c using the commitment c_i (broadcast by P_i) and the decommitment information of all other parties (broadcast in the final round) exploiting the homomorphic property of Com. We show that the above protocol is adaptively secure if the underlying commitment scheme Com is adaptively secure.

Consider the case when the initiating party P_i is tampered. In this case, the other malicious parties can launch an *input trigger attack* by sending a malformed commitment string which may serve as a wake up message to P_i. Besides, in the second round, tampered P_i can sample bad randomness and exfiltrate secrets via the commitment string c_i. When the receiving parties are corrupt, the commitment strings and their openings could also serve as a subliminal channel. The main idea of the RF is to exploit the homomorphic properties of Com to *sanitize* the incoming and outgoing messages. However, it must ensure that this mauling is consistent with the views of all parties. In particular, RF_i for P_i rerandomizes the commitment c_i to a fresh commitment $\hat{c}_i$ by choosing fresh randomness (r_i', s_i'), computing $c_i' = \mathsf{Com}(r_i'; s_i')$ and homomorphically adding them. In the final round, when all the parties send their openings (r_j, s_j), RF_i computes an additive secret sharing of r_i' and s_i' (sampled in the above step) and sanitizes each of these openings using the appropriate shares. Thus, the views of all the parties are consistent in this firewalled protocol and the final coin is also guaranteed to be random (since the offsets r_i' and s_i' were sampled randomly). Note that, the final commitment C computed by all the parties does not provide any channel to exfiltrate (since both R and S are random at the end of the firewalled execution). The detailed protocol together with the RF is in Sect. 5.1.

- Π_{zk} *using reverse firewalls* : Next, we need a ZK protocol to show conformance of each step of the protocol specification. We construct a reverse firewall for (a variant of) the adaptively secure ZK protocol of [11]. The protocol of [11] is based on the Sigma protocol of [21] where the prover sends a first message, the verifier sends a random bit string as a challenge, and the prover sends a response in a third message. Towards constructing a reverse firewall, we observe that the prover's messages can be re-randomized if the underlying primitives are homomorphic. However, the challenge string cannot be re-randomized, without also mauling the response provided by the prover. The ZK protocol of [11] does not seem to have this malleable property. Therefore, we modify the protocol, where the verifier's challenge is generated as the result of a coin-tossing protocol. This ensures that the challenge is indeed random, and after the firewall sanitizes, both the prover and the verifier have the same challenge string. Therefore, the firewall can sanitize the protocol without the need to explicitly maul the response from the prover. The modified protocol remains adaptively secure. Note that the protocol also retains the input-delayed property – only the last round of the ZK protocol depends on the statement being proven and the corresponding witness. This allows running the first two rounds of the protocol before the inputs in the MPC protocol are defined. During the MPC protocol, the parties compute the input commitments and the protocol messages which define the statement and the witness. The last round of the ZK protocol is run after this is defined, thus helping to preserve the round complexity of the underlying semi-honest adaptively-secure MPC protocol.

The idea behind a firewall for a tampered party in this modified ZK protocol, is to re-randomize the prover's first message in the coin tossing homomorphically, thus ensuring that the verifier's challenge in the sigma protocol is random. We show reverse firewalls for the prover and the verifier, and prove exfiltration resistance.

We obtain the above protocols in the urs model by instantiating the semi-honest MPC protocol and the underlying primitives in the urs model based on DDH and LWE (see Sects. 5.1 and 5.3). Next, we generate the urs using an adaptively-secure coin tossing protocol to remove the setup assumption.

Adaptively secure coin tossing in the plain model. In order to remove the setup, we construct a constant round multi-party coin tossing protocol Π_{coin} in the plain model that generates the urs required by the MPC protocol. In addition to Discrete Log (DL) and Learning With Errors (LWE) assumption, we rely on knowledge of exponent assumption (KEA) assumption in pairing groups. Since it is *impossible* to construct a constant round adaptively secure coin-tossing protocol in the plain model from black-box simulation techniques [24], our reliance on the KEA assumption seems justified. The only other adaptively secure coin-tossing protocol in the plain model by Garg and Sahai [24] uses Barak's non-blackbox technique, and it is non-trivial to extend this protocol in the RF setting. Therefore, we craft a new RF-compatible protocol from scratch.

The high-level idea behind our Π_{coin} protocol is as follows: There is an initial coin-tossing phase that sets up a public key of a homomorphic, obliviously sampleable encryption scheme. In subsequent steps, there is another coin-tossing phase where parties exchange commitments to their coins together with encryption of the commitment randomness under the public key generated in the previous coin-toss. The protocol uses the Pedersen commitment scheme – an *equivocal*, *perfectly hiding* commitment scheme, and a public key encryption scheme with additional properties. Π_{coin} consists of four phases - parameter generation phase, commitment generation phase, commitment opening phase and output phase.

In the first phase, the parties generate pairwise Pedersen commitment parameters and pairwise encryption key. For the commitment parameter, one party is the committer and the other party is the verifier; and the verifier additionally proves knowledge of the commitment trapdoor. The public key is of an encryption scheme that satisfies the following properties: oblivious ciphertext sampling, oblivious public key sampling and additive homomorphism of ciphertexts and public keys. The parameter generation is repeated by reversing the roles. In the commitment generation phase, each party generates its random coin and commits (as the committer) to it pairwise using the pairwise commitment parameters generated in the previous phase. Each party also sends two encryptions e_0 and e_1: if the committed coin is $b \in \{0,1\}$, then e_b is an encryption of the randomness used to commit to the coin, and e_{1-b} is sampled obliviously. Upon obtaining pairwise commitments to the random coins, the parties open their commitments pairwise by sending the decommitment randomness and encryption randomness for b to the pairwise verifiers. e_{1-b} is claimed to be obliviously sampled. Each party also broadcasts its random coin b. In the output phase, each party verifies the pairwise commitment openings and that correct ciphertext is an encryption of the commitment randomness. If all the openings are correct and they are consistent with the broadcasted coins then the parties output the final coin by summing up all the broadcasted coins.

This protocol is adaptively secure if the commitment is equivocal and perfectly hiding. The simulator needs to bias the output coin to a simulated coin. It is performed as follows: In the parameter generation phase, the verifier proves knowledge of trapdoor using a sub-protocol. When the verifier is corrupt, a non-black-box assumption allows extraction of the trapdoor. When the committer is corrupt, the simulator receives the commitment and the public key, samples a key pair, rewinds the committer and sets its own oblivious key such that they homomorphically combine to the honestly sampled key. Now, the simulator knows the corresponding secret key. The simulator extracts the committed coins of the malicious parties in the commitment generation phase. In the opening phase the simulator equivocates (using the extracted trapdoors) the pairwise commitments and the coins broadcasted on behalf of the honest parties such that the final output coin is equal to the simulated output coin. Once the committer opens its public key in the first coin-toss, the simulator can rewind and force the output of this coin-toss phase to be a public key for which the simulator knows the secret key. In the subsequent coin-tossing phase where parties exchange commitment to their coins together with encryption of the commitment randomness, the simulator can extract the value committed. Crucially, the simulator can extract the committed coin of the corrupt committer *before* the adversary can see the output of the coin toss allowing it to simulate. When the committer is honest, the simulator can explain the ciphertexts as encrypting the correct values.

Adding reverse firewalls to the coin tossing protocol. We exploit the homomorphism property of the underlying commitment and public-key encryption scheme to sanitize round messages. In addition to this, the RF computes pairing equations in order to verify validity of messages.

On the setup assumption. The work of [12] required a structured setup due its augmented coin-tossing protocol. In their coin tossing protocol the receiving parties obtain commitments to the sender's coin, which is different from the commitment generated by the sender. As a result, during the later part of the protocol the RF needs to maul the proofs using a controlled-malleable NIZK (cm-NIZK) as the statement being proven by the sender is different from the one being verified by the receiving parties. Unfortunately, cm-NIZKs are not known in the adaptive setting. We modify the coin-tossing protocol such that every party obtains the *same* commitment string, and hence the proof statement remains unchanged. Thus, we can use an interactive ZK protocol without needing controlled malleability (re-randomizability suffices), and this allows us to rely on urs instead of crs. Finally, we can use the coin-tossing protocol (in the plain model) to remove the need for urs.

Finally, in all our protocols we rely on the existence of broadcast channels in the RF setting. We implicitly use the protocol of [12], who showed how to implement broadcast channels in the RF setting.

1.3   Other Related Work

Besides the reverse firewall framework, other directions that address the challenge of protecting cryptosystems against different forms of subversion are reviewed below.

Algorithm Substitution Attacks. Bellare, Patterson, and Rogaway [7] initiated the study of subversion of symmetric encryption schemes in the form of algorithm-substitution attacks (ASAs). They show that such subversion of the encryption algorithm is possible in a way that is undetectable. They also show that deterministic, stateful, ciphers are secure against this type of ASAs. Subsequent works redefined and strengthened the notion in several aspects [6,17], and extended the ASA model to other contexts, like digital signatures schemes [2], public key encryption [13].

Backdooring. Motivated by the backdooring of the DUAL EC DRBG [31], a formal study of backdooring of PRGs was initiated in [19], where public parameters are surreptitiously generated together with secret backdoors by a saboteur that allows to bypass security while remaining secure to any adversary that does not know the backdoor. Parameter subversion has been considered for several primitives, including pseudorandom generators [18,19], non-interactive zero knowledge [5], and public-key encryption [3].

Watchdogs and Self-guarding. Another approach taken in [8,29,30] is to consider an external entity called a watchdog that is trusted to test whether a given cryptographic implementation is compliant with its specification via black-box access. Self-guarding is another approach to counter subversion [22]. The idea here is to not depend on external entities, instead assume a trusted initialization phase where the cryptosystem is unsubverted.

2   Preliminaries

Notation. We write PPT to denote a probabilistic polynomial time machine. We denote the security parameter by λ. For an integer $n \in \mathbb{N}$, we denote by $[n]$ the set $\{1, 2, \cdots, n\}$ and for any pair of integers $1 < i < j \leq n$, we denote by $[i, j]$ the set $\{i, i+1, \cdots, j\}$. For a distribution or random variable X, we denote $x \leftarrow X$ the action of sampling an element x according to X. For any integer $m \in \mathbb{N}$, we write U_m to denote the uniform distribution over all m-bit strings. We denote by $\mathbb{G}$ the multiplicative group where DDH assumption holds. The corresponding field is denoted by $\mathbb{Z}_q$. We denote a negligible function in λ as $\mathsf{neg}(\lambda)$.

Required Primitives. A public key encryption scheme $\mathsf{PKE} = (\mathsf{Gen}, \mathsf{Enc}, \mathsf{Dec})$ satisfies *oblivious ciphertext sampling* if there exists a polynomial time algorithm oEnc which obliviously samples a ciphertext s.t. it looks indistinguishable from a real ciphertext. Additionally, we require the PKE to satisfy *additive homomorphism* over message and randomness space, i.e. $\mathsf{Enc}(\mathsf{pk}, m; r) \cdot \mathsf{Enc}(\mathsf{pk}, m'; r') = \mathsf{Enc}(\mathsf{pk}, m + m'; r + r')$. We denote a commitment scheme as $\mathsf{Com} = (\mathsf{Gen}, \mathsf{Com}, \mathsf{Verify})$. It is *equivocal* if there exists a polynomial time algorithm Equiv that equivocates a commitment to open to any message, given the trapdoor of the commitment parameters. We need an adaptively secure commitment scheme and we use the definition of [10]. We also need the commitment scheme to satisfy additively homomorphic property like the PKE scheme. We present a version of Elgamal commitment scheme without setup as follows. Given a generator $g \in \mathbb{G}$, the committer commits to a field element $m \in \mathbb{Z}_q$ by sampling randomness $x, r \leftarrow \mathbb{Z}_q$ and sets $c = (c_1, c_2, c_3) = (g^x, g^r, g^m g^{rx}) = (h, g^r, g^m h^r)$. The tuple (x, r) serves as the decommitment information. It is *perfectly* binding and computationally hiding due to the DDH assumption. We also require an *input-delayed* (interactive) ZK protocol $\mathit{\Pi}_{zk} = (\mathsf{Gen}, \mathsf{P}, \mathsf{V})$, i.e., only the last message from the prover to the verifier should depend on the statement. We use the ZK definitions of [11].

Bilinear Groups and Knowledge of Exponent Assumption [1]. Let $\mathcal{BGG}$ denote a bilinear group generator. It takes in input the security parameter λ and outputs $(\mathbb{G}, \mathbb{H}, q, g, e)$ where $\mathbb{G}$ and $\mathbb{H}$ is a pair of groups of prime order q where g is a generator of group $\mathbb{G}$, and e is a non-degenerate bilinear map defined as $e : \mathbb{G} \times \mathbb{G} \to \mathbb{H}$ for which $e(g^a, g^b) = e(g, g)^{ab}$ for $a, b \in \mathbb{Z}_q$ and $e(g, g) \neq 1_{\mathbb{H}}$.

Definition 1. (Discrete Log Assumption) *For every non-uniform poly-time algorithm $\mathcal{A}$, the following holds:*

$$\Pr[\mathit{pub} \leftarrow \mathcal{BGG}(1^\lambda), h \leftarrow \mathbb{G}, w \leftarrow \mathcal{A}(\mathit{pub}, h) : g^w = h] \leq \mathsf{neg}(\lambda)$$

Definition 2. (Knowledge of Exponent Assumption). *For every non uniform poly-time algorithm $\mathcal{A}$ there exists a non-uniform poly-time algorithm $\mathcal{X}_{\mathcal{A}}$, the extractor such that:*

$$\Pr[\mathit{pub} \leftarrow \mathcal{BGG}(1^\lambda), x \leftarrow \mathbb{Z}_q, (A, \hat{A}; a) \leftarrow (\mathcal{A}||\mathcal{X}_{\mathcal{A}})(\mathit{pub}, g^x) :$$

$$\hat{A} = A^x \wedge A \neq g^a] \leq \mathsf{neg}(\lambda)$$

where $(A, \hat{A}; a) \leftarrow (\mathcal{A}||\mathcal{X}_{\mathcal{A}})(\mathit{pub}, g^x)$ means that $\mathcal{A}$ and $\mathcal{X}_{\mathcal{A}}$ are executed on the same input (pub, g^x) and the same random tape, and $\mathcal{A}$ outputs $(A, \hat{A})$ whereas $\mathcal{X}_{\mathcal{A}}$ outputs a.

Definition 3 ([26] Multi-party Parallel Coin-Tossing into the Well). *An n-party augmented coin-tossing into the well protocol is an n-party protocol for securely computing the functionality $(1^\lambda, \cdots, 1^\lambda) \to (U_t, U_t, \ldots, U_t)$, where U_t denotes the uniform distribution over t-bit strings.*

Definition 4 ([26] Multi-party Augmented Parallel Coin-Tossing into the Well). *An n-party augmented coin-tossing into the well protocol is an n-party protocol for securely computing the functionality* $(1^\lambda, \cdots, 1^\lambda) \rightarrow ((U_t, U_{t\cdot\lambda}), \mathsf{Com}(U_t; U_{t\cdot\lambda}), \cdots, \mathsf{Com}(U_t; U_{t\cdot\lambda}))$ *with respect to a fixed commitment scheme* $\mathsf{Com} = (\mathsf{Gen}, \mathsf{Com}, \mathsf{Verify})$ *which requires* λ *random bits to commit to each bit, and* U_t *denotes the uniform distribution over t-bit strings.*

Next, we define adaptive security for MPC in the stand-alone setting. Let us assume that an adversary $\mathcal{A}$ runs a protocol Π with parties $(P_1, \ldots, P_n)$ to compute function f on inputs $\vec{x}$. $\mathcal{A}$ adaptively corrupts parties P_i in the set C, for $i \in$ C. We denote the real world adversary view of the protocol as $\mathsf{REAL}_{\Pi,(\mathsf{C},\mathcal{A})}(\lambda, \vec{x}, z)$. Let us denote $\mathsf{REAL}_{\Pi,(\mathsf{C},\mathcal{A})}$ as the distribution ensemble $\{\mathsf{REAL}_{\Pi,(\mathsf{C},\mathcal{A})}(\lambda, \vec{x}, z)\}_{\lambda \in \mathbb{N}, \vec{x} \in (\{0,1\}^*)^n, z \in \{0,1\}^*}$. Let Sim be an ideal world adversary who interacts with the ideal functionality f and we denote the ideal world adversary view as $\mathsf{IDEAL}_{f,(\mathsf{C},\mathsf{Sim})}(\lambda, \vec{x}, \vec{r}, z)$. let $\mathsf{IDEAL}_{f,(\mathsf{C},\mathsf{Sim})}$ denote the distribution ensemble $\{\mathsf{IDEAL}_{f,(\mathsf{C},\mathsf{Sim})}(\lambda, \vec{x}, z)\}_{\lambda \in \mathbb{N}, \vec{x} \in (\{0,1\}^*)^n, z \in \{0,1\}^*}$. We say that Π adaptively securely evaluates f if for every real world adversary $\mathcal{A}$ there exists an ideal world adversary Sim, s.t. $\mathsf{REAL}_{\Pi,(\mathsf{C},\mathcal{A})}(\lambda, \vec{x}, z) \approx_c \mathsf{IDEAL}_{f,(\mathsf{C},\mathsf{Sim})}(\lambda, \vec{x}, z)$.

3   Reverse Firewalls for Adaptively Secure MPCs

In this section, we present definitions of reverse firewalls for adaptively secure MPC protocols. The existing definitions of security preservation and exfiltration-resistance for reverse firewalls are for a static adversary [12]. In the adaptive setting, while the security preservation is defined as before, exfiltration resistance now has to incorporate the adaptive power of the adversary. We first introduce some notation that will be used throughout the paper.

Notation. Let Π denote a ℓ-round MPC protocol, for some arbitrary polynomial $\ell(\cdot)$ in the security parameter λ. Let H and C denote the indices of the honest and maliciously corrupted parties respectively in the protocol Π. For a party P and reverse firewall RF we define $\mathsf{RF} \circ P$ as the "composed" party in which the incoming and outgoing messages of A are "sanitized" by RF. The firewall RF is a *stateful* algorithm that is only allowed to see the public parameters of the system, and does not get to see the inputs and outputs of the party P. We denote the tampered implementation of a party P by $\overline{P}$.

We denote the view of a party P_i by View_{P_i}, which consists of the input of P_i, its random tape and the messages received so far. We also denote the view of a party P_i till some round $k(\leq \ell)$ as $\mathsf{View}_{\overline{P}_i}^{\leq k}$. We denote the reverse firewall for party P_i as RF_i and the internal state of RF_i by $\mathsf{st}_{\mathsf{RF}_i}$. We write $\mathsf{View}_{\mathsf{RF}_i \circ P_i}$ to denote the composed view of a party P_i and its RF RF_i. Let $\mathsf{Transform}(\cdot)$ be a polynomial time algorithm that takes as input the random tape r_i of a party P_i and the internal state (or randomness) $\mathsf{st}_{\mathsf{RF}_i}$ of RF_i and returns a sanitized random tape $\mathsf{Transform}(r_i, \mathsf{st}_{\mathsf{RF}_i})^3$. Note that, the composed view $\mathsf{View}_{\mathsf{RF}_i \circ P_i}$ of

---

[3] Looking ahead, in all our constructions the function Transform will typically be a very simple function like addition or field multiplication.

P_i can be efficiently constructed from the view View_{P_i} of P_i and the state $\mathsf{st}_{\mathsf{RF}_i}$ of RF_i using the Transform function as a subroutine. We write $\Pi_{\mathsf{RF}_i \circ P_i}$ (resp. $\Pi_{\overline{P_i}}$) to represent the protocol Π in which the role of a party P_i is replaced by the composed party $\mathsf{RF}_i \circ P_i$ (resp. the tampered implementation $\overline{P_i}$).

Definition 5. (Functionality-maintaining RF). *For any reverse firewall* RF *and a party* P, *let* $\mathsf{RF}^1 \circ P = \mathsf{RF} \circ P$, *and* $\mathsf{RF}^k \circ P = \underbrace{\mathsf{RF} \circ \cdots \circ \mathsf{RF}}_{k \text{ times}} \circ P$. *For a*
protocol Π *that satisfies some functionality requirements* $\mathcal{F}$, *we say that a reverse firewall* RF *maintains functionality* $\mathcal{F}$ *for a party* P *in protocol* Π *if* $\Pi_{\mathsf{RF}^k \circ P}$ *also satisfies* $\mathcal{F}$, *for any polynomially bounded* $k \geq 1$.

Definition 6. (Security-preserving RF for Malicious Adaptively secure MPCs). *Let* Π *be a multi-party protocol run between parties* $P_1, \ldots, P_n$ *satisfying functionality requirement* $\mathcal{F}$ *and is secure against adaptive malicious adversaries. We assume that each honest party* $\{P_i\}_{i \in \mathsf{H}}$ *is equipped with its corresponding reverse firewall* $\{\mathsf{RF}_i\}_{i \in \mathsf{H}}$. *When the adversary (adaptively) corrupts a party* P_i, *it receives* $\mathsf{View}_{\mathsf{RF}_i \circ P_i}$ *as the view of* P_i. *Then, we say that the reverse firewalls* RF_i *for parties* $\{P_i\}_{i \in \mathsf{H}}$ *strongly (resp. weakly) preserves security of the protocol* Π, *if there exists a polynomial-time computable transformation of polynomial-size circuit families* $\mathcal{A} = \{\mathcal{A}_\lambda\}_{\lambda \in \mathbb{N}}$ *for the real world into polynomial-size circuit families* $\mathsf{Sim} = \{\mathsf{Sim}_\lambda\}_{\lambda \in \mathbb{N}}$ *for the ideal model such that for every* $\lambda \in \mathbb{N}$, *every subset* $\mathsf{H} \subset [n]$, *every input sequence* $\vec{x} = (x_1, \ldots, x_n) \in (\{0,1\}^\lambda)^n$, *every auxiliary information* $z \in \{0,1\}^*$ *and every arbitrary (resp. functionality-maintaining) tampered implementation* $\{\overline{P_i}\}_{i \in \mathsf{H}}$ *we have the following:* $\mathsf{REAL}_{\Pi_{\{\mathsf{RF}_i \circ \overline{P_i}\}_{i \in \mathsf{H}}}, (\mathsf{C}, \mathcal{A})}(\lambda, \vec{x}, z) \approx_c \mathsf{IDEAL}_{f, (\mathsf{C}, \mathsf{Sim})}(\lambda, \vec{x}, z)$.

We now define exfiltration resistance in terms of the game LEAK that asks the adversary to distinguish between a tampered implementation of party P_i and an honest implementation, even *given* the composed state of P_i and its RF if P_i gets adaptively corrupt in the middle of execution.[4]

Definition 7. (Exfiltration-resistant RF in the presence of adaptive corruptions). *Let* Π *be a multi-party protocol run between the parties* $P_1, \ldots, P_n$ *satisfying functionality* $\mathcal{F}$ *and having reverse firewalls* RF_i *for the set of honest parties* $\{P_i\}_{i \in \mathsf{H}}$. *When the adversary (adaptively) corrupts a party* P_i, *it receives* $\mathsf{View}_{\mathsf{RF}_i \circ P_i}$ *as the view of* P_i. *Then* $\forall i \in \mathsf{H}$, *we say that the firewall* RF_i *is exfiltration-resistant for party* P_i *against all other parties* $\{P_j\}_{j \in [n] \setminus i}$, *if for any PPT adversary* $\mathcal{A}_{\mathsf{ER}}$, *the advantage* $\mathsf{Adv}^{\mathsf{LEAK}}_{\mathcal{A}_{\mathsf{ER}}, \mathsf{RF}_i}(\lambda)$ *of* $\mathcal{A}_{\mathsf{ER}}$ *(defined below) in the game* LEAK *(see Fig. 1) is negligible in the security parameter* λ.
The advantage of any adversary $\mathcal{A}_{\mathsf{ER}}$ *in the game* LEAK *is defined as:*

$$\mathsf{Adv}^{\mathsf{LEAK}}_{\mathcal{A}_{\mathsf{ER}}, \mathsf{RF}_i}(\lambda) = \left| \Pr[\mathsf{LEAK}(\Pi, i, \{P_1, \ldots, P_n\}, \mathsf{RF}_i, \lambda) = 1] - \frac{1}{2} \right|.$$

---

[4] Note that, if we were to give P_i's internal state when it gets adaptively corrupt instead of the composed state, the adversary can trivially distinguish since the party's state does not explain the sanitized transcript.

$$\mathsf{LEAK}(\Pi, i, \{P_1, \cdots, P_n\}, \mathsf{RF}_i, \lambda)$$

W.l.o.g, let $P_\mathsf{H} = (P_1, \cdots, P_h)$ denote the set of honest parties at the onset of the protocol Π, where $h = |\mathsf{H}|$. The exfiltration-resistance game LEAK for a party $P_i \in P_\mathsf{H}$ is modelled as an interactive game between a challenger $\mathcal{C}_\mathsf{ER}$ and an adversary $\mathcal{A}_\mathsf{ER}$ described as follows:

1. The adversary $\mathcal{A}_\mathsf{ER}$ provides the tampered implementations of all the honest parties along with their inputs $\{(\overline{P_1}, \cdots, \overline{P_h}), I_\mathsf{H}\}$ to the challenger $\mathcal{C}_\mathsf{ER}$.
2. The challenger $\mathcal{C}_\mathsf{ER}$ samples a bit $b \xleftarrow{\$} \{0,1\}$ uniformly at random and does the following:
   - If $b = 1$, define $P_i^* \leftarrow \mathsf{RF}_i \circ \overline{P_i}$.
   - If $b = 0$, define $P_i^* \leftarrow \mathsf{RF}_i \circ P_i$.
3. $\mathcal{C}_\mathsf{ER}$ and $\mathcal{A}_\mathsf{ER}$ then engage in an execution of the MPC protocol Π, where the challenger $\mathcal{C}_\mathsf{ER}$ plays the role of all the honest parties P_H (with inputs I_H) and the adversary can adaptively corrupt parties in the set P_H. The $\mathcal{C}_\mathsf{ER}$ then returns the transcript T^* of Π to $\mathcal{A}_\mathsf{ER}$.
4. If $\mathcal{A}_\mathsf{ER}$ adaptively corrupts the party P_i at some point during the execution of Π (say at round k) the challenger $\mathcal{C}_\mathsf{ER}$ returns the composed view of P_i till round k, i.e., $\mathsf{View}_{\mathsf{RF}_i \circ P_i}^{\leq k}$ to $\mathcal{A}_\mathsf{ER}$. Note that, $\mathsf{View}_{\mathsf{RF}_i \circ P_i}^{\leq k}$ can be efficiently constructed from $\mathsf{View}_{\overline{P_i}}^{\leq k}$ and the state $\mathsf{st}_{\mathsf{RF}_i}$ of RF_i using the Transform function as a subroutine.
5. The challenger $\mathcal{C}_\mathsf{ER}$ also returns the views of all the other uncorrupted parties $\{\mathsf{View}_{P_k}\}_{k \in [h \setminus i]}$ to $\mathcal{A}_\mathsf{ER}$.
6. The game ends when $\mathcal{A}_\mathsf{ER}$ returns a bit b' as a guess for the bit b. Output 1 if $b' = b$.

Fig. 1. Exfiltration-resistance game LEAK for a party P_i for adaptively secure MPCs

As in prior works on RF, we consider the notion of functionality-maintaining tampering attacks. Informally, such an attack excludes all conspicuous tamperings, which would otherwise be detected by honest parties. We provide a formal definition in the full version. We also define *transparency* of reverse firewalls which was informally introduced in [20], which means that the behavior of $\mathsf{RF} \circ P$ is identical to the behavior of P if P is the honest implementation. We will also need the notion of *valid transcripts* and *detectable failures* of reverse firewalls, as presented in [20]. In this work we do not consider *input replacement tampering* attack - tampering attacks work by substituting the actual input of the honest parties with a different (possibly (un)related) value. We defer these definitions to the full version.

4   Relations Between Security Preservation and Exfiltration Resistance

In this section, we explore the relation between the notions of security preservation (SP) and exfiltration resistance (ER) for reverse firewalls in the MPC setting. Specifically, we show that ER implies SP for MPC protocols for adaptive corruptions; whereas the relation in the other direction is much less clear.

For all the implications we show in this section, we assume that security preservation be defined by the existence of a black-box simulator. We also assume that the adversaries are not computationally unbounded, and do not have access to additional oracles. Looking ahead, all of our constructions will satisfy the above requirements.

4.1 Exfiltration-Resistance Implies Security Preservation

In this section, we show that ER implies SP for adaptively-secure MPC protocols by proving the following theorem.

Theorem 4. *Let f be an n-ary functionality and let Π be a an n-party protocol that securely computes f with abort in presence of malicious adaptive adversaries. Let $C \subset [n]$ denote the indices of adaptively corrupt the corrupted parties in the protocol Π, and let $H = [n]\backslash C$ denote the indices of the honest parties at the outset of Π. Let $(\overline{P}_i)_{i \in H}$ denote the tampered implementations of the honest parties provided by the adversary. Also, let RF_i denote the RF corresponding to party P_i. Then for all $i \in H$, if RF_i is functionality maintaining, (strongly/weakly) exfiltration resistant with adaptive security for P_i against all other parties $\{P_j\}_{[n]\backslash i}$ and transparent, then for all PPT adversaries $\mathcal{A}$ and all PPT tamperings $(\overline{P}_i)_{i \in H}$ provided by $\mathcal{A}$, the firewalls RF_i for parties $\{P_i\}_{i \in H}$ (strongly/weakly) preserve security of the protocol Π according to Def. 6 in the presence of adaptive corruptions.*

Proof. We need to show that security of the MPC protocol Π is (strongly/ weakly) preserved by the reverse firewalls RF_i for parties $\{P_i\}_{i \in H}$ by relying on (strong/ weak) exfiltration-resistance of the firewalls RF_i, transparency of RF_i and the adaptive security of the underlying MPC protocol Π. More formally, we will show that there exists a simulator/ideal-world adversary Sim such that for any real-world adversary $\mathcal{A}$ participating in the protocol Π, adaptively (maliciously) corrupting parties during the execution, for all $\lambda \in \mathbb{N}$, inputs $\vec{x} \in (\{0,1\}^\lambda)^n$ and auxiliary input $z \in \{0,1\}^*$ the following two random variables are computationally indistinguishable:

$$\{\mathsf{REAL}_{\Pi_{\{\mathsf{RF}_i \circ \overline{P}_i\}_{i \in H}},(C,\mathcal{A})}(\lambda, \vec{x}, z)\} \approx_c \{\mathsf{IDEAL}_{f,(C,\mathsf{Sim})}(\lambda, \vec{x}, z)\}, \qquad (1)$$

Note that, in the above, C denotes the set of parties adaptively corrupted by the adversary. This set is allowed to grow during the execution of the protocol. H denotes the indices of honest parties at the outset of the protocol Π, i.e. the initial set of honest parties.

We prove the above theorem via a sequence of hybrids, as described below.

- Hyb_0 : This is the first hybrid which corresponds to the left hand side of Eq. 1. In particular, Hyb_0 corresponds to the real world view of the adversary $\mathcal{A}$ in the MPC protocol Π, who adaptively corrupts the subset P_C of parties. When the adversary $\mathcal{A}$ corrupts some party $P_i \in P_H$, return $\mathsf{View}_{\mathsf{RF}_i \circ P_i} = \mathsf{Transform}(\mathsf{View}_{P_i}, \mathsf{st}_{\mathsf{RF}_i})$ to $\mathcal{A}$, and move P_i to the corrupt set. All the honest parties in H are replaced with their corresponding tampered implementations composed with their firewalls, i.e., for all $i \in H$, P_i is replaced with $RF_i \circ \overline{P_i}$ in the protocol Π. The view of the real world adversary $\mathcal{A}$ consists of the following:

$$\{\mathsf{REAL}_{\Pi_{\{RF_i \circ \overline{P_i}\}_{i \in H}}, (C, \mathcal{A})}(\vec{x})\}_{\lambda \in \mathbb{N}, \vec{x} \in (\{0,1\}^\lambda)^n}\} \tag{2}$$

– Hyb_1 : Hyb_1 is same as Hyb_0, except that, in the protocol Π the implementation of the first party P_1 is replaced by its honest implementation composed with its firewall RF_1. The rest of the honest parties remain tampered, that is, $\{P_j\}_{j \in H \wedge j \in \{2, \cdots, n\}}$ are still replaced by $RF_j \circ \overline{P_j}$, and the corrupt parties remain as in Hyb_0. In particular, the view of the real world adversary is as follows:

$$\{\mathsf{REAL}_{\Pi_{(RF_1 \circ P_1, \{RF_j \circ \overline{P_j}\}_{j \in H \wedge j \in \{2, \cdots, n\}})}, (C, \mathcal{A})}(\vec{x})\}_{\lambda \in \mathbb{N}, \vec{x} \in (\{0,1\}^\lambda)^n}$$

We now present the general description of the ℓ-th hybrid for all $1 \leq \ell \leq n$ as follows:

– Hyb_ℓ : In Hyb_ℓ, in the protocol Π the implementations of the first ℓ parties $\{P_1, P_2, \cdots, P_\ell\}$ are replaced by their corresponding honest implementations composed with their firewalls. The other honest parties $\{P_j\}_{j \in H \wedge j \in \{\ell+1, \cdots, n\}}$ are still replaced by $RF_j \circ \overline{P_j}$ in the protocol Π, as in Hyb_0. When the adversary $\mathcal{A}$ corrupts a currently honest party P_j, return $\mathsf{View}_{RF_j \circ P_j} = \mathsf{Transform}(\mathsf{View}_{P_j}, \mathsf{st}_{RF_j})$ to $\mathcal{A}$, and move P_j to the set of corrupt parties as before. In particular, the adversary $\mathcal{A}$ obtains the following view:

$$\{\mathsf{REAL}_{\Pi_{(\{RF_j \circ P_j\}_{j \in [\ell]}, \{RF_j \circ \overline{P_j}\}_{j \in H \wedge j \in \{\ell+1, \cdots, n\}})}, (C, \mathcal{A})}(\vec{x})\}_{\lambda \in \mathbb{N}, \vec{x} \in (\{0,1\}^\lambda)^n} \tag{3}$$

Note that, when $\ell = 0$, we are in Hyb_0, i.e., when the implementations of all the honest parties in P_H are replaced by their corresponding tampered implementations composed with their firewalls in the protocol Π. On the other hand, when $\ell = n$, we are in Hyb_n where the implementations of all the honest parties are replaced by their honest implementations composed with their firewalls. For the sake of completeness, we present the n-th hybrid as follows:

– Hyb_n : In Hyb_n, in the protocol Π the implementations of all the honest parties $\{P_j\}_{j \in H}$ are replaced by their corresponding honest implementations composed with their firewalls. In particular, the adversary $\mathcal{A}$ obtains the following view:

$$\{\mathsf{REAL}_{\Pi_{(\{RF_j \circ P_j\}_{j \in H})}, (C, \mathcal{A})}(\vec{x})\}_{\lambda \in \mathbb{N}, \vec{x} \in (\{0,1\}^\lambda)^n} \tag{4}$$

Note that, in each subsequent hybrid we replace each party (honest and corrupt) with the fire-walled honest implementation. However this does not mean that the corrupt parties are forced to behave with honest implementation. As will be clear in the indistinguishability proof below, this approach does not enforce any restriction on the way the corrupt parties behave. We take this approach for readability and ease of proving indistinguishability.

Now, we prove the indistinguishability of consecutive hybrids.

Claim. $\forall 1 \leq \ell \leq n$, $\mathsf{Hyb}_{\ell-1} \approx_c \mathsf{Hyb}_\ell$

Proof. Note that, the two hybrids $\mathsf{Hyb}_{\ell-1}$ and Hyb_ℓ differ in the implementation of the party P_ℓ. In particular, the only change from $\mathsf{Hyb}_{\ell-1}$ to Hyb_ℓ is that $\mathsf{RF}_\ell \circ \overline{P_\ell}$ in the former is replaced by $\mathsf{RF}_\ell \circ P_\ell$ in the latter. Let $\mathcal{D}_\ell$ be an adversary that distinguishes between these two hybrids. Since the adversary is allowed to corrupt parties adaptively, assume that party P_ℓ is corrupted by $\mathcal{D}_\ell$ in round k_ℓ. Using $\mathcal{D}_\ell$, we construct an exfiltration resistant adversary $\mathcal{A}_{\mathsf{ER}}$ such that if the advantage of $\mathcal{D}_\ell$ is non-negligible, then the advantage of $\mathcal{A}_{\mathsf{ER}}$ in breaking the exfiltration-resistance game (Definition 7) is also non-negligible. At a high level, $\mathcal{A}_{\mathsf{ER}}$ interacts with $\mathcal{D}_\ell$ as the challenger for the indistinguishibility game for $\mathcal{D}_\ell$ so that ultimately $\mathcal{D}_\ell$ either sees views from $\mathsf{Hyb}_{\ell-1}$ or Hyb_l. If party P_ℓ is already in the corrupt set at the start of the protocol, then exfiltration-resistance is trivially satisfied for P_ℓ. Otherwise, for the case when P_ℓ gets adaptively corrupt in round k_ℓ, by the exfiltration guarantee, $\mathcal{D}_\ell$ cannot distinguish views till round k_ℓ.

The reduction is as follows:

- The adversary $\mathcal{A}_{\mathsf{ER}}$ receives the initial indices of honest parties (H), and the tampered implementations $\{\overline{P_j}\}_{j \in \mathsf{H} \wedge j \in \{\ell,\cdots n\}}$ corresponding to the last $(|\mathsf{H}| - \ell + 1)$ honest parties in the set P_{H} from the distinguisher $\mathcal{D}_\ell$.
- $\mathcal{A}_{\mathsf{ER}}$ then sets (1) $\overline{P_j} = \mathsf{RF}_j \circ P_j$ for all $j \in \mathsf{H} \wedge j \in [\ell-1]$, and (2) randomly samples inputs for the parties in the honest set to define I and sends it to $\mathcal{C}_{\mathsf{ER}}$. It forwards the set $\{\overline{P_j}\}_{j \in \mathsf{H}}$ (here H is set of honest parties at the outset of Π) to the challenger $\mathcal{C}_{\mathsf{ER}}$ of the exfiltration-resistance (ER) game (see the LEAK game in Fig. 1). In other words, $\mathcal{A}_{\mathsf{ER}}$ sets the tampered implementations of the first $\ell - 1$ honest parties in the set P_{H} to be simply their corresponding honest implementations with a wrapper of firewall on top of it and sets the implementations of the remaining $(|\mathsf{H}| - \ell + 1)$ honest parties as received from $\mathcal{D}_\ell$.
- Now $\mathcal{A}_{\mathsf{ER}}$ interacts with the challenger $\mathcal{C}_{\mathsf{ER}}$ and the distinguisher $\mathcal{D}_\ell$ to execute Π. $\mathcal{C}_{\mathsf{ER}}$ executes Π on the behalf of the currently honest parties, and $\mathcal{D}_\ell$ executes on behalf of the currently dishonest parties. $\mathcal{A}_{\mathsf{ER}}$ passes round messages between $\mathcal{C}_{\mathsf{ER}}$ and $\mathcal{D}_\ell$. If $\mathcal{D}_\ell$ adaptively corrupts an honest party, $\mathcal{A}_{\mathsf{ER}}$ too corrupts the same party and receives a transformed view from $\mathcal{C}_{\mathsf{ER}}$ which it passes on to $\mathcal{D}_\ell$. On corruption of an honest party, $\mathcal{C}_{\mathsf{ER}}$ moves it from the set of honest to dishonest parties. Note that if party P_ℓ is statically corrupt, the indistinguishability in the ER game trivially follows.
- Upon receiving the final views of parties from $\mathcal{C}_{\mathsf{ER}}$ as described in the LEAK game in Fig. 1, $\mathcal{A}_{\mathsf{ER}}$ constructs the view as in Eq. 3. If $\mathcal{D}_\ell$ corrupts any party post execution, $\mathcal{A}_{\mathsf{ER}}$ forwards relevant view. Note that, $\mathcal{A}_{\mathsf{ER}}$ only needs to know the views corresponding to the corrupt parties to construct the view as in Eq. 3.
- If $\mathcal{D}_\ell$ outputs a bit b', the adversary $\mathcal{A}_{\mathsf{ER}}$ outputs the same bit b'. Note that, if the challenger $\mathcal{C}_{\mathsf{ER}}$ of the ER game sampled the bit $b = 1$, then we are in

$\mathsf{Hyb}_{\ell-1}$; whereas if $b = 0$, we are in Hyb_ℓ. Hence, if the advantage of $\mathcal{D}_\ell$ in distinguishing between these hybrids is non-negligible, the advantage of $\mathcal{A}_{\mathsf{ER}}$ in breaking the ER game is also non-negligible.

□

Note that, at the end of Hyb_n, all the honest parties $\{P_j\}_{j \in \mathsf{H}}$ in the set P_H are replaced by $\mathsf{RF}_j \circ P_j$.

- Hyb_{n+1} : Hyb_{n+1} is same as Hyb_n, except that, in the protocol Π all the honest parties in H have honest implementations and there is no RF for the honest parties. In particular, the adversary $\mathcal{A}$ obtains the following view:

$$\{\mathsf{REAL}_{\Pi_{(\{P_j\}_{j \in \mathsf{H}})},(\mathsf{C},\mathcal{A})}(\vec{x})\}_{\lambda \in \mathbb{N}, \vec{x} \in (\{0,1\}^\lambda)^n}.$$

Claim. $\mathsf{Hyb}_n \approx_c \mathsf{Hyb}_{n+1}$.

Proof: It is easy to see that the hybrids Hyb_n and Hyb_{n+1} are identically distributed by relying on the transparency of the firewalls $\{\mathsf{RF}_j\}_{j \in \mathsf{H}}$. More formally, we can define a set of n hybrids (similar to the claim earlier in this section) and show that the consecutive hybrids are indistinguishable by the transparency property of each of the reverse firewalls. □

- Hyb_{n+2} : This is the final hybrid. This hybrid corresponds to the the ideal world adversary view for the MPC protocol Π where the set of corrupted parties is $\{P_i\}_{i \in \mathsf{C}}$. All the honest parties P_H have honest implementations and there is no RF for the honest parties. In particular, the adversary $\mathcal{A}$ obtains the following view:

$$\{\mathsf{IDEAL}_{f,(\mathsf{C},\mathsf{Sim})}(\vec{x})\}_{\lambda \in \mathbb{N}, \vec{x} \in (\{0,1\}^\lambda)^n} \tag{5}$$

Claim. $\mathsf{Hyb}_{n+1} \approx_c \mathsf{Hyb}_{n+2}$

Proof: Hyb_{n+2} is indistinguishable from Hyb_{n+1} due to the security of the protocol Π. Hyb_{n+1} corresponds to the real world adversary view of Π (without any RF) and Hyb_{n+2} corresponds to the ideal world adversary view of Π (without any RF). □

Thus, combining the above three claims, we obtain Eq. 1. This completes the proof of Theorem. 4. □

This implication holds in the static corruption case as well when the exfiltration resistant game, transparency game and the security preservation games are defined for static corruptions. We defer this proof to the full version.

5   Adaptively-Secure Compiler Using Reverse Firewalls in the **urs** Model

In this section, we show a compiler that transforms any semi-honest adaptively secure MPC protocol to a maliciously-secure MPC protocol in the urs model, which withstands adaptive corruptions and admits reverse firewalls. As a building block, we first present the adaptively-secure multiparty augmented coin tossing protocol using reverse firewalls.

5.1 Adaptively-Secure Augmented Coin-Tossing Using Reverse Firewalls in the urs Model

The adaptively-secure augmented coin tossing protocol $\Pi_{\text{a-coin}}$ is used to generate *random bits* (according to Definition 4) for all the parties participating in the adaptively-secure MPC protocol. The initiating party receives a random tuple (S, R) and all other parties receive a commitment $\text{Com}(S; R)$ (under the urs of party P_i) of S using commitment randomness R, where $S \in \{0,1\}^\lambda$, Com is an adaptively secure homomorphic commitment and $R \leftarrow \mathcal{R}_{\text{Com}}$. The protocol $\Pi_{\text{a-coin}}$ is presented in Fig. 2.

- **Primitives:** $(\text{Gen}, \text{Com}, \text{Verify})$ is an adaptively secure homomorphic commitment scheme where $\text{Com}(\text{urs}, a_1; b_1) \cdot \text{Com}(\text{urs}, a_2; b_2) = \text{Com}(\text{urs}, a_1 + a_2; b_1 + b_2)$ for $a_1, a_2 \in \{0,1\}^\lambda$ and $b_1, b_2 \in \mathcal{R}_{\text{Com}}$ respectively. We denote $\text{Com}_i(m; r) = \text{Com}(\text{urs}_i, m; r)$ under $\text{urs}_i \leftarrow \text{Gen}(1^\lambda)$.
- **Public Inputs:** Each party gets as input $\text{urs}_{\text{a-coin}} = \{\text{urs}_i\}_{i \in [n]}$ where $\text{urs}_i \leftarrow \text{Com.Gen}(i, 1^\lambda)$. Party P_i commits using Com_i in the protocol.

Round 1: For $j \in [n] \setminus i$, every party P_j samples $s_j \leftarrow \{0,1\}^\lambda$ and $r_j \leftarrow \mathcal{R}_{\text{Com}}$ respectively. It computes $c_j = \text{Com}_j(s_j; r_j)$, and broadcasts c_j .

Round 2: Party P_i chooses a random $s_i \leftarrow \{0,1\}^\lambda$. It then computes $c_i = \text{Com}_i(s_i; r_i)$ for a random $r_i \leftarrow \mathcal{R}_{\text{Com}}$, and broadcasts c_i.

Round 3: For $j \in [n] \setminus i$, every party P_j broadcasts (s_j, r_j) as the opening of c_j.

Local Computation:

- For $j \in [n]$, P_j aborts if $\exists k \in [n] \setminus i$ s.t. $\text{Verify}(\text{urs}_k, c_k, s_k, r_k) = \bot$.
- Party P_i sets $S = \Sigma_{i \in [n]} s_i$ and $R = \Sigma_{i \in [n]} r_i$. P_i outputs $C = \text{Com}_i(S; R)$.
- For $j \in [n] \setminus i$, Party P_j sets $S_j = \Sigma_{k \in [n] \setminus i} s_k$ and $R_j = \Sigma_{k \in [n] \setminus i} r_k$. P_j outputs $C = c_i \cdot \text{Com}_i(S_j; R_j)$.

Fig. 2. Adaptively-Secure Multi-party Augmented Coin-Tossing Protocol $\Pi_{\text{a-coin}}$ for P_i

Theorem 5. *Assuming* Com *is an adaptively secure homomorphic commitment in the* urs *model,* $\Pi_{\text{a-coin}}$ *securely implements the augmented coin-tossing functionality (Definition 4) against adaptive corruption of parties in the* urs *model.*

Next, we consider security of the protocol when honest parties are tampered. Our firewall RF_i for a tampered initiating party P_i and firewall $\{\text{RF}_k\}_{k \in [n] \setminus i}$ for a tampered receiving party $\{\mathcal{P}_k\}_{k \in [n] \setminus i}$ is presented in Fig. 3 and Fig. 4 respectively. We prove that the firewalls provide weak exfiltration resistance and preserve security.

Theorem 6. *If the commitment scheme* Com *is adaptively secure in the* urs *model and is additively homomorphic, the firewall* RF_i, *(resp.* RF_k*) is transparent, functionality-maintaining, and provides weak exfiltration resistance for initiating* P_i *(resp. receiving party* P_k*) against other parties in* $\Pi_{\text{a-coin}}$ *with valid transcripts, and detects failure for* P_i *(resp.* P_k*).*

(Gen, Com, Verify) is an additively homomorphic commitment scheme where $\mathsf{Com}(\mathsf{urs}, a_1; b_1) \cdot \mathsf{Com}(\mathsf{urs}, a_2; b_2) = \mathsf{Com}(\mathsf{urs}, a_1 + a_2; b_1 + b_2)$ for $a_1, a_2 \in \{0,1\}^\lambda$ and $b_1, b_2 \in \mathcal{R}_{\mathsf{Com}}$ respectively. We denote $\mathsf{Com}_i(m; r) = \mathsf{Com}(\mathsf{urs}_i, m; r)$ under $\mathsf{urs}_i \leftarrow \mathsf{Gen}(1^\lambda)$.

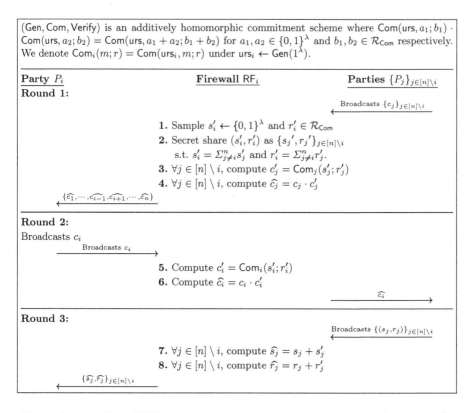

Party P_i	Firewall RF_i	Parties $\{P_j\}_{j \in [n] \setminus i}$

Round 1:

Broadcasts $\{c_j\}_{j \in [n] \setminus i}$

1. Sample $s'_i \leftarrow \{0,1\}^\lambda$ and $r'_i \in \mathcal{R}_{\mathsf{Com}}$
2. Secret share (s'_i, r'_i) as $\{s_j', r_j'\}_{j \in [n] \setminus i}$
   s.t. $s'_i = \Sigma^n_{j \neq i} s'_j$ and $r'_i = \Sigma^n_{j \neq i} r'_j$.
3. $\forall j \in [n] \setminus i$, compute $c'_j = \mathsf{Com}_j(s_j'; r_j')$
4. $\forall j \in [n] \setminus i$, compute $\widehat{c}_j = c_j \cdot c'_j$

$\{\widehat{c_1}, \cdots, \widehat{c_{i-1}}, \widehat{c_{i+1}}, \cdots, \widehat{c_n}\}$

Round 2:

Broadcasts c_i

Broadcasts c_i

5. Compute $c'_i = \mathsf{Com}_i(s'_i; r'_i)$
6. Compute $\widehat{c}_i = c_i \cdot c'_i$

$\widehat{c_i}$

Round 3:

Broadcasts $\{(s_j, r_j)\}_{j \in [n] \setminus i}$

7. $\forall j \in [n] \setminus i$, compute $\widehat{s}_j = s_j + s'_j$
8. $\forall j \in [n] \setminus i$, compute $\widehat{r}_j = r_j + r'_j$

$\{\widehat{s_j}, \widehat{r_j}\}_{j \in [n] \setminus i}$

Fig. 3. Reverse firewall RF_i for initiating party P_i involved in $\Pi_{\text{a-coin}}$ (from Fig. 2).

Now, consider $\Pi^{\mathsf{RF}}_{\text{a-coin}}$, a firewalled version of the protocol where all honest parties P_i have their respective firewalls RF_i attached to them. Now, from Theorem 6, and our implication from Theorem 4, we conclude weak security preservation; we have that $\Pi^{\mathsf{RF}}_{\text{a-coin}}$ securely implements augmented coin tossing in the presence of adaptive corruptions.

Theorem 7. $\Pi^{\mathsf{RF}}_{\text{a-coin}}$ *securely implements the augmented coin-tossing functionality (Definition 4) in the* urs *model against adaptive corruption of parties, and in the presence of functionality-maintaining tampering of honest parties.*

Instantiation. We instantiate the adaptively secure homomorphic commitment in the urs model using the recent construction of [10]. It is additively homomorphic in the message and randomness space and can be instantiated based on DDH assumption in the urs model.

5.2   Adaptively-Secure ZK in the urs$_{\text{zk}}$ Model

We construct our adaptively secure ZK protocol Π_{zk} in the common random string model based on the recent ZK protocol of [11] by incorporating a coin tossing protocol to generate the verifier's challenge. We refer to Sect. 1.2 for a

(Gen, Com, Verify) is an adaptively secure homomorphic commitment scheme where $\mathsf{Com}(\mathsf{urs}, a_1; b_1) \cdot \mathsf{Com}(\mathsf{urs}, a_2; b_2) = \mathsf{Com}(\mathsf{urs}, a_1 + a_2; b_1 + b_2)$ for $a_1, a_2 \in \{0, 1\}^\lambda$ and $b_1, b_2 \in \mathcal{R}_{\mathsf{Com}}$ respectively. We denote $\mathsf{Com}_i(m; r) = \mathsf{Com}(\mathsf{urs}_i, m; r)$ under $\mathsf{urs}_i \leftarrow \mathsf{Gen}(1^\lambda)$.

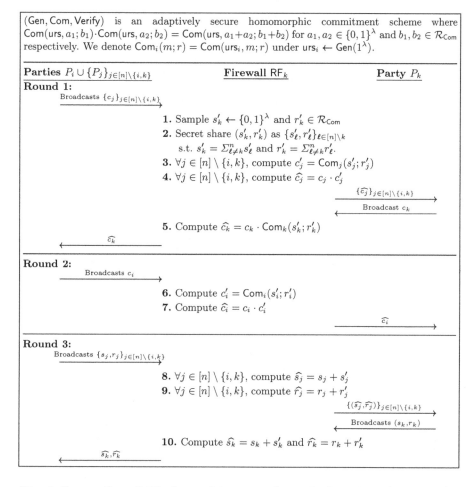

Fig. 4. Reverse firewall RF_k for receiving party P_k involved in $\Pi_{\mathsf{a\text{-}coin}}$ (from Fig. 2).

high level overview and defer the protocol to the full version. The security of our protocol is summarized below.

Theorem 8. *If* Com *is a non-interactive equivocal commitment scheme in the* urs *model and* PKE *is an IND-CPA public key encryption scheme (where the public key is statistically close to a random string) with oblivious ciphertext sampleability, then* Π_{zk} *realizes* $\mathcal{F}_{\mathsf{ZK}}$ *for all NP relations against adaptive corruptions in the* urs *model.*

We provide a firewall $\mathsf{RF}_{\mathsf{zk}}$ which provides security for a tampered prover (respectively, verifier) against a corrupt verifier (respectively, prover) in the full version. We summarize our result below.

Theorem 9. *Let* $\mathsf{RF}_{\mathsf{zk}}$ *be a reverse firewall for a tampered prover (resp. verifier) against a corrupt verifier (resp. prover) in* Π_{zk}, *and* Π_{zk} *implements* $\mathcal{F}_{\mathsf{ZK}}$ *func-*

tionality against adaptive corruption of parties. Let Com be a non-interactive equivocal commitment scheme in the urs model and PKE be an IND-CPA public key encryption scheme (where the public key is statistically close to a random string) with oblivious ciphertext sampleability. If Com and PKE are homomorphic with respect to the (addition) operation defined over the underlying spaces (i.e., the message space, randomness space) and the message space of PKE is same as randomness space of Com then the firewall RF_{zk} is transparent, functionality-maintaining and provides weak exfiltration resistance for a tampered prover (resp. verifier) against a corrupt verifier (resp. prover). The firewall also detects failures for all the parties.

From Theorem 9, and our implication from Theorem 4, we conclude weak security preservation; we have that $\Pi_{zk}^{RF_{zk}}$ securely implements $\mathcal{F}_{ZK}$ in the presence of adaptive corruptions as summarized in Theorem 10 below.

Theorem 10. $\Pi_{zk}^{RF_{zk}}$ *securely implements the* $\mathcal{F}_{ZK}$ *functionality in the* urs *model against adaptive corruption of parties, and in the presence of functionality-maintaining tampering of honest parties.*

We instantiate the commitment using the LWE-based construction of [27] and we instantiate the PKE using the LWE-based construction of [25].

5.3 Adaptively-Secure MPC in the urs_mpc Model

We present our actively-secure protocol Π_{mpc} which withstands adaptive corruption of parties in Fig. 5, 6. Adaptive security is achieved by the adaptive security of the underlying primitives and subprotocols – ZK, augmented coin-tossing, semi-honest MPC protocol and commitments.

Theorem 11. *Assuming* Com *is an adaptively secure commitment in the* urs_com *model,* $\Pi_{a\text{-}coin}$ *securely implements the augmented coin-tossing functionality against adaptive corruption of parties in the* urs_{a-coin} *model,* Π_{zk} *securely implements the* $\mathcal{F}_{ZK}$ *functionality against adaptive corruption of parties in the* urs_{zk} *model and* $\Pi_{sh\text{-}mpc}$ *is an adaptively-secure semi-honest MPC protocol in the* urs_{sh-mpc} *model,* Π_{mpc} *is an actively secure MPC protocol that withstands adaptive corruption of parties in the* urs_mpc = (urs_com, urs_zk, urs_{a-coin}, urs_{sh-mpc}) *model.*

Next, we consider a reverse firewall $RF_{mpc}^i = (RF_{zk}^i, RF_{a\text{-}coin}^i)$ to be the firewall for P_i in Π_{mpc}. RF_{mpc}^i is obtained by first applying RF_{zk}^i to the messages of Π_{zk} phase of Π_{mpc}, followed by application of $RF_{a\text{-}coin}^i$ to the messages in the $\Pi_{a\text{-}coin}$ phase, if RF_{zk}^i did not output $\bot$. We show that RF_{mpc}^i provides weak exfiltration resistance for party P_i in Π_{mpc}.

Theorem 12. *Let* Com *be an adaptively secure commitment in the* urs_com *model,* $\Pi_{a\text{-}coin}$ *securely implement the augmented coin tossing functionality against adaptive corruption of parties in the* urs_{a-coin} *model,* Π_{zk} *securely implement the* $\mathcal{F}_{ZK}$ *functionality against adaptive corruption of parties in the* urs_{zk} *model, and*

- **Primitives:** (Gen, Com, Verify) is an adaptively secure non-interactive commitment scheme and $\Pi_{zk} = (\text{Gen}, \text{P}_1, \text{V}_1, \text{P}_2, \text{V}_2)$ is an adaptively secure rerandomizable input-delayed protocol implementing $\mathcal{F}_{ZK}$ in the urs_{zk} model.

- **Subprotocols:** Adaptively secure augmented coin-tossing protocol $\Pi_{\text{a-coin}}$ in the $\text{urs}_{\text{a-coin}}$ model and adaptively secure semi-honest k-round MPC protocol $\Pi_{\text{sh-mpc}}$ in the $\text{urs}_{\text{sh-mpc}}$ model. Each invocation of $\Pi_{\text{a-coin}}$ generates λ for initiating party.

- **Inputs:** Each party gets $\text{urs}_{\text{mpc}} = (\text{urs}_{\text{com}}, \text{urs}_{zk}, \text{urs}_{\text{a-coin}}, \text{urs}_{\text{sh-mpc}})$ and security parameter 1^λ. Party P_i has private input x_i for $i \in [n]$.

- **Output:** Parties compute the ideal functionality $\mathcal{F}_{\text{mpc}}$ and output $y = \mathcal{F}_{\text{mpc}}(x_1, x_2, \ldots, x_n) = f(x_1, x_2, \ldots, x_n)$.

- **Notations:** Let $\mathcal{T}^{<T} = \bigcup_{t \in [T-1]} \{T_i^t\}_{i \in [n]}$ denote the entire transcript of $\Pi_{\text{sh-mpc}}$ until the end of round $T - 1$ for $0 < T \leq k$. We assume $\mathcal{T}^0 = \bot$. NMF is the next message function of $\Pi_{\text{sh-mpc}}$ for P_i computing $\text{NMF}(\mathcal{T}^{<t}, x_i, r_i) = T_i^t$. Let $N\lambda$ = no. of random bits required by P_i to commit $|x_i|$ bits + no. of random bits required by P_i to compute $\Pi_{\text{sh-mpc}}$. $\gamma_{\text{inp},i,j}^\ell$ denotes the ℓ-th ($\ell \in [3]$) round message in the ZK proof for $\mathcal{R}_{\text{inp}}$ where P_i is the prover and P_j is the verifier. Similarly, $\gamma_{t,i,j}^\ell$ (where $t \in [k]$) denotes the ℓ-th ($\ell \in [3]$) round message in the ZK proof for $\mathcal{R}_{\text{mpc}}$ where P_i is the prover and P_j is the verifier.

- **Relations:** Let $\mathcal{R}_{\text{inp}}((c, c^{\text{inp}}), (x, r, s)) = 1$ iff $(c = \text{Com}(x; r) \wedge c^{\text{inp}} = \text{Com}(r; s))$. Let $\mathcal{R}_{\text{mpc}}((\mathcal{T}, \mathcal{T}', c, c^{\text{inp}}, c'), (x, r, s, r', s')) = 1$ iff $(c = \text{Com}(x; r) \wedge c^{\text{inp}} = \text{Com}(r; s) \wedge c = \text{Com}(r'; s') \wedge \text{NMF}(\mathcal{T}', x, r') = \mathcal{T})$.

Offline Phase:

The parties run the following protocols in parallel:

- For $i \in [n]$, Party P_i invokes $\Pi_{\text{a-coin}}$ N times in parallel as the initiating party to obtain randomness for input commitment - $(r_i^{\text{inp}}, s_i^{\text{inp}})$ s.t. $c_i^{\text{inp}} = \text{Com}(r_i^{\text{inp}}; s_i^{\text{inp}})$, and randomness for MPC protocol $(r_i^{\text{mpc}}, s_i^{\text{mpc}})$ s.t. $c_i^{\text{mpc}} = \text{Com}(r_i^{\text{mpc}}; s_i^{\text{mpc}}) = \{r_i^{\text{mpc}}[t], c_i^{\text{mpc}}[t]\}_{t \in [k]}$. Every party obtains c_i^{inp} and c_i^{mpc}.

- For $i \in [n], j \in [n] \setminus i$, Party P_i runs $\Pi_{zk}.\text{P}_1(1^\lambda, 1^{|\mathcal{R}_{\text{inp}}|})$ as prover with P_j as verifier to obtain $\gamma_{\text{inp},i,j}^1$. Upon obtaining $\gamma_{\text{inp},i,j}^1$, P_j runs $\text{V}_2 = \Pi_{zk}(1^\lambda)$ on $\gamma_{\text{inp},i,j}^1$ to obtain $\gamma_{\text{inp},i,j}^2$. P_i and P_j obtain $(\gamma_{\text{inp},i,j}^1, \gamma_{\text{inp},i,j}^2)$. P_i aborts if $\gamma_{\text{inp},i,j}^2$ is invalid.

- For $i \in [n], j \in [n] \setminus j, t \in [k]$, Party P_i runs $\Pi_{zk}.\text{P}_1(1^\lambda, 1^{|\mathcal{R}_{\text{mpc}}|})$ as prover with P_j as verifier to obtain $\gamma_{t,i,j}^1$. Upon obtaining $\gamma_{t,i,j}^1$, P_j runs $\text{V}_2 = \Pi_{zk}(1^\lambda)$ on $\gamma_{t,i,j}^1$ to obtain $\gamma_{t,i,j}^2$. P_i and P_j obtain $(\gamma_{t,i,j}^1, \gamma_{t,i,j}^2)$. P_i aborts if $\gamma_{t,i,j}^2$ is invalid.

Online Phase:

Each party P_i (for $i \in [n]$) performs the following :

Input Commitment Phase:

- Each party P_i commits to his input x_i as $c_i = \text{Com}(x_i; r_i^{\text{inp}})$ and broadcasts c_i.

- For each $j \in [n] \setminus i$, party P_i proves honest computation of c_i using the committed randomness. P_i computes proof $\gamma_{\text{inp},i,j}^3 = \Pi_{zk}.\text{P}_2$ for $\mathcal{R}_{\text{inp}}((c_i, c_i^{\text{inp}}), (x_i, r_i^{\text{inp}}, s_i^{\text{inp}}))$ on $(\gamma_{\text{inp},i,j}^1, \gamma_{\text{inp},i,j}^2)$. P_i sends $\Gamma_{\text{inp}} = (\gamma_{\text{inp},i,j}^1, \gamma_{\text{inp},i,j}^2, \gamma_{\text{inp},i,j}^3)$ to P_j.

Fig. 5. Adaptively secure Multi-party Protocol Π_{mpc} in the urs model

---

Local Computation at the end of Input Commitment Phase:

After receiving the n commitments party P_i aborts if $\exists j \in [n]$ s.t. $\Pi_{zk}.V_2(\Gamma_{\mathsf{inp},j,i}) = 0$.

....

Round $1 \leq t \leq k$:

- If any party aborts at the end of round $t - 1$ then abort.

- P_i computes the t-th round message of the MPC protocol as $T^t = \mathsf{NMF}(T^{<t}, x_i, r_i^{\mathsf{mpc}}[t])$. P_i broadcasts T_i^t.

- For each $j \in [n] \setminus i$, party P_i proves honest computation of T_i^t to P_j using the committed input x_i and committed randomness $r_i^{\mathsf{mpc}}[t]$. P_i computes proof $\gamma_{t,i,j}^3 = \Pi_{zk}.\mathsf{P2}$ for $\mathcal{R}_{\mathsf{mpc}}((T_i^t, T^{<t}, c_i, c_i^{\mathsf{inp}}, c_i^{\mathsf{mpc}}[t]), (x_i, r_i^{\mathsf{inp}}, s_i^{\mathsf{inp}}, r_i^{\mathsf{mpc}}[t], s_i^{\mathsf{mpc}}[t]))$ on $(\gamma_{t,i,j}^1, \gamma_{t,i,j}^2)$. P_i sends $\Gamma_{t,i,j} = (\gamma_{t,i,j}^1, \gamma_{t,i,j}^2, \gamma_{t,i,j}^3)$ to P_j.

Local Computation at the end of Round t:

- Party P_i aborts if $\exists j \in [n] \setminus i$ s.t. $\Pi_{zk}.V_2(\Gamma_{t,j,i}) = \mathsf{reject}$.

- For $i \in [n]$, P_i sets $T^{<t+1} = T^{<t} \bigcup \{T_j^t\}_{j \in [n]}$ and continues to next round.

Output Computation for Party $\{P_i\}_{i \in [n]}$:

- If any party aborts at the end of round k then abort.

- P_i sets $T^{\leq k} = T^{<k} \bigcup \{T_j^k\}_{j \in [n]}$ and outputs $y = \mathsf{NMF}(T^{\leq k}, x_i, r_i^{\mathsf{mpc}}[k])$.

Fig. 6. Adaptively-Secure Multi-party Protocol in the urs model(cont.)

$\Pi_{\mathsf{sh\text{-}mpc}}$ be an adaptively-secure semi-honest MPC protocol in the $\mathsf{urs}_{\mathsf{sh\text{-}mpc}}$ model. Let RF_{zk}^i and $\mathsf{RF}_{\mathsf{a\text{-}coin}}^i$ be transparent, functionality-maintaining, and weakly exfiltration resistant for P_i in Π_{zk} and $\Pi_{\mathsf{a\text{-}coin}}$ respectively. Then, RF_{mpc}^i is a transparent, functionality-maintaining, weakly exfiltration RF for P_i in Π_{mpc} .

The proof of Theorem 12 is deferred to the full version.

We have shown in Theorem 11 that Π_{mpc} is adaptively secure. Now, consider $\Pi_{\mathsf{mpc}}^{\mathsf{RF}}$, a firewalled version of the protocol Π_{mpc} where all honest parties P_i have their respective firewalls RF_i attached to them. From Theorem 12, and our implication from Theorem 4, we conclude weak security preservation.

Theorem 13. $\Pi_{\mathsf{mpc}}^{\mathsf{RF}}$ *is an actively secure MPC protocol against adaptively corruption of parties, and in the presence of functionality maintaining tampering of honest parties.*

Instantiation. We obtain Π_{zk} and $\Pi_{\mathsf{a\text{-}coin}}$ based on LWE and DDH assumptions respectively. We assume that Π_{zk} setup consists of n setup strings $-\{\mathsf{urs}_{zk}^i\}_{i \in [n]}$, where urs_{zk}^i is used by party P_i to prove statements. Similarly, $\Pi_{\mathsf{a\text{-}coin}}$ consists of n setup strings $- \{\mathsf{urs}_{\mathsf{a\text{-}coin}}^i\}_{i \in [n]}$, where $\mathsf{urs}_{\mathsf{a\text{-}coin}}^i$ is used in a session where party P_i is the initiating party. The commitment scheme can be instantiated from the adaptively secure commitment of [10] based on DDH in the $\mathsf{urs}_{\mathsf{com}}$ model. We assume that Com consists of n setup strings $- \{\mathsf{urs}_{\mathsf{com}}^i\}_{i \in [n]}$, where $\mathsf{urs}_{\mathsf{com}}^i$ is used by party P_i to commit. We obtain an adaptively secure semi-honest MPC protocol in the urs model as follows. The work of [9] obtain a two-round semi-honest adaptively secure MPC protocol based on adaptively secure two-round

OT protocol and augmented NCE. The work of [10] construct an adaptively secure two-round OT protocol from DDH in urs model and instantiate [15] the augmented NCE from DDH; thus yielding a two-round adaptively secure MPC protocol in the urs model from DDH. We instantiate $\Pi_{\text{sh-mpc}}$ using the DDH-based MPC protocol of [10].

Round complexity. In Π_{mpc} the subprotocols $\Pi_{\text{a-coin}}$ and the first two rounds of Π_{zk} can be run in parallel during the offline phase. Thus, the offline phase requires 3 rounds in total. The input commitment phase requires 1 round and $\Pi_{\text{sh-mpc}}$ requires 2 rounds when instantiated using the protocol of [10]. We get a 6 round MPC protocol from DDH and LWE.

6   Adaptively-Secure Multi-party Coin-Tossing Protocol with Reverse Firewalls in the Plain Model

In this section we give a protocol in the plain model with reverse firewalls to generate the setup string urs_{mpc} required for Π_{mpc}. A high level overview of our construction can be found in Sect. 1.2 and our protocol is presented in Fig. 7. Our protocol satisfies security against adaptive corruptions in the plain model and its security is summarized in Theorem 14 (proven in the full version).

Theorem 14. *Let Discrete Log and Knowledge of Exponent Assumptions hold in a bilinear group $\mathbb{G}$ and PKE is a public key encryption with oblivious ciphertext sampling, oblivious public key sampling, satisfying additive homomorphism over key space, message space, randomness space and ciphertext space with public key space being $\mathbb{Z}_q$. Π_{coin}(Fig. 7) securely implements coin-tossing functionality(Definition 3) against adaptive corruptions in the plain model.*

Next, we turn to constructing a reverse firewall for Π_{coin}. We provide a reverse firewall RF_i for the tampered honest party P_i in Fig. 8. Weak ER for P_i is summarized in Theorem 15 and is proved in the full version.

Theorem 15. *Let RF_i be the reverse firewall for party P_i in Π_{coin}. If Discrete Log assumption and Knowledge of Exponent assumption holds in a bilinear group $\mathbb{G}$ and PKE is a public key encryption with oblivious ciphertext sampling and oblivious public keys sampling satisfying additive homomorphism over key space, message space, randomness space and ciphertext space and public key space of PKE be $\mathbb{Z}_q$. Then RF_i is transparent, functionality maintaining and provides weak exfiltration resistance for party P_i against every other party $\{P_j\}_{j \in [n] \setminus i}$ with valid transcripts, and detects failure for P_i.*

In the final protocol every honest party $\{P_j\}_{j \in \mathsf{H}}$ will have a firewall $\{\text{RF}_j\}_{j \in \mathsf{H}}$ and the firewalls will be composed together. By applying the result of Theorem 4 we obtain the following result.

Theorem 16. *If Discrete Log and Knowledge of Exponent assumptions hold in a bilinear group $\mathbb{G}$ and PKE is a public key encryption with oblivious ciphertext sampling and oblivious public keys sampling satisfying additive homomorphism over key space, message space, randomness space, ciphertext space and*

- **Public Inputs:** Each party gets as input the group $\mathbb{G}$ where DLP assumption holds. Every element $g' \in \mathbb{G} \setminus 1$ is a generator. Every party also receives a generator g as input and a bilinear map $e : \mathbb{G} \times \mathbb{G} \rightarrow \mathbb{H}$. Let $\mathsf{PKE} = (\mathsf{Gen}, \mathsf{Enc}, \mathsf{Dec}, \mathsf{oGen}, \mathsf{oEnc})$ is a public key encryption with oblivious ciphertext sampling and oblivious public keys sampling satisfying additive homomorphism over key space, message space, randomness space and ciphertext space. Let the public key space of PKE be $\mathbb{Z}_q$.

Parameter Generation Phase:

The following protocol steps are repeated by every party P_i for $i \in [n]$ with every party P_j for $j \in [n] \setminus i$ to generate the pair-wise commitment parameter h_{ij} where P_i is the committer and P_j is the verifier. We denote it as h and the pairwise communication without any subscript ij to avoid notation overloading.

1. P_j samples an $R \leftarrow \mathbb{G}$. P_j sends R to P_i.
2. P_i aborts if $R \in \{1, g\}$. P_i samples $a_1, u \leftarrow \mathbb{Z}_q$ and computes $A_1 = g^{a_1}$ and commits to a_1 using randomness u as $v = A_1 R^u$. P_i also samples $\mathsf{pk}_1 \leftarrow \mathsf{oGen}(1^\lambda)$ and commits to it as $v_p = g^{\mathsf{pk}_1} R^{u_p}$ for $u_p \leftarrow \mathbb{Z}_q$. P_i sends (v, v_p) to P_j.
3. P_j samples $A_2 \leftarrow \mathbb{G}, \mathsf{pk}_2 \leftarrow \mathsf{oGen}(1^\lambda)$, and sends (A_2, pk_2) to P_i.
4. P_i opens commitment v_p by sending (u_p, pk_1). P_i also sends u to P_j. P_i computes $\mathsf{pk} = \mathsf{pk}_1 + \mathsf{pk}_2$.
5. P_j aborts if (u_p, pk_1) is not a valid opening of v_p. Else, P_j computes $\mathsf{pk} = \mathsf{pk}_1 + \mathsf{pk}_2$. P_j computes $A_1 = \frac{v}{R^u}$ and sets $A = A_1 \cdot A_2$. P_j samples commitment trapdoor $t \leftarrow \mathbb{Z}_q$ and sets commitment parameter as $h = g^t$. P_j sends (h, A^t) to P_i.
6. P_i computes $A = A_1 \cdot A_2$ and aborts if $e(h, A) \neq e(g, Z)$ where P_i received (h, Z) from P_j. Else, P_i proves knowledge of discrete log of A_1 by sending a_1 to P_j. If $v \neq g^{a_1} R^u$ then P_j aborts. Else, set (g, h) as the pair-wise commitment parameter and pk as the pairwise encryption parameter.

Commitment Generation Phase:

Every party P_i chooses a random coin $s_i \leftarrow \{0, 1\}$, and commits to it pairwise. For $i \in [n]$, every party P_i and constructs $c_{ij} = g^{s_i} h_{ij}^{d_{ij}}$ where h_{ij} is the pairwise commitment parameter. P_i also encrypts the commitment randomness as $e_{ij,s_i} = \mathsf{Enc}(\mathsf{pk}_{ij}, d_{ij}; y_{ij})$ using randomness y_{ij} and samples $e_{ij,\overline{s_i}} \leftarrow \mathsf{oEnc}(\mathsf{pk}_{ij})$, where pk_{ij} is the pair-wise encryption parameter. P_i sends $(c_{ij}, e_{ij,0}, e_{ij,1})$ to P_j.

Commitment Opening Phase:

For all $i \in [n]$, party P_i broadcasts s_i. P_i opens c_{ij} pairwise (for all $j \in [n] \setminus i$) by sending (d_{ij}, y_{ij}) and claims that $e_{ij,\overline{s_i}}$ was obliviously sampled.

Output Phase:

For all $i \in [n]$, party P_i verifies the commitments $c_{ji} \stackrel{?}{=} g^{s_j} h_{ji}^{d_{ji}}$ and $e_{ji,s_j} = \mathsf{Enc}(\mathsf{pk}_{ji}, d_{ji}; y_{ji})$. If all verification checks pass then P_i sets $S = (\Sigma_{k \in [n]} s_k) \mod 2$ and outputs S as the final random coin.

Fig. 7. Adaptively-Secure Multi-party Coin-Tossing Protocol Π_{coin} using Reverse Firewalls without Setup

Parameter Generation Phase:
The following protocol steps are repeated for every party P_j for $j \in [n] \setminus i$ where P_i is the committer and P_j is the verifier:

1. When P_j sends R, RF_i samples an $r \leftarrow \mathbb{Z}_q$ and sends $\hat{R} = R^r$ to P_i.
2. When P_i sends $v = A_1 \hat{R}^u$, RF_i forwards $\hat{v} = \hat{A}_1 R^{\tilde{u}}$ to P_j where $\hat{A}_1 = A_1 \cdot \tilde{A}$, $\hat{v} = v \cdot \tilde{A} \cdot R^{\tilde{u}}$ and $\hat{u} = ru + \tilde{u}$ for random values $\tilde{a}, \tilde{u} \leftarrow \mathbb{Z}q$ and $\tilde{A} = g^{\tilde{a}}$. When P_i sends $v_p = g^{\mathsf{pk}_1}\hat{R}^{u_p}$, RF_i forwards $\hat{v}_p = g^{\hat{\mathsf{pk}}_1}R^{\hat{u}_p}$ to P_j where $\hat{\mathsf{pk}}_1 = \mathsf{pk}_1 + \tilde{\mathsf{pk}}$, $\hat{v} = v \cdot g^{\tilde{\mathsf{pk}}} \cdot R^{\tilde{u}_p}$ and $\hat{u} = ru_p + \tilde{u}_p$ for random values $\tilde{u}_p \leftarrow \mathbb{Z}q$ and $\tilde{\mathsf{pk}} = \mathsf{oGen}(1^\lambda)$.
3. When P_j sends (A_2, pk_2), RF_i forwards $\hat{A}_2 = A_2 \cdot \tilde{A}$ and $\hat{\mathsf{pk}}_2 = \mathsf{pk}_2 + \tilde{\mathsf{pk}}$ to P_i. P_i computes $\hat{\mathsf{pk}} = \mathsf{pk}_1 + \hat{\mathsf{pk}}_2 = \mathsf{pk}_1 + \mathsf{pk}_2 + \tilde{\mathsf{pk}}$.
4. When P_i sends commitment randomness (u, u_p, pk_1), RF_i drops the message if $v_p \neq g^{u_p} \hat{R}^{\mathsf{pk}_1}$. Else, RF_i forwards $(\hat{u}, \hat{u}_p, \hat{\mathsf{pk}}_1)$ to P_j.
5. P_j computes $\hat{\mathsf{pk}} = \hat{\mathsf{pk}}_1 + \mathsf{pk}_2 = \mathsf{pk}_1 + \mathsf{pk}_2 + \tilde{\mathsf{pk}}$. P_j computes $\hat{A} = A_1 \cdot A_2 \cdot \tilde{A}$. When P_j sends $(h, Z) = (h, \hat{A}^t)$ drop the message if $e(h, \hat{A}) \neq e(g, Z)$. Else, sample a $\tilde{t} \leftarrow \mathbb{Z}_q$ and compute $\hat{h} = h^{\tilde{t}}$. Send $(\hat{h}, \hat{Z}) = (\hat{h}, Z^{\tilde{t}})$ to P_i. P_j sets h as the parameter and P_i sets $\hat{h} = h^{\tilde{t}}$ as the parameter. P_i and P_j sets $\hat{\mathsf{pk}}$ as the pairwise public key parameter.
6. When P_i sends a_1, RF_i drops the message if $v \neq g^{a_1} \hat{R}^u$. Else, RF_i forwards $\hat{a}_1 = a_1 + \tilde{a}$ to P_j.

The above steps are also repeated when P_i is the verifier and P_j is the committer.
Commitment Generation Phase:
RF_i chooses a random coin $\tilde{s}_i$ and computes $\{\tilde{s}_{ji}\}_{j \in [n] \setminus i}$ randomly such that $\Sigma_{j \in [n] \setminus i} \tilde{s}_{ji} = \tilde{s}_i$. RF_i performs the following :

- *P_i is the committer:* When P_i sends a commitment $(c_{ij}, e_{ij,0}, e_{ij,1})$ compute $\hat{c}_{ij} = g^{\hat{s}_i} h_{ij}^{\hat{d}_{ij}} = c_{ij} \cdot g^{\tilde{s}_i} \cdot h_{ij}^{\tilde{d}_{ij}}$ where $\hat{s}_i = s_i + \tilde{s}_i$ and $\hat{d}_{ij} = d_{ij} \cdot \tilde{t} + \tilde{d}_{ij}$ for $\tilde{d}_{ij} \leftarrow \mathbb{Z}_q$. Set $e_{\hat{ij},0} = \tilde{t} \cdot e_{ij,0} + \mathsf{Enc}(\hat{\mathsf{pk}}, \tilde{d}_{ij}; y_{\tilde{ij},0})$ and $e_{\hat{ij},1} = \tilde{t} \cdot e_{ij,1} + \mathsf{Enc}(\hat{\mathsf{pk}}, \tilde{d}_{ij}; y_{\tilde{ij},1})$. The firewall forwards $(\hat{c}_{ij}, e_{\hat{ij},0}, e_{\hat{ij},1})$ to P_j. Here $\tilde{t}, h_{ij}$ and $\hat{\mathsf{pk}}$ correspond to the run where P_j is verifier and P_i is committer.
- *P_j is the committer:* When P_j sends a commitment $(c_{ji}, e_{ji,0}, e_{ji,1})$ compute $\hat{c}_{ji} = g^{\hat{s}_j} h_{ji}^{\hat{d}_{ji}} = c_{ji} \cdot g^{\tilde{s}_{ji}} \cdot h_{ji}^{\tilde{d}_{ji}}$ where $\hat{s}_j = s_j + \tilde{s}_{ji}$ and $\hat{d}_{ji} = d_{ji} \cdot \tilde{t} + \tilde{d}_{ji}$ for $\tilde{d}_{ji} \leftarrow \mathbb{Z}_q$. Set $e_{\hat{ji},0} = \tilde{t} \cdot e_{ji,0} + \mathsf{Enc}(\hat{\mathsf{pk}}, \tilde{d}_{ji}; y_{\tilde{ji},0})$ and $e_{\hat{ji},1} = \tilde{t} \cdot e_{ji,1} + \mathsf{Enc}(\hat{\mathsf{pk}}, \tilde{d}_{ji}; y_{\tilde{ji},1})$. The firewall forwards $(\hat{c}_{ji}, e_{\hat{ji},0}, e_{\hat{ji},1})$ to P_i. Here $\tilde{t}, h_{ji}$ and $\hat{\mathsf{pk}}$ correspond to the run where P_i is verifier and P_j is committer.

Commitment Opening Phase:

- When party P_i broadcasts s_i, RF_i broadcasts $\hat{s}_i$. When P_i opens commitments by sending (d_{ij}, y_{ij}), RF_i drops the message if $c_{ij} \neq g^{s_i} h_{ij}^{d_{ij}}$ or $e_{ij,s_i} \neq \mathsf{Enc}(\hat{\mathsf{pk}}, d_{ij}; y_{ij})$. Else, RF_i sends $(\hat{d}_{ij}, \hat{y}_{ij}) = (\tilde{t} \cdot d_{ij} + \tilde{d}_{ij}, \tilde{t} \cdot y_{ij} + y_{\tilde{ij}})$ and claims that $e_{ij,1-\hat{s}_i}$ was obliviously sampled.
- When party P_j broadcasts s_j, RF_i sends $\hat{s}_j$ to P_i. When P_j opens commitments by sending (d_{ji}, y_{ji}), RF_i drops the message if $c_{ji} \neq g^{s_j} \hat{h}_{ji}^{d_{ji}}$ or $e_{ji,s_j} \neq \mathsf{Enc}(\hat{\mathsf{pk}}, d_{ji}; y_{ji})$. Else, RF_i sends $(\hat{d}_{ji}, \hat{y}_{ji}) == (\tilde{t} \cdot d_{ji} + \tilde{d}_{ji}, \tilde{t} \cdot y_{ji} + y_{\tilde{ji}})$ and claims that $e_{ji,1-\hat{s}_j}$ was obliviously sampled.

Fig. 8. Reverse Firewall RF_i for Party P_i in Π_{coin}

public key space of PKE *be* $\mathbb{Z}_q$. *Then* Π_{coin} *(Fig. 7) securely implements the coin-tossing functionality (Definition 3) against adaptive corruption of parties in the plain model and in the presence of functionality maintaining tampering of honest parties.*

The FHE scheme of [25] based on LWE assumption satisfies all the properties required from the PKE. We consider $q = \max(q_{LWE}, q_{DL})$ where LWE holds for $q \geq q_{LWE}$ and DL holds for $q \geq q_{DL}$. Thus we get the result from Discrete Log, Knowledge of Exponent and LWE assumptions.

7   The Final Compiler

We now show our final result, i.e., an *adaptively* secure MPC protocol in the *plain* model that admits reverse firewalls. In particular, the reverse firewall for our final MPC protocol is obtained by combining the reverse firewall for our adaptively secure MPC protocol Π_{mpc} in the uniform random string (urs$_{mpc}$) model (see Sect. 5.3) along with the reverse firewall for our adaptively secure multi-party coin-tossing protocol Π_{coin} in the plain model (see Sect. 6). Let us denote the final MPC protocol (in the plain model) to be Π which is obtained by first running Π_{coin} to obtain urs$_{mpc}$ and then running Π_{mpc} using urs$_{mpc}$.

Let us consider a reverse firewall $\mathsf{RF}_i = (\mathsf{RF}_{coin}^i, \mathsf{RF}_{mpc}^i)$ to be the firewall for a party P_i in the protocol Π. RF_i is obtained by first applying RF_{coin}^i to the messages of Π_{coin}, followed by application of RF_{coin}^i to the messages of Π_{mpc}, if RF_{coin}^i did not output $\bot$. We show that RF_i provides weak ER for party P_i in Π. We defer the proof of the theorem to the full version.

Theorem 17 (Composition Theorem for Π). *Let* Π_{mpc} *be an adaptively secure MPC protocol in the uniform random string (*urs$_{mpc}$*) model,* Π_{coin} *securely implement the coin-tossing functionality (see Definition 3) against adaptive corruption of parties in the plain model. Let* RF_{mpc}^i *and* RF_{coin}^i *be transparent, functionality-maintaining, and weakly exfiltration-resistant reverse firewalls for some party* P_i *in* Π_{mpc} *and* Π_{coin} *respectively. Then* RF_i *is transparent, functionality-maintaining, and weakly exfiltration-resistant reverse firewall for party* P_i *in the protocol* Π.

References

1. Abe, M., Fehr, S.: Perfect NIZK with adaptive soundness. In: Vadhan, S.P. (ed.) TCC 2007. LNCS, vol. 4392, pp. 118–136. Springer, Heidelberg (2007). https://doi.org/10.1007/978-3-540-70936-7_7
2. Ateniese, G., Magri, B., Venturi, D.: Subversion-resilient signature schemes. In: Ray, I., Li, N., Kruegel, C. (eds.) ACM CCS 2015, pp. 364–375. ACM Press, October 2015
3. Auerbach, B., Bellare, M., Kiltz, E.: Public-key encryption resistant to parameter subversion and its realization from efficiently-embeddable groups. In: Abdalla, M., Dahab, R. (eds.) PKC 2018, Part I. LNCS, vol. 10769, pp. 348–377. Springer, Cham (2018). https://doi.org/10.1007/978-3-319-76578-5_12

4. Ball, J., Borger, J., Greenwald, G., et al.: Revealed: how us and uk spy agencies defeat internet privacy and security. Know Your Neighborhood (2013)
5. Bellare, M., Fuchsbauer, G., Scafuro, A.: NIZKs with an untrusted crs: security in the face of parameter subversion. In: Cheon, J.H., Takagi, T. (eds.) ASIACRYPT 2016, Part II. LNCS, vol. 10032, pp. 777–804. Springer, Heidelberg (2016). https://doi.org/10.1007/978-3-662-53890-6_26
6. Bellare, M., Jaeger, J., Kane, D.: Mass-surveillance without the state: Strongly undetectable algorithm-substitution attacks. In: Ray, I., Li, N., Kruegel, C. (eds.) ACM CCS 2015, pp. 1431–1440. ACM Press, October 2015
7. Bellare, M., Paterson, K.G., Rogaway, P.: Security of symmetric encryption against mass surveillance. In: Garay, J.A., Gennaro, R. (eds.) CRYPTO 2014, Part I. LNCS, vol. 8616, pp. 1–19. Springer, Heidelberg (2014). https://doi.org/10.1007/978-3-662-44371-2_1
8. Bemmann, P., Chen, R., Jager, T.: Subversion-resilient public key encryption with practical watchdogs. In: Garay, J.A. (ed.) PKC 2021, Part I. LNCS, vol. 12710, pp. 627–658. Springer, Cham (2021). https://doi.org/10.1007/978-3-030-75245-3_23
9. Benhamouda, F., Lin, H., Polychroniadou, A., Venkitasubramaniam, M.: Two-round adaptively secure multiparty computation from standard assumptions. In: Beimel, A., Dziembowski, S. (eds.) TCC 2018, Part I. LNCS, vol. 11239, pp. 175–205. Springer, Cham (2018). https://doi.org/10.1007/978-3-030-03807-6_7
10. Canetti, R., Sarkar, P., Wang, X.: Efficient and round-optimal oblivious transfer and commitment with adaptive security. In: Moriai, S., Wang, H. (eds.) ASIACRYPT 2020, Part III. LNCS, vol. 12493, pp. 277–308. Springer, Cham (2020). https://doi.org/10.1007/978-3-030-64840-4_10
11. Canetti, R., Sarkar, P., Wang, X.: Triply adaptive uc nizk. Cryptology ePrint Archive, Report 2020/1212 (2020). https://eprint.iacr.org/2020/1212
12. Chakraborty, S., Dziembowski, S., Nielsen, J.B.: Reverse firewalls for actively secure MPCs. In: Micciancio, D., Ristenpart, T. (eds.) CRYPTO 2020, Part II. LNCS, vol. 12171, pp. 732–762. Springer, Cham (2020). https://doi.org/10.1007/978-3-030-56880-1_26
13. Chen, R., Huang, X., Yung, M.: Subvert KEM to Break DEM: practical algorithm-substitution attacks on public-key encryption. In: Moriai, S., Wang, H. (eds.) ASIACRYPT 2020, Part II. LNCS, vol. 12492, pp. 98–128. Springer, Cham (2020). https://doi.org/10.1007/978-3-030-64834-3_4
14. Chen, R., Mu, Y., Yang, G., Susilo, W., Guo, F., Zhang, M.: Cryptographic reverse firewall via malleable smooth projective hash functions. In: Cheon, J.H., Takagi, T. (eds.) ASIACRYPT 2016, Part I. LNCS, vol. 10031, pp. 844–876. Springer, Heidelberg (2016). https://doi.org/10.1007/978-3-662-53887-6_31
15. Choi, S.G., Dachman-Soled, D., Malkin, T., Wee, H.: Improved non-committing encryption with applications to adaptively secure protocols. In: Matsui, M. (ed.) ASIACRYPT 2009. LNCS, vol. 5912, pp. 287–302. Springer, Heidelberg (2009). https://doi.org/10.1007/978-3-642-10366-7_17
16. Dauterman, E., Corrigan-Gibbs, H., Mazières, D., Boneh, D., Rizzo, D.: True2F: Backdoor-resistant authentication tokens. In: 2019 IEEE Symposium on Security and Privacy, pp. 398–416. IEEE Computer Society Press, May 2019
17. Degabriele, J.P., Farshim, P., Poettering, B.: A more cautious approach to security against mass surveillance. In: Leander, G. (ed.) FSE 2015. LNCS, vol. 9054, pp. 579–598. Springer, Heidelberg (2015). https://doi.org/10.1007/978-3-662-48116-5_28

18. Degabriele, J.P., Paterson, K.G., Schuldt, J.C.N., Woodage, J.: Backdoors in pseudorandom number generators: possibility and impossibility results. In: Robshaw, M., Katz, J. (eds.) CRYPTO 2016 Part I. LNCS, vol. 9814, pp. 403–432. Springer, Heidelberg (2016). https://doi.org/10.1007/978-3-662-53018-4_15

19. Dodis, Y., Ganesh, C., Golovnev, A., Juels, A., Ristenpart, T.: A formal treatment of backdoored pseudorandom generators. In: Oswald, E., Fischlin, M. (eds.) EUROCRYPT 2015, Part I. LNCS, vol. 9056, pp. 101–126. Springer, Heidelberg (2015). https://doi.org/10.1007/978-3-662-46800-5_5

20. Dodis, Y., Mironov, I., Stephens-Davidowitz, N.: Message transmission with reverse firewalls—secure communication on corrupted machines. In: Robshaw, M., Katz, J. (eds.) CRYPTO 2016, Part I. LNCS, vol. 9814, pp. 341–372. Springer, Heidelberg (2016). https://doi.org/10.1007/978-3-662-53018-4_13

21. Feige, U., Lapidot, D., Shamir, A.: Multiple noninteractive zero knowledge proofs under general assumptions. SIAM J. Comput. **29**(1), 1–28 (1999)

22. Fischlin, M., Mazaheri, S.: Self-guarding cryptographic protocols against algorithm substitution attacks. In: 2018 IEEE 31st Computer Security Foundations Symposium (CSF), pp. 76–90. IEEE (2018)

23. Ganesh, C., Magri, B., Venturi, D.: Cryptographic reverse firewalls for interactive proof systems. In: Czumaj, A., Dawar, A., Merelli, E. (eds.) ICALP 2020, volume 168 of LIPIcs, pp. 55:1–55:16. Schloss Dagstuhl, July 2020

24. Garg, S., Sahai, A.: Adaptively secure multi-party computation with dishonest majority. In: Safavi-Naini, R., Canetti, R. (eds.) CRYPTO 2012. LNCS, vol. 7417, pp. 105–123. Springer, Heidelberg (2012). https://doi.org/10.1007/978-3-642-32009-5_8

25. Gentry, C., Sahai, A., Waters, B.: Homomorphic encryption from learning with errors: conceptually-simpler, asymptotically-faster, attribute-based. In: Canetti, R., Garay, J.A. (eds.) CRYPTO 2013, Part I. LNCS, vol. 8042, pp. 75–92. Springer, Heidelberg (2013). https://doi.org/10.1007/978-3-642-40041-4_5

26. Goldreich, O., Micali, S., Wigderson, A.: How to play any mental game or A completeness theorem for protocols with honest majority. In: Aho, A., (ed.) 19th ACM STOC, pp. 218–229. ACM Press, May 1987

27. Gorbunov, S., Vaikuntanathan, V., Wichs, D.: Leveled fully homomorphic signatures from standard lattices. In: Servedio, R.A., Rubinfeld, R. (eds.) 47th ACM STOC, pp. 469–477. ACM Press, June 2015

28. Mironov, I., Stephens-Davidowitz, N.: Cryptographic reverse firewalls. In: Oswald, E., Fischlin, M. (eds.) EUROCRYPT 2015, Part II. LNCS, vol. 9057, pp. 657–686. Springer, Heidelberg (2015). https://doi.org/10.1007/978-3-662-46803-6_22

29. Russell, A., Tang, Q., Yung, M., Zhou, H.-S.: Cliptography: clipping the power of kleptographic attacks. In: Cheon, J.H., Takagi, T. (eds.) ASIACRYPT 2016, Part II. LNCS, vol. 10032, pp. 34–64. Springer, Heidelberg (2016). https://doi.org/10.1007/978-3-662-53890-6_2

30. Russell, A., Tang, Q., Yung, M., Zhou, H.-S.: Generic semantic security against a kleptographic adversary. In: Thuraisingham, B.M., Evans, D., Malkin, T., Xu, D. (eds.) ACM CCS 2017, pp. 907–922. ACM Press, October 2017

31. Shumow, D., Ferguson, N.: On the possibility of a back door in the nist sp800-90 dual ec prng. In: Procedings Crypto, vol. 7 (2007)

32. Simmons, G.J.: Authentication theory/Coding theory. In: Blakley, G.R., Chaum, D. (eds.) CRYPTO 1984. LNCS, vol. 196, pp. 411–431. Springer, Heidelberg (1984). https://doi.org/10.1007/3-540-39568-7_32

33. Young, A., Yung, M.: The dark side of "Black-Box" cryptography or: should we trust capstone? In: Koblitz, N. (ed.) CRYPTO 1996. LNCS, vol. 1109, pp. 89–103. Springer, Heidelberg (1996). https://doi.org/10.1007/3-540-68697-5_8

Enhanced Public-Key Encryption and Time-Lock Puzzles

On Time-Lock Cryptographic Assumptions in Abelian Hidden-Order Groups

Aron van Baarsen[(✉)] and Marc Stevens[(✉)]

CWI, Cryptology Group, Amsterdam, The Netherlands
{aron.van.baarsen,marc.stevens}@cwi.nl

Abstract. In this paper we study cryptographic finite abelian groups of unknown order and hardness assumptions in these groups. Abelian groups necessitate multiple group generators, which may be chosen at random. We formalize this setting and hardness assumptions therein. Furthermore, we generalize the algebraic group model and strong algebraic group model from cyclic groups to arbitrary finite abelian groups of unknown order. Building on these formalizations, we present techniques to deal with this new setting, and prove new reductions. These results are relevant for class groups of imaginary quadratic number fields and time-lock cryptography build upon them.

Keywords: Cryptographic abelian groups · Hidden order groups · Algebraic group model · Time-lock cryptography

1 Introduction

Abelian groups of hidden order have recently been gaining more attention in cryptography, due to their applications in, for example, time-lock cryptography [7,23,31], cryptographic accumulators [7] and zero-knowledge arguments [4,11]. Both RSA groups and class groups of imaginary quadratic number fields have been proposed as hidden order groups for these applications. A trusted setup is required in the RSA group setting to hide the order, but the class group setting does not suffer from this restriction. In contrast to RSA groups, class groups are abelian groups which are not always cyclic, i.e., they may require more than one generator to generate the full group. In particular, this implies prime divisors of the group order may have multiplicity larger than one. Moreover, there are no known generic efficient algorithms for hidden order abelian groups to compute a smallest set of generators or to certify a set of elements generate the full group.

There has been significantly less study of computational assumptions in abelian groups compared to cyclic groups. This paper aims to address this gap by studying the relation between various computational problems in finite abelian groups in the (strong) algebraic group model. The algebraic group model (AGM),

Research partially funded by NWO/TKI Grant 628.009.014.

© International Association for Cryptologic Research 2021
M. Tibouchi and H. Wang (Eds.): ASIACRYPT 2021, LNCS 13091, pp. 367–397, 2021.
https://doi.org/10.1007/978-3-030-92075-3_13

Table 1. Overview of the relevant computational games in cyclic groups

Name	Game $((\mathbb{G}, g) \xleftarrow{\$} \mathcal{G}_\kappa)$	Outcome
$\mathsf{MO}_\mathcal{C}$	$N \xleftarrow{\$} \mathcal{A}(g)$	$N \equiv 0 \pmod{|\mathbb{G}|}$
$\mathsf{HO}_\mathcal{C}$	$N \xleftarrow{\$} \mathcal{A}(g)$	$N = |\mathbb{G}|$
$\mathsf{DLog}/\mathsf{DLog}_1$	$X \xleftarrow{\$} \mathbb{G}, \; e \xleftarrow{\$} \mathcal{A}(g, X)$	$g^e = X$
DLog_2	$X \xleftarrow{\$} \mathbb{G}, \; Y \xleftarrow{\$} \langle X \rangle, \; e \xleftarrow{\$} \mathcal{A}(g, X, Y)$	$X^e = Y$
$\mathsf{CDH}/\mathsf{CDH}_1$	$a, b \xleftarrow{\$} \mathcal{U}_{|\mathbb{G}|}, \; Y \xleftarrow{\$} \mathcal{A}(g, g^a, g^b)$	$Y = g^{ab}$
CDH_2	$X \xleftarrow{\$} \mathbb{G}, \; a, b \xleftarrow{\$} \mathcal{U}_{|\langle X \rangle|}, \; Y \xleftarrow{\$} \mathcal{A}(g, X, X^a, X^b)$	$Y = X^{ab}$

Here $\mathcal{G} = (\mathcal{G}_\kappa)_{\kappa=1}^{\infty}$ is a cyclic group family with security parameter κ, and $\mathcal{A}$ is an adversary playing the game. Each game starts by sampling $(\mathbb{G}, g)$. See Sect. 3.

introduced by Fuchsbauer, Kiltz and Loss [17], requires algorithms to output an algebraic representation of their output elements in terms of input group elements. The strong algebraic group model (SAGM), introduced by Katz, Loss and Xu [18], additionally requires any algorithm to expose the circuit of group operations it computed for output group elements. Both these models have predominantly been used to study computational assumptions in cyclic groups, mainly those of prime order [17] and semiprime order [18]. Another aim of this paper is therefore to generalize the AGM and the SAGM to the setting of finite abelian groups which are not necessarily cyclic.

Restricted Group Models. There has been a relatively long history of studying computational problems in groups in a restricted model of computation. Starting with Nechaev [22] and Shoup [30] introducing the generic group model (GGM). The two main computational models relevant to this paper are the algebraic group model (AGM) [17] and the strong algebraic group model (SAGM) [18].

Intuitively speaking, in contrast to the GGM, an algorithm in the AGM is allowed to exploit any additional group structure and representation of group elements like in the standard model. However, the AGM is not equivalent to the standard model, as algorithms in the AGM are required to provide an algebraic representation of their output group elements in terms of input group elements. The SAGM lies between the AGM and the GGM as it requires that the algorithm exposes the circuit of group operations it computed for output group elements.

In the (S)AGM one can study the hardness of computational problems through reductions to other computational problems, just as in the standard model (SM). The generic group model also allows for the proving of information-theoretic lower bounds on the complexity of computational problems. See for instance, the lower bounds on the discrete logarithm and the computational Diffie-Hellman problem by Shoup [30], and the lower bound on any generic reduction from the discrete logarithm problem to the computational Diffie-Hellman problem when the group order has a multiple prime factor by Maurer and Wolff [21].

Since reductions in the (S)AGM are typically *generic*, i.e., the reduction itself only uses generic group operations, computational lower bounds in the GGM can imply the impossibility of efficient generic reductions in the AGM.

Table 2. Overview of the relevant computational games in finite abelian groups

Name	Game ($\mathbb{G} \xleftarrow{\$} \mathcal{G}_\kappa$, $\boldsymbol{g} := (g_1, \ldots, g_n) \xleftarrow{\$} \mathbb{G}^n$)	$\mathcal{A}$ wins if
MO	$N \xleftarrow{\$} \mathcal{A}(\boldsymbol{g})$	$N \equiv 0 \pmod{|\mathbb{G}|} \wedge N \neq 0$
HO	$N \xleftarrow{\$} \mathcal{A}(\boldsymbol{g})$	$N = |\mathbb{G}|$
LO	$(X, d) \xleftarrow{\$} \mathcal{A}(\boldsymbol{g})$	$X \neq 1_{\mathbb{G}} \wedge 1 < d < 2^\kappa \wedge X^d = 1_{\mathbb{G}}$
DLog$_1$	$X \xleftarrow{\$} \mathbb{G}$, $e \xleftarrow{\$} \mathcal{A}(\boldsymbol{g}, X)$	$\boldsymbol{g}^e = X$
DLog$_2$	$X \xleftarrow{\$} \mathbb{G}$, $Y \xleftarrow{\$} \langle X \rangle$, $e \xleftarrow{\$} \mathcal{A}(\boldsymbol{g}, X, Y)$	$X^e = Y$
CDH$_2$	$X \xleftarrow{\$} \mathbb{G}$, $a, b \xleftarrow{\$} \mathcal{U}_{|\langle X \rangle|}$, $Y \xleftarrow{\$} \mathcal{A}(\boldsymbol{g}, X, X^a, X^b)$	$Y = X^{ab}$
e-RT	$X \xleftarrow{\$} \mathbb{G}$, $Y \xleftarrow{\$} \mathcal{A}(\boldsymbol{g}, X^e)$	$Y^e = X \wedge e > 1$
StRoot	$X \xleftarrow{\$} \mathbb{G}$, $(Y, e) \xleftarrow{\$} \mathcal{A}(\boldsymbol{g}, X)$	$Y^e = X \wedge e > 1$
ARoot	$X \xleftarrow{\$} \mathcal{A}(\boldsymbol{g})$, $\ell \xleftarrow{\$} \text{Primes}(2\kappa)$, $Y \xleftarrow{\$} \mathcal{A}(X, \ell)$	$X \neq 1_{\mathbb{G}} \wedge Y^\ell = X$
T-RSW	$\mathcal{A}_2 \leftarrow \mathcal{A}_1(\boldsymbol{g})$, $X \xleftarrow{\$} \mathbb{G}$, $Y \xleftarrow{\$} \mathcal{A}_2(\boldsymbol{g}, X)$	$Y = X^{2^T} \wedge \text{ATime}(\mathcal{A}_2) < T$

Here $\mathcal{G} = (\mathcal{G}_\kappa)_{\kappa=1}^\infty$ is a group family with security parameter κ, and $\mathcal{A}$ is an adversary playing the game. Each game starts by sampling $\mathbb{G}, g_1, \ldots, g_n$. See Sect. 4.

1.1 Our Contributions

The main contributions of this paper consist of (1) a formalization of the finite abelian hidden order setting and the respective generalizations of the (S)AGM, and (2) proving security reductions in this setting as further detailed below.

In Sect. 4, we first formalize the setting of working with *finite abelian groups of hidden order* and introduce a framework to study computational problems therein. An important example are class groups of imaginary quadratic number fields. Instead of assuming the existence of a canonical set of generators, a sufficiently large set of random group elements is used to generate the full group. Hence, each game in Table 2 includes sampling a set of random generators.

We generalize both the AGM and SAGM to this setting, as earlier related works were restricted to prime order cyclic groups [17] and hidden order RSA groups [18], respectively. We will refer to these generalized models as the *abelian hidden order (strong) algebraic group model* (AHO-AGM and AHO-SAGM, respectively, for short).

An overview of the computational problems we consider in finite abelian hidden order groups is given in Table 2. These are (including some works that depend on them):

MO/HO: the *(multiple/exact) order problem* ([3,4,6,7,11,13,18,23,31]);
LO: the *low order problem* ([7,23]);
ARoot: the *adaptive root problem* ([6,7,11,31]);
StRoot: the *strong root problem* ([6,11,13]);
e-RT: the *e-th root problem* ([3,24],[9, Ch. 12]);
T-RSW: the *T-repeated squaring problem* ([7,18,23,26,31]);
DLog$_1$: the *generalized discrete logarithm problem* ([8]);
DLog$_2$: the *subgroup discrete logarithm problem* ([3], [9, Ch. 12]);
CDH$_2$: the *subgroup computational Diffie-Hellman problem* ([9, Ch. 12],[10]).

An overview of the relevant counterparts of these computational games in cyclic groups is given in Table 1.

A \ B	DLog₁	DLog₂	CDH₂	HO	MO	T-RSW	StRoot	ARoot	e-RT	LO
DLog₁				[29], 6.6	[29], 6.6	[29], 6.6	[29], 6.6	[29], 6.6	[29], 6.6	[29], 6.6
DLog₂				[29], 6.6	[29], 6.6	[29], 6.6	[29], 6.6	[29], 6.6	[29], 6.6	[29], 6.6
CDH₂		6.3		[29], 6.8	[29], 6.8	[29], 6.8	[29], 6.8	[29], 6.8	[29], 6.8	[29], 6.8
HO										
MO	6.5	6.4	7.5	Trivial		8.2	7.1	7.2	7.4	7.3
T-RSW	6.5	6.4	7.5	[18], 6.1	[18], 6.1		7.1	7.2	7.4	7.3
StRoot	6.5	6.4	7.5	[14], 6.1	[14], 6.1	8.2		7.2	7.4	7.3
ARoot	6.5	6.4	7.5	[30], 6.1	[30], 6.1	8.2	7.1		7.4	[7]
e-RT	†[3], 6.1	†[3], 6.1	†[3], 6.1	†[3], 6.1	†[3], 6.1	†[3], 6.1	†[3], 6.1	†[3], 6.1		†[3], 6.1
LO	‡6.2,6.5	‡6.2,6.4	‡6.2,7.5	‡6.2	‡6.2	‡6.2,8.2	‡6.2,7.1	‡6.2,7.2	‡6.2,7.4	

Fig. 1. Overview of the relevant reductions $A \xrightarrow{\text{AHO-GM}} B$ in the finite abelian hidden order group model, where GM is in the set $\{\text{SM}, \text{AGM}, \text{SAGM}\}$. The colors and symbols in the cells mean the following:
- new results (in SM/AGM/SAGM) ( ), partial results ( ), no *generic* reduction (■)
- †: conditioned on e coprime with group order
- ‡: assuming an oracle for small prime subdivisor of group order

For *cyclic groups of hidden order*, we show in Sect. 3 the simple reduction $\text{MO}_\mathcal{C} \Rightarrow \text{DLog}$ in the *hidden order cyclic group model* (HO-SM). Subsequently, we prove a novel reduction $\text{HO}_\mathcal{C} \Rightarrow \text{DLog}$ in the HO-SM (see Theorem 3.5).

For *finite abelian hidden order groups*, our contributions are outlined in Fig. 1 and detailed in Sects. 5, 6, 7 and 8. In the AHO-SM, we prove reductions of MO to DLog_1 and DLog_2, and of LO to MO in the case where an oracle for a small prime divisor of the group order exists. We provide an example of such an oracle for the class group setting.

In the AHO-AGM, we prove that MO is equivalent to ARoot as well as StRoot. Furthermore, we prove reductions of MO to e-RT, LO and CDH_2. Lastly, in the AHO-SAGM, we prove that T-RSW is equivalent to MO.

Overview of Techniques. The main results of this paper are reductions from the problem of computing a multiple of the order of a finite abelian group to other computational problems. A key observation here is that when $\mathbb{G}$ is a finite abelian group generated by $\boldsymbol{g} = (g_1, \ldots, g_n)$, then the integer vectors $\boldsymbol{e} = (e_1, \ldots, e_n)$ with $g_1^{e_1} \cdots g_n^{e_n} = 1_\mathbb{G}$ form a lattice, called the *relationship lattice* of $\boldsymbol{g}$. We show in Lemma 5.1 that if one can find relations $\boldsymbol{e}_1, \ldots, \boldsymbol{e}_n$ which form a full rank sublattice of $L(\boldsymbol{g})$, then $|\det(\boldsymbol{e}_1, \ldots, \boldsymbol{e}_n)|$ is an integer multiple of the order of $\mathbb{G}$.

In Lemma 5.4 we prove a template reduction to obtain a multiple of the group order with specified bounded loss in time and success probability, based on a given simple transformation from an adversary to a relation sampler with the following requirements: (1) repeated calls have independent and identical success probability, which may not hold for the underlying adversary; (2) n relations from n successful executions of the resulting relation sampler have negligible probability to be linearly dependent. The reduction succeeds when n linearly independent relations are obtained among $\lceil Sn/p \rceil$ calls to the sampler, where S is an oversampling parameter and p is the adversary's advantage. Lemmas 2.6 and 2.7 on probability distribution ensembles allow us to bound the success probability loss of the reduction.

To use the template reduction for several of our results, in each case we need to construct such a relation sampler and prove it satisfies these requirements. To show that the determinant $|\det(e_1, \ldots, e_n)|$ is non-zero, one can pick a suitable large prime p and show that the determinant is non-zero modulo p with all but negligible probability. This can be achieved by demonstrating that the relationship coefficients modulo p (i.e., the coefficients of the matrix $E = (e_1, \ldots, e_n) \bmod p$) are distributed close, i.e., at negligible statistical distance, to uniform (see Lemma 2.5). Subsequently, we can apply the Schwartz-Zippel lemma [29, 32] to conclude that the determinant of E will be zero modulo p with negligible probability.

In order to obtain these relations with close to uniformly distributed coefficients modulo p, we query an adversary $\mathcal{A}$, which solves a given computational problem G, a number of times on independent random inputs from a fixed group $\mathbb{G}$, i.e., a new set of generators and challenge group elements. Note that by each time freshly sampling a set of generators and input challenge it also satisfies the requirement for independent and identical success probabilities.

From a correct input and output instance (and algebraic representations of these instances with respect to $\boldsymbol{g}$), we need to show one can obtain a relation with respect to $\boldsymbol{g}$. To construct relations which are distributed sufficiently close to uniform modulo p, a main observation is that if we pass an element $X = g_1^{r_1} \cdots g_n^{r_n}$ to the adversary $\mathcal{A}$, and write $r_i = r_i' + r_i'' \cdot |\langle g_i \rangle|$ with $0 \leq r_i' < |\langle g_i \rangle|$, then the group element X is independent of the values of r_i'' (as $g_i^{|\langle g_i \rangle|} = 1_\mathbb{G}$) and thus any execution of $\mathcal{A}$ is independent of these r_i''. If we sample r_i uniformly from a sufficiently large set, then their modular reduction $r_i'' \bmod p$ is going to be distributed negligibly close to uniform modulo p as desired.

In the case of cyclic groups, we show one can obtain the *exact* group order with high probability from several multiples of the group order obtained from a discrete logarithm adversary (Theorem 3.5). The main ingredient in this proof is a theorem which states that independent uniformly sampled integers, shifted by some bounded independent integers, have greatest common divisor equal to one with high probability (Theorem 3.4).

1.2 Related Work

Damgård and Koprowski [14] considered a variant of the strong root problem StRoot and the e-th root problem e-RT in the GGM. The main difference is that our work considers these assumptions in the AGM, and the methods we use are mostly incomparable. This paper [14] did however introduce a version of the GGM in which the group order is *hidden* and introduced the notion of a *(hard) group family*, on which our definitions in Sect. 4 are based.

Katz et al. [18] showed a reduction from the integer factorization problem to the T-repeated squaring problem T-RSW for RSA groups in the SAGM. Their reduction is in fact a reduction from the exact order problem HO to the T-RSW problem. They show this through a reduction from HO to the multiple order problem MO, which happen to be equivalent in RSA groups [18, Lemma 1]. Although Lemma 8.1 and Theorem 8.2 of our work can be seen as a generalization of [18, Theorem 2] from the family of RSA groups to *all* finite abelian groups, the techniques we use to prove these results are distinct and novel. Additionally, our work in the finite abelian group setting investigates more relations between more computational problems. The motivation to do so is that class groups of imaginary quadratic number fields are not covered by [18], while this is one of the main candidate group families for hidden order cryptography like VDFs.

Finally, the line of work by Rotem, Segev and Shahaf [28] and Rotem and Segev [27] considers generic-group delay functions and generic-ring delay functions, respectively. In particular, they show that generically speeding up repeated squaring is equivalent to factoring [27]. Their work [27] is however again limited to rings of the form $\mathbb{Z}_N$ with $N = pq$ an RSA modulus. Moreover, the works are in the setting of the generic group model (for cyclic groups) [28] and the generic ring model [27], and their methods are unlike this work.

1.3   Applications of Hidden-Order Groups

Verifiable Delay Functions. Verifiable delay functions (VDFs) were introduced by Boneh, Bonneau, Bünz and Fisch [5] as a cryptographic primitive with proposed applications in, for example, public randomness beacons [7,16,25] and computational timestamping [7,19]. The most popular VDF constructions are those introduced by Weselowski [31] and Pietrzak [23], both are based on the notion of time-lock puzzles from Rivest, Shamir and Wagner [26]. Time-lock puzzles assume that no efficient adversary can compute X^{2^T} faster than by computing T sequential squarings, which translates to the T-RSW hardness assumption in the AHO-SAGM. We show in Theorem 8.2 that T-RSW is hard in the AHO-SAGM if it is hard to compute a multiple of the group order (i.e., MO is hard). Furthermore, these constructions assume the hardness of the adaptive root problem ARoot (for Weselowski's construction) and the low order problem LO (for Pietrzak's construction). We show in Theorem 7.2 that ARoot is hard in the AHO-AGM if MO is hard. It follows from the known standard model reduction ARoot $\Rightarrow$ LO [7] that LO is hard in the AHO-AGM if MO is hard (Corollary 7.3).

Cryptographic Accumulators. Boneh, Bünz and Fisch [6] propose a construction for a universal accumulator in a distributed setting, together with batching and aggregation techniques, in hidden order groups. The security of the accumulator is based on a variant of the strong root problem StRoot. We show in Theorem 7.1 that StRoot is hard in the AHO-AGM if MO is hard. The authors moreover construct succinct arguments for knowledge of discrete logarithms in hidden order groups based on the adaptive root problem ARoot [6].

Zero-Knowledge Arguments. Bünz et al. [11] construct transparent SNARKs based on hidden order groups, where its security depends on a variant of the strong root problem StRoot and the adaptive root problem ARoot. Block et al. [4] adapt this scheme from [11] to overcome a gap in the proof of security in order to construct time and space efficient non-interactive zero-knowledge arguments. Their construction is based on the hardness of computing a multiple of the order of a random group element, which is closely related to the MO/HO problems.

2 Preliminaries

For integers $a \leq b$, let $[a, b]$ denote the set $\{a, a + 1, \ldots, b - 1, b\}$ and for $a < b$ let $[a, b)$ denote $[a, b - 1]$. For a positive integer n, let $\text{Primes}(n)$ denote the set of the first 2^n primes.

Let $\mathbb{G}$ be a finite abelian group. For $\boldsymbol{g} = (g_1, \ldots, g_n) \in \mathbb{G}^n$ and $\boldsymbol{e} = (e_1, \ldots, e_n) \subset \mathbb{Z}^n$, we use the shorthand $\langle \boldsymbol{g} \rangle := \langle g_1, \ldots, g_n \rangle$ for the subgroup generated by $g_1, \ldots, g_n$, and $\boldsymbol{g}^{\boldsymbol{e}} := \prod_{i=1}^{n} g_i^{e_i}$ for coordinate-wise exponentiation and multiplication of the results. Furthermore, for $A = (\boldsymbol{a}_1, \ldots, \boldsymbol{a}_n) \in \mathbb{Z}^{n \times n}$, we denote $\boldsymbol{g}^A := (\boldsymbol{g}^{\boldsymbol{a}_1}, \ldots, \boldsymbol{g}^{\boldsymbol{a}_n})$.

For a finite set S, let $\mathcal{U}_S$ denote the uniform distribution on S. Moreover, for any $0 < M \leq N$, we define $\mathcal{U}_M := \mathcal{U}_{[0,M)}$ and $\mathcal{R}_{N,M} := [x \bmod M \mid x \xleftarrow{\$} \mathcal{U}_N]$ for the probability distribution on the set $[0, M)$ obtained by reducing samples from $\mathcal{U}_N$ modulo M. For sets and probability distributions, we use $\prod$ to denote the cartesian product. In particular, for probability distributions $\mathcal{D}_i$ over domains S_i, the cartesian product $\mathcal{D} = \prod_{i=1}^{n} \mathcal{D}_i$ is the probability distribution over $\prod_{i=1}^{n} S_i$ defined by the probability function: $p((x_i)_{i=1}^{n}) := \prod_{i=1}^{n} \Pr_{X_i \sim \mathcal{D}_i}[X_i = x_i]$.

We assume that all algorithms receive 1^κ as input, where κ is the security parameter. Furthermore, we assume the asymptotic runtime of our reductions is dominated by the runtime of the original adversary it calls as subroutine. To avoid unnecessary clutter, we omit asymptotic lower order additive terms in the running time analyses of our reductions. These generally include very simple operations such as sampling of integers, passing arguments between algorithms, and simple bit-wise operations. Also, we scale time units such that multiplication in the group $\mathbb{G}$ under consideration takes unit time.

2.1 Statistical Distance and Approximate Uniform Sampling

We introduce several lemmas on probability distributions that we use later on.

Lemma 2.1. *For a given positive integer $M \geq 1$, let X and Y be independent random variables on $[0, M)$ and define the random variable $Z := [X + Y \bmod M]$. If $X \sim \mathcal{U}_M$ or $Y \sim \mathcal{U}_M$, then $Z \sim \mathcal{U}_M$ is uniformly distributed on $[0, M)$ as well.*

Definition 2.2. *For given probability distributions $\mathcal{D}_1$ and $\mathcal{D}_2$ over a finite set S, the statistical distance between $\mathcal{D}_1$ and $\mathcal{D}_2$ is defined as*

$$\delta(\mathcal{D}_1, \mathcal{D}_2) := \frac{1}{2} \sum_{x \in S} \left| \Pr_{X \sim \mathcal{D}_1}[X = x] - \Pr_{Y \sim \mathcal{D}_2}[Y = x] \right|.$$

An equivalent definition we use is the maximal absolute difference that can occur between both probability distributions over all possible events:

$$\delta(\mathcal{D}_1, \mathcal{D}_2) = \max_{T \subseteq S} \left| \Pr_{X \sim \mathcal{D}_1}[X \in T] - \Pr_{Y \sim \mathcal{D}_2}[Y \in T] \right|.$$

Lemma 2.3. *Let $M \leq N$ be positive integers and let $X \sim \mathcal{U}_N$. Then*

$$\forall y \in [0, M) : |\Pr[X \equiv y \bmod M] - 1/M| \leq 1/N,$$

hence the statistical distance between $[X \bmod M] = \mathcal{R}_{N,M}$ and $\mathcal{U}_M$ is bounded as

$$\delta(\mathcal{R}_{N,M}, \mathcal{U}_M) \leq M/2N.$$

Lemma 2.4. *Let $M \leq N$ be positive integers and let $X \sim \mathcal{U}_N$. For any $x \in [0, N)$ there are unique $y \in [0, M)$, $z \in [0, \lceil N/M \rceil)$ such that $x = y + zM$. Let $Z_y := [\lfloor X/M \rfloor \mid X \equiv y \bmod M]$ be the random variable related to z obtained by dividing X by M and rounding down, conditioned on $X \equiv y \bmod M$. Then*

$$\Pr[Z_y = z] = \begin{cases} 1/\lceil N/M \rceil & \text{if } y < (N \bmod M) \wedge y + zM \in [0, N); \\ 1/\lfloor N/M \rfloor & \text{if } y \geq (N \bmod M) \wedge y + zM \in [0, N); \\ 0 & \text{otherwise.} \end{cases}$$

Hence $Z_y \sim \mathcal{U}_{\lceil N/M \rceil}$ if $y < (N \bmod M)$ and $Z_y \sim \mathcal{U}_{\lfloor N/M \rfloor}$ otherwise. Moreover, the statistical distance between those two distributions is bounded:

$$\delta(Z_y, \mathcal{U}_{\lceil N/M \rceil}) \leq \delta(\mathcal{U}_{\lfloor N/M \rfloor}, \mathcal{U}_{\lceil N/M \rceil}) \leq 1/\lceil N/M \rceil.$$

Lemma 2.5. *Let $\mathcal{U}_M$ be the uniform distribution on the set $[0, M)$ and let $\mathcal{D}_i$ be probability distributions over the same set for $i = 1, \ldots, \ell$. Assume that there exists a constant $0 < \delta \leq 1/M\ell$ such that for all instances $x \in [0, M)$*

$$\left| \Pr_{X \sim \mathcal{D}_i}[X = x] - \Pr_{Y \sim \mathcal{U}_M}[Y = x] \right| \leq \delta.$$

Then the statistical distance between the cartesian products $\prod_{i=1}^{\ell} \mathcal{D}_i$ and $\prod_{i=1}^{\ell} \mathcal{U}_M$ is upper bounded by $\frac{1}{2}\left(\delta\ell M + (\delta\ell M)^2\right)$.

Proof. See the full paper [2, App. A]. □

We prove the following Lemma that we use in reductions to analyze repeatedly calling adversaries with inputs belonging to the same group.

Lemma 2.6. *Let $\mathcal{X} = \{X_i\}_{i \in I}$ be a finite probability distribution ensemble, where $X_i \sim B(N, p_i)$ follows the binomial distribution with N samples with probability p_i. Let the set $\mathcal{X}$ itself be endowed with the uniform distribution. Given $n \geq 1$, $S \geq 4$ and the average probability $p = \mathrm{E}[p_i]$, if $N = \lceil Sn/p \rceil$ then*

$$\Pr_{X \in \mathcal{X}}[X \geq n] \geq (p/2) \cdot (1 - e^{-n \cdot C_S})$$

where $C_S := (S - 3)/2 + 1/S - \log(S/2)$. Note that $C_S \geq 1$ for $S \geq 8$.

Proof (sketch). The claim can be shown by analyzing the subset $\mathcal{X}_2 = \{X_i \in \mathcal{X} \mid p_i > p/2\}$ and bounding its size $|\mathcal{X}_2| \geq (p/2) \cdot |\mathcal{X}|$. For each $X_i \in \mathcal{X}_2$, one can then upper bound $\Pr[X_i \leq n]$ using Chernoff's bound and the fact that $p_i > p/2$. See the full paper [2, App. A] for a full version of the proof. $\qquad\square$

Lemma 2.7. *Let $B(N, p)$ and $B(N, p')$ be binomial distributions with N samples and respective success probabilities p and p'. Then the statistical distance between these distributions is bounded by $(N^2/2) \cdot |p - p'|$.*

Proof (sketch). Define $x_{i,j} := \Pr[B(i,p) = j]$, $y_{i,j} := \Pr[B(i,p') = j]$ and $\alpha_i := \max_j |x_{i,j} - y_{i,j}|$. Then the statistical distance is bounded by $1/2 \cdot N \cdot \alpha_N$. One can show that $\alpha_1 = |p - p'|$, and for $i \geq 1$ that $\alpha_{i+1} \leq \alpha_i + \alpha_1$ since for any j:

$$|x_{i+1,j} - y_{i+1,j}| =$$
$$|y_{1,1}(x_{i,j-1} - y_{i,j-1}) + y_{1,0}(x_{i,j} - y_{i,j}) + x_{i,j-1}(x_{1,1} - y_{1,1}) + x_{i,j}(x_{1,0} - y_{1,0})|$$
$$\leq y_{1,1}\alpha_i + y_{1,0}\alpha_i + x_{i,j-1}\alpha_1 + x_{i,j}\alpha_1 \leq \alpha_i + \alpha_1,$$

It follows that $\alpha_N \leq N \cdot |p - p'|$, which proves the claim. $\qquad\square$

2.2 Security Games and Adversaries

Definition 2.8. *A security game G is defined with respect to a set of parameters par (defining the group family) and an adversary $\mathcal{A}$ that plays the game. A game consists of a main procedure that receives as input a security parameter $\kappa \in \mathbb{Z}_{\geq 1}$ and at the end outputs a single bit 0 ($\mathcal{A}$ loses) or 1 ($\mathcal{A}$ wins). We denote the output of a game G executed with parameters par and adversary $\mathcal{A}$ as $\mathsf{G}^{\mathcal{A}}_{\mathrm{par}}(\kappa)$. We define the* advantage *of $\mathcal{A}$ in G as*

$$\mathsf{Adv}^{\mathsf{G}}_{\mathrm{par},\mathcal{A}}(\kappa) := \Pr[\mathsf{G}^{\mathcal{A}}_{\mathrm{par}}(\kappa) = 1].$$

We denote the (expected) running time of $\mathsf{G}^{\mathcal{A}}_{\mathrm{par}}(\kappa)$ by $\mathsf{Time}^{\mathsf{G}}_{\mathrm{par},\mathcal{A}}(\kappa)$. We extend this notation to be able to denote the advantage conditional on an event E in G:

$$\mathsf{Adv}^{\mathsf{G}}_{\mathrm{par},\mathcal{A}}|_E(\kappa) := \Pr[\mathsf{G}^{\mathcal{A}}_{\mathrm{par}}(\kappa) = 1 \mid E].$$

Definition 2.9. *Let G, H be security games. We write $\mathsf{H} \xLongrightarrow{(\Delta_\varepsilon, \Delta_t)} \mathsf{G}$ if there exists an algorithm $\mathcal{R}$ (called a $(\Delta_\varepsilon, \Delta_t)$-reduction) such that for all algorithms $\mathcal{A}$ playing game G, the algorithm $\mathcal{B} := \mathcal{R}^{\mathcal{A}}$ playing game H satisfies*

$$\mathsf{Adv}^{\mathsf{H}}_{\mathrm{par},\mathcal{B}}(\kappa) \geq \Delta_\varepsilon \cdot \mathsf{Adv}^{\mathsf{G}}_{\mathrm{par},\mathcal{A}}(\kappa) - \mathrm{negl}(\kappa), \quad \mathsf{Time}^{\mathsf{H}}_{\mathrm{par},\mathcal{B}}(\kappa) \leq \Delta_t \cdot \mathsf{Time}^{\mathsf{G}}_{\mathrm{par},\mathcal{A}}(\kappa) + T(\kappa),$$

where $T(\kappa)$ is an insignificant overhead, i.e., $\lim_{\kappa \to \infty} T(\kappa)/\mathsf{Time}^{\mathsf{G}}_{\mathrm{par},\mathcal{A}}(\kappa) \to 0$. This notation can be extended, e.g., as $\mathsf{H} \xLongrightarrow[\mathrm{AGM}]{(\Delta_\varepsilon, \Delta_t)} \mathsf{G}$ to specify the reduction holds within the mentioned restricted model (AGM in the example).

2.3 Algebraic Group Model

The *algebraic group model* (AGM) is a simplified model of computation introduced by Fuchsbauer et al. [17]. It lies between the generic group model (GGM),
first introduced by Nechaev [22] and Shoup [30], and the standard (Turing
machine) model. In the AGM all algorithms are modeled as *algebraic*. This
means that for any group element $X \in \mathbb{G}$ an algorithm may output, it addi-
tionally has to output an algebraic representation $\boldsymbol{a} = (a_1, \ldots, a_\ell) \in \mathbb{Z}^\ell$ such
that $X = \prod_{i=1}^\ell g_i^{a_i}$ in terms of the group elements $\boldsymbol{g} = (g_1, \ldots, g_\ell) \in \mathbb{G}^\ell$ the
algorithm has received as input. We will denote such a representation by $[X]_g$.
In the GGM every algorithm only receives random identifiers of group elements
and can only perform group operations through oracle queries. In contrast to the
generic group model GGM, the AGM does not let us prove information-theoretic
lower bounds on the complexity of algebraic adversaries trying to solve a given
problem. Just as in the standard model, security implications in the AGM are
proven through reductions.

The AGM has originally only been defined for *cyclic groups* $\mathbb{G}$ of *known*
prime order [17]. In this work, we will generalize this to the setting where $\mathbb{G}$
is an arbitrary *finite abelian group* of *unknown* order $|\mathbb{G}|$. The formal definition
will be given in Subsect. 4.1.

2.4 Strong Algebraic Group Model

The *strong* algebraic group model (SAGM) has been introduced by Katz et
al. [18] as a strengthened version of the algebraic group model (AGM). The
SAGM lies between the GGM and the AGM. Any SAGM algorithm is algebraic,
but it must expose the algebraic representation of output group elements instead
as an algebraic circuit more similar to the GGM. More specifically, algorithms
in the SAGM may use one or more output rounds, where in each output round
any output group element must be described as a primitive group operation on
one or two group elements that were input or were output in a previous round.
Our definition of the SAGM is completely identical to the definition from Katz
et al. [18]. However, since the definition depends on our generalized definition of
the AGM, we will postpone giving the formal definition until Sect. 4.2.

3   Hidden Order Cyclic Group Model (HO-SM)

As a stepping stone to the theory of finite (not necessarily cyclic) abelian groups,
we first consider a simple reduction of the multiple order problem $\mathsf{MO}_\mathcal{C}$ to the
discrete logarithm problem DLog for *cyclic groups of unknown order*. Then we
prove a novel reduction from $\mathsf{HO}_\mathcal{C}$ to DLog in Theorem 3.5, which will also
illustrate some of the main techniques used in the rest of this paper.

Definition 3.1. *A cyclic group family* $\mathcal{G} = (\mathcal{G}_\kappa)_{\kappa=1}^\infty$ *is a family of probability
distributions over finite cyclic groups defined with:*

1. An efficient sampling algorithm GGen that, on input 1^κ, randomly samples a group $\mathbb{G} \in \mathcal{G}_\kappa$ and outputs a group description of $\mathbb{G}$, a generator g and $1_\mathbb{G}$.
2. An efficient sampling algorithm GSample which, given a group description of $\mathbb{G}$, outputs a group element $x \in \mathbb{G}$ sampled uniformly at random.
3. Efficient algorithms GMul and GInv that, respectively, multiplies two group elements, and inverts a group element.
4. A group order upper bound $U(\kappa)$: $\forall \kappa \forall \mathbb{G} \in \mathcal{G}_\kappa : U(\kappa) \geq |\mathbb{G}|$, such that $\log U(\kappa) \in \text{poly}(\kappa)$ and $1/U(\kappa) \in \text{negl}(\kappa)$.

Remark 3.2. Note that the bit size of the representations of the group elements of all $\mathbb{G} \in \mathcal{G}_\kappa$ should be polynomial in the security parameter κ, since otherwise it would not be possible to construct efficient algorithms on $\mathbb{G}$. If we assume that an upper bound $p(\kappa)$ on the bit size of the representations is known, this automatically gives an upper bound $U_\kappa = 2^{p(\kappa)}$ on the order of $\mathbb{G}$, for which $\log(U_\kappa)$ is polynomial in κ.

Lemma 3.3. For any cyclic group family $\mathcal{G} = (\mathcal{G}_\kappa)_{\kappa=1}^\infty$:

$$\mathsf{MO}_\mathcal{C} \xrightarrow[\text{HO-SM}]{1,1} \mathsf{DLog}.$$

Proof. Given a DLog adversary $\mathcal{A}$, we construct an $\mathsf{MO}_\mathcal{C}$ adversary $\mathcal{B}^\mathcal{A}$ as follows, which takes inputs $\mathbb{G}, g, U$.

> $r \xleftarrow{\$} \mathcal{U}_{U^2}, \quad d \leftarrow \mathcal{A}(g, g^r)$
>
> if $g^d = g^r$ then return $|r - d|$ else return $\perp$

By Lemma 2.3, the statistical distance between $r \bmod |\mathbb{G}|$ and the uniform distribution on $[0, |\mathbb{G}|)$ has negligible bound $\varepsilon_1 := 1/U \in \text{negl}(\kappa)$. Since $\mathcal{A}$ succeeds with probability $p := \mathsf{Adv}^{\mathsf{DLog}}_{(\mathbb{G},g),\mathcal{A}}$ when g^r is distributed uniformly in $\mathbb{G}$, it follows that $\mathcal{A}$ succeeds on each instance (g, g^r) with probability at least $p - \varepsilon_1$. Moreover, if $\mathcal{A}$ succeeds and $g^d = g^r$, then $\mathcal{B}^\mathcal{A}$ outputs $|r - d|$ which is indeed an integer multiple of the group order, but potentially zero if $r = d$.

To bound the probability that $r = d$, write $r = r' + r''|\mathbb{G}|$ with $0 \leq r' < |\mathbb{G}|$ and $r'' \in [0, N)$, where $N := \lceil U^2/|\mathbb{G}| \rceil \geq U$. Then $g^r = g^{r'}$ only depends on r', thus the execution and output d of $\mathcal{A}$ only depends on r' as well. This implies that we can view the experiment as if r is sampled, conditioned on $r \equiv r' \bmod |\mathbb{G}|$, only after we receive the output d of $\mathcal{A}(g, g^{r'})$. Note that $r'' = (r - r')/|\mathbb{G}|$ is distributed as Z_y in Lemma 2.4, and thus r'' has statistical distance at most $1/N$ to $\mathcal{U}_N$. Since furthermore, the probability that any particular value is sampled from $\mathcal{U}_N$ is at most $1/N$, it follows that $\Pr[r = d] = \Pr[r'' = (d - r')/|\mathbb{G}|] \leq 2/N =: \varepsilon_2$, then $\varepsilon_2 \leq 2/U \in \text{negl}(\kappa)$. Hence, $\mathcal{B}^\mathcal{A}$ outputs a non-zero multiple of the group order with probability at least $(p - \varepsilon_1)(1 - \varepsilon_2) = p - \text{negl}(\kappa)$ and with the same Time complexity as $\mathcal{A}$ plus some insignificant overhead. $\qquad \square$

The above Lemma shows that we can leverage a DLog adversary to obtain a multiple of the group order with non-negligible probability. By repeating this process with independently randomly chosen g^r, we can obtain various multiples of the group order, and using the following theorem we can show that in this way we can obtain the *exact* group order with high probability.

Theorem 3.4. *Let $k \geq 2$, $n \geq 2^{23}$, and $1 \leq d < n$ be positive integers, and let $s_1, \ldots, s_k$ be arbitrary integers with $|s_i| \leq n^d$. Let $X_1, \ldots, X_k$ be independent random variables with distribution $\mathcal{U}_n$, then:*

$$\Pr[\gcd(s_1 + X_1, \ldots, s_k + X_k) = 1] \geq (1 - (d/n)^{k-1}) \cdot (1 - \epsilon_k) \cdot 1/\zeta(k) =: \sigma(k, d/n),$$

where $\zeta(k)$ is the Riemann zeta function, $\epsilon_k \leq .077$ for $k = 2$ and $\epsilon_k \leq 2.9 \cdot 10^{-5}$ for $k \geq 3$. When $d \leq n/10$, this probability is at least .505 for $k \geq 2$, at least .92 for $k \geq 4$, and at least .99 for $k \geq 7$.

Proof. The proof is given in the full paper [2, App. A]. $\qquad\square$

Theorem 3.5. *For any cyclic group family $\mathcal{G} = (\mathcal{G}_\kappa)_{\kappa=1}^\infty$, integers $k \geq 2$, $S \geq 4$:*

$$\mathsf{HO}_\mathcal{C} \xrightarrow[\text{HO-SM}]{c_k(1-e^{-k \cdot C_S})/2, \lceil Sk/p \rceil} \mathsf{DLog}, \quad e.g., \quad \mathsf{HO}_\mathcal{C} \xrightarrow[\text{HO-SM}]{.49, \lceil 56/p \rceil} \mathsf{DLog},$$

where $p := \mathsf{Adv}_{\mathcal{G}, \mathcal{A}}^{\mathsf{DLog}}(\kappa)$, C_S as in Lemma 2.6, and $c_k := \sigma(k, 1/10) \geq 0.505$. The example uses $S = 8$ and $k = 7$.

Proof. Given a DLog adversary $\mathcal{A}$ with advantage $p(\kappa) := \mathsf{Adv}_{\mathcal{G}, \mathcal{A}}^{\mathsf{DLog}}(\kappa)$, then given $k \geq 2$, $S \geq 4$ we construct an $\mathsf{HO}_\mathcal{C}$ adversary $\mathcal{B}^\mathcal{A}$ which takes input $(1^\kappa, \mathbb{G}, g)$ with $(\mathbb{G}, g) \in \mathcal{G}_\kappa$ as follows.

$$\boxed{\begin{array}{l} M := \emptyset \\ \textbf{for } i = 1, \ldots, \lceil Sk/p(\kappa) \rceil \\ \quad r_i \xleftarrow{\$} \mathcal{U}_{U^2}, \quad d_i \leftarrow \mathcal{A}(g, g^{r_i}) \\ \quad \textbf{if } g^{r_i} = g^{d_i} \textbf{ then } M \leftarrow M \cup \{|d_i - r_i|\} \\ \textbf{if } M \neq \emptyset \textbf{ then return } \gcd(M) \textbf{ else return } \perp \end{array}}$$

This adversary is similar to the one in the proof of Lemma 3.3, except it performs $\lceil Sk/p(\kappa) \rceil$ such sample & queries and returns the gcd of the obtained differences $|r_i - d_i|$. This corresponds to the time complexity factor $\lceil Sk/p(\kappa) \rceil$ in the claim.

We have already shown that for each sample & query the probability that $g^r = g^d$ depends on $(\mathbb{G}, g)$ and is $p'_\mathbb{G} := p_\mathbb{G} - \text{negl}(\kappa)$, where $p_\mathbb{G} := \mathsf{Adv}_{(\mathbb{G}, g), \mathcal{A}}^{\mathsf{DLog}}$. Let $p' := E_{\mathbb{G} \in \mathcal{G}_\kappa}[p'_\mathbb{G}]$ be the average success probability of a successful sample & query for a random group $\mathbb{G} \in \mathcal{G}_\kappa$, then $p' = p(\kappa) - \text{negl}(\kappa)$.

Next we bound the probability we find at least k successful samples for a random group $\mathbb{G} \in \mathcal{G}_\kappa$. We apply Lemma 2.6 on $\mathcal{X} = \{B(\lceil Sk/p(\kappa) \rceil, p_\mathbb{G})\}_{\mathbb{G} \in \mathcal{G}_\kappa}$ and use Lemma 2.7 to find that

$$\Pr_{\mathbb{G} \in \mathcal{G}_\kappa}[|M| \geq k] = \Pr_{X \in \mathcal{X}}[X \geq k] - \text{negl}(\kappa) \geq p \cdot (1 - e^{-k \cdot C_S})/2 - \text{negl}(\kappa).$$

For any given $(\mathbb{G}, g)$, consider any successful sample & query $g^{r_i} = g^{d_i}$ and let $N := \lceil U^2/|\mathbb{G}| \rceil$. As the size of the outputs d_i of $\mathcal{A}$ are polynomially bounded in κ, there is an integer K such that for all $\kappa \geq K$ the outputs of $\mathcal{A}$ are bounded by $|d_i| \leq N^{N/10}$. Assume that indeed $|d_i| \leq N^{N/10}$ and $N \geq U \geq |\mathbb{G}| \geq 2^{23}$.

We have already shown that $r_i'' = \lfloor r_i/|\mathbb{G}| \rfloor$ is distributed independently from d_i and has negligible statistical distance ε_1 to $\mathcal{U}_N$. By Theorem 3.4 it follows that if we have k successful samples $|r_1 - d_1|, \ldots, |r_k - d_k|$ then

$$\Pr\left[\gcd\left(|r_1 - d_1|/|\mathbb{G}|, \ldots, |r_k - d_k|/|\mathbb{G}|\right) = 1\right] \geq \sigma(k, 1/10) - k\varepsilon_1 = c_k - \text{negl}(\kappa).$$

Finally, we can conclude that indeed:
$$\Pr_{(\mathbb{G},g)\in\mathcal{G}_\kappa}\left[\mathcal{B}^{\mathcal{A}}(1^\kappa, \mathbb{G}, g) = |\mathbb{G}|\right] \geq p \cdot (c_k(1 - e^{-k \cdot C_S})/2) - \text{negl}(\kappa). \qquad \square$$

4   Abelian Hidden Order Standard Model (AHO-SM)

In this section we propose a computational framework for working in finite abelian groups of hidden order. We first generalize the notion of a (hard) group family from Damgård and Koprowski [14], and later introduce generalized notions of the algebraic group model from Fuchsbauer et al. [17] as well as of the strong algebraic group model from Katz et al. [18].

In our definition of an abelian group family below we do not assume sampled groups come with a canonical set of generators. Instead a sufficiently large set of random group elements can always be used as generator set. Hence, for the computational problems considered in Table 2, each game starts with sampling a group $\mathbb{G}$ as well as a set of random generators $(g_1, \ldots, g_n)$.

Definition 4.1. *An* abelian group family $\mathcal{G} = (\mathcal{G}_\kappa)_{\kappa=1}^{\infty}$ *is a family of probability distributions over finite abelian groups defined with:*

1. *An efficient sampling algorithm* GGen *that, on input* 1^κ, *samples uniformly at random a group* $\mathbb{G} \in \mathcal{G}_\kappa$ *and outputs a group description of* $\mathbb{G}$ *and* $1_{\mathbb{G}}$.
2. *An efficient sampling algorithm* GSample *which, given a group description of* $\mathbb{G}$, *outputs a group element* $x \in \mathbb{G}$ *sampled uniformly at random.*
3. *Efficient algorithms* GMul *and* GInv *that, respectively, multiplies two group elements, and inverts a group element.*
4. *A group order upper bound* $U(\kappa)$: $\forall\kappa\forall\mathbb{G} \in \mathcal{G}_\kappa : U(\kappa) \geq |\mathbb{G}|$, *such that* $\log U(\kappa) \in \text{poly}(\kappa)$ *and* $1/U(\kappa) \in \text{negl}(\kappa)$.
5. *A random group generator count* $n(\kappa) \in \mathbb{Z}_{>0}$ *and* $n(\kappa) \in \text{poly}(\kappa)$ *such that*

$$\Pr[\langle g \rangle \neq \mathbb{G} \mid \mathbb{G} \xleftarrow{\$} \mathcal{G}_\kappa, g \xleftarrow{\$} \mathbb{G}^{n(\kappa)}] \in \text{negl}(\kappa).$$

When the security parameter κ *is clear from the context, we will usually omit* κ *and simply denote* U *and* n *instead of* $U(\kappa)$ *and* $n(\kappa)$, *respectively.*

Note that by the same arguments as in Remark 3.2, for any tuple of abelian group family algorithms (GGen, GSample, GMul, GInv) there always exists a candidate $U(\kappa)$ that satisfies Definition 4.1. Moreover, the following Lemma also provides a candidate $n(\kappa)$.

Lemma 4.2. *For any abelian group* $\mathbb{G}$ *and* $U \geq |\mathbb{G}|$, *let* $n := \lceil \log_2 U \rceil$. *Then there exist* $g_1, \ldots, g_n$ *such that* $\langle g_1, \ldots, g_n \rangle = \mathbb{G}$. *Moreover,* $2n$ *random elements fail to generate the full group with exponentially small probability in* n, *i.e.,*

$$\Pr[\langle \boldsymbol{g} \rangle \neq \mathbb{G} \mid \boldsymbol{g} \xleftarrow{\$} \mathbb{G}^{2n}] \leq 2^{-n}(\leq 1/U).$$

Proof. The first part of the lemma follows directly from the observation that if $g_{i+1} \notin \langle g_1, \ldots, g_i \rangle$ then we have that $|\langle g_1, \ldots, g_{i+1} \rangle| = k \cdot |\langle g_1, \ldots, g_i \rangle|$ with $k \in \mathbb{Z}_{\geq 2}$. The second part of the lemma follows from two observations. First, that for all $g_1, \ldots, g_i$ that generate a strict subgroup $\mathbb{G}' := \langle g_1, \ldots, g_i \rangle \neq \mathbb{G}$ the probability that a randomly sampled element lies in the subgroup is bounded as $\Pr[x \in \mathbb{G}' \mid x \xleftarrow{\$} \mathbb{G}] \leq 1/2$. Second, for $\boldsymbol{g} \in \mathbb{G}^{2n}$ with $\langle \boldsymbol{g} \rangle \neq \mathbb{G}$, it follows that for at least n indices i it holds that $g_{i+1} \in \langle g_1, \ldots, g_i \rangle \neq \mathbb{G}$. $\square$

We generalize the notion of a *hard group family* from Damgård and Koprowski [14, Definition 1] to the abelian hidden order setting as follows.

Definition 4.3. *Let* $\mathsf{lp}(N)$ *denote the largest prime divisor of* N. *Sampling a group* $\mathbb{G} \xleftarrow{\$} \mathcal{G}_\kappa$ *and considering* $\mathsf{lp}(|\mathbb{G}|)$, *induces a distribution* $\mathcal{D}_\kappa$ *on the primes. Define* $\alpha(\mathcal{G}_\kappa) := \max_p \Pr_\mathbb{G}[p = \mathsf{lp}(|\mathbb{G}|)]$ *to be the maximal probability in* $\mathcal{D}_\kappa$. *For a positive integer* M, *define the probability* $\beta(\mathcal{G}_\kappa, M) := \Pr_\mathbb{G}[\mathsf{lp}(|\mathbb{G}|) \leq M]$ *that the largest prime divisor of the group order is at most* M.

Definition 4.4. *A* hard abelian group family *is an abelian group family* $(\mathcal{G}_\kappa)_{\kappa \in \mathbb{Z}_{>0}}$ *which satisfies the following conditions:*

1. $\alpha(\mathcal{G}_\kappa)$ *is negligible in* κ;
2. *There exists* $B(\kappa)$ *such that* $\forall \mathbb{G} \in \mathcal{G}_\kappa : B(\kappa) \leq |\mathbb{G}|$ *and* $1/B(\kappa) \in \mathrm{negl}(\kappa)$.

Moreover, Damgård and Koprowski noted that if $(\mathcal{G}_\kappa)_{\kappa \in \mathbb{Z}_{>0}}$ is a hard abelian group family, then setting $M_\kappa := 1/\sqrt{\alpha(\mathcal{G}_\kappa)}$ leads to $\beta(\mathcal{G}_\kappa, M_\kappa)$ as well as $1/M_\kappa$ being negligible [14, Fact 1].

The order of elements sampled uniformly at random will in general be superpolynomially large, which we will show using the following two lemmas.

Lemma 4.5. *Let* $|\mathbb{G}| = \prod_p p^{e(p)}$ *be the prime factorization of* $|\mathbb{G}|$. *Then the probability for a prime* $p \mid |\mathbb{G}|$ *to divide the order of a uniformly random element of* $\mathbb{G}$ *is* $1 - 1/p^{e(p)}$.

Proof. By the fundamental theorem of finite abelian groups we can write $\mathbb{G} \cong \bigoplus_{i=1}^t (\mathbb{Z}/p_i^{e_i}\mathbb{Z})$, where $p_1, \ldots p_t$ are (not necessarily distinct) prime numbers. The order of an element $X \in \mathbb{G}$ is *not* divisible by a prime $p \mid |\mathbb{G}|$ if and only if X has trivial components in all subgroups corresponding to $(\mathbb{Z}/p_i^{e_i}\mathbb{Z})$ with $p_i = p$. There are exactly $\prod_{p_i \neq p} p_i^{e_i} = |\mathbb{G}|/p^{e(p)}$ such elements. $\square$

Lemma 4.6. *Let* $(\mathcal{G}_\kappa)_{\kappa=1}^\infty$ *be a hard abelian group family. Then there exists a superpolynomial bound* M_κ *such that the order of a random element* $X \in \mathbb{G} \in \mathcal{G}_\kappa$ *will have order greater than* M_κ *with all but negligible probability, i.e.:*

$$\Pr\left[|\langle X \rangle| < M_\kappa \mid X \xleftarrow{\$} \mathbb{G}, \mathbb{G} \xleftarrow{\$} \mathcal{G}_\kappa\right] \in \mathrm{negl}(\kappa).$$

Proof. As mentioned above, for $M_\kappa := 1/\sqrt{\alpha(\mathcal{G}_\kappa)}$, the probability $\beta(\mathcal{G}_\kappa, M_\kappa)$ is negligible and the bound M_κ is superpolynomial [14, Fact 1]. Assume that the largest prime divisor p of $|\mathbb{G}|$ is at least M_κ, which thus happens with probability $1 - \mathrm{negl}(\kappa)$. Now, sampling $X \xleftarrow{\$} \mathbb{G}$, we see that p divides the order of X with probability $\geq 1 - 1/p$ by Lemma 4.5, i.e., with all but negligible probability. $\square$

Note that even without knowing the exact group structure or the exact group order we can efficiently sample group elements as g^r close to uniform, as shown in the following two lemmas.

Lemma 4.7. *Let $\mathbb{G}$ be a finite abelian group and let $g_1, \ldots, g_n \in \mathbb{G}$ be a system of generators. Put $O_i := |\langle g_i \rangle|$ for $i = 1, \ldots, n$. If we sample $(r_i)_{i=1}^n \xleftarrow{\$} \prod_{i=1}^n \mathcal{U}_{O_i}$ and set $X := g_1^{r_1} \cdots g_n^{r_n}$, then X is uniformly distributed in $\mathbb{G}$.*

Lemma 4.8. *Let $\mathbb{G}$ be a finite abelian group and $\langle g_1, \ldots, g_n \rangle = \mathbb{G}$, and let ℓ, v be positive integers. If we sample $(r_{ij})_{i,j=1}^{\ell,n} \xleftarrow{\$} (\mathcal{U}_{U^v})^{\ell n}$ and set $X_i := g_1^{r_{i1}} \cdots g_n^{r_{in}}$ for $i = 1, \ldots, \ell$. Then the statistical distance between the distribution of $(X_i)_{i=1}^\ell$ and the uniform distribution $\mathcal{U}_{\mathbb{G}^\ell}$ is upper bounded by $\ell n / 2U^{v-1} + \ell^2 n^2 / 2U^{2v-2}$.*

Proofs of Lemmas 4.7 and 4.8 can be found in the full paper [2, App. A].

4.1   Abelian Hidden Order Algebraic Group Model (AHO-AGM)

In this subsection we generalize the algebraic group model (AGM) of Fuchsbauer et al. [17] to the setting of finite abelian groups of hidden order. We call this model the *abelian hidden order algebraic group model* (AHO-AGM). In the AHO-AGM, all algorithms must satisfy the following definition.

Definition 4.9. *An algorithm $\mathcal{A}$ executed in an algebraic game G is called algebraic if for all group elements $X \in \mathbb{G}$ that $\mathcal{A}$ outputs, it also outputs a representation $\boldsymbol{a} = (a_1, \ldots, a_\ell) \in \mathbb{Z}^\ell$ such that $X = \prod_{i=1}^\ell g_i^{a_i}$, where $\boldsymbol{g} = (g_1, \ldots, g_\ell) \in \mathbb{G}^\ell$ is the list of all group elements that have been given to $\mathcal{A}$ so far. We will denote such a representation by $[X]_{\boldsymbol{g}}$. (Here, typically, $g_1, \ldots, g_n$ are the uniformly randomly chosen generators for $\mathbb{G}$.)*

Surprisingly, a standard model reduction and an algebraic group model reduction can compose to a standard model reduction under certain conditions. That is $\mathsf{Z} \xRightarrow[\text{AHO-SM}]{} \mathsf{X}$ may follow from $\mathsf{Z} \xRightarrow[\text{AHO-AGM}]{} \mathsf{Y}$ and $\mathsf{Y} \xRightarrow[\text{AHO-SM}]{} \mathsf{X}$. For instance, note that *any* standard model algorithm for any game $\mathsf{X} \in \{\mathsf{MO}, \mathsf{HO}, \mathsf{DLog}_1, \mathsf{DLog}_2\}$ is by definition also algebraic, since no group elements are output. In that case any *generic* or *algebraic* reduction $\mathsf{Y} \Rightarrow \mathsf{X}$ results in an algebraic adversary for Y. Hence, such generic reductions $\mathsf{Y} \Rightarrow \mathsf{X}$ in the standard model can be composed with any algebraic group model reduction from $\mathsf{Z} \Rightarrow \mathsf{Y}$ to obtain a *standard model* reduction $\mathsf{Z} \Rightarrow \mathsf{X}$. (See e.g., Corollary 6.4.)

4.2 Abelian Hidden Order Strong Algebraic Group Model (AHO-SAGM)

In this subsection we extend the strong algebraic group model (SAGM) to finite abelian (not necessarily cyclic) groups. In the SAGM the running time of an algorithm is measured by the number of algebraic rounds and the "normal" running time measured in some underlying computational model (e.g., the Turing machine model). The SAGM is similar to the AGM, but in the case of the repeated squaring problem with timing parameter T, an adversary can simply output g^{2^T} in one algebraic round. Therefore the AGM is not the right model to study the hardness of the repeated squaring problem. This is made formal in [18, Theorem 3]. Moreover, note that this model allows for arbitrary parallelism, since strongly algebraic algorithms are allowed to output multiple tuples per round. Of course efficient algebraic algorithms are only allowed to output a polynomial number of tuples in each round.

Note that a strong algebraic algorithm is automatically an algebraic algorithm. Conversely, assuming that the output length is polynomial, any algebraic algorithm can be turned into a strongly algebraic algorithm with a polylogarithmic time loss (see [18, Theorem 1]).

Our definition is a generalization of the original definition introduced by Katz et al. [18]. Contrary to Katz et al. [18], we let $\mathbb{G}$ be any *finite abelian group*, which is sampled according to some group family $\mathcal{G} = (\mathcal{G}_\kappa)_{\kappa=1}^\infty$. Here κ can be seen as the security parameter of the corresponding game. We call this model the *abelian hidden order strong algebraic group model* (AHO-SAGM). In the AHO-SAGM, all algorithms must satisfy the following definition.

Definition 4.10. *An algorithm $\mathcal{A}$ over a group $\mathbb{G}$ is called* strongly algebraic *if it has one or more output rounds (between which it may perform arbitrary local computation). An output round is called algebraic if it contains one or more group elements. For each group element X it outputs it must also output a tuple of one of the following forms:*

1. $(X, X_1, X_2) \in \mathbb{G}^3$ *such that* $X = X_1 X_2$, *where* X_1, X_2 *were either previously given to $\mathcal{A}$ or previously output by $\mathcal{A}$.*
2. $(X, X_1) \in \mathbb{G}^2$ *such that* $X = X_1^{-1}$, *where* X_1 *was either previously given to $\mathcal{A}$ or previously output by $\mathcal{A}$.*

In the AHO-SAGM, we will denote a tuple of one of the above forms by $[X]$. The algebraic running time of $\mathcal{A}$ is the number of algebraic rounds it takes, and is denoted by ATime. We denote the running time of $\mathcal{A}$ by a pair (ATime, Time).

5 Computing (a Multiple Of) the Group Order

Following [8], given a system of generators $\boldsymbol{g} = (g_1, \ldots, g_n)$ of a finite abelian group $\mathbb{G}$, we call any vector $\boldsymbol{e} = (e_1, \ldots, e_n) \in \mathbb{Z}^n$ with the property that $\boldsymbol{g}^{\boldsymbol{e}} = 1_{\mathbb{G}}$

a *relation* for g. The relations for g form a lattice in $\mathbb{Z}^n$, which we will denote by $L(g)$. Since this lattice is the kernel of the surjective homomorphism

$$\mathbb{Z}^n \to \mathbb{G}, \quad e \mapsto g^e, \tag{1}$$

its dimension is n. Let $B = (b_1, \ldots, b_n)$ be a basis for the lattice $L(g)$, then $\mathbb{Z}^n / B\,\mathbb{Z}^n \cong \mathbb{G}$ by (1), from which it follows that [8, Lemma 3.1]

$$|\det(B)| = |\mathbb{Z}^n / B\,\mathbb{Z}^n| = |\mathbb{G}|. \tag{2}$$

We can show that if you find a full rank *sublattice* of $L(g)$, then you obtain a *multiple* of the group order:

Lemma 5.1. *Let $\mathbb{G}$ be a finite abelian group, let $g = (g_1, \ldots, g_n)$ be a system of generators of $\mathbb{G}$, and let $B = (b_1, \ldots, b_n)$ be a basis for the relationship lattice $L(g)$. Let $R = (r_1, \ldots, r_n)$ be a system of relations for g, which are linearly independent as vectors over $\mathbb{R}$. This implies these form a full rank sublattice $\Lambda := R\mathbb{Z}^n \subset L(g)$. Then $|\det(R)|$ is an integer multiple of $|\mathbb{G}|$.*

Proof. Since both lattice bases B and R generate $\mathbb{R}^n$ as a vector space, we know that there is a matrix $T = (t_{ij})_{i,j=1}^n$ such that $R = BT$, with $d := \det(T) \neq 0$. Since a change of basis on either $L(g)$ or Λ multiplies d by ± 1, the absolute value of d is uniquely determined by $L(g)$ and Λ, and we will also refer to this as the *relative determinant* $d(\Lambda/L(g)) := |d|$. Since $r_i \in \Lambda \subset L(g)$, we can write $r_i = \sum_{j=1}^n a_{ij} b_j$ for some $a_{ij} \in \mathbb{Z}$. Hence from the expression $r_i = \sum_{j=1}^n t_{ij} b_j$, we deduce that $t_{ij} \in \mathbb{Z}$ (since otherwise we would obtain a linear relation between the b_j). This implies that $d = \det(T) \in \mathbb{Z}$. Together with equation (2), we see that $|\det(R)| = |d \cdot \det(B)|$ is an integer multiple of $|\mathbb{G}|$.   □

Given a distribution over $\mathbb{Z}^{n \times n}$ resulting in the uniform distribution over $\mathbb{Z}_p^{n \times n}$ when reducing matrices modulo a prime p, then one can use the Schwartz-Zippel lemma [29,32] to upper bound the probability of sampling a singular matrix.

Lemma 5.2 ([29,32]). *Let p be prime. Let $F(X_1, \ldots, X_k) \in \mathbb{Z}_p[X_1, \ldots, X_k]$ be a nonzero polynomial of total degree d. Then for uniformly random $x_1, \ldots, x_k \xleftarrow{\$} \mathbb{Z}_p$, the probability that $F(x_1, \ldots, x_k) = 0$ is at most d/p.*

Corollary 5.3. *Let p be a prime and $n \geq 1$ an integer. Then we have $\Pr[\det(x_1, \ldots, x_n) = 0 \mid x_1, \ldots, x_n \xleftarrow{\$} \mathbb{Z}_p^n] \leq n/p$.*

5.1 Reduction Template for MO

Using the previous results, we construct a template reduction $\mathsf{MO} \Rightarrow \mathsf{G}$ for some computational game G, and specify certain conditions G needs to satisfy in order for such a reduction to succeed with sufficiently high probability.

We have seen in Lemma 5.1 that if we can find n linearly independent relations $R = (r_1, \ldots, r_n)$ w.r.t., some system of generators g for $\mathbb{G}$, then $|\det(R)|$

$$
\begin{array}{|l|}
\hline
E := () \\
\textbf{for } i = 1, \ldots, \lceil Sn/p \rceil \\
\quad e_i \leftarrow \mathsf{Rel}^{\mathcal{A}}(\mathbb{G}, \boldsymbol{g}) \\
\quad \textbf{if } e_i \neq \bot \textbf{ then} \\
\qquad E \leftarrow (E \| e_i^T) \\
\qquad \textbf{if } \mathsf{Columns}(E) = n \textbf{ then return } |\det(E)| \\
\textbf{return } \bot \\
\hline
\end{array}
$$

Fig. 2. Template for MO adversary $\mathcal{B}^{\mathcal{A}}(\mathbb{G}, \boldsymbol{g})$

is going to be an integer multiple of the order of $\mathbb{G}$. Therefore to show that we can reduce the multiple order problem MO to some computational problem G, it suffices to show that we can use any adversary $\mathcal{A}$ for game G to obtain n linearly independent relations for a given system of generators with a reasonable probability.

We are now ready to formulate the necessary conditions on the game G for a reduction MO $\Rightarrow$ G to exist, and construct a template for such a reduction.

Lemma 5.4. *Let $\mathcal{G} = (\mathcal{G}_\kappa)_{\kappa=1}^{\infty}$ be a group family with security parameter $\kappa \in \mathbb{Z}_{>0}$. Let G be some computational game, which, given κ, is based on sampling a group $\mathbb{G} \xleftarrow{\$} \mathcal{G}_\kappa$ and $\boldsymbol{g} = (g_1, \ldots, g_n) \xleftarrow{\$} \mathbb{G}^n$ uniformly at random. Let $\mathsf{Rel}^{\mathcal{A}}$ be a relation sampler that takes as input a group $\mathbb{G} \in \mathcal{G}_\kappa$, $\boldsymbol{g} = (g_1, \ldots, g_n) \in \mathbb{G}^n$, and has oracle access to an adversary $\mathcal{A}$ for game G. Assume $\mathsf{Rel}^{\mathcal{A}}$ satisfies the following properties for any given adversary $\mathcal{A}$ in a given group model AHO-GM (i.e., AHO-SM, AHO-AGM, AHO-SAGM):*

(i) *$\mathsf{Rel}^{\mathcal{A}}(\mathbb{G}, \boldsymbol{g})$ outputs either $\bot$ (failure) or a relation e s.t. $\boldsymbol{g}^e = 1_{\mathbb{G}}$ (success).*
(ii) *When $\mathbb{G} = \langle \boldsymbol{g} \rangle$, each execution of $\mathsf{Rel}^{\mathcal{A}}(\mathbb{G}, \boldsymbol{g})$ is independent and has identical success probability $p'_{\mathbb{G},g}$ with $|p'_{\mathbb{G},g} - p_{\mathbb{G},g}| \leq \varepsilon_1 \in \mathsf{negl}(\kappa)$.*
(iii) *When $\mathbb{G} = \langle \boldsymbol{g} \rangle$, given n relation outputs $e_1, \ldots, e_n$ of n independent and successful executions of $\mathsf{Rel}^{\mathcal{A}}(\mathbb{G}, \boldsymbol{g})$, then $\Pr[\det(e_1, \ldots, e_n) = 0] \in \mathsf{negl}(\kappa)$.*
(iv) *$\mathsf{Time}_{\mathcal{G},\mathsf{Rel}} \sim \mathsf{Time}_{\mathcal{G},\mathcal{A}}^{\mathsf{G}}$, i.e., the time complexity of Rel is asymptotically equivalent to that of $\mathcal{A}$.*

Then for $S \geq 4$:

$$
\mathsf{MO} \xrightarrow[\mathrm{AHO\text{-}GM}]{(1-e^{-n \cdot C_S})/2, \lceil Sn/p \rceil} \mathsf{G},
$$

where $p := \mathsf{Adv}_{\mathcal{G},\mathcal{A}}^{\mathsf{G}}(\kappa)$, $p_{\mathbb{G},g} := \mathsf{Adv}_{\mathcal{G},\mathcal{A}}^{\mathsf{G}}|_{\mathbb{G},g}(\kappa)$ and C_S is defined as in Lemma 2.6.

Proof. Given an adversary $\mathcal{A}$ for game G, we construct an MO adversary $\mathcal{B}^{\mathcal{A}}$ which takes input $(1^\kappa, \mathbb{G}, \boldsymbol{g})$ where $\mathbb{G} \in \mathcal{G}_\kappa$, $\boldsymbol{g} \in \mathbb{G}^n$ as given in Fig. 2. The adversary $\mathcal{B}$ calls $\mathcal{A}$ exactly $l := \lceil Sn/p \rceil$ times, which explains the time factor. For the advantage of $\mathcal{B}$ our proof is based on the following inequality:

$$\mathsf{Adv}^{\mathsf{MO}}_{\mathcal{G},\mathcal{B}}(\kappa) \geq \Pr_{\mathbb{G},g}[\mathcal{B}^{\mathcal{A}}(1^{\kappa}, \mathbb{G}, g) \in \mathbb{Z}_{>0} \mid \mathsf{Columns}(E) = n \wedge \langle g \rangle = \mathbb{G}]$$

$$\cdot \Pr_{\mathbb{G},g}[\mathsf{Columns}(E) = n \mid \langle g \rangle = \mathbb{G}] \cdot \Pr_{\mathbb{G},g}[\langle g \rangle = \mathbb{G}]$$

$$\geq p \cdot (1 - e^{-n \cdot C_S})/2 - \mathsf{negl}(\kappa) \tag{3}$$

First, recall that by Definition 4.1(5.):

$$\Pr_{\mathbb{G},g}[\langle g \rangle = \mathbb{G}] = 1 - \mathsf{negl}(\kappa). \tag{4}$$

Second, by condition (iii), over all $\mathbb{G}, g$ with $\langle g \rangle = \mathbb{G}$:

$$\Pr_{\mathbb{G},g}[\mathcal{B}^{\mathcal{A}}(1^{\kappa}, \mathbb{G}, g) \in \mathbb{Z}_{>0} \mid \mathsf{Columns}(E) = n \wedge \langle g \rangle = \mathbb{G}] = 1 - \mathsf{negl}(\kappa). \tag{5}$$

Third, for any given $\mathbb{G}, g$ with $\langle g \rangle = \mathbb{G}$, the success probability of each call to Rel is $p'_{\mathbb{G},g}$ and the amount of successful calls has distribution $B(l, p'_{\mathbb{G},g})$ by condition (ii). From condition (ii) and Lemma 2.7 it follows that the statistical distance between $B(l, p'_{\mathbb{G},g})$ and $B(l, p_{\mathbb{G},g})$ is at most $\varepsilon_2 := (l^2/2) \cdot \varepsilon_1 \in \mathsf{negl}(\kappa)$. By applying Lemma 2.6 on $\mathcal{X} = \{B(l, p_{\mathbb{G},g})\}_{\mathbb{G} = \langle g \rangle}$, we find that

$$\Pr_{\mathbb{G},g}[\mathsf{Columns}(E) = n \mid \mathbb{G} = \langle g \rangle] \geq \Pr_{X \in \mathcal{X}}[X \geq n] - \varepsilon_2 \geq p \cdot (1 - e^{-n \cdot C_S})/2 - \varepsilon_2. \tag{6}$$

The desired inequality (3) is obtained by multiplying Eqs. (4), (5) and (6). $\quad\square$

6 Security Reductions in the AHO-SM

In this section we prove reductions in the abelian hidden order standard model. Firstly, $\{\mathsf{StRoot}, \mathsf{ARoot}, e\text{-}\mathsf{RT}, T\text{-}\mathsf{RSW}\} \Rightarrow \mathsf{MO}$ were previously shown. Using an assumed small prime divisor of group order oracle $\mathcal{O}$, we can prove $\mathsf{LO}^{\mathcal{O}} \Rightarrow \mathsf{MO}$ as well. Followed by reductions $\mathsf{MO} \Rightarrow \mathsf{DLog}_1$ and $\mathsf{MO} \Rightarrow \mathsf{DLog}_2$, where the latter follows from the straightforward reduction $\mathsf{CDH}_2 \Rightarrow \mathsf{DLog}_2$ and the reduction $\mathsf{MO} \Rightarrow \mathsf{CDH}_2$ from Theorem 7.5. An impossibility of efficient *generic* reductions in the opposite direction for DLog_1, DLog_2 and CDH_2 is treated in Sect. 6.1.

Lemma 6.1 ([3,14,18,31]).

$$\{\mathsf{StRoot}, \mathsf{ARoot}, T\text{-}\mathsf{RSW}, e\text{-}\mathsf{RT}\} \xrightarrow[\mathsf{AHO\text{-}SM}]{1,1} \mathsf{MO}, \quad for \ \gcd(e, |\mathbb{G}|) = 1.$$

Proof (sketch). Let N denote the multiple of the group order $|\mathbb{G}|$. For $e\text{-}\mathsf{RT}$ this is a trivial generalization over [3,14]. Given N, one can determine $N' = N/\gcd(e^{\lfloor \log_e(N) \rfloor}, N)$. The resulting value N' will still be a multiple of $|\mathbb{G}|$ and coprime with e, hence one can compute an e-th root of $X \in \mathbb{G}$ as $Y := X^d$ where $ed \equiv 1 \bmod N'$. Now the first two reductions can be easily shown using the $e\text{-}\mathsf{RT}$ reduction: For StRoot one can pick an exponent coprime to N (e.g., by picking a prime $> N$); For ARoot the adversary receives a random large prime e which is coprime to N with all but negligible probability. Finally, $T\text{-}\mathsf{RSW} \Rightarrow \mathsf{MO}$ since $\log_2(2^T) \gg \log_2(2^T \bmod N)$ for any $T \gg \log_2(N)$. $\quad\square$

Note that for e-RT with $\gcd(e, |\mathbb{G}|) > 1$ the situation is less straightforward. For cyclic groups and some more general forms of finite abelian groups, Shank's algorithm can be extended to compute e-th roots [20, Chapter 3]. However, this holds in the known group order setting, and it remains an open question whether it is possible to compute e-th roots given only a multiple of the order.

The situation for the reduction $\mathsf{LO} \Rightarrow \mathsf{MO}$ is also complex. First of all, there need to be elements or order $< 2^\kappa$ in the group $\mathbb{G}$ in order for the reduction to be possible at all. An algebraic method that works in any finite abelian group which contains elements of low order, is not known to the authors at this time. However, if one has access to an oracle which provides a small prime divisor of the group order, then it is possible to construct such a reduction as we prove below. Note that a concrete example of such an oracle can be given in the setting of class groups of imaginary quadratic number fields. Here the Cohen-Lenstra heuristics [12] predict that the group order is divisible by an odd prime q with probability $\mho(q) = 1 - \prod_{n=1}^{\infty} (1 - 1/q^n)$. For example: $\mho(3) \approx 0.439874$.

Proposition 6.2. *Let $\mathcal{O}$ be an oracle that on input a finite abelian group $\mathbb{G} \in \mathcal{G}_\kappa$, outputs a prime $q < 2^\kappa$ which divides the order $|\mathbb{G}|$ with non-negligible probability p. Let $\mathsf{LO}^{\mathcal{O}}$ denote the low order game where an adversary playing the game has access to $\mathcal{O}$. Then*

$$\mathsf{LO}^{\mathcal{O}} \xrightarrow[\text{AHO-SM}]{p/2,\, 1} \mathsf{MO}.$$

Proof. Given an MO adversary $\mathcal{A}$, we construct an LO adversary $\mathcal{B}^{\mathcal{A},\mathcal{O}}$, which takes input $(\mathbb{G}, \boldsymbol{g})$ with $\mathbb{G} \in \mathcal{G}_\kappa$ and $\boldsymbol{g} \in \mathbb{G}^n$, as defined below:

$q \leftarrow \mathcal{O}(\mathbb{G}), \quad N \leftarrow \mathcal{A}(\boldsymbol{g}), \quad \boldsymbol{r} \xleftarrow{\$} (\mathcal{U}_{U^2})^n, \quad X := \boldsymbol{g}^{\boldsymbol{r}}$

for $i = 1, \dots, \lfloor \log_q(N) \rfloor$

    if $N \not\equiv 0 \bmod q^i$ **then return** $\perp$

    if $X^{N/q^i} \neq 1_{\mathbb{G}}$ **then return** $(X^{N/q^i}, q)$

return $\perp$

For random $\mathbb{G} \xleftarrow{\$} \mathcal{G}_\kappa$ and $\boldsymbol{g} \xleftarrow{\$} \mathbb{G}^n$, if the output of $\mathcal{A}$ is correct and q divides the order of X, then we claim that $\mathcal{B}^{\mathcal{A},\mathcal{O}}$ outputs a correct element of low order. Indeed, we know that $X^N = 1_{\mathbb{G}}$ and since $N/q^{\lfloor \log_q(N) \rfloor}$ is not divisible by q, there must be an $1 \leq i \leq \lfloor \log_q(N) \rfloor$ for which $X^{N/q^i} \neq 1_{\mathbb{G}}$. Let i^* be the first i for which this happens, then $(X^{N/q^{i^*}})^q = X^{N/q^{i^*-1}} = 1_{\mathbb{G}}$, so the output of $\mathcal{B}^{\mathcal{A},\mathcal{O}}$ is indeed correct in this case.

By definition of the oracle $\mathcal{O}$, the group order $|\mathbb{G}|$ is divisible by q with probability p. If q divides the group order, then by Lemma 4.5 the probability that q divides the order of a uniformly chosen $X \in \mathbb{G}$ is at least $1 - 1/q \geq 1/2$.

By Lemma 4.8, the distribution of X has negligible statistical distance to the uniform distribution $\mathcal{U}_{\mathbb{G}}$ when $\boldsymbol{g}$ forms a system of generators for $\mathbb{G}$, and we assume the latter to happen with all but negligible probability. Hence $\mathcal{B}^{\mathcal{A},\mathcal{O}}$

succeeds with probability $\mathsf{Adv}^{\mathsf{LO}}_{\mathcal{G},\mathcal{B}^{\mathcal{A}},\mathcal{O}}(\kappa) \geq (p/2 + \varepsilon) \cdot \mathsf{Adv}^{\mathsf{MO}}_{\mathcal{G},\mathcal{A}}(\kappa)$, for some negligible ε. $\qquad\square$

Lemma 6.3.

$$\mathsf{CDH}_2 \xrightarrow[\text{AHO-SM}]{1,1} \mathsf{DLog}_2$$

Proof (sketch). Given a CDH_2 instance (X, A, B), one can simply query a DLog_2 adversary on (X, A) and raise B to the resulting output. $\qquad\square$

Note that any standard model DLog_2 adversary is algebraic as well, hence the above generic reduction produces an algebraic CDH_2 adversary which can be composed with the algebraic reduction in Theorem 7.5 to obtain:

Corollary 6.4.

$$\mathsf{MO} \xrightarrow[\text{AHO-SM}]{(1-e^{-n \cdot C_S})/2, \, \lceil Sn/p \rceil} \mathsf{DLog}_2, \quad \text{for } S \geq 4,$$

where $p := \mathsf{Adv}^{\mathsf{DLog}_2}_{\mathcal{G},\mathcal{A}}(\kappa)$ and C_S is defined as in Lemma 2.6.

Theorem 6.5.

$$\mathsf{MO} \xrightarrow[\text{AHO-SM}]{(1-e^{-n \cdot C_S})/2, \, \lceil Sn/p \rceil} \mathsf{DLog}_1, \quad \text{for } S \geq 4,$$

where $p := \mathsf{Adv}^{\mathsf{DLog}_1}_{\mathcal{G},\mathcal{A}}(\kappa)$ and C_S is defined as in Lemma 2.6.

Proof. Given a DLog_1 adversary $\mathcal{A}$, we construct an MO adversary $\mathcal{B}^{\mathcal{A}}$, which takes input $(\mathbb{G}, \boldsymbol{g})$ with $\mathbb{G} \in \mathcal{G}_\kappa$ and $\boldsymbol{g} \in \mathbb{G}^n$, according to the template in Lemma 5.4. We define a relation sampler $\mathsf{Rel}^{\mathcal{A}}$ as follows, where we assume that a state is maintained in which all internal variables are stored and which is passed between the subroutines.

$\mathsf{Rel}^{\mathcal{A}}(\mathbb{G}, \boldsymbol{g})$	$\mathsf{Samp}(\mathbb{G})$	$\mathsf{Ext}(\mathbb{G}, \boldsymbol{g}, \text{state})$
$(\tilde{\boldsymbol{g}}_i, X_i) \leftarrow \mathsf{Samp}(\mathbb{G})$	$A_i \xleftarrow{\$} (\mathcal{U}_{U^2})^{n^2}$	if $\tilde{\boldsymbol{g}}_i^{\tilde{d}_i} = X_i$ then
$\tilde{d}_i \leftarrow \mathcal{A}(\tilde{\boldsymbol{g}}_i, X_i)$	$r_i \xleftarrow{\$} (\mathcal{U}_{U^3})^n$	$\quad$ return $r_i - A_i \tilde{d}_i$
return $\mathsf{Ext}(\mathbb{G}, \boldsymbol{g}, \text{state})$	return $(\boldsymbol{g}^{A_i}, \boldsymbol{g}^{r_i})$	else return $\perp$

Assume $\mathbb{G} \xleftarrow{\$} \mathcal{G}_\kappa$ and $\boldsymbol{g} \xleftarrow{\$} \mathbb{G}^n$ are sampled uniformly at random. It is straightforward to check that $r_i - A_i \tilde{d}_i$ do indeed form relations with respect to $\boldsymbol{g}$; hence Lemma 5.4(i) is satisfied.

By assumption, $\boldsymbol{g}$ forms a system of generators with all but negligible probability. Conditioned on the event that $\mathbb{G} = \langle \boldsymbol{g} \rangle$, the instances $(\tilde{\boldsymbol{g}}_i, X_i)$ have negligible statistical distance to the uniform distribution $\mathcal{U}_{\mathbb{G}^{n+1}}$ by Lemma 4.8, which is the way problem instances are distributed in the definition of DLog_1. Hence each execution of $\mathsf{Rel}^{\mathcal{A}}(\mathbb{G}, \boldsymbol{g})$ is independent and has identical success probability

$$p'_{\mathbb{G},\boldsymbol{g}} := \mathsf{Adv}^{\mathsf{DLog}_1}_{\mathcal{G},\mathcal{A}}|_{\mathbb{G},\boldsymbol{g}}(\kappa) + \varepsilon_1$$

for some negligible ε_1; thus Lemma 5.4(ii) is satisfied. Moreover, Lemma 5.4(iv) is also clear under the assumption that the runtime of Rel is asymptotically dominated by the runtime of $\mathcal{A}$.

It remains to show that Lemma 5.4(iii) is satisfied. Let $O_j := |\langle g_j \rangle|$ and write $r_{ij} = r'_{ij} + r''_{ij} O_j$ with $0 \le r'_{ij} < O_j$. Furthermore, write $A_i = (a_{i1}, \ldots, a_{in})$ and let $d_{ij} = \sum_{k=1}^{n} a_{ikj} \tilde{d}_{ik}$. We can split the relationship coefficients as

$$\hat{r}_{ij} - \hat{d}_{ij} \quad \text{with} \quad \hat{r}_{ij} := r''_{ij} O_j, \quad \hat{d}_{ij} := d_{ij} - r'_{ij}.$$

Without loss of generality, we assume $\mathcal{A}$ succeeds on the instances $i = 1, \ldots, n$. Our goal will be to show that the $\hat{r}_{ij}$ are distributed negligibly close to uniform modulo p given arbitrary values of the shifts $\hat{d}_{ij}$, so that we can conclude that the coefficients $\hat{r}_{ij} - \hat{d}_{ij} = r_{ij} - d_{ij}$ are distributed negligibly close to uniform modulo p by Lemma 2.1. Ultimately, we conclude that the probability that $\det(r_{ij} - d_{ij})_{i,j=1}^{n} = 0$ is negligible by Corollary 5.3.

Since $g_j^{r_{ij}} = g_j^{r'_{ij}}$, the execution of $\mathcal{A}$ is independent from the r''_{ij}. So despite the distribution of the r_i being conditioned on $\mathcal{A}$ succeeding on input (g^{A_i}, g^{r_i}), the distribution of the r''_{ij} is independent from that of the d_{ij}. It therefore suffices to show that the $\hat{r}_{ij}$ are distributed negligibly close to uniform modulo p given arbitrary values of the $r'_{ij} \in [0, O_j)$. We pick p to be a prime $|\mathbb{G}|/2 < p < |\mathbb{G}|$, which exists by Bertrand's postulate (see e.g., [1, Chapter 2]), so that p is coprime to O_j for each $j = 1, \ldots, n$. Hence it suffices to show that the r''_{ij} are distributed negligibly close to uniform modulo p given arbitrary values of the $r'_{ij} \in [0, O_j)$.

Let $y \in [0, p)$ and fix $x \in [0, O_j)$. We can bound the probability as

$$\frac{1}{p} - \frac{O_j}{U^3 - O_j} \le \Pr[r''_{ij} \equiv y \bmod p \,|\, r'_{ij} = x] \le \frac{1}{p} + \frac{O_j}{U^3 - O_j},$$

and denote this distribution by $\mathcal{R}_{U^3, ij, p, x}$. Hence we can apply Lemma 2.5 with $\delta = O_j / (U^3 - O_j)$ to find that, for fixed $(x_{ij})_{i,j=1}^{n} \in \prod_{i,j=1}^{n} [0, O_j)$, the statistical distance Δ between $(\mathcal{U}_p)^{n^2}$ and $\prod_{i,j=1}^{n} \mathcal{R}_{U^3, ij, p, x_{ij}}$ is bounded as

$$\Delta \le \frac{1}{2} \left(\frac{n^2 p O_j}{U^3 - O_j} + \left(\frac{n^2 p O_j}{U^3 - O_j} \right)^2 \right) \le \frac{1}{2} \left(\frac{n^2}{U - 1} + \left(\frac{n^2}{U - 1} \right)^2 \right)$$

which is negligible. Hence the probability that $\det(E) = \det(r_{ij} - d_{ij})_{i,j=1}^{n} = 0$ is negligible by Corollary 5.3; thus Lemma 5.4(iii) is satisfied. $\square$

6.1   Impossibility Results for Generic Reductions

Corollary 6.6. *There do not exist efficient generic reductions from* DLog$_1$ *to* MO *and from* CDH$_1$ *to* MO: *solving these problems in the generic group model for prime cyclic groups* $\mathbb{G}$ *takes time* $\sqrt{|\mathbb{G}|}$ *with known group order [30, Theorem 1 and 3]. Since* DLog$_2$ *is equivalent to* DLog$_1$ *in the case of cyclic groups of prime order, it also follows that no efficient generic reduction from* DLog$_2$ *to* MO *exists.*

Lemma 6.7. *For a group family of (hidden) cyclic large prime order, we have*

$$\mathsf{CDH}_1 \xrightarrow[\text{HO-SM}]{1,1} \mathsf{CDH}_2$$

Proof (sketch). On CDH_1 input tuple (g, g^a, g^b), choose random exponent r and let $s = r^{-1} \bmod p$. Let $X = g^r$, $Y = (g^a)^r = X^a$, $Z = g^b = X^{bs}$ and we return $R = \mathcal{A}(g, X, Y, Z)$. If $\mathcal{A}$ is successful then $R = X^{abs} = g^{absr} = g^{ab}$ as desired. Note that it does not need to know the prime order p. □

Corollary 6.8. *There does not exist an efficient generic reduction from CDH_2 to MO, as otherwise this would contradict Corollary 6.6 using Lemma 6.7.*

7 Security Reductions in the AHO-AGM

Theorem 7.1.

$$\mathsf{MO} \xrightarrow[\text{AHO-AGM}]{(1-e^{-n \cdot C_S})/2,\; \lceil Sn/p \rceil} \mathsf{StRoot}, \quad \textit{for } S \geq 4,$$

where $p := \mathsf{Adv}_{\mathcal{G}, \mathcal{A}}^{\mathsf{StRoot}}(\kappa)$ and C_S is defined as in Lemma 2.6.

Proof. Again we will use the template from Lemma 5.4 to construct an MO adversary $\mathcal{B}^{\mathcal{A}}$, which takes input $(\mathbb{G}, \boldsymbol{g})$ with $\mathbb{G} \in \mathcal{G}_\kappa$ and $\boldsymbol{g} \in \mathbb{G}^n$, given an *algebraic* StRoot adversary $\mathcal{A}$. We define a relation sampler $\mathsf{Rel}^{\mathcal{A}}$ as follows, where we assume that a state is maintained in which all internal variables are stored and which is passed between the subroutines.

$\mathsf{Rel}^{\mathcal{A}}(\mathbb{G}, \boldsymbol{g})$	$\mathsf{Samp}(\mathbb{G})$	$\mathsf{Ext}(\mathbb{G}, \boldsymbol{g}, \mathsf{state})$
$(\tilde{g}_i, X_i) \leftarrow \mathsf{Samp}(\mathbb{G})$	$A_i \xleftarrow{\$} (\mathcal{U}_{U^2})^{n^2}$	**if** $(Y_i^{e_i} = X_i \wedge e_i > 1)$ **then**
$([Y_i]_{(\tilde{g}_i, X_i)}, e_i) \leftarrow \mathcal{A}(\tilde{g}_i, X_i)$	$r_i \xleftarrow{\$} (\mathcal{U}_{U^3})^n$	$\quad$ **return** $r_i(1 - c_i e_i) - e_i A_i \boldsymbol{b}_i$
$(\boldsymbol{b}_i, c_i) := [Y_i]_{(\tilde{g}_i, X_i)}$	**return** (g^{A_i}, g^{r_i})	**else return** $\bot$
return $\mathsf{Ext}(\mathbb{G}, \boldsymbol{g}, \mathsf{state})$		

Assume $\mathbb{G} \xleftarrow{\$} \mathcal{G}_\kappa$ and $\boldsymbol{g} \xleftarrow{\$} \mathbb{G}^n$ are sampled uniformly at random. Again it is straightforward to check that $r_i(1 - c_i e_i) - e_i A_i \boldsymbol{b}_i$ do indeed form relations with respect to $\boldsymbol{g}$; hence Lemma 5.4(i) is satisfied. Completely analogous to Theorem 6.5 conditions (ii) and (iv) of Lemma 5.4 are satisfied.

Our approach to show that Lemma 5.4(iii) is satisfied will be similar to the one in Theorem 6.5. Without loss of generality, we assume that $\mathcal{A}$ succeeds on instances $i = 1, \ldots, n$. Write $A_i = (\boldsymbol{a}_{i1}, \ldots, \boldsymbol{a}_{in})$ and $r_{ij} = r'_{ij} + r''_{ij} O_j$ with $0 \leq r'_{ij} < O_j$, and split the relationship coefficients as

$$\hat{r}_{ij} - \hat{d}_{ij} \quad \text{with} \quad \hat{r}_{ij} := r''_{ij}(1 - c_i e_i) O_j, \quad \hat{d}_{ij} := e_i \sum_{k=1}^{n} a_{ikj} b_{ik} + r'_{ij}(c_i e_i - 1).$$

We claim that we can now pick a prime p such that it is coprime to each O_j for $j = 1, \ldots, n$, and additionally coprime to $1 - c_i e_i$ for all $i = 1, \ldots, n$ (note that $1 - c_i e_i \neq 0$ since $e_i > 1$). This is possible since by [15, Théorème 1.10: 4 & 5], for $|\mathbb{G}| \geq 120368 \approx 2^{17}$, there are superpolynomially many, namely at least

$$\frac{|\mathbb{G}| \left(\log(|\mathbb{G}|/4) - 1.2\right)}{2(\log |\mathbb{G}| - 1)(\log(|\mathbb{G}|/2) - 1.1)},$$

primes between $|\mathbb{G}|/2$ and $|\mathbb{G}|$. As mentioned before, these are coprime to each O_j for $j = 1, \ldots, n$. Moreover, the number of prime factors of $1 - c_i e_i$ is bounded polynomially for each $i = 1, \ldots, n$, and n is bounded polynomially; hence there are superpolynomially many primes meeting our criteria.

From Theorem 6.5 we know that the distribution of $(r''_{ij} \bmod p)^n_{i,j=1}$, conditioned on arbitrary values of $(r'_{ij})^n_{i,j=1} \in \prod^n_{i,j=1}[0, O_j)$, has negligible statistical distance to $(\mathcal{U}_p)^{n^2}$ and is independent of e_i, b_i and c_i for $i = 1, \ldots, n$. Hence we can conclude that $(\hat{r}_{ij} - \hat{d}_{ij} \bmod p)^n_{i,j=1}$ has negligible statistical distance to $(\mathcal{U}_p)^{n^2}$, and thus that the probability that $\det(E) = \det(\hat{r}_{ij} - \hat{d}_{ij})^n_{i,j=1} = 0$ is negligible by Corollary 5.3; hence Lemma 5.4(iii) is satisfied.   □

Theorem 7.2.

$$\mathsf{MO} \xrightarrow[\text{AHO-AGM}]{(1-e^{-n\cdot C_S})/2,\, \lceil Sn/p \rceil} \mathsf{ARoot}, \quad for\ S \geq 4,$$

where $p := \mathsf{Adv}^{\mathsf{ARoot}}_{\mathcal{G}, \mathcal{A}}(\kappa)$ and C_S is defined as in Lemma 2.6.

Proof. Given an *algebraic* ARoot adversary $\mathcal{A}$, we will again use the template from Lemma 5.4 to construct an MO adversary $\mathcal{B}^{\mathcal{A}}$, which takes input $(\mathbb{G}, \boldsymbol{g})$ with $\mathbb{G} \in \mathcal{G}_\kappa$ and $\boldsymbol{g} \in \mathbb{G}^n$. We define a relation sampler $\mathsf{Rel}^{\mathcal{A}}$ as follows, where we assume that a state is maintained in which all internal variables are stored and which is passed between the subroutines.

$\mathsf{Rel}^{\mathcal{A}}(\mathbb{G}, \boldsymbol{g})$	$\mathsf{Samp}(\mathbb{G})$	$\mathsf{Ext}(\mathbb{G}, \boldsymbol{g}, \text{state})$
$(\tilde{g}_i, X_i, \ell_i) \leftarrow \mathsf{Samp}(\mathbb{G})$	$A_i \overset{\$}{\leftarrow} (\mathcal{U}_{U^3})^{n^2}$	if $(Y_i^{\ell_i} = X_i \wedge X_i \neq 1_{\mathbb{G}})$ then
$[Y_i]_{(\tilde{g}_i, X_i)} \leftarrow \mathcal{A}(\tilde{g}_i, X_i, \ell_i)$	$[X_i]_{g_i^{A_i}} \leftarrow \mathcal{A}(g^{A_i})$	$\quad$ return $A_i(b_i(1 - d_i\ell_i) - c_i\ell_i)$
$(c_i, d_i) := [Y_i]_{(\tilde{g}_i, X_i)}$	$b_i := [X_i]_{g_i^{A_i}}$	else return $\bot$
return $\mathsf{Ext}(\mathbb{G}, \boldsymbol{g}, \text{state})$	$\ell_i \overset{\$}{\leftarrow} \mathsf{Primes}(2\kappa)$	
	return (g^{A_i}, X_i, ℓ_i)	

It is straightforward to check that $A_i(b_i(1 - d_i\ell_i) - c_i\ell_i)$ do indeed form relations with respect to $\boldsymbol{g}$; hence Lemma 5.4(i) is satisfied. Completely analogous to Theorem 6.5 conditions (ii) and (iv) of Lemma 5.4 are satisfied.

To show that Lemma 5.4(iii) is satisfied, we again take a similar approach as in the proof of Theorem 6.5. Without loss of generality, we assume that

$\mathcal{A}$ succeeds on instances $i = 1, \ldots, n$. Write $A_i = (\boldsymbol{a}_{i1}, \ldots, \boldsymbol{a}_{in})$ and $a_{ikj} = a'_{ikj} + a''_{ikj} O_j$ with $0 \leq a_{ikj} < O_j$. Note that for every $i = 1, \ldots, n$, there is at least one $k \in \{1, \ldots, n\}$ for which $b_{ik} \neq 0$ since $\mathcal{A}$ needs to output a non-trivial X_i to succeed. For each $i = 1, \ldots, n$, pick such a $k \in \{1, \ldots, n\}$, and denote it by k_i. Put $\delta_{ik} := b_{ik}(1 - d_i \ell_i) - c_{ik} \ell_i$, expand and split the relation coefficients as

$$\hat{r}_{ij} + \hat{d}_{ij} \quad \text{with} \quad \hat{r}_{ij} := a''_{ik_i j} \delta_{ik_i} O_j, \quad \hat{d}_{ij} := a'_{ik_i j} \delta_{ik_i} + \sum_{k \neq k_i} a_{ikj} \delta_{ik}.$$

As before, our goal is to show that the $\hat{r}_{ij}$ are distributed negligibly close to uniform modulo some prime p given arbitrary values of the shifts $\hat{d}_{ij}$. We first claim that the δ_{ik_i} can only be zero with negligible probability, so that we can pick the prime p coprime to δ_{ik_i} for all $i = 1, \ldots, n$, just as in the proof of Theorem 7.1. Then it suffices to show that the distribution of $(a''_{ik_i j} \bmod p)^n_{i,j=1}$, conditioned on arbitrary values of the $(a'_{ik_i j})^n_{i,j=1} \in \prod^n_{i,j=1} [0, O_j)$, has negligible statistical distance to $(\mathcal{U}_p)^{n^2}$. The latter follows completely analogous as in the proof of Theorem 6.5. So it remains to show the first claim.

Recall that $\delta_{ik_i} = b_{ik_i}(1 - d_i \ell_i) - c_{ik_i} \ell_i$ with $b_{ik_i} \neq 0$. If $c_{ik_i} = 0$, then $\delta_{ik_i} = b_{ik_i}(1 - d_i \ell_i) \neq 0$ since $\ell_i > 1$. If $c_{ik_i} \neq 0$ and $\delta_{ik_i} = 0$, this implies that ℓ_i divides b_{ik_i}, which can only happen with negligible probability since b_{ik_i} is chosen before ℓ_i is picked uniformly from a superpolynomially large set of primes.

Ultimately we can conclude analogous to Theorem 7.1 that Lemma 5.4(iii) is satisfied, which concludes our proof. □

Boneh, Bünz and Fisch [7] previously established the standard model reduction $\mathsf{ARoot} \underset{\mathrm{SM}}{\Longrightarrow} \mathsf{LO}$. (That is, given an element $X \in \mathbb{G}$ whose order divides d, one can compute an ℓ-th root as $Y = X^e$ where $e\ell \equiv 1 \bmod d$.) We note that this reduction is generic, and thus $\mathsf{ARoot} \xrightarrow[\text{AHO-AGM}]{} \mathsf{LO}$ as well. Composing this reduction with Theorem 7.2, we obtain the following corollary.

Corollary 7.3.

$$\mathsf{MO} \xrightarrow[\text{AHO-AGM}]{(1-e^{-\mu \cdot C_S})/2, \lfloor Sn/p \rfloor} \mathsf{LO}, \quad \text{for } S \geq 4,$$

where $p := \mathsf{Adv}^{\mathsf{LO}}_{\mathcal{G}, \mathcal{A}}(\kappa)$ and C_S is defined as in Lemma 2.6.

Theorem 7.4.

$$\mathsf{MO} \xrightarrow[\text{AHO-AGM}]{(1-e^{-n \cdot C_S})/2, \lceil Sn/p \rceil} e\text{-}\mathsf{RT}, \quad \text{for } S \geq 4,$$

where $p := \mathsf{Adv}^{e\text{-}\mathsf{RT}}_{\mathcal{G}, \mathcal{A}}(\kappa)$ and C_S is defined as in Lemma 2.6.

Proof. Given an *algebraic* e-RT adversary $\mathcal{A}$ for some fixed $e \in \mathbb{Z}_{>1}$, we use the template from Lemma 5.4 to construct an MO adversary $\mathcal{B}^{\mathcal{A}}$, which takes input $(\mathbb{G}, \boldsymbol{g})$ with $\mathbb{G} \in \mathcal{G}_\kappa$ and $\boldsymbol{g} \in \mathbb{G}^n$. We define a relation sampler $\mathsf{Rel}^{\mathcal{A}}$ as follows, where we assume that a state is maintained in which all internal variables are stored and which is passed between the subroutines.

$\mathsf{Rel}^{\mathcal{A}}(\mathbb{G}, \boldsymbol{g})$	$\mathsf{Samp}(\mathbb{G})$	$\mathsf{Ext}(\mathbb{G}, \boldsymbol{g}, \text{state})$
$(\tilde{g}_i, X_i) \leftarrow \mathsf{Samp}(\mathbb{G})$	$A_i \xleftarrow{\$} (\mathcal{U}_{U^2})^{n^2}$	if $Y_i^{e_i} = X_i$ then
$[Y_i]_{(\tilde{g}_i, X_i)} \leftarrow \mathcal{A}(\tilde{g}_i, X_i)$	$r_i \xleftarrow{\$} (\mathcal{U}_{U^3})^n$	$\quad$ return $r_i(e - c_i e^2) - A_i b_i e$
$(b_i, c_i) := [Y_i]_{(\tilde{g}_i, X_i)}$	return $(g^{A_i}, g^{r_i e})$	else return $\perp$
return $\mathsf{Ext}(\mathbb{G}, \boldsymbol{g}, \text{state})$		

It is straightforward to check that $r_i(e - c_i e^2) - A_i b_i e$ do indeed form relations with respect to $\boldsymbol{g}$; hence Lemma 5.4(i) is satisfied. Again, completely analogous to Theorem 6.5, conditions (ii) and (iv) of Lemma 5.4 are satisfied.

We can show almost completely analogous to the proof of Theorem 7.1 that Lemma 5.4(iii) is satisfied, with the only difference being that we now pick the prime p coprime to $e - c_i e^2$ for $i = 1, \dots, n$ (where we again assume without loss of generality that $\mathcal{A}$ succeeds on the instances $i = 1, \dots, n$). Note that $e - c_i e^2$ is nonzero since $e > 1$. $\qquad\square$

Theorem 7.5.

$$\mathsf{MO} \xrightarrow[\mathsf{AHO\text{-}AGM}]{(1 - e^{-n \cdot C_S})/2, \lceil Sn/p \rceil} \mathsf{CDH}_2, \quad \text{for } S \geq 4,$$

where $p := \mathsf{Adv}_{\mathbb{G}, \mathcal{A}}^{\mathsf{CDH}_2}(\kappa)$ and C_S is defined as in Lemma 2.6.

Proof. Given an *algebraic* CDH_2 adversary $\mathcal{A}$, we construct an MO adversary $\mathcal{B}^{\mathcal{A}}$, which takes input $(\mathbb{G}, \boldsymbol{g})$ with $\mathbb{G} \in \mathcal{G}_\kappa$ and $\boldsymbol{g} \in \mathbb{G}^n$, using the template from Lemma 5.4. We define a relation sampler $\mathsf{Rel}^{\mathcal{A}}$ as shown in Fig. 3, where we assume that a state is maintained in which all internal variables are stored and which is passed between the subroutines. It is again straightforward to check that $r_i(d_i + a_i e_i + b_i f_i - a_i b_i) + H_i c_i$ do indeed form relations with respect to $\boldsymbol{g}$; hence Lemma 5.4(i) is satisfied. Conditions (ii) and (iv) of Lemma 5.4 hold up analogous to Theorem 6.5.

To show that Lemma 5.4(iii) is satisfied, we again follow a similar approach to Theorem 6.5, only with a few more subtleties. Without loss of generality, we assume that $\mathcal{A}$ succeeds on instances $i = 1, \dots, n$. Write $H_i = (h_{i1}, \dots, h_{in})$ and $r_{ij} = r'_{ij} + r''_{ij} O_j$ with $0 \leq r'_{ij} < O_j$, put $\delta_i := d_i + a_i e_i + b_i f_i - a_i b_i$, and split the relation coefficients as

$$\hat{r}_{ij} + \hat{d}_{ij} \quad \text{with} \quad \hat{r}_{ij} := r''_{ij} \delta_i O_j, \quad \hat{d}_{ij} := r'_{ij} \delta_i + \sum_{k=1}^{n} h_{ikj} c_{ik}.$$

Similar to the proof of Theorem 7.2, we want to pick our prime p coprime to δ_i for all $i = 1, \dots, n$. We claim that δ_i can only be zero with negligible probability, and show this using a similar argument as for that the determinant of the relationship matrix can only be zero with negligible probability.

Write $a_i = a'_i + a''_i |\langle X_i \rangle|$ and $b_i = b'_i + b''_i |\langle X_i \rangle|$ with $0 \leq a'_i, b'_i \leq |\langle X_i \rangle|$. Pick a prime $|\mathbb{G}|/2 < p' < |\mathbb{G}|$ so that it is coprime to $|\langle X_i \rangle|$ for each $i = 1, \dots, n$.

$\mathsf{Rel}^{\mathcal{A}}(\mathbb{G}, \boldsymbol{g})$	$\mathsf{Samp}(\mathbb{G})$
$(\tilde{\boldsymbol{g}}_i, X_i, A_i, B_i) \leftarrow \mathsf{Samp}(\mathbb{G})$	$H_i \xleftarrow{\$} (\mathcal{U}_{U^2})^{n^2}$
$[Y_i]_{(\tilde{\boldsymbol{g}}_i, X_i, A_i, B_i)} \leftarrow \mathcal{A}(\tilde{\boldsymbol{g}}_i, X_i, A_i, B_i)$	$(\boldsymbol{r}_i, a_i, b_i) \xleftarrow{\$} (\mathcal{U}_{U^3})^{n+2}$
$(\boldsymbol{c}_i, d_i, e_i, f_i) := [Y_i]_{(\tilde{\boldsymbol{g}}_i, X_i, A_i, B_i)}$	**return** $(\boldsymbol{g}^{H_i}, \boldsymbol{g}^{\boldsymbol{r}_i}, \boldsymbol{g}^{\boldsymbol{r}_i a_i}, \boldsymbol{g}^{\boldsymbol{r}_i b_i})$
return $\mathsf{Ext}(\mathbb{G}, \boldsymbol{g}, \mathsf{state})$	

$\mathsf{Ext}(\mathbb{G}, \boldsymbol{g}, \mathsf{state})$
if $Y_i = X_i^{a_i b_i}$ **then**
$\quad$ **return** $\boldsymbol{r}_i(d_i + a_i e_i + b_i f_i - a_i b_i) + H_i \boldsymbol{c}_i$
else return $\perp$

Fig. 3. The MO relation sampler $\mathsf{Rel}(\mathbb{G}, \boldsymbol{g}, \mathcal{A})$ given CDH_2 adversary $\mathcal{A}$.

Completely analogous to the proof of Theorem 6.5, the distribution of $(a_i'' \bmod p', b_i'' \bmod p')_{i=1}^n$, conditioned on arbitrary values of $(a_i', b_i') \in \prod_{i=1}^n [0, |\langle X_i \rangle|)^2$, has negligible statistical distance to $(\mathcal{U}_{p'})^{2n}$. Moreover, it is independent from d_i, e_i and f_i since a_i'' and b_i'' are completely hidden from the point of view of the adversary. By Lemma 5.2, the probability that $(z_{1i}, z_{2i})_{i=1}^n \xleftarrow{\$} (\mathcal{U}_{p'})^{2n}$ are a zero modulo p' of the polynomial $F(Z_{11}, \ldots, Z_{1n}, Z_{21}, \ldots, Z_{2n})$, defined as

$$\prod_{i=1}^n d_i + (a_i' + Z_{1i}|\langle X_i \rangle|)\, e_i + (b_i' + Z_{2i}|\langle X_i \rangle|)\, f_i - (a_i' + Z_{1i}|\langle X_i \rangle|)\,(b_i' + Z_{2i}|\langle X_i \rangle|),$$

is at most $2n/p'$ (note that F reduces to a nonzero polynomial of degree $2n$ over $\mathbb{F}_{p'}$), which is negligible. It follows that any of the δ_i can only be zero with negligible probability since $F(a_1'', \ldots, a_n'', b_1'', \ldots, b_n'') = \prod_{i=1}^n \delta_i$.

Now analogous to the proof of Theorem 7.2, we can conclude that Lemma 5.4(iii) is satisfied. $\qquad\square$

8   Security Reductions in the AHO-SAGM

In this section we will show, using similar arguments as before, that it is possible to reduce the multiple order problem MO to the T-repeated squaring problem T-RSW in the AHO-SAGM. Our result can be seen as a generalization of that of [18, Theorem 2] from the family of *cyclic* RSA groups to *all finite abelian groups*. The proof in the abelian case is more complex due to the additional complications that arise from having to run the T-RSW adversary multiple times in order to extract several group relations, which have to be shown to be independent enough. Furthermore, our security definition of T-RSW in AHO-SAGM is weaker by giving the adversary $\mathcal{A}_1$ more power: (1) in contrast to [18], $\mathcal{A}_1$ itself may be standard model and does not have to be strongly algebraic; (2) in contrast to

[18], $\mathcal{A}_1$ is given $\mathbf{g}$ (i.e., the same generators $\mathbf{g}$ as the strongly algebraic online algorithm $\mathcal{A}_2$ output by $\mathcal{A}_1$).

We have already seen the reduction in the opposite direction T-RSW $\Rightarrow$ MO; hence this shows the T-repeated squaring and the multiple order game are (asymptotically) equivalent in the AHO-SAGM. Before we show this reduction, we first prove a useful lemma bounding the size of the representation coefficients of the output elements of strongly algebraic algorithms.

Lemma 8.1. *Let $\mathbb{G}$ be a finite abelian group and let $\mathbf{g} = (g_1, \dots, g_n)$ be a tuple of elements of $\mathbb{G}$. Let $\mathcal{A}$ be any strongly algebraic algorithm running in at most t rounds on input $\mathbf{g}$ and $X = \mathbf{g}^{\mathbf{r}} = g_1^{r_1} \cdots g_n^{r_n}$ for $\mathbf{r} = (r_1, \dots, r_n) \in \mathbb{Z}_{\geq 1}^n$ (i.e., $\mathsf{ATime}(\mathcal{A}(\mathbf{g}, X)) \leq t$). Let Y be any output of $\mathcal{A}$ and let $(Y_s, Y_{s,1}, Y_{s,2})$ or $(Y_s, Y_{s,1})$ be the corresponding tuples for each element Y_s being output at round $1 \leq s \leq t$. (Note that $\mathcal{A}$ is in fact allowed to output arbitrary many tuples in each round, but we can always pick a path of sequential computation leading to Y.) Then the following two statements hold.*

1. *The generalized discrete logarithm $\mathsf{DLog}_{\mathcal{A}}(\mathbf{g}, Y)$ of Y with respect to $\mathbf{g}$ and $\mathcal{A}$, can be recursively computed as follows:*
   - *$\mathsf{DLog}_{\mathcal{A}}(\mathbf{g}, g_i) = \mathbf{1}_i$ (the vector with a 1 on the i-th place and 0 on all others) for $1 \leq i \leq n$, $\mathsf{DLog}_{\mathcal{A}}(\mathbf{g}, X) = \mathbf{r}$;*
   - *For $s = 1, \dots, t$, let*

$$\mathsf{DLog}_{\mathcal{A}}(\mathbf{g}, Y_s) = \begin{cases} \mathsf{DLog}_{\mathcal{A}}(\mathbf{g}, Y_{s,1}) + \mathsf{DLog}_{\mathcal{A}}(\mathbf{g}, Y_{s,2}) & \text{if } Y_s = Y_{s,1} Y_{s,2} \\ -\mathsf{DLog}_{\mathcal{A}}(\mathbf{g}, Y_{s,1}) & \text{if } Y_s = Y_{s,1}^{-1} \end{cases}$$

2. *The generalized discrete logarithm $\mathbf{d} = (d_1, \dots, d_n) := \mathsf{DLog}_{\mathcal{A}}(\mathbf{g}, Y)$ satisfies $|d_i| \leq 2^t r_i$ for all $1 \leq i \leq n$.*

Proof. The first statement is clear. For the second statement we note that if $t = 1$, the only elements $\mathcal{A}$ can output are:

$$g_i = \mathbf{g}^{\mathbf{1}_i}, \quad g_i^2 = \mathbf{g}^{2 \cdot \mathbf{1}_i}, \quad g_i g_j = \mathbf{g}^{\mathbf{1}_i + \mathbf{1}_j}, \quad g_i^{-1} = \mathbf{g}^{-\mathbf{1}_i},$$
$$X = \mathbf{g}^{\mathbf{r}}, \quad g_i X = \mathbf{g}^{\mathbf{r} + \mathbf{1}_i}, \quad X^2 = \mathbf{g}^{2\mathbf{r}}, \quad X^{-1} = \mathbf{g}^{-\mathbf{r}}$$

for $1 \leq i \neq j \leq n$; hence the statement holds for $t = 1$. We proceed to prove the statement by induction. Suppose that the lemma holds for $t - 1$. Now suppose that $\mathcal{A}$ outputs (Y, Y_1, Y_2) in round t. Then Y_1 and Y_2 are either equal to one of the g_i ($1 \leq i \leq n$), $X = \mathbf{g}^{\mathbf{r}}$, or one of the outputs of $\mathcal{A}$ in rounds $1, \dots, t - 1$. Hence we see that for $1 \leq i \leq n$:

$$|\mathsf{DLog}_{\mathcal{A}}(\mathbf{g}, Y)_i| = |\mathsf{DLog}_{\mathcal{A}}(\mathbf{g}, Y_1)_i + \mathsf{DLog}_{\mathcal{A}}(\mathbf{g}, Y_2)_i|$$
$$\leq |\mathsf{DLog}_{\mathcal{A}}(\mathbf{g}, Y_1)_i| + |\mathsf{DLog}_{\mathcal{A}}(\mathbf{g}, Y_2)_i| \leq 2^{t-1} r_i + 2^{t-1} r_i = 2^t r_i.$$

Similarly, if $\mathcal{A}$ outputs (Y, Y_1) in round t, then for $1 \leq i \leq n$ we have that $|\mathsf{DLog}_{\mathcal{A}}(\mathbf{g}, Y)_i| = |\mathsf{DLog}_{\mathcal{A}}(\mathbf{g}, Y_1)_i| \leq 2^{t-1} r_i$, which completes the proof of the second statement. □

Theorem 8.2.

$$\mathsf{MO} \xrightarrow[\text{AHO-SAGM}]{(1-e^{-n \cdot C_S})/2,\, \lceil Sn/p \rceil} T\text{-RSW}, \quad \text{for } S \geq 4,$$

where $p := \mathsf{Adv}_{\mathcal{G}, \mathcal{A}}^{T\text{-RSW}}(\kappa)$ and C_S is defined as in Lemma 2.6.

Proof. Let $\mathcal{A}_1$ be an adversary which runs in the *standard model* in the preprocessing phase and produces $\mathcal{A}_2 \leftarrow \mathcal{A}_1(\mathbb{G}, \boldsymbol{g})$ which runs as a *strongly algebraic* algorithm in the online phase. We use the template from Lemma 5.4 to construct an adversary $\mathcal{B}^{\mathcal{A}_1}$, which takes input $(\mathbb{G}, \boldsymbol{g})$ with $\mathbb{G} \in \mathcal{G}_\kappa$ and $\boldsymbol{g} \in \mathbb{G}^n$. We define a relation sampler $\mathsf{Rel}^{\mathcal{A}_1}$ as follows, where we assume that a state is maintained in which all internal variables are stored and which is passed between the subroutines, and use the shorthand $t_i := \mathsf{ATime}(\mathcal{A}_2(\tilde{\boldsymbol{g}}_i, X_i))$.

$\mathsf{Rel}^{\mathcal{A}_1}(\mathbb{G}, \boldsymbol{g})$	$\mathsf{Samp}(\mathbb{G})$	$\mathsf{Ext}(\mathbb{G}, \boldsymbol{g}, \text{state})$
$(\tilde{\boldsymbol{g}}_i, X_i) \leftarrow \mathsf{Samp}(\mathbb{G})$	$A_i \xleftarrow{\$} (\mathcal{U}_{U^3})^{n^2}$	**if** $\left(Y_i = X_i^{2^T} \wedge t_i < T\right)$ **then**
$\mathcal{A}_2 \leftarrow \mathcal{A}_1(\mathbb{G}, \tilde{\boldsymbol{g}}_i)$	$r_i \xleftarrow{\$} (\mathcal{U}_{U^3})^n$	$\quad d_i \leftarrow \mathsf{DLog}_{\mathcal{A}_2}(\tilde{\boldsymbol{g}}_i, Y_i)$
$(Y_i, ([Y_{i,s}])_{s=1}^{t_i}) \leftarrow \mathcal{A}_2(\tilde{\boldsymbol{g}}_i, X_i)$	**return** $(g^{A_i}, g^{A_i r_i})$	$\quad$ **return** $2^T A_i r_i - A_i d_i$
return $\mathsf{Ext}(\mathbb{G}, \boldsymbol{g}, \text{state})$		**else return** $\perp$

It is straightforward to check that $2^T A_i r_i - A_i d_i$ do indeed form relations with respect to $\boldsymbol{g}$; hence Lemma 5.4(i) is satisfied. Conditions (ii) and (iv) of Lemma 5.4 again hold up completely analogous to Theorem 6.5.

We once more show similar to the proof of Theorem 6.5 that Lemma 5.4(iii) is satisfied. Without loss of generality, we assume that $\mathcal{A}$ succeeds on instances $i = 1, \ldots, n$. Write $A_i = (\boldsymbol{a}_{i1}, \ldots, \boldsymbol{a}_{in})$ and $a_{ikj} = a'_{ikj} + a''_{ikj} O_j$ with $0 \leq a'_{ikj} < O_j$, and expand the relationship coefficients as:

$$\sum_{k=1}^n a''_{ikj}(2^T r_{ik} - d_{ik}) O_j + \sum_{k=1}^n a'_{ikj}(2^T r_{ik} - d_{ik}).$$

Then by Lemma 8.1 and the fact that $\mathcal{A}_2$ runs in $t_i < T$ rounds on input $(\tilde{\boldsymbol{g}}_i, X_i)$, we see that $|d_{ik}| < 2^T r_{ik}$ and thus that $\delta_{ik} := 2^T r_{ik} - d_{ik} \neq 0$ for all $i = 1, \ldots, n$ and $k = 1, \ldots, n$. Now we can pick an arbitrary $k_i \in \{1, \ldots, n\}$ for each $i = 1, \ldots, n$ (e.g., $k_i = 1$ for all $i = 1, \ldots, n$ suffices), and split the coefficients as $\hat{r}_{ij} + \hat{d}_{ij}$ with $\hat{r}_{ij} := a''_{ik_ij} \delta_{ik_i} O_j$, $\hat{d}_{ij} := a'_{ik_ij} \delta_{ik_i} + \sum_{k \neq k_i} a_{ikj} \delta_{ik}$. Then, similar to the proof of Theorem 7.2, we can pick our prime p coprime to δ_{ik_i} for all $i = 1, \ldots, n$. Analogous to the proof of Theorem 6.5 it follows that the distribution of $(a''_{ik_ij} \mod p)_{i,j=1}^n$, conditioned on arbitrary values of $(a'_{ik_ij})_{i,j=1}^n \in \prod_{i,j=1}^n [0, O_j)$, has negligible statistical distance to $(\mathcal{U}_p)^{n^2}$. Hence we conclude as in the proof of Theorem 6.5 that $(\hat{r}_{ij} - \hat{d}_{ij} \mod p)_{i,j=1}^n$ has negligible statistical distance to $(\mathcal{U}_p)^{n^2}$ and thus that Lemma 5.4(iii) is satisfied. $\qquad \square$

References

1. Aigner, M., Ziegler, G.: Proofs from the Book, vol. 274. Springer (2010). https://link.springer.com/book/10.1007/978-3-642-00856-6
2. van Baarsen, A., Stevens, M.: On time-lock cryptographic assumptions in abelian hidden-order groups. Cryptology ePrint Archive, Report 2021/1184 (2021)
3. Biehl, I., Buchmann, J., Hamdy, S., Meyer, A.: A signature scheme based on the intractability of computing roots. Des. Codes Cryptogr. **25**(3), 223–236 (2002)
4. Block, A.R., Holmgren, J., Rosen, A., Rothblum, R.D., Soni, P.: Time- and space-efficient arguments from groups of unknown order. In: CRYPTO (4). LNCS, vol. 12828, pp. 123–152. Springer (2021). https://link.springer.com/chapter/10.1007/978-3-030-84259-8_5
5. Boneh, D., Bonneau, J., Bunz, B., Fisch, B.: Verifiable delay functions. In: Shacham, H., Boldyreva, A. (eds.) Advances in Cryptology. LNCS, vol. 10991. Springer, Cham (2018). https://doi.org/10.1007/978-3-319-96884-1_25
6. Boneh, D., Bunz, B., Fisch, B.: Batching techniques for accumulators with applications to IOPs and stateless blockchains. In: Boldyreva, A., Micciancio, D. (eds.) Advances in Cryptology. LNCS, vol. 11692. Springer, Cham (2019). https://doi.org/10.1007/978-3-030-26948-7_20
7. Boneh, D., Bünz, B., Fisch, B.: A survey of two verifiable delay functions. Cryptology ePrint Archive, Report 2018/712 (2018)
8. Buchmann, J., Schmidt, A.: Computing the structure of a finite abelian group. Math. Comput. **74**(252), 2017–2026 (2005)
9. Buchmann, J., Vollmer, U.: Binary quadratic forms - an algorithmic approach, Algorithms and computation in mathematics, vol. 20. Springer (2007). https://link.springer.com/book/10.1007/978-3-540-46368-9
10. Buchmann, J., Williams, H.C.: A key-exchange system based on imaginary quadratic fields. J. Cryptol. **1**(2), 107–118 (1988)
11. Bünz, B., Fisch, B., Szepieniec, A.: Transparent snarks from DARK compilers. In: EUROCRYPT (1). LNCS, vol. 12105, pp. 677–706. Springer (2020). https://link.springer.com/chapter/10.1007/978-3-030-45721-1_24
12. Cohen, H., Lenstra, H.: Heuristics on class groups of number fields. In: Number Theory Noordwijkerhout 1983, pp. 33–62. Springer (1984). https://link.springer.com/chapter/10.1007/BFb0099440
13. Damgard, I., Fujisaki, E.: A statistically-hiding integer commitment scheme based on groups with hidden order. In: Zheng, Y. (eds.) Advances in Cryptology. LNCS, vol. 2501. Springer, Heidelberg (2002). https://doi.org/10.1007/3-540-36178-2_8
14. Damgard, I., Koprowski, M.: Generic lower bounds for root extraction and signature schemes in general groups. In: Knudsen, L.R. (eds.) Advances in Cryptology. LNCS, vol. 2332. Springer, Heidelberg (2002). https://doi.org/10.1007/3-540-46035-7_17
15. Dusart, P.: Autour de la fonction qui compte le nombre de nombres premiers. Ph.D. thesis, Université de Limoges (1998)
16. Ephraim, N., Freitag, C., Komargodski, I., Pass, R.: Continuous verifiable delay functions. In: Canteaut, A., Ishai, Y. (eds.) Advances in Cryptology. LNCS, vol. 12107. Springer, Cham (2020). https://doi.org/10.1007/978-3-030-45727-3_5

17. Fuchsbauer, G., Kiltz, E., Loss, J.: The algebraic group model and its applications. In: Shacham, H., Boldyreva, A. (eds.) Advances in Cryptology. Lecture Notes in Computer Science, vol. 10992. Springer, Cham (2018). https://doi.org/10.1007/978-3-319-96881-0_2

18. Katz, J., Loss, J., Xu, J.: On the security of time-lock puzzles and timed commitments. In: Pass, R., Pietrzak, K. (eds.) Theory of Cryptography. TCC 2020. LNCS, vol. 12552. Springer, Cham (2020). https://doi.org/10.1007/978-3-030-64381-2_14

19. Landerreche, E., Stevens, M., Schaffner, C.: Non-interactive cryptographic timestamping based on verifiable delay functions. In: Financial Cryptography. LNCS, vol. 12059, pp. 541–558. Springer (2020). https://link.springer.com/chapter/10.1007/978-3-030-51280-4_29

20. Lindhurst, S.: Computing roots in finite fields and groups, with a jaunt through sums of digits. Ph.D. thesis, The University of Wisconsin–Madison (1997)

21. Maurer, U., Wolf, S.: Lower bounds on generic algorithms in groups. In: Nyberg, K. (eds.) Advances in Cryptology. LNCS, vol. 1403. Springer, Heidelberg (1998). https://doi.org/10.1007/BFb0054118

22. Nechaev, V.: Complexity of a determinate algorithm for the discrete logarithm. Math. Notes 55(2), 165–172 (1994)

23. Pietrzak, K.: Simple verifiable delay functions. In: ITCS. LIPIcs, vol. 124, pp. 1–15. Schloss Dagstuhl - Leibniz-Zentrum für Informatik (2019)

24. Rabin, M.O.: Digitalized signatures and public-key functions as intractable as factorization. Tech. Rep. Massachusetts Inst. Technol. Cambridge Lab Comput. Sci. (1979)

25. Rabin, M.O.: Transaction protection by beacons. J. Comput. Syst. Sci. 27(2), 256–267 (1983)

26. Rivest, R., Shamir, A., Wagner, D.: Time-lock puzzles and timed-release crypto. Tech. Rep. Massachusetts Inst. Technol. (1996)

27. Rotem, L., Segev, G.: Generically speeding-up repeated squaring is equivalent to factoring: sharp thresholds for all generic-ring delay functions. In: Micciancio, D., Ristenpart, T. (eds.) Advances in Cryptology. Lecture Notes in Computer Science, vol. 12172. Springer, Cham (2020). https://doi.org/10.1007/978-3-030-56877-1_17

28. Rotem, L., Segev, G., Shahaf, I.: Generic-group delay functions require hidden-order groups. In: EUROCRYPT (3). LNCS, vol. 12107, pp. 155–180. Springer (2020). https://link.springer.com/chapter/10.1007/978-3-030-45727-3_6

29. Schwartz, J.T.: Fast probabilistic algorithms for verification of polynomial identities. J. ACM 27(4), 701–717 (1980)

30. Shoup, V.: Lower bounds for discrete logarithms and related problems. In: Fumy, W. (eds.) Advances in Cryptology. LNCS, vol. 1233. Springer, Heidelberg (1997). https://doi.org/10.1007/3-540-69053-0_18

31. Wesolowski, B.: Efficient verifiable delay functions. In: Ishai, Y., Rijmen, V. (eds.) Advances in Cryptology. LNCS, vol. 11478. Springer, Cham (2019). https://doi.org/10.1007/978-3-030-17659-4_13

32. Zippel, R.: Probabilistic algorithms for sparse polynomials. In: Ng, E.W. (eds.) Symbolic and Algebraic Computation. LNCS, vol. 72. Springer, Heidelberg (1979). https://doi.org/10.1007/3-540-09519-5_73

Astrolabous: A Universally Composable Time-Lock Encryption Scheme

Myrto Arapinis[✉], Nikolaos Lamprou[✉], and Thomas Zacharias[✉]

The University of Edinburgh, Edinburgh, UK
n.lamprou@ed.ac.uk, {marapini,tzachari}@inf.ed.ac.uk

Abstract. In this work, we study the *Time-Lock Encryption* (TLE) cryptographic primitive. The concept of TLE involves a party initiating the encryption of a message that one can only decrypt after a certain amount of time has elapsed. Following the *Universal Composability* (UC) paradigm introduced by Canetti [IEEE FOCS 2001], we formally abstract the concept of TLE into an ideal functionality. In addition, we provide a standalone definition for secure TLE schemes in a game-based style and we devise a hybrid protocol that relies on such a secure TLE scheme. We show that if the underlying TLE scheme satisfies the standalone game-based security definition, then our hybrid protocol UC realises the TLE functionality in the random oracle model. Finally, we present *Astrolabous*, a TLE construction that satisfies our security definition, leading to the first UC realization of the TLE functionality.

Interestingly, it is hard to prove UC secure any of the TLE construction proposed in the literature. The reason behind this difficulty relates to the UC framework itself. Intuitively, to capture semantic security, no information should be leaked regarding the plaintext in the ideal world, thus the ciphertext should not contain any information relating to the message. On the other hand, all ciphertexts will eventually open, resulting in a trivial distinction of the real from the ideal world in the standard model. We overcome this limitation by extending any secure TLE construction adopting the techniques of Nielsen [CRYPTO 2002] in the random oracle model. Specifically, the description of the extended TLE algorithms includes calls to the random oracle, allowing our simulator to equivocate. This extension can be applied to any TLE algorithm that satisfies our standalone game-based security definition, and in particular to Astrolabous.

Keywords: Time-lock encryption · Universal composability · Fairness

1 Introduction

The concept of encryption involves a party, the encryptor, who encrypts a message, and a designated party, the decryptor, who can retrieve that message. The decryptor can retrieve the message because she holds a piece of secret information which is called the secret key. There are two well known and studied types

© International Association for Cryptologic Research 2021
M. Tibouchi and H. Wang (Eds.): ASIACRYPT 2021, LNCS 13091, pp. 398–426, 2021.
https://doi.org/10.1007/978-3-030-92075-3_14

of encryption schemes in the literature, namely *symmetric encryption* [34] and *public key encryption* [18].

Another special type of encryption is called *time-lock encryption* (TLE). The concept of TLE involves a party that initiates the encryption of a message that can be decrypted only after a certain amount of time has elapsed.

There are two main approaches to how TLE can be defined. In the first approach [14,38], a party, called the *manager*, releases the decryption keys at specific times in the future.

In the second approach [36,37,43] a *computational puzzle*, which is a mathematical problem, needs be solved so that the message can be revealed. We distinguish *relativistic time* constructions [37,43] designed so that a puzzle can be solved only after a certain amount of computations have been performed; and *absolute time* constructions [36] designed so that the solution of the puzzle can be delegated to external entities which try to solve the puzzle independently of the TLE protocol (e.g. Bitcoin miners in [36]), giving an essence of absolute time. In either case, the message can be decrypted only after a *puzzle* has been solved or its solution has been published. The solution of the puzzle is used as the secret key in the decryption algorithm so that the message can be revealed.

In contrast to "standard" encryption, TLE differs in one but major point. The message can be retrieved without the encryptor having to reveal any secret information; the decrypting parties can actually construct the secret information themselves after some time. In standard encryption this is computationally infeasible.

The number of applications TLE finds its own space are mostly related to a security requirement called *fairness* [27]. Informally, the fairness condition states that the initial decisions of a party are not affected by the way the protocol execution progresses. There are many cryptographic protocols where fairness is violated and TLE can find an application. For example, in e-voting and specifically in self-tallying election protocols (STE) [1,33], due to access to intermediate results some parties might change their mind and vote something different from their initial choice to favour another candidate (e.g., the winning one). Another example where fairness is important is in coin flipping protocols [16], where the party that initiates the coin flip decides to abort right after the other party reveals her coin, without revealing her share to the other party. Moreover, in secret sharing protocols [41], the party that reveals her share last holds a considerable advantage over the other parties. Similar is the case of *Distributed Key Generation* protocols (DKG) [23]. By utilizing TLE, we can tackle all of the aforementioned limitations.

Unfortunately, all of the mentioned limitations cannot be solved with standard encryption or a commitment scheme. For example, the self-tallying protocols in [28,33,40,44] do not satisfy the fairness condition as already mentioned by the authors. The limitation lies fundamentally in the way encryption works. Specifically, if we use encryption only the holder of the secret key can retrieve the hidden message. So either that key is a priori known, where fairness is violated trivially as every party can decrypt the message, or not known, where the protocol cannot terminate as the message cannot be retrieved. Similar is the case if we use a commitment scheme. TLE comes to fill the gap and keep the best of both of situations mentioned, which means, *semantic security* [25,34] until some time, and then the possibility of decryption without any a priori secret information neither further interaction with the encryptor.

The state-of-the-art of composable security framework in the literature is provided by the *Universal Composability* framework (UC) [12] introduced by Canetti, where security can be maintained even if many instances of the studied protocol are executed concurrently or the protocol is composed as a subroutine of a bigger protocol. Although there are formal treatments of TLE in the literature [36], these mainly provide standalone models of security while our work aims to provide a composable treatment of the TLE primitive. The only other such attempt to our knowledge is a recently published paper [5] that we discuss in details in Sect. 2.1.

In this work, we abstract the notion of TLE into an ideal functionality $\mathcal{F}_{\mathsf{TLE}}^{\mathsf{leak},\mathsf{delay}}$, that captures the concept of TLE naturally. Moreover, we introduce a security definition exploring the one-wayness of TLE algorithms. We show that the one-way property of a TLE scheme is enough so that we have a UC realization of $\mathcal{F}_{\mathsf{TLE}}^{\mathsf{leak},\mathsf{delay}}$ after extending the TLE algorithm in the random oracle model. Although UC is the state-of-the- for arguing about security, sometimes standalone definitions are more usable and intuitive. Furthermore, many UC functionalities can only be realized in idealized models such as the RO model, suggesting that UC definitions may be "too strong" (*e.g.*, unachievable). For this reason, we further provide a new TLE game based definition in IND-CPA security style. Last, we provide a novel TLE construction, named *Astrolabous*, and show that it satisfies both of our security definitions.

Contributions. Our contributions can be summarised as follows:

1. We present a UC definition of secure TLE via an ideal functionality $\mathcal{F}_{\mathsf{TLE}}^{\mathsf{leak},\mathsf{delay}}$ that captures naturally the concept of TLE as it provides the necessary security guarantees a TLE scheme should provide. Specifically, it captures *semantic security* as the encryption of a message is not correlated with the message itself. Instead, it is correlated only with the length of the message similarly to the standard encryption functionality in [12]. In addition, it captures *correctness* [25,34], i.e., if $\mathcal{F}_{\mathsf{TLE}}^{\mathsf{leak},\mathsf{delay}}$ finds two different messages with the same ciphertext in its record, then it aborts. Finally, we note that in the literature, there are TLE constructions [36] where the adversary holds an advantage in comparison with the other parties and which might allow him to decrypt a message earlier than the intended time. To cater for such constructions, we parameterise $\mathcal{F}_{\mathsf{TLE}}^{\mathsf{leak},\mathsf{delay}}$ with a leakage function leak which specifies the exact advantage (in decryption time) of the adversary compared to the honest parties. Ideally, the leak function offers no advantage to the adversary. It is worth mentioning that TLE constructions in which the adversary holds an advantage in comparison with the honest parties in the decryption time, are still useful to study in the UC framework because the computational burden for

solving the puzzle can be transferred to external entities of the protocol (e.g., Bitcoin miners), making the decryption more client friendly [36].

2. We define a hybrid TLE protocol and a standalone basic security definition in a game-based fashion. We show that if the pair of TLE algorithms that our protocol uses satisfies our basic security definition then we have a UC realization of $\mathcal{F}_{\mathsf{TLE}}^{\mathsf{leak,delay}}$.

   Our TLE protocol does not use the vanilla version of a TLE algorithm (e.g. a TLE algorithm as defined in [36]). Instead, it relies on an extended one based on techniques introduced in [11,39] in the random oracle model. Our extension was necessary for the proof of UC realization. Specifically, in both real and ideal world, all the messages eventually can be decrypted by any party. To avoid trivial distinctions[1], the simulator must be able to equivocate so that the ciphertext opens to the correct message. As a result, the simulator programs the random oracle so that the ciphertext opens to the target message, something that is not feasible with the vanilla version of a TLE scheme without the equivocation feature which our extension provides.

   In our hybrid protocol, we defined both a functionality wrapper $\mathcal{W}_q$ and an evaluation functionality $\mathcal{F}_{\mathsf{eval}}$, to model the computation that is necessary for solving the time-lock puzzle. In our case, this computation is a random oracle query, thus $\mathcal{F}_{\mathsf{eval}}$ is the random oracle. Like in [3], the main function of a functionality wrapper is to restrict the access to $\mathcal{F}_{\mathsf{eval}}$ and thus to model the limited computational resources a party has at her disposal in each round. In our case, the limited amount of computation a party has in order to solve the time-lock puzzle through queries to $\mathcal{F}_{\mathsf{eval}}$.

   Our basic security definition of TLE schemes consists of two properties, named **Correctness** and **qSecurity**. The **Correctness** property states that the decryption of an encrypted message m leads to the message m again with high probability, similar to the definition of *correctness* in the standard encryption's case. We define the **qSecurity** property in a game-based style, between a challenger and an adversary where the latter tries to guess the *challenged message* with less than the required oracle queries. A TLE scheme satisfies the **qSecurity** property if the above happens with negligible probability, capturing the fact that a message can only be decrypted when "the time comes".

3. We provide a novel construction, named *Astrolabous*, and we show that it satisfies our basic security definition, thus it supports the UC realisation of $\mathcal{F}_{\mathsf{TLE}}^{\mathsf{leak,delay}}$ (in the random oracle model). Astrolabous combines ideas from both the constructions in [43] and in [37]. Nevertheless, we did not use either of them for the following reasons. A critical drawback of [37] is that parts of the plaintext are revealed through the process of solving the time-lock puzzle, which is based on a hash evaluation, as the message is hidden in the puzzle itself. On the other hand, the construction in [43] encrypts a message with a symmetric encryption scheme [34] and then hides the encryption key into the

---

[1] Recall that in the ideal world, to capture semantic security, ciphertexts do not contain any information about the actual message except its length.

time-lock puzzle which is based on repeated squaring. The first problem with the latter construction was that the procedure for solving the puzzle is deterministic (repeated squaring) and thus a party can bypass the functionality wrapper and solve any time-lock puzzle in a single round, in contrast with the construction in [37] where the procedure for solving the puzzle is randomized (hash evaluation which is modeled as random oracle). The second problem with the construction in [43] was that even if a party provides the solution of the puzzle but the puzzle issuer does not provide the trapdoor information that is used by the time the time-lock puzzle was created (in this case, the factorization of a composite number N) then, in order to verify the validity of the provided solution, all the verifying parties must resolve the time-lock puzzle. Thus, the *optimal complexity* scenario is hard to achieve. In contrast, the time-lock puzzle in [37] is easily verifiable without the need of any trapdoor information from the puzzle issuer.

These were our motivations for defining Astrolabous that tackles all of the above-mentioned limitations. Specifically, Astrolabous uses a symmetric key encryption scheme to hide the message like in [43] and then "hides" the symmetric key in a time-lock puzzle similar to the one in [37].

4. We introduce an additional stronger game-based definition, named IND-CPA-TLE, to capture semantic security of TLE schemes in the spirit of IND-CPA security. Our stronger definition may serve as a standard for analysing TLE schemes in the standalone setting. To demonstrate the usefulness of our stronger definition and constructions, we prove that Astrolabous and an enhanced version of the construction in [37] achieve IND-CPA-TLE security.

2   Related Work

TLE is a cryptographic primitive that allows a ciphertext to be decrypted only after a specific time period has elapsed. One way of achieving this is by "hiding" the decryption key in a puzzle [43] that can be solved after a set period of time. The reward for solving the puzzle is the decryption key. So the main purpose of the puzzle is to delay the party in opening the message before a specific amount of computation has been performed. In some proposals, decryption can further be performed without requiring knowledge of any secret information [36,43].

Previously proposed constructions are based either on *witness encryption* [22] or symmetric encryption [34]. The authors of these works provide game-based definitions to argue about the security of their constructions. Unfortunately, game-based definitions do not capture the variety of adversarial behavior the UC framework [12] does. For example, in the ideal world the capabilities of the adversary are defined explicitly. So, proving that our real protocol and the ideal one are indistinguishable (UC realization) from the environment's perspective, is like proving that whatever the adversary can do against the real protocol it can also do it in the ideal world. In contrast, in a game-based approach, we try to capture the capabilities of an adversary via an experiment without being certain if the experiment captures all the adversarial behaviours possible in the real protocol. Moreover, the task of transferring these definitions to the UC setting is quite challenging due to some incompatibilities between the two settings. More details can be found in Supporting Material B.1 of the extended version of this paper [2].

A particular TLE construction proposed in [43] is based on a block cipher, e.g., *Advanced Encryption System* (AES) [17], and repeated squaring. Specifically, first, a party encrypts a message m by using AES and a secret key sampled from a key space uniformly at random. Then the party chooses the time that finding the key should require and creates a "puzzle". The ciphertext is the encrypted message with AES under the solution to the puzzle that serves as the key. No formal proof of the security of this scheme is however provided in [43]. One drawback of this construction is that, to solve the puzzle, a party must be engaged in mathematical computations. The only way that these computations could be avoided for the puzzles to be solved is the issuer of the puzzle to announce the solution along with the trapdoor information (optimal case scenario), which is the factorization of a composite number N. Without the provision of the trapdoor information, even if a party announces the solution of the puzzle, the only way for verifying the solution is to solve the puzzle again.

A similar TLE construction is that in [37]. Here, the time-lock puzzle is based on hash evaluations. Specifically, the solver of the puzzle is engaged in serial hash evaluations until solving the puzzle. Unlike [43], if some party presents the solution of the puzzle any other party can verify it efficiently by doing all the hash evaluations in parallel. A drawback of this construction is that parts of the plaintext are revealed before the full solution of the puzzle. There are also TLE proposals [14,15,38] that instead of relying on computational puzzles, assume a *Trusted Third Party* (TTP) responsible for announcing the decryption keys. Most of these constructions are based on *Public Key Infrastructure* (PKI). An obvious drawback then is the fact that we ground a big part of the security of the scheme in the TTP, which in turn leads to weaker threat models.

There are other time-lock puzzle constructions [7,10] but none of them provide composable security guarantees. A generalization of time-lock puzzles are *Verifiable Delayed Functions* (VDF) [9,42,46] with the only addition that they require the solution of the puzzle to be publicly verifiable without having to solve the puzzle, something that is desirable but not obligatory with time-lock puzzles. Again, the constructions in [9,42,46] are not analyzed in the UC framework and thus security cannot be guaranteed either when composed as part of bigger protocols or in parallel execution (e.g. in on-line network conditions).

2.1 Comparison With [5] and [4]

A concurrent and independent work closely related to ours was very recently published at EUROCRYPT 2021 [5], with a subsequent work seemingly in preparation [4]. In particular, [5] proposes a composable treatment in the UC framework of time-lock puzzles whose security is captured by the ideal functionality $\mathcal{F}_{\mathsf{tlp}}$. It further proves how the scheme proposed by Rivest *et al.* in [43] can be used to

UC realise $\mathcal{F}_{\mathsf{tlp}}$ in both the random oracle and generic group models. Their realisation, as ours, relies on techniques for equivocation borrowed from [39] and [11]. They further show that no time-lock puzzle is UC realizable outside the random oracle model. Finally, they show that time-lock puzzles can be used to ensure fairness in coin flipping protocols.

The time-lock scheme proposed in [5] is not verifiable. This is addressed in the subsequent pre-print [4] where they adapt the scheme to include the trapdoor information along the message to be time-lock encrypted, rendering it verifiable.

There are some key differences between these two works and ours, rendering the proposed treatments of time-lock primitives orthogonal. The premises and assumptions are intrinsically different and capture different concepts and security notions. We discuss these differences here and argue why our formal treatment of time-lock encryption, and our proposed TLE scheme, namely Astrolabous, are preferable in some respects and more suited to many scenarios.

Apprehending Time with Computational Puzzles In [5] and [4], a resolutely different approach to ours is taken, when it comes to real time. In particular, they introduce the global $\mathcal{G}_{\mathsf{ticker}}$ functionality to capture delays without referring to a global *"wall clock"*, and thus without referring to real time.

We, on the other hand, insist on the importance of closely relating computational time and real time, and propose an alternative treatment in the global clock model ($\mathcal{G}_{\mathsf{clock}}$). Our approach is directly motivated by the seminal paper [43], in which R. L. Rivest, A. Shamir, and D. Wagner introduce the very concept of *time-release cryptography* to capture encryption schemes that ensure encrypted messages cannot be decrypted until a set amount of time has elapsed. The goal being to, as they put it, *"send information into the future [...] by making CPU time and real time agree as closely as possible"*.

This is key to explaining why and how time-release cryptography is used in an increasing number of distributed applications, and in particular schemes hinged on *computational puzzles*, *i.e.* puzzles that can only be solved if certain computations are performed continuously for at least a set amount of time. Indeed, the cryptographic protocols underlying these applications often rely on temporally disjoint phases. Time-release cryptographic primitives, as primitives apprehending real time through computations, allow thus these temporally disjoint stages of the protocol to be enforced yet in an asynchronous manner.

This is reflected in our protocol realising the proposed ideal TLE functionality $\mathcal{F}_{\mathsf{TLE}}^{\mathsf{leak,delay}}$. Parties only read the time from the global clock $\mathcal{G}_{\mathsf{clock}}$ to compute the amount of time the ciphertext needs to be protected for, and infer the corresponding puzzle difficulty. Decryption however requires continuous computations being performed until the set opening time is reached, and no read command being ever issued to $\mathcal{G}_{\mathsf{clock}}$. This protocol clearly demonstrates how time-lock puzzles apprehend real time through computations.

In contrast, the protocol π_{tlp} realising the ideal time lock-puzzle functionality $\mathcal{F}_{\mathsf{tlp}}$ proposed in [5] does not instruct parties to continuously work towards solving received puzzles (the scheduling of each step for solving a puzzle is left to the environment). So the treatment proposed in [5] and [4] leaves it to the protocol using π_{tlp} or $\mathcal{F}_{\mathsf{tlp}}$ as a subroutine to correctly takes care of appropriately enforcing relative delays between key events.

Ideal Functionality and Realisation $\mathcal{F}_{\mathsf{TLE}}^{\mathsf{leak,delay}}$ is more general than $\mathcal{F}_{\mathsf{tlp}}$. $\mathcal{F}_{\mathsf{tlp}}$ only captures constructions that rely on computational-puzzles for "hiding" a message and not the general concept of TLE. Specifically, the puzzle solution is provided not after some time has elapsed but after some computations have been performed (similar to Proof of Work (PoW)). In contrast, our time-lock encryption functionality $\mathcal{F}_{\mathsf{TLE}}^{\mathsf{leak,delay}}$ does not. This is why our protocol instructs parties to continuously work towards solving received puzzles. For that reason the works in [4,5] fail to capture the connection between absolute time ($\mathcal{G}_{\mathsf{clock}}$ model) and puzzle solving, something naturally expected when studying time-lock primitives. As such our functionality can cater for TLE schemes that do not rely on time-lock puzzles at all, such as the centralized solutions proposed in [14,38] where a TTP releases the solution in specific time-slots.

Moreover, some constructions such as [36] allow the adversary an unavoidable advantage in solving TLE puzzles (*e.g.*, the adversary synchronizes faster than the honest parties in the Bitcoin network [3,21]). $\mathcal{F}_{\mathsf{tlp}}$ does not capture such constructions. Our $\mathcal{F}_{\mathsf{TLE}}^{\mathsf{leak,delay}}$ functionality is parameterized with a leakage function, which specifies exactly the advantage of the adversary in each case.

Turning now to the realisations of UC secure time-lock primitives, the realisation of $\mathcal{F}_{\mathsf{tlp}}$ proposed in [5] relies on stronger assumptions as it relies both on the random oracle model and the generic group model. In contrast, our realisation of $\mathcal{F}_{\mathsf{TLE}}^{\mathsf{leak,delay}}$ only relies on the random oracle model.

On Public Verifiability While the time-lock encryption scheme proposed in [4] is publicly verifiable in the sense that given a puzzle, the verifying party does not need to solve the puzzle for themselves to verify that an announced solution for that puzzle is valid. This is not enough in some scenarios. For instance, consider the scenario with a dedicated server to be the puzzle solver and all other parties to be "lite" verifiers. This is very realistic given the computational requirements for solving puzzles. For efficiency, one would let a server solve the puzzles and only check that the solutions it provided are valid ones. Now in such a scenario parties *i)* would not trust the server, *ii)* would not trust the issuer of the puzzle either, but *iii)* are also not willing to solve the puzzle themselves.

Now, in [4] public verifiability is achieved because the issuer of the puzzle concatenates the message and the trapdoor information, which is the factorization of N. Given the trapdoor, one can efficiently verify that the announced solution to the puzzle is valid. However, the trapdoor announced (dishonest server) or the trapdoor included (dishonestly generated ciphertext) might not be valid for the puzzle. The only way to identify the dishonest party is to solve the puzzle for oneself and check it against the solution to the puzzle announced by the server. If they match, then the ciphertext was dishonestly generated, otherwise the server is dishonest.

This is reflected in the public verifiability notion that $\mathcal{F}_{tlp}$ captures that is one sided: if an announced solution to a puzzle is valid, then the verification is successful. But if the verification fails, then some party has deviated from the protocol but it could either be the server or the issuer of the ciphertext.

In contrast, the solution of our puzzle is publicly verifiable as it does not rely on any trapdoor information from the puzzle issuer being included in the ciphertext for fast verification. So dishonestly generated ciphertexts are not meaningful anymore, and only dishonest servers need to be considered. Now if the server announces an invalid solution to a given puzzle, it gets detected.

Standalone Security Along with the composable definition of secure time lock encryption schemes provided by our ideal functionality $\mathcal{F}_{\mathsf{TLE}}^{\mathsf{leak,delay}}$, we further provide two game-based definitions of security. A weaker one, capturing one-way hardness of a TLE scheme; and a stronger one that captures semantic security of a TLE scheme, in the spirit of IND-CPA security. We show that a TLE scheme that satisfies the weaker definition suffices for UC realising the $\mathcal{F}_{\mathsf{TLE}}^{\mathsf{leak,delay}}$ functionality through our protocol π_{TLE}. The stronger game-based definition serves as a standard for the security analysis of TLE schemes in the stand-alone setting. To demonstrate the usefulness of our stronger definition, we show that Astrolabous and an enhanced version of Mahmoody et al.'s construction [37] satisfy the said security standard. This result further validates our UC treatment and in particular our ideal functionality of time-lock encryption schemes.

2.2 Asymptotic vs Concrete Definitions

Time-lock puzzles have also previously been studied in the game-based framework [8,19,30]. These prior works provide standalone definitions of security of time-lock puzzles in a concrete setting. Specifically, they consider adversaries that are allowed to perform a fixed number of computational steps with each step being arbitrarily parallelizable. In this way, they capture both the privacy guarantees a time-lock puzzle should satisfy (no information leaked before a certain number of computations have been performed) and the resilience against parallel computation (the problem should not be parallelizable). They further introduce definitions that capture another important security property, namely *non-malleability*. Similar to public-key encryption, non-malleability for time-lock puzzles states that the adversary given a time-lock puzzle should not be able to generate another one in which the underlying solution is related without solving it first. While, our UC definition captures non-malleability, both our game-based definitions do not. This was out of the scope of this study and we leave it for future work.

In contrast, our approach in both game-based definitions we have introduced is an asymptotic one, similarly to the definitions of Proof of Work primitives provided in [20,21]. This was necessary to bridge UC security which is in the asymptotic setting, with the game-based approach [11]. This was not something necessary for prior standalone game-based definitions as these do not argue about security in a composable framework like UC.

3   Preliminaries

We use λ as the security parameter. We write $\mathsf{negl}(\lambda)$ to denote that a function is negligible in λ. When referring to a polynomial function we use the term p or p_x where x is an integer.

3.1   Universal Composability

The *Universal Composability (UC)* paradigm introduced by Canetti in [12] is the state-of-the-art cryptographic model for arguing about the security of protocols when run under concurrent sessions. More details about the UC framework can be found in Supporting Material A of the extended version of this paper.

Setup functionalities. In the UC literature, hybrid functionalities do not only play the role of abstracting some UC-secure real-world subroutine (e.g. a secure channel), but also formalize possible setup assumptions that are required to prove security when this is not done (and in many cases even impossible to achieve) in the "standard model". For example, this type of setup functionalities may capture the concept of a trusted source of randomness, a clock, or a Public Key Infrastructure (*PKI*). Moreover, these setup functionalities can be *global*, i.e. they act as shared states across multiple protocol instances and they can be accessed by other functionalities and even the environment that is external to the current session (recall that standard ideal functionalities do not directly interact with the environment). The extension of the UC framework in the presence of global setups has been introduced by Canetti *et al.* in [13]. In Supporting Material A.1 of the extended version of this paper. we present the setup functionalities that we consider across this work. Namely, the *Global clock* (GC) $\mathcal{G}_{\mathsf{clock}}$ [3,31], the *Random Oracle* (RO) $\mathcal{F}_{\mathsf{RO}}$ [39] and the *Broadcast* (BC) $\mathcal{F}_{\mathsf{BC}}$ [29,32] functionalities.

4   Definition of $\mathcal{F}_{\mathsf{TLE}}^{\mathsf{leak,delay}}$

We provide our UC treatment of TLE in the $\mathcal{G}_{\mathsf{clock}}$ model by defining the functionality $\mathcal{F}_{\mathsf{TLE}}$, following the approach of [12]. The functionality is described in Fig. 1, and at a high level operates as follows. The functionality is parameterized by a delay variable delay. This variable shows the time that a ciphertext needs to be created. There are settings where the ciphertetext generation needs some time, in some cases this time is very small or zero ($\mathsf{delay} = 0$) or noticeable ($\mathsf{delay} = 1$). The simulator $\mathcal{S}$ initially provides $\mathcal{F}_{\mathsf{TLE}}$ with the set of corrupted parties. Each time an encryption query issued by an honest party is handed to $\mathcal{F}_{\mathsf{TLE}}$, the functionality forwards the request to $\mathcal{S}$ without any information about the actual message except the size of the message and the party's identity. The simulator returns the token back to $\mathcal{F}_{\mathsf{TLE}}$ which replies with the message ENCRYPTING to the dummy party. This illustrates both the fact that the ciphertext does not contain any information about the message and that encryption might require some time to be completed. The environment can access the ciphertexts that this party has generated so far by issuing the command RETRIEVE, where $\mathcal{F}_{\mathsf{TLE}}$ returns all the ciphertexts that are created by that party back to it. It is worth mentioning, that the time labelling that is used in the encryption command refers to an absolute time rather than relative. On the other hand, the construction that we propose for realising $\mathcal{F}_{\mathsf{TLE}}$ is relativistic. That is why, as we see in detail in Sect. 5, the algorithm accepts the difference between the current time Cl and the time labelling τ as an input. In this way, the algorithm computes the difficulty for the puzzle such that the message can be decrypted when time τ has been reached. In addition, $\mathcal{F}_{\mathsf{TLE}}$ handles the decryption queries in the usual way, unless it finds two messages recorded along the same ciphertext, in which case it outputs $\bot$. This enforces that the encryption/decryption algorithms used by $\mathcal{S}$ should satisfy Correctness. In addition, if $\mathcal{F}_{\mathsf{TLE}}$ finds the requested ciphertext in its database, the recorded time is smaller than the current one (which means that the ciphertext can be decrypted), but the party that requested the decryption of that ciphertext provided an invalid time labelling (labelling smaller than the one recorded in $\mathcal{F}_{\mathsf{TLE}}$'s database), it returns the message INVALID_TIME to that party. In the case where the encryption/decryption queries are issued by corrupted parties, $\mathcal{F}_{\mathsf{TLE}}$ responds according to the instructions of $\mathcal{S}$. When a party receives a decryption request from $\mathcal{Z}$, except from the ciphertext c, it receives as input a time labelling τ. Ideally, τ is the time when c can be decrypted. Of course, the labelling τ can also be different to the decryption time of c. Nevertheless, this does not affect the soundness of $\mathcal{F}_{\mathsf{TLE}}$. Without the labelling, $\mathcal{F}_{\mathsf{TLE}}$ or the engaging party in the real protocol would have to find the decryption time of c which is registered either in the functionality's database (ideal case) or in the party's list of received ciphertexts (real case) and then compare it with the current time Cl.

When a party P advances $\mathcal{G}_{\mathsf{clock}}$, the simulator $\mathcal{S}$ is informed. Then, $\mathcal{S}$ can generate ciphertexts for each tag[2] received from $\mathcal{F}_{\mathsf{TLE}}$ from P and send them to $\mathcal{F}_{\mathsf{TLE}}$ issuing the UPDATE command. Later, $\mathcal{F}_{\mathsf{TLE}}$ will return these to P. This illustrates the fact that after some time ciphertexts are created. In TLE constructions where the encryption and decryption time is equal, $\mathcal{S}$ will force a delay on the ciphertext generation equal to the number of rounds that the ciphertext needs to be decrypted. Thus, the way we model $\mathcal{F}_{\mathsf{TLE}}$ allows us to capture a broader spectrum of TLE constructions (not necessarily efficient) in the context of the Global Clock (GC) model.

Naturally, after some time, ciphertexts are eventually opened and every party, including $\mathcal{S}$, can retrieve the underlying plaintext. For that task, we include the command LEAKAGE. In the vanilla case, $\mathcal{S}$ can retrieve all the messages that can be opened by the current time Cl. However, there are cases where $\mathcal{S}$ can retrieve messages before their time comes. This advantage of $\mathcal{S}$ can be specified by the function leak. This function accepts as input an integer (e.g., the current

---

[2] The simulator gives back the ciphertext as this is the case in most encryption functionalities [11,12]. Now, because we allow the simulator to delay the delivery of messages, the simulator needs a handle for updating the functionality's database. Here the tag comes into play and works as a receipt for that call.

time Cl) and outputs a progressive integer (e.g., the time that the adversary can decrypt ciphertexts, which is the same or greater than Cl). For more details see Supporting Material C.1 of the extended version of this paper.

The time-lock encryption functionality $\mathcal{F}_{\mathsf{TLE}}^{\mathsf{leak,delay}}$.

It initializes the list of recorded messages/ciphertexts L_{rec} as empty and defines the tag space TAG.

- Upon receiving $(\mathsf{sid}, \mathrm{CORRUPT}, \mathbf{P}_{\mathsf{corr}})$ from $\mathcal{S}$, it records the corrupted set $\mathbf{P}_{\mathsf{corr}}$.
- Upon receiving $(\mathsf{sid}, \mathrm{ENC}, m, \tau)$ from $P \notin \mathbf{P}_{\mathsf{corr}}$, it reads the time Cl and does:

  1. If $\tau < 0$, it returns $(\mathsf{sid}, \mathrm{ENC}, m, \tau, \bot)$ to P.
  2. It picks $\mathsf{tag} \xleftarrow{\$} \mathsf{TAG}$ and it inserts the tuple $(m, \mathsf{Null}, \tau, \mathsf{tag}, \mathsf{Cl}, P) \to L_{\mathsf{rec}}$.
  3. It sends $(\mathsf{sid}, \mathrm{ENC}, \tau, \mathsf{tag}, \mathsf{Cl}, 0^{|m|}, P)$ to $\mathcal{S}$. Upon receiving the token back from $\mathcal{S}$ it returns $(\mathsf{sid}, \mathrm{ENCRYPTING})$ to P.

- Upon receiving $(\mathsf{sid}, \mathrm{UPDATE}, \{(c_j, \mathsf{tag}_j)\}_{j=1}^{p(\lambda)})$ from $\mathcal{S}$, for all $c_j \neq \mathsf{Null}$ it updates each tuple $(m_j, \mathsf{Null}, \tau_j, \mathsf{tag}_j, \mathsf{Cl}_j, P)$ to $(m_j, c_j, \tau_j, \mathsf{tag}_j, \mathsf{Cl}_j, P)$
- Upon receiving $(\mathsf{sid}, \mathrm{RETRIEVE})$ from P, it reads the time Cl from $\mathcal{G}_{\mathsf{clock}}$ and returns $(\mathsf{sid}, \mathrm{ENCRYPTED}, \{(m, c \neq \mathsf{Null}, \tau)\}_{\forall (m,c,\tau,\cdot,\mathsf{Cl}',P) \in L_{\mathsf{rec}} : \mathsf{Cl}-\mathsf{Cl}' \geq \mathsf{delay}})$ to P.
- Upon receiving $(\mathsf{sid}, \mathrm{DEC}, c, \tau)$ from $P \notin \mathbf{P}_{\mathsf{corr}}$:

  1. If $\tau < 0$, it returns $(\mathsf{sid}, \mathrm{DEC}, c, \tau, \bot)$ to P. Else, it reads the time Cl from $\mathcal{G}_{\mathsf{clock}}$ and:
     (a) If $\mathsf{Cl} < \tau$, it sends $(\mathsf{sid}, \mathrm{DEC}, c, \tau, \mathrm{MORE\_TIME})$ to P.
     (b) If $\mathsf{Cl} \geq \tau$, then
        – If there are two tuples $(m_1, c, \tau_1, \cdot, \cdot, \cdot), (m_2, c, \tau_2, \cdot, \cdot, \cdot)$ in L_{rec} such that $m_1 \neq m_2$ and $c \neq \mathsf{Null}$ where $\tau \geq \max\{\tau_1, \tau_2\}$, it returns to P $(\mathsf{sid}, \mathrm{DEC}, c, \tau, \bot)$.
        – If no tuple $(\cdot, c, \cdot, \cdot, \cdot, \cdot)$ is recorded in L_{rec}, it sends $(\mathsf{sid}, \mathrm{DEC}, c, \tau)$ to $\mathcal{S}$ and returns to P whatever it receives from $\mathcal{S}$.
        – If there is a unique tuple $(m, c, \tau_{\mathsf{dec}}, \cdot, \cdot, \cdot)$ in L_{rec}, then if $\tau \geq \tau_{\mathsf{dec}}$, it returns $(\mathsf{sid}, \mathrm{DEC}, c, \tau, m)$ to P. Else, if $\mathsf{Cl} < \tau_{\mathsf{dec}}$, it returns $(\mathsf{sid}, \mathrm{DEC}, c, \tau, \mathrm{MORE\_TIME})$ to P. Else, if $\mathsf{Cl} \geq \tau_{\mathsf{dec}} > \tau$, it returns $(\mathsf{sid}, \mathrm{DEC}, c, \tau, \mathrm{INVALID\_TIME})$ to P.

- Upon receiving $(\mathsf{sid}, \mathrm{LEAKAGE})$ from $\mathcal{S}$, it reads the time Cl from $\mathcal{G}_{\mathsf{clock}}$ and returns $(\mathsf{sid}, \mathrm{LEAKAGE}, \{(m, c, \tau)\}_{\forall (m,c,\tau \leq \mathsf{leak}(\mathsf{Cl}),\cdot,\cdot,\cdot) \in L_{\mathsf{rec}}})$ to $\mathcal{S}$.

- Whatever message it receives from $P \in \mathbf{P}_{\mathsf{corr}}$, it forwards it to $\mathcal{S}$ and vice versa.

Fig. 1. Functionality $\mathcal{F}_{\mathsf{TLE}}^{\mathsf{leak,delay}}$ parameterized by λ, a leakage function leak, a delay variable delay ,interacting with simulator $\mathcal{S}$, parties in $\mathbf{P}$, and global clock $\mathcal{G}_{\mathsf{clock}}$.

5   Realization of $\mathcal{F}_{\mathsf{TLE}}^{\mathsf{leak,delay}}$ via Time-Lock Puzzles

In this section, we present the realization of $\mathcal{F}_{\mathsf{TLE}}$ via a protocol that uses a pair of encryption/decryption algorithms that satisfy a specific security notion that we formally define in Definition 1. We prove that our construction which is based on [37] and [43] is secure with respect to the required security notion.

The general idea of a time-lock puzzle scheme is that the parties have restricted access to a specific computation in any given period of time for solving a puzzle. In [43]'s case that computation is repeated squaring, and in [37] the computation is sequential hash evaluations. Of course, the underlying assumption here is that there is no "better" way to solve that puzzle except for sequentially applying the specific computation. Some of the most prominent proposed time-lock constructions are based on such assumption [3,36,37,43].

In the UC framework, to construct a time-lock protocol we need to abstract such computations through an oracle $\mathcal{F}_{\mathcal{O}_{\mathsf{eval}}}$. The reasoning behind this modelling is simple. In the UC framework, all the parties are allowed to run polynomial time with respect to the protocol's parameter. As a result, it is impossible to impose on a party the restriction that in a specific period of time they can only execute a constant number of computations. This is why we abstract such computations as a functionality/oracle and wrap the oracle with a *functionality wrapper* that restricts the access to the oracle. The approach is similar to the one proposed in [3], for modelling Proof of Work in the Bitcoin protocol.

In the following paragraphs, we present the evaluation oracle $\mathcal{F}_{\mathcal{O}_{\mathsf{eval}}}$, the functionality wrapper $\mathcal{W}_q(\mathcal{F}_{\mathcal{O}_{\mathsf{eval}}})$ and the protocol Π_{TLE}. We provide a security definition that captures both *correctness* and *one-wayness* of TLE constructions. The latter is illustrated via an experiment in a game-based style described in Fig. 5. We prove that Π_{TLE} UC realises $\mathcal{F}_{\mathsf{TLE}}$ given that the underlying TLE construction satisfies our security definition. Having at hand a UC realisation and given that our ideal functionality $\mathcal{F}_{\mathsf{TLE}}$ captures accurately the concept of what we expect from a TLE scheme, this validates the definition of security of TLE algorithms.

In the following section, we propose a new TLE construction and prove it satisfies our security definition, completing our construction argument. Finally, we provide a stand-alone security definition in the same spirit as *IND-CPA* security, named *IND-CPA-TLE*, which is captured via an experiment. We prove that Astrolabous satisfies this as well.

Our security definition that captures the one-wayness of a TLE construction was enough for having a UC realization. Although one-wayness as a property is very weak when arguing about the security of an encryption scheme, in our case was enough as we do not use the actual construction but we extend it in the random oracle model. On the other hand, such definition in the stand alone model is weak. That was the reason of why we introduced IND-CPA-TLE.

The evaluation functionality $\mathcal{F}_{\mathcal{O}_{\mathsf{eval}}}$ The evaluation functionality captures the computation that is needed for a time-lock puzzle to be solved by the designated parties. An explanatory example can be found bellow.

Initially, the functionality $\mathcal{F}_{\mathcal{O}_{\text{eval}}}$, as described in Fig. 2, creates the list L_{eval} for keeping a record of the queries received so far. Then, upon receiving a query from a party in $\mathbf{P}$, $\mathcal{F}_{\mathcal{O}_{\text{eval}}}$ checks if this query has been issued before. If this is the case, it returns the recorded pair. If not, then for the query x it samples the value y from the distribution $\mathbf{D}_x$ and returns to that party the pair (x, y).

The distribution $\mathbf{D}_x$ in cases such as in [3,36,37] is a random value over a specific domain. Thus, $\mathcal{F}_{\mathcal{O}_{\text{eval}}}$ is the random oracle in these cases. More precisely, $\mathbf{D}_x = \mathcal{U}\{0, 2^n - 1\}$ where $\mathcal{U}$ is the uniform distribution and $[0, 2^n - 1]$ is its domain, in our example the domain of the random oracle. In that case, the parametrization of $\mathbf{D}$ with x is unnecessary. On the other hand, if we study other time-lock puzzles such as the one in [43], where the computation to solve a puzzle is the repeated squaring, the parametrization of $\mathbf{D}$ with x becomes necessary. More intuition for $\mathbf{D}$ can be found in Supporting Material C.2 of the extended version of this paper.

Example 1. Adapting the relative time-lock puzzle of [37] to our modelling approach, the evaluation functionality is instantiated by the random oracle. Let us consider that the solution of the puzzle is the value r. The creator of the puzzle P chooses the desired difficulty of the puzzle, τ. Then, P splits the puzzle r into $q\tau$ equal pieces $r_0, \ldots, r_{q\tau}$ such that $r = r_0 || \ldots || r_{q\tau}$. Here, q is the maximum number of evaluation queries that the party can make to the oracle in one round. Remember that the essence of round can be defined with respect to the functionality $\mathcal{G}_{\text{clock}}$. Next, P makes one call to the random oracle functionality with the values $(r_0, \ldots, r_{q\tau-1})$ and receives back $(y_{r_0}, \ldots, y_{r_{q\tau-1}})$. Note that this call is counted as one. Finally, P creates the puzzle $(r_0, y_{r_0} \oplus r_1, \ldots, y_{r_{q\tau-1}} \oplus r_{q\tau})$ for the secret r. Now, if some party P^* wants to solve the puzzle, it needs to send the query r_0 to the random oracle functionality. Upon receiving the value y_{r_0} back from the random oracle functionality, P^* computes $r_1 = y_{r_0} \oplus (y_{r_0} \oplus r_1)$. Next, it repeats the procedure with the value r_1. Note that, the maximum number of evaluation queries to the functionality oracle in one round is q and thus the puzzle to be solved needs τ rounds. It is worth mentioning that for capturing the limited access to the functionality in the UC framework, a functionality wrapper needs to be defined as it is described in a dedicated Paragraph below.

The evaluation functionality $\mathcal{F}_{\mathcal{O}_{\text{eval}}}(\mathcal{D}, \mathbf{P})$.

Initializes an empty evaluation query list L_{eval}.

- Upon receiving (sid, EVALUATE, x) from a party $P \in \mathbf{P}$, it does:

  1. It checks if $(x, y) \in L_{\text{eval}}$ for some y. If no such entry exists, it samples y from the distribution $\mathbf{D}_x$ and inserts the pair (x, y) to L_{eval}. Then, it returns (sid, EVALUATED, x, y) to P. Else, it returns the recorded pair.

Fig. 2. Functionality $\mathcal{F}_{\mathcal{O}_{\text{eval}}}$ parameterized by λ, a family of distributions $\mathcal{D} = \{\mathbf{D}_x | x \in \mathbf{X}\}$ and a set of parties $\mathbf{P}$.

Functionality wrapper $\mathcal{W}_q(\mathcal{F}_{\mathcal{O}_{\text{eval}}}, \mathcal{G}_{\text{clock}}, \mathbf{P})$.

■ Upon receiving (sid, CORRUPT, $\mathbf{P}_{\text{corr}}$) from $\mathcal{S}$, it records the corrupted set $\mathbf{P}_{\text{corr}}$.

■ Upon receiving (sid, EVALUATE, $(x_1, \ldots, x_j)$) from $P \in \mathbf{P} \setminus \mathbf{P}_{\text{corr}}$ it reads the time Cl from $\mathcal{G}_{\text{clock}}$ and does:

1. If there is not a list L^P it creates one, initially as empty. Then it does:
   (a) For every k in $\{1, \ldots, j\}$, it forwards the message (sid, EVALUATE, x_k) to $\mathcal{F}_{\mathcal{O}_{\text{eval}}}$.
   (b) When it receives back all oracle queries, it inserts the tuple-(Cl, 1) $\in L^P$.
   (c) It returns (sid, EVALUATE, $((x_1, y_1), \ldots, (x_j, y_j))$) to P.
2. Else if there is a tuple-(Cl, j_c) $\in L^P$ with $j_c < q$, then it changes the tuple to (Cl, $j_c + 1$), and repeats the above steps 1a,1c.
3. Else if there is a tuple-(Cl*, j_c) $\in L^P$ such that Cl* $<$ Cl, it updates the tuple as (Cl, 1), and repeats the above steps 1a,1b,1c.

■ Upon receiving (sid, EVALUATE, $(x_1, \ldots, x_j)$) from $P \in \mathbf{P}_{\text{corr}}$ it reads the time Cl from $\mathcal{G}_{\text{clock}}$ and repeats steps 1,3 except that it maintains the same list, named L^{corr}, for all the corrupted parties.

Fig. 3. The Functionality wrapper $\mathcal{W}_q(\mathcal{F}_{\mathcal{O}_{\text{eval}}})$ parameterized by λ, a number of queries q, functionality $\mathcal{F}_{\mathcal{O}_{\text{eval}}}$, $\mathcal{G}_{\text{clock}}$ and parties in $\mathbf{P}$.

The functionality wrapper $\mathcal{W}_q(\mathcal{F}_{\mathcal{O}_{\text{eval}}})$ Our wrapper is defined along the lines of [3]. The functionality wrapper is an ideal functionality parameterized by another ideal functionality, mediating the access to the latter functionality only possible through the wrapper. Moreover, the wrapper restricts the access to the parameter functionality allowing parties to access it only a certain number of times per round. Here, the notion of round is defined with respect to the $\mathcal{G}_{\text{clock}}$ functionality defined in Fig. 3. In a nutshell, the wrapper models in the UC setting the limited resources a party has at their disposal for solving the underlying puzzle. Because in UC every party is a PPT ITM, the same holds for the adversary. So, the adversary can interact with any functionality polynomially many times in each round. There are several protocols that hinge their security on the limited computational capabilities of the participants [3,21]. Next, follows the description of $\mathcal{W}_q(\mathcal{F}_{\mathcal{O}_{\text{eval}}})$. The description of $\mathcal{W}_q(\mathcal{F}_{\mathcal{O}_{\text{eval}}})$ and insightful comments behind its design can be found in Supporting Material C.4 of the extended version of this paper. In the rest of this work we use the abbreviation $\mathcal{W}_q(\mathcal{F}_{\mathcal{O}_{\text{eval}}})$ instead of $\mathcal{W}_q(\mathcal{F}_{\mathcal{O}_{\text{eval}}}, \mathcal{G}_{\text{clock}}, \mathbf{P})$ when it is obvious from the context.

The protocol Π_{TLE} We are now ready to present the protocol Π_{TLE} which is proved in later Sections that it UC realises the $\mathcal{F}_{\text{TLE}}$ functionality. The protocol consists of the functionality wrapper $\mathcal{W}_q(\mathcal{F}_{\mathcal{O}_{\text{eval}}})$ as described in Fig. 3, the global clock $\mathcal{G}_{\text{clock}}$, the random oracle $\mathcal{F}_{\text{RO}}$, the broadcast functionality $\mathcal{F}_{\text{BC}}$ and a set of parties $\mathbf{P}$ (the descriptions can be found in Supporting Material A.1 of the extended version of this paper).

Example 2. Recall Example 1 and assume the time-lock puzzle $c = (r_0, y_0 \oplus r_1, \ldots, y_{r_{q\tau_{dec}-1}} \oplus r_{q\tau_{dec}})$. If the function wit_con is given less than $q\tau_{dec}$ oracle responses (e.g. $(y_0, \ldots, y_{q\tau_{dec}-3})$) for the puzzle c, it returns $\bot$ else it returns $w_{dec} = (r_0, y_0, \ldots, y_{r_{q\tau_{dec}-1}}, c)$. Note that here, the ciphertext and the puzzle coincide as there is no actual encryption of a message. Thus, f_{puzzle} is simply the identity function.

Necessity of extending the TLE algorithms: In order to realise $\mathcal{F}_{TLE}$ with some TLE construction we need to extend a given TLE algorithm in the random oracle model ($\mathcal{F}_{RO}$). Recall that in $\mathcal{F}_{TLE}$ all the ciphertexts eventually open. To capture semantic security, the ciphertext contains no information about the actual message, in contrast to the real protocol that contains the encryption of the actual message. So, for the simulator to simulate this difference when the messages are opened, $\mathcal{S}$ must be able to *equivocate* the opening of the ciphertext, else the environment $\mathcal{Z}$ can trivially distinguish the real from the ideal execution of the protocol. When we say that $\mathcal{S}$ equivocates the opening of the ciphertext, it means that $\mathcal{S}$ can open a ciphertext to whatever plaintext message needs to be opened. Equivocation has also been used for other cryptographic primitives, such as bit commitments, where the simulator can equivocate because it knows the trapdoor information related to the *common reference string* (CRS) [35]. This is actually fundamental, unless we restrict the environment's running time. But then we lose the composition theorem.

Our extension, that can be applied to any TLE construction, offers the feature of equivocation but at the expense of assuming the random oracle model. More information and insightful comments can be found in Supporting Material C.5 of the extended version of this paper.

Description of protocol Π_{TLE}: Each party P maintains the list of recorded messages/ciphertexts L_{rec}^P, in which the requested messages for encryption by $\mathcal{Z}$ are stored along with the ciphertext of that message (initially stored as Null), a random identifier of the message tag, the time τ that the message should open, the time CI that it is recorded for the first time and a flag which shows if that message has been broadcast or not to the other parties. When a party receives the broadcast ciphertext, she extracts the underlying puzzle with the function f_{puzzle} from that ciphertext and stores it along with its difficulty τ_{dec}, the set of oracle queries/responses issued to the oracle $\mathcal{F}_{\mathcal{O}_{eval}}$ so that puzzle to be solved with the help of the preparation function state, the time CI that this tuple was last time updated, a counter j that shows how many queries are issued for that puzzle this turn and a counter j_t that shows the total number of queries issued for that puzzle.

If party accepts encryption requests by $\mathcal{Z}$, she returns the message ENCRYPTING, delaying the encryption for one round. When a party either receives a clock advancement command or decryption, she performs the procedure

Table 1. Functions and list each party holds in Π_{TLE}.

Functions/Lists	Description
$\mathbf{P}, \mathbb{N}, \mathbf{Q}, \mathbf{R}, \mathbf{C}, \mathbf{M}, \mathbf{W}$	The space of time-lock puzzles, integers, oracle queries and responses to/from $\mathcal{F}_{\mathcal{O}_{\mathsf{eval}}}$, ciphertexts, plaintexts and witnesses
$e_{\mathcal{F}_{\mathcal{O}_{\mathsf{eval}}}} : \mathbf{M} \times \mathbb{N} \times \mathbf{Q}/\mathbf{R} \to \mathbf{C}$	The encryption algorithm takes as input the plaintext, the puzzle difficulty and the pair of oracle queries/responses so that the puzzle can be created
$d_{\mathcal{F}_{\mathcal{O}_{\mathsf{eval}}}} : \mathbf{C} \times \mathbf{W} \to \mathbf{M}$	The decryption algorithm takes as input the ciphertext and the secret key
$f_{\mathsf{state}} : \mathbf{P} \times \mathbb{N} \times \mathbf{Q}/\mathbf{R} \to \mathbf{Q}$	It prepares the next oracle query to $\mathcal{F}_{\mathcal{O}_{\mathsf{eval}}}$. Specifically, it accepts a puzzle, the number of queries that need to be prepared and all the previous queries and responses from the oracle
$f_{\mathsf{puzzle}} : \mathbf{C} \to \mathbf{P}$	It extracts the time-puzzle from a ciphertext
$\mathsf{puz\_cr} : \mathbf{M} \times \mathbb{N} \to \mathbf{Q}$	The puzzle creation function takes as input the plaintext and the desired difficulty and creates the oracle queries so that a puzzle for that plaintext of that difficulty can be created
$\mathsf{wit\_con} : \mathbf{Q}/\mathbf{R} \times \mathbb{N} \times \mathbf{P} \to \mathbf{W}$	The witness construction function that returns the solution of the puzzle or the witness if that is possible
L^P_{rec}	The list of the generated ciphertexts
L^P_{puzzle}	The list of the recorded oracle queries for puzzle solving
$(z, \tau, \{(\mathsf{state}^z_k, y_k)\}^{j_t}_{k=0}, j_c, j_t)$	The tuple contains a puzzle z, the difficulty of the puzzle τ, the pairs of oracle queries/responses to solve puzzle z, the current number j_c of oracle queries in that round and the total number of oracle queries j_t

PuzzleEncryption, in which the party issues all her q oracle queries both for solving and encrypting the pending messages for that round. More details on the description of Π_{TLE} can be found in Supporting Material C.6 of the extended version of this paper.

$\Pi_{\mathsf{TLE}}(\mathcal{W}_q(\mathcal{F}_{\mathcal{O}_{\mathsf{eval}}}), e_{\mathcal{F}_{\mathcal{O}_{\mathsf{eval}}}}, d_{\mathcal{F}_{\mathcal{O}_{\mathsf{eval}}}}, \mathsf{f}_{\mathsf{state}}, \mathsf{wit\_con}, \mathsf{f}_{\mathsf{puzzle}}, \mathsf{puz\_cr}, \mathcal{G}_{\mathsf{clock}}, \mathcal{F}_{\mathsf{RO}}, \mathcal{F}_{\mathsf{BC}}, \mathbf{P}).$

Each party maintains the list of recorded messages/ciphertexts L_{rec}^P and the list of the recorded oracle queries for puzzle solving L_{puzzle}^P, initially as empty, a tag space **TAG** and the algorithms $(e_{\mathcal{F}_{\mathcal{O}_{\mathsf{eval}}}}, d_{\mathcal{F}_{\mathcal{O}_{\mathsf{eval}}}})$. Moreover, she follows the procedure described below:

Puzzle:

1. *Preparing queries for puzzle creation:* She collects all tuples $\{(m_j, \mathsf{Null}, \tau_j, \mathsf{tag}_j, \mathsf{CI}_j, 0) \in L_{\mathsf{rec}}^P\}_{j=1}^{p_1(\lambda)}$ for $\mathsf{CI}_j = \mathsf{CI}$. She picks $\{r_1^j \xleftarrow{\$} \{0,1\}^{p^*(\lambda)}\}_{j=1}^{p_1(\lambda)}$. For each j she computes $\mathsf{puz\_cr}(r_1^j, \tau_j - (\mathsf{CI}+1)) \to \{x_k\}_{k=1}^{p_2(\lambda)}$.

2. *Puzzle solving:* For $(j_l = 0, j_l < q, j_l{+}{+})$ she collects all $\{\mathsf{state}_{j_t}^{z_n}\}_{n=1}^{p_3(\lambda)}$ such that $(z_n, \tau_{\mathsf{dec}}, \{(\mathsf{state}_k^{z_n}, y_k)\}_{k=0}^{j_t}, \mathsf{CI}, 0, j_t) \in L_{\mathsf{puzzle}}^P$ (see command 5 for initialization).

   (a) *Parallelize puzzle creation queries and puzzle solve:* If $j_l = 0$, she sends $(\mathsf{sid}, \mathsf{EVALUATE}, \{\mathsf{state}_{j_t}^{z_n}\}_{n=1}^{p_3(\lambda)} \cup \{x_k\}_{k=1}^{p_2(\lambda)})$ to $\mathcal{W}_q(\mathcal{F}_{\mathcal{O}_{\mathsf{eval}}})$ and receives back $(\mathsf{sid}, \mathsf{EVALUATE}, \{(\mathsf{state}_{j_t}^{z_n}, y_{j_t}^*)\}_{n=1}^{p_3(\lambda)} \cup \{(x_k, y_k)\}_{k=1}^{p_2(\lambda)})$. Else she sends $(\mathsf{sid}, \mathsf{EVALUATE}, \{\mathsf{state}_{j_t}^{z_n}\}_{n=1}^{p_3(\lambda)})$ to $\mathcal{W}_q(\mathcal{F}_{\mathcal{O}_{\mathsf{eval}}})$.

   (b) *Parallelize puzzle creation queries and puzzle solve:* If $j_l = 0$, she sends $(\mathsf{sid}, \mathsf{EVALUATE}, \{\mathsf{state}_{j_t}^{z_n}\}_{n=1}^{p_3(\lambda)} \cup \{x_k\}_{k=1}^{p_2(\lambda)})$ to $\mathcal{W}_q(\mathcal{F}_{\mathcal{O}_{\mathsf{eval}}})$ and receives back $(\mathsf{sid}, \mathsf{EVALUATE}, \{(\mathsf{state}_{j_t}^{z_n}, y_{j_t}^*)\}_{n=1}^{p_3(\lambda)} \cup \{(x_k, y_k)\}_{k=1}^{p_2(\lambda)})$. Else she sends $(\mathsf{sid}, \mathsf{EVALUATE}, \{\mathsf{state}_{j_t}^{z_n}\}_{n=1}^{p_3(\lambda)})$ to $\mathcal{W}_q(\mathcal{F}_{\mathcal{O}_{\mathsf{eval}}})$.

   (c) *Update the record:* In each case, she updates each tuple as $(z_n, \tau_{\mathsf{dec}}, \{(\mathsf{state}_k^{z_n}, y_k)\}_{k=0}^{j_t+1}, \mathsf{CI}, j_t{+}{+}, j_t{+}{+})$ where $\mathsf{state}_{j_t+1}^{z_n} = \mathsf{f}_{\mathsf{state}}(z_n, j_t, \{(\mathsf{state}_k^{z_n}, y_k)\}_{k=0}^{j_t+1})$, $y_{j_t+1} = \mathsf{Null}$ and $y_{j_t} \leftarrow y_{j_t}^*$. In case that $j_l = q$, she changes the CI in the tuple to $\mathsf{CI}+1$ and $j_l = 0$.

Encryption:

1. *Time-lock encryption:* She computes $\{c_1^j \leftarrow e_{\mathcal{F}_{\mathcal{O}_{\mathsf{eval}}}}(r_1^j, \{(x_k, y_k)\}_{k=1}^{p_2(\lambda)}, \tau_j - (\mathsf{CI}+1))\}_{j=1}^{p_1(\lambda)}$.

2. *Extended encryption:* For each r_1^j, she sends $(\mathsf{sid}, \mathsf{QUERY}, r_1^j)$ to $\mathcal{F}_{\mathsf{RO}}$. Upon receiving $(\mathsf{sid}, \mathsf{RANDOM\_ORACLE}, r_1^j, h^j)$ from $\mathcal{F}_{\mathsf{RO}}$, P sends $(\mathsf{sid}, \mathsf{QUERY}, r_1^j \| m_j)$ to $\mathcal{F}_{\mathsf{RO}}$. Upon receiving $(\mathsf{sid}, \mathsf{RANDOM\_ORACLE}, r_1^j \| m_j, c_3^j)$ from $\mathcal{F}_{\mathsf{RO}}$, she computes $c_j \leftarrow (c_1^j, h \oplus m, c_3^j)$ and updates the tuple $(m_j, c_j, \tau_j, \mathsf{tag}_j, \mathsf{CI}_j, 0) \to L_{\mathsf{rec}}^P$.

- Upon receiving $(\mathsf{sid}, \mathsf{ENC}, m, \tau)$ from $\mathcal{Z}$, P reads the time CI from $\mathcal{G}_{\mathsf{clock}}$ and if $\tau < 0$ she returns $(\mathsf{sid}, \mathsf{ENC}, m, \tau, \bot)$ to $\mathcal{Z}$. Else, it does:

  1. She picks $\mathsf{tag} \xleftarrow{\$} \mathbf{TAG}$ and she inserts the tuple $(m, \mathsf{Null}, \tau, \mathsf{tag}, \mathsf{CI}, 0) \to L_{\mathsf{rec}}^P$.
  2. She returns $(\mathsf{sid}, \mathsf{ENCRYPTING})$ to $\mathcal{Z}$.

- Upon receiving $(\mathsf{sid}, \mathsf{ADVANCE\_CLOCK})$ from $\mathcal{Z}$, P reads the time CI from $\mathcal{G}_{\mathsf{clock}}$. She executes both *Puzzle* and *Encryption* procedure. Then, she sends $(\mathsf{sid}, \mathsf{BROADCAST}, \{(c_j, \tau_j)\}_{j=1}^{p_1(\lambda)})$ to $\mathcal{F}_{\mathsf{BC}}$. Upon receiving $(\mathsf{sid}, \mathsf{BROADCASTED}, \{(c_j, \tau_j)\}_{j=1}^{p_1(\lambda)})$ from $\mathcal{F}_{\mathsf{BC}}$, for each j she updates each tuple $(m_j, \mathsf{Null}, \tau_j, \mathsf{tag}_j, \mathsf{CI}_j, 0)$ to $(m_j, c_j, \tau_j, \mathsf{tag}_j, \mathsf{CI}_j, 1)$ and sends $(\mathsf{sid}, \mathsf{ADVANCE\_CLOCK})$ to $\mathcal{G}_{\mathsf{clock}}$.

- Upon receiving $(\mathsf{sid}, \mathsf{RETRIEVE})$ from $\mathcal{Z}$, P reads the time CI from $\mathcal{G}_{\mathsf{clock}}$ and returns $(\mathsf{sid}, \mathsf{ENCRYPTED}, \{(m_j, c_j, \tau_j) : (m_j, c_j, \tau_j, \cdot, \mathsf{CI}_j, 1) \in L_{\mathsf{rec}}^P : \mathsf{CI} - \mathsf{CI}_j \geq 1\})$ to $\mathcal{Z}$.

- Upon receiving $(\mathsf{sid}, \mathsf{BROADCAST}, \{(c_j, \tau_j)\}_{j=1}^{p_1(\lambda)})$ from $\mathcal{F}_{\mathsf{BC}}$ where $c_j = (c_1^j, c_2^j, c_3^j)$, P reads the time CI from $\mathcal{G}_{\mathsf{clock}}$ and does for every j:

  1. She computes $\mathsf{state}_0^{\mathsf{f}_{\mathsf{puzzle}}(c_1^j)} \leftarrow \mathsf{f}_{\mathsf{state}}(\mathsf{f}_{\mathsf{puzzle}}(c_1^j), 0, \mathsf{Null})$.
  2. She creates the tuple $(\mathsf{f}_{\mathsf{puzzle}}(c_1^j), \tau_{\mathsf{dec}}, \{(\mathsf{state}_0^{\mathsf{f}_{\mathsf{puzzle}}(c_1^j)}, \mathsf{Null})\}, \mathsf{CI}, 0, 0)$ and stores it in L_{puzzle}^P.

- Upon receiving $(\mathsf{sid}, \mathsf{DEC}, c := (c_1, c_2, c_3), \tau_{\mathsf{dec}})$ from $\mathcal{Z}$, P reads the time CI from $\mathcal{G}_{\mathsf{clock}}$. Then she does:

  1. If $\tau_{\mathsf{dec}} < 0$, she returns $(\mathsf{sid}, \mathsf{DEC}, c, \tau_{\mathsf{dec}}, \bot)$ to $\mathcal{Z}$.
  2. If $\mathsf{CI} < \tau_{\mathsf{dec}}$, she returns $(\mathsf{sid}, \mathsf{DEC}, c, \tau_{\mathsf{dec}}, \mathsf{MORE\_TIME})$.
  3. She searches for a tuple $(\mathsf{f}_{\mathsf{puzzle}}(c_1), \tau, \{(\mathsf{state}_k^{\mathsf{f}_{\mathsf{puzzle}}(c_1)}, y_k)\}_{k=0}^{j_t}, \mathsf{CI}, q, j_t)$ in L_{puzzle}^P. If $\tau_{\mathsf{dec}} < \tau \leq \mathsf{CI}$ then she returns $(\mathsf{sid}, \mathsf{DEC}, c, \tau_{\mathsf{dec}}, \mathsf{INVALID\_TIME})$ to $\mathcal{Z}$.
  4. She computes $w_{\tau_{\mathsf{dec}}} \leftarrow \mathsf{wit\_con}(\{(\mathsf{state}_k^{\mathsf{f}_{\mathsf{puzzle}}(c_1)}, y_k)\}_{k=0}^{j_t}, \tau_{\mathsf{dec}}, \mathsf{f}_{\mathsf{puzzle}}(c_1))$.
  5. She runs $x \leftarrow d_{\mathcal{F}_{\mathcal{O}_{\mathsf{eval}}}}(c_1, w_{\tau_{\mathsf{dec}}})$ and she sends $(\mathsf{sid}, \mathsf{QUERY}, x)$ to $\mathcal{F}_{\mathsf{RO}}$. Upon receiving $(\mathsf{sid}, \mathsf{RANDOM\_ORACLE}, x, h)$ from $\mathcal{F}_{\mathsf{RO}}$, she computes $m \leftarrow h \oplus c_2$. She sends $(\mathsf{sid}, \mathsf{QUERY}, x \| m)$ to $\mathcal{F}_{\mathsf{RO}}$. Upon receiving $(\mathsf{sid}, \mathsf{RANDOM\_ORACLE}, x \| m, c_3^*)$ from $\mathcal{F}_{\mathsf{RO}}$: If $c_3 \neq c_3^*$, she returns to $\mathcal{Z}$ $(\mathsf{sid}, \mathsf{DEC}, c, \tau_{\mathsf{dec}}, \bot)$. Else, she returns to $\mathcal{Z}$ $(\mathsf{sid}, \mathsf{DEC}, c, \tau_{\mathsf{dec}}, m)$.
  6. If such tuple does not exist then she returns $(\mathsf{sid}, \mathsf{DEC}, c, \tau_{\mathsf{dec}}, \bot)$ to $\mathcal{Z}$.

Fig. 4. The Protocol Π_{TLE} in the presence of a functionality wrapper $\mathcal{W}_q$, an evaluation functionality $\mathcal{F}_{\mathcal{O}_{\mathsf{eval}}}$, a random oracle $\mathcal{F}_{\mathsf{RO}}$, a broadcast functionality $\mathcal{F}_{\mathsf{BC}}$, a global clock $\mathcal{G}_{\mathsf{clock}}$, where $e_{\mathcal{F}_{\mathcal{O}_{\mathsf{eval}}}}, d_{\mathcal{F}_{\mathcal{O}_{\mathsf{eval}}}}, \mathsf{f}_{\mathsf{state}}, \mathsf{wit\_con}$ and $\mathsf{f}_{\mathsf{puzzle}}$ are hard-coded in each party in $\mathbf{P}$.

5.1   Security Definitions of (Computational-Puzzle-Based) Time-Lock Encryption

In this Subsection we turn to standalone security and focus only on TLE schemes based on computational puzzles. We identify minimal standalone requirements sufficient for a computational-puzzles-based construction to provide a UC realization of our $\mathcal{F}_{\mathsf{TLE}}$ functionality. We specify these minimal requirements, namely Correctness and qSecurity, in the game-base style. In Sect. 6, we define IND-CPA security for (computational-puzzle-based) TLE schemes.

Intuitively, the Correctness property states that the decryption of the ciphertext with underlying plaintext m results in the message m itself with high probability provided that the underlying time-lock puzzle has been solved. The qSecurity property is described in a game-based style via the experiment in Fig. 5 and states that an adversary can win the experiment only with a very small probability. Specifically, the experiment captures the one-way security of a TLE scheme as in the concept of *one-way functions* security [25,26]. Although indistinguishability, like in *IND-CPA* security [25,34], is stronger than the hardness

---

The experiment $\mathbf{EXP}_{\mathsf{TLE}}(\mathcal{B}, \mathcal{O}_{\mathsf{eval}}, e_{\mathcal{O}_{\mathsf{eval}}}, d_{\mathcal{O}_{\mathsf{eval}}}, \mathsf{f}_{\mathsf{state}}, \mathsf{f}_{\mathsf{puzzle}}, q)$

Initialization Phase.

■ Ch is initialized with $e_{\mathcal{O}_{\mathsf{eval}}}, d_{\mathcal{O}_{\mathsf{eval}}}$ and sends them to $\mathcal{B}$. In addition it creates a local time counter $\mathsf{Cl}_{\mathsf{exp}}$.

Learning Phase.

■ When $\mathcal{B}$ issues the query (EVALUATE, x) to $\mathcal{O}_{\mathsf{eval}}$ through the Ch, he gets back (EVALUATE, x, y).

■ $\mathcal{B}$ can request the encryption of a message $m \in \mathbf{M}_\lambda$ with time label τ_{dec} by sending (ENC, m, τ_{dec}) to Ch.

■ When Ch receives a (ENC, m, τ_{dec}) request from $\mathcal{B}$, it runs the algorithm $e_{\mathcal{O}_{\mathsf{eval}}}(m, \tau_{\mathsf{dec}}) \to c$ and returns c to $\mathcal{B}$.

■ Ch increases $\mathsf{Cl}_{\mathsf{exp}}$ by 1 for every q queries $\mathcal{B}$ issues to $\mathcal{O}_{\mathsf{eval}}$.

■ $\mathcal{B}$ can request the decryption of a ciphertext c by sending (DEC, c, w_τ) to Ch. Then, Ch just runs the algorithm $d_{\mathcal{O}_{\mathsf{eval}}}(c, w_\tau) \to y \in \{m, \bot\}$ and returns to $\mathcal{B}$ (DEC, c, w_τ, y).

Challenge Phase.

■ $\mathcal{B}$ can request for a single time a challenge from Ch by sending (CHALLENGE, τ). Then, Ch picks a value $r \xleftarrow{\$} \mathbf{M}_\lambda$ and sends (CHALLENGE, $\tau, c_r \leftarrow e_{\mathcal{O}_{\mathsf{eval}}}(r, \tau - \mathsf{Cl}_{\mathsf{exp}})$) to $\mathcal{B}$. Then, $\mathcal{B}$ is free to repeat the *Learning Phase*.

■ $\mathcal{B}$ sends as the answer of the challenge the message (CHALLENGE, τ, c_r, r^*) to Ch.

■ If $(r^* = r) \wedge (\tau > \mathsf{Cl}_{\mathsf{exp}})$ (i.e. $\mathcal{B}$ manages to decrypt c_r before the decryption time comes) then $\mathbf{EXP}_{\mathsf{TLE}}$ outputs 1. Else, $\mathbf{EXP}_{\mathsf{TLE}}$ outputs 0.

Fig. 5. Experiment $\mathbf{EXP}_{\mathsf{TLE}}$ for a number of queries q, function $\mathsf{f}_{\mathsf{state}}$, message domain $\mathbf{M}_\lambda$, algorithms $e_{\mathcal{O}_{\mathsf{eval}}}, d_{\mathcal{O}_{\mathsf{eval}}}$ in the presence of an adversary $\mathcal{B}$, oracle $\mathcal{O}_{\mathsf{eval}}$ and a challenger Ch all parameterized by 1^λ.

to reverse a function, for our purpose of achieving UC realization (Theorem 1) it is enough. This is possible because we extend our TLE construction into a bigger one in the random oracle model and we rely on the hardness of inverting the underlying TLE construction. Because of that, in Subsect. 6.3, we provide an indistinguishability game-based definition, similar to IND-CPA but in the context of TLE so that we can argue about the security of a TLE construction even in the standalone model.

In Fig. 5, we present the experiment $\mathbf{EXP}_{\mathsf{TLE}}$ in the presence of a challenger Ch and an adversary $\mathcal{B}$. More details on the description of $\mathbf{EXP}_{\mathsf{TLE}}$ can be found in Supporting Material C.7 of the extended version of this paper.

Definition 1. *A one-way secure time-lock encryption scheme with respect to an evaluation oracle $\mathcal{O}_{\mathsf{eval}}$, a relation $\mathsf{R}_{\mathcal{O}_{\mathsf{eval}}}$, a state function $\mathsf{f}_{\mathsf{state}}$, puzzle function $\mathsf{f}_{\mathsf{puzzle}}$ and a witness construction function $\mathsf{wit\_con}$ for message space $\mathbf{M}$ and a security parameter λ is a pair of PPT algorithms $(e_{\mathcal{O}_{\mathsf{eval}}}, d_{\mathcal{O}_{\mathsf{eval}}})$ such that:*

- $e_{\mathcal{O}_{\mathsf{eval}}}(m, \tau_{\mathsf{dec}})$: *The encryption algorithm takes as input message a $m \in \mathbf{M}$, an integer $\tau_{\mathsf{dec}} \in \mathbb{N}$ and outputs a ciphertext c.*
- $d_{\mathcal{O}_{\mathsf{eval}}}(c, w_{\tau_{\mathsf{dec}}})$: *The decryption algorithm takes as input $w_{\tau_{\mathsf{dec}}} \in \{0,1\}^*$ and a ciphertext c, and outputs a message $m \in \mathbf{M}$ or $\perp$.*

The pair $(e_{\mathcal{O}_{\mathsf{eval}}}, d_{\mathcal{O}_{\mathsf{eval}}})$ satisfies the following properties:

1. **Correctness:** *For every $\lambda, \tau_{\mathsf{dec}} \in \mathbb{N}, m \in \mathbf{M}$ and $w_{\tau_{\mathsf{dec}}}$, it holds that*

$$\Pr\left[\begin{array}{l} m' \leftarrow d_{\mathcal{O}_{\mathsf{eval}}}(e_{\mathcal{O}_{\mathsf{eval}}}(m, \tau_{\mathsf{dec}}), w_{\tau_{\mathsf{dec}}}) \\ \mathsf{R}_{\mathcal{O}_{\mathsf{eval}}}(w_{\tau_{\mathsf{dec}}}, (\mathsf{f}_{\mathsf{puzzle}}(c), \tau_{\mathsf{dec}})) \end{array} : m' = m \right] > 1 - \mathsf{negl}(\lambda)$$

where $w_{\tau_{\mathsf{dec}}}$ can be constructed from the received responses of $\mathcal{O}_{\mathsf{eval}}$ and function $\mathsf{wit\_con}$ as it is described in both Table 1 and Fig. 4.

2. **qSecurity:** *For every PPT adversary $\mathcal{B}$ with access to oracle $\mathcal{O}_{\mathsf{eval}}$, the probability to win the experiment $\mathbf{EXP}_{\mathsf{TLE}}$ and thus output 1 in Fig. 5 is $\mathsf{negl}(\lambda)$.*

5.2 Proof of UC Realizing $\mathcal{F}_{\mathsf{TLE}}^{\mathsf{leak},\mathsf{delay}}$

In this Subsection we show that if the TLE scheme used in protocol Π_{TLE} in Fig. 4 is a secure time-lock encryption scheme according to Definition 1 then the protocol Π_{TLE} UC realizes $\mathcal{F}_{\mathsf{TLE}}$. We provide the proof of the theorem below in Supporting Material C.8 of the extended version of this paper.

Theorem 1. *Let $(e_{\mathcal{O}_{\mathsf{eval}}}, d_{\mathcal{O}_{\mathsf{eval}}})$ be a pair of encryption/decryption algorithms that satisfies Definition 1. Then, the protocol Π_{TLE} in Fig. 4 UC-realizes functionality $\mathcal{F}_{\mathsf{TLE}}^{\mathsf{leak},\mathsf{delay}}$ in the $(\mathcal{W}_q(\mathcal{F}_{\mathsf{RO}}^*), \mathcal{G}_{\mathsf{clock}}, \mathcal{F}_{\mathsf{RO}}, \mathcal{F}_{\mathsf{BC}})$-hybrid model with leakage function $\mathsf{leak}(x) = x + 1$, $\mathsf{delay} = 1$, where $\mathcal{F}_{\mathsf{RO}}$ and $\mathcal{F}_{\mathsf{RO}}^*$ are two distinct random oracles.*

On the importance of instantiating $\mathcal{F}_{\mathcal{O}_{\mathsf{eval}}}$ with $\mathcal{F}_{\mathsf{RO}}^*$: In our proof, we instantiate the functionality $\mathcal{F}_{\mathcal{O}_{\mathsf{eval}}}$ with $\mathcal{F}_{\mathsf{RO}}^*$, so that $\mathcal{Z}$ cannot bypass the interaction with the functionality wrapper and thus breach the security argument of our proof. For more information and insightful comments see Supporting Material C.9 of the extended version of this paper.

Efficiency cost for UC security: As we have seen, to provide UC security we need to extend a secure TLE construction (according to Definition 1) in the RO model. Specifically, in step 2 of the **Encryption** procedure of Fig. 4, the party makes two extra calls to the $\mathcal{F}_{RO}$ functionality. In reality, this means two extra hash function evaluations, which is very efficient [24]. Thus, the performance is not affected by providing UC security.

Relation between absolute and relativistic time: Our $\mathcal{F}_{TLE}$ captures naturally the concept of TLE in absolute time (messages are encrypted at time t_0 so that they open at time t_m). On the other hand, the construction that UC realizes our functionality is a relativistic one in the sense that a message is protected for a period of time $(t_m - t_0)$.

6   Astrolabous: A UC-Secure TLE Construction

We present and prove that our relative TLE construction is a secure time-lock encryption scheme according to Definition 1. Our scheme combines the construction of [37] and [43].

First, we present our TLE construction, namely *Astrolabous*, and the proof of security, i.e. Astrolabous satisfies Definition 1. Finally, for the sake of completeness, we present the equivocable Astrolabous algorithm, which is the algorithm that is used in the hybrid protocol in Fig. 4.

We did not adopt any of the TLE constructions provided in [43] and [37] because they can not provide us with the necessary security properties we are seeking in our theoretical framework so that we can UC realise $\mathcal{F}_{TLE}$. More details and insightful comments can be found in Supporting Material C.9 of the extended version of this paper.

Description of the* Astrolabous *scheme Initially, we provide the necessary glossary in Table 2. We name our construction Astrolabous from the ancient Greek clock device Astrolabe, which was used by the astronomers of that era to perform different types of calculations including the measurement of the altitude above the horizon of a celestial body, identification of stars and the determination of the local time.

We refer to the encryption/decryption algorithms of the Astrolabous scheme in Subsect. 6.1 as AST.enc, AST.dec where AST is the abbreviation of Astrola—bous. In Subsect. 6.2, we refer to the equivocable encryption/decryption algorithms as EAST.enc, EAST.dec where the letter E indicates the extended algorithms of the Astrolabous scheme.

Table 2. The glossary of Astrolabous scheme.

Notation	Description
$E = (enc, dec)$	A symmetric key encryption scheme
$\mathcal{H}, \mathcal{G}$	Two hash functions (modelled as random oracles)
$b \xleftarrow{\$} D$	b is sampled uniformly at random from D
$X.enc, X.dec$	Encryption and decryption algorithm respectively of scheme X
$\oplus$	The XOR bit operation, e.g. $0 \oplus 1 = 1, 1 \oplus 1 = 0$
$x \| y$	The concatenation of two bit strings x and y

6.1   AST Scheme Description ($AST.enc_{E,\mathcal{H}}$, $AST.dec_{E,\mathcal{H}}$)

$AST.enc_{E,\mathcal{H}}(m, \tau_{dec})$: The algorithm accepts as input the message m and the time-lock's puzzle difficulty τ_{dec}[3] and does:

- Picks $k_E \xleftarrow{\$} K_E$, where K_E is the key space of the symmetric encryption scheme E and the size of the key is equal to the domain of the hash function $\mathcal{H}$ equal to $p_1(\lambda)$. Then compute $c_{m,k_E} \leftarrow enc(m, k_E)$.
- It picks $r_0 \| r_1 \| \ldots \| r_{q\tau_{dec}-1} \xleftarrow{\$} \{0,1\}^{p_2(\lambda)}$ and computes $c_{k_E, \tau_{dec}} \leftarrow (r_0, r_1 \oplus \mathcal{H}(r_0), r_2 \oplus \mathcal{H}(r_1), \ldots, k_E \oplus \mathcal{H}(r_{q\tau_{dec}-1})$[4].
- It outputs $c = (\tau_{dec}, c_{m,k_E}, c_{k_E, \tau_{dec}})$ as the ciphertext.

$AST.dec_{E,\mathcal{H}}(c, w_{\tau_{dec}})$: The algorithm accepts as input the ciphertext c of the form $(\tau_{dec}, c_{m,k_E}, c_{k_E, \tau_{dec}})$ and the witness $w_{\tau_{dec}} = (r_0, \mathcal{H}(r_0), \mathcal{H}(r_1), \ldots, \mathcal{H}(r_{q\tau_{dec}-1}), c)$ that can be computed by issuing $q\tau_{dec}$ random oracle queries. Specifically, to solve the puzzle the first oracle query is r_0 and the response $\mathcal{H}(r_0)$. Then, the decryptor computes the value r_1 from c_{k_E} by using the *XOR* operation such as $r_1 \leftarrow c_{k_E, \tau_{dec}}[1] \oplus \mathcal{H}(r_0)$. Similarly, it computes the pair of values $(r_2, \mathcal{H}(r_2)), \ldots, (r_{q\tau_{dec}-1}, \mathcal{H}(r_{q\tau_{dec}-1}))$. Then it does:

- It computes $k_E = \mathcal{H}(r_{q\tau_{dec}-1}) \oplus c_{k_E, \tau_{dec}}[q\tau_{dec}]$, where $c_{k_E, \tau_{dec}}[j]$ indicates the jth element in vector $c_{k_E, \tau_{dec}}$.
- It computes and outputs $m \leftarrow dec(c_{m,k_E}, k_E)$.

In Table 3, we summarize the oracle, algorithms, functions and relation that define a TLE scheme as in Definition 1. We instantiate these to specify our TLE construction.

We instantiate the items from Table 3 based on our construction as shown below.

---

[3] Note that this time difficulty is relative, that means that it specifies the duration for solving the puzzle rather than the specific date at which the puzzle should be solved.

[4] To do this efficiently all the hash queries can be performed simultaneously as k_E and $r_0 \| r_1 \| \ldots \| r_{q\tau_{dec}-1}$ are known. In the UC setting, the party sends $(sid, \text{EVALUATE}, \tau_{dec})$ to $\mathcal{W}_q$ and receives back $(sid, \text{EVALUATE}, \tau_{dec}, \{(r_j, y_j)\}_{j=0}^{q\tau_{dec}-1})$.

1. The oracle $\mathcal{O}_{\mathsf{eval}}$ is the random oracle RO.
2. The encryption and decryption algorithms $(e_{\mathcal{O}_{\mathsf{eval}}}, d_{\mathcal{O}_{\mathsf{eval}}})$ are described as AST.enc$_{\mathsf{E},\mathcal{H}}$, AST.dec$_{\mathsf{E},\mathcal{H}}$. Our algorithm is relative, meaning that we define the difficulty of the time-lock puzzle rather than the specific time that the message will eventually open. For our algorithms to be compatible with the UC setting, for a given time τ_{dec} we must define the difficulty of the puzzle. In that case, given the current time is CI, the puzzle complexity is $\tau_{\mathsf{dec}} - \mathsf{CI}$. The time τ_{dec} gives us the essence of absolute time that a ciphertext should be opened. On the other hand, both constructions in [37, 43] function in relative time. To compute relative time, both values CI and τ_{dec} are provided to $e_{\mathcal{F}_{\mathcal{O}_{\mathsf{eval}}}}$.

Table 3. Oracle, algorithms, functions and relation that define a TLE construction.

TLE items	Description
$\mathcal{O}_{\mathsf{eval}}$	The oracle to which the parties issue queries for solving/creating time-lock puzzles
$(e_{\mathcal{O}_{\mathsf{eval}}}, d_{\mathcal{O}_{\mathsf{eval}}})$	The pair of encryption/decryption algorithms with respect to the oracle $\mathcal{O}_{\mathsf{eval}}$
$\mathsf{f}_{\mathsf{state}}$	The state function that prepares the next oracle query to $\mathcal{O}_{\mathsf{eval}}$
$\mathsf{f}_{\mathsf{puzzle}}$	The puzzle function that extracts the time-lock puzzle from a given ciphertext
wit_con	The witness construction function that returns the solution of the puzzle or the witness if that is possible
$\mathsf{R}_{\mathcal{O}_{\mathsf{eval}}}$	The relation that specifies when a witness w is a solution to a puzzle c with difficulty τ

3. The state function $\mathsf{f}_{\mathsf{state}}$ for a ciphertext $c = (\tau_{\mathsf{dec}}, c_{m,k_{\mathsf{E}}}, c_{k_{\mathsf{E}}, \tau_{\mathsf{dec}}})$ as described previously, is defined as:

$$\mathsf{f}_{\mathsf{state}}(c, 0, \mathsf{Null}) = c_{k_{\mathsf{E}}, \tau_{\mathsf{dec}}}[0] \tag{1}$$

and $\forall j \in \{1, \ldots, q(\tau_{\mathsf{dec}} - \mathsf{CI}) - 1\}$ it holds that:

$$\mathsf{f}_{\mathsf{state}}(c, j, y = \mathcal{H}(r_{j-1})) = y \oplus c_{k_{\mathsf{E}}, \tau_{\mathsf{dec}}}[j] \tag{2}$$

4. The puzzle function $\mathsf{f}_{\mathsf{puzzle}}$ for a ciphertext $c = (\tau_{\mathsf{dec}}, c_{m,k_{\mathsf{E}}}, c_{k_{\mathsf{E}}, \tau_{\mathsf{dec}}})$ is defined as:

$$\mathsf{f}_{\mathsf{puzzle}}(c) = c_{k_{\mathsf{E}}, \tau_{\mathsf{dec}}} \tag{3}$$

5. The witness construction function wit_con accepts the input described in Fig. 4 and outputs the witness described in the same figure. More details can be found in Supporting Material C.6 of the extended version of this paper.
6. A pair $(w_{\tau_{\mathsf{dec}}} = (r_0, \mathcal{H}(r_0), \mathcal{H}(r_1), \ldots, \mathcal{H}(r_{q(\tau_{\mathsf{dec}}-\mathsf{CI})-1})), (\mathsf{f}_{\mathsf{puzzle}}(c), \tau))$ is in $\mathsf{R}_{\mathcal{F}_{\mathcal{O}_{\mathsf{eval}}}}$, where $w_{\tau_{\mathsf{dec}}}$ and c as appeared in the description of AST.dec$_{\mathsf{E},\mathcal{H}}$, if $|w_{\tau_{\mathsf{dec}}}| = |\mathsf{f}_{\mathsf{puzzle}}(c)|$ and $w[j] = c_{k_{\mathsf{E}}, \tau_{\mathsf{dec}}}[j] \oplus \mathcal{H}(w[j-1])$ for all $j \in [0, q(\tau_{\mathsf{dec}} - \mathsf{CI}) - 2]$, where $w[-1] = 1$.

The following theorem states that our TLE construction satisfies Definition 1. The proof is provided in Supporting Material D.1 of the extended version of this paper.

Theorem 2. *Let* $\mathsf{AST.enc}_{\mathsf{E},\mathcal{H}}, \mathsf{AST.dec}_{\mathsf{E},\mathcal{H}}$ *be the pair of* encryption/decryption *algorithms just described. If the underlying symmetric encryption scheme* E *satisfies* $\mathsf{IND-CPA}$ *security and* correctness, *then the pair* $(\mathsf{AST.enc}_{\mathsf{E},\mathcal{H}}, \mathsf{AST.dec}_{\mathsf{E},\mathcal{H}})$ *is a secure TLE scheme according to Definition 1 in the random oracle model.*

Verifiability and efficiency of Astrolabous: Astrolabous is efficiently verifiable. Solvers can present all the hash evaluations and, similar to puzzle creation, the verifier can in parallel evaluate them and recreate the puzzle. If both puzzles match it accepts the solution. So for a puzzle set for computation time τ, *i.e.* requiring $q\tau$ sequential hash evaluations to be solved, the verification can be parallelized, *i.e.* $q\tau$ parallel hash evaluations.

6.2 Equivocable Astrolabous Scheme Description ($\mathsf{EAST.enc}_{\mathsf{E},\mathcal{H},\mathcal{G}}, \mathsf{EAST.dec}_{\mathsf{E},\mathcal{H},\mathcal{G}}$)

For our purposes, it is not enough to directly adopt a TLE construction such as Astrolabous and make security claims in the UC framework because we cannot equivocate, which is essential. For that reason, in our hybrid protocol in Fig. 4 we extend the input TLE construction in order for our security claims to be compatible with the UC framework and in particular with the UC treatment of time. Specifically, in Fig. 4, in procedure **Puzzle**, the party prepares the time-lock puzzles for encrypting a random string in step 1 of the **Encryption** procedure. Then, in step 2 the party makes two calls to the random oracle and extends the previously resulting ciphertext by two arguments for equivocation and non-malleability as explained above. This procedure is initiated by the party every time she advances the clock. So the execution of the Extended Astrolabous, as it appeared in Fig. 4 in both procedures, needs to be interleaved with the interaction of parties with the global clock. Because of this interaction, extended Astrolabous cannot be given black-box (*e.g.* as protocol input), it rather needs to be described as part of the Π_{TLE} protocol itself. However, outside of the UC framework, parties will actually use the extended algorithms as they do not actually interact with any global clock. This is merely the result of the way time is treated in the UC $\mathcal{G}_{\mathsf{clock}}$ model. So morally, the Equivocable Astrolabous TLE scheme satisfies the UC security notion captured by our $\mathcal{F}_{\mathsf{TLE}}$. The full specification of the corresponding extended algorithms is given in the Supporting Material D.2 of the extended version of this paper.

6.3 IND-CPA-TLE Security

Game-based definitions are often natural and easy to use. Unfortunately, the experiment $\mathbf{EXP}_{\mathsf{TLE}}$ presented in Figure: 5 is not enough to argue about the security of a TLE scheme on its own, and is only useful in the context of the

Theorem: 1. The reason is that **EXP**$_{\text{TLE}}$ argues about only the onewayness of a TLE scheme, leaving aside any semantic security. On the other hand, it is enough for the proof of Theorem: 1 as we use an extension of the TLE scheme in the random oracle model and not the scheme as it is.

Below, we present the analogous experiment of the IND-CPA security notion in the time-lock setting. In a nutshell, this experiment is the same as the one in Figure: 5 except that the adversary in the CHALLENGE command specifies two messages (m_0, m_1) as in the classical IND-CPA game. Again, in order to win the game, the adversary $\mathcal{B}$ must guess correctly which of the two messages is encrypted by the challenger Ch without engaging with the oracle more than the desired amount of times. In case he wins, that would mean that he managed to "break" the TLE scheme in the sense that he decrypted the message before its decryption time.

The experiment **EXP**$_{\text{IND-CPA-TLE}}(\mathcal{B}, \mathcal{O}_{\text{eval}}, e_{\mathcal{O}_{\text{eval}}}, d_{\mathcal{O}_{\text{eval}}}, \mathsf{f}_{\text{state}}, \mathsf{f}_{\text{puzzle}}, q)$

Initialization Phase.

■ Ch is initialized with $e_{\mathcal{O}_{\text{eval}}}, d_{\mathcal{O}_{\text{eval}}}$ and sends them to $\mathcal{B}$. In addition, it creates a local time counter Cl_{exp}.

Learning Phase.

■ When $\mathcal{B}$ issues the query (EVALUATE, x) to $\mathcal{O}_{\text{eval}}$ through the Ch, he gets back (EVALUATE, x, y).

■ $\mathcal{B}$ can request the encryption of a message $m \in \mathbf{M}_\lambda$ with time label τ_{dec} by sending (ENC, m, τ_{dec}) to Ch.

■ When Ch receives a (ENC, m, τ_{dec}) request from $\mathcal{B}$, it runs the algorithm $e_{\mathcal{O}_{\text{eval}}}(m, \tau_{\text{dec}}) \rightarrow c$ and returns c to $\mathcal{B}$.

■ Ch increases Cl_{exp} by 1 every time $\mathcal{B}$ queries $\mathcal{O}_{\text{eval}}$ q times.

■ $\mathcal{B}$ can request the decryption of a ciphertext c by sending (DEC, c, w) to Ch. Then, Ch just runs the algorithm $d_{\mathcal{O}_{\text{eval}}}(c, w) \rightarrow y \in \{m, \perp\}$ and returns to $\mathcal{B}$ (DEC, c, w, y).

Challenge Phase.

■ $\mathcal{B}$ can request for a single time a challenge from Ch by sending (CHALLENGE, $(m_0, m_1), \tau$). Then, Ch picks a value $b \xleftarrow{\$} \{0, 1\}$ and sends (CHALLENGE, $\tau, c \leftarrow e_{\mathcal{O}_{\text{eval}}}(m_b, \tau - \mathsf{Cl}_{\text{exp}})$) to $\mathcal{B}$. Then, $\mathcal{B}$ is free to repeat the *Learning Phase.*

■ $\mathcal{B}$ sends as the answer of the challenge the message (CHALLENGE, τ, c, m_{b^*}) to Ch.

■ If $(m_{b^*} = m_b) \wedge (\tau > \mathsf{Cl}_{\text{exp}})$ (i.e. $\mathcal{B}$ manages to decrypt c_τ before the decryption time comes) then **EXP**$_{\text{TLE}}$ outputs 1. Else, **EXP**$_{\text{TLE}}$ outputs 0.

Fig. 6. Experiment **EXP**$_{\text{IND-CPA-TLE}}$ for a number of queries q, function $\mathsf{f}_{\text{state}}$, message domain $\mathbf{M}_\lambda$, algorithms $e_{\mathcal{O}_{\text{eval}}}, d_{\mathcal{O}_{\text{eval}}}$ in the presence of an adversary $\mathcal{B}$, oracle $\mathcal{O}_{\text{eval}}$ and a challenger Ch all parameterized by 1^λ.

Definition 2. *A pair of TLE algorithms* $(e_{\mathcal{O}_{\text{eval}}}, d_{\mathcal{O}_{\text{eval}}})$ *as described in Definition 1 is* IND-CPA-TLE, *if for every PPT adversary* $\mathcal{B}$ *the probability to win the experiment described in Fig. 5 is* $1/2 + negl(\lambda)$.

Mahmoody et al. construction is not IND-CPA-TLE: Recall the construction in [37] for encrypting a message m or a secret in general. It can be easily seen that it does not satisfy Definition 2, as the secret is spread across the puzzle, and thus part of it is leaked as the puzzle is solved (see Supporting Material D.3 of the extended version of this paper). In contrast, next we show both Astrolabous and an enhanced version of the construction in [37], we called it MMV 2.0 from the first letter of each author, are IND-CPA-TLE.

MMV 2.0: As we explained above, the construction in [37] does not satisfy IND-CPA-TLE security because it spreads the message all over the puzzle. A natural question is if it satisfies our game based definition when the message is not spread across all over the puzzle, but instead, it is XORed in the last hash evaluation. Specifically, $e_{\text{MM0.1}}(m, \tau) \rightarrow (r_0, r_1 \oplus \mathcal{H}(r_0), \ldots, m \oplus \mathcal{H}(r_{\tau q - 1}))$, where $r = r_0 \| \ldots \| r_{\tau q - 1}$ is a random string. In that case, as we see next, the MMV 2.0 satisfies IND-CPA-TLE. The proof can be found in Supporting Material D.4 of the extended version of this paper.

Theorem 3. *The construction MMV 2.0 as described above is IND-CPA-TLE secure in the random oracle model.*

Next we show that Astrolabous is also IND-CPA-TLE secure. The reasoning again is exactly the same as the one in Theorem 2 except that the IND-CPA adversary sends the messages m_0, m_1 received from the IND-CPA-TLE adversary to the challenger instead of choosing his own. The rest are exactly the same and thus we omit the proof.

Theorem 4. *Astrolabous, i.e. the pair* $(\mathsf{AST}.\mathsf{enc}_{\mathsf{E},\mathcal{H}}, \mathsf{AST}.\mathsf{dec}_{\mathsf{E},\mathcal{H}})$, *is IND-CPA-TLE secure given that the underlying symmetric encryption scheme* E *satisfies* $\mathsf{IND} - \mathsf{CPA}$ *security.*

Even if both Astrolabous and MMV 2.0 are IND-CPA-TLE secure, Astrolabous has a potential advantage in terms of efficiency. Namely, Astrolabous hides the key of the symmetric cryptosystem that it uses into the puzzle, instead of the message itself as in MMV 2.0. As a result, many messages can be encrypted under the same key and be opened at the same time solving just one puzzle. In contrast, with MMV 2.0, for every message, a new puzzle must be generated, making the encryption more time-consuming. For example, for a puzzle with difficulty that should last 24 h, an 8-core CPU can generate it in 3 h (24/8). The total time for encrypting two messages with MMV 2.0 with the above difficulty is 3 h for the first message and 2.625 h (24–1.5/8) for the second, in total 5.625 h. With Astrolabous one puzzle can be used for both messages, making the total encryption time just 3 h. The gap becomes even bigger if we consider several encryptions instead of just two. In both examples with did not consider the time to perform AES, as in practice is very efficient.

Asymmetry of puzzle generation and puzzle solving time with Astrolabous: A natural question is if the puzzle generation time is significantly smaller than the time that is required for solving the puzzle. The answer is positive. Specifically, there are hash functions that are not meant to have an efficient evaluation, such as *Argon2* [6]. Equipped with such function we can create puzzles that are small (in terms of space) and fast, but at the same time difficult enough. For example, Argon2 can be parameterized in such a way that a single hash evaluation can take roughly 60 s [45], meaning that an 8-core processor can generate a puzzle that meant to be solved in 4 h (equably 14.400 s or $14.400/60 = 240$ hash evaluations) in just 30 min (puzzle generation is parallelizable so an 8-core processor can do 8 hash evaluation simultaneously which each one of them takes 60 s. So 240 hash evaluations can be done in 30 min.). As the number of CPU cores increases the puzzle generation can become even smaller but at the same time, the time for solving the puzzle remains unchanged (no parallelization for puzzle solving).

References

1. Arapinis, M., Lamprou, N., Zacharias, T.: E-cclesia: universally composable self-tallying elections. Cryptology ePrint Archive, Report 2020/513 (2020)
2. Arapinis, M., Lamprou, N., Zacharias, T.: A universally composable time-lock encryption scheme. Cryptology ePrint Archive, Astrolabous (2021)
3. Christian, B., et al.: A composable treatment. In: CRYPTO, Bitcoin as a Transaction Ledger (2017)
4. Baum, C., et al.: Craft: composable randomness and almost fairness from time. Cryptology ePrint Archive, Report 2020/784 (2020)
5. Baum, C. et al.: A foundation of time-lock puzzles in uc. Advances in Cryptology - EUROCRYPT (2021)
6. Biryukov, A., Dinu, D., Khovratovich, D.: Argon2: new generation of memory-hard functions for password hashing and other applications. In: 2016 IEEE European Symposium on Security and Privacy (EuroS P) (2016)
7. Bitansky, N., et al.: Time-lock puzzles from randomized encodings. In: ITCS (2016)
8. Boneh, D., Naor, M.: Timed commitments. In: CRYPTO (2000)
9. Boneh, D., Bonneau, J., Bunz, B., Fisch, B.: Verifiable delay functions. In: CRYPTO 2018 (2018)
10. Bellare, M.: Timed commitments. In: Bellare, Mihir (ed.) Advances in Cryptology – CRYPTO 2000. Springer, Berlin Heidelberg (2000)
11. Camenisch, J., Lehmann, A., Neven, G., Samelin, K.: Uc-secure non-interactive public-key encryption. In: CSF 2017 (2017)
12. Canetti, R.: Universally composable security: a new paradigm for cryptographic protocols. In: FOCS (2001)
13. Canetti, R., Dodis, Y., Pass, R., Walfish, S.: Universally composable security with global setup. In: TCC (2007)
14. Cheon, J.H., Hopper, N., Kim, Y., Osipkov, I.: Timed-release and key-insulated public key encryption. In: Di Crescenzo, G., Rubin, A. (eds.) Financial Cryptography and Data Security. FC 2006. LNCS, vol. 4107. Springer, Heidelberg (2006). https://doi.org/10.1007/11889663_17

15. Cheon, J.H., Hopper, N., Kim, Y., Osipkov, I.: Provably secure timed-release public key encryption. ACM Trans. Inf. Syst. Secur., **11**(2), (2008)
16. Dachman-Soled, D., Mahmoody, M., Malkin, T.: Can optimally-fair coin tossing be based on one-way functions?. In: Lindell, Y. (eds.) Theory of Cryptography. TCC 2014. LNCS, vol. 8349. Springer, Heidelberg (2014). https://doi.org/10.1007/978-3-642-54242-8_10
17. Daemen, J., Rijmen, V.: The design of Rijndael. Springer-Verlag (2002). https://doi.org/10.1007/978-3-662-60769-5
18. ElGamal, T.: A public key cryptosystem and a signature scheme based on discrete logarithms. In: Blakley, G.R., Chaum, D. (eds.) CRYPTO 1984. LNCS, vol. 196, pp. 10–18. Springer, Heidelberg (1985). https://doi.org/10.1007/3-540-39568-7_2
19. Ephraim, N., Freitag, C., Komargodski, I., Pass, R.: Non-malleable time-lock puzzles and applications. Cryptology ePrint Archive, Report 2020/779 (2020)
20. Garay, J., Kiayias, A., Panagiotakos, G.: Proofs of work for blockchain protocols. IACR Cryptol. ePrint Arch., 2017 (2017)
21. Juan, A.: Garay, Aggelos Kiayias, and Nikos Leonardos. analysis and applications. In: EUROCRYPT, The Bitcoin Backbone Protocol (2015)
22. Garg, S., Gentry, C., Sahai, A., Waters, B.: Witness encryption and its applications. In: STOC (2013)
23. Gennaro, R., Jarecki, S., Krawczyk, H., Rabin, T.: Secure distributed key generation for discrete-log based cryptosystems. J. Cryptol. **20** (2007)
24. Gilbert, H., Handschuh, H.: Security analysis of SHA-256 and sisters. In: Matsui, M., Zuccherato, R.J. (eds.) Selected Areas in Cryptography. SAC 2003. LNCS, vol. 3006. Springer, Heidelberg (2004). https://doi.org/10.1007/978-3-540-24654-1_13
25. Goldreich, O.: The foundations of modern cryptography. In: Modern Cryptography, Probabilistic Proofs and Pseudorandomness. Algorithms and Combinatorics, vol. 17. Springer, Heidelberg (1999). https://doi.org/10.1007/978-3-662-12521-2_1
26. Goldreich, O.: Foundations of cryptography:, vol. 1. Cambridge University Press, USA (2006)
27. Gordon, D., Ishai, Y., Moran, T., Ostrovsky, R., Sahai, A.: On complete primitives for fairness. In: Micciancio, D. (eds.) Theory of Cryptography. TCC 2010. LNCS, vol. 5978. Springer, Heidelberg (2010). https://doi.org/10.1007/978-3-642-11799-2_7
28. Groth, J.: Evaluating security of voting schemes in the universal composability framework. In: Jakobsson, M., Yung, M., Zhou, J. (eds) Applied Cryptography and Network Security. ACNS 2004. LNCS, vol. 3089. Springer, Heidelberg (2004). https://doi.org/10.1007/978-3-540-24852-1_4
29. Hirt, M., Zikas, V.: Adaptively secure broadcast. In: Gilbert, H. (ed.) EUROCRYPT 2010. LNCS, vol. 6110, pp. 466–485. Springer, Heidelberg (2010). https://doi.org/10.1007/978-3-642-13190-5_24
30. Katz, J., Loss, J., Xu, J.: On the security of time-lock puzzles and timed commitments. In: Pass, R., Pietrzak, K. (eds.) Theory of Cryptography. TCC 2020. Lecture Notes in Computer Science, vol. 12552. Springer, Cham (2020). https://doi.org/10.1007/978-3-030-64381-2_14
31. Katz, J., Maurer, U., Tackmann, B., Zikas, V.: Universally composable synchronous computation. In: TCC (2013)
32. Khisti, A., Tchamkerten, A., Wornell, G. W.: Secure broadcasting over fading channels. IEEE Trans. Inf. Theory, **54**(6) (2008)
33. Kiayias, A., Yung, M.: Self-tallying elections and perfect ballot secrecy. In: Naccache, D., Paillier, P. (eds.) PKC 2002. LNCS, vol. 2274, pp. 141–158. Springer, Heidelberg (2002). https://doi.org/10.1007/3-540-45664-3_10

34. Kościelny, C., Kurkowski, M., Srebrny, M.: Foundations of symmetric cryptography. In: Modern Cryptography Primer, pp. 77–118. Springer, Heidelberg (2013). https://doi.org/10.1007/978-3-642-41386-5_3
35. Lindell, Y.: Highly-efficient universally-composable commitments based on the DDH assumption. In: EUROCRYPT 2011 (2011)
36. Liu, J., Jager, T., Kakvi, S.A., Warinschi, B.: How to build time-lock encryption. Designs, Codes and Cryptography (2018)
37. Mahmoody, M., Moran, T., Vadhan, S.: Time-lock puzzles in the random oracle model. In: Rogaway, P. (eds.) Advances in Cryptology. LNCS, vol. 6841. Springer, Heidelberg (2011). https://doi.org/10.1007/978-3-642-22792-9_3
38. Timothy, C.: May. Timed-release crypto (1993)
39. Nielsen, J.B.: Separating random oracle proofs from complexity theoretic proofs: the non-committing encryption case. In: CRYPTO (2002)
40. Okamoto, T.: Receipt-free electronic voting schemes for large scale elections. In: Security Protocols (1998)
41. Pedersen, T.P.: Non-interactive and information-theoretic secure verifiable secret sharing. In: Feigenbaum, J. (ed.) Advances in Cryptology. LNCS, vol. 576. Springer, Heidelberg (1992). https://doi.org/10.1007/3-540-46766-1_9
42. Pietrzak, K.: Simple verifiable delay functions. In: Blum, A., (ed.) 10th Innovations in Theoretical Computer Science Conference (ITCS 2019), of Leibniz International Proceedings in Informatics (LIPIcs). Schloss Dagstuhl-Leibniz-Zentrum fuer Informatik, vol. 124 (2018)
43. Rivest, R.L., Shamir, A., Wagner, D.A.: Time-lock puzzles and timed-release crypto. Technical report (1996)
44. Szepieniec, A., Preneel, B.: New techniques for electronic voting. USENIX Association (2015)
45. Toponce, A.: Further investigation into scrypt and argon2 password hashing (2016)
46. Wesolowski, B.: Efficient verifiable delay functions. In: Ishai, Y., Rijmen, V. (eds.) Advances in Cryptology. LNCS, vol. 11478. Springer, Cham (2019). https://doi.org/10.1007/978-3-030-17659-4_13

Identity-Based Encryption for Fair Anonymity Applications: Defining, Implementing, and Applying Rerandomizable RCCA-Secure IBE

Yi Wang[1], Rongmao Chen[1(✉)], Xinyi Huang[2(✉)], Jianting Ning[2,3],
Baosheng Wang[1], and Moti Yung[4,5]

[1] School of Computer, National University of Defense Technology, Changsha, China
{wangyi14,chromao,bswang}@nudt.edu.cn
[2] Fujian Provincial Key Laboratory of Network Security and Cryptology,
College of Computer and Cyber Security, Fujian Normal University, Fuzhou, China
{xyhuang,jtning}@fjnu.edu.cn
[3] State Key Laboratory of Information Security, Institute of Information
Engineering, Chinese Academy of Sciences, Beijing, China
[4] Google LLC, New York, NY, USA
[5] Columbia University, New York, USA
moti@cs.columbia.edu

Abstract. Our context is anonymous encryption schemes hiding their receiver, but in a setting which allows authorities to reveal the receiver when needed. While anonymous Identity-Based Encryption (IBE) is a natural candidate for such fair anonymity (it gives trusted authority access by design), the *de facto* security standard (a.k.a. IND-ID-CCA) is incompatible with the ciphertext rerandomizability which is crucial to anonymous communication. Thus, we seek to extend IND-ID-CCA security for IBE to a notion that can be meaningfully relaxed for rerandomizability while it still protects against active adversaries. To the end, inspired by the notion of replayable adaptive chosen-ciphertext attack (RCCA) security (Canetti *et al.*, Crypto'03), we formalize a new security notion called Anonymous Identity-Based RCCA (ANON-ID-RCCA) security for rerandomizable IBE and propose the first construction with rigorous security analysis. The core of our scheme is a novel extension of the double-strand paradigm, which was originally proposed by Golle *et al.* (CT-RSA'04) and later extended by Prabhakaran and Rosulek (Crypto'07), to the well-known Gentry-IBE (Eurocrypt'06). Notably, our scheme is the first IBE that simultaneously satisfies adaptive security, rerandomizability, and recipient-anonymity to date. As the application of our new notion, we design a new universal mixnet in the identity-based setting that does not require public key distribution (with fair anonymity). More generally, our new notion is also applicable to most existing rerandomizable RCCA-secure applications to eliminate the need for public key distribution infrastructure while allowing fairness.

Keywords: Replayable CCA security · Identity-based encryption · Rerandomizability

© International Association for Cryptologic Research 2021
M. Tibouchi and H. Wang (Eds.): ASIACRYPT 2021, LNCS 13091, pp. 427–455, 2021.
https://doi.org/10.1007/978-3-030-92075-3_15

1 Introduction

Anonymity of encryption is a useful tool for building applications (such as various anonymous channels to unknown receivers). Anonymity typically is incorporated into systems in two ways: unconditional anonymity (without accountability), and fair anonymity (where a trusted authority may upon abuse revoke the anonymity). In this work, we are mainly interested in encryption schemes for the latter which gives a fair balance of privacy vs. anti-abuse measures (i.e., balancing individual privacy against societal safety). Anonymous Identity-Based Encryption (IBE) is a natural candidate for such a setting (it gives trusted authority access by design). Yet, other properties of such systems put some extra constraints: (1) ciphertext rerandomization: which is often used to hide connections of incoming and outgoing messages in various applications (in cryptographic applications such as anonymous communication protocol [3,25], mixnet [12,21], controlled function encryption [20] and cryptographic reverse firewalls [6,8,19]); and (2) protection against active attackers since often servers in the system can be probed with ciphertexts by anonymous parties.

The above combination of requirements, putting aside the accountability, points at the notion of replayable adaptive chosen ciphertext attack (RCCA) security, originally defined by Canetti *et al.* for public-key encryption (PKE) [4]. It is widely considered as a meaningful relaxation of CCA security, especially for its compatibility with ciphertext rerandomizability. Essentially, RCCA security is as strong as CCA security except that adversaries might have capability of mauling a ciphertext into a new one without changing the underlying plaintext. Such a relaxation makes the ciphertext possibly rerandomizable while still secure against active attackers. However, as it turns out, achieving rerandomizable RCCA (Rand-RCCA) security is quite challenging, and various specific efforts have been made to construct RCCA-secure PKE schemes for different anonymous applications (without accountability) [4,5,9,10,12,14,17,23,26].

As mentioned above, our goal of fair anonymity points at IBE. Thus, inspired by the RCCA security notion for PKE, we turn to study RCCA security in the context of IBE which, perhaps surprisingly, remains unsolved to date. Note that IBE was introduced by Shamir [24] in 1980s and has received extensive attentions in real-world applications since the first efficient realization in 2000s [2]. In an IBE system, the public key of a user is some unique information about his/her identity (e.g. email address). Thus, compared with typical PKE, IBE eliminates the need of public key distributions, making it also most desirable in applications which suffer costly public key certificate management.

Our main results. Starting with the *de facto* security notion—indistinguishability against adaptive chosen identity and ciphertext attack (IND-ID-CCA)—for typical IBE, we concretely seek how to define and realize a meaningful relaxation of IND-ID-CCA security for enabling rerandomizability. To the end, we come up with new results—in theoretical and practical aspects—as follows.

- We formalize a new security notion called "anonymous identity-based RCCA" (ANON-ID-RCCA) security for rerandomizable IBE, which is essentially the same as the notion of IND-ID-CCA except that, (i) adversaries may be able to maul a ciphertext into a new one of the same plaintext and recipient; and (ii) the recipient is anonymous given the ciphertext.

- We show that our new notion is achievable via designing an IBE scheme that satisfies ANON-ID-RCCA security and (universal) rerandomizability. A rigorous analysis which turns out to be quite challenging is carefully conducted to prove the security and rerandomizability of our proposed scheme.
- To demonstrate the usefulness of our new notion, we present an identity-based universal mixnet where our proposed rerandomizable ANON-ID-RCCA secure IBE plays as the core building block. Our proposed mixnet could serve as a desirable tool to balance individual privacy against societal safety.

Remark. We note that in the sequel we do not discuss opening of ciphertexts by the authorities for fair anonymity and we do not try to optimize it. We simply assume the authority knows all active identities which were enabled to receive ciphertexts, and can try all private keys; further, the message has enough redundancy so the authority can identify the correct receiver. Optimizing this aspect further is left for future work.

2   Results Overview and Related Work

In this section we provide an overview of the results presented in this work.

Relaxing IND-ID-CCA security. Note that existing RCCA security notion—by Canetti et al. [4]—is originally defined for PKE scheme and thus can not be straightforwardly adopted for IBE schemes. Nevertheless, inspired by the definition of RCCA security, we first formalize the notion of identity-based RCCA (ID-RCCA) security by relaxing the decryption oracle of IND-ID-CCA game in the sense that the adversary is allowed to query any ciphertext but gets "`replay`" if the decryption result equals to either of the two challenge plaintexts. Further, we enhance ID-RCCA security with the notion of recipient-anonymity, which roughly says that an IBE ciphertext does not leak any information about the underlying recipient identity. We name such a new notion as anonymous identity-based RCCA (ANON-ID-RCCA) security and show it is achievable via proposing an ANON-ID-RCCA secure IBE scheme that is rerandomizable.

An overview of our construction. The core of our construction is a novel extension of the double-strand paradigm by Golle et al. [12] to the well-known Gentry-IBE construction [11] which satisfies recipient-anonymity. We provide an overview of our construction below and the full scheme is given in Sect. 4.2.

THE DOUBLE-STRAND PARADIGM BY GOLLE et al. [12]. Recall that the ciphertext of message m in the ElGamal-based universal cryptosystem by Golle et al. [12] is $\zeta_y(m) = (g^{r_0}, m \cdot y^{r_0}, g^{r_1}, y^{r_1}) \in \mathcal{G}^4$ where g is a random generator of group $\mathcal{G}$, $y = g^x$ is the public key corresponding to secret key x and r_0, r_1 are randomnesses. In fact, this ciphertext is composed of two strands of ElGamal encryptions: $E_y(m) = (g^{r_0}, m \cdot y^{r_0})$ and $E_y(1) = (g^{r_1}, y^{r_1})$. By the homomorphic property of the ElGamal encryption, $E_y(1)$ can be used to rerandomize both $E_y(m)$ and itself correctly. The double-strand paradigm offers an elegant way to re-encrypt ciphertext without any public parameters.

Unfortunately, this paradigm cannot be applied to the well-known Gentry-IBE [11] directly, as it is of IND-ID-CCA security which contradicts to the homomorphic property. To overcome this issue, inspired by the Rand-RCCA-secure scheme of Prabhakaran and Rosulek [23], we conduct further specific treatments on adjusting the original Gentry-IBE. Before the further explanation of our proposed approaches, we first brief describe the Gentry-IBE scheme.

OVERVIEW OF THE GENTRY-IBE SCHEME. Let $e : \mathbb{G} \times \mathbb{G} \rightarrow \mathbb{G}_T$ be a symmetric bilinear map where $\mathbb{G}$ and $\mathbb{G}_T$ are groups of prime order p. Let P be a random generator of $\mathbb{G}$, $[a]$ denote aP and $[a]_T$ denote $e(P,P)^a$ for any $a \in \mathbb{Z}_p^*$. In the Gentry-IBE scheme, the ciphertext under identity $\mathsf{ID} \in \mathbb{Z}_p$ and public parameters $([\alpha], [\vec{h}] = ([h_1], [h_2], [h_3]))$ is

$$E_{\mathsf{ID}}(m) = ([X_1], [\vec{X}_{2,4}]_T) = (\ \underbrace{[s\alpha_{\mathsf{ID}}], [s]_T}_{\text{key ciphertext}}, \ \underbrace{m \cdot [-sh_1]_T}_{\text{data ciphertext}}, \ \underbrace{[s\vec{\beta}\vec{h}_{2,3}^{\top}]_T}_{\text{validity checking}}\ )$$

where $s \in \mathbb{Z}_p$, $\alpha_{\mathsf{ID}} = \alpha - \mathsf{ID}$, $[\vec{h}_{2,3}] = ([h_2], [h_3])$, $\beta = H([X_1], [\vec{X}_{2,3}]_T)$ and $\vec{\beta} = (1, \beta)$. $\alpha \in \mathbb{Z}_p$ is the master key and H is a collision-resistant hash function. At the high level, ciphertext in the Gentry-IBE scheme consists of three parts: key ciphertext, data ciphertext and validity checking. During the decryption procedure, the validity checking part is used to test the validity of ciphertext, while the key ciphertext is decrypted to obtain the session key for recovering the encrypted data. Below we show how to adjust the Gentry-IBE scheme towards ANON-ID-RCCA security with (universal) rerandomizability.

THE FIRST ATTEMPT. One can note that the first three elements $([X_1], [\vec{X}_{2,3}]_T)$ in $E_{\mathsf{ID}}(m)$ are analogous to the ElGamal encryption $E_y(m)$, and the value of last element $[X_4]_T$ varies with $([X_1], [\vec{X}_{2,3}]_T)$. Due to the collision resistance of hash function H, the value of β in $E_{\mathsf{ID}}(m)$ is different from that in $E_{\mathsf{ID}}(1)$. Thus, re-encrypting $E_{\mathsf{ID}}(m)$ with $E_{\mathsf{ID}}(1)$ would not derive a valid Gentry-IBE ciphertext. Consider that re-encryption does not change the underlying message m, we set the value of β in $E_{\mathsf{ID}}(m)$ and $E_{\mathsf{ID}}(1)$ as hash value $H(m)$, and obtain a Gentry-IBE-based universal cryptosystem with ciphertext $\zeta_{\mathsf{ID}}(m) = (\vec{X}, \vec{Y})$ where

$$\vec{X} = ([s\alpha_{\mathsf{ID}}], [s]_T, m \cdot [-sh_1]_T, [s\vec{\mu}\vec{h}_{2,3}^{\top}]_T),$$
$$\vec{Y} = ([t\alpha_{\mathsf{ID}}], [t]_T, [-th_1]_T, \quad [t\vec{\mu}\vec{h}_{2,3}^{\top}]_T)$$

and $s, t \in \mathbb{Z}_p$, $\vec{\mu} = (1, H(m))$. A re-encryption of $\zeta_{\mathsf{ID}}(m)$ is $(\vec{X}', \vec{Y}') = (\vec{X} + s'\vec{Y}, t'\vec{Y})$ where $s', t' \in \mathbb{Z}_p$. One can verify that $(\vec{X}', \vec{Y}')$ is valid ciphertext with randomnesses $s + s't$ and $t't$.

Unfortunately, the above ID-based universal cryptosystem does not satisfy ID-RCCA security. Let $\zeta_{\mathsf{ID}}(m_b) = (\vec{X}, \vec{Y})$ be the challenge ciphertext in the ID-RCCA security game with $b \xleftarrow{\$} \{0, 1\}$. Adversary $\mathcal{A}$ guesses the bit b', computes a new strand $\vec{X}^* = \left([s'X_1], [s'X_2]_T, [s'X_3]_T/(m_{b'}^{s'-1}), [s'X_4]_T\right)$ from $\vec{X}$ where $s' \in \mathbb{Z}_p$ and queries $(\vec{X}^*, \vec{Y})$ to the decryption oracle. If $b = b'$, then $(\vec{X}^*, \vec{Y})$ is a valid ciphertext and the oracle outputs `replay`; otherwise, it is invalid and the oracle outputs $\perp$. Thus, $\mathcal{A}$ can verify the guess and win the security game with overwhelming advantage.

RESTRICTING THE RERANDOMIZATION MANNER. We remark that a similar issue as above also occurs when Prabhakaran and Rosulek tried to apply the double-strand paradigm for the first realization of Rand-RCCA-secure PKE scheme in the standard model [23]. They proposed a clever idea of restricting the rerandomization of ciphertext by placing fixed vector $\vec{z} = (z_1, z_2, z_3, z_4)$ and random mask u on the key ciphertext part. Specifically, let $\mathbb{G}$ be a cyclic group of prime order p, g_1, g_2, g_3, g_4 are generators of $\mathbb{G}$ and $C, D, E \in \mathbb{G}$ belong to the public key, the first two strands in the ciphertext of message m are as follows.

$$(X_1, X_2, X_3, X_4, m \cdot C^x, (DE^{H(m)})^x, Y_1, Y_2, Y_3, Y_4, C^y, (DE^{H(m)})^y)$$

where $X_i = g_i^{(x+z_i)u}$ and $Y_i = g_i^{yu}$ for $i = 1, 2, 3, 4$. Unfortunately, while Prabhakaran and Rosulek's construction sheds some light on restricting the rerandomization manner, their approach requires the key ciphertext part to be extended to a vector, and thus is not feasible for the Gentry-IBE. Therefore, as it turns out as follows, further specific treatments are required for our construction.

To defend against the aforementioned attack, we disable the manner of rerandomization on strand $\vec{X}$ by introducing extra component in the validity checking part of both strands and perturbing the randomness in strand $\vec{X}$ with additional vector (z_0, z_1), and the strands in ciphertext $\zeta_{\mathsf{ID}}(m)$ are as follows.

$$\vec{X} = ([s\alpha_{\mathsf{ID}}], [s]_T, m \cdot [-sh_1]_T, [(s+z_0)\vec{\mu}\vec{h}_{2,3}^\top]_T, [(s+z_1)\vec{\mu}\vec{h}_{4,5}^\top]_T);$$
$$\vec{Y} = ([t\alpha_{\mathsf{ID}}], [t]_T, [-th_1]_T, [t\vec{\mu}\vec{h}_{2,3}^\top]_T, [t\vec{\mu}\vec{h}_{4,5}^\top]_T),$$

where $\vec{h}_{4,5} = ([h_4], [h_5])$ are newly added public parameters. Although the aforementioned re-encryption is prohibited by the vector (z_0, z_1), it is still possible to rerandomize strand $\vec{X}$ by performing multiplication. Concretely, let b' be the guess of adversary $\mathcal{A}$, then $\mathcal{A}$ can compute a new strand $\vec{X}^*$ from $\vec{X}$ as follows:

$$\vec{X}^* = ([X_1 + s'\alpha_{\mathsf{ID}}], \quad [X_2 + s']_T, \quad [X_3 - s'h_1]_T,$$

$$[X_4 + s'\vec{\mu}_{b'}\vec{h}_{2,3}^\top]_T, \quad [X_5 + s'\vec{\mu}_{b'}\vec{h}_{4,5}^\top]_T),$$

where $s' \in \mathbb{Z}_p$ and $\vec{\mu}_{b'} = (1, H(m_{b'}))$. If $b = b'$, then the strand $\vec{X}^*$ is valid; otherwise, it is invalid.

To restrict the manner of rerandomization further, we mask the validity checking part with a secret value $u \in \mathbb{G}_T$, and encapsulate u with another two strands (i.e., $\vec{U}$ and $\vec{V}$). The ciphertext $\zeta_{\mathsf{ID}}(m)$ now consists of following four strands.

$$\vec{X} = ([s\alpha_{\mathsf{ID}}], [s]_T, m \cdot [-sh_1]_T, [\sigma(s + z_0)\vec{\mu}\vec{h}_{2,3}^{\top}]_T, [\sigma(s + z_1)\vec{\mu}\vec{h}_{4,5}^{\top}]_T);$$
$$\vec{Y} = ([t\alpha_{\mathsf{ID}}], [t]_T, [-th_1]_T, \qquad [\sigma t\vec{\mu}\vec{h}_{2,3}^{\top}]_T, \qquad [\sigma t\vec{\mu}\vec{h}_{4,5}^{\top}]_T);$$
$$\vec{U} = ([\hat{s}\alpha_{\mathsf{ID}}], [\hat{s}]_T, u \cdot [-\hat{s}h_6]_T, [\sigma\hat{s}h_7]_T);$$
$$\vec{V} = ([\hat{t}\alpha_{\mathsf{ID}}], [\hat{t}]_T, [-\hat{t}h_6]_T, \qquad [\sigma\hat{t}h_7]_T),$$

where $\hat{s}, \hat{t} \in \mathbb{Z}_p$, $\sigma = H(u) \in \mathbb{Z}_p$, $[h_6]$ and $[h_7]$ are newly added public parameters. It is worth mentioning that $[\sigma\hat{s}h_7]_T$ and $[\sigma\hat{t}h_7]_T$ are used to obstruct any ad-hoc multiplication operations on strands $\vec{U}$ and $\vec{V}$. The random mask u shared among $\vec{X}$, $\vec{Y}$, $\vec{U}$ and $\vec{V}$ prevents adversary from obtaining valid ciphertext by mixing strands in different ciphertexts (with same underlying plaintext) or rerandomizing strand with public key. Consequently, the only way to rerandomize ciphertext $\zeta_{\mathsf{ID}}(m)$ is as follows.

$$\vec{X}' = \vec{X} + s'\vec{Y}; \quad \vec{Y}' = t'\vec{Y}; \quad \vec{U}' = \vec{U} + \hat{s}'\vec{V}; \quad \vec{V}' = \hat{t}'\vec{V},$$

where $s', t', \hat{s}', \hat{t}' \in \mathbb{Z}_p$. We remark that the current Gentry-IBE-based universal cryptosystem is ANON-ID-RCCA secure. First, the ciphertext alone does not reveal any information about underlying message m and identity ID. Second, since the manner of re-encryption is restricted and adversary $\mathcal{A}$ cannot (partially) re-encrypt the ciphertext with challenge messages and identities correctly, the decryption oracle would not leak the bits picked by challenger.

To prove the ANON-ID-RCCA security, we make negligible modifications to the simulation of security game step by step. First, the setup and extraction algorithms are modified to generate secret keys without master key. Then, the challenge ciphertext is computed using alternative encryption algorithm such that its distribution is independent of the underlying identity and plaintext. Finally, the challenger answers all the decryption queries via a time-unbounded decryption algorithm that uses public parameters and challenge ciphertext only to decrypt ciphertext. At this time, the extraction and decryption queries do not provide extra information about master key and private keys to the adversary, and challenge ciphertext perfectly hides the identity and plaintext. So the advantage of adversary is 0. More details will be given in the proof of Theorem 2.

Applications of rerandomizable ANON-ID-RCCA security. To show the usefulness of our new notion, we present an ID-based universal mixnet based on rerandomizable ANON-ID-RCCA secure IBE. The notion of universal mixnet was defined by Golle et al. [12] and has various applications such as anonymous communication and RFID tag anonymization. Roughly, a universal mix network mainly consists of a list of mix-servers which perform rerandomization and shuffle to break the linkability between incoming and outgoing messages. Universal mixnet is attractive due to its elimination of public key distribution among on-path mix-servers when sending message. In this work, based on rerandomizable ANON-ID-RCCA secure IBE, we design an ID-based universal mixnet which could be viewed as an extension of universal mix network in the identity-based setting to further eliminate the public key certificate management and to provide a more covert way of communication for end users. Also, our proposed mixnet enjoys fair anonymity where a trusted authority may upon abuse revoke the anonymity and thus gives a fair balance of privacy vs. anti-abuse measures. Compared with previous work [15], our construction satisfies stronger unlinkability where the adversary is allowed to probe the system with ciphertexts.

It is worth noting that our notion could be generally applicable to extend other Rand-RCCA-secure applications to the identity-based setting to eliminate the public-key certification management and support fair anonymity.

Other related work. The first perfect Rand-RCCA-secure scheme, where one cannot link a ciphertext to its re-encryptions, is proposed by Groth [14] under the generic group model. The ciphertext size of this scheme grows linearly with the bit-length of the plaintext. Phan and Pointcheval [22] presented an efficient framework for RCCA-secure PKE, whereas the rerandomizability of its instantiation in [21] suffers from active attacks. Then, inspired by the Cramer-Shoup encryption [7], Prabhakaran and Rosulek [23] proposed the first perfect Rand-RCCA-secure PKE in the standard model. Their scheme is universally rerandomizable—no public key is involved for ciphertext rerandomization—due to the adoption of double-strand structure by Golle et al. [12]. Chase et al. [5] designed a perfect Rand-RCCA-secure scheme satisfying public verifiability from malleable NIZKs. Libert et al. [17] improved the scheme of Chase et al., but the ciphertext size of their scheme is still large due to the usage of NIZK. Faonio et al. [10] presented a structure-preserving Rand-RCCA-secure PKE based on matrix Diffie-Hellman assumption. Their scheme does not consider universal rerandomizability and thus is more efficient than the construction by Prabhakaran and Rosulek [23]. Faonio and Fiore [9] presented an efficient Rand-RCCA-secure PKE achieving weak rerandomizability under the random oracle model. Badertscher et al. [1] found that RCCA security cannot achieve the confidentiality benchmark in the setting of constructive cryptography [18], and proposed three natural variants of RCCA security that correspond to different benchmark applications.

Recently, Wang et al. [26] proposed a generic framework for receiver-anonymous Rand-RCCA-secure PKE and solved the open problem left by [23]. In fact, although our construction is not trivially implied by their framework, our core idea could be viewed as a novel extension of their construction to the identity-based setting. It is worth noting that while our scheme only achieves computational rerandomizability, it is sufficient for some privacy-related applications.

3 Preliminaries

Let $n \in \mathbb{N}$ denote the security parameter and $\mathsf{negl}(n)$ denote the negligible function. Let $\vec{a} = (a_1, \cdots, a_n)$ be a n-tuple vector. We use $\vec{a}_{i,j}$ to denote vector $(a_i, \cdots, a_j)$ for any $i, j \in \{1, \cdots, n\}$ with $i < j$. A symmetric bilinear group is a tuple $(p, \mathbb{G}, \mathbb{G}_T, e, P)$ where $\mathbb{G}$ and $\mathbb{G}_T$ are groups of prime order p, P is a generator of $\mathbb{G}$, $e : \mathbb{G} \times \mathbb{G} \to \mathbb{G}_T$ is an efficiently computable, non-degenerate bilinear map. For clarity, we use $[a]$ to denote element aP in $\mathbb{G}$ and $[a]_T$ to denote element $e(P, P)^a$ in $\mathbb{G}_T$. Given $a, b \in \mathbb{Z}_p$, we define $[ab] := abP$ and

$$\begin{array}{l|l}
\textbf{Exp}^{\text{IR}}_{\mathcal{A},\mathcal{IBE}}(n) & \mathcal{O}_\text{D}(\text{ID}_i, \zeta_i) \\
\hline
(\text{msk}, \text{params}) \leftarrow\!\!\$ \text{Setup}(1^n); \ \mathcal{Q} := \emptyset & \text{sk}_{\text{ID}_i} \leftarrow\!\!\$ \text{Extract}(\text{msk}, \text{ID}_i) \\
(m_0, m_1, \text{ID}^*) \leftarrow \mathcal{A}^{\mathcal{O}_\text{KG}, \mathcal{O}_\text{D}}(\text{params}) & \textbf{return } \text{Dec}(\text{sk}_{\text{ID}_i}, \zeta_i) \\
\textbf{if } m_0 = m_1 \vee \text{ID}^* \in \mathcal{Q}: & \\
\quad \textbf{return } \bot & \mathcal{O}'_\text{KG}(\text{ID}_i) \\
b \leftarrow\!\!\$ \{0, 1\} & \textbf{if } \text{ID}_i = \text{ID}^*: \\
\zeta_b \leftarrow\!\!\$ \text{Enc}(\text{ID}^*, m_b) & \quad \textbf{return } \bot \\
b' \leftarrow \mathcal{A}^{\mathcal{O}'_\text{KG}, \mathcal{O}'_\text{D}}(\zeta_b) & \textbf{return } \text{Extract}(\text{msk}, \text{ID}_i) \\
\textbf{return } [b = b'] & \\
& \mathcal{O}'_\text{D}(\text{ID}_i, \zeta_i) \\
\hline
\mathcal{O}_\text{KG}(\text{ID}_i) & \text{sk}_{\text{ID}_i} \leftarrow\!\!\$ \text{Extract}(\text{msk}, \text{ID}_i) \\
\hline
\mathcal{Q} := \mathcal{Q} \cup \{\text{ID}_i\} & m := \text{Dec}(\text{sk}_{\text{ID}_i}, \zeta_i) \\
\textbf{return } \text{Extract}(\text{msk}, \text{ID}_i) & \textbf{if } m \in \{m_0, m_1\}: \\
& \quad \textbf{return replay} \\
& \textbf{return } m
\end{array}$$

Fig. 1. The ID-RCCA security game.

$[a] \cdot [b] := e([a], [b]) = [ab]_T$. Given $\vec{a} \in \mathbb{Z}_p^n$, we define $[\vec{a}] := ([a_1], \cdots, [a_n])$ and $[\vec{a}]_T := ([a_1]_T, \cdots, [a_n]_T)$.

Definition 1 (Truncated Decision Augmented Bilinear Diffie-Hellman Exponent Assumption [11]). *The truncated decision q-ABDHE assumption holds for $(\mathbb{G}, \mathbb{G}_T, e)$ if for any PPT adversary $\mathcal{A}$,*

$$\begin{vmatrix} \Pr\left[\mathcal{A}\left([\beta], [\beta\alpha^{q+2}], [1], [\alpha], \cdots, [\alpha^q], [\beta\alpha^{q+1}]_T\right) = 0\right] \\ - \Pr\left[\mathcal{A}\left([\beta], [\beta\alpha^{q+2}], [1], [\alpha], \cdots, [\alpha^q], Z\right) = 0\right] \end{vmatrix} \leq \text{negl}(n),$$

where the probability is over random generators $[1], [\beta] \leftarrow\!\!\$ \mathbb{G}$, random $\alpha \leftarrow\!\!\$ \mathbb{Z}_p$, random $Z \leftarrow\!\!\$ \mathbb{G}_T$ and the coin tosses of adversary $\mathcal{A}$. We use $\mathcal{P}_{ABDHE}$ to denote the distribution on the left and $\mathcal{R}_{ABDHE}$ to denote the distribution on the right.

4   Rerandomizable ANON-ID-RCCA IBE: Definitions and Construction

4.1   Definitions

Identity-Based Encryption (IBE). An IBE scheme $\mathcal{IBE}$ is specified by four algorithms: Setup, Extract, Enc and Dec.

- Setup takes as input 1^n where n is the security parameter and returns master key msk and system parameters params including message space $\mathcal{M}$ and ciphertext space $\mathcal{C}$.

$\mathbf{Exp}^{\mathsf{AIR}}_{\mathcal{A},\mathcal{IBE}}(n)$	$\mathcal{O}'_{\mathsf{KG}}(\mathsf{ID}_i)$
$(\mathsf{msk},\mathsf{params}) \leftarrow\!\!\$\,\mathsf{Setup}(1^n); \; \mathcal{Q} := \emptyset$	if $\mathsf{ID}_i \in \{\mathsf{ID}_0^*, \mathsf{ID}_1^*\}$:
$(m_0, m_1, \mathsf{ID}_0^*, \mathsf{ID}_1^*) \leftarrow \mathcal{A}^{\mathcal{O}_{\mathsf{KG}}, \mathcal{O}_{\mathsf{D}}}(\mathsf{params})$	$\quad$ return $\perp$
if $m_0 = m_1 \vee \{\mathsf{ID}_0^*, \mathsf{ID}_1^*\} \cap \mathcal{Q} \neq \emptyset$:	return $\mathsf{Extract}(\mathsf{msk}, \mathsf{ID}_i)$
$\quad$ return $\perp$
$\mathsf{sk}_{\mathsf{ID}_0^*} \leftarrow\!\!\$\,\mathsf{Extract}(\mathsf{msk}, \mathsf{ID}_0^*)$	$\mathcal{O}'_{\mathsf{D}}(\mathsf{ID}_i, \zeta_i)$
$\mathsf{sk}_{\mathsf{ID}_1^*} \leftarrow\!\!\$\,\mathsf{Extract}(\mathsf{msk}, \mathsf{ID}_1^*)$	if $\mathsf{ID}_i \in \{\mathsf{ID}_0^*, \mathsf{ID}_1^*\}$:
$(b, c) \leftarrow\!\!\$\,\{0, 1\}^2$	$\quad m_0^* := \mathsf{Dec}(\mathsf{sk}_{\mathsf{ID}_0^*}, \zeta_i)$
$\zeta^* \leftarrow\!\!\$\,\mathsf{Enc}(\mathsf{ID}_b^*, m_c)$	$\quad m_1^* := \mathsf{Dec}(\mathsf{sk}_{\mathsf{ID}_1^*}, \zeta_i)$
$(b', c') \leftarrow \mathcal{A}^{\mathcal{O}'_{\mathsf{KG}}, \mathcal{O}'_{\mathsf{D}}}(\zeta^*)$	$\quad$ if $m_0^* \in \{m_0, m_1\} \vee m_1^* \in \{m_0, m_1\}$:
return $[(b, c) = (b', c')]$	$\quad\quad$ return replay
	$\quad \mathsf{sk}_{\mathsf{ID}_i} \leftarrow\!\!\$\,\mathsf{Extract}(\mathsf{msk}, \mathsf{ID}_i)$
	$m := \mathsf{Dec}(\mathsf{sk}_{\mathsf{ID}_i}, \zeta_i)$
$\mathcal{O}_{\mathsf{KG}}(\mathsf{ID}_i)$	if $m \in \{m_0, m_1\}$:
	$\quad$ return replay
$\mathcal{Q} := \mathcal{Q} \cup \{\mathsf{ID}_i\}$	return m
return $\mathsf{Extract}(\mathsf{msk}, \mathsf{ID}_i)$
$\mathcal{O}_{\mathsf{D}}(\mathsf{ID}_i, \zeta_i)$
$\mathsf{sk}_{\mathsf{ID}_i} \leftarrow\!\!\$\,\mathsf{Extract}(\mathsf{msk}, \mathsf{ID}_i)$
return $\mathsf{Dec}(\mathsf{sk}_{\mathsf{ID}_i}, \zeta_i)$

Fig. 2. The ANON-ID-RCCA security game.

- Extract takes as input params, msk and arbitrary $\mathsf{ID} \in \{0, 1\}^*$, and returns a private key $\mathsf{sk}_{\mathsf{ID}}$.
- Enc takes as input params, ID and $m \in \mathcal{M}$, and returns a ciphertext $\zeta \in \mathcal{C}$.
- Dec takes as input params, $\mathsf{sk}_{\mathsf{ID}}$ and $\zeta \in \mathcal{C}$, and returns $m \in \mathcal{M}$ or $\perp$.

We omit the system parameters from the input to Extract, Enc and Dec. The scheme is *correct* if for $(\mathsf{msk}, \mathsf{params}) \leftarrow\!\!\$\,\mathsf{Setup}(1^n)$, any $m \in \mathcal{M}$, any $\mathsf{ID} \in \{0, 1\}^*$ and $\mathsf{sk}_{\mathsf{ID}} = \mathsf{Extract}(\mathsf{msk}, \mathsf{ID})$, $\Pr\left[\mathsf{Dec}(\mathsf{sk}_{\mathsf{ID}}, \mathsf{Enc}(\mathsf{ID}, m)) \neq m\right] \leq \mathsf{negl}(n)$.

Below we define a new notion named ID-RCCA security for IBE. It can be viewed as a slight relaxation of ID-CCA security.

Definition 2 (ID-RCCA Security). *Let $\mathcal{IBE} = (\mathsf{Setup}, \mathsf{Extract}, \mathsf{Enc}, \mathsf{Dec})$ be an IBE scheme. Consider the security game $\mathbf{Exp}^{\mathsf{IR}}_{\mathcal{A},\mathcal{IBE}}$ in Fig. 1, we say $\mathcal{IBE}$ is secure against replayable chosen ciphertext attacks (ID-RCCA secure) if for any PPT adversary $\mathcal{A}$,*

$$\mathbf{Adv}^{\mathsf{IR}}_{\mathcal{A},\mathcal{IBE}}(n) := \left|\Pr\left[\mathbf{Exp}^{\mathsf{IR}}_{\mathcal{A},\mathcal{IBE}}(n) = 1\right] - 1/2\right| \leq \mathsf{negl}(n).$$

We say that an IBE scheme is "anonymous" if for any PPT adversary two ciphertexts generated under different identities are computationally indis-

$$\begin{array}{ll}
\mathbf{Exp}^{\mathsf{Re}}_{\mathcal{A},\mathcal{IBE}}(n) & \mathcal{O}_\mathsf{D}(\mathsf{ID}_i, \zeta_i) \\
\hline
(\mathsf{msk}, \mathsf{params}) \leftarrow\!\!\$\, \mathsf{Setup}(1^n);\ \mathcal{Q} := \emptyset & \mathsf{sk}_{\mathsf{ID}_i} \leftarrow\!\!\$\, \mathsf{Extract}(\mathsf{msk}, \mathsf{ID}_i) \\
(\zeta^*, \mathsf{ID}^*) \leftarrow \mathcal{A}^{\mathcal{O}_\mathsf{KG}, \mathcal{O}_\mathsf{D}}(\mathsf{params}) & \mathbf{return}\ \mathsf{Dec}(\mathsf{sk}_{\mathsf{ID}_i}, \zeta_i) \\
\mathsf{sk}_{\mathsf{ID}^*} \leftarrow\!\!\$\, \mathsf{Extract}(\mathsf{msk}, \mathsf{ID}^*) & \\
m^* := \mathsf{Dec}(\mathsf{sk}_{\mathsf{ID}^*}, \zeta^*) & \mathcal{O}'_\mathsf{KG}(\mathsf{ID}_i) \\
\mathbf{if}\ \mathsf{ID}^* \in \mathcal{Q} \vee m^* = \bot: & \hline \\
\quad \mathbf{return}\ \bot & \mathbf{if}\ \mathsf{ID}_i = \mathsf{ID}^*: \\
b \leftarrow\!\!\$\, \{0,1\} & \quad \mathbf{return}\ \bot \\
\zeta_0 \leftarrow\!\!\$\, \mathsf{Enc}(\mathsf{ID}^*, m^*) & \mathbf{return}\ \mathsf{Extract}(\mathsf{msk}, \mathsf{ID}_i) \\
\zeta_1 \leftarrow\!\!\$\, \mathsf{Rerand}(\zeta^*) & \\
b' \leftarrow \mathcal{A}^{\mathcal{O}'_\mathsf{KG}, \mathcal{O}'_\mathsf{D}}(\zeta_b) & \mathcal{O}'_\mathsf{D}(\mathsf{ID}_i, \zeta_i) \\
\mathbf{return}\ [b = b'] & \hline \\
& \mathsf{sk}_{\mathsf{ID}_i} \leftarrow\!\!\$\, \mathsf{Extract}(\mathsf{msk}, \mathsf{ID}_i) \\
\mathcal{O}_\mathsf{KG}(\mathsf{ID}_i) & m := \mathsf{Dec}(\mathsf{sk}_{\mathsf{ID}_i}, \zeta_i) \\
\hline & \mathbf{if}\ m = m^*: \\
\mathcal{Q} := \mathcal{Q} \cup \{\mathsf{ID}_i\} & \quad \mathbf{return}\ \bot \\
\mathbf{return}\ \mathsf{Extract}(\mathsf{msk}, \mathsf{ID}_i) & \mathbf{return}\ m
\end{array}$$

Fig. 3. The security game of rerandomizability.

tinguishable. Formally, we incorporate the property of anonymity into game $\mathbf{Exp}^{\mathsf{IR}}_{\mathcal{A},\mathcal{IBE}}$ and obtain the game for ANON-ID-RCCA security as shown in Fig. 2.

Definition 3 (ANON-ID-RCCA Security). *Let $\mathcal{IBE} = (\mathsf{Setup}, \mathsf{Extract}, \mathsf{Enc}, \mathsf{Dec})$ be an IBE scheme. Consider the security game $\mathbf{Exp}^{\mathsf{AIR}}_{\mathcal{A},\mathcal{IBE}}$ in Fig. 2, we say $\mathcal{IBE}$ is anonymous and ID-RCCA secure (ANON-ID-RCCA secure) if for any PPT adversary $\mathcal{A}$,*

$$\mathbf{Adv}^{\mathsf{AIR}}_{\mathcal{A},\mathcal{IBE}}(n) := \left| \Pr\left[\mathbf{Exp}^{\mathsf{AIR}}_{\mathcal{A},\mathcal{IBE}}(n) = 1 \right] - 1/4 \right| \le \mathsf{negl}(n).$$

We now define rerandomizability for ID-RCCA secure IBE. In fact, it can be viewed as the weak rerandomizability by Faonio and Fiore [9] in the identity-based setting. Besides, we mainly consider "universal rerandomizability" [12,23] which essentially means that no public key is involved for rerandomization.

Definition 4 (Rerandomizability). *Let $\mathcal{IBE}$ be an ID-RCCA secure IBE, we say $\mathcal{IBE}$ is rerandomizable if following conditions are satisfied.*

- **(Correctness)** *There exists a PPT algorithm* Rerand *that takes as input ciphertext ζ and outputs a new ciphertext ζ'; and for $(\mathsf{msk}, \mathsf{params}) \leftarrow\!\!\$\, \mathsf{Setup}(1^n)$, any $\mathsf{ID} \in \{0,1\}^*$, $\mathsf{sk}_\mathsf{ID} = \mathsf{Extract}(\mathsf{msk}, \mathsf{ID})$, any ciphertext ζ,*

$$\Pr\left[\mathsf{Dec}(\mathsf{sk}_\mathsf{ID}, \zeta') \neq \mathsf{Dec}(\mathsf{sk}_\mathsf{ID}, \zeta) : \zeta' \leftarrow\!\!\$\, \mathsf{Rerand}(\zeta)\right] \le \mathsf{negl}(n);$$

Setup(1^n)	Extract(msk, ID)
$[\boldsymbol{h}] := ([h_1], \cdots, [h_7]) \leftarrow\!\$\, \mathbb{G}^7$	if ID $= \alpha$, **return** $\perp$
$\alpha, z_0, z_1 \leftarrow\!\$\, \mathbb{Z}_p$; msk $:= \alpha$	$\boldsymbol{r}_{\mathsf{ID}} := (r_{\mathsf{ID},1}, \cdots, r_{\mathsf{ID},7}) \leftarrow\!\$\, \mathbb{Z}_p^7$
params $:= ([1], [\alpha], [\boldsymbol{h}], z_0, z_1)$	$\alpha_{\mathsf{ID}} := \alpha - \mathsf{ID}$; $\boldsymbol{h}_{\mathsf{ID}} := (\boldsymbol{h} - \boldsymbol{r}_{\mathsf{ID}})/\alpha_{\mathsf{ID}}$
return (msk, params)	**return** $\mathsf{sk}_{\mathsf{ID}} := (\boldsymbol{r}_{\mathsf{ID}}, [\boldsymbol{h}_{\mathsf{ID}}])$

Enc(ID, $m \in \mathbb{G}_T$)

$s, t, \hat{s}, \hat{t} \leftarrow\!\$\, \mathbb{Z}_p$; $u \leftarrow\!\$\, \mathbb{G}_T$; $\sigma := H(u)$; $\boldsymbol{\mu} := (1, H(m))$; $(s^\dagger, s^\ddagger) := (s + z_0, s + z_1)$

$\boldsymbol{X} := ([X_1], [\boldsymbol{X}_{2,5}]_T) := ([s\alpha_{\mathsf{ID}}], [s]_T, m \cdot [-sh_1]_T, [\sigma s^\dagger \boldsymbol{\mu} \boldsymbol{h}_{2,3}^\top]_T, [\sigma s^\ddagger \boldsymbol{\mu} \boldsymbol{h}_{4,5}^\top]_T)$

$\boldsymbol{Y} := ([Y_1], [\boldsymbol{Y}_{2,5}]_T) := ([t\alpha_{\mathsf{ID}}], [t]_T, [-th_1]_T, [\sigma t \boldsymbol{\mu} \boldsymbol{h}_{2,3}^\top]_T, [\sigma t \boldsymbol{\mu} \boldsymbol{h}_{4,5}^\top]_T)$

$\boldsymbol{U} := ([U_1], [\boldsymbol{U}_{2,4}]_T) := ([\hat{s}\alpha_{\mathsf{ID}}], [\hat{s}]_T, u \cdot [-\hat{s}h_6]_T, [\sigma \hat{s} h_7]_T)$

$\boldsymbol{V} := ([V_1], [\boldsymbol{V}_{2,4}]_T) := ([\hat{t}\alpha_{\mathsf{ID}}], [\hat{t}]_T, [-\hat{t}h_6]_T, [\sigma \hat{t} h_7]_T)$; **return** $\zeta := (\boldsymbol{X}, \boldsymbol{Y}, \boldsymbol{U}, \boldsymbol{V})$

Dec($\mathsf{sk}_{\mathsf{ID}}, \zeta$)

$\boldsymbol{K} := (\boldsymbol{h}_{\mathsf{ID}}^\top, \boldsymbol{r}_{\mathsf{ID}}^\top)^\top$; $\boldsymbol{X}_{1,2}^\dagger := \boldsymbol{X}_{1,2} + (z_0\alpha_{\mathsf{ID}}, z_0)$; $\boldsymbol{X}_{1,2}^\ddagger := \boldsymbol{X}_{1,2} + (z_1\alpha_{\mathsf{ID}}, z_1)$

$m := [X_3 + \boldsymbol{X}_{1,2}\boldsymbol{K}_1]_T$; $u := [U_3 + \boldsymbol{U}_{1,2}\boldsymbol{K}_6]_T$; $\mu := H(m)$; $\boldsymbol{\mu} := (1, \mu)$; $\sigma := H(u)$

$[\boldsymbol{V}_{3,4}']_T := ([-\boldsymbol{V}_{1,2}\boldsymbol{K}_6]_T, [\sigma \boldsymbol{V}_{1,2}\boldsymbol{K}_7]_T)$; $[U_4']_T := [\sigma \boldsymbol{U}_{1,2}\boldsymbol{K}_7]_T$

if $([\boldsymbol{V}_{3,4}']_T, [U_4']_T) \neq ([\boldsymbol{V}_{3,4}]_T, [U_4]_T)$, **return** $\perp$

$[\boldsymbol{X}_{4,5}']_T := ([\sigma \boldsymbol{X}_{1,2}^\dagger \boldsymbol{K}_{2,3} \boldsymbol{\mu}^\top]_T, [\sigma \boldsymbol{X}_{1,2}^\ddagger \boldsymbol{K}_{4,5} \boldsymbol{\mu}^\top]_T)$

$[\boldsymbol{Y}_{4,5}']_T := ([\sigma \boldsymbol{Y}_{1,2}\boldsymbol{K}_{2,3} \boldsymbol{\mu}^\top]_T, [\sigma \boldsymbol{Y}_{1,2}\boldsymbol{K}_{4,5} \boldsymbol{\mu}^\top]_T)$; $[Y_3']_T := [-\boldsymbol{Y}_{1,2}\boldsymbol{K}_1]_T$

if $([\boldsymbol{X}_{4,5}']_T, [\boldsymbol{Y}_{4,5}']_T, [Y_3']_T) \neq ([\boldsymbol{X}_{4,5}]_T, [\boldsymbol{Y}_{4,5}]_T, [Y_3]_T)$, **return** $\perp$; **else** , **return** m

Rerand(ζ)

$s', t', \hat{s}', \hat{t}' \leftarrow\!\$\, \mathbb{Z}_p$

$\boldsymbol{X}' := ([X_1 + s'Y_1], [\boldsymbol{X}_{2,5} + s'\boldsymbol{Y}_{2,5}]_T)$; $\boldsymbol{Y}' := ([t'Y_1], [t'\boldsymbol{Y}_{2,5}]_T)$

$\boldsymbol{U}' := ([U_1 + \hat{s}'V_1], [\boldsymbol{U}_{2,4} + \hat{s}'\boldsymbol{V}_{2,4}]_T)$; $\boldsymbol{V}' := ([\hat{t}'V_1], [\hat{t}'\boldsymbol{V}_{2,4}]_T)$

return $\zeta' := (\boldsymbol{X}', \boldsymbol{Y}', \boldsymbol{U}', \boldsymbol{V}')$

Fig. 4. Our rerandomizable ANON-ID-RCCA secure IBE scheme.

- **(Indistinguishability)** *For any PPT adversary $\mathcal{A}$ in Fig. 3,*

$$\mathbf{Adv}_{\mathcal{A},\mathcal{IBE}}^{\mathsf{Re}}(n) := \left| \Pr\left[\mathbf{Exp}_{\mathcal{A},\mathcal{IBE}}^{\mathsf{Re}}(n) = 1 \right] - 1/2 \right| \leq \mathsf{negl}(n);$$

- **(Tightness of Decryption)** *For* (msk, params) $\leftarrow\!\$\,$ Setup(1^n), *any* ID $\in \{0,1\}^*$, $\mathsf{sk}_{\mathsf{ID}} = $ Extract(msk, ID) *and any (possibly unbounded) adversary $\mathcal{A}$,*

$$\Pr\left[m \neq \perp \wedge \zeta \notin \mathsf{Enc}(\mathsf{ID}, m) : \begin{matrix} \zeta \leftarrow \mathcal{A}(\mathsf{params}, \mathsf{ID}) \\ m := \mathsf{Dec}(\mathsf{sk}_{\mathsf{ID}}, \zeta) \end{matrix} \right] \leq \mathsf{negl}(n),$$

where $\zeta \notin$ Enc(ID, m) means ζ is not in the range of Enc(ID, m).

4.2 Our Proposed Scheme

We are now ready to describe our full scheme with security analysis. Let $(p, \mathbb{G}, \mathbb{G}_T, e, P)$ denote a symmetric bilinear group and $H : \mathbb{G}_T \to \mathbb{Z}_p$ be a collision-resistant hash function. Our rerandomizable ANON-ID-RCCA secure IBE scheme $\mathcal{IBE}$ is shown in Fig. 4. Below we analyse the correctness and security of our proposed scheme.

Theorem 1 (Decryption Correctness). *For* $(\mathsf{msk}, \mathsf{params}) \leftarrow_\$ \mathsf{Setup}(1^n)$, *any identity* $\mathsf{ID} \in \mathbb{Z}_p$ *and private key* $\mathsf{sk_{ID}} = \mathsf{Extract}(\mathsf{msk}, \mathsf{ID})$, *any* $m \in \mathcal{M}$, *we have*

$$\Pr\left[\mathsf{Dec}(\mathsf{sk_{ID}}, \mathsf{Enc}(\mathsf{ID}, m)) \neq m\right] \leq \mathsf{negl}(n).$$

Proof. Assume that $\zeta = (\vec{X}, \vec{Y}, \vec{U}, \vec{V}) = \mathsf{Enc}(\mathsf{ID}, m)$. We consider the retrieval of plaintext m. That is, $[X_3 + \vec{X}_{1,2}\vec{K}_1]_T = [X_3 + s\alpha_{\mathsf{ID}}h_{\mathsf{ID},1} + sr_{\mathsf{ID},1}]_T = [X_3]_T \cdot [s(h_1 - r_{\mathsf{ID},1}) + sr_{\mathsf{ID},1}]_T = m$. Similarly, we have $[\dot{U}_3 + \vec{U}_{1,2}\vec{K}_6]_T = u$. As for the validity checking part, we take $[\vec{X}_{4,5}]_T$ for example.

$$
\begin{aligned}
&([\sigma \vec{X}_{1,2}^\dagger \vec{K}_{2,3}\vec{\mu}^\top]_T, [\sigma \vec{X}_{1,2}^\ddagger \vec{K}_{4,5}\vec{\mu}^\top]_T) \\
&= ([\sigma((s + z_0)\alpha_{\mathsf{ID}}(h_{\mathsf{ID},2} + \mu h_{\mathsf{ID},3}) + (s + z_0)(r_{\mathsf{ID},2} + \mu r_{\mathsf{ID},3}))]_T, \\
&\quad [\sigma((s + z_1)\alpha_{\mathsf{ID}}(h_{\mathsf{ID},4} + \mu h_{\mathsf{ID},5}) + (s + z_1)(r_{\mathsf{ID},4} + \mu r_{\mathsf{ID},5}))]_T) \\
&= ([\sigma(s + z_0)(h_2 + \mu h_3)]_T, [\sigma(s + z_1)(h_4 + \mu h_5)]_T) \\
&= ([\sigma s^\dagger \vec{\mu} \vec{h}_{2,3}^\top], [\sigma s^\ddagger \vec{\mu} \vec{h}_{4,5}^\top]) = [\vec{X}_{4,5}]_T.
\end{aligned}
$$

One also can verify that checks on $[\vec{Y}_{4,5}]_T$, $[\vec{V}_{3,4}]_T$, $[Y_3]_T$, $[U_4]_T$ are valid. ∎

Theorem 2 (ANON-ID-RCCA Security). *Let* q_{ID} *be the times of extraction queries and* $q = q_{\mathsf{ID}} + 2$. *Assume that the truncated decision q-ABDHE assumption holds for* $(\mathbb{G}, \mathbb{G}_T, e)$. *The proposed* $\mathcal{IBE}$ *is ANON-ID-RCCA secure.*

Proof. We prove the ANON-ID-RCCA security of scheme $\mathcal{IBE}$ by constructing a serial of games G_0-G_4 and demonstrating the indistinguishability between them.

Game G_0: This is game $\mathbf{Exp}^{\mathsf{AIR}}_{\mathcal{A}, \mathcal{IBE}}$. Let S_i denote the event that $(b, c) = (b', c')$ in game G_i, we have $\mathbf{Adv}^{\mathsf{AIR}}_{\mathcal{A}, \mathcal{IBE}}(n) = |\Pr[S_0] - 1/4|$. We describe the modifications in each game G_1-G_4 as below.

Game G_1: This game is the same as G_0 except that the challenger runs AltSetup and AltExtract in Fig. 5 to generate system parameters and private key for adversary. Note that params is derived from tuple $\mathcal{G} = ([\beta], [\beta\alpha^{q+2}], [1], [\alpha], \cdots, [\alpha^q], Z)$ sampled from $\mathcal{R}_{ABDHE}$, which enables the challenger to compute the private keys without master key α. Particularly, $f_i(x)$ is a polynomial of degree q and $F_{\mathsf{ID},i}(x) = (f_i(x) - f_i(\mathsf{ID}))/(x - \mathsf{ID})$ is a $(q-1)$-degree polynomial. The values of $[f_i(\alpha)]$ and $[F_{\mathsf{ID},i}(\alpha)]$ could be derived from $[1], [\alpha], \cdots, [\alpha^q]$. The private key generated from AltExtract is valid, as $[h_{\mathsf{ID},i}] = [(f_i(\alpha) - f_i(\mathsf{ID}))/(\alpha - \mathsf{ID})] = [(h_i - r_{\mathsf{ID},i})/(\alpha - \mathsf{ID})]$.

Since tuple $\mathcal{G}$, randomness z_0, z_1 and polynomial $f_i(x)$ are uniformly picked at random, the distribution of params is identical to that in game G_0. Let $\mathcal{Q}$

AltSetup($1^n, \mathcal{G}$)	AltExtract(ID, $\mathcal{G}$)
$z_0, z_1 \leftarrow\!\!\$\ \mathbb{Z}_p$	**if** ID $= [\alpha]$, **return** $\perp$
$\vec{f}(x) \leftarrow\!\!\$\ (\mathbb{Z}_p[x])^7;\ [\vec{h}] := [\vec{f}(\alpha)]$	$\vec{r}_{\text{ID}} := \vec{f}(\text{ID});\ [\vec{h}_{\text{ID}}] := [\vec{F}_{\text{ID}}(\alpha)]$
params $:= ([1], [\alpha], [\vec{h}], z_0, z_1)$	$\text{sk}_{\text{ID}} := (\vec{r}_{\text{ID}}, [\vec{h}_{\text{ID}}])$
return params	**return** sk_{ID}

Fig. 5. Alternative setup algorithm AltSetup and extraction algorithm AltExtract.

denote all the identities queried by $\mathcal{A}$ and $\mathcal{I} = \{\alpha, \text{ID}_b\} \cup \mathcal{Q}$. Since $f_i(x)$ is a uniformly random q-degree polynomial and $|\mathcal{I}| = q$, the values in $\{f_i(a)\}_{a \in \mathcal{I}}$ are uniformly random and independent in $\mathcal{A}$'s view. Thus, the distribution of private keys generated from AltExtract is identical to that in game G_0. Besides, $[\text{ID}] = [\alpha]$ if and only if $\text{ID} = \alpha$. So, game G_1 is actually identical to G_0.

We call a ciphertext ζ under identity ID bad if 1) it cannot pass the validity check of Dec or 2) ID $\notin \mathcal{Q}$ and at least one tuple in $\{([X_1], [X_2]_T), ([Y_1], [Y_2]_T), ([U_1], [U_2]_T), ([V_1], [V_2]_T)\}$ is randomly sampled from $\mathbb{G} \times \mathbb{G}_T$ unless ζ is a rerandomization of challenge ciphertext ζ^*.

Lemma 1. *The decryption oracles $\mathcal{O}_D$ and $\mathcal{O}'_D$ in game G_1 reject all the bad ciphertexts except with negligible probability.*

Proof. Querying a valid ciphertext generated using Enc under identity ID or generated with sk_{ID} does not reveal more information about master key α. Let ζ be the first bad ciphertext queried by the adversary.

If $([X_1], [X_2]_T), ([Y_1], [Y_2]_T), ([U_1], [U_2]_T)$ or $([V_1], [V_2]_T)$ is randomly sampled from $\mathbb{G} \times \mathbb{G}_T$ and underlying ID $\notin \mathcal{Q}$, we assume that $([X_1], [X_2]_T) \leftarrow\!\!\$\ \mathbb{G} \times \mathbb{G}_T$. The probability of $X_1 = \alpha_{\text{ID}} X_2$ is negligible. Recall that $h_{\text{ID},1} = (h_1 - r_{\text{ID},1})/\alpha_{\text{ID}}$, then $[\vec{X}_{1,2}\vec{K}_1]_T = [(X_1/\alpha_{\text{ID}})h_1 + (X_2 - X_1/\alpha_{\text{ID}})r_{\text{ID},1}]_T$. Since $f_1(x)$ is a q-degree polynomial, $r_{\text{ID},1} = f_1(\text{ID})$ is uniformly random in $\mathcal{A}$'s view. Thus, $[\vec{X}_{1,2}\vec{K}_1]_T$ is uniformly distributed in $\mathcal{A}$'s view. Similarly, $[\vec{Y}_{1,2}\vec{K}_1]_T$ (resp. $[\vec{U}_{1,2}\vec{K}_6]_T$, $[\vec{V}_{1,2}\vec{K}_6]_T$) is also uniformly random in $\mathcal{A}$'s view when $([Y_1], [Y_2]_T)$ (resp. $([U_1], [U_2]_T)$, $([V_1], [V_2]_T)$) is randomly sampled from $\mathbb{G} \times \mathbb{G}_T$. In this case, the probability that ciphertext ζ is valid is negligible.

If ζ cannot pass the validity check of Dec, the oracles reject it, which rules out one possible value of master key α. Note that the number of decryption query is polynomial, while the size of master key space is superpolynomial, the probability of generating a valid bad ciphertext is negligible.

Game G_2: This game is the same as G_1 except that challenge ciphertext ζ^* is generated by alternative encryption algorithm AltEnc as shown in Fig. 6. Comparing to Enc, algorithm AltEnc picks random elements from $\mathbb{G} \times \mathbb{G}_T$ for $([X_1], [X_2]_T), ([Y_1], [Y_2]_T), ([U_1], [U_2]_T)$ and $([V_1], [V_2]_T)$, and uses private key sk_{ID} to compute corresponding values.

$$\begin{array}{l}
\hline
\mathsf{AltEnc}(\mathsf{ID}, \mathsf{sk}_{\mathsf{ID}}, m \in \mathbb{G}_T) \\
\hline
([X_1], [X_2]_T), ([Y_1], [Y_2]_T), ([U_1], [U_2]_T), ([V_1], [V_2]_T) \leftarrow\!\$\, \mathbb{G} \times \mathbb{G}_T \\
u \leftarrow\!\$\, \mathbb{G}_T; \ \mu := H(m); \ \boldsymbol{\mu} := (1, \mu); \ \sigma := H(u) \\
\boldsymbol{X} := ([X_1], [X_2]_T, m \cdot [-\boldsymbol{X}_{1,2}\boldsymbol{K}_1]_T, [\sigma \boldsymbol{X}_{1,2}^{\ddagger} \boldsymbol{K}_{2,3}\boldsymbol{\mu}^{\top}]_T, [\sigma \boldsymbol{X}_{1,2}^{\ddagger} \boldsymbol{K}_{4,5}\boldsymbol{\mu}^{\top}]_T) \\
\boldsymbol{Y} := ([Y_1], [Y_2]_T, [-\boldsymbol{Y}_{1,2}\boldsymbol{K}_1]_T, [\sigma \boldsymbol{Y}_{1,2}\boldsymbol{K}_{2,3}\boldsymbol{\mu}^{\top}]_T, [\sigma \boldsymbol{Y}_{1,2}\boldsymbol{K}_{4,5}\boldsymbol{\mu}^{\top}]) \\
\boldsymbol{U} := ([U_1], [U_2]_T, u \cdot [-\boldsymbol{U}_{1,2}\boldsymbol{K}_6]_T, [\sigma \boldsymbol{U}_{1,2}\boldsymbol{K}_7]_T) \\
\boldsymbol{V} := ([V_1], [V_2]_T, [-\boldsymbol{V}_{1,2}\boldsymbol{K}_6]_T, [\sigma \boldsymbol{V}_{1,2}\boldsymbol{K}_7]_T); \ \textbf{return } \zeta := (\boldsymbol{X}, \boldsymbol{Y}, \boldsymbol{U}, \boldsymbol{V}) \\
\hline
\end{array}$$

Fig. 6. Alternative encryption algorithm AltEnc.

Lemma 2. *Games* G_1 *and* G_2 *are computationally indistinguishable if truncated decision q-ABDHE assumption holds for* $(\mathbb{G}, \mathbb{G}_T, e)$.

Proof. Let $\mathsf{G}_{1,0}$ denote the game that generates challenge ciphertext ζ^* using private key $\mathsf{sk}_{\mathsf{ID}_b^*}$. Game $\mathsf{G}_{1,1}$ is the same as $\mathsf{G}_{1,0}$ except that $([X_1^*], [X_2^*]_T)$ in ζ^* is randomly sampled from $\mathbb{G} \times \mathbb{G}_T$. Game $\mathsf{G}_{1,2}$ is the same as $\mathsf{G}_{1,1}$ except that $([Y_1^*], [Y_2^*]_T)$ is randomly sampled. Game $\mathsf{G}_{1,3}$ is the same as $\mathsf{G}_{1,2}$ except that $([U_1^*], [U_2^*]_T)$ is randomly sampled. Game $\mathsf{G}_{1,4}$ is the same as $\mathsf{G}_{1,3}$ except that $([V_1^*], [V_2^*]_T)$ is randomly sampled. Obviously, game $\mathsf{G}_{1,0}$ is identical to G_1 by the decryption correctness, and game $\mathsf{G}_{1,4}$ is identical to G_2.

Next, we prove that game $\mathsf{G}_{1,0}$ is computationally indistinguishable from $\mathsf{G}_{1,1}$. Consider a random instance $([\beta], [\beta\alpha^{q+2}], [1], [\alpha], \cdots, [\alpha^q], Z)$ of truncated decision q-ABDHE assumption. The challenger simulates the Setup phase, decryption and extraction oracles as in game $\mathsf{G}_{1,0}$. In Challenge phase, only the computation of $[X_1^*]$ and $[X_2^*]_T$ in ζ^* is different from that in $\mathsf{G}_{1,0}$. Specifically, let $f'(x) = x^{q+2}$ and $F'_{\mathsf{ID}_b^*}(x) = (f'(x) - f'(\mathsf{ID}_b^*))/(x - \mathsf{ID}_b^*)$, the challenger sets

$$[X_1^*] = [\beta(f'(\alpha) - f'(\mathsf{ID}_b^*))] \qquad [X_2^*]_T = Z \cdot \left[\beta \sum_{i=0}^{q} F'_{\mathsf{ID}_b^*, i} \alpha^i\right]_T$$

where $F'_{\mathsf{ID}_b^*, i}$ is the coefficient of x^i in $F'_{\mathsf{ID}_b^*}(x)$. Let $s = \beta F'_{\mathsf{ID}_b^*}(\alpha)$, we have $[X_1^*] = [s(\alpha - \mathsf{ID}_b^*)]$. Since β is uniformly distributed over $\mathbb{Z}_p$, s and $[X_1^*]$ are uniformly distributed over $\mathbb{Z}_p$ and $\mathbb{G}$ respectively. If $Z = [\beta\alpha^{q+1}]_T$, then $[X_2^*]_T = [s]_T$. The simulation is actually game $\mathsf{G}_{1,0}$. If Z is a random element uniformly sampled from $\mathbb{G}_T$, $[X_2^*]_T$ is uniformly distributed over $\mathbb{G}_T$. The simulation is game $\mathsf{G}_{1,1}$. Then, the indistinguishability between game $\mathsf{G}_{1,0}$ and $\mathsf{G}_{1,1}$ is reduced to the hardness of truncated decision q-ABDHE problem. Similarly, game $\mathsf{G}_{1,1}$(resp. $\mathsf{G}_{1,2}, \mathsf{G}_{1,3}$) is computationally indistinguishable from $\mathsf{G}_{1,2}$(resp. $\mathsf{G}_{1,3}, \mathsf{G}_{1,4}$). Finally, game G_1 is computationally indistinguishable from G_2.   □

Lemma 3. *Given system parameters* params *and set of private keys* $\{\mathsf{sk}_{\mathsf{ID}_i}\}_{\mathsf{ID}_i \in \mathcal{Q}}$ *in game* G_2, *for* $([X_1], [X_2]_T), ([Y_1], [Y_2]_T) \leftarrow\!\$\, \mathbb{G} \times \mathbb{G}_T$, *any* $\mathsf{ID} \notin \mathcal{Q}$, *any* $\mu, \sigma \in \mathbb{Z}_p$ *and any PPT adversary* $\mathcal{A}$, $([\vec{X}_{1,2}\vec{K}_1]_T, [\vec{Y}_{1,2}\vec{K}_1]_T)$ *and* $([\vec{X}_{4,5}]_T, [\vec{Y}_{4,5}]_T)$ *in algorithm* AltEnc *are uniformly distributed in* $\mathcal{A}$'s *view*.

Proof. Recall that $h_{\mathsf{ID},1} = (h_1 - r_{\mathsf{ID},1})/\alpha_{\mathsf{ID}}$, then we rewrite $[\vec{X}_{1,2}\vec{K}_1]_T$ and $[\vec{Y}_{1,2}\vec{K}_1]_T$ as follows.

$$[\vec{X}_{1,2}\vec{K}_1]_T = [(X_1/\alpha_{\mathsf{ID}})h_1 + (X_2 - X_1/\alpha_{\mathsf{ID}})r_{\mathsf{ID},1}]_T$$
$$[\vec{Y}_{1,2}\vec{K}_1]_T = [(Y_1/\alpha_{\mathsf{ID}})h_1 + (Y_2 - Y_1/\alpha_{\mathsf{ID}})r_{\mathsf{ID},1}]_T$$

Since $f_1(x)$ is a q-degree polynomial and $|\{\alpha, \mathsf{ID}\} \cup \mathcal{Q}| = q$, then $r_{\mathsf{ID},1} = f_1(\mathsf{ID})$ is uniformly random in $\mathcal{A}$'s view. Thus, $([\vec{X}_{1,2}\vec{K}_1]_T, [\vec{Y}_{1,2}\vec{K}_1]_T)$ is uniformly distributed in $\mathcal{A}$'s view.

Let $\bar{\Theta} = \Theta_1/\alpha_{\mathsf{ID}}$, $\bar{\Theta}^\dagger = \bar{\Theta}_1 + z_0$, $\bar{\Theta}^\ddagger = \bar{\Theta}_1 + z_1$, $\hat{\Theta} = \Theta_2 - \bar{\Theta}_1$ for $\Theta \in \{X, Y\}$ and $\vec{\mu} = (1, \mu)$. We rewrite $[\vec{X}_{4,5}]_T$ and $[\vec{Y}_{4,5}]_T$ as follows.

$$[\vec{X}_{4,5}]_T = ([\sigma\bar{X}^\dagger\vec{\mu}\vec{h}_{2,3}^\top + \sigma\hat{X}\vec{\mu}\vec{r}_{\mathsf{ID},2,3}^\top]_T, [\sigma\bar{X}^\ddagger\vec{\mu}\vec{h}_{4,5}^\top + \sigma\hat{X}\vec{\mu}\vec{r}_{\mathsf{ID},4,5}^\top]_T)$$
$$[\vec{Y}_{4,5}]_T = ([\sigma\bar{Y}\vec{\mu}\vec{h}_{2,3}^\top + \sigma\hat{Y}\vec{\mu}\vec{r}_{\mathsf{ID},2,3}^\top]_T, [\sigma\bar{Y}\vec{\mu}\vec{h}_{4,5}^\top + \sigma\hat{Y}\vec{\mu}\vec{r}_{\mathsf{ID},4,5}^\top]_T)$$

Consider that $\vec{\mu}\vec{r}_{\mathsf{ID},2,3}^\top = \vec{\mu}\vec{f}_{2,3}^\top(\mathsf{ID})$, $\vec{\mu}\vec{r}_{\mathsf{ID},4,5}^\top = \vec{\mu}\vec{f}_{4,5}^\top(\mathsf{ID})$ and $\mathcal{A}$ knows $[\vec{h}_{2,5}] = [\vec{f}_{2,5}(\alpha)]$ and $\{[\vec{f}_{2,5}(\mathsf{ID}_i)]\}_{\mathsf{ID}_i \in \mathcal{Q}}$, we represent these values as matrix product.

$$[\vec{c}_2\ \vec{c}_3\ \vec{c}_4\ \vec{c}_5] \underbrace{\begin{bmatrix} \mathbf{V} & 0 & 0 & 0 & \vec{\gamma}_{\mathsf{ID}} & 0 \\ 0 & \mathbf{V} & 0 & 0 & \mu\vec{\gamma}_{\mathsf{ID}} & 0 \\ 0 & 0 & \mathbf{V} & 0 & 0 & \vec{\gamma}_{\mathsf{ID}} \\ 0 & 0 & 0 & \mathbf{V} & 0 & \mu\vec{\gamma}_{\mathsf{ID}} \end{bmatrix}}_{:=\mathbf{P}},$$

where $\mathbf{V} = [\vec{\gamma}_{\mathsf{ID}_1}\ \vec{\gamma}_{\mathsf{ID}_2}\ \cdots\ \vec{\gamma}_{\mathsf{ID}_{q-2}}\ \vec{\gamma}_\alpha]$, $\vec{\gamma}_x = (1, x, \cdots, x^q)^\top$ for $x \in \mathcal{Q} \cup \{\alpha, \mathsf{ID}\}$, $\vec{c}_i = (c_{i,0}, c_{i,1}, \cdots, c_{i,q})$ and $c_{i,j}$ is the coefficient of x^j in $f_i(x)$. Note that matrix $\mathbf{P}$ contains four $(q+1)\times(q-1)$ Vandermonde matrices whose columns are linearly independent. Since $\mathsf{ID} \notin \mathcal{Q} \cup \{\alpha\}$, $\vec{\gamma}_{\mathsf{ID}}$ is linearly independent of columns in $\mathbf{V}$. The columns of $\mathbf{P}$ are linearly independent. Thus, $([\vec{X}_{4,5}]_T, [\vec{Y}_{4,5}]_T)$ is uniformly distributed over $\mathbb{G}_T^2$ in $\mathcal{A}$'s view, as $\vec{\mu}\vec{r}_{\mathsf{ID},2,3}^\top$ and $\vec{\mu}\vec{r}_{\mathsf{ID},4,5}^\top$ are uniformly distributed in $\mathcal{A}$'s view. $\qquad\square$

Lemma 4. *If the decryption oracles in game* G_2 *reject all the bad ciphertexts except with negligible probability, given system parameters* params *and set of private keys* $\{\mathsf{sk}_{\mathsf{ID}_i}\}_{\mathsf{ID}_i \in \mathcal{Q}}$, *challenge ciphertext* ζ^* *in game* G_2 *is distributed independently of* ID_b^*, m_c *and* u.

Proof. Since $([X_1^*], [X_2^*]_T), ([Y_1^*], [Y_2^*]_T), ([U_1^*], [U_2^*]_T)$ and $([V_1^*], [V_2^*]_T)$ are uniformly sampled from $\mathbb{G} \times \mathbb{G}_T$, by Lemma 3, $([X_3^*]_T/m_c, [Y_3^*]_T), ([U_3^*]_T/u, [V_3^*]_T), ([\vec{X}_{4,5}^*]_T, [\vec{Y}_{4,5}^*]_T)$ and $([U_4^*]_T, [V_4^*]_T)$ are uniformly distributed over appropriate domains in $\mathcal{A}$'s view, from which the lemma follows. $\qquad\square$

Game G_3: This game is the same as G_2 except that the challenger handles all the decryption queries with alternative decryption algorithm AltDec, as shown in Fig. 7, that only uses system parameters params, identity ID, challenge ciphertext $\zeta^* = (\vec{X}^*, \vec{Y}^*, \vec{U}^*, \vec{V}^*)$ and underlying identity ID_b^* to decrypt ciphertext. We now prove that G_2 and G_3 are statistically indistinguishable. In this case, AltDec in game G_3 is allowed to run in unbounded time, which is also the reason why AltDec could decrypt ciphertext with params, ID, ID_b^* and ζ^*.

Alternative Decryption Algorithm AltDec(ID, ζ, ID$_b^*$, ζ^*)

(i) Check that there exist $\hat{s}, \hat{t} \in \mathbb{Z}_p$ such that $[U_2]_T = [\hat{s}]_T$, $[V_2] = [\hat{t}]_T$, $[U_1] = [\hat{s}\alpha_{\mathsf{ID}}]$ and $[V_1] = [\hat{t}\alpha_{\mathsf{ID}}]$. If not, go to (ii). Otherwise, compute $u = [U_3 + \hat{s}h_6]_T$, $\sigma = H(u)$ and check that $[V_{3,4}]_T = ([-\hat{t}h_6]_T, [\sigma\hat{t}h_7]_T)$ and $[U_4]_T = [\sigma\hat{s}h_7]_T$ holds. If not, output $\perp$. Otherwise, check that there exist plaintext m, randomness $s, t \in \mathbb{Z}_p$ such that

$$X = ([s\alpha_{\mathsf{ID}}], [s]_T, m \cdot [-sh_1]_T, [\sigma s^\dagger \boldsymbol{\mu} h_{2,3}^\top]_T, [\sigma s^\ddagger \boldsymbol{\mu} h_{4,5}^\top]_T)$$
$$Y = ([t\alpha_{\mathsf{ID}}], [t]_T, [-th_1]_T, [\sigma t \boldsymbol{\mu} h_{2,3}^\top]_T, [\sigma t \boldsymbol{\mu} h_{4,5}^\top]_T),$$

where $\boldsymbol{\mu} = (1, H(m))$. If not, output $\perp$. If $m \notin \{m_0, m_1\}$, output m; otherwise output replay.

(ii) If AltDec is called in Phase 1, output $\perp$. Otherwise, check that there exist $\hat{s}', \hat{t}', s', t' \in \mathbb{Z}_p$ such that

$$U = ([U_1^* + \hat{s}'V_1^*], [U_{2,4}^* + \hat{s}'V_{2,4}^*]_T); \quad V = ([\hat{t}'V_1^*], [\hat{t}'V_{2,4}^*]_T)$$
$$X = ([X_1^* + s'Y_1^*], [X_{2,5}^* + s'Y_{2,5}^*]_T); \quad Y = ([t'Y_1^*], [t'Y_{2,5}^*]_T).$$

If not, output $\perp$. Otherwise, check that ID $=$ ID$_b^*$. If not, output $\perp$; otherwise, output replay.

Fig. 7. The alternative decryption algorithm AltDec.

Lemma 5. *Given system parameters* params, *set of private keys* $\{\mathsf{sk}_{\mathsf{ID}_i}\}_{\mathsf{ID}_i \in \mathcal{Q}}$, $([X_1^*], [X_2^*]_T), ([Y_1^*], [Y_2^*]_T) \in \mathbb{G} \times \mathbb{G}_T$ *and* $[\vec{X}_{4,5}^*]_T$, $[\vec{Y}_{4,5}^*]_T$ *with* $\mathsf{ID}^* \notin \mathcal{Q}$ *and* $\mu^*, \sigma^* \in \mathbb{Z}_p$ *in game* G_3, *for any* $([X_1], [X_2]_T) \in \mathbb{G} \times \mathbb{G}_T$, *any* $\mu, \sigma \in \mathbb{Z}_p$ *with* $([X_1], [X_2]_T) \notin \{([X_1^* + s'Y_1^*], [X_2^* + s'Y_2^*]_T)\}_{s' \in \mathbb{Z}_p}$, $\mu \neq \mu^*$ *or* $\sigma \notin \{\sigma'\sigma^*\}_{\sigma' \in \mathbb{Z}_p}$ *and any PPT adversary* $\mathcal{A}$, $[\vec{X}_{4,5}]_T$ *with* ID^*, μ *and* σ *is uniformly distributed in* $\mathcal{A}$*'s view with overwhelming probability.*

Proof. Let $\bar{\Theta} = \Theta_1/\alpha_{\mathsf{ID}^*}$, $\bar{\Theta}^\dagger = \bar{\Theta}_1 + z_0$, $\bar{\Theta}^\ddagger = \bar{\Theta}_1 + z_1$ and $\hat{\Theta} = \Theta_2 - \bar{\Theta}_1$ for $\Theta \in \{X^*, Y^*, X\}$. We rewrite $[\vec{X}_{4,5}^*]_T$, $[\vec{Y}_{4,5}^*]_T$ and $[\vec{X}_{4,5}]_T$ as follows.

$$[\vec{X}_{4,5}^*]_T = ([\sigma^*(\bar{X}^*)^\dagger \vec{\mu}^* \vec{h}_{2,3}^\top + \sigma^* \hat{X}^* \vec{\mu}^* \vec{r}_{\mathsf{ID}^*,2,3}^\top]_T, [\sigma^*(\bar{X}^*)^\ddagger \vec{\mu}^* \vec{h}_{4,5}^\top + \sigma^* \hat{X}^* \vec{\mu}^* \vec{r}_{\mathsf{ID}^*,4,5}^\top]_T)$$
$$[\vec{Y}_{4,5}^*]_T = ([\sigma^* \bar{Y}^* \vec{\mu}^* \vec{h}_{2,3}^\top + \sigma^* \hat{Y}^* \vec{\mu}^* \vec{r}_{\mathsf{ID}^*,2,3}^\top]_T, [\sigma^* \bar{Y}^* \vec{\mu}^* \vec{h}_{4,5}^\top + \sigma^* \hat{Y}^* \vec{\mu}^* \vec{r}_{\mathsf{ID}^*,4,5}^\top]_T)$$
$$[\vec{X}_{4,5}]_T = ([\sigma \bar{X}^\dagger \vec{\mu} \vec{h}_{2,3}^\top + \sigma \hat{X} \vec{\mu} \vec{r}_{\mathsf{ID}^*,2,3}^\top]_T, [\sigma \bar{X}^\ddagger \vec{\mu} \vec{h}_{4,5}^\top + \sigma \hat{X} \vec{\mu} \vec{r}_{\mathsf{ID}^*,4,5}^\top]_T$$

Besides, $\mathcal{A}$ also knows $[\vec{h}_{2,5}] = [\vec{f}_{2,5}(\alpha)]$ and $\{\vec{f}_{2,5}(\mathsf{ID}_i) : \mathsf{ID}_i \in \mathcal{Q}\}$. We represent these values as following matrix product.

$$\vec{c} \underbrace{\begin{bmatrix} \mathbf{V} & 0 & 0 & 0 & \sigma^* \vec{\Gamma}_{X^*}^\dagger & 0 & \sigma^* \vec{\Gamma}_{Y^*} & 0 & \sigma \vec{\Gamma}_X^\dagger & 0 \\ 0 & \mathbf{V} & 0 & 0 & \mu^* \sigma^* \vec{\Gamma}_{X^*}^\dagger & 0 & \mu^* \sigma^* \vec{\Gamma}_{Y^*} & 0 & \mu \sigma \vec{\Gamma}_X^\dagger & 0 \\ 0 & 0 & \mathbf{V} & 0 & 0 & \sigma^* \vec{\Gamma}_{X^*}^\ddagger & 0 & \sigma^* \vec{\Gamma}_{Y^*} & 0 & \sigma \vec{\Gamma}_X^\ddagger \\ 0 & 0 & 0 & \mathbf{V} & 0 & \mu^* \sigma^* \vec{\Gamma}_{X^*}^\ddagger & 0 & \mu^* \sigma^* \vec{\Gamma}_{Y^*} & 0 & \mu \sigma \vec{\Gamma}_X^\ddagger \end{bmatrix}}_{:=\mathbf{P}},$$

where $\vec{c} = [\vec{c}_2\ \vec{c}_3\ \vec{c}_4\ \vec{c}_5]$, $\vec{c}_i = (c_{i,0}, c_{i,1}, \cdots, c_{i,q})$ and $c_{i,j}$ is the coefficient of x^j in $f_i(x)$, $\mathbf{V} = [\vec{\gamma}_{\mathsf{ID}_1}\ \vec{\gamma}_{\mathsf{ID}_2}\ \cdots\ \vec{\gamma}_{\mathsf{ID}_{q-2}}\ \vec{\gamma}_\alpha]$, $\vec{\gamma}_x = (1, x, \cdots, x^q)^\top$ for $x \in \mathcal{Q} \cup \{\alpha, \mathsf{ID}^*\}$, $\vec{\Gamma}_\Theta^\dagger = \bar{\Theta}^\dagger \vec{\gamma}_\alpha + \hat{\Theta} \vec{\gamma}_{\mathsf{ID}^*}$, $\vec{\Gamma}_\Theta^\ddagger = \bar{\Theta}^\ddagger \vec{\gamma}_\alpha + \hat{\Theta} \vec{\gamma}_{\mathsf{ID}^*}$ for $\Theta \in \{X^*, X\}$ and $\vec{\Gamma}_{Y^*} = \bar{Y}^* \vec{\gamma}_\alpha + \hat{Y}^* \vec{\gamma}_{\mathsf{ID}^*}$. Next, we discuss the linear independence of columns in matrix $\mathbf{P}$ as follows.

- If $\mu \neq \mu^*$, it is obvious that columns in $\mathbf{P}$ are linearly independent.
- If $\mu = \mu^*$ and $\sigma \notin \{\sigma'\sigma^*\}_{\sigma' \in \mathbb{Z}_p}$. Assume that columns in $\mathbf{P}$ are linearly dependent. Recall that $\vec{\gamma}_{\mathsf{ID}^*}$ is not a linear combination of columns in $\mathbf{V}$, then there must exist $\sigma' \in \mathbb{Z}_p$ such that $\sigma = \sigma'\sigma^*$, which is contradict to current case. Thus, $\mathbf{P}$ is non-singular.
- If $\mu = \mu^*$, $\exists \sigma' \in \mathbb{Z}_p$ s.t. $\sigma = \sigma'\sigma^*$ and $([X_1], [X_2]_T) \notin \{([X_1^* + s'Y_1^*], [X_2^* + s'Y_2^*]_T)\}_{s' \in \mathbb{Z}_p}$. Assume that $([X_1], [X_2]_T) = ([aX_1^* + bY_1^* + (\alpha - \mathsf{ID}^*)s], [aX_2^* + bY_2^* + s]_T)$ with $a \neq 1$ or $s \neq 0$, we have

$$\sigma \vec{\Gamma}_X^\dagger = a\sigma'\sigma^* \vec{\Gamma}_{X^*}^\dagger + b\sigma'\sigma^* \vec{\Gamma}_{Y^*} + \sigma(s + (1-a)z_0)\vec{\gamma}_\alpha$$
$$\sigma \vec{\Gamma}_X^\ddagger = a\sigma'\sigma^* \vec{\Gamma}_{X^*}^\ddagger + b\sigma'\sigma^* \vec{\Gamma}_{Y^*} + \sigma(s + (1-a)z_1)\vec{\gamma}_\alpha$$

Note that σ^* is uniformly distributed in $\mathcal{A}$'s view. Coefficients $(s + (1-a)z_0)$ and $(s + (1-a)z_1)$ should equal to 0 simultaneously, which is contradict to $a \neq 1$ or $s \neq 0$. In this case, columns in $\mathbf{P}$ are linearly independent.   □

Lemma 6. *Given system parameters* params, *set of private keys* $\{\mathsf{sk}_{\mathsf{ID}_i}\}_{\mathsf{ID}_i \in \mathcal{Q}}$, $([Y_1^*], [Y_2^*]_T) \in \mathbb{G} \times \mathbb{G}_T$ *and* $[\vec{Y}_{4,5}^*]_T$ *with* $\mathsf{ID}^* \notin \mathcal{Q}$ *and* $\mu^*, \sigma^* \in \mathbb{Z}_p$, *for any* $([Y_1], [Y_2]_T) \in \mathbb{G} \times \mathbb{G}_T$, *any* $\mu, \sigma \in \mathbb{Z}_p$ *with* $([Y_1], [Y_2]_T) \notin \{([t'Y_1^*], [t'Y_2^*]_T)\}_{t' \in \mathbb{Z}_p}$, $\mu \neq \mu^*$ *or* $\sigma \notin \{\sigma'\sigma^*\}_{\sigma' \in \mathbb{Z}_p}$ *and any PPT adversary* $\mathcal{A}$, $[\vec{Y}_{4,5}]_T$ *with* ID^*, μ *and* σ *is uniformly distributed in* $\mathcal{A}$'s *view with overwhelming probability.*

Proof. Let $\bar{\Theta} = \Theta_1/\alpha_{\mathsf{ID}^*}$ and $\hat{\Theta} = \Theta_2 - \bar{\Theta}_1$ for $\Theta \in \{Y^*, Y\}$. We rewrite $[\vec{Y}_{4,5}^*]_T$ and $[\vec{Y}_{4,5}]_T$ as follows.

$$[\vec{Y}_{4,5}^*]_T = ([\sigma^*\bar{Y}^*\vec{\mu}^*\vec{h}_{2,3}^\top + \sigma^*\hat{Y}^*\vec{\mu}^*\vec{r}_{\mathsf{ID}^*,2,3}^\top]_T, [\sigma^*\bar{Y}^*\vec{\mu}^*\vec{h}_{4,5}^\top + \sigma^*\hat{Y}^*\vec{\mu}^*\vec{r}_{\mathsf{ID}^*,4,5}^\top]_T)$$
$$[\vec{Y}_{4,5}]_T = ([\sigma\bar{Y}\vec{\mu}\vec{h}_{2,3}^\top + \sigma\hat{Y}\vec{\mu}\vec{r}_{\mathsf{ID}^*,2,3}^\top]_T, [\sigma\bar{Y}\vec{\mu}\vec{h}_{4,5}^\top + \sigma\hat{Y}\vec{\mu}\vec{r}_{\mathsf{ID}^*,4,5}^\top]_T)$$

Besides, $\mathcal{A}$ also knows $[\vec{h}_{2,5}] = [\vec{f}_{2,5}(\alpha)]$ and $\{\vec{f}_{2,5}(\mathsf{ID}_i)\}_{\mathsf{ID}_i \in \mathcal{Q}}$. We represent these values as following matrix product.

$$[\vec{c}_2\ \vec{c}_3\ \vec{c}_4\ \vec{c}_5] \underbrace{\begin{bmatrix} \mathbf{V} & 0 & 0 & 0 & \sigma^*\vec{\Gamma}_{Y^*} & 0 & \sigma\vec{\Gamma}_Y^\dagger & 0 \\ 0 & \mathbf{V} & 0 & 0 & \mu^*\sigma^*\vec{\Gamma}_{Y^*} & 0 & \mu\sigma\vec{\Gamma}_Y^\dagger & 0 \\ 0 & 0 & \mathbf{V} & 0 & 0 & \sigma^*\vec{\Gamma}_{Y^*} & 0 & \sigma\vec{\Gamma}_Y^\ddagger \\ 0 & 0 & 0 & \mathbf{V} & 0 & \mu^*\sigma^*\vec{\Gamma}_{Y^*} & 0 & \mu\sigma\vec{\Gamma}_Y^\ddagger \end{bmatrix}}_{:=\mathbf{P}},$$

where $\vec{c}_i = (c_{i,0}, c_{i,1}, \cdots, c_{i,q})$ and $c_{i,j}$ is the coefficient of x^j in $f_i(x)$, $\vec{V} = [\vec{\gamma}_{\mathsf{ID}_1}\ \vec{\gamma}_{\mathsf{ID}_2}\ \cdots\ \vec{\gamma}_{\mathsf{ID}_{q-2}}\ \vec{\gamma}_\alpha]$, $\vec{\gamma}_x = (1, x, \cdots, x^q)^\top$ for $x \in \mathcal{Q} \cup \{\alpha, \mathsf{ID}^*\}$ and $\vec{\Gamma}_\Theta = \bar{\Theta}\vec{\gamma}_\alpha + \hat{\Theta}\vec{\gamma}_{\mathsf{ID}^*}$ for $\Theta \in \{Y^*, Y\}$. Next, we discuss the linear independence of columns in matrix $\mathbf{P}$ as follows.

- If $\mu \neq \mu^*$, it is obvious that columns in $\mathbf{P}$ are linearly independent.
- If $\mu = \mu^*$ and $\sigma \notin \{\sigma'\sigma^*\}_{\sigma' \in \mathbb{Z}_p}$. Assume that columns in $\mathbf{P}$ are linearly dependent. Recall that $\vec{\gamma}_{\mathsf{ID}^*}$ is not a linear combination of columns in $\mathbf{V}$, then there must exist $\sigma' \in \mathbb{Z}_p$ such that $\sigma = \sigma'\sigma^*$, which is contradict to current case. Thus, $\mathbf{P}$ is non-singular.
- If $\mu = \mu^*$, $\exists \sigma' \in \mathbb{Z}_p$ s.t. $\sigma = \sigma'\sigma^*$ and $([Y_1],[Y_2]_T) \notin \{([t'Y_1^*],[t'Y_2^*]_T)\}_{t' \in \mathbb{Z}_p}$. Assume that $([Y_1],[Y_2]_T) = ([aY_1^* + s\alpha_{\mathsf{ID}}^*],[aY_2^* + s]_T)$ with $s \neq 0$, we have $\sigma \vec{\Gamma}_Y = a\sigma'\sigma^*\vec{\Gamma}_{Y^*} + \sigma s \vec{\gamma}_\alpha$. Note that σ^* is uniformly distributed in $\mathcal{A}$'s view, so is coefficient σs. In this case, columns in $\mathbf{P}$ are linearly independent in $\mathcal{A}$'s view. □

Lemma 7. *The response of challenger to decryption query in game* G_3 *agrees with the response to decryption query in game* G_2.

Proof. In the cases where the response to decryption query in G_3 is plaintext m, the response in G_2 is also m by the correctness of decryption. Analogously, in the cases where the response to decryption query in G_3 is `replay`, the response in G_2 is also `replay` by the correctness of decryption and rerandomization.

We now prove that when challenger answers decryption query in G_3 with special symbol $\perp$, challenger in G_2 would also return $\perp$ with overwhelming probability. That is, when AltDec outputs $\perp$, Dec would also output $\perp$ with overwhelming probability. Let $\zeta^* = (\vec{X}^*, \vec{Y}^*, \vec{U}^*, \vec{V}^*)$ denote the challenge ciphertext under identity ID_b^* and $\langle \mathsf{ID}, \zeta = (\vec{X}, \vec{Y}, \vec{U}, \vec{V}) \rangle$ denote the decryption query input. We consider all the possible cases where AltDec outputs $\perp$ as follows.

In step (i), there are four cases where AltDec rejects ζ under ID.

- Checks on $[\vec{V}_{3,4}]_T$ and $[U_4]_T$ do not hold. Obviously, Dec would reject ζ.
- $(X_1, Y_1) \neq (X_2\alpha_{\mathsf{ID}}, Y_2\alpha_{\mathsf{ID}})$ in Phase 1. By Lemma 3, $[\vec{X}_{4,5}]_T$ or $[\vec{Y}_{4,5}]_T$ is uniformly distributed in $\mathcal{A}$'s view.
- $(X_1, Y_1) \neq (X_2\alpha_{\mathsf{ID}}, Y_2\alpha_{\mathsf{ID}})$ in Phase 2. If there exist $s', t' \in \mathbb{Z}_p$ such that $([X_1],[X_2]_T) = ([X_1^* + s'Y_1^*],[X_2^* + s'Y_2^*]_T)$ and $([Y_1],[Y_2]_T) = ([t'Y_1^*],[t'Y_2^*]_T)$, then the underlying u of ζ would be related to u^* in ζ^*. However, u^* is uniformly distributed over $\mathbb{G}_T$. The correct value of u is unknown to $\mathcal{A}$. Thus, the validity check on ζ would fail. Otherwise, given $[\vec{X}_{4,5}^*]_T$, $[\vec{Y}_{4,5}^*]_T$, the value of $[\vec{X}_{4,5}]_T$ is uniformly distributed over $\mathbb{G}_T^2$ in $\mathcal{A}$'s view by Lemma 5.
- $(X_1, Y_1) = (X_2\alpha_{\mathsf{ID}}, Y_2\alpha_{\mathsf{ID}})$ but checks on $[\vec{X}_{4,5}]_T$, $[\vec{Y}_{4,5}]_T$ and $[Y_3]_T$ do not hold in Phase 1 and 2 for any $m \in \mathbb{G}_T$. The validity check on ζ in Dec fails.

In step (ii), there are following cases where AltDec rejects ζ under ID.

- $(U_1, V_1) \neq (U_2\alpha_{\mathsf{ID}}, V_2\alpha_{\mathsf{ID}})$ in Phase 1. By Lemma 3, $[U_3]_T/u$ or $[V_3]_T$ is uniformly distributed over $\mathbb{G}_T$ in $\mathcal{A}$'s view.
- $([U_1],[U_2]_T) \neq ([aU_1^* + bV_1^* + \alpha_{\mathsf{ID}^*}s],[aU_2^* + bV_2^* + s]_T)$ or $([V_1],[V_2]_T) \neq ([aV_1^* + \alpha_{\mathsf{ID}^*}s],[aV_2^* + s]_T)$ for any $a, b, s \in \mathbb{Z}_p$. By Lemma 3, $[U_3]_T/u$, $[U_4]_T$ or $[\vec{V}_{3,4}]_T$ is uniformly distributed in $\mathcal{A}$'s view.

- $([U_1], [U_2]_T) = ([aU_1^* + bV_1^* + \alpha_{\text{ID}^*}s], [aU_2^* + bV_2^* + s]_T)$ with $a \neq 1$ or $s \neq 0$. If $a \neq 1$, then $[U_3]_T = [aU_3^* + bV_3^* - sh_6]_T/(u^*)^{a-1}$ is uniformly distributed in $\mathcal{A}$'s view, as u^* is uniformly distributed over $\mathbb{G}_T$. If $a = 1$ and $s \neq 0$, then $[U_4]_T = [\sigma'(U_4^* + bV_4^* + \sigma^* sh_7)]_T$ is also uniformly distributed in $\mathcal{A}$'s view, as $\sigma^* = H(u^*)$ is uniformly distributed over $\mathbb{Z}_p$.
- $([V_1], [V_2]_T) = ([aV_1^* + \alpha_{\text{ID}^*}s], [aV_2^* + s]_T)$ with $s \neq 0$. Similarly, $[V_4]_T = [aV_4^* + \sigma^* sh_7]_T$ is uniformly distributed in $\mathcal{A}$'s view, as σ^* is uniformly distributed over $\mathbb{Z}_p$.
- $[\vec{U}_{3,4}]_T$, $[V_4]_T$ do not hold for any $u' \in \mathbb{G}_T$. In this case, Dec would reject ζ.
- s' or $t' \in \mathbb{Z}_p$ does not exist. By Lemma 5 and 6, $[\vec{X}_{4,5}]_T$ or $[\vec{Y}_{4,5}]_T$ is uniformly distributed in $\mathcal{A}$'s view.
- $\text{ID} \neq \text{ID}_b^*$. Obviously, Dec would reject ζ.

In conclusion, the output of AltDec in G_3 is the same as that of Dec in G_2 in every case with overwhelming probability. $\qquad\square$

Lemma 8. $\Pr[S_3] = 1/4$.

Proof. Note that AltExtract does not use the master key to generate the private key and AltDec does not use the private key to perform the decryption. The extraction and decryption queries do not provide extra information about master key and private keys to adversary $\mathcal{A}$. Lemma 4 shows that ζ^* is distributed independently of bits b, c, from which the lemma follows. $\qquad\square$

Putting it all together, the theorem follows. $\qquad\blacksquare$
Below we analyse the rerandomizability of $\mathcal{IBE}$.

Theorem 3 (Rerandomizability). *Let q_{ID} be the times of extraction queries in game $\mathbf{Exp}_{\mathcal{A},\mathcal{IBE}}^{\text{Re}}$, as shown in Fig. 3, and $q = q_{\text{ID}} + 2$. If the truncated decision q-ABDHE assumption holds for $(\mathbb{G}, \mathbb{G}_T, e)$, the proposed $\mathcal{IBE}$ is rerandomizable.*

Proof. Below we prove the three conditions specified in Definition 4.

(Correctness). For $(\text{msk}, \text{params}) \leftarrow_\$ \text{Setup}(1^n)$, any $\text{ID} \in \mathbb{Z}_p$ and $\text{sk}_{\text{ID}} = \text{Extract}(\text{msk}, \text{ID})$, any ciphertext $\zeta = (\vec{X}, \vec{Y}, \vec{U}, \vec{V})$, $\zeta' = (\vec{X}', \vec{Y}', \vec{U}', \vec{V}') = \text{Rerand}(\zeta)$ and $m = \text{Dec}(\text{sk}_{\text{ID}}, \zeta)$, if $m \neq \bot$, then ζ passes the validity check in Dec. Also, we have $m = [X_3 + \vec{X}_{1,2}\vec{K}_1]_T$ and $u = [U_3 + \vec{U}_{1,2}\vec{K}_6]_T$. One can verify that $m = [X_3' + \vec{X}_{1,2}'\vec{K}_1]_T$ and $u = [U_3' + \vec{U}_{1,2}'\vec{K}_6]_T$. ζ' also can pass the validity check and $\text{Dec}(\text{sk}_{\text{ID}}, \zeta') = m$. If $m = \bot$, ζ fails the validity check. One can verify that ζ' also would not pass the validity check. Thus, $\text{Dec}(\text{sk}_{\text{ID}}, \zeta') = \bot$.

(Tightness of Decryption). The proof of Lemma 1 shows that conditioned on system parameters, the probability of adversary $\mathcal{A}$ generating a valid bad ciphertext is negligible, from which the tightness of decryption follows.

(Indistinguishability). We construct a serial of games to prove that the advantage of adversary $\mathcal{A}$ winning game $\mathbf{Exp}_{\mathcal{A},\mathcal{IBE}}^{\text{Re}}$ is negligible. Let S_i denote the event that $b = b'$ in game G_i.

Alternative Decryption Algorithm $\mathsf{AltDec}^*(\mathsf{ID}_i, \zeta_i := (\boldsymbol{X}, \boldsymbol{Y}, \boldsymbol{U}, \boldsymbol{V}))$

Check that there exist $\hat{s}, \hat{t} \in \mathbb{Z}_p$ such that $[U_2]_T = [\hat{s}]_T$, $[V_2] = [\hat{t}]_T$, $[U_1] = [\hat{s}\alpha_{\mathsf{ID}_i}]$ and $[V_1] = [\hat{t}\alpha_{\mathsf{ID}_i}]$. If not, output $\perp$. Otherwise, compute $u = [U_3 + \hat{s}h_6]_T$, $\sigma = H(u)$ and check that $[\boldsymbol{V}_{3,4}]_T = ([-\hat{t}h_6]_T, [\sigma\hat{t}h_7]_T)$ and $[U_4]_T = [\sigma\hat{s}h_7]_T$ holds. If not, output $\perp$. Otherwise, check that there exist plaintext m', randomness $s, t \in \mathbb{Z}_p$ such that

$$\boldsymbol{X} = ([s\alpha_{\mathsf{ID}_i}], [s]_T, m' \cdot [-sh_1]_T, [\sigma s^\dagger \boldsymbol{\mu} \boldsymbol{h}_{2,3}^\top]_T, [\sigma s^\ddagger \boldsymbol{\mu} \boldsymbol{h}_{4,5}^\top]_T)$$
$$\boldsymbol{Y} = ([t\alpha_{\mathsf{ID}_i}], [t]_T, [-th_1]_T, [\sigma t \boldsymbol{\mu} \boldsymbol{h}_{2,3}^\top]_T, [\sigma t \boldsymbol{\mu} \boldsymbol{h}_{4,5}^\top]_T),$$

where $\boldsymbol{\mu} = (1, H(m'))$. If not, output $\perp$. If $m' \neq m^*$, output m'; otherwise output $\perp$.

Fig. 8. The alternative decryption algorithm AltDec^*.

Game G_0: This is the game $\mathbf{Exp}_{\mathcal{A}, \mathcal{IBE}}^{\mathsf{Re}}$. Let S_i denote the event that $b = b'$ in game G_1. In game G_0, the advantage of PPT adversary $\mathcal{A}$ is $|\Pr[S_0] - 1/2|$.

Game G_1: This game is the same as G_0 except that the challenger runs $\mathsf{AltSetup}$ and $\mathsf{AltExtract}$ in Fig. 5 to generate system parameters and private key for $\mathcal{A}$. According to the analysis in Theorem 2, game G_1 is identical to G_0.

Game G_2: This game is the same as G_1 except that ciphertext ζ_0 is generated using AltEnc in Fig. 6. By Lemma 2 in Theorem 2, games G_1 and G_2 are computationally indistinguishable if truncated decision q-ABDHE assumption holds for $(\mathbb{G}, \mathbb{G}_T, e)$.

Game G_3: This game is the same as G_2 except that ciphertext ζ_0 is generated by AltEnc^*. The only difference between AltEnc and AltEnc^* is the choice of mask u. Specifically, u in AltEnc is randomly sampled from $\mathbb{G}_T$, while u in AltEnc^* equals to the underlying mask of ζ generated by $\mathcal{A}$. That is, u in AltEnc^* is determined by $\mathcal{A}$. By Lemma 4, we have ζ_0 in G_2 is distributed independently of underlying ID, m and u, which implies that $\mathcal{A}$'s choice of u would not affect the distribution of ζ_0 in G_3. Thus, game G_3 is identical to G_2.

Game G_4: This game is the same as G_3 except that the challenger handles all the decryption queries with AltDec^* that only uses system parameter params, identity ID_i and challenge ciphertext ζ_b under identity ID to decrypt ciphertext. In this case, AltDec^* in G_4 is allowed to run in unbounded time, which is also the reason why AltDec^* could decrypt ciphertext ζ_i with params and ID_i. Let m denote the underlying plaintext of ζ. For any decryption query ID_i and ζ_i, we describe algorithm AltDec^* as shown in Fig. 8.

Lemma 9. *The output of alternative decryption algorithm AltDec^* in game G_4 agrees with the output of decryption oracles $\mathcal{O}_\mathsf{D}$ and $\mathcal{O}'_\mathsf{D}$ in game G_3.*

Proof. In the cases where the output of AltDec^* in game G_4 is plaintext $m'(m' \neq m^*)$, the output of oracle $\mathcal{O}_\mathsf{D}(\mathcal{O}'_\mathsf{D})$ is also m' by the correctness of decryption. Now we prove that when the output of AltDec^* in game G_4 is special symbol $\perp$, decryption oracle in G_3 would also return $\perp$ with overwhelming probability.

Let $\zeta_b = (\vec{X}^*, \vec{Y}^*, \vec{U}^*, \vec{V}^*)$ denote the challenge ciphertext under identity ID and $\langle \mathsf{ID}_i, \zeta_i = (\vec{X}, \vec{Y}, \vec{U}, \vec{V}) \rangle$ denote the decryption query input. We consider all the possible cases where AltDec^* outputs $\perp$ as follows.

- Validity checking failed. In this case, decryption oracle in G_3 also outputs $\perp$.
- Decryption result equals to m^*. Obviously, oracle in G_3 also outputs $\perp$.
- $s, t, \hat{s}$ or $\hat{t}$ does not exist. That is, $([X_1], [Y_1], [U_1], [V_1]) \neq ([X_2\alpha_{\mathsf{ID}_i}], [Y_2\alpha_{\mathsf{ID}_i}], [U_2\alpha_{\mathsf{ID}_i}], [V_2\alpha_{\mathsf{ID}_i}])$.
    - If $b = 0$, then $([X_1^*], [Y_1^*], [U_1^*], [V_1^*]) \neq ([X_2^*\alpha_{\mathsf{ID}}], [Y_2^*\alpha_{\mathsf{ID}}], [U_2^*\alpha_{\mathsf{ID}}], [V_2^*\alpha_{\mathsf{ID}}])$, as ζ_b is generated using AltEnc^*.
        * If $([X_1], [X_2]_T) \neq ([aX_1^*+bY_1^*+\alpha_{\mathsf{ID}}s], [aX_2^*+bY_2^*+s]_T)$, $([Y_1], [Y_2]_T) \neq ([aY_1^*+\alpha_{\mathsf{ID}}s], [aY_2^*+s]_T)$, $([U_1], [U_2]_T) \neq ([cU_1^*+dV_1^*+\alpha_{\mathsf{ID}}t], [cU_2^*+dV_2^*+t]_T)$ or $([V_1], [V_2]_T) \neq ([cV_1^*+\alpha_{\mathsf{ID}}t], [cV_2^*+t]_T)$ for any $a, b, c, d, s, t \in \mathbb{Z}_p$. By Lemma 3, $[X_3]_T/m'$, $[\vec{X}_{4,5}]_T$, $[\vec{Y}_{3,5}]_T$, $[U_3]_T/u$, $[U_4]_T$ or $[\vec{V}_{3,4}]_T$ is uniformly distributed in $\mathcal{A}$'s view.
        * Otherwise, ζ_i is derived from ζ_b and the underlying plaintext of ζ_i must be m^*.
    - If $b = 1$, then ζ_b is a rerandomization of ζ^* generated by $\mathcal{A}$. Since $m^* = \mathsf{Dec}(\mathsf{sk}_{\mathsf{ID}}, \zeta^*) \neq \perp$, we have $([X_1^*], [Y_1^*], [U_1^*], [V_1^*]) = ([X_2^*\alpha_{\mathsf{ID}}], [Y_2^*\alpha_{\mathsf{ID}}], [U_2^*\alpha_{\mathsf{ID}}], [V_2^*\alpha_{\mathsf{ID}}])$, otherwise, $[\vec{X}_{4,5}]_T$, $[\vec{Y}_{3,5}]_T$, $[U_4^*]_T$ or $[\vec{V}_{3,4}^*]_T$ is uniformly distributed over appropriate domains by Lemma 3. Again, since $s, t, \hat{s}$ or $\hat{t}$ does not exist, $[\vec{X}_{4,5}]_T$, $[\vec{Y}_{3,5}]_T$, $[U_4]_T$ or $[\vec{V}_{3,4}]_T$ is uniformly distributed in $\mathcal{A}$'s view from Lemma 3.

In conclusion, the output of AltDec^* in G_4 is the same as that of decryption oracles in G_3 in every case with overwhelming probability.   □

Lemma 10. $\Pr[S_4] = 1/2$.

Proof. Note that $\mathsf{AltExtract}$ does not use master key to generate private key and AltDec does not use private key to perform decryption. The extraction and decryption queries do not provide extra information about master key and private keys to adversary $\mathcal{A}$. The distribution of the encryptions of particular message is determined by randomnesses $s, t, \hat{s}, \hat{t}$ and mask u. One can note that in algorithms Rerand, randomnesses are rerandomized to $s + s't$, $t't$, $\hat{s} + \hat{s}'\hat{t}$, $\hat{t}'\hat{t}$ respectively. Since $s', t', \hat{s}', \hat{t}'$ are uniformly picked from appropriate domains and ζ_0, ζ_1 share same mask u, the distribution of ζ_1 is identical to that of ζ_0, from which the lemma follows.   □

Put it all together, the theorem follows.   ■

5   An Application: Identity-Based Universal Mixnet

In this section, we show that rerandomizable ANON-ID-RCCA secure IBE scheme could be useful in practice by presenting an application example.

5.1   Definitions

Universal mixnet is usually constructed for providing externally anonymous communications among parties [12,13,16]. That is, a set of senders intends to communicate with their recipients in such a way that nobody could identify a particular communication except the sender and recipient of this communication.

Here we consider an ID-based universal mix network with ℓ mix-servers $\{M_i\}_{i=1}^{\ell}$, n senders $\{S_i\}_{i=1}^{n}$ and n receivers $\{R_i\}_{i=1}^{n}$. We abuse notations and denote both party itself and its identity as M_i, S_i or R_i. All the parties share a bulletin board to upload/download ciphertexts in turn. We assume that every sender knows the identities of his receiver and all the mix-servers, and there is a trusted key generator center (KGC) responsible for generating private key for every user and mix-server.

Definition 5 (Identity-based Universal Mixnet). *An identity-based universal mixnet* Ω *with* ℓ *mix-servers* $\{M_i\}_{i=1}^{\ell}$, n *senders* $\{S_i\}_{i=1}^{n}$ *and* n *receivers* $\{R_i\}_{i=1}^{n}$ *consists of following algorithms.*

- Init $(1^n, ID)$ *takes as input security parameter* n *and the identities of all the parties* $ID := \{M_i\}_{i=1}^{\ell} \cup \{S_i, R_i\}_{i=1}^{n}$, *and outputs master key* msk, *system parameters* params *and a set of private keys* SK $:= \{\text{sk}_{ID}\}_{ID \in ID}$;
- PktGen $\left(\{(R_{\phi(i)}, m_i)\}_{i=1}^{n}\right)$ *takes as input a set of (recipient, message) tuples* $\{(R_{\phi(i)}, m_i)\}_{i=1}^{n}$, *where* ϕ *is a permutation of* $\{1, \cdots, n\}$, *and outputs a packet set* $\{P_{1,i}\}_{i=1}^{n}$;
- Mix $\left(\{P_{j,i}\}_{i=1}^{n}, \text{sk}_{M_j}\right)$ *takes as input the packet set* $\{P_{j,i}\}_{i=1}^{n}$ *and mix-server* M_j's *private key* sk_{M_j}, *and outputs a set of new packet* $\{P_{j+1,i}\}_{i=1}^{n}$;
- PktDec $\left(\{P_{\ell+1,i}\}_{i=1}^{n}, \{\text{sk}_{R_j}\}_{j=1}^{n}\right)$ *takes as input the packet set* $\{P_{\ell+1,i}\}_{i=1}^{n}$ *and all the recipients' private keys* $\{\text{sk}_{R_j}\}_{j=1}^{n}$, *and outputs a set of (recipient, message) tuples* $\{(R_j, m_{\phi^{-1}(j)})\}_{j=1}^{n}$.

Definition 6 (Correctness). *Let* Ω = (Init, PktGen, Mix, PktDec) *be an identity-based universal mixnet. We say* Ω *is correct if for* (params, SK) $\leftarrow$$ Init $(1^n, ID)$, *any permutation* $\phi \in \Phi$, *any* $m_i \in \mathcal{M}$, $\{P_{1,i}\}_{i=1}^{n} \leftarrow$$ PktGen $\left(\{(R_{\phi(i)}, m_i)\}_{i=1}^{n}\right)$, $\{P_{\ell+1,i}\}_{i=1}^{n} \leftarrow$$ Mix $\left(\cdots \text{Mix} \left(\text{Mix} \left(\{P_{1,i}\}_{i=1}^{n}, \text{sk}_{M_1}\right), \text{sk}_{M_2}\right) \cdots, \text{sk}_{M_\ell}\right)$, *we have*

$$\Pr\left[\text{PktDec}\left(\{P_{\ell+1,i}\}_{i=1}^{n}, \{\text{sk}_{R_j}\}_{j=1}^{n}\right) \neq \{(R_{\phi(i)}, m_i)\}_{i=1}^{n}\right] \leq \text{negl}(n),$$

where Φ *includes all the permutation of* $\{1, \cdots, n\}$ *and* $\mathcal{M}$ *is the message space.*

Definition 7 (Unlinkability). *Let* Ω = (Init, PktGen, Mix, PktDec) *be an identity-based universal mixnet. We say* Ω *provides unlinkability if for any PPT adversary* $\mathcal{A}$ *in game* $\mathbf{Exp}_{\mathcal{A},\Omega}^{\text{Unlink}}$ *as shown in Fig. 9,*

$$\mathbf{Adv}_{\mathcal{A},\Omega}^{\text{Unlink}}(n) := \left|\Pr\left[\mathbf{Exp}_{\mathcal{A},\Omega}^{\text{Unlink}}(n) - 1/2\right]\right| \leq \text{negl}(n).$$

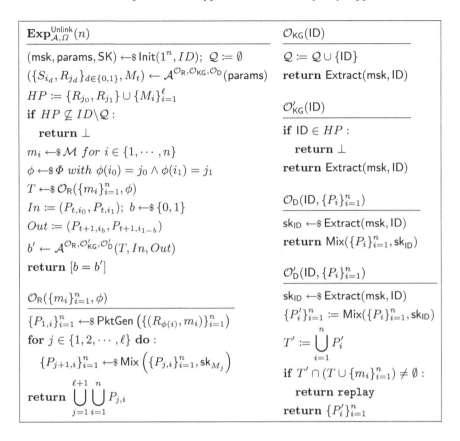

Fig. 9. The security game of unlinkability.

5.2 The Proposed Mixnet

Here we first give the definition of symmetric encryption and thereafter present the proposed ID-based universal mixnet.

Definition 8 (Semantically Secure Symmetric Encryption). *A symmetric encryption scheme* $\mathcal{SE} = (\mathsf{K}, \mathsf{E}, \mathsf{D})$ *is semantically secure if for any PPT adversary* $\mathcal{A}$ *there exists a PPT algorithm* $\mathcal{A}'$ *such that for every efficiently-sampleable distribution* X *and all efficient functions* f *and* h,

$$\left| \Pr\left[\mathcal{A}(1^n, \mathsf{E}(k, m), h(m)) = f(m)\right] - \Pr\left[\mathcal{A}'(1^n, h(m)) = f(m)\right] \right| \leq \mathsf{negl}(n),$$

where m *is chosen according to the distribution* X.

Let $\mathcal{SE} = (\mathsf{K}, \mathsf{E}, \mathsf{D})$ be a semantically secure symmetric encryption, and $\epsilon_k(m)$ denote the encryption of message m under symmetric key k. Let $\mathcal{IBE} = (\mathsf{Setup}, \mathsf{Extract}, \mathsf{Enc}, \mathsf{Dec}, \mathsf{Rerand})$ be the proposed IBE scheme and $E_{\mathsf{ID}}(m)$ denote the encryption of m under identity ID using $\mathcal{IBE}$. We present a concrete identity-based universal mixnet Ω as follows.

- Init $(1^n, ID)$: The KGC first generates master key and system parameters (msk, params) $\leftarrow\$ \text{Setup}(1^n)$, and then computes and distributes private key $\text{sk}_{\text{ID}} \leftarrow\$ \text{Extract}(\text{msk}, \text{ID})$ to every party via secure channel.
- PktGen $\left(\{(R_{\phi(i)}, m_i)\}_{i=1}^n\right)$: For $i = 1$ to n, sender S_i chooses a recipient $R_{\phi(i)}$ and then generates a packet of message m_i as follows.

$$P_{1,i} := \left\{ \epsilon_{k_{1,i}}(\cdots \epsilon_{k_{\ell,i}}(\epsilon_{k_i}(m_i))\cdots), E_{M_1}(k_{1,i}), \cdots, E_{M_\ell}(k_{\ell,i}), E_{R_{\phi(i)}}(k_i) \right\}$$

where symmetric keys $k_{1,i}, \cdots, k_{\ell,i}$ and k_i are generated by sender S_i using K. Finally, n packets are sent to the bulletin board.
- Mix $\left(\{P_{j,i}\}_{i=1}^n, \text{sk}_{M_j}\right)$: Let $P_{j,i} = \{\xi_{j,i}, \zeta_{j,i}, \cdots, \zeta_{\ell,i}, \zeta_{\ell+1,i}\}$, the mix-server M_j downloads all the packets on the bulletin board and generates a set of new packets $\{P_{j+1,i}\}_{i=1}^n$ as follows.
  For $i = 1$ to n:
  - Decrypt the IBE ciphertext $\zeta_{j,i}$ and obtains $k_{j,i} := \text{Dec}(\text{sk}_{M_j}, \zeta_{j,i})$;
  - Decrypt the symmetric ciphertext $\xi_{j,i}$ with $k_{j,i}$ and the new ciphertext is $\xi_{j+1,i} := \epsilon_{k_{j+1,i}}(\cdots \epsilon_{k_{\ell,i}}(\epsilon_{k_i}(m_i))\cdots)$;
  - Compute new IBE ciphertext $\zeta'_{s,i} \leftarrow\$ \text{Rerand}(\zeta_{s,i})$ for $s = j + 1$ to $\ell + 1$, and the new packet is $P_{j+1,i} := \{\xi_{j+1,i}, \zeta'_{j+1,i}, \cdots, \zeta'_{\ell,i}, \zeta'_{\ell+1,i}\}$.
  In the end, the mix-server M_j updates the bulletin board with new packets.
- PktDec $\left(\{P_{\ell+1,i}\}_{i=1}^n, \{\text{sk}_{R_j}\}_{j=1}^n\right)$: For $j = 1$ to n, the recipient R_j downloads the packet set $\{P_{\ell+1,i}\}_{i=1}^n$ from the bulletin board, decrypts every IBE ciphertext in the packet set to retrieve the symmetric key $k_{\phi^{-1}(j)}$, and decrypts the corresponding symmetric ciphertext to retrieve the message $m_{\phi^{-1}(j)}$.

By the correctness of $\mathcal{SE}$ and $\mathcal{IBE}$, one can verify that Ω is correct. The unlinkability of Ω is formally proved as follows.

Theorem 4. *If $\mathcal{SE}$ is of semantic security and $\mathcal{IBE}$ is of rerandomizable ANON-ID-RCCA security, the mixnet Ω above provides unlinkability.*

Proof. We use a sequence of games to prove the unlinkability of Ω as follows.

Game G_0: This is the game $\textbf{Exp}_{\mathcal{A},\Omega}^{\text{Unlink}}$. Let S_i denote the event that $b = b'$ in game G_i. In game G_0, the advantage of PPT adversary $\mathcal{A}$ is $|\Pr[S_0] - 1/2|$.

Game G_1: This game is the same as G_0 except that all the IBE ciphertexts $\{\zeta_{j,i_0}, \zeta_{j,i_1}\}_{j=t+1}^{\ell+1}$ in P_{t+1,i_0} and P_{t+1,i_1} are generated using Enc instead of Rerand. To show the gap between G_0 and G_1, we consider game $G_{0,s}$ $(s = 1, \cdots, \ell-t+1)$ that is the same as G_0 except that $\{\zeta_{j,i_0}\}_{j=t+1}^{t+s}$ in P_{t+1,i_0} are generated using Enc, and game $G_{0,s}^*(s = 1, \cdots, \ell-t+1)$ that is the same as $G_{0,\ell-t+1}$ except that $\{\zeta_{j,i_1}\}_{j=t+1}^{t+s}$ in P_{t+1,i_1} are generated using Enc. Game $G_{0,\ell-t+1}^*$ is identical to G_1.

Lemma 11. *Let $G_{0,0} = G_0$. Game $G_{0,i}$ (resp. $G_{0,i}^*$, $G_{0,\ell-t+1}$) is computationally indistinguishable from $G_{0,i+1}$ (resp. $G_{0,i+1}^*$, $G_{0,1}^*$) for $i = 0, \cdots, \ell-t$.*

Proof. If there exists a PPT adversary $\mathcal{A}$ can distinguish game $G_{0,i}$ and $G_{0,i+1}$ with non-negligible advantage, we show how to break the rerandomizability of $\mathcal{IBE}$ with $\mathcal{A}$ as follows.

Let $\mathcal{C}_{\mathsf{Re}}$ be the challenger in the game $\mathbf{Exp}_{\mathcal{A}',\mathcal{IBE}}^{\mathsf{Re}}$, and the adversary $\mathcal{A}'$ has to simulate the game $\mathsf{G}_{0,i}$ or $\mathsf{G}_{0,i+1}$ for $\mathcal{A}$. $\mathcal{A}'$ first forwards params generated by $\mathcal{C}_{\mathsf{Re}}$ to $\mathcal{A}$. Although $\mathcal{A}'$ does not know the master key chosen by $\mathcal{C}_{\mathsf{Re}}$, it can response the extraction and decryption queries from $\mathcal{A}$ with the answers provided by $\mathcal{C}_{\mathsf{Re}}$. Then, $\mathcal{A}'$ follows the description of $\mathsf{G}_{0,i}$ to generate T, In and Out, sends ζ_{t+i+1,i_0} in P_{t,i_0} and M_{t+i+1} to $\mathcal{C}_{\mathsf{Re}}$, and replaces ζ_{t+i+1,i_0} in P_{t+1,i_0} to the challenge ciphertext ζ_b. If $b = 1$, then ζ_{t+i+1,i_0} in P_{t+1,i_0} is a rerandomization of that in P_{t,i_0} and the simulation is $\mathsf{G}_{0,i}$; otherwise, it is $\mathsf{G}_{0,i+1}$.   □

Game G_2: This game is the same as G_1 except that the underlying plaintexts of all the IBE ciphertexts $\{\zeta_{j,i_0}, \zeta_{j,i_1}\}_{j=t+1}^{\ell+1}$ in P_{t+1,i_0} and P_{t+1,i_1} are changed into randomly picked symmetric keys $\{k'_{j,i_0}, k'_{j,i_1}\}_{j=t+1}^{\ell+1}$. Similarly, we consider game $\mathsf{G}_{1,s}$ $(s = 1, \cdots, \ell - t + 1)$ that is the same as G_1 except that the underlying plaintexts of $\{\zeta_{j,i_0}\}_{j=t+1}^{t+s}$ in P_{t+1,i_0} are changed into random keys $\{k'_{j,i_0}\}_{j=t+1}^{t+s}$, and game $\mathsf{G}_{1,s}^*$ $(s = 1, \cdots, \ell - t + 1)$ that is the same as $\mathsf{G}_{1,\ell-t+1}$ except that the underlying plaintexts of $\{\zeta_{j,i_1}\}_{j=t+1}^{t+s}$ in P_{t+1,i_1} are changed into random keys $\{k'_{j,i_1}\}_{j=t+1}^{t+s}$. Game $\mathsf{G}_{1,\ell-t+1}^*$ is identical to G_2.

Lemma 12. *Let $\mathsf{G}_{1,0} = \mathsf{G}_1$. Game $\mathsf{G}_{1,i}$ (resp. $\mathsf{G}_{1,i}^*$, $\mathsf{G}_{1,\ell-t+1}$) is computationally indistinguishable from $\mathsf{G}_{1,i+1}$ (resp. $\mathsf{G}_{1,i+1}^*$, $\mathsf{G}_{1,1}^*$) for $i = 0, \cdots, \ell - t$.*

Proof. We show how to break the ID-RCCA security of $\mathcal{IBE}$ with a PPT adversary $\mathcal{A}$ who can distinguish game $\mathsf{G}_{1,i}$ and $\mathsf{G}_{1,i+1}$ with non-negligible advantage.

Let $\mathcal{C}_{\mathsf{IR}}$ be the challenger in the game $\mathbf{Exp}_{\mathcal{A}',\mathcal{IBE}}^{\mathsf{IR}}$, and the adversary $\mathcal{A}'$ has to simulate the game $\mathsf{G}_{1,i}$ or $\mathsf{G}_{1,i+1}$ for $\mathcal{A}$. $\mathcal{A}'$ first forwards params generated by $\mathcal{C}_{\mathsf{IR}}$ to $\mathcal{A}$. $\mathcal{A}'$ can response the extraction and decryption queries from $\mathcal{A}$ with the answers provided by $\mathcal{C}_{\mathsf{IR}}$. Then, $\mathcal{A}'$ follows the description of $\mathsf{G}_{1,i}$ to generate T, In and Out, where k_{t+i+1,i_0} is picked by $\mathcal{A}'$. Now, $\mathcal{A}'$ samples a new key k'_{t+i+1,i_0}, sends tuple $(k_{t+i+1,i_0}, k'_{t+i+1,i_0}, M_{t+i+1})$ to $\mathcal{C}_{\mathsf{IR}}$, and replaces ζ_{t+i+1,i_0} in P_{t+1,i_0} to the challenge ciphertext ζ_b. If $b = 0$, the underlying plaintext of ζ_{t+i+1,i_0} does not change and the simulation is $\mathsf{G}_{1,i}$; otherwise, it is $\mathsf{G}_{1,i+1}$.   □

Game G_3: This game is the same as G_2 except that the underlying identity of IBE ciphertext $\zeta_{\ell+1,i_0}$ in P_{t+1,i_0} are changed into randomly picked identity R'_0.

Game G_4: This game is the same as G_3 except that the underlying identity of IBE ciphertext $\zeta_{\ell+1,i_1}$ in P_{t+1,i_1} are changed into randomly picked identity R'_1.

Lemma 13. *Game G_3 (resp. G_4) is computationally indistinguishable from G_2 (resp. G_3).*

Proof. Here we consider a variant of game $\mathbf{Exp}_{\mathcal{A}',\mathcal{IBE}}^{\mathsf{AIR}}$ where $m_0 = m_1$ and adversary $\mathcal{A}'$ only has to guess the underlying identity of challenge ciphertext. The advantage of $\mathcal{A}'$ in this game is also negligible when $\mathcal{IBE}$ is of ANON-ID-RCCA security. Below we show how to break this game with a PPT $\mathcal{A}$ who can distinguish game G_2 and G_3 with non-negligible advantage.

Let $\mathcal{C}$ be the challenger in this variant, and the adversary $\mathcal{A}'$ has to simulate game G_2 or G_3 for $\mathcal{A}$. Analogous to previous analysis, $\mathcal{A}'$ is able to response the queries from $\mathcal{A}$ correctly. $\mathcal{A}'$ then follows the description of G_2 to generate T, In and Out. Now, $\mathcal{A}'$ picks a random identity R_0', sends (k_{i_0}, R_{j_0}, R_0') to $\mathcal{C}$ and replaces $\zeta_{\ell+1,i_0}$ in P_{t+1,i_0} to the challenge ciphertext ζ_b. If $b = 0$, the simulation is G_2; otherwise, it is G_3. $\square$

Lemma 14. $\Pr[S_4] = 1/2$.

Proof. All the IBE ciphertexts in P_{t+1,i_0} and P_{t+1,i_1} are independent of those in P_{t,i_0} and P_{t,i_1}. As for symmetric ciphertext, since the underlying keys of ξ_{t+1,i_0} and ξ_{t+1,i_1} are completely changed, by the semantic security of $\mathcal{SE}$, they are also independent of ξ_{t,i_0} and ξ_{t,i_1}. $\square$

Put it all together, the theorem follows.   ∎

Comparison with Golle et al.'s Work [12]. Golle et al. [12] proposed a mixnet which is only secure against passive adversary. In contrast, due to the ID-RCCA security of the underlying $\mathcal{IBE}$, our mixnet is secure against active adversaries. In terms of system deployment, our ID-based mixnet enjoys more flexibility, as IBE scheme inherently dispenses with the issue of key distribution among servers and the universal rerandomizability of $\mathcal{IBE}$ permits server to rerandomize all the ciphertexts without public keys. Consequently, the ad-hoc enter or leave of a server (that does not locate in any mixing path) does not need complex configuration or affect the running of other servers in mix network, as mix operation on each server only requires the private key. Also, our ID-based mixnet supports fair anonymity as the trusted authority could upon abuse reveal the receiver identity.

6   Conclusions

In this work, we propose a new security notion called ANON-ID-RCCA security for rerandomizable IBE, and design a concrete IBE satisfying this security and universal rerandomizability. To illustrate the usefulness of this notion, we also present an ID-based universal mixnet where the proposed IBE plays as the core building block. With the ANON-ID-RCCA security of underlying IBE, this universal mixnet achieves both fair anonymity and strong unlinkability.

As this is the first work studying RCCA security in the identity-based setting, it naturally raises some interesting problems that deserve further investigation. Regarding the construction, reducing the ciphertext size of proposed IBE will be the top priority, as it is four times greater than the Gentry-IBE. This may require a completely new design of the ciphertext structure allowing constrained rerandomization. Also, it might be interesting to achieve perfect rerandomizability where the distribution of the rerandomization of a fixed ciphertext is identical to that of the fresh encryption of same plaintext.

As for the applications, we believe that our new notion could be also applicable to most existing rerandomizable RCCA-secure applications to eliminate the need for public key distribution infrastructure. For example, an application of rerandomizable ANON-ID-RCCA-secure IBE is achieving the first exfiltration-resilient one-round ID-based message transmission with reverse firewall [8]. More details are provided in the full version.

Acknowledgement. We thank all the anonymous reviewers for their insightful comments and suggestions on this manuscript. Rongmao Chen is support by National Natural Science Foundation of China (Grant No. 62122092, 62032005). Xinyi Huang and Jianting Ning are supported by Natural Science Foundation of China (Grant No. 61972094, 62032005), and the young talent promotion project of Fujian Science and Technology Association, and Science Foundation of Fujian Provincial Science and Technology Agency (2020J02016).

References

1. Badertscher, C., Maurer, U., Portmann, C., Rito, G.: Revisiting (R)CCA security and replay protection. In: Garay, J.A. (ed.) PKC 2021. LNCS, vol. 12711, pp. 173–202. Springer, Cham (2021). https://doi.org/10.1007/978-3-030-75248-4_7

2. Boneh, D., Franklin, M.: Identity-based encryption from the Weil pairing. In: Kilian, J. (ed.) CRYPTO 2001. LNCS, vol. 2139, pp. 213–229. Springer, Heidelberg (2001). https://doi.org/10.1007/3-540-44647-8_13

3. Camenisch, J., Lysyanskaya, A.: A formal treatment of onion routing. In: Shoup, V. (ed.) CRYPTO 2005. LNCS, vol. 3621, pp. 169–187. Springer, Heidelberg (2005). https://doi.org/10.1007/11535218_11

4. Canetti, R., Krawczyk, H., Nielsen, J.B.: Relaxing chosen-ciphertext security. In: Boneh, D. (ed.) CRYPTO 2003. LNCS, vol. 2729, pp. 565–582. Springer, Heidelberg (2003). https://doi.org/10.1007/978-3-540-45146-4_33

5. Chase, M., Kohlweiss, M., Lysyanskaya, A., Meiklejohn, S.: Malleable proof systems and applications. In: Pointcheval, D., Johansson, T. (eds.) EUROCRYPT 2012. LNCS, vol. 7237, pp. 281–300. Springer, Heidelberg (2012). https://doi.org/10.1007/978-3-642-29011-4_18

6. Chen, R., Mu, Y., Yang, G., Susilo, W., Guo, F., Zhang, M.: Cryptographic reverse firewall via malleable smooth projective hash functions. In: Cheon, J.H., Takagi, T. (eds.) ASIACRYPT 2016, Part I. LNCS, vol. 10031, pp. 844–876. Springer, Heidelberg (2016). https://doi.org/10.1007/978-3-662-53887-6_31

7. Cramer, R., Shoup, V.: Universal hash proofs and a paradigm for adaptive chosen ciphertext secure public-key encryption. In: Knudsen, L.R. (ed.) EUROCRYPT 2002. LNCS, vol. 2332, pp. 45–64. Springer, Heidelberg (2002). https://doi.org/10.1007/3-540-46035-7_4

8. Dodis, Y., Mironov, I., Stephens-Davidowitz, N.: Message transmission with reverse firewalls—secure communication on corrupted machines. In: Robshaw, M., Katz, J. (eds.) CRYPTO 2016, Part I. LNCS, vol. 9814, pp. 341–372. Springer, Heidelberg (2016). https://doi.org/10.1007/978-3-662-53018-4_13

9. Faonio, A., Fiore, D.: Improving the efficiency of re-randomizable and replayable CCA secure public key encryption. In: Conti, M., Zhou, J., Casalicchio, E., Spognardi, A. (eds.) ACNS 2020. LNCS, vol. 12146, pp. 271–291. Springer, Cham (2020). https://doi.org/10.1007/978-3-030-57808-4_14

10. Faonio, A., Fiore, D., Herranz, J., Ràfols, C.: Structure-preserving and re-randomizable RCCA-secure public key encryption and its applications. In: Galbraith, S.D., Moriai, S. (eds.) ASIACRYPT 2019, Part III. LNCS, vol. 11923, pp. 159–190. Springer, Cham (2019). https://doi.org/10.1007/978-3-030-34618-8_6

11. Gentry, C.: Practical identity-based encryption without random oracles. In: Vaudenay, S. (ed.) EUROCRYPT 2006. LNCS, vol. 4004, pp. 445–464. Springer, Heidelberg (2006). https://doi.org/10.1007/11761679_27

12. Golle, P., Jakobsson, M., Juels, A., Syverson, P.: Universal re-encryption for mixnets. In: Okamoto, T. (ed.) CT-RSA 2004. LNCS, vol. 2964, pp. 163–178. Springer, Heidelberg (2004). https://doi.org/10.1007/978-3-540-24660-2_14

13. Gomułkiewicz, M., Klonowski, M., Kutyłowski, M.: Onions based on universal re-encryption – anonymous communication immune against repetitive attack. In: Lim, C.H., Yung, M. (eds.) WISA 2004. LNCS, vol. 3325, pp. 400–410. Springer, Heidelberg (2005). https://doi.org/10.1007/978-3-540-31815-6_32

14. Groth, J.: Rerandomizable and replayable adaptive chosen ciphertext attack secure cryptosystems. In: Naor, M. (ed.) TCC 2004. LNCS, vol. 2951, pp. 152–170. Springer, Heidelberg (2004). https://doi.org/10.1007/978-3-540-24638-1_9

15. Habib, A.Y., Javad, M., Mahmoud, S.: Identity-based universal re-encryption for mixnets. Secur. Commun. Netw. **8**, 2992–3001 (2015). https://doi.org/10.1002/sec.1226

16. Klonowski, M., Kutyłowski, M., Zagórski, F.: Anonymous communication with on-line and off-line onion encoding. In: Vojtáš, P., Bieliková, M., Charron-Bost, B., Sýkora, O. (eds.) SOFSEM 2005. LNCS, vol. 3381, pp. 229–238. Springer, Heidelberg (2005). https://doi.org/10.1007/978-3-540-30577-4_26

17. Libert, B., Peters, T., Qian, C.: Structure-preserving chosen-ciphertext security with shorter verifiable ciphertexts. In: Fehr, S. (ed.) PKC 2017, Part I. LNCS, vol. 10174, pp. 247–276. Springer, Heidelberg (2017). https://doi.org/10.1007/978-3-662-54365-8_11

18. Maurer, U.: Constructive cryptography – a new paradigm for security definitions and proofs. In: Mödersheim, S., Palamidessi, C. (eds.) TOSCA 2011. LNCS, vol. 6993, pp. 33–56. Springer, Heidelberg (2012). https://doi.org/10.1007/978-3-642-27375-9_3

19. Mironov, I., Stephens-Davidowitz, N.: Cryptographic reverse firewalls. In: Oswald, E., Fischlin, M. (eds.) EUROCRYPT 2015, Part II. LNCS, vol. 9057, pp. 657–686. Springer, Heidelberg (2015). https://doi.org/10.1007/978-3-662-46803-6_22

20. Naveed, M., et al.: Controlled functional encryption. In: Ahn, G.J., Yung, M., Li, N. (eds.) ACM CCS 2014, pp. 1280–1291. ACM Press, November 2014. https://doi.org/10.1145/2660267.2660291

21. Pereira, O., Rivest, R.L., et al.: Marked mix-nets. In: Brenner, M. (ed.) FC 2017. LNCS, vol. 10323, pp. 353–369. Springer, Cham (2017). https://doi.org/10.1007/978-3-319-70278-0_22

22. Phan, D.H., Pointcheval, D.: OAEP 3-round: a generic and secure asymmetric encryption padding. In: Lee, P.J. (ed.) ASIACRYPT 2004. LNCS, vol. 3329, pp. 63–77. Springer, Heidelberg (2004). https://doi.org/10.1007/978-3-540-30539-2_5

23. Prabhakaran, M., Rosulek, M.: Rerandomizable RCCA encryption. In: Menezes, A. (ed.) CRYPTO 2007. LNCS, vol. 4622, pp. 517–534. Springer, Heidelberg (2007). https://doi.org/10.1007/978-3-540-74143-5_29

24. Shamir, A.: Identity-based cryptosystems and signature schemes. In: Blakley, G.R., Chaum, D. (eds.) CRYPTO 1984. LNCS, vol. 196, pp. 47–53. Springer, Heidelberg (1985). https://doi.org/10.1007/3-540-39568-7_5

25. Syverson, P., Dingledine, R., Mathewson, N.: Tor: the second generation onion router. In: Usenix Security (2004)
26. Wang, Y., Chen, R., Yang, G., Huang, X., Wang, B., Yung, M.: Receiver-anonymity in rerandomizable RCCA-secure cryptosystems resolved. In: Malkin, T., Peikert, C. (eds.) CRYPTO 2021. LNCS, vol. 12828, pp. 270–300. Springer, Cham (2021). https://doi.org/10.1007/978-3-030-84259-8_10

Simulation-Based Bi-Selective Opening Security for Public Key Encryption

Junzuo Lai[1]([⊠]), Rupeng Yang[2]([⊠]), Zhengan Huang[3]([⊠]), and Jian Weng[1]

[1] College of Information Science and Technology, Jinan University,
Guangzhou, China
[2] Department of Computer Science, The University of Hong Kong, Hong Kong, China
[3] Peng Cheng Laboratory, Shenzhen, China

Abstract. Selective opening attacks (SOA) (for public-key encryption, PKE) concern such a multi-user scenario, where an adversary adaptively corrupts some fraction of the users to break into a subset of honestly created ciphertexts, and tries to learn the information on the messages of some unopened (but potentially related) ciphertexts. Until now, the notion of selective opening attacks is only considered in two settings: sender selective opening (SSO), where part of senders are corrupted and messages together with randomness for encryption are revealed; and receiver selective opening (RSO), where part of receivers are corrupted and messages together with secret keys for decryption are revealed.

In this paper, we consider a more natural and general setting for selective opening security. In the setting, the adversary may adaptively corrupt part of senders and receivers *simultaneously*, and get the plaintext messages together with internal randomness for encryption and secret keys for decryption, while it is hoped that messages of uncorrupted parties remain protected. We denote it as Bi-SO security since it is reminiscent of Bi-Deniability for PKE.

We first formalize the requirement of Bi-SO security by the simulation-based (SIM) style, and prove that some practical PKE schemes achieve SIM-Bi-SO-CCA security in the random oracle model. Then, we suggest a weak model of Bi-SO security, denoted as SIM-wBi-SO-CCA security, and argue that it is still meaningful and useful. We propose a generic construction of PKE schemes that achieve SIM-wBi-SO-CCA security in the standard model and instantiate them from various standard assumptions. Our generic construction is built on a newly presented primitive, namely, universal$_\kappa$ hash proof system with key equivocability, which may be of independent interest.

Keywords: Public key encryption · Multi-user security · Selective opening security · Simulation-based security · Chosen-ciphertext security

1 Introduction

Public key encryption (PKE) is a fundamental tool to protect messages sent over a public channel. Usually, a PKE scheme is used in an open system with multi-

ⓒ International Association for Cryptologic Research 2021
M. Tibouchi and H. Wang (Eds.): ASIACRYPT 2021, LNCS 13091, pp. 456–482, 2021.
https://doi.org/10.1007/978-3-030-92075-3_16

users. The system contains multiple, say n, users, each with a public key/secret key pair, i.e., there are n public keys in the system. Anyone (even not registered in the system) can send messages over the public channel to a user securely via encrypting the message under the user's public key. Thus, each public key will be used for multiple, say k, times during the lifetime of the system.

Selective Opening Attacks. Currently, the standard security for PKE schemes is the so-called "Chosen-ciphertext attack (CCA) security", which allows the attacker to learn the decryption of its selected ciphertexts. Generally, PKE schemes are designed to guarantee security of all messages in the system against a CCA attacker under the assumption that internal status of all users are properly protected. This assumption, however, will be challenged in some real-world scenarios:

– The attacker may corrupt the senders and learn their messages and the encryption randomness.
– The attacker may corrupt the receivers and learn their secret keys. With the receivers' secret keys, the attacker is able to decrypt all ciphertexts sent to the receivers and obtain the messages.

While it is hopeless to protect those opened messages, one natural question is whether the unopened messages are still well protected. The above attacks are called selective opening attacks. Surprisingly, it is proved that standard security notion (i.e., CCA security) is *not* able to guarantee security against selective opening attacks (SO security) [2,17,18].

The notion of SO security for PKE was firstly formalized by Bellare et al. [3] at EUROCRYPT 2009. To date, two settings have been considered for SO security: sender corruption [3] and receiver corruption [2]. In the sender corruption setting, part of senders are corrupted, with the corruption exposing their coins and messages. In the receiver corruption setting, part of receivers are corrupted, with corruption exposing their secret keys and messages. We denote SO security in the sender-corruption setting and in the receiver-corruption setting by SSO security and RSO security, respectively.

Furthermore, for each setting, there are two types of definitions for SO security: indistinguishability-based (IND) SO security and simulation-based (SIM) SO security. IND-SO security requires that no efficient adversary can distinguish the uncorrupted users' ciphertexts from the encryption of fresh messages, which are sampled according to a conditional probability distribution (conditioned on the opened ciphertexts, which means the ciphertexts of the corrupted parties). In other words, IND-SO security requires that the considered message distributions should be efficiently conditionally re-samplable [3]. SIM-SO security requires that anything, which can be computed efficiently from the ciphertexts, the opened messages as well as the corrupted information, can also be computed efficiently only with the opened messages. SIM-SO security imposes no limitation on the message distributions.

Motivations. Previous works on SIM-SO-CCA secure PKE schemes only provide *either* sender selective opening security [3,9,14,16,20,21,25–27], *or* receiver selective opening security [2,11,12,19,23,32]. However, it is rarely possible to predict whether the attacker will corrupt the senders or the receivers beforehand in practice. Moreover, most of the previous works about RSO security only focused on the single-challenge setting, i.e., each public key can only be used *once* to produce a *single ciphertext*. This is very unrealistic in practice.[1]

Based on the above facts, the following question is raised naturally: *How to define security models to capture the practical requirements of selective opening security in the multi-user scenario, and provide secure PKE schemes in the new models?*

Our Contributions. In this paper, for a multi-user system with multiple public keys where each public key will be used multiple times, we give a new security definition of SO security, denoted as SIM-Bi-SO-CCA security. In the security model, the adversary may adaptively corrupt some fraction of senders and receivers *simultaneously*, and get the plaintext messages together with internal randomness for encryption and secret keys for decryption, while it is hoped that messages of uncorrupted parties remain protected. (The definition is reminiscent of Bi-Deniability [29] for PKE.) We prove that some practical PKE schemes achieve SIM-Bi-SO-CCA security in the random oracle model.

Then, we suggest a weak model of SIM-Bi-SO-CCA security, denoted as SIM-wBi-SO$_k$-CCA security ($k \in \mathbb{N}$), where (i) the adversary has to specify whether it is going to corrupt the senders or the receivers after receiving the public keys and before seeing the challenge ciphertexts, and (ii) if the adversary chooses to corrupt some fraction of the receivers, it is just allowed to corrupt the receivers whose public keys are employed for encryption *at most k times*. We stress that the weak model is still meaningful and useful because it provides the original SIM-SSO-CCA security and SIM-RSO-CCA security *simultaneously*. Furthermore, we show that SIM-wBi-SO$_k$-CCA security is strictly stronger than SIM-SSO-CCA security and SIM-RSO-CCA security. We also stress that the recently proposed SIM-RSO$_k$-CCA security notion [32] is a special case of our SIM-wBi-SO$_k$-CCA security.

Finally, we propose a generic construction of PKE that achieves SIM-wBi-SO$_k$-CCA security in the standard model and instantiate it from various standard assumptions. Our generic construction is built on a new variant of hash proof system (HPS), which should additionally satisfy the universal$_{k+1}$ property and key equivocability. The technical overview of the generic construction is given in Sect. 4.1. We also explore the existence of universal$_{k+1}$ HPS with key equivocability and provide instantiations from either the DDH assumption or the DCR assumption.

Related works. Since proposed by Bellare et al. in [3], selective opening secure PKE has been extensively studied.

For SSO security, Bellare et al. in [3] firstly showed that any lossy encryption is IND-SSO-CPA secure. IND-SSO-CCA secure PKE schemes were constructed

---

[1] Very recently, Yang et al. [32] formalized the notion of RSO security in the multi-challenge setting. But their work only considers the receiver corruption setting.

from All-But-N lossy trapdoor functions [13] or All-But-Many lossy trapdoor functions [5,16,21,25]. If this lossy encryption has an efficient opener, then the resulting PKE scheme can be proven to be SIM-SSO-CCA secure as shown in [3]. Fehr et al. [9] showed an approach, employing extended hash proof system and cross-authentication code (XAC), to build SIM-SSO-CCA secure PKE schemes. As pointed out in [20], a stronger property of XAC is needed to make the proof rigorous. Following this line of research, a generic construction of SIM-SSO-CCA secure PKE, from a special kind of key encapsulation mechanism (KEM) and a strengthened XAC, was proposed in [26] and then extended to achieve tight security in [27]. As showed in [14,15], some practical PKE constructions also enjoy SIM-SSO-CCA security.

For RSO security, Hazay et al. [12] showed that SIM-RSO-CPA secure PKE can be built from non-committing encryption for receiver (NCER) [6], and IND-RSO-CPA secure PKE can be built from a tweaked variant of NCER. IND-RSO-CCA secure PKE schemes were proposed in [23]. SIM-RSO-CCA secure PKE was constructed using indistinguishability obfuscation (iO) in [22], and constructed based on standard computational assumptions in [11,19]. Recently, Yang et al. [32] formalized the notion of multi-challenge RSO security (RSO_k security), proved that SIM-RSO security is not enough to guarantee SIM-RSO$_k$ security ($k > 1$), and showed SIM-RSO$_k$-CPA/CCA secure PKE constructions.

Roadmap. In the rest part of this work, we give some preliminaries in Sect. 2. We introduce the formal definitions for SIM-Bi-SO-CCA security and SIM-wBi-SO$_k$-CCA security ($k \in \mathbb{N}$), and show that SIM-wBi-SO$_k$-CCA security is strictly stronger than SIM-SSO-CCA and SIM-RSO-CCA security in Sect. 3. Next, we introduce the main building block, namely, universal$_\kappa$ HPS with key equivocability, and present a generic construction of PKE scheme that achieves SIM-wBi-SO$_k$-CCA security in the standard model in Sect. 4. Finally, we show that some practical PKE schemes achieve SIM-Bi-SO-CCA security in the random oracle model, in Sect. 5.

2   Preliminaries

Notations. Throughout this paper, let $\lambda \in \mathbb{N}$ denote the security parameter. For $n \in \mathbb{N}$, let $[n]$ denote the set $\{1, 2, \cdots, n\}$. For a finite set $\mathcal{S}$, we use $|\mathcal{S}|$ to denote the size of $\mathcal{S}$; we use $s \leftarrow \mathcal{S}$ to denote the process of sampling s uniformly from $\mathcal{S}$. For a distribution Dist, $x \leftarrow$ Dist denotes the process of sampling x from Dist.

We use boldface to denote vectors, e.g., $\mathbf{x}$. We use $\mathbf{x}[i]$ to denote the i-th component of $\mathbf{x}$.

For a probabilistic algorithm $\mathcal{A}$, let $\mathcal{R}_\mathcal{A}$ denote the randomness space of $\mathcal{A}$. We let $y \leftarrow \mathcal{A}(x; r)$ denote the process of running $\mathcal{A}$ on input x and inner randomness $r \in \mathcal{R}_\mathcal{A}$ and outputting y. We write $y \leftarrow \mathcal{A}(x)$ for $y \leftarrow \mathcal{A}(x; r)$ with uniformly chosen $r \in \mathcal{R}_\mathcal{A}$. We write PPT for probabilistic polynomial-time. For a function $f(\lambda)$, we write that $f(\lambda) \leq \mathsf{negl}(\lambda)$ if it is negligible.

For two distributions Dist_1 and Dist_2, the statistical distance between Dist_1 and Dist_2 is defined as

$$\Delta(\mathsf{Dist}_1, \mathsf{Dist}_2) := \frac{1}{2} \sum_x | \Pr_{X_1 \leftarrow \mathsf{Dist}_1} [X_1 = x] - \Pr_{X_2 \leftarrow \mathsf{Dist}_2} [X_2 = x]|.$$

We say that Dist_1 and Dist_2 are statistically indistinguishable (denoted by $\mathsf{Dist}_1 \overset{s}{\approx} \mathsf{Dist}_2$), if $\Delta(\mathsf{Dist}_1, \mathsf{Dist}_2)$ is negligible.

Collision-resistant hash. We recall the definition of collision-resistant hash function here.

Definition 1 (Collision-resistant hash function). A family of *collision-resistant hash function* $\mathcal{H}$, with domain Dom and range Rge, is a family of functions having the following property: for any PPT algorithm $\mathcal{A}$, its advantage $\mathsf{Adv}^{\mathrm{CR}}_{\mathcal{H},\mathcal{A}}(\lambda) := \Pr[\mathsf{H} \leftarrow \mathcal{H}; (x, x') \leftarrow \mathcal{A}(\mathsf{H}) : x \neq x' \wedge \mathsf{H}(x) = \mathsf{H}(x')]$ is negligible.

Efficiently samplable and explainable domain. In this paper, some of the domains are required to be efficiently samplable and explainable [9]. We recall its definition as follows.

Definition 2 (Efficiently samplable and explainable domain). *We say that a domain* Dom *is* efficiently samplable and explainable, *if there are two PPT algorithms* (Sample, Explain)*:*

- Sample(Dom; r): *On input a domain* Dom *with uniformly sampled* $r \leftarrow \mathcal{R}_{\mathsf{Sample}}$, Sample *outputs an element which is uniformly distributed over* Dom.
- Explain(Dom, x): *On input* Dom *and* $x \in$ Dom, Explain *outputs* r *which is uniformly distributed over the set* $\{r \in \mathcal{R}_{\mathsf{Sample}} \mid \mathsf{Sample}(\mathsf{Dom}; r) = x\}$.

This notion can be relaxed by allowing a negligibly small error probability (which includes that sampling algorithms may produce near-uniform output).

Cross-authentication code. The notion of ℓ-cross-authentication code (XAC) was proposed by Fehr et al. [9], and later adapted to strong and semi-unique XAC in [24].

Definition 3 (ℓ-Cross-authentication code). For $\ell \in \mathbb{N}$, an ℓ-cross-authentication code (ℓ-XAC) XAC, associated with a key space $\mathcal{XK}$ and a tag space $\mathcal{XT}$, consists of three PPT algorithms (XGen, XAuth, XVer). Algorithm $\mathsf{XGen}(1^\lambda)$ generates a uniformly random key $K \in \mathcal{XK}$, deterministic algorithm $\mathsf{XAuth}(K_1, \cdots, K_\ell)$ produces a tag $T \in \mathcal{XT}$, and deterministic algorithm $\mathsf{XVer}(K, T)$ outputs $b \in \{0, 1\}$. The following properties are required:

- **Correctness:** For all $i \in [\ell]$, $\mathsf{fail}_{\mathsf{XAC}}(\lambda) := \Pr[\mathsf{XVer}(K_i, \mathsf{XAuth}(K_1, \cdots, K_\ell)) \neq 1]$ is negligible, where $K_1, \cdots, K_\ell \leftarrow \mathsf{XGen}(1^\lambda)$ in the probability.

- **Security against impersonation and substitution attacks:** $\mathsf{Adv}_{\mathsf{XAC}}^{\mathrm{IMP}}(\lambda)$ and $\mathsf{Adv}_{\mathsf{XAC}}^{\mathrm{SUB}}(\lambda)$ as defined below are both negligible: $\mathsf{Adv}_{\mathsf{XAC}}^{\mathrm{IMP}}(\lambda) := \max_{i,T'} \Pr[K \leftarrow \mathsf{XGen}(1^{\lambda}) : \mathsf{XVer}(K,T') = 1]$, where the max is over all $i \in [\ell]$ and $T' \in \mathcal{XT}$, and

$$\mathsf{Adv}_{\mathsf{XAC}}^{\mathrm{SUB}}(\lambda) := \max_{i,K_{\neq i},F} \Pr \begin{bmatrix} K_i \leftarrow \mathsf{XGen}(1^k) \\ T = \mathsf{XAuth}((K_j)_{j \in [\ell]}) : \begin{matrix} T' \neq T \wedge \\ \mathsf{XVer}(K_i,T') = 1 \end{matrix} \\ T' \leftarrow F(T) \end{bmatrix},$$

where the max is over all $i \in [\ell]$, all $K_{\neq i} := (K_j)_{j \neq i} \in \mathcal{XK}^{\ell-1}$ and all possibly randomized functions $F : \mathcal{XT} \to \mathcal{XT}$.

Definition 4 (Strong and semi-unique ℓ-XAC). For $\ell \in \mathbb{N}$, we say that an ℓ-XAC XAC is strong and semi-unique, if it has the following two properties:

- **Strongness:** There is a PPT algorithm ReSamp, which takes $i \in [\ell]$, $K_{\neq i}$ and T as input (where $K_1, \cdots, K_{\ell} \leftarrow \mathsf{XGen}(1^{\lambda})$ and $T = \mathsf{XAuth}((K_j)_{j \in [\ell]})$) and outputs K_i', such that K_i' and K_i are statistically indistinguishable, i.e.,

$$\mathsf{StD}_{\mathsf{XAC}}^{\mathrm{STRN}}(\lambda) := \Delta(K_i', K_i)$$
$$= \frac{1}{2} \sum_{K \in \mathcal{XK}} |\Pr[K_i' = K|(K_{\neq i}, T)] - \Pr[K_i = K|(K_{\neq i}, T)]|$$

is negligible, where the probabilities are taken over $K_i \leftarrow \mathsf{XGen}(1^{\lambda})$, conditioned on $(K_{\neq i}, T)$, and the randomness of ReSamp.
- **Semi-uniqueness:** The key space $\mathcal{XK}$ can be written as $\mathcal{K}_a \times \mathcal{K}_b$. Given a tag $T \in \mathcal{XT}$ and $K_a \in \mathcal{K}_a$, there is at most one $K_b \in \mathcal{K}_b$ such that $\mathsf{XVer}((K_a, K_b), T) = 1$.

3 Bi-SO Security for PKE

Previous security notions of SOA for PKE only consider *either* sender corruption setting *or* receiver corruption setting. We consider a more natural and general setting for selective opening security. In the setting, the adversary may adaptively corrupt part of senders and receivers *simultaneously*. We denote it as Bi-SO security since it is reminiscent of Bi-Deniability [29] for PKE.

For a multi-user system with multiple public keys where each public key will be used many times, we firstly give the most natural security notion of Bi-SO security, denoted as SIM-Bi-SO-CCA security. Then, we suggest a weak model of SIM-Bi-SO-CCA security, denoted as SIM-wBi-SO$_k$-CCA security ($k \in \mathbb{N}$). The weak model is still meaningful and useful because it provides the original SIM-SSO-CCA security and SIM-RSO-CCA security *simultaneously*. Finally, for completeness, we show that SIM-wBi-SO$_k$-CCA security is strictly stronger than SIM-SSO-CCA and SIM-RSO-CCA security.

3.1   Security Definitions

Simulation-based Bi-SO security. In the Bi-SO setting, some of the senders and some of the receivers may be corrupted *simultaneously*, and each public key may be used to encrypt multiple messages. The formal definition is as follows.

Definition 5 (SIM-Bi-SO-CCA). *We say that a PKE scheme* $\mathsf{PKE} =$ *(Setup, Gen, Enc, Dec)[2] is SIM-Bi-SO-CCA secure, if for any PPT adversary $\mathcal{A}$, there exists a PPT simulator $\mathcal{S}$, such that for any PPT distinguisher $\mathcal{D}$,*

$$\mathsf{Adv}_{\mathsf{PKE},\mathcal{A},\mathcal{S},\mathcal{D}}^{\text{SIM-Bi-SO-CCA}}(\lambda) := |\Pr[\mathcal{D}(\mathsf{Exp}_{\mathsf{PKE},\mathcal{A}}^{\text{Bi-SO-real}}(\lambda)) = 1]$$
$$- \Pr[\mathcal{D}(\mathsf{Exp}_{\mathsf{PKE},\mathcal{S}}^{\text{Bi-SO-ideal}}(\lambda)) = 1]|$$

is negligible, where both $\mathsf{Exp}_{\mathsf{PKE},\mathcal{A}}^{\text{Bi-SO-real}}(\lambda)$ *and* $\mathsf{Exp}_{\mathsf{PKE},\mathcal{S}}^{\text{Bi-SO-ideal}}(\lambda)$ *are defined in Fig. 1.*

$\mathsf{Exp}_{\mathsf{PKE},\mathcal{A}}^{\text{Bi-SO-real}}(\lambda)$:

$\quad$ $\mathsf{pp} \leftarrow \mathsf{Setup}(1^\lambda);\ n := 0$
$\quad$ $\mathcal{C} = \emptyset;\quad (\mathcal{M}, s_1) \leftarrow \mathcal{A}_1^{\mathtt{MkRec,Dec}}(\mathsf{pp})$
$\quad$ $\boldsymbol{M} := (\mathbf{m}_1, \cdots, \mathbf{m}_n) \leftarrow \mathcal{M}$
$\quad$ For $i = 1$ to n:
$\quad\quad$ For $j = 1$ to $|\mathbf{m}_i|$:
$\quad\quad\quad$ $\mathbf{r}_i[j] \leftarrow \mathcal{R}$
$\quad\quad\quad$ $\mathbf{c}_i[j] \leftarrow \mathsf{Enc}(pk_i, \mathbf{m}_i[j]; \mathbf{r}_i[j])$
$\quad\quad\quad$ $\mathcal{C} := \mathcal{C} \cup \{(i, \mathbf{c}_i[j])\}$
$\quad$ $(\mathcal{I}_S, \mathcal{I}_R, s_2) \leftarrow \mathcal{A}_2^{\mathtt{Dec}}((\mathbf{c}_1, \cdots, \mathbf{c}_n), s_1)$
$\quad$ $out \leftarrow \mathcal{A}_3^{\mathtt{Dec}}((\mathbf{r}_i[j], \mathbf{m}_i[j])_{(i,j) \in \mathcal{I}_S},$
$\quad\quad\quad\quad\quad\quad$ $(sk_i, \mathbf{m}_i)_{i \in \mathcal{I}_R}, s_2)$
$\quad$ Return $(\boldsymbol{M}, \mathcal{M}, \mathcal{I}_S, \mathcal{I}_R, out)$

$\underline{\mathsf{MkRec}():}$

$\quad$ $n := n + 1;\ (pk_n, sk_n) \leftarrow \mathsf{Gen}(\mathsf{pp})$
$\quad$ Return pk_n

$\mathsf{Exp}_{\mathsf{PKE},\mathcal{S}}^{\text{Bi-SO-ideal}}(\lambda)$:

$\quad$ $(\mathcal{M}, s_1) \leftarrow \mathcal{S}_1^{\mathtt{SimMkRec}}(1^\lambda)$
$\quad$ $\boldsymbol{M} := (\mathbf{m}_1, \cdots, \mathbf{m}_n) \leftarrow \mathcal{M}$
$\quad$ $\mathsf{len} := ((|\mathbf{m}_i^*|, |\mathbf{m}_i^*[1]|, \cdots, |\mathbf{m}_i^*[|\mathbf{m}_i^*|]|)_{i \in [n]})$
$\quad$ $(\mathcal{I}_S, \mathcal{I}_R, s_2) \leftarrow \mathcal{S}_2(\mathsf{len}, s_1)$
$\quad$ $out \leftarrow \mathcal{S}_3((\mathbf{m}_i[j])_{(i,j) \in \mathcal{I}_S}, (\mathbf{m}_i)_{i \in \mathcal{I}_R}, s_2)$
$\quad$ Return $(\boldsymbol{M}, \mathcal{M}, \mathcal{I}_S, \mathcal{I}_R, out)$

$\underline{\mathsf{SimMkRec}():}$

$\quad$ $n := n + 1$
$\quad$ Return $\perp$

$\underline{\mathsf{Dec}(i, c):}$

$\quad$ If $(i > n) \vee ((i, c) \in \mathcal{C})$: return $\perp$
$\quad$ Return $\mathsf{Dec}(sk_i, c)$

Fig. 1. Experiments for defining SIM-Bi-SO-CCA security of PKE. In these two experiments, we require that $\mathcal{I}_S \subset \{(i,j) \mid i \in [n], j \in [|\mathbf{m}_i|]\}$ and $\mathcal{I}_R \subset [n]$.

---

[2] Note that both SIM-Bi-SO-CCA and SIM-wBi-SO$_k$-CCA security capture the security requirements in a multi-user scenario, where multiple public/secret key pairs are involved. In this setting, some global information is needed to be generated by a global algorithm Setup, as done in previous works about multi-user security, such as [1].

Note that in the real experiment, the total number of public keys and the times that each public key is used for encryption are completely determined by the adversary.

Remark 1. *One can generalize both SIM-Bi-SO-CCA and SIM-wBi-SO$_k$-CCA security to a new version that the adversary is allowed to make multiple selective opening queries adaptively. We stress that all the PKE constructions presented in this paper also achieve the generalized security.*

Simulation-based weak Bi-SO security. Now we introduce a weak model of SIM-Bi-SO-CCA security, which we denote as SIM-wBi-SO$_k$-CCA security ($k \in \mathbb{N}$). The differences between these two security models are that in the real experiment of SIM-wBi-SO$_k$-CCA security: (i) the adversary has to specify whether it is going to corrupt some fraction of the senders *or* the receivers, *before seeing the challenge ciphertexts*; (ii) if the adversary chooses to corrupt some fraction of the receivers, it is just allowed to corrupt the receivers whose public keys are used for encryption *at most k times*. The formal definition is as follows.

Definition 6. (SIM-wBi-SO$_k$-CCA). *For any $k \in \mathbb{N}$, we say that a PKE scheme PKE = (Setup, Gen, Enc, Dec) is SIM-wBi-SO$_k$-CCA secure, if for any PPT adversary $\mathcal{A}$, there exists a PPT simulator $\mathcal{S}$, such that for any PPT distinguisher $\mathcal{D}$,*

$$\mathsf{Adv}_{\mathsf{PKE},\mathcal{A},\mathcal{S},\mathcal{D}}^{\mathrm{SIM\text{-}Bi\text{-}SO\text{-}CCA}}(\lambda) := |\Pr[\mathcal{D}(\mathsf{Exp}_{\mathsf{PKE},\mathcal{A}}^{\mathrm{Bi\text{-}SO\text{-}real}}(\lambda)) = 1]$$
$$- \Pr[\mathcal{D}(\mathsf{Exp}_{\mathsf{PKE},\mathcal{S}}^{\mathrm{Bi\text{-}SO\text{-}ideal}}(\lambda)) = 1]|$$

is negligible, where both $\mathsf{Exp}_{\mathsf{PKE},\mathcal{A},k}^{\mathrm{wBi\text{-}SO\text{-}real}}(\lambda)$ and $\mathsf{Exp}_{\mathsf{PKE},\mathcal{S},k}^{\mathrm{wBi\text{-}SO\text{-}ideal}}(\lambda)$ are defined in Fig. 2.

In both $\mathsf{Exp}_{\mathsf{PKE},\mathcal{A},k}^{\mathrm{wBi\text{-}SO\text{-}real}}(\lambda)$ and $\mathsf{Exp}_{\mathsf{PKE},\mathcal{S},k}^{\mathrm{wBi\text{-}SO\text{-}ideal}}(\lambda)$, we use $\beta = 0$ (resp. $\beta = 1$) to represent that adversary $\mathcal{A}$/simulator $\mathcal{S}$ chooses to corrupt some of the senders (resp. receivers). We stress that in $\mathsf{Exp}_{\mathsf{PKE},\mathcal{A},k}^{\mathrm{wBi\text{-}SO\text{-}real}}(\lambda)$, when $\mathcal{A}_1$ outputs $\beta = 0$, the parameter k puts no restrictions on sender corruptions $\mathcal{I}$; and when $\mathcal{A}_1$ outputs $\beta = 1$, $\mathcal{A}_2$ is allowed to corrupt the receivers whose public keys are used for encryption at most k times (i.e., $\mathcal{I} \subset \{i \in [n] \mid |\mathbf{m}_i| \leq k\}$).

Note that the original SIM-SSO-CCA security [9,13] and SIM-RSO-CCA security [11,19] are both special cases of SIM-wBi-SO$_k$-CCA security. Specifically, the original SIM-SSO-CCA security is SIM-wBi-SO$_k$-CCA security when $\mathcal{A}_1$ always outputs $\beta = 0$ and queries the MkRec oracle only once,[3] and the original SIM-RSO-CCA security is SIM-wBi-SO$_k$-CCA security when $\mathcal{A}_1$ always outputs $\beta = 1$ and $|\mathbf{m}_1| = \cdots = |\mathbf{m}_n| = 1$ (note that the latter implicitly suggests $k = 1$). Hence, for a SIM-wBi-SO$_k$-CCA secure PKE scheme, it achieves the original SIM-SSO-CCA and SIM-RSO-CCA (and even SIM-RSO$_k$-CCA) security *simultaneously*.

---

[3] The SIM-SSO-CPA security notion presented in [4] allows the adversary to query the MkRec oracle multiple times.

$$\boxed{\begin{array}{ll}
\underline{\mathsf{Exp}_{\mathrm{PKE},\mathcal{A},k}^{\mathrm{wBi\text{-}SO\text{-}real}}(\lambda):} & \underline{\mathsf{Exp}_{\mathrm{PKE},\mathcal{S},k}^{\mathrm{wBi\text{-}SO\text{-}ideal}}(\lambda):} \\[2pt]
\end{array}}$$

Figure content:

$\underline{\mathsf{Exp}_{\mathrm{PKE},\mathcal{A},k}^{\mathrm{wBi\text{-}SO\text{-}real}}(\lambda):}$

$\mathsf{pp} \leftarrow \mathsf{Setup}(1^\lambda);\ n := 0$
$\mathcal{C} = \emptyset;\quad (\beta, \mathcal{M}, s_1) \leftarrow \mathcal{A}_1^{\mathsf{MkRec},\mathsf{Dec}}(\mathsf{pp})$
$\boldsymbol{M} := (\mathbf{m}_1, \cdots, \mathbf{m}_n) \leftarrow \mathcal{M}$
For $i = 1$ to n:
$\quad$ For $j = 1$ to $|\mathbf{m}_i|$:
$\quad\quad \mathbf{r}_i[j] \leftarrow \mathcal{R}$
$\quad\quad \mathbf{c}_i[j] \leftarrow \mathsf{Enc}(pk_i, \mathbf{m}_i[j]; \mathbf{r}_i[j])$
$\quad\quad \mathcal{C} := \mathcal{C} \cup \{(i, \mathbf{c}_i[j])\}$
$(\mathcal{I}, s_2) \leftarrow \mathcal{A}_2^{\mathsf{Dec}}((\mathbf{c}_1, \cdots, \mathbf{c}_n), s_1)$
If $\beta = 0$: $\textit{Open} := (\mathbf{r}_i[j], \mathbf{m}_i[j])_{(i,j)\in\mathcal{I}}$
If $\beta = 1$: $\textit{Open} := (sk_i, \mathbf{m}_i)_{i\in\mathcal{I}}$
$out \leftarrow \mathcal{A}_3^{\mathsf{Dec}}(\textit{Open}, s_2)$
Return $(\beta, \boldsymbol{M}, \mathcal{M}, \mathcal{I}, out)$

$\underline{\mathsf{MkRec}():}$

$n := n+1;\ (pk_n, sk_n) \leftarrow \mathsf{Gen}(\mathsf{pp})$
Return pk_n

$\underline{\mathsf{Exp}_{\mathrm{PKE},\mathcal{S},k}^{\mathrm{wBi\text{-}SO\text{-}ideal}}(\lambda):}$

$(\beta, \mathcal{M}, s_1) \leftarrow \mathcal{S}_1^{\mathsf{SimMkRec}}(1^\lambda)$
$\boldsymbol{M} := (\mathbf{m}_1, \cdots, \mathbf{m}_n) \leftarrow \mathcal{M}$
$\mathsf{len} := ((|\mathbf{m}_i^*|, |\mathbf{m}_i^*[1]|, \cdots, |\mathbf{m}_i^*[|\mathbf{m}_i^*|]|)_{i\in[n]})$
$(\mathcal{I}, s_2) \leftarrow \mathcal{S}_2(\mathsf{len}, s_1)$
If $\beta = 0$: $\textit{Open} := (\mathbf{m}_i[j])_{(i,j)\in\mathcal{I}}$
If $\beta = 1$: $\textit{Open} := (\mathbf{m}_i)_{i\in\mathcal{I}}$
$out \leftarrow \mathcal{S}_3(\textit{Open}, s_2)$
Return $(\beta, \boldsymbol{M}, \mathcal{M}, \mathcal{I}, out)$

$\underline{\mathsf{SimMkRec}():}$

$n := n+1$
Return $\perp$

$\underline{\mathsf{Dec}(i, c):}$

If $(i > n) \vee ((i, c) \in \mathcal{C})$: return $\perp$
Return $\mathsf{Dec}(sk_i, c)$

Fig. 2. Experiments for defining SIM-wBi-SO$_k$-CCA security. Here in both $\mathsf{Exp}_{\mathrm{PKE},\mathcal{A},k}^{\mathrm{wBi\text{-}SO\text{-}real}}(\lambda)$ and $\mathsf{Exp}_{\mathrm{PKE},\mathcal{S},k}^{\mathrm{wBi\text{-}SO\text{-}ideal}}(\lambda)$, we require that (i) $\beta \in \{0,1\}$, and (ii) when $\beta = 0$, $\mathcal{I} \subset \{(i,j) \mid i \in [n], j \in [|\mathbf{m}_i|]\}$, and when $\beta = 1$, $\mathcal{I} \subset \{i \in [n] \mid |\mathbf{m}_i| \le k\}$.

Very recently, Yang et al. [32] introduced an enhanced security notion of RSO, *SIM-RSO$_k$-CCA security* ($k \in \mathbb{N}$), for PKE. We notice that their SIM-RSO$_k$-CCA security is a special case of SIM-wBi-SO$_k$-CCA security as well. Specifically, SIM-RSO$_k$-CCA security is SIM-wBi-SO$_k$-CCA security when $\mathcal{A}_1$ always outputs $\beta = 1$.

3.2 Separation of SIM-wBi-SO$_k$-CCA and SIM-SSO-CCA and SIM-RSO-CCA

Now we show that SIM-wBi-SO$_k$-CCA security is *strictly* stronger than SIM-SSO-CCA security and SIM-RSO-CCA security. Our conclusion is derived from the fact that SIM-wBi-SO$_k$-CCA security implies SIM-SSO-CCA and SIM-RSO-CCA security simultaneously, and SIM-SSO-CCA and SIM-RSO-CCA security do not imply each other. Actually, we have stronger conclusions:

(1) Supposing that the κ-Linear assumption holds ($\kappa \in \mathbb{N}$), SIM-SSO-CCA security does not imply SIM-RSO-*CPA* security;
(2) Supposing that the DDH or DCR assumption holds, SIM-RSO-CCA security does not imply SIM-SSO-*CPA* security.

SIM-SSO-CCA $\nRightarrow$ SIM-RSO-CPA. Bellare et al. [2] introduced the notion of *decryption verifiability* for PKE, and showed that assuming the existence of a family of collision-resistant hash functions, which can be constructed under the discrete-logarithm assumption [10], any decryption-verifiable PKE scheme is not SIM-RSO-CPA secure [2, Theorem 5.1][4].

Informally, a PKE scheme PKE = (Setup, Gen, Enc, Dec) is called *decryption-verifiable*, if it is infeasible to generate $(pk, sk_0, sk_1, c, m_0, m_1)$ such that (i) $m_0 \neq m_1$, (ii) both sk_0 and sk_1 are valid secret keys corresponding to pk, and (iii) $\mathsf{Dec}(sk_0, c) = m_0$ and $\mathsf{Dec}(sk_1, c) = m_1$. We note that (i) and (iii) implicitly suggest that $sk_0 \neq sk_1$. In other words, for any PKE scheme, if each of its public key uniquely determines its corresponding secret key, then it must be decryption-verifiable.

We notice that the κ-Linear-based SIM-SSO-CCA secure PKE scheme proposed by Liu and Paterson [26] is such a decryption-verifiable PKE scheme. Generally, a public key of the κ-Linear-based Liu-Paterson scheme is of the form $(g^y, (g^{x_\theta}, g^{x_\theta \alpha_\theta}, g^{x_\theta \beta_\theta})_{\theta \in [\kappa]})$, where g is a generator of a cyclic group $\mathbb{G}$ of prime order q and $(y, (x_\theta, \alpha_\theta, \beta_\theta)_{\theta \in [\kappa]}) \in (\mathbb{Z}_q)^{3\kappa+1}$, and the corresponding secret key is $(\alpha_\theta, \beta_\theta, x_\theta^{-1} y)_{\theta \in [\kappa]}$. It's obvious that the public key uniquely determines its corresponding secret key. So the κ-Linear-based Liu-Paterson scheme is decryption-verifiable. According to [2, Theorem 5.1], we conclude that assuming the existence of a family of collision-resistant hash functions, the κ-Linear-based Liu-Paterson scheme is not SIM-RSO-CPA secure.

For completeness, we recall the formal definition of decryption verifiability [2] and the κ-Linear-based Liu-Paterson scheme [26] in the full version of this paper.

SIM-RSO-CCA $\nRightarrow$ SIM-SSO-CPA. As pointed out in [2, Theorem 4.1], the DDH-based Cramer-Shoup scheme [7] is not SIM-SSO-CPA secure. On the other hand, Huang et al. [19] and Hara et al. [11] showed that this PKE scheme (for single-bit message) achieves SIM-RSO-CCA security. This fact suggests that when the DDH assumption holds, SIM-RSO-CCA security does not imply SIM-SSO-CPA security. With similar analysis, this conclusion can be extended to the case that the DCR assumption holds.

4   PKE with SIM-wBi-SO$_k$-CCA Security

In this section, we propose a PKE scheme achieving SIM-wBi-SO$_k$-CCA security. We firstly introduce a new primitive, universal$_\kappa$ HPS with key equivocability for any polynomially bounded function κ, and provide concrete constructions for it from the DDH assumption and the DCR assumption respectively. Then, with

---

[4] Both [2, Theorem 5.1] and [2, Theorem 4.1] only hold in the the auxiliary input model (i.e., in the experiments defining SIM-RSO-CPA and SIM-SSO-CPA security, both the adversary and the simulator get an auxiliary input). So do our counterexamples in this section. These counterexamples may be modified with the technique proposed in [2, Sec. 6] to drop the auxiliary inputs.

this new primitive as a building block, we show our PKE construction and prove that it meets SIM-wBi-SO$_k$-CCA security in the standard model.

In order to make our idea more understandable, we firstly provide a technique overview before going into the details.

4.1   Technique Overview

In the real experiment of SIM-wBi-SO$_k$-CCA security, the bit β is used to indicate whether the adversary wants to corrupt some fraction of the senders ($\beta = 0$) or the receivers ($\beta = 1$), and the adversary does not specify the value of β until it sees public keys $(pk_i)_{i\in[n]}$ via querying the oracle MkRec. Hence, to prove SIM-wBi-SO$_k$-CCA security, when $\beta = 0$, we need to somehow generate malformed ciphertexts for $(pk_i)_{i\in[n]}$, such that they can be opened in the sense of SSO (i.e., exposing the messages and the corresponding randomness to the adversary); and when $\beta = 1$, we need to somehow generate malformed ciphertexts for $(pk_i)_{i\in[n]}$, such that they can be opened in the sense of RSO (i.e., exposing the messages and the corresponding secret keys to the adversary).

Our scheme, encrypting ℓ-bit messages, is inspired by the works of [9, 20,24]. The public/secret key pair is ℓ pairs of public and secret keys (i.e., $(hpk_\gamma, hsk_\gamma)_{\gamma\in[\ell]}$) of a hash proof system (HPS) HPS [8]. Informally, to encrypt a message $m = (m_1, \cdots, m_\ell) \in \{0,1\}^\ell$, the encryption algorithm sets that for each $\gamma \in [\ell]$,

$$\begin{cases} \text{If } m_\gamma = 0: \ x_\gamma \leftarrow \mathcal{X}; \ K_\gamma \leftarrow \mathcal{K}_{sp} \\ \text{If } m_\gamma = 1: \ x_\gamma \leftarrow \mathcal{L}; \ K_\gamma = \mathsf{PubEv}(hpk_\gamma, x_\gamma, w_\gamma) \end{cases}$$

where $\mathcal{L} \subset \mathcal{X}$ and $\mathcal{X}$ are both finite sets generated with a hard subset membership problem, PubEv is the public evaluation algorithm of HPS, w_γ is a witness for $x_\gamma \in \mathcal{L}$, and $\mathcal{K}_{sp}$ is the range of PubEv. Then, we use a strengthened cross-authentication code (XAC) to "glue" $x_1, \cdots, x_\ell$ together, obtaining a XAC tag T. So the generated ciphertext corresponding to m is $c = (x_1, \cdots, x_\ell, T)$. To decrypt a ciphertext $c = (x_1, \cdots, x_\ell, T)$, the decryption algorithm firstly computes that $(\overline{K}_\gamma = \mathsf{SecEv}(hsk_\gamma, x_\gamma))_{\gamma\in[\ell]}$, where SecEv is the secret evaluation algorithm of HPS, and then for each $\gamma \in [\ell]$, sets $\overline{m}_\gamma = 1$ if and only if T is verified correctly by $\overline{K}_\gamma$ (via the verification algorithm of XAC).

Now we turn to the security proof. In order to prove SIM-wBi-SO$_k$-CCA security, we need to construct a PPT simulator $\mathcal{S}$, such that the ideal experiment and the real experiment are indistinguishable. In particular, we need to generate some malformed ciphertexts (before seeing the real messages), such that they are computationally indistinguishable from the real challenge ciphertexts, and meanwhile can be efficiently opened according to the value of β.

If $\beta = 0$, we need to generate malformed ciphertexts $c = (x_1, \cdots, x_\ell, T)$, and then open them according to the real messages $m = (m_1, \cdots, m_\ell)$, by providing random coins which can be used to encrypt the real messages to recover the malformed ciphertexts. We generate the malformed ciphertexts with encryptions of ℓ ones, i.e., for each $\gamma \in [\ell]$, $x_\gamma \leftarrow \mathcal{L} \subset \mathcal{X}$ and $K_\gamma = \mathsf{PubEv}(hpk_\gamma, x_\gamma, w_\gamma) \subset$

$\mathcal{K}_{sp}$. Hence, after generating these malformed ciphertexts, to open a ciphertext, for each $\gamma \in [\ell]$, if the real message bit $m_\gamma = 1$, the random coin (i.e., w_γ) employed to generate (x_γ, K_γ) can be returned directly; if $m_\gamma = 0$, return the random coin which is generated by explaining x_γ as a random element sampled from $\mathcal{X}$, and explaining K_γ as a random key sampled from $\mathcal{K}_{sp}$.

Now, we show that a real challenge ciphertext can be substituted with the malformed ciphertext without changing the adversary's view significantly. For $\gamma = 1$ to ℓ,

1) We modify the decryption procedure of the decryption oracle, such that it does not make use of hsk_γ. More specifically, for a decryption query $c' = (x'_1, \cdots, x'_\ell, T')$, if $x'_\gamma \notin \mathcal{L}$, the decryption oracle directly sets $\overline{m}_\gamma = 0$. The statistical properties of HPS and strengthened XAC guarantee that this modification does not change the adversary's view significantly.
2) If $m_\gamma = 0$, the randomly sampled K_γ is replaced with $K_\gamma = \mathsf{SecEv}(hsk_\gamma, x_\gamma)$. The perfect universality of HPS guarantees that this change is imperceptible to the adversary.
3) If $m_\gamma = 0$, K_γ is updated again via the resampling algorithm of strengthened XAC. The statistical property of strengthened XAC guarantees that this modification does not change the adversary's view significantly.
4) The decryption procedure of the decryption oracle is changed to work with the original decryption rules. The statistical properties of HPS and strengthened XAC guarantee that this modification is imperceptible to the adversary.
5) If $m_\gamma = 0$, $x_\gamma \leftarrow \mathcal{L}$ instead of uniformly sampling from $\mathcal{X}$. The underlying subset membership problem of HPS guarantees that this change is also imperceptible to the adversary.

Note that these substitutions only consider the situation that a single public key is used to encrypt a single message. Fortunately, we can extend it to the situation that there are n public keys (for any $n \in \mathbb{N}$), and each public key is employed to encrypt multiple messages.

If $\beta = 1$, we need to generate malformed ciphertexts, and then open them according to the real messages, by providing valid secret keys which can be used to decrypt the malformed ciphertexts to obtain the messages. Note that a public key of this scheme is of the form $pk = (hpk_1, \cdots, hpk_\ell)$, and the corresponding secret key is $sk = (hsk_1, \cdots, hsk_\ell)$. Hence, informally, what we need is to generate a malformed ciphertext without seeing the message, such that for any message $m = (m_1, \cdots, m_\ell) \in \{0,1\}^\ell$, we can generate some secret key $sk' = (hsk'_1, \cdots, hsk'_\ell)$ satisfying that (i) sk' is a valid secret key corresponding to pk (i.e., for all $\gamma \in [\ell]$, hsk'_γ is a valid HPS secret key corresponding to hpk_γ); (ii) decrypting the malformed ciphertext with sk' will lead to m.

We try to generate such a malformed ciphertext $c = (x_1, \cdots, x_\ell, T)$. For each $\gamma \in [\ell]$, if $x_\gamma \in \mathcal{L}$ (with a witness w_γ), all the HPS secret keys corresponding to hpk_γ will lead to the same $\widetilde{K}_\gamma = \mathsf{PubEv}(hpk_\gamma, x_\gamma, w_\gamma) = K_\gamma$. In other words, for any fixed ciphertext $(\cdots, x_\gamma, \cdots, T)$, no matter what the secret key is, the decryption of this ciphertext will lead to the same $\overline{m}_\gamma$. So it's impossible to open the malformed ciphertext successfully when $m_\gamma = 1 - \overline{m}_\gamma$. Hence, our malformed ciphertexts focus on the case $c = (x_1, \cdots, x_\ell, T)$ that $x_1, \cdots, x_\ell \in \mathcal{X} \setminus \mathcal{L}$. On the other hand, if K_γ is uniformly sampled, it seems unlikely to decrypt the ciphertext to recover the original message when $m_\gamma = 1$ due to the property of XAC. So our malformed ciphertexts further focus on the case $c = (x_1, \cdots, x_\ell, T)$ that for all $\gamma \in [\ell]$, $x_\gamma \in \mathcal{X} \setminus \mathcal{L}$ and $K_\gamma = \mathsf{SecEv}(hsk_\gamma, x_\gamma)$.

We stress that in the real experiment of $\mathsf{SIM}\text{-}\mathsf{wBi}\text{-}\mathsf{SO}_k\text{-}\mathsf{CCA}$ security, the adversary is just allowed to corrupt the receivers whose public keys are used for encryption at most k times. So for simplicity, here we only consider the case that $pk = (hpk_1, \cdots, hpk_\ell)$ is used to encrypt *exactly* k messages (i.e., $m_j = (m_{j,1}, \cdots, m_{j,\ell}) \in \{0,1\}^\ell$ $(j \in [k])$). More specifically, for each $\gamma \in [\ell]$, hsk_γ is used k times (note that we use sk to generate the malformed ciphertexts), generating k ciphertext parts (i.e., $K_{1,\gamma} = \mathsf{SecEv}(hsk_\gamma, x_{1,\gamma}), \cdots, K_{k,\gamma} = \mathsf{SecEv}(hsk_\gamma, x_{k,\gamma})$). In other words, to generate the k malformed ciphertexts, for each $\gamma \in [\ell]$, we need to

(i) compute $\mathsf{SecEv}(hsk_\gamma, x_{1,\gamma}), \cdots, \mathsf{SecEv}(hsk_\gamma, x_{k,\gamma})$ for some $x_{1,\gamma}, \cdots, x_{k,\gamma} \in \mathcal{X} \setminus \mathcal{L}$ before seeing the messages;

(ii) generate a HPS secret key hsk'_γ such that $\mathsf{SecEv}(hsk'_\gamma, x_{j,\gamma}) = \mathsf{SecEv}(hsk_\gamma, x_{j,\gamma})$ if $m_{j,\gamma} = 1$, and $\mathsf{SecEv}(hsk'_\gamma, x_{j,\gamma}) \neq \mathsf{SecEv}(hsk_\gamma, x_{j,\gamma})$ if $m_{j,\gamma} = 0$.

However, there is no algorithm for HPS which can generate two HPS secret keys (i.e. hsk_γ and hsk'_γ) meeting the above requirements. Therefore, we introduce the following new property, which we call "key equivocability", of HPS. Informally, we require that there is an efficient algorithm $\mathsf{SampHsk}$ and a trapdoor td, such that for any $x_1, \cdots, x_k \in \mathcal{X} \setminus \mathcal{L}$, the following two distribution ensembles, Dist_0^k and Dist_1^k, are statistically indistinguishable:

$$\mathsf{Dist}_0^k := \{(hsk, K_1, \cdots, K_k, hpk) | hsk \leftarrow \mathcal{SK}; \ hpk = \mu(hsk);$$
$$\forall j \in [k]:$$
$$K_j \leftarrow \mathcal{K}_{sp} \quad \text{if } m_j = 0;$$
$$K_j = \mathsf{SecEv}(hsk, x_j) \quad \text{if } m_j = 1\}, \quad (1)$$
$$\mathsf{Dist}_1^k := \{(hsk', K_1, \cdots, K_k, hpk) | hsk \leftarrow \mathcal{SK}; \ hpk = \mu(hsk);$$
$$(K_j = \mathsf{SecEv}(hsk, x_j))_{j \in [k]};$$
$$hsk' \leftarrow \mathsf{SampHsk}(hsk, \mathsf{td}, \{x_j\}_{j \in [k]})\}. \quad (2)$$

We stress that this property requires that no information about hsk beyond hpk is leaked. Similar to the proof of case $\beta = 0$, we introduce a modification to the decryption oracle before employing the key equivocability of HPS in order to make sure that nothing about hsk beyond hpk is leaked. For any decryption query $(x'_1, \cdots, x'_\ell, T')$ and any γ, if $x'_\gamma \in \mathcal{X} \setminus \mathcal{L}$, the decryption oracle sets $\overline{m}_\gamma = 0$ directly. However, we note that in the $\mathsf{SIM}\text{-}\mathsf{wBi}\text{-}\mathsf{SO}_k\text{-}\mathsf{CCA}$ security model, each public key is used to encrypt k messages. As a result, hsk may be employed k times, i.e., to compute $\mathsf{SecEv}(hsk, x_1), \cdots, \mathsf{SecEv}(hsk, x_k)$ for some $x_1, \cdots, x_k$.

So the perfect universality$_2$ of HPS [8] is not enough to guarantee that the modification to the decryption oracle is imperceptible to the adversary. To solve this problem, we introduce another property, *perfect universality$_{k+1}$*, for HPS. Roughly speaking, HPS is called perfectly universal$_{k+1}$, if for any $x_1, \cdots, x_{k+1} \in \mathcal{X} \setminus \mathcal{L}$ and any $K' \in \mathcal{K}_{sp}$, even given $(hpk, \mathsf{SecEv}(hsk, x_1), \cdots, \mathsf{SecEv}(hsk, x_k))$, the probability that $\mathsf{SecEv}(hsk, x_{k+1}) = K'$ is $\frac{1}{|\mathcal{K}_{sp}|}$.

With the help of this new variant of HPS, we can use algorithm SampHsk to open the aforementioned equivocable ciphertexts $c = (x_1, \cdots, x_\ell, T)$ where for each $\gamma \in [\ell]$, $x_\gamma \in \mathcal{X} \setminus \mathcal{L}$ and $K_\gamma = \mathsf{SecEv}(hsk_\gamma, x_\gamma)$, successfully. Now, we show that a real challenge ciphertext can be substituted with the malformed ciphertext without changing the adversary's view significantly. A high-level description of the substitution is presented as follows.

1) We use the secret keys to generate the challenge ciphertexts, instead of the public keys. The statistical property of HPS guarantees that this change is imperceptible to the adversary.
2) All the $x_{j,\gamma}$ $(j \in [k], \gamma \in [\ell])$ are sampled from $\mathcal{X} \setminus \mathcal{L}$, instead of being sampled from $\mathcal{L}$ (when $m_{j,\gamma} = 1$). The underlying subset membership problem of HPS guarantees that this change is also imperceptible to the adversary.
3) Note that $sk = (hsk_1, \cdots, hsk_\ell)$ is employed to encrypt $m_j = (m_{j,1}, \cdots, m_{j,\ell}) \in \{0,1\}^\ell$ $(j \in [k])$, and specifically, for each $\gamma \in [\ell]$, hsk_γ is used to handle $m_{1,\gamma}, \cdots, m_{k,\gamma}$, as shown in Fig. 3. For each $\gamma \in [\ell]$, employ hsk_γ to compute $K_{j,\gamma}$ when $m_{j,\gamma} = 0$ (for all $j \in [k]$). The key equivocability of HPS guarantees that this modification does not change the adversary's view significantly.

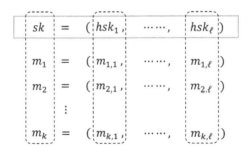

Fig. 3. Relations among sk and $m_1, \cdots, m_k$

4.2   Universal$_\kappa$ Hash Proof System with Key Equivocability

Now we introduce the main building block, namely, universal$_\kappa$ HPS with key equivocability, for any polynomially bounded κ, and show concrete constructions for it.

The definition. For any polynomially bounded function κ, we provide a definition of universal$_\kappa$ HPS with key equivocability, which enhances the standard

HPS [8] with key equivocability and universal$_\kappa$ property. It works on a strengthened version of subset membership problem SSMP, which defines some additional languages and provides a trapdoor to recognize elements from these languages.

Definition 7 (Strengthened Subset Membership Problem). *A strengthened subset membership problem (SSMP)* SSMP *consists of five PPT algorithms* (SSmpG, SSmpX, SSmpL, SSmpLS, SSmpChk):

- SSmpG($1^\lambda, k$): *On input 1^λ and polynomially bounded $k > 0$, algorithm* SSmpG *outputs a system parameter* prm *and a trapdoor* td. *The parameter* prm *defines $2k + 2$ sets $(\mathcal{X}, \mathcal{L}, \mathcal{L}_1, \cdots, \mathcal{L}_{2k})$, where $\mathcal{X}$ is an efficiently recognizable finite set, $\mathcal{L} \subset \mathcal{X}$, and $\mathcal{L}_1, \cdots, \mathcal{L}_{2k}$ are distinct subsets of $\mathcal{X} \setminus \mathcal{L}$. For simplicity of notation, we write*

$$\mathsf{prm} = (\mathcal{X}, \mathcal{L}, \mathcal{L}_1, \ldots, \mathcal{L}_{2k})$$

when employing HPS *for* SSMP *to construct PKE schemes.*
- SSmpX*(prm): On input* prm, SSmpX *outputs a uniformly chosen $x \leftarrow \mathcal{X}$.*
- SSmpL*(prm): On input* prm, SSmpL *samples $x \leftarrow \mathcal{L}$ with randomness $w \in \mathcal{R}_{\mathsf{SSmpL}}$, and outputs (x, w). We say that w is a witness for $x \in \mathcal{L}$.*
- SSmpLS(prm, $i \in [2k]$): *On input* prm *and $i \in [2k]$,* SSmpLS *outputs a uniformly chosen $x_i \leftarrow \mathcal{L}_i$.*
- SSmpChk(prm, td, x): *On input* prm, td *and x,* SSmpChk *outputs an integer $[0, 2k]$ or an abort symbol $\perp$.*

Also, it satisfies the following properties:

- **Hardness.** *For all $i \in [2k]$, for any PPT distinguisher $\mathcal{D}$, the following advantages are all negligible,*

$$\mathsf{Adv}_{\mathsf{SSMP}, \mathcal{D}, i}^{\mathsf{HARD\text{-}1}}(\lambda) := |\Pr[\mathcal{D}(\mathsf{prm}, x_{\mathcal{X}}) = 1] - \Pr[\mathcal{D}(\mathsf{prm}, x_i) = 1]|,$$

$$\mathsf{Adv}_{\mathsf{SSMP}, \mathcal{D}, i}^{\mathsf{HARD\text{-}2}}(\lambda) := |\Pr[\mathcal{D}(\mathsf{prm}, x_{\mathcal{L}}) = 1] - \Pr[\mathcal{D}(\mathsf{prm}, x_i) = 1]|,$$

where the probabilities are over prm $\leftarrow$ SSmpG($1^\lambda, k$), *$x_{\mathcal{X}} \leftarrow$ SSmpX(prm),* $(x_{\mathcal{L}}, w) \leftarrow$ SSmpL(prm), *and $x_i \leftarrow$ SSmpLS(prm, i).*[5]
- **Sparseness.** *The probability*

$$\mathsf{Spar}_{\mathsf{SSMP}}(\lambda) := \Pr[(\mathsf{prm}, \mathsf{td}) \leftarrow \mathsf{SSmpG}(1^\lambda, k); x_{\mathcal{X}} \leftarrow \mathsf{SampX}(\mathsf{prm}) : x_{\mathcal{X}} \in \mathcal{L}]$$

is negligible.
- **Explainability.** *The finite set $\mathcal{X}$ is an efficiently samplable and explainable domain (as defined in Definition 2).*
- **Sampling Correctness.** *Let* (prm, td) $\leftarrow$ SSmpG($1^\lambda, k$). *Then the distributions of the outputs of* SSmpX(prm), SSmpL(prm), *and* SSmpLS(prm, i) *($i \in [2k]$) are statistically indistinguishable from uniform distributions over $\mathcal{X}$, $\mathcal{L}$ and $\mathcal{L}_i$ ($i \in [2k]$) respectively.*

---

[5] Note that a hard SSMP is also a hard SMP, since a simple hybrid argument shows that for any PPT distinguisher $\mathcal{D}$, $|\Pr[\mathcal{D}(\mathsf{prm}, x_{\mathcal{X}}) = 1] - \Pr[\mathcal{D}(\mathsf{prm}, x_{\mathcal{L}}) = 1]| \leq \mathsf{Adv}_{\mathsf{SSMP}, \mathcal{D}, 1}^{\mathsf{HARD\text{-}1}}(\lambda) + \mathsf{Adv}_{\mathsf{SSMP}, \mathcal{D}, 1}^{\mathsf{HARD\text{-}2}}(\lambda)$.

- **Checking Correctness.** *For any* (prm, td) *generated by* SSmpG, *if* $x \in \mathcal{L}$, *then* SSmpChk(prm, td, x) = 0; *if there exists* $i \in [2k]$ *s.t.* $x \in \mathcal{L}_i$, *then* SSmpChk(prm, td, x) = i; *otherwise,* SSmpChk(prm, td, x) = $\perp$.

Remark 2. *The additional trapdoor, generated by* SSmpG, *will also be used in the key equivocability property (see Definition 10) of HPS.*

Definition 8 (Hash Proof System [8]**).** *A* hash proof system HPS *for a SSMP* SSMP *consists of three PPT algorithms* (PrmG, PubEv, SecEv):

- PrmG(prm): *Given* prm, *which is generated by* SSmpG(1^λ, k) *and defines* $2k+2$ *sets* ($\mathcal{X}, \mathcal{L}, \mathcal{L}_1, \ldots, \mathcal{L}_{2k}$), *algorithm* PrmG *outputs a parameterized instance* prmins := ($\mathcal{K}_{sp}, \mathcal{SK}, \mathcal{PK}, \Lambda_{(\cdot)}, \mu$), *where* $\mathcal{K}_{sp}, \mathcal{SK}, \mathcal{PK}$ *are all finite sets,* $\Lambda_{(\cdot)}$: $\mathcal{X} \to \mathcal{K}_{sp}$ *is a family of hash functions indexed with secret hash key* hsk $\in \mathcal{SK}$, *and* $\mu : \mathcal{SK} \to \mathcal{PK}$ *is an efficiently computable function.*
- SecEv(hsk, x): *On input* hsk $\in \mathcal{SK}$ *and* $x \in \mathcal{X}$, *the* deterministic *secret evaluation algorithm* SecEv *outputs a hash value* $K = \Lambda_{hsk}(x) \in \mathcal{K}_{sp}$.
- PubEv(hpk, x, w): *On input* hpk = μ(hsk) $\in \mathcal{PK}$, $x \in \mathcal{L}$ *and a witness* w *for* $x \in \mathcal{L}$, *the* deterministic *public evaluation algorithm* PubEv *outputs a hash value* $K = \Lambda_{hsk}(x) \in \mathcal{K}_{sp}$.

Also, it should be

- **Projective.** *For any* hsk $\in \mathcal{SK}$ *and any* $x \in \mathcal{L}$ *with witness* w, *the hash value* $\Lambda_{hsk}(x)$ *is uniquely determined by* hpk = μ(hsk) *and* x, *concretely, we require that* SecEv(hsk, x) = PubEv(hpk, x, w).
- **Perfectly Universal.** *For all* prm *generated by* SSmpG(1^λ), *all possible* prmins $\leftarrow$ PrmG(prm), *all* hpk $\in \mathcal{PK}$, *all* $x \in \mathcal{X} \setminus \mathcal{L}$, *and all* $K \in \mathcal{K}_{sp}$, *the probability* $\Pr[\Lambda_{hsk}(x) = K \mid \mu(hsk) = hpk] = \frac{1}{\mathcal{K}_{sp}}$, *where the probability is over* hsk $\leftarrow \mathcal{SK}$.

Definition 8 is the same as the original definition of HPS in [8]. In our PKE construction, we further require that $\mathcal{K}_{sp}$ is efficiently samplable and explainable. Besides, we require HPS to have the following two properties.

Definition 9 (Perfectly Universal$_\kappa$). *For any polynomial* κ, *we say that* HPS *is* perfectly universal$_\kappa$, *if for all* prm *generated by* SSmpG(1^λ, k), *all possible* prmins $\leftarrow$ PrmG(prm), *all* hpk $\in \mathcal{PK}$, *all pairwise different* $x_1, \cdots, x_\kappa \in \mathcal{X} \setminus \mathcal{L}$, *and all* $K_1, \cdots, K_\kappa \in \mathcal{K}_{sp}$,

$$\Pr\left[\Lambda_{hsk}(x_\kappa) = K_\kappa \left| \begin{array}{c} \mu(hsk) = hpk \\ \Lambda_{hsk}(x_1) = K_1, \cdots, \Lambda_{hsk}(x_{\kappa-1}) = K_{\kappa-1} \end{array}\right.\right] = \frac{1}{|\mathcal{K}_{sp}|},$$

where the probability is over hsk $\leftarrow \mathcal{SK}$.

Definition 10 (Key Equivocability). *We say that* HPS *is* key equivocable, *if there is a PPT algorithm* SampHsk, *which takes* (hsk, td, $x_1, \cdots, x_{2k}$) *as input and outputs another secret key* hsk', *such that for all possible* (prm, td) $\leftarrow$ SSmpG(1^λ, k), *all possible* prmins = ($\mathcal{K}_{sp}, \mathcal{SK}, \mathcal{PK}, \Lambda_{(\cdot)}, \mu$) $\leftarrow$ PrmG(prm), *all* *permutations* $\mathsf{P} : [2k] \to [2k]$, *and all* $(x_1, \cdots, x_{2k}) \in \mathcal{X}^{2k}$ *satisfying that* $x_i \in \mathcal{L}_{\mathsf{P}(i)}$, $\Delta(\mathsf{Dist}_0, \mathsf{Dist}_1)$ *is negligible, where* Dist_0 *and* Dist_1 *are defined in Fig. 4.*

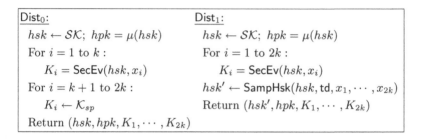

Fig. 4. Distributions for defining key equivocability of HPS.

Instantiation from DDH. Now we present our instantiation of universal$_\kappa$ HPS with key equivocability from the DDH assumption. The definition of the DDH assumption will be recalled in Appendix A.

Let λ be the security parameter and let k, κ be positive integers that are polynomial in λ. Let $\mathbb{G}$ be a multiplicative cyclic group of prime order q and let g be a generator of $\mathbb{G}$. Let $\Gamma : \mathbb{G}^{2k+1} \to \mathbb{Z}_q^{2k+1}$ be an injective function, which can be extended from the injective function in the constructions of HPS in [8] directly.

We construct a strengthened subset membership problem $\mathsf{SSMP}_1 = (\mathsf{SSmpG}, \mathsf{SSmpX}, \mathsf{SSmpL}, \mathsf{SSmpLS}, \mathsf{SSmpChk})$ as follows:

- SSmpG. On input a security parameter λ and an integer k, the parameter generation algorithm first samples $a_i \leftarrow \mathbb{Z}_q$ and computes $g_i = g^{a_i}$ for $i \in [2k+1]$. Then it sets:

$$\mathcal{X} = \{u_1, \ldots, u_{2k+1} \mid \forall i \in [2k+1], u_i \in \mathbb{G}\}$$

$$\mathcal{L} = \{g_1^w, \ldots, g_{2k+1}^w \mid w \in \mathbb{Z}_q\}$$

and for $i \in [2k]$, it sets:

$$\mathcal{L}_i = \{g_1^{w_1}, \ldots, g_{2k+1}^{w_{2k+1}} \mid w, w' \in \mathbb{Z}_q, w \neq w',$$
$$w_i = w', \forall j \in [2k+1]\backslash\{i\}, w_j = w\}$$

The public parameter $\mathsf{prm} = (\mathbb{G}, q, g, g_1, \ldots, g_{2k+1})$ and the trapdoor $\mathsf{td} = (a_1, \ldots, a_{2k+1})$
- SSmpX. On input a public parameter $\mathsf{prm} = (\mathbb{G}, q, g, g_1, \ldots, g_{2k+1})$, the algorithm samples $u_i \leftarrow \mathbb{G}$ for $i \in [2k+1]$ and outputs $x = (u_1, \ldots, u_{2k+1})$.
- SSmpL. On input a public parameter $\mathsf{prm} = (\mathbb{G}, q, g, g_1, \ldots, g_{2k+1})$, the algorithm samples $w \leftarrow \mathbb{Z}_q$ and outputs $x = (g_1^w, \ldots, g_{2k+1}^w)$ and the witness w.

- SSmpLS. On input a public parameter $\mathsf{prm} = (\mathbb{G}, q, g, g_1, \ldots, g_{2k+1})$ and an integer $i \in [2k]$, the algorithm samples $w \leftarrow \mathbb{Z}_q$ and $w' \leftarrow \mathbb{Z}_q$ s.t. $w \neq w'$. Then it computes $u_j = g_j^w$ for $j \in [2k+1]\backslash\{i\}$ and $u_i = g_i^{w'}$ and outputs $(u_1, \ldots, u_{2k+1})$.
- SSmpChk. On input a public parameter $\mathsf{prm} = (\mathbb{G}, q, g, g_1, \ldots, g_{2k+1})$, a trapdoor $\mathsf{td} = (a_1, \ldots, a_{2k+1})$, and $x = (u_1, \ldots, u_{2k+1})$, the algorithm first computes $v_j = u_j^{a_j^{-1}}$ for $j \in [2k+1]$. It outputs 0 if $v_1 = v_2 = \ldots = v_{2k+1}$. It outputs j if there exists some $j \in [2k]$ s.t. $v_j = v_{j'}$ for all $j, j' \in [2k]\backslash\{j\}$ and $v_j \neq v_{2k+1}$. Otherwise, it outputs $\perp$.

Also, we construct the HPS $\mathsf{HPS}_1 = (\mathsf{PrmG}, \mathsf{PubEv}, \mathsf{SecEv}, \mathsf{SampHsk})$ for SSMP_1 as follows:

- PrmG. On input a public parameter $\mathsf{prm} = (\mathbb{G}, q, g, g_1, \ldots, g_{2k+1})$, the algorithm defines $\mathcal{K}_{sp} = \mathbb{G}$, $\mathcal{SK} = \mathbb{Z}_q^{(2k+1)\times\kappa\times(2k+1)}$, and $\mathcal{PK} = \mathbb{G}^{(2k+1)\times\kappa}$. Then for any $hsk = (s_{h,i,j})_{h\subset[2k+1],i\subset[\kappa],j\subset[2k+1]} \in \mathcal{SK}$ and any $x = (u_1, \ldots, u_{2k+1}) \in \mathcal{X}$, it defines the map Λ from $\mathcal{SK} \times \mathcal{X}$ to $\mathcal{K}_{sp}$ as

$$\Lambda_{hsk}(x) = \prod_{h\in[2k+1],i\in[\kappa],j\in[2k+1]} u_j^{s_{h,i,j}\cdot\alpha_h^{i-1}}$$

where $(\alpha_1, \ldots, \alpha_{2k+1}) = \Gamma(x)$. Also, for any $hsk = (s_{h,i,j})_{h\in[2k+1]}, i \in [\kappa], j \in [2k+1] \in \mathcal{SK}$, it defines the map μ from $\mathcal{SK}$ to $\mathcal{PK}$ as

$$\mu(hsk) = (p_{h,i})_{h\in[2k+1],i\in[\kappa]} = (\prod_{j\in[2k+1]} g_j^{s_{h,i,j}})_{h\in[2k+1],i\in[\kappa]}$$

- SecEv. On input a secret key $hsk = (s_{h,i,j})_{h\in[2k+1],i\in[\kappa],j\in[2k+1]} \in \mathcal{SK}$ and $x = (u_1, \ldots, u_{2k+1}) \in \mathcal{X}$, the secret evaluation algorithm outputs $K = \Lambda_{hsk}(x)$.
- PubEv. On input a public key $hpk = (p_{h,i})_{h\in[2k+1],i\in[\kappa]} \in \mathcal{PK}$, $x = (u_1, \ldots, u_{2k+1}) \in \mathcal{L}$ and a witness w, the public evaluation algorithm computes $(\alpha_1, \ldots, \alpha_{2k+1}) = \Gamma(x)$ and outputs $K = \prod_{h\in[2k+1],i\in[\kappa]} p_{h,i}^{w\cdot\alpha_h^{i-1}}$.

SampHsk. On input a secret key $hsk - (s_{h,i,j})_{h\in[2k+1],i\in[\kappa],j\in[2k+1]}$, a trapdoor $\mathsf{td} = (a_1, \ldots, a_{2k+1})$, and $2k$ inputs $(x_\ell = (u_{\ell,1}, \ldots, u_{\ell,2k+1}))_{\ell\in[2k]}$, the algorithm works as follows:
  1. For $\ell \in [2k]$, it computes $\boldsymbol{p}[\ell] = \mathsf{SSmpChk}(\mathsf{prm}, \mathsf{td}, x_\ell)$.
  2. It outputs $\perp$ if there exists $\ell \in [2k]$ s.t. $\boldsymbol{p}[\ell] \notin [2k]$ or there exist distinct $\ell_1, \ell_2 \in [2k]$ s.t. $\boldsymbol{p}[\ell_1] = \boldsymbol{p}[\ell_2]$.
  3. For $h \in [2k+1], i \in [\kappa], j \in \{\boldsymbol{p}[1], \ldots, \boldsymbol{p}[k]\}$, it sets $s'_{h,i,j} = s_{h,i,j}$.
  4. For $h \in [2k+1], i \in [\kappa], j \in \{\boldsymbol{p}[k+1], \ldots, \boldsymbol{p}[2k]\}$, it samples $s'_{h,i,j} \leftarrow \mathbb{Z}_q$.
  5. For $h \in [2k+1], i \in [\kappa]$, it sets $s'_{h,i,2k+1} = (\sum_{j\in[2k+1]} a_j s_{h,i,j} - \sum_{j\in[2k]} a_j s'_{h,i,j}) \cdot a_{2k+1}^{-1}$.
  6. It outputs $hsk' = (s'_{h,i,j})_{h\in[2k+1],i\in[\kappa],j\in[2k+1]}$.

Theorem 1. *Assuming the DDH assumption holds, SSMP_1 is a strengthened subset membership problem with hardness, sparseness, explainability, and correctness.*

Theorem 2. HPS_1 *is a perfect universal$_\kappa$ HPS with key equivocability.*

Proofs of Theorem 1 and Theorem 2 are provided in the full version.

Instantiation from DCR. We present our instantiation of universal$_\kappa$ HPS with key equivocability from the DCR assumption as follows. The definition of the DCR assumption will be recalled in Appendix A.

Let λ be the security parameter and let k, κ be positive integers that are polynomial in λ. We construct a strengthened subset membership problem $SSMP_2 = (SSmpG, SSmpX, SSmpL, SSmpLS, SSmpChk)$ as follows:

- SSmpG. On input a security parameter λ and an integer k, the parameter generation algorithm first samples primes p', q', p, q s.t. $p = 2p' + 1$ and $q = 2q' + 1$. Then it computes $N = pq$ and $N' = p'q'$. Let $\mathbb{Z}_{N^2}^* = \mathbb{G}_N \cdot \mathbb{G}_{N'} \cdot \mathbb{G}_2 \cdot \mathbb{T}$, where $\mathbb{G}_N, \mathbb{G}_{N'}, \mathbb{G}_2, \mathbb{T}$ are defined as in Appendix A. Define $\mathbb{X} = \mathbb{G}_N \cdot \mathbb{G}_{N'} \cdot \mathbb{T}$ and $\mathbb{L} = \mathbb{G}_{N'} \cdot \mathbb{T}$. Define $\chi : \mathbb{Z}_{N^2} \to \mathbb{Z}_N$ as $\chi(a) = \lfloor a/N \rfloor$. Let $\Gamma : \mathbb{X}^{2k} \to \mathbb{Z}_{\lfloor N^2/2 \rfloor}^{2k}$ be an injective function, which can be extended from the injective function in the constructions of HPS in [8] directly. Also, let $g \in \mathbb{Z}_{N^2}^*$ be a fixed generator of $\mathbb{L}$.
  Then it sets:
$$\mathcal{X} = \{u_1, \dots, u_{2k} \mid \forall j \in [2k], u_j \in \mathbb{X}\},$$
$$\mathcal{L} = \{g^{r_1}, \dots, g^{r_{2k}} \mid \forall j \in [2k], r_j \in \mathbb{Z}_{2N'}\},$$
  and for $i \in [2k]$, it sets:
$$\mathcal{L}_i = \{u_1, \dots u_{2k} \mid u_i \in \mathbb{X} \backslash \mathbb{L}, \forall j \in [2k] \backslash \{i\}, r_j \in \mathbb{Z}_{2N'}, u_j = g^{r_j}\}.$$
  The public parameter $\mathsf{prm} = (N, g)$ and the trapdoor $\mathsf{td} = N'$.
- SSmpX. On input a public parameter $\mathsf{prm} = (N, g)$, the algorithm samples $u_j \leftarrow \mathbb{X}$ for $j \in [2k]$ and outputs $x = (u_1, \dots, u_{2k})$.
- SSmpL. On input a public parameter $\mathsf{prm} = (N, g)$, the algorithm samples $r_j \leftarrow \mathbb{Z}_{\lfloor N/2 \rfloor}$ for $j \in [2k]$ and outputs $x = (g^{r_1}, \dots, g^{r_{2k}})$ and the witness $(r_1, \dots, r_{2k})$.
- SSmpLS. On input a public parameter $\mathsf{prm} = (N, g)$ and an integer $i \in [2k]$, the algorithm samples $r_j \leftarrow \mathbb{Z}_{\lfloor N/2 \rfloor}$ for $j \in [2k] \backslash \{i\}$ and $u_i \leftarrow \mathbb{X}$. Then it computes $u_j = g^{r_j}$ for $j \in [2k] \backslash \{i\}$ and outputs $x = (u_1, \dots, u_{2k})$.
- SSmpChk. On input a public parameter $\mathsf{prm} = (N, g)$, a trapdoor $\mathsf{td} = N'$, and $x = (u_1, \dots, u_{2k})$, the algorithm first computes $v_j = u_j^{2N'}$ for $j \in [2k]$. It outputs 0 if $v_1 = v_2 = \dots v_{2k} = 1$. It outputs j if there exists $j \in [2k]$ s.t. $v_j = 1$ for all $j \in [2k] \backslash \{j\}$ and $v_j \neq 1$. Otherwise, it outputs $\perp$.

Also, we construct the HPS $HPS_2 = (PrmG, PubEv, SecEv, SampHsk)$ for $SSMP_2$ as follows:

- PrmG. On input a public parameter $\mathsf{prm} = (N, g)$, the algorithm defines $\mathcal{K}_{SP} = \mathbb{Z}_N$, $\mathcal{SK} = \mathbb{Z}_{\lfloor N^2/2 \rfloor}^{(2k) \times (\kappa) \times (2k)}$, and $\mathcal{PK} = \mathbb{L}^{(2k) \times (\kappa) \times (2k)}$. Then for any

$hsk = (s_{h,i,j})_{h\in[2k],i\in[\kappa],j\in[2k]} \in \mathcal{SK}$ and any $x = (u_1,\ldots,u_{2k}) \in \mathcal{X}$, it defines the map Λ from $\mathcal{SK} \times \mathcal{X}$ to $\mathcal{K}_{sp}$ as

$$\Lambda_{hsk}(x) = \chi\Big(\prod_{h\in[2k],i\in[\kappa],j\in[2k]} u_j^{s_{h,i,j}\cdot\alpha_h^{i-1}} \Big)$$

where $(\alpha_1,\ldots,\alpha_{2k}) = \Gamma(x)$. Also, for any $hsk = (s_{h,i,j})_{h\in[2k],i\in[\kappa],j\in[2k]} \in \mathcal{SK}$, it defines the map μ from $\mathcal{SK}$ to $\mathcal{PK}$ as

$$\mu(sk) = (p_{h,i,j})_{h\in[2k],i\in[\kappa],j\in[2k]} = (g^{s_{h,i,j}})_{h\in[2k],i\in[\kappa],j\in[2k]}.$$

- SecEv. On input a secret key $hsk = (s_{h,i,j})_{h\in[2k],i\in[\kappa],j\in[2k]} \in \mathcal{SK}$ and $x = (u_1,\ldots,u_{2k}) \in \mathcal{X}$, the secret evaluation algorithm outputs $K = \Lambda_{hsk}(x)$.
- PubEv. On input a public key $hpk = (p_{h,i,j})_{h\in[2k],i\in[\kappa],j\in[2k]} \in \mathcal{PK}$, $x = (u_1,\ldots,u_{2k}) \in \mathcal{L}$ and a witness $(r_1,\ldots,r_{2k})$, the public evaluation algorithm computes $(\alpha_1,\ldots,\alpha_{2k}) = \Gamma(x)$ and outputs $K = \chi(\prod_{h\in[2k],i\in[\kappa],j\in[2k]} p_{h,i,j}^{r_j\cdot\alpha_h^{i-1}})$.
- SampHsk. On input a secret key $hsk = (s_{h,i,j})_{h\in[2k],i\in[\kappa],j\in[2k]}$, a trapdoor $\mathsf{td} = N'$, and $2k$ inputs $(x_\ell = (u_{\ell,1},\ldots,u_{\ell,2k}))_{\ell\in[2k]}$, the algorithm works as follows:
  1. For $\ell \in [2k]$, it computes $\boldsymbol{p}[\ell] = \mathsf{SSmpChk}(\mathsf{prm},\mathsf{td},x_\ell)$.
  2. It outputs $\perp$ if there exists $\ell \in [2k]$ s.t. $\boldsymbol{p}[\ell] \notin [2k]$ or there exist distinct $\ell_1,\ell_2 \in [2k]$ s.t. $\boldsymbol{p}[\ell_1] = \boldsymbol{p}[\ell_2]$.
  3. For $h \in [2k], i \in [\kappa], j \in \{\boldsymbol{p}[1],\ldots,\boldsymbol{p}[k]\}$, it sets $s'_{h,i,j} = s_{h,i,j}$.
  4. For $h \in [2k], i \in [\kappa], j \in \{\boldsymbol{p}[k+1],\ldots,\boldsymbol{p}[2k]\}$, it samples $t\leftarrow\mathbb{Z}_N$ and uses the Chinese remainder theorem to compute $s'_{h,i,j} \in \mathbb{Z}_{2NN'}$ s.t. $s'_{h,i,j} = t$ mod N and $s'_{h,i,j} = s_{h,i,j}$ mod $2N'$.
  5. It outputs $hsk' = (s'_{h,i,j})_{h\in[2k],i\in[\kappa],j\in[2k]}$.

Theorem 3. *Assuming the DCR assumption holds, SSMP_2 is a strengthened subset membership problem with hardness, sparseness, explainability, and correctness.*

Theorem 4. HPS_2 *is a perfect universal$_\kappa$ HPS with key equivocability.*

Proofs of Theorem 3 and Theorem 4 are similar to proofs of Theorem 1 and Theorem 2. So, we omit the details here. Note that SSMP_2 only achieves a statistical sampling correctness while SSMP_1 achieves a perfect sampling correctness.

4.3 SIM-wBi-SO$_k$-CCA Secure PKE Construction

For any polynomially bounded function $k > 0$, we propose a PKE scheme achieving SIM-wBi-SO$_k$-CCA security. Our construction is built from a perfectly universal$_{k+1}$ HPS with key-equivocability, and a strong and semi-unique XAC. The details are as follows.

Let $\mathsf{SSMP} = (\mathsf{SSmpG},\mathsf{SSmpX},\mathsf{SSmpL},\mathsf{SSmpLS},\mathsf{SSmpChk})$ be a hard SSMP. Let $\mathsf{HPS} = (\mathsf{PrmG},\mathsf{PubEv},\mathsf{SecEv},\mathsf{SampHsk})$ be a perfectly universal$_{k+1}$ and key equivocable HPS for SSMP, such that all the $\mathcal{K}_{sp}$ generated by PrmG can be written as $\mathcal{K}_a \times \mathcal{K}_b$. For $\ell \in \mathbb{N}$ and any prmins $= (\mathcal{K}_{sp}, \mathcal{SK}, \mathcal{PK}, \Lambda_{(.)}, \mu)$ generated by PrmG, let $\text{XAC}_{\text{prmins}} = (\text{XGen}, \text{XAuth}, \text{XVer}, \text{ReSamp})$ be a strong and semi-unique $(\ell + 1)$-XAC with key space $\mathcal{XK} = \mathcal{K}_{sp} = \mathcal{K}_a \times \mathcal{K}_b$ and tag space $\mathcal{XT}$, and $\mathcal{H}_{\text{prmins}} : (\mathcal{X} \times \mathcal{PK})^\ell \to \mathcal{K}_b$ be a family of collision-resistant hash functions. Our PKE scheme $\text{PKE} = (\text{Setup}, \text{Gen}, \text{Enc}, \text{Dec})$ (for ℓ-bit messages) is defined in Fig. 5.

$\underline{\text{Setup}(1^\lambda)}$:

$\quad (\text{prm} := (\mathcal{X}, \mathcal{L}, \mathcal{L}_1, \cdots, \mathcal{L}_{2k}), \text{td}) \leftarrow \text{SSmpG}(1^\lambda, k)$

$\quad \text{prmins} = (\mathcal{K}_{sp} = \mathcal{K}_a \times \mathcal{K}_b, \mathcal{SK}, \mathcal{PK}, \Lambda_{(.)}, \mu) \leftarrow \text{PrmG}(\text{prm}); \; \mathsf{H} \leftarrow \mathcal{H}_{\text{prmins}}; \; K_a \leftarrow \mathcal{K}_a$

$\quad \text{Return pp} := (\text{prm}, \text{prmins}, \mathsf{H}, K_a)$

$\underline{\text{Gen}(\text{pp})}$:

$\quad \text{Parse prmins} = (\mathcal{K}_{sp}, \mathcal{SK}, \mathcal{PK}, \mathcal{T}, \Lambda_{(.)}, \mu)$

$\quad (hsk_\gamma)_{\gamma \in [\ell]} \leftarrow (\mathcal{SK})^\ell; \; (hpk_\gamma = \mu(hsk_\gamma))_{\gamma \in [\ell]}; \; pk := (hpk_\gamma)_{\gamma \in [\ell]}; \; sk := (hsk_\gamma)_{\gamma \in [\ell]}$

$\quad \text{Return } (pk, sk)$

$\underline{\text{Enc}(pk = (hpk_\gamma)_{\gamma \in [\ell]}, m)}$:

$\quad \text{Parse } m = (m_1, \cdots, m_\ell) \in \{0, 1\}^\ell$

$\quad r := (r_\gamma^{(\mathcal{X})}, r_\gamma^{(\mathcal{K})}, w_\gamma)_{\gamma \in [\ell]} \leftarrow (\mathcal{R}_{\text{SSmpX}} \times \mathcal{R}_{\text{Sample}} \times \mathcal{R}_{\text{SSmpL}})^\ell$

$\quad \text{For } \gamma = 1 \text{ to } \ell :$

$\qquad \text{If } m_\gamma = 0: \; x_\gamma \leftarrow \text{SSmpX}(\text{prm}; r_\gamma^{(\mathcal{X})}); \; K_\gamma \leftarrow \text{Sample}(\mathcal{K}_{sp}; r_\gamma^{(\mathcal{K})})$

$\qquad \text{If } m_\gamma = 1: \; x_\gamma \leftarrow \text{SSmpL}(\text{prm}; w_\gamma); \; K_\gamma = \text{PubEv}(hpk_\gamma, x_\gamma, w_\gamma)$

$\quad K_b = \mathsf{H}(pk, x_1, \cdots, x_\ell); \; K_{\ell+1} = (K_a, K_b); \; T = \text{XAuth}(K_1, \cdots, K_{\ell+1})$

$\quad \text{Return } c = (x_1, \cdots, x_\ell, T)$

$\underline{\text{Dec}(sk = (hsk_\gamma)_{\gamma \in [\ell]}, c = (x_1, \cdots, x_\ell, T))}$:

$\quad \overline{K}_b = \mathsf{H}(pk, x_1, \cdots, x_l)$

$\quad \text{If XVer}((K_a, \overline{K}_b), T) = 0: \; \overline{m}_1 = \cdots = \overline{m}_\ell = 0; \; \text{return } \overline{m} = (\overline{m}_1, \cdots, \overline{m}_\ell)$

$\quad \text{For } \gamma = 1 \text{ to } \ell :$

$\qquad \overline{K}_\gamma = \text{SecEv}(hsk_\gamma, x_\gamma); \; \overline{m}_\gamma = \text{XVer}(\overline{K}_\gamma, T)$

$\quad \text{Return } \overline{m} = (\overline{m}_1, \cdots, \overline{m}_\ell)$

Fig. 5. Construction of PKE.

Correctness. For $\gamma \in [\ell]$, if $m_\gamma = 1$, then $\overline{K}_\gamma = K_\gamma$ by completeness of HPS, so $\overline{m}_\gamma = \text{Xver}(\overline{K}_\gamma, \gamma, T) = 1$ except with probability $\text{fail}_{\text{XAC}}(\lambda)$ by correctness of XAC. On the other hand, if $m_\gamma = 0$, subset sparseness of SSMP and perfect universality of HPS guarantee that with overwhelming probability, $\overline{K}_\gamma$ is uniformly random, even given pk, c and m. In this case, $\overline{m}_\gamma = \text{XVer}(\overline{K}_\gamma, T) = 0$ except with probability $\text{Adv}_{\text{XAC}}^{\text{IMP}}(\lambda)$. So, correctness of PKE follows by a union bound over $\gamma \in [\ell]$.

Security. Formally, we have the following theorem, the formal proof of which is provided in the full version.

Theorem 5. *For any polynomial function $k > 0$,* PKE *is $SIM\text{-}wBi\text{-}SO_k\text{-}CCA$ secure.*

5   PKE with SIM-Bi-SO-CCA Security

In [14], Heuer et al. showed that a generic construction of DHIES [31] meets SIM-SSO-CCA security in the random oracle model. In this section, we show that a variant of the generic construction actually achieves SIM-Bi-SO-CCA security in the random oracle model.

Building blocks. We simply recall the definitions of key encapsulation mechanism (KEM) and message authentication code (MAC) as follows.

Key Encapsulation Mechanism. A KEM scheme, associated with a session key space $\mathcal{K}_{\mathsf{KEM}}$ and a ciphertext space $\mathcal{C}_{\mathsf{KEM}}$, is a tuple of PPT algorithms $\mathsf{KEM} = (\mathsf{KemGen}, \mathsf{Encap}, \mathsf{Decap})$. The key generation algorithm KemGen takes 1^λ as input, and outputs a public/secret key pair (pk, sk). The encapsulation algorithm Encap takes pk as input, outputs $(K, c) \in \mathcal{K}_{\mathsf{KEM}} \times \mathcal{C}_{\mathsf{KEM}}$. The decapsulation algorithm Decap, taking sk and c as input, outputs a value in $\mathcal{K}_{\mathsf{KEM}} \cup \{\bot\}$. Standard correctness is required. Similar to [14], without loss of generality we assume that Encap uniformly samples $K \leftarrow \mathcal{K}_{\mathsf{KEM}}$. We also assume that $|\mathcal{K}_{\mathsf{KEM}}| \geq 2^\lambda$ and $|\mathcal{C}_{\mathsf{KEM}}| \geq 2^\lambda$.

We say that KEM has *unique encapsulations*, if for any (pk, sk) generated by KemGen, and for any ciphertexts c, c' satisfying $\mathsf{Decap}(sk, c) = \mathsf{Decap}(sk, c') \neq \bot$, $c = c'$.

The security notion, one-way security in the presence of a plaintext-checking oracle (OW-PCA security) [28], is recalled in the full version.

Message Authentication Code. A MAC scheme, associated with a key space $\mathcal{K}_{\mathsf{MAC}}$, is a tuple of PPT algorithms $\mathsf{MAC} = (\mathsf{MacGen}, \mathsf{Auth}, \mathsf{Verf})$. The key generation algorithm MacGen takes 1^λ as input and outputs a key $K \in \mathcal{K}_{\mathsf{MAC}}$. The authentication algorithm Auth takes K and a message m as input, outputs a tag t. On input (K, m, t), the verification algorithm Verf outputs a bit $b' \in \{0, 1\}$. Standard correctness is also required here.

MAC is called deterministic, if Auth is deterministic. For a deterministic MAC, MAC is called *injective*, if Auth is an injective function (i.e., for any $K \in \mathcal{K}_{\mathsf{MAC}}$ and any $m \neq m'$, $\mathsf{Auth}(K, m) \neq \mathsf{Auth}(K, m')$).

The security notion of strong unforgeability under one-time chosen message attacks (sUF-OT-CMA security) is recalled in the full version.

PKE Construction. Let $\mathsf{KEM} = (\mathsf{KemGen}, \mathsf{Encap}, \mathsf{Decap})$ be an OW-PCA secure KEM scheme, having unique encapsulations, associated with a session key space $\mathcal{K}_{\mathsf{KEM}}$ and a ciphertext space $\mathcal{C}_{\mathsf{KEM}}$, where Encap uniformly samples K, $|\mathcal{K}_{\mathsf{KEM}}| \geq 2^\lambda$ and $|\mathcal{C}_{\mathsf{KEM}}| \geq 2^\lambda$. Let $\mathsf{MAC} = (\mathsf{MacGen}, \mathsf{Auth}, \mathsf{Verf})$ be a deterministic, injective MAC scheme, associated with a key space $\mathcal{K}_{\mathsf{MAC}}$, achieving

$$
\begin{array}{|l|}
\hline
\text{Setup}(1^\lambda):\\
\quad \text{Return } pp := 1^\lambda\\
\hline
\text{Gen}(pp = 1^\lambda):\\
\quad (pk^{kem}, sk^{kem}) \leftarrow \text{KemGen}(1^\lambda);\ pk := pk^{kem};\ sk := (pk^{kem}, sk^{kem})\\
\quad \text{Return } (pk, sk)\\
\hline
\text{Enc}(pk = pk^{kem}, m):\\
\quad r \leftarrow \mathcal{R}_{\text{Encap}};\ (K, c^{kem}) \leftarrow \text{Encap}(pk^{kem}; r);\ (K^{sym}, K^{mac}) = \text{H}_{\text{RO}}(K)\\
\quad c^{sym} = K^{sym} \oplus m;\ t = \text{Auth}(K^{mac}, (pk^{kem}, c^{kem}, c^{sym}))\\
\quad \text{Return } c = (c^{kem}, c^{sym}, t)\\
\hline
\text{Dec}(sk = (pk^{kem}, sk^{kem}), c = (c^{kem}, c^{sym}, t)):\\
\quad \overline{K} = \text{Decap}(sk^{kem}, c^{kem});\ (\overline{K}^{sym}, \overline{K}^{mac}) = \text{H}_{\text{RO}}(\overline{K})\\
\quad \text{If Verf}(\overline{K}^{mac}, (pk^{kem}, c^{kem}, c^{sym}), t) = 0:\ \text{return } \bot\\
\quad \text{Return } \overline{m} = c^{sym} \oplus \overline{K}^{sym}\\
\hline
\end{array}
$$

Fig. 6. Construction of $\text{PKE}_{\text{K-M}}$.

sUF-OT-CMA security. Let $\text{H}_{\text{RO}} : \mathcal{K}_{\text{KEM}} \to \{0,1\}^\ell \times \mathcal{K}_{\text{MAC}}$ be a hash function. Our PKE scheme $\text{PKE}_{\text{K-M}} = (\text{Setup}, \text{Gen}, \text{Enc}, \text{Dec})$, associated with a message space $\{0,1\}^\ell$, is defined in Fig. 6.

The correctness analysis of this scheme is trivial. Now we turn to its security analysis. Formally, we have the following theorem. Note that, in our construction, a valid ciphertext contains a tag t generated on $(pk^{kem}, c^{kem}, c^{sym})$, where in [14], the tag t is only generated on c^{sym}. We stress that this crucial modification makes our construction achieve SIM-Bi-SO-CCA security. The intuition for the security proof and details are provided in the full version.

Theorem 6. *If KEM has unique encapsulations and is OW-PCA secure, MAC is deterministic, injective and sUF-OT-CMA secure, and H_{RO} is modeled as a random oracle, then $\text{PKE}_{\text{K-M}}$ is SIM-Bi-SO-CCA secure in the random oracle model.*

Acknowledgment. We thank Fangguo Zhang for the helpful discussions. We appreciate the anonymous reviewers for their valuable comments. This work was supported by the National Natural Science Foundation of China (Grant Nos. 61922036, U2001205, 61702125, 61802078, 61825203, U1736203, 61732021), Major Program of Guangdong Basic and Applied Research (Grant No. 2019B030302008), National Key Research and Development Plan of China (Grant No. 2020YFB1005600), Guangdong Provincial Science and Technology Project (Grant No. 2017B010111005), and National Joint Engineering Research Center for Network Security Detection and Protection Technology.

A   Cryptographic Assumptions

The DDH Assumption. Let $\mathbb{G}$ be a cyclic group of prime order q with a generator g. The DDH assumption requires that it is hard to distinguish (g^a, g^b, g^c) and (g^a, g^b, g^{ab}), where $a, b, c \leftarrow \mathbb{Z}_q$.

The DCR Assumption. Now, we recall the Decision Composite Residuosity (DCR) assumption [30] and some useful facts about it shown in [8].

Let p, q, p', q' be primes such that $p = 2p' + 1$ and $q = 2q' + 1$. Let $N = pq$ and $N' = p'q'$. Then the group $\mathbb{Z}_{N^2}^*$ can be decomposed as the direct product $\mathbb{G}_N \cdot \mathbb{G}_{N'} \cdot \mathbb{G}_2 \cdot \mathbb{T}$, where $\mathbb{G}_{N'}$ and $\mathbb{G}_2$ are cyclic groups of order N' and order 2 respectively; $\mathbb{G}_N$ is a cyclic group of order N generated by $\xi = (1+N) \mod N^2$; and $\mathbb{T}$ is the order-2 subgroup of $\mathbb{Z}_{N^2}^*$ generated by $(-1 \mod N^2)$. Note that $\xi^a = (1 + aN) \mod N^2$ for $a \in \{0, 1, \cdots, N\}$.

The DCR assumption requires that it is hard to distinguish a random element in $\mathbb{Z}_{N^2}^*$ and a random element in $\mathbb{G}_{N'} \cdot \mathbb{G}_2 \cdot \mathbb{T}$.

Next, define $\mathbb{X} = \mathbb{G}_N \cdot \mathbb{G}_{N'} \cdot \mathbb{T}$. The set $\mathbb{X}$ is an efficiently samplable and explainable domain, where the sample algorithm and the explain algorithm work as follows:

- Sample: The sample algorithm proceeds as follows:
  1. For $i \in [1, 160]$:
     (a) $x \leftarrow \mathbb{Z}_{N^2}$
     (b) If the Jacobi symbol $(\frac{x}{N}) = 1$: **output** x.
  2. **Output** $\perp$.
- Explain: on input an element $x \in \mathbb{X}$, the explain algorithm proceeds as follows:
  1. Set r to be an empty string.
  2. For $i \in [1, 160]$:
     (a) Sample $b \leftarrow \{0, 1\}$.
     (b) If $b = 1$, append x to r and **outputs** r.
     (c) Otherwise, sample an element $x' \leftarrow \mathbb{Z}_{N^2}$ s.t. the Jacobi symbol $(\frac{x'}{N}) = -1$ and append x' to r.
  3. **Output** $\perp$.

Note that as $\frac{|\mathbb{X}|}{|\mathbb{Z}_{N^2}^*|} = 1/2$, the expected repetition in the sample algorithm is about 2 and the probability that the sample algorithm outputs $\perp$ is $\frac{1}{2^{160}}$, which is negligible. Also, it is easy to see the probability that the explain algorithm outputs $\perp$ is also $\frac{1}{2^{160}}$, which is negligible.

Also, define $\chi : \mathbb{Z}_{N^2} \to \mathbb{Z}_N$ as $\chi(a) = \lfloor a/N \rfloor$. For any fixed $x \in \mathbb{X}$, $\chi(x\xi^c)$ is uniform in $\mathbb{Z}_N$ if $c \leftarrow \mathbb{Z}_N$.

Finally, define $\mathbb{L} = \mathbb{G}_{N'} \cdot \mathbb{T}$. It is easy to create a generator g for $\mathbb{L}$ by first sampling a random element $\mu \in \mathbb{Z}_{N^2}^*$ and then computing $g = -\mu^{2N}$. Besides, the DCR assumption implies that a random element in $\mathbb{X}$ is computationally indistinguishable from a random element in $\mathbb{L}$.

References

1. Bellare, M., Boldyreva, A., Micali, S.: Public-key encryption in a multi-user setting: security proofs and improvements. In: Preneel, B. (ed.) EUROCRYPT 2000. LNCS, vol. 1807, pp. 259–274. Springer, Heidelberg (2000). https://doi.org/10.1007/3-540-45539-6_18

2. Bellare, M., Dowsley, R., Waters, B., Yilek, S.: Standard security does not imply security against selective-opening. In: Pointcheval, D., Johansson, T. (eds.) EUROCRYPT 2012. LNCS, vol. 7237, pp. 645–662. Springer, Heidelberg (2012). https://doi.org/10.1007/978-3-642-29011-4_38

3. Bellare, M., Hofheinz, D., Yilek, S.: Possibility and impossibility results for encryption and commitment secure under selective opening. In: Joux, A. (ed.) EUROCRYPT 2009. LNCS, vol. 5479, pp. 1–35. Springer, Heidelberg (2009). https://doi.org/10.1007/978-3-642-01001-9_1

4. Bellare, M., Yilek, S.: Encryption schemes secure under selective opening attack. Cryptology ePrint Archive, Report 2009/101 (2009). https://eprint.iacr.org/2009/101

5. Boyen, X., Li, Q.: All-but-many lossy trapdoor functions from lattices and applications. In: Katz, J., Shacham, H. (eds.) CRYPTO 2017. LNCS, vol. 10403, pp. 298–331. Springer, Cham (2017). https://doi.org/10.1007/978-3-319-63697-9_11

6. Canetti, R., Halevi, S., Katz, J.: Adaptively-secure, non-interactive public-key encryption. In: Kilian, J. (ed.) TCC 2005. LNCS, vol. 3378, pp. 150–168. Springer, Heidelberg (2005). https://doi.org/10.1007/978-3-540-30576-7_9

7. Cramer, R., Shoup, V.: A practical public key cryptosystem provably secure against adaptive chosen ciphertext attack. In: Krawczyk, H. (ed.) CRYPTO 1998. LNCS, vol. 1462, pp. 13–25. Springer, Heidelberg (1998). https://doi.org/10.1007/BFb0055717

8. Cramer, R., Shoup, V.: Universal hash proofs and a paradigm for adaptive chosen ciphertext secure public-key encryption. In: Knudsen, L.R. (ed.) EUROCRYPT 2002. LNCS, vol. 2332, pp. 45–64. Springer, Heidelberg (2002). https://doi.org/10.1007/3-540-46035-7_4

9. Fehr, S., Hofheinz, D., Kiltz, E., Wee, H.: Encryption schemes secure against chosen-ciphertext selective opening attacks. In: Gilbert, H. (ed.) EUROCRYPT 2010. LNCS, vol. 6110, pp. 381–402. Springer, Heidelberg (2010). https://doi.org/10.1007/978-3-642-13190-5_20

10. Goldreich, O.: Foundations of Cryptography: Volume 2, Basic Applications. Cambridge University Press, Cambridge (2009)

11. Hara, K., Kitagawa, F., Matsuda, T., Hanaoka, G., Tanaka, K.: Simulation-based receiver selective opening CCA secure PKE from standard computational assumptions. In: Catalano, D., De Prisco, R. (eds.) SCN 2018. LNCS, vol. 11035, pp. 140–159. Springer, Cham (2018). https://doi.org/10.1007/978-3-319-98113-0_8

12. Hazay, C., Patra, A., Warinschi, B.: Selective opening security for receivers. In: Iwata, T., Cheon, J.H. (eds.) ASIACRYPT 2015. LNCS, vol. 9452, pp. 443–469. Springer, Heidelberg (2015). https://doi.org/10.1007/978-3-662-48797-6_19

13. Hemenway, B., Libert, B., Ostrovsky, R., Vergnaud, D.: Lossy encryption: constructions from general assumptions and efficient selective opening chosen ciphertext security. In: Lee, D.H., Wang, X. (eds.) ASIACRYPT 2011. LNCS, vol. 7073, pp. 70–88. Springer, Heidelberg (2011). https://doi.org/10.1007/978-3-642-25385-0_4

14. Heuer, F., Jager, T., Kiltz, E., Schäge, S.: On the selective opening security of practical public-key encryption schemes. In: Katz, J. (ed.) PKC 2015. LNCS, vol. 9020, pp. 27–51. Springer, Heidelberg (2015). https://doi.org/10.1007/978-3-662-46447-2_2

15. Heuer, F., Poettering, B.: Selective opening security from simulatable data encapsulation. In: Cheon, J.H., Takagi, T. (eds.) ASIACRYPT 2016. LNCS, vol. 10032, pp. 248–277. Springer, Heidelberg (2016). https://doi.org/10.1007/978-3-662-53890-6_9

16. Hofheinz, D.: All-but-many lossy trapdoor functions. In: Pointcheval, D., Johansson, T. (eds.) EUROCRYPT 2012. LNCS, vol. 7237, pp. 209–227. Springer, Heidelberg (2012). https://doi.org/10.1007/978-3-642-29011-4_14

17. Hofheinz, D., Rao, V., Wichs, D.: Standard security does not imply indistinguishability under selective opening. In: Hirt, M., Smith, A. (eds.) TCC 2016. LNCS, vol. 9986, pp. 121–145. Springer, Heidelberg (2016). https://doi.org/10.1007/978-3-662-53644-5_5

18. Hofheinz, D., Rupp, A.: Standard versus selective opening security: separation and equivalence results. In: Lindell, Y. (ed.) TCC 2014. LNCS, vol. 8349, pp. 591–615. Springer, Heidelberg (2014). https://doi.org/10.1007/978-3-642-54242-8_25

19. Huang, Z., Lai, J., Chen, W., Au, M.H., Peng, Z., Li, J.: Simulation-based selective opening security for receivers under chosen-ciphertext attacks. Des. Codes Crypt. 87(6), 1345–1371 (2018). https://doi.org/10.1007/s10623-018-0530-1

20. Huang, Z., Liu, S., Qin, B.: Sender-equivocable encryption schemes secure against chosen-ciphertext attacks revisited. In: Kurosawa, K., Hanaoka, G. (eds.) PKC 2013. LNCS, vol. 7778, pp. 369–385. Springer, Heidelberg (2013). https://doi.org/10.1007/978-3-642-36362-7_23

21. Jia, D., Libert, B.: SO-CCA secure PKE from pairing based all-but-many lossy trapdoor functions. Des. Codes Crypt. 89(5), 895–923 (2021). https://doi.org/10.1007/s10623-021-00849-9

22. Jia, D., Lu, X., Li, B.: Receiver selective opening security from indistinguishability obfuscation. In: Dunkelman, O., Sanadhya, S.K. (eds.) INDOCRYPT 2016. LNCS, vol. 10095, pp. 393–410. Springer, Cham (2016). https://doi.org/10.1007/978-3-319-49890-4_22

23. Jia, D., Lu, X., Li, B.: Constructions secure against receiver selective opening and chosen ciphertext attacks. In: Handschuh, H. (ed.) CT-RSA 2017. LNCS, vol. 10159, pp. 417–431. Springer, Cham (2017). https://doi.org/10.1007/978-3-319-52153-4_24

24. Lai, J., Deng, R.H., Liu, S., Weng, J., Zhao, Y.: Identity-based encryption secure against selective opening chosen-ciphertext attack. In: Nguyen, P.Q., Oswald, E. (eds.) EUROCRYPT 2014. LNCS, vol. 8441, pp. 77–92. Springer, Heidelberg (2014). https://doi.org/10.1007/978-3-642-55220-5_5

25. Libert, B., Sakzad, A., Stehlé, D., Steinfeld, R.: All-but-many lossy trapdoor functions and selective opening chosen-ciphertext security from LWE. In: Katz, J., Shacham, H. (eds.) CRYPTO 2017. LNCS, vol. 10403, pp. 332–364. Springer, Cham (2017). https://doi.org/10.1007/978-3-319-63697-9_12

26. Liu, S., Paterson, K.G.: Simulation-based selective opening CCA security for PKE from key encapsulation mechanisms. In: Katz, J. (ed.) PKC 2015. LNCS, vol. 9020, pp. 3–26. Springer, Heidelberg (2015). https://doi.org/10.1007/978-3-662-46447-2_1

27. Lyu, L., Liu, S., Han, S., Gu, D.: Tightly SIM-SO-CCA secure public key encryption from standard assumptions. In: Abdalla, M., Dahab, R. (eds.) PKC 2018. LNCS, vol. 10769, pp. 62–92. Springer, Cham (2018). https://doi.org/10.1007/978-3-319-76578-5_3

28. Okamoto, T., Pointcheval, D.: REACT: rapid enhanced-security asymmetric cryptosystem transform. In: Naccache, D. (ed.) CT-RSA 2001. LNCS, vol. 2020, pp. 159–174. Springer, Heidelberg (2000). https://doi.org/10.1007/3-540-45353-9_13

29. O'Neill, A., Peikert, C., Waters, B.: Bi-deniable public-key encryption. In: Rogaway, P. (ed.) CRYPTO 2011. LNCS, vol. 6841, pp. 525–542. Springer, Heidelberg (2011). https://doi.org/10.1007/978-3-642-22792-9_30

30. Paillier, P.: Public-key cryptosystems based on composite degree residuosity classes. In: Stern, J. (ed.) EUROCRYPT 1999. LNCS, vol. 1592, pp. 223–238. Springer, Heidelberg (1999). https://doi.org/10.1007/3-540-48910-X_16

31. Steinfeld, R., Baek, J., Zheng, Y.: On the necessity of strong assumptions for the security of a class of asymmetric encryption schemes. In: Batten, L., Seberry, J. (eds.) ACISP 2002. LNCS, vol. 2384, pp. 241–256. Springer, Heidelberg (2002). https://doi.org/10.1007/3-540-45450-0_20

32. Yang, R., Lai, J., Huang, Z., Au, M.H., Xu, Q., Susilo, W.: Possibility and impossibility results for receiver selective opening secure PKE in the multi-challenge setting. In: Moriai, S., Wang, H. (eds.) ASIACRYPT 2020. LNCS, vol. 12491, pp. 191–220. Springer, Cham (2020). https://doi.org/10.1007/978-3-030-64837-4_7

Key Encapsulation Mechanism with Tight Enhanced Security in the Multi-user Setting: Impossibility Result and Optimal Tightness

Shuai Han[1,2]🆔, Shengli Liu[1,2,3(✉)]🆔, and Dawu Gu[1]🆔

[1] School of Electronic Information and Electrical Engineering,
Shanghai Jiao Tong University, Shanghai 200240, China
{dalen17,slliu,dwgu}@sjtu.edu.cn
[2] State Key Laboratory of Cryptology, P.O. Box 5159, Beijing 100878, China
[3] Westone Cryptologic Research Center, Beijing 100070, China

Abstract. For Key Encapsulation Mechanism (KEM) deployed in a multi-user setting, an adversary may corrupt some users to learn their secret keys, and obtain some encapsulated keys due to careless key managements of users. To resist such attacks, we formalize Enhanced security against Chosen Plaintext/Ciphertext Attack (ECPA/ECCA), which ask the pseudorandomness of unrevealed encapsulated keys under uncorrupted users. This enhanced security for KEM serves well for the security of a class of Authenticated Key Exchange protocols built from KEM.

In this paper, we study the achievability of tight ECPA and ECCA security for KEM in the multi-user setting, and present an impossibility result and an optimal security loss factor that can be obtained. The existing meta-reduction technique due to Bader et al. (EUROCRYPT 2016) rules out some KEMs, but many well-known KEMs, e.g., Cramer-Shoup KEM (SIAM J. Comput. 2003), Kurosawa-Desmedt KEM (CRYPTO 2004), run out. To solve this problem, we develop a new technique tool named rank of KEM and a new secret key partitioning strategy for meta-reduction. With this new tool and new strategy, we prove that KEM schemes with polynomially-bounded ranks have no tight ECPA and ECCA security from non-interactive complexity assumptions, and the security loss is at least linear in the number n of users. This impossibility result covers lots of well-known KEMs, including the Cramer-Shoup KEM, Kurosawa-Desmedt KEM and many others. Moreover, we show that the linear security loss is optimal by presenting concrete KEMs with security loss $\Theta(n)$. This is justified by a non-trivial security reduction with linear loss factor from ECPA/ECCA security to the traditional multi-challenge CPA/CCA security.

1 Introduction

The security of a cryptographic primitive is generally formalized by setting up a reasonable security model and defining a proper security notion. The security

© International Association for Cryptologic Research 2021
M. Tibouchi and H. Wang (Eds.): ASIACRYPT 2021, LNCS 13091, pp. 483–513, 2021.
https://doi.org/10.1007/978-3-030-92075-3_17

model formalizes resources obtained by an adversary $\mathcal{A}$ and also the attacks implemented by $\mathcal{A}$ in the real-life settings. For a primitive Π (or a computational problem P), its security model is described by an experiment (game) Exp_Π in which the environment (challenger) and an adversary interact with each other. The environment (challenger) in Exp_Π provides the resources with which $\mathcal{A}$ implements attacks, then environment detects whether $\mathcal{A}$ wins. Here $\mathcal{A}$ wins in Exp_Π means that the aim of its attacks is achieved. Without any resources for help, there also exists a threshold winning probability $\mathsf{thre}_{\mathsf{Exp}_\Pi}$ for any adversary. Then $\mathcal{A}$'s attacking advantage is given by $\epsilon_\mathcal{A} := |\Pr[\mathcal{A} \text{ wins}] - \mathsf{thre}_{\mathsf{Exp}_\Pi}|$. We call $(t_\mathcal{A}, \epsilon_\mathcal{A})$-$\mathcal{A}$ successfully attacks Π if $\mathcal{A}$'s running time is $t_\mathcal{A}$ and advantage is $\epsilon_\mathcal{A}$. Parameters $t_\mathcal{A}$ and $\epsilon_\mathcal{A}$ are measured by security parameter λ. If for all probabilistic polynomial-time (PPT) adversaries, their advantages are all negligible in the security parameter λ, then Π is (asymptotically) secure.

Security Reduction and Tightness. The security proof of primitive Π generally proceeds with a reduction algorithm $\mathcal{R}$, which transforms a $(t_\mathcal{A}, \epsilon_\mathcal{A})$-adversary $\mathcal{A}$ against Π to an algorithm $(t_\mathcal{R}, \epsilon_\mathcal{R})$-$\mathcal{R}^\mathcal{A}$ against a computational problem P (or another cryptographic primitive). Generally, we only consider simple black-box reduction [2], where $\mathcal{R}$ has oracle access to $\mathcal{A}$ by choosing the inputs for $\mathcal{A}$, running the adversary sequentially and observing its outputs (but not the codes or internal states of $\mathcal{A}$). Note that the working effort for $\mathcal{A}$ to win the security game is measured by the work factor $t_\mathcal{A}/\epsilon_\mathcal{A}$ [3], which captures the expected running time of $\mathcal{A}$ to break the security. The quotient of $\mathcal{R}$'s working factor and $\mathcal{A}$'s working factor is defined as the security loss factor $\ell_\mathcal{R}$, i.e., $\ell_\mathcal{R} := \frac{\epsilon_\mathcal{A}}{\epsilon_\mathcal{R}} \cdot \frac{t_\mathcal{R}}{t_\mathcal{A}}$. If $\ell_\mathcal{R}$ is a polynomial in the security parameter λ, then the security of Π is successfully reduced to the hardness of P. This implies that Π is secure as long as P is computationally hard. On the other hand, a large loss factor $\ell_\mathcal{R}$ will lead to a gap between Π's security level and P's hardness. To fill the gap, Π has to choose a large security parameter to make P hard enough, and this might make Π less efficient. Therefore, the smaller the security loss $\ell_\mathcal{R}$ is, the better the security reduction. If $\ell_\mathcal{R}$ is a constant, the reduction is called a *tight* one. If $\ell_\mathcal{R}$ is an a priori fixed polynomial in λ, then the reduction is called *almost tight* (or *linear-preserving* according to [33]). Such reductions (tight or almost tight) are desirable, since the loss factor is independent of adversarial behavior.

In cryptography, most of long-standing hard problem assumptions are non-interactive ones including the Decision Diffie-Hellman (DDH) assumption, the Factoring assumption, the Learning with Error (LWE) assumption, the existence of one-way function assumption, etc. If the security of a primitive can be (almost) tightly reduced to a Non-Interactive Complexity Assumption (NICA) [2], we call the primitive has (almost) tight security.

(Almost) tight security proofs for cryptographic schemes are always preferable. But the first question to be answered is whether (almost) tight reductions exist for the schemes.

KEM and Its Traditional Security. Key Encapsulation Mechanism (KEM) KEM = (Gen, Encap, Decap) is an important public-key primitive. Its key generation algorithm Gen is able to generate a pair of public key pk and secret key sk. With the public key pk, the encapsulation algorithm Encap can output an encapsulation c and an encapsulated key K. With the secret key sk, the decapsulation algorithm Decap can recover the encapsulated key K from c. KEM found wide applications in theoretic community and real world. For example, public-key encryption (PKE) schemes can always be constructed in a KEM + DEM (Data Encapsulation Mechanism) style [10,23], which include the well-known ElGamal scheme [12], Cramer-Shoup (CS) scheme [8–10], Kurosawa-Desmedt (KD) scheme [28], etc. Meanwhile, KEM usually serves as an essential building block in key exchange protocols. For example, the Diffie-Hellman key exchange protocol [11] can be regarded as exchanging $pk = g^a$, $c = g^b$ and establishing $K = g^{ab}$, with $(pk = g^a, sk = a) \leftarrow$ Gen and $(c = g^b, K = g^{ab}) \leftarrow$ Encap(pk). In [1,17,24,31], the authenticated key exchange (AKE) protocols are built from KEM and signature schemes. Due to the importance of KEM, NIST included KEM in their calling list for standards of post-quantum algorithms.

Traditionally, the security of KEM is defined in a single-user setting. In the single-user and multi-challenge Chosen-Plaintext Attack (mCPA) security model, the adversary sees the public key pk of KEM, and the environment invokes Encap multiple times to obtain $(c_i, K_i) \leftarrow$ Encap(pk). The mCPA security of KEM asks the pseudorandomness of $\{K_i\}$ given pk and $\{c_i\}$ to adversaries. Multi-challenge Chosen-Ciphertext Attack (mCCA) security of KEM can be similarly defined, except that the adversary additionally has access to a decapsulation oracle which provides decapsulation services for any c other than $\{c_i\}$.

Multi-user Security for KEM. We note that the traditional mCPA (mCCA) security notion in the single user setting does not cover the attacks in our real-life deployment of KEM. In the era of Internet, cryptographic schemes should presume to be deployed in multi-user systems. Moreover, in reality, we can never rule out the possibility that the secret keys of some users are stolen by hackers, or leaked to adversaries due to careless key management.

As for KEM, the practical attacks, including *corruption of users' secret keys* and *revealing of some encapsulated keys*, have to be considered in the security model. Concretely, in a system of n users with $(pk_i, sk_i) \leftarrow$ Gen, $1 \leq i \leq n$, the adversary may corrupt a subset I of users of its choice and obtain their secret keys $\{sk_i\}_{i \in I}$. For any uncorrupted user $j \notin I$, the adversary is able to see all the encapsulations $\{c_{j,t}\}_{1 \leq t \leq Q}$ under pk_j from a public channel, where $(c_{j,t}, K_{j,t}) \leftarrow$ Encap(pk_j), $1 \leq t \leq Q$. The adversary may reveal some encapsulated keys $\{K_{j,r}\}_{r \in R}$ for a subset $R \subseteq \{1, ..., Q\}$. The security of KEM asks pseudorandomness of the unrevealed keys $\{K_{j,t}\}_{j \notin I, t \notin R}$.

Such a security notion also meets the security requirement for KEM used as a building block in many applications. For example, in the KEM+DEM framework for constructing PKE [10], if an adversary sees a pair of plaintext & ciphertext of PKE, then the involved encapsulated key of KEM might be uniquely determined by the adversary [12] or partially leaked to the adversary [10,28]. Another example is AKE schemes built from KEM, where KEM's public/secret keys serve as (part of) AKE's long-term public/secret keys and KEM's encapsulated keys are used to derive AKE's session keys [6,24]. The security model of AKE (like the CK [5], CK+ [27], eCK [29] models) allows corruption of long-term secret keys and revealing of session keys, which in turn requires the underlying KEM supporting corruptions and key reveals.

In conclusion, the *proper* security for KEM in the multi-user setting should allow adversaries to implement corruptions & key reveals and ask the pseudorandomness of the unrevealed encapsulated keys under public keys of uncorrupted users. We name such notion *Enhanced* security, including Enhanced CPA (ECPA) security and Enhanced CCA (ECCA) security. Obviously, ECPA (resp., ECCA) security is stronger and more desirable than the traditional mCPA (resp., mCCA) security. There are two natural questions to be answered:

(1) Do the well-known KEM schemes have tight ECPA security (or ECCA security)? For example, the ElGamal-KEM [12], CS-KEM [8–10] and KD-KEM [28] are among the most efficient KEMs. The GHKW-KEM [14] and HLLG-KEM [19] are core building blocks in achieving (almost) tightly mCCA security for PKE. The Naor-Yung paradigm [35] is a generic approach to CCA-secure PKE, which further results in Naor-Yung type CCA-secure KEM (NY-KEM) by encrypting a uniformly random encapsulated key. We would like to investigate whether they achieve tight ECPA (or ECCA) security.

(2) How to identify those KEMs incapable of achieving tight ECPA or tight ECCA security?

Impossibility Results on Security Tightness of KEM. It is highly desirable to identify those KEMs for which it is impossible to reduce the ECPA (ECCA) security to any non-interactive complexity assumption (NICA) tightly.

In [2], Bader et al. made use of meta-reduction [7] to prove impossibility of tight security for some KEMs, namely, (almost) tight security reduction from multi-user mCPA (mCCA) security to NICA does not exist for a class of KEM schemes. These KEM schemes are characterized by the properties of "secret key checkability" and "secret key uniqueness/re-randomizability". "Secret key checkability" means that there exists an efficient algorithm checking whether (pk, sk) is a valid public/secret key pair output by Gen; "Secret key uniqueness" means that there is at most one valid secret key sk for each pk; "secret key re-randomizability" means that given a valid pair (pk, sk), there exists an efficient algorithm randomly choosing another secret key sk' from the set of secret keys that validly match pk.

Clearly, ECPA (resp., ECCA) security tightly implies multi-user mCPA (resp., mCCA) security, so all KEM schemes that satisfy "secret key checkability" and "secret key uniqueness/re-randomizability" do not have (almost) tight enhanced security. Recall that the ElGamal KEM [12] has public key $pk = g^a$ and secret key a, which obviously satisfies "secret key checkability" and "secret key uniqueness". This rules out the (almost) tight ECPA security of ElGamal KEM.

However, lots of other KEM schemes, including the CS-KEM [8–10] and KD-KEM [28], have neither "secret key uniqueness" nor "secret key re-randomizability". For example, for the CCA-secure CS-KEM [8–10], its public key pk contains $h = g_1^{z_1} g_2^{z_2}$ where $(z_1, z_2) \in (\mathbb{Z}_p)^2$ is part of secret key sk. For a fixed $pk = (h, \ldots)$, the set of valid secret keys is $\{(z_1', z_2', \ldots) \mid h = g_1^{z_1'} g_2^{z_2'}\}$. There are at least p valid secret keys, hence "secret key uniqueness" does not hold. Any two secret keys with distinct (z_1, z_2) and (z_1', z_2') can determine the value of $\log_{g_1} g_2 = (z_1 - z_1')(z_2' - z_2)^{-1} \mod p$, hence solving the discrete logarithm problem. So the CS-KEM does not satisfy the property of "secret key re-randomizability", unless the discrete logarithm problem is easy to solve. Therefore, determining whether tightness impossibility holds for such KEM schemes needs new techniques.

Our Contribution. We work on impossibility of tight reduction on KEM, and show that for certain KEM schemes, there exists no (almost) tight security reduction from the ECPA (ECCA) security to non-interactive complexity assumptions (NICA). We also present the optimal tightness bound of security loss factor and identify those KEM schemes that can achieve the optimal tightness bound. Our contribution is detailed as follows.

- We develop a useful tool named *rank of KEM* to identify a class of KEM schemes for which impossibility of (almost) tight reduction holds. More precisely, we proved that as long as the rank of a KEM scheme is *polynomially bounded* (in the security parameter λ), the incurred security loss factor of KEM is $\Omega(n)$ when the enhanced security of KEM is reduced to any NICA. Here n denotes the number of users.
- We compute the ranks or provide upper bounds of ranks for the well-known KEM schemes including the ElGamal-KEM [12], CS-KEM [8–10], KD-KEM [28], GHKW-KEM [14], HLLG-KEM [19], and many instantiations of NY-KEM [35]. Their polynomially-bounded ranks indicate that these KEMs suffer from a security loss factor $\Omega(n)$.
- On the other hand, we proved that any tightly mCPA (resp., mCCA) secure KEM is able to achieve ECPA (resp., ECCA) security with loss factor $O(n)$. As a result, the ElGamal-KEM [12], CS-KEM [8–10] and KD-KEM [28] all have ECPA security with security loss factor $\Theta(n)$ when reduced to the DDH assumption. Similarly, the HLLG-KEM [19] has ECCA security with security loss factor $\Theta(n)$ based on the matrix DDH (MDDH) assumption [13] (which corresponds to the standard DDH, k-Linear assumptions under different parameters). This suggests that the optimal security loss factor for ECPA (ECCA) is $\Theta(n)$ and achievable.

We highlight that our impossibility result is the first that does not impose any requirement on the (pk, sk) relation (like checkability [2,20], uniqueness, or re-randomizability [2,7,22,26,32]), nor limited to deterministic primitives [33].

1.1   Technique Overview

The Meta-Reduction Paradigm. Our impossibility result about KEM is built upon a line of research on using "meta-reductions" [2,4,7,22,26,33,36]. To the best of our knowledge, up to now all known black-box separations using the meta-reduction paradigm only apply to primitives that either embody some form of uniqueness or re-randomizability [2,7] or are deterministic ones like pseudorandom function (PRF) or message authentication code (MAC) with deterministic tagging [33].

The high-level idea of the meta-reduction paradigm for a primitive works as follows. Let $\mathcal{R}$ be any reduction algorithm from the security of the primitive to any NICA. Firstly, we construct a hypothetical (inefficient) adversary $\mathcal{A}^*$ that breaks the security of the primitive with advantage $\epsilon_{\mathcal{A}^*} \geq 1 - \alpha$. Here α means the failure probability of $\mathcal{A}^*$. Let $\epsilon_{\mathcal{R}^{\mathcal{A}^*}}$ be the advantage with which $\mathcal{R}^{\mathcal{A}^*}$ breaks the NICA via black-box access to $\mathcal{A}^*$. Secondly, we construct an efficient meta-reduction algorithm $\mathcal{B}$, which "emulates" $\mathcal{A}^*$ while running $\mathcal{R}$. Suppose that $\mathcal{B}$ emulates $\mathcal{R}^{\mathcal{A}^*}$ perfectly except with probability at most δ, then $\mathcal{B}$'s advantage $\epsilon_{\mathcal{B}}$ against NICA satisfies $|\epsilon_{\mathcal{B}} - \epsilon_{\mathcal{R}^{\mathcal{A}^*}}| \leq \delta$. Obviously, the running time $t_{\mathcal{R}^{\mathcal{A}^*}}$ is lower-bounded by $t_{\mathcal{A}^*}$. Consequently, the loss factor of reduction $\mathcal{R}$ is

$$\ell_{\mathcal{R}} \geq \frac{\epsilon_{\mathcal{A}^*}}{\epsilon_{\mathcal{R}^{\mathcal{A}^*}}} \cdot \frac{t_{\mathcal{R}^{\mathcal{A}^*}}}{t_{\mathcal{A}^*}} \geq \frac{1-\alpha}{\epsilon_{\mathcal{B}}+\delta}.$$

By the NICA assumption, $\epsilon_{\mathcal{B}}$ is negligibly small for any efficient $\mathcal{B}$. So

$$\ell_{\mathcal{R}} = \Omega(\tfrac{1-\alpha}{\delta}), \tag{1}$$

which suggests that the failure probability α of $\mathcal{A}^*$ and the failure probability δ of $\mathcal{B}$ are the key factors for the lower bound of loss factor $\ell_{\mathcal{R}}$.

Let us take [2] and [33] as examples, both of which rule out (almost) tight (i.e., linear-preserving) reductions for the multi-user security of some primitives. Let n denote the number of users.

- In [33], $\alpha = 1/\mathsf{poly}(\lambda)$ for some polynomial poly. If MAC is deterministic, then $\delta = 1/\sqrt{n}$.[1] Therefore, the security reduction for such MACs loses a factor of $\Omega(\sqrt{n})$.

  Note that the construction of $\mathcal{A}^*$ and meta-reduction $\mathcal{B}$ in [33] are tailored for deterministic primitives like PRF, deterministic MAC, deterministic signature, etc.

- In [2], $\alpha = 0$. If KEM satisfies the properties of "secret key checkability" and "secret key uniqueness/re-randomizability", then $\delta = 1/n$. Therefore, the security reduction for such KEMs loses a factor of $\Omega(n)$.

  Note that in [2] the secret keys are partitioned according to an efficient algorithm $\mathsf{SKCheck}(\cdot, \cdot)$ which checks the relation between pk and sk. For each pk, let $\mathcal{SK}_{pk}$ be the set of all secret keys corresponding to pk, i.e., $\mathcal{SK}_{pk} := \{sk' \mid \mathsf{SKCheck}(pk, sk') = 1\}$. "Secret key uniqueness" means that there is unique sk in $\mathcal{SK}_{pk}$. "Secret key re-randomizability" requires that there is another efficient algorithm for sampling sk' from $\mathcal{SK}_{pk}$ uniformly at random, given a pair of (pk, sk). The construction of $\mathcal{A}^*$ and $\mathcal{B}$ in [2] works so that $\delta = 1/n$ when (pk, sk) relation has checkability and uniqueness/re-randomizability. Such a condition is satisfied by the ElGamal-KEM [12], but

---

[1] Their results apply to more general reductions supporting rewinding and concurrency, based on bounded-round interactive complexity assumptions.

lots of other KEMs run out, including the CS-KEM [8–10], KD-KEM [28], GHKW-KEM [14], HLLG-KEM [19], etc. Therefore, we have to resort to new techniques to identity whether these KEMs have (almost) tight ECPA (ECCA) security or not.

New Partitioning Technique: Decapsulation Equivalence of Secret Keys. In this paper, we take full advantage of the resources provided to adversary in the ECPA (ECCA) game, and provide a novel technique of partitioning secret keys. We do not impose any requirement on the (pk, sk) relation (like checkability, uniqueness, or re-randomizability), and the secret keys are no longer partitioned according to public keys like [2] does. Our new strategy is partitioning secret keys according to their functionality when they are used to decapsulate a set of ciphertexts $\mathcal{X}$.

We define a decapsulation equivalence relation on the secret key space $\mathcal{SK}$ w.r.t. a subset of ciphertexts $\mathcal{X} \subseteq \mathcal{CT}$. Any two secret keys $sk, sk' \in \mathcal{SK}$ are decapsulation-equivalent w.r.t. $\mathcal{X}$ if they result in the same decapsulated key for each ciphertext in $\mathcal{X}$. In formula,

$$sk \sim_{\mathcal{X}} sk' \iff \forall c \in \mathcal{X}, \ \mathsf{Decap}(sk, c) = \mathsf{Decap}(sk', c).$$

Then the equivalence relation parameterized by ciphertext set $\mathcal{X}$ is

$$\mathsf{EquivSK}(\mathcal{X}) := \{(sk, sk') \in \mathcal{SK}^2 \mid \forall c \in \mathcal{X}, \mathsf{Decap}(sk, c) = \mathsf{Decap}(sk', c)\}.$$

Our Meta-Reduction. With the new partitioning of secret keys, we are able to present our new meta reduction. Here we give a high-level overview of the hypothetical adversary $\mathcal{A}^*$ and meta-reduction algorithm $\mathcal{B}$ in our meta-reduction. Define $[n] := \{1, 2, \cdots, n\}$ and $[n\backslash i] := \{1, 2, \cdots, n\}\backslash\{i\}$.

A high-level overview of $\mathcal{A}^*$ is presented in Fig. 1. Note that by the perfect correctness of KEM, the real secret key sk_{i^*} of user i^* also belongs to the set shown in (2), so the real secret key sk_{i^*} and the sk^* chosen by $\mathcal{A}^*$ have the same decapsulation functionality when they are used to decapsulate the set of ciphertexts $\{c_{i^*,j}\}_{j \in [Q\backslash j_{i^*}]}$. Consequently, by the equivalence relation we defined, we have

$$(sk^*, sk_{i^*}) \in \mathsf{EquivSK}(\{c_{i^*,1}, \cdots, c_{i^*,Q}\}\backslash\{c_{i^*,j_{i^*}}\}).$$

Observe that $\mathcal{A}^*$ will have advantage 1 if $\mathsf{EquivSK}(\{c_{i^*,1}, \cdots, c_{i^*,Q}\}\backslash\{c_{i^*,j_{i^*}}\}) \subseteq \mathsf{EquivSK}(\{c_{i^*,j_{i^*}}\})$, i.e., all the secret keys that have the same decapsulation results on the $Q - 1$ ciphertexts also result in the same decapsulation result on one more ciphertext $c_{i^*,j_{i^*}}$. Define

$$\alpha := \max_{c_1, c_2, \cdots, c_Q} \left(\Pr_{j \xleftarrow{\$} [Q]} \left[\mathsf{EquivSK}(\{c_1, \cdots, c_Q\}\backslash\{c_j\}) \not\subseteq \mathsf{EquivSK}(\{c_j\})\right] \right). \quad (3)$$

Then $\mathcal{A}^*$ has advantage $\epsilon_{\mathcal{A}^*} \geq 1 - \alpha$.

Now we construct a meta-reduction $\mathcal{B}$ that emulates $\mathcal{A}^*$ efficiently while running $\mathcal{R}$ as the challenger. Note that all steps of $\mathcal{A}^*$ are efficient except step 5.

Hypothetical $\mathcal{A}^*$

- STEP 1 (SETUP): $\mathcal{A}^*$ receives public keys $\{pk_1, \cdots, pk_n\}$ of n users, which are generated by $(pk_i, sk_i) \leftarrow$ Gen.
- STEP 2 (ENCAPSULATION): $\mathcal{A}^*$ issues Q encapsulation queries per user, and obtains nQ encapsulations $\{c_{i,j}\}_{i \in [n], j \in [Q]}$, where $(c_{i,j}, K_{i,j}) \leftarrow$ Encap(pk_i).
- STEP 3 (KEY REVEAL): $\mathcal{A}^*$ reveals $Q - 1$ encapsulated keys per user randomly, and obtains $n(Q - 1)$ encapsulated keys $\{K_{i,j}\}_{i \in [n], j \in [Q \setminus j_i]}$, where $j_1, j_2, \cdots, j_n \leftarrow_\$ [Q]$ are the indices of unrevealed keys.
- STEP 4 (CORRUPTION & CHECK): $\mathcal{A}^*$ corrupts all users except one, and obtains $n - 1$ secret keys $\{sk_i\}_{i \in [n \setminus i^*]}$, where $i^* \leftarrow_\$ [n]$ is the index of the uncorrupted user.
    Then $\mathcal{A}^*$ checks whether the decapsulation relation Decap$(sk_i, c_{i,j}) = K_{i,j}$ holds for each $i \in [n \setminus i^*]$ and $j \in [Q \setminus j_i]$, and aborts if the check fails.
- STEP 5 (CHALLENGE & OUTPUT): $\mathcal{A}^*$ obtains a challenge K^* w.r.t. $c_{i^*, j_{i^*}}$, which is either the real key $K_{i^*, j_{i^*}}$ encapsulated in $c_{i^*, j_{i^*}}$ or a random key. By brute-force search, $\mathcal{A}^*$ picks a random sk^* from the set

$$\{sk \in \mathcal{SK} \mid \text{Decap}(sk, c_{i^*, j}) = K_{i^*, j}, \ \forall j \in [Q \setminus j_{i^*}]\}. \tag{2}$$

    Finally, $\mathcal{A}^*$ outputs 1 if and only if $K^* = \text{Decap}(sk^*, c_{i^*, j_{i^*}})$ holds.

Fig. 1. High-level overview of the hypothetical adversary $\mathcal{A}^*$ in our meta-reduction.

So $\mathcal{B}$ can emulate steps 1–4 of $\mathcal{A}^*$ honestly. Then $\mathcal{B}$ adds a rewinding step 4.5 which rewinds the corruption procedure $n - 1$ times. With the help of information obtained from the rewindings, $\mathcal{B}$ derives a secret key to emulate $\mathcal{A}^*$ with an efficient step 5', which is different from the step 5 of $\mathcal{A}^*$. A high-level overview of $\mathcal{B}$ is presented in Fig. 2.

In step 5', as long as there exists a rewinding in which $\mathcal{R}$ responds with a corrupted secret key $sk_{i^*}^{(\iota)}$ such that (4) holds, then $\mathcal{B}$ will not abort. Since i^* is randomly chosen from $[n]$, by a similar argument as [2,20], we can bound the probability that $\mathcal{B}$ aborts by $1/n$. If (4) holds, then the $sk_{i^*}^{(\iota)}$ obtained by $\mathcal{B}$ also belongs to the set defined in (2), from which $\mathcal{A}$ chooses its sk^*, thus

$$(sk_{i^*}^{(\iota)}, sk^*) \in \text{EquivSK}(\{c_{i^*, 1}, \cdots, c_{i^*, Q}\} \setminus \{c_{i^*, j_{i^*}}\}).$$

In this case, $\mathcal{B}$ will perfectly emulate $\mathcal{A}^*$ as long as EquivSK$(\{c_{i^*, 1}, \cdots, c_{i^*, Q}\} \setminus \{c_{i^*, j_{i^*}}\}) \subseteq \text{EquivSK}(\{c_{i^*, j_{i^*}}\})$, which happens with probability at least $1 - \alpha$ according to the definition of α in (3). Taking into account the probability that $\mathcal{B}$ aborts, we know that $\mathcal{B}$ perfectly emulates $\mathcal{A}^*$ for $\mathcal{R}$ except with probability at most $\alpha + 1/n$. Therefore,

$$|\epsilon_\mathcal{B} - \epsilon_{\mathcal{R}^{\mathcal{A}^*}}| \leq \delta = \alpha + 1/n. \tag{5}$$

Meta-Reduction $\mathcal{B}$

- STEPS 1-4: $\mathcal{B}$ runs $\mathcal{R}$ as the challenger and emulates $\mathcal{A}^*$ honestly. Suppose that in step 4, the index of the uncorrupted user is i^*.
- STEP 4.5 (REWINDING): $\mathcal{B}$ rewinds the corruption procedure $n-1$ times. In the ι-th rewind ($\iota \in [n \setminus i^*]$), $\mathcal{B}$ corrupts all users except user ι and obtains the corrupted secret keys $\{sk_i^{(\iota)}\}_{i \in [n \setminus \iota]}$ from $\mathcal{R}$, where $sk_i^{(\iota)}$ denotes the corrupted secret key of user i obtained in the ι-th rewind.
- STEP 5' (CHALLENGE & OUTPUT): $\mathcal{B}$ runs $\mathcal{R}$ to obtain the challenge K^*, but has a different strategy for the output bit.

  More precisely, $\mathcal{B}$ checks whether it ever obtained a corrupted $sk_{i^*}^{(\iota)}$ of user i^* in one of the $n-1$ rewindings, such that

  $$\mathsf{Decap}(sk_{i^*}^{(\iota)}, c_{i^*,j}) = K_{i^*,j}, \quad \text{for } \forall j \in [Q \setminus j_{i^*}]. \tag{4}$$

  If $\mathcal{B}$ finds such a $sk_{i^*}^{(\iota)}$, then $\mathcal{B}$ uses $sk_{i^*}^{(\iota)}$ to test whether $K^* = \mathsf{Decap}(sk_{i^*}^{(\iota)}, c_{i^*,j_{i^*}})$, and returns 1 to $\mathcal{R}$ if and only if the equation holds.

Fig. 2. High-level overview of the meta-reduction algorithm $\mathcal{B}$ in our meta-reduction.

By plugging (5) into (1), we obtain a lower bound of the security loss factor in our meta-reduction:

$$\ell_R = \Omega(\tfrac{1-\alpha}{\delta}) = \Omega(\tfrac{1-\alpha}{\alpha+1/n}),$$

where α is defined in (3).

Observe that as long as $\alpha = O(1/n)$, the loss factor is $\ell_R = \Omega(n)$, at least linear in the number n of users. Next, we identify a class of KEMs with $\alpha = O(1/n)$ with a new technique tool called *rank of KEM*.

New Technique Tool: Rank of KEM. We define the *rank* of a KEM scheme KEM, denoted by $\mathsf{Rank}_{\mathsf{KEM}}$, as the cardinality of the largest *independent* subset $\mathcal{X}' \subseteq \mathcal{CT}$ such that $\mathsf{EquivSK}(\mathcal{X}') = \mathsf{EquivSK}(\mathcal{CT})$. Here we explain the intuitions behind this new notion and the meaning of independent set.

- $\mathsf{EquivSK}(\mathcal{X}') = \mathsf{EquivSK}(\mathcal{CT})$ indicates that, all the secret keys that have the same decapsulation functionality on $\mathcal{X}'$ also have the same decapsulation functionality on the whole ciphertext space $\mathcal{CT}$. Intuitively, this means that $\mathcal{X}'$ "determines" the decapsulation functionality of secret keys on the whole ciphertext space $\mathcal{CT}$.
- We require $\mathcal{X}'$ to be an *independent* set in the sense that every ciphertext c in $\mathcal{X}'$ contributes to $\mathsf{EquivSK}(\mathcal{X}')$, i.e., $\mathsf{EquivSK}(\mathcal{X}' \setminus \{c\}) \neq \mathsf{EquivSK}(\mathcal{X}')$.

Intuitively, the relation between $\mathcal{X}'$ and $\mathcal{CT}$ is analogous to the relation between a basis and a linear space, and the rank of KEM is analogous to the size of (the largest) basis (i.e., the dimension of linear space).

However, we note that in general the decapsulation algorithm Decap of KEM is not a linear function, especially for CCA-secure KEMs. So the rank of KEM is *different from* the dimension of $\mathcal{CT}$ even if $\mathcal{CT}$ is indeed a linear space. Moreover, we highlight that our notion of rank for KEM is more general and purely defined based on the equivalence relation "EquivSK" on secret keys, and we in fact do not require any algebraic structure from $\mathcal{CT}$.

Bounding the Security Loss with KEM's Rank. The notion of rank for KEM is a useful tool for analyzing the failure probability α defined in (3) in our meta-reduction. Let us name a ciphertext c a *bad* one in $\mathcal{X}$ if $\mathsf{EquivSK}(\mathcal{X} \setminus \{c\}) \not\subseteq \mathsf{EquivSK}(\{c\})$. We prove an important core lemma (see Lemma 3 in Subsect. 4.3). The core lemma shows that the number of bad ciphertexts in any ciphertext subset $\mathcal{X}$ is upper bounded by $\mathsf{Rank}_{\mathsf{KEM}}$. As a result, we have

$$\Pr_{c \xleftarrow{\$} \mathcal{X}} \left[\mathsf{EquivSK}(\mathcal{X} \setminus \{c\}) \not\subseteq \mathsf{EquivSK}(\{c\}) \right] \leq \frac{\mathsf{Rank}_{\mathsf{KEM}}}{\#\mathcal{X}}. \tag{6}$$

Combining (6) and (3), we have

$$\alpha \leq \frac{\mathsf{Rank}_{\mathsf{KEM}}}{Q}.$$

Note that Q is the number of encapsulation queries made by $\mathcal{A}^*$ for each user. As long as $\mathsf{Rank}_{\mathsf{KEM}}$ is bounded by an a priori fixed polynomial (in the security parameter λ), we can always choose Q such that $\alpha \leq \mathsf{Rank}_{\mathsf{KEM}}/Q < 1/n$. Then the security loss factor is $\ell_{\mathcal{R}} = \Omega(\frac{1-\alpha}{\delta}) = \Omega(\frac{1-\alpha}{\alpha+1/n}) = \Omega(n)$.

Consequently, with our new technique tool, rank of KEM, we identify a class of KEMs for which impossibility of (almost) tight reduction holds. Namely, any KEM with polynomially-bounded rank has no (almost) tight (i.e., linear-preserving) reduction from its ECPA (ECCA) security to any NICA.

A careful computation of ranks for many well-known KEM schemes (including the ElGamal-KEM [12], CS-KEM [8–10], KD-KEM [28], GHKW-KEM [14], HLLG-KEM [19] and many instantiations of NY-KEM [35]) shows that our impossibility result applies to these KEM schemes. See Subsect. 5.2 and the full version [18] for more details.

1.2 Application of Our Impossibility Result in AKE

Authenticated Key Exchange (AKE) is one of the most widely deployed protocols on Internet and it allows two parties to establish a session key over public channels. Most of AKE constructions make use of KEM explicitly or implicitly, for instance, the well-known Signed Diffie-Hellman Protocol, modular AKE constructions in [1,17,24,31,38]. Therefore, the security of AKE is closely related to the security of KEM. Defining a proper security for KEM can directly serve the security proof of AKE.

The well-known security notions of AKE are defined with the CK model [5], eCK model [29], or CK+ model [27], all of which consider both passive attacks and active attacks in the multi-user setting. Passive attacks allow the adversary to see the messages over public channel, while active attacks not only allow the adversary to modify, drop, replay, or inject messages on the public channel, but also allow the adversary to corrupt user's long-term secret key in AKE and reveal session keys of some AKE protocol instances. The security of AKE requires the pseudorandomness of session keys between two users, if the session keys are not revealed and the two users' long-term secret keys are not corrupted.

Let us consider the case that the public and secret keys (pk_{KEM}, sk_{KEM}) of KEM serve as part of a user's long-term public key $pk_{AKE} = (pk_{KEM}, \cdots)$ and secret key $sk_{AKE} = (sk_{KEM}, \cdots)$ of AKE. Furthermore, the session key of AKE is derived from the encapsulated key of KEM. As a result, the corruption of sk_{AKE} requires the security of the underlying KEM to support corruption of sk_{KEM}, and the reveal of session keys in AKE asks the underlying KEM to support reveal of encapsulated keys. Therefore, the ECPA (ECCA) security of KEM is exactly the right security notion needed by AKE in this case. Combined with our impossibility result, any KEM with polynomially-bounded rank cannot be tightly secure, hence such construction of AKE cannot be tightly secure as well.

Therefore, we have the following rules for constructing tightly secure AKE: either (i) the secret key of KEM does not appear in the long-term secret key of AKE, like [1,17,31]; or (ii) the tight security proof of AKE relies on the Random Oracle model, like [16,24,37]; or (iii) AKE avoids the usage of KEM with polynomially-bounded rank. Up to now, most of the well-known efficient KEM schemes with tight mCPA-security in the multi-user setting have polynomially-bounded rank. Hence rule (iii) eliminates the possibility of constructing tightly AKE with aforementioned KEMs if KEM's secret keys are used as AKE's long-term keys.

1.3 Related Works

Meta-reduction paradigm was proposed in [4] and used to show black-box impossibility results. Later, Coron [7] made use of meta-reductions to prove the impossibility of tight reductions for certain digital signature schemes and showed the lower bounds on security loss. This technique was further extended in [2,26,32].

Hofheinz et al. [22] showed that any black-box security proof for a signature scheme with re-randomizable signatures must have a reduction loss of at least Q, the number of signature queries from the adversary.

Lewko and Waters [30] used the technique in [22] to identify certain conditions for hierarchical identity-based encryption (HIBE) under which HIBE has an exponential loss.

Bader et al. [2] developed a new meta-reduction technique to obtain a bundle of impossibility results. Their results rule out tight reductions from non-interactive complexity assumptions (NICA) for certain class of public-key encryption (PKE), KEM and digital signatures with multi-user security allowing secret key corruptions. This class of public-key primitives is characterized by secret key's checkable relation with public key and property of secret key uniqueness or re-randomizibility.

Jager et al. [25] considered symmetric encryption schemes in multi-user setting in which adversaries can adaptively corrupt encryption keys. They ruled out linear-preserving black-box reductions from adaptive multi-user security to single-user security for any authenticated encryption scheme with a strong "key uniqueness" property.

Very recently, Morgan et al. [33] studied black-box reductions to "standard" assumptions for message authentication code (MAC). Their black-box reduction is a general one which allows reduction algorithm to concurrently run or rewind adversary, and the complexity assumption is extended from NICA to any interactive assumption with pre-defined bounded number of interactions. They showed that linear-preserving security reduction does not exist for adaptive multi-user secure deterministic stateless MACs. Their results also hold for PRFs and deterministic stateless signatures. However, the meta-reduction paradigm in [33] only applies to deterministic primitives.

2   Preliminaries

2.1   Notations

Let $\lambda \in \mathbb{N}$ denote the security parameter throughout the paper. Let $\emptyset$ denote the empty set. If x is defined by y or the value of y is assigned to x, we write $x := y$. For $n \in \mathbb{N}$, define $[n] := \{1, 2, ..., n\}$, and for $i \in [n]$, define $[n \setminus i] := [n] \setminus \{i\}$. For a set $\{x_1, ..., x_n\}$ and $i \in [n]$, define $\{x_1, ..., x_n \setminus x_i\} := \{x_1, ..., x_n\} \setminus \{x_i\}$. For a set $\mathcal{X}$, denote by $\#\mathcal{X}$ the cardinality of $\mathcal{X}$. Denote by $x \leftarrow_\$ \mathcal{X}$ the procedure of sampling x from set $\mathcal{X}$ uniformly at random. If $\mathcal{D}$ is distribution, $x \leftarrow_\$ \mathcal{D}$ means that x is sampled according to $\mathcal{D}$. All our algorithms are probabilistic unless stated otherwise. We use $y \leftarrow_\$ \mathcal{A}(x)$ to define the random variable y obtained by executing algorithm $\mathcal{A}$ on input x. We use $y \in \mathcal{A}(x)$ to indicate that y lies in the support of $\mathcal{A}(x)$. If $\mathcal{A}$ is deterministic we write $y \leftarrow \mathcal{A}(x)$. We also use $y \leftarrow \mathcal{A}(x; r)$ to make explicit the random coins r used in the probabilistic computation. Denote by $t_\mathcal{A}$ the running time of $\mathcal{A}$.

2.2   Key Encapsulation Mechanisms

Definition 1 (KEM).   *A key encapsulation mechanism (KEM) scheme* KEM = (Setup, Gen, Encap, Decap) *consists of four algorithms:*

- Setup: *The setup algorithm outputs public parameters pp, which determine public key and secret key spaces* $\mathcal{PK} \times \mathcal{SK}$, *an encapsulation key space* $\mathcal{K}$, *and a ciphertext space* $\mathcal{CT}$.
- Gen(pp): *Taking pp as input, the key generation algorithm outputs a pair of public key and secret key* $(pk, sk) \in \mathcal{PK} \times \mathcal{SK}$.
- Encap(pk): *Taking pk as input, the encapsulation algorithm outputs a pair of ciphertext* $c \in \mathcal{CT}$ *and encapsulated key* $K \in \mathcal{K}$.
- Decap(sk, c): *Taking as input sk and c, the deterministic decapsulation algorithm outputs* $K \in \mathcal{K} \cup \{\bot\}$.

We require that for all $pp \in \mathsf{Setup}$, $(pk, sk) \in \mathsf{Gen}(pp)$, $(c, K) \in \mathsf{Encap}(pk)$, it holds that $\mathsf{Decap}(sk, c) = K$.

We recall the traditional IND-CPA/CCA security notions for KEMs in the single-user and multi-challenge setting, denoted by IND-mCPA/IND-mCCA for short.

Definition 2 (IND-mCPA/IND-mCCA Security). *We say that an adversary $\mathcal{A}$ $(t_{\mathcal{A}}, \epsilon_{\mathcal{A}})$-breaks the IND-mCPA (resp., IND-mCCA) security of* KEM, *if it runs in time $t_{\mathcal{A}}$, and $\mathsf{Adv}_{\mathsf{KEM}}^{\mathsf{ind\text{-}mcpa}}(\mathcal{A}) := 2 \cdot \left| \Pr[\mathsf{Exp}_{\mathsf{KEM}}^{\mathsf{ind\text{-}mcpa}}(\mathcal{A}) \Rightarrow 1] - \frac{1}{2} \right| \geq \epsilon_{\mathcal{A}}$ (resp., $\mathsf{Adv}_{\mathsf{KEM}}^{\mathsf{ind\text{-}mcca}}(\mathcal{A}) := 2 \cdot \left| \Pr[\mathsf{Exp}_{\mathsf{KEM}}^{\mathsf{ind\text{-}mcca}}(\mathcal{A}) \Rightarrow 1] - \frac{1}{2} \right| \geq \epsilon_{\mathcal{A}}$), where the experiments are defined in Fig. 3.*

$\mathsf{Exp}_{\mathsf{KEM}}^{\mathsf{ind\text{-}mcpa}}(\mathcal{A})$, $\mathsf{Exp}_{\mathsf{KEM}}^{\mathsf{ind\text{-}mcca}}(\mathcal{A})$:	$\mathcal{O}_{\mathrm{ENC}}()$:
$pp \leftarrow_{\$} \mathsf{Setup}$	$(c, K) \leftarrow_{\$} \mathsf{Encap}(pk)$
$(pk, sk) \leftarrow_{\$} \mathsf{Gen}(pp)$	$\mathsf{EncList} := \mathsf{EncList} \cup \{c\}$
$\mathsf{EncList} := \emptyset$ //Records the encapsulation queries	$K_0 := K; \; K_1 \leftarrow_{\$} \mathcal{K}$
$b \leftarrow_{\$} \{0, 1\}$ //challenge bit	Return (c, K_b)
$b' \leftarrow_{\$} \mathcal{A}^{\mathcal{O}_{\mathrm{ENC}}(\cdot), \, \mathcal{O}_{\mathrm{DEC}}(\cdot, \cdot)}(pp, pk)$	$\mathcal{O}_{\mathrm{DEC}}(c')$:
If $b' = b$: Return 1; Else: Return 0	If $c' \notin \mathsf{EncList}$: Return $K' \leftarrow \mathsf{Decap}(sk, c')$
	Else: Return $\perp$

Fig. 3. The IND-mCPA security experiment $\mathsf{Exp}_{\mathsf{KEM}}^{\mathsf{ind\text{-}mcpa}}(\mathcal{A})$ and the IND-mCCA security experiment $\mathsf{Exp}_{\mathsf{KEM}}^{\mathsf{ind\text{-}mcca}}(\mathcal{A})$ of KEM, where in the latter the adversary has also access to a decapsulation oracle $\mathcal{O}_{\mathrm{DEC}}(\cdot)$.

2.3   Non-interactive Assumptions

We recall the definition of non-interactive complexity assumptions (NICA).

Definition 3 (NICA [2]). *A non-interactive complexity assumption (NICA) $N = (T, V, U)$ consists of three algorithms. The instance generation algorithm T outputs a problem instance x and a witness w. U is a PPT algorithm, which takes x as input and outputs a candidate solution s. The verification algorithm V takes as input (x, w) and a candidate solution s. If $V(x, w, s) = 1$, then we say that s is a correct solution to the challenge x.*

We say that an adversary $\mathcal{B}$ $(t_{\mathcal{B}}, \epsilon_{\mathcal{B}})$-breaks an NICA $N = (T, V, U)$, if it runs in time $t_{\mathcal{B}}$, and $\mathsf{Adv}_N^{\mathsf{nica}}(\mathcal{B}) := \left| \Pr[\mathsf{Exp}_N^{\mathsf{nica}}(\mathcal{B}) \Rightarrow 1] - \Pr[\mathsf{Exp}_N^{\mathsf{nica}}(U) \Rightarrow 1] \right| \geq \epsilon_{\mathcal{B}}$, where the experiment $\mathsf{Exp}_N^{\mathsf{nica}}(Z)$ $(Z \in \{\mathcal{B}, U\})$ runs $(x, w) \leftarrow_{\$} T$, executes $s \leftarrow_{\$} Z(x)$, and outputs $V(x, w, s)$.

Intuitively, U is an algorithm which implements a suitable "trivial" attack strategy for N, and $\Pr[\mathsf{Exp}_N^{\mathsf{nica}}(U) \Rightarrow 1]$ is the winning probability of trivial attacks.

3   Enhanced Security Notions for KEMs

In this section, we introduce Enhanced CPA/CCA security notions for KEM in the Multi-User and Multi-Challenge (MUMC) setting, called *MUMC-ECPA/ MUMC-ECCA*, which allow user corruptions and encapsulated key reveals.

Definition 4 (MUMC-ECPA/ECCA Security). *We say that an adversary $\mathcal{A}$ $(t_{\mathcal{A}}, \epsilon_{\mathcal{A}}, n, Q_e, Q_t)$-breaks the MUMC-ECPA (resp., MUMC-ECCA) security of KEM, if it runs in time $t_{\mathcal{A}}$, and $\mathsf{Adv}^{\mathsf{mumc\text{-}ecpa}}_{\mathsf{KEM}, n, Q_e, Q_t}(\mathcal{A}) := 2 \cdot |\Pr[\mathsf{Exp}^{\mathsf{mumc\text{-}ecpa}}_{\mathsf{KEM}, n, Q_e, Q_t}(\mathcal{A}) \Rightarrow 1] - \frac{1}{2}| \geq \epsilon_{\mathcal{A}}$ (resp., $\mathsf{Adv}^{\mathsf{mumc\text{-}ecca}}_{\mathsf{KEM}, n, Q_e, Q_t}(\mathcal{A}) := 2 \cdot |\Pr[\mathsf{Exp}^{\mathsf{mumc\text{-}ecca}}_{\mathsf{KEM}, n, Q_e, Q_t}(\mathcal{A}) \Rightarrow 1] - \frac{1}{2}| \geq \epsilon_{\mathcal{A}})$, where the experiments are defined in Fig. 4 and the scalar 2 is added so that the advantages are between 0 and 1.*

$\mathsf{Exp}^{\mathsf{mumc\text{-}ecpa}}_{\mathsf{KEM}, n, Q_e, Q_t}(\mathcal{A})$, $\mathsf{Exp}^{\mathsf{mumc\text{-}ecca}}_{\mathsf{KEM}, n, Q_e, Q_t}(\mathcal{A})$:

$pp \leftarrow_{\$} \mathsf{Setup}$

For $i \in [n]$: $(pk_i, sk_i) \leftarrow_{\$} \mathsf{Gen}(pp)$

$\mathsf{EncList} := \emptyset$ //Records the encapsulation queries

$\mathsf{RevList} := \emptyset$ //Records the reveal queries

$\mathsf{CorrList} := \emptyset$ //Records the corruption queries

$\mathsf{TestList} := \emptyset$ //Records the test queries

$\beta \leftarrow_{\$} \{0,1\}$ //Single challenge bit

$\mathsf{PKList} := \{pk_i\}_{i \in [n]}$

$\beta' \leftarrow_{\$} \mathcal{A}^{\mathcal{O}_{\mathrm{ENC}}(\cdot), \mathcal{O}_{\mathrm{DEC}}(\cdot, \cdot), \mathcal{O}_{\mathrm{REV}}(\cdot, \cdot), \mathcal{O}_{\mathrm{CORR}}(\cdot), \mathcal{O}_{\mathrm{TEST}}(\cdot, \cdot)}(pp, \mathsf{PKList})$

If $\beta' = \beta$: Return 1; Else: Return 0

$\mathcal{O}_{\mathrm{TEST}}(i, c)$:   //At most Q_t times in total

  If $(i, c, K) \in \mathsf{EncList}$ for some $K \wedge (i, c) \notin \mathsf{RevList} \cup \mathsf{TestList}$

    $\wedge\ i \notin \mathsf{CorrList}$:

      $\mathsf{TestList} := \mathsf{TestList} \cup \{(i, c)\}$

      $K_0 := K;\ K_1 \leftarrow_{\$} \mathcal{K}$

      Return K_β

  Else: Return $\perp$

$\mathcal{O}_{\mathrm{ENC}}(i)$:   //At most Q_e times in total

  $(c, K) \leftarrow_{\$} \mathsf{Encap}(pk_i)$

  $\mathsf{EncList} := \mathsf{EncList} \cup \{(i, c, K)\}$

  Return c //Only c is returned

$\mathcal{O}_{\mathrm{DEC}}(i, c')$:

  If $(i, c', \cdot) \notin \mathsf{EncList}$:

    Return $K' \leftarrow \mathsf{Decap}(sk_i, c')$

  Else: Return $\perp$

$\mathcal{O}_{\mathrm{REV}}(i, c)$:

  If $(i, c, K) \in \mathsf{EncList}$ for some K

    $\wedge (i, c) \notin \mathsf{TestList}$:

      $\mathsf{RevList} := \mathsf{RevList} \cup \{(i, c)\}$

      Return K

  Else: Return $\perp$

$\mathcal{O}_{\mathrm{CORR}}(i)$:

  If $(i, \cdot) \notin \mathsf{TestList}$:

    $\mathsf{CorrList} := \mathsf{CorrList} \cup \{i\}$

    Return sk_i

  Else: Return $\perp$

Fig. 4. The MUMC-ECPA security experiment $\mathsf{Exp}^{\mathsf{mumc\text{-}ecpa}}_{\mathsf{KEM}, n, Q_e, Q_t}(\mathcal{A})$ and the MUMC-ECCA security experiment $\mathsf{Exp}^{\mathsf{mumc\text{-}ecca}}_{\mathsf{KEM}, n, Q_e, Q_t}(\mathcal{A})$ of KEM, where in the latter the adversary has also access to a decapsulation oracle $\mathcal{O}_{\mathrm{DEC}}(\cdot, \cdot)$. In both experiments, $\mathcal{A}$ is allowed to query $\mathcal{O}_{\mathrm{ENC}}$ at most Q_e times and query $\mathcal{O}_{\mathrm{TEST}}$ at most Q_t times.

In the MUMC-ECPA and MUMC-ECCA security experiments defined in Fig. 4, the adversary $\mathcal{A}$ is allowed to make several kinds of oracle queries.

– **Encapsulation query.** Through $\mathcal{O}_{\mathrm{ENC}}(i)$ query, $\mathcal{A}$ obtains an encapsulation c under pk_i. We note that the corresponding encapsulated key K is not given out along with c through $\mathcal{O}_{\mathrm{ENC}}$, different from the IND-mCPA/mCCA experiment (cf. Fig. 3). In contrast, the key K encapsulated in c can be later revealed by Key Reveal query or tested by Test query.

– **Key Reveal query.** Upon a Key Reveal query $\mathcal{O}_{\text{REV}}(i, c)$, if c is an output of $\mathcal{O}_{\text{ENC}}(i)$, the key K encapsulated in c is returned to $\mathcal{A}$.
– **SBG-style Test query.** Upon a Test query $\mathcal{O}_{\text{TEST}}(i, c)$, if c is an output of $\mathcal{O}_{\text{ENC}}(i)$, the real key $K_0 = K$ encapsulated in c or a random key K_1 is returned to $\mathcal{A}$, depending on the challenge bit β. We note that this is defined in the Single-Bit-Guess (SBG) style [6, 24], which is desirable due to its well composability with symmetric cryptographic primitives like DEM. Such an SBG-style security of KEM also serves well as a building block for the SBG-style security of more sophisticated primitives or protocols like AKE.
– **Decapsulation query.** A decapsulation oracle $\mathcal{O}_{\text{DEC}}(i, c')$ is provided in the MUMC-ECCA security experiment to decapsulate ciphertexts c' that are not returned by $\mathcal{O}_{\text{ENC}}(i)$.
– **Corruption query.** Via $\mathcal{O}_{\text{CORR}}(i)$ query, $\mathcal{A}$ can corrupt a user and obtain its secret key sk_i.

Finally, we stress that some trivial attacks are forbidden. For example, (1) $\mathcal{A}$ is not allowed to both corrupt some user and test encapsulated keys of this user; (2) $\mathcal{A}$ is not allowed to reveal an encapsulated key and test the same key; (3) $\mathcal{A}$ is not allowed to test an encapsulated key twice due to the SBG-style definition we adopt.

The MUMC-ECPA (MUMC-ECCA) security is more reasonable than the mCPA (mCCA) notion (cf. Definition 2), since it captures the practical attacks, like corrupting users' secret keys, revealing users' encapsulated keys, in the multi-user and multi-challenge setting.

We also define the enhanced security notions in the <u>M</u>ulti-<u>U</u>ser and <u>S</u>ingle-<u>C</u>hallenge (MUSC) setting, called *MUSC-ECPA/MUSC-ECCA*, which allow at most one $\mathcal{O}_{\text{TEST}}$ query in total.

Definition 5 (MUSC-ECPA/ECCA Security). *We say that an adversary $\mathcal{A}$ $(t_{\mathcal{A}}, \epsilon_{\mathcal{A}}, n, Q_e)$-breaks the MUSC-ECPA (resp., MUSC-ECCA) security of* KEM, *if it $(t_{\mathcal{A}}, \epsilon_{\mathcal{A}}, n, Q_e, 1)$-breaks the MUMC-ECPA (resp., MUMC-ECCA) security, and we denote the corresponding advantage function by* $\mathsf{Adv}_{\mathsf{KEM}, n, Q_e}^{\text{musc-ecpa}}(\mathcal{A})$ *(resp.,* $\mathsf{Adv}_{\mathsf{KEM}, n, Q_e}^{\text{musc-ecca}}(\mathcal{A})$).

4   Decap-Equivalence of Secret Keys and Rank of KEMs

In this section, we study the equivalence of secret keys for KEM schemes when decapsulating a set of ciphertexts, and define a new notion called *rank* for KEMs. This will be our main technique tool in the establishment of the impossibility result later in Sect. 5.

"Two-Step" Decapsulation. Generally, the decapsulation algorithm $\mathsf{Decap}(sk, c)$ of KEM schemes can be decomposed into two parts according to their functionality: an (optional) verification part $\mathsf{Decap}_{\text{vrfy}}(sk, c)$ checking the well-formedness of ciphertext, and a key-derivation part $\mathsf{Decap}_{\text{kd}}(sk, c)$ deriving a decapsulated key $K \in \mathcal{K}$ from the ciphertext. If $\mathsf{Decap}_{\text{vrfy}}(sk, c) = 1$, then $K \leftarrow$

$\mathsf{Decap}_{\mathsf{kd}}(sk, c)$ is invoked and $\mathsf{Decap}(sk, c)$ will output K. If $\mathsf{Decap}_{\mathsf{vrfy}}(sk, c) = 0$, then $\mathsf{Decap}(sk, c)$ will output a fixed symbol like $\bot$ indicating the mal-formedness of c.

We note that some KEM schemes (like CPA-secure KEMs) do not have $\mathsf{Decap}_{\mathsf{vrfy}}$ and $\mathsf{Decap}(sk, c) = \mathsf{Decap}_{\mathsf{kd}}(sk, c)$. Nevertheless, $\mathsf{Decap}_{\mathsf{kd}}(sk, c)$ contributes the core of $\mathsf{Decap}(sk, c)$ in all KEM schemes. Clearly, if $\mathsf{Decap}(sk, c) = K \in \mathcal{K}$, it must hold that $\mathsf{Decap}_{\mathsf{kd}}(sk, c) = K$.

4.1   Decap-Equivalence of Secret Keys

For KEM schemes, we study the decapsulation equivalence of secret keys when they are used to decapsulate a set $\mathcal{X}$ of ciphertexts. Since $\mathsf{Decap}_{\mathsf{kd}}$ is the essential part of the decapsulation algorithm, the decapsulation equivalence is defined with $\mathsf{Decap}_{\mathsf{kd}}$, as shown below.

Definition 6 ($\mathcal{X}$-Decap-Equivalence of Secret Keys). *Let* KEM *be a KEM scheme with ciphertext space* $\mathcal{CT}$ *and secret key space* $\mathcal{SK}$. *We define a relation* $\mathsf{EquivSK}(\mathcal{X})$ *on* $\mathcal{SK}$, *parameterized by a set of ciphertexts* $\mathcal{X} \subseteq \mathcal{CT}$, *as follows:*

$$\mathsf{EquivSK}(\mathcal{X}) := \{(sk, sk') \in \mathcal{SK}^2 \mid \forall c \in \mathcal{X}, \mathsf{Decap}_{\mathsf{kd}}(sk, c) = \mathsf{Decap}_{\mathsf{kd}}(sk', c)\}.$$

We also define $\mathsf{EquivSK}(\emptyset) := \mathcal{SK}^2$ *for the empty set* $\emptyset$.

Clearly, $\mathsf{EquivSK}(\mathcal{X})$ defines an equivalence relation on $\mathcal{SK}$. We show useful properties of $\mathsf{EquivSK}$ in the following lemma.

Lemma 1 (Properties of $\mathsf{EquivSK}$). *For all* $\mathcal{X}, \mathcal{Y} \subseteq \mathcal{CT}$,

(1) $\mathsf{EquivSK}(\mathcal{X} \cup \mathcal{Y}) = \mathsf{EquivSK}(\mathcal{X}) \cap \mathsf{EquivSK}(\mathcal{Y})$.
(2) $\mathcal{X} \subseteq \mathcal{Y} \Rightarrow \mathsf{EquivSK}(\mathcal{X}) \supseteq \mathsf{EquivSK}(\mathcal{Y})$.

Proof. Note that (2) follows from (1) directly. It suffices to prove (1). By Definition 6, for any $(sk, sk') \in \mathcal{SK}^2$,

$$\begin{aligned}
&(sk, sk') \in \mathsf{EquivSK}(\mathcal{X} \cup \mathcal{Y}) \\
\Longleftrightarrow{}& \forall c \in \mathcal{X} \cup \mathcal{Y}, \mathsf{Decap}_{\mathsf{kd}}(sk, c) = \mathsf{Decap}_{\mathsf{kd}}(sk', c) \\
\Longleftrightarrow{}& \forall c \in \mathcal{X}, \mathsf{Decap}_{\mathsf{kd}}(sk, c) = \mathsf{Decap}_{\mathsf{kd}}(sk', c) \\
&\quad \wedge\ \forall c \in \mathcal{Y}, \mathsf{Decap}_{\mathsf{kd}}(sk, c) = \mathsf{Decap}_{\mathsf{kd}}(sk', c) \\
\Longleftrightarrow{}& (sk, sk') \in \mathsf{EquivSK}(\mathcal{X})\ \wedge\ (sk, sk') \in \mathsf{EquivSK}(\mathcal{Y}) \\
\Longleftrightarrow{}& (sk, sk') \in \mathsf{EquivSK}(\mathcal{X}) \cap \mathsf{EquivSK}(\mathcal{Y}). \qquad \square
\end{aligned}$$

We also define independence of a set $\mathcal{X} \subseteq \mathcal{CT}$ as follows. If $c \in \mathcal{X}$ but $\mathsf{EquivSK}(\mathcal{X} \setminus \{c\}) = \mathsf{EquivSK}(\mathcal{X})$, then the element c, compared to $\mathcal{X} \setminus \{c\}$, does not contribute to $\mathsf{EquivSK}(\mathcal{X})$. In this case we call c a *dependent element* in $\mathcal{X}$. Otherwise, if $\mathsf{EquivSK}(\mathcal{X} \setminus \{c\}) \supsetneq \mathsf{EquivSK}(\mathcal{X})$, we call c an *independent element* in $\mathcal{X}$. For set $\mathcal{X}$, we call $\mathcal{X}$ an *independent set*, if every $c \in \mathcal{X}$ is an *independent element* in $\mathcal{X}$. Below we present the formal definition.

Definition 7 (Independent Set for Decap-Equivalence). *Let $\mathcal{X} \subseteq \mathcal{CT}$ be a set of ciphertexts. $\mathcal{X}$ is called an independent set, if for all $c \in \mathcal{X}$, it holds that*

$$\mathsf{EquivSK}(\mathcal{X} \setminus \{c\}) \supsetneq \mathsf{EquivSK}(\mathcal{X}).$$

In particular, we define the empty set $\emptyset$ as an independent set.

4.2 Rank of KEMs

For set $\mathcal{X}$, there may exist many independent subsets $\mathcal{X}'$ such that $\mathcal{X}' \subseteq \mathcal{X}$ and $\mathsf{EquivSK}(\mathcal{X}') = \mathsf{EquivSK}(\mathcal{X})$. We define the rank of $\mathcal{X}$ as the cardinality of the largest subset.

Definition 8 (Rank of Set & Rank of KEM for Decap-Equivalence). *Let $\mathcal{X} \subseteq \mathcal{CT}$ be a set of ciphertexts. The rank of $\mathcal{X}$ is defined as*

$$\mathsf{Rank}(\mathcal{X}) := \max\{\#\mathcal{X}' \,|\, \mathcal{X}' \subseteq \mathcal{X} \wedge \mathsf{EquivSK}(\mathcal{X}') = \mathsf{EquivSK}(\mathcal{X}) \wedge \mathcal{X}' \text{ is independent}\}.$$

In particular, the rank of KEM scheme KEM *is defined as* $\mathsf{Rank}_{\mathsf{KEM}} := \mathsf{Rank}(\mathcal{CT})$, *where $\mathcal{CT}$ is the ciphertext space of* KEM.

Obviously, we have $\mathsf{Rank}(\mathcal{X}) \leq \#\mathcal{X}$ and $\mathsf{Rank}_{\mathsf{KEM}} = \mathsf{Rank}(\mathcal{CT}) \leq \#\mathcal{CT}$.

Here, we demonstrate that Rank is well-defined. Namely, there always exists an independent subset $\mathcal{X}' \subseteq \mathcal{X}$ such that $\mathsf{EquivSK}(\mathcal{X}') = \mathsf{EquivSK}(\mathcal{X})$. We find such an $\mathcal{X}'$ by iteration. In the first step, we set $\mathcal{X}' := \mathcal{X}$. Clearly, $\mathsf{EquivSK}(\mathcal{X}') = \mathsf{EquivSK}(\mathcal{X})$. If $\mathcal{X}'$ is independent, then we are done. Otherwise $\mathcal{X}'$ is not independent, then $\exists\, c \in \mathcal{X}'$ such that $\mathsf{EquivSK}(\mathcal{X}'\setminus\{c\}) = \mathsf{EquivSK}(\mathcal{X}')$. So, we remove c from $\mathcal{X}'$, i.e., $\mathcal{X}' \leftarrow \mathcal{X}' \setminus \{c\}$. Then $\mathsf{EquivSK}(\mathcal{X}') = \mathsf{EquivSK}(\mathcal{X})$ still holds, while $\#\mathcal{X}'$ is reduced by 1. If $\mathcal{X}'$ is independent, then we are done. Otherwise, we repeat the above procedures until $\#\mathcal{X}' = 0$. Since $\mathcal{X}$ is a finite set, we can always stop with an independent $\mathcal{X}'$ after finite steps, possibly with $\mathcal{X}' = \emptyset$ (which is also independent by definition). Therefore, we can always find an $\mathcal{X}'$ such that $\mathsf{EquivSK}(\mathcal{X}') = \mathsf{EquivSK}(\mathcal{X})$ and $\mathcal{X}'$ is independent.

We show useful properties of Rank in the following lemma.

Lemma 2 (Properties of Rank**).** *For all $\mathcal{X}, \mathcal{Y} \subseteq \mathcal{CT}$,*

(1) $\mathcal{X} \subseteq \mathcal{Y} \Rightarrow \mathsf{Rank}(\mathcal{X}) \leq \mathsf{Rank}(\mathcal{Y})$.
(2) $\mathcal{X} \subseteq \mathcal{Y}$ *and $\mathcal{Y}$ is an independent set $\Rightarrow \mathcal{X}$ is an independent set.*
(3) *If $\mathcal{X}$ is an independent set, then $\mathsf{Rank}(\mathcal{X}) = \#\mathcal{X}$.*

Proof. To show (1), it suffices to prove $\mathsf{Rank}(\mathcal{X}) \leq \mathsf{Rank}(\mathcal{X} \cup \{c\})$ for a single element $c \in \mathcal{Y} \setminus \mathcal{X}$, then (1) follows by induction. Suppose $\mathcal{X}'$ is the largest independent subset such that $\mathcal{X}' \subseteq \mathcal{X}$ and $\mathsf{EquivSK}(\mathcal{X}') = \mathsf{EquivSK}(\mathcal{X})$. By definition, $\mathsf{Rank}(\mathcal{X}) = \#\mathcal{X}'$. We consider two cases.

– In the case $\mathsf{EquivSK}(\mathcal{X}) = \mathsf{EquivSK}(\mathcal{X} \cup \{c\})$, $\mathcal{X}'$ is also an independent subset such that $\mathcal{X}' \subseteq \mathcal{X} \cup \{c\}$ and $\mathsf{EquivSK}(\mathcal{X}') = \mathsf{EquivSK}(\mathcal{X} \cup \{c\})$, so $\mathsf{Rank}(\mathcal{X} \cup \{c\}) \geq \#\mathcal{X}'$.
– In the case $\mathsf{EquivSK}(\mathcal{X}) \supsetneq \mathsf{EquivSK}(\mathcal{X} \cup \{c\})$, $\mathcal{X}' \cup \{c\}$ is an independent subset such that $\mathcal{X}' \cup \{c\} \subseteq \mathcal{X} \cup \{c\}$ and $\mathsf{EquivSK}(\mathcal{X}' \cup \{c\}) = \mathsf{EquivSK}(\mathcal{X}') \cap \mathsf{EquivSK}(c) = \mathsf{EquivSK}(\mathcal{X}) \cap \mathsf{EquivSK}(c) = \mathsf{EquivSK}(\mathcal{X} \cup \{c\})$, so $\mathsf{Rank}(\mathcal{X} \cup \{c\}) \geq \#(\mathcal{X}' \cup \{c\}) = \#\mathcal{X}' + 1$.

In either case, we have $\mathsf{Rank}(\mathcal{X}) = \#\mathcal{X}' \leq \mathsf{Rank}(\mathcal{X} \cup \{c\})$. This proves (1).

Next, we prove (2). Since $\mathcal{Y}$ is an independent set, by definition, for every $c \in \mathcal{Y}$, $\mathsf{EquivSK}(\mathcal{Y} \setminus \{c\}) \supsetneq \mathsf{EquivSK}(\mathcal{Y})$. Observe that $\mathsf{EquivSK}(\mathcal{Y}) = \mathsf{EquivSK}(\mathcal{Y} \setminus \{c\}) \cap \mathsf{EquivSK}(c)$, so it implies that $\mathsf{EquivSK}(\mathcal{Y} \setminus \{c\}) \not\subseteq \mathsf{EquivSK}(c)$. Then for every $c \in \mathcal{X}$, since $\mathcal{X} \subseteq \mathcal{Y}$, by Lemma 1, it holds $\mathsf{EquivSK}(\mathcal{Y} \setminus \{c\}) \subseteq \mathsf{EquivSK}(\mathcal{X} \setminus \{c\})$. Combining $\mathsf{EquivSK}(\mathcal{Y} \setminus \{c\}) \subseteq \mathsf{EquivSK}(\mathcal{X} \setminus \{c\})$ with $\mathsf{EquivSK}(\mathcal{Y} \setminus \{c\}) \not\subseteq \mathsf{EquivSK}(c)$, we get that $\mathsf{EquivSK}(\mathcal{X} \setminus \{c\}) \not\subseteq \mathsf{EquivSK}(c)$, and consequently, $\mathsf{EquivSK}(\mathcal{X} \setminus \{c\}) \supsetneq \mathsf{EquivSK}(\mathcal{X}) = \mathsf{EquivSK}(\mathcal{X} \setminus \{c\}) \cap \mathsf{EquivSK}(c)$. Therefore, $\mathcal{X}$ is also an independent set.

For (3), when $\mathcal{X}$ is an independent set, $\mathcal{X}$ itself is the largest independent subset of $\mathcal{X}$ such that $\mathsf{EquivSK}(\mathcal{X}) = \mathsf{EquivSK}(\mathcal{X})$, so $\mathsf{Rank}(\mathcal{X}) = \#\mathcal{X}$.   □

Lastly, we stress that we do not require any algebraic structure from the secret key space $\mathcal{SK}$ or the ciphertext space $\mathcal{CT}$. The notions (like independent set, set rank and rank of KEMs) are purely defined based on the equivalence relation "EquivSK" on secret keys.

4.3 Core Lemma

In this subsection, we develop a core lemma, which is crucial in the establishment of the impossibility result later in Sect. 5.

For the ease of notation, by $\mathsf{EquivSK}(c_1, ..., c_Q)$ we denote $\mathsf{EquivSK}(\{c_1, ..., c_Q\})$, and by $\mathsf{EquivSK}(c_1, ..., c_Q \setminus c_i)$ we denote $\mathsf{EquivSK}(\{c_1, ..., c_Q\} \setminus \{c_i\})$.

Lemma 3 (Core Lemma). *Let* KEM *be a KEM scheme with ciphertext space* $\mathcal{CT}$. *For any ciphertexts* $c_1, ..., c_Q \in \mathcal{CT}$ *with* $Q \in \mathbb{N}$,

$$\#\{ i \in [Q] \mid \mathsf{EquivSK}(c_1, ..., c_Q \setminus c_i) \not\subseteq \mathsf{EquivSK}(c_i) \} \leq \mathsf{Rank_{KEM}}. \qquad (7)$$

Proof. Denote by $\mathsf{BadIndex}$ the set in the left-hand side of (7) and denote by d the rank of KEM (i.e., $\mathsf{Rank_{KEM}} = d$).

If $Q \leq d$, the lemma trivially holds. Now, we consider the case $Q \geq d + 1$. Suppose towards a contradiction that $\#\mathsf{BadIndex} \geq d + 1$, which means that $\mathsf{BadIndex}$ contains at least $d + 1$ distinct indices, say $i_1, ..., i_{D+1}$.

We claim that $\{c_{i_1}, ..., c_{i_{d+1}}\}$ is an independent set. To prove this claim, it suffices to show $\mathsf{EquivSK}(c_{i_1}, ..., c_{i_{d+1}} \setminus c_i) \supsetneq \mathsf{EquivSK}(c_{i_1}, ..., c_{i_{d+1}})$ for any $i \in \{i_1, ..., i_{d+1}\}$. Since $\{i_1, ..., i_{d+1}\} \subseteq \mathsf{BadIndex}$, we have

$$\mathsf{EquivSK}(c_1, ..., c_Q \setminus c_i) \not\subseteq \mathsf{EquivSK}(c_i) \qquad (8)$$

for each $i \in \{i_1, ..., i_{d+1}\}$. We also have $\mathsf{EquivSK}(c_1, ..., c_Q \setminus c_i) \subseteq \mathsf{EquivSK}(c_{i_1}, ..., c_{i_{d+1}} \setminus c_i)$ by Lemma 1, then by combining it with (8), we get that

$$\mathsf{EquivSK}(c_{i_1}, ..., c_{i_{d+1}} \setminus c_i) \not\subseteq \mathsf{EquivSK}(c_i). \tag{9}$$

(9) in turn implies that

$$\mathsf{EquivSK}(c_{i_1}, ..., c_{i_{d+1}} \setminus c_i) \supsetneq \mathsf{EquivSK}(c_{i_1}, ..., c_{i_{d+1}} \setminus c_i) \cap \mathsf{EquivSK}(c_i)$$
$$= \mathsf{EquivSK}(c_{i_1}, ..., c_{i_{d+1}}).$$

This shows the independence of set $\{c_{i_1}, ..., c_{i_{d+1}}\}$.

Since $\{c_{i_1}, ..., c_{i_{d+1}}\}$ is an independent subset of $\mathcal{CT}$, by Lemma 2, we have $\mathsf{Rank}_{\mathsf{KEM}} = \mathsf{Rank}(\mathcal{CT}) \geq \mathsf{Rank}(\{c_{i_1}, ..., c_{i_{d+1}}\}) = d + 1$, which contradicts with $\mathsf{Rank}_{\mathsf{KEM}} = d$. So it must hold that $\#\mathsf{BadIndex} \leq d$ and Lemma 3 follows. □

5 Impossibility of Tight Enhanced Security for KEMs

In this section, we present an impossibility result on the tight enhanced security for a class of KEMs whose ranks are *polynomially bounded*. In Subsect. 5.1, we give the main theorem of our impossibility result. Then in Subsect. 5.2, we compute ranks for some well-known KEM schemes, and apply our impossibility result to these KEMs. The applications indicate that for these KEMs there exists no (almost) tight (i.e., linear-preserving) black-box reduction from their enhanced security to any non-interactive complexity assumption.

5.1 Impossibility of Tight Enhanced Security for KEMs

As in [2,20], we will only consider *simple* reductions, since most reductions in cryptography are simple ones. We recall the definition of simple reduction.

Definition 9 (Simple Reduction [2,20,33]). *We call an algorithm $\mathcal{R}$ a $(t_{\mathcal{R}}, \epsilon_{\mathcal{R}}, \epsilon_{\mathcal{A}}, n, Q_e)$-reduction from breaking an NICA $N = (T, U, V)$ to breaking the MUSC-ECPA security of KEM, if $\mathcal{R}$ turns an adversary $\mathcal{A}$ that $(t_{\mathcal{A}}, \epsilon_{\mathcal{A}}, n, Q_e)$-breaks the MUSC-ECPA security of KEM (cf. Definition 5) into an algorithm $\mathcal{B}$ that $(t_{\mathcal{R}}, \epsilon_{\mathcal{R}})$-breaks N (cf. Definition 3).*

We call $\mathcal{R}$ simple, if $\mathcal{R}$ has only black-box access to $\mathcal{A}$ and executes $\mathcal{A}$ only once (and in particular without rewinding).

The security loss of $\mathcal{R}$ is defined by $\ell_{\mathcal{R}} := \frac{\epsilon_{\mathcal{A}}}{\epsilon_{\mathcal{R}\mathcal{A}}} \cdot \frac{t_{\mathcal{R}\mathcal{A}}}{t_{\mathcal{A}}}$. If $\ell_{\mathcal{R}}$ is a small constant, $\mathcal{R}$ is called a fully tight *reduction; if $\ell_{\mathcal{R}}$ is an a priori fixed polynomial in the security parameter λ, $\mathcal{R}$ is called an* almost tight *reduction or a* linear preserving *reduction.*

In the following theorem, we show the impossibility of tight MUSC-ECPA security which is defined in the multi-user and *single-challenge* setting.

Theorem 1 (Impossibility of Tight MUSC-ECPA Security). *Let* $N = (T, U, V)$ *be a non-interactive complexity assumption, and let* KEM *be an MUSC-ECPA secure KEM scheme with rank* $\mathsf{Rank}_{\mathsf{KEM}} = d$. *Then any simple* $(t_{\mathcal{R}}, \epsilon_{\mathcal{R}}, \epsilon_{\mathcal{A}}, n, Q_e)$-*reduction* $\mathcal{R}$ *from breaking* N *to breaking the MUSC-ECPA security of* KEM *has to lose a factor that is at least linear in the number* n *of users, assuming* N *is hard and* $Q_e \geq 3dn(n+1)$.

Proof of Theorem 1. We prove the impossibility result by meta-reduction. Following the meta-reduction routine [2, 22, 30], we first describe a hypothetical and inefficient adversary $\mathcal{A}^*$, then we show how to construct an algorithm $\mathcal{B}$ simulating $\mathcal{A}^*$ efficiently while running the reduction $\mathcal{R}$.

THE HYPOTHETICAL ADVERSARY $\mathcal{A}^*$. Let $Q := Q_e/n$. The hypothetical adversary $\mathcal{A}^*$ attacks the MUSC-ECPA security of KEM (cf. Definition 5) as follows.

- **Setup.** $\mathcal{A}^*$ receives (pp, PKList) with $\mathsf{PKList} = \{pk_i\}_{i \in [n]}$.
  $\mathcal{A}^*$ will execute the following procedures, and in particular make the queries therein, in order.
- **Preparation.** For each user $i \in [n]$,
  (1) $\mathcal{A}^*$ makes $\mathcal{O}_{\mathrm{ENC}}(i)$ query Q times: in the j-th query $(j \in [Q])$, it receives $c_{i,j}$ from $\mathcal{O}_{\mathrm{ENC}}(i)$;
  (2) $\mathcal{A}^*$ picks an index $j_i \leftarrow_{\$} [Q]$ uniformly at random, and for each $j \in [Q \backslash j_i]$, it queries $\mathcal{O}_{\mathrm{REV}}(i, c_{i,j})$ and receives $K_{i,j}$.
- **Corruption.** $\mathcal{A}^*$ picks a user index $i^* \leftarrow_{\$} [n]$ uniformly at random, and for each $i \in [n \setminus i^*]$, it queries $\mathcal{O}_{\mathrm{CORR}}(i)$ and receives sk_i.
- **Check.** For each $i \in [n \setminus i^*]$, $\mathcal{A}^*$ checks whether $\mathsf{Decap}_{\mathsf{kd}}(sk_i, c_{i,j}) = K_{i,j}$ holds for all $j \in [Q \setminus j_i]$. It aborts immediately if one of these checks fails.
- **Test.** $\mathcal{A}^*$ queries $\mathcal{O}_{\mathrm{TEST}}(i^*, c_{i^*, j_{i^*}})$ and receives a challenge K^*.
- **Output.**
  (1) (Inefficient step) $\mathcal{A}^*$ picks a secret key sk^* uniformly at random from the set $\{sk \mid \forall j \in [Q \backslash j_{i^*}], \mathsf{Decap}_{\mathsf{kd}}(sk, c_{i^*, j}) = K_{i^*, j}\}$, which is an equivalence class of $\mathsf{EquivSK}(c_{i^*, 1}, \cdots, c_{i^*, Q} \setminus c_{i^*, j_{i^*}})$.
  (2) Using the above sk^*, $\mathcal{A}^*$ computes $K := \mathsf{Decap}_{\mathsf{kd}}(sk^*, c_{i^*, j_{i^*}})$. If $K = K^*$, it outputs $\beta' = 1$; otherwise it outputs $\beta' = 0$.

Note that $\mathcal{A}^*$ makes $nQ(= Q_e)$ $\mathcal{O}_{\mathrm{ENC}}$ queries in total and makes at most one $\mathcal{O}_{\mathrm{TEST}}$ query.

ANALYSIS OF $\mathcal{A}^*$'S ADVANTAGE. Let sk_{i^*} denote the secret key of user i^* chosen by the experiment. By the perfect correctness of KEM, it holds that $\mathsf{Decap}_{\mathsf{kd}}(sk_{i^*}, c_{i^*, j}) = \mathsf{Decap}(sk_{i^*}, c_{i^*, j}) = K_{i^*, j}$ for each $j \in [Q \setminus j_{i^*}]$. Consequently,
$$\mathsf{Decap}_{\mathsf{kd}}(sk_{i^*}, c_{i^*, j}) = K_{i^*, j} = \mathsf{Decap}_{\mathsf{kd}}(sk^*, c_{i^*, j})$$
for each $j \in [Q \setminus j_{i^*}]$, where sk^* is the secret key chosen by $\mathcal{A}^*$. It implies that
$$(sk_{i^*}, sk^*) \in \mathsf{EquivSK}(c_{i^*, 1}, \cdots, c_{i^*, Q} \setminus c_{i^*, j_{i^*}}).$$

Let bad denote the event that $\mathsf{EquivSK}(c_{i^*,1}, \cdots, c_{i^*,Q} \setminus c_{i^*,j_{i^*}}) \not\subseteq$ $\mathsf{EquivSK}(c_{i^*,j_{i^*}})$. By Lemma 3 (Core Lemma) and the uniformity of j_{i^*} over $[Q]$, we have $\Pr[\mathsf{bad}] \leq d/Q = nd/Q_e$. Let β denote the single challenge bit in the experiment.

- In the case $\beta = 0$, the K^* output by $\mathcal{O}_{\mathrm{TEST}}$ is the real key encapsulated in $c_{i^*,j_{i^*}}$. By the perfect correctness of KEM, it holds that $\mathsf{Decap}_{\mathsf{kd}}(sk_{i^*}, c_{i^*,j_{i^*}}) = \mathsf{Decap}(sk_{i^*}, c_{i^*,j_{i^*}}) = K^*$. If bad does not occur,

$$(sk_{i^*}, sk^*) \in \mathsf{EquivSK}(c_{i^*,1}, \cdots, c_{i^*,Q} \setminus c_{i^*,j_{i^*}}) \subseteq \mathsf{EquivSK}(c_{i^*,j_{i^*}}),$$

thus $K = \mathsf{Decap}_{\mathsf{kd}}(sk^*, c_{i^*,j_{i^*}}) = \mathsf{Decap}_{\mathsf{kd}}(sk_{i^*}, c_{i^*,j_{i^*}}) = K^*$. It implies $\Pr[\beta' = 1 \mid \beta = 0 \wedge \neg\mathsf{bad}] = 1$, and consequently,

$$\Pr[\beta' = 1 \mid \beta = 0] \geq \Pr[\neg\mathsf{bad}] \cdot \Pr[\beta' = 1 \mid \beta = 0 \wedge \neg\mathsf{bad}]$$
$$= \Pr[\neg\mathsf{bad}] \cdot 1 = 1 - \Pr[\mathsf{bad}] \geq 1 - nd/Q_e.$$

- In the case $\beta = 1$, the K^* output by $\mathcal{O}_{\mathrm{TEST}}$ is a random key uniformly chosen from $\mathcal{K}$, so $K = K^*$ holds with probability exactly $1/\#\mathcal{K}$. It implies $\Pr[\beta' = 1 \mid \beta = 1] = 1/\#\mathcal{K}$.

Overall, the advantage of $\mathcal{A}^*$ in the MUSC-ECPA security experiment is

$$\epsilon_{\mathcal{A}^*} = 2 \cdot \left| \Pr[\beta' = \beta] - \tfrac{1}{2} \right| = \left| \Pr[\beta' = 1 \mid \beta = 0] - \Pr[\beta' = 1 \mid \beta = 1] \right|$$
$$\geq 1 - nd/Q_e - 1/\#\mathcal{K}. \tag{10}$$

THE META-REDUCTION $\mathcal{B}$. Next, we construct an efficient algorithm $\mathcal{B}$, which runs reduction $\mathcal{R}$ as a subroutine and attempts to break the NICA N. $\mathcal{B}$ will play the role of the hypothetical adversary $\mathcal{A}^*$ to interact with $\mathcal{R}$. For the sake of efficiently emulating $\mathcal{A}^*$, $\mathcal{B}$ will rewind $\mathcal{R}$ to learn more information from the its responses. More precisely, given an instance x of N, where $(x, w) \leftarrow_\$ T$, $\mathcal{B}$ works as follows.

- **Setup.** $\mathcal{B}$ runs $\mathcal{R}(x)$ to obtain (pp, PKList) where $\mathsf{PKList} = \{pk_i\}_{i \in [n]}$. $\mathcal{B}$ initializes two arrays of n entries, $SK[\cdot]$ and $SK^*[\cdot]$, by $\emptyset$.
  $\mathcal{B}$ plays the role of adversary, executes the following procedures and makes the queries to $\mathcal{R}$ in order.
- **Preparation.** For each user $i \in [n]$,
  (1) $\mathcal{B}$ makes $\mathcal{O}_{\mathrm{ENC}}(i)$ query Q times: in the j-th $\mathcal{O}_{\mathrm{ENC}}(i)$ query ($j \in [Q]$), it receives $c_{i,j}$ from $\mathcal{R}$;
  (2) $\mathcal{B}$ picks an index $j_i \leftarrow_\$ [Q]$ uniformly at random, and for each $j \in [Q \setminus j_i]$, it queries $\mathcal{O}_{\mathrm{REV}}(i, c_{i,j})$ and receives $K_{i,j}$ from $\mathcal{R}$.
  Let the state after this preparation step be st_{prep}.
  $\mathcal{B}$ picks a user index $i^* \leftarrow_\$ [n]$ uniformly at random.
- **Rewinding.** Next, $\mathcal{B}$ will rewind $\mathcal{R}$ n times, all starting from state st_{prep}. In the ι-th rewind ($\iota \in [n]$), $\mathcal{B}$ proceeds as follows:

(1) $\mathcal{B}$ rewinds $\mathcal{R}$ to the state st_{prep}. For each $i \in [n \setminus \iota]$, $\mathcal{B}$ queries $\mathcal{O}_{\text{CORR}}(i)$ and receives $sk_i^{(\iota)}$ from $\mathcal{R}$.

(2) For each $i \in [n \setminus \iota]$, $\mathcal{B}$ checks whether or not $\mathsf{Decap}_{\mathsf{kd}}(sk_i^{(\iota)}, c_{i,j}) = K_{i,j}$ holds for all $j \in [Q \setminus j_i]$, and if so, it sets $SK[i] := sk_i^{(\iota)}$. If $\iota = i^*$, $\mathcal{B}$ additionally sets $SK^*[i] := sk_i^{(i^*)}$

(3) Let the state at the moment be $st_{\text{rewind}}^{(\iota)}$. If $\iota < n$, $\mathcal{B}$ goes to the next rewind (i.e., $\iota \leftarrow \iota + 1$).

- **Check.** For each $i \in [n \setminus i^*]$, $\mathcal{B}$ checks whether or not $SK^*[i] \neq \emptyset$ (i.e., $\mathsf{Decap}_{\mathsf{kd}}(sk_i^{(i^*)}, c_{i,j}) = K_{i,j}$ holds for all $j \in [Q \setminus j_i]$). It aborts immediately if one of these check fails, and sets a flag $\mathsf{checkfail}_1 := \mathbf{true}$.

- **Test.** $\mathcal{B}$ rewinds $\mathcal{R}$ back to the state $st_{\text{rewind}}^{(i^*)}$. $\mathcal{B}$ queries $\mathcal{O}_{\text{TEST}}(i^*, c_{i^*, j_{i^*}})$ and receives a challenge K^* from $\mathcal{R}$.

- **Output.**

(1) $\mathcal{B}$ checks whether or not $SK[i^*] \neq \emptyset$ (i.e., $SK[i^*] = sk_{i^*}^{(\iota^*)}$ for some $\iota^* \neq i^*$), s.t. $\mathsf{Decap}_{\mathsf{kd}}(sk_{i^*}^{(\iota^*)}, c_{i^*, j}) = K_{i^*, j}$ for all $j \in [Q \setminus j_{i^*}]$). It aborts if the check fails, and sets a flag $\mathsf{checkfail}_2 := \mathbf{true}$.

(2) Using $SK[i^*]$, $\mathcal{B}$ computes $K := \mathsf{Decap}_{\mathsf{kd}}(SK[i^*], c_{i^*, j_{i^*}})$. If $K = K^*$, it outputs $\beta' = 1$ to $\mathcal{R}$; otherwise it outputs $\beta' = 0$ to $\mathcal{R}$.

Finally, $\mathcal{B}$ receives a solution s from $\mathcal{R}$, and outputs s to its own challenger.

$\mathcal{B}$'S RUNNING TIME. $\mathcal{B}$ essentially runs $\mathcal{R}$ one complete run plus $(n-1)$ incomplete runs. Moreover it executes $\mathsf{Decap}_{\mathsf{kd}}$ at most $n(n-1)(Q-1)+1$ times. Thus the total running time of $\mathcal{B}$ is

$$t_{\mathcal{B}} \leq n \cdot t_{\mathcal{R}} + n^2 Q \cdot t_{\mathsf{Decap}} = n \cdot t_{\mathcal{R}} + nQ_e \cdot t_{\mathsf{Decap}},$$

where t_{Decap} denotes the running time of the Decap algorithm of KEM.

ANALYSIS OF $\mathcal{B}$'S ADVANTAGE. Denote by bad the event that $\mathsf{EquivSK}(c_{i^*,1}, \cdots, c_{i^*,Q} \setminus c_{i^*,j_{i^*}}) \not\subseteq \mathsf{EquivSK}(c_{i^*,j_{i^*}})$. We first show that in the case of $\mathsf{checkfail}_1 \vee (\neg\mathsf{checkfail}_2 \wedge \neg\mathsf{bad})$, $\mathcal{B}$ simulates the hypothetical adversary $\mathcal{A}^*$ perfectly.

- If $\mathsf{checkfail}_1$ occurs, $\mathcal{B}$ aborts, and $\mathcal{A}^*$ would also abort in the check step since $\mathsf{Decap}_{\mathsf{kd}}(sk_i^{(i^*)}, c_{i,j}) \neq K_{i,j}$ for some $i \in [n \setminus i^*]$ and some $j \in [Q \setminus j_i]$. .

- If $\neg\mathsf{checkfail}_1 \wedge \neg\mathsf{checkfail}_2 \wedge \neg\mathsf{bad}$, $\mathcal{B}$ obtains a secret key $SK[i^*]$ such that $\mathsf{Decap}_{\mathsf{kd}}(SK[i^*], c_{i^*,j}) = K_{i^*,j}$ for each $j \in [Q \setminus j_{i^*}]$. Since $\mathcal{A}^*$'s sk^* also satisfies $\mathsf{Decap}_{\mathsf{kd}}(sk^*, c_{i^*,j}) = K_{i^*,j}$ for each $j \in [Q \setminus j_{i^*}]$, it implies that

$$(SK[i^*], sk^*) \in \mathsf{EquivSK}(c_{i^*,1}, \cdots, c_{i^*,Q} \setminus c_{i^*,j_{i^*}}).$$

Since bad does not occur,

$$(SK[i^*], sk^*) \in \mathsf{EquivSK}(c_{i^*,1}, \cdots, c_{i^*,Q} \setminus c_{i^*,j_{i^*}}) \subseteq \mathsf{EquivSK}(c_{i^*,j_{i^*}}).$$

Consequently, the $K = \mathsf{Decap}_{\mathsf{kd}}(SK[i^*], c_{i^*,j_{i^*}})$ computed by $\mathcal{B}$ is identical to the $K = \mathsf{Decap}_{\mathsf{kd}}(sk^*, c_{i^*,j_{i^*}})$ computed by $\mathcal{A}^*$, so the simulation is perfect.

Therefore, $\mathcal{B}$ simulates $\mathcal{A}^*$ perfectly for $\mathcal{R}$ when $\mathsf{checkfail}_1 \vee (\neg\mathsf{checkfail}_2 \wedge \neg\mathsf{bad})$, and by the difference lemma, we have

$$|\epsilon_\mathcal{B} - \epsilon_{\mathcal{R}^{\mathcal{A}^*}}| \leq \Pr[\neg\mathsf{checkfail}_1 \wedge (\mathsf{checkfail}_2 \vee \mathsf{bad})]$$
$$\leq \Pr[\neg\mathsf{checkfail}_1 \wedge \mathsf{checkfail}_2] + \Pr[\mathsf{bad}].$$

By Lemma 3 (Core Lemma) and the uniformity of j_{i^*} over $[Q]$, we have $\Pr[\mathsf{bad}] \leq d/Q = dn/Q_e$. Next we bound the probability $\Pr[\neg\mathsf{checkfail}_1 \wedge \mathsf{checkfail}_2]$. Note that $\mathsf{checkfail}_2$ can only occur if the event $E : \exists i \in [n], SK[i] = \emptyset$ occurs. As i^* is chosen uniformly at random from $[n]$ and the view of $\mathcal{R}$ before the Test query is independent of i^*, we have $i \in [n \setminus i^*]$ with probability $1 - 1/n$. In this case $\mathsf{checkfail}_1$ occurs and thus $\Pr[\mathsf{checkfail}_1 | E] \geq 1 - 1/n$. Now since $\mathsf{checkfail}_2 \Rightarrow E$ it holds that $\Pr[\neg\mathsf{checkfail}_1 \wedge \mathsf{checkfail}_2] \leq \Pr[\neg\mathsf{checkfail}_1 \wedge E] = \Pr[\neg\mathsf{checkfail}_1 | E] \cdot \Pr[E] \leq \Pr[\neg\mathsf{checkfail}_1 | E] = 1 - \Pr[\mathsf{checkfail}_1 | E] \leq 1/n$. Overall, it holds that $|\epsilon_\mathcal{B} - \epsilon_{\mathcal{R}^{\mathcal{A}^*}}| \leq 1/n + dn/Q_e$, thus,

$$\epsilon_{\mathcal{R}^{\mathcal{A}^*}} \leq \epsilon_\mathcal{B} + 1/n + dn/Q_e. \tag{11}$$

BOUNDING THE SECURITY LOSS. Assuming that no adversary $\mathcal{B}$ is able to (t_N, ϵ_N)-break the NICA N with $t_N = t_\mathcal{B} \leq n \cdot t_\mathcal{R} + nQ_e \cdot t_{\mathsf{Decap}}$, we must have $\epsilon_\mathcal{B} \leq \epsilon_N$. By combining (10) and (11), the security loss of reduction $\mathcal{R}$ is

$$\ell_\mathcal{R} \geq \frac{\epsilon_{\mathcal{A}^*}}{\epsilon_{\mathcal{R}^{\mathcal{A}^*}}} \cdot \frac{t_{\mathcal{R}^{\mathcal{A}^*}}}{t_{\mathcal{A}^*}} \geq \frac{1 - dn/Q_e - 1/\#\mathcal{K}}{\epsilon_\mathcal{B} + 1/n + dn/Q_e} \cdot 1 \geq \frac{1 - dn/Q_e - 1/\#\mathcal{K}}{\epsilon_N + 1/n + dn/Q_e}$$
$$\geq n \cdot (1 - n\epsilon_N - dn(n+1)/Q_e - 1/\#\mathcal{K}),$$

where the last inequality holds by inspection, namely, $n \cdot (1 - n\epsilon_N - dn(n+1)/Q_e - 1/\#\mathcal{K}) \cdot (\epsilon_N + 1/n + dn/Q_e) = 1 - dn/Q_e - 1/\#\mathcal{K} - (n\epsilon_N + n^2 d/Q_e) \cdot (n\epsilon_N + dn(n+1)/Q_e + 1/\#\mathcal{K}) \leq 1 - dn/Q_e - 1/\#\mathcal{K}$. Thus, any reduction $\mathcal{R}$ from breaking N to breaking the MUSC-ECPA security of KEM loses at least a factor of

$$\ell = n \cdot (1 - n\epsilon_N - dn(n+1)/Q_e - 1/\#\mathcal{K}),$$

where n denotes the number of users, ϵ_N represents the hardness of NICA N, d is the rank of KEM, Q_e is the number of $\mathcal{O}_{\mathrm{ENC}}$ queries allowed in the MUSC-ECPA experiment, and $\#\mathcal{K}$ denotes the size of the encapsulated key space $\mathcal{K}$.

Assuming that N is hard and $Q_e \geq 3dn(n+1)$, we compute the security loss factor ℓ in two cases as examples. In the first case, we only make very *weak* assumptions, and in the second case, we make *mild* but still far more realistic assumptions.

- **Weak case (in the concrete setting).** In the case that $\epsilon_N \leq 1/(12n)$, $Q_e \geq 3dn(n+1)$ and $\#\mathcal{K} \geq 2$, we have $\ell \geq n/12$.
- **Mild case (in the asymptotic setting).** In the case that $\epsilon_N \leq 1/(\lambda n)$, $Q_e \geq \lambda dn(n+1)$ and $\#\mathcal{K} \geq \lambda$, where λ is the security parameter, we have $\ell = n(1 - 3/\lambda) = n(1 - o(1)) \approx n$.

In either case, the security loss ℓ is at least linear in n. This completes the proof of Theorem 1.   ∎

Observe that MUSC-ECPA is tightly implied by all of the MUSC-ECCA (multi-user and single-challenge *ECCA*), MUMC-ECPA (multi-user and *multi-challenge* ECPA) and MUMC-ECCA (multi-user and *multi-challenge ECCA*) securities. Hence the impossibility of tight MUSC-ECPA security shown in Theorem 1 directly yields the impossibility of tight MUSC-ECCA, tight MUMC-ECPA and tight MUMC-ECCA, as well. We conclude these in the following corollary.

Corollary 1 (Impossibility of Tight MUSC-ECCA, MUMC-ECPA & MUMC-ECCA). *Let* $N = (T, U, V)$ *be a non-interactive complexity assumption, and let* KEM *be an MUSC-ECCA (resp., MUMC-ECPA, MUMC-ECCA) secure KEM with rank* $\mathsf{Rank}_{\mathsf{KEM}} = d$. *Then any simple* $(t_\mathcal{R}, \epsilon_\mathcal{R}, \epsilon_\mathcal{A}, n, Q_e)$-*reduction* $\mathcal{R}$ *from breaking* N *to breaking the MUSC-ECCA (resp., MUMC-ECPA, MUMC-ECCA) security of* KEM *has to lose a factor that is at least linear in the number* n *of users, assuming* N *is hard and* $Q_e \geq 3dn(n+1)$.

Remark 1. Following [2], our impossibility results can be naturally generalized to reductions that may execute the adversary algorithm several times sequentially.

5.2   Applications of Our Impossibility Result to Well-Known KEMs

In the last two decades, many PKE schemes [8–10,12,14,15,19,28] (to name a few) were proposed, explicitly or implicitly, in the KEM + DEM paradigm [10] and their securities are proved in the standard model. All the KEMs inherent in these PKEs have their own charm. For example, the ElGamal-KEM [12], CS-KEM [8–10] and KD-KEM [28] are among the most efficient KEMs. The GHKW-KEM [14] and HLLG-KEM [19] are core building blocks in achieving (almost) tightly IND-mCCA security for PKE. The NY-KEM [35] is a generic approach to CCA-secure PKE/KEM from CPA-secure PKE, which in turn can be built upon CPA-secure KEM. Note that these KEMs (except the ElGamal-KEM) have neither secret key uniqueness nor re-randomizibility, so the impossibility results in existing works [2] do not apply to them.

Next, we will compute the ranks for these KEMs and apply our impossibility result on them. The computation results show that the ranks of these KEM are either small constants or upper bounded by small polynomials in λ.

- The CPA-secure ElGamal-KEM [12] has rank 1 (cf. the full version [18]).
- The CCA-secure CS-KEM in [8] has rank 1 (cf. the full version [18]) and another version in [9,10] has rank 2 (see next).
- The CCCA (constrained CCA) secure KD-KEM [28] has rank at most 4 (cf. the full version [18]).

- The PCA (plaintext check attacks) secure GHKW-KEM used in the tightly IND-mCCA secure GHKW-PKE [14] has rank at most $6k\lambda$, with k the parameter of the MDDH assumptions [13] (e.g., MDDH corresponds to the DDH assumption when $k = 1$ and includes k-Linear assumptions for a general $k \geq 2$) (cf. the full version [18]).
- The tightly mCCA-secure HLLG-KEM [19] has rank at most $2k$, with k the parameter of the MDDH assumptions (cf. the full version [18]).
- The CCA-secure NY-KEM [35] has polynomially-bounded rank, as long as the underlying CPA-secure KEM does (cf. the full version [18]). Thus many concrete instantiations of NY-KEM have polynomially-bounded rank, e.g., the NY-KEMs whose underlying CPA-secure KEMs are instantiated with the KEMs shown above (such as ElGamal).

Our impossibility result works well on these KEMs. Their polynomially-bounded ranks indicate that the MUSC-ECPA (or even MUSC-ECCA, MUMC-ECPA, MUMC-ECCA) security of these KEM schemes suffer from a security loss factor $\Omega(n)$ with n the number of users, when reducing to non-interactive complexity assumptions.

Due to space limitations, here we show how to compute rank for the CS-KEM [9,10], and put the rank computations of other KEMs in the full version [18].

Rank Computation for Cramer-Shoup's CCA-secure KEM [9,10]. Let us first recall the construction of the CS-KEM in [9,10].

Let $(\mathbb{G}, p, g_1, g_2)$ be a group of prime order p and with random generators g_1, g_2. Let H be a hash function from $\mathbb{G}^2$ to $\mathbb{Z}_p$.

- The public key is $pk := (g_1, g_2, c, d, h)$ where $c := g_1^{x_1} g_2^{x_2}$, $d := g_1^{y_1} g_2^{y_2}$ and $h := g_1^{z_1} g_2^{z_2}$ for uniformly chosen $x_1, x_2, y_1, y_2, z_1, z_2 \leftarrow_\$ \mathbb{Z}_p$, and the secret key is $sk := (x_1, x_2, y_1, y_2, z_1, z_2)$.
- $\mathsf{Encap}(pk)$ samples $r \leftarrow_\$ \mathbb{Z}_p$ uniformly, computes $u_1 := g_1^r$, $u_2 := g_2^r$, $\alpha := H(u_1, u_2)$, $v := c^r d^{r\alpha}$, $K := h^r$, and outputs $c := (u_1, u_2, v)$ and K.
- $\mathsf{Decap}(sk, c = (u_1, u_2, v))$ outputs $K := u_1^{z_1} u_2^{z_2}$ if $u_1^{x_1+y_1\alpha} \cdot u_2^{x_2+y_2\alpha} = v$ holds, where $\alpha := H(u_1, u_2)$, and outputs $\perp$ otherwise.

The secret key space is $\mathcal{SK} = \mathbb{Z}_p^6$, the ciphertext space is $\mathcal{CT} = \mathbb{G}^3$, and the key-derivation part $\mathsf{Decap}_{kd}(sk, c)$ outputs $K := u_1^{z_1} u_2^{z_2}$.

We show that the CS-KEM in [9,10] has rank 2. For a ciphertext $c = (u_1, u_2, v) \in \mathcal{CT}$, we can always write $u_1 = g_1^{r_1}$ and $u_2 = g_1^{r_2}$ with $r_1, r_2 \in \mathbb{Z}_p$. We compute $\mathsf{EquivSK}(c)$: for any $sk = (x_1, x_2, y_1, y_2, z_1, z_2)$, $sk' = (x_1', x_2', y_1', y_2', z_1', z_2') \in \mathcal{SK}$, $(sk, sk') \in \mathsf{EquivSK}(c) \iff \mathsf{Decap}_{kd}(sk, c) = \mathsf{Decap}_{kd}(sk', c) \iff u_1^{z_1} u_2^{z_2} = u_1^{z_1'} u_2^{z_2'} \iff r_1 \cdot z_1 + r_2 \cdot z_2 = r_1 \cdot z_1' + r_2 \cdot z_2'$. So, $\mathsf{EquivSK}(c) = \{(sk = (\cdots, z_1, z_2), sk' = (\cdots, z_1', z_2')) \mid r_1 \cdot z_1 + r_2 \cdot z_2 = r_1 \cdot z_1' + r_2 \cdot z_2'\}$.

Consequently, we have the following facts.

(1) $\mathsf{EquivSK}(\mathcal{CT}) = \bigcap_{c \in \mathcal{CT}} \mathsf{EquivSK}(c) = \{(sk = (\cdots, z_1, z_2), sk' = (\cdots, z_1', z_2')) \mid \bigwedge_{r_1, r_2 \in \mathbb{Z}_p} r_1 \cdot z_1 + r_2 \cdot z_2 = r_1 \cdot z_1' + r_2 \cdot z_2'\} = \{(sk = (\cdots, z_1, z_2), sk' = (\cdots, z_1', z_2')) \mid z_1 = z_1' \wedge z_2 = z_2'\}$.

(2) For any two ciphertexts $c^{(1)} = \left(u_1^{(1)} = g_1^{r_1^{(1)}}, u_2^{(1)} = g_1^{r_2^{(1)}}, v^{(1)}\right), c^{(2)} = \left(u_1^{(2)} = g_1^{r_1^{(2)}}, u_2^{(2)} = g_1^{r_2^{(2)}}, v^{(2)}\right)$, if $(r_1^{(1)}, r_2^{(1)}) \in \mathbb{Z}_p^2$ is linearly independent of $(r_1^{(2)}, r_2^{(2)})$, e.g., $(r_1^{(1)}, r_2^{(1)}) = (1, 0)$ and $(r_1^{(2)}, r_2^{(2)}) = (0, 1)$, the matrix $\begin{pmatrix} r_1^{(1)} & r_2^{(1)} \\ r_1^{(2)} & r_2^{(2)} \end{pmatrix}$ is invertible, thus

$$\mathsf{EquivSK}(c^{(1)}, c^{(2)}) = \mathsf{EquivSK}(c^{(1)}) \cap \mathsf{EquivSK}(c^{(2)})$$

$$= \left\{ (sk = (\cdots, z_1, z_2), sk' = (\cdots, z_1', z_2')) \;\middle|\; \begin{array}{l} r_1^{(1)} \cdot z_1 + r_2^{(1)} \cdot z_2 = r_1^{(1)} \cdot z_1' + r_2^{(1)} \cdot z_2' \\ \wedge\ r_1^{(2)} \cdot z_1 + r_2^{(2)} \cdot z_2 = r_1^{(2)} \cdot z_1' + r_2^{(2)} \cdot z_2' \end{array} \right\}$$

$$= \left\{ (sk = (\cdots, z_1, z_2), sk' = (\cdots, z_1', z_2')) \;\middle|\; \begin{pmatrix} r_1^{(1)} & r_2^{(1)} \\ r_1^{(2)} & r_2^{(2)} \end{pmatrix} \cdot \begin{pmatrix} z_1 \\ z_2 \end{pmatrix} = \begin{pmatrix} r_1^{(1)} & r_2^{(1)} \\ r_1^{(2)} & r_2^{(2)} \end{pmatrix} \cdot \begin{pmatrix} z_1' \\ z_2' \end{pmatrix} \right\}$$

$$= \{ (sk = (\cdots, z_1, z_2), sk' = (\cdots, z_1', z_2')) \mid z_1 = z_1' \wedge z_2 = z_2' \} = \mathsf{EquivSK}(\mathcal{CT}).$$

Clearly, we have both $\mathsf{EquivSK}(c^{(1)}, c^{(2)}) \subsetneq \mathsf{EquivSK}(c^{(1)})$ and $\mathsf{EquivSK}(c^{(1)}, c^{(2)}) \subsetneq \mathsf{EquivSK}(c^{(2)})$, thus $\{c^{(1)}, c^{(2)}\}$ is an independent set.

(3) For any three ciphertexts $c^{(1)} = \left(u_1^{(1)} = g_1^{r_1^{(1)}}, u_2^{(1)} = g_1^{r_2^{(1)}}, v^{(1)}\right), c^{(2)} = \left(u_1^{(2)} = g_1^{r_1^{(2)}}, u_2^{(2)} = g_1^{r_2^{(2)}}, v^{(2)}\right), c^{(3)} = \left(u_1^{(3)} = g_1^{r_1^{(3)}}, u_2^{(3)} = g_1^{r_2^{(3)}}, v^{(3)}\right)$, since the linear space $\mathbb{Z}_p^2$ has dimension 2, the three vectors $(r_1^{(1)}, r_2^{(1)})$, $(r_1^{(2)}, r_2^{(2)})$, $(r_1^{(3)}, r_2^{(3)})$ in $\mathbb{Z}_p^2$ must be linearly dependent. Say $(r_1^{(3)}, r_2^{(3)}) = (a \cdot r_1^{(1)} + b \cdot r_1^{(2)}, a \cdot r_2^{(1)} + b \cdot r_2^{(2)})$ for some coefficients $a, b \in \mathbb{Z}_p$. Then we have $\mathsf{EquivSK}(c^{(1)}, c^{(2)}) \subseteq \mathsf{EquivSK}(c^{(3)})$, as shown below.

For any $(sk = (\cdots, z_1, z_2), sk' = (\cdots, z_1', z_2')) \in \mathsf{EquivSK}(c^{(1)}, c^{(2)})$, it holds $r_1^{(1)} \cdot z_1 + r_2^{(1)} \cdot z_2 = r_1^{(1)} \cdot z_1' + r_2^{(1)} \cdot z_2'$ and $r_1^{(2)} \cdot z_1 + r_2^{(2)} \cdot z_2 = r_1^{(2)} \cdot z_1' + r_2^{(2)} \cdot z_2'$, thus

$$r_1^{(3)} \cdot z_1 + r_2^{(3)} \cdot z_2 = (a \cdot r_1^{(1)} + b \cdot r_1^{(2)}) \cdot z_1 + (a \cdot r_2^{(1)} + b \cdot r_2^{(2)}) \cdot z_2$$

$$= a \cdot (r_1^{(1)} \cdot z_1 + r_2^{(1)} \cdot z_2) + b \cdot (r_1^{(2)} \cdot z_1 + r_2^{(2)} \cdot z_2)$$

$$= a \cdot (r_1^{(1)} \cdot z_1' + r_2^{(1)} \cdot z_2') + b \cdot (r_1^{(2)} \cdot z_1' + r_2^{(2)} \cdot z_2')$$

$$= (a \cdot r_1^{(1)} + b \cdot r_1^{(2)}) \cdot z_1' + (a \cdot r_2^{(1)} + b \cdot r_2^{(2)}) \cdot z_2' = r_1^{(3)} \cdot z_1' + r_2^{(3)} \cdot z_2',$$

so $(sk, sk') \in \mathsf{EquivSK}(c^{(3)})$.

The fact that $\mathsf{EquivSK}(c^{(1)}, c^{(2)}) \subseteq \mathsf{EquivSK}(c^{(3)})$ implies $\mathsf{EquivSK}(c^{(1)}, c^{(2)}, c^{(3)}) = \mathsf{EquivSK}(c^{(1)}, c^{(2)}) \cap \mathsf{EquivSK}(c^{(3)}) = \mathsf{EquivSK}(c^{(1)}, c^{(2)})$. Therefore, $\{c^{(1)}, c^{(2)}, c^{(3)}\}$ is not independent for any three ciphertexts $c^{(1)}, c^{(2)}, c^{(3)}$.

Overall, the largest independent subset $\mathcal{X} \subseteq \mathcal{CT}$ such that $\mathsf{EquivSK}(\mathcal{X}) = \mathsf{EquivSK}(\mathcal{CT})$ has two ciphertexts. So, the CS-KEM in [9,10] has rank 2.

6 Enhancedly Secure KEM with Optimal Tightness

In this section, we present KEMs with enhanced security, where the security reduction has a loss factor $\Theta(n)$ with n the number of users. Combining with the impossibility result shown in Sect. 5, the enhanced security of these KEMs are *optimal* regarding tightness.

More precisely, we will prove that, any IND-mCPA/mCCA secure KEM is itself MUMC-ECPA/ECCA secure, with security reduction losing a factor of $O(n)$. Therefore, to obtain MUMC-ECPA/ECCA secure KEMs with optimal security reduction (i.e., security loss = $\Theta(n)$), it suffices to construct tightly IND-mCPA/mCCA secure KEMs (i.e., the security loss = $\Theta(1)$). Luckily, there were already a handful of such KEMs.

- The ElGamal public-key encryption (PKE) [12] is tightly IND-mCPA secure based on the DDH assumption with security loss $\Theta(1)$ [34].
- In 2012, Hofheinz and Jager [21] presented the first tightly IND-mCCA secure PKE based on (matrix) DDH assumptions [13], with security loss $\Theta(1)$.
- Recent works [14,15,19] proposed efficient IND-mCCA secure PKE schemes based on (matrix) DDH assumptions [13], with security loss $O(\lambda)$.

Note that PKE can be used as KEM naturally by encrypting a random key K. These yield (almost) tightly IND-mCPA/mCCA secure KEMs with security loss $\Theta(1)$ (resp., $O(\lambda)$). Combining with our new result, the KEMs derived from [12,14,15,19,21] achieve MUMC-ECPA/ECCA security based on the standard (matrix) DDH assumptions with security loss $\Theta(n)$ [12,21] (resp., $O(\lambda n)$ [14,15,19]), thus the tightness of their MUMC-ECPA/ECCA security is optimal (resp., almost optimal).

The Non-triviality of Our Reduction. We stress that our reduction from MUMC-ECPA/ECCA security to IND-mCPA/mCCA security is non-trivial. A straightforward reduction works as follows. An IND-mCPA/mCCA adversary $\mathcal{B}$ simulates the MUMC-ECPA/ECCA experiment for $\mathcal{A}$ by guessing the set of corrupted users, generating the public keys and secret keys of the corrupted users itself, and embedding the public keys in the IND-mCPA/mCCA experiment into (one of) the uncorrupted users.

Note that guessing the set of corrupted users will incur two problems in the security reduction.

- Firstly, it will incur an exponential loss factor, since there are 2^n possibilities of corrupted users in total, which is exponentially large when $n \geq \lambda$.
- Moreover, it is hard for $\mathcal{B}$ to answer key reveal queries w.r.t. uncorrupted users for $\mathcal{A}$, since the IND-mCPA/mCCA experiment does not provide a key reveal oracle $\mathcal{O}_{\mathrm{REV}}$.

We addressed the above two problems and provide a new reduction which loses only a linear factor $O(n)$. Our reduction goes with n hybrids. In the η-th hybrid ($\eta \in [n]$), we change the encapsulated keys in $\mathcal{O}_{\mathrm{TEST}}$ w.r.t. user η from real keys K_0 to random keys K_1.

- **One user at a time.** To avoid an exponential loss factor, our reduction focuses on only a single user at a time. In the η-th hybrid, our reduction embeds the public key in the IND-mCPA/mCCA experiment into the public key of user η. There are two cases. If $\mathcal{A}$ never corrupts user η, $\mathcal{B}$ can simulate the MUMC-ECPA/ECCA experiment perfectly for $\mathcal{A}$. So the change of $\mathcal{O}_{\text{TEST}}$ for user η is unnoticeable to $\mathcal{A}$ by the IND-mCPA/mCCA security. If $\mathcal{A}$ asks to corrupt user η, $\mathcal{B}$ aborts immediately. Note that in the latter case, $\mathcal{A}$ is not allowed to query $\mathcal{O}_{\text{TEST}}$ for user η when user η is (going to be) corrupted. So the change of $\mathcal{O}_{\text{TEST}}$ for user η is conceptual.

– **Key reveal with random keys.** To handle key reveal queries for user η, we borrow the ideas from [31]. If $\mathcal{A}$ never corrupts user η, $\mathcal{B}$ can output a random key for key reveal queries since $\mathcal{A}$ never sees the secret key of user η. If $\mathcal{A}$ asks to corrupt user η, $\mathcal{B}$ can also output a random key for key reveal queries before the corruption and aborts immediately when the corruption happens.

With only n hybrids, we change all encapsulated keys in $\mathcal{O}_{\text{TEST}}$ to random. This shows the indistinguishability of $\beta = 0$ and $\beta = 1$ in the MUMC-ECPA/ECCA experiment. Overall, our reduction only loses a linear factor $O(n)$ from MUMC-ECPA/ECCA to the IND-mCPA/mCCA security.

Formally, we have the following theorem, with proof appeared in the full version [18] due to space limitations.

Theorem 2 (IND-mCPA/mCCA $\overset{O(n)}{\Rightarrow}$ MUMC-ECPA/ECCA for KEM). *Let* KEM *be an IND-mCPA (resp., IND-mCCA) secure KEM scheme. Then* KEM *is MUMC-ECPA (resp., MUMC-ECCA) secure.*

Concretely, for any adversary $\mathcal{A}$ that $(t_{\mathcal{A}}, \epsilon_{\mathcal{A}}, n, Q_e, Q_t)$-breaks the MUMC-ECPA (resp., MUMC-ECCA) security of KEM *and makes at most Q_{total} times of queries in total, there exists an algorithm $\mathcal{B}$ that $(t_{\mathcal{B}}, \epsilon_{\mathcal{B}})$-breaks the IND-mCPA (resp., IND-mCCA) security of* KEM, *with*

$$t_{\mathcal{B}} \leq t_{\mathcal{A}} + (n + Q_{\text{total}}) \cdot t_{\text{KEM}} \quad and \quad \epsilon_{\mathcal{B}} \geq \epsilon_{\mathcal{A}}/(2n),$$

where t_{KEM} is a parameter depending only on the algorithms of KEM *and is independent of $t_{\mathcal{A}}$.*

Acknowledgments. We would like to thank the reviewers for their helpful comments. Shuai Han and Shengli Liu were partially supported by National Natural Science Foundation of China (Grant Nos. 62002223, 61925207), Guangdong Major Project of Basic and Applied Basic Research (2019B030302008), Shanghai Sailing Program (20YF1421100), and Young Elite Scientists Sponsorship Program by China Association for Science and Technology. Dawu Gu was partially supported by National Key Research and Development Project 2020YFA0712300.

References

1. Bader, C., Hofheinz, D., Jager, T., Kiltz, E., Li, Y.: Tightly-secure authenticated key exchange. In: Dodis, Y., Nielsen, J.B. (eds.) TCC 2015, Part I. LNCS, vol. 9014, pp. 629–658. Springer, Heidelberg (2015). https://doi.org/10.1007/978-3-662-46494-6_26
2. Bader, C., Jager, T., Li, Y., Schäge, S.: On the impossibility of tight cryptographic reductions. In: Fischlin, M., Coron, J.-S. (eds.) EUROCRYPT 2016, Part II. LNCS, vol. 9666, pp. 273–304. Springer, Heidelberg (2016). https://doi.org/10.1007/978-3-662-49896-5_10
3. Bellare, M., Ristenpart, T.: Simulation without the artificial abort: simplified proof and improved concrete security for waters' IBE scheme. In: Joux, A. (ed.) EUROCRYPT 2009. LNCS, vol. 5479, pp. 407–424. Springer, Heidelberg (2009). https://doi.org/10.1007/978-3-642-01001-9_24
4. Boneh, D., Venkatesan, R.: Breaking RSA may not be equivalent to factoring. In: Nyberg, K. (ed.) EUROCRYPT 1998. LNCS, vol. 1403, pp. 59–71. Springer, Heidelberg (1998). https://doi.org/10.1007/BFb0054117
5. Canetti, R., Krawczyk, H.: Universally composable notions of key exchange and secure channels. In: Knudsen, L.R. (ed.) EUROCRYPT 2002. LNCS, vol. 2332, pp. 337–351. Springer, Heidelberg (2002). https://doi.org/10.1007/3-540-46035-7_22
6. Cohn-Gordon, K., Cremers, C., Gjøsteen, K., Jacobsen, H., Jager, T.: Highly efficient key exchange protocols with optimal tightness. In: Boldyreva, A., Micciancio, D. (eds.) CRYPTO 2019, Part III. LNCS, vol. 11694, pp. 767–797. Springer, Cham (2019). https://doi.org/10.1007/978-3-030-26954-8_25
7. Coron, J.-S.: Optimal security proofs for PSS and other signature schemes. In: Knudsen, L.R. (ed.) EUROCRYPT 2002. LNCS, vol. 2332, pp. 272–287. Springer, Heidelberg (2002). https://doi.org/10.1007/3-540-46035-7_18
8. Cramer, R., Shoup, V.: A practical public key cryptosystem provably secure against adaptive chosen ciphertext attack. In: Krawczyk, H. (ed.) CRYPTO 1998. LNCS, vol. 1462, pp. 13–25. Springer, Heidelberg (1998). https://doi.org/10.1007/BFb0055717
9. Cramer, R., Shoup, V.: Universal hash proofs and a paradigm for adaptive chosen ciphertext secure public-key encryption. In: Knudsen, L.R. (ed.) EUROCRYPT 2002. LNCS, vol. 2332, pp. 45–64. Springer, Heidelberg (2002). https://doi.org/10.1007/3-540-46035-7_4
10. Cramer, R., Shoup, V.: Design and analysis of practical public-key encryption schemes secure against adaptive chosen ciphertext attack. SIAM J. Comput. **33**(1), 167–226 (2003)
11. Diffie, W., Hellman, M.E.: New directions in cryptography. IEEE Trans. Inf. Theory **22**(6), 644–654 (1976)
12. ElGamal, T.: A public key cryptosystem and a signature scheme based on discrete logarithms. In: Blakley, G.R., Chaum, D. (eds.) CRYPTO 1984. LNCS, vol. 196, pp. 10–18. Springer, Heidelberg (1985). https://doi.org/10.1007/3-540-39568-7_2
13. Escala, A., Herold, G., Kiltz, E., Ràfols, C., Villar, J.: An algebraic framework for Diffie-Hellman assumptions. In: Canetti, R., Garay, J.A. (eds.) CRYPTO 2013, Part II. LNCS, vol. 8043, pp. 129–147. Springer, Heidelberg (2013). https://doi.org/10.1007/978-3-642-40084-1_8
14. Gay, R., Hofheinz, D., Kiltz, E., Wee, H.: Tightly CCA-secure encryption without pairings. In: Fischlin, M., Coron, J.-S. (eds.) EUROCRYPT 2016, Part I. LNCS, vol. 9665, pp. 1–27. Springer, Heidelberg (2016). https://doi.org/10.1007/978-3-662-49890-3_1

15. Gay, R., Hofheinz, D., Kohl, L.: Kurosawa-Desmedt meets tight security. In: Katz, J., Shacham, H. (eds.) CRYPTO 2017, Part III. LNCS, vol. 10403, pp. 133–160. Springer, Cham (2017). https://doi.org/10.1007/978-3-319-63697-9_5

16. Gjøsteen, K., Jager, T.: Practical and tightly-secure digital signatures and authenticated key exchange. In: Shacham, H., Boldyreva, A. (eds.) CRYPTO 2018, Part II. LNCS, vol. 10992, pp. 95–125. Springer, Cham (2018). https://doi.org/10.1007/978-3-319-96881-0_4

17. Han, S., et al.: Authenticated key exchange and signatures with tight security in the standard model. In: Malkin, T., Peikert, C. (eds.) CRYPTO 2021, Part IV. LNCS, vol. 12828, pp. 670–700. Springer, Cham (2021). https://doi.org/10.1007/978-3-030-84259-8_23

18. Han, S., Liu, S., Gu, D.: Key encapsulation mechanism with tight enhanced security in the multi-user setting: impossibility result and optimal tightness. Cryptology ePrint Archive, Report 2021/1146 (2021). https://eprint.iacr.org/2021/1146

19. Han, S., Liu, S., Lyu, L., Gu, D.: Tight leakage-resilient CCA-security from quasi-adaptive hash proof system. In: Boldyreva, A., Micciancio, D. (eds.) CRYPTO 2019, Part II. LNCS, vol. 11693, pp. 417–447. Springer, Cham (2019). https://doi.org/10.1007/978-3-030-26951-7_15

20. Hesse, J., Hofheinz, D., Kohl, L.: On tightly secure non-interactive key exchange. In: Shacham, H., Boldyreva, A. (eds.) CRYPTO 2018, Part II. LNCS, vol. 10992, pp. 65–94. Springer, Cham (2018). https://doi.org/10.1007/978-3-319-96881-0_3

21. Hofheinz, D., Jager, T.: Tightly secure signatures and public-key encryption. In: Safavi-Naini, R., Canetti, R. (eds.) CRYPTO 2012. LNCS, vol. 7417, pp. 590–607. Springer, Heidelberg (2012). https://doi.org/10.1007/978-3-642-32009-5_35

22. Hofheinz, D., Jager, T., Knapp, E.: Waters signatures with optimal security reduction. In: Fischlin, M., Buchmann, J., Manulis, M. (eds.) PKC 2012. LNCS, vol. 7293, pp. 66–83. Springer, Heidelberg (2012). https://doi.org/10.1007/978-3-642-30057-8_5

23. Hofheinz, D., Kiltz, E.: Secure hybrid encryption from weakened key encapsulation. In: Menezes, A. (ed.) CRYPTO 2007. LNCS, vol. 4622, pp. 553–571. Springer, Heidelberg (2007). https://doi.org/10.1007/978-3-540-74143-5_31

24. Jager, T., Kiltz, E., Riepel, D., Schäge, S.: Tightly-secure authenticated key exchange, revisited. In: Canteaut, A., Standaert, F.-X. (eds.) EUROCRYPT 2021, Part I. LNCS, vol. 12696, pp. 117–146. Springer, Cham (2021). https://doi.org/10.1007/978-3-030-77870-5_5

25. Jager, T., Stam, M., Stanley-Oakes, R., Warinschi, B.: Multi-key authenticated encryption with corruptions: reductions are lossy. In: Kalai, Y., Reyzin, L. (eds.) TCC 2017, Part I. LNCS, vol. 10677, pp. 409–441. Springer, Cham (2017). https://doi.org/10.1007/978-3-319-70500-2_14

26. Kakvi, S.A., Kiltz, E.: Optimal security proofs for full domain hash, revisited. In: Pointcheval, D., Johansson, T. (eds.) EUROCRYPT 2012. LNCS, vol. 7237, pp. 537–553. Springer, Heidelberg (2012). https://doi.org/10.1007/978-3-642-29011-4_32

27. Krawczyk, H.: HMQV: a high-performance secure Diffie-Hellman protocol. In: Shoup, V. (ed.) CRYPTO 2005. LNCS, vol. 3621, pp. 546–566. Springer, Heidelberg (2005). https://doi.org/10.1007/11535218_33

28. Kurosawa, K., Desmedt, Y.: A new paradigm of hybrid encryption scheme. In: Franklin, M. (ed.) CRYPTO 2004. LNCS, vol. 3152, pp. 426–442. Springer, Heidelberg (2004). https://doi.org/10.1007/978-3-540-28628-8_26

29. LaMacchia, B., Lauter, K., Mityagin, A.: Stronger security of authenticated key exchange. In: Susilo, W., Liu, J.K., Mu, Y. (eds.) ProvSec 2007. LNCS, vol. 4784, pp. 1–16. Springer, Heidelberg (2007). https://doi.org/10.1007/978-3-540-75670-5_1

30. Lewko, A., Waters, B.: Why proving HIBE systems secure is difficult. In: Nguyen, P.Q., Oswald, E. (eds.) EUROCRYPT 2014. LNCS, vol. 8441, pp. 58–76. Springer, Heidelberg (2014). https://doi.org/10.1007/978-3-642-55220-5_4

31. Liu, X., Liu, S., Gu, D., Weng, J.: Two-pass authenticated key exchange with explicit authentication and tight security. In: Moriai, S., Wang, H. (eds.) ASIACRYPT 2020, Part II. LNCS, vol. 12492, pp. 785–814. Springer, Cham (2020). https://doi.org/10.1007/978-3-030-64834-3_27

32. Morgan, A., Pass, R.: On the security loss of unique signatures. In: Beimel, A., Dziembowski, S. (eds.) TCC 2018, Part I. LNCS, vol. 11239, pp. 507–536. Springer, Cham (2018). https://doi.org/10.1007/978-3-030-03807-6_19

33. Morgan, A., Pass, R., Shi, E.: On the adaptive security of MACs and PRFs. In: Moriai, S., Wang, H. (eds.) ASIACRYPT 2020, Part I. LNCS, vol. 12491, pp. 724–753. Springer, Cham (2020). https://doi.org/10.1007/978-3-030-64837-4_24

34. Naor, M., Reingold, O.: Number-theoretic constructions of efficient pseudo-random functions. In: 38th FOCS, pp. 458–467. IEEE Computer Society Press (1997)

35. Naor, M., Yung, M.: Public-key cryptosystems provably secure against chosen ciphertext attacks. In: 22nd ACM STOC, pp. 427–437. ACM Press (1990)

36. Niehues, D.: Verifiable random functions with optimal tightness. In: Garay, J.A. (ed.) PKC 2021, Part II. LNCS, vol. 12711, pp. 61–91. Springer, Cham (2021). https://doi.org/10.1007/978-3-030-75248-4_3

37. Pan, J., Qian, C., Ringerud, M.: Signed Diffie-Hellman key exchange with tight security. In: Paterson, K.G. (ed.) CT-RSA 2021. LNCS, vol. 12704, pp. 201–226. Springer, Cham (2021). https://doi.org/10.1007/978-3-030-75539-3_9

38. Xue, H., Lu, X., Li, B., Liang, B., He, J.: Understanding and constructing AKE via double-key key encapsulation mechanism. In: Peyrin, T., Galbraith, S. (eds.) ASIACRYPT 2018, Part II. LNCS, vol. 11273, pp. 158–189. Springer, Cham (2018). https://doi.org/10.1007/978-3-030-03329-3_6

Hierarchical Integrated Signature and Encryption

(or: Key Separation vs. Key Reuse: Enjoy the Best of both Worlds)

Yu Chen[1,2,3], Qiang Tang[4], and Yuyu Wang[5]

[1] School of Cyber Science and Technology, Shandong University,
Qingdao 266237, China
[2] State Key Laboratory of Cryptology, P.O. Box 5159, Beijing 100878, China
[3] Key Laboratory of Cryptologic Technology and Information Security,
Ministry of Education, Shandong University, Qingdao 266237, China
yuchen@sdu.edu.cn
[4] School of Computer Science, University of Sydney, Sydney, Australia
qiang.tang@sydney.edu.au
[5] University of Electronic Science and Technology of China, Chengdu, China
wangyuyu@uestc.edu.cn

Abstract. In this work, we introduce the notion of hierarchical integrated signature and encryption (HISE), wherein a single public key is used for both signature and encryption, and one can derive a secret key used only for decryption from the signing key, which enables secure delegation of decryption capability. HISE enjoys the benefit of key reuse, and admits individual key escrow. We present two generic constructions of HISE. One is from (constrained) identity-based encryption. The other is from uniform one-way function, public-key encryption, and general-purpose public-coin zero-knowledge proof of knowledge. To further attain global key escrow, we take a little detour to revisit global escrow PKE, an object both of independent interest and with many applications. We formalize the syntax and security model of global escrow PKE, and provide two generic constructions. The first embodies a generic approach to compile any PKE into one with global escrow property. The second establishes a connection between three-party non-interactive key exchange and global escrow PKE. Combining the results developed above, we obtain HISE schemes that support both individual and global key escrow.

We instantiate our generic constructions of (global escrow) HISE and implement all the resulting concrete schemes for 128-bit security. Our schemes have performance that is comparable to the best Cartesian product combined public-key scheme, and exhibit advantages in terms of richer functionality and public key reuse. As a byproduct, we obtain a new global escrow PKE scheme that is 12–30× faster than the best prior work, which might be of independent interest.

© International Association for Cryptologic Research 2021
M. Tibouchi and H. Wang (Eds.): ASIACRYPT 2021, LNCS 13091, pp. 514–543, 2021.
https://doi.org/10.1007/978-3-030-92075-3_18

1   Introduction

Public-key encryption (PKE) and digital signature are widely used in combination in many real-world applications, where the former is used to protect data confidentiality, and the latter is used to provide authenticity. For example, in secure communication applications such as PGP [PGP], supposing that Alice wants to send an email to Bob in a secure and authenticated manner, she first encrypts the email under Bob's public-key, and then signs the ciphertext using her signing key. In privacy-preserving cryptocurrencies such as Zether [BAZB20], to generate a confidential transaction, a sender account encrypts the transfer amount under the public keys of both the sender account and receiver account, and then signs the transaction using his secret spending key.

When using PKE and signature schemes simultaneously, we require joint security, i.e., their respective security properties are retained in the presence of additional oracles (if there is any, e.g., signing oracle and decryption oracle). The reason is that although PKE and signature schemes might have been proven to be secure individually, they may undermine each other if their respective keys are related. Typically, there are two principals for combining PKE and signature.

Key Separation vs. Key Reuse. The *key separation* principal is an engineering folklore that dictates using different keypairs for different cryptographic operations, which is best illustrated by the "Cartesian product" combined public-key (CPK) scheme: each user independently generates a keypair (ek, dk) for PKE and a keypair (vk, sk) for digital signature, concatenates the two keypairs into one, and then uses appropriate component of the compound key for each operation. Key separation allows one to flexibly choose and combine the off-the-shelf PKE and signature schemes, and the joint security follows readily from the independence of the two keypairs. However, it has an obvious shortcoming that the key size and the complexity of key management are doubled.[1]

In contrast, the *key reuse* principal is using identical keypair, e.g., for both PKE and signatures, and we refer to such cryptosystem as integrated signature and encryption (ISE). To avoid triviality, the keypair should be non-splittable, namely, it cannot be broken into two pieces for different operations respectively.

As advocated by Paterson et al. [PSST11], adopting key reuse principal is beneficial, since it can reduce key storage requirements, reduce the number of certificates needed (which in turn reduces the certificate cost[2]), and reduce the footprint of cryptographic code and development effort. These savings could be vital

---

[1] One may attempt to include the encryption key ek and verification key vk into one certificate in order to keep the certificate cost unchanged. Unfortunately this theoretically possible solution is not standard-compliant. X.509v3 as per RFC 5280 [X50] only allows a single `subjectPublicKeyInfo` field. If one wants to add more than one public key into this field, new syntax or parsing rule are needed, which would require major changes to implementations and relevant libraries. In contrast, key reuse is readily supported by X.509v3 via the `keyUsage` field.

[2] Certificate costs include but not limit to registration, issuing, storage, transmission, verification, and building/recurring fees.

in constrained environments such as embedded systems and low-end smart card applications. For instance, the globally-deployed EMV standard for authenticating credit and debit card transactions uses the same keypair for both encryption and signature precisely for these reasons (see [EMV11, Sec. 7]). Other real world instances embracing key reuse include identity management solution provider Ping Identity [Pin] and RFC 4055. We highlight that the key reuse principal also helps to simplify the design of high-level protocols. Notably, most known privacy-preserving cryptocurrencies in the account model [NVV18, BAZB20, CMTA20] either explicitly or implicitly use ISE as a core building block, which enables a clean security notion and simple constructions.

Nevertheless, key reuse is not without its issues. In an ISE scheme, the reuse of a single keypair may hinder the individual security of the PKE or the signature scheme, (consider the textbook RSA cryptosystem as a simple example and see [DLP+12] for a more sophisticated example at the protocol level). Therefore, joint security of ISE is not immediate and a rigorous proof is always needed.

Also, Haber and Pinkas [HP01] pointed out that secret keys may require different levels of protection, which becomes out of reach when sticking to key reuse principal. A more puzzling issue, as we elaborate next, is that rigid adherence to key reuse principal introduces hurdles on applications that require key escrow.

Delegation of Decryption Capability. In privacy-preserving applications enabled by PKE, a user may want to delegate his decryption capability to an agent for key recovery or usability purpose, while an authority (law-enforcement agencies as well as other organizations) may want to acquire decryption capability of users for compliance purpose. This is where key escrow comes into play. In general, there are two types of key escrow mechanisms.

The *individual key escrow* means that the user simply shares his decryption key with the escrow agent. Such delegation of decryption capability is of "one-to-one" flavor, and under the control of each individual user. The *global key escrow* means that the escrow agent has a single "master" key to decrypt any ciphertext of any user. Such delegation of decryption capability is of "all-to-one" flavor. We note that individual key escrow implies a naive solution to global key escrow by having the agent maintain a big database of all individual decryption keys. However, this naive solution comes with two deficiencies: (i) the complexity of key management grows linearly with the number of keys, which severely limits scalability, and thus being inadequate for large-scale applications; (ii) collecting a large number of valid decryption keys could be difficult to conduct in practice.

Conflict Between Key Reuse and Key Escrow. In the context of combined usage of PKE and signature, the original joint security is insufficient to enable individual key escrow, and strong joint security is needed. This is because now the adversary is directly given *the decryption key*, instead of just a decryption oracle (as we still want to ensure integrity even if escrow agent is corrupted). Clearly, the ISE schemes adhering to key reuse strategy fail to meet strong joint security as the same secret key is used for both decryption and signing, and consequently individual key escrow is insecure since a corrupted escrow agent is able sign on behalf of the user, a basic violation of the concept of digital signing [Ros] (and cannot be applied to many settings such as anonymous cryptocurrency).

From the above discussion, we are facing a dilemma between key reuse that brings performance benefit and key separation that supports key escrow mechanism. We are thus motivated to ask the following intriguing questions:

Can we enable individual key escrow mechanism while retaining the merits of key reuse? And, can we further support global key escrow mechanism?

1.1   Our Contributions

We answer the above questions affirmatively and have the following results.

Hierarchical Integrated Signature and Encryption. In an ISE scheme, a single keypair is used for both encryption and signature, thus the exposure of decryption key will completely compromise the security of signature. A closer look indicates that if there is a hierarchy between the signing key and decryption key, then stronger joint security becomes possible. We put forth a new notion called hierarchical integrated signature and encryption (HISE). In an HISE scheme, a single public key is used for both encryption and signature verification; the signing key plays the role of "master" secret key, namely, one can derive a decryption key from the signing key but not vice versa. This two-level hierarchy key derivation structure *hits a sweet balance* between key separation and key reuse, and thus allows us to enjoy the best of both worlds. It not only admits individual key escrow mechanism and classified protection of signing key and decryption key, but also retains the benefit of key reuse strategy.[3]

We specify a strong joint security model for HISE schemes by capturing multifaceted attacks in the joint sense. For confidentiality, we stipulate that the PKE component satisfies indistinguishability against chosen-ciphertext attacks (IND-CCA) even the adversary is provided with unrestricted access to a signing oracle. For authenticity, we stipulate that the signature component satisfies existentially unforgeability against chosen-message attacks (EUF-CMA) even the adversary is *directly given the associated decryption key*. We then present two generic constructions of HISE schemes.

HISE from (Constrained) IBE. Our first construction is inspired by the elegant ISE construction due to Paterson et al. [PSST11]. In their construction, they apply the Naor transform [BF03] and the tag-based version of the Canetti-Halevi-Katz (CHK) transform [BCHK07] to an identity-based encryption (IBE) scheme simultaneously, yielding a signature component and a PKE component in one shot. The two components share the same keypair, i.e., the master keypair of the underlying IBE. Note that signatures in the signature component derived from the Naor transform are private keys for messages (playing the role of identities), while these private keys can decrypt ciphertexts in the PKE component derived from the CHK transform. To attain joint security, they use a bit prefix in the identity space to provide a domain separation between the identities used

---

[3] As briefly elaborated before, the advantage of key reuse strategy mostly resides in the fact that one public key is used for both encryption and verification.

for encoding messages and the identities used as tags. However, ISE schemes from IBE do not directly lend themselves to HISE schemes, as the master secret key of IBE plays the roles of *both the signing key and decryption key.*

We resolve this problem by introducing a new notion called *constrained IBE* (see Sect. 2.2 for definition and construction) as our starting point. In a constrained IBE one can derive constrained keys sk_f for $f \in \mathcal{F}$ from the master secret key, where $\mathcal{F}$ is a predicate family defined over identity space, e.g., a family of prefix predicates. A constrained key sk_f enables the decryption of ciphertexts encrypted under id if and only if $f(id) = 1$. We are now ready to sketch our HISE construction from any constrained IBE that supports prefix predicates, which is in turn implied by binary tree encryption (BTE) [CHK03]. Suppose the identity space I of the underlying constrained IBE is $\{0, 1\}^{\ell+1}$, we use bit prefix to partition I to two disjoint sets, say, I_0 starting with bit 0 and I_1 starting with bit 1. The key generation algorithm first generates a master keypair (mpk, msk) of the constrained IBE, sets mpk as the public key and msk as the secret key, and derives a constrained key sk_{f_1} from msk, where $f_1(id) = 1$ iff $id \in I_1$. Thanks to the properties of constrained IBE, sk_{f_1} can decrypt all ciphertexts encrypted under identities in I_1, and thus could serve as the decryption key. We then build the signature component from the constrained IBE via the Naor transform by encoding messages into I_1, and build the encryption component from the constrained IBE and one-time signature via the CHK transform by using identities from I_1 as tags. The security of constrained IBE implies that the signature component remains secure even in the presence of the decryption key. In this way, we obtain HISE with strong joint security in the standard model.

We remark that if one does not insist on joint security in the standard model, then it is not necessary to resort to the CHK transform to achieve CCA security. As a result, a much simpler construction of HISE can be built from any IBE. The construction is similar to the one from constrained IBE, except that I_1 shrinks to a single identity fixed in the public parameters, and the encryption component is obtained by applying the IBE-to-PKE degradation and the Fujisaki-Okamoto transformation [FO99] sequentially.

HISE from PKE and ZKPoK. Our second construction is from PKE and zero-knowledge proof of knowledge (ZKPoK). At the heart of it is a novel hierarchical key derivation mechanism. Roughly speaking, the key generation algorithm consists of two steps: (1) choosing a random bit string as the signing key, and then map it to random coins via a uniform one-way function (OWF) F (a OWF that outputs uniform bits when input uniform bits); (2) feeding the resulting random coins to the key generation algorithm of PKE, yielding a keypair. The public key serves as both the encryption key and verification key. The encryption component is exactly the underlying PKE. In this way, the decryption key can be easily derived from the signing key, but not vice versa. The merit of the above hierarchical key derivation mechanism is that it endows great flexibility of the underlying PKE schemes, and thus is of particular interest for application scenarios where it is desirable to upgrade the PKE in use to HISE in a seamless way. However, it also gives rise to a technical challenge: how to design a signature scheme with *an unstructured bit string* as the signing key, which should remain secure even in the presence of partial leakage, say, the decryption key. We show that if the function G from random coins to public key induced by the key generation algorithm is target-collision resistant, then the composed function G ∘ F from signing key to public key is one-way even with respect to arbitrary leakage of the intermediate random coins, let alone the decryption key. Therefore, we can overcome the aforementioned difficulty by leveraging public-coin ZKPoK. A signature is a non-interactive zero-knowledge proof of the signing key, incorporating a message to be signed. This construction essentially embodies a generic approach of converting any PKE to HISE with the help of ZKPoK (we refer to it as the HI conversion hereafter).

We note that the high-level idea of using OWF and ZKPoK to build signatures had appeared in previous works [CDG+17,KKW18], but our usage of this technique is *qualitatively* different. Prior works focus on building a standalone signature scheme: the public key is simply an image $y = F(x)$ of a OWF F and secret key x. In our construction, we aim to add signature functionality to existing PKE schemes, yielding HISE schemes with strong joint security. To do so, the public key is set as the output of secret key via a function composed of a OWF and the PKE's key generation algorithm. Careful analysis of the minimal requirements on the OWF and key generation algorithm, as well as the HISE construction we propose, are new to this work.

Supporting Global Key Escrow. We then turn to the problem of equipping HISE with global key escrow mechanism. To make our techniques more general, we first take a little detour to revisit the topic in the setting of PKE.

Global Escrow PKE. In global escrow PKE there is an escrow agent holding a global escrow decryption key that can decrypt ciphertexts encrypted under any public key. The state of the art of global escrow PKE is less satisfactory, which is long overdue for formal definition and efficient construction. So far, the only known practical scheme based on standard assumption is the escrow ElGamal PKE proposed by Boneh and Franklin [BF03] from bilinear maps.

At first glance, it seems that global escrow PKE can be trivially built from broadcast encryption by having the receiver set include the real intended receiver and the escrow agent. However, the idea does not work since the sender in broadcast encryption is always assumed to be honest, while in the context of global escrow PKE the sender could be *malicious* (e.g. generate ciphertexts dishonestly) especially if he has the incentive to evade the oversight of escrow agent. To capture such misbehaving, we introduce the "consistency" notion to enforce the decryption results of any ill-formed ciphertexts yielded by the receiver's decryption key and the global escrow decryption key to be identical. We then propose two generic constructions of global escrow PKE.

Our first construction is based on PKE and non-interactive zero-knowledge proof (NIZK) (see Sect. 6.1 for details). The escrow agent generates a keypair (pk_γ, sk_γ), then publishes pk_γ as public parameters, and uses sk_γ as the global escrow decryption key. To generate a ciphertext for the receiver holding public key pk_β, the sender encrypts the plaintext under pk_β and pk_γ respectively, and then appends a NIZK proof for the validity of encryption. To decrypt a ciphertext, the receiver (resp. escrow agent) first checks if the proof is valid, and then decrypts with secret key sk_β (resp. sk_γ) if so or returns $\bot$ otherwise. The main purpose of using NIZK is to guarantee the consistency of decryption results yielded by the receiver's decryption key and global escrow decryption key, while a bonus is that the resulting global escrow PKE automatically satisfies CCA security. This construction can be interpreted as a novel usage of the celebrated Naor-Yung paradigm [NY90], which indicates that any PKE can be upgraded to support global escrow with the help of NIZK (we refer to it as the GE conversion hereafter).

Our second construction is based on three-party non-interactive key exchange (NIKE) (see Sect. 6.2 for details). Same as our first construction, the escrow agent generates a keypair (pk_γ, sk_γ), publishes pk_γ as part of public parameters, and uses sk_γ as the global escrow decryption key. To generate a ciphertext for the receiver holding public key pk_β, the sender generates a random keypair (pk_α, sk_α), and then runs the three-party NIKE *in his head* to compute a shared key among $(pk_\alpha, pk_\beta, pk_\gamma)$. The final ciphertext consists of pk_α and a symmetric encryption of plaintext under the shared key. To decrypt, the receiver (resp. escrow agent) uses secret key sk_β (resp. sk_γ) to compute the shared key among $(pk_\alpha, pk_\beta, pk_\gamma)$, and then decrypts the symmetric part. This construction suggests a generic approach of converting three-party NIKE to global escrow PKE, uncovering a connection between two seemingly unrelated notions. More interestingly, we show that the construction still works by relying on a relaxed version of three-party NIKE, leading to the most efficient global escrow PKE to date (outperforms prior scheme [BF03] in speed by a factor 12–30×), which might be of independent interest.

Global Escrow HISE. Now, we are ready to construct HISE that supports global key escrow mechanism that we dub "global escrow HISE". In a global escrow HISE, the escrow agent is capable of decrypting any ciphertext under any public key with a succinct global escrow decryption key, while the security of the signature component retains even in the presence of the associated individual decryption key and the global escrow decryption key. Combining the results developed above, we obtain two paths of building global escrow HISE from different starting points. One is to apply the Naor-Yung like transform (GE conversion) to any HISE, and the other is to add hierarchy key derivation structure (HI conversion) to any global escrow PKE meeting the mild requirement described above. Figure 1 depicts the technology roadmap for the constructions of global escrow HISE.

Applications of (Global Escrow) HISE. Besides the merit of compact public key sizes, (global escrow) HISE also helps to reduce the key management complexity and simplify the design and analysis of high-level protocols. In general, they are suitable for scenarios that simultaneously require privacy, authenticity and key escrow. Below, we give several illustrative usages.

Usage of HISE. In privacy-preserving cryptocurrencies such as Zether [BAZB20], a user may need to share his decryption key with an authority for audit purpose

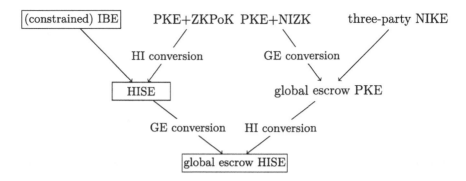

Fig. 1. Technology roadmap of global escrow HISE. The rectangles denote our newly introduced cryptographic schemes.

or delegating costly decryption operations[4] to a service. Currently, Zether is equipped with ISE and thus does not support individual key escrow. In another case, a PGP user may be required to handover his decryption key to an authority on demand for compliance purpose.[5] For the time being, PGP adopts key separation and thus naturally supports individual key escrow, but each user has to maintain at least two public key certificates. In either case, the user wants to guarantee that his signing capability remains exclusive. By deploying HISE, not only the systems can benefit from key reuse, but also the user can safely escrow his decryption key to a third party without worrying the security of signature being breached (e.g. in the cryptocurrency setting, even the auditing authority with decryption key cannot spend user's coin).

Usage of Global Escrow HISE. Enterprise applications such as Slack get increasing adoption for large-scale collaborative working, and thus has raised the demand for secure internal communication which may contain proprietary information. The employer may have the right to get access to all private communications as in traditional work emails [vox], or might be obliged to possess "super" decryption capability for various reasons such as archival purpose, litigation-related eDiscovery, or detection of malware. On the other side, the employees need to be assured that even a malicious administrator of the "super" key cannot slander them by forging signatures for fabricated communications. Global escrow HISE is perfectly suitable for these cases. By playing the role of escrow agent, the authority is able to conduct large-scale supervision efficiently with the global escrow decryption key, but unable to violate users' exclusive signing capability.

---

[4] A bunch of recent privacy-preserving cryptocurrencies [NVV18, BAZB20, CMTA20] employ lifted ElGamal like PKE schemes, and thus decryption operations require computing the discrete logarithm, which is time consuming.

[5] The government of the United Kingdom requires any PGP user to give the police both his private key and his passphrase on demand. Failure to comply is a criminal offense, punishable by a jail term of two years.

Instantiation, Implementation and Evaluation. We instantiate our generic constructions of (global escrow) HISE and implement all the resulting concrete schemes for 128-bit security. We choose the Cartesian product CPK built from the best available encryption and signature schemes as benchmark. Our (global escrow) HISE schemes have performance that is comparable to the Cartesian product CPK scheme, while exhibiting advantages in terms of richer functionality for escrow and compact key sizes. Moreover, we report the most efficient global escrow PKE known to date (12–30× faster than prior scheme), which is interesting in its own right. Our implementation is released on Github: https://github.com/yuchen1024/HISE. We summarize experimental results in Sect. 8.

1.2   Related Works

Combined Usage of PKE and Signature. Key separation is a conventional wisdom originated from real-world practice. Haber and Pinkas [HP01] investigate this security engineering folklore and initiate a formal study of key reuse. They introduce the notion of combined public key (CPK) scheme, which is a combination of a signature and encryption scheme: the existing algorithms of sign, verify, encrypt and decrypt are preserved, while the two key generation algorithms are modified into a single algorithm. This algorithm outputs two keypairs for signing and encryption operations respectively, with the keypairs no longer necessarily being independent. They also formalize the joint security of CPK scheme, i.e., the encryption component is IND-CCA secure even in the presence of an additional signing oracle, while the signature component is EUF-CMA secure even in the presence of an additional decryption oracle. Finally, they show that various well-known concrete schemes are jointly secure when their keys are partially shared. As an extreme case of CPK scheme, ISE scheme uses a single non-splittable keypair for both signature and encryption. Degabriele et al. [DLP+12] find a theoretical attack for the RSA-based ISE scheme in EMV standard version 4.1. Coron et al. [CJNP02] and Komano and Ohta [KO03] build ISE from trapdoor permutations in the random oracle model. Paterson et al. [PSST11] give an elegant construction of ISE from identity-based encryption.

In contrast to ISE, HISE is equipped with a two-level hierarchy key structure, i.e., the signing key plays the role of master secret key, and one can derive a decryption key from the signing key. The joint security of HISE stipulates that the signature component is EUF-CMA secure even in the presence of a decryption key, which is strictly stronger than that of ISE.

Key Escrow. We now briefly survey existing works on key escrow in the context of public-key encryption. As aforementioned, there are two types of key escrow: *individual key escrow* and *global key escrow*. While individual key escrow is straightforwards, global key escrow appears to be harder to attain. The earlier solutions to global key escrow are not satisfactory. They either rely on tamper-resistant devices, or require the escrow agent to get involved in interactive computations at an undesirable level. Paillier and Yung [PY99] propose a solution called self-escrowed public-key infrastructure, which requires that the relation between secret key and public key is trapdoorness. Such stringent requirement greatly limits the choice of possible candidates, and so far the only known realization of SE-PKI is based on a non-standard assumption. Until 2003, Boneh and Franklin [BF03] give the first practical scheme called escrow ElGamal based on standard assumption. Nevertheless, formal definition and generic constructions of global escrow PKE are still missing.

To our knowledge, the only work in the literature that considers key reuse and key escrow together is due to Verheul [Ver01]. Verheul considers the problem of supporting non-repudiation and individual key escrow in the single public key setting, and proposes a candidate scheme from the XTR subgroup. The author gives an indication of security, but is not aware of more rigorous security proof.[6] Therefore, this problem remains open. In this work, we resolve this open problem by proposing a new cryptographic primitive called HISE and giving efficient and provably secure constructions.

2   Preliminaries

We use the standard definitions of bilinear maps, SKE, PKE, signature, IBE, zero-knowledge proof systems, as well as non-interactive key exchange protocols. The definition of one-way functions has appeared previously, while the definition and construction of constrained IBE schemes are new. Since they are central to our work, we include their formal definitions as below.

2.1   One-Way Function

A function $F : X \to Y$ is one-way if it is efficiently computable and hard-to-invert on average. Let $\mathcal{H}$ be a family of leakage functions defined over domain X. F is leakage-resilient one-way [DHLW10] w.r.t. $\mathcal{H}$ if the one-wayness remains in the presence of leakage $h(x)$, where x is the preimage and h could be any function from $\mathcal{H}$. If $F(x)$ is uniform over Y when $x \xleftarrow{R} X$, we say that F is uniform.

2.2   Constrained Identity-Based Encryption

We introduce a new notion called constrained IBE. In a nutshell, a constrained IBE is an IBE in which master secret key allows efficient delegation with respect to a family of predicates over identity space. Formally, a constrained IBE consists of the following PPT algorithms:

- Setup(1^λ): on input a security parameter λ, outputs public parameters pp. Let $\mathcal{F}$ be a family of predicates over identity space I.
- KeyGen(pp): on input public parameters pp, outputs a master public key mpk and a master secret key msk.

---

[6] Our perspective is that a security reduction from Verheul's scheme to standard hardness problem is unlikely to be forthcoming, since it is difficult to emulate the decryption key for the adversary against the signature component.

- Extract(msk, id): on input a master secret key msk and an identity $id \in I$, outputs a user secret key sk_{id}.
- Constrain(msk, f): on input a master secret key msk and a predicate $f \in \mathcal{F}$, outputs a constrained secret key sk_f.
- Derive(sk_f, id): on input a constrained secret key sk_f and an identity $id \in I$, outputs a user secret key sk_{id} if $f(id) = 1$ or $\perp$ otherwise.
- Enc(mpk, id, m): on input mpk, an identity $id \in I$, and a message m, outputs a ciphertext c.
- Dec(sk_{id}, c): on input a user secret key sk_{id} and a ciphertext c, outputs a message m or a special reject symbol $\perp$ denoting failure.

Correctness. For any $(mpk, msk) \leftarrow$ KeyGen(pp), any identity $id \in I$, any $sk_{id} \leftarrow$ Extract(msk, id), any message m, and any $c \leftarrow$ Enc(mpk, id, m), it holds that Dec(sk_{id}, c) = m. Besides, for any $f \in \mathcal{F}$ such that $f(id) = 1$, the outputs of Extract(msk, id) and Derive(sk_f, id) have the same distribution.

Security. Roughly speaking, a secure constrained IBE should ensure the secrecy of plaintexts encrypted by id as long as id has not been queried for user secret key or related constrained secret key. We formally define IND-CPA security for constrained IBE as below. Let $\mathcal{A}$ be an adversary against the IND-CPA security of constrained IBE and define its advantage in the following experiment:

$$\Pr \left[b = b' : \begin{array}{l} pp \leftarrow \mathsf{Setup}(1^\lambda); \\ (mpk, msk) \leftarrow \mathsf{KeyGen}(pp); \\ (id^*, m_0, m_1) \leftarrow \mathcal{A}^{\mathcal{O}_{\mathsf{ext}}(\cdot), \mathcal{O}_{\mathsf{constrain}}(\cdot)}(pp, mpk); \\ b \xleftarrow{\mathrm{R}} \{0, 1\}, c^* \leftarrow \mathsf{Enc}(mpk, id^*, m_b); \\ b' \leftarrow \mathcal{A}^{\mathcal{O}_{\mathsf{ext}}(\cdot), \mathcal{O}_{\mathsf{constrain}}(\cdot)}(c^*); \end{array} \right] - \frac{1}{2}.$$

$\mathcal{O}_{\mathsf{ext}}(\cdot)$ denotes the key extraction oracle, which on input id returns $sk_{id} \leftarrow$ Extract(msk, id). $\mathcal{O}_{\mathsf{constrain}}(\cdot)$ denotes the key constrain oracle, which on input f returns $sk_f \leftarrow$ Constrain(msk, f). $\mathcal{A}$ is not allowed to query $\mathcal{O}_{\mathsf{ext}}(\cdot)$ with id^* or query $\mathcal{O}_{\mathsf{constrain}}(\cdot)$ with f such that $f(id^*) = 1$. A constrained IBE is IND-CPA secure if no PPT adversary $\mathcal{A}$ has non-negligible advantage in the above security experiment. Two weaker security notions can be defined similarly. One is OW-CPA security, in which the adversary is required to recover the plaintext from a random ciphertext. The other is selective-identity IND-CPA security, in which the adversary is asked to specify the target identity id^* before seeing mpk.

We present a generic construction of constrained IBE for prefix predicates from BTE. Please see the full version for the details.

3 Definition of HISE

An HISE scheme consists of the following PPT algorithms.

- Setup(1^λ): on input a security parameter λ, outputs public parameters pp. We assume that pp includes the description of plaintext space M and message space $\widetilde{M}$.

- KeyGen(pp): on input pp, outputs a secret key sk and a public key pk. Here, sk serves as a master secret key, which can be used to derive decryption key.
- Derive(sk): on input a secret key sk, outputs a decryption key dk.
- Enc(pk, m): on input a public key pk and a plaintext $m \in M$, outputs a ciphertext c.
- Dec(dk, c): on input a decryption key dk and a ciphertext c, outputs a plaintext m or a special reject symbol $\perp$ denoting failure.
- Sign($sk, \widetilde{m}$): on input a secret key sk and a message $\widetilde{m} \in \widetilde{M}$, outputs a signature σ.
- Vrfy($pk, \widetilde{m}, \sigma$): on input a public key pk, a message $\widetilde{m}$, and a signature σ, outputs a bit b, with $b = 1$ meaning valid and $b = 0$ meaning invalid.

Correctness. For the PKE component, we require that for any $m \in M$, it holds that $\Pr[\mathsf{Dec}(dk, c) = m] \geq 1 - \mathsf{negl}(\lambda)$, where the probability is taken over the choice of $pp \leftarrow \mathsf{Setup}(1^\lambda)$, $(pk, sk) \leftarrow \mathsf{KeyGen}(pp)$, $dk \leftarrow \mathsf{Derive}(sk)$, and $c \leftarrow \mathsf{Enc}(pk, m)$. For the signature component, we require that for any $\widetilde{m} \in \widetilde{M}$, it holds that $\Pr[\mathsf{Vrfy}(pk, \widetilde{m}, \sigma) = 1] \geq 1 - \mathsf{negl}(\lambda)$, where the probability is taken over the choice of $pp \leftarrow \mathsf{Setup}(1^\lambda)$, $(pk, sk) \leftarrow \mathsf{KeyGen}(pp)$, $\sigma \leftarrow \mathsf{Sign}(sk, \widetilde{m})$, and the random coins used by Vrfy.

The joint security of HISE stipulates that the PKE component is IND-CCA secure even in the presence of a signing oracle, while the signature component is EUF-CMA secure in the presence of the decryption key. The formal security notion is defined as below.

Definition 1 (Joint Security for HISE). *HISE is jointly secure if its encryption and signature components satisfy the following security notions. Hereafter, let $\mathcal{O}_{\mathsf{sign}}(\cdot)$ be the signing oracle that on input $\widetilde{m} \in \widetilde{M}$ returns $\sigma \leftarrow \mathsf{Sign}(sk, \widetilde{m})$, and $\mathcal{O}_{\mathsf{dec}}(\cdot)$ be the decryption oracle that on input c returns $m \leftarrow \mathsf{Dec}(dk, c)$.*

IND-CCA Security in the Presence of a Signing Oracle. *Let $\mathcal{A}$ be an adversary against the PKE component and define its advantage as:*

$$\Pr\left[b = b' : \begin{array}{l} pp \leftarrow \mathsf{Setup}(1^\lambda); \\ (pk, sk) \leftarrow \mathsf{KeyGen}(pp); \\ (m_0, m_1) \leftarrow \mathcal{A}^{\mathcal{O}_{\mathsf{dec}}(\cdot), \mathcal{O}_{\mathsf{sign}}(\cdot)}(pp, pk); \\ b \xleftarrow{\text{R}} \{0,1\}, c^* \leftarrow \mathsf{Enc}(pk, m_b); \\ b' \leftarrow \mathcal{A}^{\mathcal{O}_{\mathsf{dec}}(\cdot), \mathcal{O}_{\mathsf{sign}}(\cdot)}(c^*); \end{array} \right] - \frac{1}{2}.$$

$\mathcal{A}$ has unrestricted access to $\mathcal{O}_{\mathsf{sign}}(\cdot)$, but is not allowed to query $\mathcal{O}_{\mathsf{dec}}(\cdot)$ with c^* in Phase 2. The PKE component is IND-CCA secure in the joint sense if no PPT adversary $\mathcal{A}$ has non-negligible advantage in the above security experiment.

EUF-CMA Security in the Presence of a Decryption Key. *Let $\mathcal{A}$ be an adversary against the signature component and define its advantage as:*

$$\Pr\left[\begin{array}{c} \mathsf{Vrfy}(pk, m^*, \sigma^*) = 1 \\ \wedge \; m^* \notin \mathcal{Q} \end{array} : \begin{array}{l} pp \leftarrow \mathsf{Setup}(1^\lambda); \\ (pk, sk) \leftarrow \mathsf{KeyGen}(pp); \\ dk \leftarrow \mathsf{Derive}(sk); \\ (m^*, \sigma^*) \leftarrow \mathcal{A}^{\mathcal{O}_{\mathsf{sign}}(\cdot)}(pp, pk, dk); \end{array} \right].$$

The set Q records queries to $\mathcal{O}_{\mathsf{sign}}(\cdot)$. The signature component is EUF-CMA secure in the joint sense if no PPT adversary $\mathcal{A}$ has non-negligible advantage in the above security experiment.

Remark 1. The security notion of HISE is strictly stronger than that of ISE in the sense that the signature component remains secure even when the adversary learns the entire decryption key rather than only has access to $\mathcal{O}_{\mathsf{dec}}(\cdot)$. This strengthening is crucial for applications that require secure delegation of decryption capability. We then discuss possible weakening of joint security. It is well-known that homomorphism denies CCA security. Thus, when homomorphic property is more desirable, we can instead only require the PKE component to be CPA-secure. We refer to the corresponding security as weak joint security.

Towards a modular design, the PKE component can be defined as key encapsulation mechanism. We omit the formal definition here for straightforwardness.

Global Escrow Extension. If an HISE scheme further satisfies global escrow property, we refer to it as global escrow HISE. In global escrow HISE, the setup algorithm additionally outputs a escrow decryption key edk, and there is an alternative decryption algorithm enabled by edk, whose decryption results of any ciphertext are identical to those obtained by applying normal decryption algorithm with the decryption key of intended receiver. The joint security stipulates that the encryption component remains secure in the presence of a signing oracle, and the signature component is secure even in the presence of the decryption key and escrow decryption key. We omit the formal definition here for its straightforwardness.

4   HISE from Constrained Identity-Based Encryption

In this section, we present a generic construction of HISE. Given a constrained IBE for prefix predicates (cf. definition in Sect. 2.2) and a strong one-time signature (OTS), we create an HISE scheme as below.

- Setup(1^λ): runs $pp_{\mathsf{cibe}} \leftarrow$ CIBE.Setup(1^λ), $pp_{\mathsf{ots}} \leftarrow$ OTS.Setup(1^λ), outputs $pp = (pp_{\mathsf{cibe}}, pp_{\mathsf{ots}})$. We assume the identity space of constrained IBE is $\{0,1\}^{\ell+1}$, and the verification space of OTS is $\{0,1\}^\ell$.
- KeyGen(pp): on input $pp = (pp_{\mathsf{cibe}}, pp_{\mathsf{ots}})$, runs CIBE.KeyGen($pp_{\mathsf{cibe}}$) to generate (mpk, msk), outputs public key $pk = mpk$ and secret key $sk = msk$.
- Derive(sk): parses sk as msk, runs $sk_{f_\mathbf{v}} \leftarrow$ CIBE.Constrain($msk, f_\mathbf{v}$) where $\mathbf{v} = 1$ and $f_\mathbf{v}(id) = 1$ iff $id[1] = 1$, outputs $dk = sk_{f_\mathbf{v}}$.
- Enc(pk, m): parses $pk = mpk$. The encryption algorithm runs $(ovk, osk) \leftarrow$ OTS.KeyGen(pp_{ots}). sets $id = 1\|ovk$, computes $c_{\mathsf{cibe}} \leftarrow$ CIBE.Enc(mpk, id, m), $\sigma \leftarrow$ OTS.Sign(osk, c_{cibe}), then outputs $c = (ovk, c_{\mathsf{cibe}}, \sigma)$.
- Dec(dk, c): parses $dk = sk_{f_\mathbf{v}}$ and $c = (ovk, c_{\mathsf{cibe}}, \sigma)$. The decryption algorithm first checks if OTS.Vrfy($ovk, c_{\mathsf{cibe}}, \sigma$) = 1, if not outputs $\perp$, else sets $id = 1\|ovk$ and computes $sk_{id} \leftarrow$ CIBE.Derive($sk_{f_\mathbf{v}}, id$), outputs $m \leftarrow$ CIBE.Dec($sk_{id}, c_{\mathsf{cibe}}$).

- Sign$(sk, \widetilde{m})$: parses sk as msk, computes $sk_{id} \leftarrow$ CIBE.Extract(msk, id) where $id = 0||\widetilde{m}$, outputs $\sigma = sk_{id}$.
- Vrfy$(pk, \sigma, \widetilde{m})$: parses pk as mpk, σ as sk_{id} for $id = 0||\widetilde{m}$, picks a random plaintext $m \in M$, computes $c_{\text{cibe}} \leftarrow$ CIBE.Enc(mpk, id, m), outputs "1" if CIBE.Dec$(sk_{id}, c_{\text{cibe}}) = m$ and "0" otherwise.

Correctness follows from that of constrained IBE and OTS. For security, we have the following theorem.

Theorem 1. *If the constrained IBE scheme is IND-CPA secure and the OTS scheme is strong EUF-CMA secure, then the HISE construction is jointly secure.*

Due to space limit, we defer the security proof to the full version.

Remark 2. The above generic construction from constrained IBE enjoys joint security in the standard model. So far, we only know how to build constrained IBE for prefix predicates from BTE [CHK03]. However, in existing constructions of BTE the size of secret key and ciphertext and encryption/decryption efficiency are all linear in ℓ, which are inefficient. We leave more efficient constructions of BTE and constrained IBE as an interesting open problem.

In applications where the encryption component only has to be IND-CPA secure, or one is willing to accept IND-CCA security in the random oracle model, we have a simpler and more efficient construction of HISE from any IBE. We defer the details to the full version.

5   HISE from PKE and ZKPoK

In this section, we present a generic construction of HISE from a PKE scheme and a 3-round public-coin ZKPoK protocol. At the heart of our construction is a novel mechanism what we called hierarchical key derivation. The high-level idea is to pick a random bit string as secret key sk, then derive an encryption/decryption keypair (ek, dk) of PKE in a deterministic manner. The encryption key ek is used for both encrypting plaintexts and verifying signatures, and hence will be denoted by pk. The decryption key is only used for decrypting. The secret key sk is used for signing messages and deriving the decryption key dk. The key derivation should be one-way, namely, one can derive the decryption key from the signing key, but not vice versa. Thus, the signing key acts as master secret key. Let the randomness space R of PKE's key generation algorithm be $\{0, 1\}^{\ell}$, we describe the generic construction as below.

- Setup(1^{λ}): runs $pp_{\text{pke}} \leftarrow$ PKE.Setup(1^{λ}), $pp_{\text{zkpok}} \leftarrow$ ZKPoK.Setup(1^{λ}), picks a uniform OWF F $: \{0, 1\}^n \rightarrow \{0, 1\}^{\ell}$, outputs $pp = (pp_{\text{pke}}, pp_{\text{zkpok}}, \mathsf{F})$.
- KeyGen(pp): parses $pp = (pp_{\text{pke}}, pp_{\text{zkpok}}, \mathsf{F})$, picks $sk \xleftarrow{\text{R}} \{0, 1\}^n$, computes $r \leftarrow \mathsf{F}(sk)$, runs $(ek, dk) \leftarrow$ PKE.KeyGen$(pp_{\text{pke}}; r)$, outputs public key $pk = ek$ and secret key sk. Let PK be the public key space.
- Derive(sk): this algorithm is exactly a part of KeyGen, i.e., on input sk, computes $r \leftarrow \mathsf{F}(sk)$, runs $(ek, dk) \leftarrow$ PKE.KeyGen$(pp_{\text{pke}}; r)$, outputs the resulting decryption key dk.

- $\mathsf{Enc}(pk, m)$ and $\mathsf{Dec}(dk, c)$ are same as those of the underlying PKE.
- $\mathsf{Sign}(sk, \tilde{m})$: Let G be $\mathsf{PKE.KeyGen_1}$, i.e., the algorithm that outputs the first outcome pk of PKE.KeyGen. G and F induce an $\mathcal{NP}$ relation $\mathsf{R_{key}}$ over $PK \times \{0,1\}^n$ defined as below.

$$\mathsf{R_{key}} = \{(pk, sk) \mid pk = \mathsf{G}(\mathsf{F}(sk))\} \tag{1}$$

We are thus able to build a signature scheme with sk as the signing key and pk as the verification key from a three-round public-coin ZKPoK for $\mathsf{R_{key}}$.

1. Run the prover algorithm $P(sk)$ with randomness α to sample a random element a from the initial message space A. We assume that $|A|$ is exponential in λ.
2. Hash a with the message $\tilde{m}$ to be signed into the challenge, i.e., $e \leftarrow \mathsf{H}(a, \tilde{m})$. Here, H is a cryptographic hash function, which is modeled as a random oracle.
3. Run the prover algorithm $P(sk, \alpha, e)$ to generate a response z.

Finally, outputs the signature $\sigma = (a, z)$ for $\tilde{m}$.

- $\mathsf{Vrfy}(pk, \tilde{m}, \sigma)$: on input a public key pk, a message $\tilde{m}$ and a signature $\sigma = (a, z)$, first recovers the challenge $e \leftarrow \mathsf{H}(a, \tilde{m})$, then runs the verifier's verification algorithm $V(a, e, z)$ to decide if (a, e, z) is an accepting transcript w.r.t. $\mathsf{R_{key}}$ (Fig. 2).

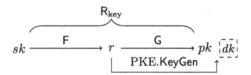

Fig. 2. The hierarchical key structure

In the above construction, the signature generation follows the same routine of crushing the ZKPoK into a non-interactive one via Fiat-Shamir heuristic. Thus, we can simplify the syntax of the construction by describing the signing procedure as $\mathsf{NIZKPoK.Prove}(pk, sk, \tilde{m})$ and the verifying procedure as $\mathsf{NIZKPoK.Verify}(pk, \tilde{m}, \sigma)$, where pk serves as the instance, sk serves as the witness, $\tilde{m}$ is treated as auxiliary input, and σ serves as the proof.

The correctness of the above construction follows from those of the underlying PKE and ZKPoK. For the security, we have the following theorem.

Theorem 2. *The above HISE construction is jointly secure assuming the security of its building blocks and modeling H as a random oracle.*

Due to space limit, we defer the security proof to the full version.

6   Global Escrow PKE

As discussed in the introduction, HISE naturally supports individual key escrow mechanism, but may not satisfy global key escrow property. To investigate how to further support global escrow mechanism for HISE in a general manner, next we make a little detour to revisit the topic of global escrow PKE, with focus on formal definition and generic construction. The obtained results can be used in a mixed way with the results in Sect. 4, yielding global escrow HISE.

Global escrow PKE is an extension of PKE. In global escrow PKE, there is a single global escrow decryption key that enables the decryption of ciphertexts encrypted under any public key. Such scheme enables government intelligence and law enforcement agencies to reveal encrypted information without the knowledge or consent of users. Formally, a global escrow PKE consists of five polynomial time algorithms (Setup, KeyGen, Enc, Dec, Dec'). KeyGen, Enc, and Dec are the same as those of ordinary PKE. The Setup algorithm outputs an additional escrow decryption key, while Dec' can decrypt ciphertexts under any public key using this escrow decryption key.

- Setup(1^λ): on input the security parameter λ, outputs global public parameters pp and a global escrow decryption key edk. This algorithm is run by a trusted party.
- Dec'(edk, c): on input an escrow decryption key edk and a ciphertext c, outputs a plaintext m or a special reject symbol $\perp$ denoting failure.

In most applications of global escrow PKE, the escrow agent needs to know the public key of the intended receiver. Therefore, we assume that the public key of the intended receiver is always provided in the clear from ciphertext.

Correctness. For all $m \in M$, we have $\Pr[\mathsf{Dec}(sk, c) = m = \mathsf{Dec}'(edk, c)] \geq 1 - \mathsf{negl}(\lambda)$, where the probability is taken over the choice of $(pp, edk) \leftarrow \mathsf{Setup}(1^\lambda)$, $(pk, sk) \leftarrow \mathsf{KeyGen}(pp)$, and $c \leftarrow \mathsf{Enc}(pk, m)$.

Consistency. The definition of correctness stipulates that the decryption results of the receiver and the escrow agent are identical when the ciphertexts are honestly generated. In applications of escrow PKE, the sender may generate the ciphertexts dishonestly to evade supervision. Therefore, in addition to correctness, we also need to consider the notion of consistency for global escrow PKE. The intuition is that the decryption results of the receiver and the escrow agent are still identical when the ciphertexts are dishonestly generated. Fix pp, we define a collection of $\mathcal{NP}$ languages indexed public key, namely, $L_{pk} = \{c \mid \exists m, r \text{ s.t. } c = \mathsf{Enc}(pk, m; r)\}$, which represents the set of all valid ciphertexts encrypted under pk. We are now ready to formally define consistency. For an adversary $\mathcal{A}$ against consistency, we define its advantage function as:

$$\mathsf{Adv}_{\mathcal{A}}(\lambda) = \Pr\left[\begin{array}{c} c \notin L_{pk} \wedge \\ \mathsf{Dec}(sk, c) \neq \mathsf{Dec}'(edk, c) \end{array} : \begin{array}{c} (pp, edk) \leftarrow \mathsf{Setup}(1^\lambda); \\ (pk, sk) \leftarrow \mathsf{KeyGen}(pp); \\ c \leftarrow \mathcal{A}(pp, pk); \end{array} \right].$$

A global escrow PKE is computationally (resp. statistically) consistent if no PPT (resp. unbounded) adversary has non-negligible advantage in the above experiment.

Security. Let $\mathcal{A}$ be an adversary against global escrow PKE and define its advantage in the following experiment.

$$\mathsf{Adv}_{\mathcal{A}}(\lambda) = \Pr \left[b = b' : \begin{array}{l} (pp, edk) \leftarrow \mathsf{Setup}(1^\lambda); \\ (pk, sk) \leftarrow \mathsf{KeyGen}(pp); \\ (m_0, m_1) \leftarrow \mathcal{A}^{\mathcal{O}_{\mathsf{dec}}(\cdot)}(pp, pk); \\ b \xleftarrow{\text{R}} \{0, 1\}, c^* \leftarrow \mathsf{Enc}(pk, m_b); \\ b' \leftarrow \mathcal{A}^{\mathcal{O}_{\mathsf{dec}}(\cdot)}(pp, pk, c^*); \end{array} \right] - \frac{1}{2}.$$

Here, $\mathcal{O}_{\mathsf{dec}}(\cdot)$ is the decryption oracle. $\mathcal{A}$ can make polynomial number of decryption queries with the restriction that $\mathcal{A}$ is not allowed to query $\mathcal{O}_{\mathsf{dec}}(\cdot)$ with c^* in Phase 2. A global escrow PKE scheme is IND-CCA secure if no PPT adversary has non-negligible advantage in the above experiment. We can define IND-CCA1 security (resp. IND-CPA security) similarly by only giving $\mathcal{A}$ access to $\mathcal{O}_{\mathsf{dec}}(\cdot)$ in Phase 1 (resp. denying access to $\mathcal{O}_{\mathsf{dec}}(\cdot)$).

6.1 Global Escrow PKE from PKE and NIZK

At first glance, it seems that global escrow PKE is trivially implied by broadcast encryption by having the receiver set include the public keys of the intended receiver and the escrow agent. However, the consistency of this construction is not guaranteed since broadcast encryption always assume that the sender generates ciphertexts honestly.

Next, we show how to make any PKE scheme satisfy global escrow property by leveraging NIZK. The idea is that when building up the system the escrow agent generates a keypair (pk_γ, sk_γ) himself, and then includes his public key pk_γ in the public parameters and uses the secret key sk_γ as escrow decryption key. To send an encrypted message to receiver with public key pk, the sender encrypts the same plaintext m twice under pk and pk_γ independently, then appends a NIZK proof for the consistency of encryption. To decrypt the ciphertext, both the receiver and the escrow agent first check the correctness of NIZK proof, then decrypts the corresponding part using their secret keys. Our construction coincides with the celebrated Naor-Yung double encryption paradigm for chosen-ciphertext security. In the Naor-Yung paradigm, the two public keys belong to the receiver, and the NIZK proof is used to achieve CCA security. In our case, one public key belongs to the receiver, the other key belongs to the escrow agent, and the NIZK proof is used to the ensure that the escrow agent has the same decryption capability as the receiver. Our construction is somewhat dual to previous solutions [YY98, YY99, PY99]. Rather than providing a proof of key recoverability to CA when registering public key, our construction provides a proof of correct encryption each time when generating ciphertexts. The advantage of our construction is that it removes the need of recoverability certificate entirely, and efficient zero-knowledge proof is relatively easy to design for most PKE schemes. Moreover, if we aim for CCA security, then the added zero-knowledge proofs do not constitute extra overhead.

For completeness, we present our construction as below.

- Setup(1^λ): runs $pp_{\mathrm{pke}} \leftarrow$ PKE.Setup(1^λ), $(pk_\gamma, sk_\gamma) \leftarrow$ PKE.KeyGen(pp_{pke}), $pp_{\mathrm{nizk}} \leftarrow$ NIZK.Setup(1^λ), generates $crs \leftarrow$ NIZK.CRSGen(pp_{nizk}), outputs $pp = (pp_{\mathrm{pke}}, pp_{\mathrm{nizk}}, crs, pk_\gamma)$ and $edk = sk_\gamma$.
- KeyGen(pp): parses $pp = (pp_{\mathrm{pke}}, pp_{\mathrm{nizk}}, crs, epk)$, then outputs $(pk, dk) \leftarrow$ PKE.KeyGen(pp_{pke}).
- Enc(pk, m): picks two random coins r_1 and r_2 independently, computes $c_1 \leftarrow$ PKE.Enc($pk, m; r_1$) and $c_2 \leftarrow$ PKE.Enc($pk_\gamma, m; r_2$), then generates $\pi \leftarrow$ NIZK.Prove($crs, (pk, c_1, c_2), (r_1, r_2, m)$), outputs $c = (pk, c_1, c_2, \pi)$. Here, π is a proof for (c_1, c_2) being encryptions of the same plaintext under pk and pk_γ, i.e., $(pk, c_1, c_2) \in L_{pk}$, where L_{pk} is defined as below:

$$L_{pk} = \{(pk, c_1, c_2) \mid \exists m, r_1, r_2 \text{ s.t.}$$
$$c_1 = \mathsf{PKE.Enc}(pk, m; r_1) \wedge c_2 = \mathsf{PKE.Enc}(pk_\gamma, m; r_2)\}$$

- Dec(sk, c): on input a decryption key sk and a ciphertext $c = (pk, c_1, c_2, \pi)$, first runs NIZK.Verify($crs, (pk, c_1, c_2), \pi$) to check if c is a valid encryption under pk; if the check fails then returns $\bot$, else returns $m \leftarrow$ PKE.Dec(dk, c_1).
- Dec$'$(edk, c): on input a global escrow decryption key $edk = sk_\gamma$ and a ciphertext $c = (pk, c_1, c_2, \pi)$, first checks if c is a valid encryption under pk_γ by running NIZK.Verify($crs, (pk_\gamma, c_1, c_2), \pi$); if the check fails then returns $\bot$, else returns $m \leftarrow$ PKE.Dec(sk_γ, c_2).

The correctness follows from that of PKE and NIZK, and the consistency holds based on the adaptive soundness of the underlying NIZK. For the security, we have the following theorem.

Theorem 3. *The above construction of global escrow PKE is CCA1-secure (resp. CCA-secure) if the underlying PKE is CPA-secure and the NIZK is adaptively secure (resp. simulation sound adaptive secure).*

Proof. The security proofs are very similar to those for Naor-Yung construction [NY90] and Sahai construction [Sah99]. We omit the details here.

Remark 3. The above generic construction encrypts the plaintext twice independently under the public keys of the intended receiver and the escrow agent. When the underlying PKE satisfies a mild property called "randomness fusion", we can safely reuse the random coins and apply twisted Naor-Yung transform [BMV16], leading to improvements in terms of both efficiency and bandwidth.

6.2 Global Escrow PKE from Three-Party NIKE and SKE

In this section, we present another generic construction of global escrow PKE from three-party NIKE and SKE. This construction follows the KEM-DEM paradigm. We start by defining the notion of global escrow KEM by adapting KEM to the escrow setting. A global escrow KEM consists of five polynomial time algorithms (Setup, KeyGen, Encaps, Decaps, Decaps'). The KeyGen, Encaps, and Decaps algorithms are same as those of an ordinary KEM. The Setup algorithm outputs an additional escrow decryption key, while Decaps' decapsulates ciphertexts using this escrow decryption key.

- Setup(1^λ): on input a security parameter λ, outputs global public parameters pp and a global escrow decryption key edk. This algorithm is run by a trusted party. We assume that pp includes the description of session key space K.
- Decaps'(edk, c): on input a global escrow decryption key edk and a ciphertext c, outputs a session key k or a special reject symbol $\bot$ denoting failure.

Correctness. We require that $\Pr[\mathsf{Decaps}(sk, c) = k = \mathsf{Decaps}'(edk, c)] \geq 1 - \mathsf{negl}(\lambda)$, where the probability is taken over the choice of $(pp, edk) \leftarrow \mathsf{Setup}(1^\lambda)$, $(pk, sk) \leftarrow \mathsf{KeyGen}(pp)$, and $(c, k) \leftarrow \mathsf{Encaps}(pk)$.

Consistency. Analogous to the setting of global escrow PKE, we also need to consider the notion of consistency for global escrow KEM. Fix pp, we define a collection of $\mathcal{NP}$ languages indexed by pk. Let $L_{pk}^{\mathrm{kem}} = \{c \mid \exists r \text{ s.t. } (c, k) = \mathsf{Encaps}(pk; r)\}$, which represents all valid ciphertexts encapsulated under pk. We are now ready to define consistency. For an adversary $\mathcal{A}$ against consistency, we define its advantage function as:

$$\mathsf{Adv}_\mathcal{A}(\lambda) = \Pr\left[\begin{array}{c} c \notin L_{pk}^{\mathrm{kem}} \wedge \\ \mathsf{Decap}(sk, c) \neq \mathsf{Decap}'(edk, c) \end{array} : \begin{array}{l} (pp, edk) \leftarrow \mathsf{Setup}(1^\lambda); \\ (pk, sk) \leftarrow \mathsf{KeyGen}(pp); \\ c \leftarrow \mathcal{A}(pp, pk); \end{array} \right].$$

We say that a global escrow KEM is computationally (resp. statistically) consistent if no PPT (resp. unbounded) adversary has non-negligible advantage in the above experiment.

Security. Let $\mathcal{A}$ be an adversary against global escrow KEM and define its advantage in the following experiment.

$$\mathsf{Adv}_\mathcal{A}(\lambda) = \Pr\left[b = b' : \begin{array}{l} (pp, edk) \leftarrow \mathsf{Setup}(1^\lambda); \\ (pk, sk) \leftarrow \mathsf{KeyGen}(pp); \\ (c^*, k_0^*) \leftarrow \mathsf{Encaps}(pk), k_1^* \leftarrow K; \\ b \xleftarrow{\mathrm{R}} \{0, 1\}; \\ b' \leftarrow \mathcal{A}^{\mathcal{O}_{\mathrm{decaps}}(\cdot)}(pp, pk, c^*, k_b^*); \end{array} \right] - \frac{1}{2}.$$

Here, $\mathcal{O}_{\mathrm{decaps}}(\cdot)$ denotes the decapsulation oracle. $\mathcal{A}$ can make polynomial number of such queries with the restriction that $c \neq c^*$, and the challenger responds with $k \leftarrow \mathsf{Decaps}(sk, c)$. A global escrow KEM is IND-CCA secure if no PPT adversary has non-negligible advantage in the above experiment. A global escrow KEM is IND-CPA secure if no PPT adversary has non-negligible advantage in the same experiment but denying access to $\mathcal{O}_{\mathrm{decaps}}(\cdot)$.

6.2.1   Global Escrow PKE from Global Escrow KEM and SKE

We build global escrow PKE from global escrow KEM and SKE as below.

- Setup(1^λ): runs $(pp_{\mathrm{kem}}, edk) \leftarrow$ KEM.Setup(1^λ), $pp_{\mathrm{ske}} \leftarrow$ SKE.Setup(1^λ), outputs $pp = (pp_{\mathrm{kem}}, pp_{\mathrm{ske}})$ and edk.
- KeyGen(pp): parses public parameters $pp = (pp_{\mathrm{kem}}, pp_{\mathrm{ske}})$, outputs $(pk, sk) \leftarrow$ KEM.KeyGen(pp_{kem}).
- Enc(pk, m): computes $(c_{\mathrm{kem}}, k) \leftarrow$ KEM.Encaps(pk), $c_{\mathrm{ske}} \leftarrow$ SKE.Enc(k, m), outputs $c = (c_{\mathrm{kem}}, c_{\mathrm{ske}})$.
- Dec(sk, c): parses $c = (c_{\mathrm{kem}}, c_{\mathrm{ske}})$, computes $k \leftarrow$ KEM.Decaps(sk, c_{ske}); if $k = \bot$ outputs $\bot$, else outputs $m \leftarrow$ SKE.Dec(k, c_{ske}).
- Dec'(edk, c): parses $c = (c_{\mathrm{kem}}, c_{\mathrm{ske}})$, computes $k \leftarrow$ KEM.Decaps'(edk, c_{ske}); if $k = \bot$ outputs $\bot$, else outputs $m \leftarrow$ SKE.Dec(k, c_{ske}).

The correctness follows from that of global escrow KEM and SKE. We analyze the consistency requirement as below. The above construction follows the KEM-DEM approach. Fix pp, we define a collection of $\mathcal{NP}$ languages indexed by pk. Let $L_{pk} = \{(c_{\mathrm{kem}}, c_{\mathrm{ske}}) \mid \exists m, r_1, r_2 \text{ s.t. } (c_{\mathrm{kem}}, k) = \text{KEM.Encaps}(pk; r_1) \wedge c_{\mathrm{ske}} = \text{SKE.Enc}(k, m; r_2)\}$. It is easy to see that no matter whether $c_{\mathrm{kem}} \in L_{pk}^{\mathrm{kem}}$ or not, the consistency of global escrow KEM guarantees that the decapsulation results are identical, and so are the final decryption results.

Theorem 4. *The above construction is IND-CPA secure (resp. IND-CCA secure) if the underlying global escrow KEM is IND-CPA secure (resp. IND-CCA secure) and the SKE is IND-CPA secure (resp. IND-CCA secure).*

Proof. The security proof is similar to that of PKE from the KEM-DEM methodology. We omit the details here.

6.2.2   Global Escrow KEM from Three-Party NIKE

We present a generic construction of global escrow KEM from three-party NIKE. The high-level idea is that the escrow agent generates a keypair (pk_γ, sk_γ), then publishes pk_γ as part of the public parameters and keeps sk_γ to itself. To send a ciphertext to the receiver with public key $pk = pk_\beta$, the sender generates a random keypair (pk_α, sk_α), then runs the three-party NIKE in his head to derive a shared key for $\{pk_\alpha, pk_\beta, pk_\gamma\}$, and finishes encapsulation by setting pk_α as the ciphertext and the shared key as the session key. According to the functionality and security of NIKE, both the escrow agent and the receiver can derive the same session key, which is pseudorandom in any PPT adversary's view. The construction is as below.

- Setup(1^λ): on input a security parameter λ, runs $pp_{\mathrm{nike}} \leftarrow$ NIKE.Setup(1^λ) and $(pk_\gamma, sk_\gamma) \leftarrow$ NIKE.KeyGen(pp_{nike}), outputs public parameters $pp = (pp_{\mathrm{nike}}, pk_\gamma)$ and sets the global escrow decryption key $edk = sk_\gamma$.
- KeyGen(pp): parses $pp = (pp_{\mathrm{nike}}, pk_\gamma)$, runs NIKE.KeyGen($pp_{\mathrm{nike}}$) to generate a keypair (pk, sk).

- Encaps(pk): parses $pk = pk_\beta$, the sender runs NIKE.KeyGen(pp_{nike}) to generate a random keypair (pk_α, sk_α), sets $S = \{pk_\alpha, pk_\beta, pk_\gamma\}$, computes $k_S \leftarrow$ ShareKey(sk_α, S), outputs ciphertext $c = (pk_\alpha, pk_\beta)$ and session key $k = k_S$. The language for valid encapsulation is: $L_{pk}^{KEM} = \{(pk_\alpha, pk) \mid pk_\alpha \in PK\}$.
- Decaps(sk, c): on input a secret key $sk = sk_\beta$ and a ciphertext $c = (pk_\alpha, pk_\beta)$, first sets $S = \{pk_\alpha, pk_\beta, pk_\gamma\}$, then computes $k_S \leftarrow$ ShareKey(sk_β, S) and outputs session key $k = k_S$.
- Decaps'(edk, c): on input $edk = sk_\gamma$ and a ciphertext $c = (pk_\alpha, pk_\beta)$, sets $S = \{pk_\alpha, pk_\beta, pk_\gamma\}$, then computes $k_S \leftarrow$ ShareKey(sk_γ, S) and outputs session key $k = k_S$.

The correctness and consistency of global escrow KEM follow from those of the underlying three-party NIKE. For security, we have the following theorem.

Theorem 5. *If the three-party NIKE is CKS-light secure in the HKR setting (resp. in the DKR setting), then the resulting global escrow KEM is IND-CPA secure (resp. IND-CCA secure).*

Due to space limit, we defer the security proof to the full version.

6.2.3 Relaxation of Three-Party NIKE

We note that the above construction of global escrow KEM does not require the full power of three-party NIKE. In fact, a relaxed version suffices for our purpose, a.k.a., there are three types of public keys in the system (say Type-A, Type-B and Type-C), and the shared key can be agreed upon if the three participants hold different types of public keys. When building global escrow KEM, we can set user's public key as Type-A, the temporary public key as Type-B (serves as the ciphertext), and the escrow agent's public key as Type-C (serves as part of the public parameters). This relaxation increases the space of the underlying protocols that can be used, and hence can potentially lead to more efficient construction of global escrow PKE. Next, we show how to build an efficient global escrow KEM from a relaxed version of Joux's protocol [Jou04] to exemplify the power of this conceptual insight.

As noticed by [GPS08, AGH15], there is a huge gap in pairing-based cryptography: schemes are usually presented in the academic literature via symmetric pairing because it is simpler and the complexity assumptions can be weaker, while schemes are preferable to be implemented via asymmetric pairing (notably Type-III pairing) since it is the most efficient choice in terms of bandwidth and computation time. Such gap also occurs in our case. The original Joux's protocol is based on symmetric pairing and cannot be easily adapted to the setting of asymmetric pairing. Consequently, it does not lend itself to an efficient global escrow KEM. We fill this gap by observing that the relaxed version of Joux's protocol described above can be realized using Type-III pairing under the co-DBDH assumption. Towards minimizing the public key size of the resulting global escrow KEM, we adapt the original Joux's protocol by designating Type-A public key of the form $g_1^b \in \mathbb{G}_1$, Type-B public key of the form $g_2^c \in \mathbb{G}_2$, and Type-C public key of the form $(g_1^a, g_2^a) \in \mathbb{G}_1 \times \mathbb{G}_2$. This yields a global escrow KEM (and hence a global escrow PKE) from asymmetric pairing based on the co-DBDH assumption. See Sect. 8 for comparison with the only known prior work called escrow ElGamal PKE [BF03].

7   Instantiations

In this section, we present instantiations of our two generic HISE constructions (described in Sect. 4 and 5) and two generic global escrow HISE constructions (yielded by mixing the general approaches for building HISE and global escrow PKE). We limit ourselves to discrete-log/pairing-based realizations since factoring-based and lattice-based realizations suffer from large key size.

7.1   Instantiation of HISE from IBE

We instantitate our first HISE construction (presented in Sect. 4) by choosing Boneh-Franklin IBE with asymmetric pairing as the underlying IBE scheme, yielding HISE scheme 1 as below.

- Setup(1^λ): runs $(\mathbb{G}_1, \mathbb{G}_2, \mathbb{G}_T, p, e) \leftarrow$ BLGroupGen(1^λ), picks $g_1 \xleftarrow{\text{R}} \mathbb{G}_1$, sets $id^* = 1^{\ell+1}$, outputs $pp = id^*$. We assume that pp also includes the descriptions of bilinear groups and a hash function H : $\{0,1\}^{\ell+1} \rightarrow \mathbb{G}_2$.
- KeyGen(pp): on input $pp = id^*$, picks $sk \xleftarrow{\text{R}} \mathbb{Z}_p$, computes $pk = g_1^{sk} \in \mathbb{G}_1$.
- Derive(sk): on input sk, outputs $dk = \mathsf{H}(id^*)^{sk} \in \mathbb{G}_2$.
- Enc(pk, m): on input pk and $m \in \mathbb{G}_T$, picks $r \xleftarrow{\text{R}} \mathbb{Z}_p$, computes $c_1 \leftarrow g_1^r \in \mathbb{G}_1$ and $c_2 \leftarrow e(pk, \mathsf{H}(id^*))^r \cdot m$, outputs $c = (c_1, c_2)$.
- Dec(dk, c): on input dk and c, outputs $m = c_2/e(c_1, dk)$.
- Sign($sk, \tilde{m}$): on input sk and $\tilde{m} \in \{0,1\}^\ell$, outputs $\sigma = \mathsf{H}(0||\tilde{m})^{sk} \in \mathbb{G}_2$.
- Vrfy($pk, \tilde{m}, \sigma$): picks $r \xleftarrow{\text{R}} \mathbb{Z}_p$, outputs "1" if $e(pk, \mathsf{H}(0||\tilde{m}))^r = e(g_1^r, \sigma)$ and "0" otherwise.

Remark 4. HISE scheme 1 is obtained by faithfully applying the generic transform to the Boneh-Franklin IBE. We note that in this case the Vrfy algorithm could be simplified by directly checking if $e(pk, \mathsf{H}(0||\tilde{m})) = e(g_1, \sigma)$, the resulting the signature component is exactly the Boneh-Lynn-Shacham signature [BLS01] from the asymmetric pairing.

We realize HISE scheme 1 atop pairing-friendly curve bls12-381 with 128-bit security level [SKSW20][7], in which $|\mathbb{G}_1| = 48$ bytes, $|\mathbb{G}_2| = 96$ bytes, $|\mathbb{Z}_p| = 32$ bytes, and $|\mathbb{G}_T| = 191$ bytes (by exploiting compression techniques [RS08]).

---

[7] Recent security evaluations show that the security level of bls12-381 is close to but less than 128-bit. As curves of 128-bit security level are currently the most widely used, BLS12-381 and BN462 are recommended in the memo [SKSW20] in order to have a more efficient and a more prudent option respectively.

7.2   Instantiation of HISE from PKE and ZKPoK

Public-Key Encryption. We choose the ElGamal PKE as the starting PKE scheme. The randomness space R for KeyGen is $\mathbb{Z}_p$. The KeyGen algorithm on input $r \xleftarrow{\text{R}} \mathbb{Z}_p$ outputs $sk = r$ and $pk = g^r$. Thus, $\mathsf{G} : \mathbb{Z}_p \to \mathbb{G}$ is defined as $r \mapsto g^r$. Clearly, G is injective, and thus it is unconditionally target-collision resistant. We assume that there is a one-to-one mapping from $\{0,1\}^\ell$ to $\mathbb{Z}_p$ for some integer ℓ. Concretely, we choose the elliptic curve secp256k1 with 128-bit security. We demonstrate the generality of our second HISE construction by providing two more eligible PKE candidates (see the full version for the details).

Uniform One-Way Function. After fixing $R = \{0,1\}^\ell$, we choose a one-way function H from $\{0,1\}^n$ to $\{0,1\}^\ell$. A popular choice is using hash function like SHA-256, in which the number of AND gates of a single call is about 25000. Motivated by applications in FHE schemes, MPC protocols and SNARKs, recently there is a trend to design lightweight symmetric encryption primitives with a low number of multiplications or a low multiplicative depth. In our instantiation, we choose the POSEIDON-128 hash [GKR+21], whose number of rank-1 constraint satisfiability (R1CS) constraints is roughly 300.

General Purpose ZKPoK. Due to the involvement of F, R_{key} defined by $\mathsf{G} \circ \mathsf{F}$ is unlikely to be an algebraic relation. As a consequence, it is difficult to prove R_{key} using simple Sigma protocols. Our solution is to resort efficient general purpose public-coin ZKPoK protocols. A flurry of recent work on zk-SNARKs with transparent setup offers plenty of candidates, including the backbone protocols that underlie almost all the known zk-SNARKs in the random oracle model. In our instantiation, we choose Spartan [Set20]. We convert the proved relation R_{key} into R1CS format using xJsnark [KPS18]; the number of R1CS constraints of is roughly $680,000 \approx 2^{20}$.

We are now ready to instantiate our second HISE construction (presented in Sect. 5) from the above building blocks, yielding HISE scheme 2.

- Setup(1^λ): on input a security parameter λ, runs $(\mathbb{G}, g, p) \leftarrow \mathsf{GroupGen}(1^\lambda)$, picks a uniform one-way function $\mathsf{F} : \{0,1\}^n \to \{0,1\}^\ell$, runs $pp_{\text{nizkpok}} \leftarrow$ NIZKPoK.Setup(1^λ), and outputs $pp = (\mathsf{F}, pp_{\text{nizkpok}})$. The plaintext space is $M = \mathbb{G}$. The message space is $\widetilde{M} = \{0,1\}^*$.
- KeyGen(pp): on input $pp = (\mathsf{F}, pp_{\text{nizkpok}})$, picks $sk \xleftarrow{\text{R}} \{0,1\}^n$, computes $pk = g^{\mathsf{F}(sk)} \in \mathbb{G}$.
- Derive(sk): on input sk, outputs $dk \leftarrow \mathsf{F}(sk) \in \mathbb{Z}_p$.
- Enc(pk, m): on input pk and $m \in \mathbb{G}$, picks $r \xleftarrow{\text{R}} \mathbb{Z}_p$, computes $X \leftarrow g^r \in \mathbb{G}$, $Y \leftarrow pk^r \cdot m$, outputs $C = (X, Y)$.
- Dec(dk, c): on input dk and $C = (X, Y)$, outputs $m \leftarrow Y/X^{dk}$.
- Sign($sk, \tilde{m}$): computes $\sigma \leftarrow$ NIZKPoK.Prove($pk, sk, \tilde{m}$).
- Vrfy($pk, \tilde{m}, \sigma$): on input pk, $\tilde{m}$ and σ, outputs $b \leftarrow$ NIZKPoK.Verify($pk, \sigma, \tilde{m}$).

7.3 Two Instantiations of Global Escrow HISE

As depicted in Fig. 1 in the introduction part, there are two paths to build global escrow HISE. Our first construction is along the path enabled by the GE conversion. Starting from the HISE scheme presented in Sect. 7.1, we compile it into a global escrow one by applying the twisted Naor-Yung transform [BMV16], yielding global escrow HISE scheme 1. Our second construction is along the path enabled by the HI conversion. Starting from the global escrow PKE based a relaxed version of Joux's three-party NIKE (sketched in Sect. 6.2.3), we add the signing functionality via the HI conversion, yielding global escrow HISE scheme 2. The joint security of the above two schemes follows from the fact that the signing key is independent of the global escrow decryption key.

Due to space limit, we defer the specification global escrow HISE scheme 1/2 to the full version.

8 Comparison and Evaluation

This section compares (global escrow) HISE with CPK and ISE in terms of security and functionality properties, then evaluates our instantiations of (global escrow) HISE and global escrow PKE.

8.1 Comparison of Security and Functionality Properties

Paterson et al. [PSST11] introduce a "Cartesian product" construction of CPK (henceforth CP-CPK for short). The construction uses arbitrary encryption and signature schemes as components, runs the key generation algorithms independently, then concatenates the keypairs of the encryption scheme and signature scheme, and uses the appropriate component of the compound keypair for each operation. CP-CPK best formalizes the principle of key separation, and hence also naturally supports individual key escrow. We choose it as a baseline to judge (global escrow) HISE schemes that use the principle of key reuse.

Table 1 offers a comparision of (global escrow) HISE against previous CP-CPK and ISE in terms of security and functionality properties as well as certificate cost. The results show that HISE supports individual key escrow in the context of key reuse, while global escrow HISE further supports global key escrow. Besides, we highlight that CP-CPK doubles the certificate cost, which should be minimized in practice.

8.2 Efficiency Evaluation of (Global Escrow) HISE

Baseline. We build a concrete CP-CPK scheme atop elliptic curve secp256k1 with 128-bit security (where $|\mathbb{G}| = 33$ bytes, $|\mathbb{Z}_p| = 32$ bytes) as a baseline. More precisely, we choose ElGamal PKE as the encryption component and Schnorr signature as the signature component, because they are among the most efficient elliptic-curve based cryptosystems with short public keys.

Table 1. Comparison between CP-CPK, ISE, and our (global escrow) HISE

Scheme	strong joint security	individual escrow	global escrow	key reuse	certificate cost
CP-CPK [PSST11]	✓	✓	✗	✗	×2
ISE [PSST11]	✗	✗	✗	✓	×1
HISE	✓	✓	✗	✓	×1
global escrow HISE	✓	✓	✓	✓	×1

For certificate cost, ×1 (resp. ×2) means the cost associated with one (resp. two) certificate(s). As aforementioned, certificate costs include but not limit to registration, issuing, storage, transmission, verification, and building/recurring fees. Take SSL certificate as an example, one certificate is roughly 1 KB, takes roughly 200∼300 ms to transmit in WAN setting with 50 Mbps network bandwidth and 8ms to verify. The monetary cost for an SSL certificate varies depending on features and business needs. While the cost of an SSL certificate for common usage is \$10∼\$2000/year, the banks and large financial institutions could spend up to \$500,000/year on an SSL certificate with high-level security guranttee.

Methodology. We implement the CP-CPK scheme and our (global escrow) HISE instantiations in C++ based on the `mcl` library [Shi]. Parameters of all schemes are set to achieve 128-bit security level. All experiments are carried on a MacBook Pro with Intel i7-9750H CPU (2.6 GHz) and 16 GB of RAM. We view the key size and the associated certificate cost as the primary metric of interest. The experimental results are presented in Table 2. As shown in this table, our (global escrow) HISE schemes have more compact key size than the CP-CPK in both asymptotic and concrete sense. Among the five schemes, global escrow HISE scheme 1 achieves joint security, while the rest schemes achieve weak joint security (the encryption component is CPA-secure).

The ciphertext size of HISE scheme 1 and global escrow HISE scheme 1 and 2 are slightly large. Nevertheless, this is not a big issue since in real-world applications long plaintexts are typically encrypted using hybrid encryption, thereby the overhead of the PKE ciphertext can be greatly amortized. The signature components of (global escrow) HISE scheme 2 are less efficient due to the involvement of general-purpose ZKPoK for large-size circuit describing the composite relation R_{key}. We hence regard (global escrow) HISE scheme 2 more of theoretical interest for the time being. We leave how to improve the efficiency as an interesting problem. A possible solution is to adapt the techniques of creating efficient NIZK for composite statement [AGM18] to the public-coin setting.

8.3 Comparison of Global Escrow PKE

As a byproduct, we obtain a global escrow PKE, which serves as the starting point of our global escrow HISE 2. Our scheme (see details in the full version) can be viewed as an adaption of Boneh-Franklin escrow ElGamal PKE [BF03, Section 7] to the setting of asymmetric pairing, and hence enjoys much better efficiency. While this may appear straightforward in hindsight, we stress again that the adaptation is non-trivial, which is leaded by our observation that global escrow PKE can be derived from a relaxed version of three-party NIKE (see discussions in Sect. 6.2.3).

Table 2. Efficiency comparison of CPK and our proposed (global escrow) HISE schemes

Scheme	efficiency (ms) [# exp, #pairing]							sizes (bytes) [& $\mathbb{G}$, & $\mathbb{Z}_p$]			
	KGen	Sign	Vrfy	Enc	Dec	Der	Dec$'$	$|pk|$	$|sk|$	$|c|$	$|\sigma|$
CP-CPK	0.015	0.064	0.120	0.118	0.056	$\oslash$	$\oslash$	66	64	66	65
	[2, 0]	[1, 0]	[2, 0]	[2, 0]	[1, 0]	$\oslash$	$\oslash$	$2\mathbb{G}$	$2\mathbb{Z}_p$	$2\mathbb{G}$	$[\mathbb{G}, \mathbb{Z}_p]$
HISE scheme 1	0.057	0.148	0.733	0.569	0.364	0.148	$\oslash$	48	32	239	96
	[1, 0]	[1, 0]	[0, 2]	[2, 1]	[0, 1]	[1, 0]	$\oslash$	$\mathbb{G}_1$	$\mathbb{Z}_p$	$[\mathbb{G}_1, \mathbb{G}_T]$	$\mathbb{G}_2$
HISE scheme 2	0.058	3.5s	250	0.115	0.056	0.0004	$\oslash$	33	32	66	40K
	[1, 0]	N/A	N/A	[2, 0]	[1, 0]	N/A	$\oslash$	$\mathbb{G}$	$\mathbb{Z}_p$	$2\mathbb{G}$	N/A
global escrow	0.057	0.148	0.733	1.462	1.505	0.148	1.505	48	32	701	96
HISE scheme 1	[1, 0]	[1, 0]	[0, 2]	[5, 2]	[4, 1]	[1, 0]	[4, 1]	$\mathbb{G}_1$	$\mathbb{Z}_p$	$[2\mathbb{G}_1, 3\mathbb{G}_T, \mathbb{Z}_p]$	$\mathbb{G}_2$
global escrow	0.057	3.5s	250	0.629	0.531	0.0004	0.532	48	32	287	40K
HISE scheme 2	[1, 0]	N/A	N/A	[2, 1]	[1, 1]	N/A	[1, 1]	$\mathbb{G}_1$	$\mathbb{Z}_p$	$[\mathbb{G}_2, \mathbb{G}_T]$	N/A

Performance of Cartesian product CPK and (global escrow) HISE schemes with 128-bit security level. $(\mathbb{G}_1, \mathbb{G}_2, \mathbb{G}_T)$ refers to asymmetric pairing groups. $\mathbb{G}$ refers to ordinary elliptic group. We report times for setup, key generation, signing, verification, key derivation, encryption, and (escrow) decryption, as well as the sizes of public key pk, secret key sk, ciphertext c and signature σ, and ignore the size of public parameters and group operations in the interests of space. The symbol $\oslash$ indicates that there is no corresponding algorithm. The symbol N/A indicates that the efficiency (or bandwidth) is hard to measure by algebra operations (or elements). At the time of this writing, the frontend tool(The frontend of a ZK proof system provides means to express statements in high-level language and compile them into low-level representation (e.g., rank 1 constraint system), then invokes a suitable ZK backend.) for Spartan [Set20] is not available, and hence we estimate the costs of signing/verification operations and signature size of (global escrow) HISE scheme 2 using the cost model provided by the authors, and mark the figures with gray color.

We build escrow ElGamal PKE on supersingular curve `ss-1536` [SKSW20] (where $|\mathbb{G}| = 193$ bytes, $|\mathbb{G}_T| = 192$ bytes, $|\mathbb{Z}_p| = 32$ bytes)[9] based on the `relic` library [AGM+]. We implement our global escrow PKE atop pairing-friendly curve `bls12-381`. To attain the same security level, our scheme could operate in elliptic groups defined on much smaller base field than the case of escrow ElGamal PKE. The comparison results in Table 3 show that our scheme outperforms escrow ElGamal PKE in all parameters, in particularly, being several orders of magnitude faster in terms of speed.

Table 3. Comparison of escrow ElGamal PKE [BF03] and our global escrow PKE

Scheme	efficiency (ms) [# exp, #pairing]					sizes (bytes) [& $\mathbb{G}$, & $\mathbb{Z}_p$]				
	Setup	KGen	Enc	Dec	Dec$'$	$|pp|$	$|edk|$	$|pk|$	$|sk|$	$|c|$
Boneh-Franklin	2.879	2.014	8.723	6.654	6.745	386	32	193	32	385
escrow ElGamal PKE	[2, 0]	[1, 0]	[2, 1]	[1, 1]	[1, 1]	$2\mathbb{G}$	$\mathbb{Z}_p$	$\mathbb{G}$	$\mathbb{Z}_p$	$[\mathbb{G}, \mathbb{G}_T]$
our proposed	0.243	0.058	0.680	0.579	0.586	288	32	48	32	287
global escrow PKE	[4, 0]	[1, 0]	[2, 1]	[1, 1]	[1, 1]	$[2\mathbb{G}_1, 2\mathbb{G}_2]$	$\mathbb{Z}_p$	$\mathbb{G}_1$	$\mathbb{Z}_p$	$[\mathbb{G}_2, \mathbb{G}_T]$

Performance of global escrow PKE schemes with 128-bit security level. $(\mathbb{G}_1, \mathbb{G}_2, \mathbb{G}_T)$ refers to asymmetric pairing groups. $(\mathbb{G}, \mathbb{G}_T)$ refers to symmetric pairing groups. We report times for setup, key generation, encryption, and (escrow) decryption, as well as the sizes of public parameters pp, global escrow decryption key edk, public key pk, secret key sk, and ciphertext c.

---

[9] So far, `ss-1536` is the only reported pairing-friendly curve with 128-bit security that supports Weil pairing.

9   Conclusion

Key reuse and key escrow are two broad issues arising from practical applications of cryptography. In this work, we investigated the interdiscipline of these two contradictory objects, an important but much-overlooked problem in prior work, aiming to enjoying the best of both worlds. We introduced a new notion called HISE featuring a novel two-level key derivation structure, which hits a sweet balance between key separation and key reuse. HISE not only admits individual key escrow, but also retains the benefit of key reuse. We then gave a black-box construction from (constrained) IBE, as well as a non-black-box construction from uniform OWF, PKE, and ZKPoK. To further attain global key escrow, we initiated a systematic study of global escrow PKE, which is long overdue for formal definition and efficient construction. We provided rigorous security notions and two generic constructions. The first uncovers a new application of the Naor-Yung paradigm. The second establishes an interesting connection to the three-party NIKE, and leads to the most efficient global escrow PKE to date. By mixing the results developed above, we suggested two paths for building global escrow HISE. The concrete (global escrow) HISE schemes instantiated from our generic constructions have competitive performance to the best CP-CPK scheme, and exhibit advantages in terms of richer functionality and public key reuse.

On the theoretical side our work resolves the problems left open in prior works [Ver01, PSST11], of reconciling the conflict between key reuse and key escrow. On the practical side our work serves as a developer guide for integrated usage of signature and encryption.

Finally, we remark that it is possible to consider a dual version of HISE, in which the hierarchy between signing key and decryption key are reversed. Such dual HISE could be useful in scenarios where decryption capability is a first priority. We leave the construction and application of dual HISE as an interesting problem.

Acknowledgments. We would like to thank the anonymous reviewers for their valuable comments on this paper. We thank Ren Zhang and Weiran Liu for helpful discussions. We thank Zhi Hu, Changan Zhao and Shiping Cai for help on implementation of pairing-based cryptography. We thank Xiangling Zhang for help on the test of certificate cost.

Yu Chen is supported by National Natural Science Foundation of China (Grant No. 61772522, No. 61932019), Shandong Provincial Key Research and Development Program (Major Scientific and Technological Innovation Project under Grant No. 2019JZZY010133), and Shandong Key Research and Development Program (Grant No. 2020ZLYS09). Yuyu Wang is supported by the National Natural Science Foundation for Young Scientists of China (Grant No. 62002049) and the Fundamental Research Funds for the Central Universities (Grant No. ZYGX2020J017).

References

[AGH15] Akinyele, J.A., Garman, C., Hohenberger, S.: Automating fast and secure translations from type-i to type-iii pairing schemes. In: ACM CCS 2015, pp. 1370–1381 (2015)

[AGM+] Aranha, D.F., Gouvêa, C.P.L., Markmann, T., Wahby, R.S., Liao, K.: RELIC is an efficient library for cryptography (2013). https://github.com/relic-toolkit/relic

[AGM18] Agrawal, S., Ganesh, C., Mohassel, P.: Non-interactive zero-knowledge proofs for composite statements. In: Shacham, H., Boldyreva, A. (eds.) CRYPTO 2018, Part III. LNCS, vol. 10993, pp. 643–673. Springer, Cham (2018). https://doi.org/10.1007/978-3-319-96878-0_22

[BAZB20] Bünz, B., Agrawal, S., Zamani, M., Boneh, D.: Zether: towards privacy in a smart contract world. In: Bonneau, J., Heninger, N. (eds.) FC 2020. LNCS, vol. 12059, pp. 423–443. Springer, Cham (2020). https://doi.org/10.1007/978-3-030-51280-4_23

[BCHK07] Boneh, D., Canetti, R., Halevi, S., Katz, J.: Chosen-ciphertext security from identity-based encryption. SIAM J. Comput. **36**(5), 1301–1328 (2007)

[BF03] Boneh, D., Franklin, M.K.: Identity-based encryption from the Weil pairing. SIAM J. Comput. **32**, 586–615 (2003)

[BLS01] Boneh, D., Lynn, B., Shacham, H.: Short signatures from the Weil pairing. In: Boyd, C. (ed.) ASIACRYPT 2001. LNCS, vol. 2248, pp. 514–532. Springer, Heidelberg (2001). https://doi.org/10.1007/3-540-45682-1_30

[BMV16] Biagioni, S., Masny, D., Venturi, D.: Naor-Yung paradigm with shared randomness and applications. In: SCN 2016, pp. 62–80 (2016)

[CDG+17] Chase, M., et al.: Post-quantum zero-knowledge and signatures from symmetric-key primitives. In: ACM CCS 2017, pp. 1825–1842 (2017)

[CHK03] Canetti, R., Halevi, S., Katz, J.: A forward-secure public-key encryption scheme. In: Biham, E. (ed.) EUROCRYPT 2003. LNCS, vol. 2656, pp. 255–271. Springer, Heidelberg (2003). https://doi.org/10.1007/3-540-39200-9_16

[CJNP02] Coron, J.-S., Joye, M., Naccache, D., Paillier, P.: Universal padding schemes for RSA. In: Yung, M. (ed.) CRYPTO 2002. LNCS, vol. 2442, pp. 226–241. Springer, Heidelberg (2002). https://doi.org/10.1007/3-540-45708-9_15

[CMTA20] Chen, Y., Ma, X., Tang, C., Au, M.H.: PGC: pretty good confidential transaction system with auditability. In: ESORICS 2020, pp. 591–610 (2020)

[DHLW10] Dodis, Y., Haralambiev, K., López-Alt, A., Wichs, D.: Cryptography against continuous memory attacks. In: FOCS 2010, pp. 511–520 (2010)

[DLP+12] Degabriele, J.P., Lehmann, A., Paterson, K.G., Smart, N.P., Strefler, M.: On the joint security of encryption and signature in EMV. In: Dunkelman, O. (ed.) CT-RSA 2012. LNCS, vol. 7178, pp. 116–135. Springer, Heidelberg (2012). https://doi.org/10.1007/978-3-642-27954-6_8

[EMV11] EMV Co: EMV Book 2 - Security and Key Management -Version 4.3 (2011). https://www.emvco.com/wp-content/uploads/2017/05/EMV_v4.3_Book_2_Security_and_Key_Management_20120607061923900.pdf

[FO99] Fujisaki, E., Okamoto, T.: Secure integration of asymmetric and symmetric encryption schemes. In: Wiener, M. (ed.) CRYPTO 1999. LNCS, vol. 1666, pp. 537–554. Springer, Heidelberg (1999). https://doi.org/10.1007/3-540-48405-1_34

[GKR+21] Grassi, L., Khovratovich, D., Rechberger, C., Roy, A., Schofnegger, M.: Poseidon: a new hash function for zero-knowledge proof systems. In: USENIX Security 2021 (2021)

[GPS08] Galbraith, S.D., Paterson, K.G., Smart, N.P.: Pairings for cryptographers. Discret. Appl. Math. **156**(16), 3113–3121 (2008)

[HP01] Haber, S., Pinkas, B.: Securely combining public-key cryptosystems. In: ACM CCS 2001, pp. 215–224 (2001)

[Jou04] Joux, A.: A one round protocol for tripartite Diffie-Hellman. J. Cryptol. **17**(4), 263–276 (2004)

[KKW18] Katz, J., Kolesnikov, V., Wang, X.: Improved non-interactive zero knowledge with applications to post-quantum signatures. In: ACM CCS 2018, pp. 525–537 (2018)

[KO03] Komano, Y., Ohta, K.: Efficient universal padding techniques for multiplicative trapdoor one-way permutation. In: Boneh, D. (ed.) CRYPTO 2003. LNCS, vol. 2729, pp. 366–382. Springer, Heidelberg (2003). https://doi.org/10.1007/978-3-540-45146-4_22

[KPS18] Kosba, A.E., Papamanthou, C., Shi, E.: xJsnark: a framework for efficient verifiable computation. In: IEEE S&P 2018, pp. 944–961 (2018)

[NVV18] Narula, N., Vasquez, W., Virza, M.: zkledger: privacy-preserving auditing for distributed ledgers. In: USENIX NSDI 2018, pp. 65–80 (2018)

[NY90] Naor, M., Yung, M.: Public-key cryptosystems provably secure against chosen ciphertext attacks. In: STOC 1990, pp. 427–437 (1990)

[PGP] PGP. https://www.openpgp.org

[Pin] Ping identity. http://www.pingidentity.com

[PSST11] Paterson, K.G., Schuldt, J.C.N., Stam, M., Thomson, S.: On the joint security of encryption and signature, revisited. In: Lee, D.H., Wang, X. (eds.) ASIACRYPT 2011. LNCS, vol. 7073, pp. 161–178. Springer, Heidelberg (2011). https://doi.org/10.1007/978-3-642-25385-0_9

[PY99] Paillier, P., Yung, M.: Self-escrowed public-key infrastructures. In: Song, J.S. (ed.) ICISC 1999. LNCS, vol. 1787, pp. 257–268. Springer, Heidelberg (2000). https://doi.org/10.1007/10719994_20

[Ros] Ross, D.E.: PGP: backdoors and key escrow. https://www.rossde.com/PGP/pgp_backdoor.html

[RS08] Rubin, K., Silverberg, A.: Compression in finite fields and torus-based cryptography. SIAM J. Comput. **37**(5), 1401–1428 (2008)

[Sah99] Sahai, A.: Non-malleable non-interactive zero knowledge and adaptive chosen-ciphertext security. In: FOCS 1999, pp. 543–553. ACM (1999)

[Set20] Setty, S.: Spartan: efficient and general-purpose zkSNARKs without trusted setup. In: Micciancio, D., Ristenpart, T. (eds.) CRYPTO 2020, Part III. LNCS, vol. 12172, pp. 704–737. Springer, Cham (2020). https://doi.org/10.1007/978-3-030-56877-1_25

[Shi] Shigeo, M.: A portable and fast pairing-based cryptography library. https://github.com/herumi/mcl

[SKSW20] Sakemi, Y., Kobayashi, T., Saito, T., Wahby, R.S.: Pairing-Friendly Curves. Internet-Draft draft-irtf-cfrg-pairing-friendly-curves-09, Internet Engineering Task Force (2020). https://datatracker.ietf.org/doc/html/draft-irtf-cfrg-pairing-friendly-curves-09

[Ver01] Verheul, E.R.: Evidence that XTR is more secure than supersingular elliptic curve cryptosystems. In: Pfitzmann, B. (ed.) EUROCRYPT 2001. LNCS, vol. 2045, pp. 195–210. Springer, Heidelberg (2001). https://doi.org/10.1007/3-540-44987-6_13

[vox] https://www.vox.com/recode/2020/1/24/21079275/slack-private-messages-privacy-law-enforcement-lawsuit

[X50] Internet X.509 Public Key Infrastructure Certificate and Certificate Revocation List (CRL) Profile. https://tools.ietf.org/html/rfc5280

[YY98] Young, A., Yung, M.: Auto-recoverable auto-certifiable cryptosystems. In: Nyberg, K. (ed.) EUROCRYPT 1998. LNCS, vol. 1403, pp. 17–31. Springer, Heidelberg (1998). https://doi.org/10.1007/BFb0054114

[YY99] Young, A., Yung, M.: Auto-recoverable cryptosystems with faster initialization and the escrow hierarchy. In: Imai, H., Zheng, Y. (eds.) PKC 1999. LNCS, vol. 1560, pp. 306–314. Springer, Heidelberg (1999). https://doi.org/10.1007/3-540-49162-7_24

Real-World Protocols

TARDIGRADE: An Atomic Broadcast Protocol for Arbitrary Network Conditions

Erica Blum[1]([✉]), Jonathan Katz[1]([✉]), and Julian Loss[2]([✉])

[1] University of Maryland, College Park, MD, USA
{erblum,jkatz2}@umd.edu
[2] CISPA Helmoltz Center for Information Security, Saarbrücken, Germany

Abstract. We study the problem of *atomic broadcast*—the underlying problem addressed by blockchain protocols—in the presence of a malicious adversary who corrupts some fraction of the n parties running the protocol. Existing protocols are either robust for any number of corruptions in a *synchronous* network (where messages are delivered within some known time Δ) but fail if the synchrony assumption is violated, or tolerate fewer than $n/3$ corrupted parties in an *asynchronous* network (where messages can be delayed arbitrarily) and cannot tolerate more corruptions even if the network happens to be well behaved.

We design an atomic broadcast protocol (TARDIGRADE) that, for any $t_s \geq t_a$ with $2t_s + t_a < n$, provides security against t_s corrupted parties if the network is synchronous, while remaining secure when t_a parties are corrupted even in an asynchronous network. We show that TARDIGRADE achieves optimal tradeoffs between t_s and t_a. Finally, we show a second protocol (UPGRADE) with similar (but slightly weaker) guarantees that achieves per-transaction communication complexity linear in n.

Keywords: Atomic broadcast · Byzantine agreement · Consensus

1 Introduction

Atomic broadcast [10] is a fundamental problem in distributed computing that can be viewed as a generalization of *Byzantine agreement* (BA) [20,32]. Roughly speaking, a BA protocol allows a set of n parties to agree on a value *once*, even if some parties are *Byzantine*, i.e., corrupted by an adversary who may cause them to behave arbitrarily. In contrast, an atomic broadcast (ABC) protocol allows parties to repeatedly agree on values by including them a totally-ordered, append-only log maintained by all parties. (Formal definitions are given

J. Katz—Work performed under financial assistance award 70NANB19H126 from the U.S. Department of Commerce, National Institute of Standards and Technology, and also supported in part by NSF award #1837517.

J. Loss—Portions of this work were done while at University of Maryland and Ruhr University Bochum.

© International Association for Cryptologic Research 2021
M. Tibouchi and H. Wang (Eds.): ASIACRYPT 2021, LNCS 13091, pp. 547–572, 2021.
https://doi.org/10.1007/978-3-030-92075-3_19

in Sect. 3. Note that ABC is not obtained by simply repeating a BA protocol multiple times; this point is discussed further below.) Atomic broadcast is used as a building block for *state machine replication*, and has received renewed attention in recent years for its applications to blockchains and cryptocurrencies.

Different network models for atomic broadcast can be considered. In a *synchronous* network [2,8,15,18,28], all messages are delivered within some known time Δ. In an *asynchronous* network [16,25], messages can be delayed arbitrarily. (Some work assumes the *partially synchronous* model [13], where messages are delivered within some time bound Δ that is unknown to the parties. We do not consider this model in our work.) Assuming a public-key infrastructure (PKI), atomic broadcast is feasible for $t_s < n$ adversarial corruptions in a synchronous network, but only for $t_a < n/3$ faults in an asynchronous network. A natural question is whether it is possible to design a protocol that can withstand strictly more than $n/3$ faults if the network happens to be synchronous, without entirely sacrificing security if the network happens to be asynchronous. More precisely, fix two thresholds t_a, t_s with $t_a \leq t_s$. Is it possible to design a *network-agnostic* atomic broadcast protocol that (1) tolerates t_s corruptions if it is run in a synchronous network and (2) tolerates t_a corruptions if it is run in an asynchronous network? Depending on one's assumptions about the probabilities of different events, a network-agnostic protocol could be preferable to either a purely synchronous protocol (which loses security if the network is asynchronous) or a purely asynchronous one (which loses security if there are $n/3$ or more faults).

We settle the above question in a model where there is a trusted dealer who distributes information to the parties in advance of the protocol execution:

- We present an atomic broadcast protocol, TARDIGRADE,[1] that achieves the above for any t_a, t_s satisfying $t_a + 2t_s < n$. We also prove that no atomic broadcast protocol can provide the above guarantees[2] if $t_a + 2t_s \geq n$, and so TARDIGRADE is optimal in terms of the thresholds it tolerates.
- We also describe a second protocol, UPGRADE, that is sub-optimal in terms of t_a, t_s but has asymptotic communication complexity comparable to state-of-the-art asynchronous atomic broadcast protocols (see Table 1).

Our work is inspired by work of Blum et al. [5], who show analogous results (with the same thresholds) for the simpler problem of Byzantine agreement. We emphasize that ABC is not realized by simply repeating a (multi-valued) BA protocol multiple times. In particular, the validity property of BA guarantees only that if a value is used as input by all honest parties then that transaction will be output by all honest parties. In the context of ABC, however, each honest party holds a local buffer containing multiple values called *transactions*. Transactions may arrive at arbitrary times, and there is no way to ensure that all

---

[1] Tardigrades, also called water bears, are microscopic animals known for their ability to survive in extreme environments.

[2] This does not contradict the existence of synchronous ABC protocols for $t_s < n$, since such protocols are insecure in an asynchronous setting even if no parties are corrupted.

Table 1. Per-transaction communication complexity of ABC protocols, for transactions of length $|\mathsf{tx}|$, assuming infinite block size and suppressing dependence on the security parameter for simplicity.

Protocol	Communication	Network model
HoneyBadger [25]	$O(n \cdot |\mathsf{tx}|)$	Asynchronous
BEAT1/BEAT2 [12]	$O(n^2 \cdot |\mathsf{tx}|)$	Asynchronous
Dumbo1/Dumbo2 [16]	$O(n \cdot |\mathsf{tx}|)$	Asynchronous
TARDIGRADE	$O(n^2 \cdot |\mathsf{tx}|)$	Network-agnostic
UPGRADE	$O(n \cdot |\mathsf{tx}|)$	Network-agnostic

honest parties will input the same transactions to some execution of an underlying BA protocol. (Although generic transformations from BA to ABC are known in other settings [9], no such transformation is known for the network-agnostic setting we consider.) Indeed, translating the approach of Blum et al. from BA to ABC introduces several additional challenges. In particular, as just noted, in the context of atomic broadcast there is no guarantee that honest parties ever use the same transaction, making it more challenging to prove liveness. A central piece of our construction is a novel protocol for the fundamental problem of *asynchronous common subset* (ACS). Our ACS protocol achieves non-standard security properties that turn out to be generally useful for constructing protocols in a network-agnostic setting; it has already served as a crucial ingredient in follow-up work [6] on network-agnostic secure computation.

1.1 Related Work

There is extensive prior work on both Byzantine agreement and atomic broadcast/SMR/blockchain protocols; we do not provide an exhaustive survey, but instead focus only on the most closely related works.

Miller et al. [25] already note that well-known SMR protocols that tolerate malicious faults (e.g., [8,18]) fail to achieve liveness in an asynchronous network. The HoneyBadger protocol [25] is designed for asynchronous networks, but only handles $t < n/3$ faults even if the network is synchronous.

Several of the most prominent blockchain protocols rely on synchrony [15,28]; Nakamoto consensus, in particular, relies on the assumption that messages will be delivered much faster than the time required to solve proof-of-work puzzles, and is insecure if the network latency is too high or nodes become (temporarily) partitioned from the network.

We focus on designing a single protocol that may be run in either a synchronous or asynchronous network while providing security guarantees in either case. Related work includes that of Malkhi et al. [24] and Momose and Ren [26], who consider networks that may be either synchronous or *partially* synchronous; Liu et al. [21], who design a protocol that tolerates a minority of malicious faults in a synchronous network and a minority of *fail-stop* faults in an asynchronous network; and Guo et al. [17] and Abraham et al. [2], who consider temporary disconnections between two synchronous network components.

A different line of work [22,23,29,30] designs protocols with good *responsiveness*. Roughly, such protocols still require synchrony, but terminate in time proportional to the actual message-delivery time δ rather than the upper bound on the network-delivery time Δ. Kursawe [19] gives a protocol for an asynchronous network that terminates more quickly if the network is synchronous (but does not tolerate more faults in that case). Finally, other work [3,11,14,31] considers a model where synchrony is available for some (known) period of time, and the network is asynchronous afterward.

1.2 Paper Organization

We describe our model in Sect. 2, and give formal definitions in Sect. 3. In Sect. 4, we describe a protocol for the asynchronous common subset (ACS) problem. Then, in Sect. 5, we show how to construct a network-agnostic atomic broadcast protocol (TARDIGRADE) achieving optimal security tradeoffs using ACS and other building blocks. In Sect. 6, we present a second atomic broadcast protocol (UPGRADE) that achieves per-transaction communication complexity linear in n at the cost of tolerating fewer corruptions. Additional constructions, formal proofs, and supplementary results are included in the full version of the paper.[3]

2 Model

We consider protocols run by n parties $P_1, \ldots, P_n$, over point-to-point authenticated channels. Some fraction of these parties are controlled by an adversary, and may deviate arbitrarily from the protocol. For simplicity, we generally assume a static adversary who corrupts parties prior to the start of the protocol; in Sect. 5.6, however, we do briefly discuss how TARDIGRADE can be modified to tolerate an adaptive adversary who may corrupt parties as the protocol is executed. Parties who are not corrupted are called *honest*.

In our model, the network has two possible states. The state is fixed prior to the beginning of the execution; however, the state is not known to the honest parties. When the network is *synchronous*, all parties begin the protocol at the same time, parties' clocks progress at the same rate, and all messages are delivered within some known time Δ after they are sent. The adversary is able to adaptively delay and reorder messages arbitrarily (subject to the bound Δ). When the network is *asynchronous*, the adversary is able to delay messages for arbitrarily long periods of time (as long as all messages are eventually delivered). The parties still have local clocks in the asynchronous setting; however, in this case their clocks are only assumed to be monotonically increasing. In particular, parties' clocks are not necessarily synchronized, and they may start the protocol at different times.

---

[3] Available at: eprint.iacr.org/2020/142.pdf.

We assume the network is either synchronous or asynchronous for the lifetime of the protocol. A more general model would consider a network that alternates between periods of synchrony and asynchrony. Our adaptively secure protocol (cf. Sect. 5.6) tolerates an asynchronous network that later becomes synchronous so long as the attacker does not exceed t_a corruptions until all iterations initiated while the network was asynchronous are complete, and does not exceed t_s corruptions overall. Handling a synchronous network that later becomes asynchronous is only interesting if some mechanism is provided to "uncorrupt" parties (as in the proactive setting). This is outside our model, and we leave treatment of this case as an interesting direction for future work.

We assume a trusted *dealer* who initializes parties with some information prior to execution of the protocol. Specifically, we assume the dealer distributes keys for threshold signature and encryption schemes, each secure for up to t_s corruptions. In a threshold signature scheme there is a public key pk, private keys $sk_1, \ldots, sk_n$, and (public) signature verification keys $(pk_1, \ldots, pk_n)$. Each party P_i receives sk_i, pk, and $(pk_1, \ldots, pk_n)$, and can use its secret key sk_i to create a signature share σ_i on a message m. A signature share from party P_i on a message m can be verified using the corresponding public verification key pk_i (and is called *valid* if it verifies successfully); for this reason, we can also view such a signature share as a signature by P_i on m. We often write $\langle m \rangle_i$ as a shorthand for the tuple (i, m, σ_i), where σ_i is a valid signature share on m with respect to P_i's verification key, and implicitly assume that invalid signature shares are discarded. A set of $t_s + 1$ valid signature shares on the same message can be used to compute a signature for that message, which can be verified using the public key pk; a signature σ on a message m is called *valid* if it verifies successfully with respect to pk. We always implicitly assume that parties use some form of domain separation when signing to ensure that signature shares are valid only in the context in which they are generated.

In a threshold encryption scheme, there is a public encryption key ek, (private) decryption keys $dk_1, \ldots, dk_n$, and public verification keys $vk_1, \ldots, vk_n$ that can be used, as above, to verify that a decryption share is correct (relative to a particular ciphertext). A party P_i can use its decryption key dk_i to generate a decryption share of a ciphertext c; any set of $t_s + 1$ correct decryption shares enable recovery of the underlying message m. Security requires that no collection of t_s parties can decrypt on their own.

We idealize the threshold signature and encryption schemes for simplicity, but they can be instantiated using any of several known protocols; in particular, we only require CPA-security for the threshold encryption scheme. We assume that signature shares and signatures have size $O(\kappa)$, where κ is the security parameter; this is easy to ensure using a collision-resistant hash function. We assume that encrypting a message m of length $|m|$ produces a ciphertext of length $|m| + O(\kappa)$, and that decryption shares have length $O(\kappa)$; these are easy to ensure using standard KEM/DEM mechanisms.

3   Definitions

In this section, we formally define atomic broadcast and relevant subprotocols. Throughout, when we say a protocol achieves some property, we include the case where it achieves that property with overwhelming probability in a security parameter κ. Additionally, in some cases we consider protocols where parties may not terminate even upon generating output; for this reason, we mention termination explicitly in our definitions when applicable.

Many of the definitions below are parameterized by a threshold t. This will become relevant in later sections, where we will often analyze a protocol's properties in a synchronous network with t_s corruptions, as well as in an asynchronous network with t_a corruptions.

3.1   Broadcast and Byzantine Agreement

A *reliable broadcast* protocol allows parties to agree on a value chosen by a designated sender. Honest parties are not guaranteed to terminate; hence, reliable broadcast is weaker than standard broadcast. However, if there is some honest party who terminates, then all honest parties terminate.

Definition 1 (Reliable broadcast). *Let Π be a protocol executed by parties $P_1, \ldots, P_n$, where a designated sender $P^* \in \{P_1, \ldots, P_n\}$ begins holding input v^* and parties terminate upon generating output.*

- **Validity:** *Π is t-valid if the following holds whenever at most t parties are corrupted: if P^* is honest, then every honest party outputs v^*.*
- **Consistency:** *Π is t-consistent if the following holds whenever at most t parties are corrupted: either no honest party outputs a value, or all honest parties output the same value v.*

If Π is t-valid and t-consistent, then we say it is t-secure.

We reserve the term "broadcast" for reliable broadcast. When a party P_i sends a message m to all parties (over point-to-point channels), we say that P_i *multicasts* m.

Byzantine agreement (BA) is closely related to broadcast. In a BA protocol, there is no designated sender; instead, each party has their own input and the parties would like to agree on an output.

Definition 2 (Byzantine agreement). *Let Π be a protocol executed by parties $P_1, \ldots, P_n$, where each party P_i begins holding input $v_i \in \{0, 1\}$.*

- **Validity:** *Π is t-valid if the following holds whenever at most t of the parties are corrupted: if every honest party's input is equal to the same value v, then every honest party outputs v.*
- **Consistency:** *Π is t-consistent if whenever at most t parties are corrupted, every honest party outputs the same value $v \in \{0, 1\}$.*
- **Termination:** *Π is t-terminating if whenever at most t parties are corrupted, every honest party terminates with some output in $\{0, 1\}$.*

If Π is t-valid, t-consistent, and t-terminating, then we say it is t-secure.

3.2 Asynchronous Common Subset

Informally, a protocol for the *asynchronous common subset* (ACS) problem [4] allows n parties, each with some input, to agree on a subset of those inputs. (The term "asynchronous" in the name is historical, and one can also consider protocols for this task in the synchronous setting.)

Definition 3 (ACS). *Let Π be a protocol executed by parties $P_1, \ldots, P_n$, where each P_i begins holding input $v_i \in \{0,1\}^*$, and parties output sets of size at most n.*

- **Validity:** Π *is t-valid if the following holds whenever at most t parties are corrupted: if every honest party's input is equal to the same value v, then every honest party outputs $\{v\}$.*
- **Consistency:** Π *is t-consistent if whenever at most t parties are corrupted, all honest parties output the same set S.*
- **Liveness:** Π *is t-live if whenever at most t parties are corrupted, every honest party generates output.*

If Π is t-consistent, t-valid, and t-live, we say it is t-secure.

For our analysis, it will be helpful to define a few additional properties.

Definition 4 (ACS properties). *Let Π be as above.*

- **Set quality:** Π *has t-set quality if the following holds whenever at most t parties are corrupted: if an honest party outputs a set S, then S contains the input of at least one honest party.*
- **Validity with termination:** Π *is t-valid with termination if, whenever at most t parties are corrupted and every honest party's input is equal to the same value v, then every honest party outputs $\{v\}$ and terminates.*
- **Termination:** Π *is t-terminating if whenever at most t parties are corrupted, every honest party generates output and terminates.*

3.3 Atomic Broadcast

Protocols for *atomic broadcast* (ABC) allow parties to maintain agreement on an ever-growing, ordered log of *transactions*. An atomic broadcast protocol does not terminate but instead continues indefinitely. We model the local log held by each party P_i as a write-once array $\mathsf{Blocks}_i = \mathsf{Blocks}_i[1], \mathsf{Blocks}_i[2], \ldots$. Each $\mathsf{Blocks}_i[j]$ is initially set to a special value $\perp$. We say that P_i *outputs a block in iteration j* when P_i writes a set of transactions to $\mathsf{Blocks}_i[j]$; similarly, for each i, j such that $\mathsf{Blocks}_i[j] \neq \perp$, we refer to $\mathsf{Blocks}_i[j]$ as the *block output by P_i in iteration j*. For convenience, we let $\mathsf{Blocks}_i[k : \ell]$ denote the contiguous subarray $\mathsf{Blocks}_i[k], \ldots, \mathsf{Blocks}_i[\ell]$ and let $\mathsf{Blocks}_i[: \ell]$ denote the prefix $\mathsf{Blocks}_i[1 : \ell]$.

For simplicity, we imagine that each party P_i has a local buffer buf_i, and that transactions are added to parties' local buffers by some mechanism external to the protocol (e.g., via a gossip protocol). Whenever P_i outputs a block, they delete from their buffer any transactions that have already been added to their log. We emphasize that a particular transaction tx may be provided as input to different parties at arbitrary times, and may be provided as input to some honest parties but not others.

Definition 5 (Atomic broadcast). *Let Π be a protocol executed by parties $P_1, \ldots, P_n$ who are provided with transactions as input and locally maintain arrays* Blocks *as described above.*

- **Completeness:** Π *is* t-complete *if the following holds whenever at most t parties are corrupted: for all $j > 0$, every honest party outputs a block in iteration j.*
- **Consistency:** Π *is* t-consistent *if the following holds whenever at most t parties are corrupted: if an honest party outputs a block B in iteration j then all honest parties output B in iteration j.*
- **Liveness:** Π *is* t-live *if the following holds whenever at most t parties are corrupted: if every honest party is provided a transaction tx as input, then every honest party eventually outputs a block that contains tx.*

If Π is t-consistent, t-live, and t-complete, then we say it is t-secure.

In the above definition, a transaction tx is only guaranteed to be contained in a block output by an honest party if *every* honest party receives tx as input. A stronger definition might require that a transaction is output even if only a *single* honest party receives tx as input; however, it is easy to achieve the latter from the former by requiring honest parties to forward new transactions they receive to the rest of the parties in the network.

4   ACS with Higher Validity Threshold

A key component of our atomic broadcast protocol is an ACS protocol for asynchronous networks that is secure when the number of corrupted parties is below a fixed threshold t_a, and guarantees validity up to a higher threshold t_s. More precisely, fix $t_a \leq t_s$ with $t_a + 2 \cdot t_s < n$; we show a t_a-secure ACS protocol that achieves t_a-termination, t_s-validity with termination, and t_a-set quality. Throughout this section, we assume an asynchronous network. (Of course, the protocol achieves the same guarantees in a synchronous network.)

Our protocol is adapted from the ACS protocol of Ben-Or et al. [4] (later adapted by Miller et al. [25]), which is built using subprotocols for reliable broadcast and Byzantine agreement. We present our construction in two steps: first, we describe an ACS protocol $\Pi_{\mathsf{ACS}*}^{t_a,t_s}$ (cf. Fig. 1) that is t_a-secure and has t_a-set quality, but is non-terminating. Then, we construct a second protocol $\Pi_{\mathsf{ACS}}^{t_a,t_s}$ (cf. Fig. 2) that uses $\Pi_{\mathsf{ACS}*}^{t_a,t_s}$ as a subprotocol. $\Pi_{\mathsf{ACS}}^{t_a,t_s}$ inherits security and set quality from $\Pi_{\mathsf{ACS}*}^{t_a,t_s}$, and additionally achieves t_a-termination and t_s-validity with termination.

Protocol $\Pi_{\mathsf{ACS}*}^{t_a,t_s}$. At a high level, an execution of $\Pi_{\mathsf{ACS}*}^{t_a,t_s}$ involves one instance of reliable broadcast and one instance of Byzantine agreement per party P_i, denoted Bcast_i and BA_i, respectively. Informally, Bcast_i is used to broadcast P_i's input v_i, and BA_i is used to determine whether P_i's input will be included in the final output. When a party receives output v_i' from Bcast_i, they input 1 to BA_i. Once a party has received output from $n - t_a$ broadcasts, they input 0 to any BA instances they have not yet initiated. Each party keeps track of which BA instances have output 1 using a local variable $S^* := \{i : \mathsf{BA}_i \text{ output } 1\}$. At the end of the protocol, if a party observes a majority value v in the set of values $\{v_i'\}_{i \in S^*}$, it outputs the singleton set $\{v\}$; otherwise, it outputs $\{v_i'\}_{i \in S^*}$, i.e., the set of all values broadcast by parties in S^*.

We assume an ABA subprotocol that is secure for $t_a < n/3$ corruptions and has communication complexity $O(n^2)$, such as the ABA protocol of Mostéfaoui et al. [27]. We also assume an asynchronous reliable broadcast protocol Bcast that is t_s-valid and t_a-consistent with communication complexity $O(n^2 |v|)$. It is straightforward to adapt Bracha's (asynchronous) reliable broadcast protocol [7] to achieve these properties; an example construction can be found in the full version of the paper.

$$\Pi_{\mathsf{ACS}^*}^{t_a, t_s}$$

- Set commit := false and $S^* := \emptyset$.
- Run Bcast_j as the sender with input v_j, and for each $i \neq j$ run Bcast_i with P_i as the sender.
- Upon Bcast_i terminating with output v_i': if P_j has not yet begun running BA_i then begin running it with input 1.
- Upon BA_i terminating with output 1: add i to S^*.
- Upon setting $|S^*|$ to $n - t_a$: for any BA_i that P_j has not yet begun running, begin running BA_i with input 0.

Predicates:
$C_1(v)$: at least $n - t_s$ executions $\{\mathsf{Bcast}_i\}_{i \in [n]}$ have output v.
   C_1: $\exists v$ for which $C_1(v)$ is true.
$C_2(v)$: $|S^*| \geq n - t_a$, all executions $\{\mathsf{BA}_i\}_{i \in [n]}$ have terminated, and a strict majority of the executions $\{\mathsf{Bcast}_i\}_{i \in S^*}$ have output v.
   C_2: $\exists v$ for which $C_2(v)$ is true.
   C_3: $|S^*| \geq n - t_a$, all executions $\{\mathsf{BA}_i\}_{i \in [n]}$ have terminated, and all executions $\{\mathsf{Bcast}_i\}_{i \in S^*}$ have terminated.

Output conditions:
(Event 1) If $C_1(v) = \mathsf{true}$ for some v and commit = false then:
         set commit := true and output $\{v\}$.
(Event 2) If $C_1 = \mathsf{false}$, $C_2(v) = \mathsf{true}$ for some v, and commit = false then:
         set commit := true and output $\{v\}$.
(Event 3) If $C_1 = C_2 = \mathsf{false}$, $C_3 = \mathsf{true}$, and commit = false then:
         set commit := true and output $\{v_i'\}_{i \in S^*}$.

Fig. 1. An ACS protocol, from the perspective of party P_j with input v_j.

Lemma 1. *Fix t_s, t_a with $t_a + 2 \cdot t_s < n$, and assume there are at most t_s corrupted parties during some execution of $\Pi_{\mathsf{ACS}^*}^{t_a, t_s}$. If an honest party P_i outputs a set S_i, then $\exists v_j \in S_i$ such that v_j was input by an honest party P_j.*

Proof. We show that P_i's output S_i always includes a value that was output from an execution of Bcast where the corresponding sender is honest. The lemma follows from t_s-validity of Bcast.

Suppose P_i generates output due to Event 1, so S_i is a singleton set $\{v\}$. P_i must have received v as output from at least $n - t_s$ executions of $\{\mathsf{Bcast}_i\}$. Because $n - 2t_s > t_a \geq 0$, at least one of those corresponds to an honest sender.

Next, suppose P_i generates output due to Event 2. Again, S_i is a singleton set $\{v\}$. P_i must have seen at least $\lfloor \frac{|S^*|}{2} \rfloor + 1$ broadcast instances terminate with output v, and furthermore $|S^*| \geq n - t_a$. Therefore, P_i has seen at least $\lfloor \frac{n - t_a}{2} \rfloor + 1 \geq \lfloor \frac{2t_s}{2} \rfloor + 1 > t_s$ executions of $\{\mathsf{Bcast}_i\}$ terminate with output v. Since there are at most t_s corrupted parties, at least one of those executions must correspond to an honest sender.

Finally, suppose P_i generates output due to Event 3, so $S_i = \{v_i'\}_{i \in S^*}$. Since there are at most t_s corrupted parties and $|S^*| - t_s \geq n - t_a - t_s > t_s \geq 0$, at least one party in S^* is honest. $\square$

Lemma 2. *If $t_a + 2 \cdot t_s < n$, then $\Pi_{\mathsf{ACS}^*}^{t_a, t_s}$ is t_s-valid.*

Proof. Assume at most t_s parties are corrupted, and all honest parties have the same input v. By t_s-validity of Bcast, at least $n - t_s$ executions of $\{\mathsf{Bcast}_i\}$ (namely, those for which the sender is honest) will eventually output v. It follows that all honest parties eventually set $C_1(v) = \mathsf{true}$, at which point they will output $\{v\}$ if they have not already generated output. It only remains to show that there is no other set an honest party can output.

If an honest party generates output S due to Events 1 or 2, then S is a singleton set. Since all honest parties have input v, Lemma 1 implies $S = \{v\}$.

To conclude, we show that no honest party can generate output due to Event 3. Assume toward a contradiction that some honest party P generates output due to Event 3. Then P must have seen Bcast_i terminate (say, with output v_i) for all $i \in S^*$. Since also $|S^*| \geq n - t_a > 2t_s$, a majority of those executions $\{\mathsf{Bcast}_i\}_{i \in S^*}$ correspond to honest senders and so (by t_s-validity of Bcast) resulted in output v. But then $C_2(v)$ would be true for P, and P would not generate output due to Event 3. $\square$

Lemma 3. *Fix $t_a \leq t_s$ with $t_a + 2 \cdot t_s < n$, and assume at most t_a parties are corrupted during an execution of $\Pi_{\mathsf{ACS}^*}^{t_a, t_s}$. If honest parties P_1, P_2 output sets S_1, S_2, respectively, then $S_1 = S_2$.*

Proof. Say P_1 generates output due to event i and P_2 generates output due to event j, and assume without loss of generality that $i \leq j$. We consider the different possibilities.

First, assume $i = 1$ so Event 1 occurs for P_1 and $S_1 = \{v_1\}$ for some value v_1. We have the following sub-cases:

- If Event 1 also occurs for P_2, then $S_2 = \{v_2\}$ for some value v_2. P_1 and P_2 must have each seen some set of at least $n - t_s > n/2$ executions of $\{\mathsf{Bcast}_i\}$ output v_1 and v_2, respectively. The intersection of these sets is non-empty; thus, t_a-consistency of Bcast implies that $v_1 = v_2$ and hence $S_1 = S_2$.
- If Event 2 occurs for P_2, then once again $S_2 = \{v_2\}$ for some v_2. P_2 must have $|S^*| \geq n - t_a$, and must have seen at least $\left\lfloor \frac{|S^*|}{2} \right\rfloor + 1 \geq \left\lfloor \frac{n-t_a}{2} \right\rfloor + 1$ executions of $\{\mathsf{Bcast}_i\}$ output v_2. Moreover, P_1 must have seen at least $n - t_s$ executions of $\{\mathsf{Bcast}_i\}$ output v_1. Since

$$n - t_s + \left\lfloor \frac{n - t_a}{2} \right\rfloor + 1 \geq n - t_s + \left\lfloor \frac{2t_s}{2} \right\rfloor + 1 > n, \tag{1}$$

  these two sets of executions must have a non-empty intersection. But then t_a-consistency of Bcast implies that $v_1 = v_2$ and hence $S_1 = S_2$.
- If Event 3 occurs for P_2 then P_2 must have seen all executions $\{\mathsf{Bcast}_i\}_{i \in S^*}$ terminate, where $|S^*| \geq n - t_a$. We know P_1 has seen at least $n - t_s$ executions $\{\mathsf{Bcast}_i\}_{i \in [n]}$ output v_1, and so (by t_a-consistency of Bcast) there are at most t_s executions $\{\mathsf{Bcast}_i\}_{i \in [n]}$ that P_2 has seen terminate with a value other than v_1. The number of executions of $\{\mathsf{Bcast}_i\}_{i \in S^*}$ that P_2 has seen terminate with output v_1 (which is at least $(n - t_a) - t_s > t_s$) is thus strictly greater than the number of executions $\{\mathsf{Bcast}_i\}_{i \in S^*}$ that P_2 has seen terminate with a value other than v_1 (which is at most t_s). But then $C_2(v_1)$ would be true for P_2. We conclude that Event 3 cannot occur for P_2.

Next, assume $i = j = 2$, so Event 2 occurs for P_1 and P_2. Then $S_1 = \{v_1\}$ and $S_2 = \{v_2\}$ for some v_1, v_2. Both P_1 and P_2 must have seen all executions $\{\mathsf{BA}_i\}_{i \in [n]}$ terminate. By t_a-consistency of BA, they must therefore agree on S^*. P_1 must have seen a majority of the executions $\{\mathsf{Bcast}_i\}_{i \in S^*}$ output v_1; similarly, P_2 must have seen a majority of the executions $\{\mathsf{Bcast}_i\}_{i \in S^*}$ output v_2. Then t_a-consistency of Bcast implies $v_1 = v_2$.

Finally, consider the case where $j = 3$ (so Event 3 occurs for P_2) but $i > 1$ (so P_1 generates output due either to Event 2 or 3). As above, t_a-consistency of BA ensures that P_1 and P_2 agree on S^*. Moreover, P_2 must have seen all executions $\{\mathsf{Bcast}_i\}_{i \in S^*}$ terminate, but without any value being output by a majority of those executions. But then t_a-consistency of Bcast implies that P_1 also does not see any value being output by a majority of those executions, and so Event 2 cannot occur for P_1; thus, Event 3 must have occurred for P_1. Therefore, t_a-consistency of Bcast implies that P_1 outputs the same set as P_2. □

Lemma 4. *If $t_a \leq t_s$ and $t_a + 2 \cdot t_s < n$, then $\Pi_{\mathsf{ACS}^*}^{t_a, t_s}$ is t_a-live.*

Proof. It follows easily from t_a-security of Bcast and BA that if any honest party generates output then all honest parties generate output, so consider the case where no honest parties have (yet) generated output. Let H denote the indices of the honest parties. By t_s-validity of Bcast, all honest parties eventually see the executions $\{\mathsf{Bcast}_i\}_{i \in H}$ terminate, and so all honest parties input a value to the executions $\{\mathsf{BA}_i\}_{i \in H}$. By t_a-security of BA, all honest parties eventually see those executions terminate and agree on their outputs. There are now two cases:

- If all executions $\{BA_i\}_{i \in H}$ output 1, then it is immediate that all honest parties have $|S^*| \geq n - t_a$.
- If BA_i outputs 0 for some $i \in H$, then (by t_a-validity of BA) some honest party P must have used input 0 when running BA_i. But then P must have seen at least $n - t_a$ other executions $\{BA_i\}$ output 1. By t_a-consistency of BA, this implies that all honest parties see at least $n - t_a$ executions $\{BA_i\}$ output 1, and hence have $|S^*| \geq n - t_a$.

Since all honest parties have $|S^*| \geq n - t_a$, they all execute $\{BA_i\}_{i \in [n]}$. Once again, t_a-termination of BA implies that all those executions will eventually terminate. Finally, if $i \in S^*$ for some honest party P then P must have seen BA_i terminate with output 1; then t_a-validity of BA implies that some honest party used input 1 when running BA_i and hence has seen $Bcast_i$ terminate. It follows that P will see $Bcast_i$ terminate. As a result, we see that every honest party can (at least) generate output due to Event 3. □

Lemma 5. *If* $t_a \leq t_s$ *and* $t_a + 2 \cdot t_s < n$, *then* $\Pi_{ACS^*}^{t_a, t_s}$ *has* t_a-*set quality.*

Proof. If an honest party P outputs $S = \{v\}$ due to Event 1, then P has seen at least $n - t_s$ executions $\{Bcast_i\}$ terminate with output v. Of these, at least $n - t_s - t_a > 0$ must correspond to honest senders. By t_s-validity of Bcast, those honest parties must have all had input v, and so set quality holds. Alternatively, say P outputs a set $\{v\}$ due to Event 2. Then P must have $|S^*| \geq n - t_a$, and at least $\lfloor \frac{|S^*|}{2} \rfloor + 1 \geq \lfloor \frac{n - t_a}{2} \rfloor + 1 > t_a$ of the executions $\{Bcast_i\}_{i \in S^*}$ output v. At least one of those executions must correspond to an honest party, and that honest party must have had input v (by t_s-validity of Bcast); thus, set quality holds. Finally, if P output a set S due to Event 3, then S contains every value output by $\{Bcast_i\}_{i \in S^*}$ with $|S^* \geq n - t_a$. Since S^* must contain at least one honest party, set quality follows as before. □

Theorem 1. *Fix* t_a, t_s *with* $t_a \leq t_s$ *and* $t_a + 2 \cdot t_s < n$. *Then* $\Pi_{ACS^*}^{t_a, t_s}$ *is* t_a-*secure and* t_s-*valid, and has* t_a-*set quality.*

Proof. Lemma 2 proves t_s-validity. Lemmas 3 and 4 together prove t_a-liveness and t_a-consistency, and Lemma 6 proves t_a-set quality. □

Lemma 6. *If* $t_a \leq t_s$ *and* $t_a + 2 \cdot t_s < n$, *then* $\Pi_{ACS^*}^{t_a, t_s}$ *has* t_a-*set quality.*

Proof. If an honest party P outputs $S = \{v\}$ due to Event 1, then P has seen at least $n - t_s$ executions $\{Bcast_i\}$ terminate with output v. Of these, at least $n - t_s - t_a > 0$ must correspond to honest senders. By t_s-validity of Bcast, those honest parties must have all had input v, and so set quality holds. Alternatively, say P outputs a set $\{v\}$ due to Event 2. Then P must have $|S^*| \geq n - t_a$, and at least $\lfloor \frac{|S^*|}{2} \rfloor + 1 \geq \lfloor \frac{n - t_a}{2} \rfloor + 1 > t_a$ of the executions $\{Bcast_i\}_{i \in S^*}$ output v. At least one of those executions must correspond to an honest party, and that honest party must have had input v (by t_s-validity of Bcast); thus, set quality holds. Finally, if P output a set S due to Event 3, then S contains every value output by $\{Bcast_i\}_{i \in S^*}$. Since $|S^*| \geq n - t_a$, S^* must contain at least one honest party, and so set quality follows as before. □

Protocol $\Pi_{ACS}^{t_a,t_s}$. Protocol $\Pi_{ACS}^{t_a,t_s}$ does not guarantee termination. We transform $\Pi_{ACS*}^{t_a,t_s}$ to a terminating ACS protocol $\Pi_{ACS}^{t_a,t_s}$ using digital signatures. The parties first run $\Pi_{ACS*}^{t_a,t_s}$. When a party P_i generates output S_i from that protocol, it then notifies the other parties by multicasting a signature share$\langle$commit, $S_i\rangle_i$ on S_i. Any party who receives enough signature shares to form a signature—or receives a signature directly—multicasts the signature to all other parties, outputs the corresponding set, and terminates.

$$\Pi_{ACS}^{t_a,t_s}$$

- Run $\Pi_{ACS*}^{t_a,t_s}$ using input v_j.
- Upon receiving output S_j from $\Pi_{ACS*}^{t_a,t_s}$, multicast $\langle$commit, $S_j\rangle_j$.
- Upon receiving $t_s + 1$ signature shares of (commit, S), form a signature σ on (commit, S), multicast (commit, S, σ), output S, and terminate.
- Upon receiving a valid signature σ of (commit, S), multicast (commit, S, σ), output S, and terminate.

Fig. 2. A terminating ACS protocol, from the perspective of party P_j with input v_j.

Lemma 7. $\Pi_{ACS}^{t_a,t_s}$ is t_a-terminating.

Proof. If one honest party terminates $\Pi_{ACS}^{t_a,t_s}$ then all honest parties will eventually receive a valid signature and thus terminate $\Pi_{ACS}^{t_a,t_s}$. But as long as no honest parties has yet terminated, t_a-liveness of $\Pi_{ACS*}^{t_a,t_s}$ implies that all honest parties will generate output from $\Pi_{ACS*}^{t_a,t_s}$; moreover, t_a-consistency of $\Pi_{ACS*}^{t_a,t_s}$ implies that all those outputs will be equal to the same set S. So the $n - t_a \geq t_s + 1$ honest parties will send signature shares on S to all parties, which means that all honest parties will terminate. □

Lemma 8. *Fix t_a, t_s with $t_a \leq t_s$ and $t_a + 2 \cdot t_s < n$. Then $\Pi_{ACS}^{t_a,t_s}$ is t_a-secure, t_a-terminating, and t_s-valid with termination, and has t_a-set quality.*

Proof. Lemma 7 implies that $\Pi_{ACS}^{t_a,t_s}$ is t_a-live as well as t_a-terminating. If an honest party outputs a set S from $\Pi_{ACS}^{t_a,t_s}$, then (as long as at most t_s parties are corrupted) at least one honest party must have output S from $\Pi_{ACS*}^{t_a,t_s}$. Thus, $\Pi_{ACS}^{t_a,t_s}$ inherits t_a-set quality, t_a-consistency, and t_s-validity (without termination) from $\Pi_{ACS*}^{t_a,t_s}$ (cf. Theorem 1). It is straightforward to extend t_s-validity to t_s-validity with termination using an identical argument as in Lemma 7. □

Communication complexity of $\Pi_{ACS}^{t_a,t_s}$. Let $|v|$ be the size of each party's input. Recall that each instance of Bcast has communication complexity $O(n^2 |v|)$, and each instance of BA has cost $O(n^2)$. Since the inner protocol $\Pi_{ACS*}^{t_a,t_s}$ consists of n parallel instances of Bcast and BA, the cost of the inner protocol is $O(n^3 |v|)$. In the remaining steps, each party sends a set of size at most n plus a signature share (or signature) to everyone else, contributing an additional $O(n^2 \cdot (n|v| + \kappa))$ communication. The total communication for $\Pi_{\mathsf{ACS}}^{t_a, t_s}$ is thus $O(n^3 |v| + n^2 \kappa)$.

5   Network-Agnostic Atomic Broadcast

In this section, we show our main result: for any $t_s \geq t_a$ with $t_a + 2t_s < n$, an atomic broadcast protocol that is t_s-secure in a synchronous network and t_a-secure in an asynchronous network.

5.1   Technical Overview

At a high level, each iteration of the protocol consists of four main steps. First, there is an information-gathering phase in which each party sends its input to all other parties, and waits for a fixed amount of time to receive inputs from others. Any party who receives enough inputs during the first phase will use them as input to a synchronous *block agreement* (BLA) protocol $\Pi_{\mathsf{BLA}}^{t_s}$. If the network is synchronous and at most t_s parties are corrupted, the BLA subprotocol will output a set of inputs that contains sufficiently many honest parties' inputs. The BLA subprotocol is run for a fixed amount of time, with the timeout chosen to ensure that (with high probability) it will terminate before the timeout if the network is synchronous. This brings us to the third phase, in which parties run the ACS protocol $\Pi_{\mathsf{ACS}}^{t_a, t_s}$. If a party received output from the BLA protocol before the timeout, they will use that as their input to the ACS subprotocol; otherwise, they wait until they have received sufficiently many inputs from other parties and use those. The final phase occurs once parties have received output from the ACS protocol. The parties use that output to form the next block.

The BLA and ACS protocols are designed to have complementary security properties. In particular, if the network is synchronous then the BLA protocol will ensure that all honest parties use the same input value B in the ACS protocol. This is exactly why $\Pi_{\mathsf{ACS}}^{t_a, t_s}$ has t_s-validity with termination: so that, in this case, all parties will be in agreement on the singleton set $\{B\}$ after running $\Pi_{\mathsf{ACS}}^{t_a, t_s}$. On the other hand, if the network is not synchronous and at most t_a parties are corrupted, it is possible that $\Pi_{\mathsf{BLA}}^{t_s}$ will not succeed, and parties may input different values to $\Pi_{\mathsf{ACS}}^{t_a, t_s}$. However, in this case t_a-security of $\Pi_{\mathsf{ACS}}^{t_a, t_s}$ ensures that the parties will agree on a set of values $B = \{\beta_1, \beta_2, \dots\}$. Moreover, the output-quality property ensures that at least a constant fraction of the values in B were contributed by honest parties.

5.2   Block Agreement

We use a block-agreement protocol to agree on objects that we call *pre-blocks*. (The name alludes to their role in our eventual atomic broadcast protocol, where they will serve as an intermediate between parties' raw inputs and the final blocks.) A pre-block is a vector of length n whose ith entry is either $\perp$ or a message along with a valid signature by P_i on that message. The *quality* of a pre-block is defined as the number of entries that are not $\perp$; we say that a pre-block is a *k-quality pre-block* if it has quality at least k.

Definition 6 (Block agreement). *Let Π be a protocol executed by parties $P_1, \ldots, P_n$, where parties terminate upon generating output.*

- **Validity:** *Π is t-valid if whenever at most t of the parties are corrupted and every honest party's input is an $(n-t)$-quality pre-block, then every honest party outputs an $(n-t)$-quality pre-block.*
- **Consistency:** *Π is t-consistent if whenever at most t of the parties are corrupted, every honest party outputs the same pre-block B.*

If Π is t-valid and t-consistent, then we say it is t-secure.

A synchronous block-agreement protocol can be constructed using a straightforward adaptation of the *synod protocol* by Abraham et al. [1]. (For completeness, a construction and security analysis can be found in the full version.)

Theorem 2. *Fix a maximum input length $|m|$. There is a block-agreement protocol Π_{BLA} with communication complexity $O(n^3\kappa^2 + n^2\kappa|m|)$ that is t-secure for any $t < n/2$ when run in a synchronous network and terminates in time $5\kappa\Delta$.*

5.3   A Network-Agnostic Atomic Broadcast Protocol

We now describe our atomic broadcast protocol TARDIGRADE (cf. Fig. 3), parameterized by thresholds t_s and t_a. Let L denote a desired maximum *block size*, i.e., the maximum number of transactions that can appear in a block. At a high level, parties agree on each new block via the following steps. First, each party P_i chooses a set V_i of L/n transactions from among the first L transactions in its local buffer. (We assume without loss of generality that parties always have at least L transactions in their buffer, since they can always pad their buffers with null transactions.) Next, P_i encrypts V_i using a (t_s, n)-threshold encryption scheme to give a ciphertext μ_i. (As in HoneyBadger [25], transactions are encrypted to limit the adversary's ability to selectively censor certain transactions.) Each party signs its ciphertext and multicasts it, then waits for a fixed period of time to receive signed ciphertexts from the other parties. Whenever a party receives a signed ciphertext during this time, they add it to a pre-block. Any party who forms an $(n - t_s)$-quality pre-block in this way within the time limit will input that pre-block to Π_{BLA}. The parties then wait for another fixed period of time to see whether Π_{BLA} outputs an $(n - t_s)$-quality pre-block. If a party receives an $(n-t_s)$-quality pre-block as output from Π_{BLA} within this time limit, it inputs that pre-block to the ACS protocol $\Pi_{\mathsf{ACS}^*}^{t_a, t_s}$. Otherwise, if some party does not receive suitable output within the time limit, it inputs a pre-block containing the signed ciphertexts it received directly from other parties. (In this case, if a party has not received enough signed ciphertexts to form an $(n - t_s)$-quality pre-block, it waits for additional ciphertexts to arrive before inputting its pre-block to $\Pi_{\mathsf{ACS}^*}^{t_a,t_s}$.) At this point, each party waits for $\Pi_{\mathsf{ACS}^*}^{t_a,t_s}$ to output a set of pre-blocks. The output of $\Pi_{\mathsf{ACS}^*}^{t_a,t_s}$ is passed into a subroutine ConstructBlock that performs threshold decryption for each ciphertext in each pre-block in the set, and combines the resulting transactions into a final block.

Each party begins iteration k when its local clock reaches time $T_k := \lambda \cdot (k-1)$, where $\lambda > 0$ is a *spacing parameter*. (The value of λ is irrelevant for the security proofs, but can be tuned to achieve better performance in practice; see further discussion in Sect. 5.4.) If the network is synchronous, parties' clocks are synchronized and so all parties begin each iteration at the same time. If the network is asynchronous, we do not have this guarantee. In either case, parties do not necessarily finish agreeing on block k prior to starting iteration $k' > k$, and so it is possible for parties to be participating in several iterations in parallel.

We implicitly assume that messages in each iteration, including messages corresponding to the various subprotocols, carry an identifier for the corresponding iteration so that parties know the iteration to which it belongs. Importantly, the executions of Π_{BLA} and $\Pi_{\mathsf{ACS}^*}^{t_a,t_s}$ associated with a particular iteration are entirely separate from those of other iterations.

$$\Pi_{\mathsf{ABC}}^{t_a,t_s}$$

For each iteration $k = 1, 2, \ldots$ do:

- At time $T_k = \lambda \cdot (k-1)$: sample $V \leftarrow$ ProposeTxs$(L/n, L)$ and encrypt V using pk to produce a ciphertext μ. Multicast (input, $\langle \mu \rangle_j$).
- Upon receiving a signed input (input, $\langle \mu \rangle_i$) from P_i (for iteration k):
  - If this is the first input received for iteration k, create a new pre-block $\beta_j^k := (\bot, \ldots, \bot)$ and set ready$_k :=$ false.
  - If $\beta_j^k[i] = \bot$: set $\beta_j^k[i] := \langle \mu \rangle_j$.
  - If B_j^k is an $(n - t_s)$-quality pre-block and ready$_k =$ false, set ready$_k :=$ true.
- At time $T_k + \Delta$: if ready$_k =$ true, run Π_{BLA} using input β_j^k.
- At time $T_k + \Delta + 5\kappa\Delta$:
  - Terminate Π_{BLA} (if it has not already terminated). If Π_{BLA} had output an $(n - t_s)$-quality pre-block β^*, run $\Pi_{\mathsf{ACS}}^{t_a,t_s}$ using input β^*. Else, wait until ready$_k =$ true and then run $\Pi_{\mathsf{ACS}}^{t_a,t_s}$ using input β_j^k.
  - When $\Pi_{\mathsf{ACS}}^{t_a,t_s}$ terminates with output B^*, run ConstructBlock(B^*) to produce a block B. Then set Blocks$[k] := B$ and delete from buf$_j$ any transactions that appear in Blocks$[k]$.

ProposeTxs(ℓ, M): choose a set V of ℓ values $\{\mathsf{tx}_1, \ldots, \mathsf{tx}_\ell\}$ uniformly (without replacement) from the first M values in buf$_j$, then output V.

ConstructBlock(B^*): participate in threshold decryption for each unique ciphertext μ in each pre-block $\beta \in B^*$. Once all decryptions have finished, output the set B of all unique transactions obtained.

Fig. 3. Our atomic broadcast protocol TARDIGRADE, from the perspective of party P_j.

Theorem 3 (Completeness and consistency). *Fix t_a, t_s with $t_a \leq t_s$ and $t_a + 2 \cdot t_s < n$. Then $\Pi_{\mathsf{ABC}}^{t_a, t_s}$ is t_a-complete/consistent when run in an asynchronous network, and t_s-complete/consistent when run in a synchronous network.*

Proof. First, consider the case where at most t_s parties are corrupted and the network is synchronous. In the beginning of each iteration k, each honest party multicasts a set of transactions, and so every honest party can form an $(n - t_s)$-quality pre-block by time $T_k + \Delta$. Thus, every honest party starts running Π_{BLA} at time $T_k + \Delta$ using an $(n - t_s)$-quality pre-block as input. By t_s-security of Π_{BLA} in a synchronous network (note $t_s < n/2$), with overwhelming probability every honest party outputs the same $(n - t_s)$-quality pre-block β^* from Π_{BLA} by time $T_k + \Delta + 5\kappa\Delta$. Therefore, each honest party inputs β^* to $\Pi_{\mathsf{ACS*}}^{t_a, t_s}$. By t_s-validity with termination of $\Pi_{\mathsf{ACS*}}^{t_a, t_s}$, every honest party obtains the same output B^* from $\Pi_{\mathsf{ACS*}}^{t_a, t_s}$. So all honest parties eventually receive $n - t_s > t_s$ valid decryption shares for each ciphertext in each pre-block of B^*, and they all output the same block.

The case where the network is asynchronous and at most t_a parties are corrupted is similar. In each iteration, each honest party multicasts a set of transactions and so every honest party eventually receives input from at least $n - t_a \geq n - t_s$ distinct parties and can form an $(n - t_s)$-quality pre-block. This means that every honest party eventually runs $\Pi_{\mathsf{ACS*}}^{t_a, t_s}$ using an $(n - t_s)$-quality pre-block as input. By t_a-security of $\Pi_{\mathsf{ACS*}}^{t_a, t_s}$, all honest parties eventually receive the same output B^* from $\Pi_{\mathsf{ACS*}}^{t_a, t_s}$. So all honest parties will eventually receive $n - t_a > t_s$ valid decryption shares for each ciphertext in each pre-block of B^*, and they all output the same block. □

In what follows, we let $\mathsf{Blocks}[k]$ denote the block output by honest parties in iteration k. We now turn our attention to liveness. We begin by proving a bound on the number of honest parties who contribute transactions to a block. Formally, we say that an honest party P_i *contributes transactions* to a block $B :=$ $\mathsf{ConstructBlock}(B^*)$ if there is a pre-block $\beta \in B^*$ such that $B[i] \neq \bot$. Using this lower bound, we show that any transaction that is at the front of most honest parties' buffers will eventually be output with overwhelming probability. Liveness follows by arguing that any transaction that is in the buffer of all honest parties will eventually move to the front of most honest parties' buffers.

Lemma 9. *Fix t_a, t_s with $t_a \leq t_s$ and $t_a + 2 \cdot t_s < n$, and assume at most t_a parties are corrupted and the network is asynchronous, or at most t_s parties are corrupted and the network is synchronous. Then in an execution of $\Pi_{\mathsf{ABC}}^{t_a, t_s}$, for any block B output by an honest party, at least $n - (t_s + t_a)$ honest parties contributed transactions to B.*

Proof. First, consider the case where at most t_a parties are corrupted and the network is asynchronous. As shown in the proof of Theorem 3, every honest party executes $\Pi_{\mathsf{ACS*}}^{t_a, t_s}$ using an $(n - t_s)$-quality pre-block as input. Thus, the input of every honest party to $\Pi_{\mathsf{ACS*}}^{t_a, t_s}$ contains at least $n - (t_s + t_a)$ ciphertexts created by honest parties. By t_a-set quality of $\Pi_{\mathsf{ACS}^*}^{t_a,t_s}$, the output of $\Pi_{\mathsf{ACS}^*}^{t_a,t_s}$ contains some honest party's input and the lemma follows.

Next, consider the case where at most t_s parties are corrupted and the network is synchronous. As shown in the proof of Theorem 3, every honest party executes $\Pi_{\mathsf{ACS}^*}^{t_a,t_s}$ using the same $(n - t_s)$-quality pre-block β as input. By t_s-validity with termination of $\Pi_{\mathsf{ACS}^*}^{t_a,t_s}$, all honest parties output $B^* = \{\beta\}$ from $\Pi_{\mathsf{ACS}^*}^{t_a,t_s}$. Because β is $(n - t_s)$-quality, it contains at least $(n - 2t_s)$ honest parties' ciphertexts; the lemma follows. $\qquad\square$

Lemma 10. *Assume the conditions of Lemma 9. Consider an iteration k and a transaction* tx *such that, at the beginning of iteration k, all but at most t_s honest parties have* tx *among the first L transactions in their buffers. Then for any $r > 0$,* tx *is in* Blocks$[k : k + r]$ *except with probability at most* $(1 - 1/n)^{r+1}$.

Proof. By Lemma 9, at least $n - (t_s + t_a)$ honest parties contribute transactions to Blocks$[k]$. So even if t_s parties are corrupted, at least one of the $n - 2t_s$ honest parties who have tx among the first L transactions in their buffers contributes transactions to Blocks$[k]$. That party fails to include tx in the set V of transactions it chooses with probability $\binom{L-1}{L/n}/\binom{L}{L/n} = 1 - \frac{1}{n}$, and so tx is in Blocks$[k]$ except with probability at most $1 - \frac{1}{n}$. (Note that this does not take into account the fact that the adversary may be able to choose which honest parties contribute transactions to B. However, because the parties encrypt their transactions, the adversary's choice has no effect on the calculation.) If tx does not appear in Blocks$[k]$, then we can repeat the argument in all successive iterations $k + 1, \ldots, k + r$ until it does. $\qquad\square$

Theorem 4 (Liveness). *Fix $t_a \le t_s$ with $t_a + 2 \cdot t_s < n$. Then $\Pi_{\mathsf{ABC}}^{t_a,t_s}$ is t_a-live in an asynchronous network, and t_s-live in a synchronous network.*

Proof. Suppose all honest parties have received a transaction tx. If, at any point afterward, tx is not in some honest party's buffer then tx must have already been included in a block output by that party (and that block will eventually be output by all honest parties). If all honest parties have tx in their buffers, then they each have a finite number of transactions ahead of tx. By completeness, all honest parties eventually output a block in each iteration. Additionally, by Lemma 9, at least $n - (t_s + t_a)$ honest parties' inputs are incorporated into each block, and so in each iteration all but at most t_s honest parties each remove at least L/n transactions from their buffers. It follows that eventually all but at most t_s honest parties will have tx among the first L transactions in their buffers. Once that occurs, Lemma 10 implies that tx is included in the next κ blocks except with probability negligible in κ. $\qquad\square$

The above shows that a transaction received by all honest parties is eventually output. This is the standard notion of liveness in asynchronous networks. When working in a synchronous model, on the other hand, it is common to analyze liveness in more concrete terms. We provide such an analysis in the full version of the paper.

5.4   Efficiency and Choice of Parameters

The communication cost per iteration is dominated by the cost of the ACS and BLA subprotocols. Both ACS and BLA are run on pre-blocks, which have size $L \cdot |\mathsf{tx}| + O(n \cdot \kappa)$. Thus, each execution of BLA incurs cost $O(n^3 \kappa^2 + n^2 L |\mathsf{tx}| \kappa)$, and an execution of ACS incurs cost $O(n^4 \kappa + n^3 L |\mathsf{tx}|)$. The overall communication per block is therefore $O(n^4 \kappa + n^3 \kappa^2 + n^3 L |\mathsf{tx}| + n^2 L |\mathsf{tx}| \kappa)$.

At the beginning of every iteration, each honest party uniformly selects L/n transactions from among the first L transactions in its buffer. The following lemma shows that the expected number of *distinct* transactions they collectively choose is $O(L)$:

Lemma 11. *Assume the conditions of Lemma 9. In any iteration of $\Pi_{\mathsf{ABC}}^{t_a, t_s}$, the expected number of distinct transactions contributed by honest parties to the block B output by the honest parties in that iteration is at least $L/4$.*

Proof. The expectation is minimized when all honest parties have the same L transactions as the first L transactions in their buffers, so we assume this to be the case. As in Lemma 10, for some particular such transaction tx, the probability that some particular honest party fails to include tx in the set V of transactions it chooses is $1 - \frac{1}{n}$. Since, by Lemma 9, at least $n - (t_s + t_a) > n/3$ honest parties contribute transactions to B, the probability that none of those parties choose tx is at most $\left(1 - \frac{1}{n}\right)^{n/3} \leq e^{-1/3} < 3/4$, and so tx is chosen by at least one of those parties with probability at least $1/4$. (Once again, we do not take into account the fact that the adversary may be able to choose which honest parties contribute transactions because honest parties encrypt the transactions they choose.) The lemma follows by linearity of expectation.   □

Because each block contains $O(L)$ transactions, the communication cost per transaction is $O((n^4 \kappa + n^3 \kappa^2)/L + n^3 |\mathsf{tx}| + n^2 |\mathsf{tx}| \kappa)$. So for $L = \Theta(n\kappa)$, the amortized communication cost per transaction is $O(n^3 |\mathsf{tx}| + n^2 |\mathsf{tx}| \kappa)$.

We remark that although each block contains at least $L/4$ distinct transactions in expectation, it is possible that some of those transactions are not new, i.e., they may have already been included in a previous block. This is possible because honest parties may sample their input in some iteration before having finished outputting blocks in all previous iterations. Thus, the actual communication cost per transaction may be higher than what we computed above. In general, the amount of overlap between blocks will depend on the spacing parameter λ as well as the actual network conditions and the parties' local clocks. If λ is too small, some space in each block may be wasted on redundant transactions; however, setting λ to be too large could introduce unnecessary delays in a synchronous network. Understanding how different choices of λ affect our protocol's performance in various network conditions is an interesting challenge for future work.

5.5   Optimality of Our Thresholds

We show that our protocol achieves the optimal tradeoff between the security thresholds. This result does not follow immediately from the impossibility result of Blum et al. [5] for network-agnostic Byzantine agreement because reductions from BA to atomic broadcast do not trivially translate to the network-agnostic setting; however, the main ideas of their proof readily extend to the case of atomic broadcast.

Lemma 12. *Fix t_a, t_s, n with $t_a + 2t_s \geq n$. If an n-party atomic broadcast protocol is t_s-live in a synchronous network, then it cannot also be t_a-consistent in an asynchronous network.*

Proof. Assume $t_a + 2t_s = n$ and fix an ABC protocol Π. Partition the n parties into sets S_0, S_1, S_a where $|S_0| = |S_1| = t_s$ and $|S_a| = t_a$. Consider the following experiment:

- Choose uniform $m_0, m_1 \leftarrow \{0,1\}^\kappa$. At global time 0, parties in S_0 begin running Π holding only m_0 in their buffer, and parties in S_1 begin running Π holding only m_1 in their buffer.
- All communication between parties in S_0 and parties in S_1 is blocked. All other messages are delivered within time Δ.
- Create virtual copies of each party in S_a, call them S_a^0 and S_a^1. Parties in S_a^b begin running Π (at global time 0) with their buffers containing only m_b, and communicate only with each other and parties in S_b.

Compare this experiment to a hypothetical execution E_{sync} of Π in a synchronous network, in which parties in S_1 are corrupted and simply abort, and the remaining parties are honest and initially hold only (uniformly chosen) m_0 in their buffer. The views of parties $S_0 \cup S_a^0$ in the experiment are distributed identically to the views of the honest parties in E_{sync}. Thus, t_s-liveness of Π implies that in the experiment, all parties in S_0 include m_0 in some block. Moreover, since parties in S_0 never receive information about m_1, they include m_1 in any block with negligible probability. By a symmetric argument, in the experiment, all parties in S_1 include m_1 in some block, and include m_0 in any block with negligible probability.

Now, consider a hypothetical execution E_{async} of Π, this time in an asynchronous network. In this execution, parties in S_0 and S_1 are honest while parties in S_a are corrupted. The parties in S_0 and S_1 initially hold $m_0, m_1 \leftarrow \{0,1\}^\kappa$, respectively. The corrupted parties interact with parties in S_0 as if they are honest and have m_0 in their buffer, and interact with parties in S_1 as if they are honest and have m_1 in their buffer. Meanwhile, all communication between parties in S_0 and S_1 is delayed indefinitely. The views of the honest parties in this execution are distributed identically to the views of $S_0 \cup S_1$ in the above experiment, yet the conclusion of the preceding paragraph shows that t_a-consistency is violated with overwhelming probability. □

5.6 Adaptive Security

Our analysis of TARDIGRADE assumes a static adversary who must choose the set of corrupted parties prior to the start of the protocol. In fact, TARDIGRADE is not secure against an adaptive adversary, since an adaptive adversary can prevent Π_{BLA} from terminating within time $5\kappa\Delta$ by corrupting the parties who are chosen as leaders. It is possible to modify TARDIGRADE to achieve adaptive security by suitably modifying Π_{BLA} in a relatively standard way: rather than choosing a leader who acts as the only proposer, each party will act as the proposer for one instance of the propose protocol, and a leader is then chosen retroactively after all instances terminate. Designing an adaptively secure network-agnostic atomic broadcast protocol with improved communication complexity is an interesting direction for future work. (Note that the committee-based approach in the following section is not adaptively secure.)

6 Improving Complexity Using Committees

In this section, we describe an extension to TARDIGRADE that achieves lower amortized communication complexity in the presence of a static adversary. The improved protocol, UPGRADE, achieves expected communication complexity per transaction that is *linear* in n; specifically, it has expected per-transaction communication complexity $O(n\kappa|\mathsf{tx}| + \kappa^2|\mathsf{tx}|)$. This is made possible by delegating the most expensive steps of TARDIGRADE to a small committee.

To prove security for TARDIGRADE, we often used the fact that any sufficiently large subset of parties contained at least some minimum number of honest parties. We cannot assume this about the committees in UPGRADE, as the committee may be constant size, and in particular may be less than the number of corrupted parties. Instead, we prove that UPGRADE is secure in a setting with $O(\epsilon)$ fewer corrupted parties, where ϵ is a positive constant parameter of the protocol. More formally, fix t_s, t_a as before, and fix $\hat{t}_s$ such that $\hat{t}_s \leq (1 - 2\epsilon) \cdot t_s$ (for some $\epsilon > 0$); with probability $1 - e^{-O(\epsilon^2\kappa)}$, the improved ABC protocol is $\hat{t}_s$-secure in a synchronous network and t_u-secure in an asynchronous network. (Unless otherwise mentioned, all of the claims in this section hold with this probability.)

As in TARDIGRADE, we assume a trusted dealer who sets up threshold encryption and signature schemes. During the setup phase, the dealer also selects a *committee* $C \subset \{P_1, \ldots, P_n\}$ of size $O(\kappa)$ and provides each committee member $P_i \in C$ with a special credential π_i that proves P_i is on the committee. (For example, π_i might be a signature $\langle i \rangle_D$ on the index i that can be checked against the dealer's public key.) We also assume that there is a collision-resistant hash function $H : \{0,1\}^* \to \{0,1\}^\kappa$ known to all the parties.

6.1 Committee-Based Reliable Broadcast

We briefly describe a committee-based reliable broadcast protocol that will prove useful in our improved ACS construction. The basis for the committee-based protocol is a plain reliable broadcast protocol Bcast that is t_s-valid and t_a-consistent with communication complexity $O(n^2 |v|)$ a hash of the sender's input. (An example construction can be found in the full version.) The sender sends their input v individually to each of the committee members. If the hash output by the reliable broadcast matches this value, the committee members propagate v to all parties (Fig. 4).

The security analysis uses standard techniques for broadcast; for completeness, proofs can be found in the full version.

$$\Pi_{\mathsf{BB}+}^{t_a,t_s}(v)$$

Throughout, let $t_\kappa := \lfloor \frac{(1-\epsilon)\cdot\kappa\cdot t_s}{n} \rfloor$.

- If $P_i = P^*$: send input v to each $P_j \in C$, and input $h = H(v)$ to $\Pi_{\mathsf{BB}}^{t_s}$.
- Run $\Pi_{\mathsf{BB}}^{t_s}$.
- If $P_i \in C$ and $\Pi_{\mathsf{BB}}^{t_s}$ has output h': upon receiving a message v' from P^* or (v', h', π_j) from some $P_j \in C$, if $H(v') = h'$, multicast (v', h', π_i).
- Upon receiving $(v'', H(v''), \pi_j)$ from at least $t_\kappa + 1$ distinct $P_j \in C$ (even if $\Pi_{\mathsf{BB}}^{t_s}$ has not yet output a value), output v'' and terminate.

Fig. 4. A reliable broadcast protocol for sender P^* and committee C, from the perspective of party P_i.

Communication complexity of $\Pi_{\mathsf{BB}+}^{t_a,t_s}$. Running the inner broadcast on hashes of size $O(\kappa)$ has communication complexity $O(n^2\kappa)$, while sending the value, hash, and credential to all parties costs $O(n\kappa(|m| + \kappa))$. Thus, sending a message of size $|m|$ using the 'wrapped' reliable broadcast costs $O(n^2\kappa + n|m|\kappa + n\kappa^2)$, while sending it using the inner reliable broadcast alone costs $O(n^2|m|)$.

6.2 Committee-Based ACS

We can construct a committee-based ACS protocol (Fig. 5) by making two minor changes to the basic ACS protocol introduced in Sect. 4. First, the inner (non-terminating) ACS protocol is modified to use the committee-based broadcast described in Sect. 6.1. Because broadcast is used opaquely by the inner ACS protocol, this change does not require any special modifications, and the claims previously proven about the inner ACS protocol still hold. Second, the termination wrapper is modified so that only the members of the committee send the output in its entirety. Upon outputting a set S from the inner (non-terminating) ACS subprotocol, each committee member P_i multicasts S and $\langle \mathsf{commit}, H(S) \rangle_i$, along with the credential they received from the dealer. The other parties will echo signature shares and hashes, but not the set S itself.

$$\Pi_{\mathsf{ACS+}}^{t_a,t_s}(v_j)$$

Throughout, let $t_\kappa := \lfloor \frac{(1-\epsilon)\cdot\kappa\cdot t_s}{n} \rfloor$.

- Input v_j to $\Pi_{\mathsf{ACS}}^{t_a,t_s}$.
- If $P_j \in C$: upon receiving output S_j from $\Pi_{\mathsf{ACS}}^{t_a,t_s}$, compute $h := H(S_j)$ and multicast $(S_j, \langle \mathsf{commit}, h \rangle_j, \pi_j)$.
- Upon receiving at least $t_\kappa + 1$ valid signature shares $\sigma_i = \langle \mathsf{commit}, h \rangle_i$ from distinct parties in C on the same value h, form a combined signature σ for h and multicast (σ, h).
- Upon receiving a valid combined signature σ for some h, multicast σ.
- Upon holding S, σ such that σ is a combined signature for h from parties in C and S is a set such that $H(S) = h$, output S and terminate.

Fig. 5. A terminating ACS protocol with predetermined committee C, shown from the perspective of party P_j with input v_j.

The proof that $\Pi_{\mathsf{ACS+}}^{t_a,t_s}(v)$ is t_a-secure and has $\hat{t}_s$-validity with termination is very similar to the security proof for the basic ACS protocol, so we omit it.

Communication complexity of $\Pi_{\mathsf{ACS+}}^{t_a,t_s}$. As before, let $|m|$ represent the size of parties' inputs. When instantiated using the committee-based broadcast protocol from Sect. 6.1, the communication complexity of the inner ACS protocol is $O(n^3\kappa + n^2|m|\kappa + n^2\kappa^2)$. Moving on to the rest of the protocol, we see that the committee members multicast their output, a signature share, and the credential they received from the dealer. (Note that the signature share is for a hash of the output rather than the entire output.) Since the signature share, credential, and hash are each of size $O(\kappa)$, this step contributes $O(n \cdot \kappa(n \cdot |m| + \kappa)) = O(n^2\kappa \cdot |m| + n\kappa^2)$. Next, all parties multicast a combined signature of size $O(\kappa)$, for a total cost of $O(n^2\kappa)$. All together, the total cost of the improved ACS protocol is $O(n^3\kappa + n^2|m|\kappa + n^2\kappa^2)$.

6.3 An ABC Protocol with Improved Communication Complexity

Here, we give an overview of UPGRADE. Because the high-level techniques are similar to TARDIGRADE, we will highlight the key differences between the two protocols and defer further details to the full version.

The first (and simplest) difference is that wherever TARDIGRADE would run an instance of the plain ACS protocol, UPGRADE runs the improved version described in Sect. 6.2. The second difference concerns how parties choose and share their inputs, and how those inputs are combined to form a final block. At the beginning of the protocol, when parties choose a set of transactions to input, they will now also choose a second, larger input set, which is encrypted and sent only to the committee members. The committee members form the large ciphertexts into a separate pre-block, which is used to construct the final block in case ACS outputs only one small pre-block is output. Sending a large pre-block all-to-all is costly, so the committee members also form a placeholder called a *block pointer*. A block pointer contains a hash of a large pre-block and a combined signature on that hash by members of the committee. In most steps, the block pointer can be sent in place of the large pre-block. Although forming and sharing the block pointer adds some extra communication, we are able to significantly increase the expected number of distinct transactions.

References

1. Abraham, I., Devadas, S., Dolev, D., Nayak, K., Ren, L.: Efficient synchronous Byzantine consensus (2017). https://eprint.iacr.org/2017/307
2. Abraham, I., Malkhi, D., Nayak, K., Ren, L., Yin, M.: Sync HotStuff: simple and practical synchronous state machine replication. In: 2020 IEEE Symposium on Security and Privacy (SP), pp. 106–118. IEEE (2020)
3. Beerliová-Trubíniová, Z., Hirt, M., Nielsen, J.B.: On the theoretical gap between synchronous and asynchronous MPC protocols. In: Proceedings of the 29th ACM SIGACT-SIGOPS Symposium on Principles of Distributed Computing (PODC), pp. 211–218 (2010)
4. Ben-Or, M., Kelmer, B., Rabin, T.: Asynchronous secure computations with optimal resilience. In: Proceedings of the 13th Annual ACM Symposium on Principles of Distributed Computing (PODC), pp. 183–192 (1994)
5. Blum, E., Katz, J., Loss, J.: Synchronous consensus with optimal asynchronous fallback guarantees. In: Hofheinz, D., Rosen, A. (eds.) TCC 2019. LNCS, vol. 11891, pp. 131–150. Springer, Cham (2019). https://doi.org/10.1007/978-3-030-36030-6_6
6. Blum, E., Liu-Zhang, C.-D., Loss, J.: Always have a backup plan: fully secure synchronous MPC with asynchronous fallback. In: Micciancio, D., Ristenpart, T. (eds.) CRYPTO 2020. LNCS, vol. 12171, pp. 707–731. Springer, Cham (2020). https://doi.org/10.1007/978-3-030-56880-1_25
7. Bracha, G.: An asynchronous [(n−1)/3]-resilient consensus protocol. In: Proceedings of the Third Annual ACM Symposium on Principles of Distributed Computing (PODC), pp. 154–162 (1984)
8. Castro, M., Liskov, B.: Practical Byzantine fault tolerance. In: Proceedings of the Third Symposium on Operating Systems Design and Implementation, OSDI 1999, pp. 173–186. USENIX Association (1999)
9. Correia, M., Neves, N., Veríssimo, P.: From consensus to atomic broadcast: time-free Byzantine-resistant protocols without signatures. Comput. J. **49**(1), 82–96 (2006)
10. Cristian, F., Aghili, H., Strong, R., Dolev, D.: Atomic broadcast: from simple message diffusion to Byzantine agreement. Inf. Comput. **118**(1), 158–179 (1995)
11. Damgård, I., Geisler, M., Krøigaard, M., Nielsen, J.B.: Asynchronous multiparty computation: theory and implementation. In: Jarecki, S., Tsudik, G. (eds.) PKC 2009. LNCS, vol. 5443, pp. 160–179. Springer, Heidelberg (2009). https://doi.org/10.1007/978-3-642-00468-1_10
12. Duan, S., Reiter, M.K., Zhang, H.: BEAT: asynchronous BFT made practical. In: Proceedings of the 2018 ACM SIGSAC Conference on Computer and Communications Security (CCS), pp. 2028–2041 (2018)
13. Dwork, C., Lynch, N., Stockmeyer, L.: Consensus in the presence of partial synchrony. J. ACM **35**(2), 288–323 (1988)

14. Fitzi, M., Nielsen, J.B.: On the number of synchronous rounds sufficient for authenticated byzantine agreement. In: Keidar, I. (ed.) DISC 2009. LNCS, vol. 5805, pp. 449–463. Springer, Heidelberg (2009). https://doi.org/10.1007/978-3-642-04355-0_46

15. Garay, J., Kiayias, A., Leonardos, N.: The bitcoin backbone protocol: analysis and applications. In: Oswald, E., Fischlin, M. (eds.) EUROCRYPT 2015. LNCS, vol. 9057, pp. 281–310. Springer, Heidelberg (2015). https://doi.org/10.1007/978-3-662-46803-6_10

16. Guo, B., Lu, Z., Tang, Q., Xu, J., Zhang, Z.: Dumbo: faster asynchronous BFT protocols. In: Proceedings of the 2020 ACM SIGSAC Conference on Computer and Communications Security (CCS), pp. 803–818 (2020)

17. Guo, Y., Pass, R., Shi, E.: Synchronous, with a chance of partition tolerance. In: Boldyreva, A., Micciancio, D. (eds.) CRYPTO 2019. LNCS, vol. 11692, pp. 499–529. Springer, Cham (2019). https://doi.org/10.1007/978-3-030-26948-7_18

18. Kotla, R., Alvisi, L., Dahlin, M., Clement, A., Wong, E.: Zyzzyva: speculative Byzantine fault tolerance. In: Proceedings of Twenty-First ACM SIGOPS Symposium on Operating Systems Principles, SOSP 2007, pp. 45–58. ACM (2007). https://doi.org/10.1145/1294261.1294267

19. Kursawe, K.: Optimistic Byzantine agreement. In: Proceedings of the 21st IEEE Symposium on Reliable Distributed Systems, SRDS 2002, p. 262. IEEE Computer Society (2002)

20. Lamport, L., Shostak, R.E., Pease, M.C.: The Byzantine generals problem. ACM Trans. Program. Lang. Syst. 4(3), 382–401 (1982)

21. Liu, S., Viotti, P., Cachin, C., Quema, V., Vukolic, M.: XFT: practical fault tolerance beyond crashes. In: 12th USENIX Symposium on Operating Systems Design and Implementation (OSDI 16), pp. 485–500. USENIX Association, Savannah, November 2016. https://www.usenix.org/conference/osdi16/technical-sessions/presentation/liu

22. Liu-Zhang, C.-D., Loss, J., Maurer, U., Moran, T., Tschudi, D.: MPC with synchronous security and asynchronous responsiveness. In: Moriai, S., Wang, H. (eds.) ASIACRYPT 2020. LNCS, vol. 12493, pp. 92–119. Springer, Cham (2020). https://doi.org/10.1007/978-3-030-64840-4_4

23. Loss, J., Moran, T.: Combining asynchronous and synchronous byzantine agreement: the best of both worlds. Cryptology ePrint Archive, Report 2018/235 (2018). https://eprint.iacr.org/2018/235

24. Malkhi, D., Nayak, K., Ren, L.: Flexible byzantine fault tolerance. In: Proceedings of the 2019 ACM SIGSAC Conference on Computer and Communications Security (CCS), pp. 1041–1053 (2019)

25. Miller, A., Xia, Y., Croman, K., Shi, E., Song, D.: The honey badger of BFT protocols. In: Proceedings of the 2016 ACM SIGSAC Conference on Computer and Communications Security (CCS), pp. 31–42 (2016)

26. Momose, A., Ren, L.: Multi-threshold Byzantine fault tolerance. In: 28th Conference on Computer and Communications Security (CCS) (2021). https://eprint.iacr.org/2017/307

27. Mostefaoui, A., Moumen, H., Raynal, M.: Signature-free asynchronous Byzantine consensus with t¡ n/3 and o (n2) messages. In: Proceedings of the 2014 ACM Symposium on Principles of Distributed Computing (PODC), pp. 2–9 (2014)

28. Pass, R., Seeman, L., Shelat, A.: Analysis of the blockchain protocol in asynchronous networks. In: Coron, J.-S., Nielsen, J.B. (eds.) EUROCRYPT 2017. LNCS, vol. 10211, pp. 643–673. Springer, Cham (2017). https://doi.org/10.1007/978-3-319-56614-6_22

29. Pass, R., Shi, E.: Hybrid consensus: efficient consensus in the permissionless model. In: 31st International Symposium on Distributed Computing (DISC 2017). Schloss Dagstuhl-Leibniz-Zentrum fuer Informatik (2017)

30. Pass, R., Shi, E.: Thunderella: blockchains with optimistic instant confirmation. In: Nielsen, J.B., Rijmen, V. (eds.) EUROCRYPT 2018. LNCS, vol. 10821, pp. 3–33. Springer, Cham (2018). https://doi.org/10.1007/978-3-319-78375-8_1

31. Patra, A., Ravi, D.: On the power of hybrid networks in multi-party computation. IEEE Trans. Inf. Theory **64**(6), 4207–4227 (2018). https://doi.org/10.1109/TIT.2018.2827360

32. Pease, M., Shostak, R.E., Lamport, L.: Reaching agreement in the presence of faults. J. ACM **27**(2), 228–234 (1980)

Onion Routing with Replies

Christiane Kuhn[1]([✉]), Dennis Hofheinz[2]([✉]), Andy Rupp[3]([✉]),
and Thorsten Strufe[1]([✉])

[1] Karlsruhe Institute of Technology, KASTEL, Karlsruhe, Germany
{christiane.kuhn,thorsten.strufe}@kit.edu
[2] ETH Zürich, Zürich, Switzerland
hofheinz@inf.ethz.ch
[3] University of Luxembourg, Esch-sur-Alzette, Luxembourg
andy.rupp@uni.lu

Abstract. Onion routing (OR) protocols are a crucial tool for providing anonymous internet communication. An OR protocol enables a user to anonymously send requests to a server. A fundamental problem of OR protocols is how to deal with replies: ideally, we would want the server to be able to send a reply back to the anonymous user without knowing or disclosing the user's identity.

Existing OR protocols do allow for such replies, but do not provably protect the payload (i.e., message) of replies against manipulation. Kuhn et al. (IEEE S&P 2020) show that such manipulations can in fact be leveraged to break anonymity of the whole protocol.

In this work, we close this gap and provide the first framework and protocols for OR with protected replies. We define security in the sense of an ideal functionality in the universal composability model, and provide corresponding (less complex) game-based security notions for the individual properties.

We also provide two secure instantiations of our framework: one based on updatable encryption, and one based on succinct non-interactive arguments (SNARGs) to authenticate payloads both in requests and replies. In both cases, our central technical handle is an *implicit* authentication of the transmitted payload data, as opposed to an explicit, but insufficient authentication (with MACs) in previous solutions. Our results exhibit a new and surprising application of updatable encryption outside of long-term data storage.

Keywords: Privacy · Anonymity · Updatable encryption · SNARGs

1 Introduction

Onion routing. Whenever we are communicating online without further security measures, personal information is leaked. While encryption can protect the content of the communication, metadata (like who communicates with whom) still allows an adversary to learn extensive sensitive information about her victim

© International Association for Cryptologic Research 2021
M. Tibouchi and H. Wang (Eds.): ASIACRYPT 2021, LNCS 13091, pp. 573–604, 2021.
https://doi.org/10.1007/978-3-030-92075-3_20

574   C. Kuhn et al.

[18]. Mix [8] and Onion Routing (OR) Networks, like Tor [13], are crucial tools to protect communication metadata for example when accessing information on web servers or during personal chat or email communication. Intuitively, in an OR protocol, the sender encrypts the message several times (e.g. using a public-key encryption scheme), which results in an "onion".[1] This onion is then sent along a path of OR relays chosen from an overlay network. Each relay removes (only) one layer of encryption and then forwards the partially-processed onion to the next relay. The last relay as the final receiver[2] removes the innermost layer of encryption and thus retrieves the plaintext.

This technique provides a certain degree of anonymity: the first relay knows the sender, but neither message plaintext nor final receiver, while the last relay as receiver knows only the message, but not the sender. These guarantees hold even if some relays are corrupt (i.e., under control of an adversary). In fact, as long as one of the involved relays is honest (and does not share its secrets), an onion cannot be distinguished from any other onion (with a possibly different sender and/or receiver).

Open problem: onion routing with replies. Most natural use cases for internet communication are bidirectional, i.e., require a receiver to respond to the sender. However, in the above simplified description, a receiver of an OR-transmitted message has no obvious way to send a *reply* back to an anonymous sender. Note that adding a sender address in plain to the payload message would of course defeat the purpose of OR. Even encrypting the sender address, say, with the public key of the receiver (so that the receiver can use another OR communication to reply), is not appropriate as we may not always trust the receiver to protect the sender's privacy (e.g., like a newspaper agency being forced to reveal whistleblowers).

Perhaps surprisingly, this problem of "OR with replies" has not been formally addressed in the OR literature with sufficient generality (with one recent exception).[3] Hence, our goal in this work is to provide definitions and instantiations for OR protocols "with an anonymous back envelope". That is, we attempt to formalize and construct OR protocols which allow the receiver to reply to the sender *without* revealing the identity of the sender to anyone.

Related work. Before detailing our own contribution, we first start by giving context. OR and Mixing have been introduced in the early years of anonymous communication. Chaum presented the first idea of a mix network, which randomly adds delays to each message at the forwarding relays to hinder linking based on timing information to the basic concept of layered encryption and

---

[1] This name stems from the fact that in order to get to the message, several layers of encryption have to be "peeled".

[2] There are also OR protocols that allow the receiver to be unaware of the protocol and provide anonymization as a service. In such a protocol, the last relay recovers both the plaintext and the receiver address. We however focus our work on the model with a protocol aware receiver.

[3] The one exception is a work by Ando and Lysyanskaya [1]. We discuss their work, and why we believe that their solution is not sufficient, below.

source routing [8]; Goldschlag, Reed and Syverson proposed a clever setup procedure together with the same basic ideas, but decided against random delays [16], which later on led to the development of the best known anonymous communication network, Tor [13]. In the following years many solutions applied the same technique [9–12,25,26]. With increasing importance of OR and understanding of the subtleties, which allow for attacks, theoretical and formal models for OR were developed. Thereby, the problem of secure onion routing and mixing is usually divided in two subproblems [4,11]: The definition of a secure onion routing/mixing packet format (to avoid simple observing and tagging attacks) and additional measures, like methods to detect dropping adversaries (against traffic analysis attacks).

For the scope of this paper, we concentrate on the first subproblem. Thus, we ignore attacks based on timings or dropping of onions, but instead aim to construct a secure packet format, which can later be combined with different measures against timing and traffic analysis attacks.[4]

Early on, Mauw et al. [23] modeled and analyzed OR. However, this work does not contain any proposal to prove future systems secure. Backes et al.'s ideal functionality [2] models Tor and hence includes sessions and reply channels. However, it is very specific to Tor and thus rather complex and can hardly be reused for general onion routing and mix networks. The Black-Box Model of Feigenbaum et al. [14] on the other hand, oversimplifies the problem and cannot support replies either. Further approaches [6,7,19] propose some security properties, but do not give any ideal functionality or similar concept that would allow to understand their concrete implications for the users' privacy.

As the most prominent formalization without replies, Camenisch and Lysanskaya [4] defined an ideal functionality in the UC-Framework and showed properties an onion routing protocol needs to fulfill to prove its security. Proving these properties has become the preferred way to prove mix and onion routing networks secure. It has been used to prove the correction [26] of Minx [12], as well as for the security proof of Sphinx [11], a fundamental protocol for onion routing and mix networks. Sphinx splits the onion in a header and payload part and elegantly includes the keys for every forwarding relay in the header, while the payload is modified with these keys at each hop. By decoupling header and payload Sphinx allows to precalculate a header for the backward direction, which can be included in the payload to send a reply. The most eminent, recently proposed practical onion routing and mix networks [9,10,25] build on Sphinx as solution for the first subproblem to subsequently tackle the second subproblem of dropping and timing attacks, while proving the security of their adaptions to Sphinx still based on the properties of Camenisch and Lysanskaya.

---

[4] For example, we accept a packet format solution that transforms a modification attack into a dropping attack, e.g. by recognizing the modification and dropping the according onion. As dropping attacks can be solved with additional measures, this does not weaken the protocol.

However, Kuhn et al. [21] recently recognized and corrected flaws in those definitions that allowed for sincere practical consequences in the form of a *malleability attack*:

An adversary that controls the internet service provision of the sender, or the first relay as well as the receiver can easily mark the onion for later recognition by flipping bits in the payload of the onion sent by her victim. She then checks if the receiver receives some message that is not in the usual message space (e.g. not containing English language). This allows the adversary to easily learn that the victim wanted to contact the receiver (if such an unusual message was received). Otherwise, the victim must be communicating with someone else. This attack requires a very weak adversary only, but ultimately breaks the anonymity of the sender, defeating the entire purpose of the protocol.

While the corrected properties are easy enough to be used, Kuhn et al. only partially fix the situation as the models do not include support for reply messages (to the anonymous sender). Sphinx and the improved version of Minx make adaptions to the properties of Camenisch and Lysyanskaya to account for replies to some extent, but thereby they build on the flawed properties and do not treat replies correctly, thus limiting the achieved privacy [21]. Even worse, nearly all of the eminent recent network proposals claim to support anonymity for replies, while relying on the flawed properties for which the practical attack [21] was introduced at the example of HORNET [9], an OR network that was proposed as the successor of Tor.

On the work of Ando and Lysyanskaya. In a recent work [1], Ando and Lysyanskaya define an ideal functionality for repliable onion routing. They also propose corresponding properties and a protocol that satisfies their ideal functionality. In this, they partition onions in header and payload and realize replies by having the senders pre-compute another header for the reply path. They alter the header and payload deterministically and check the header's integrity at each hop on the path, but they do not check the payload's integrity until the onion is at its final destination.

Thus the above malleability attack still works: Assume an adversarial first relay P_1 and receiver. P_1 modifies the payload of the (forward) onion, i.e. replaces the payload ciphertext C_2 in [1] with randomness. The next honest relays process the onion as usual without noticing this, as [1] uses *mere end-to-end* integrity protection for the payload. Only the adversarial receiver can notice the payload manipulation as the verification fails. This is the signal for the adversary that this is the onion she tampered with earlier. While the message is lost, the adversary learns critical metadata: who wanted to contact the receiver (e.g. the regime, hosting own relays and pressuring newspapers, learns who tried to anonymously contact the newspaper), unacceptable for practical protocols like [9,10].

While Ando and Lysyanskaya target the same setting, they avoid the challenge imposed by the above malleability attack [21] by explicitly allowing it in their ideal functionality, which allows them to work with traditional malleability protection: a "postponed" integrity check at the destination. This however even strengthens the simple, yet effective de-anonymizing malleability attack on the payload, as the receiver now realizes the failed integrity check and does not even have to compare with the expected message space. Therefore, the question of a *secure*, repliable OR scheme is still unanswered.

A technical challenge with practical relevance. The goal we are aiming at is not only useful, but also technically difficult to achieve. First of all, practically prominent protocols and packet formats [9, 11, 26] require that *any reply is indistinguishable from any forward request*, except at the sender and receiver. In particular, all parts of the onions in both directions should look alike, and must be treated according to the same processing rules. This is necessary to provide senders that expect replies with a sufficiently large anonymity set even if there is only a small amount of reply packets, because they are hidden under all forward traffic.

To prevent the malleability attack [21], tampering by a potentially corrupt relay must become detectable. Theoretically, conventional payload authentication for all forward layers, e.g., with MACs precalculated by the sender, is sufficient. However, both Ando and Lysyanskaya [1] and practical proposals [9] require indistinguishability of forward and reply onions. Extending authentication also to the reply payload is challenging: The original sender cannot precalculate those authentication tags as the reply payload is unknown and we cannot necessarily assume that the receiver is honest. Letting the reply sender (= original receiver) precalculate the authentication tags enables an attack similar to the malleability attack: the malicious reply sender (= receiver) together with the last relay can recognize the reply onion (without modifying its payload on the way) simply based on the known authentication tags; thus letting the attacker learn the same metadata as in the malleability attack. Hence, payload protection in the reply setting is the real challenge towards a practical solution.

Our contribution. In this work, we present a framework for repliable OR, along with two different instantiations (with different properties). Our framework protects against malleability attacks on the payload, while even guaranteeing that replies are indistinguishable from original requests. In our approach, hence, both requests and replies are authenticated *implicitly* (i.e., without MACs) at each step along the way.

From a definitional point of view, we express these requirements by an ideal functionality (in the UC framework) which does not reveal the onion's path, message or direction to the adversary (unless all involved routers are corrupt; further a corrupt receiver of course learns the message and direction). This translates to strong game-based properties, which are proven to imply the security in the sense of that ideal functionality.

We also present two protocols that realize this ideal functionality. Both of our OR protocols are in fact similar to existing protocols, and are partially inspired by the popular Sphinx approach [11] and the Shallot scheme of Ando and Lysyanskaya [1]. The main conceptual difference to previous work is that the authentication of the (encrypted) payload happens *implicitly* in our case.

Our first protocol uses updatable encryption (UE), a variant of symmetric[5] encryption that provides both re-randomizable ciphertexts (and in fact RCCA security [5] and plaintext integrity) and re-randomizable keys, as a central primitive. Intuitively, using UE for encrypting the payload message (in both communication directions) enables a form of "implicit authentication" of ciphertexts, and hence thwarts malleability attacks without explicit MACs on the payload.

Our second protocol is based on succinct non-interactive arguments (SNARGs [3,24]), a variant of zero-knowledge arguments with compact proofs. Intuitively, SNARGs enable every relay *and* the receiver to prove that they have processed (or replied to) their input onion according to the protocol. This way, no explicit authentication of the payload data is necessary, since the SNARGs guarantee that no "content-changing" modification of the payload took place.

Neither of our protocols indeed are competitive in efficiency with existing OR protocols. Further, our protocols require a trusted setup. This is due to the introduction of new concepts and techniques for qualitatively stronger security properties. Our work however represents an important conceptual first step towards an efficient *and* secure solution.

A closer look at our UE-based protocol. We start by outlining the basic ideas of our protocol based on updatable encryption (UE).

UE originally targets the scenario of securely outsourcing data to a semi-trusted cloud server. To enable efficient key rotation, i.e., updating the stored ciphertexts to a freshly chosen key, UE schemes allow the generation of update tokens based on the old and new key. Given such a token the server can autonomously lift a ciphertext encrypted with the old key to a ciphertext encrypted with the new key. Of course, the token itself may not leak information about the old nor the new key to the cloud server. Despite this update feature, UE schemes should satisfy security properties similar to regular authenticated symmetric encryption schemes like IND-CPA/RCCA/CCA type of security along with INT-PTXT or INT-CTXT security (when excluding trivial wins resulting from corrupting certain keys and tokens). An additional property, which make them especially interesting for our purposes is that some provide unlinkability of ciphertext updates, i.e., an updated ciphertext does not provide information about its old version (even given the old key).

The basic idea to exploit UE for secure onion routing with replies is simple: the sender encrypts its request using an UE scheme and provides each relay, using a header construction similar to Sphinx, with an update token to unlinkably transform this request. Similarly, the receiver is equipped with the corresponding decryption key and a fresh encryption key for the backward path.

More precisely, each onion $O = (\eta, \delta)$ consists of two components:

– a *header* η which contains encrypted key material with which routers can process and (conventionally) authenticate the header itself, and

---

[5] Although being a variant of symmetric encryption, UE schemes typically make use of public-key techniques to achieve updatability through malleability.

– the UE-encrypted *payload* δ; each router will use a UE update token to re-randomize and re-encrypt δ under a different (hidden) key.

The structure of η is similar to the Sphinx and Shallot protocols. Namely, each layer contains a public-key encryption (under the public key of the respective relay) of ephemeral keys that encrypt the next layer (including the address of the next relay), and authentication information with which to verify this layer. Additionally, in our case each layer also contains an encrypted token which can be used to update the payload ciphertext δ and we include the backward path in the header as well. All of this header information can be precomputed by the sender for both communication directions (i.e., for the path from sender to receiver, and for the return path).

After processing the header (i.e., decrypting, verifiying, and applying the UE token to the payload), each relay pads the so-extracted header for the next relay suitably with randomness, so that it is not clear how far along the onion has been processed. At some point, the decrypted header will contain a receiver symbol and a UE decryption key to indicate that processing of the onion in the forward direction has finished.

The header will then contain also a UE encryption key and enough information for the receiver to prepare a "backwards onion", i.e., an onion with the same format for the return path. We stress that all header parts of this "backwards onion", including UE tokens and authentication parts, are precomputed by the initial sender. The receiver merely UE-encrypts the payload and adds padding similarly to relays during processing.

Processing on the return path works similarly, only that eventually, the initial sender is contacted with the (still UE-encrypted) reply payload. The sender can then decrypt the payload using a precomputed UE key.

We stress that there is no explicit check that the payload δ is still intact at any point. However, the demanded UE security guarantees that re-encryption of invalid UE ciphertexts will fail.

More precisely, we require an UE scheme with strong properties, namely RCCA security, plaintext integrity and perfect re-encryption under *ciphertext-independent* re-encryption of *arbitrary* (i.e., even maliciously formed) ciphertexts. RCCA security and plaintext integrity ensure that valid payloads from an honest sender cannot be modified or replaced by adversarially generated payloads. Perfect re-encryption ensures that a payload encryption observed along the forward/backward path does not leak the position in the path. This property also implies the unlinkability of ciphertext updates. Allowing re-encryption of arbitrary ciphertexts in the UE security games (what many UE schemes do not consider) is crucial in our scenario as the relays who will perform re-encryption might be easily confronted with adversarially crafted ciphertexts which they need to reject. Also the property that update tokens can be generated independently of the ciphertext to be updated is essential for our application as otherwise the anonymous sender could not pre-compute the tokens for the backward path.

Considering the requirements from above, we are currently only aware of a single suitable UE scheme which is a construction by Klooss, Lehmann, and

Rupp [20] based on (the malleability of) Groth-Sahai proofs. Unfortunately, instantiating our protocol with their UE scheme leads to payload parts of the onion which are comparatively large: Their underlying algebraic structure is a pairing-based group setting $e : \mathbb{G}_1 \times \mathbb{G}_2 \rightarrow \mathbb{G}_T$. To encrypt a single $\mathbb{G}_1$-element, the payload part contains 58 $\mathbb{G}_1$-and 44 $\mathbb{G}_2$-elements. For realistic group (bit)sizes of, say, $|\mathbb{G}_1| = 256$ and $|\mathbb{G}_2| = 512$, we obtain a payload size of about 4.5 kilobytes for 256 bits of communicated message. The header part of the onion is about half as large for small pathlengths, and using conventional state-of-the art building blocks, a full onion (including header and payload) comes out at about $4.5 + N$ kilobytes, where N is the maximal length of a path, i.e., the number of hops between sender and receiver (cf. our extended version [22] for details). Processing an onion at a relay is dominated by the cost to perform the re-encryption of the payload which requires about 110 $\mathbb{G}_1$- and 90 $\mathbb{G}_2$-exponentiations [20].

A closer look at our SNARG-based protocol. Our SNARG-based protocol works conceptually similarly, but with two differences:

- First, the payload is enclosed by multiple symmetric encryption layers (one for each relay). This is very similar to previous approaches [1,11], but also opens the door to malleability attacks.
- Second, in order to prevent such malleability attacks, each layer contains a concise SNARG proof on top of header and payload, which proves that this onion is the result of (a) a fresh onion as constructed by a sender, (b) a fresh backwards onion as constructed by a receiver, or (c) a legitimate processing of another onion (with valid SNARG proof). In essence, this SNARG proof avoids malleability attacks by inductively proving that this onion has gone only through valid onion generation or processing steps.

We note that the SNARG proof may need to show that this onion is the result of an honest processing of another onion *with valid SNARG proof*. Hence, we need to be careful in designing the corresponding SNARG language in a recursive way while avoiding circularities. This recursive and self-referential nature of our language is also the reason why we use SNARGs (as opposed to "regular" zero-knowledge techniques with larger proofs).

Our SNARG-based onions are in fact smaller (for small pathlengths N) than the ones from our UE-based protocol. Using the SNARKs of Groth and Maller [17] (and state-of-the-art conventional building blocks), we obtain onions with an additive overhead (over the message size) of $128N^2 + 448N + 192(2N - 1) + 160$ bytes (cf. our extended version [22] for details). The perhaps surprising quadratic term in the maximal pathlength N stems from the fact that we require additional encryptions of *all* previous onion headers to enable a recursive extraction of previous onion states.

However, due to our somewhat complex SNARG language, we expect that the actual processing time of our SNARG-based approach (which involves constructing SNARG proofs at each processing step) will be considerably higher than the one from our UE-based protocol.

Performance in comparison to Ando and Lysyanskaya. While Ando and Lysyanskaya do not provide concrete efficiency calculations, conceptually their and our (time and space) overhead are similar *except* for the parts related to updatable encryption, resp. SNARGs. For realistic security parameters, these parts dominate the header overhead. This is the price one has to pay for preventing the malleability attack from [21] while making reply onions indistinguishable from request onions as desired by practical protocols like HORNET [9].

After all, this is the first paper providing immunity in this strong sense, and while we do not claim optimality of our constructions, we are convinced they are the basis for a real-world improvement in communication privacy.

2 Notation

We use the superscript $x^{\leftarrow}$ to denote the corresponding entity on the backwards path. For example, while P_1 is the first router on the forwards path, $P_1^{\leftarrow}$ is the first router on the backwards path. Further, we use the notation as summarized in the following table:

Notation	Meaning
$\|$	Concatenation of strings
λ	The security parameter
$\mathcal{P}$	An onion path
m	A message
P_i	For the i-th router name on the forward path, P_0 (usually $= P_{n+1}^{\leftarrow}$) is the forward sender and $P_{n+1}(= P_0^{\leftarrow})$ the forward receiver
PK_i	Public key of P_i
SK_i	Private key of P_i
O_i	$= (\eta_i, \delta_i)$ is the i-th forward onion layer to be processed by P_i
η_i	The header of O_i
δ_i	The payload of O_i
FormOnion	The function to build a new onion as a sender
ProcOnion	The function to process an onion at a relay
ReplyOnion	The function to reply to a received onion as receiver

3 Model and Ideal Functionality

We first define our assumptions and model for repliable OR and then describe our desired security as the ideal functionality. Our model extends the OR scheme definition of [4] as used in [21] by adding an algorithm to create replies. Our ideal functionality extends the one of [4] as used in [21] and has similarities to [1], but is strictly stronger as it requires protection against malleability attacks on the payload.

3.1   Assumptions

We make the following assumptions that result from commonly used techniques to ensure unlinkability of onion layers on criteria other than the concrete representation of the onion.

As in earlier examples, we assume the existence of public keys PK for all relays.

Assumption 1. *The sender knows the (authentic) public keys PK_i of all relays P_i it uses (e.g., by means of a PKI).*

To ensure that packets cannot be linked based on their size, all onions are padded to the same, fixed size (otherwise the largest incoming onion could trivially be linked to the largest outgoing onion). As the path information has to be encoded in the onion, fixing the size also entails an upper bound for the length of the routing path.

Assumption 2. *The protocol's maximum path length is N.*

To ensure that packets cannot be linked based on the included routing path, the sender includes the routing information encrypted for each forwarder, such that any forwarder only learns the next hop of the routing path. We assume that the routing information is included in a header, while the message is included in the payload of the onion.

Assumption 3. *Each onion O consists of a header η and a payload δ.*

To ensure that packets cannot be linked based on duplicate attacks, i.e. the onion of the victim is duplicated at the first corrupted relay and observed twice at the corresponding receiver, duplicates have to be detected and dropped. We support duplicate detection with deterministically evolving headers, which allows to also protect from duplicated replies. Thus, even though the (forward) receiver is allowed to decide on her answer arbitrarily, we can still detect if she tries to send multiple different answers to the same request[6]. As some related work wrongly adapted proof strategies for OR schemes where the duplicate detection is solely based on *parts of the onion*, we deliberately build this model for OR-schemes allowing for such protocols.[7]

---

[6] Note that our scope is a secure message format. Traffic analysis protection, like e.g. recognizing duplicated onions, has to happen *additionally* to our message format, but assuming that such a protection is in place allows for simplified proofs even for the message format.

[7] Practically, this assumption is often ensured by storing the seen headers in an efficient way, e.g. Bloom filters, until a router's key pair is changed or the current epoch expires if the protocol works in time epochs. The change of key pairs can be expressed in our framework by replacing a router identity by a fresh one ("Bob2020" becomes "Bob2025").

Assumption 4. *Duplicates, i.e. onions O_i, O'_i with the same header $\eta_i = \eta'_i$, lead to a fail for every but the first such onion that is given to $ProcOnion(SK_i, O_i, P_i)$ except with negligible probability.*

To ensure the best chances that an honest relay is on the path, the honest sender will pick a path without any repetition in the relays (acyclic).[8]

Assumption 5. *Each honestly chosen path $\mathcal{P}$ is acyclic.*

While true for, to our knowledge, all protocols, we use the following processing order as an assumption in our proofs:

Assumption 6. *Each onion is processed by the receiver, before it is replied to.*

3.2   Modeling Replies

We extend the definition of an onion routing scheme [4] as used in [21] with an algorithm to send replies, similar to [1].

Definition 1 (Repliable OR Scheme). *A Repliable OR Scheme is a tuple of PPT algorithms $(G, \text{FormOnion}, \text{ProcOnion}, \text{ReplyOnion})$ defined as:*

Key generation. *$G(1^\lambda, p, P_i)$ outputs a key pair (PK_i, SK_i) on input of the security parameter 1^λ, some public parameters p and a router identity P_i.*

Forming an onion. *$\text{FormOnion}(i, \mathcal{R}, m, \mathcal{P}^\rightarrow, \mathcal{P}^\leftarrow, (PK)_{\mathcal{P}^\rightarrow}, (PK)_{\mathcal{P}^\leftarrow})$ returns an i-th[9] onion layer O_i ($i = 1$ for sending) on input of $i \leq n+n^\leftarrow +2$ (for $i > n+1$, m is the reply message and O_i the backward onion layer), randomness $\mathcal{R}$, message m, a forward path $\mathcal{P}^\rightarrow = (P_1, \ldots, P_{n+1})$, a backward path $\mathcal{P}^\leftarrow = (P_1^\leftarrow, \ldots, P_{n^\leftarrow+1}^\leftarrow)$, public keys $(PK)_{\mathcal{P}^\rightarrow} = (PK_1, \ldots, PK_{n+1})$ of the relays on the forward path, and public keys $(PK)_{\mathcal{P}^\leftarrow} = (PK'_1, \ldots, PK'_{n^\leftarrow+1})$ of the relays on the backward path. The backward path can be empty if the onion is not intended to be repliable.*

Forwarding an onion. *$\text{ProcOnion}(SK, O, P)$ outputs the next onion layer and router identity (O', P') on input of an onion layer O, a router identity P and P's secret key SK. (O', P') equals $(\perp, \perp)$ in case of an error or $(m, \perp)$ if P is the recipient.*

Replying to an onion. *$\text{ReplyOnion}(m^\leftarrow, O, P, SK)$ returns a reply onion $O^\leftarrow$ along with the next router $P^\leftarrow$ on input of a received (forward) onion O, a reply message $m^\leftarrow$, the receiver identity P and its secret key SK. $O^\leftarrow$ and $P^\leftarrow$ attains $\perp$ in case of an error.*

Correctness. We want the onions to take the paths and deliver the messages that were chosen as the input to FormOnion resp. ReplyOnion.

---

[8] Note that our adversary model trusts the sender and hence this assumption is merely a restriction of how the protocol works and the sender does not need to prove a correct choice to anyone.

[9] During normal operation only $i = 1$ is used. The possibility to form onion layers for $i > 1$ (without using ProcOnion) is needed for our security definitions and proofs.

Definition 2 (Correctness). *Let* $(G, FormOnion, ProcOnion, \text{ReplyOnion})$ *be a repliable OR scheme with maximal path length* N. *Then for all* $n, n^{\leftarrow} < N$, $\lambda \in \mathbb{N}$, *all choices of the public parameter* p, *all choices of the randomness* $\mathcal{R}$, *all choices of forward and backward paths* $\mathcal{P}^{\rightarrow} = (P_1, \ldots, P_{n+1})$ *and* $\mathcal{P}^{\leftarrow} = (P_1^{\leftarrow}, \ldots, P_{n^{\leftarrow}+1}^{\leftarrow})$, *all* $(PK_i^{(\leftarrow)}, SK_i^{(\leftarrow)})$ *generated by* $G(1^{\lambda}, p, P_i^{(\leftarrow)})$, *all messages* $m, m^{\leftarrow}$, *all possible choices of internal randomness used by ProcOnion and* ReplyOnion, *the following needs to hold:*

Correctness of forward path. $Q_i = P_i$, *for* $1 \leq i \leq n$ *and* $Q_1 := P_1$, $O_1 \leftarrow$
   FormOnion $(1, \mathcal{R}, m, (P_1, \ldots, P_{n+1}), (P_1^{\leftarrow}, \ldots, P_{n^{\leftarrow}+1}^{\leftarrow}), (PK_1, \ldots, PK_{n+1}),$
   $(PK_1^{\leftarrow}, \ldots, PK_{n^{\leftarrow}+1}^{\leftarrow})), (O_{i+1}, Q_{i+1}) \leftarrow \text{ProcOnion}(SK_i, O_i, Q_i).$
Correctness of request reception. $(m, \perp) = \text{ProcOnion}(SK_{n+1}, O_{n+1}, P_{n+1})$
Correctness of backward path. $Q_i^{\leftarrow} = P_i^{\leftarrow}$, *for* $1 \leq i \leq n$
   and $(O_1^{\leftarrow}, Q_1^{\leftarrow}) \leftarrow \text{ReplyOnion}(m^{\leftarrow}, O_{n+1}, P_{n+1}, SK_{n+1})$, $(O_{i+1}^{\leftarrow}, Q_{i+1}^{\leftarrow}) \leftarrow$
   $\text{ProcOnion}(SK_i^{\leftarrow}, O_i^{\leftarrow}, Q_i^{\leftarrow}).$
Correctness of reply reception. $(m^{\leftarrow}, \perp) = \text{ProcOnion}(SK_{n^{\leftarrow}+1}^{\leftarrow}, O_{n^{\leftarrow}+1}^{\leftarrow}, P_{n^{\leftarrow}+1}^{\leftarrow})$

Recognizing onions. To define our security properties, we need a way to recognize if an onion O provided by the adversary resulted from processing a given onion O^*. To this end, we define the algorithm $\text{RecognizeOnion}(i, O, \mathcal{R}, m, \mathcal{P}^{\rightarrow}, \mathcal{P}^{\leftarrow}, (PK)_{\mathcal{P}^{\rightarrow}}, (PK)_{\mathcal{P}^{\leftarrow}})$, which uses the given inputs (that have been used to create the onion O^* in the first place) to form the i-th layer of the onion O_i^* using FormOnion and then compares the header of O_i^* to the header of the onion O in question. If the headers[10] are identical, it returns *True*, otherwise *False*.

Note that the "correctness" of FormOnion and RecognizeOnion for $i > 1$ is defined implicitly as part of our security properties in Sect. 4.

3.3   Ideal Functionality

Informally, as long as the sender is honest we want that the adversary can only learn the parts of the onion's path (and associated reply's path), where she corrupted all relays. This includes especially the following three facts:

1. The adversary cannot link onion layers before and after any honest relay.
2. The adversary cannot learn the included message, unless she controls the receiver.
3. The adversary cannot distinguish whether onions are on the forward or backward path, unless she controls the receiver and the onion is either the last layer before (forward) reception, or the first layer of her reply.

Note that this especially includes that she also cannot link layers based on malleability attacks on the payload. See our extended version [22] for details.

---

[10] We define RecognizeOnion and the duplicate detection on the header as this is common practice.

4   New Properties

We now define our security properties and show that if they are fulfilled, our ideal functionality is realized.

The ideal functionality requires that the adversary only learns parts of the onion's real path; the subpaths from each honest relay until the next honest relay. Our idea is to replace any real sequence of onion layers that is observed on such a subpath, with a random sequence that only is equal in the information learned by the adversary, i.e., the allowed leakage of the ideal functionality. More precisely, this information relates to the subpath the adversary controls. It extends to the plaintext of the message, and the fact if the onion is at forward or backward layers, if she also controls the receiver. For replacement, we distinguish three types of subpaths and introduce one property for each type, challenging the adversary to distinguish the real and a random layer sequence for this specific subpath type. The types are: a subpath that is part of the forward path (Forwards Layer-Unlinkability), one that is part of the backward path (Backwards Layer-Unlinkability) and one that includes parts of the forward and backward path as the receiver is corrupted (Repliable Tail-Indistinguishability).

Forward Path: We first require that the layers on the forward path can be replaced by *random* ones. Therefore, we extend Layer-Unlinkability from [21] with oracles for the creation of replies and illustrate the property in Fig. 1.

Thereby, we challenge the adversary to distinguish between (a) an onion created according to her choices from (b) a random onion that takes the same path from the sender to the first honest relay. We use oracles to allow for processing of and replying to (other) onions at the honest relays. Due to duplicate checks, these oracles only return a processed onion if no onion with this header was processed before (Assumption 4) and only return a reply onion if the onion was processed before (Assumption 6). Further, the oracle after the challenge has to treat the challenge onion with care: if it is processed or replied to (depending if the honest relay is an intermediate relay or the receiver), a onion fitting to the original choice is constructed with FormOnion and returned.

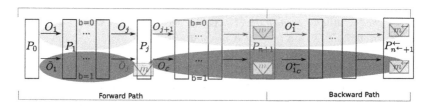

Fig. 1. Forwards Layer-Unlinkability illustrated: Red boxes are corrupted relays, black honest relays, orange ellipses are the $b = 0$ and the blue the $b = 1$ case. $\bar{m}$ is a random message. The main idea is that the adversary cannot distinguish between real and random onions *before* P_j. (Color figure online)

Definition 3 (Forwards Layer-Unlinkability $LU^{\rightarrow}$). *Forwards Layer Unlinkability is defined as:*

1. *The adversary receives the router names P_H, P_S and challenge public keys PK_S, PK_H, chosen by the challenger by letting $(PK_H, SK_H) \leftarrow G(1^\lambda, p, P_H)$ and $(PK_S, SK_S) \leftarrow G(1^\lambda, p, P_S)$.*
2. *Oracle access: The adversary may submit any number of Proc and Reply requests for P_H or P_S to the challenger. For any Proc(P_H, O), the challenger checks whether η is on the η^H- list. If not, it sends the output of ProcOnion(SK_H, O, P_H), stores η on the η^H-list and O on the O^H-list. For any Reply(P_H, O, m) the challenger checks if O is on the O^H- list and if so, the challenger sends ReplyOnion(m, O, P_H, SK_H) to the adversary. (Similar for requests on P_S with the η^S-list).*
3. *The adversary submits a message m, a position j with $1 \leq j \leq n+1$, a path $\mathscr{P}^{\rightarrow} = (P_1, \ldots, P_j, \ldots, P_{n+1})$ with $P_j = P_H$, a path $\mathscr{P}^{\leftarrow} = (P_1^{\leftarrow}, \ldots, P_{n^{\leftarrow}+1}^{\leftarrow} = P_S)$ and public keys for all nodes PK_i ($1 \leq i \leq n+1$ for the nodes on the path and $n+1 < i$ for the other relays).*
4. *The challenger checks that the chosen paths are acyclic, the router names are valid and that the same key is chosen if the router names are equal, and if so, sets $PK_j = PK_H$ and $PK_{n^{\leftarrow}+1}^{\leftarrow} = PK_S$ and picks $b \in \{0,1\}$ at random.*
5. *The challenger creates the onion with the adversary's input choice and honestly chosen randomness $\mathscr{R}$: $O_1 \leftarrow$ FormOnion$(1, \mathscr{R}, m, \mathscr{P}^{\rightarrow}, \mathscr{P}^{\leftarrow}, (PK)_{\mathscr{P}^{\rightarrow}}, (PK)_{\mathscr{P}^{\leftarrow}})$ and a replacement onion with the first part of the forward path $\bar{\mathscr{P}}^{\rightarrow} = (P_1, \ldots, P_j)$, a random message $\bar{m} \in \mathcal{M}$, another honestly chosen randomness $\bar{\mathscr{R}}$, and an empty backward path $\bar{\mathscr{P}}^{\leftarrow} = ()$: $\bar{O}_1 \leftarrow$ FormOnion$(1, \bar{\mathscr{R}}, \bar{m}, \bar{\mathscr{P}}^{\rightarrow}, \bar{\mathscr{P}}^{\leftarrow}, (PK)_{\bar{\mathscr{P}}^{\rightarrow}}, (PK)_{\bar{\mathscr{P}}^{\leftarrow}})$*
6. *If $b = 0$, the challenger gives O_1 to the adversary. Otherwise, the challenger gives $\bar{O}_1$ to the adversary.*
7. *Oracle access:*

   If $b = 0$, the challenger processes all oracle requests as in step 2).

   Otherwise, the challenger processes all requests as in step 2) except for:
   - *If $j < n+1$: Proc(P_H, O) with RecognizeOnion$(j, O, \bar{\mathscr{R}}, m, \mathscr{P}^{\rightarrow}, \mathscr{P}^{\leftarrow}, (PK)_{\mathscr{P}^{\rightarrow}}, (PK)_{\mathscr{P}^{\leftarrow}}) = True$, η is not on the η^H-list and ProcOnion$(SK_H, O, P_H) \neq \bot$:*
     The challenger outputs (P_{j+1}, O_c) with $O_c \leftarrow$ FormOnion$(j+1, \mathscr{R}, m, \mathscr{P}^{\rightarrow}, \mathscr{P}^{\leftarrow}, (PK)_{\mathscr{P}^{\rightarrow}}, (PK)_{\mathscr{P}^{\leftarrow}})$ and adds η to the η^H-list and O to the O^H-list.
   - *If $j = n+1$:*
     * *Proc(P_H, O) with RecognizeOnion$(j, O, \bar{\mathscr{R}}, m, \mathscr{P}^{\rightarrow}, \mathscr{P}^{\leftarrow}, (PK)_{\mathscr{P}^{\rightarrow}}, (PK)_{\mathscr{P}^{\leftarrow}}) = True$, η is not on the η^H-list and ProcOnion$(SK_H, O, P_H) \neq \bot$:*
       The challenger outputs $(m, \bot)$ and adds η to the η^H-list and O to the O^H-list.
     * *Reply$(P_H, O, m^{\leftarrow})$ with RecognizeOnion$(j, O, \bar{\mathscr{R}}, m, \mathscr{P}^{\rightarrow}, \mathscr{P}^{\leftarrow}, (PK)_{\mathscr{P}^{\rightarrow}}, (PK)_{\mathscr{P}^{\leftarrow}}) = True$, O is on the O^H- list and has not been replied before and ReplyOnion$(m^{\leftarrow}, O, P_H, SK_H) \neq \bot$:*

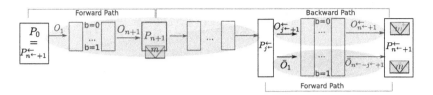

Fig. 2. Backwards Layer-Unlinkability illustrated: Red boxes are corrupted relays, black honest relays, orange ellipses are the $b = 0$ and the blue the $b = 1$ case. The main idea is that the adversary cannot distinguish between real and random onions after $P_j^\leftarrow$. (Color figure online)

> The challenger outputs $(P_1^\leftarrow, O_c)$ with $O_c \leftarrow FormOnion(j +$
> $1, \mathcal{R}, m^\leftarrow, \mathcal{P}^\rightarrow, \mathcal{P}^\leftarrow, (PK)_{\mathcal{P}\rightarrow}, (PK)_{\mathcal{P}\leftarrow})$

8. The adversary produces guess b'.

$LU^\rightarrow$ is achieved if any probabilistic polynomial time (PPT) adversary $\mathcal{A}$, cannot guess $b' = b$ with a probability non-negligibly better than $\frac{1}{2}$.

Note that by using the real processing for the oracle in step 7 for $b = 0$ and the recognition and a newly formed onion layer for $j + 1$ in $b = 1$, it follows that both RecognizeOnion and FormOnion have to adhere to their intuition, i.e. with overwhelming probability only the challenge onion is recognized and the newly formed layer has to be indistinguishable to the real processing.

Backward Path: Additionally, we build a reverse version of Layer-Unlinkability for the backward path and illustrate the property *Backwards Layer-Unlinkability* $LU^\leftarrow$ in Fig. 2. This definition is similar to $LU^\rightarrow$, but the challenge is to distinguish a reply from randomness. We thus return the challenge onion in a special case of the second oracle (step 7 in $LU^\rightarrow$) and the forward onion is always constructed to the adversary's choice (instead of step 6 in $LU^\rightarrow$). The challenge onion either contains the layers of the reply constructed to the adversary's choices (including the chosen reply message) or random *forward* layers with a random message. As these two cases are trivially distinguishable by processing the challenge onion at the honest original sender (i.e. backwards receiver), we ensure that the oracle denies to do this final processing of the challenge onion. This corresponds to the real world in which our trusted sender does not share any received message with the adversary. For a formal definition of this property see our extended version [22].

Notice that we pick the random replacements to be *forward onion layers*. Thus the property $LU^\leftarrow$ implies indistinguishability between forward and backward onions for intermediates (otherwise the adversary could distinguish the real (backward) onion from the fake (forward) onion).

Between forward and backward path: Finally, we want to replace the layers between the last honest relay on the forward and the first honest relay on the backward path with random ones. Note that the replaced part of the path contains an adversarial receiver. For the replacement in this case, we extend

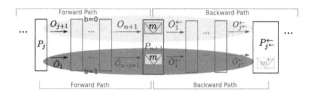

Fig. 3. Repliable Tail-Indistinguishability illustrated: Red boxes are corrupted relays, black honest relays, orange ellipses are the $b = 0$ and the blue the $b = 1$ case. While the adversary can learn the behavior between *between* P_j and $P_{j\leftarrow}^{\leftarrow}$ she cannot connect it to anything before P_j and after $P_{j\leftarrow}^{\leftarrow}$. (Color figure online)

Tail-Indistinguishability from [21] with oracles for the creation of replies and illustrate the property *Repliable Tail-Indistinguishability* $TI^{\leftrightarrow}$ in Fig. 3. As we can already replace all other layers before and after this part of the path with random ones due to the Layer Unlinkability properties, the $TI^{\leftrightarrow}$ property does not output anything for these layers. We thus, start outputting the challenge layers only *after* the honest relay P_j on the forward path and refuse processing of the challenge onion at the honest relay on the backwards path $P_{j\leftarrow}^{\leftarrow}$ in our oracle (similar to $LU^{\leftarrow}$). The challenge onion hence either contains the layers after P_j of an onion build according to the adversary's choices or random layers that take the same part of the path and carry the same message, but for an onion that actually starts at P_j and ends (with the backwards path) at $P_{j\leftarrow}^{\leftarrow}$. For a formal definition of this property see our extended version [22].

Properties imply ideal functionality. As argued in the beginning of this section, we built the properties to step by step replace the real onion layers between honest relays with random ones that only coincide with the real ones in information that the ideal functionality allows to leak. By applying one property for each subpath between honest relays at a time, similar to earlier proofs [4,21], we show that these properties imply the ideal functionality in our extended version [22]. From here on, we call any OR scheme that fulfills our properties a *secure, repliable OR scheme*.

5   Our UE-Based Scheme

5.1   Building Blocks

Our construction makes use of the generic building blocks listed below. Due to the page limit, we restrict to only elaborate on the less common and more complex building block of updatable encryption while referring to our extended version [22] for formal definitions of the more common building blocks.

- an asymmetric CCA2-secure encryption scheme (to encrypt ephemeral keys) with encryption and decryption algorithms denoted by $\mathsf{PK.Enc}_{PK_i}$ and $\mathsf{PK.Dec}_{SK_i}$ when used with public key PK_i and secret key SK_i,

- a PRP-CCA secure symmetric encryption scheme (to encrypt routing information) of length L_1 with encryption and decryption algorithms denoted by $\mathsf{PRP.Enc}_{k^\eta}$ and $\mathsf{PRP.Dec}_{k^\eta}$ when used with the symmetric key k^η,
- an SUF-CMA secure message authentication code (to protect the header) with tag generation and verification algorithm denoted by MAC_{k^γ} and Ver_{k^γ} when used with the symmetric key k^γ,
- a sufficiently secure (see below) updatable encryption scheme (to protect the payload) with encryption, decryption and re-encryption algorithms denoted by $\mathsf{UE.Enc}_{k^\Delta}$, $\mathsf{UE.Dec}_{k^\Delta}$ and $\mathsf{UE.ReEnc}_\Delta$ when used with keys k^Δ and tokens Δ. We assume that keys and tokens are of the same length or padded to the same length. Further, all messages are padded to the same length.

Updatable Encryption. Roughly speaking, an updatable encryption (UE) scheme is a symmetric encryption scheme with an extra re-encryption functionality moving ciphertexts from an old to a new key. In the following, we recapitulate the definitions of an UE scheme providing RCCA security and plaintext integrity given in [20].

Security for UE is defined based on a notion of time which evolves in epochs. Data is encrypted with respect to a specific epoch e (starting with $e = 1$) using key k_e. When time advances from epoch e to $e + 1$, first a new key k_{e+1} is generated using $\mathsf{UE.GenKey}$ and then a token Δ_e is created using $\mathsf{UE.GenTok}$ on input of k_e and k_{e+1}. This token allows to update all ciphertexts from epoch e to $e + 1$ using the re-encryption algorithm $\mathsf{UE.ReEnc}$.

Definition 4 (Updatable Encryption [20]). *An **updatable encryption scheme** UE is a tuple* $(\mathsf{GenSP}, \mathsf{GenKey}, \mathsf{GenTok}, \mathsf{Enc}, \mathsf{Dec}, \mathsf{ReEnc})$ *of PPT algorithms defined as:*

$\mathsf{UE.GenSP}(pp)$ *is given the public parameters and returns some system parameters sp. We treat sp as implicit input to all other algorithms.*

$\mathsf{UE.GenKey}(sp)$ *is the key generation algorithm which on input of the system parameters outputs a key $k \in \mathcal{K}_{sp}$.*

$\mathsf{UE.GenTok}(k_e, k_{e+1})$ *is given two keys k_e and k_{e+1} and outputs some update token Δ_e.*

$\mathsf{UE.Enc}(k_e, M)$ *is given a key k_e and a message $M \in \mathcal{M}_{sp}$ and outputs some ciphertext $C_e \in \mathcal{C}_{sp}$ (or $\bot$ in case $M = \bot$).*

$\mathsf{UE.Dec}(k_e, C_e)$ *is given a key k_e and a ciphertext C_e and outputs some message $m \in \mathcal{M}_{sp}$ or $\bot$.*

$\mathsf{UE.ReEnc}(\Delta_e, C_e)$ *is given an update token Δ_e and a ciphertext C_e and returns an updated ciphertext C_{e+1} or $\bot$.*

Given UE, we call $\mathsf{SKE} = (\mathsf{GenSP}, \mathsf{GenKey}, \mathsf{Enc}, \mathsf{Dec})$ *the **underlying (standard) encryption scheme**. UE is called **correct** if SKE is correct and it holds that* $\forall sp \leftarrow \mathsf{GenSP}(pp), \forall k^{\mathrm{old}}, k^{\mathrm{new}} \leftarrow \mathsf{GenKey}(sp), \forall \Delta \leftarrow \mathsf{GenTok}(k^{\mathrm{old}}, k^{\mathrm{new}}), \forall C \in \mathcal{C}: \mathsf{Dec}(k^{\mathrm{new}}, \mathsf{ReEnc}(\Delta, C)) = \mathsf{Dec}(k^{\mathrm{old}}, C)$.

RCCA Security. RCCA is a relaxed version of CCA where the decryption oracle ignores queries for ciphertexts containing the challenge messages m_0 or m_1. In particular, these ciphertexts could be re-randomizations of the challenge ciphertext. In the updatable encryption setting, the adversary is additionally given access to a re-encryption oracle and an oracle to adaptively corrupt secret keys and tokens of the current and past epochs. Trivial wins by means of corruption or re-encryption need to be excluded by the definition.

Definition 5 (UP-IND-RCCA [20]). UE *is called UP-IND-RCCA secure if for any PPT adversary $\mathcal{A}$ the following advantage is negligible in κ:*
$$\mathsf{Adv}^{up\text{-}ind\text{-}rcca}_{\mathsf{UE},\mathcal{A}}(pp) := \left| \Pr[\mathsf{Exp}^{up\text{-}ind\text{-}rcca}_{\mathsf{UE},\mathcal{A}}(pp,0) = 1] - \Pr[\mathsf{Exp}^{up\text{-}ind\text{-}rcca}_{\mathsf{UE},\mathcal{A}}(pp,1) = 1] \right|.$$

Experiment $\mathsf{Exp}^{up\text{-}ind\text{-}rcca}_{\mathsf{UE},\mathcal{A}}(pp,b)$

$\quad (sp, k_1, \Delta_0, \mathbf{Q}, \mathbf{K}, \mathbf{T}, \mathbf{C}^*) \leftarrow \mathsf{Init}(pp)$

$\quad (M_0, M_1, state) \leftarrow_{\mathrm{R}} \mathcal{A}^{\mathsf{Enc},\mathsf{Dec},\mathsf{Next},\mathsf{ReEnc},\mathsf{Corrupt}}(sp)$

$\quad$ proceed only if $|M_0| = |M_1|$ and $M_0, M_1 \in \mathcal{m}_{sp}$

$\quad C^* \leftarrow_{\mathrm{R}} \mathsf{UE.Enc}(k_e, M_b)$, $\mathrm{M}^* \leftarrow (M_0, M_1)$, $\mathbf{C}^* \leftarrow \{e\}$, $e^* \leftarrow e$

$\quad b' \leftarrow_{\mathrm{R}} \mathcal{A}^{\mathsf{Enc},\mathsf{Dec},\mathsf{Next},\mathsf{ReEnc},\mathsf{Corrupt}}(C^*, state)$

$\quad$ **return** b' if $\mathbf{K} \cap \widehat{\mathbf{C}}^* = \emptyset$, i.e. $\mathcal{A}$ did not trivially win. (Else abort.)

In the above definition, the global state $(sp, k_e, \Delta_{e-1}, \mathbf{Q}, \mathbf{K}, \mathbf{T}, \mathbf{C}^*)$ is initialized by $\mathsf{Init}(pp)$ as follows:

$\mathsf{Init}(pp)$: Returns $(sp, k_1, \Delta_0, \mathbf{Q}, \mathbf{K}, \mathbf{T}, \mathbf{C}^*)$ where $e \leftarrow 1$, $sp \leftarrow_{\mathrm{R}} \mathsf{UE.GenSP}(pp)$, $k_1 \leftarrow_{\mathrm{R}} \mathsf{UE.GenKey}(sp)$, $\Delta_0 \leftarrow \perp$, $\mathbf{Q} \leftarrow \emptyset, \mathbf{K} \leftarrow \emptyset$, $\mathbf{T} \leftarrow \emptyset$ and $\mathbf{C}^* \leftarrow \emptyset$.

The list $\mathbf{Q}$ contains "legitimate" ciphertexts the adversary has obtained through Enc or ReEnc calls. The challenger also keeps track of epochs in which $\mathcal{A}$ corrupted a secret key ($\mathbf{K}$), token ($\mathbf{T}$), or obtained a re-encryption of the challenge-ciphertext ($\mathbf{C}^*$).

Moreover, the oracles given to the adversary are defined as follows:

$\mathsf{Next}()$: Runs $k_{e+1} \leftarrow_{\mathrm{R}} \mathsf{UE.GenKey}(sp)$, $\Delta_e \leftarrow_{\mathrm{R}} \mathsf{UE.GenTok}(k_e, k_{e+1})$, adds (k_{e+1}, Δ_e) to the global state and updates the current epoch to $e \leftarrow e + 1$.

$\mathsf{Enc}(M)$: Returns $C \leftarrow_{\mathrm{R}} \mathsf{UE.Enc}(k_e, M)$ and sets $\mathbf{Q} \leftarrow \mathbf{Q} \cup \{(e, M, C)\}$.

$\mathsf{Dec}(C)$: If $\mathsf{isChallenge}(k_e, C) = \mathtt{false}$, it returns $m \leftarrow \mathsf{UE.Dec}(k_e, C)$, else invalid.

$\mathsf{ReEnc}(C, i)$: Returns C_e iteratively computed as $C_\ell \leftarrow_{\mathrm{R}} \mathsf{UE.ReEnc}(\Delta_{\ell-1}, C_{\ell-1})$ for $\ell = i+1, \ldots, e$ and $C_i \leftarrow C$. It also updates the global state depending on whether the queried ciphertext is the challenge ciphertext or not:
  – If $(i, M, C) \in \mathbf{Q}$ (for some m), then set $\mathbf{Q} \leftarrow \mathbf{Q} \cup \{(e, M, C_e)\}$.
  – Else, if $\mathsf{isChallenge}(k_i, C) = \mathtt{true}$, then set $\mathbf{C}^* \leftarrow \mathbf{C}^* \cup \{e\}$.

$\mathsf{Corrupt}(\{\mathsf{key}, \mathsf{token}\}, i)$: Allows corruption of keys and tokens, respectively:
  – Upon input (key, i), the oracle sets $\mathbf{K} \leftarrow \mathbf{K} \cup \{i\}$ and returns k_i.
  – Upon input (token, i), the oracle sets $\mathbf{T} \leftarrow \mathbf{T} \cup \{i\}$ and returns Δ_{i-1}.

The isChallenge predicate (used by Dec and ReEnc) is defined as:

isChallenge(k_i, C) : If UE.Dec(k_i, C) $\in M^*$, return `true`. Else, return `false`.

To exclude trivial wins, we need to define the set of *challenge-equal epochs* containing all epochs in which the adversary obtains a version of the challenge ciphertext, either through oracle queries or by up/downgrading[11] the challenge ciphertext herself using a corrupted token.

$$\widehat{\mathbf{C}}^* \leftarrow \{e \in \{1, \ldots, e_{\text{end}}\} \mid \text{challenge-equal}(e) = \text{true}\}$$
$$\text{and true} \leftarrow \text{challenge-equal}(e) \text{ iff: } (e \in \mathbf{C}^*) \vee$$
$$(\text{challenge-equal}(e - 1) \wedge e \in \mathbf{T}) \vee (\text{challenge-equal}(e + 1) \wedge e + 1 \in \mathbf{T})$$

The adversary can trivially win *UP-IND-RCCA* by corrupting the key in any challenge-equal epoch. This is excluded by the *UP-IND-RCCA* definition.

Perfect Re-encryption. Intuitively, perfect re-encryption demands that fresh and re-encrypted ciphertexts are indistinguishable. This is defined by requiring that decrypt-then-encrypt has the same distribution as re-encryption.

Definition 6 (Perfect Re-encryption [20]). *Let* UE *be an updatable encryption scheme where* UE.ReEnc *is probabilistic. We say that re-encryption (of* UE*) is* **perfect**, *if for all* $sp \leftarrow_R$ UE.GenSP(pp), *all keys* $k^{\text{old}}, k^{\text{new}} \leftarrow_R$ UE.GenKey(sp), *token* $\Delta \leftarrow_R$ UE.GenTok($k^{\text{old}}, k^{\text{new}}$), *and all ciphertexts* C, *we have*

$$\text{UE.Enc}(k^{\text{new}}, \text{UE.Dec}(k^{\text{old}}, C)) \stackrel{\text{dist}}{\equiv} \text{UE.ReEnc}(\Delta, C).$$

In particular, note that ReEnc(Δ, C) $= \perp \Leftrightarrow$ Dec(k^{old}, C) $= \perp$.

Plaintext Integrity. Plaintext integrity demands that the adversary cannot produce a ciphertext decrypting to a message for which she does not trivially know an encryption.

Definition 7 (UP-INT-PTXT [20]). UE *is called UP-INT-PTXT secure if for any PPT adversary* $\mathcal{A}$ *the following advantage is negligible in* κ:
$$\text{Adv}_{\text{UE},\mathcal{A}}^{\text{up-int-ptxt}}(pp) := \Pr[\text{Exp}_{\text{UE},\mathcal{A}}^{\text{up-int-ptxt}}(pp) = 1].$$

Experiment $\text{Exp}_{\text{UE},\mathcal{A}}^{\text{up-int-ptxt}}(pp)$

  $(sp, k_1, \Delta_0, \mathbf{Q}, \mathbf{K}, \mathbf{T}) \leftarrow \text{Init}(pp)$
  $c^* \leftarrow_R \mathcal{A}^{\text{Enc,Dec,Next,ReEnc,Corrupt}}(sp)$
  return 1 if UE.Dec($k_{e_{\text{end}}}, c^*$) $= m^* \neq \perp$ and $(e_{\text{end}}, m^*) \notin \mathbf{Q}^*$,
    and $\nexists e \in \mathbf{K}$ where $i \in \mathbf{T}$ for $i = e$ to e_{end}; i.e. if $\mathcal{A}$ does not trivially win.

The oracles provided to the adversary are defined as follows:

Next(), Corrupt({key, token}, i): as in CCA game
Enc(M): Returns $C \leftarrow_R$ UE.Enc(k_e, M) and sets $\mathbf{Q} \leftarrow \mathbf{Q} \cup \{(e, M)\}$.

---

[11] We assume that a token Δ_e also enables *downgrades* of ciphertexts from epoch $e + 1$ to epoch e.

$\mathsf{Dec}(C)$: Returns $m \leftarrow \mathsf{UE.Dec}(k_e, C)$ and sets $\mathbf{Q} \leftarrow \mathbf{Q} \cup \{(e, M)\}$.

$\mathsf{ReEnc}(C, i)$: Returns C_e, the re-encryption of C from epoch i to the current epoch e. It also sets $\mathbf{Q} \leftarrow \mathbf{Q} \cup \{(e, M)\}$ where $M \leftarrow \mathsf{UE.Dec}(k_e, C_e)$.

To exclude trivial wins, we define the set $\mathbf{Q}^*$ which contains all plaintexts (and epochs) the adversary has received a ciphertext for by means of Enc and ReEnc queries or by upgrading a ciphertext herself using a corrupted token.

> for each $(e, m) \in \mathbf{Q}$:
> set $\mathbf{Q}^* \leftarrow \mathbf{Q}^* \cup (e, m)$, and $i \leftarrow e + 1$
> while $i \in \mathbf{T}$: set $\mathbf{Q}^* \leftarrow \mathbf{Q}^* \cup (i, m)$ and $i \leftarrow i + 1$

The adversary trivially wins if her output decrypts to a message m such that (e_{end}, m) is contained in this set or if she has corrupted a secret key and all following tokens, as this allows to create valid ciphertexts for any plaintext.

5.2   Scheme Description

The basic idea is to share the update tokens for the payload with intermediate relays and the encryption key with the receiver. So, the payload in each layer is encrypted under a different key that only the sender knows (see Fig. 4). To realize this, we need to construct a header that transports the tokens and routing information while ensuring that headers of different layers of the same onion cannot be linked to each other.

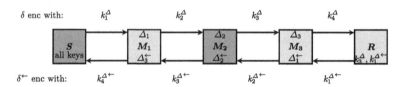

Fig. 4. Overview of the basic idea for the payload δ. Each relay gets an updatable encryption token Δ to change the key k^Δ under which the payload is encrypted.

Setup. To setup the system, $\mathsf{UE.GenSP}(pp)$ needs to be run on the public parameters pp (which, e.g., may contain a description of the group setting) by an honest party (or by using multi-party computation). The resulting system parameters sp (which, e.g., may contain a Groth-Sahai CRS) need to be made public and used by all participating parties. Usually they would be distributed along with the software package.

Header Construction. Each onion layer O_i, which is sent from P_{i-1} to P_i, is a tuple of header η_i and payload δ_i: $O_i = (\eta_i, \delta_i)$. Constructing the header is inspired by the Sphinx approach [11] and the Shallot scheme [1]. Contrary to the existing works, we however treat the payload with sufficiently secure updatable encryption.

Fig. 5. Non-repliable receiver header illustrated

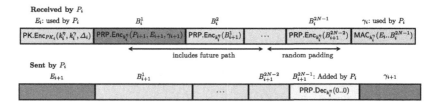

Fig. 6. Processing illustrated

Each header η_i is a tuple of encrypted temporary keys and tokens in E_i, encrypted routing information and keys for the current router P_i and later routers $P_{>i}$ in B_i^j and a MAC over the header in γ_i: $\eta_i = (E_i, B_i^1, B_i^2, \ldots, B_i^{2N-1}, \gamma_i)$. We describe a non-repliable header first and later on extend it to be repliable. The first layer's header η_1 contains:

$$\eta_1 = (\quad E_1, \qquad B_1^1, \qquad B_1^2 \quad, \ldots, \quad B_1^{2N-1}, \qquad \gamma_1 \quad)$$

$\eta_1 = (\mathsf{PK.Enc}_{PK_1}(k_1^\eta, k_1^\gamma, \Delta_1), \mathsf{PRP.Enc}_{k_1^\eta}(P_2, E_2, \gamma_2), \mathsf{PRP.Enc}_{k_1^\eta}(B_2^1), \ldots, \mathsf{PRP.Enc}_{k_1^\eta}(B_2^{2N-2}), \mathsf{MAC}_{k_1^\gamma}(E_1, B_1^1, \ldots, B_1^{2N-1}))$

The second layer's header η_2 has padding added by the first relay in B_2^{2N-1}:

$$\eta_2 = (\quad E_2, \qquad B_2^1, \qquad B_2^2 \quad, \ldots, \quad B_2^{2N-1}, \qquad \gamma_2 \quad)$$

$\eta_2 = (\mathsf{PK.Enc}_{PK_2}(k_2^\eta, k_2^\gamma, \Delta_2), \mathsf{PRP.Enc}_{k_2^\eta}(P_3, E_3, \gamma_3), \mathsf{PRP.Enc}_{k_2^\eta}(B_3^1), \ldots, \mathsf{PRP.Dec}_{k_1^\eta}(\mathbf{0} \ldots \mathbf{0}), \mathsf{MAC}_{k_2^\gamma}(E_2, B_2^1, \ldots, B_2^{2N-1}))$

The already existing relay padding is further decrypted for later layers:

$$\eta_3 = (\ldots, \quad B_3^{2N-3} \quad, \quad B_3^{2N-2} \quad, \quad B_3^{2N-1} \quad, \ldots)$$

$\eta_3 = (\ldots, \mathsf{PRP.Enc}_{k_3^\eta}(B_4^{2N-4}), \mathsf{PRP.Dec}_{k_2^\eta}(\mathsf{PRP.Dec}_{k_1^\eta}(\mathbf{0} \ldots \mathbf{0})), \mathsf{PRP.Dec}_{k_2^\eta}(\mathbf{0} \ldots \mathbf{0}), \ldots)$

The message is destined for the current processing relay P_{n+1} if $(\perp, \perp, \perp)$ is encrypted in B_{n+1}^1. All later $B_{n+1}^{>1}$ contain random bit strings chosen by the sender resp. the padding added by the earlier relays (see Fig. 5). The blocks with sender chosen padding are used for the reply path in repliable onions later.

To construct η_1 for a path $\mathcal{P} = (P_1, \ldots, P_{n+1}), n + 1 \leq N - 1$, the sender builds the onion from the center, i.e. calculates the layer for the receiver first:

1. Pick keys $k_1^\eta, \ldots, k_{n+1}^\eta$ for the block cipher, $k_1^\Delta, \Delta_1, \ldots, \Delta_n, k_{n+1}^\Delta$ for the UE and $k_1^\gamma, \ldots, k_{n+1}^\gamma$ for the MAC randomly.

2. Construct η_{n+1}:
$$E_{n+1} = \mathsf{PK.Enc}_{PK_{n+1}}(k^{\eta}_{n+1}, k^{\gamma}_{n+1}, k^{\Delta}_{n+1})$$
$$B^1_{n+1} = \mathsf{PRP.Enc}_{k^{\eta}_{n+1}}(\bot, \bot, \bot)$$
$$B^{2N-i}_{n+1} = \mathsf{PRP.Dec}_{k^{\eta}_n}(\mathsf{PRP.Dec}_{k^{\eta}_{n-1}}(\ldots \mathsf{PRP.Dec}_{k^{\eta}_{n+1-i}}(0\ldots 0)))$$

for $1 \le i \le n$ (blocks appended by relays)
$$B^{2N-i}_{n+1} \xleftarrow{R} \{0,1\}^{L_1} \text{ for } n+1 \le i \le 2N-2$$

(blocks as path length padding calculated by sender)
$$\gamma_{n+1} = \mathsf{MAC}_{k^{\gamma}_{n+1}}(E_{n+1}, B^1_{n+1}, B^2_{n+1}, \ldots, B^{2N-1}_{n+1})$$
3. Construct $\eta_i, i < n+1$ recursively (from $i = n$ to $i = 1$):
$$E_i = \mathsf{PK.Enc}_{PK_i}(k^{\eta}_i, k^{\gamma}_i, \Delta_i)$$
$$B^1_i = \mathsf{PRP.Enc}_{k^{\eta}_i}(P_{i+1}, E_{i+1}, \gamma_{i+1})$$
$$B^j_i = \mathsf{PRP.Enc}_{k^{\eta}_i}(B^{j-1}_{i+1}) \text{ for } 2 \le i \le 2N-1$$
$$\gamma_i = \mathsf{MAC}_{k^{\gamma}_i}(E_i, B^1_i, B^2_i, \ldots, B^{2N-1}_i)$$

Payload Construction. Let m be a message of the fixed message length to be sent. We add a 0 bit to the message to signal that it is not repliable $m' = 0\|m$:
$$\delta_i = \mathsf{UE.ReEnc}_{\Delta_{i-1}}(\ldots(\mathsf{UE.ReEnc}_{\Delta_1}(\mathsf{UE.Enc}_{k^{\Delta}_1}(m')))\ldots).$$

Onion Processing. The same processing is used for any forward or backward, repliable or not-repliable onion. If P_i receives an onion $O_i = (\eta_i = (E_i, B^1_i, B^2_i, \ldots, B^{2N-1}_i, \gamma_i), \delta_i))$, it takes the following steps (see Fig. 6):

1. Decrypt the first part of the header $(k^{\eta}_i, k^{\gamma}_i, \Delta_i) = \mathsf{PK.Dec}_{PK_i}(E_i)$ [resp. k^{Δ}_{n+1} instead of Δ_i, if P_i is the receiver]
2. Check the MAC γ_i of the received onion (and abort if it fails)
3. Decrypt the second part of the header $(P_{i+1}, E_{i+1}, \gamma_{i+1}) = \mathsf{PRP.Dec}_{k^{\eta}_i}(B^1_i)$ [if $P_{i+1} = E_{i+1} = \gamma_{i+1} =\bot$ (P_i is the receiver), skip processing of the header and process the payload (and check for replies as explained below)]
4. Decrypt the rest of the header $B^{j-1}_{i+1} = \mathsf{PRP.Dec}_{k^{\eta}_i}(B^j_i)$ for $j \ge 2$
5. Pad the new header $B^{2N-1}_{i+1} = \mathsf{PRP.Dec}_{k^{\eta}_i}(0\ldots 0)$
6. Construct the new payload $\delta_{i+1} = \mathsf{UE.ReEnc}_{\Delta_i}(\delta_i)$ [resp. retrieve the message in case of being the receiver ($\delta_{i+1} = \mathsf{UE.Dec}_{k^{\Delta}_{n+1}} = 0\|m$ if no reply)] and abort if this fails
7. Send the new onion $O_{i+1} = ((E_{i+1}, B^1_{i+1}, \ldots, B^{2N-1}_{i+1}, \gamma_{i+1}), \delta_{i+1})$ to the next relay P_{i+1}

Constructing a Repliable Onion. Let m be the message for the receiver, $\mathscr{P}^{\leftarrow} = (P^{\leftarrow}_1, \ldots, P^{\leftarrow}_{n^{\leftarrow}+1}), n^{\leftarrow}+1 \le N-1$ the backward path. To send a repliable onion, the sender performs the following steps:

1. Construct a (non-repliable) header $\eta^{\leftarrow}_1$ with path $\mathscr{P}^{\leftarrow}$. Let the chosen keys be $k^{\eta \leftarrow}_1, \ldots, k^{\eta \leftarrow}_{n^{\leftarrow}+1}$ and $k^{\Delta \leftarrow}_1, \Delta^{\leftarrow}_1, \ldots, \Delta^{\leftarrow}_{n^{\leftarrow}}, k^{\Delta \leftarrow}_{n^{\leftarrow}+1}$.

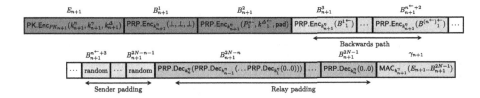

Fig. 7. Repliable receiver header illustrated

2. Construct the (repliable) header η_1 by starting to construct η_{n+1} for the receiver as before in the non-repliable case, but with the following differences (see Fig. 7) with pad being padding to the fixed blocklength:
   - Set $B_{n+1}^2 = \mathsf{PRP.Enc}_{k_{n+1}^\eta}(P_1^\leftarrow, k^{\Delta\leftarrow}_1, \mathsf{pad})$.
   - Set $B_{n+1}^i = \mathsf{PRP.Enc}_{k_{n+1}^\eta}(B^{(i-2)\leftarrow}_1)$ for $3 \leq i \leq n^\leftarrow + 2$.
   - Store the key $k^{\Delta\leftarrow}_{n^\leftarrow+1}$
3. Evolve the header η_{n+1} as before to create η_1
4. Construct the message for the repliable onion as $m' = 1\|m$.
5. Construct the payload δ_1 for m' as before.
6. The repliable onion is (η_1, δ_1).

Sending a reply. After recognizing to be the receiver (due to $(\bot, \bot, \bot)$ in B^1) of an repliable message (due to the starting bit), the receiver retrieves $P_1^\leftarrow$ and $k^{\Delta\leftarrow}_1$ from B_{n+1}^2. Let $m^\leftarrow$ be the reply message padded to the fixed message length. To send the reply the receiver performs the following steps:

1. Calculate $\delta_1^\leftarrow = \mathsf{UE.Enc}_{k^{\Delta\leftarrow}_1}(m^\leftarrow)$
2. Evolve the header (as before but shifting the header by two blocks):
   - $B^{(j-2)\leftarrow}_1 = \mathsf{PRP.Dec}_{k_{n+1}^\eta}(B_{n+1}^j)$ for $j \geq 3$
   - $B^{(2N-1)\leftarrow}_1 = \mathsf{PRP.Dec}_{k_{n+1}^\eta}(0 \dots 0)$ (i.e. receiver padding)
   - $B^{(2N-2)\leftarrow}_1 = \mathsf{PRP.Dec}_{k_{n+1}^\eta}(1 \dots 1)$ (i.e. receiver padding)
3. Send the onion $O_1^\leftarrow = (\eta_1^\leftarrow, \delta_1^\leftarrow)$ to $P_1^\leftarrow$

Decrypting a reply. After recognizing to be the receiver (due to $(\bot, \bot, \bot)$ in B^1), the relay checks whether the included key k^Δ_{n+1} for her matches a stored $k^{\Delta\leftarrow}_{n^\leftarrow+1}$s (it indeed is a reply) or not (it is just a new message). She uses the key and decrypts the message: $m = \mathsf{UE.Dec}_{k^\Delta_{n+1}}(\delta)$.

6 Security of Our Repliable OR Scheme

In this section, we prove that our scheme is secure:

Theorem 1. *Let us assume a PK-CCA2 secure PKE, a PRP-CCA secure SKE, a UP-IND-RCCA, and UP-INT-PTXT secure UE scheme with perfect Re-Encryption (of arbitrary ciphertexts), and a SUF-CMA secure MAC are given. Then our construction described in Sect. 5 satisfies $LU^\rightarrow$ security.*

Intuitively, the PK-CCA2 secure PKE ensures that the temporary keys for each relay are only learned by the intended relay, and the PRP-CCA secure SKE that the header is rerandomized and can be padded in the processing at a relay (so incoming and outgoing onions cannot be linked based on the header). Further, the SUF-CMA secure MAC protects the header against modifications. The UE scheme takes care of the payload: the UP-IND-$RCCA$ ensures that the message is hidden and that the payload is rerandomized during the processing at a relay (so incoming and outgoing onions cannot be linked based on the payload), UP-INT-$PTXT$ security that the payload cannot be maliciously modified (as in the malleability attack), while Perfect Re-Encryption guarantees that the adversary does not learn how far on the path the onion has already traveled.

Formally, we first describe FormOnion for later layers and show a detailed proof sketch for $LU^{\rightarrow}$. As the proofs for $LU^{\leftarrow}$ and $TI^{\leftrightarrow}$ are similar to the one of $LU^{\rightarrow}$, we only quickly sketch them here. All detailed proofs are provided in our extended version [22]. Further, correctness follows from inspection of our scheme.

FormOnion - later layers. FormOnion for $i > 1$ uses the k_i^{Δ} belonging to the corresponding epoch to create the payload $\delta = \mathsf{UE.Enc}_{k_i^{\Delta}}(m)$ and creates the other onion parts deterministically as described in the protocol for the current layer (with the randomness, all used keys are known and the deterministic parts of all layers can be built). For reply layers ($i > n + 1$) it combines the deterministically computed header and payload with the encrypted new message[12] (as all randomness is known, all temporary keys are).

Forwards Layer Unlinkability. Our proof for $LU^{\rightarrow}$ follows a standard hybrid argument. We distinguish the cases that the honest node is a forward relay ($j < n + 1$) and that it is the receiver ($j = n + 1$).

Case 1 – Honest Relay ($j < n + 1$). We first replace the temporary keys of the honest party included in the header, to be able to change the blocks of the header and the payload corresponding to the $b = 1$ case. For the oracles we further need to ensure, that RecognizeOnion does not mistreat any processing of e.g. modified onions. Therefore, we leverage the UE properties for the payload protection and the MAC for the header.

Proof Sketch. We assume a fixed, but arbitrary PPT algorithm $\mathcal{A}_{LU^{\rightarrow}}$ as adversary against the $LU^{\rightarrow}$ game and use a sequence of hybrid games $\mathcal{H}$ for our proof. We show that the probability of $\mathcal{A}_{LU^{\rightarrow}}$ outputting $b' = 1$ in the first and last hybrid are negligibly close to each other.

Hybrid 1) $LU^{\rightarrow}_{(b=0)}$. The $LU^{\rightarrow}$ game with b chosen as 0.

Hybrid 2) replaces the keys and token included in E_j with $0 \ldots 0$ before encrypting them and adapts the oracle of step 7 such that RecognizeOnion checks for the adapted header, but still uses the original keys as decryption of E_j.

---

[12] We use the parameter m of FormOnion for the reply message if $i > n + 1$, as the forward message is not needed to construct the reply.

We reduce this to the PK-CCA2 security of our PK encryption: We either embed $0 \ldots 0$ or the keys and token as the $CCA2$ challenge message and process other onions (for the step 7 oracle) by using the $CCA2$ decryption oracle.

Hybrid 3) rejects all onions that reuse E_j, but differ in another part of the header, in the oracle of step 7.

Due to the SUF-CMA of our MAC a successful processing of a modified header can only occur with negligible probability.

Hybrid 4) replaces the blocks (with information and keys for the future path of the onion) with random blocks and adapts the oracle of step 7 such that RecognizeOnion checks for the adapted header, but still uses the original blocks as processing result.

We reduce this to the PRP-CCA security of the PRP, by embedding the PRP-CCA challenge into these blocks, while continuing to treat these same blocks during processing as if they had the original content. (Other blocks in onions using E_j are rejected in the oracle of step 7.)

Hybrid 5) replies with a fail to all step 7 oracle requests, that use the challenge onion's header, but modified the message included in its payload.

We reduce this to the $UP\text{-}INT\text{-}PTXT$ of our UE: First, we carefully construct the secrets of the challenge onion until it is at the honest relay with the help of the $UP\text{-}INT\text{-}PTXT$-oracles. Then we wait for an onion with the challenge header to be given to the oracle in step 7. We use the payload of this onion as the ciphertext to break $UP\text{-}INT\text{-}PTXT$. Note that we do not have to answer this oracle request in our reduction, but only oracle requests for onions with a different header, which we can easily process with the knowledge of the secret keys (only the keys for the challenge onion are partially unknown in the reduction).

Hybrid 6) replaces the processing result of the challenge onion (recognized based on the header, with an unchanged message in payload) with a newly formed onion (FormOnion) that includes the same rest of the path and message.

FormOnion constructs the header deterministically as before, the only difference is the re-encryption (Hybrid 5) and the fresh encryption (Hybrid 6) of the same message in the payload. Due to the perfect Re-Encryption of our UE scheme those are indistinguishable.

Hybrid 7) replaces the message included in the payload with a random message and adapts the oracle in step 7 to expect this random message as payload, but still replies with the newly formed onion including the original message as before.

We reduce this to the $UP\text{-}IND\text{-}RCCA$ security of our UE: We carefully construct the secrets of the challenge onion until the honest relay with the help of the $UP\text{-}IND\text{-}RCCA$-oracles and either embed the original or a random message as the $UP\text{-}IND\text{-}RCCA$ challenge message. To answer the step 7 oracle, we use the knowledge of the secret keys if the requested onion does not have the challenge onion's header. If it has, we use the decryption oracle of $UP\text{-}IND\text{-}RCCA$ to detect whether the payload was maliciously modified (the $UP\text{-}IND\text{-}RCCA$

oracle returns another message m') or not (the UP-IND-$RCCA$ oracle does not process the payload). In the first case, we return a fail (as introduced in Hybrid 5), in the second we return a newly formed onion (as introduced in Hybrid 6).

Hybrid 8) - Hybrid 12) revert the hybrids 5)-2) (similar argumentation).

Case 2 – Honest Receiver ($j = n + 1$): The steps are the same as for the first case of $LU^{\rightarrow}$, but in Hybrid 6) we need to treat Reply and Proc requests separately. As the FormOnion behavior simulating the receiver is exactly the same as in the real protocol, we do not need to rely on Perfect Re-Encryption, but just on correctness of the decryption in this step. Note further that the earlier restrictions on the oracle work both for Reply and Proc requests.

Other Properties. We sketch the proofs in our extended version [22].

Theorem 2. *Let us assume a PK-CCA2 secure PKE, a PRP-CCA secure SKE and a UP-IND-RCCA secure UE scheme with perfect Re-Encryption (of arbitrary ciphertexts), and a SUF-CMA secure MAC are given. Then our construction described in Sect. 5 satisfies $LU^{\leftarrow}$ security.*

Backwards Layer Unlinkability. The steps are similar to the ones for $LU^{\rightarrow}$ Case 1: We replace the temporary keys of honest routers, before we exclude bad events (header manipulations) at the oracles and finally set the header and payload parts to correspond to the $b = 1$ case. However, this time we need to replace parts for both at the forward and backward path, as the forward layers also include information about the backward layers (but not the other way round). Notice that we can skip the steps related to the modification of the payload (and thus UP-INT-$PTXT$). As the forward message is known to the adversary anyways and the backward message (as the final processing) is never given to the adversary, she cannot exploit payload modification at the oracles to break $LU^{\leftarrow}$.

Theorem 3. *Let us assume a PK-CCA2 secure PKE, a PRP-CCA secure SKE, and a SUF-CMA secure MAC are given. Then our construction described in Sect. 5 satisfies $TI^{\leftrightarrow}$ security.*

Tail Indistinguishability. This is similar to $LU^{\leftarrow}$, except that we can skip more steps. For the same reasons as before, we do not need the payload protection in $TI^{\leftrightarrow}$. Further, the adversary does not obtain any leakage related to k_j^{η} and thus the blocks in the forward header can be replaced right away.

7   Our SNARG-Based Scheme

We now present an alternative instantiation of a secure, repliable OR scheme based on SNARGs, instead of updatable encryption.

7.1   Building Blocks and Setting

We make use of the following cryptographic building blocks and emphasize the differences compared to the UE-based scheme (see our extended version [22] for details):

- an asymmetric CCA2-secure encryption scheme with encryption and decryption algorithms denoted by $PK.Enc_{PK_i}$ and $PK.Dec_{SK_i}$ when used with public key PK_i and secret key SK_i.
- an SUF-CMA secure message authentication code with tag generation algorithm denoted by MAC_{k^γ} when used with the symmetric key k^γ.
- *two* PRP-CCA secure symmetric encryption schemes of short length L_1 (for the header) and long length L_2 (for the payload) with encryption and decryption algorithms denoted by $PRP.Enc_{k^\eta}$ and $PRP.Dec_{k^\eta}$ resp. $PRP2.Enc_{k^\delta}$ and $PRP2.Dec_{k^\delta}$ when used with the symmetric key k^η resp. k^δ.
- a *re-randomizable IND-CPA secure asymmetric encryption scheme*, with encryption, decryption, and re-randomization algorithms denoted by $PKM.Enc_{PK^M}$, $PKM.Dec_{SK^M}$, $PKM.ReRand_{PK^M}$ when used with public key PK^M and secret key SK^M. We require that re-randomization is invertible, in the sense that knowing the random coins of $PKM.ReRand$ allows to retrieve the original ciphertext.
- a *simulation-sound SNARG* with proof generation, verification, and simulation algorithms denoted by $Prove_{ZK}$, Vfy_{ZK}, and Sim_{ZK}.

We assume that all keys of honest participants are chosen independently at random.

Regarding the setting, we assume additionally that

- a master public key PK^M (for the re-randomizable IND-CPA secure encryption) and a common reference string CRS (for the SNARG) are known to all participants, while the corresponding SNARG trapdoor and secret key SK^M are not known to anyone.[13]

We will use PK^M to let participants encrypt secrets "to the sky", and the corresponding secret key SK^M will only be used as an extraction trapdoor in our proof. Hence, it is crucial that in an implementation of our scheme, both PK^M and CRS are chosen such that noone knows their trapdoors. (However, at least in the case of CRS, subversion-zero-knowledge SNARKs [15] are a promising tool to allow for adversarially chosen CRS.)

7.2 Scheme Description

Overview. Each router (publicly) proves at each step of the protocol that the *whole* current onion (including payload) is consistent, in the sense that it is the result of a faithful processing of a previous onion. This proof is realized with a succinct non-interactive argument of knowledge (SNARG [3]). This in fact presents us with a minor technical challenge, since now proving consistency involves proving that a previous onion *with a valid consistency proof* exists.

---

[13] Those public parameters can be either chosen by a trusted party, agreed upon with an initial multi-party computation, or, if SNARG and the re-randomizable encryption scheme have dense keys, be derived from a public source of trusted randomness (like, e.g., sunspots).

Why we do not use SNARK extraction. In our security proofs, such a consistency proof will be used to reconstruct previous onions (and in fact the whole past of an onion) by using the soundness of the SNARG. We stress that we will not be using any extractability properties from the SNARG (i.e., we do not rely on any knowledge soundness properties) at this point, since this would need to extract recursively. Indeed, in our proofs, we will need to simulate a ProcOnion oracle on adversarial inputs (i.e., onions) without knowing the underlying secret key. Instead, we will "reverse-process" the given onion until its creation with FormOnion, and then extract all future onions from the initial FormOnion inputs.

Our crucial tool to enable this "reverse-processing" is the soundness of the used SNARG. Intuitively, it seems possible to use a SNARK (i.e., a succinct argument of *knowledge*, which allows extraction of a witness) to prove that this onion has been created or processed honestly, with the witness being the corresponding FormOnion, resp. ProcOnion input. The problem with this approach is that each proof only certifies a single processing step, and so we would have to extract SNARK witnesses multiple times, and in fact *recursively extract* (which is notoriously difficult).

Instead, each onion will carry enough encrypted information to recreate previous onions, and the corresponding SNARG will certify the validity of that (encrypted) information. (Since the size of onions should not grow during processing, we will not be able to *fully* reconstruct the previous onion. However, we will still be able to implement the above strategy.) Like before, we rely on using MACs for a more "fine-grained" (and, most importantly, deterministic) authentication and progression of onion *headers*.

Viewed from a higher level, these consistency proofs provide a whole authentication chain for both requests and replies even with an intermediate receiver that replies with an arbitrary (and a-priori unknown) payload. This authentication chain protects against malleability attacks and payload changes along the way.

More details. In our protocol, each onion $O = (\eta, \sigma, \delta)$ consists of three main components:

- a *header* η which contains encrypted key material with which routers can process and (conventionally) authenticate the onion,
- the (SNARG-related) *authentication part* σ,
- the multiply encrypted *payload* δ; each router will decrypt one layer during processing.

While η and δ are similar to the Sphinx and Shallot protocols, σ contains several SNARG proofs $\pi_1, \ldots, \pi_N$ and an encrypted ring buffer (that consists of ciphertexts $C_1, \ldots, C_N$). Here, N denotes the maximal path length in the scheme. Intuitively, the C_i contain information that is required to reverse-process O, and the π_i prove that the information encrypted in C_1 is accurate. More specifically:

- C_1 contains a public-key encryption of the $\pi'_1, \ldots, \pi'_N$ from the *previous* onion O', as well as the last router's long-term secret key SK'. The public key used is a public parameter of the OR scheme, such that the secret key is not known by anyone. Of course, this last property is crucial to the security of the scheme. We will use this secret key as a trapdoor that allows to reverse-process onions during the proof.

- $C_2, \ldots, C_N$ are the values $C'_1, \ldots, C'_{N-1}$ from O'. Note that this implies that C'_N is lost during processing and cannot be reconstructed.
- π_i is a SNARG proof that proves that η, δ, and $C_1, \ldots, C_{N-i}$ are the result of an honest processing of some previous onion. The reason for N proofs π_i (and not just a single one) is that during repeated reverse-processing of a given onion, more and more C_i will unavoidably be lost. To check the integrity of such incomplete onions, we will use π_i in the i-th reverse-processing step.

Header Construction. Each onion layer O_i is a tuple of header η_i, SNARG-Information σ_i and payload δ_i: $O_i = (\eta_i, \sigma_i, \delta_i)$. We construct the header η_i as in the UE-based solution (see Sect. 5.2), except that instead of the Δ_i resp. k_i^Δ we now include k_i^δ of the second PRP-CCA secure symmetric encryption scheme for the relays.

SNARG Construction: The SNARG-Information σ_i consists of a ring buffer $C_i = (C_i^1, \ldots, C_i^N)$ and the SNARGs $\pi_i = (\pi_i^1, \ldots \pi_i^N)$: $\sigma_i = (C_i, \pi_i)$.

Ring buffer. The ring buffer C_i is calculated similarly to B_i, but reversed. The ring buffer for forward onions includes all information needed to undo the processing of the onion or reconstruct all input to FormOnion, encrypted under the master public key. On the reply path, we overwrite old (forward) information in C_is, as this is sufficient to achieve the forward-backward indistinguishability.

$$C_1^1 = \mathsf{PKM.Enc}_{PK^M}(\mathscr{I}) \text{ with } \mathscr{I} = (\mathtt{form}, (R, m, \mathscr{P}^\rightarrow, \mathscr{P}^\leftarrow, (PK)_{\mathscr{P}^\rightarrow}, (PK)_{\mathscr{P}^\leftarrow}))$$

$$C_1^j \xleftarrow{R} \{0,1\}^{L_3} \setminus \{\mathtt{sim}\} \text{ with } \mathtt{sim} \text{ being a special symbol}$$
$$\text{and } L_3 \text{ the fixed length of ring buffer elements}$$

$$C_i^1 = \mathsf{PKM.Enc}_{PK^M}(\mathscr{I}) \text{ with } \mathscr{I} = (\mathtt{proc}, (SK_{i-1}, \pi_{i-1}^1, \ldots, \pi_{i-1}^N, E_{i-1}, P_{i-1}))$$
$$C_i^j = \mathsf{PKM.ReRand}_{PK^M}(C_{i-1}^{j-1})$$

Note that the onion O_i is created by P_{i-1} and thus the information included in C_i is known at the time of creation. Further, information encrypted in C_i does not include the payload message or the MAC, as both an be reconstructed given the current onion layer. Finally, all C_i^j are padded to the fixed length L_3.

SNARGs. The SNARG π_i^j is calculated by P_{i-1} for the language $\mathcal{L}^j$, which consists of all partial onions $X = (\eta_i, (C_i^1, \ldots, C_i^{N-j}), \delta_i)$ for which the following holds: namely, there should exist R, M such that $C_i^1 = \mathsf{Enc}(PK^M, M; R)$, and such that M fulfills the following:

1. If M is of the form $M = (\mathtt{form}, I)$, then I is some parameter list $I = (1, \mathscr{R}, m, \mathscr{P}^\rightarrow, \mathscr{P}^\leftarrow, (PK)_{\mathscr{P}^\rightarrow}, (PK)_{\mathscr{P}^\leftarrow})$ (including random coins $\mathscr{R}$) for which

FormOnion(I) outputs an onion $O^* = (\eta^*, \sigma^*, \delta^*)$ with $\eta^* = \eta_i$ and $\delta^* = \delta_i$. In other words, in this case, M explains X as an immediate FormOnion output for a particular message m.

2. If M is of the form $M = (\text{proc}, (SK_{i-1}, \pi_{i-1}^1, \ldots, \pi_{i-1}^N, E_{i-1}, P_{i-1}, \mathcal{R}))$, then

   (a) all π_{i-1}^{N-k} (for $k > j$) are valid, in the sense that π_{i-1}^{N-k} shows that $(\eta_i, (C_i^1, \ldots, C_i^{N-k}), \delta_i) \in \mathcal{L}^k$. (Note that this is a well-defined statement if we define $\mathcal{L}^j$ for larger j first.)

   (b) $\text{ProcOnion}_{\text{partial}}^j(SK_{i-1}, (\eta_{i-1}, (C_{i-1}^1, \ldots, C_{i-1}^{N-j-1}), \delta_{i-1}), P_{i-1}; \mathcal{R}) = (\eta_i, (C_i^1, \ldots, C_i^{N-j}), \delta_i)$, where $\text{ProcOnion}_{\text{partial}}^j$ is the upcoming ProcOnion algorithm restricted to header, payload, and (partial) ring buffer processing (i.e., without any SNARG proof checks or creations), and η_{i-1}, δ_{i-1}, and the C_{i-1}^j are the previous header, payload, and (partial) ring buffer that are reverse-processed from X, SK_{i-1}, and random coins $\mathcal{R}$.[14]

3. M of any other form are not allowed.

The intuition behind $\mathcal{L}^j$ is simple: partial onions in $\mathcal{L}^j$ feature a ciphertext C_i^1 that allows to "reverse-process" the given onion to some extent. In particular, either the onion in question is the immediate output of either a FormOnion or a ProcOnion query. In case of a ProcOnion output, the whole onion cannot be reconstructed or checked (since some information in the C_i ring buffer is necessarily lost during processing). However, given an onion O_i and the secret key SK^M, the validity of π_i^N guarantees that a large portion of O_{i-1} can be reconstructed. In fact, only C_{i-1}^N cannot possibly be retrieved. However, going further, the reconstructed π_{i-1}^{N-1} now makes a statement about that "incomplete onion" O_{i-1}, and the reverse-processing can be continued.

Payload Construction. For message m, we again signal that it is not replicable by prepending a 0-bit: $m' = 0\|m$ and construct the payload as multiple encryption: $\delta_1 = \text{PRP2.Enc}_{k_1^\delta}(\text{PRP2.Enc}_{k_2^\delta}(\ldots \text{PRP2.Enc}_{k_{n+1}^\delta}(m')\ldots))$

Onion Processing. The processing of the header is done as in the UE-based scheme (see Sect. 5.2). However, the processing also checks the SNARG and treats the payload with PRP2.Dec:

If P_i receives an onion $O_i = (\eta_i = (E_i, B_i^1, B_i^2, \ldots, B_i^{2N-1}, \gamma_i), (C_i, \pi_i), \delta_i))$, it does the following steps differently:

1. Check the SNARG-Sequence π_i of the received onion (and abort if it fails)
2. Decrypt the header to retrieve $(k_i^\eta, k_i^\gamma, k_i^\delta)$ and new header blocks for $i + 1$, check the MAC, pad the header as before (see Sect. 5.2)
3. Construct the new payload $\delta_{i+1} = \text{PRP2.Dec}_{k_i^\delta}(\delta_i)$ [resp. retrieve the message in case of being the receiver $(\delta_{i+1} = 0\|m$ if no reply)]
4. Rerandomize and shift ring buffer: $C_{i+1}^{j+1} = \text{PKM.ReRand}_{PKM}(C_i^j)$

---

[14] We will describe ProcOnion only below, but it will be clear that the header, payload, and partial ring buffer part of the processing can be reversed with the secret key SK_{i-1} of the processing party. We additionally run ProcOnion$_{\text{partial}}$ to re-check MAC values.

5. Replace first ring buffer entry: $C^1_{i+1} = \mathsf{PKM.Enc}_{PK^\mathbb{M}}(\mathcal{G})$
6. Build the new SNARG-Sequence π_{i+1}
7. Send the new onion $O_{i+1} = ((E_{i+1}, B^1_{i+1}, \ldots, B^{2N-1}_{i+1}, \gamma_{i+1}), (C_{i+1}, \pi_{i+1}), \delta_{i+1})$
   to the next relay P_{i+1}

Constructing a Repliable Onion. Works as for the UE-based scheme before, except that we include $k^{\delta\leftarrow}_1$ in the header and store all chosen $k^{\delta\leftarrow}_i$ for later use.

Sending a reply. Processing the repliable onion, the receiver stores $P^\leftarrow_1, \eta^\leftarrow_1$ and k^δ_R. To reply with m (padded to the fixed message length), the receiver does the following steps:

1. Calculate $\delta_1 = \mathsf{PRP2.Enc}_{k^\delta_R}(m)$
2. Construct the SNARG-Sequence π_1,
3. Pick the ring buffer elements randomly $C^j_1 \leftarrow^R \{0,1\}^{L_3} \setminus \{\mathsf{sim}\}$ for all j
4. Send the onion $O_1 = (\eta^\leftarrow_1, (C_1, \pi_1), \delta_1)$ to $P^\leftarrow_1$

Decrypting a reply. After recognizing to have received a reply (by checking the stored $k^\delta_{n^\leftarrow+1}$), the reply is "decrypted":
$$m = \mathsf{PRP2.Dec}_{k^\delta_1}(\mathsf{PRP2.Enc}_{k^\delta_2}(\ldots(\mathsf{PRP2.Enc}_{k^\delta_{n^\leftarrow}}(\mathsf{PRP2.Enc}_{k^\delta_{n^\leftarrow+1}}(\delta)))\ldots)))$$

7.3 Security

The proofs of our onion routing properties are similar to the ones for the UE-based scheme, except that they rely on the SNARGs to protect the payload. We detail them in our extended version [22].

Theorem 4. *Our SNARG-based OR Scheme is a* secure, repliable OR scheme.

Acknowledgements. This work was supported by funding from the topic Engineering Secure Systems (Subtopic 46.23.01) of the Helmholtz Association (HGF), by the KASTEL Security Research Labs, by the Cluster of Excellence 'Centre for Tactile Internet with Human-in-the-Loop' (EXC 2050/1, Project ID 390696704), and by the ERC grant 724307.

References

1. Ando, M., Lysyanskaya, A.: Cryptographic shallots: a formal treatment of repliable onion encryption. eprint (2020). https://eprint.iacr.org/2020/215.pdf
2. Backes, M., et al.: Provably secure and practical onion routing. In: Computer Security Foundations Symposium, pp. 369–385 (2012)
3. Bitansky, N., et al.: From extractable collision resistance to succinct non-interactive arguments of knowledge, and back again. In: ITCS (2012)
4. Camenisch, J., Lysyanskaya, A.: A formal treatment of onion routing. In: Shoup, V. (ed.) CRYPTO 2005. LNCS, vol. 3621, pp. 169–187. Springer, Heidelberg (2005). https://doi.org/10.1007/11535218_11
5. Canetti, R., Krawczyk, H., Nielsen, J.B.: Relaxing chosen-ciphertext security. In: Boneh, D. (ed.) CRYPTO 2003. LNCS, vol. 2729, pp. 565–582. Springer, Heidelberg (2003). https://doi.org/10.1007/978-3-540-45146-4_33

6. Catalano, D., et al.: Fully non-interactive onion routing with forward secrecy. Int. J. Inf. Secur. **12**(1), 33–47 (2013)
7. Catalano, D., Fiore, D., Gennaro, R.: A certificateless approach to onion routing. Int. J. Inf. Secur. **16**(3), 327–343 (2016). https://doi.org/10.1007/s10207-016-0337-x
8. Chaum, D.L.: Untraceable electronic mail, return addresses, and digital pseudonyms. Commun. ACM (1981)
9. Chen, C., Asoni, D.E., Barrera, D., Danezis, G., Perrig, A.: HORNET: high-speed onion routing at the network layer. In: ACM CCS (2015)
10. Chen, C., et al.: TARANET: traffic-analysis resistant anonymity at the NETwork layer. In: IEEE EuroS&P (2018)
11. Danezis, G., Goldberg, I.: Sphinx: a compact and provably secure mix format. In: IEEE S&P (2009)
12. Danezis, G., Laurie, B.: Minx: a simple and efficient anonymous packet format. In: WPES (2004)
13. Dingledine, R., Mathewson, N., Syverson, P.: Tor: the second-generation onion router. Technical report, Naval Research Lab Washington DC (2004)
14. Feigenbaum, J., Johnson, A., Syverson, P.: Probabilistic analysis of onion routing in a black-box model. ACM TISSEC (2012)
15. Fuchsbauer, G.: Subversion-zero-knowledge SNARKs. In: Abdalla, M., Dahab, R. (eds.) PKC 2018. LNCS, vol. 10769, pp. 315–347. Springer, Cham (2018). https://doi.org/10.1007/978-3-319-76578-5_11
16. Goldschlag, D.M., Reed, M.G., Syverson, P.F.: Hiding routing information. In: Anderson, R. (ed.) IH 1996. LNCS, vol. 1174, pp. 137–150. Springer, Heidelberg (1996). https://doi.org/10.1007/3-540-61996-8_37
17. Groth, J., Maller, M.: Snarky signatures: minimal signatures of knowledge from simulation-extractable SNARKs. In: Katz, J., Shacham, H. (eds.) CRYPTO 2017. LNCS, vol. 10402, pp. 581–612. Springer, Cham (2017). https://doi.org/10.1007/978-3-319-63715-0_20
18. Hayden, M.: The price of privacy: re-evaluating the NSA. In: Johns Hopkins Foreign Affairs Symposium, April 2014
19. Kate, A., Zaverucha, G.M., Goldberg, I.: Pairing-based onion routing with improved forward secrecy. ACM TISSEC **13** (2010)
20. Klooß, M., Lehmann, A., Rupp, A.: (R)CCA secure updatable encryption with integrity protection. In: Ishai, Y., Rijmen, V. (eds.) EUROCRYPT 2019. LNCS, vol. 11476, pp. 68–99. Springer, Cham (2019). https://doi.org/10.1007/978-3-030-17653-2_3
21. Kuhn, C., Beck, M., Strufe, T.: Breaking and (Partially) fixing provably secure onion routing. In: IEEE S&P (2020)
22. Kuhn, C., Hofheinz, D., Rupp, A., Strufe, T.: Onion routing with replies. Cryptology ePrint Archive, Report 2021/1178 (2021). https://ia.cr/2021/1178
23. Mauw, S., Verschuren, J.H.S., de Vink, E.P.: A formalization of anonymity and onion routing. In: Samarati, P., Ryan, P., Gollmann, D., Molva, R. (eds.) ESORICS 2004. LNCS, vol. 3193, pp. 109–124. Springer, Heidelberg (2004). https://doi.org/10.1007/978-3-540-30108-0_7
24. Micali, S.: CS proofs (extended abstracts). In: 35th FOCS, pp. 436–453 (1994)
25. Piotrowska, A.M., Hayes, J., Elahi, T., Meiser, S., Danezis, G.: The Loopix anonymity system. In: USENIX (2017)
26. Shimshock, E., Staats, M., Hopper, N.: Breaking and provably fixing minx. In: PETS (2008)

Private Join and Compute
from PIR with Default

Tancrède Lepoint[1]([✉]), Sarvar Patel[2]([✉]), Mariana Raykova[2]([✉]), Karn Seth[2]([✉]), and Ni Trieu[3]([✉])

[1] Menlo Park, USA
[2] Google LLC, Menlo Park, USA
[3] Arizona State University, Tempe, USA
nitrieu@asu.edu

Abstract. The private join and compute (PJC) functionality enables secure computation over data distributed across different databases, and is applicable to a wide range of applications, many of which address settings where the input databases are of significantly different sizes.

We introduce the notion of private information retrieval (PIR) with default, which enables two-party PJC functionalities in a way that hides the size of the intersection of the two databases and incurs sublinear communication cost in the size of the bigger database. We provide two constructions for this functionality, one of which requires offline linear communication, which can be amortized across queries, and one that provides sublinear cost for each query but relies on more computationally expensive tools. We construct inner-product PJC, which has applications to ads conversion measurement and contact tracing, relying on an extension of PIR with default. We evaluate the efficiency of our constructions, which can enable 2^8 PIR with default lookups on a database of size 2^{25} (or inner-product PJC on databases with such sizes) with the communication of 44 MB, which costs less than 0.17c. for the client and 26.48c. for the server.

1 Introduction

Private set intersection (PSI) enables two parties who have private input sets to identify items that they have in common without learning any other information. While PSI has proven its broad applicability, there are settings which require more refined functionality that does not reveal the whole intersection but rather enables restricted computation on the data in the intersection. We refer to this functionality as *private join and compute (PJC)* [Goo19].

An important difference in the privacy requirements relevant for the PJC and the PSI settings, is that while the intersection size is inherently revealed by the PSI output, in the PJC case this is an additional privacy leakage, which should be avoided in many scenarios. The cost of the "compute" part in a private join and compute protocol is determined by the size of the intersection, which is often much smaller than the size of the input sets, thus the dominant efficiency cost

---

T. de Lepoint—Independent researcher.

© International Association for Cryptologic Research 2021
M. Tibouchi and H. Wang (Eds.): ASIACRYPT 2021, LNCS 13091, pp. 605–634, 2021.
https://doi.org/10.1007/978-3-030-92075-3_21

is the cost of the step computing the intersection. Similarly to the PSI setting, when the two input datasets are of the same size, the intersection computation is necessarily linear in the input size. However, when we have asymmetric inputs where one of the datasets is much larger than the other, the efficiency goal is to avoid linear dependence on the size of the larger input set. This raises the question whether it is possible, in the private join and compute setting, to address both the privacy requirement of hiding the intersection size and at the same time provide sublinear efficiency.

The PSI-Sum solution of Ion et al. [IKN+20], which was deployed in practice, does not provide either of the above properties, and they will be highly beneficial for that setting. First, that solution scales poorly for the party with the smaller input set, which also often has much more constrained resources, but needs to incur cost proportional to the larger set. Second, it inherently reveals the intersection size, which can be significant leakage especially when one of the inputs is small – their protocol mitigates the issue by allowing the party with the small input to learn the intersection size first and decide to abort if it is too small. Our construction addresses both of these issues. Additionally, we also allow revealing the intersection cardinality in a differentially private manner. Further, we extend the functionality that can be computed over the intersection, including allowing both parties to contribute associated values. While we mainly focus on a specific functionality (described below), we also discuss how to extend our work to generic functionalities.

We specifically consider the problem of private join and compute (Inner Product PJC) which allows computing an inner product between attribute values associated with the intersection IDs in each of the two input datasets. In this setting the two input sets are of the form $(X, W) = \{(x_1, w_1), \ldots, (x_t, w_t)\}$ and $(Y, V) = \{(y_1, v_1), \ldots, (y_n, v_n)\}$ and the computation evaluated by the PJC functionality is defined as follows: $f((X, W), (Y, V)) = \sum_{i \in [t], j \in [n], x_i = y_j} w_i v_j.$

1.1 Our Motivation

We motivate the above functionality with two practical applications. The first application involves privacy-preserving computation for the effectiveness of advertising campaigns, which is a generalization of the functionality supported by Ion et al. [IKN+20]. A transaction data provider (TDP) has a database of transaction values tdp_db which contains $(id, spending)$. Here, the customer "id" has seen an ad, and then makes a purchase with an amount "spending". The Ad tech company has a database at_db which contains $(id, type)$. Here, the customer "id" has seen an ad with a "type" supplied by the ad tech company. The "type" can be the time spent watching ads. Typically the number of ad impressions over a particular time period is orders of magnitude higher (millions) than the corresponding number of transactions on a fixed date (thousands), thus the sets are highly asymmetric. The TDP may want to partition based on user attributes such as new/returning customer, whether the customer is a loyalty card member, or some demographic information, and may want to learn an inner-product for each partition. The following query on the join of these two databases computes the sum of the transaction values of users who saw ads weighted according to the type (or weight) supplied by the ad tech company.

SELECT $sum(tdp\_db.spending * at\_db.type)$

FROM at_db INNER JOIN tdp_db

ON $at\_db.id = tdp\_db.id$

This problem can be seen as an instance of inner product PJC, where set sizes are asymmetric, and hiding the exact intersection size may be especially important, since the computation may be repeated with overlapping partitions from the TDP.

The inner product PJC functionality could also be used to enhance the privacy guarantees of exposure notification protocols in the existing decentralized contact tracing solutions [AGC20, CGH+20, TSS+20, DP320]. In such solutions, user devices broadcast BLE packets that contain pseudorandom values generated from a daily secret key. Users who test positive for COVID-19 can report their secret keys for the periods when they were infectious to a central server. Each key is accompanied with a transmission risk score based on the diagnosis and user symptoms. Anyone who downloads the server database can therefore check whether the random values that her app has received were derived from any of the reported secrets. However, this approach also allows learning information about the values transmitted in individual BLE packets. We can view the above problem as an instance of inner product PJC where the server database contains the reported pseudorandom values with their risk scores, and where the user has the pseudorandom values she has observed, and possibly with corresponding weights determined by the time elapsed since the exposure incident, the exposure duration, and other parameters. The goal is for the user to obtain the weighted sum of the transmission risks of the pseudorandom values matching all her exposures. We note that this application also has a natural input size asymmetry: the client set is much smaller than the server database.

1.2   Our Contributions

With these two applications in mind, we present two different instantiations of our approach, tailored for two distinct settings. We assume that the participants are semi-honest, they follow the protocol but attempt to obtain extra information from the execution transcript. Our first construction is in the setting allowing offline precomputation and initialization. In this setting, the server's database is fixed beforehand and can be computed on in an "offline" phase. The goal is to minimize the cost of (possibly repeated) client queries in the "online" phase when the client data becomes available. Our first construction in this setting incurs a setup time that is linear in the size of the server's (larger) dataset. The subsequent client queries are highly efficient, and have computation and communication time linear in the client's dataset and essentially independent of the size of the server dataset. This is similar to approaches taken by [KLS+17,RA18], which send an encoded server database to the client in the offline phase, allowing highly efficient "online" intersections. Our work can be seen as extending the functionality achieved by these previous works by enabling computation over the intersection but keeping the intersection itself hidden, while preserving the desirable efficiency properties for the online phase. This construction is well-suited to applications where many small PJC executions are run against a single large databases. For example, in the conversion-measurement setting, the client's dataset may arrive in small batches, or the client may want to make multiple overlapping queries based on different demographic slices. Previous works incur the costs proportional to the larger database each PJC query.

The second construction is in the fully online setting (without precomputation). In this case, we instantiate our construction using techniques derived from Private Information Retrieval (PIR). The resulting construction allows the client to incur costs that are asymptotically linear in the size of its own dataset, and logarithmic in the server's dataset size. In practice, this makes it so the bulk of the costs of executing the protocol are shifted from the client to the server. In this way, our work improves on [PSTY19] by making the costs incurred by each party more equitable in the asymmetric input size setting, This is especially beneficial when the client is a constrained device like a mobile phone, such as in the contact tracing application.

Both our constructions compose with differential privacy in a straightforward way, which allows repeated client queries on a single server database, using the differential-privacy noise to hide correlations between the outputs of the different queries. This allows our protocol to hide and/or apply differential privacy noise to the intersection size as well as the function computed over the intersection. This is an improvement over PJC [IKN+20] and related works such as [BKM+20], which require revealing the intersection size without noise.

PJC from PIR-with-Default. The main building block for one of our PJC constructions provides another primitive of independent interest which we call *private information retrieval (PIR) with default*. This is a primitive which enables PIR queries over a sparse database where the client has an input index and receives either the data stored at that index, or a default value, if there is no item with this index in the database. The server does not learn anything about the query including whether the client received a database value or a default value. The client does not learn any further information about the database or the default value apart from her output. In particular, if the database values and the default value are indistinguishable, then the client does not learn whether the query index was present in the database. We also present a multi-query PIR-with-Default construction.

PIR-with-Default on its own is sufficient to compute private set intersection-sum [IKN+20]. Another application of PIR-with-Default outside the PJC setting, is a way to distribute anonymous tokens [KLOR20] as follows: the users who belong to the database stored by the server receive one type of an authentication token (which is used as the associated value for all database entries in the PIR-with-Default execution), while every other user receives a second type of an

Table 1. Theoretical costs of PJC protocols. In Construction 2, the log factor comes from the asymptotic behavior of the underlying PIR scheme, and can be replaced with the efficiency of the specific PIR scheme. The computational complexity of [PSTY19] is slightly improved by mega-bin hashing. Poly-ROOM [SGRP19] achieves asymptotics similar to [PSTY19], thus, we group it in the circuit-based PSI. Label-PSI [CHLR18] achieves similar asymptotic efficiency as Construction-2, but has worse concrete performance (see [LPR+20]) and requires extra cost due to using a generic MPC. We denote the extra cost as $|GC(t)|$.

		Construction 1		Construction 2	Circuit-based PSI [PSTY19, SGRP19]	Labeled PSI [CHLR18]
		Offline	Online			
Communication	Client	-	$O(t)$	$O(t\log(n/t))$	$O(t+n)$	$O(t\log(n/t)) + |GC(t)|$
	Server	$O(n)$				
Computation	Client	-		$O(t\log(n/t))$	$t\log(t)$	$O(t\log(n/t)) + |GC(t)|$
	Server	$O(n)$		$O(n)$	$n\log(n)^2$	

authentication token which is used for the default value. The server does not learn which of the two groups the user belongs to, and if the two types of tokens are indistinguishable, the client does not learn which type it received.

We also introduce a small extension of the PIR-with-Default functionality, which we call Extended-PIR-with-Default, that enables both parties to contribute associated values. In this case, the parties will learn shares the product of the associated values, or the default value. If the parties sum the shares they receive from multiple queries, they will receive shares of the inner-product over the intersection, which then directly achieves the inner-product PJC functionality.

Table 1 shows the theoretical communication and computation complexity of our protocol compared with prior works. Note that [CHLR18] is secure against malicious adversaries, but only for the Labeled PSI functionality itself and not for PSI with computation. Table 1 lists the cost of semi-honest Labeled PSI [CHLR18].

Implementation Evaluation. We evaluate the concrete communication, computation and monetary costs of our constructions and present them together with comparisons to existing works in Sect. 7. For our first PJC construction, only the offline communication and computation depends (linearly) on the size of the larger dataset. The online communications and computation is determined completely by the size of the smaller set and the cost of random memory access (for datasets of size 2^8 and 2^{25}, the online computation is ~ 2.43 ms and the communication is 7MB). Our second construction is more computationally expensive but outperforms any existing constructions in terms of total communication when the differences of the two dataset sizes are significant, especially when the difference of input sizes is greater than a factor of 2^{10}. In terms of monetary cost, a PJC execution on sets of sizes 2^8 and 2^{25} costs ~ 0.17 c. for the client and ~ 26.48 c. for the server. Compared to the previous works, our online constructions lead to a significant reduction in client monetary costs with a small corresponding rise in server costs. For example, for $n = 2^{25}$ and $t = 2^8$, our client cost is 36.5× lower than that of [PSTY19], while incurring a server cost that is only 4× higher than theirs.

1.3   Improvement on Related Work

Our work is focused on privately computing a function over the intersection of two asymmetric-sized datasets, both in the setting with offline setup, and in the fully-online setting. We discuss the most important related works.

The field of private set intersection protocols is very rich, starting from the earliest PSI constructions that are based on the Diffie-Hellman assumption [Mea86]. Over the last few years, there has been a long list of works on efficient secure PSI [DCW13, CHLR18, PRTY19, PRTY20] with fast implementations, which can process millions of items in seconds. However, most of these works only allow to output the intersection itself. In our scenario we wish to compute some function of the intersection while hiding the individual elements in the intersection. There is much less related work on the more general private intersection join and compute.

In terms of works that support computing over the intersection while hiding the values, a prominent approach is *Garbled-Circuit-based PSI*. [HEK12] proposes an efficient sort-compare-shuffle circuit construction to implement PJC. [PSTY19] improves circuit-PSI using several hashing techniques. The main bottleneck in the existing circuit-based protocols is need for a large number of string comparisons, and the methods used for computing over associated values. These are done inside a generic MPC protocol, which increases the interaction round complexity, and incurs cost due to bitwise encryption of each party's dataset. Moreover, while these protocols are well-suited to symmetrically-sized input sets, they perform worse when inputs are asymmetric: both parties incur costs linear in the larger database size. Another approach in this space, which is currently used in practice by Google [Goo19], is the approach combining Diffie–Hellman and homomorphic encryption techniques [IKN+20]. While this approach has reasonable communication cost and can be extended to the PJC functionality, it also performs poorly in the asymmetric inputs setting, since both parties incur costs proportional to the other party's dataset size. In terms of work that leverages offline precomputation where one of the parties' datasets is fixed beforehand, there are several prominent works with the application of private contact discovery. Recent works [KLS+17, RA18] achieve good performance in the offline setting with asymmetric inputs. However, these works cannot be straightforwardly extended to privately compute on the intersection.

The work that achieves the closest result to ours is the protocol of [CHLR18], which uses homomorphic encryption to perform efficient PSI on sets of asymmetric sizes, with communication cost logarithmically related to the larger dataset. The authors show how to extend this construction to enable each party to retrieve labels associated to individual items in its input, with the property that the client receives "valid" labels only for the items in the intersection . They further describe how these labels can be additively masked and fed into a downstream generic MPC computation that allows privately computing a function over these labels (while hiding which specific labels were in common). This "PSI-with-Computation" extension is described mostly theoretically by [CHLR18], and is not accompanied by detailed experiments.

We see our work as improving on the approach outlined in [CHLR18] in several important ways. The first is that we use a highly tailored approach to test membership and retrieve additive shares of the labels, which greatly moderates the client cost compared to a generic approach. Secondly, the [CHLR18] protocol effectively uses a novel batched Private Information Retrieval (PIR) protocol to achieve efficiency in the asymmetric input size setting. We make the relationship to PIR explicit in our construction, which allows us to leverage techniques from the PIR literature [GR05, ACLS18, ALP+19], especially recursion and oblivious query expansion. Thirdly, our approach can be efficiently applied in the offline precomputation setting such that the client's online cost is essentially independent of the server's database size. This can provide significant gains when many queries will be made against the same database.

2   Technical Overview

Next we overview the main techniques in our constructions. We first describe the construction of PIR-with-Default, which is the core of our contributions. In particular, we show two different instantiations of PIR-with-Default: one with offline setup and one with sublinear online executions, and we describe important batching optimizations. Next, we show how to modify our constructions to achieve an extended functionality, which we call Extended-PIR-with-Default. Finally, we will describe how to build inner-product PJC from Extended-PIR-with-Default.

PIR-with-Default: In the PIR-with-Default functionality, we assume the server holds the larger input set $(Y, V) = \{(y_1, v_1), \ldots, (y_m, v_n)\}$ while the client holds a single input x. We want the client to receive v_j if $x = y_j$ for some j, and a server-chosen default value d otherwise. Neither party should learn anything extra, and in particular, the server should not learn which value was retrieved, and the client should not learn the other items in the server's database. The client should also not learn whether it received the default value (assuming the default value is chosen by the server to be indistinguishable from the w_j values.).

Our approach uses Bloom filters [Blo70], a data structure that allows efficient set membership tests over sparse sets. A Bloom filter (BF) is a binary vector that encodes a set. For each item x, one can check whether x is in the set or not by querying a constant number of locations in the BF. Specifically, Bloom filters have as public parameters a set of hash functions $H_1, \ldots, H_k$ and testing membership of x requires accessing only locations $H_1(x), \ldots, H_k(x)$ in the Bloom Filter and checking that they are all 1 (or alternatively, checking $k = \sum_{i \in [k]} \mathsf{BF}[H_i(x)]$). In order to allow retrieving associated values, we leverage the closely related notion of garbled Bloom filters (GBF) [DCW13], which allows to store not only a set but also a set of associated values. For value x present in the database, computing $\sum_{i \in [k]} \mathsf{GBF}[H_i(x)]$ will result in the associated value. However, if x is not present in the database, $\sum_{i \in [k]} \mathsf{GBF}[H_i(x)]$ will return a garbage value that needs to be transformed to the default value. We use a GBF in conjunction with a BF as we discuss next.

The first step is that the server creates a BF that contains the indices in Y and a GBF that contains its database (Y, V). The client and the server then execute a query protocol where the client has as input an index x and the output of the query protocol will be secret-shares of the membership bit for x in the BF and secret-shares of the value retrieved from the GBF for x (which is either a secret-share of some w_j, or a secret share of some garbage value). Next the client and the server will execute a Value-Or-Default protocol in which the two parties input their shares of the BF and GBF query responses and additionally the server's default value for this execution, and the client obtains either the value from the GBF query, if the BF query response was a share of 1, or the default value, otherwise.

We first describe the BF query protocol with a linear offline setup phase with a fixed server database, and client query that is available only during the online phase. We will then describe a setup-free BF query with sublinear cost in the larger database. These will constitute the difference between our two different constructions of PIR-with-Default. After that, we will describe the Value-Or-Default protocol, which will be shared by both PIR-with-Default constructions.

BF/GBF Queries with Linear Offline Cost. In the offline phase the server sends an encryption of BF and GBF, where each entry is encrypted using an additively homomorphic encryption scheme. Now for each query x, the client can compute $H_1(x), \ldots, H_k(x)$, and can locally compute the encryption of $\mathsf{Enc}(\sum_{i \in [k]} \mathsf{BF}[H_i(x)])$. The client generates a random value r_C, which it keeps as its share, and sends $\mathsf{Enc}(\sum_{i \in [k]} \mathsf{BF}[H_i(x)] - r_C)$ to the server, which the server decrypts to obtain its share r_S. The client and server then transform shares r_C and r_S of $\sum_{i \in [k]} \mathsf{BF}[H_i(x)]$ into shares of the BF membership result using a single 1-out-of-$(k+1)$ oblivious transfer (OT) [Rab05] as follows. The client chooses a bit b_C and computes $B = \{b_0, \ldots, b_k\}$ where all b_i are b_C, except $b_{(r_C + k) \bmod (k+1)}$ is the client's share which is equal to $1 \oplus b_C$. The client and the server execute 1-out-of-$(k+1)$ OT where the client is the sender with input B and the server is the receiver with input r_S. The server obtains output b_S such that $b_C \oplus b_S = 1$ if and only if $r_S + r_C = k$.

In order to obtain shares of the GBF value, the client similarly locally computes $\mathsf{Enc}(\sum_{i \in [k]} \mathsf{GBF}[H_i(x)])$, and generates a random value v_C, and sends the server $\mathsf{Enc}(\sum_{i \in [k]} \mathsf{BF}[H_i(x)] - v_C)$. The server decrypts this value to obtain its share v_S. After these steps, the server and client have shares of the BF membership bit, and the GBF evaluation, as desired.

BF/GBF Queries with Sublinear Cost. Our second construction for the BF and the GBF queries leverages constructions for symmetric private information retrieval (PIR) [GIKM00] with sublinear communication based on homomorphic encryption (HE) [Gen09]. The general idea is that instead of transferring the entire encrypted BF and GBF to the client during a setup phase, the client instead makes PIR queries to retrieve the desired entries $H_i[x]$ of the BF and GBF. We make use of the fact that in many constructions of PIR, the client sends a homomorphic encryption of its desired index, which the server uses to obliviously compute an encryption of the query response under the same homomorphic encryption scheme, and the server can therefore sum several such responses before returning them. Specifically, our client sends PIR queries for locations $H_1(x), ..., H_k(x)$, and the server evaluates the queries to obtain $\mathsf{Enc}(\mathsf{BF}[H_i(x)])$ and $\mathsf{Enc}(\mathsf{GBF}[H_i(x)])$. The server then homomorphically sums these values, and subtracts randomly chosen masks r_S and v_S to obtain $\mathsf{Enc}(\sum_{i\in[k]} \mathsf{BF}[H_i(x)] - r_S)$ and $\mathsf{Enc}(\sum_{i\in[k]} \mathsf{GBF}[H_i(x)] - v_S)$, which it sends to the client. The client decrypts these values to get r_C and v_C respectively. The client and server engage in the 1-out-of-$(k+1)$ OT described earlier to get shares b_C and b_S of the BF membership bit. These, together with the v_C and v_S values, are the desired output of the BF/GBF Queries.

Our use of PIR is heavily amenable to different kinds of optimization, which we explore in detail in Sect. 5.3 and the full version of this work [LPR+20]. Specifically, PIR constructions achieve sublinear communication either by using packing techniques leveraging the slots in a HE ciphertext to encrypt the entire selection vector in a single ciphertext [ACLS18, ALP+19], or using recursion where the selection vector is written as an outer product of several vectors of shorter length [GR05, ALP+19]. These two techniques are not compatible with each other, i.e. packing the entire selection vector for a query in a single HE ciphertext requires increased computation at the server and higher multiplicative degree from the HE, and does not provide efficiency benefits. However, in our setting we need to execute multiple PIR queries and we use the HE slots to pack coordinates of the selection vectors from different queries. This HE-slotting technique is also compatible with multi-query PIR approaches which use Cuckoo hashing [PR01, PSSZ15] to reduce the communication cost per query. Such hashing techniques partition both parties' inputs in a way that guarantees that the client queries are distributed evenly across the smaller server partitions and can be executed only over the partition without revealing anything about the query indices. We also instantiated this approach using two-choice hashing [CRS03, PRTY19] and compare it to Cuckoo hashing for different parameters. In both of these multi-query instantiations we can pack coordinates from queries for different partitions in the same HE ciphertext while preserving the efficiency of the server computation.

Value-Or-Default *protocol:* As we discussed above, after the BF/GBF queries, the client and server have XOR shares b_C and b_S of a bit (the output of the BF query) and additive shares v_C and v_S of a value (the output of the GBF query). In addition the server has as input a default value d. The goal of the Value-Or-Default phase is to take these shares and produce output received by the client, namely $v = v_C + v_S$ if $b = b_C \oplus b_S = 1$, and, d, otherwise. We execute this phase using only two 1-out-of-2 OT executions. The first OT enables the server to learn $q = \Delta_C + b \cdot v_C$ where Δ_C is a random value generated by the client. This is achieved by executing a OT where the client is the sender with messages $m_0 = \Delta_C + b_C \cdot v_C$, $m_1 = \Delta_C + (1 - b_C) \cdot v_C$ and the server is the receiver with bit b_S. The second OT enables the client to obtain $\Delta_C + b \cdot v_C + b \cdot v_S + (1 - b) \cdot d$ from which the client can subtract Δ_C to recover v if $b = 1$, and d, if $b = 0$, as desired. In the second OT the server is the sender with messages $m_0 = q + b_S \cdot v_S + (1 - b_S) \cdot d$ and $m_1 = q + (1 - b_S).v_S + b_S.d$ which the client is the receiver with input bit b_C. Combining the BF/GBF queries with the Value-Or-Default phase achieves the PIR-with-Default functionality.

Extended-PIR-with-Default *from* PIR-with-Default: Extended-PIR-with-Default has the additions: firstly, the client holds a weight w in addition to x. Secondly, the output learned by the client should be an additively masked version of the product $w \cdot v_j - s$ if $x = v_j$ for some v_j in the server's database, and the additively masked default value $d - s$, and the server should receive the additive mask s. This extension acts as a bridge between PIR-with-Default and inner-product PJC by incorporating values from both parties, and also to more easily hide from the client whether it retrieved a "real" value or the default.

We note that the mask w can be incorporated by having the party that creates the GBF sum homomorphically multiply the GBF sum by w before proceeding with the protocol. More specifically, in the PIR-with-Default protocol with offline setup, once the client homomorphically computes the GBF sum, it can homomorphically multiply the result with the scalar w before masking it. In the protocol with sublinear costs, the client additionally sends a homomorphic encryption of w to the server along with its PIR queries. The server, after computing the PIR queries and summing the results, can multiply the GBF sum with the encryption of w before masking it.

In order to additively mask the final result, the server simply replaces the values v_S and d that it uses in the Value-Or-Default phase with the values $v_S - s$ and $d - s$ respectively. This makes it so the final value retrieved by the client is either $w \cdot v_j - s$ or $d - s$ as desired.

Inner Product PJC from Extended-PIR-with-Default : In inner product PJC, the server holds larger input set $(Y, V) = \{(y_1, v_1), \ldots, (y_m, v_n)\}$ and the client holds the smaller input set $(X, W) = \{(x_1, w_1), \ldots, (x_t, w_t)\}$. In our protocol, the client and the server jointly execute t Extended-PIR-with-Default queries from the set X where the server has default value 0 for all the queries. As a result of this the client and the server have shares $\alpha_{C,i}$ and $\alpha_{S,i}$ such that $\alpha_{C,i} + \alpha_{S,i} = w_i \cdot v_j$ for all $x_i \in Y$ and $\alpha_{C,i} + \alpha_{S,i} = 0$ for all $x_i \notin Y$. Therefore, by adding their local shares $\sum_{i \in [t]} \alpha_{C,i}$ and $\sum_{i \in [t]} \alpha_{S,i}$, the client and the server obtain shares of the desired output $\sum_{i \in [t], j \in [n], x_i = y_j} w_i v_j$.

3   Preliminaries

We briefly introduce notations and cryptographic primitives in this section, and refer to the full version of this work [LPR+20] for complete definitions. We denote by κ and λ the computational and statistical security parameters respectively. For $n \in \mathbb{N}$, we write $[n] = \{1, \ldots, n\}$. We define a probabilistic polynomial time (PPT) algorithm to be a randomized algorithm that runs in polynomial time in the length of its first parameter.

Oblivious Transfer (OT) [Rab05]: 1-out-of-n OT is a two-party protocol, in which a sender with n inputs $(m_1, \ldots, m_n)$ interacts with a receiver who has an input choice $b \in [n]$. The result is that the receiver learns m_i without learning anything about others $m_j, \forall j \in [n] \setminus \{i\}$, while the sender learns nothing about the receiver's choice b.

Bloom Filter (BF) [Blo70] *and Garbled Bloom Filter (GBF)* [DCW13]: A BF is an array $\{BF[i]\}_{i \in [n]}$ of bits where each keyword x is inserted to the BF by setting $BF[h_i(x)] = 1$ for all h_i in a collection of hash functions $H = \{h_1, \ldots, h_k \mid h_i : \{0,1\}^\star \rightarrow [n]\}$. A GBF is an array of integers in $\mathbb{Z}_\ell$ that implements a key-value (x, v) store, where the value v associated with key x is $v = \sum_{i=1}^{k} GBF[h_i(x)]$.

Cuckoo Hashing [PR01] *and 2-Choice Hashing* [CRS03]: Basic Cuckoo hashing consists of m bins $B[1], \ldots, B[m]$, a stash, and k random hash functions $h_1, \ldots, h_k$ of range $[m]$. To insert an element x into a Cuckoo hash table, we place it in bin $h_i(x)$, if this bin is empty for any i. Otherwise, we choose a random $i \in [k]$ and place x in bin $h_i(x)$, evict the item currently in that bin, and recursively insert the evicted item. 2-choice hashing uses $k = 2$ random hash functions h_1, h_2 of range $[m]$, and each item x will be placed in whichever of $h_1(x), h_2(x)$ currently has fewest items.

Homomorphic Encryption (HE): HE is a form of encryption that allows to perform arbitrary computation on plaintext values while manipulating only ciphertexts. In this work, we use the BGV [BGV14] and FV [FV12] HE schemes.

Private Information Retrieval: Private information retrieval (PIR) is a cryptographic primitive that allows a client to query a database from one or multiple servers without revealing any information about the query to the database holder(s). A trivial solution suffering linear communication overhead consists in sending the whole database to the client. While the feasibility of a protocol with sublinear communication has been resolved for a long time [CKGS98], the search for concretely efficient constructions for practical applications has been an active area of research [GR05, ACLS18, ALP+19]. In this paper, we focus on the single-server setting and will use RLWE-based homomorphic encryption scheme as in [ACLS18, ALP+19].

4 Definitions

In this section, we provide the formal security definitions that we will use for our protocols. All our constructions will be proven in the semi-honest setting where the parties follow the prescribed steps in the construction.

We provide standard simulation security definitions [Gol04] for our constructions that use the following notation: $\mathsf{View}_{\mathcal{C}}^{\Pi}(1^\lambda, [X]_{\mathcal{C}}, [Y]_{\mathcal{S}})$ is the view of party $\mathcal{C}$ during the execution of protocol Π with security parameter λ between parties $\mathcal{C}$ and $\mathcal{S}$ which have inputs X and Y respectively; $\mathsf{SIM}_{\mathcal{C}}^{\Pi}(1^\lambda, O)$ is a ppt simulator algorithm, which generates the view of party $\mathcal{C}$ in the execution of a protocol Π (i.e. the messages received from the other participants) given input the security parameter λ and the output O that $\mathcal{C}$ receives at the end of Π.

PARAMETERS: Server/Sender $\mathcal{S}$ and Client/Receiver $\mathcal{R}$, agree upon
- An upper bound n on the number of key-value pairs in Server $\mathcal{S}$'s input.
- A space $\mathbb{Z}_\ell$ for the associated values and default values.
- A bound t on the number of Client $\mathcal{C}$'s queries.

INPUTS:
$\mathcal{S}$: A set of key-value pairs $\mathcal{P} = \{(y_1, v_1), \ldots, (y_n, v_n)\}$ with distinct y_i, and default values $\mathcal{D} = \{d_1, \ldots, d_t\}$.
$\mathcal{R}$: A set of t queries $\{x_i\}_{i \in [t]}$.
OUTPUTS:
$\mathcal{S}$: No output.
$\mathcal{R}$: A set $O = \{o_i\}_{i \in [t]}$ where

$$o_i = \begin{cases} v_j, & \text{if } x_i = y_j \text{ for some } j \in [n] \\ d_i, & \text{otherwise} \end{cases}$$

Fig. 1. The PIR-with-Default Functionality.

PARAMETERS: Server/Sender $\mathcal{S}$ and Client/Receiver $\mathcal{R}$, agree upon
- An upper bound n on the number of key-value pairs in Server $\mathcal{S}$'s input.
- A space $\mathbb{Z}_\ell$ for the associated values and default values.
- A bound t on the number of Client $\mathcal{C}$'s queries.

INPUTS:
$\mathcal{S}$: A set of key-value pairs $\mathcal{P} = \{(y_1, v_1), \ldots, (y_n, v_n)\}$ with distinct y_i, a set of default values $\mathcal{D} = \{d_1, \ldots, d_t\}$, and a set of additive masks $S = \{s_1, \ldots, s_t\}$. Each v_i, d_i and $s_i \in \mathbb{Z}_\ell$.
$\mathcal{R}$: A set of t pairs $\{(x_i, w_i)\}_{i \in [t]}$. Each $w_i \in \mathbb{Z}_\ell$.
OUTPUTS:
$\mathcal{S}$: No output.
$\mathcal{R}$: A set $O = \{o_i\}_{i \in [t]}$ where

$$o_i = \begin{cases} (w_i \cdot v_j) - s_i, & \text{if } x_i = y_j \text{ for some } j \in [n] \\ d_i - s_i, & \text{otherwise} \end{cases}$$

Fig. 2. The Extended-PIR-with-Default Functionality. All arithmetic is in $\mathbb{Z}_\ell$.

4.1 PIR with Default

We start by defining formally our new notion of PIR-with-Default. We first recall the different existing variants of private information retrieval and their security guarantees. The notion of PIR [CGKS95] enables a client to query a public database with a private index and to obtain the corresponding entry, while the party who holds the database learns nothing about the index during the execution of the query. *Symmetric* PIR [GIKM00] adds also a privacy guarantee for the database requiring that the client learns nothing but the queried database entry. *Keyword* PIR [CGN98] addressed the setting of sparse databases where the query index is over a keyword domain, and database is index with a subset of the same domain.

The query party in keyword PIR either obtains the requested value if present in the database, or learns that the query is not present in the database.

PIR-with-Default extends the notion of keyword PIR providing stronger privacy against the client hiding whether the query is present in the database. This is achieved by modifying the functionality to return either the database entry if the query is in the database, or a default value provided by the database holder, otherwise. This privacy property is stronger than symmetric keyword PIR assuming that the database entries and the default values are indistinguishable. In many real-world applications, the default value is a cryptographic object with natural pseudorandomness. As stand-alone applications of PIR-with-Default, we envision use-cases where clients retrieve cryptographic tokens from a server to utilize elsewhere. In Sect. 1.2, we consider the specific case of anonymous tokens [KLOR20], but this could extend to retrieving coupons (with dummy codes for non-targeted users), or a token proving allowlist-membership or blocklist-non-membership.

The precise PIR-with-Default functionality is described in Fig. 1. We note that the presentation in Fig. 1 allows the client to submit multiple queries, where the server specifies different default values for each client query. Single-query PIR-with-Default is equivalent to setting $t = 1$. Next we define the security properties for such a protocol.

Definition 1 (Semi-Honest Security for PIR-with-Default). Let $n(\lambda)$ be an upper bound on the size of server database of (index, value) pairs $\mathcal{P}$, $t(\lambda)$ be a bound on the number of queries client's set X, and $Z_{\ell(\lambda)}$ be the domain for the database values and default values $\mathcal{D}$. Let O be a vector of length $|X|$ that contains the outputs of the PIR with default functionality executed with queries from X on database $\mathcal{P}$ and default values $\mathcal{D}$.

A PIR-with-Default protocol is $(n(\lambda), t(\lambda), \ell(\lambda))$-secure, if there exist ppt algorithms $\mathsf{SIM}_\mathcal{C}$ and $\mathsf{SIM}_\mathcal{S}$ such for any probabilistic polynomial-time adversary $\mathcal{A}$, there exists a negligible function $\mathsf{negl}(\cdot)$ such that

$$
\begin{aligned}
& \big| \Pr[\mathcal{A}(1^\lambda, \mathsf{View}_\mathcal{S}^\Pi(1^\lambda, [X]_\mathcal{C}, [\mathcal{P}, \mathcal{D}]_\mathcal{S})) = 1] \\
& - \Pr[\mathcal{A}(1^\lambda, \mathsf{SIM}_\mathcal{S}(1^\lambda, n, \ell, O, [\mathcal{P}, \mathcal{D}]_\mathcal{S})) = 1] \big| < \mathsf{negl}(\lambda)
\end{aligned}
$$

and

$$
\begin{aligned}
& \big| \Pr[\mathcal{A}(1^\lambda, \mathsf{View}_\mathcal{C}^\Pi(1^\lambda, [X]_\mathcal{C}, [\mathcal{P}, \mathcal{D}]_\mathcal{S})) = 1] \\
& - \Pr[\mathcal{A}(1^\lambda, \mathsf{SIM}_\mathcal{C}(1^\lambda, [X]_\mathcal{C}, t)) = 1] \big| < \mathsf{negl}(\lambda)
\end{aligned}
$$

The above security definition formalizes the intuition that the client does not learn anything more than the output of its query (the actual value if the item is present, or the default value) and the database size, and the server does not learn anything from the executions except the number of queries.

We also define the notion that extends the computation of PIR-with-Default as follows:

1. Allowing the client to also specify associated values, such that the client will learn the product of the client and server's associated values if the client identifier is in the server database.
2. Allowing the server to specify an additive mask, such that the client will receive a *masked* associated-value or default. This enables the protocol to have additively secret-shared outputs.

Extended-PIR-with-Default is formally described in Fig. 2. The security definition for this primitive is the same as PIR-with-Default except the output O is computed with the extended functionality. While PIR-with-Default is a special case of Extended-PIR-with-Default, where the client's associated values are all 1, and the server's additive masks are all 0, we will be constructing both primitives in a non-blackbox way from building block components to achieve better efficiency. Note that one can use Extended-PIR-with-Default to output additive shares of items in the intersection, which can serve as input to any MPC protocol described in Sect. 6.2.

5   PIR with Default Construction

5.1   Construction Outline

Both of our constructions share the following three high-level steps.

The first step is a secret-shared private membership test (SS-PMT). This enables the client and server to compute a secret-share of a membership bit, i.e. the two parties obtain XOR shares of 1 or 0 if the client's query is or is not in the database.

The second step is computation of a secret-shared associated value (SS-AV). This enables the client and server to compute an additive secret share of the database value corresponding to the client's query. The outputs for the client and the server are additive shares of a value, which is the value that is in S's database if the query is in S's database. If the query is not in the database, there are no guarantees for the value underlying the secret shared output. In particular, it may be an arbitrary function of the server's database entries.

The third step is functionality called Value-Or-Default, which enables the server and the client to take their outputs from the first two steps as well as the default values on the server side, and translate them into the client's output, which is either the associated value or the default value depending on whether the output of SS-PMT was shares of 0 or of 1.

In the following sections, we will give two constructions for PIR-with-Default. These constructions will have different implementations for SS-PMT and SS-AV, but will have the same implementation of Value-Or-Default.

5.2   Construction 1: PIR-with-Default with Offline Setup

Our first construction for PIR-with-Default involves an expensive setup phase that has communication linear in the server's database. However, the remainder of the protocol is independent of the number of entries in the server's dataset. Therefore this protocol is well suited to scenarios where the server's database is fixed and the setup phase can be performed offline, and requires an efficient online phase once the client's input is available. Moreover, the setup phase can be run once and reused for multiple protocol executions, and for different clients.

The construction presented in Fig. 3 works as follows. The server inserts its database into a Bloom filter BF and a Garbled Bloom filter GBF. The server generates a public/private key pair (pk, sk) for additively homomorphic encryption, and encrypts the entries of both BF and GBF using the public key. It sends the encrypted results to the client in the setup phase. Whenever the client wants to run a PIR-with-Default query x, the client invokes the online phase of computation with the server to compute SS-PMT, SS-AV and Value-Or-Default. We describe each of these computations as follows:

SS-PMT Functionality. We instantiate SS-PMT as follows. The client first computes a sum of the encrypted entries $b = \sum_{i=1}^{k} \text{EBF}[h_i(x)]$ using the homomorphic property of the encryption scheme. It is easy to see that b is an encryption of a value p which is smaller than $k + 1$. Moreover, if the query x is in the server dataset Y, p is exactly equal to k. The client now needs to turn this into secret shares of the membership bit. A straw man solution is to homomorphically convert b to an encryption of a bit $(0/1)$ so that each party can have a secret share of the bit indicating whether $x \in Y$. The conversion can be done by homomorphically evaluating the equality circuit that has multiplicative depth $\lceil \log(k) \rceil$. However this approach is relatively inefficient.

Instead, we use a simple solution that relies on oblivious transfer. More precisely, the client randomly chooses a value $r \leftarrow \mathbb{Z}_\ell$, which will be its output share, and masks b by computing $c \leftarrow b - \text{Enc}(pk, r)$. The client sends the resulting value to the server, who decrypts it to obtain its output share $r' = \text{Dec}(sk, c) = p - r$. The parties use their output shares of p as inputs in the next OT functionality that translates these shares into shares of a single membership bit.

The client chooses a random bit $b_\mathcal{C}$ and acts as OT's sender with $(k + 1)$ OT messages $B = \{b_0, \ldots, b_k\}$ where all b_i are $b_\mathcal{C}$, except $b_{(k-r') \bmod (k+1)}$ which is equal to $1 \oplus b_\mathcal{C}$. The server acts as OT's receiver with $r \bmod (k + 1)$. The OT functionality gives the server $b_\mathcal{S}$ such that $b_\mathcal{C} \oplus b_\mathcal{S} = 1$ if $r + r' = k$ (i.e. the client's keyword is in the server's database), otherwise $b_\mathcal{C} \oplus b_\mathcal{S} = 0$. The described process exactly implements the SS-PMT functionality.

Instantiating 1-out-of-N OT. A trivial implementation of the 1-out-of-$(k+1)$ OT used above is via $\log(k+1)$ 1-out-of-2 OT instances. Recently, several works [KK13, KKRT16, PSZ18] have proposed efficient protocols to generalize 1-out-of-2 OT extension to 1-out-of-N OT. Each protocol has a different underlying encoding function to support an upper-bound number of N messages in OT. Kolesnikov and Kumaresan [KK13] employ 256-bit Walsh-Hadamard error-correcting code and achieve 1-out-of-N OT on random strings, for N up to approximately 256. For arbitrarily large N, the best 1-out-of-N OT protocol [KKRT16] uses 424–448

PARAMETERS:
- Security parameter λ.
- Server $\mathcal{S}$ input set size n, associated value space $\mathbb{Z}_\ell$, number of client $\mathcal{C}$ queries t .
- A 1-out-of-k OT primitive.
- Bloom Filter parameters: Bloom filter size η sufficient to hold n items, a number of hash functions k, a hash function family HF : $\{0,1\}^* \to [\eta]$.
- An additively HE scheme (HGen, HEnc, HDec) with message space $\mathbb{Z}_\ell$.

INPUT:
- Server $\mathcal{S}$: A set of key-value pairs $\mathcal{P} = \{(y_1, v_1), \ldots, (y_n, v_n)\}$ with distinct y_i, and a set of default values $D = \{d_1, \ldots, d_t\}$, where each $v_i, d_i \in \mathbb{Z}_\ell$. Additionally, a set of t masks $\{s_1, \ldots, s_t\}$ each $\in \mathbb{Z}_\ell$.
- Client $\mathcal{C}$: A set of t queries $\{x_1, \ldots, x_t\}$. Additionally, a set of t associated values $\{w_1, \ldots, w_t\}$, each $\in \mathbb{Z}_\ell$

PROTOCOL:
1. **Setup phase:**
   - $\mathcal{S}$ and $\mathcal{C}$ jointly select k hash functions $\{h_1, \ldots, h_k\}$ at random from HF.
   - $\mathcal{S}$ generates a HE key-pair $(pk, sk) \leftarrow \mathsf{HGen}(\lambda)$ and sends pk to $\mathcal{C}$.
   - $\mathcal{S}$ inserts a set of keys $\{y_1, \ldots, y_n\}$ into a Bloom filter BF and the set of key-value pairs $\mathcal{P}$ into a Garbled Bloom filter GBF using hash functions h_i. $\mathcal{S}$ aborts if either insertion operation fails.
   - Using pk, $\mathcal{S}$ encrypts BF and GBF as $\mathsf{EBF}[i] = \mathsf{HEnc}(pk, \mathsf{BF}[i]), \forall i \in [\eta]$ and $\mathsf{EGBF}[i] = \mathsf{HEnc}(pk, \mathsf{GBF}[i]), \forall i \in [\eta]$.
   - $\mathcal{S}$ sends EBF and EGBF to $\mathcal{C}$.
2. **Online phase:** The following steps are executed in parallel for each x_j for $j \in [t]$.
   (a) **SS-PMT computation:**
      - $\mathcal{C}$ chooses a random mask $r \leftarrow \mathbb{Z}_\ell$, homomorphically computes $z = \mathsf{Refresh}(-\mathsf{HEnc}(pk, r) + \sum_{i=1}^{k} \mathsf{EBF}[h_i(x_j)])$, and send the ciphertext z to $\mathcal{S}$
      - $\mathcal{S}$ decrypts the received ciphertext z using secret key sk, and obtains r'.
      - Parties invoke an instance of 1-out-of-$(k+1)$ OT:
         - $\mathcal{S}$ chooses a bit $b_\mathcal{S}$ at random.
         - $\mathcal{S}$ acts as OT's sender with input $\{b_0, \ldots, b_k\}$ where each b_i is equal to $b_\mathcal{S}$, except $b_{(k-r') \mod (k+1)}$ which is equal to $1 \oplus b_\mathcal{S}$.
         - $\mathcal{C}$ acts as OT's receiver with choice $r \mod (k+1)$.
         - $\mathcal{C}$ obtains $b_\mathcal{C}$ from the OT's functionality.
   (b) **SS-AV computation:**
      - $\mathcal{C}$ chooses a random mask $v_\mathcal{C} \leftarrow \mathbb{Z}_\ell$, homomorphically computes $z' = \mathsf{Refresh}(-\mathsf{HEnc}(pk, v_\mathcal{C}) + w_j \cdot \sum_{i=1}^{k} \mathsf{EGBF}[h_i(x)])$, and sends the ciphertext to $\mathcal{S}$
      - $\mathcal{S}$ decrypts the received ciphertext z' using its secret key sk, and obtains $v_\mathcal{S}$.
   (c) **Value-Or-Default computation:**
      - $\mathcal{S}$ and $\mathcal{C}$ engage in a Value-Or-Default protocol execution described in Figure 4.
      - $\mathcal{S}$ uses inputs $b_\mathcal{S}$, $v_\mathcal{S} - s_j$ and $d_j - s_j$.
      - $\mathcal{C}$ uses inputs $b_\mathcal{C}$ and $v_\mathcal{C}$.
      - Let o_j be the output received by $\mathcal{C}$ from the Value-Or-Default protocol execution
3. **Output:** $\mathcal{C}$ outputs the set $O = \{o_j\}_{j \in [t]}$.

Fig. 3. Construction 1: PIR-with-Default construction with Setup. The highlighted parts are only needed for Extended-PIR-with-Default construction.

bits codeword length, which requires 424–448 bits of communication per OT and N hash evaluations. For smaller N, the best protocols [PSZ18,OOS17] use linear BCH code, in which codeword length depends on N. Our instantiation for the BF parameters yields $N = 2^5$ to achieve a BF false-positive rate of $2^{-\lambda}$. In this case, the required codeword length and the best underlying encoding are 248 bits, which are chosen according to [min] to achieve Hamming distance of two codewords at least κ security parameter.

SS-AV Functionality. The SS-AV protocol uses similar but simplified approach as the one in SS-PMT. The client first computes a sum of all encrypted $\mathsf{EGBF}[h_i(x)], \forall i \in [k]$, using the additive HE property $z = \sum\limits_{i=1}^{k} \mathsf{EBF}[h_i(x)]$. Due to the GBF property, z is an encryption of the associated value v if $(x, v) \in \mathcal{P}$, and some unrelated value otherwise. To output SS-AV, the client chooses a random $v_{\mathcal{C}}$ and sends $z - \mathsf{Enc}(pk, v_{\mathcal{C}})$ to the server who can decrypt it and obtain $v_{\mathcal{S}}$.

The work [DCW13] observed that the GBF procedure aborts when processing item x if and only if x is a false positive for a BF containing the previous items. Therefore, to bound the probability by $2^{-\lambda}$, one can use a table with $58n$ entries to store n items. In that case, the optimal number of hash functions is $k = 31$.

In the setting of Extended-PIR-with-Default, the client homomorphically multiplies its value w_i with the sum of the encrypted GBF values before masking and sending it to the server. Then if x_i is in the server database, $v_{\mathcal{S}}$, the decryption of z, will be a share of $(v_j \cdot w_i)$. Then the server can simply add $(-s_i)$ to $v_{\mathcal{S}}$ before proceeding to the next phase: now $v_{\mathcal{C}}$ and $v_{\mathcal{S}} - s_i$ are additive shares of $(v_j \cdot w_i) - s_i$.

Finally, the server and client engage in a Value-Or-Default protocol to translate the outputs of the previous two steps into the associated value or the default value. We describe this subprotocol in the next section (Fig. 4).

Value-Or-Default Functionality. We describe our Value-Or-Default protocol for the PIR-with-Default construction and note that the only change required for the Extended-PIR-with-Default construction is that the server has to modify its inputs to Value-Or-Default, but there are no changes to the Value-Or-Default protocol itself.

After SS-AV, parties hold secret shares of the associated value v if $(x, v) \in \mathcal{P}$. To complete the PIR-with-Default functionality, the client has to either reconstruct v or obtain a default value d from the server. We translate the shares into the required output using 2 OT invocations (forward and backward) as follows.

In the "forward" OT, the client chooses a random value $\Delta_{\mathcal{C}} \leftarrow \{0, 1\}^\ell$, and acts as OT's sender with OT's messages $\{\Delta_{\mathcal{C}} + b_{\mathcal{C}} \cdot v_{\mathcal{C}}, \Delta_{\mathcal{C}} + (1 - b_{\mathcal{C}}) \cdot v_{\mathcal{C}}\}$, while the server acts as OT's receiver with a choice bit $b_{\mathcal{S}}$, and obtains q. Clearly, $q = \Delta_{\mathcal{C}} + (b_{\mathcal{C}} \oplus b_{\mathcal{S}}) \cdot v_{\mathcal{C}} = \Delta_{\mathcal{C}} + b \cdot v_{\mathcal{C}}$.

INPUT:
- Server S: A bit b_S and two strings v_S and d each $\in Z_\ell$.
- Client C: A bit b_C and a string $v_C \in Z_\ell$.

DESIRED OUTPUT:
- Server S: No output.
- Client C: $v = v_S + v_C$ if $b = 1$, or d if $b = 0$, where $b = b_S \oplus b_C$

PROTOCOL:

1. C chooses $\Delta_C \leftarrow Z_\ell$ at random.
2. Parties invoke an OT instance:
    - C acts as OT's sender with OT's messages $m_0 = \Delta_C + b_C \cdot v_C$ and $m_1 = \Delta_C + (1 - b_C) \cdot v_C$.
    - S acts as OT's receiver with a choice bit b_S, and obtains q. Note that $q = \Delta_C + b \cdot v_C$ where $b = b_S \oplus b_C$
3. Parties invoke another OT instance:
    - S acts as OT's sender with inputs $m_0 = q + (b_S \cdot v_S) + ((1 - b_S) \cdot d)$ and $m_1 = q + ((1 - b_S) \cdot v_S) + (b_S \cdot d)$.
    - C acts as OT's receiver with a choice bit b_C, and receives q'. Note that $q' = q + (b \cdot v_S) + ((1 - b) \cdot d)$ where $b = b_S \oplus b_C$
4. C outputs $q' - \Delta_C$. Note that the output is exactly $v_S + v_C$ if $b = 1$, or d if $b = 0$, where $b = b_S \oplus b_C$

Fig. 4. Our Value-Or-Default Construction. All arithmetic is implicitly in $\mathbb{Z}_\ell$.

In the "backward" OT, the server acts as OT's sender with input $\{q + b_S \cdot v + (1 - b_S) \cdot d, q + (1 - b_S) \cdot v + b_S \cdot d\}$ while the client acts as OT's receiver with a choice bit b_C, and receives q'. It is easy to see that $q' = q + b \cdot v_S + (1 - b) \cdot d$. Finally the client reconstructs it output $o = q' - \Delta_C$.

5.3 Construction 2: PIR-with-Default with Sublinear Communication

Our second construction aims to remove the expensive offline setup phase from our first construction, replacing it by (standard) Private Information Retrieval queries.

Recall that the offline Phase in Construction 1 consists of S sending encrypted BF and GBF to the client. For each query x_j C homomorphically sums the entries corresponding to $h_i(x_j)$ for each of the k hash functions h_i, additively masks the encrypted result, and sends it to the server.

In Construction 2, C will instead obliviously query the server at the locations $h_i(x_j)$, and will receive the masked sum of the corresponding values at those locations in BF and GBF. Note that if C only needed to retrieve the entries at locations $h_i(x_j)$ (without summing or masking), then C could have used standard (symmetric) PIR. In order to execute the query results summed and masked, we have C instead use a modified version of PIR, which we call Sum-PIR.

Sum-PIR Functionality. The Sum-PIR primitive allows a receiver C, holding a set of indices $p_1, \ldots, p_k$, to interact with a server holding a database $\mathcal{P}$ and receive $\sum_{i=1}^{k} \mathcal{P}[p_i] - r$, for some additive mask r held by the server. The server should not learn the entries queried by the client.

Our construction for Sum-PIR builds on standard constructions of PIR from additively homomorphic encryption, for example [ACLS18, ALP+19]. In the basic version of these constructions, the receiver $\mathcal{C}$ sends η ciphertexts $c_1, \ldots, c_\eta$ to the server, where $\eta = |\mathcal{P}|$ is the number of items held by the server. These ciphertexts all encrypt 0, except the c_i (where i is the index $\mathcal{C}$ wishes to retrieve), which encrypts 1. The server $\mathcal{S}$ receives these ciphertexts and performs a homomorphic dot-product between these ciphertexts and its database $\mathcal{P}$. This results in a ciphertext $c^* = \sum_{j=1}^{\eta} \mathcal{P}[j] \cdot c_j$, which is an encryption of exactly $\mathcal{P}[i]$. $\mathcal{S}$ then sends c^* to the client who decrypts to receive its desired value.

We observe that if the client wishes to instead receive the sum of k entries, then it can send k PIR queries simultaneously to the server, who executes the computation described above, and *homomorphically sums* the resulting ciphertexts before returning the result to the client. The result will then contain exactly the sum of the k queried items. If we additionally want the result to be masked, then the server can homomorphically add a chosen mask r to the result before returning it to the client.

While the basic construction described has high client communication costs, we can perform several optimizations to reduce the communication and computation costs, which we describe in Sect. 7. We also note that the description above only requires additively homomorphic encryption. However, some of our optimizations will additionally require homomorphic multiplications. Therefore, our construction will be from RLWE-based somewhat-HE [BGV14].

We present our Sum-PIR functionality and its construction in Fig. 5. The security of our Sum-PIR construction follows in a straightforward way from the security of its building block (e.g. PIR).

Building PIR-with-Default from Sum-PIR. Our second PIR-with-Default construction is presented in Fig. 6 and works as follows. In the setup phase, the server inserts its database into a Bloom filter BF and a Garbled Bloom filter GBF. The online execution starts the SS-PMT phase, which now consists of a Sum-PIR execution. For each item $x_{i \in [t]}$, the client inputs a set of indices $\{h_1(x_i), \ldots, h_k(x_i)\}$ while the server inputs BF and a random mask r. Similar to Construction 1, the parties obtain secret share of the value p which is smaller than $k+1$. The parties then use their obtained values as inputs to the 1-out-of-$(k+1)$ OT that translates these shares into output of SS-PMT functionality.

For SS-AV computation, the parties also invoke Sum-PIR. We observe that the client can *reuse* the queries from the SS-PMT phase in the SS-AV phase, since it is querying the same indices (i.e., $\mathcal{C}$ does not need to send PIR.Query to the server in Step (2,a) of Fig. 5) while the server inputs GBF and a random mask $v_{\mathcal{S}}$. Sum-PIR directly gives parties SS-AV's outputs as desired.

In the setting of Extended-PIR-with-Default , for each $j \in [t]$, the client additionally sends encryption of w_j to the server who homomorphically multiplies it with the PIR results in Step (2,c) of Fig. 5 before masking the result with the additive mask $v_{\mathcal{S}}$ in Step (2,d) of Fig. 5.

INPUT:
- Server $\mathcal{S}$: A database D of size η and an additive mask r
- Client $\mathcal{C}$: a set of indices $p_1, \ldots, p_k$.

DESIRED OUTPUT:
- Server $\mathcal{S}$: no output
- Client $\mathcal{C}$: $v = \sum_{i=1}^{k} D[p_i] - r$

PROTOCOL:

1. $\mathcal{C}$ generates a public-secret key pair (pk, sk) with PIR.Gen, and sends pk to $\mathcal{S}$
2. $\mathcal{S}$ and $\mathcal{C}$ invoke multi-query PIR. For each $i \in [k]$,
   - (a) $\mathcal{C}$ uses PIR.Query(pk, p_i) to generate a query q_i and sends it to $\mathcal{S}$
   - (b) $\mathcal{S}$ uses PIR.Answer(pk, q_i, D) to generate the answer d_i.
   - (c) $\mathcal{S}$ homomorphically computes $c = \sum_{i=1}^{k} d_i$
   - (d) $\mathcal{S}$ homomorphically masks c^* with r as $c^* \leftarrow c - \mathsf{HEnc}(pk, r)$.
   - (e) $\mathcal{S}$ sends c^* to $\mathcal{C}$.
3. $\mathcal{C}$ outputs PIR.Extract(sk, c^*)

Fig. 5. Our Sum-PIR Construction.

Finally, the server and client engage in the Value-Or-Default protocol as before to translate the outputs of the previous two steps into the associated value or the default value. This protocol is the same as in Construction 1.

Hashing Based Multi-query PIR-with-Default Construction. Construction 2 based on Sum-PIR relies heavily on several PIR queries (see Step 2 of Fig. 5), with one query for each client input, which is executed against the server's data at the same time. However, standard PIR techniques require the server to touch each item in its dataset for each client query, which quickly becomes expensive. In this section, we describe an optimization based on hashing to bins that enables large cost savings when executing multiple parallel PIR executions. Variants of this idea have appeared in previous work: [ACLS18, ALP+19] proposed a new PIR construction for sparse databases based on Cuckoo hashing to amortize CPU cost when making multiple PIR queries. We also show how to leverage a hashing technique [KMP+17, PRTY19] to speed up the computational cost of Construction 2.

Our main idea is that the parties use hashing to partition its items into m bins. Each bin contains a smaller fraction of inputs, which allows the parties to evaluate PIR-with-Default or Extended-PIR-with-Default bin-by-bin. The amount of data the server has to touch per query is now only the items that were mapped to the same bin as the client query, which is much more efficient computationally.

Our hashing based PIR-with-Default construction is presented in the full version of this work [LPR+20]. In this construction, parties hash their items to bins using one of the hashing schemes described above, and execute PIR-with-Default bin-by-bin. We note that when we use this hashing technique, we are able to achieve a weakened version of PIR-with-Default. Specifically, the server cannot assign a particular default value specifically to the ith client query since it does not know which

PARAMETERS:
- Security parameter λ.
- Server $\mathcal{S}$ input set size n, associated value space $\mathbb{Z}_\ell$, number of client $\mathcal{C}$ queries t .
- A 1-out-of-k OT primitive and a Sum-PIR primitive.
- Bloom Filter parameters: Bloom filter size η sufficient to hold n items, a number of hash functions k, a hash function family HF : $\{0,1\}^* \to [\eta]$.

INPUT:
- Server $\mathcal{S}$: A set of key-value pairs $\mathcal{P} = \{(y_1, v_1), \ldots, (y_n, v_n)\}$ with distinct y_i, and a set of default values $D = \{d_1, ..., d_t\}$, where each $v_i, d_i \in \mathbb{Z}_\ell$. Additionally a set of t masks $\{s_1, ..., s_t\}$ each $\in \mathbb{Z}_\ell$.
- Client $\mathcal{C}$: A set of t queries $\{x_1, ..., x_t\}$. Additionally a set of t associated values $\{w_1, ..., w_t\}$, each $\in \mathbb{Z}_\ell$.

PROTOCOL:
1. **Setup phase:**
   - $\mathcal{S}$ and $\mathcal{C}$ jointly select k hash functions $\{h_1, ..., h_k\}$ at random from HF.
   - $\mathcal{S}$ inserts a set of keys $\{y_1, \ldots, y_n\}$ into a Bloom filter BF and the set of key-value pairs $\mathcal{P}$ into a Garbled Bloom filter GBF using hash functions h_i. $\mathcal{S}$ aborts if either insertion operation fails.
2. **Online phase:** The following steps are executed in parallel for each x_j for $j \in [t]$.
   (a) SS-PMT computation:
      - $\mathcal{S}$ selects a mask $r \leftarrow \mathbb{Z}_\ell$.
      - $\mathcal{C}$ and $\mathcal{S}$ execute a Sum-PIR query. $\mathcal{C}$ uses inputs $h_1 x_j, ..., h_k(x_j)$. $\mathcal{S}$ uses BF and r as input.
      - $\mathcal{C}$ receives $r' = -r + \sum_{i=1}^{k} BF[h_i(x_j)]$ as output.
      - Parties invoke an instance of 1-out-of-$(k+1)$ OT:
         - $\mathcal{S}$ chooses a bit $b_\mathcal{S}$ at random.
         - $\mathcal{S}$ acts as OT's sender with input $\{b_0, \ldots, b_k\}$ where each b_i is equal to $b_\mathcal{S}$, except $b_{(-r+k) \mod (k+1)}$ which is equal to $1 \oplus b_\mathcal{S}$.
         - $\mathcal{C}$ acts as OT's receiver with choice $r' \mod (k+1)$.
         - $\mathcal{C}$ obtains $b_\mathcal{C}$ from the OT's functionality.
   (b) SS-AV computation:
      - $\mathcal{C}$ sends HEnc(pk, w_j) to $\mathcal{S}$.
      - $\mathcal{S}$ selects a mask $v_\mathcal{S} \leftarrow \mathbb{Z}_\ell$.
      - $\mathcal{C}$ and $\mathcal{S}$ execute a Sum-PIR query. $\mathcal{C}$ uses inputs $h_1 x_j, ..., h_k(x_j)$. $\mathcal{S}$ uses GBF and $v_\mathcal{S}$ as input.
      - Prior to additively masking the Sum-PIR result c with $v_\mathcal{S}$ to compute c^*, $\mathcal{S}$ homomorphically multiplies c with HEnc(pk, w_j)
      - $\mathcal{S}$ receives mask $v_\mathcal{S}$ as output. $\mathcal{C}$ receives $v_\mathcal{C} = -v_\mathcal{S} + w_j \cdot \sum_{i=1}^{k} GBF[h_i(x_j)]$ as output.
   (c) Value-Or-Default computation:
      - $\mathcal{S}$ and $\mathcal{C}$ engage in a Value-Or-Default protocol execution described in Figure 4.
      - $\mathcal{S}$ uses inputs $b_\mathcal{S}$, $v_\mathcal{S} - s_j$ and $d_j - s_j$.
      - $\mathcal{C}$ uses inputs $b_\mathcal{C}$ and $v_\mathcal{C}$.
      - Let o_j be the output received by $\mathcal{C}$ from the Value-Or-Default protocol execution
3. **Output:** $\mathcal{C}$ outputs the set $O = \{o_j\}_{j \in [t]}$.

Fig. 6. Construction 2: PIR-with-default construction with sublinear communication. Portions with changes highlighted are needed for achieving Extended-PIR-with-Default

bin this query got assigned to. Rather, the server must assign defaults to the ith client query *per-bin*. That is, default values must be assigned bin-wise. The same holds true for masks in the case of Extended-PIR-with-Default . We observe that this does not impact any of our applications, since they have $\mathcal{S}$ choose all default values (and masks) the same way (as a random share of 0), independent of which specific client query is being responded to. Therefore these applications lose nothing from assigning default values and masks by bin.

An additional difference is that the hashing-based modification needs both the client and server to pad their inputs with dummy values so that each bin is of the same size. These dummy values need to be chosen carefully so that they are distinct for the client and server, and never occur in either party's input set. Our formulation [LPR+20] makes it so whenever $\mathcal{C}$ uses a dummy value, it always receives the default value. $\mathcal{S}$ therefore has to provide additional default values to allow for the increased number of client queries due to padding. We also note that in the case of PIR-with-Default, the client can just discard the values received for dummy items. However, for Extended-PIR-with-Default , the client must preserve these values, since the server has received a mask-share for them, and may use it in downstream computation. This implies another caveat for using hashing: the downstream computation for Extended-PIR-with-Default must also be able to smoothly handle additional default values corresponding to dummy client inputs. We observe that our applications are all able to smoothly do so, since their defaults and masks all correspond to random shares of 0, and computation that follows can accommodate additional shares of 0 while remaining correct.

We now discuss concrete hashing schemes and parameters. If there are m bins, each with maximum load γ items on the client's side, then the number of default values the server must provide is $m\gamma$. In the setting of Extended-PIR-with-Default, the number of additive masks the server must provide is also $m\gamma$.

Concretely, the client uses Cuckoo hashing or 2-choice hashing with k hash functions, and inserts her items into m bins. The server maps his points into m bins using the same set of k hash functions (i.e., each of the server's items appears k times across all over bins). Using a standard ball-and-bin analysis based on k, m, and the input size of client $|X|$, one can deduce an upper bound β such that no server bin contains more than β items with high probability $(1 - 2^{-\lambda})$.

In our protocol, we use Cuckoo hashing, the client can place its set into a Cuckoo table of size $m = 1.27t$ using $k = 3$ hash functions. There are only 3% dummy items [PSTY19] required per bin on the server's side. Therefore, the client and server maximum bin size are $\gamma = 1$ and $\beta = 1.03\lceil 3n/m\rceil$, respectively.

5.4   Correctness and Security Proofs

We observe that our constructions are correct by observation, except with the negligible probability of Bloom Filter failure. In particular, our constructions fail to be correct if the server is unable to hash its items into a BF or GBF, or if the

Bloom filter returns a false positive on a client query. However, we note that we can set parameters so that the probability of such failures is negligible.

The security proof of the following theorem is given in Appendix 5.4.

Theorem 1. *The* PIR-with-Default *constructions 1 and 2 described in Fig. 3 and Fig. 6 securely implement the* PIR-with-Default *functionality defined in Fig. 1 in the semi-honest setting, given the OT, HE, and* Sum-PIR *functionalities described in Sect. 5.3.*

Because the client's associated values w_j are either masked with random or encrypted before sending to the server, the security of our Extended-PIR-with-Default constructions follows straightforwardly from the security of PIR-with-Default and the encryption scheme. Thus, we omit the proof of the following theorem.

Theorem 2. *The* Extended-PIR-with-Default *constructions 1 and 2 described in Fig. 3 and Fig. 6 securely implement the* Extended-PIR-with-Default *functionality defined in Fig. 2 in the semi-honest setting, given the OT, HE, and* Sum-PIR *functionalities described in Sect. 5.3.*

6   Two Party PJC

6.1   Inner-Product Private Join and Compute

The functionality of Extended-PIR-with-Default provides directly a protocol for inner-product private join and compute. In particular, a client with input $(X, W) = \{(x_1, w_1), \ldots, (x_t, w_t)\}$ and a server with input $(Y, V) = \{(y_1, v_1), \ldots, (y_n, v_n)\}$ execute the Extended-PIR-with-Default protocol where the server uses 0 as the default value for all queries. The two parties receives as outputs additive shares of $w_i \cdot v_i$ is $x_i \in Y$, or shares of 0 otherwise. Now each of the parties sums locally all the shares they have obtained, and in doing so they obtain shares of the value $\sum_{i \in [t], j \in [n], x_i = y_j} w_i v_j$, which is the desired output.

Private set intersection-SUM is a special case of inner-product PJC can also be obtained in the same way as above except that the client uses weight equal to 1 in the execution of the Extended-PIR-with-Default protocol. For a slightly more efficient implementation the parties can use a *plain* PIR-with-Default execution, where for the i-th client query, the server additively masks all values with the same mask s_i, and sets s_i to be the default value, and uses these values as input to the protocol. The client then receives effectively an additive share of the associated value or of 0, with the server's share being $-s_i$. Parties can sum their shares locally to get additive shares of the intersection-sum.

If the server sets $v_i = 1$ for all $i \in [n]$, this protocol computes the cardinality of the intersection for the two input sets. Since the two parties obtain shares of the cardinality they can further execute a two-party protocol that checks whether the cardinality is above a threshold.

6.2   General PJC

The Extended-PIR-with-Default functionality enables the two parties to obtain shares of the associated values for the server's records included in the intersection, or shares of zero for the records with identifiers in $Y \setminus X$. We note we can obtain such shares for multiple attributes values associated with record.

We can also enable the two parties to obtain shares of the client's attribute values (or vectors of attribute values) for the intersection records (and shares of 0 for the records in $Y \setminus X$) as follows: The client executes PIR-with-Default with an input x_i to receive a share of the server's associated attribute(s). The client and the server execute a 1-out-of-2 OT similar to Step 2 of the Value-Or-Default protocol, using the shares of membership bit b_C and b_S from the SS-PMT phase of the preceding PIR-with-Default, where the client uses inputs $m_0 = r_i + b_C \cdot w_i$, $m_1 = r_i + (1 - b_C) \cdot w_i$ for a random mask r_i, and the server uses b_S as its choice bit. The result will be an additive sharing of either w_i or 0.

At this point the two parties can run any general two-party computation protocol which takes as input the shares of the attribute values for the records in $X \cap Y$ and shares of 0 for records in $Y \setminus X$, and evaluates a function on these attribute values.

6.3   Supporting Differentially Private Outputs

The above approach to compute general functions on the inner-join data can also be extended easily to support differential privacy (DP) [DMNS06] for the output by having the two parties compute jointly DP noise that will be added to the output. Since we are constructing semi-honest protocols each party can locally compute noise with the magnitude required for the resulting output. This means that the noise will be double the standard amount of noise, but this is needed in order to prevent either of the parties from subtracting its noise contribution from the output. The ability to add noise is important when the records in the input data sets are records of individuals and the PJC output is aggregate statistics over the users in the inner-join database, which should not reveal information about individuals.

7   Implementation

In the full version of this work [LPR+20], we revisit the state of the art constructions and optimizations of single-server PIR based on RLWE-based homomorphic encryption: SealPIR [ACLS18] and MulPIR [ALP+19]. Then, we explain how to apply the optimizations of the latter works to the application setting of our new PIR-with-Default construction. In particular, note that we achieve sublinear communication using recursion and multiplicative homomorphism, and use oblivious expansion to compress the upload as in [ALP+19]. Finally, we explain how to embed weights in PIR queries for the Extended-PIR-with-Default construction. The communication cost of all protocols is calculated according to Sect. 7.2 (Fig. 8).

Table 2. Communication and computation costs of PIR-with-Default with elements of 32 bits. Running time is amortized over the number of client queries.

Parameters		Construction 1				Construction 2		Circuit PSI [PSTY19]		Poly-ROOM [SGRP19]		PJC+RLWE [IKN+20]	
		Setup		Online		Online		Online		Online		Online	
		Comm.	Time	Comm.	Time	Comm.	Time	Comm.	Time	Comm.	Time	Comm.	Time
n	t	(MB)	(/query)	(MB)	(/query)	(MB)	(/query)	(MB)	(/query)	(MB)	(/query)	(MB)	(/query)
2^{16}	2^8	29	35 ms	7	2.43 ms	27	673 ms	5	11.79 ms	55	59 ms*	3†	44.8 ms†
	2^{12}	29	2.19 ms	112	1.03 ms	120	34 ms	30	0.93 ms	863	3.5 ms*	3†	2.97 ms†
	2^{16}	29	0.14 ms	1794	0.72 ms	801	2 ms	472	0.13 ms	13788	2.2 ms*	6†	0.36 ms†
2^{20}	2^8	465	539 ms	7	2.43 ms	29	11821 ms	51	178 ms	71	–	40†	713 ms†
	2^{12}	465	34 ms	112	1.03 ms	213	521 ms	76	11.31 ms	878	–	40†	44.7 ms†
	2^{16}	465	2.11 ms	1794	0.72 ms	1821	34 ms	522	0.78 ms	13837	–	44†	2.97 ms†
2^{25}	2^8	14885	17252 ms	7	2.43 ms	44	370s	1582	5668 ms	591	–	1272†	22838 ms†
	2^{12}	14885	1078 ms	112	1.03 ms	379	15.8s	1607	354 ms	1401	–	1272†	1427 ms†
	2^{16}	14885	67 ms	1794	0.72 ms	3704	1.1s	2180	22.22 ms	14391	–	1276†	89 ms†

Machine: single core of Intel(R) Xeon(R) CPU E5-2696 v3 @ 2.30GHz. For all constructions and $n = 2^{25}$, times have been estimated from microbenchmarks of the core operations, and fixed cost for a random access was assumed.

* The times for Poly-ROOM are taken from [SGRP19, Fig. 17], initially provided for a database $n = 50,000$ and a number of queries $t = 5,000$ and $50,000$. Unknown machine.

† Although PJC+RLWE does not achieve the PIR-with-Default functionality, we report it for comparison purpose. Timings are estimated from microbenchmarks of NIST-P256, and RLWE-encryption with degree 2048 and 62 bit modulus.

7.1   Communication and Computation

Asymptotically, Construction 2 (Fig. 6) achieves sublinear communication per client query with respect to the server database size. In our benchmarking, we will make use of the hashing-based multi-query PIR-with-Default Construction described in Sect. 5.3 to reduce server costs. For both our constructions (and related work), we report the communication cost of t queries against a database of key-value pairs of size n with 32-bit values, for $2^8 \leq t \leq 2^{16}$ and $2^{16} \leq n \leq 2^{25}$, and the computational cost amortized over the number of queries t, in Table 2.

For Construction 1 (Fig. 3), we report the cost of encrypting a Bloom Filter and Garbled Bloom Filter of dimension $58n$ with an homomorphic encryption scheme. We use the Shell homomorphic encryption library [she20] with HE parameters $d = 1024$, $\log_2(q) = 15$ for the encryption of the Bloom filter, and $d = 2048$, $\log_2(q) = 46$ for the encryption of the Garbled Bloom filter, both ensuring more than 128 bits of security [APS15] and allowing $k = 31$ homomorphic additions. Each coefficient of the polynomials embeds a cell of the (Garbled) Bloom Filter, and rotations are performed by multiplications with x^i. As expected, the setup communication grows linearly with n and becomes larger than 15GB when $n > 2^{25}$. On the computation side, it is important to note that, assuming fixed cost for a random access, the online time *only depends on* t (and not on n).

For Construction 2 (Fig. 6), we try different combinations of the optimizations and for each input size, we report the cost for the combination with smallest communication cost. In particular, we use Cuckoo hashing with three hash functions, as described in Sect. 5.3, and loop over 5 recursions levels (1 to 5 homomorphic multiplications). Concretely, for $n = 2^{20}$ and $t = 2^8 = 256$, we

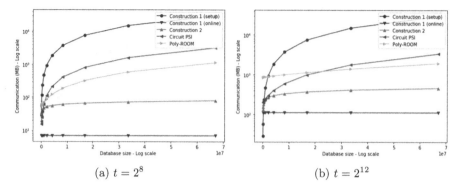

Fig. 7. Communication cost of t PIR-with-Default queries, for increasing database sizes n and fixed number t.

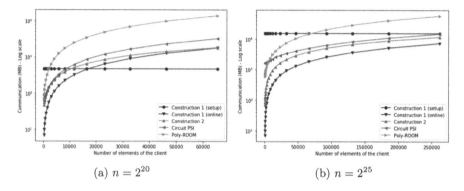

Fig. 8. Communication cost of t PIR-with-Default queries, for increasing number t and fixed database sizes n.

obtain 326 buckets for the Cuckoo hashing, each of size $576,461$. We perform $k = 31$ queries over each bucket, and use 4 homomorphic multiplications for recursion. The total number of elements transmitted is therefore approximately $5 \cdot B^{1/5} \cdot 31 \cdot 326 = 717,305$, which fits in 88 ciphertexts using oblivious expansion [ACLS18, ALP+19]. The HE parameters are $d = 8192$, $\log_2(q) = 255$, and each ciphertext is about 250 kB. The key information is about 6 MB, and the upload ciphertexts account for about 29MB of communication. Finally, the amortized time per query is 11.8s.

As illustrated in Fig. 7, for a fixed number t of elements, Construction 2 has the smallest communication footprint as the database size n increases. For database of moderate sizes $n \leq 2^{25}$ and very few elements t, our solutions use less communication than alternatives. We note that Construction 2 becomes more communication efficient relative to other solutions as the gap between n and t grows larger, with the advantage appearing when the server size is a factor of 2^{10} larger than the client dataset. Finally, we note that the computation cost is relatively higher for Construction 2 than related works, but the bulk of the cost is incurred by the server instead of shared between client and server.

7.2 Comparison to Previous Work

We compare the resulting communication of our protocols to those of the best Circuit PSI protocol [PSTY19] and ROOM [SGRP19]. The run-time comparison of the protocols is illustrated in Table 2.

We first compute the communication complexity of [PSTY19]. The communication is composed of (a) the OPRF evaluations for each of the m bins which has an amortized communication of at most 450 bits; (b) the communication of $1.03kn$ coefficients of size $\tau + \ell$ bits each where τ is approximately equal to $\lambda + \log(knt) - \log(m)$; (c) the weighted sum garbled circuit which contains m comparison of two τ-bit elements, m multiplications of two ℓ-bit associated values, and $m - 1$ additions of two ℓ-bit associated values. Using circuit compiler [MGC+16], the weighted sum garbled circuit has $m(\tau + \ell - 1) + 993m\ell + (m - 1)(\ell - 1)$ AND gates in total. Note that each AND requires 256 bits. The communication cost of garbled circuit also requires $m(\tau + \ell)$ OT instances, each requiring 256 bits of communication.

In ROOM [SGRP19], the communication is composed of (a) the communication of n coefficients of size 128 bits each; (b) m garbled AES executions, each requiring 6400 AND gates; (c) and the same weighted sum garbled circuit as that of [PSTY19], which has $t(\tau + \ell - 1) + 993t\ell + (t - 1)(\ell - 1)$ AND gates and $m(\tau + \ell)$ OT instances.

For PJC [IKN+20], we use the NIST-P256 elliptic curve, which requires 32B to represent an element. We also use RLWE-based encryption for the associated values, with degree $d = 2048$ and $\log_2(q) = 62$-bit modulus. We use their packing technique to pack 2048 associated values into a single RLWE ciphertext, together with homomorphic rotation and addition.

Note that the labeled PSI protocol proposed in [CHLR18] can be extended to perform PJC. However, the extended protocol either reveals the intersection size, or incurs extra cost due to using a generic MPC. [CHLR18] only provide experimental numbers for their implementation of a similar functionality of keyword PIR (e.g. retrieve the associated value of an intersection item) for the server's dataset of size $n = 2^{20}$ records and the 256 queries. Their protocol takes 340 ms and 20.9 ms per query in the offline and online phases, respectively. To extend their functionality to PIR-with-Default, the sender needs to mask labeled (associated) message with random value using HE, and send it to the receiver. When the receiver decrypts the ciphertext, parties hold a secret share of a correct associated value, or of a random value. These shares are forwarded to a secondary MPC protocol to perform the functionality of PIR-with-Default. Indeed, the last extended step is similar to the garbled circuit phase of [PSTY19], which takes about 40% of [PSTY19]'s total cost. Therefore, we estimate that [CHLR18] requires an extra 71.2 ms in the online phase to implement a PIR-with-Default query. In contrast, Construction 1 only takes 2.43 ms online time to perform an instance of PIR-with-Default, a 37× improvement. However, Construction 1 is 1.5× slower than [CHLR18] in the offline phase. In terms of communication/storage cost, [CHLR18] requires at least 66.56 MB transmitted without storage from the offline phase while ours needs only 7 MB transmitted but 465 MB storage from the offline phase. We present the performance comparison of ours and [CHLR18] for $n = 2^{20}$ and $t = 2^8$ in the full version of this work [LPR+20].

7.3   Monetary Costs

We estimate the monetary costs of our protocol compared to other works [IKN+20, PSTY19] using the same cost model. The cost is charged by Google Platform for pre-emptible virtual machines (including CPU and RAM). More details of the estimation of the monetary costs are shown in the full version of this work [LPR+20].

We observe that Construction 2 enables much lower client monetary costs compared to other protocols. However, due to the expensive server computation, we notice that the server monetary cost is higher than that of alternative protocols. However, the relative changes in cost make the comparison attractive. For example for $n = 2^{25}$ and $t = 2^8$, our client cost is $36.5\times$ lower than that of [PSTY19], while incurring a server cost that is only $4\times$ higher than theirs.

Acknowledgement. The last author is partially supported by NSF awards #2031799, #2101052, and #2115075. Part of this work was done while the first and last authors worked at Google.

References

[ACLS18] Angel, S., Chen, H., Laine, K., Setty, S.T.V.: PIR with compressed queries and amortized query processing. In: 2018 IEEE Symposium on Security and Privacy (2018)

[AGC20] Privacy-preserving contact tracing (2020)

[ALP+19] Ali, A., et al.: Communication-computation trade-offs in PIR. IACR Cryptology ePrint Archive 2019:1483 (2019)

[APS15] Albrecht, M.R., Player, R., Scott, S.: On the concrete hardness of learning with errors. Cryptology ePrint Archive, Report 2015/046 (2015). http://eprint.iacr.org/2015/046

[BGV14] Brakerski, Z., Gentry, C., Vaikuntanathan, V.: (leveled) fully homomorphic encryption without bootstrapping. TOCT **6**(3), 13:1–13:36 (2014)

[BKM+20] Buddhavarapu, P., Knox, A., Mohassel, P., Sengupta, S., Taubeneck, E., Vlaskin, V.: Private matching for compute. ePrint (2020)

[Blo70] Bloom, B.H.: Space/time trade-offs in hash coding with allowable errors. Commun. ACM **13**(7), 422–426 (1970)

[CGH+20] Chan, J., et al.: Pact: Privacy sensitive protocols and mechanisms for mobile contact tracing (2020)

[CGKS95] Chor, B., Goldreich, O., Kushilevitz, E., Sudan, M.: Private information retrieval. In: 36th FOCS, pp. 41–50. IEEE Computer Society Press, October 1995

[CGN98] Chor, B., Gilboa, N., Naor, M.: Private information retrieval by keywords. Cryptology ePrint Archive, Report 1998/003 (1998). http://eprint.iacr.org/1998/003

[CHLR18] Chen, H., Huang, Z., Laine, K., Rindal, P.: Labeled PSI from fully homomorphic encryption with malicious security. In: ACM CCS 2018 (2018)

[CKGS98] Chor, B., Kushilevitz, E., Goldreich, O., Sudan, M.: Private information retrieval. J. ACM **45**(6), 965–981 (1998)

[CRS03] Czumaj, A., Riley, C., Scheideler, C.: Perfectly balanced allocation. In: Arora, S., Jansen, K., Rolim, J.D.P., Sahai, A. (eds.) APPROX/RANDOM -2003. LNCS, vol. 2764, pp. 240–251. Springer, Heidelberg (2003). https://doi.org/10.1007/978-3-540-45198-3_21

[DCW13] Dong, C., Chen, L., Wen, Z.: When private set intersection meets big data: an efficient and scalable protocol. In: Sadeghi, A.-R., Gligor, V.D., Yung, M. (eds.) ACM CCS 2013, pp. 789–800. ACM Press, November 2013

[DMNS06] Dwork, C., McSherry, F., Nissim, K., Smith, A.: Calibrating noise to sensitivity in private data analysis. In: Halevi, S., Rabin, T. (eds.) TCC 2006. LNCS, vol. 3876, pp. 265–284. Springer, Heidelberg (2006). https://doi.org/10.1007/11681878_14

[DP320] Decentralized privacy-preserving proximity tracing (2020). https://github.com/DP-3T

[FV12] Fan, J., Vercauteren, F.: Somewhat practical fully homomorphic encryption. Cryptology ePrint Archive 2012:144 (2012)

[Gen09] Gentry, C.: A fully homomorphic encryption scheme. Ph.D. thesis, Stanford, CA, USA (2009)

[GIKM00] Gertner, Y., Ishai, Y., Kushilevitz, E., Malkin, T.: Protecting data privacy in private information retrieval schemes. J. Comput. Syst. Sci. (2000)

[Gol04] Goldreich, O.: The Foundations of Cryptography - Volume 2: Basic Applications. Cambridge University Press (2004)

[Goo19] GoogleBlogPost (2019). https://security.googleblog.com/2019/06/helping-organizations-do-more-without-collecting-more-data.html

[GR05] Gentry, C., Ramzan, Z.: Single-database private information retrieval with constant communication rate. In: Caires, L., Italiano, G.F., Monteiro, L., Palamidessi, C., Yung, M. (eds.) ICALP 2005. LNCS, vol. 3580, pp. 803–815. Springer, Heidelberg (2005). https://doi.org/10.1007/11523468_65

[HEK12] Huang, Y., Evans, D., Katz, J.: Private set intersection: are garbled circuits better than custom protocols? In: NDSS 2012. The Internet Society, February 2012

[IKN+20] Ion, M., et al.: On deploying secure computing commercially: private intersectionsum protocols and their business applications. In: EuroSP (2020)

[KK13] Kolesnikov, V., Kumaresan, R.: Improved OT extension for transferring short secrets. In: Canetti, R., Garay, J.A. (eds.) CRYPTO 2013. LNCS, vol. 8043, pp. 54–70. Springer, Heidelberg (2013). https://doi.org/10.1007/978-3-642-40084-1_4

[KKRT16] Kolesnikov, V., Kumaresan, R., Rosulek, M., Trieu, N.: Efficient batched oblivious PRF with applications to private set intersection. In: ACM CCS 2016 (2016)

[KLOR20] Kreuter, B., Lepoint, T., Orru, M., Raykova, M.: Efficient anonymous tokens with private metadata bit. Cryptology ePrint Archive, Report 2020/072 (2020)

[KLS+17] Kiss, Á., Liu, J., Schneider, T., Asokan, N., Pinkas, B.: Private set intersection for unequal set sizes with mobile applications. In: PoPETs (2017)

[KMP+17] Kolesnikov, V., Matania, N., Pinkas, B., Rosulek, M., Trieu, N.: Practical multi-party private set intersection from symmetric-key techniques. In: ACM CCS 2017 (2017)

[LPR+20] Lepoint, T., Patel, S., Raykova, M., Seth, K., Trieu, N.: Private join and compute from PIR with default. Cryptology ePrint Archive, Report 2020/1011 (2020). https://ia.cr/2020/1011

[Mea86] Meadows, C.A.: A more efficient cryptographic matchmaking protocol for use in the absence of a continuously available third party. In: IEEE Symposium on Security and Privacy, pp. 134–137 (1986)

[MGC+16] Mood, B., Gupta, D., Carter, H., Butler, K.R.B., Traynor, P.: Frigate: a validated, extensible, and efficient compiler and interpreter for secure computation. In: IEEE European Symposium on Security and Privacy, EuroS&P 2016, Saarbrücken, Germany, 21–24 March 2016, pp. 112–127. IEEE (2016)

[min] http://mint.sbg.ac.at

[OOS17] Orru, M., Orsini, E., Schol, P.: Actively secure 1-out-of-N OT extension with application to private set intersection. In: CT-RSA (2017)

[PR01] Pagh, R., Rodler, F.F.: Cuckoo hashing. In: auf der Heide, F.M. (ed.) ESA 2001. LNCS, vol. 2161, pp. 121–133. Springer, Heidelberg (2001). https://doi.org/10.1007/3-540-44676-1_10

[PRTY19] Pinkas, B., Rosulek, M., Trieu, N., Yanai, A.: SpOT-Light: lightweight private set intersection from sparse OT extension. In: Boldyreva, A., Micciancio, D. (eds.) CRYPTO 2019. LNCS, vol. 11694, pp. 401–431. Springer, Cham (2019). https://doi.org/10.1007/978-3-030-26954-8_13

[PRTY20] Pinkas, B., Rosulek, M., Trieu, N., Yanai, A.: PSI from PaXoS: fast, malicious private set intersection. In: Canteaut, A., Ishai, Y. (eds.) EUROCRYPT 2020. LNCS, vol. 12106, pp. 739–767. Springer, Cham (2020). https://doi.org/10.1007/978-3-030-45724-2_25

[PSSZ15] Pinkas, B., Schneider, T., Segev, G., Zohner, M.: Phasing: private set intersection using permutation-based hashing. In: USENIX Security 2015 (2015)

[PSTY19] Pinkas, B., Schneider, T., Tkachenko, O., Yanai, A.: Efficient circuit-based PSI with linear communication. In: Ishai, Y., Rijmen, V. (eds.) EUROCRYPT 2019. LNCS, vol. 11478, pp. 122–153. Springer, Cham (2019). https://doi.org/10.1007/978-3-030-17659-4_5

[PSZ18] Pinkas, B., Schneider, T., Zohner, M.: Scalable private set intersection based on OT extension. In: ACM TOPS (2018)

[RA18] Resende, A.C.D., Aranha, D.F.: Faster unbalanced private set intersection. In: Meiklejohn, S., Sako, K. (eds.) FC 2018. LNCS, vol. 10957, pp. 203–221. Springer, Heidelberg (2018). https://doi.org/10.1007/978-3-662-58387-6_11

[Rab05] Rabin, M.O.: How to exchange secrets with oblivious transfer. ePrint 2005/187 (2005)

[SGRP19] Schoppmann, P., Gascón, A., Raykova, M., Pinkas, B.: Make some ROOM for the zeros: data sparsity in secure distributed machine learning. In: ACM Conference on Computer and Communications Security, pp. 1335–1350. ACM (2019)

[she20] Simple homomorphic encryption library with lattices (2020). https://github.com/google/shell-encryption

[TSS+20] Trieu, N., Shehata, K., Saxena, P., Shokri, R., Song, D.: Epione: lightweight contact tracing with strong privacy, arXiv (2020)

Generalized Channels from Limited Blockchain Scripts and Adaptor Signatures

Lukas Aumayr[1](✉), Oguzhan Ersoy[2](✉), Andreas Erwig[3](✉),
Sebastian Faust[3](✉), Kristina Hostáková[4](✉), Matteo Maffei[1](✉),
Pedro Moreno-Sanchez[5](✉), and Siavash Riahi[3](✉)

[1] Technische Universität Wien, Vienna, Austria
{Lukas.Aumayr,Matteo.Maffei}@tuwien.ac.at
[2] Delft University of Technology, Delft, Netherlands
o.ersoy@tudelft.nl
[3] Technische Universität Darmstadt, Darmstadt, Germany
{Andreas.Erwig,Sebastian.Faust,Siavash.Riahi}@tu-darmstadt.de
[4] ETH Zürich, Zürich, Switzerland
kristina.hostakova@inf.ethz.ch
[5] IMDEA Software Institute, Madrid, Spain
pedro.moreno@imdea.org

Abstract. Decentralized and permissionless ledgers offer an inherently low transaction rate, as a result of their consensus protocol demanding the storage of each transaction on-chain. A prominent proposal to tackle this scalability issue is to utilize off-chain protocols, where parties only need to post a limited number of transactions on-chain. Existing solutions can roughly be categorized into: (i) application-specific channels (e.g., payment channels), offering strictly weaker functionality than the underlying blockchain; and (ii) state channels, supporting arbitrary smart contracts at the cost of being compatible only with the few blockchains having Turing-complete scripting languages (e.g., Ethereum).

In this work, we introduce and formalize the notion of *generalized channels* allowing users to perform any operation supported by the underlying blockchain in an off-chain manner. Generalized channels thus extend the functionality of payment channels and relax the definition of state channels. We present a concrete construction compatible with any blockchain supporting transaction authorization, time-locks and constant number of Boolean ∧ and ∨ operations – requirements fulfilled by many (non-Turing-complete) blockchains including the popular Bitcoin. To this end, we leverage *adaptor signatures* – a cryptographic primitive already used in the cryptocurrency literature but formalized as a standalone primitive in this work for the first time. We formally prove the security of our generalized channel construction in the Universal Composability framework.

As an important practical contribution, our generalized channel construction outperforms the state-of-the-art payment channel construction, the Lightning Network, in efficiency. Concretely, it halves the off-chain communication complexity and reduces the on-chain footprint in case of disputes from linear to constant in the number of off-chain applications funded by the channel. Finally, we evaluate the practicality of our

© International Association for Cryptologic Research 2021
M. Tibouchi and H. Wang (Eds.): ASIACRYPT 2021, LNCS 13091, pp. 635–664, 2021.
https://doi.org/10.1007/978-3-030-92075-3_22

construction via a prototype implementation and discuss various applications including financially secured fair two-party computation.

Keywords: Blockchain · Adaptor signatures · Off-chain protocols and channels

1   Introduction

One of the most fundamental technical challenges of decentralized and permissionless blockchains is scalability. Since transactions are processed via a costly distributed consensus protocol run among a set of parties (so-called miners), transaction throughput is limited and transaction confirmation is slow. There has been a plethora of work on improving scalability of blockchains, with off-chain protocols being one of the most promising solutions.

Intuitively, off-chain protocols build a second layer over the blockchain (often referred to as the *layer-1*) by allowing the vast majority of transactions to be processed directly between the involved participants, with the blockchain being used only in the initial setup and in case of disputes, thereby drastically improving transaction throughput and confirmation time.

While there exists a large variety of different off-chain (or layer-2) solutions (see, e.g., [6,30,32,53] and many more), *payment channels* [10,19,47] are by far the most prominent one. Intuitively, a payment channel works in three phases. First, the two users *open* a channel by locking a certain amount of coins on-chain into an account controlled by both users. Then they perform an arbitrary amount of payments by exchanging authenticated messages *off-chain*. Finally, they *close* the channel by announcing the outcome of their trades to the ledger.

Off-chain computations in Ethereum. Ethereum supports on-chain transactions specified in a *Turing-complete scripting language*, which enables the execution of arbitrarily complex programs, also called smart contracts, thereby going beyond simple payments. The underlying blockchain is organized accordingly in the account-based model, in which the balance associated to an account is explicitly stored in its memory and programmatically updated via smart contracts. By leveraging the expressiveness of Turing-complete scripting languages, payment channels can be generalized into so-called *state channels* [22,23,43], whose functionality goes far beyond simple payments. Namely, state channels enable users to execute arbitrarily complex smart contracts in an off-chain manner, thereby making their execution faster and cheaper.

Turing-complete vs restricted scripting. The majority of current blockchains (e.g., Bitcoin, Zcash, Monero, and Cardano's ADA) only support a restricted scripting language and are based on the Unspent Transaction Output (UTXO) model: intuitively, they enable a restricted class of transactions, possibly conditioned to some events, that transfer money from an unspent transaction to a new unspent transaction. There are several reasons behind the choice of a limited scripting language. First, the simplicity of design and usage, which is believed to be beneficial for security: countless examples of smart contract vulnerabilities on Ethereum show that complex contract logic and increased expressiveness pave the way for critical bugs, which may have severe consequences for the stability of the underlying currency as shown by the infamous DAO hack [48]. Second, blockchains with simple transaction logic are less costly to maintain: this is important as transaction execution is done by many parties, and even normal users. Finally, restricted scripting languages are expressive enough to encode many interesting computations (e.g., lotteries [2], auctions [21], and more [7,8,37]).

Unfortunately, current state channel constructions are not applicable without a Turing-complete scripting language, thereby excluding the majority of blockchains. In this work, we investigate the following question: *Can we generically lift any transaction logic offered by layer-1 to layer-2 even for blockchains with restricted transaction logic?* Besides its practical importance, we believe that this question is theoretically interesting. It may constitute a first step towards a more general research agenda exploring the feasibility (or impossibility) of generic off-chain computation from blockchains with limited expressiveness.

1.1 Our Contribution

Our main contribution is to put forward the notion of *generalized channels* – a generic extension of payment channels to support off-chain execution of *arbitrary transaction logic* supported by the underlying blockchain. State channels can hence be seen as a special case of generalized channels for blockchains with Turing-complete scripting languages. We briefly outline our main contributions below. A technical overview of our construction is given in Sect. 2.

Generalized Channels. We show that if the underlying UTXO-based blockchain supports transaction authorization, time-locks and basic Boolean logic (constant number of $\wedge$, $\vee$ operations), then *any* transaction logic available on layer-1 can be lifted to layer-2 securely and generically.

As most cryptocurrencies, including the by far most prominent Bitcoin, satisfy the assumptions of our construction, they can benefit from generalized channels as a scalability solution. This, in particular, implies that our construction directly enables to execute *any* Bitcoin transaction off-chain. Moreover, we stress that our construction can also be deployed over any blockchain that can simulate a UTXO-based system, which, in particular, includes blockchains with support for Turing-complete smart contracts, e.g., Ethereum or Hyperledger Fabric [1].

A novel revocation mechanism for generalized channels. The main technical challenge in our generalized channel design is to propose an efficient mechanism for old channel state revocation while putting minimal assumptions on the scripting language of the underlying blockchain. The state-of-the-art approach, put forward by the Lightning Network [47], uses a punishment mechanism which allows the cheated party to claim all coins from the channel. As we argue, a straightforward generalization of the Ligthning-style revocation is unsuitable for generalized channels. Firstly, the blockchain communication complexity in case of misbehavior depends on the number of parallel conditional payments funded by the channel. This significantly increases the blockchain overhead when processing a punishment (if triggered). Secondly, the security of the revocation mechanism relies on state duplication, hence each off-chain transaction funded by the channel has to be performed twice (once on each duplicate). This is particularly problematic when channels are built on top of channels [26] as the off-chain communication complexity grows exponentially with the number of channel layers.

To overcome these drawbacks, we design a novel revocation mechanism reducing the on-chain complexity in case of a dispute from linear to constant, and the off-chain communication complexity from exponential to linear.

Formalization of adaptor signatures. A key idea of our novel revocation mechanism is to utilize an *adaptor signature scheme* [46] – a cryptographic primitive introduced by the cryptocurrency community to tie together the authorization of a transaction and the leakage of a secret value. Although adaptor signatures have been used in previous works (e.g. [29, 41, 45]), a formal definition has never been presented. We fill this gap by providing the first formalization of adaptor signatures and their security (in terms of cryptographic games), and proving that ECDSA and Schnorr-based schemes satisfy our notions. We believe that our formalization and security analysis of adaptor signatures is of independent interest (see details on the impact of our work below).

Formalization of generalized channels. In order to formally define the security guarantees of a generalized channel protocol, we utilize the extended Universal Composability model allowing for global setup (the GUC model for short) put forward by Canetti et al. [15]. More precisely, we model money mechanics of an UTXO-based blockchain via a global ledger ideal functionality and provide an ideal specification of a generalized channel protocol via a novel ideal functionality. Thereafter, we prove that our generalized channel construction satisfies this ideal specification. The key challenges of our security analysis are to ensure the consistency of timings imposed by the blockchain processing delay, and to ensure that no honest party can ever lose coins by participating in a channel.

Evaluation and applications. We implemented our protocols and conducted an experimental evaluation, demonstrating how to use generalized channels as a building block for popular off-chain applications, like payment routing through a payment channel network (PCN) [41, 42, 47] and channel splitting [26]. Concretely, our evaluation demonstrates that, already when routing *one* payment through a channel, the amount of blockchain fees in case of a dispute is reduced by 28% compared to the state-of-the-art Lightning network solution. In practice, there have been cases of disputes in channels with 50 concurrent payments [40], which currently costs 553.66 USD in fees to resolve in Lightning and only 17.47 USD with generalized channels. For channel splitting, we reduce the transactions to be exchanged off-chain per sub-channel from exponential to constant.

Moreover, we discuss how to use generalized channels to realize the Claim-or-Refund functionality of Bentov and Kumaresan [8]. This functionality, can be used to build a fair two-party computation protocol over Bitcoin, where fairness is achieved by financially penalizing malicious parties. Realizing the Claim-or-Refund functionality, in particular, implies that generalized channels allow parties to execute any two-party computation off-chain.

1.2   Other Related Work

We briefly discuss related work on off-chain protocols and adaptor signatures, where the latter is an important building block in our construction.

Off-chain protocols. As already mentioned before, there has been an extensive line of work on various types of payment channels [10, 19, 47] and payment channel networks (PCNs) [41, 42, 47]. However, these constructions only support simple payments and do not extend to support more complex transaction logic. The authors in [34] provide a formalization of the Lightning Network (LN) in the UC framework. This formalization is, however, tailored to the details of the current LN and cannot be leveraged to formalize generalized channels as we propose here. Most related to our work is the research on state channels [22, 23, 43], as these constructions allow to lift any transaction logic supported by the underlying blockchain off-chain. However, state channels crucially rely on the underlying blockchain to support smart contracts and hence do not work for blockchains with restricted scripting language. Finally, eltoo [20] is a payment channel construction which does not rely on a punishment mechanism, yet requires Bitcoin to adapt a new scripting command (op-code). This op-code, however, has not been included to Bitcoin's scripting language in the past due to security concerns. In the case of address reuse or lazy wallet designs, funds can be stolen by replaying transactions [52]. Moreover, the security of the eltoo protocol has not been formally proven and it only supports simple payments.

Apart from payment and state channels, numerous other solutions have been proposed in order to perform heavy on-chain computation off-chain. For instance, various previous works (e.g., [17, 18, 35]) focus on realizing on-chain functionality off-chain by using Trusted Execution Environments which, however, inherently add an additional trust assumptions that may not hold in practice (e.g., [12, 13, 16]). A proposal to remove these assumptions is to use MPC protocols [8, 37], which however require collateral linear in the number of conditional payments. In contrast, generalized channels only require constant collateral for the execution of an arbitrary number of such payments. There have been proposals to remedy the collateral requirement in MPC protocols [9, 36, 38] but they are incompatible with many existing UTXO blockchains, including Bitcoin.[1]

Adaptor signatures. Poelstra [46] introduced the notion of adaptor signatures (AS), which intuitively allows to create partial signatures whose completion is conditioned on solving a cryptographic hard problem – a feature that has been proven useful in off-chain applications such as PCNs [41] and payment-channel hubs [49]. For instance, Malavolta et al. [41] use AS as building block to define and realize multi-hop payments in PCNs. Moreover, AS have been used as an off-the-shelf cryptographic building block for multi-path payments [25] and Monero-compatible PCNs [51]. Banasik et al. [5] construct a scheme satisfying a similar notion to AS in order to allow two parties to exchange a digital asset using cryptocurrencies that do not support Turing-complete programs. None of these works, however, define AS as a stand-alone primitive. Concurrently to our work, Fournier [29] attempts to formalize AS as an instance of one-time verifiable encrypted signatures [11]. Yet, the definition of [29] is weaker than the one we give in this work and does not suffice for the channel applications. Also concurrent to this work, Thyagarajan and Malavolta [50] define *lockable signatures*. While

---

[1] These solutions require the underlying blockchain to either support verification of signatures on arbitrary messages or Turing-complete smart contracts.

similar to AS in spirit, lockable signatures are a weaker primitive as the partial signature must be created honestly (e.g., through MPC) and the solution to the cryptographic hardness problem must be known beforehand. On the other hand, lockable signatures can be built from any signature scheme while AS cannot be constructed from unique signatures [27].

2   Background and Solution Overview

Blockchain transactions. We focus on blockchains based on the Unspent Transaction Output (UTXO) model, such as Bitcoin. In the UTXO model, coins are held in *outputs*. Formally, an output θ is a tuple (cash, φ), where cash denotes the amount of coins associated to the output and φ defines the conditions (also known as scripts) that need to be satisfied to spend the output.

A *transaction* transfers coins across outputs meaning that it maps (possibly multiple) existing outputs to a list of new outputs. The existing outputs that fund the transactions are called *transaction inputs*. In other words, transaction inputs are those tied with previously unspent outputs of older transactions. Formally, a transaction tx is a tuple of the form $(\mathsf{txid}, \mathsf{In}, \mathsf{Out}, \mathsf{Witness})$, where $\mathsf{txid} \in \{0,1\}^*$ is the unique identifier of tx and is calculated as $\mathsf{txid} := \mathcal{H}([\mathsf{tx}])$, where $\mathcal{H}$ is a hash function modeled as a random oracle and $[\mathsf{tx}]$ is the *body of the transaction* defined as $[\mathsf{tx}] := (\mathsf{In}, \mathsf{Out})$; In is a vector of strings identifying all transaction inputs; $\mathsf{Out} = (\theta_1, \ldots, \theta_n)$ is a vector of new outputs; and $\mathsf{Witness} \in \{0,1\}^*$ contains the witness allowing to spend the transaction inputs.

To ease the readability, we illustrate the transaction flows using charts (see Fig. 1 for examples). We depict transactions as rectangles with rounded corners. Doubled edge rectangles represent transactions published on the blockchain, while single edge rectangles are transactions that could be published on the blockchain, but they are not (yet). Transaction outputs are depicted as a box inside the transaction. The value of the output is written inside the output box and the output condition is written above the arrow coming from the output.

Conditions of transaction outputs might be fairly complex and hence it would be cumbersome to spell them out above the arrows. Instead, for frequently used conditions, we define the following abbreviated notation. If the output script contains (among other conditions) signature verification w.r.t. some public keys $pk_1, \ldots, pk_n$ on the body of the spending transaction, we write all the public keys *below* the arrow and the remaining conditions *above* the arrow. Hence, information below the arrow denotes "who *owns* the output" and information above denotes "additional spending conditions". If the output script contains a check of whether a given witness hashes to a predefined h, we express this by writing the hash value h *above* the arrow. Moreover, if the output script contains a relative time-lock, i.e., a condition that is satisfied if and only if at least t rounds passed since the transaction was published, we write "$+t$" *above* the arrow. Finally, if the output script φ can be parsed as $\varphi = \varphi_1 \vee \cdots \vee \varphi_n$ for some $n \in \mathbb{N}$, we add a diamond shape to the corresponding transaction output. Each of the sub-conditions φ_i is then written above a separate arrow.

Payment channels. A payment channel [47] enables several payments between two users without submitting every single transaction to the blockchain. The

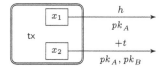 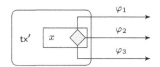

Fig. 1. (Left) tx is published on the blockchain. The output of value x_1 can be spent by a transaction containing a preimage of h and signed w.r.t. pk_A. The output of value x_2 can be spent by a transaction signed w.r.t. pk_A and pk_B but only if at least t rounds passed since tx was accepted by the blockchain. (Right) tx' is not published yet. Its only output can be spent by a transaction whose witness satisfies $\varphi_1 \vee \varphi_2 \vee \varphi_3$.

cornerstone of payment channels is depositing coins into an output controlled by two users, who then authorize new deposit balances in a peer-to-peer fashion while having the guarantee that all coins are refunded at a mutually agreed time.

First, assume that Alice and Bob want to create a payment channel with an initial deposit of x_A and x_B coins respectively. For that, Alice and Bob agree on a *funding transaction* (that we denote by TX_f) that sets as inputs two outputs controlled by Alice and Bob holding x_A and x_B coins respectively and transfers them to an output controlled by both Alice and Bob (i.e., its spending condition mandates both Alice's and Bob's signature). When TX_f is added to the blockchain, the payment channel between Alice and Bob is effectively *open*.

Assume now that Alice wants to pay $\alpha \leq x_A$ coins to Bob. For that, they create a new *commit transaction* TX_c representing the commitment from both users to the new channel state. The commit transaction spends the output of TX_f into two new outputs: (i) one holding $x_A - \alpha$ coins owned by Alice; and (ii) the other holding $x_B + \alpha$ coins owned by Bob. Finally, parties exchange the signatures on the commit transaction, thereby complete the channel *update*. Alice (resp. Bob) could now add TX_c to the blockchain. Instead, they keep it locally in their memory and overwrite it when they agree on another commit transaction, let us denote it $\overline{TX}_c$, representing a newer channel state. This, however, leads to several commit transactions that can possibly be added to the blockchain. Since all of them are spending the same output, only one can be accepted. As it is impossible to prevent a malicious user from publishing an old commit transaction, payment channels require a mechanism punishing such behavior.

Lightning Network [47], the state-of-the-art payment channel for Bitcoin, implements such mechanism by introducing *two* commit transactions, denoted TX_c^A and TX_c^B, per channel update, each of which contains a punishment mechanism for one of the users. In more detail (see also Fig. 2), the output of TX_c^A representing Alice's balance in the channel has a special condition. Namely, it can be spent by Bob if he presents a preimage of a hash value h_A or by Alice if certain number of rounds passed since the transaction was published. During a channel update, Alice chooses a value r_A, called the *revocation secret*, and presents the hash $h_A := \mathcal{H}(r_A)$ to Bob. Knowing h_A, Bob can create and sign the commit transaction TX_c^A with the built-in punishment for Alice (analogously for Bob and TX_c^B). During the next channel update, parties first commit to the new state by creating and signing $\overline{TX}_c^A$ and $\overline{TX}_c^B$, and then *revoke* the old state by

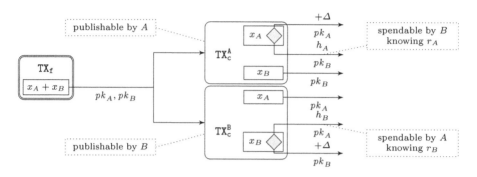

Fig. 2. A Lightning style payment channel where A has x_A coins and B has x_B coins. The values h_A and h_B correspond to the hash values of the revocation secrets r_A and r_B. Δ upper bounds the time needed to publish a transaction on a blockchain.

sending the revocation secrets to each other thereby enabling the punishment mechanism. If a malicious Alice now publishes the old commit transaction TX_c^A, Bob can spend both of its outputs and claim all coins locked in the channel.

2.1 Solution Overview

The goal of our work is to extend the idea of payment channels such that parties can agree on *any* conditional payment that they could do on-chain and not only direct payments. Technically, this means that we want the commit transaction to contain arbitrary many outputs with arbitrary conditions (as long as they are supported by the underlying blockchain). The main question we need to answer when designing such channels, which we call *generalized channels*, is how to implement the revocation mechanism.

Revocation per update. The first idea would be to extend the revocation mechanism explained above such that *each output* of TX_c^A contains a punishment mechanism for Alice (analogously for Bob). While this solution works, it has several disadvantages. If one party, say Alice, cheats and publishes an old commit transaction TX_c^A, Bob has to spend all outputs of TX_c^A to punish Alice. Although Bob could group some of them within a single transaction (up to the transaction size limit), he might be forced to publish multiple transactions thereby paying high transaction fees. Moreover, such revocation mechanism requires a high on-chain footprint not only for TX_c^A, but also for Bob getting coins from the outputs.

Our goal is to design a punishment mechanism whose on-chain footprint and potential transaction fees are *independent of the channel state*, i.e., the number and type of outputs in the channel. To this end, we propose the *punish-then-split* mechanism which separates the punishment mechanism from the actual outputs. In a nutshell, the commit transaction TX_c^A has now only one output dedicated to the punishment mechanism which can be spent (i) immediately by Bob, if he proves that the commit transaction was old (i.e., he knows the revocation secret r_A of Alice); or (ii) after certain number of rounds by a *split transaction*

TX_s^A owned by both parties and containing all the outputs of the channel (i.e. representing the channel state). Hence, if TX_c^A is published on the blockchain, Bob has some time to punish Alice if the commit transaction was old. If Bob does not use this option, any of the parties can publish the split transaction TX_s^A representing the channel state. Analogously for TX_c^B.

One commit transaction per channel update. Another drawback of the Lightning-style revocation mechanism is the need for two commit transactions for the same channel state. While this is not an issue for simple payment channels, for generalized channels it might cause undesirable redundancy in terms of communication and computational costs. This comes from the fact that generalized channels support arbitrary output conditions and hence can be used as a source of funding for other off-chain applications, e.g., a fair two-party computation or another off-chain channel as we discuss later in this work (see Sect. 7). Such off-chain application would, however, have to "exist" twice. Once considering TX_c^A being eventually published on-chain and once considering TX_c^B. Especially when considering channels built on top of channels, the overhead grows exponentially. Our goal is to construct generalized channels that require only one commit transaction and hence avoid any redundancy.

A naive approach to design such a single commit transaction TX_c would be to "merge" the transactions TX_c^A and TX_c^B. Such TX_c could be spent (i) by Alice if she knows Bob's revocation secret; (ii) by Bob if he knows Alice's revocation secret or (iii) by the split transaction TX_s representing the channels state after some time. Unfortunately, this simple proposal allows parties to misuse the punishment mechanism as follows. A malicious Alice could publish an old commit transaction TX_c and since she knows Bob's revocation secret, she could immediately try to punish Bob. To prevent such undue punishment of honest Bob, we need to make sure that Alice can use the punishment mechanism only if Bob published TX_c.

The main idea of how to implement this additional requirement is to force the party publishing TX_c to reveal some secret, which we call *publishing secret*, that the other party could use as proof. We achieve this by leveraging the concept of an *adaptor signature scheme* – a signature scheme that allows a party to *presign* a message w.r.t. some statement Y of a hard relation (at a high level, a statement/witness relation is hard, if given a statement Y is it computationally hard to find a witness y). Such pre-signature can be adapted into a valid signature by anyone knowing a witness for the statement Y. Also, it is possible to extract a witness y for Y by knowing both the pre-signature and the adapted full signature. In our context, adaptor signatures allow users of a generalized channel to express the following: "I give you my *pre-signature* on TX_c that you can turn into a full signature and publish TX_c, which will reveal your publishing secret to me."

To conclude, our solution, depicted in Fig. 3, requires only one commit transaction TX_c per update. The commit transaction has one output that can be spent (i) by Alice if she knows Bob's revocation secret r_B *and* publishing secret y_B; (ii) by Bob if he knows Alice's revocation secret r_A *and* publishing secret y_A or (iii) by the split transaction TX_s representing the channels state after some time. In the depicted construction, we assume that statement/witness pairs used for

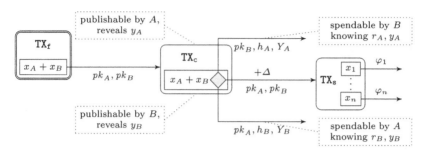

Fig. 3. A generalized channel in the state $((x_1, \varphi_1), \ldots, (x_n, \varphi_n))$. In the figure, pk_A denotes Alice's public key, (h_A, r_A) her revocation public/secret values, and (Y_A, y_A) her publishing public/secret values (analogously for Bob). The value of Δ upper bounds the time needed to publish a transaction on a blockchain.

the adaptor signature scheme are public/secret keys of the blockchain signature scheme. Hence, testing if a party knows a publishing secret can be done by requiring a valid signature w.r.t. this public key. Let use emphasize that public/secret keys can also be used for the revocation mechanism instead of the hash/preimage pairs. This is actually preferable (not only in our construction but also in the Lightning-style channels) since the punishment output script will only consist of signature verification, thereby requiring less complex scripting language. As a result, our solution does not only work over Bitcoin, but over any UTXO based blockchain that supports transaction authorization (if there exists an adaptor signature scheme w.r.t. the considered digital signature), relative time-locks and constant number of ∧ and ∨ in output scripts.

3   Preliminaries

We denote by $x \leftarrow_\$ \mathcal{X}$ the uniform sampling of the variable x from the set $\mathcal{X}$. Throughout this paper, n denotes the security parameter and all our algorithms run in polynomial time in n. By writing $x \leftarrow A(y)$ we mean that a *probabilistic polynomial time* algorithm A (or PPT for short) on input y, outputs x. If A is a *deterministic polynomial time* algorithm (DPT for short), we use the notation $x := A(y)$. A function $\nu \colon \mathbb{N} \to \mathbb{R}$ is *negligible* in n if for every $k \in \mathbb{N}$, there exists $n_0 \in \mathbb{N}$ s.t. for every $n \geq n_0$ it holds that $|\nu(n)| \leq 1/n^k$. Throughout this work, we use the following notation for *attribute tuples*. Let T be a tuple of values which we call attributes. Each attribute in T is identified using a unique keyword attr and referred to as T.attr. Let us now briefly recall the cryptographic primitives used in this paper to establish the used notation.

A signature scheme consists of three algorithms $\Sigma = (\mathsf{Gen}, \mathsf{Sign}, \mathsf{Vrfy})$, where: (i) $\mathsf{Gen}(1^n)$ gets as input 1^n and outputs the secret and public keys (sk, pk); (ii) $\mathsf{Sign}_{sk}(m)$ gets as input the secret key sk and a message $m \in \{0, 1\}^*$ and outputs the signature σ; and (iii) $\mathsf{Vrfy}_{pk}(m; \sigma)$ gets as input the public key pk, a message m and a signature σ, and outputs a bit b. A signature scheme must fulfill correctness, i.e. it must hold that $\mathsf{Vrfy}_{pk}(m; \mathsf{Sign}_{sk}(m)) = 1$ for all messages m

and valid key pairs (sk, pk). In this work, we use signature schemes that satisfy the notion of strong existential unforgeability under chosen message attack (or SUF–CMA). At a high level, SUF–CMA guarantees that a PPT adversary on input the public key pk and with access to a signing oracle, cannot produce a *new* valid signature on any message m.

We next recall the definition of a hard relation R with statement/witness pairs (Y, y). Let L_R be the associated language defined as $\{Y \mid \exists y \text{ s.t. } (Y, y) \in R\}$. We say that R is a *hard relation* if the following holds: (i) There exists a PPT sampling algorithm GenR that on input 1^n outputs a statement/witness pair $(Y, y) \in R$; (ii) The relation is poly-time decidable; (iii) For all PPT $\mathcal{A}$ the probability of $\mathcal{A}$ on input Y outputting a valid witness y is negligible.

Finally, we recall the definition of a non-interactive zero-knowledge proof of knowledge (NIZK) with online extractors as introduced in [28]. The online extractability property allows for extraction of a witness y for a statement Y from a proof π in the random oracle model and is useful for models where the rewinding proof technique is not allowed, such as UC. We need this property to prove our ECDSA-based adaptor signature scheme secure. More formally, a pair (P, V) of PPT algorithms is called a NIZK with an online extractor for a relation R, random oracle $\mathcal{H}$ and security parameter n if the following holds: (i) *Completeness*: For any $(Y, y) \in R$, it holds that $\mathsf{V}(Y, \mathsf{P}(Y, y)) = 1$ except with negligible probability; (ii) *Zero knowledge*: There exists a PPT simulator, which on input Y can simulate the proof π for any $(Y, y) \in R$. (iii) *Online Extractor*: There exist a PPT online extractor K with access to the sequence of queries to the random oracle and its answers, such that given (Y, π), the algorithm K can extract the witness y with $(Y, y) \in R$. An instance of such proof system is in [28].

4 Generalized Channels

4.1 Notation and Security Model

To formally model the security of generalized channels, we use the global UC framework (GUC) [15] which extends the standard UC framework [14] by allowing for a global setup. Here we discuss our security model (which follows previous works on off-chain channels [22–24]), only briefly and refer the reader to the full version of this paper [4] for more details.

We consider a protocol π that runs between parties from a fixed set $\mathcal{P} = \{P_1, \ldots, P_n\}$. A protocol is executed in the presence of an *adversary* $\mathcal{A}$ who can *corrupt* any party P_i at the beginning of the protocol execution (so-called static corruption). Parties and the adversary $\mathcal{A}$ receive their inputs from a special entity – called the *environment* $\mathcal{Z}$ – which represents anything "external" to the current protocol execution. We assume a synchronous communication network meaning that protocol execution happens in rounds, formalized via a global ideal functionality $\mathcal{F}_{clock}$ representing "the clock" [33]. Parties in the protocol are connected with authenticated communication channels with guaranteed delivery of exactly one round, formalized via an ideal functionality $\mathcal{F}_{GDC}$. For simplicity, we assume that all other communication (e.g., messages sent between the adversary and the environment) as well as local computation take zero rounds. Monetary transactions are handled by a global ideal ledger functionality $\mathcal{L}(\Delta, \Sigma, \mathcal{V})$, where Δ is an upper bound on the blockchain delay (number of rounds it takes to publish a transaction), Σ defines the signature scheme and $\mathcal{V}$ defines valid output conditions. Furthermore, the global ledger maintains a PKI.

Generalized channel syntax. A *generalized channel* γ is an attribute tuple $(\gamma.\mathsf{id}, \gamma.\mathsf{users}, \gamma.\mathsf{cash}, \gamma.\mathsf{st})$, where $\gamma.\mathsf{id} \in \{0,1\}^*$ is the channel identifier, $\gamma.\mathsf{users} \in \mathcal{P} \times \mathcal{P}$ defines the identities of the channel users, $\gamma.\mathsf{cash} \in \mathbb{R}^{\geq 0}$ represents the total amount of coins locked in γ, and $\gamma.\mathsf{st} = (\theta_1, \ldots, \theta_n)$ is the state of γ composed of a list of *outputs*. Each output θ_i has two attributes: the value $\theta_i.\mathsf{cash} \in \mathbb{R}^{\geq 0}$ representing the amount of coins and the function $\theta_i.\varphi \colon \{0,1\}^* \to \{0,1\}$ defining the spending condition. For convenience, we use $\gamma.\mathsf{otherParty} \colon \gamma.\mathsf{users} \to \gamma.\mathsf{users}$ defined as $\gamma.\mathsf{otherParty}(P) := Q$ for $\gamma.\mathsf{users} = \{P, Q\}$.

4.2   Ideal Functionality

We capture the desired functionality of a generalized channel protocol as an ideal functionality $\mathcal{F}$. As a first step towards defining our functionality, we informally identify the most important security and efficiency notions of interest that a generalized channel protocol should provide.

Consensus on creation: A generalized channel γ is successfully created only if all parties in $\gamma.\mathsf{users}$ agree with the creation. Moreover, parties in $\gamma.\mathsf{users}$ reach agreement whether the channel is created or not after an a-priori bounded number of rounds.

Consensus on update: A generalized channel γ is successfully updated only if both parties in $\gamma.\mathsf{users}$ agree with the update. Moreover, parties in $\gamma.\mathsf{users}$ reach agreement whether the update is successful or not after an a-priori bounded number of rounds.

Instant finality with punish: An honest party $P \in \gamma.\mathsf{users}$ has the guarantee that either the current state of the channel can be enforced on the ledger, or P can enforce a state where she gets all $\gamma.\mathsf{cash}$ coins. A state st is called *enforced* on the ledger if a transaction with this state appears on the ledger.

Optimistic update: If both parties in $\gamma.\mathsf{users}$ are honest, the update procedure takes a constant number of rounds (independent of the blockchain delay Δ).

Having the guarantees identified above in mind, we now design our ideal functionality $\mathcal{F}$. It interacts with parties from the set $\mathcal{P}$, with the adversary $\mathcal{S}$ (called the simulator) and the ledger $\mathcal{L}(\Delta, \Sigma, \mathcal{V})$. In a bit more detail, if a party wants to perform an action (such as open a new channel), it sends a message to $\mathcal{F}$ who executes the action and informs the party about the result. The execution might leak information to the adversary who may also influence the execution which is modeled via the interaction with $\mathcal{S}$. Finally, $\mathcal{F}$ observes the ledger and can verify that a certain transaction appeared on-chain or the ownership of coins.

To keep $\mathcal{F}$ generic, we parameterized it by two values T and k – both of which must be independent of the blockchain delay Δ. At a high level, the value

T upper bounds the maximal number of consecutive off-chain communication rounds between channel users. Since different parts of the protocol might require different amount of communication rounds, the upper bound T might not be reached in all steps. For instance, channel creation might require more communication rounds than old state revocation. To this end, we give the power to the simulator to "speed-up" the process when possible. The parameter k defines the number of ways the channel state γ.st can be published on the ledger. As discussed in Sect. 2, in this work we present a protocol realizing the functionality for $k = 1$ (see Fig. 3). A generalized channel construction using Lightning style revocation mechanism (see Fig. 2) would be a candidate protocol for $k = 2$.

We assume that the functionality maintains a set Γ of created channels in their latest state and the corresponding funding transaction tx. We present $\mathcal{F}^{\mathcal{L}(\Delta, \Sigma, \mathcal{V})}(T, k)$ formally in Fig. 4. Here we discuss each part of the functionality at a high level and argue why it captures the aforementioned security and efficiency properties identified above. We abbreviate $\mathcal{F} := \mathcal{F}^{\mathcal{L}(\Delta, \Sigma, \mathcal{V})}(T, k)$.

Create. If $\mathcal{F}$ receives a message of the form (CREATE, γ, tid_P) from both parties in γ.users within T rounds, it expects a channel funding transaction to appear on the ledger $\mathcal{L}$ within Δ rounds. Such a transaction must spend both funding sources (defined by transaction identifiers tid_P, tid_Q) and contain one output of the value γ.cash. If this is true, $\mathcal{F}$ stores this transaction together with the channel γ in Γ and informs both parties about the successful channel creation via the message CREATED (how this can be done within the UC model is discussed in the full version of this paper [4]). Since a CREATE message is required from both parties and both parties receive CREATED, "consensus on creation" holds.

Close. Any of the two parties can request closure of the channel via the message (CLOSE, id), where id identifies the channel to be closed. In case both parties request closure within T rounds, *peaceful closure* is expected. This means that a transaction, spending the channel funding transaction and whose output corresponds to the latest channel state γ.st, should appear on $\mathcal{L}$ within Δ rounds. If only one of the parties requests closing, $\mathcal{F}$ executes the ForceClose subprocedure in which case such transaction is supposed to appear on $\mathcal{L}$ within 3Δ rounds modelling possible dispute resolution. In both cases, if the funding transaction is not spent before a certain round, an ERROR is returned to both users.

Update. The channel update is initiated by one of the parties P (called the *initiating party*) via a message (UPDATE, $id, \vec{\theta}, t_{\text{stp}}$). The parameter id identifies the channel to be updated, $\vec{\theta}$ represents the new channel state and t_{stp} denotes the number of rounds needed by the parties to set up off-chain applications (e.g., new channels or fair two-party computation) that are being built on top of the channel via this update request. The update is structured into two phases: (i) the prepare phase, and (ii) the revocation phase. Intuitively, the prepare phase models the fact that both parties first agree on the new channel state and get time to set up the off-chain applications on top of this new state. The revocation phase models the fact that an update is only completed once the two parties invalidate the previous channel state. We detail the two phases in the following.

The prepare phase starts when $\mathcal{F}$ receives a vector of transaction identifiers $\vec{tid} = (tid_1, \ldots, tid_k)$ from $\mathcal{S}$.[2] In the optimistic case, it is completed within $3T + t_{\mathsf{stp}}$ rounds and ends when the initiating party P receives an UPDATE–OK message from $\mathcal{F}$. The setup phase can be aborted by both the initiating party P and the other party Q. This is achieved by P not sending the SETUP–OK and by Q not sending the UPDATE–OK message, respectively. This models two things. Firstly, the fact that Q might not agree with the proposed update and secondly, that setting up off-chain objects might fail in which case parties want to abort the channel update. The abort may also result in a forceful closing of the channel via the subprocedure ForceClose. It happens when one of the parties has sufficient information to enforce the new state on-chain, while the other does not.

In order to complete the update, the revocation phase is executed. The functionality expects to receive the REVOKE message from both parties within $2T$ rounds, in which case $\mathcal{F}$ updates the channel state in Γ accordingly and informs both parties about the successful update via the message UPDATED. If one of the messages does not arrive, the subprocedure ForceClose is called.

To conclude, the possibility for forceful closing guarantees the security property "consensus on update" as it ensures termination of the update process and allows both parties see the state in which the channel was closed. Moreover, in case both parties are honest, the update duration is independent of the ledger delay Δ, hence the efficiency property "optimistic update" is satisfied.

Punish. In order to guarantee "instant finality with punishments", parties continuously monitor the ledger and apply the punishment mechanism if misbehavior is detected. This is captured by the functionality in the part "Punish" which is executed at the end of each round. The functionality checks if a funding transaction of some channel was spent. If yes, then it expects one of the following to happen: (i) a punish transaction appears on $\mathcal{L}$ within Δ rounds, assigning γ.cash coins to the honest party $P \in \gamma$.users; or (ii) a transaction whose output corresponds to the latest channel state γ.st appears on $\mathcal{L}$ within 2Δ rounds, meaning that the channel is peacefully or forcefully closed. If none of the above is true, ERROR is returned. Hence, under the condition that no ERROR was returned, the security property "instant finality with punish" is satisfied.

In summary, our functionality satisfies the identified security and efficiency properties if no ERROR occurs. Otherwise, all guarantees may be lost. Hence, we are interested only in those protocols realizing $\mathcal{F}$ that never output an ERROR.

Notation used in the formal description in Fig. 4. Messages sent between parties and $\mathcal{F}$ have the following format: (MESSAGE_TYPE, *parameters*). To shorten the description, we use following arrow notation: by $m \overset{t}{\hookrightarrow} P$, we mean "send the message m to party P in round t." and by $m \overset{t}{\hookleftarrow} P$, we mean "receive a message m from party P in round t". To indicate that a message should be sent/received before/after a certain round, we use inequality symbols above the arrows. When $\mathcal{F}$ expects $\mathcal{S}$ to set certain values (such as the vector of tid's during the update

---

[2] For technical reasons, ideal functionality cannot sign transactions and thus it can also not prepare the transaction ids (which is the task of the simulator).

process or the exact round in which a message should be sent to parties) and it does not do so, we implicitly assume that ERROR is returned. Since we do not aim to make any claims about privacy, we implicitly assume that every message that $\mathcal{F}$ receives/sends from/to a party is directly forwarded to $\mathcal{S}$. In the formal description, we treat the channel set Γ as a function which on input id outputs (X, tx), where X is a set of channels s.t. for every $\gamma \in X$ $\gamma.\mathsf{id} = id$, if such channel exists and $\perp$ otherwise. We denote the script requiring signature of (only) P as $\mathsf{One\text{-}Sig}_{pk_P}$. Moreover, we omit several natural checks that one would expect $\mathcal{F}$ to make. For example, messages with missing parameters should be ignored, channel instruction should be accepted only from channel users, etc. We formally define all checks as a functionality wrapper in the full version of this paper [4]. Finally, we omit the read queries that $\mathcal{F}$ sends to $\mathcal{L}$ in order to learn its state.

5 Adaptor Signatures

Our goal is to realize the ideal functionality for generalized channel for $k = 1$, meaning that there is only one way to publish the channel state on-chain. As explained at a high level in Sect. 2.1, we achieve our goal by utilizing an adaptor signature scheme – a cryptographic primitive that we discuss in this section.

Adaptor signatures have been introduced by the cryptocurrency community to tie together the authorization of a transaction and the leakage of a secret value. An adaptor signature scheme is essentially a two-step signing algorithm bound to a secret: first a partial signature is generated such that it can be completed only by a party knowing a certain secret, with the complete signature revealing such a secret. More precisely, we define an adaptor signature scheme with respect to a digital signature scheme Σ and a hard relation R. For any statement $Y \in L_R$, a signer holding a secret key is able to produce a *pre-signature* w.r.t. Y on any message m. Such pre-signature can be *adapted* into a valid signature on m if and only if the adaptor knows a witness for Y. Moreover, it must be possible to extract a witness for Y given the pre-signature and the adapted signature.

Despite the fact that adaptor signatures have been used in previous works (e.g. [29, 41, 45]), none of these works has given a formal definition of the adaptor signature primitive and its security. In the following, we fill this gap and provide the first game-based formalization of adaptor signatures. As already mentioned, Erwig et al. [27] recently extended our definition to a two-party case.

Definition 1 (Adaptor signature scheme). *An adaptor signature scheme w.r.t. a hard relation R and a signature scheme $\Sigma = (\mathsf{Gen}, \mathsf{Sign}, \mathsf{Vrfy})$ consists of four algorithms $\Xi_{R,\Sigma} = (\mathsf{pSign}, \mathsf{Adapt}, \mathsf{pVrfy}, \mathsf{Ext})$ with the following syntax: $\mathsf{pSign}_{sk}(m, Y)$ is a PPT algorithm that on input a secret key sk, message $m \in \{0,1\}^*$ and statement $Y \in L_R$, outputs a pre-signature $\tilde{\sigma}$; $\mathsf{pVrfy}_{pk}(m, Y; \tilde{\sigma})$ is a DPT algorithm that on input a public key pk, message $m \in \{0,1\}^*$, statement $Y \in L_R$ and pre-signature $\tilde{\sigma}$, outputs a bit b; $\mathsf{Adapt}(\tilde{\sigma}, y)$ is a DPT algorithm that on input a pre-signature $\tilde{\sigma}$ and witness y, outputs a signature σ; and $\mathsf{Ext}(\sigma, \tilde{\sigma}, Y)$ is a DPT algorithm that on input a signature σ, pre-signature $\tilde{\sigma}$ and statement $Y \in L_R$, outputs a witness y such that $(Y, y) \in R$, or $\perp$.*

Upon $(\texttt{CREATE}, \gamma, tid_P) \xleftarrow{\tau_0} P$, distinguish:

Both agreed: If already received $(\texttt{CREATE}, \gamma, tid_Q) \xleftarrow{\tau} Q$, where $\tau_0 - \tau \leq T$: If tx s.t. $\mathsf{tx.In} = (tid_P, tid_Q)$ and $\mathsf{tx.Out} = (\gamma.\mathsf{cash}, \varphi)$, for some φ, appears on $\mathcal{L}$ in round $\tau_1 \leq \tau + \Delta + T$, set $\Gamma(\gamma.\mathsf{id}) := (\{\gamma\}, \mathsf{tx})$ and $(\texttt{CREATED}, \gamma.\mathsf{id}) \xrightarrow{\tau_1} \gamma.\mathsf{users}$. Else stop.

Wait for Q: Else wait if $(\texttt{CREATE}, id) \xleftarrow{\tau \leq \tau_0 + T} Q$ (in that case "Both agreed" option is executed). If such message is not received, stop.

Upon $(\texttt{UPDATE}, id, \boldsymbol{\theta}, t_{\mathsf{stp}}) \xleftarrow{\tau_0} P$, parse $(\{\gamma\}, \mathsf{tx}) := \Gamma(id)$, set $\gamma' := \gamma$, $\gamma'.\mathsf{st} := \boldsymbol{\theta}$:

1. In round $\tau_1 \leq \tau_0 + T$, let $\mathcal{S}$ define $\boldsymbol{tid}$ s.t. $|\boldsymbol{tid}| = k$. Then $(\texttt{UPDATE-REQ}, id, \boldsymbol{\theta}, t_{\mathsf{stp}}, \boldsymbol{tid}) \xrightarrow{\tau_1} Q$ and $(\texttt{SETUP}, id, \boldsymbol{tid}) \xrightarrow{\tau_1} P$.

2. If $(\texttt{SETUP-OK}, id) \xleftarrow{\tau_2 \leq \tau_1 + t_{\mathsf{stp}}} P$, then $(\texttt{SETUP-OK}, id) \xrightarrow{\tau_3 \leq \tau_2 + T} Q$. Else stop.

3. If $(\texttt{UPDATE-OK}, id) \xleftarrow{\tau_3} Q$, then $(\texttt{UPDATE-OK}, id) \xrightarrow{\tau_4 \leq \tau_3 + T} P$. Else distinguish:
   - If Q honest or if instructed by $\mathcal{S}$, stop *(reject)*.
   - Else set $\Gamma(id) := (\{\gamma, \gamma'\}, \mathsf{tx})$, run $\texttt{ForceClose}(id)$ and stop.

4. If $(\texttt{REVOKE}, id) \xleftarrow{\tau_4} P$, send $(\texttt{REVOKE-REQ}, id) \xrightarrow{\tau_5 \leq \tau_4 + T} Q$. Else set $\Gamma(id) := (\{\gamma, \gamma'\}, \mathsf{tx})$, run $\texttt{ForceClose}(id)$ and stop.

5. If $(\texttt{REVOKE}, id) \xleftarrow{\tau_5} Q$, $\Gamma(id) := (\{\gamma'\}, \mathsf{tx})$, send $(\texttt{UPDATED}, id, \boldsymbol{\theta}) \xrightarrow{\tau_6 \leq \tau_5 + T} \gamma.\mathsf{users}$ and stop *(accept)*. Else set $\Gamma(id) := (\{\gamma, \gamma'\}, \mathsf{tx})$, run $\texttt{ForceClose}(id)$ and stop.

Upon $(\texttt{CLOSE}, id) \xleftarrow{\tau_0} P$, distinguish: **Both agreed:** If already received $(\texttt{CLOSE}, id)$ $\xleftarrow{\tau} Q$, where $\tau_0 - \tau \leq T$, run $\texttt{ForceClose}(id)$ unless both parties are honest. In this case let $(\{\gamma\}, \mathsf{tx}) := \Gamma(id)$ and distinguish:

   - If tx', with $\mathsf{tx'.In} = \mathsf{tx.txid}$ and $\mathsf{tx'.Out} = \gamma.\mathsf{st}$ appears on $\mathcal{L}$ in round $\tau_1 \leq \tau_0 + \Delta$, set $\Gamma(id) := \bot$, send $(\texttt{CLOSED}, id) \xrightarrow{\tau_1} \gamma.\mathsf{users}$ and stop.
   - Else output $(\texttt{ERROR}) \xrightarrow{\tau_0 + \Delta} \gamma.\mathsf{users}$ and stop.

Wait for Q: Else wait if $(\texttt{CLOSE}, id) \xleftarrow{\tau \leq \tau_0 + T} Q$ (in that case "Both agreed" option is executed). If such message is not received, run $\texttt{ForceClose}(id)$ in round $\tau_0 + T$.

At the end of every round τ_0: For each $id \in \{0, 1\}^*$ s.t. $(X, \mathsf{tx}) := \Gamma(id) \neq \bot$, check if $\mathcal{L}$ contains tx' with $\mathsf{tx'.In} = \mathsf{tx.txid}$. If yes, then define $S := \{\gamma.\mathsf{st} \mid \gamma \in X\}$, $\tau := \tau_0 + 2\Delta$ and distinguish: **Close:** If tx'' s.t. $\mathsf{tx''.In} = \mathsf{tx'.txid}$ and $\mathsf{tx''.Out} \in S$ appears on $\mathcal{L}$ in round $\tau_1 \leq \tau$, set $\Gamma(id) := \bot$ and $(\texttt{CLOSED}, id) \xrightarrow{\tau_1} \gamma.\mathsf{users}$ if not sent yet.

Punish: If tx'' s.t. $\mathsf{tx''.In} = \mathsf{tx'.txid}$ and $\mathsf{tx''.Out} = (\gamma.\mathsf{cash}, \texttt{One-Sig}_{pk_P})$ appears on $\mathcal{L}$ in round $\tau_1 \leq \tau$, for P honest, set $\Gamma(id) := \bot$, $(\texttt{PUNISHED}, id) \xrightarrow{\tau_1} P$ and stop.

Error: Else $(\texttt{ERROR}) \xrightarrow{\tau} \gamma.\mathsf{users}$.

$\texttt{ForceClose}(id)$: Let τ_0 be the current round and $(X, \mathsf{tx}) := \Gamma(id)$. If within Δ rounds tx is still unspent on $\mathcal{L}$, then $(\texttt{ERROR}) \xrightarrow{\tau_0 + \Delta} \gamma.\mathsf{users}$ and stop. *Note that otherwise, message $m \in \{\texttt{CLOSED}, \texttt{PUNISHED}, \texttt{ERROR}\}$ is output latest in round $\tau_0 + 3 \cdot \Delta$.*

Fig. 4. The ideal functionality $\mathcal{F}^{\mathcal{L}(\Delta, \Sigma, \mathcal{V})}(T, k)$. We abbreviate $Q := \gamma.\mathsf{otherParty}(P)$.

An adaptor signature scheme $\Xi_{R,\Sigma}$ must satisfy pre-signature correctness *stating that for every $m \in \{0,1\}^*$ and every $(Y,y) \in R$, the following holds:*

$$\Pr \left[\begin{array}{l} \mathsf{pVrfy}_{pk}(m,Y;\tilde{\sigma}) = 1, \\ \mathsf{Vrfy}_{pk}(m;\sigma) = 1, (Y,y') \in R \end{array} \middle| \begin{array}{l} (sk,pk) \leftarrow \mathsf{Gen}(1^n),\ \tilde{\sigma} \leftarrow \mathsf{pSign}_{sk}(m,Y) \\ \sigma := \mathsf{Adapt}_{pk}(\tilde{\sigma},y),\ y' := \mathsf{Ext}_{pk}(\sigma,\tilde{\sigma},Y) \end{array} \right] = 1.$$

The first security property, *existential unforgeability under chosen message attack for adaptor signature* (aEUF–CMA security for short), protects the signer. It is similar to EUF–CMA for digital signatures but additionally requires that producing a forgery σ for some message m is hard even given a pre-signature on m w.r.t. a random statement $Y \in L_R$. Let us stress that allowing the adversary to learn a pre-signature on the forgery message m is crucial since, for our applications, signature unforgeability needs to hold even in case the adversary learns a pre-signature for m without knowing a witness for Y.

Definition 2 (Existential unforgeability). *An adaptor signature scheme $\Xi_{R,\Sigma}$ is* aEUF–CMA *secure if for every PPT adversary $\mathcal{A} = (\mathcal{A}_1, \mathcal{A}_2)$ there exists a negligible function ν such that:* $\Pr[\mathsf{aSigForge}_{\mathcal{A},\Xi_{R,\Sigma}}(n) = 1] \leq \nu(n)$, *where the experiment* $\mathsf{aSigForge}_{\mathcal{A},\Xi_{R,\Sigma}}$ *is defined as follows:*

$\mathsf{aSigForge}_{\mathcal{A},\Xi_{R,\Sigma}}(n)$	$\mathcal{O}_\mathsf{S}(m)$	$\mathcal{O}_\mathsf{pS}(m,Y)$
$1: \mathcal{Q} := \emptyset, (sk,pk) \leftarrow \mathsf{Gen}(1^n)$	$1: \sigma \leftarrow \mathsf{Sign}_{sk}(m)$	$1: \tilde{\sigma} \leftarrow \mathsf{pSign}_{sk}(m,Y)$
$2: (Y,y) \leftarrow \mathsf{GenR}(1^n)$	$2: \mathcal{Q} := \mathcal{Q} \cup \{m\}$	$2: \mathcal{Q} := \mathcal{Q} \cup \{m\}$
$3: (m,\mathsf{st}) \leftarrow \mathcal{A}_1^{\mathcal{O}_\mathsf{S}(\cdot),\mathcal{O}_\mathsf{pS}(\cdot,\cdot)}(pk,Y)$	$3: \mathbf{return}\ \sigma$	$3: \mathbf{return}\ \tilde{\sigma}$
$4: \tilde{\sigma} \leftarrow \mathsf{pSign}_{sk}(m,Y)$		
$5: \sigma \leftarrow \mathcal{A}_2^{\mathcal{O}_\mathsf{S}(\cdot),\mathcal{O}_\mathsf{pS}(\cdot,\cdot)}(\tilde{\sigma},\mathsf{st})$		
$6: \mathbf{return}\ \left(m \notin \mathcal{Q} \wedge \mathsf{Vrfy}_{pk}(m;\sigma)\right)$		

The reason why the game computes $\tilde{\sigma}$ in step 4 (although $\mathcal{A}$ could obtain it by querying $\mathcal{O}_\mathsf{pS}$) is that it allows $\mathcal{A}$ to learn $\tilde{\sigma}$ without m being added to $\mathcal{Q}$.

The second property, called *pre-signature adaptability*, protects the verifier. It guarantees that any valid pre-signature w.r.t. Y (possibly produced by a malicious signer) can be completed into a valid signature using a witness y with $(Y,y) \in R$. Notice that this property is stronger than the pre-signature correctness property from Definition 1, since we require that even pre-signatures that were not produced by pSign but are valid, can be completed into valid signatures.

Definition 3 (Pre-signature adaptability). *An adaptor signature scheme $\Xi_{R,\Sigma}$ satisfies* pre-signature adaptability *if for any message $m \in \{0,1\}^*$, any statement/witness pair $(Y,y) \in R$, any public key pk and any pre-signature $\tilde{\sigma} \in \{0,1\}^*$ with $\mathsf{pVrfy}_{pk}(m,Y;\tilde{\sigma}) = 1$, we have $\mathsf{Vrfy}_{pk}(m;\mathsf{Adapt}(\tilde{\sigma},y)) = 1$.*

The last property that we are interested in is *witness extractability* which protects the signer. Informally, it guarantees that a valid signature/pre-signature pair $(\sigma,\tilde{\sigma})$ for message/statement (m,Y) can be used to extract a witness y for Y. Hence a malicious verifier cannot use a pre-signature $\tilde{\sigma}$ to produce a valid signature σ without revealing a witness for Y.

Definition 4 (Witness extractability). *An adaptor signature scheme $\Xi_{R,\Sigma}$ is witness extractable if for every PPT adversary $\mathcal{A} = (\mathcal{A}_1, \mathcal{A}_2)$, there exists a negligible function ν such that the following holds:* $\Pr[\mathsf{aWitExt}_{\mathcal{A}, \Xi_{R,\Sigma}}(n) = 1] \leq \nu(n)$, *where the experiment* $\mathsf{aWitExt}_{\mathcal{A}, \Xi_{R,\Sigma}}$ *is defined as follows*

$\mathsf{aWitExt}_{\mathcal{A}, \Xi_{R,\Sigma}}(n)$	$\mathcal{O}_{\mathsf{S}}(m)$	$\mathcal{O}_{\mathsf{pS}}(m, Y)$
$1: \mathcal{Q} := \emptyset, (sk, pk) \leftarrow \mathsf{Gen}(1^n)$	$1: \sigma \leftarrow \mathsf{Sign}_{sk}(m)$	$1: \tilde{\sigma} \leftarrow \mathsf{pSign}_{sk}(m, Y)$
$2: (m, Y, \mathsf{st}) \leftarrow \mathcal{A}_1^{\mathcal{O}_{\mathsf{S}}(\cdot), \mathcal{O}_{\mathsf{pS}}(\cdot, \cdot)}(pk)$	$2: \mathcal{Q} := \mathcal{Q} \cup \{m\}$	$2: \mathcal{Q} := \mathcal{Q} \cup \{m\}$
$3: \tilde{\sigma} \leftarrow \mathsf{pSign}_{sk}(m, Y)$	$3: \mathbf{return}\ \sigma$	$3: \mathbf{return}\ \tilde{\sigma}$
$4: \sigma \leftarrow \mathcal{A}_2^{\mathcal{O}_{\mathsf{S}}(\cdot), \mathcal{O}_{\mathsf{pS}}(\cdot, \cdot)}(\tilde{\sigma}, \mathsf{st})$		
$5: \mathbf{return}\ ((Y, \mathsf{Ext}_{pk}(\sigma, \tilde{\sigma}, Y)) \notin R \land m \notin \mathcal{Q} \land \mathsf{Vrfy}_{pk}(m; \sigma))$		

Let us stress that while the experiment aWitExt looks fairly similar to the experiment aSigForge, there is one crucial difference; namely, the adversary is allowed to choose the forgery statement Y. Hence, we can assume that they know a witness for Y so they can generate a valid signature on the forgery message m. However, this is not sufficient to win the experiment. The adversary wins *only* if the valid signature does not reveal a witness for Y.

Definition 5. *An adaptor signature scheme $\Xi_{R,\Sigma}$ is secure, if it is* aEUF–CMA *secure, pre-signature adaptable and witness extractable.*

Note that none of the security definitions explicitly states that pre-signatures are unforgeable. However, it is implied by the definitions as we discuss in the full version of this paper [4].

5.1 ECDSA-based Adaptor Signature

We now construct a provably secure adaptor signature scheme based on ECDSA digital signatures that are commonly used by blockchains. The construction presented here is similar to the construction put forward by [45], however some modifications are needed for the security proof. In addition to the ECDSA-based adaptor signature scheme presented here, we show a scheme based on Schnorr digital signatures, including correctness and security proofs, in the full version of this paper [4].

Recall the ECDSA signature scheme $\Sigma_{\mathsf{ECDSA}} = (\mathsf{Gen}, \mathsf{Sign}, \mathsf{Vrfy})$ for a cyclic group $\mathbb{G} = \langle g \rangle$ of prime order q. The key generation algorithm samples $x \leftarrow_{\$} \mathbb{Z}_q$ and outputs $g^x \in \mathbb{G}$ as the public key and x as the secret key. The signing algorithm on input a message $m \in \{0, 1\}^*$, samples $k \leftarrow_{\$} \mathbb{Z}_q$ and computes $r := f(g^k)$ and $s := k^{-1}(\mathcal{H}(m) + rx)$, where $\mathcal{H}: \{0, 1\}^* \rightarrow \mathbb{Z}_q$ is a hash function modeled as a random oracle and $f: \mathbb{G} \rightarrow \mathbb{Z}_q$ (i.e., f is typically defined as the projection to the x-coordinate since in ECDSA the group $\mathbb{G}$ consists of elliptic curve points). The verification algorithm on input a message $m \in \{0, 1\}^*$ and a signature (r, s) verifies that $f(g^{s^{-1}\mathcal{H}(m)} X^{s^{-1}r}) = r$. One of the properties of

$\mathsf{pSign}_{sk}(m, I_Y)$	$\mathsf{pVrfy}_{pk}(m, I_Y; \tilde{\sigma})$	$\mathsf{Adapt}(\tilde{\sigma}, y)$	$\mathsf{Ext}(\sigma, \tilde{\sigma}, I_Y)$
$x := sk, (Y, \pi_Y) := I_Y$	$X := pk, (Y, \pi_Y) := I_Y$	$(r, \tilde{s}, K, \pi) := \tilde{\sigma}$	$(r, s) := \sigma$
$k \leftarrow_\$ \mathbb{Z}_q, \tilde{K} := g^k$	$(r, \tilde{s}, K, \pi) := \tilde{\sigma}$	$s := \tilde{s} \cdot y^{-1}$	$(\tilde{r}, \tilde{s}, K, \pi) := \tilde{\sigma}$
$K := Y^k, r := f(K)$	$u := \mathcal{H}(m) \cdot \tilde{s}^{-1}$	**return** (r, s)	$y' := s^{-1} \cdot \tilde{s}$
$\tilde{s} := k^{-1}(\mathcal{H}(m) + rx)$	$v := r \cdot \tilde{s}^{-1}$		**if** $(I_Y, y') \in R'_g$
$\pi \leftarrow \mathsf{P}_Y((\tilde{K}, K), k)$	$K' := g^u X^v$		**then return** y'
return $(r, \tilde{s}, K, \pi)$	**return** $((r = f(K)) \wedge \mathsf{V}_Y((K', K), \pi))$		**else return** $\bot$

Fig. 5. ECDSA-based adaptor signature scheme.

the ECDSA scheme is that if (r, s) is a valid signature for m, then so is $(r, -s)$. Consequently, Σ_{ECDSA} does not satisfy SUF–CMA security which we need in order to prove its security. In order to tackle this problem we build our adaptor signature from the *Positive ECDSA* scheme which guarantees that if (r, s) is a valid signature, then $|s| \leq (q - 1)/2$. The positive ECDSA has already been used in other works such as [5,39]. This slightly modified ECDSA scheme is not only assumed to be SUF–CMA but also prevents having two valid signatures for the same message after the signing process, which is useful in practice, e.g., for threshold signature schemes based on ECDSA. As the ECDSA verification accepts valid positive ECDSA signatures, these signatures can be used by any blockchain that uses ECDSA, e.g., Bitcoin.

The adaptor signature scheme in [45] is presented w.r.t. a relation $R_g \subseteq \mathbb{G} \times \mathbb{Z}_q$ defined as $R_g := \{(Y, y) \mid Y = g^y\}$. The main idea of the construction is that a pre-signature (r, s) for a statement Y is computed by embedding Y into the r-component while keeping the s-component unchanged. This embedding is rather involved, since the value s contains a product of k^{-1}, r and the secret key. More concretely, to compute the pre-signature for Y, the signer samples a random k and computes $K := Y^k$ and $\tilde{K} := g^k$. It then uses the first value to compute $r := f(K)$ and sets $s := k^{-1}(\mathcal{H}(m) + rx)$. To ensure that the signer uses the same value k in K and $\tilde{K}$, a zero-knowledge proof that $(\tilde{K}, K) \in L_Y := \{(\tilde{K}, K,) \mid \exists k \in \mathbb{Z}_q \text{ s.t. } g^k = \tilde{K} \wedge Y^k = K\}$ is attached to the pre-signature. We denote the prover of the NIZK as P_Y and the corresponding verifier as V_Y. The pre-signature adaptation is done by multiplying the value s with y^{-1}, where y is the corresponding witness for Y. This adjusts the randomness k used in s to ky, and hence matches with the r value.

Unfortunately, it is not clear how to prove security for the above scheme. Ideally, we would like to reduce both the unforgeability and the witness extractability of the scheme to the strong unforgeability of positive ECDSA. More concretely, suppose there exists a PPT adversary $\mathcal{A}$ that wins the aSigForge (resp. aWitExt) experiment. Having $\mathcal{A}$, we want to design a PPT adversary (also called the simulator) $\mathcal{S}$ that breaks the SUF–CMA security. The main technical challenge in both reductions is that $\mathcal{S}$ has to answer queries (m, Y) to the pre-signing oracle $\mathcal{O}_{\mathsf{pS}}$ by $\mathcal{A}$. This has to be done with access to the ECDSA signing oracle, but without knowledge of sk and the witness y. Thus, we need a method to "transform" full signatures into valid pre-signatures without knowing y, which seems to go against the aEUF–CMA-security (resp. witness extractability).

Due to this reason, we slightly modify this scheme. In particular, we modify the hard relation for which the adaptor signature is defined. Let R'_g be a relation whose statements are *pairs* (Y, π), where $Y \in L_{R_g}$ is as above, and π is a non-interactive zero-knowledge proof of knowledge that $Y \in L_{R_g}$. Formally, we define $R'_g := \{((Y, \pi), y) \mid Y = g^y \wedge V_g(Y, \pi) = 1\}$ and denote by P_g the prover and by V_g the verifier of the proof system for L_{R_g}. Clearly, due to the soundness of the proof system, if R_g is a hard relation, then so is R'_g.

It might seem that we did not make it any easier for the reduction to learn a witness needed for creating pre-signatures. However, we exploit the fact that we are in the ROM and the reduction answers adversary's random oracle queries. Upon receiving a statement $I_Y := (Y, \pi)$ for which it must produce a valid pre-signature, it uses the random oracle query table to extract a witness from the proof π. Knowing the witness y and a signature (r, s), the reduction can compute $(r, s \cdot y)$ and execute the simulator of the NIZK_Y to produce a consistency proof π. This concludes the protocol description and the main proof idea. We refer the reader to the full version of the paper [4] for the detailed proof of the following theorem.

Theorem 1. *If the positive ECDSA signature scheme Σ_{ECDSA} is SUF–CMA-secure and R_g is a hard relation, $\Xi_{R'_g, \Sigma_{\mathsf{ECDSA}}}$ from Fig. 5 is a secure adaptor signature scheme in the ROM.*

6   Generalized Channel Construction

We now present a concrete protocol, denoted Π, that requires only one commit transaction, i.e., implements the punish-then-split mechanism. This is achieved by utilizing an adaptor signature scheme $\Xi_{R, \Sigma} = (\mathsf{pSign}, \mathsf{Adapt}, \mathsf{pVrfy}, \mathsf{Ext})$ for signature scheme $\Sigma = (\mathsf{Gen}, \mathsf{Sign}, \mathsf{Vrfy})$ used by the underlying ledger and a hard relation R. Throughout this section, we assume that statement/witness pairs of R are public/secret key of Σ. More precisely, we assume there exists a function ToKey that takes as input a statement $Y \in L_R$ and outputs a public key pk. The function is s.t. the distribution of $(\mathsf{ToKey}(Y), y)$, for $(Y, y) \leftarrow \mathsf{GenR}$, is equal to the distribution of $(pk, sk) \leftarrow \mathsf{Gen}$. We emphasize that both ECDSA and Schnorr based adaptor signatures satisfy this condition as discussed in the full version of the paper [4], where we also explain how to modify our protocol when this condition does not hold. Our protocol consists of four subprotocols: Create, Update, Close and Punish. We discuss each subprotocol separately at a high level here and refer the reader to the full version of the paper [4] for the pseudo-code description.

Channel creation. In order to create a channel γ, the users of the channel, say A and B, have to agree on the body of the funding transaction $[\mathsf{TX_f}]$, mutually commit to the first channel state defined by $\gamma.\mathsf{st} = ((x_A, \mathsf{One\text{-}Sig}_{pk_A}),$ $(x_B, \mathsf{One\text{-}Sig}_{pk_B}))$, and sign and publish the funding transaction $\mathsf{TX_f}$ on the

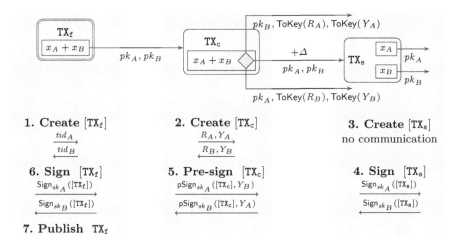

Fig. 6. Schematic description of the generalized channel creation protocol.

ledger. Recall that $\mathsf{One\text{-}Sig}_{pk}$ represents the script that verifies that the transaction is correctly signed w.r.t. the public key pk. Once $\mathsf{TX_f}$ is published, the channel creation is completed. Looking at Fig. 6, one can summarize the creation process as a step-by-step creation of transaction bodies from left to right, and then a step-by-step signature exchange on the transaction bodies from right to left. Let us elaborate on this in more detail.

Step 1: To prepare $[\mathsf{TX_f}]$, parties need to inform each other about their funding sources, i.e., exchange the transaction identifiers tid_A and tid_B. Each party can then locally create the body of the funding transaction $[\mathsf{TX_f}]$ with $\{tid_A, tid_B\}$ as input and output requiring the signature of both A and B. **Step 2:** Parties can now start committing to the initial channel state. To this end, each party $P \in \{A, B\}$ generates a *revocation public/secret* pair $(R_P, r_P) \leftarrow \mathsf{GenR}$ and *publishing public/secret* pair $(Y_P, y_P) \leftarrow \mathsf{GenR}$, and sends the public values R_P, Y_P to the other party. Parties can now locally generate $[\mathsf{TX_c}]$ which spends $\mathsf{TX_f}$ and can be spent by a transaction satisfying one of these conditions:

Punish A: It is correctly signed w.r.t. $pk_B, \mathsf{ToKey}(Y_A), \mathsf{ToKey}(R_A)$;
Punish B: It is correctly signed w.r.t. $pk_A, \mathsf{ToKey}(Y_B), \mathsf{ToKey}(R_B)$;
Channel state: It is correctly signed w.r.t. pk_A and pk_B, and at least Δ rounds have passed since $\mathsf{TX_c}$ was published.

Steps 3+4: Using the transaction identifier of $\mathsf{TX_c}$, parties can generate and exchange signatures on the body of the split transaction $\mathsf{TX_s}$ which spends $\mathsf{TX_c}$ and whose output is equal to initial state of the channel $\gamma.st$. **Step 5:** Parties are now prepared to complete the committing phase by *pre-signing* the commit transaction to each other. This means that party A executes the pSign_{sk_A} on message $[\mathsf{TX_c}]$ and statement Y_B and sends the pre-signature to B (analogously for B). **Step 6:** If valid pre-signatures are exchanged (validity is checked using the pVrfy algorithm), parties exchange signatures on the funding transaction and post it on the ledger in **Step 7**. If the funding transaction is accepted by the ledger, channel creation is successfully completed.

The question is what happens if one of the parties misbehaves during the creation process by aborting or sending a malformed message (w.l.o.g. let B be the malicious party). If the misbehavior happens before A sends her signature on TX_f (i.e., before step 6), party A can safely conclude that the creation failed and does not need to take any action. If the misbehavior happens during step 6, A is in a hybrid situation. She cannot post TX_f on-chain as she does not have B's signature needed to spend tid_B. However, since she already sent her signature on TX_f to B, she has no guarantee that B will not post TX_f later. To resolve this issue, our protocol instructs A to spend her output tid_A. Now within Δ rounds, tid_A is spent – either by the transaction posted by A (in which case creation failed) or by TX_f posted by B (in which case creation succeeded).

To conclude, channel creation as described above takes 5 off-chain communication rounds and up to Δ rounds are needed to publish the funding transaction. Our formal protocol description contains two optimizations that reduce the number of off-chain communication rounds to 3. The optimizations are based on the observations that messages sent during steps 1 and 2 can be grouped into one as well as the messages sent during steps 4 and 5.

Channel closure. The purpose of the closing procedure is to collaboratively publish the latest channel state on the blockchain. The naive implementation is to let parties publish the latest agreed upon commit transaction and thereafter the corresponding split transaction representing the latest channel state. However, due to the punishment mechanism built-in the commit transaction, parties have to wait for Δ rounds after such a transaction is accepted by the ledger to publish the split transaction. To realize our ideal functionality, we need to design a more efficient solution eliminating the redundant waiting for honest parties.

When parties want to close a channel, they first run a "final update". In short, the final update preserves the latest channel state, but removes the punishment layer. More precisely, parties agree on a new split transaction that has exactly the same outputs as the last split transaction but spends the funding transaction TX_f directly (i.e., **Steps 2+5** from Fig. 6 are skipped). Once parties jointly sign the split transaction, they can publish it on the ledger which completes the channel closure. If the final update fails, parties close the channel forcefully. Namely, they first publish the latest commit transaction, wait until the time for punishments expires. Then they post the split transaction representing the final channel state. It takes at most Δ rounds to publish the commit transaction and at most 2Δ rounds to publish the split transaction once the commit transaction is accepted which corresponds to the upper bound dictated by our ideal functionality. Since forceful closing might also be triggered during a channel update (as we discuss next), we define forceful closure as a separate subprocedure `ForceClose`.

Channel Update. To update a channel γ to a new state, given by a vector of output scripts $\vec{\theta}$, parties have to (i) agree on the new commit and split transaction capturing the new state and (ii) invalidate the old commit transaction.

Part (i) is very similar to the agreement on the initial commit and split transaction as described in the creation protocol (**Steps 2–5** in Fig. 6). There is one major difference coming from the fact that the new channel state $\vec{\theta}$ can contain outputs that fund other off-chain applications (such as sub-channels).[3] In order to set up these applications, the identifier of the new split transaction is needed. To this end, parties first prepare the commit (**Steps 2+3**) to learn the desired identifier and set up all applications off-chain. Once this is done, which is signaled by "SETUP–OK" and takes at most t_{stp} rounds, parties execute the second part of the committing phase (**Steps 4+5**).

To realize part (ii), in which the punishment mechanism of the old commit transaction is activated, parties simply exchange the revocation secrets corresponding to the previous commit transaction which completes the update. Note that in this optimistic case when both parties are honest, the update is performed entirely off-chain and takes at most $5 + t_{\mathsf{stp}}$ rounds.

We now discuss what happens if one party misbehaves during the update. As long as none of the parties pre-signed the new commit transaction, i.e., before **Step 5**, misbehavior simply implies update failure. A more problematic case is when the misbehavior occurs after at least one of the parties pre-signed the new commit transaction. This happens, e.g., when one party pre-signs the new commit but the other does not; or when one party revokes the old commit and the other does not. In each of these situations, an honest party ends up in a hybrid state when the update is neither rejected nor accepted. In order to realize our ideal functionality requiring consensus on update in bounded number of rounds, our protocol instructs an honest party to ForceClose the channel. This means that the honest party posts the latest commit transaction that both parties agreed on to the ledger guaranteeing that $\mathtt{TX_f}$ is spent within Δ rounds. If the transaction spending $\mathtt{TX_f}$ is the new commit transaction, the channel is closed in the updated state. Otherwise, the update fails and either the channel is closed in the state before the update, or the punishment mechanism is activated and the honest party gets financially compensated (as discussed in the next paragraph).

Punish. Since we are in the UTXO model, nothing can stop a corrupted party from publishing an old commit transaction, thereby closing the channel in an old state. However, the way we designed the commit transaction enables the honest party to punish such malicious behavior and get financially compensated. If an honest party A detects that a malicious party B posted an old commit transaction $\overline{\mathtt{TX}}_{\mathsf{c}}$, it can react by publishing a *punishment transaction* which spends $\overline{\mathtt{TX}}_{\mathsf{c}}$ and assigns all coins to A. In order to make such punishment transaction valid, A must sign it under: (i) her secret key sk_A, (ii) B's publishing secret key $\bar{y}_B$, and (iii) B's revocation secret key $\bar{r}_B$. The knowledge of the revocation secret $\bar{r}_B$ follows from the fact that $\overline{\mathtt{TX}}_{\mathsf{c}}$ was old, i.e., parties revealed their revocation secrets to each other. The knowledge of the publishing secret $\bar{y}_B$ follows from the fact that it was B who published $\overline{\mathtt{TX}}_{\mathsf{c}}$. Let us elaborate on this in more detail. Since $\overline{\mathtt{TX}}_{\mathsf{c}}$ was accepted by the ledger, it had to include a signature of A.

---

[3] This is not the case during channel creation since we assume that the initial channel state consists of two accounts only.

The only signature A provided to B on $\overline{\text{TX}}_c$ was a *pre-signature* w.r.t. $\bar{Y}_B$. The unforgeability and witness extractability properties of $\Xi_{R,\Sigma}$ guarantee that the only way B could produce a valid signature of A on $\overline{\text{TX}}_c$ was by adapting the pre-signature and hence revealing the secret key $\bar{y}_B$ to A.

Security analysis. We now formally state our main theorem, which essentially says that the Π protocol is a secure realization, as defined according to the UC framework, of the $\mathcal{F}(3,1)$ ideal functionality.

Theorem 2. *Let Σ be a SUF–CMA secure signature scheme, R a hard relation and $\Xi_{R,\Sigma}$ a secure adaptor signature scheme. Let $\mathcal{L}(\Delta, \Sigma, \mathcal{V})$ be a ledger, where $\mathcal{V}$ allows for transaction authorization w.r.t. Σ, relative time-locks and constant number of Boolean operations $\wedge$ and $\vee$. Then the protocol Π UC-realizes the ideal functionality $\mathcal{F}^{\mathcal{L}(\Delta,\Sigma,\mathcal{V})}(3,1)$.*

The formal UC proof of the Theorem 2 can be found in the full version of this paper [4]. Let us here just argue at a high level, why our protocol satisfies the most complex property defined by the ideal functionality, i.e., instant finality with punishment.

We first argue that instant finality holds after the channel creation, meaning that each of the two parties (alone) is able to unlock her coins from a created channel if it was never updated. The pre-signature adaptability property of $\Xi_{R,\Sigma}$ guarantees that after a successful channel creation, each party P is able to adapt the pre-signature of the other party Q on $[\text{TX}_c]$ by using the publishing secret value y_P (corresponding to Y_P). Party P can now sign $[\text{TX}_c]$ herself and post TX_c on the ledger. Since parties never signed any other transaction spending TX_f, the posted TX_c will be accepted by the ledger within Δ rounds. Note that here we rely on the unforgeability of the signature scheme and the unforgeability of the adaptor signature scheme. Let us stress that parties have not revealed their revocation secrets, i.e., the values r_P and r_Q, to each other yet. Hardness of the relation R implies that none of the two parties is able to use the punishment mechanism of the published commit transaction. Thus, after Δ rounds, P can post the split transaction TX_s on the ledger by which she unlocks her x_P coins.

After a successful update, each party P possesses a pre-signature of the other party Q on the new commit transaction TX_c and the revocation secret of the other party on the previous commit transaction. The former implies that P is able to complete Q's pre-signature, sign $[\text{TX}_c]$ herself and post TX_c on-chain. Assume first that the funding transaction of the channel TX_f is not spent yet, hence TX_c is accepted by the ledger within Δ rounds. Since party Q does not know the revocation secret of party P corresponding to TX_c, by hardness of the relation R, the only way how TX_c can be spent is by publishing TX_s representing the latest channel state. Hence, instant finality holds in this case.

Assume now that TX_f is already spent and hence TX_c is rejected by the ledger. The only transaction that could have spent TX_f is one of the old commit transactions. This is because P never signed or pre-signed any other transaction spending TX_f. Let us denote the transaction spending TX_f as $\overline{\text{TX}}_c$. Since $\overline{\text{TX}}_c$ is an old transaction P knows Q's revocation secret r_Q. Moreover, the extractability property of the adaptor signature scheme implies that P can extract Q's publishing secret y_Q from the pre-signature that she gave to Q on this transaction and the completed signature contained in $\overline{\text{TX}}_c$. Hence, P can create a valid punishment transaction spending $\overline{\text{TX}}_c$. As our protocol instructs an honest party P to constantly monitor the blockchain and publish the punishment transaction immediately if $\overline{\text{TX}}_c$ appears on-chain, the punishment transaction will be accepted by the blockchain before the relative time-lock of $\overline{\text{TX}}_c$ expires. Hence, P receives all the coins locked in the channel which is what we needed to show.

7   Applications

Our generalized channels support a variety of applications such as PCNs [41,42,47], payment channel hubs [31,49], multi-path payments in PCNs [25], financially fair two-party computation [8], channel splitting [26], virtual payment channels [3] or watchtowers [44]. Furthermore, generalized channels prove to be highly versatile in interoperable applications, i.e., applications that run across multiple blockchains. As generalized channels rely only on on-chain signature verification, time-locked transactions and basic Boolean logic, they can be implemented on a multitude of different blockchains, easing thus the design and execution of cross-chain applications. Here, we first generally discuss which applications can be built on top of generalized channels and then focus on several concrete examples.

Suitable applications. We are interested in applications that are executed among two parties (i.e., two-party applications) and whose goal is to redistribute coins between them. We call the initial transaction outputs holding coins of the two parties the *funding source* of the application. If all outputs of the funding source are contained in already published transactions, we say that the application is *funded directly by the ledger*. If the outputs are part of a generalized channel state, we say that the application is *funded by a generalized channel*.

In principle, any two-party application that can be funded directly by the underlying ledger can also be funded by a generalized channel. There are, however, two subtleties one should keep in mind. Firstly, generalized channels provide "only" instant finality with punishment. This implies that generalized channels are suitable for two-party applications in which parties are willing to accept financial compensation in exchange for an off-chain state loss. Secondly, it takes up to 3Δ rounds to publish the funding source of the application. Hence, the protocol implementing the application needs to adjust the dispute timings accordingly (if applicable). We summarize this statement in the full version of this paper [4], where we also explain how to add applications to a generalized channel. Here we now discuss several concrete applications that benefit from generalized channels.

Fair two-party computation. One important example of an application that can be built on top of generalized channels is the *claim-or-refund* functionality introduced by Bentov and Kumaresan [8], and used in a series of work to realize multiple applications over Bitcoin [37]. At a high level, claim-or-refund allows one party, say A, to lock β coins that can be claimed by party B if she presents a witness satisfying a condition f. After a predefined number of rounds, say t, the payment of β coins is refunded back to A if the witness is not revealed.

In their work, Bentov and Kumaresan demonstrated how to utilize this simple functionality to realize secure two-party protocol with penalties over a blockchain. Hence, the fact that claim-or-refund can be built on top of generalized channels naturally implies that two parties can execute any such protocol *off-chain*. Off-chain execution offers several advantages if both parties collaborate: (i) they do not have to pay fees or wait for the on-chain delay when deploying and funding the claim-or-refund as well as when one of the parties rightfully claims (resp. refunds) coins; (ii) they can run several simultaneous instances of claim-or-refund fully off-chain, thus improving efficiency; and (iii) a blockchain observer is oblivious to the fact that the claim-or-refund functionality has been executed off-chain. In case of misbehavior during the execution of a claim-or-refund instance, the channel punishment procedure ensures that the honest party is financially compensated with all funds locked in the channel.

Channel splitting. A generalized channel can be split into multiple subchannels that can be updated independently in parallel. This idea appears already in [26] where two users A and B want to split a channel γ with coin distribution (α_A, α_B) into two sub-channels γ_0 and γ_1 with the coin distributions (β_A, β_B) and $(\alpha_A - \beta_A, \alpha_B - \beta_B)$ respectively.

Executing multiple applications without prior channel splitting requires all applications to share a single funding source (i.e., that provided by the channel) and thus to be adjusted with every single channel update (i.e., even if the update is required for a single application), which might significantly increase the off-chain communication complexity. However, first splitting the channel into sub-channels effectively makes the execution of applications in each sub-channel independent of each other. For instance, two applications that benefit from channel splitting are *payment channels with watchtower* [44] and *virtual channels* [3] – both of which rely on generalized channels, and which we discuss next.

We elaborate on further applications in the full version of this paper [4].

8   Performance Analysis

We implemented a proof of concept for our generalized channels construction, creating the necessary Bitcoin transactions. We successfully deployed these transactions on the Bitcoin testnet, demonstrating thereby the compatibility

Table 1. Costs of lightning (LC) and generalized channels (GC) funding m HTLCs.

	on-chain (dispute)			off-chain (update)	
	# txs	size (bytes)	cost (USD)	# txs	size (bytes)
LC	$2 + m$	$513 + m \cdot 410$	$13.52 + m \cdot 10.80$	$2 + 2 \cdot m$	$706 + 2 \cdot m \cdot 410$
GC	2	663	17.47	2	$695 + m \cdot 123$

with the current Bitcoin network. The source code is available at https://github.com/generalized-channels/gc. For the different operations, we measure the (i) number and (ii) byte size for off- and on-chain transactions required for the protocol. On-chain, we additionally measure the current estimated fee cost (May 2021). Note that the transaction fee in Bitcoin is dependent on the transaction size. We compare these numbers to Lightning-based channels.

Evaluation of multiple HTLCs. Users in a PCN typically take part in several multi-hop payments at once inside one channel. We evaluate the costs of performing m parallel payments, over both Lightning channels (LC) and generalized channels (GC). To realize multiple payments in a channel, there needs to be $2 + m$ outputs: Two of which account for the balances of each user, and m representing one payment each in a "Claim-or-Refund" contract (HTLC).

To update to a channel with m parallel payments, parties need to exchange $2+2 \cdot m$ transactions in LC and only 2 transactions in GC. The advantage of GC is two-fold: The state is not duplicated and the HTLCs do not require an additional transaction. The difference in off-chain transaction size is $706 + 2 \cdot m \cdot 410$ bytes for LC compared to $695 + m \cdot 123$ bytes for GC.

In case of a dispute, the difference in on-chain cost is even more pronounced. To punish in LC, the honest party needs to spend $m + 1$ outputs: the one representing the balance of the malicious party and one per HTLC. This is in contrast to GC, where the honest party publishes the punishment transaction only. As a result, the total size of on-chain transactions in the LC is $513 + m \cdot 410$ bytes, which cost around $13.52 + m \cdot 10.80$ USD. In GC, the on-chain transaction size is 663 bytes resulting in a cost of 17.47 USD. There have already been disputes for channels with 50 active HTLCs [40]. To settle such a dispute in LC, transactions with 21013 bytes or a cost of 553.66 USD have to be deployed. In GC, again we only need 663 bytes or 17.47 USD. GC thus reduce the on-chain cost from linear on m to constant in the case of a dispute as shown in Table 1.

Evaluation of channel splitting. The state duplication impacts other applications as well, e.g., channel splitting (see Sect. 7). For a LC, two commit transactions need to be exchanged per update. Hence, if we split a LC into two sub-channels, parties need to create these sub-channels for both commit transactions. Moreover, for each sub-channel two commit transactions are required. This is a total of 4 commit transactions per sub-channel. GC needs only one commitment and one split transactions per sub-channel.

After a channel split, sub-channels are expected to behave as normal channels. If we want to split a LC sub-channel further, we would need eight commit transactions (two for each of the four commitments) per sub-channel. Observe, that for every recursive split of a channel, the amount of LC commit transactions for the new subchannel doubles. For the mth split, we need 2^{m+1} additional commit transactions in the LC setting. In the GC setting, there is no state duplication, therefore the amount of transactions per sub-channel is always one commit and one split transaction. We reduce the complexity for additional transactions on the mth split from exponential to constant.

Acknowledgment. This work was partly supported by the German Research Foundation (DFG) Emmy Noether Program *FA 1320/1-1*, by the *DFG CRC 1119 CROSSING* (project S7), by the German Federal Ministry of Education and Research (BMBF) *iBlockchain project* (grant nr. 16KIS0902), by the German Federal Ministry of Education and Research and the Hessen State Ministry for Higher Education, Research and the Arts within their joint support of the *National Research Center for Applied Cybersecurity ATHENE*, by the European Research Council (ERC) under the European Unions Horizon 2020 research (grant agreement No 771527-BROWSEC), by the Austrian Science Fund (FWF) through PROFET (grant agreement P31621) and the Meitner program (grant agreement M 2608-G27), by the Austrian Research Promotion Agency (FFG) through the Bridge-1 project PR4DLT (grant agreement 13808694) and the COMET K1 projects SBA and ABC, by the Vienna Business Agency through the project Vienna Cybersecurity and Privacy Research Center (VISP), by CoBloX Labs and by the ERC Project PREP-CRYPTO 724307.

References

1. Androulaki, E., et al.: Hyperledger fabric: a distributed operating system for permissioned blockchains. In: EuroSys, pp. 30:1–30:15 (2018). https://doi.org/10.1145/3190508.3190538

2. Andrychowicz, M., et al.: Secure multiparty computations on bitcoin. Commun. ACM **59**(4), 76–84 (2016)

3. Aumayr, L., et al.: Bitcoin-compatible virtual channels. In: IEEE S&P, Matteo Maffei (2021)

4. Aumayr, L., et al.: Generalized channels from limited blockchain scripts and adaptor signatures. Cryptology ePrint Archive, Report 2020/476 (2020). https://ia.cr/2020/476

5. Banasik, W., et al.: Efficient zero-knowledge contingent payments in cryptocurrencies without scripts. In: ESORICS, pp. 261–280 (2016)

6. Bano, S., et al.: SoK: Consensus in the age of blockchains. In: ACM AFT, pp. 183–198. ACM (2019)

7. Bartoletti, M., Zunino, R.: Bitml: A calculus for bitcoin smart contracts. In: David, L., Mohammad, M., Michael, B., XiaoFeng, W. (eds.) CCS, pp. 83–100 (2018)

8. Bentov, I., Kumaresan, R.: How to use bitcoin to design fair protocols. In: Garay, J.A., Gennaro, R. (eds.) CRYPTO 2014. LNCS, vol. 8617, pp. 421–439. Springer, Heidelberg (2014). https://doi.org/10.1007/978-3-662-44381-1_24

9. Bentov, I., Kumaresan, R., Miller, A.: Instantaneous decentralized poker. In: ASIACRYPT, pp. 410–440 (2017)

10. Bitcoin wiki: Payment channels. https://tinyurl.com/y6msnk7u

11. Boneh, D., et al.: Aggregate and verifiably encrypted signatures from bilinear maps. In: Biham, E. (ed.) EUROCRYPT 2003. LNCS, vol. 2656, pp. 416–432. Springer, Heidelberg (2003). https://doi.org/10.1007/3-540-39200-9_26

12. Brasser, F., et al.: Software grand exposure: SGX cache attacks are practical. In: 11th USENIX Workshop on Offensive Technologies (2017)

13. Bulck, J.V., et al.: Foreshadow: Extracting the keys to the intel SGX kingdom with transient out-of-order execution. In: USENIX (2018)

14. Canetti, R.: Universally composable security: A new paradigm for cryptographic protocols. In: 42nd FOCS, pp. 136–145. IEEE Computer Society Press, October 2001

15. Canetti, R., et al.: Universally composable security with global setup. In: Vadhan, S.P. (ed.) TCC 2007. LNCS, vol. 4392, pp. 61–85. Springer, Heidelberg (2007). https://doi.org/10.1007/978-3-540-70936-7_4
16. Chen, G., et al.: Pectre attacks: Leaking enclave secrets via speculative execution. In: IEEE Euro S&P, pp. 142–157 (2018)
17. Cheng, R., et al.: Ekiden: A platform for confidentiality-preserving, trustworthy, and performant smart contracts. In: IEEE EuroS&P, pp. 185–200 (2019)
18. Das, P., et al.: Fastkitten: Practical smart contracts on bitcoin. In: USENIX 2019, pp. 801–818 (2019)
19. Decker, C., Wattenhofer, R.: A fast and scalable payment network with bitcoin duplex micropayment channels. In: Stabilization, Safety, and Security of Distributed Systems 2015, pp. 3–18 (2015)
20. Decker, C., et al.: eltoo: A simple layer2 protocol for bitcoin. https://blockstream.com/eltoo.pdf
21. Deuber, D., et al.: Minting mechanisms for blockchain - or - moving from cryptoassets to cryptocurrencies. Cryptology ePrint Archive, Report 2018/1110 (2018). https://eprint.iacr.org/2018/1110
22. Dziembowski, S., et al.: General state channel networks. In: ACM CCS 18, pp. 949–966 (2018)
23. Dziembowski, S., et al.: Multi-party virtual state channels. In: Ishai, Y., Rijmen, V. (eds.) EUROCRYPT 2019, Part I. LNCS, vol. 11476, pp. 625–656. Springer, Cham (2019). https://doi.org/10.1007/978-3-030-17653-2_21
24. Dziembowski, S., et al.: Perun: Virtual payment hubs over cryptocurrencies. In: IEEE S&P 2019, pp. 106–123 (2019)
25. Eckey, L., et al.: Splitting payments locally while routing interdimensionally. ePrint Archive (2020). https://eprint.iacr.org/2020/555
26. Egger, C., et al.: Atomic multi-channel updates with constant collateral in bitcoin-compatible payment-channel networks. In: ACM CCS 19, pp. 801–815. ACM (2019)
27. Erwig, A., et al.: Two-party adaptor signatures from identification schemes. In: PKC (2021)
28. Fischlin, M.: Communication-efficient non-interactive proofs of knowledge with online extractors. In: Shoup, V. (ed.) CRYPTO 2005. LNCS, vol. 3621, pp. 152–168. Springer, Heidelberg (2005). https://doi.org/10.1007/11535218_10
29. Fournier, L.: One-time verifiably encrypted signatures a.k.a. adaptor signatures, October 2019. https://tinyurl.com/y4qxopxp
30. Gudgeon, L., et al.: Off the chain transactions. In: FC, Sok (2020)
31. Heilman, E., et al.: Tumblebit: An untrusted bitcoin-compatible anonymous payment hub. In: NDSS, 01 2017. 10.14722/ndss.2017.23086
32. Jourenko, M., et al.: Sok: A taxonomy for layer-2 scalability related protocols for cryptocurrencies. Cryptology ePrint Archive, Report 2019/352 (2019). https://eprint.iacr.org/2019/352
33. Katz, J., et al.: Universally composable synchronous computation. In: Amit, S., (ed.) TCC 2013, volume 7785 of LNCS, pp. 477–498. Springer, Heidelberg, March 2013. https://doi.org/10.1007/978-3-642-36594-2_27
34. Kiayias, A., Litos, O.S.T.: A composable security treatment of the lightning network. In: IEEE CSF 2020, pp. 334–349 (2020)
35. Kosba, A., et al.: Hawk: The blockchain model of cryptography and privacy-preserving smart contracts. In: IEEE S&P, pp. 839–858 (2016)
36. Kumaresan, R., Bentov, I.: Amortizing secure computation with penalties. In: ACM CCS 2016, pp. 418–429 (2016)

37. Kumaresan, R., Bentov, I.: How to use bitcoin to incentivize correct computations. In: Ahn, G.J., Yung, M., Li, N. (eds.) ACM CCS 14, pp. 30–41. ACM Press, November 2014

38. Kumaresan, R., et al.: How to use bitcoin to play decentralized poker. In: ACM CCS, pp. 195–206 (2015)

39. Lindell, Y.: Fast secure two-party ECDSA signing. In: Katz, J., Shacham, H. (eds.) CRYPTO 2017. LNCS, vol. 10402, pp. 613–644. Springer, Cham (2017). https://doi.org/10.1007/978-3-319-63715-0_21

40. lnchannels. https://ln.bigsun.xyz/ (2020)

41. Malavolta, G., et al.: Anonymous multi-hop locks for blockchain scalability and interoperability. In: NDSS 2019. https://www.ndss-symposium.org/ndss-paper/anonymous-multi-hop-locks-for-blockchain-scalability-and-interoperability/

42. Malavolta, G., et al.: Concurrency and privacy with payment-channel networks. In: Bhavani, M., Thuraisingham, D.E., Tal, M., Dongyan, X., (eds.) ACM CCS 17, pp. 455–471. ACM Press, October/November 2017

43. Miller, A., et al.: Sprites and state channels: Payment networks that go faster than lightning. In: Ian, G., Tyler, M., (eds.) FC 2019, volume 11598 of Lecture Notes in Computer Science, pp. 508–526 (2019)

44. Mirzaei, A., et al.: A fair and privacy preserving watchtower for bitcoin. In: FC, Fppw (2021)

45. Moreno-Sanchez, P., Kate, A.: Scriptless scripts with ecdsa. https://tinyurl.com/yxtjo47l

46. Poelstra, A.: Scriptless scripts. https://tinyurl.com/ludcxyz, May 2017

47. Poon, J., Dryja, T.: The bitcoin lightning network: Scalable off-chain instant payments. https://tinyurl.com/q54gnb4 (2016)

48. Siegel, A.: Understanding the dao attack. https://tinyurl.com/2bzxkn7a (2016)

49. Tairi, E., et al.: A^2l: Anonymous atomic locks for scalability in payment channel hubs. In: IEEE S&P (2021)

50. Thyagarajan, S.A.K., Malavolta, G.: Lockable signatures for blockchains: Scriptless scripts for all signatures. In: IEEE S&P (2021)

51. Thyagarajan, S.A.K., et al.: Paymo: Payment channels for monero. Cryptology ePrint Archive (2020). https://eprint.iacr.org/2020/1441

52. Transcripts from coredev.tech amsterdam 2019 meeting on sighash noinput. https://tinyurl.com/49ryfutr

53. Wang, G., et al.: Sharding on blockchain. In: ACM AFT, Sok, pp. 41–61 (2019)

ConTra Corona: Contact Tracing against the Coronavirus by Bridging the Centralized–Decentralized Divide for Stronger Privacy

Wasilij Beskorovajnov[1], Felix Dörre[2], Gunnar Hartung[2],
Alexander Koch[2(✉)] ⓘ, Jörn Müller-Quade[2], and Thorsten Strufe[2]

[1] FZI Research Center for Information Technology, Karlsruhe, Germany
beskorovajnov@fzi.de
[2] Competence Center for Applied Security Technology (KASTEL),
Karlsruhe Institute of Technology (KIT), Karlsruhe, Germany
{felix.doerre,gunnar.hartung,alexander.koch,joern.mueller-quade,
thorsten.strufe}@kit.edu

Abstract. Contact tracing is among the most important interventions to mitigate the spread of any pandemic, usually in the form of manual contact tracing. Smartphone-facilitated *digital contact tracing* may help to increase tracing capabilities and extend the coverage to those contacts one does not know in person. Most implemented protocols use local Bluetooth Low Energy (BLE) communication to detect contagion-relevant proximity, together with cryptographic protections, as necessary to improve the privacy of the users of such a system. However, current decentralized protocols, including DP3T [T+20], do not sufficiently protect infected users from having their status revealed to their contacts, which raises fear of stigmatization.

We alleviate this by proposing a new and practical solution with stronger privacy guarantees against active adversaries. It is based on the upload-what-you-observed paradigm, includes a separation of duties on the server side, and a mechanism to ensure that users cannot deduce which encounter caused a warning with high time resolution. Finally, we present a simulation-based security notion of digital contact tracing in the real–ideal setting, and prove the security of our protocol in this framework.

Keywords: Digital contact tracing · Privacy · Transmissible diseases · Active security · Anonymity · Security modeling · Ideal functionality

1 Introduction

During the early stages of a pandemic, when a vaccine is not yet available, one of the most important interventions to contain its spread, is – besides the reduction of face-to-face encounters in general – the consequent isolation of infected persons, as well as those who have been in close contact with them ("contacts") to

© International Association for Cryptologic Research 2021

M. Tibouchi and H. Wang (Eds.): ASIACRYPT 2021, LNCS 13091, pp. 665–695, 2021.
https://doi.org/10.1007/978-3-030-92075-3_23

break the chain of infections. In phases with low case numbers of the SARS-CoV-2 pandemic, contact tracing has been the used to keep case numbers in check (for a longer time). However, tracing contacts manually (by interviews with infected persons) is not feasible when the number of infections is too high. Hence, more scalable and automated solutions are needed to safely relax restrictions of personal freedom imposed by a strict lockdown, without the risk of returning to a phase of exponential spread of infections. *Digital contact tracing* using off-the-shelf smartphones is used as an additional measure that is more scalable, does not depend on infected persons' ability to recall their location history during the days before the interview, and can even track contacts between strangers.

In many digital contact tracing protocols, e.g. [AHL18, C+20, R+20, CTV20, R+, T+20, P20a, BRS20, CIY20, BBH+20, AG20], users' devices perform automatic proximity detection via short-distance wireless communication mechanisms, such as Bluetooth Low Energy (BLE), and jointly perform an ongoing cryptographic protocol which enables users to check whether they have been colocated with contagious users. However, naïve designs for digital contact tracing pose a significant risk to users' privacy, as they process confidential information about users' location history, meeting history, and health condition [KBS21].

This has sparked a considerable research effort to design protocols for privacy-preserving contact tracing, most of which revolve around the following idea: Participating devices continuously broadcast ephemeral, short-lived pseudonyms and record pseudonyms broadcast by close-by devices. When a user is diagnosed, she submits either all the pseudonyms her device used while she was contagious or all the pseudonyms her device has recorded (during the same period) to a server. The first approach is the *upload-what-you-sent* paradigm, while the second is called *upload-what-you-observed* paradigm. Users' devices are then either actively notified by the server, or they regularly query the server for pseudonyms uploaded by infected users.

Some of the designs that received the most attention are the centralized PEPP-PT proposals [P20c, P20b], as well as the more decentralized approach of [CTV20] and DP3T [T+20], which served as sketches for the subsequently proposed Apple/Google-API (GAEN) [AG20]. While the "centralized" approaches of PEPP-PT do not provide any privacy guarantees towards the users against the central server infrastructure [D20b, D20c] (unless they are augmented by, e.g. mix-nets), the DP3T approach [T+20], as well as the similar protocol by Canetti, Trachtenberg, and Varia [CTV20], expose the ephemeral pseudonyms of every infected user, which enables her contacts to learn whether she is infected. A detailed comparison is given in [F20].

We argue that both, *protection against a centralized actor*, as well as *protection of infected users from being stigmatized for their status*[1], is important for any real-world solution. By specifying a protocol that achieves both of these goals and detailing the corresponding design choices, we aim to contribute to the ongoing discussion on privacy-preserving digital contact tracing.

---

[1] See https://coronadetective.eu for a service that detects the contacts that caused a warning for DP3T-based approaches.

1.1 Contribution

We propose a strong and encompassing simulation-based security notion via an ideal contact tracing functionality (in Sect. 5) that allows us to capture the following privacy and security guarantees.

- It makes the exact leakage an attacker would gather explicit. This leakage can be described by a partially anonymized, partially pseudonymized contact graph (described and motivated in detail in Sect. 5 and Fig. 3), a list of positively tested and corrupted participants, and their warning status. This (minimal) leakage is inherent to BLE-based contact tracing schemes.
- It captures that the locally exchanged identifiers do change quickly (each "short-term epoch") in an unlinkable fashion, but the time of an encounter causing a warning can only be narrowed down on a more coarse-grained timescale. In other words, while observed identifiers change, e.g. every 15 min, a warning does only give away the day (or another globally-fixed "long-term epoch") of the encounter.
- It captures the worst-case guarantees in the sense that our guarantees hold, no matter how history unfolds, people meet, move and get infected, i.e., the environment can fully control the (directed) contact graph and infection status per short-term epoch.
- It provides guarantees against not being warned despite a (BLE-detectable) risk contact with an honest user (false negatives). For this, we assume that an attacker does not jam any local communication.
- It provides guarantees against being warned without a corresponding risk contact (false positives), *unless* the user was in proximity to a corrupted user *and* a corrupted user is infected or in proximity to an infected user. (This restriction is necessary, as in any protocol not protecting against malicious replays of proximity beacons, any attacker can cause a false positive under these conditions. However, protecting against replays would require processing time and location information, which is deemed undesirable.)

As a second part, we specify a privacy-preserving contact tracing protocol that achieves this security notion. It follows the upload-what-you-observed paradigm and achieves its goals by the following mechanisms:

- We split up the identifiers into short-lived *public identifiers* (pids) used for broadcasting, and longer-lived secret identifiers used for querying for warnings (cf. Sects. 3.1 and 3.2).
- We employ a strict server separation concept, where the servers (for uploading the lookup table for this split-up identifiers, for matching, and for warning queries) carry out different functions (cf. Sect. 3.3). For reasons of complexity reduction, the ideal functionality in the main body does not include server corruptions. However, the case of passive server corruptions is given informally in Sect. 6.2 and formally in the full version [BDH+20].
- We employ strong, but anonymous anti-Sybil protections coupled to, e.g., an SMS challenge, to ensure that the guarantees cannot be circumvented by registering multiple Sybil identities (cf. Sect. 3.4).

Additionally, we argue that our protocol is similar in efficiency to DP3T, on the side of the smartphone used, see our efficiency analysis on p. 18. While our protocol was designed with the current COVID-19 pandemic in mind, note that it can easily be generalized to perform contact tracing for other transmissible diseases and enable an effective containment in case a new virus is about to hit a population without any immunity from prior exposition.

The full version also includes an appendix that identifies the timing of Bluetooth beacons as a side-channel that can be exploited to link distinct public identifiers, and using secret sharing to ensure a lower bound on necessary contact time for a warning.

1.2   Outline

We define our informal security model for BLE-based contact tracing in Sect. 2, the formal version is given in Sect. 5. For this protocol, Sect. 3 proposes a number of core security mechanisms in a modular way, which are applied to obtain our overall protocol presented in Sect. 4. An informal security and privacy analysis of the protocol follows in Sect. 6.

2   Security Model

Our main goals are *privacy*, i.e. limiting disclosure of information about participating individuals, and *security*, i.e. limiting malicious users' abilities to produce "wrong protocol outcomes", such as being warned without a (BLE-detectable) risk contact (false negatives), or not being warned despite a risk contact (false positives). For privacy, we consider the following types of private information: (i) where users have been at which point in time, (ii) whom they have met (and when and where), (iii) whether a user has been infected, (iv) whether a user has received a warning because she was colocated with an infected user. We have a precise analysis of which of these goals are achieved under which conditions, and refer to Sects. 5 and 6 for details. We refer the interested reader to [KBS21] for a systematization of different privacy desiderata.

Ideal–Real Paradigm. Formally, we cast our security guarantees in the ideal–real paradigm [MR91,B92], to obtain strong, simulation-based security definitions, as is also common in proofs in the Universal Composability framework [C01]. In contrast to a fixed list of security properties, which might leave doubt about whether everything the system should guarantee is captured, this has the advantage that the correctness guarantees and exact privacy leakage (dependent on the behavior of the adversary) are made explicit. We refer the interested reader to [L17]. Slightly more specific, we consider a scenario in which an interactive distinguisher $\mathcal{Z}$ (also called *environment*) that can choose the parties' inputs, observe their outputs and can communicate with the adversary arbitrarily during the execution, has to find out if it is running within a "real" experiment ("real world") or an "ideal" experiment ("ideal world").

In the "real" experiment, the protocol is executed and an attacker interferes with it. In the "ideal" experiment, the attacker is replaced by a Simulator $\mathcal{S}$ (which simulates protocol messages so that they look like in the real experiment) and all honest parties calculate their result via an ideal (contact tracing) functionality $\mathcal{F}_{CT}$ (later given in Sect. 5). The real-world protocol is considered secure if no PPT distinguisher $\mathcal{Z}$ has a non-negligible advantage in distinguishing an execution of the real protocol (in the "real" setting) from an execution in the ideal setting. In this sense, the real world only permits attacks that would also be possible in the ideal world, which behaves perfectly as prescribed/is secure by definition. Hence, $\mathcal{F}_{CT}$ formalizes the security guarantees we require for a contact tracing protocol.

Modeling Time. We assume time is divided into disjoint, consecutive intervals called *epochs* (or *short-term epochs*). A *long-term epoch* is the union of a fixed number of consecutive short-term epochs. Again, all long-term epochs are disjoint and consecutive. In the following, we assume each short-term epoch corresponds to a 15 min interval, and each long-term epoch corresponds to a day. Hence, there are 96 short-term epochs in a long-term epoch, and a tuple from $\mathbb{N} \times \mathbb{Z}_{96}$ specifies a short-term epoch. (These durations are parameters, but for concreteness we describe our protocol with these parameters fixed.)

Allowing the Distinguisher to Define Reality. We let the distinguisher $\mathcal{Z}$ define the physical reality for each epoch $t \in \mathbb{N} \times \mathbb{Z}_{96}$, i.e. who meets whom (defined by a contact graph G_t) and who is infected (a set of parties $\mathcal{P}_{infected,t}$). Nodes in G_t correspond to participating parties, and G_t contains an edge (P_1, P_2) if P_2 registered a contact with P_1. Since who registered a contact with whom might not be a symmetric relation (e.g. due to noise in the wireless signal), each G_t is a *directed graph*.[2] (We do not impose any restrictions on G_t or $\mathcal{P}_{infected,t}$, the environment may set these arbitrarily, even in ways that would be impossible in the physical world.) The distinguisher $\mathcal{Z}$ defines these values by sending them to a party P_{mat} (named after the ideal functionality $\mathcal{F}_{mat}$ as explained below). Each such input marks the beginning of a new short-term epoch. In the ideal experiment, this is a dummy party which forwards these inputs to $\mathcal{F}_{CT}$. In the real experiment, P_{mat} sends $\mathcal{P}_{infected}$ to $\mathcal{F}_{med}$ and G to $\mathcal{F}_{mat}$. This *hybrid* (i.e. ideal, but used in the real world to abstract from a realization of it) functionality $\mathcal{F}_{mat}$ represents the "world state" or "material world"[3], including a representation of who met whom (controlable by the environment), and a synchronized "epoch-wise" clock. This functionality is used for local broadcast and to decide which participant receives a particular public identifier pid. Here, Servers constitutes a set of centralized servers, see Sect. 3.3.

---

[2] This captures a relaxed notion of "proximity", as high-gain antennas could be used to register a contact, although not physically being in proximity.

[3] Internally, the author(s) humorously prefer to read the name of $\mathcal{F}_{mat}$ as "the matrix".

$$\mathcal{F}_{\text{mat}}(\mathcal{P}, P_{\text{mat}}, \text{Servers})$$

State:

- Current contact graph $G = (\mathcal{P}, E)$
- Current time $e = (e_{lt}, e_{st}) \in \mathbb{N} \times \mathbb{Z}_{96}$.

Set Neighborhood:

1. Receive and store directed contact graph $G = (\mathcal{P}, E)$ from party P_{mat}.
2. Increment e_{st} (in $\mathbb{Z}_{96}$). If $e_{st} = 0$, increment e_{lt} and send (*newLongTermEpoch*) to all servers, and then to all parties except P_{mat}.

Receiving Broadcasts:

1. Receive (pid) from a participant P, where pid is a public identifier.
2. Send (pid) to all P' with $(P, P') \in E$.

As mentioned above, the incorruptible party P_{mat} just forwards the contact graph G and the set of infected parties $\mathcal{P}_{infected}$ to the relevant functionalities $\mathcal{F}_{\text{mat}}$ and $\mathcal{F}_{\text{med}}$ (which represents the medical professional that is informed about who is infected, and will be given in Sect. 4 on p. 14), respectively.

Protocol of P_{mat} in the Real Setting

Update Neighborhood and Infections:

1. Receive a contact graph G and a set of infected parties $\mathcal{P}_{infected}$ from the environment as input.
2. Send G to $\mathcal{F}_{\text{mat}}$.
3. Send $\mathcal{P}_{infected}$ to $\mathcal{F}_{\text{med}}$.

Communication Channels. Channels between the parties, functionalities and the servers are assumed to be confidential and authentic (in the fitting direction). We assume the attacker does not jam any wireless communication between honest parties. (The distinguisher $\mathcal{Z}$ can emulate a suppression of broadcasts by leaving out edges in the contact graph.)

When a user, e.g. uploads data used in the protocol that should not be linked to the person (e.g. public or secret identifiers), the server can easily link these pairs with communication metadata (such as the user's IP address), which might be used to ultimately link this data to a specific individual. We therefore use an anonymous communication channel for all communication with the servers. In practice, one can communicate via publicly available proxies that are managed by operators separate from the protocol servers. Alternatively, one might also employ the TOR onion routing network [TOR]. (We analyze the load that would be placed on TOR on p. 18.)

Corruption Model. In the formal modeling and our security proofs – to keep the complexity of the description and proofs manageable – centralized servers are perfectly trusted. However, the protocol was designed in a way that the information leakage to the servers is still acceptable in the case of a passive (honest-but-curious) server corruption, as will be explained in Sect. 6.2. (A formal security notion with passive server corruptions is given in the full version.)

Regarding the users, we do only consider static corruptions, i.e. corruptions that happen at the beginning the protocol execution. We do not distinguish between "the attacker" and corrupted, malicious, or compromised parties.

Modeling Medical Professionals. Furthermore, we trust medical professionals to not disclose data regarding the users who are under their care, as is their duty under standard medical confidentiality. This is abstracted by introducing a hybrid functionality $\mathcal{F}_{\text{med}}$, which represents medical professionals who are aware about the infection status of all users. $\mathcal{F}_{\text{med}}$ is defined in Sect. 4 on p. 14.

3   Core Security Mechanisms

We start by giving a relatively generic, abstract template of contact tracing protocols, which are characterized by send-what-you-observed upon infection. This allows us to put our core security mechanisms in context and serve as a starting point for describing them.

Generation of "Random" Identifiers. For every time period t, the user's device generates an identifier pid_t. (These identifiers can look uniformly random and be computationally unlinkable, unless they incorporate additional time/location information for replay/relay protections.)

Broadcasting and Recording. During the time period t the identifier pid_t is repeatedly broadcast so nearby participants can record it, together with the date/time (maybe involving additional postcomputation before storing).

Warning Co-located Users. When a user is tested positive, one extracts a list of all *recorded* pid' from the infected user's device (assuming that old ones are periodically deleted). The user is then given a TAN code that she can use to send this list to a central server. The server marks the respective pids as potentially infected, and then allows users to query for a given pid, answering whether it is marked as potentially infected.

We now describe the security mechanisms our protocol is built upon:

3.1   Splitting of Identifiers

We propose to use, instead of just one public identifier pid that is used for both, broadcasts and warning queries, two versions of identifiers: public identifiers pid that are used for broadcasting, and a secret identifiers sid which are used to query the server for warnings. The server internally keeps a table linking sids to pids, where users can submit new entries to. This split-up of identifiers achieves better privacy, because malicious users cannot just use public identifiers they have observed to query the server for the warning status of the pids' owners. Note that later mechanisms from Sects. 3.2 and 3.3 will further modify this.

Generation of "Random" Identifiers. For every time period t, the device generates pid_t, sid_t in a such way that one cannot efficiently derive sid_t from pid_t. Moreover, given a set of pids which are either all from the same user, or all from different users, it should not be possible to distinguish which is the case. Finally, we require that only the user to whom these ids belong can submit them, e.g. by her knowing a preimage that is used to generate both in tandem and also submitting the preimage.[4]

Broadcasting and Recording. Proceeds as above.

Warning Co-Located Users. When an infected user sends a list of all recorded pid' as above, the server looks up the respective sids in his database of (sid, pid) tuples and marks them as potentially infected. The server then allows users to query for sids, answering whether they are marked as potentially infected.

3.2   Lower-Resolution Secret Identifiers for Improved Infection-Status Privacy

In the protocol sketch described in Sect. 3.1, users receiving a warning can immediately observe which of their secret identifiers sid was published. By correlating this information with the knowledge on when they used which public identifier pid, they can learn at which time they have met an infected person, which poses a threat to the infected person's privacy. Note that the DP3T protocol [T+20] and [CTV20] succumb to analogous problems, see [V20a].

To mitigate this risk, we propose to associate a secret identifier sid with many public identifiers pid, i.e. we use the same sid during a long-term epoch, but change pids per short-term epoch. As the example of deriving $(\mathsf{sid}_t, \mathsf{pid}_t)$ pairs for time epoch t from Footnote 4 does not allow such longer-term secret identifiers, we modify this procedure as follows:

Generation of "Random" Identifiers. The user generates a single random key, now called *warning identifier*, once per long-term epoch. More concretely, a user generates a random warning identifier $\mathsf{wid}_{e_{lt}} \leftarrow\!\!\!{\scriptstyle\$}\, \{0,1\}^n$ per long-term epoch e_{lt} (e.g. a day), and encrypts it with the server's public key $\mathsf{pk}_\mathcal{W}$ to obtain $\mathsf{sid} := \mathsf{Enc}(\mathsf{pk}_\mathcal{W}, \mathsf{wid}_{e_{lt}})$, using a *rerandomizable* public-key encryption scheme. For each shorter time period t (e.g., 15 min), the user generates a

---

[4] We give a simple example of how this might be done. Note however, our protocol uses a different method, see Sect. 3.2. For this example, let H be a hash function, such that $\mathsf{H}(k\|x)$ is a pseudorandom function (PRF) with key $k \in \{0,1\}^n$ evaluated on input x. For every time period t, the device generates a random key $k_t \leftarrow\!\!\!{\scriptstyle\$}\, \{0,1\}^n$, and computes $\mathsf{sid}_t := \mathsf{H}(k_t\|0)$ and $\mathsf{pid}_t := \mathsf{H}(k_t\|1)$, stores them, and anonymously uploads k_t to the central server, who recomputes $\mathsf{sid}_t, \mathsf{pid}_t$ in the same way. Both parties store $(\mathsf{sid}_t, \mathsf{pid}_t)$.

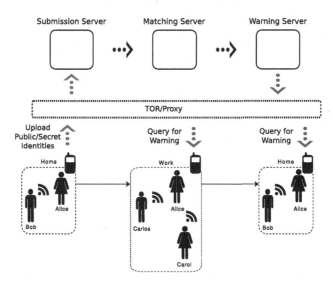

Fig. 1. Overview of the application's infrastructure. The figure depicts different possible scenarios: In the morning, Alice uploads her daily public/secret identifiers to the submission server, and periodically queries the warning server for warnings. Throughout the day, while she is in proximity to Bob, Carlos and Carol, the application exchanges public identifiers with their phones.

rerandomization sid'_t of sid, where the randomness is derived from a PRG, and computes $\mathsf{pid}_t := \mathsf{H}(\mathsf{sid}'_t)$. Once per long-term epoch, the user uploads sid and the PRG seed to the server, who performs the same rerandomization, obtaining the same pid_t values, and the corresponding $\mathsf{wid}_{e_{lt}}$ by decryption.

The user then broadcasts the pid_t in random order during the current long-term epoch. The warning of co-located users proceeds as before, with the only change that the server maintains a database of $(\mathsf{wid}, \mathsf{pid})$ tuples, and allows users to query for wids (instead of sids).

There is a trade-off regarding the length of the long-term epochs: While warnings are more precise for shorter long-term epochs, they also give more information about when the encounter of the warning happened. In practice, choosing a long-term epoch of a day is reasonable.

3.3   Splitting-Up the Server into a Pipeline

The change introduced in Sect. 3.2 allows to split the process of warning co-located users into three tasks for three non-colluding[5] servers, the submission server, the matching server, and the warning server:

- The *submission server* collects the uploaded secret and public identifiers from different users (more precisely, it receives sid and the seed for the PRG) and then computes the $(\mathsf{sid}'_i, \mathsf{pid}_i)$ pairs using the PRG with the given seed. It rerandomizes the sid'_i values another time with fresh, non-reproducible randomness (obtaining sid''_i), and stores $(\mathsf{sid}''_i, \mathsf{pid}_i)$ for a short period of time. When the submission server has a sufficient number of submissions, it shuffles them and sends them to the matching server. For ease of notation, we assume that this transaction happens at the beginning of the next long-term epoch. (We assume that enough users participate, for the batching to make sense.)
- The *matching server* collects the $(\mathsf{sid}''_i, \mathsf{pid}_i)$ pairs and stores them. Upon receiving the pids recorded by the devices of infected users, which we call a *match request*, the matching server looks up the respective sid''_is of all potentially infected users and sends them to the warning server.
- The *warning server* decrypts sid''_i to recover $\mathsf{wid} := \mathsf{Dec}_{\mathsf{sk_W}}(\mathsf{sid}''_i)$ for all potentially infected users. It then allows to query for warning ids by the users, which we call *warning query* in the following.

For illustration, see Fig. 1. We assume all communication between the servers uses confidential and authenticated channels. Section 6.2 contains a privacy analysis in case of compromised, honest-but-curious and partly colluding servers.

3.4   Protecting from Encounter-Wise Warning Identifiers and Sybil Attacks

Our measures from Sect. 3.2, namely having a lower resolution for the secret/warning identifiers are not yet sufficient to hide the infection against the following, more motivated attack: An attacker that is able to upload an unlimited number of sid and PRG seed values to the submission server, can change to a set of pids that belong to a different warning identifier, after each short-term epoch. Upon warning, the attacker can then deduce which of the warning identifiers have been warned, and from that deduce the exact short-term epoch the encounter happened. A simple rate-limiting on the side of the app is ineffective against malicious attackers, and a simple traffic-based rate-limiting on the side of the servers per app instance is not possible due to the anonymized communication. Moreover, the above attacker can run a so-called *Sybil attack*, i.e. creating multiple (seemingly) independent app instances. Hence, we aim to prevent this

---

[5] To make sure servers do not collude, they should be run by different organizations whose independence is guaranteed by law, e.g. supervisory agencies on privacy (ideally multiple different ones per nation-state) and non-governmental organisations that are widely trusted by the general public.

type of attack and ideally to ensure a limitation of uploads to the submission server to one per user (identifier) per day. For this, it is helpful to use a users identifier that is difficult to obtain in larger numbers, to force the adversary to invest additional resources for spawning Sybil instances. While there are a number of solutions, for concreteness, we propose to bind each app instance to a phone number (as the aforementioned user identifier) and require a registration process using an SMS challenge. (Note that this approach does not prevent an attacker from performing a Sybil attack on lower scale, as the attacker might own multiple phone numbers.[6])

Binding an app to an identifiable resource (such as a valid phone number) while ensuring the user's anonymity, requires a bit of care. For this, we use the periodic n-times anonymous authentication scheme from [CHK+06]. In such a scheme, *token dispensers* are issued to parties using an Obtain protocol. These dispensers can be used n times in a Show protocol in a given epoch. The server participating in the Obtain protocol can not link these requests to the executions of the Show protocol. The formal definition is given as follows, where the security notions are included in the full version (alternatively, see [CHK+06]).

Definition 1 (E-token dispenser scheme [CHK+06]).

- $\mathsf{Gen}_{\mathcal{I}}(1^k)$ *is the key generation algorithm of the e-token issuer $\mathcal{I}$. It outputs a key pair* $(\mathsf{pk}_{\mathcal{I}}, \mathsf{sk}_{\mathcal{I}})$.
- $\mathsf{Gen}_{\mathcal{U}}$ *creates the user's key pair* $(\mathsf{pk}_{\mathcal{U}}, \mathsf{sk}_{\mathcal{U}})$ *analogously.*
- $\mathsf{Obtain}(\mathcal{U}(\mathsf{pk}_{\mathcal{I}}, \mathsf{sk}_{\mathcal{U}}, n), \mathcal{I}(\mathsf{pk}_{\mathcal{U}}, \mathsf{sk}_{\mathcal{I}}, n))$ *is a protocol between a user $\mathcal{U}$ and an issuer $\mathcal{I}$. At the end of this protocol, the user $\mathcal{U}$ obtains an e-token dispenser D, usable n times per time period.*
- $\mathsf{Show}(\mathcal{U}(D, \mathsf{pk}_{\mathcal{I}}, t, n), \mathcal{V}(\mathsf{pk}_{\mathcal{I}}, t, n))$ *is a protocol between a user $\mathcal{U}$ and a verifier $\mathcal{V}$. The verifier outputs a token serial number (TSN) S and a transcript τ. The user's output is an updated e-token dispenser D'.*
- $\mathsf{Identify}(\mathsf{pk}_{\mathcal{I}}, S, \tau, \tau')$. *Given two records (S, τ) and (S, τ') output by honest verifiers in the Show protocol, where $\tau \neq \tau'$, computes a value $s_{\mathcal{U}}$ that can identify the owner of the dispenser D that generated the TSN S.*

In our setting, we choose $n = 1$ and choose as time period the long-term epoch period, i.e. the user can obtain one "e-token" per long-term epoch to upload a new sid and PRG seed to the submission server. The submission server validates the "e-tokens" and only accepts submissions with valid tokens while checking for double-spending. The token dispenser is then issued to the user during a registration process, which uses the aforementioned SMS challenges. Formally, we define the hybrid functionality $\mathcal{F}_{\mathrm{reg}}$, which represents the party towards which parties run the registration protocol, and which keeps a list of registered parties, and is given below. This is e.g. for obtaining a token dispenser to perform the regular uploads. To keep the model simple, we do not incorporate SMS challenges into $\mathcal{F}_{\mathrm{reg}}$. (An SMS challenge, as well as the upload TAN, might be modeled via an authenticated channel from the party, for which an adversary can break authentication by guessing. See [AGH+19] for a formalization).

---

[6] One might use remotely verifiable electronic ID cards instead.

$$\mathcal{F}_{\mathrm{reg}}(\mathcal{P})$$

State:

- Set of registered parties and their public keys as pairs $\mathcal{RP}$.
- Issuer secret and public key for e-token dispensers $(\mathsf{sk}_\mathcal{I}, \mathsf{pk}_\mathcal{I})$

Registering a Party:

1. Upon $(register, \mathsf{pk}_\mathcal{U})$ from party P: if P is not already in a pair in $\mathcal{RP}$, store $(P, \mathsf{pk}_\mathcal{U})$ in $\mathcal{RP}$, else abort.
2. Issue a new e-token dispenser for P acting as $\mathcal{U}$ by participating as $\mathcal{I}$ in the protocol $\mathsf{Obtain}(\mathcal{U}(\mathsf{pk}_\mathcal{I}, \mathsf{sk}_\mathcal{U}, 1), \mathcal{I}(\mathsf{pk}_\mathcal{U}, \mathsf{sk}_\mathcal{I}, 1))$.

4   Our Contact-Tracing Protocol

We can now describe the full protocol. For this, let n denote the security parameter, $\mathbb{G}$ be a group of prime order such that the decisional Diffie-Hellman problem in $\mathbb{G}$ is intractable. We assume a IND-CPA secure, rerandomizable public key encryption scheme $(\mathsf{Gen}, \mathsf{Enc}, \mathsf{Dec}, \mathsf{ReRand})$ having message space $\mathcal{M} = \mathbb{G}$. (We propose standard ElGamal for instantiation.) Let PRG be a secure pseudorandom generator, and H be a one-way function. Finally, let $\Sigma_{\mathsf{tok}} = (\mathsf{Gen}_\mathcal{I}, \mathsf{Gen}_\mathcal{U}, \mathsf{Obtain}, \mathsf{Show}, \mathsf{Identify})$ be an anonymous e-token dispenser scheme as in [CHK+06]. The exact definitions can be found in the full version.

App Setup. When the proximity tracing software is first installed on a user's device, for anti-Sybil measures as described in Sect. 3.4, the application proves possession of a phone number (e.g. via an SMS challenge) and obtains an e-token dispenser.

Creating Secret Warning Identifiers. For each long-term epoch, the application generates a random *warning identifier* $\mathsf{wid} \leftarrow_\$ \mathbb{G}$.

Deriving Public Identifiers. For each warning identifier wid, the app computes $\mathsf{sid} := \mathsf{Enc}(\mathsf{pk}_\mathcal{W}, \mathsf{wid})$, where Enc is the encryption algorithm of a rerandomizable, IND-CPA-secure public-key encryption scheme, and $\mathsf{pk}_\mathcal{W}$ is the warning server's public key. Additionally, the app chooses a random $\mathsf{seed} \leftarrow_\$ \{0,1\}^n$ *(rerandomization seed)* per warning identifier.

The app (interactively) presents an e-token τ to the submission server via an anonymous channel, and uploads $(\mathsf{sid}, \mathsf{seed})$ to the submission server via the same channel. If the e-token is invalid (or the server detects double-spending of this e-token), the server refuses to accept $(\mathsf{sid}, \mathsf{seed})$. Both the submission server and the app compute 96 rerandomization values $r_1, \ldots, r_{96} = \mathsf{PRG}(\mathsf{seed})$, and rerandomize sid using these values, obtaining $\mathsf{sid}_i := \mathsf{ReRand}(\mathsf{sid}; r_i)$ for $i \in \{1, \ldots, 96\}$. The ephemeral public identifiers of the user are defined as $\mathsf{pid}_i := \mathsf{H}(\mathsf{sid}_i')$ for all i. The app saves the public identifiers for broadcasting during the day of validity of wid. The submission server rerandomizes each sid_i' again (using non-reproducible randomness) to obtain sid_i'' and stores the $(\mathsf{sid}_i'', \mathsf{pid})$ pairs.

Broadcasting and Recording. During each time period i, the device repeatedly broadcasts pid_i. When it receives a broadcast value pid' from someone else, it stores (e_{lt}, pid'), where e_{lt} is the current long-term epoch. Every long-term epoch, the device deletes all pid's that are old enough to no longer be epidemiologically relevant.

Sending a Warning. When a user is tested positive, the medical personnel generates a TAN and registers it at the matching server. The user collects a list of public identifiers pid' that have been received by his device while the user was likely infectious, and sends this list together with the TAN to the matching server, see p. 16.

The medical professional is modeled by the hybrid functionality $\mathcal{F}_{\mathrm{med}}$, which gives out a TAN to parties which are deemed infected, as given below. In a bit more detail, $\mathcal{F}_{\mathrm{med}}$ stores a set $\mathcal{P}_{infected}$ of infected/positively tested participants as provided by the environment $\mathcal{Z}$. If such a participant $P \in \mathcal{P}_{infected}$ requests a TAN (using *warningRequest*), $\mathcal{F}_{\mathrm{med}}$ chooses a TAN, registers its hash value with the matching server and sends it to P. For an illustration, see Fig. 2.

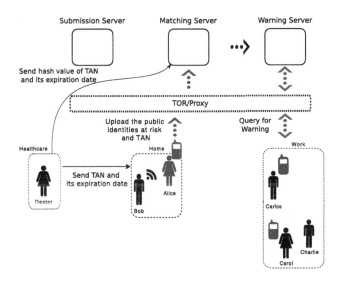

Fig. 2. Information flow upon issuing a warning. When the doctor is informed about a positive test, she generates a new TAN and sends it to the matching server and then communicates it to positively tested Alice. Then, using this TAN, Alice uploads all public identifiers she observed during her infectious period. The application regularly queries for its warnings to its the warning server. In the case of Carlos and Carol, who have been in contact with Alice in Fig. 1, this check will turn out to be positive.

$$\mathcal{F}_{\mathrm{med}}(P_{\mathrm{mat}}, \textit{Matching Server})$$

State:

- Set of infected parties $\mathcal{P}_{infected}$.

Set Infected:

1. Receive and store the set of infected parties $\mathcal{P}_{infected}$ from a party P_{mat}.

Handling Warning Request:

1. Upon $(warningRequest)$ from $P \in \mathcal{P}_{infected}$.
2. Generate tan $\leftarrow_{\$} \{0,1\}^{2n}$.
3. Send $(\mathsf{H}(\mathrm{tan}))$ to the *Matching Server*.
4. Send (tan) to P.

Retrieving Warnings. The application regularly queries the warning server for the warning identifiers it has used during the last 28 days itself. This is done via an anonymous channel with proper authentication of the warning server. If the query returns that the warning identifier has been marked as at-risk, it informs the user she has been in contact with an infected person during the long-term epoch when the warning identifier was used.

Protocol of the App/Users

State:

- Current epoch $e = (e_{lt}, e_{st}) \in \mathbb{N} \times \mathbb{Z}_{96}$
- Current token dispenser D.
- Set of recorded broadcasts of pids.
- Let $\mathsf{pk}_{\mathcal{W}}$ and $\mathsf{pk}_{\mathcal{I}}$ be the hardwired public key of the warning server, and e-token dispenser issuer, respectively.
- Let $(\mathsf{sk}_{\mathcal{U}}, \mathsf{pk}_{\mathcal{U}})$ be the generated user secret/public key pair during the registration.
- Current Warning identifier wid
- Set of earlier warning identifiers (wid, k), where k is the according long-term epoch.
- The public identifiers of the current long-term epoch $(\mathsf{pid}_j)_{j \in [1,\ldots,96]}$

Register:

1. When a new party is created by the environment, it first generates a token-dispenser secret/public key pair $(\mathsf{sk}_{\mathcal{U}}, \mathsf{pk}_{\mathcal{U}})$ and then sends $(register, \mathsf{pk}_{\mathcal{U}})$ to $\mathcal{F}_{\mathrm{reg}}$.
2. Obtain a token dispenser D by participating as $\mathcal{U}$ in $\mathsf{Obtain}(\mathcal{U}(\mathsf{pk}_{\mathcal{I}}, \mathsf{sk}_{\mathcal{U}}, 1), \mathcal{I}(\mathsf{pk}_{\mathcal{U}}, \mathsf{sk}_{\mathcal{I}}, 1))$ with $\mathcal{F}_{\mathrm{reg}}$ acting as $\mathcal{I}$.
3. Initialize the state and run "Upload Submission".

Upload Submission:

1. Generate fresh $(\mathsf{wid}, \mathsf{seed}, \mathsf{sid})$ and the according list of $\{(\mathsf{sid}'_j, \mathsf{pid}_j)\}_{j \in [1,\cdots,96]}$.
2. Enqueue the current (wid, e_{lt}).
3. Submit a token by participating as $\mathcal{U}$ in $\mathsf{Show}(\mathcal{U}(D, \mathsf{pk}_\mathcal{I}, e_{lt}, 1), \mathcal{V}(\mathsf{pk}_\mathcal{I}, e_{lt}, 1))$ to the *Submission Server*, which acts as $\mathcal{V}$.
4. Send $(\mathsf{seed}, \mathsf{sid})$ over the same channel to the *Submission Server*.

Scheduled Upload:

1. Upon $(newLongTermEpoch)$ from $\mathcal{F}_{\mathrm{mat}}$.
2. Increment e_{lt}.
3. Dequeue outdated wids and recorded pids.
4. Continue as in "Upload Submission".

Sending Broadcasts:

1. Upon $(sendBroadcast)$ from the environment.
2. Send $(\mathsf{pid}_{e_{st}})$ to $\mathcal{F}_{\mathrm{mat}}$ and increment e_{st}.

Recording Broadcasts:

1. Upon (pid) from $\mathcal{F}_{\mathrm{mat}}$.
2. Enqueue (pid, e_{lt}).

Match Request:

1. Upon $(positive)$ from the environment.
2. Send $(warningRequest)$ to $\mathcal{F}_{\mathrm{med}}$.
3. Receive (tan) from $\mathcal{F}_{\mathrm{med}}$.
4. Extract the list L of all recorded/received public identifiers from the queue.
5. Send (L, tan) to the *Matching Server*.

Querying a Warning:

1. Upon $(query, t)$ from the environment.
2. Find the corresponding wid for long-term epoch t and send (wid) to the *Warning Server*.
3. Receive bit b from the warning server.
4. Output b to the environment.

Collecting Daily Submissions. The submission server rerandomizes all the sid'_i values using fresh randomness, obtaining $\mathsf{sid}''_i := \mathsf{ReRand}(\mathsf{sid}'_i)$, and saves a list of the $(\mathsf{sid}''_i, \mathsf{pid}_i)$ tuples. When the submission server has accumulated a sufficiently large list, originating from sufficiently many submissions, it shuffles the list, forwards all tuples to the matching server and clears the list.

Protocol of the Submission Server

State:

- Current epoch e_{lt}.
- The current batch of $\{(\mathsf{sid}_j''^k, \mathsf{pid}_j^k)\}_{j\in[1,\cdots,96]}$.

Handling Submissions:

1. Verify the token by participating as $\mathcal{V}$ in $\mathsf{Show}(\mathcal{U}(D, \mathsf{pk}_\mathcal{I}, e_{lt}, 1), \mathcal{V}(\mathsf{pk}_\mathcal{I}, e_{lt}, 1))$.
2. Detect possible double spending.
3. Receive $(\mathsf{seed}, \mathsf{sid})$ from $\mathcal{U}$.
4. Generate $\{(\mathsf{sid}_j', \mathsf{pid}_j)\}_{j\in[1,\cdots,96]}$ with the help of seed.
5. Rerandomize the sid_j' using fresh randomness, i.e. $\mathsf{sid}_j'' = \mathsf{ReRand}(\mathsf{sid}_j')$
6. Add the generated tuples (with rerandomization) $\{(\mathsf{sid}_j'', \mathsf{pid}_j)\}_{j\in[1,\cdots,96]}$ to the batch of e_{lt}.

Forwarding Submissions:

1. Upon (*newLongTermEpoch*) from $\mathcal{F}_{\mathrm{mat}}$.
2. Shuffle the last batch and send the complete batch to the *Matching Server* together with e_{lt}.
3. Increment e_{lt}.
4. Create a new empty batch for the new epoch.

Performing Contact Matching. The matching server maintains a list of hash values of all TANs issued by medical professionals and all tuples it has received from the submission server, deleting each tuple after three weeks.[7] When a user submits a list of public identifiers together with a valid TAN, the matching server marks the TAN's hash value as invalid by deleting it from its list. The server looks up the corresponding secret identifiers sid and sends them to the warning server.

Protocol of the Matching Server

State:

- The current epoch e_{lt}.
- Per long-term epoch t a set $\mathcal{B}_t$ of $(\mathsf{sid}', \mathsf{pid})$ pairs.
- Set of TANs of pending matching requests $T_{corrupted}$.

Removing Outdated Information:

1. Upon (*newLongTermEpoch*) from $\mathcal{F}_{\mathrm{mat}}$.
2. Increment e_{lt} and delete all sets $\mathcal{B}_t$ where $0 \leq t \leq e_{lt} - 14$.

---

[7] If a user A has been in contact with an infected user B, and if B takes up to three weeks to show symptoms and have a positive test result, the data retention on the matching server is sufficient to deliver a warning to A.

Handling Submissions:

1. Receive a set of $(\mathsf{sid}', \mathsf{pid})$ tuples and an epoch t from the *Submission Server* and store it as $\mathcal{B}_t$.

Preparing Match Request:

1. Receive (h_{tan}) from $\mathcal{F}_{\mathsf{med}}$ and insert $(h_{\mathsf{tan}}, e_{lt})$ into $T_{corrupted}$.

Handling Match Request:

1. Receive (S, tan) from party P, where S is a set of pids.
2. If there is an index $t \in \mathbb{N}$ such that there is an entry $(\mathsf{H}(\mathsf{tan}), t) \in T_{corrupted}$, remove this entry from $T_{corrupted}$, otherwise abort.
3. Let $M := \{(\mathsf{sid}'_l, t_l) : \exists \mathsf{pid}_l \in S, t_l \in \mathbb{N} \text{ such that } (\mathsf{sid}'_l, \mathsf{pid}_l) \in \mathcal{B}_{t_l} \wedge t_l \leq t\}$.
4. Rerandomize all the $\mathsf{sid}'_l \in M$ from the previous step and send $\{(\mathsf{sid}''_l := \mathsf{ReRand}(\mathsf{sid}'_l), t_l) : (\mathsf{sid}'_l, t_l) \in M\}$ to the warning server.

Processing of Warnings. The warning server decrypts the secret identifiers received from the matching server to recover the warning identifier wid contained in them. Users may query the warning server for specific wids. On such queries, the warning server returns either 1 (if this wid was recovered by decryption during the last two weeks) or 0 (otherwise).

Protocol of the Warning Server

State:

- The current epoch e_{lt}.
- PKE key pair $(\mathsf{sk}_{\mathcal{W}}, \mathsf{pk}_{\mathcal{W}})$.
- Set $\mathcal{WL}$ of released wids and their validity epoch t.

Removing Outdated Information:

1. Upon $(newLongTermEpoch)$ from $\mathcal{F}_{\mathsf{mat}}$.
2. Increment e_{lt} and delete all $(\mathsf{wid}, t) \in \mathcal{WL}$, with $0 \leq t \leq e_{lt} - 14$.

Issuing Warnings:

1. Receive a list $\{(\mathsf{sid}''_l, t_l)\}$ from the *Matching Server*.
2. Decrypt, deduplicate and add the received warning identifiers $\{(\mathsf{wid}_l = \mathsf{Dec}_{\mathsf{sk}_{\mathcal{W}}}(\mathsf{sid}''), t_l)\}$ to $\mathcal{WL}$.

Warning Query:

1. Receive warning identifier (wid).
2. Search all finished *epoch* for wid and return 1 if a match is found, 0 otherwise.

This concludes the description of our protocol, cf. Figs. 1 and 2 for illustration.

4.1 Efficiency

Our protocol incurs computation, communication and storage cost on the smartphone, submission server, matching server and the warning server.

First of all we argue that the application on the smartphone does not incur significantly larger costs than currently deployed solutions. Computation-wise, the most expensive operations, i.e. operations needed for using the token-dispenser scheme and 96 reencryptions, have to be performed only once a day (long-term epoch). These are 12 multi-base exponentiations in the domain group of a pairing and 23 multi-base exponentiations in the target group as was shown in [CHK+06]. The remaining computations, i.e. 96 hashes for the pids and the generation of seed, wid, sid, are cost-wise similar to currently deployed solutions for contact tracing and thus the overall battery consumption and CPU load are comparable. The application has to store a constant amount of information of several kilobytes, i.e. $28 \times$ wid, $96 \times$ pid. The only growing variable is the set of recorded/observed pids. We argue that the number of received pids will be rather small as current studies suggest, i.e. [FM21]. The communication comprises several small requests a day to different servers and the broadcast/reception of a pid, which we deem overall negligible.

Next, we analyze the computational cost on the submission server. Considering that the population of the EU is approximately 448 Mio. and current experience with the German contact-tracing application CWA shows that 30% of the German population have adopted the application, we may assume for further considerations 134 Mio. users in our protocol. The submission server must perform $2 \cdot 96$ reencryptions of the sids per day and user, which means that $2 \cdot 96 \cdot 134 \cdot 10^6 \approx 2.6 \cdot 10^{10}$ reencryptions a day or ≈ 300000 a second. Using the ElGamal scheme, the dominant part of the reencryption are two modular exponentiations or scalar multiplications if we use the ECC variant of ElGamal. For an upper bound we may use current benchmarks for the verification algorithm of ECDSA, which has two dominant scalar multiplications on elliptic curves as well. According to [BL21] the verification of ecdonaldp256 on an (2018) AMD EPYC 7371 with 16×3100MHz requires 425723 cycles, which means that we are able to verify $\frac{16 \cdot 3100 \cdot 10^6}{425723} \approx 116507$ signatures a second. We argue therefore that ≈ 300000 reencryptions per second is a realistic requirement and the computational load on the submission server—while undeniably high—can be handled with a realistic amount of equipment.

Next, we analyze the amount of data uploaded from the users' devices to the submission server. Our estimation shows that a daily upload by our protocol is at most 240 kbit. With 138 Mio. users the submission server has to handle 33Tbit a day. By scattering uploads across the span of the day we achieve a lower bound of 0.3Gbit/s, which we deem realistic. While the server may be able to handle this amount of requests, our protocol requires that the uploads are performed through an anonymous channel. To this end one may use TOR and we argue that the EU-wide deployment of our protocol relying on TOR is within TOR's capacities. As of 2020 the advertised bandwidth of the TOR network is approx. 500 Gbit/s and the consumed bandwidth is approx. 250Gbit/s (cf. https://metrics.torproject.

org/bandwidth.html), which is sufficient for our 0.3Gbit/s. Another important restriction of TOR is the number of active users, which currently is around 2Mio users (cf. https://metrics.torproject.org/userstats-relay-country.html). If our server is able to handle 0.3Gbit/s then the amount of users served per second will be 1550, which is a rather small delta to the overall number of TOR users. The latency added by using TOR is in the magnitude of seconds and has no impact on the protocol, as a warning delivered a few seconds later is acceptable. Similar considerations can be made for the matching and the warning server. However, the costs of computation and communication are overall smaller than on the submission server and are hence tamable in the same fashion.

5   Formal Security Notion

Before we are ready to state our ideal contact-tracing functionality, let us begin with several assumptions that allow us to simplify our proof and reduce complexity: (i) In this section, we assume that the servers are uncorruptible. However, we provide a discussion on security against server corruptions in Sect. 6.2 and give a strengthened ideal functionality in the full version. (ii) The per-day uploads are synchronous. We assume that before any pid is broadcast, all parties have made their per-day upload.[8] (iii) All parties, even corrupted ones, send exactly one broadcast per epoch. (The distinguisher can emulate a single corrupted party making multiple broadcasts by using additional corrupted parties with similar/equal sets of recipients.) (iv) For formal reasons, parties can only perform computations and broadcasts when they receive an input. Hence, we assume the distinguisher $\mathcal{Z}$ inputs a dummy message (*sendBroadcast*) to all honest participants at the beginning of a new epoch. (v) Contacts happening on the day an infected person is uploading their list do not incur immediate warnings. These are delayed until the next long-term epoch. This is also a privacy feature, ensuring that no one can learn the time of an encounter with an infected person with precision higher than a long-term epoch.

We are now ready to describe important aspects and notions used in our ideal functionality $\mathcal{F}_{CT}$, which formalizes our security and privacy guarantees: Whenever the environment $\mathcal{Z}$ starts a new short-term epoch by sending $G_i = (\mathcal{P}, E_i)$ and $\mathcal{P}_{infected}$ to $\mathcal{F}_{CT}$ (via P_{mat}), $\mathcal{F}_{CT}$ creates two derived graphs G_i' and $(\mathcal{P}, \hat{E}_i)$. G_i' is a partially anonymized, partially pseudonymized version of G_i. We let $\mathcal{F}_{CT}$ output G_i' and $\mathcal{P}_{infected} \cap \mathcal{P}_{corrupted}$ to the simulator, hence this is the information leakage of our protocol. The edge set $\hat{E}_i$ represents who will receive warnings from whom, hence the simulator's abilities to modify $\hat{E}_i$ represent the attacker's abilities to induce and suppress warnings.

Information Leakage on the Contact Graph. We now describe the anonymization and pseudonymization process for G_i' in detail, cf. Steps 3 to 5 in

---

[8] In practice, parties can make their uploads a few days ahead of time without incurring additional risk.

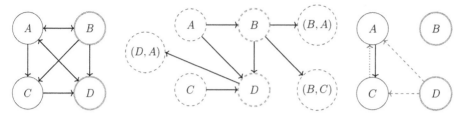

Fig. 3. *Left:* An example of a contact graph $G_t = (\mathcal{P}, E_t)$ with two honest parties A and C and two corrupted parties B and D. The edges indicate where a broadcast is delivered. *Middle:* The pseudonymized graph $G'_t = (\mathcal{Q}_t, E'_t)$ of G_t as leaked by $\mathcal{F}_{\mathrm{CT}}$ to the simulator. Dashed node borders indicate that the node name is replaced with an opaque pseudonym. *Right:* An example for $(\mathcal{P}, \hat{E}_t)$. This graph is initialized with all edges from G_t between honest parties (shown in solid black). The adversary has already inserted edges using the commands $(relay, t, \text{pseudonymize}(C), D, B, \text{pseudonymize}((B, A)))$ as in "Replay/Relay" (shown in dotted purple) and $(sendBroadcast, t, t, B, D)$ as in "Broad-casts From Corrupted User" (shown in dashed green). Note that warnings from honest parties are delivered *against* the direction of all the edges. So an infected A would warn C and D, an infected C would warn A and D.

"Set Neighborhood/Infected" below. The process is exemplified by the graphs G_t and G'_t shown in Fig. 3 (left and middle, respectively). Nodes corresponding to uncorrupted parties are renamed to a pseudonym chosen independently for each epoch (in the example, the nodes of A and C are shown as dashed). This means that an attacker cannot re-identify participants encountered earlier and hence cannot track them over time. Edges between uncorrupted parties are removed entirely (in the example the edge (A, C) is removed), hence the attacker is completely oblivious of contacts between honest parties. Edges between corrupted parties (in the example (B, D)) are preserved without modifications, since we assume they are fully controlled by the attacker and hence the attacker is completely aware of any contacts between them. Before the pseudonymization takes place, nodes corresponding to honest receivers are duplicated for each incoming edge, leaving only the outgoing edges on the original node, since corrupted senders cannot detect if they are broadcasting to the same participant. This step anonymizes edges to honest nodes. In the example the newly introduced nodes by this step are: (D, A), (B, A) and (B, C). The outgoing edges are left at their original node (for example from A), since corrupted receivers (in the example B and D) can easily detect they were in contact with the same person at approximately the same time by comparing the broadcast values. Note that this disadvantage is shared by many contact tracing protocols.

Additionally, all users of the protocol can query $\mathcal{F}_{\mathrm{CT}}$ to check if they have received a warning, which might enable them to infer additional information about the infection status of other participants. (However, this information is inherent to all contact tracing protocols.)

Manipulation of Warnings. We now discuss the attacker's ability to manipulate warnings, i.e. the attacker's options to influence $\hat{E}_i$. Note that $\hat{E}_i$ is initialized to contain all edges between honest parties (step 7 in "Set Neighborhood/Infected" below). The simulator does not have the ability to remove edges from $\hat{E}_i$, but it can introduce new edges (under certain conditions) by causing $\mathcal{F}_{CT}$ to execute "Replay/Relay" and "Broadcasts From Corrupted User".

"Replay/Relay" models a situation where a corrupted user re-broadcasts a value previously broadcast by an honest party: In this scenario – see the dotted purple edges of Fig. 3 (right) – an honest party C broadcasted certain value during an epoch t, received by the corrupted party D. D cooperates with B and B re-broadcasts the same value in the presence of A. Hence, in our protocol, if A was infected, it would cause a warning to be delivered to C (regarding a contact during epoch t), even if those parties did not meet.

"Broadcasts From Corrupted User" models a situation, see the dashed green edges of Fig. 3 (right), where a corrupted user B broadcasts a pid potentially uploaded by another corrupted user D, or potentially not even uploaded, yet. Broadcasting another user's pid causes warnings to be delivered to that user (D), as if D had been performing the broadcast instead of B, hence we add corresponding edges to $\hat{E}_i$. Note that the time of broadcast can be different from the long-term epoch for which the pid was (or will be) uploaded.

In addition to the ability to manipulate $\hat{E}_i$ discussed above, the attacker is able to directly send warnings in case a corrupted party is infected. $\mathcal{F}_{CT}$ enforces that the attacker can only send warnings to honest parties who have been in contact with any corrupted party during the last 14 long-term epochs and a corrupted party is infected after this encounter took place (see step 6 of "Handling Match Requests" on p. 23). The simulator is allowed to specify honest parties fulfilling these conditions (via their pseudonyms). $\mathcal{F}_{CT}$ will add these parties to the set $\mathcal{WP}$ of parties who have received a warning. When these parties next send $(query, t)$ for the corresponding long-term epoch t to $\mathcal{F}_{CT}$, $\mathcal{F}_{CT}$ will find the warning in $\mathcal{WP}$ and return 1, indicating a warning has been issued.

$$\mathcal{F}_{CT}(\mathcal{P}, \mathcal{P}_{mat})$$

State:

- Current epoch $(e_{lt}, e_{st}) \in \mathbb{N} \times \mathbb{Z}_{96} =: I$.
- Set of corrupted parties $\mathcal{P}_{corrupted}$.
- Set of honest parties $\mathcal{P}_{honest} = \mathcal{P} \setminus \mathcal{P}_{corrupted}$.
- A sequence $(\mathcal{P}_{infected,i})_{i \in I}$ of sets of infected parties, i.e. the history of infected parties.
- Set of currently infected parties $\mathcal{P}_{infected}$
- A sequence of all contact graphs so-far $(G_i = (\mathcal{P}_i, E_i))_{i \in I}$, i.e. the global meeting history.
- Current contact graph $G = (\mathcal{P}, E) = G_{(e_{lt}, e_{st})}$ and its pseudonymized version $G' = (\mathcal{Q}, E')$

- Parties at risk $\mathcal{WP} \subseteq \mathcal{P} \times \mathbb{N}$, which signifies which parties have encountered a positive participant (that generated a warning) in the last 14 long-term epochs and during which long-term epochs the encounters took place.
- A sequence of edge sets $(\hat{E}_i)_{i \in I}$ on $\mathcal{P}_i$ which does some bookkeeping necessary to know who is to be warned. Let $\hat{E}$ be the edge set of the current epoch.

Set Neighborhood/Infected:

1. Receive a contact graph $G = (\mathcal{P}, E)$ and a set of infected parties $\mathcal{P}_{infected}$ from party P_{mat}.
2. Add G to the global meeting history, and $\mathcal{P}_{infected}$ to the history of infected parties.
3. Set $E' = \{(P_0, P_1) \in E \mid P_0 \in \mathcal{P}_{corrupted} \vee P_1 \in \mathcal{P}_{corrupted}\}$.
4. For all $\alpha = (P_0, P_1) \in E'$ with $P_0 \in \mathcal{P}_{corrupted}$, $P_1 \in \mathcal{P}_{honest}$, replace α with $\alpha' = (P_0, \alpha)$.
5. Select a random, injective mapping $\mathrm{pseudonymize}_i \colon \mathcal{P}_{honest} \cup (\mathcal{P} \times \mathcal{P}) \to \{0,1\}^{2n}$ where $i = (e_{lt}, e_{st})$. Extend it by $\mathrm{pseudonymize}_i(P) = P$ for all $P \in \mathcal{P}_{corrupted}$. Set $E' := \{(\mathrm{pseudonymize}_i(x), \mathrm{pseudonymize}_i(y)) \colon (x, y) \in E'\}$, i.e. rename all nodes in E'. Let $\mathcal{Q}$ be the set of nodes used in the set of edges E'.
6. Leak $(\mathcal{Q}, E'), \mathcal{P}_{infected} \cap \mathcal{P}_{corrupted}$ to the adversary.
7. Let $\hat{E} := (\mathcal{P}_{honest} \times \mathcal{P}_{honest}) \cap E$.
8. Increment e_{st} (in $\mathbb{Z}_{96}$).
9. If $e_{st} = 0$ then increment e_{lt} and delete all (P, t) pairs from $\mathcal{WP}$ where $0 \leq t \leq e_{lt} - 14$.

Send Broadcast:

1. Receive and ignore $(sendBroadcast)$ from a participant P.

Broadcasts From Corrupted User:

1. Receive $(sendBroadcast, t_1, t_2, P_1, P_2)$ from the adversary, with $t_1, t_2 \in [e_{lt} - 14, e_{lt}] \times \mathbb{Z}_{96}$, $P_1, P_2 \in \mathcal{P}_{corrupted}$ (with the meaning that P_1 broadcasts in the name of (i.e. the pids registered by) P_2).
2. For each $(P_1, x) \in E_{t_1}$, add edge (P_2, x) to $\hat{E}_{t_2}$.

Replay/Relay:

1. Receive $(relay, t, P_1', P_2', P_3', P_4')$ from the adversary, where $P_1' \in \mathrm{pseudonymize}(\mathcal{P})$, $P_2', P_3' \in \mathcal{P}_{corrupted}$, $P_4' \in \mathrm{pseudonymize}(\mathcal{P}_{corrupted} \times \mathcal{P}_{honest})$.
2. Let $P_j := \mathrm{pseudonymize}_i^{-1}(P_j')$ for $j = 1, 2, 3, 4$. (Note that $P_2 = P_2'$, $P_3 = P_3'$.)
3. If $(P_1, P_2) \in E_t$, $(P_3', P_4') \in E'$, let $\hat{P}_4 \in \mathcal{P}$ be the node such that $P_4 = (P_3, \hat{P}_4)$, and add the new edge $(P_1, \hat{P}_4)$ to $\hat{E}_t$.

Handling Match Requests:

1. Receive (*positive*) from party P.
2. If $P \in \mathcal{P}_{corrupted}$, skip to step 6.
3. If $P \notin \mathcal{P}_{infected}$, return. Otherwise, continue:
4. Let $R := \mathbb{N} \cap [e_{lt} - 14, e_{lt})$. For each epoch $i \in R \times \mathbb{Z}_{96}$ (the relevant time period), determine the set $\Delta\mathcal{WP}_i$ (new parties at risk) of nodes P' such that $(P', P) \in \hat{E}_i$.
5. Skip to step 7.
6. Let $lastInfected_{lt} := \max\{i \in \mathbb{N} : \exists j \in \mathbb{Z}_{96}, \text{ such that } P \in \mathcal{P}_{infected,(i,j)}\}$. (Let $lastInfected_{lt} := -\infty$ if this set is empty.) Let $R := \mathbb{N} \cap [e_{lt} - 14, e_{lt}) \cap [0, lastInfected_{lt}]$. Send (*forceWarning*) to the adversary, asking for subsets S_i of (the pseudonyms of) uncorrupted parties which have been in proximity to a corrupted party during epochs in R, i.e. $S_i \subseteq \{q \in \text{pseudonymize}_i(\mathcal{P}_{honest}) \mid \exists q' \in \mathcal{P}_{corrupted} \text{ where } (\text{pseudonymize}_i^{-1}(q), q') \in E_i\}$. After the response, set $\Delta\mathcal{WP}_i = \text{pseudonymize}_i^{-1}(S_i)$ as the set of parties that will be warned for the current epoch.
7. For each $i = (i_{lt}, i_{st}) \in R \times \mathbb{Z}_{96}$, add $\{(P', i_{lt}) \mid P' \in \Delta\mathcal{WP}_i\}$ to the list of active warnings $\mathcal{WP}$.

Handling Warning Query:

1. Receive (*query*, t) from party P
2. Return 1 if $(P, t) \in \mathcal{WP}$, otherwise return 0.

---

6 Security and Privacy Analysis

Our protocol's security is summarized as follows.

Theorem 1. *Under the following list of assumptions, the real protocol (as specified in Sect. 4) realizes the ideal protocol $\mathcal{F}_{CT}$ (cf. Sect. 5) in the $\mathcal{F}_{med}, \mathcal{F}_{mat}, \mathcal{F}_{reg}$-hybrid model and with static corruptions, assuming that P_{mat} as well as the submission, matching and warning server are honest. Assumptions:*

- *Let $\Sigma_R = (\text{Gen}_R, \text{Enc}_R, \text{Dec}_R, \text{ReRand})$ be an IND-CPA-secure, rerandomizable encryption scheme with message space $\mathcal{M} = \mathbb{G}$, ciphertext space $\mathcal{C}$.*
- *Let PRG be a secure pseudorandom generator.*
- *Let $H: \mathcal{C} \to \{0,1\}^{2n}$ be a one-way function.*
- *Let $\Sigma_{tok} = (\text{Gen}_{\mathcal{I}}, \text{Gen}_{\mathcal{U}}, \text{Obtain}, \text{Show}, \text{Identify})$ be a sound, anonymous e-token dispenser scheme with identification of double-spending.*

Having stated the formal security guarantee that we capture with this theorem, we proceed to discuss the interpretation and limitations on what we achieve exactly. For exact definitions of the required primitives and the proof see the full version. For example, the extensive powers of the environment, also in determining the number and place of corrupted users, make it less clear what, e.g. our anti-Sybil protections actually achieve w.r.t. the privacy of the users. While in our argumentation in the full version we state that the e-token dispenser is meant to guarantee that not too many malicious users/Sybils exists because they are hard to create, in our formal terms this only corresponds to the guarantee that the number of daily uploads is bounded by the number of users. Hence, for real-word security we believe that we can exclude excessive Sybil attacks.

Note that this points at a larger aspect that is typical for security modeling in general, but also relevant to fully understand the scope of our modeling: Giving the environment a lot of power to shape the scenarios in which the protocols are used, is an instance of a strong worst-case modelling. By quantifying over all environments (and implicitly over all computable "real world" scenarios of contact graphs and infection statuses), without a proper analysis of the costs and impracticalities of achieving this in the real, physical world[9], we simplify the analysis and abstract from the many scenarios that may arise in its actual use. In the light of this, we give, in the following, an interpretation of our security guarantees and a discussion of guarantees and limitations not captured by our model, in the following:

6.1   Privacy

For our privacy analysis, we assume corrupted users can link some public identifiers they directly observe to the real identities of the corresponding user, e.g. by accidentally meeting someone they know. This pessimistic approach yields a worst-case analysis regarding the information available to corrupted users.

Privacy of Positively Tested Participants. In the ideal functionality ($\mathcal{F}_{\mathrm{CT}}$ in Sect. 5), the attacker is provided with $\mathcal{P}_{infected} \cap \mathcal{P}_{corrupted}$, so the infection status of honest parties is protected here. The pseudonymized contact graph is independent of the infection status. Apart from the inherent leakage about the infection status from warning queries, this models that the protocol does not introduce any additional information leaks on the infection status of honest participants. (For example, a motivated "paparazzi" attacker might take a "group testing" approach in that he tries to get near several subgroups of a larger group to later single out positively tested participants upon warning.) Note that is in contrast to DP3T, where short-term identifiers of a whole day can be linked together, upon uploading data in case of an infection.

Privacy of Warned Participants. Our protocol naturally protects the privacy of warned participants and their social graph as the published warning identifier

---

[9] While it would be perfectly possible for an environment to use as a contact graph a fresh, and independently sampled random graph on $\mathcal{P}$ for each short-term epoch, the costs of implementing this in real time for 15 min epochs would be quite challenging.

is computationally unlinkable to any information that can be recorded locally (i.e. pids), and also deciding whether some identifiers belong to the same user, is impossible. Thus, a wid does not help the attacker in breaking the users' privacy.

6.2   Privacy in the Case of Compromised Servers

This section presents an analysis of the privacy guarantees offered by our protocol if servers are compromised. See the full version for the formal guarantees in case of passively corrupted servers.

Linking Public Identifiers from the Long-Term Epoch. If the submission server is compromised, the attacker will be able to link different public identifiers pid to the same secret sid, and hence can link the public identifiers the user is using during the same long-term epoch. This poses a privacy threat, if the attacker additionally has observed some of the targeted public identifiers pid, which requires users colluding with the server.

Similarly, if both the matching server and the warning server are corrupted, the attacker can decrypt the sid values stored by the matching server to recover the wid value, and hence again link public identifiers to the secret identifiers sid and the respective warning identifier wid. Such an attacker that also colludes with corrupted users may be able to link public identifiers to times and places where these identifiers have been broadcast, and hence observe parts of the user's location history and track a user for up to one day. We stress that even if all servers are compromised, an attacker will not be able to link public identifiers used on different days (assuming the use of anonymous channels).

Contact Information of Infected Users. Information about encounters between users is stored strictly on the user's devices. Only the meeting history, i.e. the list of encountered public identifiers, without times and places of meetings, of infected users is transmitted to the central servers.

If the attacker has compromised the matching server *and* is able to link public identifiers used on the same long-term epoch (as in the previous scenario), the attacker might be able to infer repeated meetings of the infected user, i.e. she can learn how many encounters with the same persons the infected user's device has registered within each day. If the attacker has additionally observed some of the warned public identifiers at specific times and places, the attacker will also learn where and when the encounter took place, and hence learn parts of the location history of the infected user as well as the warned users.

Warnings Issued. If the attacker has compromised the matching server, she can immediately observe the public identifiers of all users who have been colocated with infected users. If the attacker can additionally link a public identifier to a specific individual, the attacker can conclude this person has received a warning. (Note that a similar attack is possible in the DP3T protocol [T+20], but even without compromising a server.)

6.3 Security

We now analyze an attacker's ability to cause false negatives or false positives. As above, we assume central servers to follow the protocol. See the full version for the formal guarantees in case of passively corrupted servers.

Creating False Negatives. A false negative occurs when an uncorrupted user A has been in colocation with an uncorrupted infected user B but A does not receive a warning. These false negatives are not possible in our protocol. In $\mathcal{F}_{\mathrm{CT}}$ this property is modeled by, $\hat{E}$ initially containing all edges between honest users, and during the protocol edges can only be added and never removed. (Note that we excluded jamming of the BLE signal by the adversary, as motivated in Sect. 2.)

Only in the case of a (passively) corrupted matching server can the adversary evade these guarantees regarding false negatives. This is because a corrupted matching server will learn the TANs at the time when honest users upload their list of observed identifiers. Exactly during (in parallel to) this step, an adversary may "use up" (and thereby invalidate) this TAN (after the matching server learned it), but before the honest user's request is finished. However, note that in this case, it is evident to the honest user that the TAN has been invalidated, pointing towards a passive corruption of the matching server (which is hence incentivised to not use this attack.)

False Positives Regarding Honest Users. An honest user A is subject of a false positive if she has not been colocated with an infected user, but she nonetheless receives a warning. Our security goal is to prevent false positives, unless i) A was in proximity to a corrupted user, *and* ii) the attacker is in proximity to an infected user, or has been infected themselves.

This is captured by the following fact: In order for an honest party A to be warned, the party has to be included in $\mathcal{WP}$. It can only be included in $\mathcal{WP}$, if there is an outgoing edge from A in $\hat{E}$ (warning triggered from an honest party) or there is an outgoing edge from A to a corrupted party in E (warning triggered from a corrupt party).

If A was not in proximity to a corrupted user, the attacker cannot use "Replay/Relay" to add new outgoing edges to $\hat{E}$ (as $(P_3', P_4') \notin E'$ in Step 3, because P_3' is corrupted and $\hat{P}_4 = A$ is not in proximity to a corrupted user) and hence cannot trigger a false warning from an honest party (unless the submission or the matching server is passively corrupted, as in this case the adversary learns otherwise unobserved pids to use for this). The attacker cannot trigger a warning for an honest that has not been in contact with a corrupt party, as Step 6 of "Handling Match Requests" requires all S_i to be empty in this case (unless the submission or the matching server is passively corrupted).

If the attacker has not been in proximity to an infected user and no corrupted party has been infected, the attacker can only insert edges into $\hat{E}$ using "Replay/Relay" where the target will never be infected. So a false warning cannot be triggered from an honest party. Regarding warnings triggered from a corrupt party, *lastInfected*$_{lt}$ will always be $-\infty$ in Step 6 of "Handling Match Requests" and parties can be added to $\mathcal{WP}$. This concludes our argument that producing a false positive for an honest user requires proximity of the attacker to both, the honest user and to an infected user (or the a corrupted user is infected).

7   Related Work

Canetti et al. [CTV20] mention an extension of their protocol using private set intersection protocols in order to protect the health status of infected individuals. However, it is unclear how feasible such a solution is with regard to the computational load incurred on both, the smartphone and the server, cf. [D20d, P3]. Whereas DP3T [T+20] claims that protecting the infection status of individuals in decentralized protocols is impossible by [D20a, IR 1] and therefore does not address further countermeasures.

Chan et al. [C+20, Sect. 4.1] include a short discussion of protocols in the upload-what-you-observed paradigm, and propose a form of rerandomization of identifiers at the side of the smartphone. In this protocol, a user downloads all published identifiers and checks whether they are a rerandomization of their own identifier (requiring one exponentiation). Hence, this approach puts a regular heavy computation cost on the user's device, and is likely not practical. Bell et al. [BBH+20] propose a solution for digital contact tracing based on homomorphic equality tests, aimed at protecting the infection status. However, there the central server learns the full contact graph for infected and non-infected users alike, as all users periodically upload their observations.

Besides BLE-based approaches, there are also proposals that use GPS traces of infected individuals to discover hot spots as well as colocation, such as [BBV+20, FMP+20]. However, there is a consensus that GPS-based approaches do not offer a sufficient spatial resolution to estimate the distance between two participants with sufficient precision.

The protocols of Garofalo et al [GhP+21], and DESIRE [CBB+20] (another hybrid approach, constituting concurrent work), broadcast public keys and compute Diffie-Hellman shared secret upon receiving a broadcast. Both are very similar to a proposal from Cho, Ippolito, and Yu [CIY20]. Both constructions compute two separate hashes of a shared secret, which constitutes an encounter, and use one for reporting contacts at risk and another one for querying their status. An advantage of registering an encounter by computing a shared secret from a Non-Interactive Key Exchange is the protection against certain kinds of replay attacks as observing a public key is not enough for impersonation. The main disadvantage, is that a public key does usually not fit into a single advertisement packet and therefore additional workarounds are necessary. Also, the security model of DESIRE is different from ours, e.g. if two corrupted users would like to know whether and when they met the same honest non-infected user, they could cooperate with the DESIRE server (which can link all encounter tokens of a user together, because a user has to upload all of them at once when querying for a warning) to link both encounters. Garofalo et al. introduce a Central Health Authority server, and a matching server that has some similarities to our server pipeline.

Instead of broadcasting large public keys, the protocol Pronto-C2 by [ABI+20] broadcasts addresses, where the public keys can be retrieved from. This requires the public keys to be anonymously uploaded in advance, which is similar to the submission routine in our protocol. Pronto-C2 separates the task for authenticating app requests from the central server and leaves the task for matching and risk-computation to the smartphone, which might incur a significant workload on the smartphone. On the other hand, our protocol utilizes a dedicated party for every privacy-sensitive task, i.e. submission, matching, warning and registering, and leaves only the task of risk-computation to the smartphone. The interested reader is referred to [V20b] for a general discussion on hybrid approaches.

The protocol Epione by [TSS+20], as well as the protocol Catalic by [DPT20] make use of private set intersection to improve on the privacy side.

Canetti et al. [CKL+20] introduce two protocols and also feature a universal composability (UC) modeling of contact tracing functionalities, which constitutes concurrent and independent work. While their modelling takes broad strokes by employing a global functionality for interacting with the physical world, via a set of allowable measurement functions and faking functions to the physical world, we specifically model the aspect of people being in relevant closeness to each other using a contact graph, and can hence model the leakage and e.g. relay attacks by certain operations on the graph – yielding a more easy-to-handle criterion. Moreover, only an extension of one of their protocols, called CertifiedCleverParrot, incorporates anti-Sybil protections, but this is not modeled and proven secure in their UC setting. For an alternative modelling and analysis of security notions using game-based definitions, such as forward security, see the concurrent work of Danz et al. [DDL+20].

8   Summary

Our protocol "ConTra Corona" provides a new and "hybrid" approach to digital contact tracing that protects both, the contact graph/encounter history, and the infection status. For this, it is important to fully understand, what security and privacy of contact tracing protocols mean, and to formalize this in a rigorous manner, with a simulation-based security notion in the real–ideal paradigm constituting a gold standard for such an endeavour in the cryptography landscape. Our notion makes the exact leakage and the attacker capabilities (in terms of inducing false positives/negatives) explicit. In the full version we present a proof that our protocol fulfills this security notion.

In order to reduce the required trust into the central server components, we described how the server's functions may be separated by distributing core functions to different organizations. In conclusion, we argue that our protocol represents an overall improvement regarding security and privacy and remains practical.

Acknowledgements. We would like to express our gratitude to Michael Klooß and Jeremias Mechler for helpful comments. This work was supported by funding from the topic Engineering Secure Systems of the Helmholtz Association (HGF) and by KASTEL Security Research Labs. We thank Serge Vaudenay for his comments.

References

[ABI+20] Avitabile, G., Botta, V., Iovino, V., Visconti, I.: Towards defeating mass surveillance and SARS-CoV-2: the Pronto-C2 fully decentralized automatic contact tracing system. Cryptology ePrint Archive, Report 2020/493 (2020)

[AG20] Apple and Google: Privacy-Preserving Contact Tracing (2020). http://www.apple.com/covid19/contacttracing

[AGH+19] Achenbach, D., et al.: Your money or your life—modeling and analyzing the security of electronic payment in the UC framework. In: Goldberg, I., Moore, T. (eds.) FC 2019. LNCS, vol. 11598, pp. 243–261. Springer, Cham (2019). https://doi.org/10.1007/978-3-030-32101-7_16

[AHL18] Altuwaiyan, T., Hadian, M., Liang, X.: EPIC: efficient privacy- preserving contact tracing for infection detection. In: ICC 2018, pp. 1–6 IEEE (2018). https://doi.org/10.1109/ICC.2018.8422886

[B92] Beaver, D.: How to break a "Secure" oblivious transfer protocol. In: Rueppel, R.A. (ed.) EUROCRYPT 1992. LNCS, vol. 658, pp. 285–296. Springer, Heidelberg (1993). https://doi.org/10.1007/3-540-47555-9_24

[BBH+20] Bell, J., Butler, D., Hicks, C., Crowcroft, J.: TraceSecure: towards privacy preserving contact tracing. In: ArXiv e-prints (2020). id: 2004.04059 [cs.CR]

[BBV+20] Berke, A., Bakker, M., Vepakomma, P., Raskar, R., Larson, K., Pentland, A.: Assessing disease exposure risk with location data: a proposal for cryptographic preservation of privacy. In: ArXiv e-prints (2020). id: 2003.14412 [cs.CR]

[BDH+20] Beskorovajnov, W., Dörre, F., Hartung, G., Koch, A., Müller-Quade, J., Strufe, T.: ConTra corona: contact tracing against the coronavirus by bridging the centralized decentralized divide for stronger privacy (2020). Cryptology ePrint Archive, Report 2020/505

[BL21] Bernstein, D.J., Lange, T. (eds.): eBACS: ECRYPT Benchmarking of Cryptographic Systems (2021). https://bench.cr.yp.to/results-sign.html

[BRS20] Brack, S., Reichert, L., Scheuermann, B.: CAUDHT: decentralized contact tracing using a DHT and blind signatures. In: Tan, H., Khoukhi, L., Oteafy, S. (eds.) 2020. https://doi.org/10.1109/LCN48667.2020.9314850

[C+20] Chan, J., et al.: PACT: privacy sensitive protocols and mechanisms for mobile contact tracing. ArXiv e-prints (2020). id: 2004.03544 [cs.CR]

[C01] Canetti, R.: Universally composable security: a new paradigm for cryptographic protocols. In: FOCS 2001, pp. 136–145. IEEE Computer Society (2001). https://doi.org/10.1109/SFCS.2001.959888

[CBB+20] Castelluccia, C., et al.: DESIRE: a third way for a european exposure notification system (2020). https://github.com/3rd-ways-for-EU-exposure-notification/project-DESIRE

[CHK+06] Camenisch, J., Hohenberger, S., Kohlweiss, M., Lysyanskaya, A., Meyerovich, M.: How to win the clone wars: efficient periodic n-times anonymous authentication. In: Juels, A., Wright, R.N., di Vimercati, S.D.C. (eds.) CCS 2006, pp. 201–210. ACM (2006). https://doi.org/10.1145/1180405.1180431

[CIY20] Cho, H., Ippolito, D., Yu, Y.W.: Contact tracing mobile apps for COVID-19: privacy considerations and related trade-offs. ArXiv e-prints (2020). id: 2003.11511 [cs.CR]

[CKL+20] Canetti, R., et al.: Privacy-preserving automated exposure notification. Cryptology ePrint Archive, Report 2020/863 (2020)

[CTV20] Canetti, R., Trachtenberg, A., Varia, M.: Anonymous collocation discovery: harnessing privacy to tame the coronavirus. ArXiv e-prints (2020). id: 2003.13670 [cs.CY]

[D20a] DP-3T Project: Privacy and Security Risk Evaluation of Digital Proximity Tracing Systems (2020). https://github.com/DP-3T/documents/blob/master/Security%20analysis/Privacy%20and%20Security%20Attacks%20on%20Digital%20Proximity%20Tracing%20Systems.pdf

[D20b] DP-3T Project: Security and privacy analysis of the document 'PEPP- PT: Data Protection and Information Security Architecture' (2020). https://github.com/DP-3T/documents/blob/master/Security%20analysis/PEPP-PT_%20Data%20Protection%20Architecture%20-%20Security%20and%20privacy%20analysis.pdf

[D20c] DP-3T Project: Security and privacy analysis of the document 'ROBERT: ROBust and privacy-presERving proximity Tracing' (2020). https://github.com/DP-3T/documents/blob/master/Security%20analysis/ROBERT%20-%20Security%20and%20privacy%20analysis.pdf

[D20d] DP3T Project: FAQ: Decentralized Proximity Tracing (2020). https://github.com/DP-3T/documents/blob/master/FAQ.md

[DDL+20] Danz, N., Derwisch, O., Lehmann, A., Pünter, W., Stolle, M., Ziemann, J.: Provable security and privacy of decentralized cryptographic contact tracing. Cryptology ePrint Archive, Report 2020/1309 (2020)

[DPT20] Duong, T., Phan, D.H., Trieu, N.: Catalic: delegated PSI cardinality with applications to contact tracing. In: Moriai, S., Wang, H. (eds.) ASI-ACRYPT 2020. LNCS, vol. 12493, pp. 870–899. Springer, Cham (2020). https://doi.org/10.1007/978-3-030-64840-4_29

[F20] Fraunhofer AISEC: Pandemic Contact Tracing Apps: DP-3T, PEPP-PT NTK, and ROBERT from a Privacy Perspective. Cryptology ePrint Archive, Report 2020/489 (2020)

[FM21] Feehan, D.M., Mahmud, A.S.: Quantifying population contact patterns in the United States during the COVID-19 pandemic. Nat. Commun. **12**(1), 1–9 (2021). https://doi.org/10.1038/s41467-021-20990-2

[FMP+20] Fitzsimons, J.K., Mantri, A., Pisarczyk, R., Rainforth, T., Zhao, Z.: A note on blind contact tracing at scale with applications to the COVID-19 pandemic. In: Volkamer, M., Wressnegger, C. (eds.) ARES 2020, pp. 92:1–92:6. ACM (2020). https://doi.org/10.1145/3407023.3409204

[GhP+21] Garofalo, G., Hamme, T.V., Preuveneers, D., Joosen, W., Abidin, A., Mustafa, M.A.: PIVOT: PrIVate and effective cOntact Tracing. Cryptology ePrint Archive, Report 2020/559 (2021)

[KBS21] Kuhn, C., Beck, M., Strufe, T.: Covid notions: towards formal definitions - and documented understanding - of privacy goals and claimed protection in proximity-tracing services. In: Online Social Networks Media, vol. 22 (2021). https://doi.org/10.1016/j.osnem.2021.100125

[L17] Lindell, Y.: How to simulate it – a tutorial on the simulation proof technique. In: Tutorials on the Foundations of Cryptography. ISC, pp. 277–346. Springer, Cham (2017). https://doi.org/10.1007/978-3-319-57048-8_6

[MR91] Micali, S., Rogaway, P.: Secure computation. In: Feigenbaum, J. (ed.) CRYPTO 1991. LNCS, vol. 576, pp. 392–404. Springer, Heidelberg (1992). https://doi.org/10.1007/3-540-46766-1_32

[P20a] PePP-PT e.V.: Pan-European Privacy-Preserving Proximity Tracing (2020). https://www.pepp-pt.org/content

[P20b] PePP-PT e.V.: PEPP-PT NTK High-Level Overview (2020). https://github.com/pepp-pt/pepp-pt-documentation/blob/master/PEPP-PT-high-level-overview.pdf

[P20c] PePP-PT e.V.: ROBust and privacy-presERving proximity Tracing protocol (2020). https://github.com/ROBERT-proximity-tracing/documents

[R+] Rivest, R.L., et al.: A Global Coalition for Privacy-First Digital Contact Tracing Protocols to Fight COVID-19. https://tcn-coalition.org/

[R+20] Rivest, R.L., et al.: The PACT protocol specification (2020). https://pact.mit.edu/wp-content/uploads/2020/04/The-PACT-protocol-specification-ver-0.1.pdf

[T+20] Troncoso, C., et al.: Decentralized privacy-preserving proximity tracing. IEEE Data Eng. Bull. **43**(2), 36–66 (2020). First published 3 April 2020 on https://github.com/DP-3T/documents. http://sites.computer.org/debull/A20june/p36.pdf

[TOR] The Tor Project, Inc.: TOR Project. https://www.torproject.org/

[TSS+20] Trieu, N., Shehata, K., Saxena, P., Shokri, R., Song, D.: Epione: lightweight contact tracing with strong privacy. IEEE Data Eng. Bull. **43**(2), 95–107 (2020). http://sites.computer.org/debull/A20june/p95.pdf

[V20a] Vaudenay, S.: Analysis of DP3T. Cryptology ePrint Archive, Report 2020/399 (2020)

[V20b] Vaudenay, S.: Centralized or Decentralized? The Contact Tracing Dilemma. Cryptology ePrint Archive, Report 2020/531 (2020)

Cryptographic Analysis of the Bluetooth Secure Connection Protocol Suite

Marc Fischlin[(✉)] and Olga Sanina[(✉)]

Cryptoplexity, Technische Universität Darmstadt, Darmstadt, Germany
{marc.fischlin,olga.sanina}@tu-darmstadt.de
https://www.cryptoplexity.de

Abstract. We give a cryptographic analysis of the Bluetooth Secure Connections Protocol Suite. Bluetooth supports several subprotocols, such as Numeric Comparison, Passkey Entry, and Just Works, in order to match the devices' different input/output capabilities. Previous analyses (e.g., Lindell, CT-RSA'09, or Troncoso and Hale, NDSS'21) often considered (and confirmed) the security of single subprotocols only. Recent practically verified attacks, however, such as the Method Confusion Attack (von Tschirschnitz et al., S&P 21), against Bluetooth's authentication and key secrecy property often exploit the bad interplay of different subprotocols. Even worse, some of these attacks demonstrate that one cannot prove the Bluetooth protocol suite to be a secure authenticated key exchange protocol. We therefore aim at the best we can hope for and show that the protocol still matches the common key secrecy requirements of a key-exchange protocol if one assumes a trust-on-first-use (TOFU) relationship. This means that the adversary needs to mount an active attack during the initial connection, otherwise the subsequent reconnections remain secure. Investigating the cryptographic strength of the Bluetooth protocol, we also look into the privacy mechanism of address randomization in Bluetooth (which is only available in the Low Energy version). We show that the cryptography indeed provides a decent level of address privacy, although this does not rule out identification of devices via other means, such as physical characteristics.

1 Introduction

Bluetooth has become an omnipresent standard for short-range wireless communication. It is used in billions of products today, from powerful devices like computers and smartphones to more limited devices like headsets. The standard is maintained by the Bluetooth Special Interest Group and its latest specification of more than 3,000 pages describes version 5.2 [9].

The Bluetooth protocol comes in two major versions, the classical version (BR/EDR, for basic rate/enhanced data rate) and the low-energy version (BLE).[1] The BR/EDR variant is usually used for connections with continuous

---

[1] Strictly speaking, there is another mode, the AMP (Alternative MAC/PHY) alias HS (high speed) mode, which is also associated to the classical version. We follow the common terminology to call the classical Bluetooth protocol BR/EDR instead of BR/EDR/AMP.

© International Association for Cryptologic Research 2021
M. Tibouchi and H. Wang (Eds.): ASIACRYPT 2021, LNCS 13091, pp. 696–725, 2021.
https://doi.org/10.1007/978-3-030-92075-3_24

data streams like headphones. In contrast, BLE is typically used when power consumption is a concern and data is only transferred periodically, e.g., for fitness trackers. The modes are not compatible but dual-mode devices are able to use both technologies.

1.1 Connecting Securely with Bluetooth

To transfer data between two Bluetooth devices securely and bidirectionally, they need to initially establish the link on a physical and logical level. If this has happened, then both devices establish a cryptographic key, called the link key in BR/EDR resp. long-term key in BLE. This key is used to derive a channel key for communication following the link establishment and to authenticate devices and derive a new channel key in later reconnections. In the latest version 5.2 of the standard [9], the strongest method to establish such a key is the Secure Connections (for BR/EDR) resp. LE Secure Connections (for BLE). Previous versions of (more or less secure) connection methods are nowadays called legacy protocols.

We note that the main part of the Secure Connections protocol, so-called Secure Simple Pairing (SSP), has been added to BR/EDR already with version 2.1. With version 4.1, the SSP protocol has been upgraded to the Secure Connections protocol, using FIPS-approved cryptographic algorithms. BLE has been introduced in version 4.0, and has not inherited the protocol (and security) from classical Bluetooth. Only since version 4.2 BLE supports the Secure Connections pairing. The main difference between the Secure Connections methods in BR/EDR and BLE in terms of cryptographic operations is that Secure Connections for BR/EDR uses HMAC for message authentication and key derivation in the key exchange part, whereas the LE version uses AES-CMAC. In the following high-level discussion we thus lump both protocols together under the term Secure Connections.

The Secure Connections protocol itself is a protocol family, all members sharing an elliptic curve Diffie-Hellman key exchange with key confirmation. Only the authentication stages differ, depending on the input/output capabilities of the connecting devices. For example, some devices may be able to display numbers, some only allow for a yes/no confirmation, and some may not support any interaction. Hence, there are four connection modes, also called association models:

Numeric Comparison: The devices display a short 6-digit number which the user should compare and confirm by pressing a button.

Passkey Entry: The user enters a 6-digit passkey on both devices (or, one device displays the passkey and the user enters the value into the other device).

Out-of-Band: Some device data is exchanged via an alternative channel, e.g., via a separate NFC connection between the two devices before the protocol execution.

Just Works: The devices connect without any further form of user involvement.

The first three modes (NumCom, PasskeyEntry, and OOB) are referred to as authenticated, whereas the JustWorks mode is called unauthenticated in the Bluetooth standard [9].

1.2   A Short History of Attacks

The Bluetooth protocol family has been repeatedly shown to be vulnerable to attacks. We only discuss here the most recent attacks, especially on the latest standards, which are also most relevant for our result. One goal of the adversary is to fool the authentication property of Bluetooth, ideally also allowing to learn the session key between the devices.

As pointed out by Zhang et al. [27], for example, the PasskeyEntry method is susceptible to man-in-the-middle attacks. It is based on the different input/output capabilities of devices. In the attack, the user aims to connect a KeyboardOnly device (in this case, a keyboard) to a DisplayOnly device (in this case, a screen), allowing the attacker to connect its own keyboard to the user's screen, without being detected. This means that PasskeyEntry does not allow to authenticate devices reliably.

With the Bluetooth Impersonation AttacksS (BIAS) Antonioli et al. [1] have demonstrated that an adversary can enforce a reconnection for classic Bluetooth to any of two parties sharing a link key, without the adversary actually knowing the key. The attack exploits that legacy authentication of BR/EDR does not enforce mutual authentication of partners and that the request to switch master and slave role is not protected under the shared key. If this is case, then the adversary can connect to any of the two parties by asking one to switch roles and relaying the authentication information. For Secure Connections, the attack works if the devices support downgrades to legacy security because the request is not authenticated.

Another problem with the PasskeyEntry protocol has been pointed out by Troncoso and Hale [23]. They discuss that the initiator- or responder-generated passkey protocol allows a man-in-the-middle attacker to make two devices connect with the help of the user, but such that the two devices are cryptographically not partnered. For the user-generated PasskeyEntry case they discuss a "role confusion" attack wherein both parties accept and believe to be the initiator of the connection.

The recent paper of von Tschirschnitz et al. [24] introduced the Method Confusion Attack, which allows the adversary to place itself in the middle between two devices. The adversary establishes two connections with the devices by running the PasskeyEntry mode in one session and the NumCom mode in the other one. Since it can ask the user in the first connection (PasskeyEntry mode) to enter exactly the value used in the second connection (NumCom mode), the user(s) will confirm both connections. Eventually, the devices are thus considered to be connected, although they are each paired with the adversary. The attack is based on the fact that the passkeys both in NumCom and PasskeyEntry use the same length and alphabet, making it impossible for the user to distinguish the two modes.

Another active attack on the initial connection has been presented by Claverie and Lopes-Esteve [12], called BlueMirror. In this attack, the adversary mounts a man-in-the-middle attack on the passkey subprotocol, reflecting the data in the execution with the initiator, and eventually making the responder believe to communicate with the original initiator. Still, the adversary holds the key in the execution with the responder.

The bad interplay of Bluetooth Classic and Bluetooth Low energy has been exploited in the so-called BLUR attack [3]. If the devices establish a key in the classic or in the low-energy mode, then they can convert it to another key for the complementary mode (cross-transport key derivation), enabling a potential switch to the other architecture later. In [3], however, it has been demonstrated that an adversary can use this feature to overwrite the securely established key by an unauthenticated just-works key via the other connection mode.

The lack of authentication of the negotiation data enabled the "Key Negotiation of Bluetooth" (KNOB) attack [2,4] where the man-in-the-middle adversary modifies the requested key length. It sets the entry to 1 byte (for session keys in BR/EDR) resp. 7 bytes for long-term keys in BLE, making the devices use weak keys that can be recovered by exhaustive search. This attack, as most of the previously mentioned ones, has also been demonstrated in practical scenarios.

Another downgrade attack is the Bluetooth LE Spoofing Attack (BLESA), described in [26]. The attack comes in two versions and has also been shown feasible in practice. One attack version of BLESA is on reactive authentication and lets the adversary make the partner device switch to an encryption-free transfer in reconnections. The other version is against proactive authentication, exploiting that some implementations do not correctly close connections when being asked to downgrade the encryption level in reconnections. The former is a shortcoming in the design of the protocol, the latter in the implementations.

We conclude this section by noting that, so far, the OOB mode has not displayed major vulnerabilities. But this may have to do with the fact that any such attack, likewise any positive security result, would need to make additional assumptions about the extra communication channel. Furthermore, this mode seems to be also much less prominent than the other modes, as it requires additional communication means like NFC or optical components to scan QR codes.

1.3   A Short History of Analyses

Despite the attacks above, the literature also reveals a number of affirmative security results. The mismatch to the above attacks often relies on the fact that the attacks exploit vulnerabilities between different pairing modes (e.g., associating PASSKEYENTRY and NUMCOM in the Method Confusion Attack [24]), or between the classic and low energy cross-modes (like the BLUR attack [3]), or forcing the devices to switch to weak legacy modes (like the BIAS attack [1]). In contrast, most cryptographic analysis focus on a single mode only.

In [19] Lindell studies Bluetooth's Numeric Comparison protocol as a key-exchange protocol (in Bluetooth specification v2.1 but the cryptographic differences to the current version are minor). He shows that the NUMCOM protocol—as a standalone protocol—is a secure (comparison-based) key exchange protocol under the DDH assumption and further modest assumptions about the underlying primitives. Noteworthy, the model somehow assumes that user confirmation of the comparison value also authenticates the Bluetooth addresses, although these data are transmitted unprotected over the network and are not displayed to the user.

Sun and Sun [21] extended the result of Lindell to BR/EDR in version v5.0, for NUMCOM and OOB as standalone protocols. They reach the same conclusions in terms of security as [19] for these protocols. Yet, their security model is more restrictive (e.g., the adversary is not allowed to communicate with parties after the test query).

We have already mentioned the analysis of Troncoso and Hale [23] in the attack section above. Noting the insecurities in the PASSKEYENTRY sub protocol, they give a security proof for two modified versions of PASSKEYENTRY, also as a standalone protocol. The first modification, secure hash modification, includes more data in the hash computation. The other modification, the dual passkey entry, presumes that both devices allow entering and displaying a passkey. Both versions are shown to be secure under the DDH assumption, reasonable assumptions about the other cryptographic primitives, and a single-query version of the PRF-ODH assumption [17].

1.4   Bluetooth as a TOFU Key Exchange Protocol

The starting point of our approach originates from the observation that known attacks show Bluetooth, as a full protocol suite, does not provide authentication of keys. There is no chance to show security in the common sense of authenticated key exchange. This either leaves us with analyzing a modified protocol (as in [23])—and strictly speaking thus not giving any security guarantees for Bluetooth— or to switch to the best security claim "we can hope for". We decided for the latter.

We analyze Bluetooth as a *trust-on-first-use* (TOFU) authenticated key exchange protocol according to a BR-like security model. This means we assume that the adversary is passive in the initial connection and can only mount active attacks on devices that have been bonded before. Of course, the adversary may on top bond arbitrarily with all the devices, but such interactions are, by definition, not protected since no trust-relationship has been established. Besides capturing all possible pairing methods simultaneously, we note that this also extends previous analyses by the reconnection step.

While the guarantees as a TOFU protocol appear to be quite weak, superficially viewed, it gives quite assuring guarantee for "minimalistic" modes of operations. That is, suppose that one significantly reduces attack vectors by turning off the compatibility features: specifically, no legacy protocols but only Secure Connections, sufficient key lengths, no cross-transport key derivation between

BR/EDR and BLE. Then the TOFU result says that successful attacks against session keys can only be mounted if the adversary is present when the devices are initially connecting.

Our analyses assumes to be "close to the standard". For instance, the security analyses in [19,21,23] assume that the parties use a fresh Diffie-Hellman share in each execution. The Bluetooth v5.2 standard, however, allows the Diffie-Hellman key to be re-used in several executions [9, Vol 2, Part H, Sect. 5.1]:

> "...a device should change its private key after every pairing (successful or failed). Otherwise, it should change its private key whenever S + 3F > 8, where S is the number of successful pairings and F the number of failed attempts since the key was last changed."

Note that this explicitly refers to the Elliptic Curve Diffie-Hellman (ECDH) public-private key pair generated in the first step of the SSP protocol [9, Vol 2, Part H, Sect. 7.1]. In particular, in [19] Lindell identifies partnered sessions via the public Diffie-Hellman shares of the partners. Since two devices may reuse their shares multiple times but choose different nonces in these initial connections (and thus derive different keys), strictly speaking, Lindell's result cannot even guarantee basic correctness properties for the real Bluetooth protocol.

Another deviation from the standard is that the analyses in [19,21] assume the entire Diffie-Hellman curve point enters the protocol computations, whereas the standard only uses the x-coordinate of the elliptic curve point. Being aware of the possibility to enable attacks by this mapping, such as the fixed coordinate invalid curve attack [7], Troncoso and Hale [23] correctly use the x-coordinate in some of the protocol steps.

1.5   Privacy

Bluetooth Low Energy supports a privacy mechanism that should help to disguise the device's Bluetooth address BD_ADDR during discovery. Essentially, instead of sending the physical MAC address, BLE permits to send a randomized address, either randomly generated only once during fabrication or each time when powering up the device, or refreshed in short time intervals. The latter type are called non-resolvable private random addresses. The protocol also has an advanced feature called resolvable private random addresses where a previously bonded device can recognize the pseudorandom address and link it to a physical address.

In contrast, classic Bluetooth does not support address randomization or any other other privacy mechanism. According to [14], it was believed that tracking devices is hard, due to the larger number of communication channels and highly frequent channel hopping. This belief has recently been shown to be false in [14]. The authors demonstrate that one can track devices even over large distances. Since the (de-)anonymization of BR/EDR devices escapes a cryptographic treatment, we focus here on the privacy mechanisms in BLE.

We are interested in the address randomization technique and privacy on a protocol (i.e. transcript) level. Sun et al. [22] provide an analysis of the BLE protocol, pointing out correctly that re-using the Diffie-Hellman key share in Secure Connections allows linking executions of different devices. They also provide a cryptographic analysis of privacy guarantees on the protocol layer, under the assumption that a fresh Diffie-Hellman value is used in each session. This analysis, however, neglects that other connection data (such as transmitting the Bluetooth address) may also allow the adversary to link executions of the same party. In particular, they do not consider BLE's address resolution technique but focus on pairing stage only.

Of course, besides inspecting the payload, an attacker may be able to distinguish devices according to physical characteristics. This question recently gained attention in light of contact tracing via Bluetooth. For instance, Ludant et al. [20] showed that dual-mode devices supporting classic Bluetooth (sending the plain address BD_ADDR) and BLE (potentially using randomized addresses) can be cross-linked by their channel characteristics for each of the two services with high accuracy. This implies that the privacy mechanism of BLE effectively becomes void because of the lack of privacy for classic Bluetooth. Countermeasures may be to temporarily turn off either of the two unused protocols or to reduce the transmission power in order to limit the attack radius.

Jouans et al. [18] demonstrated that the address randomization technique itself can actually be used against privacy: the frequency with which devices change their addresses can be used to differentiate them. Celosia and Cunche [10] discuss that between 0.06% and 1.7% of devices using address randomization nonetheless transmit linkable cleartext names of devices. Another often encountered entry in the advertisement data is the Universally Unique Identifier (UUID) field to identify services and characteristics of the device. These 16, 32 or 128-bit values are usually available in the generic attribute profile (GATT) of the device and can be transmitted as part of the advertisement. Following similar attacks on Wi-Fi [25] and BLE [5], it has been pointed out in [11] that the UUIDs can be used to fingerprint devices and overcome privacy techniques with address randomization.

Our analysis does not aim to protect against attacks based on the physical characteristics, but only to ensure that the cryptographic and privacy mechanisms do not support privacy breaches. The other distinctive characteristics must be taken care of by different means, e.g., using identical address randomization intervals on each device, or switching off clear name advertisements. We show that if the Diffie-Hellman values are chosen afresh in each execution, then the cryptographic technique of address randomization indeed provides the decent level of privacy.

2   Bluetooth

We start by giving an overview over the Bluetooth protocol along the standard [9]. The Bluetooth protocol comes in several versions with minor differences.

The most common protocols are Bluetooth *Basic Rate/Enhances Data Rate* (BR/EDR), also called Bluetooth classic, and *Low Energy* (BLE). From a high-level cryptographic view point, the only differences are that in the pairing step BR/EDR uses HMAC-SHA256 to compute the link key whereas BLE uses AES-CMAC for this computation. In the reconnection step, however, the two protocols diverge in the way they derive the session keys. Finally, BLE supports a privacy mechanism to hide the devices' addresses. We discuss the latter in Sect. 5.

We note that both protocols, BR/EDR and BLE, gradually converge to one protocol, while previous versions ("legacy versions") had major differences. For instance, earlier versions of BLE did not use elliptic curve DH mechanisms. Both subprotocols are incompatible from a technological viewpoint, e.g., they use a different number of communication channels. Dual-mode devices, which support both technologies simultaneously, are becoming more and more ubiquitous.

2.1 High-Level Protocol Flow

The flow of two devices connecting in both versions, BR/EDR and BLE, is identical from an abstract viewpoint but differs in the technological aspects. We give a description of the relevant protocol parts in Fig. 1. Initially both devices need to connect physically and logically. This is done in an inquiry or discovery phase and involves the devices exchange their Bluetooth addresses. The address itself is a 48-bit value. To distinguish cleartext addresses from randomized ones in BLE, the devices uses the `TxAdd` and `RxAdd` (transmission/reception) flags which we discuss in more detail when investigating the privacy feature.

Then the devices connect on the link layer and can start exchanging device-specific information, especially the input/output capabilities. Here BR/EDR and BLE use different commands for this, but we neglect these details here. In this step, the devices also exchange information about the strength of the connection (e.g., the *SC* flag in the feature vector in BLE to request Secure Connections, see Sect. 5.1). We assume that both devices only allow the strongest version called Secure Connections.

Based on the available IO capabilities, the devices decide on the subprotocol for Secure Simple Pairing (SSP) protocol, also called the association model. These IO capabilities determine how the device is able to interact with users. It can be either of the following five options: `DisplayOnly` (no input capability, numeric output), `DisplayYesNo` (yes/no input and numeric output), `KeyboardOnly` (keyboard input, no output), `NoInputNoOutput` (neither output nor input capabilities, or yes/no input and no output). The BLE protocol also supports `KeyboardDisplay` (keyboard input, numeric output). We note that one sometimes considers the exchange of the IO capabilities to be part of the SSP protocol, but this distinction is irrelevant for us here. The combination of the capabilities of the two devices determines the SSP subprotocol according to Table 1 (for Secure Connections only).

We note that either device may set the out-of-band (*OOB*) flag as part of the features. In BR/EDR this is part of the *IOcap* structure, whereas in BLE

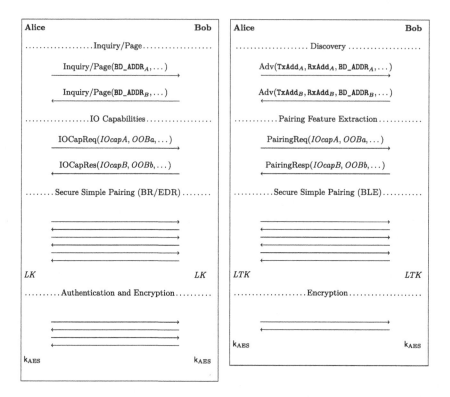

Fig. 1. Bluetooth protocol flow (left: BR/EDR, right: BLE)

this is a flag in the pairing features. If either devices sets the *OOB* flag, then the parties use the OOB association model. We note that only one of the two devices may set this flag, in which case only this device transmit out-of-band information. The data in the OOB association model contains the Bluetooth address of a device, commitments of the public keys, and random values that are used in further execution.

Next, the two devices execute the SSP protocol in the corresponding association model to establish a shared key. The steps are very similar and only differ in some cryptographic operations. We discuss the details in Sect. 2.2. For BR/EDR the derived key is called a link key *LK*, for BLE it is called a long-term key *LTK*. We note that both versions allow to convert the key for future use in the other type of connection (cross-transport key derivation), but we do not consider this conversion here. This concludes the initial connection procedure.

The final step is to derive the key for the authenticated encryption scheme. We note that this is also the protocol that is executed if the devices have bonded and created a shared key (i.e. during reconnection), and in this case they skip the SSP step. Here the two protocols differ, as BR/EDR involves an additional authentication step. We discuss this part in more detail in Sect. 2.3.

Table 1. Mapping of IO capabilities to association models. The last column and row KeyboardDisplay is only available in BLE.

Responder	Initiator				
	DisplayOnly	DisplayYesNo	KeyboardOnly	NoInputNoOutput	KeyboardDisplay
DisplayOnly	JUSTWORKS	JUSTWORKS	PASSKEYENTRY	JUSTWORKS	PASSKEYENTRY
DisplayYesNo	JUSTWORKS	NUMCOM	PASSKEYENTRY	JUSTWORKS	NUMCOM
KeyboardOnly	PASSKEYENTRY	PASSKEYENTRY	PASSKEYENTRY	JUSTWORKS	PASSKEYENTRY
NoInputNoOutput	JUSTWORKS	JUSTWORKS	JUSTWORKS	JUSTWORKS	JUSTWORKS
KeyboardDisplay	PASSKEYENTRY	NUMCOM	PASSKEYENTRY	JUSTWORKS	NUMCOM

2.2   Secure Simple Pairing

We next describe Secure Simple Pairing and its four variants: JUSTWORKS, OOB, NUMCOM, and PASSKEYENTRY. At this point the parties have already exchanged their 48-bit addresses A and B, their *IOcap* values (leading to the agreement on the variant), and the elliptic curve to be used. In BR/EDR, if both devices agree on the Secure Connections mode, then the devices use the P-256 elliptic curve, else the P-192 curve. Both curves are FIPS-approved and defined in the Bluetooth standard. In BLE, only P-256 elliptic curve is used (in Secure Connections mode). For the elliptic curve operations we use the "simple" multiplicative presentation. That is, we write g^a for the a-fold application of the group operation to the generator g specified in the standard, without giving any further reference to the group. When processing elliptic curve points in HMAC or CMAC in Authentication stage 1 of the SSP protocol, the standard uses the x-coordinate, i.e., we write $[g^a]_x$ for the x-coordinate of g^a. This x-coordinate is a 256-bit value for Secure Connections.

To capture both versions of the SSP protocol for BR/EDR and BLE simultaneously, we use abstract cryptographic procedures for computing the commitment value (Com), hashing (Hash), MAC key computation (MACKey), MAC computation (MAC), and link key/long-term key computation (KDF). Roughly, for BR/EDR these algorithms are initialized by HMAC-SHA256 (except for Hash, which uses SHA256 directly), and for BLE one uses AES-CMAC. The different implementations of the primitives for BR/EDR and BLE are displayed in Table 2. For the MAC key computation we note that in BR/EDR the Diffie-Hellman value, here denoted W, can be used directly as a key in the HMAC computation MAC, since HMAC is able to process large keys. For AES-CMAC in BLE, however, the MAC key is computed via CMAC(Salt, W) for a constant Salt and then used as a 128-bit key in the AES-CMAC computation of MAC.

Figure 2 shows the Numeric Comparison protocol with the abstract operations. The NUMCOM protocol starts with the devices exchanging the Diffie-Hellman values, followed by Authentication stage 1 wherein the parties exchange random nonces and involve the user to confirm a 6-digit number Va resp. Vb. For this the device truncates the hash value over the (x-coordinates of the) public key parts and the nonces to 32 bits and then converts this to a decimal number. The last 6 digits correspond to the check values. It is followed by Authentication

Table 2. Cryptographic operations of BR/EDR and BLE in SSP. Note that $T =$ CMAC(Salt, W) for a fixed constant Salt in the standard; $\text{kID}_{\text{BR/EDR}} = 0x62746C6B$ is a 4-octet representing the ASCII string 'btlk'; $\text{kID}_{\text{BLE}} = 0x62746C65$ is a 4-octet representing the ASCII string 'btle'; for an address A in BLE the address A' is A extended by another octet $0x01$ for a random address and $0x00$ for a public address; the notation $/2^{128}$ for BR/EDR means that one takes the leftmost 128 bits of the SHA256 output.

Function	BR/EDR	BLE
Com(U, V, X, Y)	HMAC($X, U\|V\|Y)/2^{128}$	CMAC($X, U\|V\|Y$)
Hash(U, V, X, Y)	SHA($U\|V\|X\|Y$)	CMAC($X, U\|V\|Y$)
MACKey($W, N1, N2, A1, A2$)	W	CMAC($T, 0x00\|\text{kID}_{\text{BLE}}\|N1\|N2\|A1\|A2\|0x0100$)
MAC($W, N1, N2, R, I, A1, A2$)	HMAC($W, N1\|N2\|R\|I\|A1\|A2)/2^{128}$	CMAC($W, N1\|N2\|I\|A1'\|A2'$)
KDF($W, N1, N2, A1, A2$)	HMAC($W, N1\|N2\|\text{kID}_{\text{BR/EDR}}\|A1\|A2)/2^{128}$	CMAC($T, 0x01\|\text{kID}_{\text{BLE}}\|N1\|N2\|A1\|A2\|0x0100$)

stage 2 in which the parties confirm the shared Diffie-Hellman key. Finally, both parties compute the link key (in BR/EDR) resp. the long-term key (in BLE).

We give more details on the other association models in the full version. These protocols only differ in the Authentication stage 1 of the SSP framework which turns out to be irrelevant for our TOFU security analysis. We merely remark that all association models, among others, exchange random nonces Na and Nb. We note that, technically, BLE computes the MAC key and long-term key in one step. We have moved the computation of the long-term key to the end of the protocol in order to comply with the BR/EDR step for computing the link key there.

2.3 Deriving the Encryption Key

The encryption key is derived differently in classic Bluetooth and in the Low Energy version. In the classic setting it corresponds to a mutual challenge-response authentication protocol for the link key, which also enters the derivation of the session key (usually called AES encryption key in the Bluetooth context, although it serves as input to the AES-CCM authenticated encryption scheme). That is, the parties exchange the 128-bit random values (AU_RAND) for authentication, and each party computes the so-called 32-bit signed response (SRES) for authentication. In BLE instead one simply derives the session key from (concatenated) 64-bit nonces, called session key diversifier (SKD), without further authentication.

BLE also uses AES-CCM for authenticated encryption of data. Both procedures also produce some initial nonce offset of 64 bits for the encryption process, denoted as ACO in BR/EDR and IV in BLE. In the latter case, the IV is given by the concatenation of the two random 32-bit values IVm, IVs, chosen by either party. From a security viewpoint, while ACO is not transmitted in clear, the IV in BLE is known by the adversary.

The steps for BR/EDR are described in Table 3 and Fig. 3, and for BLE in Fig. 4. We use the common notation of *master* and *slave* since the devices may change roles for reconnections. We note that in BLE the key derivation step and the data ($SKDm, IVm$ resp. $SKDs, IVs$) are transmitted as part of an encryption

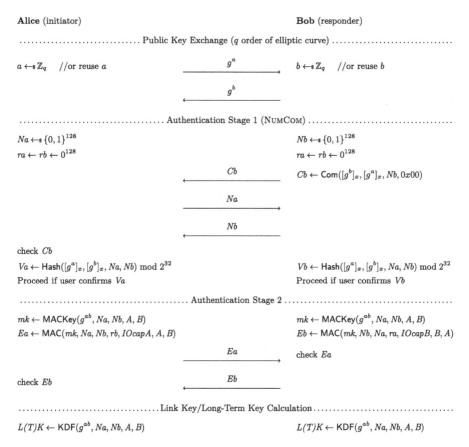

Alice (initiator)   Bob (responder)

.... Public Key Exchange (q order of elliptic curve) ....

$a \leftarrow_\$ \mathbb{Z}_q$ //or reuse a g^a $b \leftarrow_\$ \mathbb{Z}_q$ //or reuse b

                                                    g^b

.... Authentication Stage 1 (NUMCOM) ....

$Na \leftarrow_\$ \{0,1\}^{128}$ $Nb \leftarrow_\$ \{0,1\}^{128}$
$ra \leftarrow rb \leftarrow 0^{128}$ $ra \leftarrow rb \leftarrow 0^{128}$

                                                    Cb $Cb \leftarrow \mathsf{Com}([g^b]_x, [g^a]_x, Nb, 0x00)$

                                                    Na

                                                    Nb

check Cb
$Va \leftarrow \mathsf{Hash}([g^a]_x, [g^b]_x, Na, Nb) \bmod 2^{32}$ $Vb \leftarrow \mathsf{Hash}([g^a]_x, [g^b]_x, Na, Nb) \bmod 2^{32}$
Proceed if user confirms Va Proceed if user confirms Vb

.... Authentication Stage 2 ....

$mk \leftarrow \mathsf{MACKey}(g^{ab}, Na, Nb, A, B)$ $mk \leftarrow \mathsf{MACKey}(g^{ab}, Na, Nb, A, B)$
$Ea \leftarrow \mathsf{MAC}(mk, Na, Nb, rb, IOcapA, A, B)$ $Eb \leftarrow \mathsf{MAC}(mk, Nb, Na, ra, IOcapB, B, A)$

                                                    Ea check Ea

check Eb Eb

.... Link Key/Long-Term Key Calculation ....

$L(T)K \leftarrow \mathsf{KDF}(g^{ab}, Na, Nb, A, B)$ $L(T)K \leftarrow \mathsf{KDF}(g^{ab}, Na, Nb, A, B)$

Fig. 2. Bluetooth Secure Simple Pairing in mode Numeric Comparison. The session identifier, here and in all other association models, is given by sid = (g^a, g^b, A, B, Na, Nb).

request and response message. In BR/EDR the sequence must be preceded by an encryption_mode request and response. Noteworthy, in contrast to BLE, where the key length is negotiated as part of the pairing feature extraction, the BR/EDR protocol may negotiate the key length only here as well. We assume in the following that only the maximal key size is enforced by the devices, in order to prevent attacks like the KNOB attack [2, 4].

3   Security Model

In this section we define our security model for TOFU key exchange protocols. Given the history of successful attacks against Bluetooth, especially against authentication, we aim at very basic security of key secrecy. Since Bluetooth does not achieve forward secrecy—if the link key resp. long-term key is available then

Table 3. Secure authentication and computation of encryption key in BR/EDR secure connections. HMAC is HMAC with SHA256; $\text{kID}_{\text{Dev}} = 0x6274646B$ is a 4-octet representing the ASCII string 'btdk' (Bluetooth Device Key); $\text{kID}_{\text{AES}} = 0x6274616B$ is a 4-octet representing the ASCII string 'btak' (Bluetooth AES Key); $SRESm$, $SRESs$ are 32 bits each, and ACO (Authentication Ciphering Offset) is 64 bits; the notation $/2^{128}$ means that one takes the leftmost 128 bits of the SHA256 output.

Value	Function
Device key	$\text{dk} \leftarrow \text{HMAC}(LK, \text{kID}_{\text{Dev}}|\text{BD\_ADDR}_A|\text{BD\_ADDR}_B)/2^{128}$
Confirmation	$SRESm|SRESs|\text{ACO} \leftarrow \text{HMAC}(\text{dk}, AU\_RANDm|AU\_RANDs)/2^{128}$
AES key	$\text{k}_{\text{AES}} \leftarrow \text{HMAC}(LK, \text{kID}_{\text{AES}}|\text{BD\_ADDR}_A|\text{BD\_ADDR}_B|\text{ACO})/2^{128}$

Master   Slave

··Authentication···

dk ←   dk ←
HMAC($LK,'btdk'|\text{BD\_ADDR}_A|\text{BD\_ADDR}_B)/2^{128}$ HMAC($LK,'btdk'|\text{BD\_ADDR}_A|\text{BD\_ADDR}_B)/2^{128}$

$AU\_RANDm \leftarrow_\$ \{0,1\}^{128}$ $\xrightarrow{\quad AU\_RANDm \quad}$ $AU\_RANDs \leftarrow_\$ \{0,1\}^{128}$

                                           $\xleftarrow{\quad AU\_RANDs \quad}$

$SRESm|SRESs|\text{ACO} \leftarrow$ $SRESm|SRESs|\text{ACO} \leftarrow$
HMAC(dk, $AU\_RANDm|AU\_RANDs)/2^{128}$ HMAC(dk, $AU\_RANDm|AU\_RANDs)/2^{128}$

                                           $\xrightarrow{\quad SRESm \quad}$ check $SRESm$

check $SRESs$ $\xleftarrow{\quad SRESs \quad}$

··AES Key Computation···

$\text{k}_{\text{AES}} \leftarrow$ $\text{k}_{\text{AES}} \leftarrow$
HMAC($LK,'btak'|\text{BD\_ADDR}_A|\text{BD\_ADDR}_B|\text{ACO})/2^{128}$ HMAC($LK,'btak'|\text{BD\_ADDR}_A|\text{BD\_ADDR}_B|\text{ACO})/2^{128}$
(output also ACO as IV)   (output also ACO as IV)

Fig. 3. Bluetooth BR/EDR secure authentication and encryption key derivation. The session identifier for this subprotocol is given by $\text{sid} = (AU\_RANDm, AU\_RANDs)$.

all previous connections become insecure—we do not incorporate this feature into our model. We also note that it is convenient to model the initial connection step with the derivation of the link key resp. long-term key as a separate session (creating an empty session key but initializing a permanent connection key), even though usually computation of an encryption key would immediately follow the initial connection. We let the adversary decide when and how often devices reconnect.

The TOFU property indicates if the session key should be considered to be secure. When initializing a new session we declare this session to be not trustworthy, and only change this later if there is a honest partner session to which the session here is connected to, i.e., if the adversary has been passive. All subsequent reconnections of the session then inherit this flag. Overall, we thus have three flags for keys: isTested for session keys which have been tested, isRevealed for session keys which have been revealed, and isTOFU for session keys

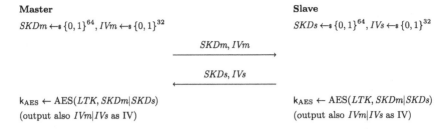

Fig. 4. Bluetooth BLE encryption key derivation. The session identifier is given as $\mathsf{sid} = (SKDm, SKDs)$.

which have been derived from a trustworthy initialization step. The latter flags refine the usual freshness condition for session keys.

3.1 Attack Model

We give a game-based security model in the Bellare-Rogaway style [6]. We assume that parties have some identity. For Bluetooth this will be the 48-bits Bluetooth device address BD_ADDR of the device, which can be either public or random. According to the Bluetooth protocol description we sometimes denote the identities of connecting devices as A and B. Parties know their identity and also know the intended partner's id when the cryptographic protocol starts (via device discovery). We note that Bluetooth addresses can be easily changed on a device and are usually not authenticated.

As explained in the introduction we are interested in the trust-on-first-use security of the protocol. We model this by declaring a trustworthy relationship if two sessions of honest parties are partnered, indicating that the adversary has been passive in the initial connection. From then on the (now active) adversary can interact with either of the two parties. We note that the adversary can still start initial connections with any party and actively participate in these connection. We do not aim to protect the session keys in such connections but since parties may re-use secret information like the Diffie-Hellman shares in multiple executions, we need to account for such attack vectors.

For the re-usable Diffie-Hellman key we assume that each party i, at the beginning of the game, is initialized with a key pair $(\mathsf{sk}_i, \mathsf{pk}_i) \leftarrow \mathsf{KGen}(1^\lambda)$. To model that the key may or may not be used in several sessions we grant the adversary access to a $\mathsf{NextPK}(i)$ oracle which renews the key pair of party i. We note that the new key pair will only be used in future sessions, not in the currently running ones. This means that each session is assigned a unique key pair. This is modeled by having a counter value pkctr_i, initialized to 0, which is incremented with each key rolling.

Sessions. A protocol session $\mathsf{lbl} = (i, k)$ is given by a pair consisting of the k-th session in a protocol run of party with identity i. When the adversary initiates a new session the game assigns the next available integer k. Each such session lbl holds a set of entries:

- id is the identity i of the party.
- mode, either init or reconnect, describes if this is a new initial connection or a reconnection.
- aux denotes some auxiliary information like the association model JUSTWORKS, PASSKEYENTRY, NUMCOM or OOB which should be used, and further data like passkey $\in \{0, 1, \ldots, 9\}^* \cup \{\bot\}$ in the passkey entry mode or information transmitted out of band.
- LinkKey describes the connection or link key (called link key in Bluetooth Classic and long-term key in Bluetooth Low Energy) which is set during the initial connection and used later to derive further session keys when reconnecting. Initialized to $\bot$.
- The variable state determines if the session is running, or has accepted or rejected.
- The Boolean variable isTested determines if the session key has been tested before. Initialized to false.
- The Boolean variable isRevealed defines if the session has been revealed. Initialized to false.
- The Boolean variable isTOFU determines if the session key has been derived following a trustworthy initial connection. Initialized to false.
- pkctr denotes the counter value of key pair used by party i in the session. When performing protocol steps the party always uses the key pair identified by this counter value. But the party may actually use different keys in different sessions concurrently.
- key $\in \{0, 1\}^* \cup \{\bot\}$ describes the session key, initialized to $\bot$. Note that for a successful initial connection in Bluetooth, the session key coincides with the connection key.
- sid $\in \{0, 1\}^* \cup \{\bot\}$ is the session identifier, the initial value is $\bot$. The session identifier is set only once during an execution.

A central property in key exchange protocols is to define when two sessions belong to each other. We use here the common approach to say that two (distinct) sessions are partnered if they hold the same (non-trivial) session identifier:

Definition 1 (Partnered Sessions). *We say that two sessions* $\mathsf{lbl}, \mathsf{lbl}'$ *are partnered if* $\mathsf{lbl} \neq \mathsf{lbl}'$ *and* $\mathsf{lbl}.\mathsf{sid} = \mathsf{lbl}'.\mathsf{sid} \neq \bot$.

Note that sid $\neq \bot$ presumes that the session has accepted.

Adversarial Queries. We consider an active adversary $\mathcal{A}$ interacting with the protocol. The adversary has an access to the following oracle queries:

- InitSession(i, [aux]) establishes a new session at party i (with number k). Assigns the corresponding values to the entries in lbl $= (i, k)$, i.e., lbl.id $\leftarrow i$, the mode is set to lbl.mode $\leftarrow$ init, and the optional parameter [aux], if present, is stored in lbl.aux (and otherwise this entry is set to $\perp$). We set lbl.state $\leftarrow$ running, lbl.pkctr $\leftarrow$ pkctr$_i$, as well as lbl.isTested, lbl.isRevealed, lbl.isTOFU $\leftarrow$ false, since this establishes a new session in which the active adversary may interact with party i. Return lbl.

- Reconnect(lbl, [aux]) checks if there exists a session with lbl.LinkKey $\neq \perp$. If so it establishes a new session lbl$'$ $= (i, k')$ via calling InitSession(i, [aux]) but immediately overwrites lbl$'$.mode $\leftarrow$ reconnect. The new session inherits the TOFU characteristic of the preceding session, that is, one sets lbl$'$.isTOFU $\leftarrow$ lbl.isTOFU, and copies the previous connection key, lbl$'$.LinkKey $\leftarrow$ lbl.LinkKey. Return lbl$'$.

- Send(lbl, m) sends a protocol message m to the session lbl. Returns $\perp$ if the session does not exist or is not established, and the party's protocol reply otherwise. When executing the command, the protocol party may set lbl.sid or change the state lbl.state to accepted or rejected. If lbl.state turns to accepted then check the following:
  - If lbl.mode = init and there exists a partnered session lbl$'$ to lbl then set lbl.isTOFU $\leftarrow$ true and lbl$'$.isTOFU $\leftarrow$ true.
  - If there exists a partnered session lbl$'$ with lbl$'$.isTested = true then set lbl.isTested $\leftarrow$ true. This mirrors the property for partnered sessions.
  - If there exists a partnered session lbl$'$ with lbl$'$.isRevealed = true then set lbl.isRevealed $\leftarrow$ true.

- NextPK(i) updates the key pair of party i. That is, increment pkctr$_i$ and compute a new key pair $(\mathsf{sk}_i[\mathsf{pkctr}_i], \mathsf{pk}_i[\mathsf{pkctr}_i]) \leftarrow \mathsf{KGen}(1^\lambda)$.

- Reveal(lbl) returns the session key key of session lbl, or $\perp$ if the session does not exist, or if lbl.state $\neq$ accepted, or if lbl.isRevealed = true. Sets lbl.isRevealed $\leftarrow$ true and also lbl$'$.isRevealed $\leftarrow$ true for all partnered sessions lbl$'$ with lbl$'$.sid = lbl.sid.

- Test(lbl) tests the session key key of the session lbl. If the session does not exist, lbl.isRevealed = true, or lbl.isTOFU = false, or key $= \perp$, or lbl.state $\neq$ accepted, or lbl.isTested = true, then immediately returns $\perp$. Else returns either the real key key or a random string of length |key|, depending on the random bit b chosen by the challenger $\mathcal{C}$. Sets lbl.isTested $\leftarrow$ true to make sure that the adversary potentially does not get another random key when testing this session again. For the same reason it also sets lbl$'$.isTested $\leftarrow$ true for all partnered sessions lbl$'$ with lbl$'$.sid = lbl.sid.

When considering attacks against the Bluetooth protocol we assume a set $\mathcal{I}$ of admissible identities. We denote by $\mathcal{L}$ the set of session labels lbl activated by the adversary.

3.2 Security Properties

We state the two common security properties of key exchange protocols. One is Match-security, covering basic functional guarantees such as honest executions deriving the same session key, and that the partnering condition is not "too loose". The other one is key secrecy. We note that we often define the properties in the asymptotic sense for sake of simplicity. But we give concrete security bounds when analyzing the Bluetooth security suite.

In the definition we give the adversary access to the same oracles as for key secrecy, e.g., including a Test oracle, albeit not oracles may be relevant for the attack. This is only to unify both attacks.

Match-Security. Intuitively, Match-security states that, if two sessions are partnered then they also hold the same session key (1), and at most two sessions are partnered (2). For reconnections the former should only hold for sessions which have been connected before and thus hold the same connection key. We therefore stipulate that the LinkKey-entry in both executions must be identical if one of the sessions is in mode mode = reconnect, and split the first requirement into one for initial connections (if at least one party is in mode mode = init) and one for reconnections.

Definition 2 (Match-Security). *We say that a key exchange protocol Π provides Match-security if for any PPT adversary $\mathcal{A}$ and identity set $\mathcal{I}$ we have*

$$\boldsymbol{Adv}_{\mathcal{A},\Pi,\mathcal{I}}^{Match}(\lambda) := \Pr\left[\boldsymbol{Exp}_{\mathcal{A},\Pi,\mathcal{I}}^{Match}(\lambda) = 1\right]$$

is negligible, where

$\boldsymbol{Exp}_{\mathcal{A},\Pi,\mathcal{I}}^{Match}(\lambda)$
_____

$b \leftarrow\!\!\!{}_\$ \{0,1\}$

forall $i \in \mathcal{I}$ **do**

   $\mathsf{pkctr}_i \leftarrow 0$

   $(\mathsf{sk}_i[0], \mathsf{pk}_i[0]) \leftarrow\!\!\!{}_\$ \mathsf{KGen}(1^\lambda)$

$\mathcal{A}^{\mathsf{InitSession,Reconnect,Send,NextPK,Reveal,Test}}(\{(i, \mathsf{pk}_i[0])\}_{i\in\mathcal{I}})$

return 1 **if**

   $\exists$ *pairwise distinct* $\mathsf{lbl}, \mathsf{lbl}', \mathsf{lbl}'' \in \mathcal{L}$:

      (1a) $\mathsf{lbl}.\mathsf{sid} = \mathsf{lbl}'.\mathsf{sid} \neq \bot$ *and* $\mathsf{lbl}.\mathsf{mode} = \mathsf{init}$ *and* $\mathsf{lbl}.\mathsf{key} \neq \mathsf{lbl}'.\mathsf{key}$

      (1b) $\mathsf{lbl}.\mathsf{sid} = \mathsf{lbl}'.\mathsf{sid} \neq \bot$ *and* $\mathsf{lbl}.\mathsf{mode} = \mathsf{reconnect}$

            and $\mathsf{lbl}.\mathsf{LinkKey} = \mathsf{lbl}'.\mathsf{LinkKey}$ *and* $\mathsf{lbl}.\mathsf{key} \neq \mathsf{lbl}'.\mathsf{key}$

      (2) $\mathsf{lbl}.\mathsf{sid} = \mathsf{lbl}'.\mathsf{sid} = \mathsf{lbl}''.\mathsf{sid} \neq \bot$

Key Secrecy. Next we define what it means that a session key, derived after a trustworthy initialization step, remains secret. This should hold even if the adversary mounts an active attack after the TOFU step. We note that we only need to check eventually that no session has been tested and revealed (or its partner session has been revealed). The TOFU property, that only keys which have been created in a trustworthy way should be kept secret, is ensured by the attack model (e.g., the Test oracle immediately rejects requests for session keys with isTOFU = false).

Definition 3 (Key Secrecy). *We say that a key exchange protocol Π provides Secrecy if for any PPT adversary $\mathcal{A}$ and identity set $\mathcal{I}$ we have*

$$Adv_{\mathcal{A},\Pi,\mathcal{I}}^{Secrecy}(\lambda) := \Pr\left[Exp_{\mathcal{A},\Pi,\mathcal{I}}^{Secrecy}(\lambda) = 1\right] - \frac{1}{2}$$

is negligible, where

$Exp_{\mathcal{A},\Pi,\mathcal{I}}^{Secrecy}(\lambda)$

$b \leftarrow_\$ \{0,1\}$

forall $i \in \mathcal{I}$ **do**

    $\mathsf{pkctr}_i \leftarrow 0$

    $(\mathsf{sk}_i[0], \mathsf{pk}_i[0]) \leftarrow_\$ \mathsf{KGen}(1^\lambda)$

$a \leftarrow_\$ \mathcal{A}^{\mathsf{InitSession},\mathsf{Reconnect},\mathsf{Send},\mathsf{NextPK},\mathsf{Reveal},\mathsf{Test}}(\{(i, \mathsf{pk}_i[0])\}_{i \in \mathcal{I}})$

return 1 **if**

    $a = b$ **and** *there are no sessions* $\mathsf{lbl}, \mathsf{lbl}' \in \mathcal{L}$ *with*

        $\mathsf{lbl}.\mathsf{sid} = \mathsf{lbl}'.\mathsf{sid}$ *but* $\mathsf{lbl}.\mathsf{isRevealed} = \mathsf{false}$ *and* $\mathsf{lbl}'.\mathsf{isTested} = \mathsf{true}$

4 Security of Bluetooth

In this section we show that the Bluetooth protocol suite (for both BR/EDR and BLE) provides a secure TOFU key exchange protocol. In the security statements below we usually refer to the Bluetooth protocol Π, capturing either $\Pi_{\mathrm{BR/EDR}}$ or Π_{BLE}, and only refine the concrete security bounds with respect to the specific protocol. We note that we view the initial pairing phase as creating a permanent key, equal to the link key resp. long-term key, but formally no session key. Session keys are then derived via the corresponding mechanisms in the protocol. This is valid since the model also allows empty session keys, which trivially satisfy correctness and security properties.

4.1 Security Assumptions

For our security results we merely need two assumptions. One is the PRF-ODH assumption to draw conclusions about the re-used Diffie-Hellman value in the SSP protocol, and the other one is the key derivation in the reconnection steps.

PRF-ODH Assumption. The PRF-ODH assumption states that applying a pseudorandom function PRF to a Diffie-Hellman key g^{uv} and an adversarial chosen string x^* looks random, even if the adversary learns related outputs of PRF. The only restriction is that the adversary cannot ask for $\mathsf{PRF}(g^{uv}, x^*)$ directly. We work here with the so-called mm setting [8] where the adversary can make multiple queries for both Diffie-Hellman keys g^u and g^v. This is necessary since either Bluetooth device may reuse the key in other sessions. We also assume that the adversary has access to both Diffie-Hellman parts and oracles at the outset.

Definition 4 (PRF-ODH Assumption). *Let* $\mathbb{G}$ *be a cyclic group of prime order* $q = q(\lambda)$ *generated by* g. *Let* $\mathsf{PRF} : \mathbb{G} \times \{0,1\}^* \to \{0,1\}^*$ *be a pseudorandom function, taking a key* $k \in \mathbb{G}$ *and a string* s *as input, and producing a string* $\mathsf{PRF}(k,s)$ *as output. For a given* $w \in \mathbb{Z}_q$ *let* $\mathsf{ODH}_w : \mathbb{G} \times \{0,1\}^* \to \{0,1\}^*$ *be the function which takes as input* $X \in \mathbb{G}$ *and string* s *and returns* $\mathsf{PRF}(X^w, s)$.

We say that the PRF-ODH assumption holds relative to $\mathbb{G}$ *if for any PPT adversary* $\mathcal{A}$ *we have*

$$\mathbf{Adv}_{\mathcal{A},\mathsf{PRF},\mathbb{G}}^{PRF\text{-}ODH}(\lambda) := \Pr\left[\mathbf{Exp}_{\mathcal{A},\mathsf{PRF},\mathbb{G}}^{PRF\text{-}ODH}\right] - \tfrac{1}{2}$$

is negligible, where

$$
\begin{array}{l}
\mathbf{Exp}_{\mathcal{A},\mathsf{PRF},\mathbb{G}}^{PRF\text{-}ODH} \\
\hline
u, v \leftarrow_\$ \mathbb{Z}_q, b \leftarrow_\$ \{0,1\} \\
U \leftarrow g^u, V \leftarrow g^v \\
(x^*, st) \leftarrow_\$ \mathcal{A}^{\mathsf{ODH}_u(\cdot,\cdot),\mathsf{ODH}_v(\cdot,\cdot)}(U, V) \\
y_0 \leftarrow \mathsf{PRF}(g^{uv}, x^*), y_1 \leftarrow \{0,1\}^{|y_0|} \\
a \leftarrow_\$ \mathcal{A}^{\mathsf{ODH}_u(\cdot,\cdot),\mathsf{ODH}_v(\cdot,\cdot)}(st, V, y_b) \\
\textbf{return } a = b
\end{array}
$$

where we assume that $\mathcal{A}$ *never makes a query* $(A, x) = (V, x^*)$ *to oracle* ODH_u *resp.* $(B, x) = (U, x^*)$ *to* ODH_v.

We note that for Bluetooth Classic the pseudorandom function $\mathsf{PRF}(W, x)$ is $\mathsf{HMAC}(W, x)$. For BLE it is a nested CMAC computation, $\mathsf{PRF}(W, x) = \mathsf{CMAC}(\mathsf{CMAC}(Salt, W), x)$. It seems plausible to assume that the PRF-ODH assumption holds for these instantiations. We also note that the PRF-ODH assumption implicitly stipulates that the Diffie-Hellman problem is hard, i.e., small subgroup attacks such as in [7] must be prevented. This is usually done by checking the validity of the curve points.

Pseudorandom Function. For the reconnection steps we require that the underlying function HMAC in BR/EDR and AES in BLE, from which the encryption keys are derived, behave like pseudorandom functions. For an adversary $\mathcal{C}$ let $\mathbf{Adv}_{\mathcal{C},\mathsf{PRF}}^{\mathsf{PRF}}(\lambda)$ denote the common security advantage of $\mathcal{C}$ distinguishing a $\mathsf{PRF}(k, \cdot)$ oracle from a random function oracle, the choice which oracle is used made at a random.

4.2   Match Security

We first argue Match-security of the Bluetooth protocol. Recall that we set the session identifiers to consist of $\mathsf{sid} = (g^a, g^b, A, B, Na, Nb)$ for the initial connection, and $\mathsf{sid} = (AU\_RANDm, AU\_RANDs, A, B)$ for BR/EDR reconnections resp. sid = $(SKDm, SKDs)$ for BLE. Also note that the parties may reuse their Diffie-Hellman secret across multiple executions; the nonces, however, are fresh 128-bit values, chosen randomly in each session and present in each of the SSP subprotocols. Furthermore, recall that the initial connection derives an empty session key and that the link key resp. long-term key is stored as the permanent key in entry LinkKey of the session.

Proposition 1 (Match-Security). *The Bluetooth protocol Π provides Match-security. That is, for any adversary $\mathcal{A}$ calling at most q_s sessions we have*

$$\boldsymbol{Adv}^{Match}_{\mathcal{A},\Pi,\mathcal{I}}(\lambda) \leq q_s^2 \cdot 2^{-|nonce|},$$

where $|nonce| = 128$ for BR/EDR *and $|nonce| = 64$ for* BLE.

The reason for having different bounds stems from the distinct key derivation when reconnecting. Both protocol versions use 128-bit nonces for initial connection, but only BR/EDR uses 128 bit values for reconnections; BLE instead uses the 64-bit session key diversifiers.

Proof. For the first properties, (1a) and (1b), that partnered sessions have the same session key, note that the link/long-term key in an initial connection is computed as $\mathsf{KDF}(g^{ab}, Na, Nb, A, B)$ such that the output of the (deterministic) key derivation matches for equal session identifiers. Also, session identifiers for the initial connection and reconnections differ in length such that they cannot match the other type (in both BR/EDR and BLE). For reconnections the session identifiers $(AU\_RANDm, AU\_RANDs, A, B)$ resp. $(SKDm, SKDs)$ fully specify the derived session keys together with the same link/long-term key, implying a match as well.

For the second property note that if there were three sessions with the same session identifier sid, then two of them must be in the role of Alice (or Bob). If we have at most q_s sessions in total, there are at most q_s^2 such pairs of two Alice- or Bob-sessions. The honest party picks a fresh nonce Na resp. Nb in each of these two executions (for initial connections in either mode), and fresh values AU_RANDm, AU_RANDs for reconnections in BR/EDR resp. 64-bit values $SKDm, SKDs$ in BLE. it follows that each pairs yields a nonce collision with probability at most $2^{-|nonce|} = 2^{-128}$ in BR/EDR resp. $\leq 2^{-64}$ in BLE. The overall threefold collision probability for session identifiers is thus at most $q_s^2 \cdot 2^{-|nonce|}$ as stated. □

4.3   Key Secrecy

As it turns out, key secrecy does not depend on the Authentication stages 1 and 2 of the protocol. As such the analysis easily works for all modes of the protocol simultaneously.

Proposition 2 (Key Secrecy). *The Bluetooth protocol Π provides trust-on-first-use Secrecy. That is, for any adversary $\mathcal{A}$ initiating at most q_s sessions* *there exists adversaries $\mathcal{B}$ and $\mathcal{C}$ (with roughly the same run time as $\mathcal{A}$, and $\mathcal{C}$ making at most q_s oracle queries) such that*

$$\boldsymbol{Adv}_{\mathcal{A},\Pi,\mathcal{I}}^{Secrecy}(\lambda) \leq q_s^3 \cdot \boldsymbol{Adv}_{\mathcal{B},\mathsf{PRF},\mathsf{G}}^{PRF\text{-}ODH}(\lambda) + q_s \cdot \boldsymbol{Adv}_{\mathcal{C},\mathsf{PRF'}}^{PRF}(\lambda) + q_s^2 \cdot 2^{-|nonce|}.$$

where $|nonce| = 128$, and PRF in the PRF-ODH case is HMAC for BR/EDR resp. $\mathsf{CMAC}(\mathsf{CMAC}(Salt, \cdot), \cdot)$ for BLE, and $\mathsf{PRF'}$ for reconnections is HMAC for BR/EDR resp. AES for BLE.

We note that the reduction factor q_s^3 is indeed large but follows other analyses. A factor q_s comes from the multiple test queries which our model allows, and the quadratic term q_s^2 from the need to guess the correct insertion points of the Diffie-Hellman keys. For instance, Troncoso and Hale [23] also have the quadratic loss factor for the model with a single-test query. Tighter security bounds usually require other techniques as used in Bluetooth [16] or to use and program a random oracle [13,15]. The latter may nonetheless be a viable way to reduce the loss factor in Bluetooth as well. On the other hand, since Bluetooth is a short-range technique mounting attacks with an extensive number of sessions seems to be hard. Indeed, a factor q_s^2 would disappear if the adversary had to announce the target in advance.

Proof. The proof proceeds via game hopping. We start with the original attack on the Bluetooth protocol. Then we gradually change the game till we reach the point where, independently of the challenge bit b, the adversary only gets to see random keys. We denote by $\Pr[\mathsf{Game}_j]$ the probability that the adversary wins in the corresponding game (over the guessing probability). In particular, $\Pr[\mathsf{Game}_0] = \mathbf{Exp}_{\mathcal{A},\Pi,\mathcal{I}}^{Secrecy}(\lambda) - \frac{1}{2}$.

Game 0. Is the original attack on the protocol. We assume in the following without loss of generality that the adversary never reveals or tests an empty session key of a session in mode $\mathsf{mode} = \mathsf{init}$.

Game 1. In Game_1 we assume that there are no three sessions (in mode $\mathsf{mode} = \mathsf{init}$) with the same session identifier.

It follows as in the case of Match-security that this happen with probability at most $q_s^2 \cdot 2^{-|nonce|}$. Note that we here have $|nonce| = 128$ (and not 64) because both versions, BR/EDR and BLE, use 128-bit nonces in the pairing step.

Game 2. In Game_2 we replace the connection key $\mathsf{LinkKey}$ in each session lbl in mode $\mathsf{lbl.mode} = \mathsf{init}$ upon acceptance as follows: If there is a partnered session $\mathsf{lbl'}$ which has accepted before—there can be at most one by the previous game hop—set $\mathsf{lbl.LinkKey} \leftarrow \mathsf{lbl'.LinkKey}$. Else, replace $\mathsf{lbl.LinkKey}$ by a random string of the same length.

Observe that the sessions where we replace keys are those which are considered to be trustworthy in the sense that they completed an initial execution with a passive adversary ($\mathsf{isTOFU} = \mathsf{true}$). We note that the former step in the replacement above only ensures consistency; in the protocol execution in Game_1 the parties would derive the same $\mathsf{LinkKey}$ by construction.

We argue that $\Pr[\mathsf{Game}_1] \leq \Pr[\mathsf{Game}_2] + q_s^3 \cdot \mathbf{Adv}_{\mathcal{B},\mathsf{PRF},\mathsf{G}}^{\mathrm{PRF\text{-}ODH}}(\lambda)$. The argument is via an (interactive) hybrid argument against the PRF-ODH assumption. Details are omitted here for space reasons; they appear in the full version.

Game 3. In Game_3 we can now replace all session keys in sessions lbl.mode = reconnect and lbl.isTOFU = true by random values, ignoring any consistency requirement.

Note that such sessions are exactly those where we have replaced the connection key LinkKey by a fresh random value. Also observe that the security game ensures that the key of the partner session of a revealed session key or any tested session key cannot be obtained again, such that we do not need to take care of consistency here. It follows now via a straightforward reduction to the pseudorandomness of HMAC resp. AES, with a hybrid argument over all at most q_s connection keys, that this is indistinguishable from the adversary's point of view.

In game Game_3 the adversary gets to see a random and independent session key in either of the two cases of the challenge bit b. Hence, the probability of predicting b correctly is exactly $\frac{1}{2}$. The claim now follows from collecting all probabilities.   □

5   Privacy in Bluetooth LE

Bluetooth Low Energy supports address randomization technique to provide privacy. We show here that this mechanism indeed achieves privacy (against outsiders) if one neglects other attack possibilities based on physical features or other observable data.

5.1   Details on Privacy Mechanisms in Bluetooth Low Energy

For the BLE protocol we dive into the Link Establishment process to understand better the privacy mechanisms.

Private Addresses. To support the privacy mechanism, the standard specifies four types of Bluetooth addresses BD_ADDR in LE:

Public Addresses: A globally unique device identifier MAC, consisting of a 24-bit vendor identifier and a local identifier chosen by the vendor.

Static Random Address: A random address which is set once for the device's lifetime or can be changed upon reboots. Such addresses carry the most significant bit values '11', what allows distinguishing them from the next two types.

Non-Resolvable Random Private Addresses: A frequently changed random address (with the most significant bits set to '00'). The standard recommends to renew random addresses, including this type and the next one, at least every 15 min [9, Vol 3, Part C, App. A].

Resolvable Random Private Addresses: A random address wherefrom a trusted device can extract the Public or Static Random Addresses. It consists of 24 bits *prand* that are set randomly—effectively only 22 random bits since the most significant bits correspond to '10'— and the other 24 bits are computed as a (pseudorandom) hash from *prand* for an Identity Resolving Keys (*IRK*). This Identity Resolving Key must have been shared with the trusted device in a previous connection.

Generating Resolvable Random Private Addresses. The Identity Resolving Key *IRK* is a device-specific 128-bit value. It can be assigned or generated randomly during manufacturing, but the standard also allows any other methods to create the *IRK*. It can be also generated from a 128-bit Identity Root *IR* as $IRK \leftarrow$ $\text{AES}(IR, 0x00000000|0x01|0x00)$. Noteworthy, unlike the *IRK*, the identity root *IR* is supposed to have 128 bits of entropy according to the standard. In fact, if the *IRK* is all-zero, then the device does not support resolvable private address. We assume in the following that the *IRK* is created randomly and non-zero.

With an *IRK*, the device can generate a (pseudo)random address as follows:

$$\text{BD\_ADDR} \leftarrow [\text{AES}(IRK, 0^{104}|prand) \bmod 2^{24}] \mid prand,$$

where the 24-bit value *prand* consists of the 22 random bits and '10'. In order to resolve the obtained random private address BD_ADDR, the receiving device extracts *prand* out of the received address. Then the device goes through its list of stored *IRK*s and for each entry checks whether the AES-computation with that *IRK* for the (padded) value *prand* matches the BD_ADDR. If so, it can look up the actual address of the device and the long-term key, stored together with the *IRK*. If the device does not find a matching *IRK* in the list, then it ignores the PDU from the other party.

Devices achieve privacy only if they have bonded and exchanged the necessary keys, *IRK* and *CSRK*, as well as the identities (either static random addresses or a public addresses). The exchange of these data happens after the devices have performed the initial connection and enabled encryption. First the slave sends its *IRK*, address, and *CSRK*. Then the exchange is followed by the master sending the information in the same order. This means that both parties share their *IRK* with any other bonded device, but the exchange is done over a secured communication channel. The specification also allows IRKs to be pre-distributed. However, we do not consider this case here since it requires assumptions on the channel during the pre-distribution procedure.

Discovery Phase. Link Establishment starts with a discovery process. During this process, two devices in proximity synchronize, by one device advertising and the other scanning for potential connections. The link layer master is called the initiator, and the link layer slave is called the responder. The advertising protocol data unit (PDU) has the following format:

Structure	Header						Payload			
Field	*PDU* type	*RFU*	*ChSel*	TxAdd	RxAdd	*Length*	*AdvA*	AD_1	AD_2	...
Bits	4	1	1	1	1	8	48	Variable	Variable	...

The important for privacy information contained in the packets are the Bluetooth addresses BD_ADDR in the *AdvA* field in the payload, which can be one of the four aforementioned types. The flags TxAdd and RxAdd in the header indicate whether the transmission address (TxAdd) resp. reception address (RxAdd) is random (= 1) or public (= 0). The Payload may contain additional advertisement data (AD) elements, like the AD type flag and AD data. The latter can be for example a human-readable "complete local name". We simply write $AD_1, AD_2, \ldots$ for these data elements.

The entries *PDUtype* contain the advertisement type, *RFU* is reserved for future use, *ChSel* determines whether the device supports an alternative channel selection algorithm, *Length* describes the length of the payload.

Pairing Feature Extraction. Once the devices have established the link, the pairing starts with the pairing request and response. This information determines the features how the two devices can pair. The pairing requests contain the following information:

Field	Code	IOcap	OOB	AuthReq						MaxEnc	InitKey					RespKey
Sub				BF	MITM	SC	KP	CT2	Rsrv		LTK	IRK	CSRK	LK	Rsrv	
Bits	8	8	8	2	1	1	1	1	2	8	1	1	1	1	4	8

The most relevant for privacy entries here are *SC*: the bit that indicates whether the device supports the "Secure Connections" mode. If both parties have this flag set, then the devices use the P-256 elliptic curve, else they go for the legacy mode. Bit *BF* defines whether two pairing devices will create a bond (i.e. store the security and identity information, such as *LTK, IRK CSRK*) or not. The other important entry is the *IOcap* byte, which describes the input/output capabilities of the device.

The entry *MaxEnc* sets the number of octets for encryption keys. The lack of authentication of the entries enabled the "Key Negotiation of Bluetooth" (KNOB) attack [2,4] where the man-in-the-middle adversary sets the entry to 7 bytes for long-term keys in BLE, making the devices use a weak key. To prevent this downgrade attack, devices should only support 128-bit keys. We presume that this countermeasure is in place.

The further entries are as follows: the entry *Code* determines whether this is a request or response, *OOB* specifies whether OOB data is available; *BF* says whether the device supports bonding; *MITM* determines whether the device requests to use man-in-the-middle protection (e.g., if neither *OOB* nor *MITM* are set on the devices, then they revert to JustWorks connections; if the *OOB* flags are not set and at least one device sets *MITM*, then they use *IOcap* to determine the connection method); *KP* is the keypress flag used in the passkey entry mode, *CT2* defines what is used as input to AES-CMAC for generation of an intermediate key when conversing *LTK* to *LK* and the other way around.

The initiator and responder distribution key entries *InitKey* and *RespKey* contain information used in the optional "Transport Specific Key Distribution" phase that determines the data exchanged when bonding. For Secure Connections, the master or the slave can later send either of the following information: the "Identity Resolving Key" *IRK* to resolve pseudorandom addresses when reconnecting; the public, or static random address; and the "Connection Signature Resolving Key" *CSRK* to authenticate (unencrypted) data. We stress that the flags here only indicate which keys should be distributed; the actual data is exchanged later.

We note that all these data are sent in clear. This potentially allows distinguishing devices based on their features. This is inevitable, therefore we aim in the following to protect only devices with identical features and focus only on the cryptographic transcript part.

5.2   Privacy Requirements

The Bluetooth protocol aims to hide a device's identity if private address resolution is used and against outsiders with which the private address resolution has not been established [9, Vol 3, Part H, Sect. 2.4.2.1]:

> "The privacy concept only protects against devices that are not part of the set to which the IRK has been given."

Since any communication with the adversary controlling some device would reveal the *IRK*, we thus only consider executions between devices in which the adversary is passive.

To capture this behavior, we give the adversary only a Test oracle which it can query about three devices. One device serves as the communication partner with one of the other two devices, where the choice is made at random according to some challenge bit b. The devices either start a new initial connection or reconnect, and the adversary gets to learn the transcript of the communication. The task of the adversary is to predict the bit b. To avoid trivial attacks, we assume that two devices in question either both share an *IRK* with the other device or neither of them.

Formally, the Test oracle takes as input three identities $i_0, i_1, j \in \mathcal{I}$ of devices and a value mode, either equal to init or to reconnect, and some auxiliary information aux (e.g., describing the requested SSP protocol). The oracle, holding the random challenge bit b, runs an execution between device i_b and j according to the parameters and returns the transcript to the adversary.

As mentioned before, the distribution of *IRK* and BD_ADDR happens after the devices have enabled encryption. Therefore, we extend the initial connection procedure by forcing the devices to enable encryption and perform the key distribution step. If this does not happen, the pairing step (and hence the initial connection) fails and the devices are not considered bonded.

To strengthen the definition, we assume that the adversary learns all actual addresses of the devices at the outset. We may for simplicity assume that the identity i of a device equals this address. For initialization we also assume that a secret key, called *IRK* here as well, is generated at the beginning of the security experiment.

Definition 5 (Outsider Privacy). *The key exchange protocol Π provides outsider privacy if for any PPT adversary $\mathcal{A}$*

$$\boldsymbol{Adv}_{\mathcal{A},\Pi}^{Privacy}(\lambda) := \Pr\left[\boldsymbol{Exp}_{\mathcal{A},\Pi}^{Privacy}(\lambda) = 1\right] - \frac{1}{2}$$

is negligible, where

$$\underline{\boldsymbol{Exp}_{\mathcal{A},\Pi,\mathcal{I}}^{Secrecy}(\lambda)}$$

$b \leftarrow_\$ \{0,1\}$

forall $i \in \mathcal{I}$ **do**

$IRK \leftarrow_\$ \{0,1\}^{128} \setminus \{0\}$

$a \leftarrow_\$ \mathcal{A}^{Test}(\mathcal{I})$

return 1 *if* $a = b$

5.3   Privacy Guarantees of BLE

We say that a device running BLE is in *full privacy mode* if it uses a non-resolvable random private address when establishing an initial connection to some other device, and a resolvable one when reconnecting to that device. Furthermore, we assume devices use a fresh Diffie-Hellman value in each SSP execution.

Proposition 3 (Outsider Privacy). *The Bluetooth LE protocol Π_{BLE} in full privacy mode provides outsider privacy. That is, for any adversary $\mathcal{A}$ calling at most q_s test sessions, there exists an adversary $\mathcal{B}$ (with roughly the same run time as $\mathcal{A}$) such that*

$$\boldsymbol{Adv}_{\mathcal{A},\Pi_{\mathrm{BLE}},\mathcal{I}}^{Privacy}(\lambda) \leq q_s^2 \cdot 2^{-|prand|+2} + q_s \cdot \boldsymbol{Adv}_{\mathcal{B},\mathsf{AES}}^{PRF}(\lambda).$$

where $|prand| = 24$.

Note that two bits of *prand* are reserved to signal the address type such that *prand* only consists of 22 random bits. We remark that the bound is tight in the sense that there is an adversary that can link a device (and thus predict the challenge bit) with probability $q_s^2 \cdot 2^{-|prand|+2}$. For this the adversary considers one device (with identity j) and one target device (with identity t) and initializes q_s other devices. It connects each of the $q_s + 1$ devices to j such that they all share an individual *IRK* with device j. Then it calls the Test oracle to reconnect device j to either device t, or to the next unused additional device. If at some point the same random address appears twice then the adversary concludes that the secret bit b is 0 and the target device t is communicating. If no such collision occurs then the attacker outputs a random bit.

For the analysis note that if the Test oracle always picks the device t with the same IRK, i.e., $b = 0$, then a collision on $prand$ implies a collision on the full address. Hence this happens with probability roughly $q_s^2 \cdot 2^{-22}$. For different devices and fresh IRKs this happens rarely, with probability approximately $q_s^2 \cdot 2^{-46}$, even if the $prand$ values collide. The difference in probabilities is thus still in the order of $q_s^2 \cdot 2^{-22}$. If neither case occurs, then our attacker succeeds with probability $\frac{1}{2}$ by the random guess, such that the overall advantage is close to $q_s^2 \cdot 2^{-22}$.

Proof (of Proposition 3). We proceed once more by a game-hopping argument. We denote again by $\Pr[\mathsf{Game}_j]$ the probability that the adversary wins in the corresponding game (over the guessing probability).

Game 0. Game Game_0 is the original attack on the privacy.

Game 1. We declare the adversary to lose if the $prand$ parts of the initially transmitted resolvable addresses in any pair of reconnection calls to Test collide.

Note that since each device chooses 22-bits of the value $prand$ randomly the probability of such a collision, independently of the question whether the test oracle uses the left or right device, is given by at most $q_s^2 \cdot 2^{-22}$. Hence, $\Pr[\mathsf{Game}_0] \leq \Pr[\mathsf{Game}_1] + q_s^2 \cdot 2^{-22}$.

Game 2. In Game_2 we replace the most significant 24 pseudorandom bits in this resolvable private random addresses transmitted or used in a reconnection step by independent random bits (chosen randomly once but fixed in this execution). Internally, the receiving party of such a modified address will be told the correct entry in the list.

Starting with Game_1 we first replace the pseudorandom functions $\mathsf{AES}(IRK, \cdot)$ for each distinct IRK by a random function (but using the same random function for re-appearing IRK's). We can do this by a hybrid argument among the (at most) q_s different keys IRK, simulating the other game steps. Note that we can identify re-appearing IRKs by looking at the identities of devices. This step occurs a loss of $q_s \cdot \mathbf{Adv}_{\mathcal{B},\mathsf{AES}}^{\mathrm{PRF}}(\lambda)$, where $\mathcal{B}$ is the game-simulating adversary. We now apply a random function to different inputs, since all $prand$ values are distinct by the previous game hop. This effectively means that all the 24-bit outputs are random. This corresponds now exactly to Game_2.

We finally note that all the cryptographic parts in transcripts generated by the Test oracle are independent of the device. In initial connections the device i_b in a Test query uses a non-resolvable private random address and a fresh Diffie-Hellman value, by the assumption about the full privacy mode of the device. All other protocol steps of an SSP run are neither device-specific. (Note that the addresses used in the protocol are the now updated values, and that we assume that the IO capablities of the devices i_0, i_1 in a Test query must be equal.)

In each reconnection step, the resolvable private random address is now purely random, and otherwise the parties only exchange random values $SKDm, IVm$ and $SKDs, IVs$. It follows that this step does not depend on the device in question. Since each Test oracle query in the final game is therefore independent of any device-specific data, the adversary cannot do better in the final game than guessing the challenge bit b.   □

6 Conclusion

Our results complement the long list of successful attacks on the Bluetooth protocol suite. These attacks exploit dependencies between different subprotocols or even between the BR/EDR and BLE technology, or the possibility to downgrade the data. We show that if one sticks to the strongest connection model, then the only attack possibility against key secrecy is to be active during the initial connection step. Otherwise the encryption keys are secret, albeit the role of the parties nor their identity is authenticated.

Based on our experience with the analysis of the Bluetooth standard, we would like to conclude that the standard is hard to digest, both in terms of size as well as in terms of clarity. Especially when it comes to the desired security properties, the standard is rather vague in the sense that the requirements are not specified or subsumed under imprecise terms. To give an example, the term "authentication" is used in several contexts with different meanings. It could be entity authentication in the sense that the devices' identities are confirmed, or key authentication in the sense that only intended partner derive the session key, or a form of protection against man-in-the-middle attacks. The Authentication Stage 2 in the SSP protocol rather seems to be a key confirmation step.

Acknowledgments. We thank the anonymous reviewers for extremely comprehensive and helpful comments. This research work has been funded by the German Federal Ministry of Education and Research and the Hessian Ministry of Higher Education, Research, Science and the Arts within their joint support of the National Research Center for Applied Cybersecurity ATHENE. It has also been funded by the Deutsche Forschungsgemeinschaft (DFG, German Research Foundation)— 251805230/GRK 2050.

References

1. Antonioli, D., Tippenhauer, N.O., Rasmussen, K.: BIAS: Bluetooth impersonation AttackS. In: 2020 IEEE Symposium on Security and Privacy, pp. 549–562. IEEE Computer Society Press, San Francisco, May 2020
2. Antonioli, D., Tippenhauer, N.O., Rasmussen, K.: Key negotiation downgrade attacks on Bluetooth and Bluetooth low energy. ACM Trans. Priv. Secur. **23**(3), 141–1428 (2020). https://doi.org/10.1145/3394497
3. Antonioli, D., Tippenhauer, N.O., Rasmussen, K., Payer, M.: BLURtooth: Exploiting Cross-Transport Key Derivation in Bluetooth Classic and Bluetooth Low Energy (2020)
4. Antonioli, D., Tippenhauer, N.O., Rasmussen, K.B.: The KNOB is broken: exploiting low entropy in the encryption key negotiation of Bluetooth BR/EDR. In: Heninger, N., Traynor, P. (eds.) USENIX Security 2019: 28th USENIX Security Symposium. pp. 1047–1061. USENIX Association, Santa Clara, 14–16 August 2019
5. Becker, J.K., Li, D., Starobinski, D.: Tracking anonymized Bluetooth devices. Proc. Priv. Enhanc. Technol. **2019**(3), 50–65 (2019)
6. Bellare, M., Rogaway, P.: Entity authentication and key distribution. In: Stinson, D.R. (ed.) CRYPTO 1993. LNCS, vol. 773, pp. 232–249. Springer, Heidelberg (1994). https://doi.org/10.1007/3-540-48329-2_21

7. Biham, E., Neumann, L.: Breaking the Bluetooth pairing – the fixed coordinate invalid curve attack. In: Paterson, K.G., Stebila, D. (eds.) SAC 2019. LNCS, vol. 11959, pp. 250–273. Springer, Cham (2020). https://doi.org/10.1007/978-3-030-38471-5_11

8. Brendel, J., Fischlin, M., Günther, F., Janson, C.: PRF-ODH: relations, instantiations, and impossibility results. In: Katz, J., Shacham, H. (eds.) CRYPTO 2017, Part III. LNCS, vol. 10403, pp. 651–681. Springer, Cham (2017). https://doi.org/10.1007/978-3-319-63697-9_22

9. Bluetooth Core Specification, version 5.2, December 2019,

10. Celosia, G., Cunche, M.: Fingerprinting Bluetooth-low-energy devices based on the generic attribute profile. In: Liu, P., Zhang, Y. (eds.) Proceedings of the 2nd International ACM Workshop on Security and Privacy for the Internet-of-Things, IoT S&P@CCS 2019, London, 15 November 2019, pp. 24–31. ACM (2019). https://doi.org/10.1145/3338507.3358617

11. Celosia, G., Cunche, M.: Saving private addresses: an analysis of privacy issues in the Bluetooth-low-energy advertising mechanism. In: Poor, H.V., Han, Z., Pompili, D., Sun, Z., Pan, M. (eds.) MobiQuitous 2019, Proceedings of the 16th EAI International Conference on Mobile and Ubiquitous Systems: Computing, Networking and Services, Houston, Texas, USA, 12–14 November 2019, pp. 444–453. ACM (2019), https://doi.org/10.1145/3360774.3360777

12. Claverie, T., Lopes-Esteves, J.: Bluemirror: reflections on bluetooth pairing and provisioning protocols. In: IEEE Security and Privacy Workshops, SP Workshops 2021, San Francisco, CA, USA, 27 May 2021, pp. 339–351. IEEE (2021). https://doi.org/10.1109/SPW53761.2021.00054

13. Cohn-Gordon, K., Cremers, C., Gjøsteen, K., Jacobsen, H., Jager, T.: Highly efficient key exchange protocols with optimal tightness. In: Boldyreva, A., Micciancio, D. (eds.) CRYPTO 2019, Part III. LNCS, vol. 11694, pp. 767–797. Springer, Cham (2019). https://doi.org/10.1007/978-3-030-26954-8_25

14. Cominelli, M., Gringoli, F., Patras, P., Lind, M., Noubir, G.: Even black cats cannot stay hidden in the dark: full-band de-anonymization of Bluetooth classic devices. In: 2020 IEEE Symposium on Security and Privacy, SP 2020, San Francisco, CA, USA, 18–21 May 2020, pp. 534–548. IEEE (2020). https://doi.org/10.1109/SP40000.2020.00091

15. Diemert, D., Jager, T.: On the tight security of TLS 1.3: Theoretically-sound cryptographic parameters for real-world deployments. Cryptology ePrint Archive, Report 2020/726 (2020). https://eprint.iacr.org/2020/726

16. Gjøsteen, K., Jager, T.: Practical and tightly-secure digital signatures and authenticated key exchange. In: Shacham, H., Boldyreva, A. (eds.) CRYPTO 2018, Part II. LNCS, vol. 10992, pp. 95–125. Springer, Cham (2018). https://doi.org/10.1007/978-3-319-96881-0_4

17. Jager, T., Kohlar, F., Schäge, S., Schwenk, J.: On the security of TLS-DHE in the standard model. In: Safavi-Naini, R., Canetti, R. (eds.) CRYPTO 2012. LNCS, vol. 7417, pp. 273–293. Springer, Heidelberg (2012). https://doi.org/10.1007/978-3-642-32009-5_17

18. Jouans, L., Viana, A.C., Achir, N., Fladenmuller, A.: Associating the randomized Bluetooth MAC addresses of a device. In: 18th IEEE Annual Consumer Communications and Networking Conference, CCNC 2021, Las Vegas, NV, USA, 9–12 January 2021, pp. 1–6. IEEE (2021). https://doi.org/10.1109/CCNC49032.2021.9369628

19. Lindell, A.Y.: Comparison-based key exchange and the security of the numeric comparison mode in Bluetooth v2.1. In: Fischlin, M. (ed.) CT-RSA 2009. LNCS, vol. 5473, pp. 66–83. Springer, Heidelberg (2009). https://doi.org/10.1007/978-3-642-00862-7_5

20. Ludant, N., Vo-Huu, T.D., Narain, S., Noubir, G.: Linking Bluetooth LE and classic and implications for privacy-preserving Bluetooth-based protocols. In: 2021 IEEE Symposium on Security and Privacy, SP 2021, San Francisco, CA, USA, 24–27 May 2021. IEEE (2021)

21. Sun, D.Z., Sun, L.: On secure simple pairing in Bluetooth standard v5.0-part I: authenticated link key security and its home automation and entertainment applications. Sensors **19**(5), 1158 (2019). https://www.mdpi.com/1424-8220/19/5/1158

22. Sun, D., Sun, L., Yang, Y.: On secure simple pairing in Bluetooth standard v5.0-part II: privacy analysis and enhancement for low energy. Sensors **19**(15), 3259 (2019). https://doi.org/10.3390/s19153259

23. Troncoso, M., Hale, B.: The Bluetooth cyborg: Analysis of the full human-machine passkey entry AKE protocol. Cryptology ePrint Archive, Report 2021/083 (2021). https://eprint.iacr.org/2021/083

24. von Tschirschnitz, M., Peuckert, L., Franzen, F., Grossklags, J.: Method confusion attack on Bluetooth pairing. In: 2021 IEEE Symposium on Security and Privacy (SP), pp. 213–228. IEEE Computer Society, Los Alamitos, CA, USA, May 2021. https://doi.ieeecomputersociety.org/10.1109/SP40001.2021.00013

25. Vanhoef, M., Matte, C., Cunche, M., Cardoso, L.S., Piessens, F.: Why MAC address randomization is not enough: an analysis of Wi-Fi network discovery mechanisms. In: Chen, X., Wang, X., Huang, X. (eds.) Proceedings of the 11th ACM on Asia Conference on Computer and Communications Security, AsiaCCS 2016, Xi'an, China, 30 May – 3 June 2016, pp. 413–424. ACM (2016). https://doi.org/10.1145/2897845.2897883

26. Wu, J., et al.: BLESA: spoofing attacks against reconnections in Bluetooth low energy. In: 14th USENIX Workshop on Offensive Technologies (WOOT 20). USENIX Association, August 2020. https://www.usenix.org/conference/woot20/presentation/wu

27. Zhang, Y., Weng, J., Dey, R., Jin, Y., Lin, Z., Fu, X.: Breaking secure pairing of Bluetooth low energy using downgrade attacks. In: Capkun, S., Roesner, F. (eds.) USENIX Security 2020: 29th USENIX Security Symposium, pp. 37–54. USENIX Association, 12–14 August 2020

Author Index

Printed in the United States
by Baker & Taylor Publisher Services